*The Gospel
according to*
Matthew

The Gospel according to

Matthew

LEON MORRIS

WILLIAM B. EERDMANS PUBLISHING COMPANY
GRAND RAPIDS, MICHIGAN

INTER-VARSITY PRESS
LEICESTER, ENGLAND

Copyright © 1992 by Wm. B. Eerdmans Publishing Co.
255 Jefferson Ave. S.E., Grand Rapids, Michigan 49503
All rights reserved.

First published 1992 in the United States of America by
Wm. B. Eerdmans Publishing Co.

First British edition 1992 by Inter-Varsity Press,
38 De Montfort Street, Leicester, England LE1 7GP

Printed in the United States of America

Library of Congress Cataloging-in-Publication Data

Morris, Leon, 1914–
The Gospel according to Matthew / Leon Morris.
p.   cm.   — (A Pillar commentary)
Includes bibliographical references and indexes.
ISBN 0-8028-3696-8 (cloth)
1. Bible. N.T. Matthew — Commentaries.
I. Bible. N.T. Matthew. English. Morris. 1992. II. Title. III. Series.
BS2575.3.M677   1992
226.2'077 — dc20   92-15806
                                                 CIP

British Library Cataloguing in Publication Data

A catalogue record for this book is
available from the British Library.

ISBN 0-85111-338-9

Contents

CONTENTS

CONTENTS

Preface

According to R. Polzin, "Traditional biblical scholarship has spent most of its efforts in disassembling the works of a complicated watch before our amazed eyes without apparently realizing that similar efforts by and large have not succeeded in putting the parts back together again in a significant or meaningful way."[1] This criticism may not unfairly be directed against a good deal of New Testament scholarship, which has been more concerned to discern the sources that underlie our Gospels and to study the methods used by the Evangelists as they have worked through their sources and put their Gospels together than it has been to discover what the Evangelists meant. I do not want to say anything derogatory about such activities. They have their importance, and I have spent a good deal of time doing them throughout the years. But it can scarcely be denied that much recent scholarship has been preoccupied with pulling the watch to pieces and explaining how and why it came to be put together in the way it has.

Important as such work is, it is not the task I have set for myself in writing this commentary. Rather, I have chosen to look at the watch as it has come to us. I want to find out what sense can be made of our first Gospel if we simply take it as it is. Clearly its author intended it to be read by people who had no access to his sources. He expected them to make sense of it as it stood. Surely it is not asking too much to suggest that it may be profitable to attempt to do the same in our age. We may not find our task as easy as the first readers did, but in this commentary we will take a good look at the Gospel as it stands and keep searching until we find the author's meaning.

Many commentaries spend a lot of time examining the relationship of this Gospel to Q, to Mark, to Luke, and sometimes to other possible sources. I must confess to a certain scepticism about the possibility of being at all certain how the author went about his task of putting his material together. To cite nothing else, the revival of the Griesbach hypothesis (i.e., the view that Matthew was written first, that Mark was an abbreviation of Matthew, and that Luke depended on Matthew) shows that there are great difficulties in handling questions of order and sources. Whatever

---

1. Cited by T. D. Alexander in *The Evangelical Quarterly,* LXI (1989), p. 5.

view we decide on, we will find that many competent critics do not agree. In this commentary I have, of course, taken some notice of Synoptic relationships, but this is not a major feature. I have tried to take this Gospel as a work in its own right and to see what it says to us as it is, no matter how it came to be put together.

Nor have I been greatly concerned with Matthew's *Sitz im Leben*. Now I realize that I will be taken to task for this omission, but again I must reply that with the information at our disposal we cannot be sure of either the date or the place of this Gospel, nor of the precise opponents of the Evangelist. Without such knowledge we may engage in more or less plausible speculation, but we can do no more. While I recognize that much can be learned from discussions of such matters, I feel that I have nothing significant to contribute to them. My basic concern is with meaning. I have had in mind the reader who uses his commentaries to answer questions like "What do these words mean?" Throughout I have been concerned with making as clear as I can what I consider to be the meaning of the Greek text that Matthew has bequeathed to the church.

Some readers will object that we cannot know this Evangelist's real meaning unless we take notice of what he has done to his sources: his alterations give us significant insights into his meaning. But if this is true, we can scarcely be sure of his meaning anywhere, for, despite the confidence with which some scholars put forward their hypotheses of the way Matthew worked, the Synoptic problem has not been solved. J. A. Fitzmyer is not being unreasonable or obscurantist when he points out that "the history of Synoptic research reveals that the problem is *practically insoluble*."[2] Nobody knows for sure what Matthew's sources were. Most of us agree that he used Mark (though some deny even this), and a few hold that he used Luke. Most scholars accept the Q hypothesis, but some are happy to dispense with Q, and of those who accept it there is no agreement as to its contents. Given such uncertainties, I think it best to focus on what Matthew has written, while keeping an open mind as to where he got it and how he used his sources.

For this commentary I have made my own translation of the text of Matthew from the Greek. Though it may not be the most elegant rendering, I have used it simply to let the reader know something of what I see in the Greek.

I am grateful to William B. Eerdmans, Jr., for the invitation to write this commentary; to Milton Essenburg for his consideration and expertise in editing a number of my books, including this one; and to many friends who have given me encouragement and help.

LEON MORRIS

2. *Jesus and Man's Hope* (Pittsburgh, 1970), p. 132; Fitzmyer's italics.

Chief Abbreviations

AB	*The Anchor Bible:* W. F. Albright and C. S. Mann, *Matthew* (New York, 1971)
Allen	W. C. Allen, *A Critical and Exegetical Commentary on the Gospel according to Matthew* (Edinburgh, 1907)
Argyle	A. W. Argyle, *The Gospel according to Matthew* (Cambridge, 1963)
AS	G. Abbott-Smith, *A Manual Greek Lexicon of the New Testament* (Edinburgh, 1954)
ASV	*The American Standard Version*
Augustine	Augustine, *Our Lord's Sermon on the Mount* (NPNF, 1st ser., vol. VI)
BAGD	Walter Bauer, *A Greek-English Lexicon of the New Testament and Other Early Christian Literature,* rev. and aug. by William F. Arndt, F. Wilbur Gingrich, and Frederick W. Danker from the 5th edn. (Chicago, 1979)
Barclay	William Barclay, *The Gospel of Matthew,* 2 vols. (Edinburgh, 1958)
BDF	F. Blass and A. Debrunner, *A Greek Grammar of the New Testament,* trans. and rev. by R. W. Funk (Chicago, 1961)
Beare	F. W. Beare, *The Gospel according to Matthew* (San Francisco, 1981)
BEB	W. A. Elwell, ed., *Baker Encyclopedia of the Bible* (Grand Rapids, 1988)
Bengel	J. A. Bengel, *Gnomon of the New Testament,* I (Edinburgh, 1866)
Black	Matthew Black, *An Aramaic Appoach to the Gospels and Acts* (Oxford, 1946)
Bonnard	P. Bonnard, *L'Evangile selon Saint Matthieu,* 2nd edn. (Neuchâtel, 1970)
Bruce	*The Expositor's Greek Testament:* A. B. Bruce, *The Synoptic Gospels* (Grand Rapids, 1979 rpt.)
Bruner	F. D. Bruner, *The Christbook, Matthew 1–12* (Waco, 1987)
BS	A. Deissmann, *Bible Studies* (Edinburgh, 1901)
Burton, *MT*	E. de W. Burton: *Syntax of the Moods and Tenses in New Testament Greek* (Edinburgh, 1955)
Buttrick	*The Interpreter's Bible,* VII: G. A. Buttrick, *The Gospel according to St. Matthew, Exposition* (Nashville, 1951)

Calvin	J. Calvin, *A Harmony of the Gospels, Matthew, Mark and Luke*, 3 vols. (Grand Rapids, 1980 rpt.)
Carr	*Cambridge Greek Testament:* A. Carr, *The Gospel according to St Matthew* (Cambridge, 1892)
Carson	D. A. Carson, *Matthew*, in F. E. Gaebelein, ed., *The Expositor's Bible Commentary*, vol. 8 (Grand Rapids, 1984)
Carson, *SM*	D. A. Carson, *The Sermon on the Mount* (Grand Rapids, 1982)
Cassirer	H. W. Cassirer, *God's New Covenant: A New Testament Translation* (Grand Rapids, 1989)
Chamberlain	W. D. Chamberlain, *An Exegetical Grammar of the Greek New Testament* (New York, 1941)
Chrysostom	John Chrysostom, *Homilies on St. Matthew* (NPNF, 1st ser., vol. X)
Danby	H. Danby, *The Mishnah* (Oxford, 1933)
Daube	D. Daube, *The New Testament and Rabbinic Judaism* (London, 1956)
Davies and Allison	W. D. Davies and D. C. Allison, *A Critical and Exegetical Commentary on the Gospel according to Saint Matthew*, vol. I (Edinburgh, 1988)
DB	F. C. Grant and H. H. Rowley, eds., *Dictionary of the Bible* (Edinburgh, 1963)
Derrett	J. D. M. Derrett, *Law in the New Testament* (London, 1970)
Diétrich	S. de Diétrich, *Saint Matthew* (London, 1962)
DM	H. E. Dana and J. R. Mantey, *A Manual Grammar of the Greek New Testament* (New York, 1927)
ET	*The Expository Times*
Fenton	J. C. Fenton, *The Gospel of St Matthew* (Harmondsworth, 1963)
Filson	F. V. Filson, *A Commentary on the Gospel according to St. Matthew* (London, 1960)
France	R. T. France, *The Gospel according to Matthew* (Leicester and Grand Rapids, 1985)
Glover	R. Glover, *A Teacher's Commentary on the Gospel of St. Matthew* (London, 1956)
GNB	*Good News Bible* (London and New York, 1976)
Green	H. B. Green, *The Gospel according to Matthew* (Oxford, 1975)
Green, M.	M. Green, *Matthew for Today* (London, 1988)
GT	*A Greek-English Lexicon of the New Testament*, trans. J. H. Thayer (Edinburgh, 1888)
GTJ	*Grace Theological Journal*
Grammatical Insights	Nigel Turner, *Grammatical Insights into the New Testament* (Edinburgh, 1965)
Gundry	R. H. Gundry, *Matthew* (Grand Rapids, 1982)
Gutzwiller	R. Gutzwiller, *Day by Day with Saint Matthew's Gospel* (London, 1964)
Hamann	H. P. Hamann, *The Gospel according to Matthew* (Adelaide, 1984)

Hendriksen	W. Hendriksen, *New Testament Commentary: Exposition of the Gospel according to Matthew* (Grand Rapids, 1973)
Hill	D. Hill, *The Gospel of Matthew* (London, 1972)
Horsley	G. H. R. Horsley, *New Documents Illustrating Early Christianity*, vols. 1-5 (Sydney, 1981-89)
IBD	*The Illustrated Bible Dictionary*, 3 vols. (Leicester, 1980)
IBNTG	C. F. D. Moule, *An Idiom Book of New Testament Greek* (Cambridge, 1953)
ICC	*The International Critical Commentary*
IDB	*The Interpreter's Dictionary of the Bible*, 4 vols. (Nashville, 1962; supplementary volume, 1976)
ISBN	*The International Standard Bible Encyclopedia*, 4 vols. (Grand Rapids, 1979-88)
JB	*The Jerusalem Bible* (London, 1966)
JBL	*The Journal of Biblical Literature*
Johnson	*The Interpreter's Bible*, VII: S. E. Johnson, *The Gospel according to St. Matthew, Exegesis* (Nashville, 1951)
JTS	*The Journal of Theological Studies*
Kingsbury	
Matthew	J. D. Kingsbury, *Matthew* (Philadelphia, 1986)
Story	J. D. Kingsbury, *Matthew as Story* (Philadelphia, 1988)
Structure	J. D. Kingsbury, *Matthew: Structure, Christology, Kingdom* (Philadelphia, 1975)
KJV	*The King James Version*
Knox	R. Knox, *The Holy Bible: A Translation from the Latin Vulgate* (London, 1955)
LAE	A. Deissmann, *Light from the Ancient East* (London, 1927)
Law	J. D. M. Derrett, *Law in the New Testament* (London, 1970)
LB	*The Living Bible*
Lenski	R. C. H. Lenski, *The Interpretation of St. Matthew's Gospel* (Minneapolis, 1964)
L'ÉSM	M. Didier, *L'Évangile selon Matthieu* (Gembloux, 1972)
Lightfoot	John Lightfoot, *A Commentary on the New Testament from the Talmud and Hebraica*, 4 vols. (Grand Rapids, 1979 rpt.)
Lloyd-Jones	D. M. Lloyd-Jones, *Studies in the Sermon on the Mount* (Grand Rapids, 1976)
LSJ	*A Greek-English Lexicon*, comp. by H. G. Liddell and R. Scott, rev. by H. S. Jones and R. McKenzie, 2 vols. (Oxford, 1940)
LXX	*The Septuagint*
M, I	J. H. Moulton, *A Grammar of New Testament Greek*, vol. 1, *Prolegomena* (Edinburgh, 1906)
M, II	*Ibid.*, II, *Accidence and Word Formation*, ed. W. F. Howard (Edinburgh, 1919)
M, III	*Ibid.*, III, *Syntax*, by Nigel Turner (Edinburgh, 1963)
M, IV	*Ibid.*, IV, *Style*, by Nigel Turner (Edinburgh, 1976)

McNeile	A. H. McNeile: *The Gospel according to St. Matthew* (London, 1915)
Meier	J. P. Meier, *Matthew* (Wilmington, 1980)
Melinsky	H. Melinsky, *Matthew* (London, 1965)
Metzger	B. M. Metzger, *A Textual Commentary on the Greek New Testament* (London and New York, 1971)
MM	J. H. Moulton and G. Milligan, *The Vocabulary of the Greek Testament* (London, 1914-29)
Moore	G. F. Moore, *Judaism*, 2 vols. (Cambridge, 1958), vol. 3 (1959)
Morgan	G. C. Morgan, *The Gospel according to Matthew* (London, n.d.)
Mounce	R. H. Mounce, *Matthew* (San Francisco, 1985)
NASB	*New American Standard Bible* (La Habra, 1972)
NBCR	*New Bible Commentary, Revised* (London, 1970)
NIDNTT	C. Brown, ed., *The New International Dictionary of New Testament Theology*, 3 vols. (Exeter, 1975-78)
NIV	*The Holy Bible, New International Version* (Grand Rapids, 1978)
Nixon	R. E. Nixon, *Matthew*, in D. Guthrie, J. A. Motyer, A. M. Stibbs, and D. J. Wiseman, eds., *The New Bible Commentary Revised* (London, 1970)
NPNF	Nicene and Post-Nicene Fathers
NRSV	*The Holy Bible: New Revised Standard Version* (Nashville, 1990)
NTS	*New Testament Studies*
ODCC	F. L. Cross, ed., *The Oxford Dictionary of the Christian Church* (London, 1958)
OED	*The Shorter Oxford English Dictionary*, 2 vols. (London, 1944; rpt. with corrections, 1959)
Patte	D. Patte, *The Gospel according to Matthew* (Philadelphia, 1987)
Phillips	J. B. Phillips, *The Gospels in Modern English* (London, 1957)
Plummer	A. Plummer, *An Exegetical Commentary on the Gospel according to S. Matthew* (London, 1910)
REB	*The Revised English Bible* (Oxford and Cambridge, 1989)
Redating	J. A. T. Robinson, *Redating the New Testament* (London, 1976)
Ridderbos	H. N. Ridderbos, *Matthew* (Grand Rapids, 1987)
Robertson	A. T. Robertson, *A Grammar of the Greek New Testament in the Light of Historical Research* (London, n.d.)
Robinson	T. H. Robinson, *The Gospel of Matthew* (London, 1928)
RSV	*The Revised Standard Version*
RThR	*The Reformed Theological Review*
Ryle	J. C. Ryle, *Expository Thoughts on the Gospels: Matthew* (London, 1965)
SBk	H. L. Strack and P. Billerbeck, *Kommentar zum Neuen Testament aus Talmud und Midrasch*, 4 vols. (Munich, 1922-28)
Schweizer	E. Schweizer, *The Good News according to Matthew* (London, 1976)

Sermon	W. D. Davies, *The Sermon on the Mount* (Cambridge, 1966)
SJT	*Scottish Journal of Theology*
SM	W. D. Davies, *The Setting of the Sermon on the Mount* (Cambridge, 1964)
Stanton	G. Stanton, ed., *The Interpretation of Matthew* (London and Philadelphia, 1983)
Stendahl	K. Stendahl, in *Peake's Commentary on the Bible*, ed. M. Black and H. H. Rowley (London, 1962)
Stonehouse	
Witness	N. B. Stonehouse, *The Witness of Matthew and Mark to Christ* (London, 1944)
Origins	N. B. Stonehouse, *Origins of the Synoptic Gospels* (London, 1964)
Stott	J. R. W. Stott, *The Message of the Sermon on the Mount* (Leicester, 1978)
Tasker	R. V. G. Tasker, *The Gospel according to St. Matthew* (London, 1961)
TDNT	*Theological Dictionary of the New Testament*, trans. G. W. Bromiley (Grand Rapids, 1964-76)
TIM	G. Bornkamm, G. Barth, and H. J. Held, *Tradition and Interpretation in Matthew* (London, 1963)
Trench	R. C. Trench, *Synonyms of the New Testament* (London, 1880)
Turner	N. Turner, *Grammatical Insights into the New Testament* (Edinburgh, 1965)
UBS[3]	United Bible Societies' *Greek New Testament*, eds. Kurt Aland et al., 3rd edn. (New York, 1975)
Use of the OT	R. H. Gundry, *The Use of the Old Testament in St. Matthew's Gospel* (Leiden, 1975)
Vermes	G. Vermes, *The Dead Sea Scrolls in English* (Harmondsworth, 1968)
Zahn	T. Zahn, *Das Evangelium des Matthäus* (Leipzig, 1922)

JEWISH TRACTATES

ʿAbod. Zar.	ʿAboda Zara	Dem.	Demai
ʾAbot	ʾAbot	ʿEduy.	ʿEduyyot
ʿArak.	ʿArakin.	ʿErub.	ʿErubin
B. Bat.	Baba Batra	Giṭ.	Giṭṭin
B. Meṣ.	Baba Meṣiʿa	Ḥag.	Ḥagiga
B. Qam.	Baba Qamma	Ḥul.	Ḥullin
Bek.	Bekorot	Ker.	Keritot
Ber.	Berakot	Ketub.	Ketubot

Ma'aś. Sh.	*Ma'aśer Sheni*	*Sanh.*	*Sanhedrin*
Mak.	*Makkot*	*Shab.*	*Shabbat*
Meg.	*Megilla*	*Shebu.*	*Shebu'ot*
Menaḥ.	*Menaḥot*	*Sheqal.*	*Sheqalim*
Ned.	*Nedarim*	*Soṭa*	*Soṭa*
Ohol.	*Oholot*	*Ta'an.*	*Ta'anit*
Pes.	*Pesaḥim*	*Ṭohar.*	*Ṭoharot*
Pesiq.	*Pesiqta Rabbati*	*Yad.*	*Yadaim*
Qidd.	*Qiddushin*	*Yebam.*	*Yebamot*
Rosh. Hash.	*Rosh. Ha-Shana*	*Yoma*	*Yoma*

Introduction

"In grandness of conception and in the power with which a mass of material is subordinated to great ideas no writing in either Testament, dealing with a historical theme, is to be compared with Matthew. In this respect the present writer would be at a loss to find its equal also in the other literature of antiquity."[1] In these words a great scholar of an earlier day brought out something of the majesty of our first Gospel.[2] We should bear this in mind when we recall how much this Gospel has suffered in modern discussions in comparison with the others. Mark is usually seen as the earliest of the four and as having a freshness about it that demands attention if we are looking for accurate information about Jesus. Luke is much fuller, and the beauty of his writing is so impressive that E. Renan called it "the most beautiful book that there is."[3] John is very different from the other three and more theological. The result is that in modern times Matthew has often been slighted. It is good that such views are becoming outmoded.[4]

To disparage Matthew is a great mistake. Nobody should minimize the importance of the Gospel that contains the infancy stories, the Sermon on the Mount, and a rich collection of parables (many of which we find in this Gospel only), to name but a few of its contents. All four Gospels emphasize the passion narratives (giving rise to the view that they are all passion narratives with extensive introductions). But each has its own way of doing this, and while Matthew is usually held to rely heavily on Mark, his Gospel includes matter not found elsewhere (e.g., Jesus' threefold prayer in Gethsemane, Jesus' confidence that he could call on more than twelve legions of angels, and the suicide of Judas). This Evangelist makes it clear that the death of Jesus was in fulfilment of the plan of God;

---

1. Zahn, cited in Lenski, p. 20.
2. Mounce remarks, "Matthew is the Gospel that over the years has shaped the life and thought of the church"; he cites Renan's view that it is the most important book ever written (p. xiii).
3. *Les Évangiles* (Paris, 1877), p. 283.
4. Graham Stanton points to the recent spate of books and articles on Matthew and sees debate now as "keener than ever. So many of the distinctive features of this Gospel continue to fascinate and to puzzle scholars that it is no exaggeration to suggest that Matthew is a new storm centre in contemporary scholarship" (Stanton, p. 1).

1

sometimes he brings out its meaning explicitly, as when he says that Jesus came to give his life "a ransom for many" (20:28) or when he reports that Jesus spoke of the wine at the Last Supper as "my blood of the covenant, which is poured out for many for the forgiveness of sins" (26:28).

We should not overlook the fact that throughout most of the centuries of the Christian church this Gospel has been held to be the most important we have. In the ancient MSS it is the first of the four, and in common use it was clearly held to be the most important.[5] R. T. France writes, "it is a fact that mainstream Christianity was, from the early second century on, to a great extent Matthean Christianity."[6] We must not read back our prejudices into the early church; while few interpreters these days would endorse the verdict of the early church on the importance of this Gospel, we should not minimize the force of the considerations that produced that verdict.[7] The contribution our first Gospel has made to the church throughout the centuries must not be overlooked nor minimized. And it still has much to say to the church today.

I. DISTINCTIVE CHARACTERISTICS

Matthew shares many features with the other Gospels, but some of them are especially characteristic of the first Gospel.

A. Jewishness

The writer seems concerned throughout to show that Christianity is the true continuation of the Old Testament — the true Judaism, if we may put it that way. He was clearly a knowledgeable Jew, well acquainted with the kind of teaching we find in the Mishnah and the Talmud, and some would

---

5. Not only in ancient times. Johnson points out that "in the 1929 revision of the American Book of Common Prayer Matthew is favored over Luke with thirty-seven to thirty-three pericopes, John being used twenty-seven times and Mark six times." He goes on to say that the layman may claim that John or Luke is his favorite but he will probably "make actual use more often of Matthew" (p. 231).

6. *Matthew: Evangelist and Teacher* (Exeter, 1989), p. 20. He cites E. Massaux, "Matthew seems to have been the only one to have had a normative role, and to have created the climate of Christianity at large" (p. 16).

7. Curiously F. W. Beare calls this Gospel "a grim book," "singularly lacking in those notes of joy that sound through the writings of Luke. The Christ that he presents is on the whole a terrifying figure. . . . There is little trace here of a gospel of grace abounding to the chief of sinners" (p. viii). He speaks of Matthew as paving the way for "a new legalism" (p. 6). Has he not noticed the note of joy at the beginning and end of the Gospel (2:10; 28:8) and, of course, in between as well (e.g., 5:12; 13:44, etc.)? And what sort of legalism is it of which even Beare can say, "Wealth cannot purchase an entrance (i.e. into the kingdom). . . . It is not a reward for virtue or for any kind of human achievement" (p. 36)? There can be no greater emphasis on the significance of love, love to God and love to people, than we find in Matthew 22:37-40. Such a misunderstanding of Matthew as Beare's is not helpful.

say not averse to the use of Midrash. He does not find it necessary to explain Jewish customs (compare 15:1-9 with Mark 7:1-13). He begins his genealogy with Abraham, the great ancestor of the Jewish race (1:1-2). He alone tells us that Jesus was sent to "the lost sheep of the house of Israel" (15:24; cf. 10:5-6). He writes of matters that would interest Jews, such as the Sabbath (12:1-14) and the temple tax (17:24-27).[8] Not all his comments, of course, are favorable to the Jews. There are some strong criticisms, notably in chapter 23, and we should notice his use of expressions like "their" scribes (7:29) and "their" synagogues (9:35), which distance the author from official Judaism.[9]

But most of all he was a genuine follower of Jesus, a convinced Jewish Christian. A striking example of his Jewishness is his emphasis on the fulfilment of prophecy. He has a formula, "that it might be fulfilled which was spoken by the Lord through the prophet — ," which we find as early as 1:22 and which recurs throughout the Gospel. From another angle, the United Bible Societies' *The Greek New Testament* (3rd edn.) lists 61 quotations from the Old Testament in this Gospel compared with 31 in Mark, 26 in Luke, and 16 in John. Clearly the writer has a special interest in what the Old Testament Scripture says and the way it applies to Jesus. And it is not only the number of quotations that is important; it is the way they are used. Running throughout this Gospel is the thought that God is working his purpose out and that one way in which that purpose is to be discerned is the manner in which what God has inspired his prophets to say can be seen to have been fulfilled in the life and teaching of Jesus. And this Gospel ends with the great commission to make disciples from all the nations (28:16-20). Matthew has a Jewish background and he is deeply interested in Jews, but he is also interested in the relevance of Jesus for all the nations.

B. Fulfilment in Christianity

As we have indicated, the idea that what God was promising in the Old Testament scriptures is fulfilled in Christianity runs throughout this Gospel. This is to be seen in the many references to the fulfilment of prophecy, but, as Albright and Mann point out, "It was of the essence of the Gospel — supremely exemplified in Matthew and in Paul's teaching — that all Israel's experience had been gathered up, fulfilled, in Jesus."[10] We find it, for example, in the theme of kingship that features so prominently in this book. Jesus is seen as the Messiah (Matthew has the term

8. In this Gospel "we see, as we could see nowhere else, how believers of the same race as Jesus, brought up in the same religious tradition, with the same spiritual ancestry, looked upon the Christ" (Robinson, pp. x-xi).

9. S. van Tilborg puts great emphasis on Matthew's criticisms of Judaism, so much so that he views the author as a Gentile (*The Jewish Leaders in Matthew* [Leiden, 1972], p. 171).

10. *AB*, p. XXII. They also say, "Matthew seems to have been influenced most by the theological idea of fulfillment" (p. XXVI).

"Christ" 17 times, whereas Mark, whom he follows so closely, has it 7 times, and Luke 12 times; John, however, uses it most,[11] with 19 references). Matthew refers to Jesus as "the Son of David" 8 times (with another use of the term for Joseph [1:20]), an expression with overtones of royalty. This is brought out especially in a passage where Matthew emphasizes that Jesus is greater than David (22:41-45). He also refers to "the kingdom of heaven" 32 times, "the kingdom of God" 5 times, "the kingdom" 6 times, and "the kingdom of the Son of man" 3 times. But however it is expressed, the thought is that the divine kingdom has drawn near in the person of Jesus. It is another way of bringing out the fulfilment of the divine purpose, and it is a Jewish way of doing this.

In addition, it is a way of emphasizing that the blessing of God that the Jews had looked for had now passed to the followers of Jesus. The Jews had not recognized the divine visitation when the Son of God came among them: "Many will come from the East and the West and will recline with Abraham and Isaac and Jacob in the kingdom of heaven" (8:11). With this we should take the many passages that speak of those who will or who will not enter the kingdom. There can be no doubt that these point to a Jewish way of thinking, but no doubt either that this Evangelist looks for them to be fulfilled in the followers of Jesus, not the Jewish nation.

C. Ecclesiastical Interest

By the time this Gospel was written the followers of Jesus were clearly distinct from the Jews (and not merely a group among the Jews as they had been in Jesus' lifetime). Matthew is interested in them as a separate group, and it may be significant that he is the only one of our Evangelists to use the word "church" (16:18; 18:17). This can be exaggerated, and not too much should be built on the use of this particular word. But throughout the Gospel there is clearly an interest in the church as an organization. Its relationship to Jesus Christ is brought out in the incident in which Jesus spoke of building his church on Peter's confession of his messiahship and the fact of its continuing existence in the passage in which Jesus tells his followers what to do when a brother offends and when he speaks of the power of binding and loosing (18:15-18). Matthew is very interested in Peter, and he has this apostle appear frequently in his narrative (even if it may be going a trifle too far to say, "if he had named his own book he might well have called it 'The Good News According to Peter'").[12]

Perhaps we should notice here Kilpatrick's view that this Gospel is to be understood as a lectionary. He argues that the church would have

11. That is, most in the Gospels; Paul is the big user of the term, employing it 379 times.

12. Johnson, p. 234.

4

taken over the synagogal custom of the regular reading of Scripture, that Mark had been used in Christian services of worship, and that Matthew was written "as a kind of revised gospel book, conveniently incorporating into one volume the three documents Mark, Q, and M."[13] He holds that Matthew "was intended primarily to serve a liturgical purpose," and he concludes his book with "The revision, if so we may describe it, was carried out so successfully that the Gospel, itself the most used of the four, has had no successors."[14] The case is argued with learning and skill, but few have been persuaded. There are some grievous weaknesses. For example, Kilpatrick assumes far too easily that we know what was done in first-century synagogues. We should not assume that the church was taking over a well-known custom of the Jews, for we at any rate do not know what the Jews did by way of lectionary, if indeed they had a lectionary.[15] And he ignores the New Testament indications that there was a strong charismatic element in early Christian worship. It is hard to fit a lectionary into the worship of which we read in 1 Corinthians (where it was not even known for certain who would preach, 1 Cor. 14:30). That this Gospel came to be used in church services is clear enough. That it was written to be used as a lectionary is not and is highly unlikely.

Krister Stendahl refers to Kilpatrick's work and proceeds to sum up his own notable contribution to Matthean studies in this way: "We have elsewhere suggested a somewhat broader and yet more specific interpretation of the nature of Mt. by calling it a handbook for teaching and administration within the church, and we have compared its form with the Manual of Discipline from Qumrân."[16] Stendahl stresses Matthew's use of the Old Testament and speaks of a "school" with its own methods of interpretation. Not many scholars today accept his entire theory, but the comparison of Matthew to the Manual of Discipline is often accepted.

D. Anti-Pharisaism

Matthew also has a strong polemic against the Pharisees. These men formed a highly regarded sect among the Jews and were insistent that the traditions that came from the great ones of the past must be adhered to. They could not recognize the hand of God in what Jesus was doing, but opposed him at every turn. Matthew reports Jesus' criticisms of the

13. G. D. Kilpatrick, *The Origins of the Gospel according to St. Matthew* (Oxford, 1946), p. 70. This may be a simplistic view of what Matthew has done.

14. *Ibid.*, pp. 77, 141.

15. I have examined this problem in *The New Testament and the Jewish Lectionaries* (London, 1964). We should not forget that the account in Luke 4 is the oldest one we have of a synagogue service, nor that it is still not clear when either of the two principal lectionary systems, the one-year cycle and the three-year cycle, made its appearance. It is hazardous to argue from Jewish practice when we know so little about it.

16. K. Stendahl, p. 769.

Pharisees as well as the attempts of these Jewish leaders to defeat the purposes of God he discerned in what Jesus taught and did.

E. The Gentiles

Matthew is interested in the way Gentiles were drawn in to follow Jesus. We do not find here the universalism of Paul or of Luke, but there is an insistence that Gentiles have their place in the divine scheme of things, and specifically in receiving the teaching and the help of Jesus. Thus Matthew reports the coming of the Magi to see the infant Jesus, he centers much of what he has to say on "Galilee of the Gentiles," and he recounts stories like that of the healing of the centurion's slave and of the daughter of the Canaanite woman.

F. Teaching

Matthew has a great interest in the teaching of Jesus,[17] and he expresses what he says very clearly.[18] Thus the Sermon on the Mount is one of five great discourse sections, many parables are recorded, and from time to time there are statements that Jesus taught, without his teaching being expressly included in the Gospel. It is plain that Matthew valued the teaching of Jesus and made a point of passing a good deal of it on to his readers. He was also, it would seem, both a good teacher himself and a man with a great interest in the teachers in the church. There is little doubt that he wrote in such a way as to be of help to them (cf. Filson, "His immediate aim is to provide the Church's teachers with a basic tool for their work").[19] Writing in a day when the possession of books was not common, he puts a good deal of teaching in a form easily memorized.[20] He also arranges things in threes (three messages to Joseph, three denials of Peter), sevens (seven parables in ch. 13, seven woes in ch. 23), and other numerical groups that could be readily memorized.

Matthew has a great gift for economy of words; where he shares a narrative with Mark he is almost always shorter. Thus France points out that to tell the story of the woman with a haemorrhage Mark takes 154 words and Luke 114, but Matthew uses only 48 words. "Yet Matthew's bare account contains all the essential elements: the length of her illness,

17. G. Bornkamm heads his discussion of this Gospel "The Teacher of the Church (Matthew)" and finds a "didactic concern" that "stamps the whole Gospel" (*The New Testament: A Guide to its Writings* [London, 1974], pp. 57, 60).

18. Johnson can say, "His prose differs from that of Plato to approximately the extent that the English in the news columns of a well-written metropolitan daily differs from that of Shakespeare and the King James Version. The Greek of the Gospel is fluent and clear, easily read by simple people but generally without offensive colloquialisms" (p. 239).

19. Filson, p. 20.

20. E. von Dobschütz says that Matthew "likes echoes"; he points to this apostle's penchant for using formulas repeatedly and for saying the same thing twice (Stanton, p. 20).

her conviction that a mere touch of his garment would suffice, Jesus' declaration, 'Take heart, daughter, your faith has made you well', and the fact of her instant healing."[21] But where he has additional information that he sees as important he can be longer than the others, as when he adds the words about Jesus being sent only to the lost sheep of the house of Israel to the story of the Canaanite woman (15:24).

Matthew has five considerable sections of teaching (chs. 5–7, 10, 13, 18, 23–25) — a fact that B. W. Bacon made the basis of a view that attracted a good deal of support, namely, that Matthew is replacing the five books of Moses with five books of the messianic Torah.[22] Sometimes this notion is linked with suggestions of a New Moses or a New Exodus, but this does not seem to be what Matthew is driving at. W. D. Davies has examined Bacon's view and concluded that Matthew's "fivefold structure cannot certainly be held to have any theological significance, that is, it does not necessarily point to a deliberate interpretation of the Gospel in terms of a new Pentateuch, as, in its totality, a counterpart to the five books of Moses."[23] Anyone who works with this Gospel must come to some conclusion about the sections into which it may be divided, but the difficulty in doing this is brought out by the fact that Filson comes up with three different outlines, each based on a way of looking at the Gospel as a whole.[24]

We should also bear in mind that seeing Jesus' teaching merely in five discourses may be a trifle too confident. Furthermore, it involves lumping together chapters 23–25, whereas most students regard chapter 23 as a discourse distinct from chapters 24 and 25. H. B. Green also draws attention to the importance of chapter 11 and speaks of seven discourses.[25]

---

21. *Matthew: Evangelist and Teacher*, p. 134.

22. This view was accepted, for example, by R. H. Fuller, who could write, "The clue to Mt's theology is the five discourses. These correspond with the 5 books of the Pentateuch. Jesus is the second Moses, the founder and lawgiver of the new Israel, the church" (*A Critical Introduction to the New Testament* [London, 1966], p. 117). But in this Gospel Jesus is not the second Moses; as W. D. Davies puts it, "He is not Moses come as Messiah, if we may so put it, so much as Messiah, Son of Man, Emmanuel, who has absorbed the Mosaic function" (*Sermon*, p. 27).

23. *SM*, p. 107. There are problems in detail, such as the difficulty of finding anything corresponding to Leviticus in Matthew's arrangement.

24. Filson, pp. 22-23. Davies questions "the extreme scepticism" about our knowledge of the life and teaching of Jesus. "First, the milieu within which Jesus appeared was conditioned for the faithful reception and transmission of tradition" (he draws attention to the oral transmission of matter now in the Mishnah). "Secondly, the technical formulae describing the reception and transmission of tradition emerge so clearly in the NT documents that we must believe that the early Christian communities handed on a tradition." Thirdly, Jesus may have been bilingual and certainly many early Christians were, so that teaching could be transferred to Greek accurately. "Fourthly, it is highly pertinent to note that there was frequent intercourse between figures such as Peter, and other apostolic guardians of the tradition, and Christian communities in various places, so that the transmission and development of the tradition were not unchecked" (*Sermon*, pp. 127-28; cf. also *SM*, pp. 416-17).

25. F. L. Cross, ed., *Studia Evangelica*, IV (Berlin, 1968), pp. 48-49.

The resemblance to the Pentateuch has to be read into this Gospel; it is not the most natural way of understanding it.

G. The Kingdom

An important feature of Matthew's Gospel is his emphasis on God's kingdom. As we noted earlier, he uses the expression "the kingdom of heaven" most frequently (32 times), though he also has the expression favored in the other Gospels, "the kingdom of God" (5 times), as well as "the kingdom" (5 times), and once also (in prayer) "your kingdom." He uses expressions like "the kingdom of their Father" and "the kingdom of my Father," and he refers to the kingdom of the "Son of man" (13:41, etc.). Ten times he introduces parables with "The kingdom of heaven is like —." Sometimes the kingdom is clearly future (25:31), but sometimes it is thought of as coming in the person of Jesus (4:17; 12:28). For Matthew it is important that God is sovereign over all and that his rule will one day be brought to a glorious consummation. The present or the future aspect of the kingdom underlies a great deal of what is written in this Gospel.

Kingsbury draws attention to the importance of the expression "the gospel of the kingdom" (4:23; 9:35, etc.) and regards it as Matthew's own designation of "the contents of his work . . . an expression that enables him to summarize in the same terms both the pre-Easter message of Jesus and the post-Easter message of his church."[26] This may be going too far; after all, Matthew does head his work "The book of the story of Jesus Christ" (1:1). But it does draw attention to the importance of the kingdom for Matthew.

II. DATE

The testimony of antiquity is unanimous that the author of this Gospel was Matthew the apostle and that this was the first Gospel to be written. If this is accepted, the Gospel will have been written quite early. After examining the evidence from the patristics, France concludes: "Altogether, then, the patristic evidence seems unanimous that Matthew was written not later than the early sixties."[27]

But modern scholarship finds this conclusion more than a little difficult. It is generally held that this Gospel shows evidence of dependence on Mark (the passages common to the two Gospels are such that it is highly improbable that Mark used Matthew). Since Mark is thought to have been written not before about A.D. 65, this means that Matthew would

---

26. *Structure,* p. 10.

27. *Matthew: Evangelist and Teacher,* p. 83. Irenaeus says that this Gospel was written while Peter and Paul were preaching in Rome (*Adv. Haer.* 3.1.1). We are not aware of these two apostles preaching in Rome together, but clearly Irenaeus thinks of this Gospel as written in the 60s.

be dated at the earliest in the 70s. This evidence would be stronger if Mark could be dated with certainty.[28]

Many scholars find evidence for a somewhat late date in the use of expressions like "until now," "until today" (11:12; 27:8; 28:15). But it is fairly countered that such expressions might well be used of something that happened twenty or thirty years ago, which would still enable us to date the Gospel in the 50s or 60s. Again, Matthew has a number of references to the destruction of Jerusalem, from which it has been concluded that he wrote after that city had been overthrown. Similarly it is suggested that the reference in the parable to the king who sent his armies and burned up the city refers to the destruction of Jerusalem (22:7).[29] But those who speak so confidently of this verse as referring to the fall of Jerusalem usually overlook the fact that the city was not in fact burned. Josephus tells us that the temple was burned (*War* 6.249-50), but he does not speak of the city as destroyed by fire.[30] Some expressions in Jesus' eschatological discourse are also said to reflect the overthrow of that city (e.g., 24:15-19). But all these references are general and point to the kind of thing that was common when armies captured cities, so that they scarcely amount to more than predictions that Jerusalem would be destroyed. And with the continuing strife between Jewish hotheads and the Romans, together with the well-known Roman attitude toward rebellion, to forecast that Jerusalem would be destroyed, and more specifically that it would be burned, would require no supernatural insight. We should not overlook Jesus' "immediately" (24:29); it is curious that Matthew should be reporting without qualification that Jesus said the end of the age would follow "immediately" after the destruction of Jerusalem if he is writing after the city has fallen.[31]

The references to the church (16:18-19; 18:17-18) are adduced as pointing to a development that must have taken time to bring about. To

---

28. Gundry, p. 601, points out that we have less evidence for the dating of Mark than we have for that of Matthew, so that we should date Mark from Matthew, not the reverse.

29. That these words were written after the destruction of the city is not at all obvious, despite the arguments of scholars who accept this point of view. J. A. T. Robinson is not persuaded, and he cites K. H. Rengstorf and Sigfried Pedersen as others who do not accept it (*Redating*, p. 20).

30. He points out that the Romans apparently did not try to burn the temple and makes this the responsibility of the Jews: "The flames, however, owed their origin and cause to God's own people" (*War* 6.251); the defenders themselves kindled the flames, at least in part. The Romans then set the surrounding buildings alight (*War* 6.281). But it was at a later time that the city as a whole was captured and Titus entered it (*War* 6.409), and later still that "the whole city" and what was left of the temple were "razed to the ground" (*War* 7.1).

31. C. C. Torrey long ago argued that "all four Gospels were written before the year 70"; he pointed out that "The supposed references" to the overthrow of Jerusalem by the Romans "are in every word and without exception merely repeated from Old Testament prophecies." He proceeds to cite the relevant prophecies (*The Four Gospels* [London, n.d.], p. 256). More recently J. A. T. Robinson has also argued that the Gospels must have been written before A.D. 70 (*Redating*, ch. 2).

which it is countered that there is no indication of any significant development of church order; the organization presupposed in these passages is of the simplest sort and does not require anything more complex than is revealed in the Pauline letters. Unless we read later ideas into them, the references do not demand anything beyond the primitive Palestinian communities from what we know of them. So with the allegation that the apostles are highly reverenced and that the writer softens or omits derogatory references. Paul insisted on the dignity of an apostle at a date earlier than any usually adduced for any of the Gospels. It has been suggested that the appearance of false prophets (7:15, 22) indicates a late date, but once again Paul shows that false prophets made their appearance quite early.

With this we should take the anti-Jewish tone of some parts of the Gospel (cf. 8:10-12; 21:43; 23, etc.). This is said to be the kind of thing we might expect in the period from A.D. 85 on, when the Jewish authorities were excluding Christians from their synagogues. Not as much is known about this process of exclusion and its precise dating as is sometimes claimed, but in any case the situation reflected in this Gospel is not that of a definite break. Rather, it is the sort of thing we would expect when different kinds of Jews were arguing with one another, with the messianic Jews still hoping that other Jews would come to see things their way. Acts provides evidence that from quite early days orthodox Jews took action against Christians (Acts 4:1-3, 17-18; 5:40; 13:50, etc.).

Some aspects of this Gospel do point to an early date. Thus it was clearly the favorite Gospel in the early church, but it lacked the prestige of a center like Rome or Ephesus and there was no suggestion of a Peter (as in the case of Mark) or other outstanding figure behind it; Matthew was always a comparatively unimportant apostle. Again, the Judaic elements in the Gospel would have discredited it if it had appeared when the separation between church and synagogue had progressed beyond the early stages. We should not miss the point that the references to the destruction of Jerusalem are all forward looking and therefore should be taken to point to a time before it occurred. Some interpreters point out that there is no reference to the Pauline epistles, whereas it might be expected that a late writing would show knowledge of, for example, the list of resurrection appearances (1 Cor. 15:5-8). It has further been pointed out that Matthew's story of the temple tax (17:24-27) implies that it is proper for Jewish followers of Jesus to pay that tax. This would apply before A.D. 70, for during that period the tax went to maintain the temple at Jerusalem. But after that date the Romans insisted that, while the tax must be paid by all Jews, it was to be used for the support of idol temples. It is not easy to see why the story should be included without qualification if it was written after A.D. 70. Matthew refers to the Sadducees 7 times (as many as all the other books of the New Testament put together; Mark and Luke have the term once each). This reflects the time before A.D. 70; after that date we hear little of the Sadducees. Jesus' warning against flight in winter or on a Sabbath (24:20) reads strangely if the flight had already taken place. Gundry gives further indication of an early date when he points out that this Gospel evidences in its quotations a "working upon the Hebrew text of the OT," for after the church broke from the synagogue "access to Hebrew scrolls must have been difficult."[32] J. A. T. Robinson argues that there was probably a "proto-Matthew" (reflected in some parts of the Didache) and that this was later enlarged. He says, "The final stages of the three synoptic gospels as we have them would then have occupied the latter 50s or early 60s."[33]

From all this it is clear that there is little hard evidence to determine the date of this Gospel. Most modern scholars date it somewhere in the period from the 70s to the 90s, but there is good reason for seeing it as appearing before A.D. 70, perhaps the late 50s or early 60s. We can scarcely be more definite.[34]

III. PLACE OF ORIGIN

Very little can be said about the provenance of this writing. The indications that it was written for a Jewish Christian community might point to a place in Palestine, and this is supported by the tradition recorded by Papias that it was written for Hebrews. This would apply to Palestine, but also to such a center as Antioch in Syria.[35] That city had a sizeable number of Jews in it, and we know from Acts that quite early there was a Christian church there, a church that was very active, for example, in sending out missionaries like Paul and Barnabas (Acts 13:1-3). It is not unlikely that it was in this center that our first Gospel was written. This view is supported by the fact that Ignatius, bishop of Antioch in the early second century, almost certainly refers to this Gospel when he speaks of Christ as having been baptized by John, "that all righteousness might be fulfilled by him" (*Smyrn.* 1.1; this appears to be a quotation from Matt. 3:15). G. D. Kilpatrick has difficulties with Antioch and prefers one of the Phoenician cities, perhaps Tyre or Sidon.[36] Another suggestion is that some place in Palestine itself was the origin, perhaps Caesarea.[37] A few interpreters have thought

32. *Use of the OT*, pp. 178-79.

33. *Redating*, p. 116; cf. pp. 99, 107.

34. B. Reicke can say, "The situation presupposed by Matthew corresponds to what is known about Christianity in Palestine between A.D. 50 and ca. 64, but not after the flight of the Christians in ca. 64 and the start of the Jewish war in A.D. 66" (D. E. Aune, ed., *Studies in New Testament and Early Christian Literature* [Leiden, 1972], p. 133).

35. B. H. Streeter argued strongly for Antioch as the place of origin (*The Four Gospels* [London, 1930], pp. 500-527).

36. *Origins*, ch. VII; the conclusion is reached on p. 134.

37. The case for Caesarea was persuasively argued by B. T. Viviano (*CBQ*, 41 [1979], pp. 533-46).

that Alexandria is likely the place where this Gospel came into being.[38] Certainty is impossible, but most commentators agree that a place in Syria (or perhaps even Palestine) is likely.

IV. AUTHORSHIP

The external evidence is unanimous that the author was Matthew, one of the twelve apostles. Thus Irenaeus says, "Matthew also issued a written Gospel among the Hebrews in their own dialect, while Peter and Paul were preaching at Rome, and laying the foundations of the Church" (*Adv. Haer.* 3.1.1). According to Eusebius, Origen held that Matthew was the first of the Gospels to be written and that it was written in Hebrew (*Eccl. Hist.* 6.25.4), and Eusebius himself held that Matthew, having first preached to Hebrews, wrote his Gospel for them "in his native language" when he was on the point of leaving them (*Eccl. Hist.* 3.24.6). Eusebius also refers to the writings of Papias, bishop of Hierapolis c. 60-130 (so *ODCC*), and says that according to Papias: "Matthew collected the oracles in the Hebrew language, and each interpreted them as best he could" (*Eccl. Hist.* 3.39.16).[39] Eusebius denies that Papias was a hearer of the apostles, but the passage he quotes from Papias to show this says that that worthy proposed to set down "all that I ever learnt well from the presbyters." He goes on to speak of "the words of the presbyters, what Andrew or Peter or Philip or Thomas or James or John or Matthew, or any other of the Lord's disciples, had said," and further, "what Aristion and the presbyter John, the Lord's disciples, were saying" (*Eccl. Hist.* 3.39.3-4). Papias is claiming that he had information from people who had heard a number of the apostles, and he speaks of two disciples as still speaking. Papias is thus an early witness. Irenaeus says that he was a hearer of John and a companion of Polycarp (*Adv. Haer.* 5.33.4).[40]

---

38. van Tilborg argues this (*The Jewish Leaders*, p. 172).

39. Unfortunately Papias's work is no longer extant; therefore we must depend on the quotations made in Eusebius. Allen thinks that Papias's work may well have been "a book containing sayings, discourses, and parables." He points out that about two-fifths of Matthew consists of sayings and suggests that someone took the sayings from Papias and worked them into a larger book, our Gospel. It then came to be named from the author of the sayings book that had been incorporated in it (pp. lxxx-lxxxi). Barclay has much the same view (I, p. xxi). T. W. Manson (*Sayings*, pp. 27-30) and others argue that Papias is referring to the document we call Q. Robinson holds that " 'logia' means the Old Testament," so that Papias may have been referring to a "collection of 'oracles' dealing with the Messiah, such as might be used by the Christian to prove to the Jew that Jesus was the Christ. We know that such collections were current in the third century, and that they passed in the western church under the name of 'Testimonies,' but in the Jewish church the need for them would be immediate and urgent" (p. xv).

40. C. S. Petrie argues strongly that Papias must be taken seriously and that he testifies to Matthew as the author of the Gospel composed in the Hebrew language (*NTS*, XIV [1967-68], pp. 15-32).

Gundry devotes a good deal of attention to the statements of Papias, which he dates before A.D. 110 and which he understands to mean that "John the elder and apostle ascribes the first gospel to the Apostle Matthew."[41] Gundry denies that we should understand Papias to be saying that Matthew wrote in Hebrew; rather, in describing Matthew, " 'a Hebrew dialect' means a Hebrew way of presenting Jesus' messiahship."[42] Not everyone will be convinced by Gundry's argument, but at least he makes it clear that Papias does not rule out Matthean authorship of our first Gospel as decisively as some critics hold. Rather, he should be understood as strengthening the evidence for Matthew as the author.

A puzzle is posed, on the one hand, by the fact that there is widespread agreement in antiquity that Matthew was an early Semitic writing and, on the other, by the fact that the Gospel we have must be regarded as originally written in Greek, not as a translation. This may be why some scholars hold that our Greek Matthew is not a translation of a Hebrew or Aramaic original but a new recension of it.[43]

It is widely agreed by critical orthodoxy that this Gospel was not written by Matthew or for that matter by any close personal follower of Jesus. It is pointed out that the writer makes use of earlier written documents, such as Mark and Q (the symbol to denote a source containing the matter common to Matthew and Luke but not in Mark). M is also included to denote the matter peculiar to this Gospel, which is also understood as coming from a written source. Attention is also drawn to the omission of words and phrases that seem to belittle Jesus or to emphasize the limitations of the Twelve. These are important considerations and must be given due weight.

There remains the fact that in ancient tradition this book is universally ascribed to Matthew. To name anyone else as the author is to affirm that the name of its true author was forgotten within a comparatively short time (about 50 years?) and another name substituted, especially since Matthew was not, as far as our information goes, especially prominent either among the Twelve or in the early church. Accordingly, there seems to be no reason for assigning to him such an important writing unless in fact he wrote it. But against Matthean authorship it is pointed out that just as ancient tradition is unanimous in saying that Matthew was the author, so is it unanimous in saying that he wrote it in Hebrew. Now this Gospel is written in good idiomatic Greek, and there is no indication that it was translated from a Semitic original.[44] If the tradition was wrong about the

41. Gundry, p. 620.
42. *Ibid.*, pp. 619-20.
43. See Hendriksen, p. 91. C. F. D. Moule suggests that "the oracles" point us to some "early Semitic source lying behind both Matt. and Lk." and thinks that Papias's reference to each translating them as best he could may explain some of the differences between Matthew and Luke (*The Birth of the New Testament* [London, 1962], p. 89).
44. A. Wikenhauser remarks, "It may be taken as certain that an Aramaic original of

book's being a translation, it is argued, it could also be wrong about its author. It could, of course, but the one does not necessarily imply the other. Perhaps Matthew wrote a Gospel in Aramaic that later was lost. Or perhaps one of the sources that lie behind this Gospel was in Aramaic.

It is routinely pointed out that none of the ancient MSS of this Gospel says that Matthew was the author. This argument should be looked at more closely than it usually is, despite the fact that it is almost universally accepted by modern scholarship. It takes no note of the fact that, whether in ancient or modern times, few books give any indication of authorship beyond the title page (other than autobiographies or books in which the author plays a prominent part). The title page indicates the author quite clearly, and there is no reason for repeating the information anywhere else in the book. Now none of the oldest MSS of this Gospel has been preserved with the title page intact, but from the earliest ones that do have it onward the book is invariably ascribed to Matthew. This point is of greater weight than is usually recognized. We must face the fact that throughout antiquity it is accepted that Matthew wrote this Gospel and that there is no other name in the tradition.[45]

This argument is sometimes supported by the fact that Matthew was a tax collector[46] and therefore would necessarily have had literary skills. He would certainly have had some experience in writing and would have known Greek, but we can scarcely go beyond that, as far as his occupation is concerned.[47] An objection to Matthew as the author is that an apostle would not have used the work of one who did not belong to the apostolic

---

the Gospel of St. Matthew can be defended only if we regard Greek Mt. not as a literal translation of the Aramaic, but as a thorough revision made with frequent use of the Gospel of St. Mark." He adds that this "is consistent with the decision of the Biblical Commission" (*New Testament Introduction* [New York, 1958], p. 195).

45. Fenton remarks, "It is possible that this Gospel was from the first published with the title *According to Matthew*" (p. 136).

46. Matthew is said to be a tax collector in 9:9; 10:3 and a member of the Twelve in 10:3; Mark 3:18; Luke 6:15. The tax collector is called Levi in Mark 2:14; Luke 5:27, but, although it is unusual for the same man to have two Hebrew names (though he might have a Hebrew and a Greek name, like Saul who was called Paul), it seems that all these references are to the same man. He uses the general word for money, *nomisma*, and the words for "gold" 5 times, "silver" 10 times (two words), and "talent" 14 times, a total of 29, whereas Mark refers to "silver" once and Luke has it 4 times; they have none of the other words for big currency. Matthew also has references to coins such as the *assarion*, the *chalkos*, the *denarius*, the *didrachma*, the *kodrantes*, and the *stater*. Mark and Luke mention some of these coins, but not as many as Matthew.

47. C. F. D. Moule remarks, "Is it not conceivable that the Lord really did say to that tax-collector Matthew: You have been a 'writer' (as the Navy would put it); you have had plenty to do with the commercial side of just the topics alluded to in the parables — farmer's stock, fields, treasure-trove, fishing revenues; now that you have become a disciple, you can bring all this out again — but with a difference?" (F. L. Cross, ed., *Studia Evangelica*, II [Berlin, 1964], p. 98). Gundry argues that Matthew "was a notetaker during the earthly ministry of Jesus and that his notes provided the basis for the bulk of the apostolic gospel tradition," citing the practice in "ancient schools" by which notes taken by students "became the common possession of the schools and circulated without the name of the author" (*Use of the OT*, p. 182).

band, namely Mark. To that two things could be said. One is that while it is likely that this Evangelist used Mark's Gospel, we must bear in mind that this has never been proved beyond any doubt and that some great names are ranged against the view. The other is that no reason appears to be adduced to rule out an apostle's using the work of a nonapostle.[48] Why should this not happen? In an age when authors seem to have copied from one another far more than they do today there seems to be no objection to the view, provided that Matthew thought the source reliable. And he would be especially ready to use it if he was aware of the tradition that Peter was associated with Mark in the writing of his book.[49]

In the last resort it appears that the authorship of this Gospel will remain in dispute. In my opinion there is more to be said for the apostle Matthew than recent scholarship commonly allows and more for Matthew than for any other candidate. But the evidence certainly falls short of complete proof, and in the end divergent views will continue to be held.[50]

V. SOURCES

Most of the content of Mark is also found in this Gospel, though generally in a shorter form.[51] Most scholars have concluded that our author was apparently glad to use the earlier Gospel, but did not appreciate the length at which Mark wrote his stories. It is also clear that he shared with Luke a source with a good deal of information that we do not find in Mark.[52] There is a problem in the fact that sometimes Matthew and Luke agree against Mark, and when they differ from one another sometimes one and sometimes the other agrees with Mark. In my opinion critics generally have paid too little attention to Luke's express statement that "many" have taken it on themselves to write on this subject (Luke 1:1). While not everybody could read and write in the first century, many people could, and the

48. Cf. R. M. Grant, "This claim does not seem very convincing. We cannot tell whether or not an apostle would have followed such a procedure. An apostle might have believed that Mark's outline was largely correct but needed some revision and some supplementation" (A Historical Introduction to the New Testament [London, 1963], p. 129).

49. N. B. Stonehouse argues strongly for Matthean authorship in Origins of the Synoptic Gospels (London, 1964), pp. 1-47.

50. A. F. J. Klijn finds many questions about the authorship of this Gospel undecided, but does not consider this very important, "For none of the other gospels bear less the personal imprint of their authors than does this one" (An Introduction to the New Testament [Leiden, 1967], p. 34).

51. I have discussed the Synoptic problem, the way the three Synoptic Gospels relate to one another, in Luke: An Introduction and Commentary² (Leicester and Grand Rapids, 1988), pp. 51-63.

52. An exception is M. D. Goulder, who holds that Matthew was composed as a lectionary. He agrees that the author had Mark before him but "no Q, no M, and very little oral tradition" (Midrash and Lection in Matthew [London, 1974], p. xiii). His suggestion has attracted a good deal of attention but seems to me to be inadequately based. I have discussed his work with other lectionary hypotheses in "The Gospels and the Jewish Lectionaries," in R. T. France and David Wenham, eds., Gospel Perspectives, III (Sheffield, 1983), pp. 129-56.

Pauline correspondence, for example, is evidence that Paul knew that in every congregation there were people who could read what he wrote. It is in the highest degree likely that others than our four Evangelists and the authors of such sources as Q wrote about the life and teaching of Jesus. But since their writings have perished we have no way of knowing what was in them. We should not presume that everything that has come down to us was originally in Mark, Q, M (Matthew's special source), and L (Luke's special source). There must have been many other writings about Jesus, and we have no way of knowing whether Matthew used any of them or not.

Critical orthodoxy works on the "Two Document" theory, the view that Matthew and Luke had before them two documents, Mark and Q.[53] Sometimes this is expressed as a "Four Document" theory, adding M (the source of what Matthew alone has) and L (what Luke alone has). A good deal can be accounted for on this basis, but there are some difficulties, such as the agreements of Matthew and Luke against Mark. How could this happen if there were no more than four sources and the final two Evangelists followed their sources reasonably closely? Such problems have caused some scholars to rethink the process, and in recent years there has been a revival of the hypothesis of J. J. Griesbach. This view dispenses with Q and takes Matthew to be the first Gospel to have been written, followed by Luke and then Mark.[54] On this view Mark was produced by reworking some of the material in the two longer Gospels. Perhaps there was some rivalry between supporters of Matthew and Luke, and this Gospel was produced to take up a mediating position.[55] More can be accounted for on this hypothesis than a good number of critics have conceded, but it still remains unsatisfactory.[56] It is not easy to understand why Mark in abbreviating Matthew should so consistently come up with narratives that are longer as well as more lifelike.

It appears that many writers are all too ready to ignore Luke's express statement (to which we have already referred) that "many" had written before him. In the first century literacy was reasonably widespread, and the New Testament gives ample evidence that writing was congenial to the early Christians. Why should we limit the accounts of Jesus' teaching

53. Many scholars have been too confident about Q, and there have been criticisms. O. Linton, to name but one, has subjected the hypothesis that there was such a source to critical examination. He agrees that there was such a source, but it does not account for anything like all the non-Markan matter that is common to Matthew and Luke (D. E. Aune, ed., *Studies in the New Testament and Early Christian Literature*, pp. 43-59).

54. Hamann thinks that the order was Matthew, Mark, and Luke (p. 306).

55. There are, of course, still other theories. F. Neirynck, for example, has given close attention to the theory of A. Gaboury which puts heavy emphasis on the order of the pericopes: "One guiding principle pervades the whole study of the phenomenon of order: the evangelists never altered the order of incidents they found in their sources. This principle is extremely simple indeed, but it forces the author to an unnecessary multiplication of sources" (*L'ÉSM*, pp. 37-69; the quotation is from p. 68). Such theories are unsatisfactory.

56. For example, there is B. H. Streeter's objection to the view that Mark has abbreviated Matthew: "only a lunatic would leave out Matthew's account of the Infancy, the Sermon on the Mount, and practically all the parables, in order to get room for purely verbal expansion of what was retained" (*The Four Gospels* [London, 1930], p. 158).

to the four Gospels plus three hypothetical sources? It seems much more likely that many did write about Jesus but that in time most of their works perished. When the four Gospels were produced they evidently were so superior to the other writings about Jesus in circulation that in time they drove the rest out of business. Why go to all the trouble of copying a source when you could have it incorporated with other material in a satisfying Gospel? It seems to me not only that have we not solved the Synoptic Problem, but also that we are not likely ever to solve it. Too much of the writing of the early church has perished.[57]

It is suggested that Matthew's infancy narratives give evidence of a Hebrew source. Thus there is a play on the words "Jesus" and "Savior" in 1:21,[58] which is natural in Hebrew but impossible in Aramaic. This suggestion may be supported by some of the quotations from the Old Testament. Many come from LXX, but there is a group of quotations introduced by "that it might be fulfilled which was spoken through the prophet" or similar words (1:22-23; 2:5-6, etc.). Except for 3:3 all are found in Matthew only. These are not as close to LXX as other quotations in this Gospel and may be independent translations from the Hebrew. Some differ from our Hebrew text (as 1:23; 2:6; 4:15; 13:35). Such considerations may point us to a source or sources. But we can scarcely say more.

I cannot leave this section on sources without drawing attention to a point made so well by Patte: "Some may be surprised that I do not pay more attention to Matthew's sources and to the way in which he modifies them. I simply take seriously the fact that when an author duplicates a source and makes it part of his or her own discourse, he or she has appropriated that source. In other words, even when Matthew duplicates exactly what one of his sources says, the passage has to be viewed as expressing *Matthew's* convictions and views."[59] Many commentaries spend a good deal of time on what Matthew has done to his sources. While I concede that much can be learned from such exercises, I agree with Patte that when Matthew incorporates a source it is because he has made it his own and wants to express what that source is saying. It is more important to understand what the words mean in their new situation than to engage in scholarly niceties about how they came to be there.[60]

---

57. Albright and Mann further draw attention to the vitality of oral tradition and open the possibility that "Mark and Matthew may represent two quite separate collections of tradition" (*AB*, p. XLVIII). We should not let our familiarity with a multiplicity of printed books hide from us the importance of oral tradition in a day when all books had to be laboriously written by hand.

58. "Jesus" is יֵשׁוּעַ and "will save" is יוֹשִׁיעַ; "since such a play is not possible in Aramaic, a Hebrew original must underlie the verse" (McNeile).

59. Patte, p. 12.

60. Cf. Brevard S. Childs, "the assumption that the many tensions within the Gospel are to be resolved by sharply distinguishing between tradition and redaction (cf. Strecker, Schulz) renders impossible a canonical reading of the Gospel as a whole. Thus the judgment that portions of ch. 5 are 'traditional ballast' which distort Matthew's real intention, is a highly tendentious approach" (*The New Testament as Canon: An Introduction* [London, 1984], p. 62).

17

Matthew 1

I. THE BIRTH AND INFANCY OF JESUS, 1:1–2:23

The opening to this Gospel[1] is quite different from that of any of the others. Its prologue is the shortest of the four, except for that of Mark. Indeed, it is best regarded as no more than a heading. Immediately and without further discussion the narrative launches into the genealogy of Jesus.

> [1]*The book of the story of Jesus Christ, the son of David, the son of Abraham.*

1. Matthew has his own way of beginning a Gospel: none of the other Evangelists begins like this. His opening word is the normal word for "book,"[2] though BAGD notes that in later writings it was especially used of a "sacred, venerable book," which thus makes it very suitable for the kind of book that Matthew was writing. That lexicon does not note its use for anything other than a book of some sort, which makes it unlikely that we should take Matthew to be referring to a short section such as the nativity stories. The word I have translated *story*[3] is difficult. The term is

---

1. Kingsbury argues strongly that the canonical Gospels are to be understood as biographies, albeit "of the nature of ancient biography" rather than biography of the modern type (*Matthew*, pp. 9-13). But this is to ignore the fact that from the earliest days εὐαγγέλιον is applied to them; whatever else we may say about these books, they are "Jesus Christ's good news" (Mark 1:1). Kingsbury shows a better appreciation of what Matthew is doing when he writes, "Matthew's document is of the nature of a 'gospel,' that is to say, a kerygmatic story. Its purpose is, again, to announce the news that saves or condemns which is revealed in and through Jesus Messiah, the Son of God, and is proclaimed first to Israel and then to the gentiles to the effect that in him the eschatological rule of God has drawn near to humankind" (*Matthew*, p. 29).
2. βίβλος, here only in Matthew, occurs 10 times in the New Testament. The original form was βύβλος, which denoted "the Egyptian papyrus, Cyperus Papyrus" (LSJ; it suggests that the form βιβλ- arose "by assimilation in βιβλίον"). It lacks the article since this is a heading (cf. M, I, p. 82). In the plural βίβλος came to denote strips of the plant, which were made into the writing material papyrus. Thus it came to mean a roll of papyrus, a book.
3. γένεσις has about it the idea of "origin" or "source" (BAGD notes its use "in the subscription of the infancy narrative of Pythagoras"); it is understood in this way by most translators and commentators, who often translate it by "genealogy." But its use in Genesis 2:4 is surely in the sense "This is the account of the heavens and the earth when they were created" (*NIV; NRSV*'s "These are the generations of the heavens and the earth . . ." is scarcely

used of birth or origin or existence, but none of these meanings is easy to see in the present passage. There is evidence that the word was already used as the title of the first book of the Old Testament in LXX,[4] and it may well be that Matthew used it as the title of the book in which he would write about the new genesis, the new creation in Jesus Christ. The two opening words are combined elsewhere in Scripture only twice. In Genesis 2:4 the combination seems clearly to be used as the heading for the history that follows, and that seems the best way to take it also in Genesis 5:1. These examples may well give us the clue to its meaning here. The expression is best seen as the heading for the whole Gospel. It has usually been regarded as simply introducing the genealogy, but it would be curious to have a heading for the first half chapter and not one for the book as a whole.[5] Zahn was surely right when he saw the meaning as "Book of the History of Jesus Christ."[6] Beare thinks that the expression was intended to be "the title of the entire Gospel," and he says that it conveys the thought "that this will be the story of the New Creation."

Matthew is saying, then, that his book is the story *of Jesus Christ*. He does not use the full name *Jesus Christ* very often; indeed, this is the only place where it certainly occurs in this Gospel (it is read by many MSS in v. 18 and 16:21, but in each case omitted by others). Matthew probably saw it as appropriate in the heading of his book. His normal custom is to use the personal name *Jesus*,[7] which he does 150 times (Mark has this name 81 times, Luke 89, and John 237). We should perhaps notice that he uses the term only in narrative; no one in this Gospel addresses Jesus by his name. Matthew uses *Christ* only 17 times (Mark 7, Luke 12, and John 19). The word is, of course, a title; it means "anointed" and is the Greek way of referring to "Messiah." The title was used so often by Christians that in time it came to be a proper name, but Matthew's sparing use of it probably reflects the fact that this was not the case in Jesus' lifetime.[8] It

---

intelligible); "account" or "history" is the meaning. It occurs also in Genesis 5:1, where *NIV* has "This is the written account of Adam's line." The emphasis in Genesis 5:1 is on Adam who began the line, but in Matthew it is on Jesus in whom the line reached its consummation.

4. Davies and Allison draw attention to the earliest MSS of LXX and to early writers like Justin and Origen for this title.

5. See Bonnard for the idea that the words form a heading for both the genealogy and the whole book. Fenton regards it as telescopic, referring first to the genealogy, then the birth, then the life-story, and finally "the whole new creation which begins at the conception of Jesus and will be completed at his second coming." R. L. Overstreet writes, "it seems best to understand it as not being a reference to the birth alone of Christ, but rather as an introduction to his life and acts. In other words, the phrase seems to introduce the complete book of Matthew" (*GTJ*, 2 [1981], p. 306). See also Davies and Allison, and Davies, *SM*, pp. 67ff.

6. Cf. W. Marxsen, "By means of this phrase therefore the work is presented almost as 'Holy Scripture' — by analogy with the Old Testament — to which one can appeal and from which one can take one's bearings if one wishes to observe or teach others to observe what Jesus commanded" (*Introduction to the New Testament* [Philadelphia, 1974], p. 151).

7. *Jesus* is the Latin form of the name = Ἰησοῦς, the Greek form of the Hebrew *Jeshua*, a shorter form of *Jehoshua*, which means "Yahweh is salvation."

8. See further my *New Testament Theology* (Grand Rapids, 1986), pp. 125-26.

surely has messianic significance in the way this Evangelist uses it. Normally he has the definite article with the name *Jesus*, but its omission here in the heading to the book should not unduly surprise us (he omits the article with this name in all 19 times).

He goes on to speak of Jesus as the *son of David*;[9] he was of royal descent. Matthew uses the name of the great king 17 times, which is more than in any other book of the New Testament (next is Luke with 13). The expression "son of David" is probably a messianic title.[10] David was the greatest of the kings of Israel. Since he was a mighty warrior, the title would have pointed to a conquering Messiah, one who would destroy the enemies of Israel and establish God's kingdom with its capital at Jerusalem. It may well be that its militaristic associations account for the sparing use of the title among the Christians. To have made it central would have been to invite misunderstanding among those who dwelt on David's military feats. Matthew has *son of David* 9 times (one referring to Joseph, 1:20; Mark and Luke each have it 3 times, and no other New Testament writer uses it). Its use here shows that Matthew plans to bring out what is meant by the Davidic Messiah. Interestingly, he uses it most frequently when people are appealing to Jesus for help (9:27; 15:22; 20:30-31). But it also appears in the story of the triumphal entry (21:9, 15), indicating that Matthew is not unaware of the royal associations of the term. His book is to be about one who fulfilled all that is meant in being the descendant of Israel's greatest king.[11]

Jesus was also the *son of Abraham*, "to whom the divine promises were first given and with whom 'sacred history' may be said to have begun" (Tasker). It was Abraham with whom God made the covenant that set Israel apart in a special sense as the people of God (Gen. 12:2-3; 15:17-21; 17:1-14). All Israelites took pride in being descendants of the great patriarch, and the Christians were especially fond of him as the classic example of one who believed (Paul brings this out particularly in Romans). His Hebrew name means "father of a multitude" (Gen. 17:5), and it had been prophesied that all nations would be blessed through him (Gen. 12:3).[12]

---

9. Both *son of David* and *son of Abraham* lack the article; this is probably because we are still involved in the title of the book. υἱός can mean "son" in the sense of a direct male offspring, or, as here, of a more remote male descendant. It may also be used of followers (as in "the sons" of the Pharisees, 12:27), or of members of a large group (cf. "the sons of men," Mark 3:28), or of those who share similar ideas or experiences such as "the sons of the kingdom," 8:12), or of "the sons of light" (Luke 16:8). It is, of course, frequently used of Jesus, as in a special sense "the Son of God."

10. It occurs in the *Psalms of Solomon*, "raise up to them their king, the Son of David" (17:23). It is not found often in pre-Christian days, but in post-Christian times it was common as a designation of the Messiah (SBk, I, p. 525). That this goes back to the time of Jesus seems clear from 22:41-45.

11. G. Dalman has an important discussion of "Son of David" in *The Words of Jesus* (Edinburgh, 1902), pp. 316-24. See also my *New Testament Theology*, pp. 126-27.

12. Many interpreters view this as the wrong way to interpret Gen. 12:3, but Robinson points out that it "goes back at least to the LXX and dominated all later exegesis."

We find the idea of a universal blessing at the end of this Gospel as well as at the beginning (28:19). In combining David and Abraham Matthew is drawing attention to two strands in Jesus' Hebrew ancestry and implying that he fulfilled all that would be expected in a Messiah with such connections.

A. THE GENEALOGY OF JESUS, 1:2-17

²*Abraham fathered Isaac, and Isaac fathered Jacob, and Jacob fathered Judas and his brothers,* ³*and Judas fathered Phares and Zara from Thamar, and Phares fathered Esrom, and Esrom fathered Aram,* ⁴*and Aram fathered Aminadab, and Aminadab fathered Naasson, and Naasson fathered Salmon,* ⁵*and Salmon fathered Boes from Rachab, and Boes fathered Jobed from Ruth, and Jobed fathered Jessai,* ⁶*and Jessai fathered David the king.*

And David fathered Solomon from the wife of Ourias, ⁷*and Solomon fathered Roboam, and Roboam fathered Abia, and Abia fathered Asaph,* ⁸*and Asaph fathered Josaphat, and Josaphat fathered Joram, and Joram fathered Ozias,* ⁹*and Ozias fathered Joatham, and Joatham fathered Achaz, and Achaz fathered Ezekias,* ¹⁰*and Ezekias fathered Manasses, and Manasses fathered Amos, and Amos fathered Josias,* ¹¹*and Josias fathered Jechonias and his brothers at the removal to Babylon.*

¹²*And after the removal to Babylon Jechonias fathered Salathiel, and Salathiel fathered Zorobabel,* ¹³*and Zorobabel fathered Abioud, and Abioud fathered Eliakim, and Eliakim fathered Azor,* ¹⁴*and Azor fathered Sadok, and Sadok fathered Achim, and Achim fathered Elioud,* ¹⁵*and Elioud fathered Eleazar, and Eleazar fathered Matthan, and Matthan fathered Jacob,* ¹⁶*and Jacob fathered Joseph the husband of Mary, from whom was fathered Jesus who is called Christ.*

¹⁷*All the generations from Abraham to David were fourteen generations, and from David to the removal to Babylon were fourteen generations, and from the removal to Babylon to the Christ were fourteen generations.*

Matthew begins with a genealogy. This seems to us a strange way to begin a book, but the Jews were very interested in records of descent. There are many examples of this in the Old Testament, the early chapters of 1 Chronicles forming a notable example (Matthew's genealogy seems to depend on 1 Chronicles 1–3, with a little help from Ruth 4; from Zerubbabel on the source is unknown — perhaps it was a family record). Nearer to New Testament times Josephus begins his autobiography by tracing the names of his ancestors, whom, he says, "I cite as I find it recorded in the public registers" (*Life* 1); his reference to the "public registers" is significant and points to widespread interest. Jesus' genealogy shows that he is of royal descent.

Matthew takes his genealogy back no farther than Abraham (Luke goes back to Adam). From Abraham to David the genealogy is much the same as in Luke, though, of course, the two arrange the names differently: Luke goes from son to father and Matthew from father to son. The striking differences in the genealogies from David on present a difficult problem. Some commentators suggest that Matthew gives us the genealogy of Joseph (the legal father) and Luke that of Mary (the actual line). This is unlikely, for genealogies were not reckoned through the mother (though, of course, we must reckon with the fact that we have no information about what would happen when there was no human father). In any case Luke speaks of "Joseph the son of Eli" (Luke 3:23), which certainly does not read as though he were giving Mary's genealogy. Another supposition is that there had been a levirate marriage when Eli died childless; Jacob, with the same mother but a different father, married the widow, and Joseph was his son. This is ingenious, but it lacks evidence. The best suggestion is that Matthew's list represents the legal descendants of David, those who would actually have reigned had the kingdom continued, while Luke gives the descendants of David in the line to which Joseph belonged.[13] But we have no way of being certain.

A feature of Matthew's genealogy is his arrangement, as he tells us, in three groups of fourteen (v. 17). The reason for this is not clear, but it must have been important because Matthew has to omit some names to get his numbers. His second group lacks Ahaziah, Joash, and Amaziah after Joatham (v. 9),[14] and his third group has only thirteen (since it covers some 500 years, there have clearly been omissions).[15] The omissions need not worry us since "father" might be used when speaking of any descendants and not only those in the immediate family (e.g., 3:9).[16] As it stands

---

13. See J. G. Machen, *The Virgin Birth of Christ* (London, 1958), p. 204.

14. From his understanding of 1 Chronicles 3:11-12 (LXX) Allen argues that the three omitted are Joash, Amaziah, and Azariah. This involves accepting Οζεια or Οζιας (which normally in LXX = Uzziah) in 1 Chronicles 3:11 (Rahlfs reads Οχοζια, which normally in LXX = Ahaziah), and assuming that Matthew or a copyist has passed from Οζεια to Uzziah's son, Jotham. *AB* accepts this view and further posits "an editor assimilating Matthew's list to the LXX record." Nothing appears to be gained by this hypothesis, and it is simpler to see an omission of Ahaziah, Joash, and Amaziah. Marshall D. Johnson argues for an accidental scribal omission of the names Azariah, Joash, and Amaziah and "that accident was turned into virtue — that after the accidental omission the scribe discovered a second pattern of fourteens which came to determine the structure of the genealogy" (*The Purpose of the Biblical Genealogies* [Cambridge, 1969], p. 182).

15. Schweizer holds that, since ancient reckoning always included the first and last names in series, we should probably understand the sequence as "from Abraham to David, fourteen; from David (counted a second time) to Josiah, the last free king, fourteen; from the first king of the captivity, Jehoiakim, to Jesus, fourteen." Or we may be meant to count Jeconiah twice, once as the last name in the second division and once as the first name in the third. Another suggestion is that we should take one "Jeconiah" as really "Jehoiakim," who is not otherwise mentioned in the list.

16. That the Jews shortened genealogies is seen by comparing Ezra 7:1-5 with 1 Chronicles 6:3-15 (Ezra has even omitted his own father!). Overstreet comments, "Apparently to the Jewish mind this was a proper thing to do, and it is not unusual to find Matthew omitting names in his genealogy" (*GTJ*, 2 [1981], p. 310).

the list certainly highlights Abraham the founder of the line, David the ideal king, and the exile to Babylon. The fourteens may come about through gematria, which takes the numbers signified by the letters as significant. Thus many interpreters point out that the numbers indicated by the letters of the Hebrew word for David add up to fourteen and detect an emphasis on the royal kingship which reaches its climax in Jesus. A less likely suggestion is that three times fourteen (= 6 × 7) means six weeks of people leading up to the age of the Messiah. Diétrich understands fourteen (2 × 7) as "the symbol of plenitude, of something complete."

It is unusual, though not unexampled (see 1 Chron. 2:4; 3:5), to find names of women in a genealogy, but here we have four. In Jewish writings it is not uncommon to find four women singled out for special mention: Sarah, Rebecca, Rachel, and Leah. But Matthew's four — Tamar, Rahab, Ruth, and Bathsheba — are probably all Gentiles; and since Ruth was a Moabitess, we should not overlook the fact that to the tenth generation a Moabite was not to be admitted to the congregation (Deut. 23:3). Three of the four are of morally dubious reputation. Matthew is surely saying that the gospel is for all people, not Jews only, and that the gospel is for sinners. It is a sinful world, and Matthew is writing about grace.[17] Stendahl thinks the mention of these women is a preparation for the "holy irregularity" of the virgin birth.

The comparative disuse in modern times of the verb "beget" presents a problem in translation; Matthew's verb denotes the action of the male parent, but the repetition of "begot" sounds strange today. *NRSV* and others render it "was the father of," which refers to a state rather than an event. I have used the word "fathered," which is not an ideal translation but gives us the general idea. Throughout the genealogy Matthew has the article with the names; this appears to have been a colloquial usage since it is neither the classical nor the normal New Testament custom (cf. BDF, 260). He mostly uses the forms of names in LXX rather than those in the Hebrew and seems to depend largely on 1 Chronicles 2–3.

2-6. Matthew here employs the form Ἰακώβ for Jacob, a form he uses for the father of Joseph in verses 15 and 16 and which elsewhere in the New Testament always denotes the patriarch.[18] Judah's *brothers* do not

---

17. "The number and the choice are intentional, not accidental. The Evangelist has a point to make through them. He wishes to show that the genealogy of Christ, embracing the whole history of Israel, bears witness not only to its high points but also to the sin and unworthiness which run through this history even at its high points, i.e., in the age of the patriarchs and the house of David. . . . the history of the people elected to be the people of the Messiah is one of grace rather than glory" (G. Kittel, *TDNT*, III, p. 1). Barclay envisions a grand sweep, "In his genealogy Matthew shows us the royalty of kingship gained; the tragedy of freedom lost; the glory of liberty restored. And that, in the mercy of God, is the story of mankind, and of each individual man."

18. Cf. BAGD, "This, the un-Grecized form of the OT, is reserved for formal writing, and esp. for the patriarch"; for other people the Grecized form Ἰάκωβος is usual (Matthew has it 6 times).

feature in the genealogy, but they are important in the Old Testament. And brotherhood is an important concept for Matthew (he has the word "brother" 39 times, the same number as in 1 Corinthians and the most in any book in the New Testament apart from Acts, which has it 57 times). Thamar is the first woman to be mentioned in the genealogy;[19] this is curious not only because she was a woman but because the children were conceived out of wedlock. This is the first point at which the genealogy differs from that in Luke. There Esrom's son is Arni, Arni's son is Admin, and Admin's son is Aminadab (Matthew omits Admin and agrees with Ruth 4:19-20). Only here do we find Rahab featured in David's ancestry. This fact is not recorded elsewhere in Scripture, nor in other Jewish writings.[20] And the information about Ruth is not found in Chronicles; it is recorded in Ruth 4:13-22. When he comes to David, Matthew adds *the king;* this is where kingship is attained in the line he is tracing. Now Matthew is very interested in kingship and uses the word "king" 22 times, more than any other book in the New Testament. He uses it in a variety of ways, referring to King Herod, the king in a parable, and the Son of man as King on Judgment Day. Here he is making it clear that there is royalty in Jesus' line so that he is rightly called "King of the Jews" (2:2; 27:11, 29, 37, 42).

7-11. Problems arise in that the name of Jehoiakim is omitted and there is no mention of any brothers of Jeconiah (= Jehoiachin) in the Old Testament. But Matthew's interest in brothers accounts for the inclusion of the reference even though we do not know where he got it (Ridderbos thinks that they were mentioned not because of their importance but because of their unimportance! It is that kind of genealogy). The second section of the genealogy concludes with the deportation to Babylon,[21] a very significant happening in the history of the nation.

12-16. Had Jehoiakim been included, we would have had fourteen names in this third section, so the omission is curious.[22] The genealogy concludes with Joseph, described as *the husband of Mary* but not as the father of Jesus. Matthew will tell us a little later that the child was conceived as a result of the activity of the Holy Spirit (v. 20).[23] The passive form here is probably the "divine passive," indicating an activity of God;

19. Just as γεννάω is normally used of the action of the father, so ἐκ is used of the mother.

20. See Marshall D. Johnson, *The Purpose of the Biblical Genealogies,* pp. 162-65.

21. The genitive Βαβυλῶνος illustrates the indefiniteness of the genitive. The form denotes no more than "a Babylon-type removal" and could denote a removal to Babylon or from Babylon or even of Babylon. But our knowledge of history shows us that the meaning must be "to Babylon." Moule sees this as a "strongly adjectival use" (*IBNTG,* p. 38).

22. One factor may be that the names Jehoiakim and Jehoiachin are both rendered Ιωαχιμ in LXX.

23. The Sinaitic Syriac MS reads "Joseph, to whom was betrothed Mary the virgin, begot Jesus who is called the Christ," and this is occasionally accepted (as, e.g., by Moffatt). But Metzger's discussion shows that there is no reasonable doubt that this reading should be rejected.

it certainly points to something different from what precedes and it prepares us for the narrative of the virgin birth. That the virginal conception
is in mind in the genealogy is probably another way of bringing out the
truth that Jesus was the "son of David."[24] There is another passive in verse
20, and twice Matthew speaks of Jesus' conception as due to the Holy
Spirit (vv. 18, 20). He also cites prophecy to show the real significance of
the child who was to be born (vv. 22-23); further, he tells us that Mary was
a virgin (v. 23) and that Joseph had no sexual relations with her before the
birth of Jesus (v. 25). All this combines to make it clear that Matthew is
writing about the coming into the world not simply of another baby, but
of the very Son of God.

17. Matthew explains what he is about by referring to his three
groups of fourteen. Clearly the number is significant for him, but unfortunately he does not explain why. But the note of fulfilment is strong, and
perhaps Marshall D. Johnson gives us the answer: "The function of the
genealogy — the note of fulfillment — explains the lack of a precise and
exact parallel with contemporary sources: *the two genealogies of Jesus in the
NT are the only extant Messianic genealogies* which are written to prove that
the Messiah has come."[25] We should perhaps bear in mind also the point
made by L. Finkelstein that the number fourteen was regarded as significant in contemporary Judaism. He says, "The number, 'fourteen', is not
accidental. It corresponds to the number of high priests from Aaron to the
establishment of Solomon's Temple; the number of high priests from the
establishment of the Temple until Jaddua, the last high priest mentioned
in Scripture. It is clear that a mystic significance attached to this number,
in both the Sadducean and the Pharisaic traditions."[26] Matthew would
have been aware of this and may be producing an argument that would
impress Jews.

B. THE BIRTH OF JESUS, 1:18-25

> [18]Now the birth of Jesus Christ was like this. Mary his mother was
> engaged to Joseph, but before they came together she was found to be
> pregnant by the Holy Spirit. [19]And Joseph her husband, being a just man
> and not wishing to expose her publicly, decided to divorce her secretly. [20]But

---

24. Cf. Patte, "A son of David is not someone primarily characterized by a certain
biological descendance but someone whose existence has been brought about by the intervention of God. A child of David and of Abraham is someone who owes his or her origin
(*genesis*) to God." He notes that in 3:9 the Pharisees and Sadducees cannot really claim to be
children of Abraham, and that God can raise up children to Abraham out of the very stones.

25. *The Purpose of the Biblical Genealogies,* p. 208 (Johnson's italics). Cyrus H. Gordon
has a note in which he points out that there are many examples in antiquity of people who
claimed to have a divine father as well as a human father. He does not dispute that Jesus'
fatherhood was special, but simply points out that dual fatherhood did not sound as paradoxical in the first century as it does to us (*JBL,* 96 [1977], p. 101).

26. Cited in *SM,* pp. 303-4.

when he had made up his mind to do this, look, an angel of the Lord appeared
to him in a dream and said, "Joseph, son of David, don't be afraid to take
Mary your wife, for what has been conceived in her is from the Holy Spirit.
21She will give birth to a son, and you will call his name Jesus; for he will
save his people from their sins." 22Now all this happened so that it might
be fulfilled which was spoken by the Lord through the prophet, saying,
23"Look, the virgin will conceive and bear a son, and they will call his name
'Emmanuel,' which means, 'God with us.'" 24And Joseph, when he had
awakened from his sleep, did as the Lord's angel directed and took his wife;
25and he had no intercourse with her until she had given birth to a son.
And he called his name Jesus.

Matthew tells the story of the birth of Jesus from the standpoint of
Joseph rather than that of Mary, as Luke does. Luke accordingly has such
stories as the appearance of the angel to Mary, but Matthew simply says
that Mary became pregnant due to an activity of the Holy Spirit and goes
on to tell his readers what Joseph did. It would have been expected that
he would have divorced Mary, but an angelic visitor told him not to do
so. Matthew tells us how Joseph obeyed the angel. Matthew's account is
clearly quite independent of that of Luke, but it emphasizes equally the
virgin birth.27 We should notice (a) the emphasis on the place of Joseph,
(b) the important place of divine guidance given in dreams, and (c) the
repeated references to the fulfilment of prophecy.

18. Matthew has a kind of subheading to let the reader know that
he will now tell us about the birth28 of *Jesus Christ* (see on v. 1; this seems
to be the probable reading, though some MSS have "Jesus" or "Christ").
The formal name and title are suited to the opening of the narrative proper,
and the unusual use of the article points back to the Jesus Christ already
referred to.29 He does not tell the reader who Joseph and Mary were;
evidently he can presume that they will know this. Similarly, he does not
speak explicitly of the virginal conception; that, too, he evidently presumes
is known. The word I have translated *engaged*30 indicates a firm commit-

27. Gundry holds that "We only have to suppose that Matthew had the traditions that
later went into Luke 1–2 to see what happens under his artistry." Matthew, he thinks, "turns
the annunciation to Mary before her conceiving Jesus (Luke 1:26-38) into an annunciation to
Joseph after her conceiving Jesus." Plummer, by contrast, holds that neither narrative "can
have been based on the other." He finds "signs of historic reality" in the "delicacy and sobriety
of both narratives" in sharp contrast to pagan legends, Jewish stories (as in the Book of
Enoch), and Christian apocryphal Gospels (p. 4).

28. For γένεσις see on verse 1. Here it signifies "coming into being" and thus "birth."
The δέ is continuative; it links the account with the preceding.

29. Most MSS read τοῦ δὲ Ἰησοῦ Χριστοῦ, but the article is very rare with Ἰησοῦς Χριστός.
Χριστοῦ is read by a number of Western sources, but Metzger points out that this may be no
more than an assimilation to the reading of the preceding sentence. Similarly, Ἰησοῦ (W) may
conform this passage to the words of the angel (v. 21). It seems better to retain the harder
reading.

30. μνηστεύω, elsewhere in the New Testament only in Luke 1:27; 2:5, signifies "woo

ment, normally undertaken a year before marriage. During that year the girl remained with her own family, but the tie established was a strong one and was really the first part of marriage. A betrothed woman could be punished as an adulteress (Deut. 22:23-24; the punishment of "a virgin who is not betrothed" was different, vv. 28-29). The second part took place when the man took the woman to his home (cf. v. 20; cf. also 25:1-13). That Mary became pregnant *before they came together*[31] was thus very serious, as Joseph's attitude makes clear. Some translations read "she found out" *(GNB, REB)*, but the passive more likely refers to Joseph's becoming aware of the situation. The whole story is written from his point of view. But before speaking of Joseph's attitude Matthew explains that the pregnancy was due to an activity of the Holy Spirit. He speaks with reverent reserve and says no more.[32] The Spirit is called "Holy," an adjective not applied to him in Philo or Josephus (so BAGD, 5c). The idea that the Spirit is holy is distinctively Christian. Matthew often has the expression without the article (as here).[33]

19. Joseph, Mary's husband,[34] is called *just,* which probably means that he was careful in his observance of the law.[35] The passage that covered

---

and win, betroth" (BAGD). It was a binding arrangement, and the betrothed could be called "the wife" of her fiancé (Gen. 29:41; Deut. 22:23-24), as is the case with Mary here (v. 20); the young man could similarly be called the girl's "husband" (e.g., Joel 1:8), as is Joseph here (v. 19). To break a betrothal, divorce proceedings were necessary. On the genitive absolute BDF remarks, "The harshest and at the same time rarest case is where the 'antecedent' follows as subject . . . but here the inserted infinitive with πρίν (with another subject) mitigates the ensuing anacolouthon, for which classical parallels may be found" (423[4]). The use of the genitive absolute when the participle could have agreed with a noun gives it emphasis (Robertson, pp. 1131-32).

31. συνέρχομαι, here only in Matthew, may be used of assembling but also "of coming together in a sexual sense"; it is used in the papyri in marriage contracts with the meaning "marry" (BAGD).

32. Bonnard points out that Luke speaks of the Spirit coming "upon" (ἐπί) Mary, but Matthew is "more reserved, more Jewish"; he indicates only that there was a miraculous conception without speaking of a movement of the Spirit toward or in Mary. Cf. Barclay, ". . . has come from the Holy Spirit."

33. It is sometimes argued that the omission of the article points to the power rather than the person, but it is difficult to justify this from the usage. Turner points out further that the omission of the article in prepositional expressions, as here, does not make the word indefinite (M, III, pp. 175-76). Cf. *AB,* "In Aramaic at this time there was no differentiation between the definite and the indefinite article. The absence of the definite article in Greek at this point is therefore not significant."

34. The word is ἀνήρ, which Matthew uses only 8 times. It means "man" in contrast to woman, and thus "husband"; by contrast he uses ἄνθρωπος 112 times, which is more than in any other book in the New Testament.

35. AS differentiates δίκαιος (used here) from ἀγαθός in that this latter term in Rom. 5:7 "implies a kindliness and attractiveness not necessarily possessed by the δίκαιος, who merely measures up to a high standard of rectitude" (*sub* ἀγαθός; under ἀγαθωσύνη he cites Armitage Robinson for the view that ἀ. represents "the kindlier, as δικαιοσύνη the sterner, element in the ideal character"). David Hill holds that here it refers "quite simply to Joseph's decision to observe the Jewish law faithfully and conscientiously" (*ET,* LXXVI [1964-65], p. 134). Matthew uses δίκαιος 17 times, which is more than in any other New Testament book (next is Luke with 11) and equals the total in all the Pauline letters.

the situation was that of the betrothed woman who has had sexual inter-course (Deut. 22:23-27). Where the woman is a consenting partner, both are to be put to death (vv. 23-24); where she has been violated, only the guilty man is to be executed (vv. 25-27). But the violation has taken place: the girl is no longer a virgin. Angelo Tosato cites evidence that she is no longer eligible to be married to her betrothed; she must be given a bill of divorce.[36] Joseph, being *just,* saw that he was unable to consummate the marriage, but he did not want[37] to be harsh. Perhaps we should say that for Joseph being just before God included an element of mercy (the "just man" is compassionate, Ps. 37:21). Probably also he preferred to act in a way that would avoid an open scandal. He could have made a public display of his indignation by taking Mary before the law court and making an example of her.[38] But his concern for the law did not lead him to the conclusion that he must humiliate the young lady who, he thought, had offended. He preferred to *divorce her secretly.* Divorce was no great problem for an Israelite man: he simply had to give the lady "a bill of divorce" before two witnesses and send her away (the procedure is given in Deut. 24:1).[39]

20. But[40] he did not go through with it. He gave the matter thought, and the aorist indicates that he apparently came to a conclusion: he *had made up his mind*[41] (despite *GNB,* "While he was thinking about this"). *Look* is a favorite interjection of Matthew's (62 times out of 200 in the NT); it enlivens a narrative and makes what follows more vivid. An *angel* appeared. The word means a messenger: occasionally in the New Testa-ment it is used of a human messenger (Luke 7:24), but more often it refers to a messenger from God, as is made clear here by the addition *of the Lord.* Curiously, when it is used in the singular in the New Testament it almost always lacks the article, as here (though cf. v. 24), but the plural

36. *CBQ,* 41 (1979), pp. 547-51. The Mishnah says explicitly that the woman is "for-bidden" to both the husband and the paramour (*Soṭa* 5:1).

37. The verb is θέλω (which Matthew uses 42 times, the most in any New Testament book). It conveys the notion of the exercise of the will, though sometimes this is attenuated to mere wishing. In New Testament times it seems not to have differed greatly from βούλομαι (the word rendered *decided*). καί is probably used here in the sense "and yet" (BAGD, I.2.g) —Joseph as a pious upholder of the law might well have seen the right course as that of making a public example of an erring fiancée.

38. That is the force of the rare verb δειγματίζω, connected with δεῖγμα, "a proof," "an example."

39. The bill of divorce must contain the formula "Lo, thou art free to marry any man," or according to R. Judah, "Let this be from me thy writ of divorce and letter of dismissal and deed of liberation, that thou mayest marry whatsoever man thou wilt" (*Giṭ.* 9:3). It should be signed by two or more witnesses (*Giṭ.* 6:7).

40. δέ here has adversative force. The conjunction is found at the beginning of each of the verses 18-22, though with somewhat variable meaning. But at least it serves to link the various parts of the narrative.

41. ἐνθυμέομαι occurs again in the New Testament only in 9:4. It has the meaning "reflect on, consider."

28

form "the angels of God" invariably has it except in one quotation from the Old Testament (in Heb. 1:6). Matthew specifies that this angel appeared to Joseph *in a dream,* an expression used 6 times by Matthew and by no one else in the New Testament.[42] Nothing is said about the appearance of the angel or anything he did; attention is concentrated on his message. He addresses Joseph as *son of David,* an expression used of Jesus in verse 1 (where see note). The expression is one of dignity, and Matthew perhaps records it as emphasizing the royal line of Jesus. *Don't be afraid* does not necessarily indicate fear; the word may be used in the sense "shrink from doing something," and it is this sense that is required here (cf. BAGD, φοβέω, 1.c). We might have expected the present, giving the sense "Stop being afraid," but the aorist may give the sense "Never fear."[43] *Take* is used of receiving one's wife into one's home a number of times (BAGD), and this is obviously the meaning. Notice that Mary is called Joseph's *wife.* Davies and Allison observe that throughout chapters 1 and 2 "It is Joseph who does what needs to be done." They think that this can be explained "by a christological interest: by his actions, Joseph, the Davidid, proves that he has made Jesus his own." The angel gives a reason[44] for Joseph's reception of Mary: the Holy Spirit has brought about the conception. The verb is that normally used of the action of the male parent (= "that which was begotten"), but it is sometimes used of the female, so that there is nothing very unusual about the expression. For *Holy Spirit* see on verse 18.

21. Mary's child[45] will be *a son,* and Joseph is instructed to *call his name Jesus.* This is a Hebraic construction; it would have been possible to say simply, "call him — ." By giving the name Joseph officially accepted the child (cf. "I have called you by name, you are mine," Isa. 43:1); this gave the child the status of a descendant of David.[46] On this occasion the name is not to be left to the discretion of the parent, for this child is special and has a destiny that is to be expressed in the meaning of the name. So the angel goes on to say, *he* (the word is emphatic: "He and no other")

---

42. BAGD notes that the expression κατ᾽ ὄναρ is rejected by Photius as a barbarism but that it is attested from the time of Conon. But Matthew uses it several times for divine revelations (2:12, 13, 19, 22; 27:19).

43. So Turner, M, III, p. 77; he also says that the words mean "Never at any time in the future be afraid to take her to wife" (*Grammatical Insights,* p. 25). Matthew uses μή with the aorist imperative 29 times (he has it with the present imperative 12 times). Except for this passage and 3:9 all are in sayings of Jesus (M, I, pp. 123-24).

44. Matthew uses γάρ 124 times, which is more than any of the other Evangelists (Mark has it 64 times, Luke 97, and John 64). Turner points out that Matthew's use of γάρ "is about the same as in Mark (one in 15 lines), less frequent than Paul and Hebrews, more so than Luke-Acts and the Johannine writings" (M, IV, p. 38). Matthew likes to bring out logical connections.

45. τίκτω is the usual verb for the action of the female parent. Matthew has it 4 times.

46. In his essay "Quis et Unde," K. Stendahl says, "The genuine point is that the angel encourages Joseph, the son of David, to make this child a Davidic child. Thereby Jesus' place in the genealogy is explained. God has ordered this engrafting" (Stanton, p. 61).

will save his people from their sins (cf. Ps. 130:8). The word *save* may mean deliver from troubles and afflictions of various kinds, but the addition here shows that what is in mind is the salvation that reckons with the plight in which people involve themselves by their evil deeds.[47] *People*[48] may be used of the populace generally, but it is often used more specifically of the people of God, and this in the sense of ancient Israel or of Christians. Matthew does not use the word "sin"[49] very often (7 times), but the expression here shows that he regarded it as an important concept. Jesus came to deal with *sins*, and his name gives expression to a very significant truth. Barclay aptly says, "Jesus was not so much The Man born to be King, as He was The Man born to be Saviour." We should not miss the point that the note of grace is struck so early in this Gospel. The impression is sometimes given that Matthew stresses upright living whereas Paul speaks of saving grace. It is true that these two writers have their own emphases, and we should not interpret either as though he were setting forth the other's thoughts. But neither should we overlook the fact that all the New Testament writers refer to the same Savior. And all stress the importance of grace. Matthew will later return to the idea that Jesus brings forgiveness (e.g., 20:28; 26:28).

22. It is characteristic of Matthew to appeal to prophecy and to see in it a fulfilment of what God had said long ago. *All*[50] *this*, he says, happened so that[51] prophecy would be fulfilled. This formula, when appealing to the fulfilment of prophecy, is found again (sometimes with small variations) in 2:15, 17, 23; 4:14; 8:17; 12:17; 13:35; 21:4; 26:56; 27:9.

Matthew is very interested in the way the ancient prophecies found their fulfilment in Jesus. But though the formula is common in Matthew, the inclusion of *all* is not (again in 26:56); here Matthew emphasizes that all the items mentioned were fulfilled and not only some of them. Notice that he speaks of the words in question not as spoken by the prophet, but

---

47. For the wordplay here see Introduction, p. 17, n. 58.

48. λαός.

49. ἁμαρτία meant first a missing of the mark, and Trench notes that Aristotle "sometimes withdraws it, almost, if not altogether, from the region of right and wrong. . . . The ἁμαρτία is a mistake . . ." (*Synonyms*, p. 241). G. Stählin points out that in LXX sin is considered much more serious, and the word comes "to express the divine reference of sin much more purely than, e.g., such primarily ethical concepts as ἀδικία and κακία." The New Testament follows LXX, and there "It is almost always a matter of 'offence in relation to God with emphasis on guilt,' i.e., of 'sin'" (*TDNT*, I, p. 295).

50. ὅλος occurs in Matthew more often than in any other New Testament writing (22 times). It means "whole, entire, complete" (BAGD) and is not often found as it is here with a pronoun.

51. ἵνα usually denotes purpose. It is possible to see something like result because purpose and result are so closely connected when it is a matter of the divine will. But the conjunction normally indicates purpose, and there is no real reason for departing from that meaning here. Cf. Burton, "The writer of the first gospel never uses ἵνα to express result, either actual or conceived; and that he by this phrase at least intends to express purpose is made especially clear by his employment of ὅπως (which is never ecbatic) interchangeably with ἵνα" (*MT*, 222).

30

as spoken by the Lord through the prophet. Matthew takes inspired prophecy very seriously.[52]

23. The prophecy comes from Isaiah 7:14 and is exactly as in LXX, except that the verb *call* is plural in place of Isaiah's singular. For *Look* see on verse 20. The definite article points to a particular *virgin*.[53] The point of the plural is not obvious; it may be a way of linking both parents in the giving of the name, or perhaps of associating other people with this. *Emmanuel* is found here only and is the transliteration of the Hebrew word meaning *God with us*, as Matthew goes on to explain.[54] As far as our information goes, nobody ever called Jesus "Emmanuel"; it was not the child's name in the same sense as "Jesus" was. Matthew surely intends his readers to understand that "Emmanuel" was his name in the sense that all that was involved in that name found its fulfilment in him.[55] The quotation and the translation of the Hebrew name underline the fact that in Jesus none less than God came right where we are. And at the end of this Gospel there is the promise that Jesus will be with his people to the end of the age (28:20) — God with us indeed.

24. In due course Joseph woke up and did what the angel told him to do. *Angel* has the definite article (unusually; see on v. 20), which signifies "the aforementioned angel." Matthew picks out the central part of the angelic command: Joseph *took his wife*, that is, publicly accepted Mary as his wife.

25. But though he married Mary, they had no sexual relations[56] before

---

52. It is sometimes suggested that Matthew has manufactured a narrative to fit a number of prophecies, but M. J. Down has argued convincingly that "the evangelist did not start with prophecy and invent a story; he started with a story and slipped in certain prophecies" (*ET*, XC [1978-79], p. 52).

53. Isaiah uses the word עַלְמָה, which is usually understood to mean a woman of marriageable age. The word occurs 7 times and is apparently not used for women who are married (though Prov. 30:19 may be an exception). France points out that the word is not elsewhere used where childbirth is in mind (and where "wife" would be expected) and that it may have been this indication that Isaiah had in mind a birth that did not conform to the usual pattern that caused the LXX translators to use παρθένος. This word in biblical Greek normally means "virgin" (though not in Gen. 34:3); it means "virgin" in Isaiah and here. Isaiah is speaking of happenings in the time of Ahaz, but Matthew perceives a fuller meaning. "Clearly the LXX translators, with their striking use of *parthenos,* understood it to refer to more than an ordinary birth, and the choice of *'almâ* in the Hebrew as well as the symbolic name 'Immanuel' suggests that they were right" (France).

54. עִמָּנוּאֵל.

55. The Hebrew text of Isaiah reads, "she will call his name Emmanuel," in LXX it is a command, "you (singular) shall call . . . ," while Matthew has "they will call. . . ." Matthew's impersonal plural signifies people in general. Bruner comments, "There is some point in Matthew's plural rendering because we never hear Jesus called Emmanu-El by his mother or by any particular person in the Gospels or Epistles. But if one were to ask the faithful through the centuries what they believe Jesus *means* to them, and thus in this sense what they *call* him, 'God with us' is as good an answer as it is possible to give in three words" (pp. 34-35).

56. The verb γινώσκω means "come to know, know," and is used of knowing in a wide variety of contexts. BAGD says that here it is "euphem. of sex relations"; it cites classical and late authors as well as LXX for this usage. The subject may be a man, as here, or a woman (Luke 1:34).

the birth of the son. *Until* is a Matthean word;[57] the passage makes it clear that there was no sexual intercourse before the birth of the baby. It does not say whether or not this took place thereafter, but the natural way of taking the passage would indicate that it did (Allen holds that the imperfect tense here "is against the tradition of perpetual virginity"). It is also true that in both Old and New Testaments such intercourse is approved and viewed as an integral part of marriage (Gen. 1:28; 9:1; Prov. 5:18; 1 Cor. 7:3-5). The singular *called* almost certainly means "Joseph called" (though grammatically the subject of the verb might be "she"). The story is told throughout from his point of view; thus it is natural that it concludes with him naming the child Jesus. His naming of the child means that he adopted him legally.

57. ἕως occurs 48 times in this Gospel, which is more than in any other New Testament book (next is Luke with 28). It may be used as a temporal conjunction or, as here, as an improper preposition with the genitive οὗ. BAGD sees the relative as used with prepositions "whereby a kind of conjunction is formed" (ὅς, ἥ, ὅ, I.11; for this passage I.11.f). McNeile says that in the New Testament a negative followed by ἕως οὗ ἕως, or ἕως ὅτου "always implies that the negatived action did, or will, take place after the point of time indicated by the particle." Matthew uses ἕως οὗ 5 times.

Matthew 2

C. THE INFANT JESUS, 2:1-23

Matthew's infancy stories are quite different from those of Luke and are peculiar to this Gospel. Matthew tells of the visit of Magi from the East, the flight of the holy family into Egypt, and Herod's slaughter of the children of Bethlehem. He is clearly interested in the divine protection of the child Jesus, and his stories bring out the truth that God works his will despite the opposition of sinful people.

1. The Visit of the Magi, 2:1-12

1When Jesus was born in Bethlehem of Judea in the days of Herod the king, see, wise men from the East came to Jerusalem, 2saying, "Where is he who has been born King of the Jews? For we saw his star at its rising and we have come to worship him." 3Now when King Herod heard this he was troubled, and all Jerusalem with him. 4And he gathered all the high priests and scribes of the people and inquired of them, "Where is the Messiah to be born?" 5And they said to him, "In Bethlehem of Judea; for so it is written through the prophet:

6'And you, Bethlehem, land of Judah,
are by no means least among the leaders of Judah;
for out of you will go forth a leader
who will shepherd my people Israel.'"

7Then Herod secretly called the wise men and ascertained from them exactly the time when the star appeared. 8And he sent them to Bethlehem and said, "Go, search diligently for the little child; and when you have found him tell me, so that I, too, may come and worship him. 9And when they had heard the king, they went on their way and, look, the star that they had seen at its rising went before them until it came and stood over the place where the little child was. 10And when they saw the star, they rejoiced with exceedingly great joy. 11And when they had come into the house, they saw the little child with Mary his mother, and they fell down and worshipped him, and they opened their treasures and offered him gifts, gold and frankincense and myrrh. 12And having been warned in a dream

33

not to return to Herod, they went back to their own country by another way.

Many scholars have declined to see anything historical in this chapter. They point to the fact that all kinds of legends were in circulation about the infant Moses and that while the heyday of such legends came later, Josephus is evidence that wonderful stories about Moses were in circulation at this time (*Ant.* 2.205-7, 215-16). These scholars suggest that the author of this Gospel, moved by such stories, is manufacturing tales to bring out the greatness of Jesus.[1] Matthew is simply concerned to improve on previous models ("anything they can do we can do better"!). Others hold that the Old Testament quotations in the chapter form the clue to what went on. They think that there was a collection of testimonia circulating in the early church, passages taken from the Old Testament to show that Jesus was the Messiah and that everything in his life was done in accordance with the plan of God. The author of this Gospel, they hold, started from such a collection and manufactured fulfilments of prophecy in the birth at Bethlehem, importantly in the place of Gentiles from the first, and in general improving on the Moses stories.

Clearly there is a large subjective element in such reconstructions. That there were stories about Moses does not require us to think that a writer about Jesus would manufacture similar stories (and anyway, apart from the protection of the child, the resemblances are minor). We may agree with some scholars that Matthew regards Moses as in some respects a "type" of Christ, but we can scarcely say more. The existence of testimonia, while held by many, is far from certain. And even if they did exist, we have no evidence that the writer of this Gospel used them as a basis for composing stories about Jesus. It is much more probable that he started from what he knew had happened (the account of the visit of the Magi "has on the face of it all the elements of historical probability," *AB*)[2] and brought forward passages from Scripture to show that all was in accordance with prophecy than that the prophecy led to the creation of beautiful stories that lacked factual foundation.[3]

Matthew may well have included this story to bring out the truth that Jesus is Lord of all peoples; since this is so, it was appropriate that at the time of his infancy people came from a distant Gentile country to pay their homage. In this narrative the Jews and their king are ranged against the infant Jesus, but Gentiles do him homage.[4] There will also be the motif

---

1. But Plummer's comment is still relevant: "The examples cited are more remarkable for their differences than for their resemblances" (p. 12).

2. Cf. Allen, "The main outline of the story of the Magi is in many respects noteworthy for its historical probability."

3. For a careful examination of these scriptural quotations see R. T. France, *NTS,* 27 (1980-81), pp. 233-51.

4. "In this chapter, Matthew introduces the major theme of his Gospel: the Jews have

that the purposes of God cannot be overthrown. Earthly kings like Herod
may try to circumvent the divine purpose, but in the end they are always
defeated. And, of course, there is the strong motif of the fulfilment of
Scripture; Matthew finds events in the life of Jesus from the earliest days
foretold in the holy writings.

1. *When Jesus was born* indicates that this narrative took place after the
birth of Jesus, but Matthew does not say how long after. When he was telling
us about Jesus' birth Matthew did not say where it took place, but he now
informs his readers that it was at *Bethlehem of Judea*. This distinguishes it from
another Bethlehem in Galilee (Josh. 19:15), and more importantly directs
attention to the fact that it was the royal city, the place where the great David
was born. This is part of the way Matthew indicates Jesus' messiahship. The
location was not important for what he had to say in chapter 1 (in the birth
story he does not say where Jesus was born), but it matters a great deal for
what comes before us now. The name Bethlehem means "House of Bread,"
that is, a granary. Matthew speaks of Bethlehem 5 times, but Luke (twice)
and John (once) are the only other New Testament writers to refer to it. It
was evidently not considered an important place. It was located about 5
miles (or 8 kilometers) south of Jerusalem. Judea, here as in most places,
indicates the southern part of Palestine (in contrast to Samaria, etc.); it can
mean the region occupied by the Jewish nation (Luke 1:5), and it may be
used in such a way as to include territory on the east of the Jordan (19:1).

In addition to the information about the place we have a general
indication of time: *in the days of Herod the king*. This Herod is Herod the
Great, and he is correctly called "the king" (the title was sometimes accorded the tetrarch, but he was not a king; this Herod was). He was not
a Jew, his father being an Idumean and his mother an Arabian, but the
Romans made him King of Judea in 40 B.C. He is generally thought to have
died in 4 B.C. (there is some dispute about this).[5] He was an unscrupulous
tyrant, but his achievements were such that he merited the epithet "the
Great." He was a great builder and was responsible for the erection of the
temple in Jerusalem, the rebuilding of Samaria (which he called Sebaste
in honor of the emperor), and other significant works. And, in the words
of Barclay, "He was the only ruler of Palestine who ever succeeded in
keeping the peace and in bringing order into disorder."

Wise men[6] are not people endowed with wisdom in general, but

---

rejected the offer of salvation, but the Gentiles will accept it. . . . The Gentiles will be brought
into the place which the Jews had forfeited by their unbelief, and the Church will be the
Israel of the last days, destined to share in the joys of the age to come" (Fenton).

5. Our system of dating (with years B.C. and A.D.) was worked out by Dionysius Exiguus
at the beginning of the sixth century; he appears to have been about four years off in his
calculations.

6. μάγος seems originally to have meant a member of the tribe of the Magoi; later it
was used of a member of a sacred caste who carried on with Magian practices, and then it
was used of sorcerers in general (Acts 13:6, 8). We derive our word "magic" from it.

students of the stars: "a (Persian . . . then also Babylonian) wise man and priest, who was expert in astrology, interpretation of dreams and various other secret arts" (BAGD). *REB* renders the term "astrologers." *From the East*[7] is very general; many interpreters hold that these wise men came from Babylon, and they may have done so, but we cannot be sure. Their study of the stars had led them to believe that a great leader had been born in Judea. That being so, they naturally directed their steps to Jerusalem,[8] the capital city. These men would have been Gentiles, but Matthew gives this no emphasis. Tradition says that there were three of them, but Matthew gives no number and it appears to be a deduction from the number of the gifts. Tradition also makes them kings, but this is highly unlikely.

2. This sentence is the only utterance of the Magi that Matthew records. These wise men describe the leader they are looking for as *King of the Jews* (again in this Gospel at 27:11, 29, 37) and ask where he has been born. The words they use mean "born king," not "born to be king," as is often said;[9] they are talking about what he is, not what he will be. They explain that they *saw his star.* Many attempts have been made to explain the phenomenon of the star, such as that there was a conjunction of planets or the explosion of a supernova or the appearance of a comet, but none carries conviction.[10] What is clear is that the Magi reported some astronomical phenomenon that they had some way of linking with a particular king, the king of the Jews.[11] But they do not say what the link was. It is not completely certain whether we should translate "at its rising" or "in the East," but the expression here differs slightly from that in verse

---

7. ἀνατολή occurs 5 times in Matthew, twice in Luke, and 3 times in Revelation in the New Testament. The word means "rising," specifically the rising of the sun, and thus the East. In this sense it may be singular or plural. It lacks the article, for "The points of the compass, found only with prepositions, never take the article" (BDF, 253[5]). Turner divertingly points out that we could understand the expression to mean "Wise men from the west," for "in modern Greek the plural of *Anatol* is a proper name signifying 'various parts of Asia Minor [i.e., *Anatolia*]' " (*Grammatical Insights*, p. 25), which would be west, not east, of Herod's kingdom. This could be supported by the use of the expression in Genesis 13:11, for Lot must have traveled eastward. But "from the East" is more probable, especially in view of the connection of magi with Persia and Babylon.

8. There are two Greek forms of the name Jerusalem. Matthew here uses Ἱεροσόλυμα, which he has 11 times, as against twice for Ἰερουσαλήμ. For Mark the figures are 10 and 0, for Luke 4 and 27, for John 12 and 0, for Acts 23 and 26, and for the rest of the New Testament 3 and 11. There appear to be no reasons other than personal preference for the use of either name.

9. Nigel Turner argues from the word order and the tense that we should understand this phrase as "the new-born King of the Jews." He further thinks that "It is not so much *who* the Person is, as *where* He is, that matters to them at the moment of their question" (*ET*, LXVIII [1956-57], p. 122).

10. There is evidence that astral phenomena were widely held to be connected with the birth of great men; see *TDNT*, I, p. 505.

11. Davies and Allison cite evidence that "at the turn of the era" there was a widespread "expectation of a world-ruler to come from Judea."

1[12] and it appears that the wise men are telling of the astronomical feature that carried conviction to them rather than calling attention to the direction in which they saw it. They say that they have come *to worship him,* where the verb may indicate an act of reverence toward a great man or an act of worship of God.[13] The Magi probably intended an act of homage, but Matthew may well be giving the expression its fullest meaning — the attitude of the Magi in the presence of the Baby was the attitude proper in the presence of God. The worship of the Christ was important to Matthew, and he refers to this worship 10 times (2:2, 8, 11; 8:2; 9:18; 14:33; 15:25; 20:20; 28:9, 17).

3. "Having heard" is a participle indicating cause: "because he heard this, he was troubled." Matthew does not say how Herod heard this, only that he did hear. But with such visitors no doubt reports were flying through Jerusalem, and it would be strange if some of Herod's people did not pick up the news. There is an article with *King Herod,* perhaps to distance this king from "the King of the Jews." Herod *was troubled;* he was an Edomite, not a Jew, and he had been made king by the Romans. The news that the Magi were bringing sounded suspiciously like the emergence of a genuine descendant of the royal line of David as a claimant to the throne (Glover points out that Herod was more interested in saving his throne than in saving his soul!). And if Herod was troubled, the whole[14] city was troubled with him. When Herod the Great trembled the whole city shook.

4. The king proceeded to gather his experts. Matthew has more references to high priests (25) and to scribes (22) than has anyone else in the New Testament. There is a problem about the exact force of the term "high priest" because in a number of places, as here, we have the plural, whereas there was only one high priest, for the office was held for life. But the rulers sometimes deposed the legitimate high priest, and the title was then applied both to the man who had formerly exercised the office (and who in the opinion of many was the real high priest) and the one who currently filled the post. J. Jeremias has shown that the term was used also to cover a number of officials such as the captain of the temple, the

---

12. The earlier expression was ἀπὸ ἀνατολῶν, while here we have ἐν τῇ ἀνατολῇ. The singular and the article seem more probably to refer to an astronomical "rising."

13. προσκυνέω is used of homage to men (18:26), to God (4:10), to the devil (4:9), to idols (Acts 7:43), to the church at Philadelphia (Rev. 3:9), and to an angel (Rev. 22:8). Abbott notes that the dative is regular in LXX and the accusative in classical Greek: "the dative emphasizes the notion of 'prostrating oneself *to* a person, idol, or God,' while the accusative means 'adore' without this emphasis" (*Johannine Grammar,* 2019). The infinitive conveys the thought of purpose. The verb occurs 13 times in this Gospel, whereas Mark and Luke each have it twice (John uses it 11 times and Revelation 24 times). In Matthew the word mostly seems to signify "worship."

14. The feminine πᾶσα is curious since Ἰεροσόλυμα is neuter. It may be that "city" is understood, but more likely the name is treated as feminine (as happens elsewhere occasionally).

leader of the weekly course of priests, those who had charge of financial affairs, and so on.[15] It thus covered a group of important people. Our problem is that the extension of the term from the incumbent high priest, while clear, is never defined. "Scribe" might refer to a secretary or "clerk" but could also denote a scholar who had made a study of the law, and thus the meaning might be much like our "lawyer." In Matthew the term "scribes" is linked with "high priests" on 5 occasions (again in 16:21; 20:18; 21:15; 27:41), and it is linked with "Pharisees" 6 times (5:20; 12:38; 15:1; 23:2, 13, 15; 7 times if 23:14 be accepted). Many of the scribes were Pharisees, which is natural enough, for both groups were zealous for the law, but not all Pharisees were scribes. The passages that link scribes with the high-priestly party warn us that we should not see too strong a link with the Pharisees. The Sadducean high-priestly party needed legal experts, and it is these who are in mind in this passage. Here the one article links them closely. *All* shows that Herod was being thorough; he did not content himself with asking one or two outstanding men. *Of the people* may indicate that the scribes had a closer connection with people at large than the high priests did. The verb for *inquired* is in the imperfect tense, which Turner thinks "means that he scarce expected his demand to be implemented. Tentative requests are often described in that tense."[16] The inquiry concerned the place where the Messiah (or the Christ) would be born. The article shows that the expression is used of an official title, while the present tense in the verb referring to something future puts some emphasis on the certainty that it will happen.

5. Herod's experts came up with a speedy reply. This is interesting, for we read in John's Gospel of an opinion that nobody knows where the Christ will come from (John 7:27).[17] But such views were not found among Herod's men; for them it was quite clear that Bethlehem was the place, and they were able to quote Scripture to make their point.[18] They thus showed, as Ridderbos points out, that their failure to believe was not due to ignorance: "Israel knew precisely where the King of the Jews would be born, but it was the Gentiles who worshiped him first" (on v. 4). When they say that it was written *through* the prophet they are reasoning that God is the author of Scripture; the prophet was no more than his instrument. The reference is to Micah 5:2 (with the last line from 2 Sam. 5:2; 1 Chron. 11:2). It is interesting that, although they could say immediately

---

15. *Jerusalem in the Time of Jesus* (London, 1967), pp. 160-81. He can say, "The chief priests permanently employed at the Temple formed a definite body who had jurisdiction over the priesthood and whose members had seats and votes on the council" (p. 180).

16. *Grammatical Insights*, p. 27.

17. For a discussion of the view that the place of origin of the Christ is completely unknown see my *The Gospel according to John* (Grand Rapids, 1971), pp. 411-12.

18. Matthew introduces the words with γέγραπται, where the perfect indicates the permanence of the record. Matthew has this verb 10 times, and except for 27:37 it is always in the form γέγραπται. Deissmann shows that the term is a legal one (*BS*, pp. 112-14, 249-50), but here the stress is rather on the fulfilment of what is written in Scripture.

where the Messiah would be born, they apparently did nothing about the report that the Magi brought. "They fail by being passive" (Filson).[19]

6. The Jewish leaders may have quoted these words from the prophet or, as Tasker thinks, they may be "an annotation by the evangelist himself" (the Jews would have kept closer to the Hebrew text). The quotation is not particularly close to either LXX or the Hebrew. For example, "land of Judah" replaces LXX "house of Ephratha," while the Hebrew has "Bethlehem Ephratah." But it preserves the sense.[20] The last section, about shepherding the people, may come from 2 Samuel 5:2 or Micah 5:4. The city of *Bethlehem* is addressed and is then equated with *land of Judah*. Matthew uses *land* (γῆ) more often than anyone else in the New Testament except the author of Revelation, a total of 43 times. The word means "earth" and may be used of soil, ground, land, earth in contrast to heaven, or the inhabited globe. Here it is "land" in the sense of "territory." *By no means* is not in the text of Micah that we know; therefore some interpreters suggest that Matthew has contradicted the prophet by inserting it. But if he did insert it, there is no real contradiction. The passage is saying that Bethlehem's greatness consists only in that it is the birthplace of the great leader, and this is as plain in Micah as in Matthew. On the next section the translation is rather free, or else it presupposes a different Hebrew text. Our text refers to *the leaders of Judah* and goes on to *a leader*.[21] The leader is not said to be the Messiah, but the one who[22] was to shepherd the people certainly qualifies for the title. The verb may be used of the activities of a shepherd with a flock of animals (1 Cor. 9:7), but here the symbolic meaning emphasizes the care the leader would show as he looked after those he led.

7. Armed with this information,[23] Herod summoned the Eastern

---

19. Mounce comments, "All this time the religious leaders of Jerusalem know from their own Scriptures where the Messiah is to be born. But not even the visit of foreign dignitaries piques their curiosity enough to travel six miles to Bethlehem to find out if there is any truth in the report" (p. 11).

20. Calvin comments, "We must always observe the rule, that as often as the Apostles quote a testimony from Scripture, although they do not render it word for word, in fact may move quite a way from it, they adapt it suitably and appropriately to the case in hand."

21. *The leaders* is τοῖς ἡγεμόσιν and *a leader* is the participle ἡγούμενος. There is not a great difference in meaning. *NIV* and *REB* have "rulers," while *GNB* reads "leading cities."

22. Matthew uses ὅστις more often than any other New Testament writer (29 times; next is Acts with 24). It often does not differ significantly from ὅς, but here a certain emphasis on the quality (who will be of such a sort) is probable.

23. Matthew makes a good deal of use of τότε; he has it 90 times out of its 159 New Testament occurrences (next most frequent is Acts with 21). It can refer to time past or to time future, but also "to introduce that which follows in time (not in accordance w. class. usage) *then, thereupon*" (BAGD, 2). BDF notes that "the use of τότε as a connective particle to introduce a subsequent event, but not one taking place at a definite time ('thereupon' not 'at that time'), is unclassical" (459[2]). D. Senior cites McNeile for the information that this usage occurs 61 times in Matthew and is thus this Evangelist's most frequent use. Senior points out that this may refer to the past or that it may be used "for current narrative" or "in reference to a future sequence of events" (*L'ÉSM*, p. 351, n. 28).

sages. He wanted no undue publicity, so he called them secretly and found out from them exactly ("the exact date," *JB*) when the star made its appearance. He does not say why he wanted this information, but to know the time when the star appeared would obviously give an indication of the age of this new King of the Jews.

8. Herod apparently shared with the Magi the information he had acquired about the birthplace of the Messiah, then despatched them to Bethlehem. He instructed them to search diligently[24] for the baby, and when they had found him to let him know where the child was so that he could go along too and worship him. It must have rung true for the Magi; they had come so far to find the new king, and the old king gave evidence of sharing their enthusiasm and their pious purpose. There is some emphasis in his *I:* "I, as well as you."[25] He says that he intends[26] to worship as they planned to do. The word for *little child*[27] may be used of children of various ages, but mostly of the young (though in familiar address it can be used even of grown men, John 21:5). Here it clearly refers to a very small child. It is perhaps surprising that he did not send someone with the Magi. But soldiers would have been inappropriate, and he may have felt that anyone linked to him would raise problems for the search. He had no reason for thinking that the Magi would not report back.

9. When they[28] heard this they set out. Matthew's favorite *look* (see on 1:20) introduces a touch of vividness; he sees it as he writes. As they went on their way they saw the star again. It may be that they had given up looking for the star when they got to Jerusalem, feeling that their journey was over. But now they realized that they had still some distance to go, and once again they saw the star. We could understand the Greek to mean that the star was the one that they had seen "in the East," but as in verse 2 it is more likely that Matthew is referring to the way the star appeared *(at its rising)* than to the place where they first saw it. It is not easy to understand how the star *went before them* nor how it *stood* over any one place here on earth. But Matthew is apparently saying that in some way the star kept going ahead of them until[29] it came to the place where[30] the baby was and that it then stood (still).

---

24. ἀκριβῶς, "with exactness, carefully" (AS).

25. κἀγώ. Matthew uses the expression 9 times, a total exceeded only by John (30) and 1 Corinthians (10; 2 Corinthians also has 9).

26. ὅπως introduces a clause of purpose.

27. παιδίον, diminutive of παῖς. Matthew is the most frequent New Testament user of the word with 18 occurrences.

28. οἱ δέ is the article used as a demonstrative pronoun "To indicate the progress of the narrative" (BAGD, I.3).

29. This is the conjunction ἕως (not the preposition) used with the aorist indicative, "until it stood still" (BAGD, I.1.a).

30. Matthew has no word here meaning *place*, simply οὗ, the genitive of ὅς, used as an adverb of place. Matthew has it 3 times.

10. When the Magi "caught sight of the star,"[31] they were more than a little joyful. It had been the star that had brought them to the land of Judea, and now that they were not sure of their destination within that land they were reassured by the evidence that the star was still leading them. Matthew's expression indicates that when they saw their star again they were more than mildly pleased.[32] "Deliriously happy" may be an overstatement, but it was something like that.

11. Matthew does not say that they journeyed on or that they followed the star. It was enough to say that the star appeared and went before them; it could be assumed that they followed it. Matthew resumes his story with their entry into *the house*.[33] There they saw the little child and his mother (in each place in this passage where the two are mentioned the child comes first, vv. 13, 14, 20, 21; Matthew's main interest is in Jesus). Interestingly Joseph is not mentioned, though in these opening chapters he takes a more prominent place than anywhere else in the New Testament. But it would be natural to mention the mother with the baby and perhaps not as natural to include the father. The Magi prostrated themselves before the baby in lowly worship. They proceeded to open their treasure chests[34] and offer gifts (the verb is used of offering in general, but is especially frequent for sacrifices). Matthew specifies three gifts (from which some deduce that there were three Magi; legend has made them three kings (an idea which Bruce calls "beautiful but baseless"), and even given them names. The gifts were *gold* (which Matthew has in more than half its New Testament occurrences, 5 out of 9), *frankincense* ("a white resinous gum, obtained fr. several kinds of a certain tree in Arabia, used both medicinally and for cult purposes," BAGD), and *myrrh* ("the resinous gum of the bush 'balsamodendron myrrha,'" BAGD). Clearly all three were valuable, and together they formed a munificent gift, suitable for offering to a king. Christians have often seen symbolical meanings in them, gold for royalty, frankincense for deity, and myrrh pointing to suffering and death, but Matthew says nothing about this.

12. *Warned* is a verb used often to indicate a divine utterance, a revelation;[35] here this divine command is given in a dream, as on a number

---

31. M, I, p. 117.

32. σφόδρα occurs 7 times in Matthew out of its New Testament total of 11. It may be used with an adjective or a verb, here with the adjective μεγάλην.

33. οἰκία, which Matthew and Luke each have 25 times, more than anyone else in the New Testament (Mark is next with 18). Matthew also has οἶκος 10 times, which Luke has 33 times, with another 25 in Acts. AS notes that οἶκος "in Attic law denoted the whole *estate*, οἰκία the *dwelling* only," but adds that the distinction is not always observed in late Greek. We can scarcely say more than that Matthew prefers οἰκία. Luke speaks of the child as in a manger (Luke 2:12, 16); the holy family may have moved, or the house may have been that of poor people with the animals living under the same roof as the family.

34. θησαυρός (9 times in Matthew out of 17 times in the New Testament) derives from τίθημι and signifies a place for putting things, for keeping them safe, then for what is kept safe, treasure.

35. χρηματίζω may have the basic meaning of "impart a revelation," from which the

of occasions in Matthew (see on 1:20). This time there is no mention of an angel. They were instructed not to go back to Herod. No reason for this is given, but the informed reader will know that Herod was a bloodthirsty and unreliable man, and more may well have been said to the Magi than Matthew records. At any rate we are informed that they were obedient and went back home by another way.

2. The Flight into Egypt, 2:13-15

> [13]*Now when they had gone away, look, an angel of the Lord appears to Joseph in a dream, saying, "Get up and take the little child and his mother, and flee into Egypt, and be there till I tell you; for Herod is going to look for the little child to destroy him." [14]So he got up, took the little child and his mother by night, and went away into Egypt. [15]And he was there until Herod's death, in order that what was spoken by the Lord through the prophet might be fulfilled, saying: "Out of Egypt I have called my son."*

Since there is no information about the flight into Egypt other than what we read here, some reject it. But there is nothing improbable about it. Throughout history many Jews had taken refuge in Egypt; it was almost a traditional country to which to flee when there was trouble in Palestine. There was a considerable Jewish minority in that land and, for example, there were as many as a million Jews in Alexandria and the country beyond.[36]

13. The Magi departed. With some vivid touches (Matthew's characteristic *look* and the present tense in the verb) once again we have an angel appearing to Joseph; as before, he does so in a dream. Luke has angels appearing to Zechariah, to Mary, and to the shepherds, but there are no references to dreams. Matthew has an angel appearing in a dream several times (1:20; 2:13, 19), and when there is no angel he still speaks of divine communications taking place in dreams (1:12, 22; 27:19). *Get up* can refer to waking from sleep (cf. 1:24), but here it rather means getting up after one has awakened. Joseph is told to take the child and his mother (specified separately and, as elsewhere, the child mentioned first) and to seek safety in flight to Egypt. They are to stay there until[37] they receive further orders from on high;[38] a divine commandment would come to

---

idea of giving a name derives (see BAGD). Or the basic meaning may be "transact business," from which there are two lines of development: the one refers to the anwering of questions in the course of business that leads to the concept of "answer as an oracle," the other to getting a name (from one's business activities; see AS). W. F. Howard held that two distinct words were involved (M, II, p. 265). See also B. Reicke, *TDNT,* IX, pp. 480-82.

36. Philo, *Flaccus* 43.

37. This use of ἕως followed by ἄν and the aorist subjunctive is a construction used "to denote that the commencement of an event is dependent on circumstances" (BAGD, I.1.b).

38. BAGD notes as one meaning of εἰμί "to denote a sojourn, *stay, reside*" (I.3); that is

them in Egypt. *For* introduces the reason for the foregoing. Herod is going[39] to make a search for the baby in order[40] to kill him. Flight was imperative.

14. And flight was taken. Joseph's actions in getting up and taking the child are described in the exact terms of the command given him (v. 13). Matthew adds that this happened *by night*. This probably means that Joseph acted immediately following the dream (the little family was evidently poor, there would not be a great deal involved in their preparations, and the dream would have conveyed a sense of urgency). Or it may possibly mean that he chose a time for their departure when they could leave unobserved. He went away[41] to Egypt.

15. Joseph *was there*, which means that he remained in Egypt; he resided there for a time, until the death of Herod.[42] Matthew puts some emphasis on the fulfilment of the divine purpose in his use of both the conjunction for "in order that" and his characteristic formula for introducing quotations from Scripture (for both see on 1:22). Matthew quotes from Hosea 11:1 with some variants from LXX. He uses the uncompounded form of the verb *called*,[43] and he has *my son* (as the Hebrew does) where LXX has "his children" (which means that Matthew may be making his own translation from the Hebrew). But where Hosea is referring to the Exodus, Matthew is thinking of Jesus' flight into Egypt.[44] Consistently he sees Scripture as fulfilled in Jesus; thus the outworking of the divine purpose is accomplished in him. Carson points out that "The NT writers insist that the OT can be rightly interpreted only if the entire revelation is kept in perspective as it is historically unfolded." He argues that there is a pattern in revelation and that "Jesus himself is the locus of true Israel." In a kind of Israel-Jesus typology, what could be said of the old Israel

---

the meaning here. ἐκεῖ occurs more often in Matthew than in any other New Testament book (28 times). It means "there," which may signify "to that place" (as v. 22) or "in that place," which is the meaning here.

39. μέλλω is used of futurity of various kinds, here to denote intention. "It is usually employed of an action which one intends to do, or of that which is certain, destined to take place" (*MT*, 72). Herod will certainly decide to look for the little child.

40. τοῦ with the infinitive normally denotes purpose, as here. Matthew uses the verb ἀπόλλυμι 19 times, a total exceeded only by Luke (27). On its use here and in 27:20 where the Jewish leaders persuade the mob to have Jesus killed, Gundry remarks, "what Herod failed to do with their help they succeeded in doing at a later time without his help."

41. ἀναχωρέω is used in the sense "withdraw," and is often used of avoiding danger: "The connotation of 'taking refuge' from some peril will suit most of the NT passages remarkably well" (MM). There is a rabbinic tradition that Jesus was in Egypt (*Sanh.* 107b).

42. On ἕως, "until," BAGD remarks, "a historical event forms the boundary" (II.1.a). τελευτή occurs here only in the New Testament. It means "a finishing," "an end," and here, of course, refers to the "end of Herod," that is, his death.

43. Matthew has ἐκάλεσα, LXX has μετεκάλεσα.

44. Commenting on Hosea 11:1 J. B. Hindley remarks, "The NT use (Mt. 2:15) indicates that as Israel had forfeited their privilege of divine sonship, the prophecy would have to be fulfilled by Another (cf. Rom. 11:29)" (*NBCR in loc.*). There are some resemblances to Numbers 23:22; 24:8, where the nation is said to be "out of Egypt."

could on occasion have its application to Jesus.[45] In other words, the divine purpose runs through the whole of Scripture, and it all points in some way to the climax, the coming of Christ. This is the first time that Matthew speaks of Jesus as "Son" with reference to God. That Jesus is the Son of God is a very important concept for Matthew,[46] and it is interesting that it makes its appearance so early.

3. The Killing of the Children of Bethlehem, 2:16-18

> [16]Then Herod, when he had seen that he had been tricked by the wise men, was furiously angry, and he sent and killed all the boys in Bethlehem and in all the neighborhood two years of age and under in accordance with the time that he had carefully ascertained from the wise men. [17]Then was fulfilled what was spoken through Jeremiah the prophet, saying:

> [18]"A voice was heard in Ramah,
> Weeping and great lamentation,
> Rachel weeping for her children,
> And she would not be comforted,
> Because they are no more."

Some commentators have discounted the story of the slaughter of the children, partly because it is not attested elsewhere and partly because of the character of the narrative. It is felt that such a horrifying happening as this slaughter of little boys would be referred to elsewhere if it really happened. It may fairly be countered that Herod's declining years were so full of bloodshed that an incident of this kind might well have gone unreported in our sources. Bethlehem was a small place and may well have had no more than twenty or so boys below the age of two years. With Herod's ferocious killings this one may well not have attracted much notice. And we cannot reject a narrative simply because only one of the Evangelists records it.

16. For Matthew's characteristic *then* see on verse 7; here it means "at that time." Since Bethlehem is only about six miles from Jerusalem, Herod would have expected the Magi to be back with him within a day or two of his sending them on their way. *Seen*, of course, is used in the sense "perceived," "came to know," rather than of direct sight. It is not easy to find an adequate equivalent for the word I have rendered *tricked;* most of its New Testament occurrences are used for the mockery of Jesus

---

45. W. D. Davies can say, "Matthew sees in the history of Jesus a recapitulation of that of Israel" (*SM*, p. 78).

46. Kingsbury emphasizes the significance of the concept for Matthew (*Structure*, pp. 40-83). While he perhaps exaggerates a little (not all see a reference to the Son of God in every place where Kingsbury finds it), he makes it clear that the understanding of Jesus as uniquely the Son of God is a major concept throughout this Gospel.

after his arrest, and this is the only place in the New Testament where the sense is something like "deceive." The verb for "make angry" is used here only in the New Testament, and it is strengthened with an adverb meaning "very much, exceedingly."[47] The combination signifies furious anger.

When the verb "send" is used with other verbs "it often means simply that the action in question has been performed by someone else, like . . . *he had (them) killed.*"[48] The act of killing[49] was performed by someone else; the responsibility belonged to Herod. He saw to it that all the boys up to two years of age were killed. This extreme reaction accords with what we know of Herod: "the cruelty of Herod had become proverbial even in Rome" (Stendahl). He had three of his own sons killed, and when he was himself near death he left orders that one member of each family should be executed on his death so that the whole nation would really be in mourning[50] (the orders were not carried out). The word "boy" is used here with reference to age and signifies the very young; it can also refer to descent (son), to social position (servant), to religious standing (servant of God), and in other ways. Herod's orders covered Bethlehem itself and *all the neighborhood;*[51] he was taking no chances. The specification of *two years of age and under* corresponds to the time he had ascertained from the Magi, the time of the appearance of the star. Matthew repeats the verb he used in verse 7 for accurate inquiry. Clearly he wants his readers to be in no doubt that Herod had accurate knowledge of the time the star appeared.[52] He was determined that no child within the area and the time frame indicated by the Magi would remain alive. We wonder that God would allow such cruelty and in the end cannot fully understand it. But we must remember, as Diétrich reminds us, "that the history of the People of God is all strewn with blood and tears. . . . The rage of man is unfurled upon the Elect of God. . . . Our own time has seen massacres equally shameless. The testimony of the evangelist is that God nonetheless pursues the purpose of salvation."

17. Most of this verse repeats what was said in 1:22 (where see notes). The one new thing in the formula of quotation is the attribution of this prophecy to Jeremiah (in 1:22 the prophet is not named). Matthew will later tell us that some of the Jews thought that Jesus was Jeremiah come back again (16:14), but here the name simply indicates the source of the

47. The verb is θυμόω and the adverb λίαν (which Matthew uses 4 times). The aorist is ingressive with the meaning "he became angry."

48. BAGD, ἀποστέλλω, 1.d.

49. ἀναιρέω, used here only in Matthew (Acts has it 19 times), means "take up, take away" and thus "do away with, murder."

50. Josephus, *Ant.* 17.181.

51. ὅριον (6 times in Matthew, 5 in Mark, 1 in Acts only in the New Testament) is always plural in the New Testament and signifies "boundaries." This enables it to be used to signify the region surrounding a city.

52. His verb ἀκριβόω conveys the idea of exactness or accuracy. κατά is classified here as "of the norm, of similarity, homogeneity . . . of a standard of any other kind" (BAGD, II.5.a and γ).

quotation. The repetition of the reference to fulfilled prophecy brings out once more a thought that means a lot to Matthew, namely that God acts in accordance with the revelation he has made in Scripture. In what happened to Jesus even in his infancy we may see the outworking of what God knew would happen.

18. The words are from Jeremiah 31:15 (LXX 38:15), with significant differences from LXX.[53] *A voice* may denote an utterance expressing any one of a variety of moods, but here clearly mourning is in mind. Ramah seems to have been in the area allotted to the tribe of Benjamin and about six miles north of Jerusalem. This, of course, raises the question of why a prophecy about a voice in Ramah should be related to a happening in Bethlehem. There seems to have been a tradition that Rachel was buried near Bethlehem (though another view was that it was at Ramah, and there is a further view that the site was Zelzah, 1 Sam. 10:2). But certainly Jeremiah speaks of Rachel as weeping for her children as the Israelites went off into exile (Rachel is taken symbolically as the mother of the nation, though, of course, Leah gave birth to more of the tribes than did Rachel),[54] and relates this to the fact that the infant Jesus went off into exile in Egypt. Matthew relates Rachel's grief to the situation in Bethlehem after Herod's men were through. Neither the prophet nor Matthew says whose voice was heard: the emphasis is on the mourning, not the mourners, and the language stresses the depths of the grief.[55] It is this sort of bitter grief that Matthew sees in Bethlehem. *Her children* in a passage like this means "descendants," and Rachel's grief is such that she will[56] not be comforted. The reason? *Because they are no more.* Nothing can alter the fact of the exile and nothing can alter the fact of the killings at Bethlehem. Thus the grief remains.[57] Yet we should add that Jeremiah's prophecy goes on to the note of hope (Jer. 31:17) and to the making of a new covenant (Jer. 31:31-34); further, the Israelites did in time return from their exile. All

---

53. Matthew has no equivalent of LXX's θρήνου, while he has a πολύς that is lacking in LXX. The nouns are nominative in Matthew and genitive in LXX. He has the simple κλαίουσα, LXX the compound ἀποκλαιομένη. LXX reads ἐπὶ τοῖς υἱοῖς αὐτῆ and puts it later in the sentence than Matthew's τὰ τέκνα αὐτῆς. LXX reads παύσασθαι for Matthew's παρακληθῆναι. In this verb Matthew is closer to the Hebrew than is LXX, but elsewhere LXX has the advantage. But over all in this quotation "we have evidence favouring the evangelist's knowledge of Hebrew" (Davies and Allison).

54. In Jeremiah there is "An imaginative prophetic touch: Rachel in her grave weeping afresh over the exile of her sons Joseph and Benjamin" (F. Cawley and A. R. Millard, *NBCR* on Jer. 31:15-17).

55. κλαυθμός is found in Matthew in 7 of its 9 New Testament occurrences. It describes a loud weeping. ὀδυρμός (again in the New Testament only in 2 Cor. 7:7) signifies lamentation, which would again be done loudly.

56. The use of θέλω points to an act of will; in the greatness of her grief Rachel is not willing to be consoled.

57. Robinson has some difficulty understanding the relevance of the quotation, and reasons "it is clear that it is the tradition which has led to the selection of the proof-text, not the proof-text which is responsible for the tradition."

this points to the fact that the child Jesus would in due course come back from his exile in Egypt.

4. The Return from Egypt, 2:19-23

> [19]But when Herod had died, look, an angel of the Lord appears in a dream to Joseph in Egypt, [20]and said, "Get up, take the young child and his mother, and go into the land of Israel; for those who sought the young child's life are dead." [21]And he rose, took the young child and his mother, and went into the land of Israel.
>
> [22]Now when he heard that Archelaus was reigning over Judea in the place of his father Herod, he was afraid to go there. And having been warned in a dream, he went off into the region of Galilee. [23]And he came and settled in a city called Nazareth, so that what was spoken through the prophets might be fulfilled, that he will be called a Nazarene.

Matthew goes on to tell his readers of the holy family's return to Palestine and how they came to settle in Nazareth.

19. It was not until *Herod had died* that there was any change in the situation. As long as the tyrant lived, there was danger in Palestine, but his death removed the threat. Matthew records a divine message conveyed in a dream and uses almost the same words as in 1:20 (where see notes). The exception is that he uses the present tense for *appears* (as in v. 13), which makes it all a little more vivid. The Evangelist is making clear that God's power and God's oversight extended to Egypt. His angel appeared there and gave Joseph directions.

20. The words of the angel are almost the same as those in verse 13, the only difference being that "flee into Egypt" is replaced by *go*[58] *into the land of Israel*. The return, like the flight, was undertaken at divine direction. An explanation is added, characteristically introduced by *for*; Matthew loves to give reasons. He does not name Herod, but refers (in Old Testament language; cf. Exod. 4:19) to the death of *those who sought*[59] *the young child's life*.[60] It is only Herod who has been named as dying, but the plural here draws attention to the passing from power of those associated with the tyrant.[61] The angel is saying that there is nothing to fear, no barrier to their going back to their own country.

---

58. Turner sees the use of the present πορεύου "where the rule demands aor." as "perhaps for politeness, as less peremptory" (M, III, p. 75).

59. Burton takes this as an example of the use of the present participle as an imperfect "to denote a continued action antecedent to that of the principal verb" (*MT,* 127). They kept seeking his life.

60. ψυχή, which Matthew uses 16 times, the most in any one book in the New Testament, has a wide range of meaning and is frequently used in the sense "soul." Here, however, it clearly means this earthly life.

61. Unless it is what Turner calls "The allusive pl.," which "is sometimes used when a class or variety rather than number is stressed" (M, III, pp. 25-26).

21. For the fourth time we have a reference to Joseph rising and taking the young child and his mother (vv. 13, 14, and 20). Joseph was obedient. He had received the divine instruction, so he entered the land of Israel.

22. The return to Israel was due to the divine direction, but the precise location arose from Joseph's fear, together with another dream. Matthew says nothing about where Joseph and Mary's home was previously, but Luke tells us that they had lived in Nazareth before going to Bethlehem (Luke 1:26; 2:4). Perhaps they would have liked to make their home in the city of David, especially in view of the circumstances attending Jesus' birth. But there was a difficulty arising from the fact that that area was now ruled[62] by Archelaus. This son of Herod was made ethnarch of Judea, Idumea, and Samaria when Herod died, but it did not take long for his incompetence to become apparent, and the Romans deposed him in A.D. 6. He was noted for his cruelty even in an age when cruel men were not scarce, so it is not surprising that Joseph feared to settle in this man's dominions. His fear was reinforced by further divine direction in a dream, though on this occasion we are not told what precise instructions he was given. But the upshot of it all was that he went to *the region*[63] *of Galilee*[64] to live. When Herod died, this area was in the tetrarchy of Herod Antipas.

23. Matthew often says "he came and did — "; here Joseph *came and settled*,[65] his new home being in Nazareth.[66] Luke locates both Joseph and Mary in this town (Luke 1:26-27; 2:4), but Matthew has not said anything so far about where either lived; he has said only that Jesus was born in Bethlehem. We should not read too much into *city*; the Greek language does not have a word equivalent to our "town," and it makes do with "city" or "village." We should understand that Nazareth was more than a hamlet, but not that it was a bustling metropolis. It was apparently not an important place; it is not mentioned in the Old Testament, the Talmud, the Midrashim, or Josephus (so BAGD). Matthew finds another fulfilment

---

62. Matthew's verb βασιλεύει strictly refers to the rule of a king. Herod left Judea, Idumea, and Samaria to him with the title "king," so Matthew's statement is accurate for this time. But the Romans refused him this title until he proved worthy of it, which he never did. It is perhaps relevant also that Archelaus ruled "in the place of" (ἀντί) his father. Josephus uses the same verb of this man (*Life* 5).

63. μέρος means "part"; in the plural it can denote the parts of a country and thus "region, district." With this meaning it is followed by a genitive.

64. Galilee is the Greek form of גָּלִיל, "circle, district," and was used of "the district of the Gentiles"; "after the Exile the northern part of Palestine, bounded by Syria, Sidon, Tyre, Ptolemais, Carmel, the plain of Jezreel, and the Jordan" (BAGD derives these limits from Josephus, *War* 3.35-40).

65. The verb κατοικέω means "settle down" and signifies a permanent dwelling as against sojourning (παροικέω).

66. There is variation in the name: Ναζαρά, Ναζαρέτ, and Ναζαρέθ are all found, and in some MSS Ναζαράθ and Ναζαράτ. Howard comments, "The exact Greek name of this obscure little place, which was never heard of till the Gospel story was current, might easily fluctuate in oral and written sources" (M, II, p. 149).

of prophecy in this choice of domicile. They lived there *so that*[67] prophecy might be fulfilled. On this occasion there are some small differences from the way Matthew usually cites prophecy; thus he uses the plural *prophets,* he omits "saying," and he inserts the word I have translated *that* (and which is taken by many interpreters as the equivalent of quotation marks, by others as meaning "because"). All this may be connected with the fact that it is not easy to find the words *he will be called a Nazarene*[68] in any of the prophetical books, or for that matter, anywhere in the Old Testament.[69] No passage even resembles this. It appears that Matthew is drawing attention to the thrust of Old Testament prophecy about the Christ rather than to any one passage. Jesus went to Galilee so that what was written about him in the prophets would be fulfilled, and we see this in his being called a Nazarene, a citizen of an obscure and unimportant town.[70] Had he been known as "Jesus of Bethlehem" he would have had the aura of one who came from the royal city; there would have been overtones of messianic majesty. But "Jesus the Nazarene" carried with it overtones of contempt.[71] We are to understand the prophets as pointing to one who would be despised and rejected, and Jesus as fulfilling this by his connection with obscure Nazareth.

67. ὅπως occurs 17 times in Matthew, the most in any one book. He uses it to bring out the sense of purpose, as here.

68. Matthew and John use the form Ναζωραῖος, which Luke has once in his Gospel and invariably in Acts. Mark always has Ναζαρηνός, and Luke has it twice. There is no difference in meaning. BAGD points out that "linguistically the transition fr. Ναζαρέτ to Ναζωραῖος is difficult . . . and it is to be borne in mind that Ναζωραῖος meant someth. different before it was connected w. Nazareth." But the transition was certainly made, for there can be no doubt that in the New Testament the word means "from Nazareth."

69. The most favored suggestions point to נצר (a "shoot" or "branch," Isa. 11:1) and to נזיר ("Nazirite," Num. 6:2). But, despite the confident assertions of many commentators, it is not easy to understand the connection between the branch or the Nazirite and the present passage. Cf. Hamann, "The word sounds a little like 'Nazirite', but the two should not be confused, for they are quite different in derivation and meaning." Matthew's own explanation is that the term refers to Nazareth, and for an understanding of his Gospel it is best to accept his explanation.

70. Cf. R. Knox, "No such prophecy has survived to us. But an obscure village is often regarded by its more important neighbours as typical of an unfashionable or provincial outlook; cf. Jn. 1.46. The prophecy (Is. 53.3) that our Lord would be despised by men was fulfilled when his contemporaries spoke of him scornfully as 'a prophet from Nazareth' (like our 'wise men of Gotham')" (*The New Testament,* p. 2, n. 4). Zahn has a somewhat similar view, but he takes ὅτι as causal, "because." Lenski, Ridderbos, and Plummer also take it as causal.

71. "When Christians were referred to in Acts as the 'Nazarene sect' (24:5), the expression was meant to hurt" (Carson).

Matthew 3

II. PRELIMINARIES TO JESUS' MINISTRY, 3:1-4:11

A. JOHN THE BAPTIST, 3:1-17

1. John's Preaching, 3:1-12

> ¹Now in those days John the Baptist appears, preaching in the wilderness of Judea ²and saying, "Repent, for the kingdom of heaven has drawn near. ³For this is he who was spoken of through Isaiah the prophet, saying,
>
> 'A voice of someone crying out in the wilderness,
> "Prepare the way of the Lord.
> Make his paths straight." ' "
>
> ⁴Now John had his clothing made of camel's hair and a leather belt around his waist, and his food was locusts and wild honey. ⁵Then there went out to him Jerusalem and all Judea and all the country by the Jordan, ⁶and they were baptized by him in the river Jordan, confessing their sins.
> ⁷And when he saw many of the Pharisees and Sadducees coming to his baptism, he said to them, "You offspring of snakes, who warned you to flee from the coming wrath? ⁸Produce therefore fruit worthy of repentance. ⁹And do not think to say within yourselves, 'We have Abraham as Father.' For I tell you that God is able to raise up children to Abraham from these stones! ¹⁰And already the axe is lying at the root of the trees; any tree therefore that does not produce good fruit will be cut down and thrown into the fire.
> ¹¹"I indeed baptize you in water for repentance, but he that comes after me is greater than I, whose sandals I am not worthy to carry. He will baptize you with the Holy Spirit and fire. ¹²His winnowing fork is in his hand, and he will thoroughly cleanse his threshing floor and gather his wheat into the barn; but he will burn up the chaff with fire that cannot be put out."

In common with the other Evangelists Matthew tells us that Jesus' ministry was preceded by that of John the Baptist. To bring out John's significance he cites Isaiah 40:3, but in a shorter form than does Luke, and he does not precede it with words from Malachi 3:1 as Mark does. He has quite a different approach from that of John, who simply gives us the testimony the Baptist bore to Jesus. For Matthew the important thing is that the Baptist came prophesying the doom that awaited sinners and calling on his hearers to repent.[1]

1. Matthew's *in those days* is a very general indication of time (and contrasts with Luke's precise dating, with reference to the time of the emperor, the prefect, the tetrarchs, and the high priest). It is puzzling since it follows immediately on the infancy narratives, but *those* cannot refer to that time. It may be an example of the use of "that"[2] to indicate without precision some time in the past (cf. 24:38; Luke 2:1, etc.), or perhaps better Matthew means "'in those crucial days' or 'in that critical time'" (Hill, who draws attention to Gen. 38:1; Exod. 2:11, etc.). Matthew calls John[3] *the Baptist,* a usage he employs 7 times (Mark has it twice, and Luke 3 times). It puts some emphasis on John's activity in baptizing people,[4] whereas he might simply have been designated a preacher of repentance. John, he says, *appears,* where his present tense makes it somewhat vivid; John appeared on the scene with his preaching and his baptizing. *Preaching* is a characteristic Christian activity (though, of course, not confined to Christians). The word properly means something like "make known by a herald"[5] and indicates a message given by authority to the proclaimer, not a free composition of his own.

Before giving the content of John's message Matthew proceeds to locate him. He was *in the wilderness of Judea,* a term that is sometimes understood in the sense "desert" (*GNB, NIV,* etc.). But while the word can sometimes be used of a sandy or stony waste, it often denotes land that is less inhospitable (e.g., 15:33; Luke 15:4; etc.). Since John did so much baptizing he cannot have been in what we would call a desert. This particular wilderness is that *of Judea,* the country from the watershed in

1. Cf. Davies, "not for the Baptist was it to call upon a select group to leave the world for the wilderness, as was the intent of the Teacher of Righteousness of the Dead Sea Sect, but to broadcast a challenge" (*SM,* p. 33).

2. Matthew uses ἐκεῖνος 54 times in all, which is more than anyone else in the New Testament except John with 70.

3. The name is spelled Ἰωάννης in many MSS, but there is only one ν in others. In D the doubled ν is used in Matthew and Mark, but the single ν in Luke and Acts (so BDF, 40). Matthew and Luke use the word for the Baptist 23 times each, which is more than anyone else. Matthew has the article 7 times and the nonarticular form 16 times, but there seems to be no difference in meaning.

4. In many baptisms in antiquity people baptized themselves, perhaps before witnesses. G. R. Beasley-Murray speaks of "the novelty of administering baptism to others, instead of leaving them to baptize themselves, as happened with all OT ablutions and in Jewish proselyte baptism" (*NIDNTT,* I, p. 150). Evidently John was distinguished by his activity during the process. The word is distinctive and is cited only from Christian writers apart from one reference in Josephus, where it also refers to John (see BAGD).

5. κηρύσσω is clearly connected with κῆρυξ, "a herald." The Christian message was designated by the cognate κήρυγμα: it was an authoritative proclamation of a message that was given, not the bright thoughts that occurred to an individual preacher. Bonnard remarks, "When a κῆρυξ appeared people did not ask whether he was intelligent or original, but 'What has taken place?' or 'What is going to happen?'"

the Judean hills eastward to the river Jordan. Its rainfall is light and its slopes steep; thus it offers little scope for agriculture. John will have been located toward the south of the area, where there were fords and people could come out to meet him.[6] At a later time Herod Antipas arrested John; since his dominion did not extend to the west of the Jordan at that time, however, John was working on the east side of the river.

2. Matthew strikes the note of John's preaching with his first word: *Repent* (Mark and Luke speak of him as "preaching a baptism of repentance for the forgiveness of sins," but Matthew's imperative is striking).[7] This is the first word also in the preaching of Jesus (4:17), and when Jesus sent the disciples out they called on people to repent (Mark 6:12). Repentance is of fundamental importance in the Christian message; what is not always noticed is that it is distinctive. In Greek writings generally "repent" means "change one's mind" — from a good purpose to a bad one just as much as from a bad one to a good one. Further, the idea that people should turn from a whole evil way of life to a new kind of living is not found.[8] That is a new teaching, though, of course, in the Old Testament there are constant calls to repent and return to God. With this demand John places himself in the prophetic tradition.[9]

John gives a reason[10] for his call to repentance: *the kingdom of heaven*[11] has approached. In all three Synoptists "the kingdom" is the most impor-

6. See further Charles H. Scobie, *John the Baptist* (London, 1964), pp. 41-48. Since the Qumran community was located not far from this area, it has been speculated by some that John had been a member of some such community. His parents were old when he was born, it is known that some Essene communities brought up children, and there are many points of contact between what we know of the preaching of John and the teachings in the Qumran scrolls. It would fit what we know if John had been a member of such a community but then had rebelled and left it. But this is speculation. There is no real evidence (despite the confident statement of *AB:* "There would seem to be no reason to doubt that John grew up in Qumran").

7. "He came with no theology; he came with no philosophy to discuss; he came with no new cult to introduce; he did not come to ask men to consider a position which they could accept or reject as they pleased; he came with the thundering voice of a great inspiration — "Repent' (Morgan).

8. Cf. J. Behm, "The change of opinion or decision, the alteration in mood or feeling, which finds expression in the terms, is not in any sense ethical. It may be for the bad as well as the good. . . . For the Greeks μετάνοια never suggests an alteration in the total moral attitude, a profound change in life's direction, a conversion which affects the whole of conduct" (*TDNT*, IV, p. 979).

9. William L. Lane has a fine note on repentance in the rabbinic literature (*The Gospel according to Mark* [Grand Rapids, 1974], pp. 593-600). He finds that "The preaching of John and of Jesus belongs to the prophetic tradition in which there is a radical demand for a once-for-all commitment to God, a 'turning' of one's whole self to the fulfilment of his will," whereas "In the Pharisaic and later rabbinic tradition repentance is conceived in terms of legal observance, while provision for forgiveness is made through such repeated practices as prayer, fasting and almsgiving" (p. 600). This verdict should perhaps be modified in accordance with such rabbinic statements as Barclay has collected. But there is no doubt that the rabbis tended to think of individual sins that might be repented over rather than the wholehearted commitment to God that John and Jesus demanded.

10. γάρ (see on 1:20) gives the reason for the foregoing.

11. Matthew has βασιλεία 55 times, while Mark has it 20 times and Luke 46. No other

tant topic in Jesus' teaching. In Matthew it is usually *the kingdom of heaven* (32 times), while "the kingdom of God," which is the most usual expression in Mark and Luke, occurs but 5 times. Sometimes it is simply "the kingdom" (6 times), or that of the Son of man (3 times), or that of the Father (twice). It is generally agreed that *the kingdom of heaven* in this Gospel means much the same as "the kingdom of God" in the others, and that it is a Jewish expression with the word "God" avoided out of motives of reverence. Matthew may, however, mean by it that we should keep open the possibility that the kingdom extends beyond this earth, and further that the Son has part in it as well as the Father.[12] It is also accepted that we should understand *kingdom* as meaning "rule" rather than "realm";[13] that is to say, the expression is dynamic: it points us to God as doing something, as actively ruling, rather than to an area or a group of people over whom he is sovereign. The kingdom is something that happens rather than something that exists. It was not a commonplace of Jewish teaching; in fact, the expression cannot be found prior to Jesus' use of it (that God rules in the affairs of all people is, of course, frequent in the Old Testament, but the expression "the kingdom of God [heaven]" is not). The kingdom is closely connected with the person of Jesus, and this is what is in mind with John's use of the expression. He is pointing to the truth that Jesus will shortly appear, and with him the kingdom. There is a sense in which the kingdom is future[14] (cf. 25:31, 34; 26:29), and another sense in which it is present. It is this latter to which John points.

3. John explains that what is happening is spoken of in prophecy. With an expression similar to Matthew's normal formula for introducing prophecy (see on 1:22; this one, however, does not refer specifically to fulfilment) the Baptist quotes some words from Isaiah 40:3 (almost exactly as in LXX except for "his paths" where LXX has "the paths of our God"). But where Matthew's formula has a reference to "that which was spoken," on this occasion the masculine participle shows that it is the person spoken of who is in mind. Jesus is closely identified with the kingdom. The expression is used in all three Synoptists, but Matthew has it in the shortest form (Mark precedes Isaiah with some words from Mal. 3:1, and Luke carries the Isaiah passage further). The passage begins with *a voice:* the

---

book has it more than Revelation's 9 times. Matthew is thus the most prolific user of the concept. He also uses οὐρανός, "heaven," more than does anyone else (82 times; Revelation is next with 52 times); it may refer to a part of the atmosphere, the sky, or to the dwelling of God and the angels, or, as here, it may be a reverent way of referring to God. He mostly uses the word in the plural, except when he refers to "heaven and earth" (see on 5:18). But he seems to mean much the same by "heavens" as by "heaven."

12. Cf. Schweizer, " 'Kingdom of heaven' suggests both God and Christ as the Lord."

13. Joel Marcus has defended this view in an article entitled "Entering into the Kingly Power of God" (*JBL*, 107 [1988], pp. 663-75).

14. But cf. Stonehouse, "Of all the instances where Matthew refers to the kingdom, only a few demand an exclusive reference to the coming of the kingdom at the consummation of the age" (*Witness*, p. 233).

message is important, the messenger is not.[15] This voice is crying out *in the wilderness* (*crying out* may point to loudness, as *GNB*, "shouting," or solemnity, 27:46; for *in the wilderness* see also v. 1).[16] This is not where we expect a voice to be sounding; we look for it in the great city, where there will be many to hear. But there is often sinfulness and vice in the city, and there are passages in Scripture where the Lord's people are in the wilderness. It may be that the language here is not simply geographical but also theological: it is there, in the lonely wilderness, the place of openness to the message of God, that preparation is being made to receive the Lord.

Prepare may be used of making a thing ready or keeping it ready. Here the imagery is of a road that needs to be repaired so that it may be ready for the Lord to travel over it smoothly. *Way*[17] may be used in the literal sense of a road; here the imagery is that of the road over which a king will approach. In antiquity when it was known that the sovereign was coming, every effort would be made to ensure that the road was as smooth as it could be. The great one must be able to travel easily and quickly. "The Lord"[18] refers in Isaiah to Yahweh, but the Baptist is applying the passage to Jesus. When Matthew records this use of Scripture he is revealing something of his Christology. To ascribe to Jesus words that in Holy Scripture applied to God shows that for the writer Jesus occupies the highest of places. The use of the same prophecy in the other Synoptists indicates that this was an accepted practice among the Christians, not something peculiar to Matthew. *Make his paths straight* continues the metaphor, but it is not quite clear whether straightening the path means eliminating bends or removing bumps. It is perhaps more likely to be making the path[19] level (cf. Moffatt, "level the paths") than altering it to have fewer

15. BAGD thinks that we should take φωνή as no more than "hark!" (2.e).

16. Most scholars hold that if we follow the Massoretic accentuation we should understand the Hebrew as "A voice crying: 'In the wilderness. . . .' " This was also the way the Qumran community took it as it applied the words to itself (1QS 8:13ff.). But LXX favors "A voice of one crying in the wilderness, 'Prepare. . . .' " Gundry holds that "the MT is probably unoriginal" here.

17. ὁδός is a Matthean word (22 times; Mark has it 16 times and Luke 20, with another 20 in Acts; no other book has it more than 4 times). The word means "a road, a highway" and then a journey (10:10). It is also used figuratively, as when Matthew refers to "the way of righteousness" (21:32) and the early Christians spoke of Christianity as "the Way" (e.g., Acts 9:2).

18. κύριος means the owner of possessions and thus the lord or master who has complete control. Hence it means someone in high position, and from this it comes to be used as a polite form of address (like our "sir"). It is commonly used for someone in the highest place of all (Festus referred to the emperor in this way, Acts 25:26). It is thus used as a designation of God, who is supreme over all, and it comes to be used of Jesus in like manner, especially in Acts and the Epistles. The word is used 718 times in the New Testament, so it is frequent on Christian lips. Of these, 80 occur in Matthew but only 18 in Mark; there are 103 in Luke and 107 in Acts, the most in any one book.

19. *Path* translates τρίβος (connected with τρίβω, "to rub"), which means *"worn or beaten track"* (LSJ). Such a path was bound to have potholes and would require leveling.

bends. All is to be made ready for the coming of God's chosen one. John's announcement of the coming of the kingdom and his call to repentance were ways of preparing the path for the coming of Jesus.

4. Attention is now directed to John's[20] clothing[21] and diet, for these tell us something important about the man. His garments were made of *camel's hair*, which would have been somewhat coarse and presumably cheap, and he wore a leather (or perhaps dried skin) belt. The impression we get is that there was nothing elaborate or attractive in the way John dressed. He was to do his work by preaching effectively, not by sartorial splendor. Moreover, such clothing had been worn by Elijah (2 Kings 1:8), so John was dressing in the prophetic tradition (cf. also Zech. 13:4). *Locusts* (permitted food in Lev. 11:22) are still eaten by the poor in many areas, and accompanied by *wild honey* (i.e., honey produced by bees in the wild, as against honey sold by beekeepers; cf. 1 Sam. 14:25-29) they point to a diet that could be obtained locally without difficulty. The picture we get is of a man who lived simply. His clothing was far from splendid or elaborate, and his food such as could be obtained in the wild.

5. *Then* (see on 2:7) does not follow logically from the description of John's clothing and food; it means "at that time," signifying in a general fashion the time of John's ministry, long past when these words were written. *Jerusalem*, of course, indicates here the inhabitants of that city, and we must understand *all Judea* and the region[22] *by the Jordan* similarly. Matthew is saying that large numbers of people went out from the centers of population to John's lonely area. Such a prophetic figure was a rarity, and people wanted to see and hear the man. So, though he was in the wilderness, John did not lack an audience.

6. John's characteristic act was that of baptism, and it is this that gives him his title "the Baptist." Since Christians are familiar with baptism only as a religious ceremony, we are apt to miss some of its meaning. But the verb means "dip, plunge" and in the passive "be drowned"; it is used of ships in the sense "sink" (LSJ; it notes Josephus's use for the crowds who flocked into Jerusalem at the time of the siege: they "flooded" the

---

20. The verse begins with αὐτός, which is very difficult to translate (*JB* tries with "This man John"). It "is used for emphasis" (BDF, 277[3]) and means "*self*, intensive, setting the individual off fr. everything else, emphasizing and contrasting," and in the usage here, "the mng. *even, very* directs attention to a certain pers. or thing to the exclusion of the others, so that αὐ. can almost take on a demonstrative sense" (BAGD, 1 and 1.h). Howard suggests "John in his person" or "As to himself, John" or "Perhaps simply 'John'" (M, II, p. 431).

21. Matthew's word is ἔνδυμα, a term he uses 7 times; elsewhere in the New Testament it is found only in Luke 12:23. Bengel remarks, "Even the dress and food of John preached, being in accordance with his teaching and office."

22. περίχωρος is an adjective meaning "round about"; it is often used as a substantive (with γῆ understood) for "the region round about" and, as here, for the people of the region round about. Josephus makes it clear that John had a large following and that he headed a significant movement (*Ant.* 18.116-19).

city). We should not miss the significance of this violent imagery. Baptism signifies death to a whole way of life (cf. Rom. 6:3).[23] The Jews employed baptism in admitting Gentiles as proselytes, but the sting in John's practice was that he applied it to Jews! *By him* indicates that John actually administered the baptism and did not simply act as a witness while the penitents baptized themselves. What they did do was confess their sins (see on 1:21). Matthew depicts John's whole ministry as a calling on people to repent of their sins in preparation for the coming of God's Messiah (who would save them from their sins, 1:21). Confession is an integral part of that process. When people really repent they say so.

7. Matthew turns to John's reaction to some of the people who came to be baptized.[24] *Saw* may be used of various kinds of perception, but here it is clearly direct sight. *Many* is interesting; there were a great number more than the handful of people who might have been expected to be interested in a rough man of the deserts. Matthew singles out those of *the Pharisees and Sadducees,* where the one article indicates that they formed a single group (the two are linked also in 16:1, 6, 11, and 12). Outside Matthew they are linked in this way only in Acts 23:7; evidently for Matthew the expression stands for the groups of leading Jews who opposed the Christian movement. We should not reason from the use of the single article that he perceived the two as wholehearted allies; he knew that they were different parties with different teachings (22:34). He is saying no more than that from the Christian standpoint there was not much to choose between them. They were united in their opposition to John and then to Jesus, whatever differences they might have in other respects.

This Evangelist uses the term "Pharisee" more often than anyone else (29 times; Luke has 27). The Pharisees were a religious party who delighted to derive their name from a word meaning "separated"; they viewed themselves as God's separated ones. They studied the law very carefully and made a determined attempt to put it into practice. In doing this they paid close attention to a multitude of rules (the tradition of the elders) meant to help people avoid breaking any command of God. There were so many of these that most people gave up the attempt to follow them. The result was that the Pharisees tended to see themselves as a cut above other people while at the same time they gave such attention to

23. The verb may be followed by ἐν as here, by εἰς (Mark 1:9), or by a simple dative (Mark 1:8).

24. This passage is absent from Mark but is closely paralleled in Luke 3:7-9. The introductory words are different: Matthew refers to Pharisees and Sadducees as coming to his baptism, while Luke speaks of the crowds who went out to be baptized. But what John said is almost identical in the two accounts. Matthew has 63 words, Luke 64 (he puts καί before ἡ ἀξίνη in v. 9), and the only differences are Matthew's singular in the words "fruit worthy" (v. 8) where Luke has the plural, and Matthew's δόξητε (v. 9) where Luke has ἄρξησθε. Clearly they are following the same source closely, or one is using the other. Matthew is the only Evangelist who tells of John's denunciation of the Pharisees and Sadducees (John has an inquiry from the Pharisees [John 1:19, 24], but not a denunciation).

outward minutiae that they sometimes lost sight of weightier matters. Since Jesus was impatient of this approach, they tended to oppose him vigorously. There were some very fine Pharisees, but unfortunately too many of the other kind.

"Sadducee" (7 times in Matthew out of 14 in the New Testament) denoted a member of the high-priestly party. The name was probably derived from Zadok, the man made high priest by David at the time of Solomon's accession to the throne (1 Kings 1:8; 2:35); the Sadducees thus regarded themselves as "Zadokites," true descendants of the great priest. None of their writings survives, so we are left to deduce their positions from the writings of their opponents. It is often said that they accepted only the Pentateuch as sacred Scripture (as some of the early Christian fathers say), but it is difficult to find evidence for this and it seems most unlikely. The fact that the Septuagint was in existence indicates that the Jews widely accepted the canon of Scripture; there seems to be no reason why a prominent Jewish party should reject most of it. But the Sadducees did reject the oral tradition that the Pharisees valued so highly; Josephus tells us that they accepted only written Scripture (*Ant.* 13.297). The Sadducees tended to be aristocratic (they had "the confidence of the wealthy alone but no following among the populace," Josephus, *Ant.* 13.298) and contemptuous of movements like that represented by John and Jesus. They cooperated with the Romans and thus had political power; they saw Jesus as something of a danger, for he might provoke a movement in opposition to Rome and bring a strong reaction from their overlords.

Matthew makes it clear that many from the more important religious parties came to John. This would not have been anticipated, for they were the more "respectable" members of society and John would not have been expected to make much of an appeal to people like this. It is interesting that even people from groups like these should seek baptism.[25] At the same time we should bear in mind that from the way he addressed them John evidently suspected that their "repentance" was not very deep.

John addressed[26] this group of candidates[27] for baptism in forthright

25. ἐπί here indicates purpose (cf. Chamberlain, p. 121; BAGD, "of purpose, goal, result," here "to have themselves baptised," III.1.b.η). ἐπί can signify "*against* w. hostile intent" (BAGD, III.1.a.ε); if we take it in this way we can think of the Pharisees and Sadducees as coming to John with hostile intentions. But John's words seem addressed to candidates for his baptism. βάπτισμα, found twice in Matthew and 20 times in the New Testament, is apparently used only in Christian writers (βαπτισμός is used elsewhere). It denotes John's baptism as here, Christian baptism, and, figuratively, martyrdom.

26. Notice the string of imperfects telling of John's dress (v. 4), his audience (v. 5), and his baptizing (v. 6). This sequence, leading up to the aorists in John's address, "all contributes to a vivid picture against the background of which John utters his rebukes (v. 7 aor.)" (Turner, M, III, p. 66).

27. Allen sees in this address to the Pharisees and Sadducees a mark of genuineness, for "it is very unlikely that the Baptist should have spoken words like these to the common people who crowded to his baptism."

terms, calling them *offspring of snakes* (serpents sprung from serpents).[28] This is scarcely complimentary, and it is backed up with the question, *who warned*[29] *you to flee from the coming wrath?* The implication is that they had no real repentance but only a desire to escape divine retribution. The word rendered *coming* indicates not only futurity but certainty.[30] That God will act in opposition to sin is certain, as John sees things, the only question being when. This is Matthew's only use of *wrath*,[31] but it is an important New Testament concept. It stands for the settled opposition of God's holy nature to everything that is evil. We are not to think that God is mildly displeased when people sin. He is totally and vigorously opposed to evil, and the Bible expresses this by speaking of his wrath. It is the consistent teaching of Scripture that this wrath will be manifested in all its vigor at the end of the age, when evil will finally be punished. John is linking this wrath with the coming of God's kingdom and accusing the Pharisees and Sadducees of simply looking for a way of escaping the punishment that their deeds had deserved (cf. 23:33). They lacked a determination to abandon evil ways.

8. *Produce,* more literally "make," is a word often used of plants when they "make" fruit[32] and is thus a good word for producing the "fruit" of life. *Therefore* is perhaps not the connective we would have anticipated, but it may well be that it is here used in the sense "*certainly, in fact,* confirming something, freq. in contrast with something which is not confirmed . . . *really*" (LSJ). John wants to see not simply the words that express repentance but the *fruit* that befits it, fruit that is *worthy*[33] *of repentance.* The singular is important.[34] John is not inviting people to pile up good works; he is looking for a change in the orientation of the whole of life that will result in fruitful living. For the meaning and the distinctive-

---

28. The expression occurs 4 times in the New Testament, 3 in this Gospel, the other 2 being directed at the Pharisees (12:34; 23:33). It is often translated "viper," and this may be right, though it sometimes apparently denotes "a constrictor snake" (LSJ).

29. ὑποδείκνυμι means "to show secretly" and then generally "to teach, make known" (see AS). Stendahl thinks that the meaning is "who gave you the idea. . . ?" Teaching about coming wrath is clearly a warning.

30. For μέλλω see on 2:13.

31. ὀργή occurs 36 times in 12 different books. It is the usual word for the divine wrath, θυμός being used a number of times in Revelation but rarely elsewhere other than for human wrath. There is often little difference between them, but θυμός is a passionate outburst whereas ὀργή proceeds from a settled disposition. Translations like "retribution" (*NEB*) miss this. See further my *The Apostolic Preaching of the Cross*³ (London and Grand Rapids, 1965), pp. 179-84. On the present passage Gutzwiller remarks, "Not a generation is to pass before the temple will be destroyed, Jerusalem burned, and Israel driven out of its homeland." Perhaps it is worth adding that among the rabbis it was held that "wrath" signifies Gehenna (e.g., *B. Bat.* 10a).

32. ποιέω is frequent in Matthew (84 times). It is used of trees producing fruit in 7:17 and elsewhere. Of course, the word is used of "making" in a variety of other senses as well.

33. AS derives ἄξιος from ἄγω in the sense "to weigh"; it comes to mean "of weight" and thus "worthy, befitting."

34. Bruce comments on this singular, "Any one can do . . . acts externally good, but only a good man can grow a crop of right acts and habits."

ness of the Christian idea of repentance see the note on verse 2. John is making with some vigor the point that being present at a fashionable religious center is not enough. Lives must be changed. In view of the certainty of the wrath to come people must forsake evil ways and live rightly before God.

9. The demand is hammered in with a reference to Jewish pride in descent from Abraham. To many Jews it was unthinkable that the great patriarch's descendants should ever be excluded from God's blessing.[35] Thus they thought that because they could say, *We have Abraham* (see on 1:1) *as Father,* they had eternal security. But John tells them not to think like that.[36] No place of privilege counts in the face of the demands of an all-holy and all-powerful God. For John it was crystal clear that God looked for more from people than a complacent claim of kinship with Abraham ("God, he says, is not interested in family-trees which bear no fruit in changed lives," Melinsky). *To say within yourselves* indicates personal conviction rather than public profession. John is speaking about the way this section of his hearers might justify their refusal to repent: that did not matter, they would reason, for their connection with their great forefather ensured their deliverance and his merits availed for them. This John strongly opposes. His *For I tell you* puts some emphasis on what follows: the words are important. Being children of Abraham is no great matter, for God can[37] *raise up children to Abraham from these stones.*[38] The Jews thought of themselves as being in a unique position: they were the descendants of Abraham in a way nobody else was. Therefore they had a wonderful privilege. But they underestimated the power of God. God did not need the children of Abraham in order to accomplish his purposes. John tells them that it is within God's power to raise up privileged people at any time out of the most unpromising material. The reference to *these* stones probably means that stones were visible; the area where they were was a rugged place. But even out of stones God could raise up those who were effectively children of Abraham, true sons over against those who could claim no more than physical descent (cf. Gal. 3:7).

---

35. Cf. R. Levi: "In the Hereafter Abraham will sit at the entrance to Gehenna, and permit no circumcised Israelite to descend therein" (*Gen. Rab.* 48:8). Matthew has Ἀβραάμ 7 times, but in only this verse does it have the article. This singles him out as *the* Abraham, the great, well-known Abraham.

36. δοκέω occurs 10 times in Matthew and Luke, the most in any New Testament book. It derives from δόκος, "opinion," and thus has the meaning "be of opinion, think." Moulton compares this with Luke's version; in Matthew "we find δόξητε for ἄρξησθε, 'do not presume to say,' which is thoroughly idiomatic Greek, and manifestly a deliberate improvement of an original preserved more exactly by Luke" (M, I, p. 15).

37. δύναμαι is an important word in all four Gospels (Matthew has it 27 times, Mark 33, Luke 26, and John 36); outside the Gospels it is used much less freely. All the Evangelists are interested in what is and what is not possible. They often speak of God's ability to do great things, as here. The placing of the verb first in its clause puts emphasis on it.

38. There is a play on words: in Aramaic the word for "stones" is similar in sound to that for "sons."

10. John proceeds to bring out the seriousness of the position of those who did not genuinely repent. *Already* points to what has occurred; John is not referring only to the remote future; for those who have eyes to see things were already happening. This is reinforced by the present tense in the three verbs of this verse. *The axe* (here and in Luke 3:9 only in the New Testament) was a symbol of destruction, and *lying at the root of the trees*[39] paints a grim picture of impending doom (cf. Isa. 10:34; Jer. 46:22). It is not easy to understand why the axe is pictured as lying at "the root" of the trees; if one is using an axe a tree is generally cut down some little distance up from the ground. But the root is that from which the tree draws its sustenance; therefore, the picture suggests that not only will the tree be overthrown, but its source of nourishment will be taken away.[40] There is no hope for such a tree. *Any tree* makes it universal — there are no exceptions.[41] The sinner must not think that he can get away with his sin. *Therefore* links this up in logical sequence; John regards the destruction as inevitable. In verse 8 he has spoken of fruit befitting repentance; now it is simply *good*[42] *fruit*. The tree that lacks such fruit will be totally destroyed — not only *cut down* but also *thrown into the fire.* "Does John seem too stern? Jesus spoke with similar sternness; no gospel is needed if there is no judgment" (Filson).

11. In this little paragraph there are parallels to Mark, and especially to Luke (both of whom have the words spoken to the people generally rather than to the Pharisees and Sadducees). Of Matthew's 57 words Mark has 16 (not always in the same order) and Luke 43. There is very little that any of the Synoptists has that does not appear in one or both of the others. At this point John turns to his practice of baptism and relates it to another baptism that would follow. *I indeed* is emphatic; it sets John in contrast with the stronger one who is to come[43] (there is also a less emphasized contrast with the immediately following *you*: John sets himself over against those whom he baptizes). His baptism is *in water,*[44] to which

---

39. Moule views this as an example of the "pregnant" sense of πρός with the accusative, "seemingly combining 'linear' motion with 'punctiliar' rest on arrival" (*IBNTG*, p. 53). *RSV* and *NEB* try to bring this out with "to the root" (*NRSV* alters this to "at the root"). However we translate it, there is the thought that the axe is not only available but that it is so placed that an assault on the trees is imminent.

40. Lenski sees the significance as "Not even a stump will be left; judgment will be complete."

41. "πᾶς before an anarthrous noun means *every* in the sense of *any*; not every individual, like ἕκαστος, but any you please" (M, III, p. 199).

42. *Good* is καλός; Matthew uses it more than anyone (21 times; next is 1 Timothy with 16 occurrences). If the word can be differentiated from ἀγαθός, it will refer to "goodliness as manifested in form: ἀ. to inner excellence" (AS, *sub* ἀγαθός); it may thus point to fruit which can be seen as good.

43. Matthew uses μέν 20 times, a total exceeded only in Acts (47) and 1 Corinthians (21); thus it is a Matthean word. He always follows it with δέ, marking a contrast brought out in the second clause. Here he places the Baptist in marked contrast with Jesus.

44. ἐν ὕδατι. Sometimes the simple dative is used to indicate the material in which baptism takes place (as Mark 1:8); it may also be εἰς + accusative (Mark 1:9).

Matthew adds (as the others do not) *for*[45] *repentance* (see on v. 2). This term follows naturally on what John has just been saying about the importance of changed lives and the certainty of coming judgment.

John moves to his contrast with *but*. The verb "come" may be used in the sense "appear, make an appearance . . . esp. of the Messiah," and here it is *"come after* of Christ in relation to his forerunner" (BAGD, I.1.a.η). John's successor, then, would come on the scene as one *greater than I.* The word *greater* contains the idea of strength, of power; the Christ would be more powerful than his predecessor. Then John moves on to fitness. He sees himself as *not worthy* to perform the most menial service for the coming great one and selects the carrying[46] of the sandals to bring this out. Mark and Luke have the loosing of the sandal thong, but since the sandals were then carried off this means no more than references to two stages of the same process. The important point is that dealing with the sandals was the menial task of a slave. Teachers in Palestine at that time were not paid, but it was usual for disciples to help their rabbi in whatever way they could. There is a rabbinic saying: "Every service which a slave performs for his master shall a disciple do for his teacher except the loosing of his sandal-thong."[47] It is a mark of John's humility that he says he is not worthy of the service that no one but a slave would perform.

The great one, John says, *will baptize you with the Holy Spirit and fire.*[48] Jesus will do much more for those baptized than John could. John could demand that they repent, but Jesus would bring them the Holy Spirit. It is unlikely that John would think of the Third Person of the Trinity, but he would have in mind the outpouring of the Holy Spirit promised by Joel (Joel 2:28; in v. 30 there is a reference to fire). And Matthew would surely see a deeper meaning in John's words. John at the very least is saying that Jesus' baptism is no mere ritual affair, but one that involves the effective gift of the Spirit. We do well not to inquire too closely into

---

45. Baptism is often followed by εἰς, but only here with a reference to repentance. We might expect the construction to denote purpose ("with a view to"), but this is surely not what is meant, for repentance should precede baptism. More likely it means "because of" (so DM, p. 104); baptism is the seal that marks repentance (cf. Bonnard). Elsewhere baptism εἰς is "into the name" (28:19), "into the Jordan" (Mark 1:9), "into Christ" (Rom. 6:3), "into his death" (Rom. 6:3), "into one body" (1 Cor. 12:13), and "into" Moses (1 Cor. 10:2).

46. Cf. MM, "The firmly established vernacular use determines the meaning of Mt 3¹¹ as 'whose sandals I am not worthy to *take off'*: the phrase is an excellent example of Mt's skilful abbreviation, for one word fully expresses all that Mk 1⁷ tells us in four" (*sub* βαστάζω).

47. SBk, I, p. 121. In its present form the saying dates from c. A.D. 250, but it is probably much older. Daube (p. 266) thinks that Matthew is differentiating carrying the sandals (which a disciple might do) from taking them off (which was the task of a slave). But this is surely "too ingenious," as Davies and Allison say.

48. ἐν is used of baptism "in" the Holy Spirit just as it was used of John's baptism "in" water. H. J. Flowers argues that we should take πνεῦμα here in the sense of "wind"; he thinks that John is predicting a judgment of wind and fire (*ET,* LXIV [1952-53], pp. 155-56). E. Schweizer supports this view (*ET,* LXV [1953-54], p. 29). But in the New Testament πνεῦμα consistently refers to the Holy Spirit, and no adequate reason is given for allowing an exception here.

the relationships between the Persons of the Trinity, but at least we can say that the coming Messiah will bring his followers into vital contact with the Holy Spirit and thus inject a new force into their lives. With this is linked *fire;* the connection is close, for there is no separate preposition. Baptizing with the Holy Spirit goes along with baptizing with fire, which here stands for purification. Some interpreters understand fire to refer to judgment (as it often does; Ridderbos, e.g., accepts this view here),[49] but the link with the Holy Spirit makes it more likely that the same people are referred to and that they are purified as well as indwelt (fire was linked with the coming of the Spirit on the Day of Pentecost, Acts 2:3).

12. The thought of judgment is pursued and enlarged. John pictures the Messiah as having a *winnowing fork* in his hand. At harvesttime the grain was threshed, for example, by having oxen tread it out, a process that shook the grain free from the husks but left them in the same heap. It was then winnowed: the threshed grain was separated from the husks by throwing it into the air, at first with a fork and later with a shovel (cf. Isa. 30:24). The heavier grain would fall straight down, but the lighter husks would be blown further away. If the winnowing fork is already in hand, the process of separation is about to begin (*REB* has "his winnowing shovel," which would indicate that the last stage in winnowing is about to begin). The picture is one of imminent activity; judgment will not be delayed. And it will be wholehearted, for *he will thoroughly cleanse his threshing floor*. The verb is unusual,[50] but it clearly points to a complete cleaning out of the *threshing floor*. It is possible to understand this as meaning that the threshing floor will be cleaned by the removal of all the husks so that only the grain is left. But the further imagery of fire suggests that the cleansing will be by burning up the chaff. *And*[51] he will *gather his wheat* signifies the preservation of those who are right with God, just as *burn up the chaff* the severe judgment of those who are in the wrong. Fire is often used in connection with the last judgment. *That cannot be put out*[52] points to the impossibility of averting the punishment of evil. The putting of the wheat into the barn (Matthew has "his[53] wheat" and Luke "his

---

49. L. W. Barnard suggests that the background to John's preaching was Iranian eschatology, which teaches that all, good and bad alike, are destined to be immersed in a fiery stream. "John's water baptism is then the pledge that the individual is prepared to face this baptism. The man who immerses himself in the Jordan pre-enacts his own Judgment" (*JTS*, n.s. VIII [1957], p. 107). This is an interesting suggestion, but there is no reason for thinking that John's teaching and practice derived from Iranian eschatology.

50. διακαθαρίζω seems not to occur anywhere but here and as a variant reading in Luke 3:17. ἅλων, "threshing floor," is found in the New Testament only here and in Luke 3:17.

51. καί is used regularly simply as a way of connecting clauses, and this may be its significance here. But it may also be used as "explicative; i.e., a word or clause is connected by means of καί w. another word or clause, for the purpose of explaining what goes before it, *and so, that is, namely*" (BAGD, 3); "that is" would make excellent sense here.

52. ἄσβεστος, again in the New Testament only in Mark 9:43; Luke 3:17, signifies "inextinguishable"; it seems to have much the same meaning as αἰώνιος in 18:8; 25:41.

53. αὐτοῦ is repeated three times, "his hand," "his threshing floor," and "his wheat"

barn") and the burning up of the chaff picture the satisfactory completion of the harvest.

2. Jesus' Baptism, 3:13-17

13*Then Jesus comes from Galilee to the Jordan to John to be baptized by him.* 14*But John tried to stop him, saying, "I have need to be baptized by you, and are you coming to me?"* 15*But Jesus answered him, "Let it be so now, for in this way it is fitting for us to fulfil all righteousness." Then he allowed him.* 16*And when Jesus was baptized, he came up from the water straightaway; and, look, the heavens were opened, and he saw the Spirit of God descending like a dove and coming on him.* 17*And look, a voice out of heaven, saying, "This is my Son, the Beloved, in whom I am well pleased."*

While there are resemblances between this passage and the corresponding sections in Mark and Luke, they are not nearly as many or as close as in the preceding passage. Indeed, the differences are so many that it is not easy to see Matthew as using the same source as either of the others; the changes are too many and too significant. There is no parallel to Matthew 13:14-15, with John's attempt to dissuade Jesus from baptism, and there are significant differences in verse 16. The words of the voice from heaven are closer, but Matthew has "This is" where the others have "You are." We should regard this section as independent of the parallel passages in the other Synoptists.

13. For Matthew's characteristic *Then* see on 2:7. Here it denotes that which follows next in sequence. For *comes* we have the same verb and the same tense as that used of the Baptist in verse 1 (both Mark and Luke prefer the aorist in their equivalent expressions); the present gives it greater vividness, and we get the thought that Jesus makes his appearance on the scene. Matthew mentions both his starting point and his destination,[54] but he says nothing about the journey. He further tells us that Jesus came specifically *to John to be baptized by him.* The construction[55] indicates purpose; Jesus came to John in order to undergo the baptism John was administering.

14. *But* sets John's purpose over against that of Jesus. Jesus came with the purpose of being baptized, *but* John objected.[56] A further contrast

---

(in some MSS also "his barn"; this should, however, probably be rejected). But there is no "his" with the chaff.

54. *To the Jordan* is ἐπὶ τ.'Ι., an unusual construction (the verb is followed by ἐπί elsewhere in the New Testament only in a variant reading in Luke 22:52). But ἐπί may be used "of motion that comes close to someth. or someone *to, up to, in the neighborhood of, on*" (BAGD, III.1.a.γ), which will be the sense of it here.

55. τοῦ with the infinitive usually, though not invariably, conveys the notion of purpose. Matthew has the construction 6 times (2:13; 3:13; 11:1; 13:3; 21:32; 24:45); it is much more common in Paul and in Luke. "It belongs . . . to a higher stratum of Koine" (BDF, 400).

56. The imperfect διέχωλυεν is conative, "tried to stop." Howard sees the διά as perfective, "John was for stopping him altogether" (M, II, p. 302).

is brought out with the use of the emphatic pronouns for *I* and *you*. John
sets himself over against Jesus and says that any baptism should be the
other way around: he should be baptized by Jesus and not Jesus by him.
He points to his *need;* it is not a question of what he wants (or what Jesus
wants) but of need. This is a further illustration of John's humility and of
his recognition of his own sinfulness, for a baptism like John's was for
penitent sinners, not for people who needed no repentance.[57] His *and* is
in the sense "emphasizing a fact as surprising or unexpected or noteworthy: *and yet, and in spite of that*" (BAGD, καί, I.2.g). John is surprised at
finding Jesus among his baptizands. It does not seem right and therefore
he does not want this baptism to proceed. The Fourth Evangelist tells us
that the Baptist did not know Jesus until he saw the Spirit descend on him
like a dove (John 1:33), which may mean that he did not know Jesus or
that he did not know him to be the Messiah. But Matthew does not address
himself to this question. He simply tells us that John recognized his inferior
place without going into the question of how he came to know it or for
that matter how he understood it. Since John does not speak of Jesus as
Messiah, he may have meant only that he knew that Jesus had greater
authority than he or was morally superior to him.

15. Another *but* carries on the contrast. Jesus answers[58] not so much
the question John asked as the problem that lay behind it for John. *Let it
be so now* clearly means "Let us get on with the baptism at this point"; the
words negate John's request not to proceed to baptize Jesus (the word *now*
leaves room for something different in the future and thus for some recognition of John's lower place than that of Jesus). *It is fitting* also presents
no great problem. Jesus is saying that it is seemly or proper that they
should go ahead. What is not so clear is how we should understand the
words *for us to fulfil all righteousness.*[59] Suggestions such as taking the
expression "in the sense of fulfilling the divine statutes" (BAGD, 2.a; Carr

---

57. Unless he had in mind that Jesus would baptize with the Holy Spirit and fire (v. 11),
as McNeile and Bonnard, for example, think; John certainly needed that baptism. He may
be saying in effect, "I need your baptism of the Spirit and fire, but you do not need my
baptism of repentance in water."

58. In Matthew the verb ἀποκρίνομαι is almost always followed by a verb of saying
(here εἶπεν; there are exceptions at 15:23; 22:46; 26:62), a Hebraistic way of carrying on a
narrative. Moulton speaks of it as one of his "pure Hebraisms" (M, I, p. 14; cf. also M, II,
p. 453). KJV translates both words, here "answering said," but modern translations generally
content themselves with "answered." Usually the expression is a reply to a question, but it
may be used when no question has been asked (e.g., 8:8) or in carrying on a discourse (11:25;
12:38, etc.).

59. δικαιοσύνη occurs 7 times in Matthew as against 3 in all the other Gospels put
together. Clearly it is an important concept for him. But the big user of "righteousness" in
the New Testament is Paul with 57 examples. Paul uses the word for the "right standing"
that believers have before God when they are saved in Christ. This, of course, is the basic
New Testament teaching, but the word can also be used of the conduct befitting one who is
"right" with God. See further my *The Apostolic Preaching of the Cross*[3] (London and Grand
Rapids, 1965), chs. VIII and IX.

is similar with "the requirements of the law") should be rejected; what divine statute was fulfilled when Jesus was baptized? The view that it is the righteousness of the whole life that is in mind is somewhat better, though it is not easy to understand how Jesus and John were fulfilling that in this baptism.[60] The expression is undoubtedly difficult and has aroused a great deal of discussion. But in this Gospel "fulfil" is often used of the fulfilment of prophecy, and this is surely in mind here. We should probably understand righteousness as in Isaiah 53:11: "by the knowledge of himself shall my righteous servant justify many; and he shall bear their iniquities."[61] Matthew is not averse to referring to Isaiah (e.g., 1:23; 12:18-21; he cites this very chapter in 8:17), and a reference to the righteousness of the Servant would suit the present passage admirably. Jesus might well have been up there in front standing with John and calling on sinners to repent. Instead he was down there with the sinners, affirming his solidarity with them, making himself one with them in the process of the salvation that he would in due course accomplish.[62] If there is a reference to Isaiah 53, it is relevant to note that in that chapter we read: he "was numbered with the transgressors" (Isa. 53:12). There may also be something of the Israel typology here. Jesus himself had no need of repentance, but Israel certainly did; in submitting to John's baptism Jesus is pointing to the people's need. Matthew pictures Jesus as dedicating himself to the task of making sinners righteous, an appropriate beginning of his public ministry. John understood enough of what Jesus was saying to play his part; despite his initial hesitation he baptized Jesus.

16. Matthew does not describe the baptism, but takes up his narrative from the time when it was completed. He says that Jesus immediately went up from the water,[63] and he follows this with *look, the heavens were*

60. Hill comments "by submitting to John's baptism, Jesus acknowledged this standard of righteousness as valid both for himself and for others, and affirms that he will realize and establish it ('fulfil') as the will of God in the Kingdom." But it is not easy to see how all this can be gotten out of the word "righteousness" and the fact of the baptism.

61. Such a reference is understood by A. E. Garvie (*The Expositor*, VI, 5 [1902], p. 375), O. Cullmann (*Baptism in the New Testament* [London, 1950], p. 18), C. E. B. Cranfield (*SJT*, VIII [1955], p. 54), and others. Cf. Albright and Mann, " 'Righteousness' must be seen as the whole purpose of God for his people, and not . . . as a moral quality only" *(AB)*. It may also be relevant that in the Gospel tradition Jesus speaks of his death as a baptism (Mark 10:38; Luke 12:50).

62. Cf. F. D. Coggan, "But, Jesus points out in this pregnant saying, the purpose of His Advent and Ministry will never be fulfilled unless He identifies Himself with those He came to rescue" and again, "Here is *God with us.* 'Being found in fashion as a man, he humbled himself and became obedient even unto' — Baptism, that symbol of death without which there can be no Resurrection-life" *(ET,* LX [1948-49], p. 258). Hamann comments, "in being baptized, the Messiah, God's Son, shows his solidarity with mankind whom he came to save, a sinner (by imputation) among sinners. But, at the same time, as God's agent for salvation, he brings it about that people have the righteousness God demands of them, but which they themselves could not produce or effect for themselves."

63. He uses the preposition ἀπό (which he uses 113 times), whereas Mark has ἐκ (Mark 1:10). But Matthew has no dislike for ἐκ, for he uses it 82 times, so he is not simply avoiding

opened. His characteristic *look* (see on 1:20) draws attention to what follows and makes it all more vivid. It is not easy to see what is meant by the opening of the heavens, but we should probably think that for a short time the barrier between this world and heaven was set aside so that there could be some form of intercourse between the two. But it is not easy to understand whether Matthew is referring to a vision Jesus had which was personal to himself, or whether he is saying that all present shared in the experience. The manuscripts do not agree; many have "to him"[64] after *were opened* (so *GNB*), and if we accept this reading Matthew is writing about what Jesus alone experienced (which would accord with Mark's "he saw the heavens opened," Mark 1:10). But if we follow the MSS that do not include "to him," Matthew is saying that others, too, saw the opened heavens. He goes on to say that Jesus saw the Spirit coming down on him, but he does not say whether this vision was shared by others (Mark agrees with Matthew, Luke does not say who saw it, while John does not record the opening of heaven). On the whole it appears that Matthew is putting his emphasis on the experience of Jesus. The sight of the opened heavens and the visible manifestation of the Spirit would have been an encouragement to Jesus, and this is the way Matthew records it. Whether other people shared in the experience or not was apparently not so important to him, and he leaves us to puzzle about it.

This Evangelist alone says that it was *the Spirit of God*[65] who came down (Mark and John have "the Spirit," and Luke "the Holy Spirit"). Usually the Spirit is referred to as "the Holy Spirit," but "God's Spirit" is found in a number of places (e.g., 12:28), as are "my Spirit," "his Spirit," and "the Spirit of the Lord." The Spirit descended on Jesus "like a dove."[66] There are two problems here. One is the precise nature of the bird. I have translated the word "dove," but we must bear in mind that until comparatively recent times animals and birds seem not to have been named with great precision, apart from a few outstanding forms. Matthew's word[67] can refer to any one of a variety of pigeons and doves. It is

---

Mark's preposition. He may, of course, use ἀπό to indicate "more clearly Jesus' complete departure from the waters of the Jordan" than does Mark's ἐκ (Gundry). Hendriksen, Ridderbos, and others connect εὐθύς with the opening of the heavens rather than the going out from the water (cf. Moffatt, "the moment he rose out of the water, the heavens opened"), but the word order makes this very difficult to hold. For the opening of heaven cf. Ezekiel 1:1.

64. αὐτῷ is read by most MSS but omitted by א* B syr^{s.c} sah Ir, a strong combination which may mean that the shorter text is original. But, as Metzger points out, it is also possible that αὐτῷ was there from the first but was omitted by copyists who did not consider it necessary.

65. The article is omitted before πνεῦμα and before θεοῦ in some MSS, but the meaning does not appear to be affected.

66. Calvin points out that the Spirit "is diffused everywhere and fills heaven and earth," and that in any case he is invisible. Thus "John does not see the essence of the Spirit, which does not fall within the sight of the eyes . . . but he sees the form of a dove, under which God revealed the presence of His Spirit."

67. περιστερά (3 times in Matthew and John, 10 times in the New Testament) is usually

impossible to attain certainty, but it is usually held that a dove is in mind and there is no reason to quarrel with this. The other problem is the meaning of the symbolism.[68] In modern times it is often urged that the dove was an accepted symbol of the Holy Spirit, but this is not supported by the evidence. That the Spirit "was moving over the face of the waters" at the creation (Gen. 1:2) may be relevant, but there is no mention of "dove" in that passage. The dove was sometimes a symbol for Israel[69] (cf. Hos. 7:11), and it is possible that this is in mind here. If so, Jesus is seen as the true, ideal Israelite when he receives the Spirit of God at the threshold of his public ministry. Morgan further points out that the dove "is the emblem of weakness," so that "the Spirit of God in the form of a dove is an emblem of power in gentleness." Matthew is the only one of the Evangelists who adds to the Spirit's descent the fact that he "came" on Jesus. This apparently means that what looked like a dove alighted on Jesus and the Spirit of God now rested on him. It should not be overlooked that John linked the Holy Spirit and fire, whereas when the Spirit came on Jesus it was in the form of a harmless dove. Both pieces of symbolism, of course, point to truth and neither can be neglected.

17. Once again Matthew has his *And look;* he is fond of the expression and the emphasis it can give to what follows. All three Synoptists tell us of the *voice out of heaven,* which, of course, means the voice of God, "heaven" being a reverent periphrasis for the deity.[70] Mark and Luke have the words addressed to Jesus, "You are my Son . . . ," but Matthew's *This is my Son* makes the words relevant to the bystanders; they are an open testimony to the Father's approval of his Son (cf. 17:5 and see the note on 4:3), and we should view "Son" as a messianic title. The heavenly voice points to a relationship shared by no other. *Beloved*[71] tells us of the strong affection the Father has for the Son; it is probably (as Allen thinks) "an independent title = 'the Beloved' = the Messiah" (see further the note on the same expression in 17:5). It is reinforced with *in whom I am well pleased.*[72]

---

translated "dove," but many versions have "pigeon" in Luke 2:24. E. W. G. Masterman says that seven varieties of the *Columbae* are found in Palestine, and further that "Dove" is "a favourite name of affection" and that "to-day it is one of the commonest names given to girls by Eastern Jewish parents" (*DB,* p. 221).

68. "The dove which, fr. the viewpoint of natural science in ancient times, has no bile, was for the early Christians the symbol of all kinds of virtues" (BAGD, *sub* περιστερά). Thus it symbolized harmlessness (10:16) and helplessness (Ps. 74:19). This association with virtue may have led to the view that it was a useful symbol for the Spirit, but this can be no more than speculation. Davies and Allison list 16 possibilities, so there is no unanimity on the matter.

69. See the passages in SBk, I, pp. 123-24.

70. This is sometimes said to be a *Bath Qol* ("the daughter of the Voice"), an expression the rabbis used for an echo of the divine voice at a time when direct inspiration had ceased. But this is not an echo; it is the voice of God himself.

71. ἀγαπητός occurs 3 times in Matthew, all referring to Christ. Its 61 occurrences are spread pretty widely through the New Testament, but the greatest user of the word is Paul with 27.

72. The aorist is unusual in such a sentence (we would have expected the perfect).

The verb has the meaning "to think it good, give consent" and thence "to be well pleased, take pleasure in"; the latter is, of course, the meaning here. The divine voice gives approval to Jesus as he begins his public ministry. The words are reminiscent of Psalm 2:7 and Isaiah 42:1; they show us that right at the beginning of his ministry Jesus was identified with both the Messiah and the Suffering Servant,[73] "and this strange combination exactly describes the nature of the Lord's ministry soon to begin" (Melinsky). We should perhaps notice the mention of the three Persons of the Trinity in this passage; Matthew has a certain trinitarian interest (cf. 28:19).[74]

Burton has a long note in which he surveys the possibilities and says, "It may be described, therefore, as an Inceptive Aorist equivalent to an English Perfect, and may be rendered *I have become well pleased*. . . . The Aorist affirms the becoming pleased and leaves the present pleasure to be suggested" (*MT*, 55). Filson and others think that it refers to approval of Jesus' submission to baptism.

73. I. Howard Marshall examines the saying in its Marcan form (which differs from that in Matthew only by the use of the second person rather than the third) and concludes, "it can be claimed with a fair degree of probability that these three passages [i.e., Gen. 22:2; Ps. 2:7; Isa. 42:1) must be regarded as the background for its interpretation, and that a denial of the presence of ideas from either Ps. ii.7 or Isa. xlii.1 is to be rejected" (*NTS*, XV [1968-69], p. 335). Vincent Taylor comments on "the striking and original combination of ideas in i.11. Here the idea of the Messianic Son is combined with that of the Servant, and . . . this fusion . . . is to be traced to the mind and experience of Jesus rather than to the Evangelist" (*The Gospel according to St. Mark* [London, 1959], p. 162).

74. Cf. Ryle, "It was the whole Trinity, which at the beginning of the creation said, 'Let us make man'; it was the whole Trinity again, which at the beginning of the Gospel seemed to say, 'Let us save man.' "

Matthew 4

B. JESUS' TEMPTATION, 4:1-11

After telling his readers about Jesus' baptism Matthew goes on to let them know of the way their leader began his ministry. He tells us that Jesus was tempted by the devil and makes clear how he overcame the temptation. Then he goes on to some preliminary work in Galilee and relates the call of the first disciples.

> ¹*Then Jesus was led up by the Spirit into the wilderness to be tempted by the devil.* ²*And after fasting forty days and forty nights he was hungry.* ³*And the tempter approached and said to him, "If you are the Son of God, tell these stones to become bread."* ⁴*But he replied, "It stands written, 'Not on bread alone will man live, but on every word that goes out through God's mouth.'"*
>
> ⁵*Then the devil takes him along into the holy city and stood him on the wing of the temple;* ⁶*and he says to him, "If you are the Son of God, throw yourself down, for it stands written,*
>
> *'Because to his angels he will give command about you,*
> *and they will hold you on their hands,*
> *lest you strike your foot against a stone.'"*
>
> ⁷*Jesus said to him: "Again it stands written, 'You shall not put the Lord your God to the test.'"*
> ⁸*Again, the devil takes him to a very high mountain and shows him all the kingdoms of the world and their splendor,* ⁹*and he said to him, "All these things I will give you if you fall down and worship me."* ¹⁰*Then Jesus says to him, "Go away, Satan, for it stands written, 'The Lord your God you will worship, and him only you will serve.'"* ¹¹*Then the devil leaves him, and, look, angels drew near and took care of him.*

There is a short temptation narrative in Mark 1:12-13 and significantly longer accounts in Matthew and Luke. These two are very similar, though the second and third temptations are in the reverse order, a fact that has never been explained satisfactorily. All the suggestions seem to give psychological reasons for the variation, and in the end these must remain subjective estimates. There are many slight linguistic differences, and if they are following a common source one of these writers (or perhaps both) has made significant alterations. The account must go back to Jesus himself: nobody else was present when the temptations took place.[1]

All three accounts speak of the Holy Spirit in the opening of the story, which means that there was a divine purpose in it all. Jesus has just had the wonderful experience at his baptism of seeing the heavens opened and hearing the voice of God greet him as Son and as the Beloved. Clearly he is marked out for special service. Some discussions of the temptation suggest that Jesus found it difficult to believe that he was the Son of God and that he was tempted accordingly to work a miracle to prove it.[2] But this seems to be reading something into the narrative. There is no evidence that Jesus doubted the heavenly voice for one moment, and no probability. Even on a purely human level we may ask, What more is needed to bring conviction than having the heavens opened, the Spirit descending on one like a dove, and the voice of God coming from heaven? When the Father spoke to Jesus he accepted what was said. The temptations must be understood as the consequence of Jesus' acceptance of his divine sonship, not of doubts about it.

The temptations proceed from the fact that he is the Son of God, and that accordingly he must live as the Son of God. The temptation narratives picture Jesus asking what that means. Is he to be a wonder-worker, using his powers to meet his own needs (and possibly those of others, too)? Is he to do spectacular but pointless miracles? Is he to establish a mighty empire ruling over the whole world? Matthew tells us that right at the beginning of his ministry Jesus looked at each of these and rejected them all as the temptations of the devil. It is significant that Jesus rejected each of the temptations by quoting Scripture: anything that goes against what is written there must be resisted. Each temptation was defeated by citing a passage of Scripture that had reference to the temptations that confronted Israel in the wilderness. Again we have the thought that Jesus fulfilled Israel's vocation. Where Israel failed in the wilderness Jesus succeeded in the wilderness.[3]

1. Plummer points out that had the early Christians made up the story "they would have imagined quite different temptations for Him, as various legends of the saints show." P. Pokorny misses this when he says, "the dialogue was composed by a learned Christian" (*NTS*, 20 [1973-74], p. 125); he cites no evidence that "learned Christians" of the time ever composed stories like this one. Plummer also makes the point that "the temptations assume that our Lord could work miracles. . . . It is incredible that any one should have told such a story about himself to persons who knew that he had never done any mighty work." We could make the same point by reflecting that turning stones into bread is not a temptation to us; it is a temptation only to someone who knows he can do it.
2. "We find him struggling with the question: Can it really be that I am the Son of God? . . . 'Why not satisfy yourself once and for all?' tempts Satan" (J. A. T. Robinson, *Twelve New Testament Studies* [London, 1962], p. 55).
3. France objects to calling this "the temptation of Jesus," arguing that πειράζω in this

1. *Then* (see on 2:7) is sometimes used rather loosely in Matthew, but on this occasion it surely places what follows as next in time: after the baptism came the temptation. Jesus *was led up,* where *up* is probably very much to the point: the Jordan where Jesus was baptized is well below sea level, but *the wilderness* (see on 3:1) seems to mean the high country. The term covers a wide area, but the meaning here is surely not that Jesus remained in that part of the wilderness which adjoins the Jordan but that he went up into the lonely mountainous area to the west. All three Synoptists speak of the activity of *the Spirit,* though they put it in different ways. Luke says simply that Jesus was "full of the Holy Spirit" (Luke 4:1), but Mark says that the Spirit "drives" him into the wilderness.[4] We must surely see that the temptation had its place in God's plan for his Son. The Spirit had just come on Jesus at the baptism when Jesus was assured of his divine sonship, and that same Spirit now leads him into the place where some important truths about the nature of that sonship would become clear through the process of resisting temptation. At the baptism it was made clear that Jesus would be serving God in a special way, with a special mission. But what did that mean? How would he go about that mission? The temptation was apparently the process that cleared that up.

Jesus then went to the wilderness *to be tempted,* where the construction seems to signify purpose: this took place in the plan of God.[5] This does not mean that God initiated the temptation, for God tempts no one (Jas. 1:13). It means rather that God can use the efforts of evil people and even of Satan himself to set forward his purposes. The verb means "to test" and may be used in a good sense, a test applied with the intention that people will pass the test (e.g., Heb. 11:17). But much more often it is used where the intention is that the person will fail the test, and thus it comes to mean "to tempt"; indeed, in the New Testament that is its charac-

---

Gospel always means testing, not tempting; he understands the episode as "The Testing of God's Son."I am not sure that his linguistics will stand up. When the participle of the verb is used in this very incident to refer to Satan (v. 3), are we to think that Satan was no more than a neutral applier of tests? H. Seesemann surely has the rights of it when he says: "The πειράζων . . . attempts to turn Jesus from the task which God has laid upon Him in His baptism, and therewith to render His mission impossible. He exerts himself in every possible way to deflect Jesus from obedience to God" (*TDNT,* VI, p. 34). Bonnard says that of the verbs *tenter* and *éprouver,* "il faut préférer ici le premier," and he emphasizes that Satan was intent not on testing Jesus but on overcoming him. Matthew surely means that the evil one was there in the role of a persuader to do wrong; he was tempting Jesus. It was a test, certainly. But it was also a temptation. France is on surer ground when he denies that this occasion "was the sum-total of Jesus' struggle against Satanic suggestions"; temptations are part of life, and Jesus experienced them accordingly (cf. Heb. 4:15).

4. W. Lane comments, "it is the same Spirit who descended upon Jesus at his baptism who now forces him to penetrate more deeply into the wilderness" (*The Gospel according to Mark* [Grand Rapids, 1974], p. 59).

5. The simple infinitive does not always indicate purpose, but it can do so and this seems to be its meaning here. Turner sees a "simple infin. of purpose" (M, III, p. 134).

teristic meaning, and the participle of the verb has the meaning "tempter" (so in v. 3).[6] Matthew is telling us that immediately after the experience in which Jesus, so to speak, was commissioned for his work as Messiah Satan tried to deflect him from doing the will of God.[7] On this occasion the evil one is called *the devil*,[8] the one who opposes God and tries to lead the people of God, and here the Son of God, away from the right path. Jesus has been called into the service of God. The devil will then try to seduce him into the service of evil.

2. None of the Evangelists indicates why Jesus fasted,[9] but fasting was a natural accompaniment of serious thinking and prayer. It was a common practice among the Jews of those days and a suitable accompaniment of reflection on the new life that was opening out before Jesus. Matthew goes on to spell out the length of the fast as *forty days and forty nights* (the same period that Moses fasted at the time of the giving of the Law, Exod. 34:28; cf. also Elijah, 1 Kings 19:8). Mark and Luke speak of the same length of time (though they do not mention the nights), but refer to it as the time of temptation, not the length of a fast (though after speaking of the temptation Luke adds that Jesus ate nothing in those days). Matthew speaks of the fast first, then goes on to the temptation. At the end of the abstention from food he says that Jesus *was hungry*, the natural result of the long fast (*JB* has "he was very hungry," and *REB* "he was famished," but such translations are the result of reflecting on the length of the fast rather than a strict rendering of the Greek).

3. The evil one is seen in his capacity as *the tempter* (see on v. 1): he came[10] to tempt Jesus to do what was wrong. He begins with *If you are the*

---

6. The verb is πειράζω (in Matthew 6 times). Cf. Trench, "The melancholy fact that men so often break down under temptation gives to πειράζειν a predominant sense of putting to the proof with the intention and the hope that the 'proved' may not turn out 'approved,' but 'reprobate'; may break down under the proof; and thus the word is constantly applied to the solicitations and suggestions of Satan . . . which are always made with such a malicious hope, he himself bearing the name of 'The Tempter'" (p. 281). C. F. D. Moule says, "the New Testament seems to stand alone, up to its date, in widening the use of the *peirazein*-group to embrace deliberate enticement to sin" (*RThR*, XXXIII [1974], p. 70). But the word group is so widened, as its application to Satan shows.

7. H. Seesemann sees the essence of the temptations as "that Jesus should be unfaithful to His Messianic task" (*TDNT*, VI, p. 34).

8. διάβολος, which derives from διαβάλλω, = 1. to throw across, 2. to slander, and thus to accuse. The noun seems to have meant "calumniator," "accuser." This being is consistently opposed to God and Christ, and indeed to the best interests of people.

9. νηστεύω occurs 8 times in Matthew, the most in any one book. It denotes abstaining from food and perhaps mourning, as an accompaniment of prayer and for other religious reasons. The only fast commanded in the Bible is that for the Day of Atonement, but by New Testament times the Jews fasted much more often; many pious people fasted twice a week (cf. Luke 18:12). The participle assumes the fast, and Matthew takes it up from there.

10. For some reason Matthew has an overwhelming preponderance of the occurrences of προσέρχομαι; he has it 52 times out of its New Testament total of 87, more than the rest of the New Testament put together (next highest is Luke with 10 in both his Gospel and Acts). The word may be used of approaching a deity in worship (e.g., Heb. 4:16), but in Matthew

Son of God. There is a certain subtlety here, for the first-class conditional[11] seems to assume the reality of the case: "If you are the Son of God (as you are) . . ." while yet the "if" suggests a little doubt: it might be well to bring some proof of this. Jesus' special position is implied in *the* Son of God;[12] that Son should be able to do a small thing like make stones into bread (and was he not very hungry?). And has not the Son of God the right to meet his basic needs by the use of his powers? *These stones,* that is, stones in the very area, indicates rocky surroundings. It was a desolate place, and food would not have been obtainable by ordinary means. The stones may well have been small ones, resembling in size and general appearance the small loaves that were often used. We could translate the word "loaves of bread" (as *NRSV,* Knox), though this would present a problem when the same word occurs in the singular in the next verse and we could scarcely say "loaf" there. It is better to retain the kinship between the two verses. The important thing in any case is not the precise terminology, but the temptation for a hungry man, who knew he could do it, to turn[13] stones into food, food that would satisfy his hunger then and there[14] (and, of course, repeated on a larger scale, would provide many hungry people with food). At a later time, it is true, Jesus did use his powers to provide food for multitudes (14:15-21; 15:32-38), but these were special and exceptional occasions. There was no use of his powers for his own gratification or as a means of impressing people. His multiplication of loaves on those occasions was consistent with his God-ordained mission, just as was his refusal to do it here. He had come to take a lowly place and in the end die on a cross to save others; to use his powers to satisfy personal needs

---

it is mostly the literal use, as here. This Evangelist does not often use it for Jesus approaching people; mostly he uses it of people who come to him. J. Schneider says that in this Gospel the verb "is used to give us a vivid picture of the men surrounding Jesus. The circle of powers, men, groups and classes which came to Jesus with differing concerns is brought out with astonishing clarity" (*TDNT,* II, p. 683). Davies and Allison may well be right in holding that, as Matthew uses it, the verb "may serve the function of emphasizing Jesus' majesty."

11. εἰ with the indicative. Matthew has εἰ 55 times in all, but the simple εἰ as here (i.e., without such an addition as μή) 35 times, which is the most in any New Testament book. On the form of the conditional cf. BDF, 371(1): "Εἰ with the indicative of all tenses denotes a simple conditional assumption with emphasis on the reality of the assumption (not of what is being assumed); the condition is considered 'a real case.'" J. L. Boyer has examined about 300 examples of the construction in the New Testament and concludes that in about half of them the condition is undetermined (*GTJ,* 2 [1981], pp. 75-114). He construes the meaning of the construction to be "If this . . . then that. . . . It is saying that the result (the apodosis) is as sure as the condition (the protasis)" (p. 82). Lenski comments, "While he uses a condition of reality . . . the 'if' really questions the fact, for Satan demands that Jesus furnish the proof." Hendriksen takes the reality seriously, translating "Since you are God's Son. . . ."

12. There is no article, but this is a case where Colwell's rule applies that the preceding predicate is definite even though it lacks the article. The expression means "the," not "a," Son of God. See the note in my *The Gospel according to John* (Grand Rapids, 1971), p. 77, n. 15.

13. *Become* renders the verb γίνομαι, which is used of "things which change their nature, to indicate their entering a new condition" (BAGD, I.4).

14. Hill sees the temptation as that of "breaking the vow of fasting," but this goes beyond the text; Matthew says nothing about a "vow."

would be to deny all this. Many draw attention to the contrast with Adam. Cf. Glover, "With *'every tree of the garden'* for food, Adam fell; with desert stones mocking His hunger, the second Adam conquered." It is perhaps worth noting that Luke seems to bring out the contrast with Adam; between the baptism and the temptation he has his genealogy, which ends with Jesus' relationship to Adam.

4. *But*[15] sets Jesus in contrast: over against the tempter's suggestion comes this reply. *It stands written* (see on 2:5) points to the reliability and unchangeability of Scripture. For Jesus, to have found a passage in the Bible that bears on the current problem is to end all discussion. He proceeds to quote Deuteronomy 8:3 in a form that agrees exactly with LXX (Luke stops at "will man live"). *Not on*[16] *bread alone* does not deny the importance of bread (in Palestine it was almost synonymous with "food"), but it does deny its exclusive importance. A life sustained by food only is a very poor life.[17] So Jesus goes on to a *but* that employs the strong adversative,[18] and makes a sharp contrast with the preceding. *Every word* is comprehensive: Jesus is not suggesting that parts of Scripture may safely be neglected, but affirming that it is profitable in its entirety. The reason is apparent in the words *that goes out through God's mouth.* Jesus views God as the author of Scripture, and because of this it must be heeded carefully. *Through* is unusual in such a connection; it perhaps hints that what has been spoken is more than a casual utterance. It does not originate on the lips, so to speak, but comes from the inner being. We should not overlook the fact that, while Jesus was tempted to do something quite beyond our ability, he does not cite a text that applies to the Messiah alone; what he quotes is valid for the whole race. Jesus overcame temptation with resources open to each of his followers. Obedience was important for him, and it is important for them.

5. The second temptation is the third in Luke, and there are considerable differences. In this opening up to *and says to him* Matthew has seventeen words of which only nine are in Luke, who has twelve words. Thus Matthew has most of what is in Luke, together with matter of his own. For *then* see on 2:7; it brings us to the next in Matthew's sequence. Jesus had rejected the first temptation because he trusted God to supply his need; now he is tempted through that very assurance. Matthew reverts to *the devil* as his name for the evil one and says that he now *takes* (the present tense gives greater vividness) Jesus *along into the holy city* (i.e., Jerusalem; this

---

15. δέ.

16. ἐπί is the use for "that upon which a state of being, an action, or a result is based . . . *live on bread*" (BAGD, II.1.b.γ).

17. Buttrick brings out the point: "The famished Bedouin, finding treasure in the desert, cried, 'Alas, it is only diamonds.' Man in his deepest hunger always cries, 'Alas, it is only bread.' He lives by bread, but not mainly by bread. The bread is the means, not the end."

18. ἀλλά, which Matthew uses 37 times, is commonly employed in the New Testament for a strong contrast.

term occurs again in 27:53 and 4 times in Revelation only in the New Testament). Neither Matthew nor Luke makes it clear whether this is a physical removal of Jesus from the wilderness or whether it means a vivid suggestion to the mind such that he saw himself in the position mentioned. But in any case we should remember that the essence of temptation is inward: it does not depend on the physical location of the person tempted. The devil *stood*[19] *him on the wing of the temple.* The word translated *wing*[20] seems to have been used for the extremity of anything; it is used of the fins of a fish, the tail flaps of a lobster, and the tip of a rudder (LSJ). It seems that here it means the peak, the point of a roof, or, as some think, a battlement or turret ("parapet," *JB, REB*). But there is a problem in that we do not know what roof. The definite article shows that it was a well-known place, but we can scarcely do more than say that it was obviously something at a great height, so that a leap from it would be spectacular.

6. As in the first temptation, the devil begins with *If you are the Son of God,* and this time follows it with *throw yourself down;* he implies that Jesus can do this quite safely. It does not need to be said that this would be a spectacular miracle; the evil one simply suggests the leap. In the first temptation he had been repelled by the quotation of Scripture, but this time he does some quoting of his own, appealing to Psalm 91:11-12 with the strong formula of quotation *it stands written* accompanied by *for,* which gives the reason: Jesus should do this, Satan suggests, *because* the angels are there to help him.[21] For the most part Matthew records the quotation as in LXX. The words in the Psalm, "to guard you in all your ways," are omitted, but we should not see something sinister in that. It may well have been done to concentrate attention on the bearing up in the hands of the angels: it is safe descent from a height that is in mind, not angelic protection through the varied vicissitudes of every day. For *angel* see on 1:20. None less than the angels have received a command from the Father; the implication is that a command emanating from such a quarter and addressed to such agents will surely be carried out. Holding him *on their hands* means that he will be given close protection and that in the case of a fall from a height he will come to no harm. This will be done, the Psalm

---

19. Matthew has the verb ἵστημι 21 times but the transitive use as here only 4 times; it is not characteristic.

20. πτερύγιον (found only here and in Luke 4:9 in the New Testament) is a diminutive of πτέρυξ, "wing," but our trouble is that we do not know which "little wing" was named in this way. Robertson was in no doubt: "Here the whole point lies in the article, the wing of the Temple overlooking the abyss" (p. 756). Josephus speaks of the Royal Portico overlooking the ravine: "the height of the portico standing over it was so very great that if anyone looked down from its rooftop, combining the two elevations, he would become dizzy and his vision would be unable to reach the end of so measureless a depth" (*Ant.* 15.412). There was a rabbinic view that the land of Israel was higher than other lands and that the temple was the highest place in Israel (*Qidd.* 69a).

21. Many translations take ὅτι as recitative, introducing the quotation, but γέγραπται is not followed by ὅτι elsewhere in this narrative and it does occur at this point in the Psalm.

says, *lest*[22] *you strike your foot against a stone.* Satan is suggesting that the care of the angels will be such that the smallest mishap is quite impossible. There would not even be a stubbed toe!

7. Jesus' reply[23] begins with *Again,*[24] and once more it features *it stands written.* Jesus had defeated the first temptation by citing Scripture, and he uses the same method this time. He raises no objection to Satan's quoting from the Psalm, but simply goes on to another passage that shows that the application the evil one has made of the Scripture he cites is faulty. Jesus draws attention to Deuteronomy 6:16 (Matthew has it exactly as LXX), *"You shall not put the Lord your God to the test."* In Deuteronomy the words refer to the incident at Massah, where the Israelites were short of water and complained about Moses. That patriarch asked the grumblers, "Why do you put the LORD to the proof?" (Exod. 17:2), which is further explained in the question they had asked, "Is the LORD among us or not?" (Exod. 17:7). On that occasion God ordered Moses to strike the rock with his rod. When he did so, water came out and the people's need was fully met. But the way the incident is reported makes it clear that a demand for the miraculous, such as the one the Israelites made, is not acceptable. The servants of God cannot demand that God should keep on intervening with miraculous provision for their needs.[25] To jump from a height and then look to God to avert the natural consequences of such an act is just such an offense. Furthermore, it is worse than what happened at Massah, for at least the people there were in real need of water. What Satan is suggesting is that Jesus should needlessly thrust himself into danger; he would be creating a hazard where none previously existed. And for what? To compel God to save him miraculously. It is a temptation to manipulate God, to create a situation not of God's choosing in which God would be required to act as Jesus dictated. Jesus rejects the suggestion with decision. He prefers the way of quiet trust in the heavenly Father, a trust that needs no test, and a ready acceptance of his will. He refuses to demand a miracle even if from the perspective of someone on earth that might seem desirable, even compelling.

8. *Again* together with the following verb repeats an expression from verse 5: once more Satan takes Jesus along, but this time to *a very high mountain.*[26] There are frequent references to mountains in the Gospels (as

---

22. μήποτε may be an emphatic form of μή, but here it is a conjunction denoting purpose. Matthew uses it more than does any other New Testament writer (8 times).

23. This is Matthew's first use of φημί, a verb he employs 17 times in all. The meaning "say, declare" is much the same as that of λέγω.

24. πάλιν means "back"; the word can signify "back to a previous state" and thus "again." There may be some adversative force here; thus BAGD gives the meaning "on the other hand."

25. In that case "Religion would become a divine service done to man, not a human service done to God" (Gutzwiller).

26. Luke's account diverges considerably from that of Matthew. Of the words in this verse Luke has only 5, while in the next verse Luke has 19 words not in Matthew, though of Matthew's 11 words 7 are in Luke.

also in the Apocalypses). This one was *very high*.[27] From this standpoint the devil *shows*[28] Jesus all earth's *kingdoms*. The word means territory ruled over by a king, but here the emphasis is on the territory rather than the method of government. *The world* makes the expression as extensive as it can possibly be, and *splendor* brings out the attractiveness of those kingdoms at their best. The fact that there is no mountain from which all the world may be seen literally favors the view that the tempter brings all this before the mind of Jesus. Satan holds out before him the prospect of a mighty empire, one that would embrace the whole world. When we contemplate the evils that flourish in even the best states we know and the wickedness that abounds in high places, we can see that to establish a worldwide empire that would be ruled with perfect justice was a real temptation, not a sham parade. Nor should we dismiss the whole episode as something that happened to Jesus but has no relevance to anyone else. Many who profess to follow the Christ have purchased their own "empires" at the cost of the acceptance of evil.

9. But the price for *all these things* was a very high one. To obtain such an empire[29] Jesus would be required to *fall down and worship*[30] the evil one (Goodspeed translates "fall on your knees and do homage to me," but this sounds too much like the honor that may be accorded humans in high position; Matthew is thinking of the honor that is to be given only to God). Filson explains it this way: "Serve the devil and rule the world. In modern terms, be practical, realistic, ready to compromise; 'the end justifies the means'. To help people you must get position and power." The expression signifies not a passing gesture but a real acceptance of Satan's ways; it means yielding the chief place to Satan. It meant that if Jesus was to obtain these kingdoms he would have to accord to the evil one the place that belongs to God alone. Jesus would obtain the mighty empire only by doing what Satan wanted.

27. ὑψηλός, used again of a mountain in 17:1, may mean "exalted" in the sense of "haughty," but clearly here it is altitude that is in mind. λίαν (see on 2:16) intensifies the idea: it was not simply a "high" mountain, but a "very high" one. Cf. the instruction to Baruch, "Go up to the top of this mountain, and all countries of this earth will pass before you, as well as the likeness of the inhabited world . . ." (2 Bar. 76:3).

28. δείκνυμι (3 times in Matthew) may mean "point out, show" in the sense of literal sight or "explain" in the sense of making the meaning clear.

29. The condition is introduced by ἐάν, which usually takes the subjunctive (as here) and does not assume anything about the fulfilment or otherwise of the condition. Satan leaves it open whether he thinks Jesus will do as he suggests: he simply makes the promise of what will happen if he does.

30. πίπτω is a Matthean word (19 times, a total exceeded only by Revelation, a book with a great deal about worship, with 23). The verb may mean no more than descending suddenly from a higher to a lower point, but it may also be used in the sense "*fall down, throw oneself to the ground* as a sign of devotion, before high-ranking persons or divine beings" (BAGD, 1.b.α). προσκυνέω was "used to designate the custom of prostrating oneself before a person and kissing his feet, the hem of his garment, the ground, etc.; the Persians did this in the presence of their deified king, and the Greeks before a divinity or someth. holy" (BAGD). See further on 2:2.

10. Jesus rejects this temptation with decision and, as he rejected the earlier temptations, by citing a passage of Scripture. Matthew begins this part of his account with his habitual *then* (see on 2:7) and again uses the present tense, which gives greater vividness. *Go away*[31] is a decisive rejection of the proposition Satan has made; Jesus will have nothing to do with it nor with him who suggested it. *Satan* is used here for the first time in this Gospel (Matthew has it 4 times in all). The word has the meaning "adversary" and is used for the being who is strongly opposed to God and to the best interests of the people God has made. For *it stands written* see the note on 2:5. Jesus proceeds to quote from Deuteronomy again, this time from 6:13.[32] In this passage *the Lord your God* stands first with emphasis; not Satan but God is to be the object of worship, and the prefix *the Lord* points to something of his majesty. *You will worship* is a future with the force of an imperative; the passage gives instruction on the object of worship. Divine honors are for God alone. With *worship* the passage links *serve*,[33] another word that points to service offered to God. Worship and this kind of service are not to be offered to humans, nor to angelic beings, however high. The terms refer to what is proper for God alone. *Only* is an important word. It is worth reflecting that, while Satan offered Jesus sovereignty over all the earth if he would but worship him, Jesus worshipped God only and all power in heaven and on earth was given him (28:18).

11. *Then* (see on 2:7) denotes what is next in sequence. Satan was defeated and he left Jesus. Matthew says no more than that the evil one went away, leaving us to infer that the temptation was over, at any rate for the time being. Bruce comments, "Nothing was to be made of one who would not do evil that good might come." Luke says that the evil one left Jesus "until a suitable time" (Luke 4:13), for which Matthew has no equivalent.[34] This does not mean, of course, that Matthew thought that his Lord was never tempted again; there was a notable occasion when Jesus addressed Peter as "Satan," clearly recognizing the evil one behind the words Peter had been speaking (16:23). Matthew rounds off this narrative with the information that *angels* (see on 1:20) *came and took care of* Jesus.

31. ὑπάγω is mostly transitive in classical Greek, meaning "bring under" or the like, but in the New Testament it is predominantly intransitive with the meaning "go, go away" (BAGD).

32. There are significant differences from LXX, but the quotation is almost identical in Luke, even though in the narrative as a whole the two Gospels have many differences.

33. λατρεύω, "to serve," is derived from λάτρις, "a hired servant" (AS, who notes that the verb properly means "to serve for hire, LXX (as sometimes in cl.), always of service to the deity on the part of both priests and people"; sub λειτουργέω). λατρεύω may be used of either priests or people, but it is always the service of God; λειτουργέω denotes the service of priests (in the New Testament that of apostles, prophets, and other officers of the church), not laypeople, but it may be the service of God or of people.

34. The only words common to Matthew and Luke in this verse are "the devil." The two Evangelists have their own ways of rounding off the story.

He does not elaborate, and the verb *took care* is quite general and could denote any one of a wide variety of services.[35] The imperfect tense denotes a sustained action.

III. JESUS' MINISTRY IN GALILEE, 4:12–13:52

A. INTRODUCTION, 4:12-17

> [12]*And having heard that John had been arrested, he withdrew into Galilee.* [13]*And he left Nazara and came and lived in Capernaum, which is by the sea in the regions of Zebulon and Naphthali;* [14]*so that what was spoken through Isaiah the prophet might be fulfilled, saying,*
>
> [15]*"Land of Zebulon and land of Naphthali,*
> *way of the sea, beyond the Jordan,*
> *Galilee of the Gentiles —*
> [16]*the people that sit in darkness*
> *saw a great light,*
> *and on those sitting in the region and shadow of death*
> *light has dawned."*
>
> [17]*From then on Jesus began to preach and to say, "Repent, for the kingdom of heaven has drawn near."*

Matthew here begins his story of Jesus' ministry, characteristically stressing the note of fulfilled prophecy. He leaves the impression that Jesus was in Judea for some time after his baptism, moving to Galilee only after the arrest of the Baptist. Of course John may have been arrested immediately after he had baptized Jesus, but unless this happened Jesus remained in Judea for some time (which would agree with John's account of activities of Jesus in that area). Matthew prefers to start his account of Jesus' ministry with the fulfilment of prophecy.

12. Matthew does not tell us how Jesus heard that John the Baptist had been *arrested* (for the story see 14:3-12), where his verb is a technical term for handing someone over into custody. It is often used of Judas, when it is usually translated "betray."[36] Matthew contents himself with saying that Jesus heard this news and goes on to the information that he

---

35. διακονέω originally meant the service of a table waiter, and this kind of thing may be meant by *REB*'s "attended to his needs" (Gundry makes it explicit: "The ministering of angels to Jesus includes the serving of food"); others understand the service to be more general, translating "helped him" *(GNB)* or "attended him" *(NIV)*. The imperfect points to an ongoing service.

36. παραδίδωμι occurs 31 times in Matthew, the most in any one book. In addition to meanings connected with arrests, the word may mean "commit, commend," and, when used of oral or written tradition, "hand on."

then *withdrew into Galilee*. The verb was used of the Magi (2:12); it often has something of the notion of withdrawing from danger. The point of this withdrawal is sometimes said to be that after John had been arrested it was prudent for those who had been associated with the Baptist to place themselves at some distance from the area of his work. There may be something in this, but we must bear in mind that Herod Antipas ruled both regions. It is more likely that with John's ministry completed Jesus saw that it was time to begin his own; whereas John had done his work in the wilderness Jesus would do his largely among the people of Galilee.[37] Matthew says essentially what Mark and Luke say, but with very few coincidences of language (only "John" and "into Galilee"). *Galilee* (see on 2:22) was the region west of the Jordan and the Sea of Galilee bounded on the west and north by Phoenicia and Syria and on the south by Samaria. It was thus not large in area, but it was very fertile and had a considerable population. Josephus observes that it had all been cultivated, that there was no waste land, and that the smallest village had more than 15,000 inhabitants (*War* 3.43). Even allowing for exaggeration Galilee must have been well populated. Important roads passed through the area (Barclay quotes a saying: "Judaea is on the way to nowhere: Galilee is on the way to everywhere"), and whereas Judea was mountainous and isolated, Galilee was open to trade and ideas. History had seen foreign conquerors make their mark on the region and, of course, had brought an influx of people from many races. All this means that Galilee was the kind of country where new teachings might be heard and even welcomed.

13. *He left Nazara,*[38] where the verb sometimes means no more than leave behind, but where it can also signify "abandon" (cf. its use in 19:5). However we translate, the fact is that Jesus seems not to have lived any longer in Nazara[39] where he had been brought up. Luke tells us that the people of this town rejected Jesus when he preached in their synagogue (Luke 4:16-31), but that incident can scarcely have been the cause of his removal, for he had already exercised a ministry in Capernaum when he preached in Nazareth (Luke 4:23). Little is known about Capernaum, but Matthew tells us that it occupied a seaside position and that it was in the general area of Zebulon and Naphtali (these tribes are mentioned again in the New Testament only in v. 15 and Rev. 7:6-8). The name Capernaum means "Nahum's village," but this does not help us because it is not known who the Nahum in question was. It is generally accepted that the

37. "When Jesus went to Galilee, his move was an answer to Herod; he took up in Herod's territory the work which Herod had tried to stop by arresting John; he began his ministry with a challenge rather than with a retreat" (Filson).

38. The form Ναζαρά (indeclinable) is found here and in Luke 4:16. It is a variant of "Nazareth" (see on 2:23).

39. Fenton comments, "the rejection of God's word in one place leads to the preaching of it in another place; and in particular . . . the rejection of it by the Jews leads to its offer to the Gentiles."

site of the city is that known as "Tell Hum" at the northwest corner of the Sea of Galilee. It was of a fair size (J. P. Kane says that its area was c. 800 by 250 m.),[40] but it was not a great city and there are few references to it outside the Gospels. For whatever reason, Jesus made Capernaum the center of his ministry rather than his hometown; *JB*'s "settled in Capernaum" brings this out (cf. 9:1).

14. Characteristically Matthew finds that all this was done in order to fulfil prophecy (the construction expresses purpose), this time some words in Isaiah 9:1-2. For the formula of quotation see on 1:22. What is written in Scripture must, Matthew holds, find its fulfilment, and thus the Messiah made his dwelling in a place mentioned by the prophet. It might have been expected that the Messiah would do his work mainly in the capital city, Jerusalem. But Jesus spent most of his time in despised Galilee. Why? Matthew tells us that this was in order to fulfil the divine purpose expressed in the prophecy.

15. The prophecy agrees with neither the Hebrew nor LXX; Matthew may have had access to a translation no longer extant. The prophet goes on to speak of the birth of the Messiah (Isa. 9:6), but Matthew is not dealing with this at the moment, so he confines his reference to information about the land. He passes over the prophecy that gloom will vanish and that the Lord "will make glorious the way of the sea" (Isa. 9:1) and concentrates on the fact that this is where Messiah lives. *Land of Zebulon* and *land of Naphthali* referred originally to the tribal lands where the joy would be, but for Matthew they refer to the place where Jesus would live. *Way of the sea*[41] is a natural enough expression, for Capernaum was situated by the sea of Galilee, but *beyond the Jordan* is puzzling (*NIV* has "along the Jordan," but this does not seem correct). As far as our information goes, Jesus was in the region beyond the Jordan only occasionally, but our knowledge is incomplete and Jesus may have worked there more than we know. Certainly people from trans-Jordan came to know his teaching and were included among those who followed him (v. 25; cf. 19:1). *Galilee of the Gentiles*[42] points to the fact that many non-Israelites lived in the area (cf. *NEB*, "heathen Galilee"). The inhabitants had been forcibly Judaized and compelled to accept circumcision in about 104 B.C.,[43] which means

40. *IDB*, I, p. 248.
41. BAGD points out that the accusative ὁδόν, "following the Hebr. דֶּרֶךְ, and contrary to Gk. usage . . . is used as a prep. *toward*" (1.a). It means "seawards" rather than referring to a road leading to the sea (M, III, p. 247).
42. Gundry comments, "The description of Galilee as 'of the Gentiles' provides the key point in the quotation. Though Jesus will minister in Galilee mainly to Jews, this description makes that ministry prefigure his disciples' wider mission to Gentiles."
43. Josephus tells us that Aristobulus I defeated the Itureans, annexed a large part of their land, and compelled the inhabitants to be circumcised (*Ant.* 13.318). The Itureans ruled Galilee, and thus the Galileans were included in the process of Judaizing. B. Reicke remarks, "Although the larger cities remained Hellenistic, the general population kept the Jewish laws that Aristobulus had forced upon them" (*The New Testament Era* [London, 1969], p. 69).

that their commitment to Judaism was probably less than wholehearted.[44] The extent of this operation has been questioned, but it must have had some effect. The mixed population in Galilee caused the Jews in Jerusalem to look down on the Galileans, but for Matthew it was important that the Messiah came to despised Galilee. This fits in with his general approach: God does not act in accordance with the expectations of people, even religious people; he does his great work among the lowly and the despised. While Jesus did not mingle much with Gentiles,[45] the salvation he came to bring was just as much for them as for the Jews. It was important accordingly that he lived in an area greatly influenced by Gentiles.

16. The prophecy goes on to refer to *people*[46] *that sit in darkness,* where *sit* indicates more than a passing moment. The people in question are habitually in darkness, a darkness of the mind or spirit.[47] And it is those benighted people who came to see a *great light* (the position of *great* seems to give it emphasis; it was no usual light that they came to see). The thought is repeated in the second couplet with some variations. They are still *sitting,* so the thought of a continuing state is repeated. But they are now seen as *in the region and shadow of death;* a territory is assigned to death, and that is where they sit. They are close to death, for they are in its *shadow,* a term that also points to lack of light (cf. *GNB,* "the dark land of death"). The people in mind are those whose horizon is bounded by death. Death is a tyrant, and their whole life is lived in its shadow, subject to its nearness, under its threat. This is evidently the way the people in Jerusalem regarded their country cousins in Galilee. Matthew's recording of it is part of the way he brings out the truth that Jesus' ministry was in the first instance to those whom the religious leaders of his day had neglected. For those people *Light has dawned.* They are not seen as producing light; the light dawned for them as a new day dawns. The light that dispels their darkness is God's good gift.

17. Having pointed out the significance of prophecy for the location

44. Davies brings evidence to show that "Galilean Judaism can be differentiated from Judaean Judaism even among the rabbis. . . . R. Johannan b. Zakkai, for example, found the spiritual climate in Galilee much less congenial than in Jerusalem" (*SM,* p. 450).

45. There is no record of Jesus visiting places like Sepphoris or Tiberias, centers where Hellenistic culture flourished. With the church so strongly Gentile when the Evangelists wrote, it is unlikely that such visits would have been ignored if they had taken place. "There is no trace of a planned effort to reach the Gentiles who were all about him. The mission to Gentiles had roots in the teaching and attitudes of Jesus, but its actual inauguration waited until the Apostolic Age" (G. E. Wright and F. V. Filson, eds., *The Westminster Historical Atlas to the Bible* [London, 1946], p. 86).

46. λαός often refers to Israel the people of God, but here the reference seems to be wider than that to one nation. Matthew is surely referring to all in darkness, be they Jew or Gentile.

47. Hendriksen points out that when *darkness* is used figuratively it mostly means delusion, depravity, or despondency; he holds that while all three may be in mind here, the emphasis is on the last mentioned.

of Jesus' ministry, Matthew goes on to summarize his first preaching. *From then*[48] points to a new departure: "from the time that Jesus moved to Capernaum there was a difference." He now *began to preach,*[49] and Matthew mentions two points in that preaching, repentance and the coming of the kingdom (for both see the notes on 3:2). Jesus began with the same emphasis as John the Baptist had. The two go together: if the kingdom of God is near, then clearly people cannot be complacent. They must prepare for that kingdom, and that means repenting of their sins. Jesus calls on them to realize that they are unfit for the kingdom of heaven and to repent accordingly. Such preaching is a clarion call to action, not a recipe for slothful complacency. We should not overlook the importance of this call to repentance at the very beginning of Jesus' ministry; everything else follows from that. Matthew has often been seen as one who stresses the importance of good works, and of course he does. But this must not be held in such a form that his emphasis on grace is missed. From the beginning Jesus took it for granted that people are sinners, and accordingly his first message was that they must repent. Only so would they know the forgiveness he came to bring.

There has been a great deal of discussion on whether we should see the kingdom as having arrived in the person of Jesus or whether he proclaimed a kingdom yet to come. But a good deal of this is misplaced ingenuity, for both surely have a place in the teaching of Jesus. That the expression does not mean that the kingdom is already here is surely indicated by the fact that John the Baptist used exactly the same verb and on his lips the expression cannot mean that the kingdom is a present reality. There is a sense in which God has acted decisively in sending his Son: the kingdom is here in his words and deeds. But there is another sense in which the culmination of the kingdom in all its fulness is a future reality: the best is yet to be. Both truths are important.

B. The First Disciples and the First Teaching, 4:18-25

> [18]Now as he was walking by the Sea of Galilee he saw two brothers, Simon who was called Peter and Andrew his brother, casting a net into the sea, for they were fishers. [19]And he says to them, "Come after me, and I will make you fishers of men." [20]And straightaway they left their nets and

48. ἀπὸ τότε also occurs elsewhere; some regard its occurrences in 16:21 and 26:16 as marking the major divisions of the Gospel. Carson is probably right in rejecting this, but the expression does lead into something significantly new.

49. The redundant ἄρχω (which Matthew has 13 times) is an Aramaism. Turner notes that, in passages common to Matthew and Mark, our first Evangelist has reduced the number of examples from 26 to 6 (M, IV, p. 32). But here he has added it to Mark, so it is surely meaningful: it marks the beginning of a new state of affairs, while κηρύσσω (see on 3:1) characterizes it as basically concerned with proclamation. McNeile remarks that in Matthew it "is never quite superfluous" (as sometimes in Mark or Luke); "it either describes the beginning of a continuous action or marks a fresh start or phase in the narrative."

followed him. [21]*And he went on from there and saw two other brothers,*
James the son of Zebedee and John his brother, in the boat with Zebedee
their father preparing their nets; and he called them. [22]*And immediately*
they left the boat and their father and followed him.

[23]*And he went about in all Galilee, teaching in their synagogues, preach-*
ing the gospel of the kingdom, and healing every disease and every illness
among the people.

[24]*And the report about him went out into all Syria, and they brought to*
him all who were ill with various diseases and those gripped with torments,
and demoniacs and lunatics and paralytics, and he healed them. [25]*And great*
crowds followed him from Galilee and Decapolis and Jerusalem and Judea
and Trans-Jordan.

Presently Matthew will give us an extensive account of Jesus' preaching in the Sermon on the Mount and proceed with stories of individual
healings. But he begins with a short account of the way Jesus called his
first disciples and a summary statement of the effect of his teaching and
healing. We need not think of the call of the disciples as anything more
than a sample account — Jesus had other disciples than these four — but
Matthew did not find it necessary to say how they were all called. It is
noteworthy that Jesus called those he wanted; in Judaism the disciple
chose his rabbi.

18. Mark also has an account of the call of the first disciples,[50] but
there are verbal differences throughout. For example, where Matthew
speaks of *two brothers,*[51] *Simon who was called Peter and Andrew his brother,*
Mark has "Simon and Andrew the brother of Simon" (Mark 1:16). The
differences do not amount to much, but they indicate that neither has
copied the other. The words of Jesus are almost verbatim, but the rest of
the story has variations.[52] Matthew seems to imply that Jesus was not
deliberately looking for particular people; he simply says that *as he was*
walking by he saw the men. This does not, of course, rule out the possibility

50. We should not miss the point that Jewish teachers did not normally "call" their
disciples. We read in the Mishnah, "Rabban Gamaliel said: Provide thyself with a teacher
and remove thyself from doubt" (*'Abot* 1:16). It was something new that Jesus took the
initiative and called those whom he would have as disciples. Cf. Davies, "there was a marked
difference between a life dedicated to study at the feet of a Rabbi, in which the aim was an
increasing knowledge of the Law, which would eventually 'qualify' a student himself to
become a rabbi, and the life of the Christian disciple (often not markedly studious by nature!)
called to personal loyalty to Jesus in His way" (*Sermon,* p. 133).

51. For Matthew's interest in brothers see on 1:2. He manages to use the word *brother*
4 times in verses 18 and 21.

52. Matthew has 89 words and Mark 82, of which 54 are common. This points to a
good deal of resemblance, and indeed Fenton can say that there are "almost no alterations."
But when we allow for the verbatim words of Jesus and bear in mind that the story could
scarcely be told without the names and words like "brother" and "father," the differences
are not inconsiderable. Matthew may well have based his account on that of Mark, but he
has made significant alterations.

of previous contacts.[53] We are not required to think that Jesus had no knowledge of these men (nor they of him), or that he did have knowledge but by supernatural means. Matthew simply ignores all that had gone before and goes right to the critical time. He tells us that the name of one man was *Simon* and that he was called *Peter*. This latter name means "stone" or "rock," but Matthew does not stop to explain this, nor does he say when or why the name was given. He states that the brother's name was *Andrew*, and he adds that the brothers were casting a hand net[54] into the sea. He explains that they were fishermen.[55]

19. Jesus calls them (Matthew uses the present tense), saying something like "Here, after me."[56] This call clearly points to a lasting association; Jesus is not inviting them to a pleasant stroll along the seashore but inviting them to discipleship; there is the thought of personal attachment. Jesus adds a promise, *"I will make you fishers of men."* This is a somewhat cryptic saying (Carr calls it "a condensed parable"), for it is not immediately clear what *fishers of men* means. Stendahl reminds us that "used in a good sense" there is "no known precedent" for this expression. At this early stage the men could not have known Jesus well, nor could they have had any depth of insight into his mission. But clearly fishing for men has a greater dignity than fishing for fish so that in this allegorical connecting of their present and future ways of life they must have discerned that Jesus was inviting them to something very worthwhile.[57] Diétrich puts it well: "It is no longer a question of taking fish from the lake, but of drawing men up out of the abyss of sin and death, catching them in the great net of God!" Jesus' disciples would not only learn from him but would bring others into living contact with God. The call to discipleship clearly meant separation from the kind of life they had been living hitherto, but it did not mean that they had to sell everything and break every earthly tie (as 8:14 shows).

20. The two knew enough about Jesus to realize that his call was not to be taken lightly; they obeyed immediately.[58] They *left their nets,* which

---

53. Bruce comments, "we naturally postulate previous knowledge in explanation. But all indications point to the uniquely impressive personality of Jesus."

54. The ἀμφίβληστρον (which I have seen in use near Sidon) was a circular net with weights on the circumference and lines from the circumference to an opening in the middle. The net was thrown out so that it fell flat on the water, the weights took it to the bottom, the lines were pulled to draw in the circumference, and any fish underneath the net were trapped.

55. ἁλιεύς is connected with ἅλς, "the sea." The word occurs again in the New Testament only in verse 19; Mark 1:16, 17; and Luke 5:2.

56. His imperative is δεῦτε, an adverb used as the plural of another adverb, δεῦρο. Matthew uses it 6 times out of 12 in the New Testament.

57. BAGD cites Diogenes Laertius (3rd cent. A.D.) for the use of the metaphor of hunting with the meaning "catch someone for one's point of view" (*sub* ἁλιεύς). This may be relevant, though it is from a later time as well as employing a different metaphor. But clearly the fishermen understood what Jesus meant.

58. εὐθύς indicates immediate action. It is a favorite word of Mark's (42 times); Matthew has it 7 times, which is second only to Mark's total. Matthew frequently omits the word in matter he shares with Mark, but here he retains it.

means that they stopped doing what they had been occupied with. But there is more to it than that. The action is symbolic. The word *left*[59] can have the meaning "abandoned" (cf. 26:56), and whether Matthew means it in this sense or not he is speaking of a decisive action. Until then these men had been fishermen; now they were committing themselves to becoming disciples of Jesus. They left their nets[60] and all that those nets meant behind. And they *followed*[61] Jesus. The verb may be used in the literal sense of walking behind (21:9), but it also means "accompany" (v. 25). This idea of association may intensify into that of being a disciple, which is clearly what is in mind here. It is often pointed out that students used to follow their teachers literally as they walked from place to place.

21. Jesus *went on*. Matthew does not say whether he was specifically looking for James and John, but as he went on his way he came to them. *James* is mentioned first and related to Zebedee,[62] after which we hear of *John* who was *his brother*. James appears to be the more important of the two and probably the elder. The brothers were in *the* boat, where the article points to a definite boat. Since we find elsewhere, however, that the family had at least an interest in another boat (Luke 5:7), it is not easy to see what this means. The brothers were with their father and were *preparing*[63] *their nets*. As they were busy about their craft, Jesus *called them*.[64] Matthew does not give the words Jesus used, but clearly he means that the two brothers were called into discipleship in the same way that the brothers already mentioned were called.

22. Just as the first pair did, these two responded. Their response was prompt: as in the case of Peter and Andrew they acted straightaway. In the Marcan account when Jesus saw this pair he "immediately" called them (Mark 1:20), but Matthew transfers "immediately" to the brothers' response; his emphasis is on their prompt obedience to the call. And their response was wholehearted, for they left the nets that symbolized their whole way of life. Matthew tells us further that this pair left not only their

---

59. ἀφίημι is used by Matthew more than by any other New Testament writer (47 times; next is Mark with 34). It has a wide range of meaning including "let go," "pardon," "permit," etc., but here leaving the nets is in view.

60. The word this time is δίκτυον; it is a general word for "net" and not the specific hand net of verse 18. The plural covers all the nets they would have used in their profession as fishermen. They now left them all.

61. ἀκολουθέω is another favorite word of our Evangelist. Matthew has it 25 times, which is more than in any other book (next is John with 19).

62. The word *son* is not included (the Greek means literally "the of Zebedee"), but in this expression it is readily understood. Interestingly, when Zebedee is mentioned with one of his sons his name always has the article as here, τὸν τοῦ Ζεβεδαίου, but the article is lacking in the plural "sons of Zebedee" except in John 21:2.

63. καταρτίζω means "make ἄρτιος," that is, "fit, complete"; they were making their nets ready for a further fishing expedition. This would involve any necessary repairs, and cleaning and folding the nets. *NEB* has "overhauling."

64. Glover comments, "We read of no one being called to the apostleship while *standing idle in the markets.'* No indolent man will make either an apostle or a teacher."

boat but *their father,* thus breaking the strongest family tie. Allegiance to Jesus is stronger than any earthly attachment. But we should not think that they left their father to manage on his own; he had hired hands who worked for him (Mark 1:20).

23. In verse 17 Matthew has told us that Jesus began to preach; now he tells us a little more of what the Master's ministry involved.[65] That this is of importance for Matthew is shown by the fact that he repeats it essentially in 9:35. Matthew emphasizes healings of a variety of kinds and speaks of people coming from a number of places to be cured. This was a period when Jesus was popular and greatly sought after. He *went about in all Galilee,* which points to a wandering ministry where *all* makes it clear that Jesus did not confine himself to any particular area: he was active throughout the region. Bonnard detects a marked difference from the rabbis (who set themselves to instruct a small group of disciples) and from the men of Qumran (who withdrew the pure into the desert). Jesus' concern was for all the people in all the country.

Matthew speaks of a triple function: teaching, preaching, and healing. Jesus' *teaching* was carried out in *their synagogues.* We usually think of the synagogue as a place of worship, which, of course, it was, but it was many other things as well.[66] The word means "a gathering place" and could be used for gatherings of various kinds. It could, for example, be used of the gathering together of waters (Gen. 1:9), but predominantly in Scripture it means the gathering together of people. The synagogue was in a special sense the place where people came together to study the law of God. It was the center of Jewish life: the place where Jews assembled, where Jewish law was administered and punishment was inflicted (10:17), and where Jewish teaching was given. Somewhat later the word could be used of Christian assemblies (Jas. 2:2), but in the Gospels it always refers to Jewish assemblies. There would have been no great difficulty in Jesus giving teaching in the synagogues, for any Israelite might be invited to address the people. Matthew speaks of *their* synagogues, but with no indication as to who "they" may have been. It is not the way of referring to the synagogues that we might have expected, for Jesus was a Jew and a synagogue was his as much as anyone's. But this may be meant as a way of differentiating him from the people who ran the synagogues, all the more so since Matthew often speaks of synagogues in this way (see 9:35; 10:17; 12:9; 13:54; cf. 23:34). From quite early times the Jewish authorities set themselves in opposition to Jesus, and Matthew is mindful of this. An interesting feature of Matthew's presentation is that he records no discourse of Jesus as given in a synagogue or even in a house. It seems that for him the essential message

---

65. Luke 6:17-19 is usually seen as parallel to this passage, but it is a very rough parallel at best; coincidences of language are few.

66. For differences between the syngagogue and the church see chapter II of my *The New Testament and the Jewish Lectionaries* (London, 1964).

of Jesus was given as he moved about — in the countryside, on the sea-shore, and in similar places.

Jesus also engaged in *preaching* (for this word with its emphasis on proclamation see on 3:1); this is not the systematic instruction indicated by *teaching* but a forthright proclamation, a setting forth of certain facts whether people want to take notice of them or not. The content in this case is given shortly as *the gospel*,[67] the good news. In a Christian context the good news is always the good news of what God has done for sinful people in sending his Son to be their Savior. Here it is the gospel *of the kingdom*, which, as Jesus has said, has drawn near (v. 17). The good news is that God is at work bringing in the kingdom that will be associated with the work his Son is doing. *The gospel of the kingdom* is an expression found in this Gospel only (9:35; 24:14). It matters to Matthew that the gospel was concerned with God's sovereign rule.

The third component in Jesus' initial ministry was healing, and Matthew tells us that he was *healing every disease and every illness*. Matthew is very interested in healing,[68] and has many references to the subject. It is important for him that Jesus brought wholeness to people; he met their spiritual need but he also dealt with their physical ailments. Carson reminds us that "both Scripture and Jewish tradition take sickness as resulting directly or indirectly from living in a fallen world" (on v. 24). Jesus' defeat of sickness is part of his overcoming of evil. Here Matthew speaks of healing from *every disease* (a very general term) and *every illness* (which basically means "softness" and comes to signify "weakness, sickness."[69] Matthew does not say how Jesus healed, only that he did, and this puts him in contrast with various "healers" of antiquity. Whatever their therapeutic merits such people normally made a great fuss of their techniques. In contrast "the mode of healing practised by Jesus is infinitely simple, externally unimpressive, but inwardly so much the more powerful."[70] *People* often refers specifically to the people of God, and some commentators think that that is the meaning here: Jesus confined his healing to Jews. But this is hard to square with the repeated *every*; the impression Matthew leaves is that of the breadth of Jesus' ministry at this time, not of its narrowness. It is better to understand it

---

67. εὐαγγέλιον is found 4 times in this Gospel and 8 times in Mark; in the New Testament it is basically not a Gospel word but Pauline (Paul has it in 60 of its 76 New Testament occurrences). It is a compound of εὐ and ἀγγελία, "good" and "message." It meant originally the reward given to the messenger, but came to be used for the good news he brought.

68. He has the verb θεραπεύω 16 times out of 43 in the New Testament, which is more than anyone else. The word actually means "to do service" (as in Acts 17:25), but in the New Testament the particular service is mostly the service of the sick, healing. Here it is used with the accusative of the disease, in verse 24 with the accusative of the person healed.

69. *Disease* is νόσος, which Matthew has 5 times, and *illness* is μαλακία, which he alone uses in the New Testament (3 times), The repeated πᾶσαν emphasizes Jesus' complete mastery over all forms of illness, and that whether we take it to mean "every kind of" or "every case of."

70. A. Oepke, *TDNT*, III, p. 209.

as a reference to the general populace. Matthew stresses that Jesus healed them all, a fact that differentiates him from the healers of antiquity (or, for that matter, in modern times). Those healers had their successes and their failures, but Jesus had complete mastery over illness; he healed all who came to him.[71]

24. What Jesus was doing could not remain unnoticed, and *the report*[72] went out about him. We would have expected that the report would go into all Galilee (and it probably did), but Matthew surprises us by mentioning Syria (here only in this Gospel). He probably means that the news of what Jesus was doing spread very widely and went into the neighboring country as well as throughout the one in which Jesus was working. But Syria was the name of the Roman province that covered all Palestine (cf. Luke 2:2; Acts 15:23, 41), and he may be referring to the province. Either way the expression covers a wide area. Matthew does not supply a subject for his verb *brought*,[73] but there is no difficulty in understanding that family or friends would perform this service. He refers to people who *were ill* (more literally, "had [it] badly"), a general term covering all kinds of physical complaints,[74] and he proceeds to elaborate on this. The adjective *various*, which Matthew uses only here, means "many-colored" and is sometimes employed, as here, in the sense "manifold." *Diseases* is the word used in the previous verse, after which Matthew goes on to those in the grip of *torments*.[75] To these he adds *demoniacs*, a very important group in an age when so much was attributed to demon possession. All three Synoptic Gospels make a great deal of Jesus' power over demons. Matthew goes on to *lunatics* (apparently different from the demoniacs); these are often held to be epileptics in modern discussions (*NRSV* and other translations have "epileptics"), and some of the cases may indeed be those of epilepsy. But we should bear in mind that the word is the exact etymological equivalent of "lunatic"[76] and that there is no reason for denying

---

71. Davies and Allison comment on the passage 4:23–5:2: "Before the crowds hear the Messiah's word they are the object of his compassion and healing. Having done nothing, nothing at all, they are benefited. So grace comes before task, succour before demand, healing before imperative" (I, p. 427). We should not miss the note of grace that runs through Matthew's Gospel.

72. ἀκοή means "the sense of hearing" or "the organ of hearing," the ear, but it comes also to have the meaning "what is heard," whether this be a message or, as here, a report.

73. The verb προσφέρω is often used in the sense "offer" (as in 2:11), but here it is used in its literal sense "bring to."

74. The expression is κακῶς ἔχοντας, which Matthew has 5 times in this sense.

75. Matthew has the verb συνέχω only here; it means "hold together" and then "hold fast" (of a prisoner, Luke 22:63). It may be used of constraining someone to do something, and in the passive, as here, it is used of people held fast by ills of one sort or another (and unable to break free from them). The noun βάσανος also occurs only here in this Gospel. It is a word of Oriental origin that meant properly "a touchstone," a stone used in the testing of metals. It evidently was regarded as a very stringent test, for it came to be used of examination of people by torture and then of the torture itself (AS). It thus seems to denote painful diseases.

76. The word is σεληνιάζω (again in 17:15 and nowhere else in the New Testament), which in the passive means "to be moonstruck." AS says that epilepsy was supposed to be

that meaning here. Matthew rounds off his list with *paralytics*, people for whom there was no cure in the first century. It meant a great deal to Matthew, as to the sufferers, that Jesus healed these people too.

25. Clearly the healings made a deep impression, for great crowds[77] followed Jesus. This, of course, does not mean that they followed him as disciples (as did the men in vv. 20 and 22), but simply that, as curiosity seekers, they did not want to miss the latest sensation. In Matthew the crowds occupy a middling position: they are not opposed to Jesus as the Jewish leaders are (though they can be found in opposition, as in 26:55; 27:20), but they are not adherents as the disciples are (though they can support him, 21:9). Matthew lists the places from which these crowds came. We would have expected *Galilee,* for that was the area in which Jesus was moving, but the others in the list show that some of the people came a good distance. *Decapolis* means "ten cities"; these were all east of the Jordan except Scythopolis. *Jerusalem* was quite a distance away, as was *Judea,* which here denotes the region in the south of Palestine and not the broad concept that took in the whole of the area. *Trans-Jordan* means much of the country to the east of the Jordan, so this adds to the impression Matthew is conveying that people were attracted to Jesus from very great distances. For this Evangelist Jesus was more than a petty healer in a tiny province.

---

influenced by the moon, which is the reason for the widespread understanding of the term as "epileptic." Phillips has "the insane" (so also LB), Filson and Knox "lunatics."

77. More literally "many crowds," ὄχλοι πολλοί, which Matthew employs often for "a great crowd" (8:1, 12 v.l.; 13:2; 15:30; 19:2); despite the plural we are not to think of several crowds.

Matthew 5

C. THE SERMON ON THE MOUNT, 5:1–7:29

Matthew's method is to give some important teaching of Jesus in the form of comparatively lengthy discourses (he has five major discourses), interspersed with other aspects of his ministry, such as healing and the instruction of disciples. Now that he has introduced Jesus' ministry with the call of disciples and with the explanation that Jesus taught, preached, and healed, Matthew comes to the first great section of teaching, usually called "The Sermon on the Mount." There has been a great deal of discussion of this sermon, and the literature on it is enormous.

A good deal of the discussion turns on the achievability of the ethical teaching Jesus gives here. For some this is an impossible ideal, demanding such a lofty ethical standard that no one can possibly attain it; as a result they dismiss it from the world of practical living. Others view it as something that people can and should attain. There are all sorts of variations on these two basic positions, both of which seem to have truth in them. Part of our problem is Jesus' method: he keeps making strong, paradoxical statements without the qualifications that we must supply in some situations. To make those qualifications would take away the impact of his words, but he clearly expects his hearers to apply his words in the right way. For example, he says that they are to let their light shine before men (5:16) and that they are not to do their righteousness before men (6:1); clearly both injunctions must be interpreted carefully. He says that they are not to swear oaths (5:34), but he himself made a statement under oath (26:63-64). To interpret these woods in a wooden, literalistic manner is to repeat the method of the scribes whom he denounces so strongly.[1]

The teaching in this sermon certainly sets a high standard. If we take it seriously we realize that we cannot attain it and therefore cannot merit salvation. It is the end of the way of law and drives us to seek salvation

---

1. Ridderbos has a wise comment: "In many respects His words have the character of a (Heb.) *māšāl (mashal)* or proverb, that is, an unexpected, paradoxical, and absolute manner of speaking that sharply accentuates a particular side of the truth without considering the possible exceptions to the rule (cf. 5:16 to 6:1). The hearer then has to ponder the matter himself" (Ridderbos, p. 112, n. 12).

in Christ.[2] But when we have received this salvation as God's free gift, the sermon shows us how we should live in the service of our gracious God. It shows us what life is like in the kingdom of God. The sermon removes all complacency. The follower of Christ cannot say, "I have done all I should; I am the complete servant of God." No matter how far we have gone along the Christian road the sermon tells us that there is more ahead of us.

But if it stretches our horizons in this way, it also enables us to understand more of what the grace of God means. Dale C. Allison, Jr., brings this out when he sums up his examination of the structure of the Sermon in these words: "The Sermon on the Mount sets forth God's grace in the past (4:23–5:2), in the present (6:25-34; 7:7-11), and in the future (5:3-12); and this is the context in which 5:13–7:12 is to be heard. Amos Wilder was right on target when he wrote that Matthew 5–7 offers 'not so much ethics of obedience as ethics of grace.' "[3] We miss the point if we see the Sermon on the Mount as nothing other than a series of far-reaching demands. The demands are there, certainly. But the love and the mercy of God are there, too.

Most critics hold that this is not the account of any one sermon, but that Matthew has gathered (and adapted) material used on several occasions.[4] We need not doubt that some of what we find in this sermon was delivered on other occasions, but I wonder whether some commentators have paid sufficient attention to the fact that an itinerant preacher normally makes repeated use of his material, often with minor or even major changes. He adapts what he has used elsewhere to the situation now confronting him. That we find somewhat similar statements in other parts of the Gospels does not mean that Jesus did not use them on this occasion. We should be on our guard against thinking that it is Matthew's sermon rather than that of Jesus. The introductory and concluding verses (5:1-2; 7:28-29) read like the beginning and ending of an address. The best solution to a difficult problem seems to be that Matthew has taken a sermon Jesus delivered, and expanded it by including matter given on other occasions. He may be giving a summary of an extended session of teaching given over several hours (or even stretching into days; on one occasion at any rate people were with Jesus without food for three days, evidently to absorb his teaching, 15:32). It can scarcely be a verbatim report, for it is too long for anyone to have remembered the exact words, and there is no suggestion that it was written down as Jesus delivered it. But for us the

2. "No man can live the Sermon on the Mount in and of himself, and unaided"; "There is nothing that so leads to the gospel and its grace as the Sermon on the Mount" (Lloyd-Jones, I, pp. 14, 18).

3. *JBL*, 106 (1987), p. 441.

4. Cf. Johnson, "Jesus would not have given all this teaching on a single occasion. The sermon is made up of aphorisms, maxims, and illustrations which were remembered and treasured out of many discourses."

important thing is that here we are brought into contact with Jesus' teaching on important aspects of the life of the servant of God.

This discourse displays many resemblances to Luke's "Sermon on the Plain" (Luke 6:17-49), and many interpreters hold that they are variant accounts of the same discourse. Luke's use of "plain" does not rule this out, for it means no more than "a level place" and may well indicate a rather flat area in the mountains (though against this is the fact that a great multitude came to be healed, Luke 6:18, and it is unlikely that the sick would have climbed a mountain). Both sermons begin with beatitudes, go on to significant ethical teaching, and conclude with the little parable of the men building houses. But the differences between the two are such that it is not easy to regard them as variant accounts of the same sermon. It is better to think that Jesus used similar material on more than one occasion.[5]

1. Introduction, 5:1-2

> 1And when he saw the crowd, he went up into the mountain; and when he had sat down, his disciples came to him. 2And he opened his mouth and taught them, saying, . . .

Matthew has made it clear that great crowds of people were following Jesus at this stage of his public ministry; here he moves to one occasion when the Master went up into a mountain and taught the people in the open air.

1-2. Jesus saw the great crowds that were following him, so he went up into a mountain.[6] Some commentators draw attention to the fact that Moses went up into a mountain to receive the Law (Exod. 19:20) and couple this with the five great discourses in this Gospel, which parallel the five books of the law. They suggest that Matthew is depicting Jesus as the new Moses (cf. Diétrich, "Jesus, the new Moses, promulgates the new law for the children of the Kingdom"). But this is highly unlikely. Matthew is concerned with gospel, not law, and while Moses went up into his

---

5. For a helpful introduction to the Sermon see Carson, pp. 122-28. The number of *Interpretation* for April 1987 (vol. 41, no. 2) is given over to the Sermon on the Mount and has a useful discussion of a wide range of views.

6. He actually says "the" mountain, but it is not easy to understand the significance of the article. Matthew has a similar article in 8:1; 14:23; 15:29; 17:9; was there a particular mountain that the disciples knew as "the" mountain? (Plummer thinks this possible). This may be so, but the article need mean no more than the mountain that was nearby, or the mountainous area as opposed to the plain. Matthew uses ὄρος 16 times, which is more than in any other New Testament book. Perhaps we should notice Kingsbury's view: "can we assume that Matthew, at 5:1 and 15:29, is likewise employing the mountain to point to Jesus as the Son of God? All indications are that this is indeed the case" (*Structure*, p. 57; so also p. 58). But this is unreasonable. Being on a mountain does not carry such a far-reaching implication.

mountain alone, Jesus had a crowd of people with him. In addition, Moses gave the Law for the whole people, while Jesus' teaching was addressed to the disciples.[7]

Matthew says that Jesus went "up," which points to a climb, though we need not think that he went to the summit. He *sat down,* which is the normal posture for a teacher,[8] and his followers[9] responded by coming to him. Matthew refers to "his" disciples (so also in 8:23; 9:10, 11, 19; 10:1, etc.), which is an early way of speaking. When the Christian faith became established, it was enough to speak of "the disciples"; everyone knew who were meant. But in Jesus' day there were many teachers, each with his own group of learners, so it was necessary to say whose disciples were in mind. Matthew's use is the early one rather than the later (overall Matthew has about the same numbers of the early and the later usages). We should bear in mind that the teaching that follows is addressed to disciples rather than the general public. For example, throughout the whole sermon there is no call to repent, the first note in Jesus' preaching to the people (4:17; cf. the description of the hearers in vv. 13 and 14). This does not mean that no one other than disciples heard Jesus' teaching, only that it was addressed primarily to people committed to him. Gundry thinks that there were many of these and that *the crowd* were crowds of disciples. It was not necessary to say *he opened his mouth,* but it makes for a solemn introduction and prepares the reader for some significant teaching.[10]

2. The Beatitudes, 5:3-12

3"*Blessed are the poor in spirit, for theirs is the kingdom of heaven.* 4*Blessed are the mourners, for they will be comforted.* 5*Blessed are the meek, for they will inherit the earth.* 6*Blessed are those who hunger and thirst after righteousness, for they will be filled.* 7*Blessed are the merciful, for mercy will be shown to them.* 8*Blessed are the pure in heart, for they will see God.* 9*Blessed are the peacemakers, for they will be called God's sons.* 10*Blessed are those who have been persecuted for the sake of righteousness,*

7. Davies, who has examined the concepts of the new Exodus and the new Moses, allows that such motifs may be discernible in some places, but he concludes that they are not dominant (*SM*, pp. 25-108). He says that "the context of the Sermon in the totality of the Gospel's thought on the nature of the Christian life forbids any exclusive or even predominant 'Mosaic' approach to it" (*SM*, p. 99). Davies and Allison, however, "are moved" to accept a Mosaic motif in verses 1-2.

8. The posture, the verb, and the reference to disciples combine to show that Matthew is referring to teaching rather than proclamation. Davies holds that Matthew "has, with unmistakable deliberateness and with massive and majestic impressiveness, placed the teaching of Jesus in the forefront of his Gospel" (*SM*, p. 107),

9. This is Matthew's first use of μαθητής, a term he will use 73 times (John has it 78 times). Its 262 New Testament uses are confined to the Gospels and Acts. For discipleship in this Gospel see my *New Testament Theology* (Grand Rapids, 1986), pp. 136-40.

10. Barclay takes the imperfect ἐδίδασκεν in the sense "This is what He used to teach" and sees evidence that this is not one sermon but a summary of what Jesus habitually taught.

for the kingdom of heaven is theirs. [11]*Blessed are you when they upbraid you and persecute you and falsely say all kinds of evil about you for my sake.* [12]*Rejoice and be very glad because your reward is great in heaven; for in this way they persecuted the prophets who were before you."*

Luke has four beatitudes (Luke 6:20-22), but they are very different from those in this Gospel, and they are followed by four "Woes" for which Matthew has no parallel. Luke's four beatitudes are in the second person, while Matthew has eight in the third person (he has the second person in v. 11). It is not easy to see these as simple variants of the same original. It is more likely that Jesus used the "beatitude" approach on more than one occasion.[11] It is significant that this sermon begins with beatitudes rather than imperatives. Jesus will go on to make great demands on his followers, but these demands are to be understood in a context of grace.

3. For *blessed* many translations use expressions of a somewhat secular nature, such as "fortunate" *(AB)* or "happy" *(JB)*. These bring out the joy that is conveyed by Jesus' word, but not its full religious content.[12] There is more to blessedness than happiness. Bruner has "God bless," but this sounds too much like a prayer, while Jesus is making a strong affirmation. The first of the blessed ones are *the poor in spirit*.[13] This is not to be understood in the sense of "abject" or "mean spirited," as the English might perhaps convey. Nor is it the kind of poverty against which people rebel, but rather one that the poor in spirit accept, as pointing to the reality that they can bring nothing to God. *The poor in spirit* in the sense of this beatitude are those who recognize that they are completely and utterly destitute in the realm of the spirit. They recognize their lack of spiritual resources and therefore their complete dependence on God (cf. Goodspeed, "those who feel their spiritual need"; *NEB,* "know their need of God"). It is the opposite of the Pharisaic pride in one's own virtue with which Jesus was so often confronted (and which has all too often made its appearance in later times). "This is the man to whom I will look," the Lord says, "he that is humble and contrite in spirit, and trembles at my word" (Isa. 66:2). These are the poor in spirit.

---

11. According to *AB,* the two accounts "may well represent two versions uttered by Jesus on two different occasions."

12. μακάριος means "blessed, fortunate, happy" but "usu. in the sense *privileged recipient of divine favor*" (BAGD), "*O, the happiness of,* or *hail to those* . . . may be exactly right for the Aramaic original (= Hebr. אַשְׁרֵי), but it scarcely exhausts the content that μακάριος had in the mouths of Gk.-speaking Christians" (BAGD, 1.b). Curiously Morgan regards "happy" as more accurate than "blessed." F. Hauck in a felicitous expression says that the beatitudes "are not just intimations of the future or consolations in relation to it. They see the present in the light of the future" (*TDNT,* IV, p. 369).

13. The word πτωχός means a person so poor that he "lives not by his own labour or industry, but on other men's alms . . . being one therefore whom Plato would not endure in his ideal State"; it contrasts with πένης (which also means "poor"): "The πένης has nothing superfluous, the πτωχός nothing at all" (Trench, p. 129).

There are strong protests in modern times against "spiritualizing" and "psychologizing" interpretations of this beatitude, and it is insisted that it must be seen for what it is, a radical reversal of the world's values. We are told that it is the poor and the distressed as such of whom Jesus speaks. But we must exercise care at this point. Jesus is not saying that poverty is a blessing in itself; to canonize a state of life in which people find themselves against their will (real poverty does not mean voluntarily choosing to live simply) and from which they would escape if they could is scarcely Christian. Now it is true that it is easy for the interpreter smugly to transform the meaning of what Jesus says into an understanding of which the interpreter approves and avoid any real contact with the poverty-stricken. A rediscovery of Jesus' interest in the poor is long overdue. But I cannot rid myself of the feeling that much modern writing proceeds from the comfortable, people for whom poverty is an interesting subject for discussion but who have never themselves experienced what real poverty is. I have. And poverty is not a blessing, nor is powerlessness. Whatever Jesus meant, it was surely not that these states are blessed in themselves. He knew poverty, and he knew powerlessness in the face of a government that did not care. Any interpretation of his teaching that makes these things *in themselves* a blessing simply fails to take notice of reality. Jesus is pronouncing a blessing on those empty of any spiritual resource, poor as they often were in material things as well.

There may well be a reminiscence of Old Testament teaching on the poor, but we must bear in mind that the poor in this sense are not the poverty stricken as such, but God's poor, people oppressed by tyrants but trusting God, people who have nothing, no resource but God. "This poor man cried, and the LORD heard him, and saved him out of all his troubles" (Ps. 34:6). The Old Testament has many references to "the poor," but we are to understand these not merely of people who lack in worldly goods but of the faithful though downtrodden poor, those who look to God for their deliverance.[14]

Of these lowly people Jesus says, *theirs is the kingdom of heaven*.[15] We should understand this in the sense of consequence rather than reward. In no sense do they merit the kingdom, but being what they are they possess it. We should understand this in the sense, "theirs alone."[16] Those who are not poor in spirit can never have membership in the kingdom.

14. We find "the poor in spirit" also in later Jewish writings such as the Qumran scrolls (see Vermes, p. 142).

15. Cf. Lloyd-Jones, "I would say that there is no more perfect statement of the doctrine of justification by faith only than this Beatitude: 'Blessed are the poor in spirit: for theirs (and theirs only) is the kingdom of heaven.' Very well then, this is the foundation of everything else" (I, p. 42).

16. Davies comments, "The repeated αὐτοί in the second clause in each part of the Beatitudes in vv. 3, 4, 5, 6, 7, 8, 10 has an antithetical effect. It is not reading too much into these verses to find that it is 'these' people rather than 'those' who are blessed" (*SM*, p. 289).

In the basic sense, of course, the kingdom belongs to God, and it is often said to be his. But in another sense membership in the kingdom belongs to all the people of God, and it is something like this that is in mind here. Jesus is saying that the lowly are especially characteristic of the kingdom. The riches of the kingdom belong to them in the fullest measure. The present tense is used for the blessing pronounced on them here and again in verse 10, but in the intermediate beatitudes the tense is future. We should not press this point too far, for the full blessing in all the beatitudes is future. But this present points to a significant blessing for the poor in spirit right now.

4. A benediction for *the mourners* is most unexpected. We generally regard mourners as the most unfortunate of people. We see them as people to be pitied, helped, comforted, but not as those to be envied as the recipients of God's blessing. And they are blessed, Jesus says, because they *will be comforted.*[17] It is this that makes the reference to ordinary mourning as we know it so very difficult. It is not easy to think that Jesus is speaking of those who have suffered bereavement, for example, and saying that they are not really in an unhappy situation because one day they will be consoled. It is much more likely that he is referring to a more fundamental kind of mourning.[18] Perhaps we should bear in mind that typically the worldly take a lighthearted attitude to the serious issues of life, a fact that is very evident in our modern pleasure-loving generation. In their seeking after self-gratification and pleasure they do not grieve over sin or evil. Because they do not grieve over what is wrong in themselves, they do not repent; and because they do not grieve over the wrong they share with others in the communities in which they live, they take few steps to set things right. Because they are not moved by the plight of the poor and the suffering, they make no move to help the world's unfortunates. It may be that Jesus is saying that our values are wrong and that it is those[19] who mourn in the face of the evils that are part and parcel of life as we know it, those who mourn over the way God's cause is so often neglected and his people despised, who are the truly blessed ones. The Psalmist could say: "My eyes shed streams of tears, because men do not keep thy law" (Ps. 119:136). It is to such that Jesus holds out the prospect of ultimate consolation. Now they mourn; but now is not always. God's ultimate

---

17. The verb παρακαλέω can have the meaning "encourage" (cf. Heb. 3:13), and that may possibly be in mind here. Many interpreters find here the "divine passive," that is, the passive used when the real doer of the action is God. Thus *GNB* has "God will comfort them" (and so in vv. 6, 7, 9, etc.). E. M. Sidebottom has shown that the construction is perhaps not as widely used as some suggest (*ET*, LXXXVII [1975-76], pp. 200-203), but we can scarcely doubt that this is the way the present verse is to be understood.

18. "It is not the sorrow of bereavement to which Christ refers, but the sorrow of repentance" (Stott, pp. 40-41).

19. αὐτοί resumes the subject and puts some emphasis on it: *they* and not others are the ones who will be comforted.

triumph, and with it the comforting of those who have grieved over evil, is sure.

5. Now *the meek* come in for attention[20] (*JB* and *REB* have "gentle"). Meekness is another word for self-effacement. We should not miss the point that in all three of the opening beatitudes the truth is brought out that the follower of Jesus does not aggressively insist on his own rights[21] but displays genuine humility. Meekness is not to be confused with weakness: the meek are not simply submissive because they lack the resources to be anything else.[22] Meekness is quite compatible with great strength and ability as humans measure strength, but whatever strength or weakness the meek person has is accompanied by humility and a genuine dependence on God. True meekness may be a quality of the strong, those who could assert themselves but choose not to do so. The strong who qualify for this blessing are the strong who decline to domineer. Self-assertion is never a Christian virtue; rather, it is Christian to be busy in lowly service and to refuse to engage in the conduct that merely advances one's personal aims.

The reward of the meek is that *they will inherit the earth* (cf. Ps. 37:11). The verb[23] points to firm possession; clearly there is no thought here of inheriting on the death of a testator or the like. There may be a reference to the psalm that contrasts the wicked, who "will be no more," with the meek, who "shall possess the land" (Ps. 37:10-11). The sense in which they will do this is not obvious. Tolstoy and others have spoken of "the terrible meek" apparently because there are so many of the downtrodden that in the end the strong are not able to budge the inert mass and accomplish what they want to get done. But it is impossible to think that Jesus' meaning is anything like that. Rather, the thought is eschatological; Jesus is looking forward to the coming of the messianic kingdom. In the end it is the meek, not the self-assertive, who will have a place in God's kingdom. It has often been pointed out that the future in this and the following verses indicates certainty and not simply futurity.

6. Next Jesus turns to people's attitude to uprightness. Matthew uses the verb "to *hunger*" 9 times, but in all the other 8 it refers to literal hunger while here the meaning is clearly metaphorical (as it is twice in Luke and

---

20. This verse precedes verse 4 in D 33 it[mss] syr[c] etc. But it follows so naturally on verse 3 that it is hard to see why any scribe should have interposed verse 4 if this had been the original order. It is much more likely that scribes altered the original sequence to bring verses 3 and 5 together.

21. "Others claim their rights, but the meek are concerned about their duties" (Buttrick).

22. "These are not the weak in character, the meekly submissive or the fearful compromisers. Christianity is not a crutch for the sick or a parapet for the dizzy, a substitute for those who have missed something else. Therefore the gospel is not a hymn in praise of people without stuffing or strength" (Gutzwiller).

23. κληρονομέω, which means "receive by lot" (κλῆρος) and then "inherit," and thus "possess."

once in John). With it is linked *thirst,* which is more often used in the metaphorical sense (cf. Ps. 42:2). Jesus is speaking of an intense longing after *righteousness* that may be likened to both hunger and thirst.[24] Everyone now and then does what is right, but Jesus is pointing his hearers not to occasional acts but to a passionate concern for the right. *Righteousness* is often used in the New Testament for the right standing believers have before God because of Christ's atoning work, but this is often said to be a Pauline concept rather than one that Matthew sets forth. Now it is plain that Matthew has a strong interest in the upright living that should characterize the servant of Christ, and we must not try to turn him into a pale shadow of Paul. But we must not minimize his emphasis on grace either (cf. v. 3). Specifically we should notice that he is not suggesting that people can make a strong effort and achieve the righteousness of which he is writing: it is a given righteousness, not an achieved righteousness. The blessed do not achieve it but *hunger and thirst* for it. They *will be filled,* which surely means that God will fill them (cf. 6:33, "his righteousness"). We need not doubt that the term here includes the doing of right, an indication that we are expected to live in full accordance with the will of God. How could anyone have a strong desire for a right standing before God without at the same time strongly wanting to do the right? Today there is a strong emphasis on social righteousness, the liberation of people from oppression, and that can scarcely be out of mind either. *Righteousness* is a rich and full concept, but whichever way we understand it, it is a righteousness that people cannot produce of themselves. We are to do our best and we may be able to avoid "the gutters of life," but this righteousness is a gift of God.[25] And of those who have this wholehearted longing for the right Jesus says, *they will be filled.*[26] They do not achieve it of themselves, but God fulfils their longing. God will not disappoint anyone who has this deep desire to do his will. Those who long for righteousness will have a full measure, not a mere trace. There are two thoughts here, the first of which insists on the disposition of the seeker. The good gift of God does not come indiscriminately to all the race, but only to those who seek it wholeheartedly. The second is that, for all their

24. "To believe oneself to be in possession of righteousness, like the Pharisee in the parable, is fatal. To know oneself to be in want of it is not enough. One must feel the want of it, and have a passionate and persistent longing for it . . ." (Plummer, p. 65).

25. Cf. G. Schrenk, "in opposition to the Jewish thought of merit, δικαιοσύνη is plainly regarded as a gift which God gives to those who ask for it" (*TDNT,* II, p. 198). Johnson denies that the saying can be "reconciled with rabbinical Judaism" and understands the meaning to be "they depend, not upon their own power to achieve righteousness, but upon God." R. Bultmann says that this verse "obviously does not mean those who 'ever striving, endeavor' to attain ethical perfection, but those who long to have God pronounce the verdict 'righteous' as His decision over them in the judgment" (*Theology of the New Testament,* I [London, 1952], p. 273).

26. The verb χορτάζω is used of animals in the sense "feed, fatten," so that when it comes to be used of persons it means "fill," "satisfy fully."

intense longing, the seekers do not fill themselves with righteousness, but are filled; righteousness is a gift of God.

7. The first four beatitudes express in one way or another our dependence on God; the next three the outworking of that dependence. This beatitude is relatively straightforward: people who show mercy on others will themselves be the recipients of mercy. The adjective for *merciful* (found elsewhere in the New Testament only in Heb. 2:17) means those whose bent is to show mercy, not those who engage in an occasional merciful impulse. Such people will receive mercy, a truth we often observe in this life. But Jesus is surely referring basically to an eschatological truth. There are people who show by their habitual merciful deeds that they have responded to God's love and are living by his grace. They will receive mercy on the last day.

8. Matthew does not often use the word for *pure* (three times only); it signifies "clean" and thus pure. This is the one place in the New Testament where purity is predicated of the *heart*. With us heart is used of the physical organ and as a way of referring to the emotions, but we must not read that way of understanding the term back into Scripture. There it stands for the whole of our inner state, thought and will as well as emotions: "In a psychological sense, the seat of man's collective energies, the focus of personal life, the seat of the rational as well as the emotional and volitional elements in human life, hence that wherein lies the moral and religious condition of the man" (AS).[27] This beatitude thus leads us to purity at the very center of our being. This is no truism. Jesus later said, "out of the heart proceed evil thoughts, murders, adulteries, fornications, thefts, false witness, blasphemies" (15:19). The heart is not the place where we naturally expect purity,[28] but Jesus demands purity right there. To be pure in heart is to be pure throughout (cf. Ps. 24:4). And the consequence of this kind of purity is that *they will see God* (cf. Ps. 73:1). There is a sense and a measure in which this is true of life here and now. The pure in heart see God in a way that the impure never know. But the main thought is surely eschatological; it points us to a vision too wonderful to be fully experienced in this life but that will come to its consummation in the world to come.

9. The word *peacemakers* is found only here in the New Testament. It is quite general and is not qualified in any way, so that we are left wondering whether the primary reference is to the large scale (dealing with wars and the like) or the small scale (quarrels). That it is left general probably means that both are in mind.[29] There is a quality of peaceableness, a

---

27. According to BAGD, καρδία is used "as center and source of the whole inner life, w. its thinking, feeling, and volition . . . in the case of the natural man as well as the redeemed man." They note its use of thought, of the will, of moral decisions ("pure in heart"), of the emotions (esp. love; 22:37), and of the disposition.

28. "All agree that purity of heart is the mother of all virtues, but there is scarcely a man in a hundred who does not put smart dealing in the place of the highest virtue" (Calvin, I, p. 171).

29. Billy Graham brings out the fact that this world sorely needs peacemakers by citing

disinclination to engage in disputes, that is admirable, but Jesus is talking about more than that. He refers not to peace-*keepers* but to peace-*makers*, people who end hostilities and bring the quarrelsome together. Argyle points out that these are "not appeasers, but those who actively overcome evil with good." A person may be known as one who ends hostilities throughout his whole sphere of life, whether that sphere be great or small.[30]

It is people like this who will be called *God's sons*. There is something godlike in bringing peace to people and people to peace.[31] There is, of course, a sense in which all believers are members of the family of God, whether they are distinguished as makers of peace or not. But those who make peace are fulfilling what membership in the family really means, and this is something to which all the members of the family must aspire. The verb "to call" may be used in a variety of ways, but here the point is that the call signifies that the person called really is what the name indicates.

10. We come now to a most unexpected beatitude, one for the persecuted. Matthew's first readers, who probably had some experience of persecution, would no doubt have been surprised at this statement, for it is never pleasant to experience suffering (cf. Heb. 12:11). Matthew uses his verb "persecute"[32] four times in this chapter and twice elsewhere. It can denote putting to flight, driving away (10:23), or even following without hostile intent (Luke 17:23). It may even be used of pursuing virtues like love (1 Cor. 14:1) or generally what is good (1 Thess. 5:15). But in the New Testament it is mostly used of inflicting suffering on people who hold beliefs that the establishment frowns on, and it is this kind of persecution of which Jesus speaks here. He does not speak of persecution as such, but of persecution *for the sake of righteousness*. People may suffer for doing evil, but such suffering is punishment, not persecution, and in any case believers are not to suffer that way (cf. 1 Pet. 4:15). Jesus is speaking of those committed to God's cause, and *righteousness* is the kind of conduct appropriate for those who have been given right standing before God.[33] Salvation is all of grace, but there is a kind

---

the numbers of wars fought by various nations from 1480 to 1941: Great Britain 78 wars, France 71, Spain 64, Russia 61, Austria 52, Germany 23, China 11, Japan 9, U.S.A. 13 plus 110 against the Indians within U.S.A. He adds, "Someone has pointed out that in the past four thousand years there has been less than three hundred years of peace" (*The Secret of Happiness* [New York, 1955], p. 85). In a race like ours peacemakers have plenty of scope for action.

30. The Jews lauded peacemaking, and Hillel, for example, said, "Be of the disciples of Aaron, loving peace and pursuing peace" (*'Abot* 1:12). But he adds, "loving mankind and bringing them nigh to the Law." The reverence for peace and the love of mankind are noteworthy, but the emphasis on the law strikes a different note.

31. "*Sons of God*, then, are those who manifest the God-life, do as God does, perform God's task in the world" (Robinson).

32. διώκω. The perfect tense points to a persecution in the past that endures into the present.

33. Lenski points out that this "means more than that they suffered innocently. . . . They suffered because of what they were in their character and their lives, for the divine approval that rested upon them."

of conduct that is expected of those who have received God's good gift and it is that kind of conduct on which Jesus pronounces a blessing. Those who undergo persecution for God's cause and not for any fault of their own receive a blessing like that for "the poor in spirit" (v. 3), and it is given in exactly the same words: *the kingdom of heaven is theirs.* There is the same underlying attitude and the same ultimate reward.[34]

11. Many of the benedictions have been surprising, but none more than this; it is an intensification of the statement in verse 10. Persecution is universally regarded as evil (except by the persecutors). To have it pronounced as a blessing is surprising indeed. But God's people have always been rejected by the worldly: persecution puts us in good company. There is a change from the third person in the beatitudes up to this point to direct address in this one. *When* is a general term; we could understand it as "whenever."[35] *Upbraid* refers to verbal abuse, reproaching, insulting, and the like, but *persecute* refers to actions as well as words. With *falsely say all kinds of evil* we are back at words, but we are to bear in mind the qualification *falsely.*[36] Believers are not to engage in the kind of conduct that enables people to accuse them genuinely; their lives are to be above reproach. *All kinds* is comprehensive; believers must expect a great variety of evil comments. *For my sake* links the whole saying with the Christian profession. Jesus is not pronouncing a blessing on those in general who receive criticism, but on those who are upbraided for following him. For them reproach, persecution, and slander are occasions of blessing.

12. Far from being despondent and depressed, saddened or enraged, Christians who find themselves in this situation are bidden, *Rejoice* (cf. Acts 5:41). This call for joy is reinforced with *be very glad.*[37] There is a twofold reason for this joy. *Because* introduces the first. The word for *reward*[38] properly signifies a "wage" (20:8), but it is also used in the sense "reward," and this is in order in the present passage, though we should bear in mind that the word often has something of equivalence in its

34. Filson comments, "God will preserve and welcome into the Kingdom those who in the conflict of life pay the cost of discipleship."

35. ὅταν, which is used "of an action that is conditional, possible, and, in many instances, repeated" (BAGD, which goes on to point out that when the aorist subjunctive is used the action of the subordinate clause precedes that of the main clause, here "when they have reviled"). Matthew has it 19 times.

36. ψευδόμενοι is read by many important MSS (א B C mss of OL syr^c sah Boh etc.) but omitted by a significant group (D mss of OL syr^s). It is a nice point whether the word was original but omitted by some scribes who thought it scarcely necessary (it could be assumed that if the followers of Jesus were accused it would be falsely) or whether it was absent from the original text but was supplied by scribes to make sure there was no doubt about the point. On the whole I think it should be read. But if it is not read it is implied, for what the enemy say would not really be evil if it were true.

37. ἀγαλλιᾶσθε is a strong term, "exult." The verb is found only here in Matthew; it is "a new formation in H. Gk., found only in Bibl. and ecc. wr. for ἀγάλλω" (BAGD). Cf. *KJV*, "be exceeding glad."

38. μισθός is used 10 times by Matthew, the most in any New Testament book.

meaning. This does not mean that the pious have merited a heavenly reward, for "the reward is so far beyond anything which men could possibly attain by their own goodness that the very word 'reward' has something of irony about it" *(AB)*; it is rather that God's goodness overflows toward the persecuted. *Great* shows that the reward in question is far from meager, and *in heaven* locates it.[39] Jesus is not talking about a reward in the here and now. Whatever compensations they receive in this world, the full reward of the persecuted is reserved for the next.

The second reason for joy is that this is the way *the prophets* were treated. Persecuted believers are in good company. The plural brings all the prophets together as one godly company. The persecutions they received no doubt varied greatly, but the point is that persecution is the lot of the people of God while they walk this earth. In three consecutive verses Matthew has used the verb "persecute," which puts emphasis on the concept. Here even the prophets, whom everyone now accepts as the servants of God par excellence, were treated badly in their own day. It is a privilege for the servants of God in later days to share in some measure in the lot of these great men of God.

3. Salt and Light, 5:13-16

> 13"You are the salt of the earth; but if the salt has lost its taste, with what will it be salted? It is good for nothing any longer but to be thrown out and be trodden under foot by men. 14You are the light of the world. A city set on a hill cannot be hidden. 15Nor do people light a lamp and put it under the measuring bowl, but on the lampstand, and it gives light to all who are in the house. 16Let your light so shine before men that they may see your good works and give glory to your Father who is in heaven."

Now comes a paragraph that points to the penetrating power of the gospel and of people who are transformed by it. They are likened to salt and to light. Morgan points to the permanent applicability of what Jesus said, for people continue to be "in circumstances of corruption and darkness." While these circumstances last, there will still be the need of this teaching of Jesus. The Master is conveying a warning: salt must salty or it will be thrown out; light must shine.[40] The section comes fittingly after the beatitudes: it is the little people, those with no merit of their own to

---

39. Cf. Allen, "Here the thought is not that of reward for piety, but of future recompense for a present condition of persecution and reproach."

40. There is a similar saying about salt in Mark 9:50 but with considerable differences (of Mark's 21 words only 6 are in Matthew), so that dependence is not easy to demonstrate. Luke also has a saying about salt (Luke 14:34-35), but adds only μωρανθῇ to the words common to Mark. Luke has words about throwing out worthless salt, but they are different from those here, and he adds, "he who has ears to hear, let him hear." Mark and Luke also have a saying about a covered light (Mark 4:21; Luke 8:16).

plead but who have been accepted by God in all their lowliness, who are the salt and the light. Jesus has spoken of their blessedness; now he turns to their responsibility.

13. *You* is emphatic and restrictive: Jesus is not talking about people in general but specifically about his followers. He says, *you are:* he is making a statement, not giving a promise. He does not explain *the salt*[41] *of the earth,* but we should bear in mind that "Salt has no beneficial effect upon soil" (McNeile; cf. Deut. 29:23; Judg. 9:45; Ps. 107:34); Jesus is not talking about what happens when salt is put into soil. We should take *salt* as a metaphor and *the earth* as referring to people. Jesus is apparently thinking of the function of salt as a preservative, as the enemy of decay, and as giving taste to food. What is good in society his followers keep wholesome. What is corrupt they oppose; they penetrate society for good and act as a kind of moral antiseptic. And they give a tang to life like salt to a dish of food.[42] *Of the earth* makes the application a wide one; their influence is not to be confined to a narrow circle. *Has lost its taste*[43] presents us with a bit of a problem, for sodium chloride does not lose its taste. But the salt in use in first-century Palestine was very impure and it was quite possible for the sodium chloride to be leached out, so that what remained lacked "saltness,"[44] and specifically the salty taste. This remainder was literally useless; what could possibly be done with it? Jesus asks, *with what will it be salted?* It was not possible to put salt back into it. Jesus says of this residual mass: "it has power for nothing";[45] its force was given it by its saltiness; lacking that it had no power. Its fate accordingly was to be thrown out and trampled, testimony to its uselessness.

14. Again we have an emphatic *You* as words are introduced that apply not to people at large but to those committed to Jesus. *The light of the world* implies that the world is in darkness (despite its continuing claims to enlightenment!). It is an expression applied to Jesus (John 8:12; 9:5; cf. John 12:35); thus it is interesting to find it used also of his fol-

---

41. BDF sees the article here as "inserted if the predicate noun is presented as something well known or as that which alone merits the designation" (273[1]). On *salt* Stendahl comments, "The connotation of 'salt' in rabbinic metaphorical language is mainly 'wisdom.' " Such a reference may be favored by the use of the verb μωραίνω (see n. 39 above).

42. "While Christians are not challenged to *become* salty — their saltiness is a gift of Jesus' Word — they are obliged to *stay* salty, that is, they are challenged to be real Christians" (Bruner, p. 160).

43. The verb so translated, μωραίνω, means "to be foolish" (cf. Rom. 1:22) and comes to have a causal sense "to make foolish." It is not what we expect with *salt,* but foolishness easily leads to insipidity and this results from the lack of salt. Carson comments, "It is hard not to conclude that disciples who lose their savor are in fact making fools of themselves."

44. L. G. Herr says that the Dead Sea was the main source of salt for Palestine, but "the salt from the Dead Sea region was generally contaminated with other minerals; thus the salt could be dissolved out of this mixture, leaving a tasteless substance" (*ISBE,* IV, p. 287; so also *TDNT,* I, p. 229).

45. ἰσχύω has the meaning "be strong"; in passages like this it signifies "avail," "be serviceable" (cf. Gal. 5:6; Heb. 9:17).

lowers.[46] The sense is, of course, quite different; Christ is himself the light, whereas his followers are no more than pointers to and reflectors of Christ the Light (they are "light in the Lord," Eph. 5:8, and they shine "as lights in the world," Phil. 2:15). But in this way they bring the light to the world and the world to the light in a way that would not take place apart from them. *World* in this verse, like earth in the previous verse, points to no small and mean task. The task of the disciples is to bring light to the whole world. Jesus goes on to point out that, being who and what they are, giving light is inevitable. It is quite impossible for a city *set on*[47] *a hill* to be hidden. Its situation makes concealment impossible. The disciples are not to be worldly people, indistinguishable from the people among whom they live.[48]

15. A further example of visibility is added: the point is clearly important. Jesus refers to people lighting[49] a lamp.[50] Literally he says, "they light," but "they" does not refer to any particular group of people; the verb is quite general. The present tense likewise points to continuous activity: this is what people habitually do, or in this case do not do. When they light a lamp people do not put it under *the measuring bowl*,[51] the implement the household would use for measuring grain (the word could also denote a specific quantity of grain, but that is not in mind here). That would defeat the purpose of lighting the lamp. Instead they put it on *the lampstand*, with the result[52] that everyone in the house[53] has light. This homely illustration brings out an important function of discipleship. The very purpose of being a follower of Jesus is to give light. Giving light is not an option, so to speak, which the disciple may or may not choose. It is part of being a disciple, just as much part of discipleship as giving light is of a lighted lamp. Jesus has chosen his own so that they may give light. It is the nature of light to shine, and when people have received the light of the gospel they will shine in a dark world. That is the point of both comparisons. It is of the very nature of light that it brings illumination.

---

46. The Qumran scrolls refer to members of the community as "the sons of light" and say things like "All the children of righteousness are ruled by the Prince of Light and walk in the ways of light" (Vermes, p. 75).

47. ἐπάνω signifies that the city is on top of the hill.

48. Cf. Tasker, "The most obvious *general* characteristic of salt is that it is essentially different from the medium into which it is put. Its power lies precisely in this difference. So is it, says Jesus, with His disciples. Their power in the world lies in their difference from it."

49. καίω means "light," "kindle," and "in contrast to ἅπτω, κ. lays the emphasis less upon the act of lighting than on keeping a thing burning" (BAGD, 1.a).

50. AS understands λύχνος as "*a lamp* (portable, and usually set on a stand, λυχνία)."

51. The μόδιος, Latin *modius*, was a measure of grain comprising 16 sextarii = "about 8.75 liters, almost exactly one peck" (BAGD). The article here points to the measure in the house.

52. καί here is consecutive, "and so": καὶ λάμπει = ὥστε λάμπειν (BDF, 442[2]).

53. οἰκία strictly means "the house" as opposed to οἶκος, the whole estate (see on 2:11). This obviously fits the present passage. A typical house of the poor would have only one room, so that one lamp would lighten the whole house.

16. The point of all this is explicitly brought out. *Your light* is, of course, a borrowed light. It is because they have received light from Jesus that the disciples can shine in the world. *So* refers back to the preceding: "let your light shine in the aforementioned way." This light will issue in *good*[54] *works* that are seen by people, a provision that must be understood carefully, for there were people like the Pharisees who made sure that their good deeds were seen by others and it is not this Pharisaic attitude that Jesus is commending. The good works are to be seen, not in order that the doers may be congratulated as fine, upstanding servants of God, but in such a way that the observers will *give glory to your Father*. There is to be no parade of virtue, no attempt to win praise for oneself. It is the *light* that is to shine, not those privileged to be the bearers of the light. People will always see the deeds that disciples do, and disciples are to make sure that when that takes place it is the light that they will see. And that they will see it in such a way that they will praise God. This is the first time in this Gospel that God is called *Father*, a usage that will recur (44 times, a total exceeded only by John; in this sermon it occurs 16 times); the divine fatherhood meant much to Matthew. God was sometimes called Father in the Old Testament and by the Jews, but it was not characteristic. It was characteristic for Jesus and for his followers after him. Matthew often qualifies *Father* with a reference to heaven (v. 45; 6:1, 9; 7:11, 21; 10:32, 33; 12:50; 16:17; 18:10, 14, 19).[55] We are so accustomed to referring to God as "the Father" that we do not stop to reflect that this is a revolutionary way of thinking of "the high and lofty One who inhabits eternity, whose name is Holy" (Isa. 57:15). Jesus altered forever the way we think of God.

4. Fulfilling the Law, 5:17-20

> [17]"*Do not think that I came to abolish the law or the prophets; I did not come to abolish but to fulfil.* [18]*For truly I tell you, until heaven and earth pass away, one iota or one little stroke will not pass away from the law until all has taken place.* [19]*Whoever therefore relaxes one of the least of these commandments, and teaches men so, will be called least in the kingdom of heaven; but whoever does and teaches them, this person will be called great in the kingdom of heaven.* [20]*For I tell you that unless your righteousness exceeds that of the scribes and Pharisees, you certainly will not enter the kingdom of heaven.*"

The law, the books from Genesis to Deuteronomy, was Scripture par excellence for the Jews, and they examined it with minute thoroughness.

---

54. *Good* is καλός; over against ἀγαθός and δίκαιος, it signifies the goodness that is attractive. Some "good" people are very unattractive. That is not the goodness of which Jesus is speaking.

55. The adjective οὐράνιος qualifies *Father* in verse 48; 6:14, 26, 32; 15:13; 18:35; 23:9, a construction found in Matthew only. He also has some references to the Father as "in secret" (6:4, 6, 18). For οὐρανός see on 3:2.

They discovered, for example, that there are 613 commandments in this part of Scripture (248 positive and 365 negative), and this opened up wonderful possibilities for those of a legalistic turn of mind. They could easily concentrate on discussions of those commandments and on keeping the letter of the law in such a way as to find little place for weightier matters. Jesus had a continuing dispute with people with this approach (see ch. 23), and from their point of view it was easy to accuse him of not taking the law seriously. From the point of view of his own followers there was also a problem. He taught them that salvation is all of grace; people do not merit salvation by their own good works. What then was the place of the commands that Scripture conveys so clearly? It was important for Matthew's readers (as well as for the Jews and the disciples at the time of Jesus) that Jesus' attitude to the law be made plain, and in this section of the Sermon Matthew includes important teaching about the law. He shows that Jesus affirmed its continuing validity and that he came to fulfil it. There are some strong words for anyone prepared to break even the least of the commandments and to teach other people to do the same. The statement that the righteousness of those who enter the kingdom must exceed that of the scribes and Pharisees must have come as a very surprising piece of information.

17. Jesus directs his hearers as to how they should *think*[56] about the law and his relationship to it. There is a great deal in this Gospel about the law, and this section is very important for Jesus' understanding of the law and its implications. He makes clear that "He is in no way contradicting the Mosaic law, though He is opposed to the legalistic type of religion that the scribes had built upon it" (Tasker). *I came* is a significant expression; it is not one that a person would normally use of himself. It will have a meaning like "came into the world," "came from God" and points to a consciousness of mission. Jesus had a special place and a special function, and that was not concerned with abolishing the law. His verb *abolish* is a strong one[57] and indicates doing away entirely with the law. *The law* strictly denotes the Pentateuch, and that is its meaning here. With it Jesus joins *the prophets.*[58] The Jews spoke of "the former prophets," under which heading they included the books from Joshua to 2 Kings, and "the latter prophets," which were the books we speak of as prophecy. The combination is a way of referring to the whole of Old Testament Scripture (cf. 7:12; 22:40). Jesus firmly disclaims any intention of doing away with any part

---

56. There is a play on words. The verb νομίζω is related to νόμος and in fact is derived from it. AS gives its meaning as "1. *to practise, hold by custom* . . . 2. *to deem, consider, suppose.*" Turner regards the command as categorical: "Do not think *for one moment* that . . ." (*Grammatical Insights*, p. 32).

57. καταλύω = "loose down"; it is used of demolishing the temple, for example (24:2; 26:61; 27:40).

58. The two are linked with ἤ, a disjunctive. Conceivably a different attitude might be taken to one than to the other. Jesus fulfils both.

of the Bible. His program had some resounding novelties about it, but he did not abandon Scripture, as his habit of referring to it shows. Rather, he fulfilled it. He did not have a negative approach to it but a positive one.

To fulfil[59] has been understood in three main ways: (1) It may mean that he would do the things laid down in Scripture. (2) It may mean that he would bring out the full meaning of Scripture. (3) It may mean that in his life and teaching he would bring Scripture to its completion. Each points to an aspect of the truth, and Jesus may well have meant that he would fulfil Scripture in more ways than one.[60] Davies and Allison well remark: "First, he who fulfils the law and the prophets displaces them in so far as he must become the centre of attention: the thing signified (Jesus) is naturally more important than the sign (the law and the prophets). . . . Secondly, if the law is fulfilled, it cannot on that account be set aside. Fulfilment can only confirm the Torah's truth, not cast doubt upon it." But however we interpret it, we must not forget that the law may be summed up in the two commandments of love (22:37-40) and that "love is the fulfilment of the law" (Rom. 13:10). We must bear in mind that "fulfil" does not mean the same as "keep"; Jesus is speaking of more than obedience to regulations. Nor should we forget that the way in which Jesus fulfilled the law could not be fully appreciated until after his death and resurrection. Not till then could it be seen how he had "fulfilled all righteousness" (3:15), nor how he would send the Holy Spirit to enable his followers to attain a higher standard of righteousness than they ever could in their own strength. We should also bear in mind that the verb "fulfil" applies here not only to the law but also to the prophets. As Robert Banks puts it, "The prophetic teachings point forward (principally) to the actions of Christ and have been realized in them in an incomparably greater way. The Mosaic laws point forward (principally) to the teachings of Christ and have also been realized in them in a more profound manner."[61]

18. *For* introduces the reason, and *truly* is regularly followed by *I tell you*. It adds up to a very solemn formula of affirmation and indicates that the words that follow are important. *Truly* represents the word we trans-

59. The infinitive expresses the purpose of Jesus' coming (*MT*, 366).

60. The meaning of *fulfil* has aroused a great deal of discussion (see Carson for a useful summary). That Jesus did not insist on the whole ceremonial law is evident, but he makes no distinction between the ceremonial and the moral law here. Cf. Carson, "The best interpretation of these difficult verses says that Jesus fulfills the Law and the Prophets in that they point to him, and he is their fulfillment. The antithesis is not between 'abolish' and 'keep' but between 'abolish' and 'fulfill.' " According to Davies, the verb is best taken as "to bring to its destined end" (*SM*, p. 100). *JB* has a note: "Jesus is speaking not of carrying into effect each single injunction of the old Law but of bestowing on that Law a new and definitive form by raising it to a higher place through the spirit of the gospel." Calvin argues with regard to the ceremonies laid down in the law that "it is only their practice that was abrogated: their significance was actually given more confirmation" (I, p. 180). McNeile holds that the reference is to Jesus' teaching: "He came to *fill* the Law, to reveal the full depth of meaning that it was intended to hold." This is true but inadequate.

61. *JBL*, 93 (1974), p. 231.

literate as "amen." The normal use of the term was as a congregational response to words uttered by someone leading the congregation, for example, at worship. The peculiarity of Jesus' use is that he put it at the beginning of important sayings. Matthew has the word 31 times, and with the exception of the "amen" at the end of the Lord's Prayer in some manuscripts he always has it in words of Jesus.[62] All the Evangelists have Jesus using the word in this way; in John it is invariably doubled, but in each of the others it is single, a phenomenon that has never been convincingly explained. John has the actual word 50 times (i.e., on 25 occasions), but Matthew has it on more occasions than anyone else. It is used to give solemn emphasis to the words that follow. The solemn protestation of what is true implies that the Person who has made it has high claims to reliability, so that the expression has christological implications.[63] Bengel points out that the prophets tend to say "saith the Lord" and the apostles "It is written," but Jesus uses "I say unto you."

Until[64] *heaven*[65] *and earth pass away* points to the end of created things. *Heaven* does not here denote the permanent abode of the blessed but part of the physical universe; it is used with *earth* in this expression to convey the thought of the totality of creation. It will all in due course *pass away*, but what God has said in Scripture is more permanent than that. Jesus says emphatically that it will certainly not[66] pass away. He is referring to written Scripture, as the terms he employs show clearly. The *iota* was the smallest letter of the Greek alphabet, but here it is usually understood to refer to the *yodh*, the smallest letter of the Hebrew alphabet.[67] The *little stroke*[68] was probably a tiny projection on some letters (that helped distin-

62. Stonehouse points out that in this Gospel Jesus is recorded as using the expression "I say" 55 times, whereas in Mark this happens 18 times, in Luke 43 times, and in John 34 times (*Witness*, p. 210). Clearly Matthew is more than a little interested in the solemn pronouncements Jesus makes.

63. Cf. H. Schlier, "The point of the Amen before Jesus' own sayings is rather to show that as such they are reliable and true, and that they are so as and because Jesus Himself in His Amen acknowledges them to be His own sayings and thus makes them valid. . . . Thus in the ἀμήν preceding the λέγω ὑμῖν of Jesus we have the whole of Christology *in nuce*" (*TDNT*, I, p. 338).

64. For ἕως see the note on 1:25.

65. Matthew usually has οὐρανός in the plural, but in the expression "heaven and earth" he prefers the singular (see v. 34; 6:10; 11:25; 24:35; 28:18).

66. The double negative οὐ μή is emphatic. Moulton points out that the words of Jesus and quotations from LXX account for nearly 90 percent of the New Testament examples of the construction; he detects "a feeling that inspired language was fitly rendered by words of a decisive tone not needed generally elsewhere" (M, I, p. 192). The aorist subjunctive is used here in the sense of the future indicative (*MT*, 172). Matthew has it about 20 times, almost all in words of Jesus.

67. Bengel says that there are 66,420 yodhs in the Hebrew Scriptures. Just one of such a number would not seem to be important, but even that will not pass away, Jesus says.

68. The word is κεραία, found again in the New Testament only in Luke 16:17. It derives from κέρας, "a horn," and means "a little horn." Precisely what the "little horn" meant in New Testament days is not certain, but it may well have been used "of the *point* or extremity which distinguishes some Heb. letters from others" (AS).

guish similar letters). Jesus is saying "Not the smallest letter, not the tiniest part of a letter — ." It forms a very emphatic assertion of the permanent validity of Scripture. None of it will pass away, Jesus says, until *all has taken place.*[69] The divine purpose in Scripture will be fully worked out.[70]

19. *Therefore* introduces the consequence of this permanence of Scripture, and *whoever*[71] makes its application general. Since Scripture is of continuing validity and Jesus is to fulfil it, the breaking of the least of the commandments is not unimportant. The verb for *relaxes*[72] more literally means "looses" and points to more than an isolated breaking of a commandment. As the words about teaching men show, the attitude condemned is one of doing away with the commandment in question, regarding it as nonexistent, as null and void. Even to nullify just *one* commandment is serious. The rabbis distinguished between "light" and "heavy" commandments (though both should be kept, *'Abot* 2:1), but it is unlikely that Jesus is accepting such a distinction. He simply refers to the fact that some of the commandments are not as weighty as others, and he selects the *least* of them for notice.[73] Even this one is to be kept. Verses 21-48 show that this does not mean the literal interpretation of every injunction. There must be careful interpretation. But no commandment is to be taken lightly. The person of whom Jesus is speaking not only fails to keep the light commandment but teaches others to take up the same attitude. Such a person qualifies to *be called*[74] least in God's kingdom. A wrong attitude to God's commandments means a lowly position in God's kingdom. The other side of this coin concerns the person who both obeys the commandments and teaches others to do the same. This is the person who attains honor, who is called *great* in the kingdom. Apparently both are in the kingdom, but the former has just made it (cf. 1 Cor. 3:15) whereas the latter is held in honor.

20. *For* links the following on and is possibly explanatory, "for, as

69. γίνομαι may be used in the sense "be," "become," but here it has the meaning "happen, take place" (BAGD, I.3.a); "until all has taken place" signifies "until all is past."

70. Lloyd-Jones sees this as "the central claim which is made by our Lord. It is, in other words, that all the law and all the prophets point to Him and will be fulfilled in Him down to the smallest detail. Everything that is in the law and the prophets culminates in Christ, and He is the fulfilment of them. It is the most stupendous claim that He ever made" (I, p. 187). France remarks, "The law is unalterable, but that does not justify its application beyond the purpose for which it is intended."

71. "Relative clauses which can be converted into conditional clauses usually make no assertions about concrete realities, but rather general assertions or suppositions, so that ὅς . . . ἄν, corresponding to the ἐάν of the conditional clause proper, appears as a rule" (BDF, 380[1]).

72. λύω means "loose" in a variety of senses; of such things as commandments or laws it means "repeal, annul, abolish" (BAGD, 4).

73. There is notice of an opinion that the "least" commandment was that about taking the mother bird and its young (Deut. 22:6-7) in SBk, I, p. 249.

74. Of this use of καλέω BAGD notes, "Very oft. the emphasis is to be placed less on the fact that the name is such and such, than on the fact that the bearer of the name actually is what the name says about him" (1.a.δ).

you see." *I tell you* puts some emphasis on the surprising statement that follows: Jesus calls for his followers to have a *righteousness* that *exceeds that of the scribes and Pharisees.* He is surely using the term *righteousness* in a sense different from that which the scribes and Pharisees attached to it. They looked for strict legal correctness, whereas Jesus looked for love. They stressed the keeping of the law, and from the standpoint of the lawkeeper it is not easy to see how anyone could exceed their righteousness.[75] Along the lines of lawkeeping who could possibly exceed the righteousness of those who tithed mint, dill, and cummin (23:23)? But Jesus has already spoken of a different kind of righteousness (3:15), and it is central to the Christian gospel that Jesus would fulfil all that Scripture means in making a new way, a way in which he would bring those who believe in him to salvation. This does not mean cheap grace, for the words of this verse bring out the truth that those who have been touched by Jesus live on a new plane, a plane in which the keeping of God's commandments is important.[76] Their righteousness is a given righteousness. Nowhere do we get the idea that the servant of God achieves in his own strength the kind of living that gives him standing before God. But when he is given that standing, Jesus looks to him to live in accordance with that standing. Later in this sermon Jesus will emphasize the spirit rather than the letter of the law. The Pharisees put a tremendous emphasis on the letter of the law, but Jesus was looking for something very different from the Pharisaic standard. For them it was a matter of observing regulations (and softening them where possible), but for him it was keeping the commandments in depth; he taught a radical obedience.[77]

The *scribes* were learned people, and the term could be used for a high official (Acts 19:35). Among the Jews it meant the experts in the law, scholars who spent their time on learning more and more about Scripture. They are often mentioned with others, such as the elders or the high priests; here they are linked with the Pharisees. They had their place in the Sanhedrin. They were not necessarily Pharisees (and Pharisees were not necessarily scribes), but many of them did belong to that party.[78] They are often mentioned along with the Pharisees (7 times in Matthew). Both had a great knowledge of trivia (such as the number of letters or words

75. Barclay quotes some scribal interpretations of the law that show plainly the way they understood "righteousness" and its distance from the teaching of Jesus.

76. "This verse challenges us to be good if we will be God's. There is no cheap grace in Matthew" (Bruner, p. 172).

77. "There has been much talk since Freud of a 'depth-psychology'; the concern of Jesus was for a 'depth-morality'. Pharisees were content with an external and formal obedience, a rigid conformity to the the letter of the law; Jesus teaches us that God's demands are far more radical than this" (Stott, p. 75).

78. D. B. Wallace has pointed out that, while Granville Sharp's Rule applies when one article governs two singular nouns, that is, that the same person is meant by both, this does not follow with plurals. Then there is a variety of possibilities; he sees τῶν γραμματέων καὶ Φαρισαίων here as signifying "the scribes and *other* Pharisees" (*GTJ*, 4 [1983], p. 73).

in a given book), which was sometimes coupled with a lack of insight into the real meaning of what was written. When he says *you certainly will not enter* the kingdom, Jesus uses an emphatic negative.[79] The verb *enter* is used of entering life (18:8, 9; 19:17). This verse makes it clear that the commandments of God are very important and that there are wrong ways of viewing them. The Pharisees were almost universally praised in Jesus' day and were regarded as outstanding examples of people who lived by the law of God. Jesus warns his hearers that the Pharisaic way is the wrong way. If they are to enter the kingdom of God they must come by a different way. He does not say at this point how the Messiah will produce this righteousness in his people, only that it must be produced. The Pharisaic way is the wrong way.

5. Applying the Law, 5:21-48

Jesus' understanding of keeping the law meant a great deal more than making sure that the letter of the law was not infringed. For him it was important that the deeper implications of what God had commanded be understood and put into practice. He brings this out with reference to specific commands that the Pharisees had no difficulty in keeping in the literal sense. He shows that in each case a principle is involved. When this is understood, keeping the commands is far from the simple thing the Pharisees understood. He is not abrogating the law but exposing the limitations of the way some provisions in it had been understood.

Daube has drawn attention to a rabbinic method of teaching which may lie behind this passage. He points out that a rabbi might say, "I hear," and go on to a passage of Scripture giving a wrong, though literal, interpretation. He cites an exposition of the fifth commandment which begins, "Honour thy father and thy mother. I might understand. . . . Honour them with words only." The Midrash, he says, goes on to refute this and to show that the commandment goes beyond speech. He says that the expression " 'he who hears', is used in the sense of 'he who sticks to the superficial, literal meaning of Scripture'." The point of all this is that "in Matthew, we have before us, not a scholarly working out by some Rabbis of a progressive interpretation as against a conceivable narrow one, but a laying down by Jesus, supreme authority, of the proper demand as against a view, be it held by friends or enemies, which would still take the exact words of the Scriptural precept as a standard of conduct. Jesus, supreme authority, lays down the proper demand."[80] Jesus is protesting against a strictly literal interpretation of the commands, an interpretation that indicates an

79. For the double negative οὐ μή see on verse 18. The Evangelists often use it in reporting the words of Jesus as though they felt it appropriate to the solemn words of a great person. Here, however, there is real emphasis. There is no question of entrance into the kingdom for the person of whom Jesus speaks.

80. Daube, pp. 55-62.

apparent willingness to obey what God has said, but which imposes a strict limit on obedience and leaves scope for a good deal of ungodly behavior. He is laying down authoritatively how these commands of God should be understood.

a. Murder, 5:21-26

21*"You have heard that it was said to the people of old, 'You shall not murder'; and, 'Whoever murders will be subject to the judgment.'* 22*But I say to you, 'Everyone who is angry with his brother will be subject to the judgment; and whoever says to his brother, "Raka," will be subject to the Sanhedrin; and whoever says, "You fool," will be subject to the Gehenna of fire.'* 23*If therefore you are offering your gift on the altar and there remember that your brother has something against you,* 24*leave there your gift before the altar and first go; be reconciled to your brother, and then come and offer your gift.* 25*Make friends with your opponent quickly while you are still with him on the way, lest your opponent hand you over to the judge, and the judge to the officer, and you be thrown into prison.* 26*Truly, I say to you, you will certainly not come out from there until you have paid the last penny."*

21. The first of the commands Jesus considers is that which prohibits murder. *You have heard* reflects an age in which many could not read; most of Jesus' audience depended on what they heard. *It was said to*[81] *the men of old* is a most unusual way of citing Scripture,[82] but there is no doubt as to what it means, for a quotation from Exodus 20:13 follows (with an interpretative addition). *The people of old* refers to those who lived long ago and were the original recipients of the commandments (*JB* renders "our ancestors" and *REB* "our forefathers," but it is their relationship to the original commandment that is in view, not their relationship to Jesus' hearers). The commandment was, *You shall not murder;*[83] the words *Whoever murders* (Moulton holds that the aorist gives the meaning "*has* committed murder," M, I, p. 186) *will be subject to the judgment* are not in the Exodus passage. This was evidently the way the passage was understood;[84] it puts

81. This could be translated "It was said by the men of old," as does *KJV.* Ridderbos, Hendriksen, and others accept this rendering, reasoning that Jesus is not citing Scripture but scribal tradition.

82. The form used is ἐρρέθη, whereas Jesus' own formula of quotation is γέγραπται (4:4, 6, 7, etc.). Matthew also uses the participle ῥηθέν in such quotations (1:22; 2:17, etc.).

83. The future indicative renders "the categorical injunctions and prohibitions (negative οὐ) in the legal language of the OT . . . but the future is nowhere used in this chapter in independent injunctions of Jesus" (BDF, 362). An apparent exception is in verse 48, but it takes this as going back to such passages as Deuteronomy 18:13 and Leviticus 19:2.

84. "Moses said it truly; the interpreters of Moses said it with altered meaning: the hearers did not distinguish the meaning of Moses from that of his interpreters" (Bengel). Perhaps we should notice that Gundry does not see any reference to Jewish tradition, but holds that Matthew is giving his "own summary of the OT penalty for murder."

some emphasis on the legal position.[85] *The judgment* can be understood of a local court (cf. *GNB*, "will be brought to trial"; for local courts cf. Deut. 16:18; Josephus, *Ant.* 4.214, etc.; Matthew, however, does not use the word elsewhere for a local court). It is also possible that there is a reference to "the" judgment, God's judgment at the last day. Either way the murderer is accountable.

22. *But I say to you* sets Jesus emphatically[86] over against this view. He, being who and what he is, can issue directives that rank with the honored law. It is not correct to say that he replaces the law with his own commands, for in no case does he relax a provision of the law. Rather, he shows that, rightly understood, the law goes much further than his hearers had reckoned. For them it was enough not to put somebody to death; for Jesus that was just the beginning. He goes to the cause of murder and includes being angry[87] in the scope of the command. *Brother* here is surely "brother man"; it is impossible to limit the expression to a male sibling.[88] *Subject to the judgment* is exactly the same expression as that used in the previous verse for the sin of murder. Since it is hard to imagine anyone being charged in a court of law with the crime of anger, a strong case can be made that the judgment of God is in mind.

A second possible violation that Jesus deprecates is that of saying to one's brother, "*Raka.*" The precise meaning of this word is uncertain,[89] but it is clearly an expression of contempt that evidently was used by angry people. This form of anger, Jesus says, renders a person *subject to the Sanhedrin* (which would support the view that *the judgment* in the earlier

85. ἔνοχος (5 times in Matthew out of 10 in the New Testament) is a legal term meaning "liable to," "answerable to" with a dative of the court. κρίσις (which Matthew also has more than anyone else, 12 times; John with 11 is next) is obviously a legal term as well. Strictly it denotes the process of judging, but it may also be used of a court.

86. He uses the emphatic ἐγώ. France comments, "This is not a new contribution to exegetical debate, but a definitive declaration of the will of God. It demands (and receives, 7:28-29) the response, 'Who is this?' Thus this passage contributes another aspect to the presentation of Jesus as the Messiah which is Matthew's overriding purpose."

87. *KJV* adds "without a cause," a reading supported by אᶜ D K L etc. but not found in 𝔭67vid א* etc. Most interpreters agree that it should not be accepted. But it does give a correct understanding of Jesus' words, for there are situations in which anger is quite proper (cf. Mark 3:5).

88. To Jewish ears "brother" meant "fellow Jew." Recent commentators often draw attention to the Qumran sect with its gradations of punishment for offenses against fellow members and suggest that the passage refers to discipline practiced among Christians (cf. Davies, for whom brother means "a Christian"; *SM*, p. 98; so Gundry and others). But to limit its meaning in this way is surely to fall into the same error as that of the Pharisees; it would allow anger against all non-Christians. Is this really Jesus' meaning?

89. It is usually held to be derived from the Aramaic רֵיקָא, "a shortened form of רֵיקָן, 'empty,' as vocalized in the Galilaean dialect" (AS). But BAGD notes its use "as an uncomplimentary, perh. foul epithet in a Zenon pap. of 257 B.C." when it is unlikely to be Aramaic. It also finds it in the Talmud. It notes that Jerome and others take it as equivalent to κενός, "empty-head, numbskull, fool." Compare Chrysostom, who said, "this word 'Raca,' is not an expression of great insolence, but rather of some contempt and slight on the part of the speaker." It is like talking to servants or "any very inferior person" (p. 110).

part of the verse means that of the law court). Sanhedrin means "council" (e.g., 10:17), but it is used mostly in the New Testament for the high council of the Jews. It comprised priests, elders, and scribes, and the high priest was its president. It was the highest authority among the Jews, not only in religious affairs, but in governmental and legal matters also. Here the term may be used of a local council. Jesus is saying that the insolent and insulting person is not guiltless: he must give account of himself.

The third form of murder is to say, "*You fool.*"[90] It has been suggested that this expression means "obstinate," or that it is the equivalent of the Hebrew word for "rebel," or that it is the Greek translation of *Raka*. On the whole it appears that "fool" is the most likely understanding and that it is an angry and critical ejaculation.[91] Jesus is censuring the attitude that brings forth the epithet. The person who is angry enough to utter this derogatory word "is guilty enough to go into the hell of fire" (BAGD).[92]

23. *If* introduces another supposition, and *therefore* shows that it arises from the preceding statements. Because of the dangerous position in which he finds himself, the angry person must take care how he worships. The change from everyone to *you* sharpens the personal application. The word for *are offering* is the verb normally used for the offering of sacrifice, and *gift* is often used of what is sacrificed (though both words are used of other offerings as well). *Altar* is sometimes used metaphorically, but here the literal altar in the temple at Jerusalem is meant. Jesus is depicting a man in the solemn act of sacrifice. The present tense pictures the worshiper as in the act of offering. And right there, at the altar, he remembers. *Something* is a very general expression; the brother is thought of as having a legitimate complaint against the worshiper. Interestingly, it is not the anger of the

90. If we are to distinguish between the two words it will probably be as Bruce puts it: "Raca expresses contempt for a man's head = you stupid! *Mōre* expresses contempt for his heart and character = you scoundrel." But Ridderbos regards the three sins of murder here "as virtually equivalent." It is difficult to think that Jesus would engage in a hair-splitting distinction between "Raka" and "you fool."

91. μωρός occurs 6 times in Matthew out of a New Testament total of 12; it is not found in any other Gospel or in Acts. It is normally an adjective, but here it seems to be a noun. It is possible that it is a transliteration of the Hebrew מוֹרֶה, "rebel" or "apostate" (cf. Deut. 21:18). Then we might see a gradation of offense, from being angry, to calling the brother stupid, to calling him a rebel, coupled with a gradation of punishment, first that of the local council, then the Sanhedrin, and finally the judgment of God. This distinction has its attractions, but it falls short of being demonstrated. Albright and Mann, by contrast, detect "a descending scale of offences" *(AB)*.

92. *Sub* ἔνοχος 2.a. γέεννα occurs 7 times in Matthew out of a New Testament total of 12 (Mark with 3 is the only other book to have it more than once). It refers to the valley of Hinnom, a ravine to the south of Jerusalem. During the monarchy it was the center of an idolatrous cult that involved passing children through the fire (2 Kings 23:10, etc.). There are prophecies of judgment on this dreadful place (Jer. 7:32; 19:6), and it came to be linked with the final place of torment. There is some evidence that the place was used as a rubbish dump where fires burned continually. Among the Jews there was the idea that the Last Judgment would take place there, and before New Testament times the name was used for the place of fiery torment that awaits the wicked (cf. *TDNT*, I, pp. 657-58).

person Jesus is addressing of which he speaks, but anger provoked by that person. It is not enough to control one's temper (though that is important); one must not arouse other people's anger.

24. *Leave your gift* is a sharp command; there is something more urgent than completing the act of sacrifice. The worshiper is to leave the animal right there, in front of the altar, and *go*. The interruption of so solemn an act emphasizes the overriding importance of reconciliation. *First*[93] has a time reference: "in the first place, before doing anything else." It is important that the worshiper get his priorities right, and the first thing to do is to effect reconciliation.[94] He must take whatever steps are needed to restore harmony, and only when this is done[95] may he come back and resume his offering. The act of sacrifice is not as important as the spirit in which it is done.

25. *Make friends*[96] carries on the thought; reconciliation leads to the idea of being in continuing friendly relations even with one's *opponent*. This word strictly means an adversary in a lawsuit;[97] it is thus the appropriate word in this context. *Quickly* points to the importance of haste in such a matter; there is to be no delay in establishing friendly relations.[98] Jesus pictures a brief encounter in the street or on the way to the court and says that the most is to be made of the opportunity. Friendship can be established there: it is too late when they reach the law court. Prudential considerations dictate urgency, and Jesus opens up the possibility of initiating a series of happenings that lead remorsely to a prison sentence. If reconciliation fails, the opponent may *hand* one *over* (the verb is a technical term for "hand over into custody"; see BAGD) to the judge, and he in turn may hand him over to the officer[99] who puts offenders in jail.

---

93. πρῶτον is to be taken with what precedes (as in 6:33; 7:5; so *NIV, REB,* "First go") rather than with what follows (as *NRSV,* "first be reconciled)."

94. διαλλάσσομαι occurs here only in the New Testament; it has the meaning "become reconciled to." J. B. Lightfoot sees it as denoting "mutual concession after mutual hostility" (*Notes on Epistles of St Paul* [London, 1904], p. 288); this may be the case, or it may be reading a little too much into the word. The emphasis is on the offender putting things right with the offended brother. Turner comments on the tenses: "First be reconciled once and for all (aorist) to your brother, and then come and offer as many gifts as you like (present)" (*Grammatical Insights,* p. 30).

95. For τότε see on 2:7. This is another example of its use in the nonclassical sense of what follows in time rather than "at that time" (so also in 7:5; 12:29, etc.).

96. The "seemingly periphrastic" tense (BDF, 353[1]), ἴσθι εὐνοῶν, is unexpected. It perhaps indicates the continuing state ("be habitually well disposed," Chamberlain, p. 72); Jesus is speaking of something more than a momentary impulse. εὐνοέω occurs only here in the New Testament.

97. ἀντίδικος. MM calls it "this common legal word" and cites examples from the papyri of its use in lawsuits. Its only New Testament occurrences are twice each in Matthew and Luke, and once in 1 Peter.

98. The combination ἕως ὅτου is found only here in Matthew; it is not common. The meaning is generally "until," but here it is clearly "while." BAGD classes this use of μετά as signifying "accompaniment for a short time" (A.II.1.c.α).

99. ὑπηρέτης may denote a helper or servant in any one of a variety of ways; here it is the servant of the court who looks after imprisonment.

26. For the emphatic *Truly, I say to you* see the note on verse 18; it indicates that the following statement is true and important. The double negative is emphatic and points to the impossibility of release from the place of confinement[100] until[101] the condition is fulfilled. The condition in question is the full payment[102] that the penalty requires, and the specification of *the last penny*[103] emphasizes the completion of the punishment. Failure to take advantage of the opportunity of reconciliation means that one must bear the penalty of being unreconciled.

b. Adultery, 5:27-30

27"You have heard that it was said, 'You shall not commit adultery.' 28But I say to you that everyone who looks at a woman to lust after her has already committed adultery with her in his heart. 29And if your right eye makes you sin, gouge it out and throw it away from you, for it is expedient for you that one of your members should perish and not that your whole body be thrown into Gehenna. 30And if your right hand makes you sin, cut it off and throw it away from you, for it is expedient for you that one of your members should perish and not that your whole body go off into Gehenna."

Jesus cites the prohibition of adultery and goes on to point out the significance of the lustful look. It is the look that leads to the physical act and thus comes under condemnation. Just as with the command not to murder, Jesus is concerned with the inner state that leads to action and does not simply prohibit the outward deed.

27. The opening formula is as in verse 21 (where see note) except that the reference to the ancients is omitted (so again in vv. 31, 38, and 43). The prohibition is exactly as in the Old Testament (Exod. 20:14; Deut. 5:17), which is not surprising in a two-word quotation. In the ancient world generally it was held that a married man could have sexual adventures as long as they did not involve a married woman (which would mean violating the rights of her husband). A woman, however, was expected to have no such relations; she should be chaste before marriage and faithful after it.[104] The command Jesus cites makes no distinction; people of both

100. *From there* renders ἐκεῖθεν, a favorite expression of Matthew's (he has it 12 times; nobody else has it more than Mark's 5).

101. ἕως "w. the aor. subj. and, as the rule requires . . . ἄν . . . to denote that the commencement of an event is dependent on circumstances" (BAGD, I.1.b).

102. ἀποδίδωμι is found 18 times in Matthew (out of a New Testament total of 47). It basically means "give away" and is often used in the sense "give back," "recompense," which may be in a good sense or a bad one. It may also mean "sell." Here, of course, the meaning is "repay."

103. κοδράντης is found again in the New Testament only in Mark 12:42. It is a loanword from the Latin *quadrans,* which was the Roman copper coin with the smallest value (BAGD speaks of a quarter of a cent).

104. O. J. Baab puts the accepted view in these terms: "Because of the nature of marriage, adultery was not so much evidence of moral depravity as the violation of a

117

sexes were to remain faithful. Specifically he speaks of the man as the adulterer (v. 32; 19:9).

28. Again we have an authoritative word from Jesus (for *I say to you* see on v. 22). He says that the lustful look (which the rabbis sometimes mentioned[105]) is wrong in itself; to lust[106] after a woman is already to have broken the commandment. This might be deduced from the tenth commandment, but Jesus finds it also in this one. The *heart* is the center of a person's life and may denote thought, emotions, and will. Jesus is saying that the person who lusts has committed adultery in the center of his being (contrast "the pure in heart" in v. 8); in all that matters he is an adulterer. This is a startling extension of the commandment. Great rabbis like Hillel and Shammai might debate over the causes that justified a man in divorcing his wife, but they did not approach Jesus in seeing the binding nature of the marriage bond and the importance of complete fidelity on the part of both partners.

29. Since the look can be so significant, it is important to use the eye rightly, and Jesus uses hyperbolical language in speaking of the exercise of sight. His *if* clause puts the case strongly; for the sake of discussion it implies that the condition is met. The *right* eye was thought of as especially valuable, for a warrior would be gravely handicapped if he lacked sight in this member.[107] Jesus envisages the possibility that this valuable member may in fact be the cause of sin.[108] He does not define this further, but

husband's right to have sole sexual possession of his wife and to have the assurance that his children were his own" (*IDB*, I, p. 51). It was not seen as adultery, for example, for an Israelite to have intercourse with a female slave or with a Gentile woman. Adultery for him involved infringing the rights of another Israelite male.

105. There is a complaint about men who "gratified their eyes with lewdness," for "Whoever looks upon a woman's little finger is as though he gazed upon the pudenda" (*Shab.* 64b). Elsewhere the leg, the voice, and the hair of a woman are added to the little finger as objects that may be sexual incitements (*Ber.* 24a). The Book of Jubilees urges "that we should keep ourselves from all fornication and pollution . . . let them not fornicate with her after their eyes and hearts" (Jub. 20:3-4).

106. BAGD interpreters πρός as used here "of the result that follows a set of circumstances *(so that)*"; it translates, "the one who looks at a woman in such a way that desire for her is aroused in him" (III.3.b; cf. BDF 402[5], "with respect to"). Chamberlain also considers result as possible (p. 192). Turner finds "hardly any telic force, but simple accompaniment *(and)*" (M, III, p. 144). ἐπιθυμέω may be used of a good desire (Luke 22:15), but mostly it means evil desires, as here.

107. Josephus speaks of a king who put out the right eyes of subjugated warriors; "since the left eye was covered by the shield" this rendered them "utterly unserviceable" (*Ant.* 6.69-70).

108. σκανδαλίζω is from σκάνδαλον, the bait stick of a trap, and properly denotes the putting of a trap or snare in the way. In the New Testament it is always used metaphorically and may mean anything that leads people away from right conduct into sin. Matthew has almost half the total New Testament occurrences of the verb (14 out of 29; he also has most occurrences of σκάνδαλον). AS notes that the word occurs in LXX, other Greek translations of the Old Testament, once in the Psalms of Solomon, and "not elsewhere except NT and eccl." MM favors the view that the emphasis is "on the idea of 'snare' rather than of 'stumbling-block.' "

the lustful look of which he has just spoken makes clear the kind of way in which an invaluable member of the body may be the cause of bringing evil to the whole. Under those circumstances Jesus advises that it be gouged out and thrown away.[109] This picturesque repudiation of a prized part of the body shows vividly that there is to be no compromise with evil. It is better to lose one member now than to lose the whole in Gehenna in due course.[110]

30. The same argument is applied to the right hand, the hand favored by most people for all activities.[111] As in the previous verse the nature of the possible sin is not explained; the reference is left quite general. But if the right hand leads one into sin, it is better to cut it off.[112] Mark has a saying similar to this (though with differences),[113] and he adds similar statements about the foot and the eye (Mark 9:43-48). Matthew has much the same in 18:8-9. It is not easy to understand why Matthew has included the reference to the hand here; the eye is immediately relevant, but the hand is difficult. It is, of course, not unlikely that Jesus used similar material on a number of occasions. He is not, of course, advocating self-mutilation, nor is he suggesting that if people engage in this kind of surgery their evil desires will be exorcised. But this vivid imagery "emphasizes the crucial importance of taking whatever measures are necessary to control natural passions that tend to flare out of control" (Mounce).[114]

c. Divorce, 5:31-32

31*"And it was said, 'Whoever divorces his wife, let him give her a bill of divorce.'* 32*But I say to you that everyone who divorces his wife except for a matter of fornication makes her commit adultery, and whoever marries her that was put away is made to commit adultery."*

---

109. Bengel remarks, "Not the organ itself, but the *concupiscence* which animates the eye or hand is meant. . . . a man might pluck out his material eye, and yet cherish concupiscence within." Cf. Bruce, "Mutilation will not serve the purpose; it may prevent the outward act, but it will not extinguish desire."

110. Cf. Bruner, "in sexual purity decisiveness is everything"; "Better to go limping into heaven than leaping into hell" (p. 186).

111. Derrett points out that among many Eastern peoples "the left hand is used for lavatory and inauspicious purposes (the left index finger is used in cursing), the right exclusively for blessing" (*Law*, p. xlv). He holds that the right hand here refers to actions like taking (stealing, etc.) and giving (bribes).

112. ἐϰϰόπτω (4 times in Matthew, the most in one book) means "cut off or down." It is used of cutting down trees (3:10) or metaphorically of removing the pretext of Paul's opponents (2 Cor. 11:12). Josephus uses it of putting out eyes (*Ant.* 10.140).

113. Thus Matthew specifies the right hand as Mark does not, while Mark has the article with γέενναν, which Matthew lacks. But both have σϰανδαλίζω (Matthew has εἰ with the present indicative and Mark ἐάν with the present subjunctive), a compound of ϰόπτω (Matthew uses ἐϰ, Mark ἀπό), and the verb ἀπέρχομαι (Matthew aorist subjunctive, Mark aorist infinitive). Clearly the two are related, but it is not easy to derive the one from the other.

114. *It is expedient* etc. is identical with the wording in verse 29 except that ἀπέλθῃ replaces βληθῇ and εἰς γέενναν precedes the verb here, whereas it followed it in verse 29.

In the other passages in this section Jesus is dealing with a specific command of God. But people were not commanded to get divorced; this passage assumes the practice of divorce and speaks of the way it was regulated in the Mosaic law.[115] The *bill of divorce* was a protection for the woman; a capricious husband could not drive her from his home and afterward claim that she was still his wife. He must give her the document that set out her right to marry someone else. It was accepted throughout Judaism that a man was entitled to divorce his wife (the procedure is given in Deut. 24:1-4). A wife was not permitted to divorce her husband, though she could petition the court, and if her plea was accepted the court would direct the husband to divorce her. The husband's right was regarded as inalienable, and the only question was the ground on which he based his action. The school of Shammai took a hard line and saw the meaning of "some indecency" (Deut. 24:1) as adultery,[116] whereas the school of Hillel allowed a much wider range of interpretation, and, for example, permitted a man to divorce his wife if she spoiled his dinner (Mishnah *Giṭ.* 9.10; it adds the further information that R. Akiba allowed divorce "Even if he found another fairer than she").[117] Against such a background Jesus calls on people to appreciate the true meaning and solemnity of marriage. We should bear in mind that he is laying down great principles that should guide conduct; he is not making laws or giving a precise list of occasions when divorce might take place.

31. *It was said* is the same way of introducing Scripture as in the previous sections, but in an abbreviated form. It is a summary of the way the passage was understood rather than an exact quotation, which accords with the fact that Jesus is opposing scribal interpretations rather than Scripture. Among the Jews divorce was a simple procedure for a man. He must write a bill of divorce in the correct form (it must include words that expressly permit the divorced woman to marry), and there must be proper witnesses; there is to be no doubt as to what is taking place (see the note on 1:19 for the requirements in wording and witnesses).[118] The verb rendered *divorces*[119] means more literally "releases," but it is the usual word

---

115. "Whatever grounds for divorce the Mosaic enactment may have had in view, the thrust of the passage in its original setting is not to establish grounds for divorce, but, presupposing the practice of divorce on various grounds, to provide some protection for the woman from the harshness of her husband. The aim of the legislation is not to condone divorce as such, but to mitigate its evil consequences" (Stonehouse, *Witness*, p. 204).

116. This is surely an incorrect understanding of Scripture, for the punishment for adultery was death (Deut. 22:22); in Deuteronomy there is no question of divorce on the ground of adultery.

117. Cf. Josephus, "He who desires to be divorced from the wife who is living with him for whatsoever cause — and with mortals many such may arise — must certify in writing . . ." (*Ant.* 4.253).

118. The Mishnah devotes a whole tractate to the bills of divorce. Clearly the precise requirements meant a great deal to the Jews in the early centuries, and there was a good deal of discussion. But as to the central point, that it was a man's right to divorce his wife, there was no dispute.

119. ἀπολύω occurs 19 times in Matthew, which is nearly a third of its 65 New Testament

for sending a wife away in divorce. The *bill of divorce*[120] is a general word for relinquishing rights, but it was commonly used for divorce, the giving up of one's claim on a wife.

32. With the emphatic *But I say to you* Jesus moves to his own understanding of the position. For him marriage was intended to be a lifelong union of one man and one woman, and it was not to be dissolved lightly. He recognizes that *a matter of fornication*[121] is a reason for divorce, and tells his hearers that divorce for any other reason is invalid (cf. Mal. 2:16). A man who divorces his wife and thus, in a Jewish situation, compels her to marry someone else (in first-century Jewish society how else could she live?) makes her an adulteress. There is a problem in that the prohibition of divorce in Mark 10:11-12; Luke 16:18 is absolute. There is no provision there for divorce on account of sexual sin. Many scholars hold that Mark and Luke tell us what Jesus said and that Matthew is giving us the position held in the church in his day. But it is more likely that Matthew is simply spelling out what was implicit in the first century. There is evidence that among the Jews a man was not so much allowed as required to divorce an adulterous wife,[122] so that Mark and Luke did not need to mention it specifically. But there is no doubt about Matthew's inclusion, and we must reckon with it if we are to study the thought of this Gospel.

The word rendered *fornication*[123] strictly denotes sexual intercourse between unmarried people, and some have seen that meaning here. On this view Jesus is saying that if two people get married and it is subsequently found that prior to the marriage one of them had committed fornication, then the marriage may be dissolved. But that seems to be confining the meaning in a way that is not common in the New Testament; the word is used for all sorts of sexual sins. It is much more likely that in this passage

---

occurrences. It is used of releasing a prisoner (27:15) or a debtor (18:27), and of forgiveness (Luke 6:37). It comes to mean "let go, dismiss," and it is in this sense that it is used of divorce. Moulton says that the aorist tense here, "denotes not so much the carrying into effect as the determination" (M, I, p. 186).

120. ἀποστάσιον occurs again only in 19:7; Mark 10:4 in the New Testament. MM notes its use in the papyri for documents of relinquishing rights to property after sale and the like.

121. λόγου πορνείας. λόγος among other things may be used of "*the subject* under discussion, *matter, thing*" and may have meanings like "reckoning, account" or "reason, motive" (BAGD). I have taken the meaning here as "matter," but "motive" is a possibility.

122. "The penalty for proven adultery, when the capital punishment was abolished, was mitigated into the divorce of the woman (the husband having no option)" (Israel Abrahams, *Studies in Pharisaism and the Gospels*, 1st ser. [rpt. New York, 1967], p. 74). So also G. F. Moore, *Judaism*, II [Cambridge, 1958], p. 125). The Mishnah provides that if a woman "was found unchaste . . . he may not continue [his union] with her" (*Ketub.* 3.5). Markus Bockmuehl cites Qumran and other evidence that "adultery (and rape) requires divorce" (*NTS*, 35 [1989], p. 295). See also Mishnah, *Soṭa* 5:1.

123. πορνεία properly means the use of a harlot (πόρνη) and is sometimes distinguished from adultery (15:19). But it is also used of sexual sin in general (1 Cor. 5:1; Col. 3:5), and that seems to be its meaning here. Bonnard argues that it signifies marriage within the prohibited degrees (Lev. 18:6-18), but there is no good reason for understanding the term in this way.

it signifies adultery[124] than something that happened before the marriage. Improper sexual relations on the part of a married person mean that the marriage may be dissolved. If *fornication* is interpreted in the way murder is understood in verse 22, the ground for divorce may be somewhat wider than appears in most of our translations.[125] It is important to understand that the divorced woman is made to commit adultery and that the man who marries her is also made to commit adultery.[126] Among the Jews a man was not held to have committed adultery by engaging in sexual acts outside marriage unless his partner was herself a married woman. But Jesus does not distinguish between the man and the woman: either may commit adultery. It seems to have been a Christian idea that a man could commit adultery; others regarded sexual adventures as a normal part of life for a man. Jesus lays down the highest standard for both sexes. Divorce might happen, but it was not meant to be. Marriage is for life.

d. Oaths, 5:33-37

> [33]*"Again, you have heard that it was said to the men of old, 'You shall not break your oath, but you shall keep your oaths to the Lord.'* [34]*But I say to you, 'Do not swear at all; neither by heaven because it is the throne of God, [35]nor by the earth because it is the footstool of his feet, nor by Jerusalem because it is the city of the great king. [36]Nor shall you swear by your head because you cannot make one hair white or black. [37]But let your statement be "Yes, yes; no, no"; what is more than these is of the evil one.'"*

This passage is peculiar to Matthew (who returns to the theme with somewhat different statements in 23:16-22). Clearly he was interested in the fact that people seemed very ready to swear oaths. He regarded it as important that what his disciples said could always be relied on; it should not be necessary for them to back up their statements with oaths. This is in striking contrast to a good deal of Judaism, in which oaths evidently played a large part in life. The Mishnah has a complete tractate on oaths (*Shebu'ot*), dividing them into classes, giving examples of valid and invalid oaths, etc. Another tractate on vows (*Nedarim*) is also relevant.

---

124. The word is used of an adulterous wife (Sir. 23:23).

125. *NIV* translates "except for marital unfaithfulness," which, of course, clearly includes adultery. But it is a wider term and perhaps captures for us a little more of Jesus' meaning. It is perhaps relevant that Paul cites Jesus' teaching (1 Cor. 7:10), but goes on to deal with other situations (vv. 12-15) and claims to have "the Spirit of God" in this discussion (v. 40). Clearly he did not understand the words of Jesus to exclude the possibility of divorce on other grounds than literal adultery.

126. The two passives are to be noted: the man who puts away his wife wrongfully makes her commit adultery, as most translations note. They do not note that he also makes her future husband commit adultery. Lenski puts emphasis on these two passives and translates, he "brings about that she is stigmatized as adulterous" and the new husband "is stigmatized as adulterous." Again, "Neither 'commits' anything, both have had something committed upon them." The guilt attaches to the one who broke the marriage.

33. *Again* leads into the next subject. The term is used to connect similar items such as a series of quotations from Scripture (here) or a series of parables. It is often used when a speaker takes up a form of words he has used previously; here we have the form employed in verse 21 and in a modified way in verses 27 and 31. The command not to break an oath[127] is not given in exactly the words of the Old Testament, but words very similar to them are to be found (Lev. 19:12; Num. 30:2; Deut. 23:21; Ps. 50:14; Zech. 8:17). In any case Jesus is giving us the way in which Scripture was understood. The use of both the negative (*"You shall not break your oath"*) and the positive (*"you shall keep*[128] *your oaths"*) gives emphasis to the importance of respecting sworn testimony.[129] GNB draws attention to something a bit different when it renders "Do not break your promise" and in the next verse, "do not use any vow when you make a promise." It is true that promises must be kept, but at this point Jesus is speaking of sworn testimony. A similar comment might be made about "You shall not break your vows to God" *(LB)*; while this is true, it narrows unduly what Jesus is saying. An oath is a solemn statement (not necessarily a promise or a vow) affirmed to be true before God. When anyone invokes the deity, the truth must be spoken. Robinson points out that this goes back to a time when people thought that a lie between people did not concern God, whereas if the divine name were invoked "His dignity and honour were at stake"; people would expect perjury to be punished.

34. As throughout this section, Jesus' command is in emphatic contrast: *"Do not swear at all."* To swear means "To make a solemn declaration or statement with an appeal to God or a superhuman being, or to some sacred object, in confirmation of what is said" *(Shorter Oxford Dictionary)*.[130] J. Schneider understands swearing to be "primarily self-cursing should one not be speaking the truth" *(TDNT*, V, p. 458). Such a solemn statement is sometimes called for, but Jesus is saying that it should not be necessary for his followers.[131] He is not forbidding the taking of an oath in a law

---

127. Or not to commit perjury; ἐπιορκέω can mean either.

128. ἀποδίδωμι (see on v. 26) is a favorite Matthean word. It has about it the idea of paying what is due. Here it means that whatever is sworn must be performed. Davies thinks that the passage refers to vows rather than oaths *(SM,* p. 240); if this were so, the verb would be very appropriate.

129. Matthew has ὅρκος, "oath," 4 times, Hebrews twice, and no other writing more than once. This Evangelist is interested in oaths.

130. ὀμνύω (a variant form of ὄμνυμι) is found in Matthew in 13 of its 26 occurrences. It is followed by the accusative of the person or thing by whom one swears or by ἐν with the dative, εἰς with the accusative, or κατά with the genitive. The repeated μήτε divides the preceding negative into its component parts (BAGD).

131. The swearing of oaths is forbidden in the *Damascus Document* of the Qumran sect (Vermes, p. 108). But those who joined the community must first swear "a binding oath to return with all his heart and soul to every commandment of the Law of Moses in accordance with all that has been revealed of it to the sons of Zadok . . ." (Vermes, p. 79). Josephus says of the Essenes, "Any word of theirs has more force than an oath; swearing they avoid, regarding it as worse than perjury, for they say that one who is not believed without an

court or the like. The law said, "you shall . . . swear by his name" (Deut.
6:13; 10:20), and Jesus himself responded when the high priest put him on
oath (26:63-64). He is saying in the strongest terms that those who follow
him must speak the truth. They must never take the line that only when
an oath is sworn need they be truthful. *At all*[132] with the negative excludes
the oath altogether. There must never be the need for it. Jesus brings this
out by referring to the way oaths were commonly sworn. The Jews held
that unless the name of God was specifically mentioned the oath was not
binding; there were lengthy discussions about when an oath is or is not
binding, and people would sometimes swear by heaven or earth or a
similar oath and later claim that they were not bound by that oath because
God was not mentioned. Jesus rejects such casuistry. People should not
swear oaths at all, certainly not *by heaven*, for that is *the throne of God*; to
substitute *heaven* for God does not in fact avoid a reference to the deity,
for heaven is his *throne*.

35. Nor should an oath be sworn *by the earth*. It seems a curious form
of oath, but it is perhaps meant as a contrast to the preceding reference
to heaven. Since the name of God was not used, many Jews cheerfully
swore "by earth" (an oath "by heaven and by earth" is mentioned in
Shebuʿot 4:13, and regarded as not binding). There may be a reminiscence
of Isaiah 66:1, where God speaks of heaven as his throne and the earth as
his footstool. Swearing *by the earth* does not avoid the link with God, for
the earth is *the footstool of his feet* (cf. Isa. 66:1). At one and the same time
the footstool brings out subjection and nearness. It is perhaps relevant
that God's footstool is associated with worship (Ps. 99:5). Nor should an
oath be sworn *by Jerusalem*[133] (which also may be seen as God's footstool,
Lam. 2:1). The city is linked with God as being *the city of the great king* (cf.
Ps. 48:1-2; for *king* see on 1:6).[134] The point of all this is that by their
hair-splitting differences the Jews could not escape between this form of
oath or vow and that. God is present in all his creation. The important
thing, Jesus is saying, is to tell the truth and keep one's pledges without
insisting that a certain form of words must be used if it is to be binding.
No oath is necessary for the truthful person.

36. The first three rejected oaths all in one way or another refer to

---

appeal to God stands condemned already" (*War* 2.135). But to join the sect they had to swear
"tremendous oaths" (139).

132. ὅλως has a meaning like "altogether," and with a negative, "not at all."

133. *By* here is εἰς, which is unusual in such a context. Ἱεροσόλυμα is Matthew's usual
form of the name. A vow that included the words "as Jerusalem" was binding, but if "as"
was lacking it was not binding (*Ned.* 1:3). A number of commentators refer to the rabbinic
view that an oath "by Jerusalem" is nothing, but an oath "to Jerusalem" is binding (*Tos. Ned.*
1).

134. For examples of oaths sworn in all these ways see SBk, I, pp. 332-36. Philo advises
swearing by one's father or mother, but permits swearing by "earth, sun, stars, heaven, the
whole universe" (*De Spec. Leg.* 2.2, 5). Such oaths avoid the use of the divine name and
therefore taking God's name in vain.

God, but now comes an oath that centers on the person of the swearer. You are not to swear *by your head*,[135] Jesus says. For this final example the verb *swear* is repeated, which may be for emphasis, but more probably in order to give balance to the sentence. To swear by the head means that the swearer "would give his head (i.e., his life) if he were not speaking the truth" (Ridderbos). The reason for not swearing moves from the greatness of God to the littleness of people: no one is able[136] to change the color of even *one hair*, a very small part of the human body. Such an impotent being is not one by whom to swear oaths!

37. The conclusion of the matter is that it is never necessary for Christ's people to swear an oath before they utter the truth. Their word should always be so reliable that nothing more than a statement is needed from them. God is in all of life, and every statement is made before him. *Your statement*[137] will refer to anything you say. I have translated the Greek fairly literally, but the meaning may well be as in *REB*, "Plain 'Yes' or 'No' is all you need to say." That would suit the context. Another possibility is that the words signify much what James says: "Let your 'yes' be yes, and your 'no' no" (Jas. 5:12), that is, your statement should be thoroughly reliable and thus make an oath unnecessary. Some interpreters suggest that a doubled "yes" or "no"[138] (which is more than the single word) is the limit of what is permissible,[139] but it is unlikely that Jesus would engage in such casuistry, especially when he is opposing that of the Jews. Anything more[140] than these expressions *is of the evil one*.[141] This may mean that it originates in evil or, more probably, that it comes from the devil (so Lenski).

e. Retaliation, 5:38-42

38"*You have heard that it was said, 'An eye for an eye and a tooth for a tooth.'* 39*But I say to you, 'Do not resist the evil person; but whoever slaps*

135. ἐν is a reversion to the previous construction after just one εἰς. Matthew uses κεφαλή more often than does any other book except Revelation (12 times; Revelation has 19). Matthew means the literal head, apart from one reference in a quotation to "the head of the corner" (21:42). The rabbis regarded a vow "by the life of thy head" as binding, though a dissentient opinion says that it is not (*Sanh.* 3:2).

136. For δύναμαι see on 3:9. The use of dyes, of course, changes only the appearance of the hair, not its real color.

137. ὁ λόγος ὑμῶν. This noun may be used in any one of a variety of ways, but here it signifies "what you say," "any statement you make."

138. Both times we have accented οὔ. Matthew has this term 4 times, the most in any New Testament book.

139. The rabbis regarded the doubled word as more significant than the single use. Thus a *bath qol* might be recognized "only if it says, yes, yes, or no, no" (*Meg.* 32a). R. Eleazar held that "no" or "yes" was an oath, but it was countered that either word must be doubled if it was to be an oath (*Shebu.* 36a).

140. περισσός = "exceeding the usual number or size," here in the comparative sense (BAGD). BDF sees this with the following τούτων as "the so-called *abbreviated comparison*" and with περισσός finds it equivalent to πλείων (185[1]).

141. ἐκ τοῦ πονηροῦ.

you on the right cheek, turn to him the other one also. ⁴⁰And let him who wants to go to law with you and take your tunic have your cloak too. ⁴¹And whoever compels you to go one mile, go with him two. ⁴²Give to him who asks you, and do not turn away from him who wants to borrow from you.' "

Revenge comes easily to the human race. We have a natural tendency to retaliate when anyone harms us (or even when the harm is in our imagination!). But Jesus instructs his followers to eschew hitting back in all its forms; we should even go the "second mile" in doing more than the enemy asks. This is a radically new approach to the question of grievances. Jesus is, of course, still dealing with great principles, not laying down rules. We must not think that he held that his followers should never right wrongs, for example, nor that he felt that they must give to every beggar who approaches them. Were this so, all Christians would live under tyranny and in a state of destitution. But the principles that we are to refrain from asserting our rights and that we should put the needs of others before our own run through all of life and mark the difference between the servant of God and the worldling. There are some parallels in Luke 6:29-30, but mostly in the general sense. Almost every significant word is different, which makes it difficult to derive either account from the other.

38. The formula is the same as that in verse 27, that is, it lacks the reference to "the men of old." The quotation (from Exod. 21:24; Lev. 24:20; Deut. 19:21) inserts "and" to join the two members, but is otherwise exact. The *eye*, of course, is a very important organ of sense perception, and its loss would be felt keenly. So when an eye is damaged or lost, a similar punishment is to be inflicted on whoever caused the loss. So with the *tooth*. In both cases the punishment is precisely equivalent.[142] The precept is an ancient one and is expressed, for example, in the Code of Hammurabi (18th cent. B.C.). In its day this *lex talionis* was, of course, a great advance. It meant evenhanded justice without respect of persons. No matter how great the offender, he could not escape just punishment, and no matter how small, no more could be exacted of him than his offense merited. It took punishment out of the realm of private vengeance, but Jewish practice tended to put it back. By contrast, Jesus teaches that his people should not be noted for insisting on their just deserts. They must be ready to forego private vengeance, as indeed the law provided if people would only heed it (Lev. 19:17-18; cf. Prov. 24:29).

39. Again the emphatic formula is used to introduce striking new teaching. *"Do not resist the evil person"*[143] does not mean that we should let

142. ἀντί is the preposition of substitution: it means "in place of," "in the stead of." It shows that the punishment is an exact requital.

143. As in verse 34 we have the infinitive, but the meaning is plainly imperative. ἀνθίστημι, here only in Matthew, has the meaning of setting oneself against someone; "it has the notion of hostility" (Chamberlain, p. 133). τῷ πονηρῷ could mean "the evil one" or "evil," but in this context it is much more likely to refer to an evil person ("those who wrong you,"

evil triumph throughout our communities. Jesus is referring to private retaliation, not to public order, and he is instructing his followers not to be intent on getting their own back when someone wrongs them. To be the victim of some form of evil does not give us the right to hit back. Jesus proceeds to give an example, and his *but* is the strong adversative,[144] a word that introduces a sharp contrast; he says, *whoever*[145] slaps you, "hits you with the open hand."[146] The traditional understanding is that the slap is on the cheek, and this may well be right, though the word properly means the jawbone.[147] The proper conduct in such a case is not retaliation, but readiness to endure a further blow. This contrasts with the teaching of the Mishnah, where we find that "If a man cuffed his fellow he must pay him a *sela*" (B. Qam. 8:6; the tractate goes on to lay down the penalties for slapping, hitting with the back of the hand, etc.). There will be occasions when protest is in order, as when Jesus himself drew attention to an illegality at his trial (John 18:22-23). But such occasions are never for the purpose of revenge or the like.

40. Jesus envisages a further indignity and loss, the oppressor[148] who wants to take the disciple's *tunic*. This is not outright robbery, but the process whereby the enemy adopts legal means of depriving the follower of Jesus of part of his clothing. Normally a person would seem to have worn a loincloth, a tunic, a cloak (outer garment), a girdle, a head covering, and sandals.[149] Jesus envisages a situation in which someone adopts legal measures to deprive the disciple of his *tunic*. *Take* means here "take into one's possession"; the verb can be used of seizing by force (21:35, 39). The proper response is not to fight back, but to be ready to let him have the outer garment[150] as well, a more expensive garment and one that even the

---

REB). Knox understands it of "the evil thing" and renders "you should not offer resistance to injury."

144. ἀλλ'.

145. ὅστις (see on 2:6) is the relative of quality, but it often has a meaning like "whoever, everyone who," and that will be its significance here. Most translations have "if anyone," and this certainly gives the general sense; this is a "conditional relative clause" (BDF, 380; it also cites this as an example of Matthew's correct use "in sentences of general reference" (293[1]). But the word draws attention to the kind of person, "one who slaps," rather than to a conditional possibility.

146. ῥαπίζω (ῥαπίς, "a rod") in secular writers seems to mean "hit with a rod or a club"; in the New Testament, however, it seems always to mean "hit with the open hand," "slap" (though some think a rod is in mind in 26:67). If a right-handed person hits another on the right cheek it is probably with the back of the hand, which was regarded by the Jews as more serious than a slap with the open hand; it carried double the fine (B. Qam. 8:6).

147. σιαγών (again in the New Testament only in Luke 6:29), which AS defines as "the jawbone, jaw, cheek." MM notes its use in the papyri and remarks that it "is not of learned origin."

148. τῷ θέλοντι is a *casus pendens*, resumed by the pronoun αὐτῷ (cf. M, II, p. 424).

149. See S. Daniel-Rops, *Daily Life In Palestine at the Time of Christ* (London, 1962), pp. 211-18.

150. "Here the order is χιτ.-ί; the situation is that of a lawsuit, in which the defendant is advised to give up not only the indispensable χιτών demanded by his opponent, but the

poorest had the right to keep (Exod. 22:26-27; Deut. 24:12-13). A person had an inalienable right to his cloak; it could not be taken away from him permanently. Its voluntary surrender is thus significant.

41. As in verse 39 *whoever* is the generalizing use of the pronoun (though this time the verb is in the future, there the present). The verb[151] was used in the sense "requisition"; originally it was used of the Persian post, but it came to be used of forced service of various kinds. In its only other New Testament occurrences it refers to the pressing into service of Simon the Cyrenian to carry Jesus' cross (27:32; Mark 15:21). The word *mile* was a Roman mile, that is, 1,000 paces, but it came to be used of a fixed measure, 8 stades (i.e., 4,854 feet or 1,478.5 meters, BAGD). Jesus tells his followers that when they are compelled to drop what they are doing and go a mile for the authority, they should show their willingness by going another.[152] *Two* points to the importance of going well beyond what is required. The right thing, Jesus says, is not only to put up cheerfully with the unreasonable and disliked demand, but to go well beyond what is asked.

42. *Give*[153] is unqualified; Jesus looks for generosity without condition. *Asks* is a general term for making requests, and it, too, is unqualified. Jesus is saying that his people must be ready to give to anyone who asks, deserving or undeserving (as in Deut. 15:7-8; Ps. 112:9); they should not reject anyone who wants to borrow from them. The verb *turn away*[154] is used in a variety of senses, but here it clearly points to a refusal that should have no place in the life of the Christian. The follower of Jesus may perhaps not be in a position to give the borrower exactly what he asks, but that does not mean that he rejects him. It may be only a kind word or good advice, but he gives what he can in the circumstances in which he finds himself.[155]

---

i. as well." In Luke 6:29, however, "the order is i.-χ., a sequence that suggests highway robbery, in which the robber first deprives his victim of his outer garment" (BAGD, sub ἱμάτιον 2).

151. ἀγγαρεύω. MM cites its use from 252 B.C. The word is discussed by Deissmann, *BS*, pp. 86-87.

152. Matthew is fond of μετά, which he uses 70 times, the most in any one book. Overall it is used with the genitive about 3½ times as often as the accusative (364 to 103), but Matthew has it 6 times as often (60 to 10).

153. Turner comments on the aorist: δός "of a definite occasion and person, where Lk 6³⁰ δίδου to *anyone* who asks" (M, III, p. 76).

154. ἀποστρέφω may be transitive or intransitive; it can mean "repudiate," "reject" (2 Tim. 1:15; Heb. 12:25), which is the meaning here. *AB* understands the text to mean "do not refuse one who is unable to pay interest," emphasizing that δανίζω means "lend at interest." But in the middle this verb means "borrow"; *AB*'s interpretation seems unduly limiting.

155. Buttrick comments on the injunctions in this section: "A literal obedience raises problems in our ambiguous world, but is better far than the evasion which says, 'This is figurative language.'" Calvin reminds us that "Christ's purpose was to make His disciples generous, not prodigal. There is stupid prodigality, which pours away the Lord's gifts recklessly. . . ."

f. Love for Enemies, 5:43-48

43"*You have heard that it was said, 'You shall love your neighbor and hate your enemy.' 44But I say to you, 'Love your enemies and pray for those who persecute you, 45so that you may be sons of your Father who is in heaven, for he makes his sun rise on evil people and good ones and sends rain on just and unjust. 46For if you love those who love you, what reward do you have? Do not even the tax collectors do the same? 47And if you greet your brothers only, what are you doing more (than others)? Do not the Gentiles also do the same? 48You shall therefore be perfect, even as your heavenly Father is perfect.'*"

This section is of fundamental importance for an understanding of the Christian ideal of love. We all love our friends, but love of our enemies is quite another matter. But the followers of Jesus are not to take their standards from the communities in which they live. The God they serve is a loving God, and therefore they are to be loving people. Jesus points out that they must learn from God's love. God's good gifts, the sunshine and the rain, are given to all alike, the bad as well as the good. Those who serve God should show a similar generous attitude to enemies as well as to friends.[156]

43. Jesus introduces the scribal teaching with the same introductory formula as in verses 27 and 38. *"You shall love your neighbor"* is from Leviticus 19:18, though the omission of "as yourself" may indicate that the scribes set the standard rather lower than did Leviticus. Jesus appears to be summarizing the way the interpreters of his day saw the teaching about enemies rather than citing Scripture itself, for the Old Testament nowhere says, *"you shall hate your enemy."*[157] Indeed, its teaching about enemies is complex. There certainly are passages that inculcate a stern attitude to one's foes (Exod. 34:12; Deut. 7:2; 23:6), and the Psalmist speaks

---

156. Luke 6:27-28, 32-36 are similar to this passage, but there are not unimportant differences. Schweizer indeed finds "only three points of agreement" (p. 113). The introductory formula is different in Luke 6:27-28, and "pray" is the only word in common after "love your enemies." It is not much better with Luke 6:32-36. "Those who love you" is the same in both accounts, but Matthew has ἐάν, the aorist, and τίνα μισθὸν ἔχετε where Luke has εἰ, the present, and ποία ὑμῖν χάρις ἐστίν. In verse 46 Matthew has a question introduced by οὐχί concerning οἱ τελῶναι and referring generally to τὸ αὐτὸ ποιοῦσιν where Luke has a statement that sinners love those who love them. Matthew's statement about a greeting in verse 47 is paralleled by one about doing good, though we are a trifle closer with οἱ ἐθνικοί (Matthew) and οἱ ἁμαρτωλοί (Luke), both followed by τὸ αὐτὸ ποιοῦσιν. At the end Matthew refers to being perfect as (ὡς) the heavenly Father is perfect, and Luke to being compassionate as (καθὼς) your Father is compassionate. Many interpreters regard these as variants of the same set of sayings, but it is better to see them as going back to the variants normal for an itinerant preacher.

157. ἐχθρός means "hated, hateful" and thus in an active sense, "hating, hostile" and as subst. "enemy" (LSJ). Matthew has it 7 times and Luke 8 times, but nobody else in the New Testament has it more than 3 times. It is the ordinary word for "enemy," but on occasion it is opposed to ἀγαπητός.

of hating those who hate God (Ps. 139:21-22). But other Old Testament passages extend love at least to the resident alien (Lev. 19:34) and call for an attitude of helpfulness that extends even to the "enemy" (Exod. 23:4-5; Prov. 25:21-22). We must also bear in mind that on occasion "hate" can be used in the sense "love less" (6:24; cf. 10:37 with Luke 14:26; Gen. 29:31; Deut. 21:15). All this means that those who summed up Old Testament teaching as calling for love for neighbors and hatred for enemies were oversimplifying. The call for hatred is certainly the kind of addition to the command that many have put into practice.[158] The verb love[159] points to the warmest of attitudes, and from ancient times this is the way the Israelite was taught to view his neighbor,[160] that is, his fellow Israelite. A foreigner who lived nearby did not qualify. But with this regard for fellow Israelites there went a hatred for one's enemies.[161] And with this mind-set it was easy to distinguish between good Israelites (Pharisees?) and bad Israelites (tax collectors? were bad Israelites enemies?). As Hendriksen says, "In such an atmosphere it was impossible for hatred to starve. It had plenty to feed on."

44. Again we have the formula that sets Jesus' words in emphatic contrast. *Love* is not simply praised but commanded. As the passage goes on to show, God's love comes first, and love both to God and to our fellows is our appropriate response to that love. *Enemies* is plural over against the singular in the previous verse; this may be no more than the reflection of the plural verb *love,* but it is an all-inclusive term. Jesus had quoted a precept in the singular, but his response is entirely in the plural. He proceeds to an example of what he means with the injunction to

158. The Qumran sect's Community Rule enjoined members "that they may love all that He has chosen and hate all that He has rejected" (Vermes, p. 72); they are to "hate all the sons of darkness, each according to his guilt in God's vengeance" *(ibid.).* There are other such passages in the scrolls. This "eschatology of vengeance" (Davies, *SM,* p. 248) is in marked contrast to Jesus' teaching. But there were other views. Thus we read in 2 Enoch, "if you are able to take vengeance with a hundredfold revenge, do not take vengeance, neither on one who is close to you nor on one who is distant from you" (2 Enoch 50:4).

159. ἀγαπάω is used 8 times in Matthew out of 141 times in the New Testament. It is the usual verb for "to love" in these writings (φιλέω occurs only 25 times, 5 in Matthew). It is used of a variety of loves, here of the love of one person for another, but it is used also of love for God, for Jesus, and for things. It is used of God's love for Jesus and Jesus' love for God, and of the divine love for people. Cf. 6:24; 19:19; 22:37-39, and for the idea in other language, 7:12.

160. πλησίον is the neuter of the adjective πλησίος. It was used as an adverb meaning "near," and with the article to mean "the one who is near," "the neighbor," and thus one's fellow, often in the sense fellow countryman. In the New Testament it is often used, as here, in the quotation from Leviticus 19:18.

161. μισέω is found only 5 times in Matthew (39 times in the New Testament); it may be used of hating people or things. The word for "enemy," ἐχθρός, appears 7 times in Matthew out of 32 in the New Testament. It is really an adjective meaning "hostile," but it is used as a substantive with the meaning "enemy." This may mean the enemies of God or of people; it may refer to the devil (13:39) or to death (1 Cor. 15:26). Here it is used with the genitive of the person who is the object of the enmity.

pray[162] for (or "on behalf of") the persecutors. The verb "to persecute" (see on v. 10) can indicate persecution in any form, but here it is persecution specifically directed at Jesus' followers (you). It may be possible to regard in a detached way persecution of others; it is not so easy when one is the object of the persecution. "Persecutors are the most difficult enemies to love" (Nixon). But it is precisely in a situation of persecution that Jesus' followers are to show their love by praying for those who are harming them.[163]

45. So that is a construction that expresses purpose. But we should probably understand it not in the sense that our love is to be nothing more than the means to an end — our membership in the heavenly family. Rather, our membership in that family will be so important to us that we pursue love avidly. We will see that to be[164] God's children means to love. Love and membership in God's family go together. Sons here are members of the heavenly family. There is a sense in which those members are infinitely diverse and another sense in that they are all characterized by dependence on and likeness to the Father; in this sense sons are "those who are bound to a personality by close, non-material ties; it is this personality that has promoted the relationship and given it its character" (BAGD, 1.c.γ; for "Father in heaven" see on v. 16). The conduct Jesus has enjoined in the previous verse is the conduct that characterizes those in close relationship with the heavenly Father. God loves like that, and his sons come to love in some measure like that, too.

The love of God for all the people he has created is shown in the way he gives good gifts indiscriminately to all (there are some gifts that cannot be appropriated without the right spiritual approach, but that is another matter). The sun does not shine exclusively on the good; the rain does not pass over the evil. The shining of the sun is not viewed as something that occurs naturally; God makes the sun rise. There is a divine volition. There is no article with evil or good;[165] it is not "the bad" and "the

---

162. The verb προσεύχομαι is frequent in the New Testament (Matthew has it 15 times). It is always used of prayer to God (or the gods). The construction with ὑπέρ is not common (again in Col. 1:9; BAGD cites it in a number of nonbiblical passages). This is Matthew's one use of the preposition with the genitive (it occurs 130 times in the New Testament).

163. Cf. Barclay, "We cannot go on hating another man in the presence of God. The surest way of killing bitterness is to pray for the man we are tempted to hate."

164. γένησθε might be understood as "become" (so GNB); disciples are not to be content with what they are but to "become" increasingly God's children. It is not only that they act in love to show what they are now (Zahn); that is true, but they also go on to become what they are not yet. This does not mean that they qualify for membership in the family by their deeds, but rather that they continually progress in the service of God. Cf. Bruner, "that we might really be in act what we have been made in fact — sons and daughters of the Father" (p. 221).

165. ἀγαθός occurs 18 times in Matthew (only Romans with 21 has it more often). It is used in both physical and moral senses and may refer to persons, things, or deeds. AS thinks it refers to "inner excellence" as against καλός, which signifies "goodliness as manifested in form." AS also differentiates it from δίκαιος in that it "implies a kindliness and attractiveness

good" viewed as classes, but people generally seen as characterized by evil or goodness. God's provision extends to the whole race and is not limited by the moral standards people accept. With the sunshine Jesus links the *rain*. Just as the sunlight, the rain comes on good and bad alike. Jesus changes his terminology, but in this context there is not a great deal of difference between the *evil* and the *good* on the one hand, and the *just* and the *unjust* on the other.[166] The point being emphasized is that God does not limit his blessings to those who serve him faithfully. Even to those who oppose him he gives many good things.

46. *For* introduces the consequence: the goodness of God has its implications for Christian conduct. The *if* implies nothing as to the fulfilment or otherwise of the condition; it simply puts a hypothetical case. To love those who love one is nothing wonderful, and Jesus brings this out by asking what *reward* they can expect for this kind of conduct. He spoke earlier about the heavenly reward his followers could expect (see on v. 12), and here he makes it clear that there is no reward for doing what is commonplace. To behave in this way is to act like the world; it is the natural response of worldly people, and Jesus singles out the *tax collectors*[167] as people who do this. The form of the question[168] looks for an affirmative answer: "of course they do." Tax collectors have never been popular in any culture, but in first-century Palestine they were especially unpopular. Partly this was because they gathered taxes for the Romans, and anything that helped the conquerors was anathema to the subject Jews. Partly also it was because they tended to be extortionate. In the eyes of Jesus' audience there were no more wicked people than tax collectors

---

not necessarily possessed by the δίκαιος, who merely measures up to a high standard of rectitude."

166. Both *NEB* and *JB* make the distinction here between the "honest" and the "dishonest."

167. τελώνης occurs 8 times in Matthew out of a New Testament total of 21 (Luke has it 10 times). The Roman system was to invite bids for the taxing rights of a given area. The successful bidder would then employ people to do the actual work of collecting the taxes. Strictly speaking the τελώνης was the man who had the tax-farming contract (Lat. *publicanus*), but the term came to be used also for his underlings. A certain amount over and above the tax was legitimate, since the people who did the collecting were entitled to their wages and salaries. But human nature being what it is, there was a great temptation to collect more than was justified and a vicious circle developed. The more the tax collectors collected the more they were hated, and the more they were hated the more they collected. Among the Jews a further count was ceremonial uncleanness. The contacts the tax men had with Gentiles made it almost inevitable that they would be unclean. In the Mishnah we find that if tax gatherers enter a house, everything in it becomes unclean (*Tohar.* 7:6). This will mean those who did the actual collecting of taxes; those who held the taxing rights were further removed from contact with uncleanness and were not regarded as unclean (J. Jeremias, *New Testament Theology*, I [London, 1971], p. 111). They are linked with "sinners" (9:10-11), Gentiles (18:17), and harlots (21:31), and in the Mishnah with murderers and robbers (*Ned.* 3:4).

168. Introduced by the emphatic οὐχί. The ascensive καί has a meaning like "even"; since one would expect this of anyone, if the tax collectors, the worst possible people in the view of most people of the day, do this, then anyone might be expected to respond in the same way.

as a class. If even they would respond to love with love, then anyone would. They are the last people one would expect to show love, but they do — to their own kind. This example shows that there is nothing wonderful about this kind of love.

47. Jesus gives a further example, this one taken from the usage of his hearers. Again there is the *if* construction with no indication of fulfilment or otherwise. *Greet*[169] strictly means no more than exchange pleasantries on meeting. But the Jewish greeting was "Peace," and this was in fact a prayer. Doubtless many people used it with no more thought of praying than we do when we say "Good-bye" without remembering that we are really saying "God be with you." But to take it seriously implied a certain warmth; the greeting would have the note of goodwill and of welcome. For *brother* see on 1:2; here it refers to others than siblings and points to people belonging to the same group. Such people are normally greeted warmly. When Jesus' people do this and do not greet others in the same way, then what are they doing other than what is common practice? For *more* see the note on verse 37; here it will mean "more than is common," "more than other people"; it is never enough that believers do the good that unbelievers do; always it is necessary that they do more. If they only equal the deeds of worldly people, we may well ask, "What is so wonderful about that?" Jesus picks out *the Gentiles*[170] as folk who do this. If even they do this, then why should the people of God pride themselves on doing no more? There is no merit in such greetings. Even Gentiles manage them.

48. Jesus ends this part of his discourse with a future normally understood as a command: *You shall be* (for this construction see on v. 21). This is surely correct: there is a command here. But may we not also see something of a promise?[171] Jesus puts his command in such a way that disciples may look for divine help as they press toward God's goal for them. His *therefore* relates this future to what has gone before: because of the importance of showing in their lives that they are doing more than is required of people in general, more than the tax collectors or the Gentiles do, more than they themselves do when they greet one another, they must look for perfection. *You* is emphatic. Jesus is not saying what the Gentiles ought to be or the Jews who do not follow him. He is referring to his followers; they must be *perfect*.[172] That their standard is to be the highest

169. ἀσπάζομαι in the New Testament is mostly a Pauline word (40 times out of 59); Matthew has it twice only.
170. The expression here, οἱ ἐθνικοί, is the masculine plural of the adjective meaning "Gentile"; Matthew has it in 3 of its 4 New Testament occurrences, and each time he uses it as a noun with an implied contrast to "the Jews" (6:7; 18:17; so also in 3 John 7).
171. Cf. Schweizer, "Of course, the formulation, both in Greek and in Hebrew, includes the promise 'You will be' as well as the summons 'You must be'" (p. 135).
172. τέλειος has the meaning "having attained the end (τέλος) or aim"; if anything has fully attained that for which it is designed it is perfect. It can refer to the maturity of an adult

possible ("no limit to your goodness," *REB*) is shown by the words that follow: *even as your heavenly Father is perfect*.[173] When Matthew uses the adjective *heavenly* it always refers to God (he has the word 7 times out of its 9 New Testament occurrences). In this he contrasts with Luke, who uses it of the heavenly host (Luke 2:13) and of the heavenly vision (Acts 26:19). Matthew thus employs the term to stress the difference between God and others, just as *Father* brings out his nearness and his love. To set this kind of perfection before his followers means that Jesus saw them as always having something for which to strive. No matter how far along the path of Christian service we are, there is still something to aim for. There is a wholeheartedness about being Christian; all that we have and all that we are must be taken up into the service of the Father.

man — the end or aim of that to which the boy points. Jesus is calling on his followers to be mature people, attaining the end for which God has made them. God has set before us the highest of standards; it is expected that we will press on to attain them. We find the expression τέλειος ἔσῃ in Deuteronomy 18:13 (LXX).

173. The Jews, too, could take notice of the divine example. Abba Saul said: "Be thou like Him: just as He is gracious and compassionate, so be thou gracious and compassionate" (*Shab.* 133b). But Jesus is saying something more than this; "perfect, even as your heavenly Father is perfect" sets the highest possible standard. Who would ever claim to have reached it?

Matthew 6

6. Practicing Piety, 6:1-34

The previous section has made it very clear that Jesus was not opposed to the keeping of the law; rather, he was firmly committed to it and in a much more wholehearted way than his Pharisaic opponents. But the service of God included a good deal more than could be determined by a reference to the law; therefore, he turns now to some of the practical matters that appear when people are trying to put their professed willingness to serve God into practice. The three activities he mentions — the giving of alms, prayer, and fasting — were particularly important in Jewish piety (cf. Tob. 12:8, "Prayer is good when accompanied by fasting, almsgiving, and righteousness"). Jesus insists on the importance of a deep sincerity in those who follow him.

a. Almsgiving, 6:1-4

> [1] *"Take care not to parade your righteousness before men in order to be seen by them; if you do, you have no reward with your Father who is in heaven. [2] Whenever then you give alms, do not sound a trumpet before you, as the hypocrites do in the synagogues and in the streets, in order that they may be praised by men; truly I tell you, they have their reward. [3] But when you are giving alms, let your left hand not know what your right hand is doing, [4] so that your almsgiving may be in secret; and your Father who sees in secret will reward you."*

Jesus begins with the giving of alms, a most important part of piety in a day when poverty was very widespread and when the lot of the poor was so hard.[1] Everybody accepted the fact that it was a religious duty to help the poor, but Jesus points out that it was possible to do this in an objectionable way. Some people made a public display of their generosity

---

1. The Jews took giving to the poor very seriously, and in each community there were officials who made weekly collections of goods or money for the poor (Moore, II, pp. 174-79). Gifts were obligatory; a man residing in a town for thirty days became "liable for contributing to the soup kitchen, three months for the charity box . . ." (*B. Bat.* 8a). But more than this compulsory levy was needed, and almsgiving over and above the charity box was commended.

(a phenomenon that has been repeated in every age). They were more interested in ensuring that they were known as benefactors than in genuinely helping the poor; reputation rather than relief of poverty was what mattered to them. Jesus teaches that it is important to give, not to be known to give. So he suggests that precautions be taken to ensure that, while gifts are indeed given, the identity of the givers is kept secret.

1. *Take care* renders a verb that has the meaning "turn (your mind) to" and thus "give careful attention to," "concentrate on." Jesus is inviting his hearers to concentrate on the central thing when they perform any act of *righteousness.*[2] This word may be used in any one of a variety of ways, but here it refers to any good deed that a person may do as part of his service of God (Jesus goes on to illustrate with the examples of almsgiving, prayer, and fasting). The believer must always keep in mind that the act is righteous only if it is what it purports to be — the service of God. When instead it is done as a means of enhancing the reputation of the doer of the deed, then it is no longer a simple act of divine service. It is thus important that the aim should never be that people may observe it. Occasions may arise when publicity is unavoidable, but the deed must never be done in order to be made public. If it is so done,[3] then there is no *reward* (see on 5:12) *with your Father who is in heaven* (see on 5:16). Why should there be? The deed was done in order to secure a reputation, not in order to serve God. Already the doer has secured his *reward*. He aimed at reputation. He got it. He has no right to expect the further benefit of divine approval.

2. *Whenever* is comprehensive; Jesus is not pointing to an occasional happening, but to the regular practice.[4] *You* is singular, which makes the application personal (in the previous verse the plural was used). Jesus assumes that his hearers will assist the poor;[5] the question is not "Whether?" but "How?" Almsgiving is commanded in Scripture (e.g., Deut. 15:11), and all who serve God must take this seriously. Jesus tells his hearers not to *sound*[6] *a trumpet* before them. This lively piece of imagery

2. For δικαιοσύνη see on 3:15. ἐλεημοσύνην is read by L W Z Θ etc., but this can scarcely be original. It seems to be an explanation made by a scribe who thought the verse was concerned only with almsgiving instead of being the introduction to the succeeding sections as well.

3. γέ is an enclitic particle "appended to the word it refers to; it serves to emphasize this word"; the expression εἰ δὲ μή γε signifies "otherwise" (BAGD).

4. ὅταν is employed "Usually of an iterative action, indefinite, in the past or future" (M, III, p. 112).

5. ἐλεημοσύνη is connected with the idea of mercy (ἔλεος) and points to any deed of compassion. In LXX and other Jewish writings it came to be used specifically of the gift of money for the poor (the English "alms" goes back to a corruption of this Greek word; see *OED*). This usage was apparently not common among the Greeks, and only one example is cited (*TDNT*, II, p. 486, n. 4). Davies and Allison remark, "The Greeks had no word for alms" (*ICC*, I, p. 578, n. 12). Lightfoot cites examples of Jewish approval of the practice (II, pp. 136-38).

6. Turner understands this imperative to mean "*On no account* sound a trumpet . . ." (*Grammatical Insights*, p. 32).

(surely there cannot be anything more public than the sounding of a trumpet!) at one and the same time burlesques the attitude of publicity seekers and denounces it.[7] That is the method of the *hypocrites*.[8] The word was used for actors who, of course, play a part and whose words are spoken for effect and not in order to convey the truth. These hypocrites were people who acted a concern for the poor whereas their real concern was to establish a reputation for piety. The synagogue (see on 4:23) was, of course, a place of worship, but it was also the center of life for the community and functions like the administration of justice were carried on there. The synagogue was a public place, and a generous gift made there would certainly be noticed. So it was with *the streets*.[9] Jesus selects two very public places where hypocritical gifts may be given and warns his followers against following the practice. People who engage in that kind of giving are interested in being *praised by men;*[10] it is the praise and not the helping of the needy in which they are primarily interested. For *truly I tell you* see on 5:18; it is an expression that recurs in this sermon. Such people *have*[11] *their reward.* This expression employs the ordinary commercial term for a receipt and is a lively way of bringing out the truth that these hypocrites have received all the reward they are going to get

---

7. Those who think there was a literal blowing of trumpets vary in their understanding. Hill sees a reference to the blowing of trumpets when alms were collected in the temple and cites Bonnard as his authority. But while Bonnard does say that trumpets were blown to announce the time of collection of money for the poor, he also raises a question about the attestation of the blowing of the trumpet and suggests that the expression may be a piece of imagery. The fact is that no evidence seems to be cited for blowing a trumpet when alms were given. Others are reminded of the trumpet-shaped receptacles into which money was put when given at the temple, but these were not trumpets at all and could not be "blown." Carson accepts A. Büchler's suggestion that it refers to the blowing of trumpets when fasts were proclaimed, and it was widely held that almsgiving was a suitable accompaniment of fasts and prayers. But Lenski points out that trumpets would not have been blown in synagogues. The language is figurative.

8. ὑποκριτής occurs 13 times in this Gospel, but elsewhere in the New Testament only 3 times in Luke and once in Mark. AS derives it from ὑποκρίνομαι, a variant of ἀποκρίνομαι = "answer (on the stage), play a part." The word was used mostly for the actors in a play, from which it is an easy step to those who speak words for effect and without regard to what is true. Bruce remarks sardonically, "There are religious actors still, and they draw good houses." Albright and Mann argue for the meaning "overscrupulous" (*AB,* pp. CXV-CXXIII), but they do not deny that the word was used of one who was "an actor or was consciously playing a part" (p. CXVII). In any case, it is the hypocritical rather than the overscrupulous who blow a trumpet to draw attention to their deeds. It is surely the one who is playing a part who is in mind here. A. W. Argyle argues that there can scarcely have been an Aramaic word for "actor" since "theatre was forbidden among the Jews"; he finds in the use of this word evidence that Jesus sometimes spoke Greek (*ET,* LXXV [1963-64], pp. 113-14).

9. ῥύμη denotes a narrow street or lane. In such a street a person would be very close to others; he could not make a gift without it being noticed.

10. ὅπως introduces the real purpose of the hypocrites. Chamberlain says that it is used to introduce purpose about 50 times in the New Testament, of which 17 are in Matthew (Chamberlain, p. 186).

11. The verb ἀπέχω (5 times in Matthew) is used as a technical term in commerce with the meaning "*receive* a sum *in full* and give a receipt for it" (BAGD).

for this "good" deed. They sought the praise of men. They received the praise of men. There is nothing more to come. They cannot expect a heavenly reward in addition, for they have already been "paid in full."

3. *But* is adversative; it sets the follower of Jesus in contrast to the hypocrites. The present tense of the verb pictures the act as in progress; while it is taking place there must be the utmost secrecy. The figure of the *left hand* being unaware of what the *right hand* is doing (again the tense points to the action in progress) is a striking expression for complete secrecy.[12] And it forbids the giver to gloat over how good he or she is! "Christian giving is to be marked by self-sacrifice and self-forgetfulness, not by self-congratulation" (Stott, p. 131). The motive deep down is important.[13]

4. *So that* introduces the purpose. In giving alms what is one really aiming at? Jesus says that the person must aim at doing this good deed *in secret*.[14] But though almsgiving is done in the right way, that is, done without ostentation and in secret, that does not mean that it is entirely unnoticed. *Your Father* (an expression found again in the first three Gospels only in vv. 6 and 18; the plural is more common) sees it and takes notice of it (for *Father* see on 5:16). The verb may be used of various kinds of seeing, literal and metaphorical; here it indicates that human secrecy is no bar to God's complete knowledge. God sees what is given and will take action, rewarding the donor. This does not mean that good deeds should be done with a view to obtaining a reward;[15] that would mean that the deeds would no longer be good. It is a way of saying that in the end justice will be done.[16] In our anxiety to make sure that we do not serve God for what we can get out of it we must not go to the other extreme and think of God as not caring what we do, or if he does, as not doing anything about it. God notices what his children do and responds to it. We should bear in mind the nature of the reward. To respond to love is to obtain a

12. The Jews at their best surpassed the Pharisees. The Mishnah speaks of a "Chamber of Secrets" in the temple (*Sheqal.* 5:6) where the devout could leave gifts in privacy and go away; the poor of good family would later come and receive help without knowing who their benefactor was. In the Talmud we read, "A man who gives charity in secret is greater than Moses our Teacher" (*B. Bat.* 9b).

13. Cf. Lenski, "The whole matter is in the heart, it is not a mechanical rule about hiding our gifts. For one might hide all his giving in the secret hope of eventually being discovered and then being praised for the saintly secrecy of his gifts" (on v. 4).

14. κρυπτός occurs 5 times in Matthew, more than in any other book; it may point to what is hidden or, as here, what is secret. ἐν τῷ κρυπτῷ is applied to the Father again in verses 4 and 6 (twice) only in the New Testament.

15. For ἀποδίδωμι see on 5:26; it means "recompense" and is used both in the good sense of rewarding (as here) and the bad sense of punishing.

16. Cf. Barclay, "To banish all rewards and punishments from the idea of religion is in effect to say that injustice has the last word. It cannot reasonably be held that the end of the good man and the end of the bad man are one and the same" (I, p. 179); "the person who looks for reward, and who calculates that it is due to him, does not receive it; the person whose only motive is love, and who never thinks that he has deserved any reward, does, in fact, receive it" (I, p. 181).

wonderful reward even if the reward cannot be quantified in any way nor regarded as merited. But it is very real. As Plummer puts it, "There is nothing degrading in working for the reward of a good conscience here, and of increased holiness hereafter, both enriched by God's love and blessing" (p. 91). Cf. Gutzwiller, "God himself is the reward of Christians."

b. Prayer, 6:5-15

5"And whenever you pray, you shall not be like the hypocrites, for they love to pray standing in the synagogues and on the street corners in order that they may be seen by men; truly I tell you, they have their reward. 6But you, whenever you are praying, go into your room, and when you have shut your door, pray to your Father who is in secret; and your Father who sees in secret will reward you.

7"And when you are praying, do not babble like the Gentiles do, for they think that they will be heard for their many words. 8Therefore do not be like them; for your Father knows what you need before you ask him. 9You then pray like this:

'Our Father in heaven,
may your name be kept holy,
10may your kingdom come,
may your will be done,
    as in heaven also on earth.
11Give us today our daily bread,
12and forgive us our debts,
    as we also have forgiven our debtors.
13And do not bring us into temptation,
    but deliver us from evil.'

14For if you forgive men their offenses, your heavenly Father will forgive you too; 15but if you do not forgive men, neither will your Father forgive your offenses."

It would seem that, just as was the case with helping the poor, so there was a tendency for people to use their prayers as a means of impressing others with their piety. But prayer is to be communion with God, not a means of increasing one's reputation. To pray with a view to impressing people is wrongheaded. Jesus calls on praying people to consider what they are doing. They should concentrate on the matter in hand and forget the plaudits of people.

5. *And* links on another example. *Whenever,* as in verse 2, gives a general instruction suitable for all times of prayer. For *pray* see on 5:44; Matthew has a good deal to say about prayer. There is a change from the singular to the plural, but this does not seem to have great significance. *You shall not be* is another example of the use of the future with imperatival force; Jesus is not so much uttering a prophecy as giving a direction. For *hypocrites* see on verse 2; again the word signifies those who profess to do a pious action, but do so with their eye on people when they should be concerned with God only. *For* is not used here in a causal sense; it rather has a meaning like "seeing that."[17] *Standing*[18] was a normal posture for prayer (cf. Mark 11:25), though when the worshiper wished to adopt an especially lowly position he might prostrate himself, as Jesus did in Gethsemane (26:39). People might pray kneeling (Acts 21:5) or sitting (2 Sam. 7:18). Clearly the posture is unimportant. As we have seen before, the synagogue (see on 4:23) was the center of community life as well as the place of worship. Here it is the place where God is worshipped, and it is singled out as a place where there would be many people. To pray standing in a synagogue was to take up a very public posture. The same must be said about praying on street[19] corners. The junction of two streets would be a very public place and to pray there, in a place not especially given over to religious exercises and with many people to observe what was going on, was to court notice and to win the approbation of people who liked to observe religious activities in progress. There were prayers that were offered at prescribed times (cf. Ps. 55:17; Dan. 6:10; Acts 3:1),[20] and it was not beyond the ingenuity of some to order their affairs so that they were in a public place at the time of prayer and thus "compelled" to pray where they would be seen. *In order that* introduces the purpose of the activity: the public exercise of which Jesus speaks was nominally aimed at addressing God, but it actually sought to achieve visibility to men (the masculine, of course, is inclusive and means "people"). The words about reward are repeated exactly from verse 2. Like the demonstrative givers of alms, those who pray merely to put on a show have been "paid in full" for their efforts. In all this Jesus is not condemning public prayer or praying in a public place; it is praying in such a way as to maximize its effect on other people that he condemns.

6. *But* is adversative and marks a contrast, while *you* is emphatic. The followers of Jesus will not pray in that demonstrative fashion. *Whenever* means that this is the way they must always pray. Jesus is not, of

---

17. ὅτι here "hardly states why we are not to be 'as the hypocrites' . . . but in what respect we are not to be like them" (Lenski).

18. The perfect ἑστῶτες may possibly point to lengthy prayers, though the emphasis here is on publicity rather than length.

19. The word is not ῥύμη, as in verse 2, but πλατεῖα (the feminine of πλατύς, "broad"), which means a wide road or street. *Ta'anit* 2:1-2 refers to prayer in "the open space in the town" on certain fast days.

20. The Mishnah tractate *Berakot* goes into detail. For example, the *Shema'* is to be recited in the morning "So soon as one can distinguish between blue and white" (another opinion is "between blue and green," *Ber.* 1:2). Directions are given as to what is to be done if a man were on top of a tree or a heap of stones when the hour of prayer arrived (*Ber.* 2:4) or if he were riding an ass or journeying on a ship or raft (*Ber.* 4:5, 6). Even if the king greeted a man while he was saying his prayer, he must not interrupt it (*Ber.* 5:1). It is clear that the saying of prayers at the prescribed times was taken seriously.

course, forbidding prayer in public, for example, in services of public worship or on other occasions when united praying is required. Rather, he is giving direction for one's own prayers and indicating that they are to be undertaken with a single eye on God, not with a side glance at people who could be impressed.[21] *Go into your room*[22] (the word means an inner room) prescribes a private place for such prayer. The room itself is secure from observation from the street, and shutting the door secures it from the observation of those who have legitimate business in the house. Every precaution is to be taken that the prayer should be unobserved.[23] "The secret of religion is religion in secret" (McNeile). *Pray* is a command; prayer is not simply desirable but necessary. In verse 4 the giving of alms is said to be in secret and the Father is said to see in secret, but here we have the interesting expression *your Father who is in secret.* The secret place will exclude other people but not God; he is there, in the secret place.[24] The expression may also hint that the essential nature of God is hidden from those he created. For his seeing in secret and rewarding see on verse 4.

7. Jesus has significant teaching on the importance of conciseness in prayer. His followers are not to *babble,* where the unusual word forbids prolixity.[25] To pray at length was regarded by *the Gentiles* as the way to make sure that one's prayer was appreciated by deity, and there is no reason for thinking that this error was confined to the Gentiles; Jews could also err in this way (cf. Mark 12:40; the Talmud speaks of pious men who prayed for nine hours a day! *Ber.* 32b, though we should remember that

21. "Prayer does not exist where man's aim is self-promotion; such parade is not prayer to God but self-worship" (Filson).

22. ταμεῖον means a storeroom and thus a room in the inner part of a house. With houses made of mud brick it was possible for thieves to "dig through" an outer wall (cf. v. 19); thus anything valuable was stored in an inner room. In many houses this was the only room that could be locked. In the present context the emphasis is on a room that cannot be observed. Cf. 24:26. The threefold *your* (*your* room, *your* door, *your* Father) emphasizes the personal character of it all.

23. Lloyd-Jones points out that "it is possible for a man to pray in secret in such a way that everybody knows he is praying in secret, because he gives the impression that by spending so much time there he is a great man of prayer" (II, p. 26). There are many ways of being ostentatious about our praying.

24. A. Oepke remarks, "Jesus restores lost modesty to piety by directing it to the place of concealment" (*TDNT,* III, p. 974). Carr comments, "Christ was the first to enjoin clearly secret and silent prayer," and he points to praying aloud as the practice in a number of religions.

25. βατταλογέω is found only here in the New Testament, and BAGD finds it in writers dependent on this passage and in only two other places in all the rest of Greek literature (it lacks attestation in one of these). They think that it is a hybrid form possibly deriving from Aramaic words meaning "talk idly"; they give the meaning as "*babble,* speak without thinking." AS thinks that it may be onomatopoeic, meaning "stammer, repeat idly." MM points out that in D the word is βλαττολογέω, "the form of which suggests an approximation towards the Latin *blatero* [query — cf. provincial English *blether,* with the same meaning . . .]." The word is discussed in M, II, p. 272. A Jewish injunction reads, "Do not prattle in the assembly of the elders, nor repeat yourself in your prayer" (Sir. 7:14).

Jews, too, could advocate short prayers, following Eccl. 5:2). Over against the conviction that the multitude of words indicates piety, Jesus points out that babbling is not the way to the heart of God. For *Gentiles* see on 5:47; it stands for Gentiles over against the Jews, the people of God. Such people do not understand the way to pray. *For* introduces the reason for their practice and *that* the content of their thinking. The Gentiles think of prayer as effective only if long (cf. 1 Kings 18:26-29).[26] They agree that God hears and answers, but hold that he does so in proportion to their wordiness.

8. *Therefore* introduces the reason: there is a fallacy in the position of the Gentiles, which is obvious as soon as it is stated. *Do not be like them* means, of course, "Do not pray as they do," "Do not make the error they make." Jesus justifies this by going on to refer to the knowledge the Father[27] has of his children. Before they offer any prayer, he knows exactly what their need is. They pray, not to inform the Father on matters of which he is ignorant, but to worship him.[28] Jesus is not, of course, forbidding long prayers; he himself on occasion could pray all night (Luke 6:12) and on one occasion he taught his followers "that they should always pray and not grow weary" (Luke 18:1). Nor does he forbid repetition, for in Gethsemane he repeated his prayer (26:39-44). It is prayer based on the view that length will persuade God that he discourages.

9. Many recent scholars hold that the prayer that we commonly call "the Lord's Prayer" should be understood in eschatological terms. In this Gospel we have already found that the kingdom of heaven has come near in the person of Jesus (3:2; 4:17), and the suggestion is that Jesus is teaching his followers a prayer that they should pray mindful of the fact that the end of all things is upon them. It may well be granted that these words are suitable for use in the last days as in others, but there is nothing in the language of the prayer that shows that those days alone are in view; if that is what Jesus meant, why did he not use at least one expression that unambiguously gives expression to it? The experience of the church throughout the centuries makes it abundantly clear that the prayer applies

---

26. BDF sees ἐν here as probably used to give the reason (BDF, 219[2]). Moule thinks that its significance is "by means of" (*IBNTG*, p. 77).

27. There is some textual variation. *Your Father* is read by most MSS (ℵ* D K L W etc., "our Father" by f1 1253 1546, "God your Father" by ℵª B sah Origen, and "your heavenly Father" by 28 892^mg 1195 etc. Metzger regards the use of "our" in place of "your" as due to "scribal inadvertence," "God our Father" as "a scribal intrusion reflecting a characteristically Pauline collocation of θεός and πατήρ," and "your heavenly Father" as assimilation to the text of verse 9. UBS³ gives an A rating to "Your Father."

28. Calvin remarks that Christians pray "to alert themselves to seek Him, to exercise their faith by meditating upon His promises, unburdening their cares by lifting themselves into His bosom, and finally to testify that from Him alone, all good for themselves and for others is hoped and asked." Plummer quotes Augustine, "Prayer calms and purifies the heart, and makes it more capacious for receiving the Divine gifts. God is always ready to give us His light, but we are not always ready to receive." He proceeds, "By prayer we open channels through which blessings, which are always ready, may flow" (p. 94).

well to the here and now. We should understand it as a model prayer to guide disciples in their devotional life.[29]

As Matthew records it, the giving of the prayer is quite spontaneous, but in Luke it comes in response to a question of the disciples. Jesus had been praying, and the disciples asked him to teach them to pray as John the Baptist had taught his followers. There are differences in the two versions of the prayer that we will notice as we come to them, but both forms "have simplicity, conciseness, intellectual clarity, and spiritual comprehensiveness" (Filson). Comparisons are made between the two versions, often with a view to determining which is the older. The usual conclusion is that on the whole the Lucan form is the more primitive, but that in some details Matthew has preserved what is nearer to the original. This enterprise seems to me mistaken.[30] If Jesus seriously meant this to be a form to be used verbatim or as a model, it is highly unlikely that he would have enunciated it once only. And if it was to be used as a pattern rather than as a rigid form, nothing is more probable than that it should vary somewhat on different occasions.[31] *Like this*[32] indicates that what follows is meant as a guide, a model, rather than as a set form of words (cf. Zahn). This does not mean that the Lord's Prayer may not usefully and meaningfully be used exactly as it is enunciated, but it points us to the truth that Jesus is giving us a model that may usefully be employed in fashioning other prayers. The present imperative *pray* points to the habitual practice. *You* is emphatic; in verses 5-8 we have seen that the Gentiles pray in an unacceptable fashion, as do the hypocrites among the Jews, but Jesus' followers are set in sharp contrast. This was taken seriously by the early church, where the use of the prayer was confined to full members of the church (it appears to have been taught as part of baptismal instruction). Others were not to use it.

Jesus starts with the address, *"Our Father*[33] *in heaven"* (see on 5:16;

---

29. This does not exclude the possibility that the prayer "is to be seen in the light of the expectation of the new world where all evil will be destroyed" (Hamann, p. 76; he has just rejected the limiting of "lead us not into temptation" "to the great trial at the end of this age").

30. For that reason I have not discussed it. There is a useful summary in Carson, pp. 166-68. Stendahl sees the difference as "one between two different 'theologies': In Mt. the setting is thoroughly eschatological; in Lk. there is more concern for the daily life, the End is not in the process of breaking in, the eschatological tension is relatively low." J. Jeremias agrees that it is possible that Jesus "spoke the 'Our Father' on different occasions in a slightly differing form," though he prefers the view that the Lucan form is the older one and that in Matthew we have a form used liturgically (*ET*, LXXI [1959-60], p. 143).

31. "It may well have been taught by Jesus more than once and in more than one form" (Tasker, p. 72).

32. οὕτως is common in Matthew. It means "thus, in this way" and may refer to what precedes (5:19), or, as here, to what follows.

33. The vocative Πάτερ is found 4 times only in Matthew (out of 64 occurrences), all being in prayers of Jesus. The nominative, of course, may be used in the vocative sense (e.g., 11:26). We are often reminded that this is equivalent to the Aramaic *Abba* (Mark 14:36; Rom.

143

in Luke the prayer begins simply with "Father"). *Our* links the praying person to other believers; while the prayer may be used in private it is meant to be prayed in community, which means that it may have had a liturgical use from the first (though this, of course, does not mean that it cannot be profitably used in private prayer). Jesus addressed God simply as "Father" (11:25; Mark 14:36; Luke 23:46; John 17:1), and taught his followers to do the same. Bonnard points out that when God is called "Father" in the Synoptic Gospels the word is always on the lips of Jesus. This is not a commonplace of ancient religion, but a new understanding of the nature of God Jesus taught his disciples. It is characteristic that his followers should address God as "Father," and distinctive because others, both Jews and Gentiles, even if they addressed God as "Father," tended to begin their prayers with titles stressing God's greatness, lordship, and the like.[34] But, while the address expresses love and devotion,[35] the one whom we call *Father* is at the same time supremely great, as the fact that he is *in heaven* reminds us ("God is in heaven, and you upon earth," Eccl. 5:2). We should not miss the balance in this opening to the prayer. We address God intimately as *Father*, but we immediately recognize his infinite greatness with the addition *in heaven*.

The *name*[36] in antiquity meant a good deal more than it does with us. We use it for a personal designation, and that is about all. But in antiquity the name was held to be bound up with the person in some way;[37] the name and the qualities associated with the name went together.

8:15; Gal. 4:6), the language of the little child to its Father, but Gundry points out that *Abba* was also used when adults addressed their male parent. On the use of *our*, G. Bornkamm points to the fact that Jesus frequently uses "my Father" and "your Father" but never joins the disciples with "our Father" and goes on, "The consistency with which the tradition has retained this particular feature is at least an unmistakable proof that the believing community looked upon the secret of the fatherhood of God and the secret of our being the children of this father as a miracle, not as a natural fact" (*Jesus of Nazareth* [London, 1960], p. 129).

34. In the 4th and the 6th of the Eighteen Benedictions God is addressed simply as "our Father," but in all of them we find "O Lord." See Moore, II, pp. 201-11 for a discussion of the use of "Father" with regard to God. But he concludes that all this "does not indicate that the age had a new conception of God"; the expressions he cites simply express "a characteristic attitude of piety" (p. 211).

35. Cf. Diétrich, "The whole miracle of divine grace is contained in this single word." Barclay comments that the heathen "lives in a world crowded with gods . . . all these gods are jealous, and grudging, and hostile. They must all be placated, and a man can never be sure that he has not omitted the honour due to some of these gods." To find that there is but one God and that he is to be called "Father" is a liberating discovery: "We need no longer shiver before a horde of jealous gods; we can rest in a father's love" (pp. 200-201).

36. ὄνομα is found 22 times in Matthew (and as many as 60 times in Acts and 34 in Luke). The use of the name was important in Jewish prayer: "any benediction in which the Divine Name is not mentioned is no benediction." In view of a later petition in this prayer we may notice also, "Any benediction in which (God's) Kingship is not mentioned is no benediction" (*Ber.* 40b).

37. In the New Testament period people generally saw in the name "someth. real, a piece of the very nature of the personality whom it designates, that partakes in his qualities and his powers" (BAGD, 4).

Thus in the opening of this Gospel we find that the baby was to be called Jesus, for he would save his people from their sins (1:21); the name and the activity went together. The prayer then means more than that we should use the divine name with suitable reverence. It includes that, and is thus a standing witness against every age that uses the name of God (or Jesus or Christ) lightly in oaths or jests. But it also means that we should be reverent before all that God is and stands for. If God's name is *kept holy*,[38] it is held in proper reverence. This prayer is not so much a petition that God will do some great act that will show everyone who and what he is, as a prayer that he will bring people to a proper attitude toward him. It expresses an aspiration that he who is holy will be seen to be holy and treated throughout his creation as holy.

10. The *kingdom* of God is a most important concept in this Gospel (see on 3:2). There is a sense in which the kingdom is a present reality, but here it is the future kingdom that is in mind.[39] The petition looks to the coming of the time when all evil will be done away and people will gladly submit to the divine Sovereign (cf. Rev. 11:15). Davies and Allison point out that "kingdom of God" is never the subject of the verb "come" in Jewish writings or in the New Testament outside the Gospels; they find here the thought of the "coming" of God (which, of course, includes the coming of his kingdom). The prayer looks for God to take action, not for worshipers to bring the kingdom into being (cf. Stendahl, "It asks for the establishment of the Kingdom of God, by God for us, not by us for God"). The prayer looks for the full realization of all that the kingdom means[40] and for the will of God to be perfectly done (the words *your will be done* are absent from the Lukan version). The word *will* may be used of the act of willing (e.g., Rom. 1:10) or of the thing that is willed to happen; that which takes place may be done either by oneself (e.g., Eph. 1:9) or by others (21:31). It is this latter use that we see here. The prayer looks for the perfect accomplishment of what God wills, and that in the deeds of those he has created as well as in what he does himself. It points to no passive acquiescence but to an active identification of the worshiper with the working out of the divine purpose; if we pray that way we must live

---

38. ἁγιάζω "belongs almost exclusively to biblical Greek or Greek influenced by the Bible" (O. Procksch, *TDNT*, I, p. 111). It occurs 3 times in Matthew out of a New Testament total of 27 (6 times in Hebrews is the most in any one book). It is used of "sanctifying" objects set apart for use in worship in the temple and the like, and when used of people signifies that they have been consecrated in some way to the service of God. Further, "the logical subject of sanctifying is God alone and not man. . . . God's name is as little hallowed by man as His kingdom comes or His will is done. . . . When God's deity is revealed to man in the mystery of worship (cf. Is. 6:3), then God is sanctified to him" (*ibid.*).

39. Unless with Turner we take ἐλθάτω to mean "*continue to come* . . . (the Kingdom being present already as a grain of seed)" (M, III, p. 75).

40. Cf. Calvin, "So the sum of this supplication is that God will illuminate the heart by the light of His Word, bring our hearts to obey His righteousness by the breathing of His Spirit, and restore to order at His will, all that is lying waste upon the face of the earth."

that way. We see something of the cost of praying this prayer by reflecting on the way Jesus used it (Luke 22:42). In heaven God's will is perfectly done now, for there is nothing in heaven to hinder it, and the prayer looks for a similar state of affairs here on earth.[41]

11. Until now the petitions have concerned the great causes of God and his kingdom; at this point Jesus' attention moves to the personal needs of the worshiper. It is interesting that immediately following the prayer for the perfect establishment of the kingdom of heaven and the accomplishment of the will of God we have a prayer for *bread*[42] here and now. This was so incredible to many in the early church that they spiritualized the expression and understood it of Holy Communion or "the invisible bread of the Word of God" (Augustine, p. 42; he finds other meanings as well). In modern times we often find scholars claiming that the expression refers to the messianic banquet in the coming age. Both miss the point that Jesus takes seriously our physical needs. The word translated *daily*[43] is difficult, but a survey of the evidence indicates that the ancient understanding "daily" fits the facts as well as any; "for the coming day" has essentially the same meaning. The prayer prayed in the morning seeks bread for the day opening out before the praying person, while prayed at night it seeks bread for the coming day. Both ways of taking the word see it as looking to God for the supply of one's immediate needs, not those of the indefinite future. Jesus says that we should do no more than ask

---

41. Bonnard holds that the aorist γενηθήτω more naturally refers to a decisive action; the reference will then be to the final decisive act. But France points out that "To view these three petitions as purely eschatological is to defuse one of the most demanding prayers disciples can be called on to offer, with far-reaching consequences for the daily conduct of our lives"; but he also adds, "to view them as purely ethical is to ignore the 'blessed hope' which is the mainspring of New Testament discipleship." Both thoughts are surely there.

42. ἄρτος is a Gospel word, being found 21 times in Matthew and Mark, 15 times in Luke, and 24 times in John, a total of 81 times out of its 97 New Testament occurrences. It may denote bread in the literal and specific sense or it may be used (as here) for food generally. It may also be used figuratively — for example, "the living bread" (John 6:51).

43. ἐπιούσιος, an extremely rare word found again in the New Testament only in Luke 11:3, and with no undisputed example of its use in early documents outside these two passages (B. M. Metzger examines the evidence that it occurs in two secular documents and shows that there is no good reason for holding that the word occurs in either, *ET*, LXIX [1957-58], pp. 52-54). Origen may well be right in saying that the word was "coined by the evangelists" (BAGD). The meaning is thus sought from its derivation, and a number of possibilities have been suggested. (1) ἐπί + οὐσία, "necessary for existence"; cf. *GNB*, "the food we need"; Patte, "essential"; so W. Foerster, *TDNT*, II, p. 599. Against this view MM objects that in the papyri οὐσία generally means "property." (2) ἐπὶ τὴν οὖσα, sc. ἡμέραν, "for this day," "today"; cf. *NRSV*, "daily" ("conceptually and grammatically the most plausible explanation," BDF, 123[1]). (3) ἡ ἐπιοῦσα, sc. ἡμέρα, "for the following day"; cf. Moffatt, "for the morrow" (Howard accepts this view, M, II, pp. 313-14). (4) Deriving from ἐπιέναι, which may yield "bread for the future," "bread that comes to it, i.e., that belongs to it," "next," or "bread of the coming kingdom" (BAGD). MM considers it probable that the word is connected with ἐπιέναι and that it denotes "the *immediately* following day." Chrysostom asks, "What is *daily bread*?" and answers, "That for one day." He also says that this prayer is "so that we may not, beyond this, wear ourselves out with the care of the following day."

for food sufficient for the day on the day. *Give*⁴⁴ recognizes that our basic food is not the result of our unaided endeavor; it is the gift of God, while today is important as pointing to a day-by-day reliance on God. The prayer encourages a continuing dependence on God; it does not countenance a situation in which the disciple asks God for a supply for a lengthy period, after which prayer he can go on for some time in forgetfulness of God. He depends on God constantly, and this dependence is expressed in this prayer.

12. *Forgive* (see on 12:31) recognizes that sinning puts people in the wrong with God and that only he can cancel out the offense and pardon it. The offense is here seen as a *debt* (in Luke 11:4 we have "sins"), which recognizes that we owe to God our full obedience. When we do not pay it we are debtors to God, and only he can remit the debt.⁴⁵ The prayer for forgiveness is qualified by *as we also have forgiven our debtors*. This must surely be taken as an aspiration rather than a limitation, or none of us would be forgiven; our forgivenesses are so imperfect. But the prayer recognizes that we have no right to seek forgiveness for our own sins if we are withholding forgiveness from others, and perhaps even that we cannot really seek it (cf. Buttrick, if anyone says, "I'll never forgive you!" that person "is not penitently aware of his sins, but only vengefully aware of another man's sins"; Robinson remarks, "The spirit open to receive love is of necessity open to bestow love"). *We also* is emphatic; it underlines the significance of forgiving action on the part of those seeking forgiveness.⁴⁶ *Have forgiven*⁴⁷ expresses more than a resolution for future action. The person seeking forgiveness must first have taken forgiving action with respect to those who have sinned against him; "as 5:23-24 shows, mere good intentions are not enough" (Schweizer). We should notice that it is *debtors* that are forgiven, not "debts." Both, of course, are involved, but it is the person on whom the emphasis falls. *Debtor* may be used of literal, monetary debts (18:24), or it may be used metaphorically of various kinds of obligation, and of those who owe something to people (here) or to God (Luke 13:4). Sin may be viewed in any one of a variety of ways. Here it is

44. In Luke we have the present δίδου, "keep on giving" (with τὸ καθ᾽ ἡμέραν, "day by day"), where Matthew has the aorist δός, "give" (with σήμερον, "today").
45. M. Black points out that the word is the equivalent of an Aramaic term that may mean "debt" or "sin"; "'Sin' was conceived of in terms of a debt; we may compare the parable of the Unforgiving Debtor. Examples of the words in these senses are common" (Black, p. 102).
46. Jewish writings sometimes come close to this; Sirach 28:2-4, for example, puts it this way: "Forgive your neighbor the wrong he has done, and then your sins will be pardoned when you pray. Does a man harbor anger against another, and yet seek for healing from the Lord?"
47. Reading the aorist ἀφήκαμεν. Some MSS have the present, but most of Metzger's committee favored the aorist. Luke has καὶ γὰρ αὐτοὶ ἀφίομεν, which is a different way of emphasizing the subject; he goes on to use the continuous tense, "as we keep forgiving." After the verb Luke puts the emphasis on the offender rather than the offense, παντὶ ὀφείλοντι ἡμῖν, "everyone indebted to us."

147

seen as arising from the fact that we have obligations to God. When we fail to do what we should, we owe God a debt and are in need of help, namely the cancellation of the debt because we cannot repay it.

13. The big question here is the meaning of the word I have translated *temptation.* The word has the basic meaning "test," and, when used of Satan's testing of people with a view to their failing in the test (see the note on the corresponding verb, 4:1), it comes to mean "temptation." It has usually been understood in this way in this prayer (*KJV;* so *NIV,* etc.). But in recent years there has been an increasing tendency to interpret it as pointing to the fiery trial associated with the coming of the End, and it is taken that way in translations like "do not put us to the test" *(REB).* Against this is the absence of the definite article (there is no "the" in the Greek); the expression seems to point to testing in general rather than one specific test. In any case, no evidence seems to be cited that the word, by itself, signifies the test at the climax of all things. Others understand it as a time of trial rather than of temptation, "do not bring us to hard testing" *(GNB).* The eschatological meaning is unlikely, but a prayer that we may not undergo difficult tests is a possibility. On the whole the traditional view that the word means "temptation" seems most probable, though not, of course, in the sense that the worshiper may feel that God will present him with temptation (cf. Jas. 1:13).[48] God tempts no one. But the worshiper knows his own weakness and in this prayer seeks to be kept far from anything that may bring him to sin.[49] *But* is the strong adversative;[50] it sets the following course of action in marked contrast to the preceding. There is a question whether we should take the final expression in the verse in the sense "the evil one" *(NIV* and most recent translations) or "evil" (Knox): the Greek could mean either. It is argued that in the first century it is more likely that the evil one would be in mind than a general reference to evil, but the translation "evil" may be supported by appeal to 5:39 where the expression cannot mean "the evil one." It could also be contended that to take it as meaning "the evil one" would make the two parts of the verse say much the same thing and further that this would

---

48. Carson suggests that the petition may be an example of litotes (expressing a positive by negating the opposite; e.g., "not a few" means "many"). The meaning will then be "Lead us, *not* into temptation, but away from it, into righteousness . . ." (*SM,* p. 70).

49. C. F. D. Moule asks, "Is it, then, true humility not to intellectualize, not to be over-logical, but, realizing one's own weakness, to pray for escape even from what seems inevitable . . . while, at the same time, offering one's obedience: 'thy will be done'?" He goes on to suggest "that nearly all who pray the Lord's Prayer probably interpret it, often unconsciously, to mean 'Let us not succumb to temptation when we are tested'" (*RThR,* XXXIII [1974], p. 75). This may possibly be so, but there are certainly some who pray from a sense of their own weakness and simply express a firm desire not to undergo temptation. "We ask our Father . . . to keep us out of some situations because our faith could not endure them (example, Peter)" (Lenski). "Whoever prays the Lord's Prayer is not outstandingly pious, not a religious superstar; he does not ask God for opportunity to prove his faith, but asks not to be put to the test" (Schweizer).

50. ἀλλά. The words "but deliver us from evil" are absent from Luke.

mean there is "no express prayer for deliverance from moral evil" (Glover). Perhaps the decisive point is one made by Hill: "since neither Hebrew nor Aramaic uses 'the evil (one)' to denote Satan, it is probably better to regard the word as neuter. . . ." Either way of taking the expression makes good sense, but on the whole it seems that the reference is to "evil."

In the form in which the prayer is commonly used it concludes with the doxology "for thine is the kingdom, and the power, and the glory for ever and ever. Amen." This is lacking in the oldest MSS (in Luke as in Matthew), though it has considerable early attestation.[51] But it may be argued that it is unlikely that a first-century Jewish prayer should conclude without a doxology and that its absence in many MSS may be because it was simply assumed, while in others it was explicitly included. On the whole it seems probable that it was a liturgical addition made early in the life of the church, but we should not regard this as certain. The case for the doxology is stronger than many students assume.[52]

14. *For* introduces a reason for praying in the way Jesus has just outlined: first, those who forgive in the way suggested in the prayer will find forgiveness themselves, whereas those who do not forgive will not be forgiven. The conditional implies nothing as to the fulfilment or otherwise of the condition; it simply suggests a hypothetical possibility. *Men,* of course, is quite general and has no particular reference to adult members of the male sex; it means "people." *Offenses*[53] are activities in which other people really take action against us in some way; forgiveness of such sins is not automatic. But Jesus expects it of his people, and he assures them that such forgiveness means that the forgiveness of God is certain. It is not that the act of forgiving merits an eternal reward, but rather it is evidence that the grace of God is at work in the forgiving person and that that same grace will bring him forgiveness in due course.

15. *But* is the adversative conjunction that introduces the other side of the coin. The change that puts *offenses* in the second clause in this verse instead of in the first clause as in verse 14 is largely stylistic, but it perhaps emphasizes the activity of forgiving rather than the nature of the offenses. Forgiveness is important for the followers of Jesus, whereas the nature of the offenses committed against them is not. Jesus is saying that to fail to forgive others is to demonstrate that one has not felt the saving touch of God.

---

51. It is absent from ℵ B D etc., but it is found with variations in K L W Δ Θ etc., it has strong support in the versions, and it is attested in writings such as the *Didache* and the *Apostolic Constitutions.*

52. Davies has a useful discussion of the doxology (*SM,* pp. 451-53). J. Jeremias says, "according to contemporary analogies Jesus must have intended that the Our Father should conclude with a doxology, but would have left the user to fill it in for himself" (*Unknown Sayings of Jesus* [London, 1958], p. 28, n. 1).

53. In verse 12 our sins were called "debts"; now they are *offenses.* παράπτωμα ("a falling beside") is used of a false step, and thus a transgression. It is mostly used of offenses against God, but here of those against people.

c. Fasting, 6:16-18

16"*And whenever you fast, do not be like the hypocrites, putting on a gloomy look, for they disfigure their faces so that they may appear to men as fasting; truly I tell you, they have their reward. 17But you, when you fast, anoint your head and wash your face, 18so that you do not appear to men as fasting, but to your Father who is in secret; and your Father who sees in secret will recompense you.*"

This is another Matthean section without parallels. It fits in with the kind of teaching given earlier in the chapter where the demand is for complete sincerity in praying and giving. So is it with fasting. This is no concern of anyone except the fasting person and God. Anyone who fasts should take care to keep it that way; he should make no display of his fasting. Jesus and his disciples apparently fasted rarely, if at all (9:14-15, though cf. 4:2).

16. The one fast prescribed in the law was the Day of Atonement (Lev. 16:29-31; "afflict yourselves" is generally understood to include fasting). But other fasts came to be observed (Zech. 8:19; cf. Neh. 9:1; Ps. 35:13, etc.; private fasting was also practiced, Neh. 1:4; Dan. 9:3; for New Testament times cf. Luke 18:12). *Whenever*[54] indicates that people will fast, but leaves the times open. No particular significance is attached to fasting here, as though the fast were for a specific object; it is simply a normal religious, disciplinary activity, one of three pious practices held in special esteem among the Jews (with almsgiving and prayer). But Jesus says that whenever it takes place certain precautions should be observed, for fasting readily gives an opening for those who like to make a show of their piety (for *hypocrites* see on v. 2). Fasters could put on *a gloomy look*[55] to go with their physical discomfort, or they might *disfigure*[56] *their faces*. It is not quite certain what form the disfigurement took, but evidently some act of disfigurement was recognized as a common accompaniment of fasting so that these people not only fasted but appeared to fast;[57] they made it plain to those who saw them that they were engaged in a serious and onerous religious duty. They were more interested in appearing to fast than in the actual fasting itself. Such people, Jesus says, *have their reward* (i.e., they have received in full all the reward they are going to get; see on verses

---

54. ὅταν; see the note on verse 2. δέ is used "in lists of similar things, to bring about a clearer separation betw. the things listed" (BAGD, 1.c). For νηστεύω see on 4:2.

55. σκυθρωπός combines σκυθρός, "sullen," and ὤψ, "face"; clearly some who fasted were determined to let everyone know about it.

56. ἀφανίζω can mean "render invisible," which might point to any one of a number of ways of doing away with one's normal appearance. Those who think that this is meant literally hold that it means covering the head or using so much ashes or dirt that the person is unrecognizable. But that would defeat the hypocrite's purpose; he had to be known or his ostentatious show of humility would be wasted.

57. BAGD gives one use of φαίνω as, with the participle, "to denote the role that one plays before men" (2.c).

1-2). They aimed at making an impression rather than at religious excellence. They succeeded in their aim and should not expect any further recompense than the applause they had attained.

17. *But you*[58] puts the follower of Jesus in contrast; that way is not for the disciple. Jesus implies that those who follow him will fast from time to time, but he says nothing about frequency, occasion, or method. He is concerned only with the motive behind the fasting and indeed primarily with the requirement that fasting be done secretly, as a matter between the religious person and God. So the faster is told *anoint your head;* this points to a normal social custom of the day, but evidently those who fasted sometimes omitted the practice. So with washing the face.[59] It is pleasant to be clean, and evidently it was felt by some who fasted that they should forego this pleasure. And, of course, an untended face is very obvious.

18. The purpose of this *(so that)* is that those fasting should not make a display of their disciplinary activity, The hypocrites fasted in order to make an impression on others ("a sacred means is being corrupted by an unholy purpose," Gutzwiller); Jesus prescribes the exact opposite: his followers are not to appear to fast. Fasting is a matter between them and the Father. The thought of being "in secret" is repeated from verses 4 and 6, though with a slightly different vocabulary.[60] With fasting, as with almsgiving and prayer, it is important that the activity be done in secret. As with those activities the Father will *recompense* the person who fasts rightly (in the end justice will be done), but the emphasis is not on the recompense; it is on keeping one's religious activities religious and not making them a means of self-glorification.[61]

d. Possessions, 6:19-24

> [19]*"Do not lay up for yourselves treasures on the earth, where moth and rust destroy, and where thieves break in and steal;* [20]*but lay up for yourselves treasures in heaven, where neither moth nor rust destroys, and where thieves do not break in nor steal.* [21]*For where your treasure is, there your heart will be also.*
>
> [22]*"The light of the body is the eye. If therefore your eye is healthy, your whole body will be illuminated;* [23]*but if your eye is evil, your whole body*

---

58. σὺ δέ.

59. The rabbis forbade washing on the Day of Atonement (and other fasts?) unless one is soiled "with mud or excrement." They similarly forbade anointing (*Yoma* 77b). Washing and anointing were, however, permitted at some times of fasting (*Ta'an.* 1:4-5).

60. In the earlier passages we have κρυπτός, here κρυφαῖος (the only place in the New Testament where this word occurs). There appears to be no significant difference in meaning.

61. How easy it is for a wrong attitude to fasting to invade Christianity is to be seen in the *Didache* (which may be as early as the first century); it instructs believers: "Let not your fasts be with the hypocrites, for they fast on Mondays and Thursdays, but do you fast on Wednesdays and Fridays" (8:1).

*will be darkened. If therefore the light that is in you be darkness, how great
is the darkness!*

24"*No one can be a slave to two owners; for either he will hate the one
and love the other, or he will hold to the one and despise the other. You
cannot be a slave to God and to mammon.*"

Jesus demands that his followers be wholehearted; it is important
that they should not set their minds on anything earthly; he forbids what
Stott calls "the materialism which tethers our hearts to the earth" (Stott,
p. 155). Real treasure is in heaven; it does not consist in material things
of any sort. The eye and the slave are brought into service to emphasize
from different angles the importance of single-minded adherence to
God.[62]

19. Jesus draws attention to what people prize above all else. Some put
their emphasis on *treasures*[63] here and now to the exclusion of eternal values;
Jesus points out that that means putting all one's emphasis on what may
well be lost. He instructs his followers not to lay up their treasures on this
earth because treasures located here are liable to loss. He is not, of course,
saying that they must not go about their daily work with due care, or that
they must not run their businesses profitably. It is worldly-mindedness to
which he is objecting, the concentration on prosperity in this world to the
neglect of all else. Jesus is saying that his followers must have a right sense
of values and not see earthly success, however that be understood, as the
aim of all their labor (a temptation to which the rich are especially vulnerable, but which also may afflict the poor; it is the attitude to possessions that
is important, not their amount). Glover reminds us that "avarice is the vice
of respectability." Whether they are rich or poor, people see no harm in
concentrating on getting more. Everyone has some "treasure," the main
object in life. Jesus is asking whether that is to be the transient or the eternal,[64]
and he warns that earthly riches may disappear. Jesus specifies *moth and
rust*[65] as the destroying agents, where *moth* refers to what destroys cloth of

62. There is a partial parallel in Luke 12:33-34, but it is not easy to derive either saying
from the other and it looks as though Jesus gave similar teaching on more than one occasion.

63. Matthew has quite an interest in treasure; he has the noun θησαυρός 9 times out of
17 in the New Testament and the verb θησαυρίζω twice out of 8 (the only book to have it more
than once). The noun can denote a treasure box (2:11) or a storehouse (13:52), and it may be
used figuratively of the heart as the treasury where heavenly possessions are stored up
(12:35). Or it may refer to what is stored, treasure itself, either earthly or heavenly (19:21).
The imperative here may signify "Quit laying up treasures" (Chamberlain, p. 86).

64. Lloyd-Jones points to the insidious nature of treasure on earth by saying, "Many
a preacher has been ruined by his congregation." The congregation's praise leads him "almost
unconsciously to be controlled by the desire to have his people's good opinion and praise,
and the moment that happens a man is laying up treasures on earth" (II, p. 82).

65. σής is found in this passage and Luke 12:33 only in the New Testament. It denotes
a moth whose larvae will eat clothing. βρῶσις is a little more common (11 times, 2 in Matthew).
It means "eating" and can mean "what is eaten" ("food," as in John 6:27), but here it is "the
act of eating" that is meant, which may be the eating away of metals, corrosion or rust (cf.

any sort, especially fine clothing (which was valued as a form of wealth). *Rust* is more of a problem. It may mean the corrosion that attacks metallic objects or the "eating" that vermin of any kind may carry out; "worm" (*RSV* mg.) carries on the thought of destroying cloth). Another suggestion is the mice or other vermin that eat grain. The point is that material possessions appear substantial and lasting, but they are subject to decay in a variety of ways, and that means loss to the owner. It is foolish to regard them as lasting. The verb *destroy* is that rendered "disfigure" in verse 16; it means "render invisible," here by ruining the articles in question. And there is a further problem with earthly valuables, namely that they may be stolen. This is not accidental (as with the moth), but a deliberate action, for these thieves *break in and steal*.[66] There are hazards connected with earthly possessions; they may be lost in more ways than one.

20. By contrast,[67] there are riches that cannot be lost in such ways. Jesus speaks first of the place where they may be laid up, namely *in heaven*, and then points out that the various factors he has spoken of as doing away with earthly riches do not apply there. In heaven neither moth nor rust is at work, and there are no thieves to break in or steal. The treasures in heaven are described in language that exactly negates what is predicated of earthly treasures.

21. Jesus points out that the place we choose for our treasures tells something about ourselves. He does not describe *treasure* in any way, but clearly it means here that which one prizes most, that which one values above all else. The place where we choose to store up what we value most shows what our values are deep down. The *heart* may be used in any one of a variety of ways; BAGD uses it here "of the emotions, wishes, desires," but it is surely more. Jesus is not speaking of passing emotions but of that on which the life centers.[68] In the two previous verses "you" is plural, but in this one it is singular: the application is personal.

22. We find the little section on the eye difficult; we no longer speak of the "single"[69] or the "evil"[70] eye; therefore the meaning is not at all

---

Jas. 5:2-3; a different word is used), or the action of vermin of some kind eating crops, timber, or, indeed, any form of wealth.

66. κλέπτης means a thief "who steals in secret, by fraud and cunning," as against λῃστής, "a brigand who plunders, openly, with violence" (AS). διορύσσω has the idea of "dig through" and refers to digging through the mud brick wall of a building to get at what is inside.

67. The adversative δέ.

68. Plummer points out that the treasure and the heart "act and react upon one another; where our treasure is, there will our hearts be; and where our hearts are, there is our treasure" (p. 106). Robinson says of the miser, "Instead of lifting his heart to heaven, he has buried it with his savings."

69. ἁπλοῦς occurs in the New Testament again only in Luke 11:34 (and only once in LXX). It means "single, simple"; cognate words have the idea of generosity about them, which may mean that the word should be understood here in the sense "generous." Here it is opposed to πονηρός (cf. 20:15, "is your eye evil because I am good?").

70. In the Old Testament an evil eye points to a miserly person (e.g., Deut. 15:9; Prov.

obvious to us. But the eye is a useful illustration of spiritual possibilities. When the eye is functioning normally, the light it perceives means illumination of benefit to the whole body. All sorts of bodily functions may then be performed satisfactorily. There is a spiritual parallel. Jesus speaks of the eye as the *light*[71] of the body. The meaning appears to be that the eye is the organ that means light to the body; whether we are sighted or blind depends entirely on the eye. The eye is the source of light to the whole body. Apart from the eye the body would receive no light; thus the eye functions much as a lamp does. It is therefore important that the eye be *healthy*,[72] singly concentrating on its proper function. In that case the proper functioning of one small member means illumination for the whole body.

23. The contrary supposition is that the eye *is evil*, which presumably means that it is diseased or impaired in some way.[73] An eye that is not functioning properly does not bring to the body the benefit of light and, lacking a healthy eye, the whole body is envisaged as in darkness. Nothing can compensate for the lack of light at the one point of entrance. *If therefore*[74] brings out the consequence of all this. Granted that the entrance of light is so important, then, there is disaster if the light within anyone is in fact darkness. Such a person may well think he has light, but to walk in darkness is to lack vision, to demonstrate that one has no light. Filson comments, "If man divides his interest and tries to focus on both God and possessions, he has no clear vision, and will live without clear orientation or direction. Life not focused on God's claim and command is lost in spiritual darkness."

23:6; 28:22; see *KJV* — modern translations generally paraphrase). Lightfoot says that among the Jews "a good eye" means "a bountiful mind" and "an evil eye" likewise "a covetous mind"; he cites the Mishnah, *Terumot* 4:3, which says of the offering made to the priests: "A good eye yieldeth one out of forty [i.e., the fortieth part]. . . . A middling eye, one out of fifty. . . . And an evil eye, one out of sixty."

71. λύχνος, which properly denotes a lamp. Turner points out that the predicate is usually anarthrous but the article "may be inserted if the predicate noun is supposed to be a unique or notable instance"; he cites this passage to illustrate his point: "*the eye* alone *is the light of the body*" (M, III, p. 183). Davies and Allison argue that in antiquity it was held that the eye contains a fire or light, not that it receives light. This would make sense in the present passage, but it raises the question why people could not see in the dark (which these commentators do not face).

72. ἐάν introduces a clause in which there is no implication as to the fulfilment or otherwise of the condition. ἁπλοῦς (see on v. 22) means "single," "simple," and thus as applied to the eye "sound" or "healthy."

73. πονηρός is used in Matthew twice as often as in any other New Testament book (26 times; next is Luke with 13). It is usually employed in the ethical sense, "evil," but it may be used in the physical sense with the meaning "in poor condition, sick" (BAGD, 1.a). *JB* has "diseased"; Hill thinks that it "probably denotes the eye that is 'focussed on evil' and draws a man into evil ways." As we saw in the previous verse, there may be the thought of "ungenerous," "miserly."

74. εἰ with the indicative assumes the fulfilment of the condition and tells us what follows in that case. οὖν introduces the result of the previous chain of reasoning.

The climax of this saying is concerned with the spiritual rather than the physical meaning of vision; *the light that is in you* is surely not the light that strikes the eye. We might call it the brightness of goodness within. Perhaps we should think of something like "the eye of the soul"; just as a healthy physical eye means illumination for the bodily functions, so a healthy eye of the soul means enlightened living. Jesus is talking about the enlightenment that comes to the person who lives close to God.[75] When that light is *darkness* there is disaster! Jesus is supposing that where there should be light in a person there is in fact darkness, a perversion at the very heart and center of the person's life, a complete lack of vision. When that happens, "the darkness — how great!"

24. The service of God must be wholehearted. This is the thrust of the teaching about light and darkness (it is to be one or the other, not both), and this is further brought out with the forthright statement that it is impossible to give one's first allegiance to both God and money. *No one*[76] can belong completely to two owners. It is true that the ancient world knew of slaves with a shared ownership (e.g., Acts 16:16),[77] but in this case the slave belonged completely to neither. Jesus is making the point that in the full sense of the term to be a slave meant to belong wholly. This is a relationship that cannot exist in duplicate: to belong wholly to one owner means that all other owners are ruled out. Where there is an attempt at shared ownership, Jesus goes on, there is failure. The slave in such a position will regard the two "owners" differently. Jesus speaks of no half measures; the slave will be linked to the two by hatred or love, by devotion[78] or contempt, and in each case the one attitude rules out the other. There can be no half measures.

The climax of this saying is that it is impossible to be simultaneously a slave of both God and *mammon*. *Cannot* is a strong term; it signifies a sheer impossibility. *Slave* is another strong term;[79] it points to complete devotion. It is possible to devote oneself wholly to the service of God and it is possible to devote oneself wholly to the service of money,[80] but it is

---

75. Cf. BAGD, "light that illuminates the spirit and soul of man, is gener. the element in which the redeemed person lives, rich in blessings without and within" (φῶς 3.a; they place the use here, however, under "the eye as an organ of light," 1.b.α). Philo says, "what the intellect is in the soul, this the eye is in the body" (*On the Creation*, 53).

76. This verse is almost word for word the same as Luke 16:13, but Luke has οἰκέτης after οὐδείς. A household slave is especially close to the master and cannot share this close servitude with slavery to anyone else.

77. K. H. Rengstorf points to the practice; one master might free the slave, who would then be half slave and half free (*TDNT*, II, p. 270). *Pesaḥim* 8:1 provides that a slave owned by two masters must not eat the Passover meal of both.

78. Chamberlain sees the meaning of ἀντέχομαι as "I hold myself over against another," "I hold to" (p. 134).

79. Matthew has the verbal form δουλεύειν, "serve as a slave."

80. The term is μαμωνᾶς, elsewhere in the New Testament only 3 times in Luke. It transliterates an Aramaic term whose derivation is uncertain but which probably comes from a root meaning "that in which one trusts" (F. Hauck, *TDNT*, IV, p. 388), and which comes to

not possible to devote oneself wholly to the service of both. The stark alternatives make it clear that the service of God is no part-time affair but something that calls for one's fullest devotion. Since money tends to draw people away from God, Jesus warns about it.[81] It is no sin to have money, but it is sin to serve ("be a slave to") money.

e. Anxiety and Trust, 6:25-34

25"*For this reason I say to you: 'Do not be anxious about your life, what you eat [or what you drink], nor for your body, what you put on. Is not the life more than food and the body than clothing?* 26*Look at the birds of the air, that they do not sow nor reap nor gather into barns, and yet your heavenly Father feeds them; are you not worth more than they are?* 27*And which of you by being anxious can add one cubit to his height?* 28*And why are you anxious about clothing? Consider the flowers of the field, how they grow; they do not work, nor do they spin;* 29*but I tell you, that not even Solomon in all his glory clothed himself like one of these.* 30*Now if God so clothes the grass of the field, which today is and tomorrow is thrown into the furnace, will he not much more clothe you, you people of little faith?* 31*Therefore do not be anxious, saying, "What shall we eat?" or "What shall we drink?" or "With what shall we clothe ourselves?"* 32*For the Gentiles seek all these things: for your heavenly Father knows that you need all these things.* 33*But seek first his kingdom and righteousness, and all these things will be given to you as well.* 34*Therefore do not be anxious about tomorrow, for tomorrow will be anxious about itself. Sufficient for the day is its own trouble.'*"

Jesus underlines the pointlessness of anxiety and the sound reasons for trusting the heavenly Father. There is more to life than food and clothing, so one's attention should not be concentrated on them but should be focused elsewhere. As we read his words we must remember that he lived in a society where shortage of food was much more common than in modern Western states (despite the problems in their slum areas). Even so he sees the Father as active throughout his creation, caring even for birds and flowers; there is accordingly no reason for those who call him

---

signify "wealth, property." It is used in *'Abot* 2:12, "Let the property of thy fellow be dear to thee as thine own." Black notes a number of its occurrences (Black, p. 102). Some translations read "money" (*REB, GNB, NIV,* etc.). Cf. Melinsky, "Certainly to be devoted to the increase of wealth . . . rules out that devotion to God which alone is the ground of human integrity or wholeness."

81. Cf. Calvin, "it is not impossible for men who are rich to serve God, but whoever hands himself over as a slave to riches must leave the service of God, since greed always engages us in bondage to the devil" (p. 219). Carson quotes from the diary of Matthew Henry (1662-1714) a prayer written after that pious man had been robbed: "Lord, I thank you that I have never been robbed before; that although they took my money, they spared my life; that although they took everything, it wasn't very much; that it was I who was robbed, not I who robbed" (Carson, *The Sermon on the Mount* [Grand Rapids, 1982], p. 81). This is the kind of attitude Jesus is urging his followers to take up.

"Father" to be anxious. God will surely meet all their real needs. Worry is pointless; trust is well based.[82]

25. *For this reason* connects this paragraph to the preceding; because it is impossible to be a slave to both God and mammon, we should not act as though possessions were the be-all and the end-all of life. The new thought is that people "can be unfaithful to God through care as well as through covetousness" (Bruce). We are to rely on God, not on our money-making abilities. *"Do not be anxious*[83] *about your life,"* Jesus says, and specifies food and clothing (and possibly drink[84]) as things about which people might worry. The *life*[85] seems to mean this earthly life, for it is life that may be sustained by nourishment. This is strengthened by the reference to the *body;* it is this physical life here and now of which Jesus is talking. And when he comes to the body he proceeds to its need for clothing. Food and drink and clothing are the basic necessities, and these things may well have been a cause of anxiety for many of his hearers, who would have come from the poorer classes. The question introduced by *Is not* looks for a positive answer.[86] Put this way, even the poorest must agree that, important as are food and clothing, they are not the most important things of all. There is more[87] to life than food;[88] there is more to the body than its clothing. This attitude removes people from preoccupation with their own worldly success; it discourages the wealthy and the comfortable from concentrating on their own success and the poor and uncomfortable from concentrating on their own misery. We belong together, whatever our worldly goods, and this encourages the idea of sharing.

26. The birds with their absence of care can teach people something about reliance on God. There is some disagreement about the meaning of

---

82. There is a parallel passage in Luke 12:22-32. The sense is the same as in this passage, though there are continuous minor variations. Matthew has 183 words, of which 106 are in Luke. The resemblances may be close (v. 29 is almost exactly the same as in Luke), or there may be considerable differences (as in v. 34). For the thought cf. Philippians 4:6; Hebrews 13:5; 1 Peter 5:7.

83. Matthew uses μεριμνάω 7 times, which is more than in any other book in the New Testament. It conveys the thought of anxious care, or worry, here used with the dative of that which occasions the worry. Six of Matthew's 7 uses of the verb occur in verses 25-34; there is strong emphasis on anxiety in this passage.

84. ἢ τί πίητε is read by B W f13 33 etc., but the words are not found in ℵ f1 892 some OL etc. They form a natural correlative to the preceding and may well have been added by scribes who wanted to complete the thought or to assimilate the passage to verse 31, but it is hard to suggest a reason for their omission if original (though, of course, it may have been accidental). Matthew has πίνω 15 times (a total exceeded only by Luke with 17), so it is a verb he may well have used.

85. It is generally agreed that ψυχή here means life as a whole, and not "soul" as it sometimes does.

86. οὐχί is used "to emphasize the expectation of an affirmative answer" (Chamberlain, p. 207).

87. The neuter πλεῖον in the predicate arises because the subject, ψυχή, refers to a whole class and not one individual life (cf. BDF, 131).

88. τροφή is a general term for food or nourishment.

Jesus' verb,[89] but clearly he was inviting his hearers to give attention to God's creatures.[90] *Birds* do not engage in agricultural processes like sowing crops or reaping them, but that does not mean that they starve. Nor, of course, does it mean that they are idle (is anything busier than a sparrow?); they search for their food. Jesus is not counseling his followers to be indolent. The processes of sowing and reaping are elementary for the careful farmer, as is the storing of the crop in *barns*. But although[91] birds have no part in any such process, they are fed. Jesus does not say that "*their*" *heavenly Father* feeds them, but *your* heavenly Father; the very Father in whom the anxious have ceased to trust provides[92] even for improvident birds. *You* is emphatic; the disciples stand in strong contrast with the birds, as having much greater worth. The question looks for a positive answer: of course they are worth more[93] than the birds. And since they so obviously excel the well-cared-for birds, why should they not trust the Father?

27. The folly of worry is tackled from another angle, as Jesus draws attention to the limitations of human achievement, even when anxiety is given full rein. We have the same verb for *being anxious* as in verse 25; there is still the thought of the worrying that comes so easily to the human race. But all the worrying in the world produces little in the way of achievement. There is uncertainty as to whether Jesus goes on to speak of time or of height. The word I have translated *height* can mean either "age" (as in John 9:21) or "height" (Luke 19:3). The *cubit* was originally the forearm, and from this it came to be a measure of length, the distance from the fingertip to the elbow. It is used rarely if at all as a measure of time (LSJ does not cite it as measuring time; they think it may be metaphorical in this passage); perhaps there is something of an analogy in the words of the Psalmist: "thou hast made my days a few handbreadths" (Ps. 39:5). We could translate: which of you "by taking thought can add one cubit

89. ἐμβλέπω (in the New Testament 11 times, twice in Matthew) is used in the sense "look at, fix the gaze on" but also in the sense "consider." The latter meaning suits the context here, but it is not unlikely that an open air preacher pointed to birds flying (*GNB* translates, "Look at the birds flying around").

90. It is not clear whether ὅτι is to be taken as meaning "for" (*KJV*) or "that" (*NASB*); either is possible, but most recent translations simply omit it. For the thought cf. R. Simeon b. Eleazar: "Hast thou ever seen a wild animal or a bird practising a craft? — yet they have their sustenance without care" (*Qidd.* 4:14).

91. καί here is used to emphasize "a fact as surprising or unexpected or noteworthy: *and yet, and in spite of that, nevertheless*" (BAGD, 1.2.g).

92. τρέφω means "provide with food (τροφή)" and is used of food for people or animals or even plants.

93. διαφέρω means literally "carry through"; it is used intransitively in the sense "differ." Where things differ one may well be better than the other, and the meaning "excel" is common (it is not unlike our use of "different"). Morgan comments, "The Lord's argument here is not that we are to cease our sowing and reaping and gathering, but that if He takes care of those who cannot do such things, much more will He take care of those who can" (p. 68).

unto his stature" (KJV) or "by being anxious can add one cubit to your span of life" (NRSV). These days we reason that few people are anxious to increase their height by the length of their forearm,[94] whereas many would like to increase their length of life. Most modern translations accordingly go along with NRSV. But we must beware of making Jesus reason along lines congenial to us, and it is not at all impossible that he was ridiculing worrying by putting a spectacular limit to its powers of increasing height.[95] Sometimes he used humorous exaggeration to make his point, as when he spoke of the difficulty a camel would have in getting through the eye of a needle (19:24). It is impossible to be absolutely sure which piece of imagery Jesus is using, but it is clear that he is putting a firm limit to what worrying can do. Worry is futile. Why engage in it?

28. Jesus turns attention to clothing; he asks why people worry about what they wear. While the question is perhaps not as urgent as that of food, it is serious enough; in all ages people have seen clothing as one of the basic necessities of life. This time Jesus tells people to learn[96] from the flowers.[97] He is probably thinking of wild flowers (flowers "of the field") rather than those which have had the benefit of human cultivation. Such flowers do not toil,[98] and specifically they do not spin. Beautiful as they are, they do not work; they produce no cloth of any sort to account for their "clothing."

29. *But I tell you* is a solemn introduction to the words that follow and indicates that they are important. Matthew speaks of Solomon five times, which is more than in any other New Testament book; here the point is that that king was proverbial for magnificence.[99] But not even that

94. Stott reminds us that "God does it to all of us between our childhood and adult life" (Stott, p. 163).

95. *NEB* has "who by anxious thought can add a foot to his height?"; in one way or another this view is found in the Vulgate, and in the translations of Knox and Phillips. McNeile supports this understanding of the text. It is perhaps significant that this is the way Chrysostom in antiquity took it.

96. καταμανθάνω, found here only in the New Testament, may refer to "a fully learnt lesson, and not the process of study," though it is also possible to see the meaning as "understand, take in this fact about" (M, I, pp. 117-18). Turner thinks that the aorist imperative is "a command now, once and for all, to look at the lilies . . ." (M, III, p. 76).

97. κρίνον clearly denotes a flower, but it is not clear which one. BAGD mentions the autumn crocus, the Turk's cap lily, the anemone, and the gladiolus, and in the end suggests that Jesus perhaps "had no definite flower in mind, but was thinking of all the wonderful blooms that adorn the fields of Galilee." Modern translations mostly retain the traditional "lilies" or go for the general term "flowers" (GNB, "wild flowers").

98. κοπιάω means "become weary" (11:28) and thus "work hard." Flowers perform no hard labor. It is possible that we should take "toil" as referring to work normally done by men in the fields and "spin" as referring to women's work. The birds do neither. A further possibility arises from the reading of ℵ: οὐ ξαίνουσιν οὐδὲ νήθουσιν οὐδὲ κοπιῶσιν. Peter Katz argued that there was a primitive corruption and that we should read οὐ ξαίνουσιν οὐδὲ νήθουσιν: "they do not card [i.e., wool] nor do they spin" (JTS, n.s. V [1954], pp. 207-9). But not many have been persuaded.

99. δόξα is used for "glory" of any sort; here the thought is of kingly splendor, and specifically the glorious clothing that the great king wore.

magnificence can compare to the way the flowers are clothed. *One* points to the basic unit; Solomon's clothes could not compare to that of even one of the flowers.

30. *If* casts no doubt on the proposition that follows: "if (as has been said)" is the force of it ("the truth of a general principle," *MT*, 243). The "clothing" of the flowers is not something they achieve of themselves; God provides them with clothing. This time the plants are not called "flowers" but *grass*, a term that mostly refers to ordinary green grass (which fits the addition *of the field* used once more at this point; it indicates that it is wild growth, not cultivated, of which Jesus is speaking). Whereas before he had spoken of the beauty of the wild flowers, now he speaks of no more than "grass"; for all their beauty, flowers do not rank high in the scale of living creatures. This is further brought out by the transitoriness of plant life; the "grass" is alive today and is thrown into the furnace[100] tomorrow. Some translations have "oven" (e.g., *KJV*), but if it be taken in this way the meaning will be that the plants serve as fuel for the fire around the oven, not for the oven itself (why else would plants be put into an oven?). Jesus is emphasizing the transitoriness and the small value of the plants. They soon pass away and then are of no more use than fuel for a fire. Since God does so much for the transitory plants, will he not *much more* look after the clothing of his servants? A final rebuke of those anxious about clothing is found in the word that greets them as *of little faith*.[101] Wherever this term occurs in the New Testament, it is always applied to the disciples. More might have been expected of them.

31. *Therefore* leads on to the logical consequence. Since God takes such care of the lower orders of creation, certain consequences follow for his people. Jesus is not saying that his followers may be as careless as the birds and the flowers, doing no work and simply looking to our Father to provide everything. It is a condition of our life here and now that we work for our daily bread. But there is all the difference in the world between doing this in anxiety and fear and doing it in trust in a loving Father. Jesus then utters a firm imperative, *do not be anxious*.[102] He goes on to pose three questions that might be asked, one concerning food, a second with respect to drink, and a third with regard to clothing. In each case

---

100. κλίβανος may be defined as "*covered earthen vessel*, wider at bottom than at top, wherein bread was baked by putting hot embers round it" (LSJ); others say that the fire was kindled in the oven and when it was heated the coals were scraped out. MM notes the use of the word for "furnace."

101. ὀλιγόπιστος is not attested in the classics or LXX, or indeed in any pre-Christian writing. It seems to have been coined by the early Christians. In the New Testament it occurs 4 times in Matthew and once in Luke (cf. 17:20).

102. The same verb was used in verse 25, but there in the present; here we have the aorist. If there is a difference, Jesus is now telling them not to begin to be anxious about anything, whereas in the earlier verse he spoke of the continuing attitude. In the corresponding passage Luke has μὴ ζητεῖτε (Luke 12:29); Matthew concentrates on the attitude, whereas Luke is concerned with the deed.

there is a deliberative subjunctive, giving expression to the kind of thing a worried person might ask, filled with concern about how his basic needs are to be supplied.

32. The first *for* locates the anxiety Jesus is deprecating where it belongs. The questions he has suggested are questions that the Gentiles, those outside the people of God, might well ask. Such people cannot claim to be members of the heavenly family, and it is not surprising, accordingly, that they should be anxious and ask questions like these. As they see it, they must seek[103] the supply of these necessities by their own efforts and out of their own resources. Anxiety is natural for them. But worry should not characterize God's children. The second *for* goes on to introduce the reason the disciples should not ask such questions. They have a *heavenly Father,* and that Father knows all[104] their needs. Since God knows them all, there is not the slightest reason for anxiety. Perhaps we should notice that it is *need* of which Jesus speaks. His followers may expect their needs to be met, but not necessarily their desires.

33. Disciples are to *seek*[105] as their first priority, not the things they would like to have or even the things they are sure they need, but God's *kingdom and righteousness. First* does not here mean "first in time" but "of first importance"; the kingdom is not one among many competing aims for the disciples, but that which comes first of all (cf. Bengel, "He who seeks that first, will soon seek that only"). For *kingdom* see on 3:2. Matthew mostly speaks of "the kingdom of heaven," though he sometimes has "the kingdom of God" (which some MSS read here; Davies and Allison accept this reading) or "his kingdom" or "the kingdom." It is generally agreed that here we should read "his kingdom and righteousness." Jesus is clearly saying that the disciple's first and best effort is to be directed toward God's kingdom, not any personal needs. The kingdom has both present and future significance, and we should seek to exclude neither from the present passage. Kingdom points to rule, and the expression is to be understood in terms of doing the will of God now as well as looking for the coming of his final kingdom. The important thing for the disciple is to be con-

---

103. ἐπιζητέω is sometimes said to be intensive, but J. Armitage Robinson comments on the preposition ἐπί in compounds: "It seems to fix the verb upon a definite object. . . . The preposition is not *intensive,* but *directive.* . . . It prepares us to expect the limitation of the verb to a particular object" (*St Paul's Epistle to the Ephesians* [London, 1907], p. 249).

104. The first *all* represents πᾶς, a word Matthew uses 128 times; Luke has it 152 times and Acts 170 times, but no other book exceeds Matthew's total. Clearly he is fond of the word. The second *all* is ἅπας (3 times in Matthew and 32 times in the whole New Testament). "The Att. distinction that πᾶς follows vowels and ἅπας consonants . . . cannot be applied consistently even to Lk . . . although ἅπας is found prevailingly after a consonant" (BDF, 275).

105. The verb ζητέω basically means "to look for" something, to try to find it. This usage is somewhat different; the meaning is "somewhat removed fr. the basic mng. of seeking — a. *try to obtain, desire to possess*" (BAGD, 2). JB has, "Set your hearts on his kingdom first." The present imperative conveys the idea "Keep seeking." Lloyd-Jones says that Jesus "is not telling His hearers how to make themselves Christian; but He is telling them how to behave because they are Christian" (II, p. 143).

stantly seeking to do the things that God wills, that is, to be submissive to the King. In this context seeking God's *righteousness* (not our righteousness)[106] will mean seeking that righteousness which God only can give (there is no thought that the believer by his own efforts can attain a righteousness that may fitly be called "God's"). This will include the "right standing" before God that comes about as the result of Christ's saving work and also the right conduct that befits the servant of God. But we should be on our guard against understanding the text in purely ethical terms: Jesus does not say "your righteousness," or "to be as righteous as you can," or anything of the sort. It is God's righteousness that disciples must seek. Then, Jesus says, *all these things* will be given you, where *these things* are the things the Gentiles worry about. They will come to the trusting disciple, so there is no need for anxiety. The word rendered *given* is more literally "added": the things in question will be added to what the disciple already has.

34. Another *therefore* carries on the argument in logical sequence. Since the preceding is true, it follows that there is no point in worrying about tomorrow (cf. Prov. 27:1). A number of commentators point out that something like the words of this verse is found in commonsense proverbs in antiquity. This may indeed be so, but what distinguishes this passage from similar ones is that Jesus is not teaching fatalism but trust in God. It is trust that is important. The aorist imperative does not imply anything about the present state and perhaps signifies that disciples should not start being anxious.[107] There is no need to be anxious even about tomorrow, let alone the days ahead. *Tomorrow will be anxious about itself* does not mean that, while we must not worry today, tomorrow we may do so. It is a forceful way of saying that worry must always be deferred. Tomorrow's worry is only in the sense "tomorrow never comes"; if worry is confined to tomorrow we are free, for it is always today. And Jesus finishes this part of his subject with the reminder that each day has sufficient *trouble*[108] to keep us occupied; there is no point in anticipating tomorrow's quota of trouble today. "Today's trouble is enough for today" *(NRSV).*[109] This, of course, is a counsel that defeats worry. We are rarely anxious for today; it

---

106. Cf. Bruner, "at this point Matthew and Paul agree. The righteousness we are taught to seek here is an alien righteousness, the Father's righteousness, and not first of all our own" (p. 269). Filson asks, "is righteousness used here, as in Second Isaiah, of the vindicating salvation by which God saves those who seek him?" Hendriksen sees both imputed and imparted righteousness.

107. Turner thinks that the meaning is "never be anxious" in contrast to "cease being anxious" in verse 25 (M, III, p. 76).

108. This is Matthew's one use of κακία (11 times in the New Testament). The word means "badness" and thus "wickedness"; it comes to mean "evil" or "trouble." The neuter ἀρκετόν is perhaps used because no one day is in mind; it is a general reference.

109. The rabbis could advise one not to fret about tomorrow, for "peradventure tomorrow he is no more: thus he shall be found grieving over a world that is not his" *(Sanh.* 100b).

is the future that bothers us. If we restrict our concern to today, we defeat anxiety. The plain statement that there is trouble each day, however, is important. A shallow thinker might gather from the previous words about trust that the believer will have a smooth path through life. That is not what Jesus is saying. All people have trouble, believers among them. But he is making it clear that there is all the difference in the world between facing the problems we will certainly meet with firm faith in our heavenly Father and facing them with anxiety.[110]

110. Barclay remarks, "There may be greater sins than worry, but very certainly there is no more disabling sin" (I, p. 264).

Matthew 7

7. Judging, 7:1-6

> [1]"Do not judge, in order that you be not judged; [2]for with what judgment you judge you will be judged, and with whatever measure you measure it will be measured to you. [3]And why do you look at the speck in your brother's eye and do not notice the plank in your own eye? [4]Or how will you say to your brother, 'Let me take the speck out of your eye,' while, look, there is the plank in your own eye? [5]Hypocrite! First take the speck out of your own eye and then you will see clearly to take the plank out of your brother's eye.
>
> [6]"Do not give what is holy to the dogs, and do not throw your pearls in front of pigs, lest they trample them with their feet and turn and tear you to pieces."

Jesus turns from a negative attitude in one's own affairs (worry) to a negative attitude in one's attitude to others (censoriousness). He points to a bad habit all too characteristic of the human race, and instructs his followers not to be hasty in making negative judgments on their fellows. It is a dangerous procedure because it invites a similar judgment in return. And it is a difficult procedure because our own faults make it hard for us to see precisely what is amiss in our fellows.[1] Jesus is not, of course, forbidding all judgments (cf. "judge righteous judgment," John 7:24, and the judgments required in this very chapter); he is warning against the hasty condemnations that are so easy to make, and so characteristic of the human race.[2]

1. *Do not judge* refers to the passing of harsh, adverse verdicts on the conduct of our fellows; it does not forbid the use of our best critical thinking (which may be done in a spirit of tolerance and helpfulness and which Jesus elsewhere commands as a help to others, 18:15; for that matter how can we avoid casting pearls before pigs [v. 6] without a process of discrimination?). "Don't judge" does not mean "don't think" (Stott remarks that the com-

---

1. Luke 6:37-42 is similar, but the the degree of resemblance varies.
2. Augustine comments that here "we are taught nothing else, but that in the case of those actions respecting which it is doubtful with what intention they are done, we are to put the better construction on them" (p. 154).

164

mand "is not a requirement to be blind, but rather a plea to be generous," p. 177). The verb is used not only generally of passing a verdict, but specifically of passing an adverse verdict, condemning, and it is this that Jesus is forbidding. The present imperative gives the sense "Don't make a practice of judging."[3] The habit is easy to form. But it is to be avoided, and Jesus points to the disastrous consequences that follow. It is possible to take *that*[4] *you be not judged* to point to the judgment others will pass on us; to be sharply critical of others is to invite others to be sharply critical of us. But what other people do is not to be our criterion, and in the end it does not matter greatly. What matters is the judgment of God; Jesus' words surely refer to the divine tribunal. To be quick to call others to account is to invite God to call us to account.[5] That judgment in some form is required of his followers is clear from the demand that they cast not what is holy to dogs (v. 6); what is forbidden is censoriousness, the readiness to find fault.[6]

2. *For*[7] introduces the reason. The word *judgment*, here only in Matthew, may be used with any one of a variety of meanings.[8] In this passage it denotes the standards people use in passing judgments on their fellows. There is the same double meaning as in verse 1. Those who so readily pass judgment on their peers will find that their peers pass similar judgment on them, and they face the further reality that they will be called to account by God for their harsh attitude to other people (cf. Chrysostom, "thou art making the judgment-seat dreadful to thyself, and the account strict," p. 158).[9] The lesson is reinforced by being repeated in other terms. The *measure*[10] means much the same as *judgment* earlier in the verse; it points

---

3. "The present tense of μὴ κρίνετε does not merely prohibit *habitual* judging, as though *occasional* judging meets no disapproval, but carries the force 'Stop judging' or 'Don't ever judge' " (Gundry). Contrast the aorist imperatives in verse 6.

4. ἵνα indicates purpose.

5. Cf. Lenski, "The punctiliar aorist κριθῆτε refers to God's final judgment; if the judgment of men were referred to, the durative present subjunctive would have been used." *GNB* paraphrases with "so that God will not judge you" to make this meaning clear.

6. "This verse does not forbid all judging of any kind, for moral distinctions drawn in the Sermon on the Mount require that decisive judgments be made" (Carson).

7. For γάρ see on 1:20.

8. κρίμα may mean a lawsuit, a decision, or a judicial judgment, especially a negative verdict. Strictly it points to the sentence of judgment as against κρίσις, the process of judging. κρίνω is used 6 times in this Gospel, not a large proportion of its 114 New Testament occurrences. ἐν is used of means or instrument in Greek generally, but its frequency in the New Testament is generally ascribed to LXX, reflecting a Hebrew construction. In this passage there is an abbreviated construction with a single use of the preposition instead of repeating it: ἐν ᾧ κρίματι κρίνετε = ἐν τῷ κρίματι ἐν ᾧ κρίνετε. The sentiment is found in the Old Testament (Ps. 18:25-26) and in Judaism, for example, "With what measure a man metes it shall be measured to him again" (*Soṭa* 1:7). Hillel said, "judge not thy fellow until thou art come to his place" (*'Abot* 2:5).

9. BDF sees the use of the passive as an attempt "to avoid the divine name" (130[1]). This may indeed be the reason, but a better reason seems to be that it is a double application of the words: people who rush into judging others find that they are the objects of other people's judgments now, though the emphasis is surely on that of God at the last day.

10. μέτρον means an instrument for measuring, of whatever kind. Thus it is used of

to the standard people use in passing their judgments on others. God does not act arbitrarily, but there is an appropriateness about his judgment. *NRSV* brings out the force of this saying very neatly: "the measure you give will be the measure you get." Cf. also Mark 4:24.

3. The facile passing of adverse judgments is attacked from another angle. This time Jesus asks *why* his hearers do this sort of thing; what is their reason? He speaks of a *speck in your brother's eye,* where some translators become more specific with "speck of sawdust" (*NEB, NIV*), or think of a "splinter" (*JB*). Jesus' word[11] is not specific, but can mean any small object; if it fits into the eye it is very small indeed. He pictures a person who fixes his gaze on something quite unimportant in someone else and who does not *notice*[12] what is much more significant in himself. The *plank*[13] was a considerable piece of timber and was used for a main beam in either the floor or the roof of a building. The meaning is not that in every case the person passing judgment is a worse sinner than the one he criticizes. It is rather that what he finds wrong in his brother is a very small matter compared with the sin God sees in him. The hyperbole effectively demolishes the position of the critic in a blaze of ridicule. *Your own*[14] is emphatic; it puts some emphasis on the contrast. Jesus is using a humorous method of bringing out the contrast between our excellence in picking up the faults of others and our myopia in discerning our own.

4. *Or* leads into another possibility, or rather impossibility, for it is scarcely possible for anyone, plank in eye, to pose the question that follows to someone whose eye is incommoded by only a speck.[15] *"How will you say,"* Jesus begins, introducing a question that contains an inbuilt improbability.[16] Luke has "How can you say. . . ?" in his equivalent. It is, of course, physically possible for the person to say these words, but the plank and the speck make it utterly impossible for the words to carry conviction. The polite request to be allowed to help[17] is shown to be ridiculous by the *plank*

---

capacity (Luke 6:38) or length (Rev. 21:15). It can also denote a quantity, the result of measuring.

11. κάρφος can denote a little piece of anything, especially of sticks or straw; it points to what is quite insignificant.

12. κατανοέω, here only in Matthew, means "notice, observe carefully" (BAGD).

13. δοκός is not frequent in the New Testament (3 times each in Matthew and Luke). LSJ gives its meaning as *"bearing-beam, main beam,* esp. in the roof or floor of a house"; it means no small piece of timber.

14. Matthew might have used σοῦ or σεαυτοῦ, but σός points up the contrast.

15. Jewish teachers could make much the same points. Thus R. Tarfon said: "if one says to him: Remove the mote from between your eyes, he would answer: Remove the beam from between your eyes!" ('*Arak.* 16b). This may, of course, be a rabbinic misuse of what Jesus said: when someone was told to deal with a mote he tended to retort with a reference to his critic's "beam."

16. πῶς is used "in questions denoting disapproval or rejection" to give meanings like "With what right?" "How dare you?" (BAGD, 1.c).

17. BDF notes the use of the subjunctive with ἄφες so that "an invitation is extended to another to *permit* the speaker to do something" (BDF, 364[1]).

that totally excludes any possibility of effective assistance, while *look* introduces something relevant to the situation that has not yet been taken into consideration. When it is, it becomes apparent that such an offer of help is completely ridiculous. While the passage rebukes hypocrisy, we should not overlook the implication that one brother will certainly try to help another.

5. For *hypocrite* see on 6:2 (*AB* has "casuist," but this is not the meaning of the word).[18] The word is singularly appropriate here where someone with a large fault is pictured as offering to help another whose disability is the most minor that could be imagined. Jesus is drawing attention to a curious feature of the human race in which a profound ignorance of oneself is so often combined with an arrogant presumption of knowledge about others, especially about their faults. *First* gets the priorities right; that which matters most is to deal with the plank. The would-be helper's first priority must be to remove the obstacle to clear-sightedness from his own eye. That done, he is equipped to bring aid to his *brother*. We should not overlook the point that the speck is to be removed (Jesus does not say that because it is only a speck it does not matter); it is not unimportant that even this small defect be rectified.[19] But this cannot be done until the plank is taken out of the way; only then is the would-be helper qualified. *See clearly*[20] points to the importance of unimpaired vision for the person whose concern is to remove specks. This humorous treatment of a serious subject is not unlike those referring to the camel going through the eye of a needle (19:24), or being swallowed (23:24). Jesus made effective use of humor in his teaching.

6. This little section is peculiar to Matthew. It is perhaps put here as the opposite extreme to what has occupied us in the preceding verses: there Jesus dealt with the error of being too harsh in judging those who ought not to be judged, here with that of being too lax in giving what is holy to dogs. It may well be the adaptation of a proverbial saying that stresses the value of holy things and warns against profaning them. *Do not give* is a firm command; this is not a tentative suggestion.[21] *What is holy* is not defined with any exactness. It may refer to meat from a sacrificial offering (that is the "holy thing" in which dogs might be thought to be interested). The fundamental idea in "holy" is that of being set apart for the service of God, and the saying brings out the truth that that is a solemn process. What is so set apart must be used only for the holy purpose that led to its being set apart. Dogs were regarded as unclean animals; therefore they must not be made the recipients of holy things.[22] The "holy things"

18. "He is a hypocrite because his unkind criticism takes the outward form of a kindly act" (McNeile).

19. J. D. M. Derrett sees Jesus as meaning "that a brother *should* rebuke a brother. Only he should remember before whom he himself stands" (*NTS*, 34 [1988], p. 276).

20. There is a change from βλέπω (v. 3) to διαβλέπω here.

21. "*On no account* give . . ." (Turner, *Grammatical Insights*, p. 32).

22. Some scholars point out that "holy things" make an imperfect parallel to "pearls"

may be the reproofs of verses 1-4; care should be taken in the way they are used. But we should keep in mind that for the followers of Jesus there is nothing more holy than the gospel. This message is to be offered to all (cf. 28:18-20), but there is a limit to the time that is to be given to its obstinate rejecters.[23] Disciples are not to be judgmental, but that does not mean that they are to lack discernment. They must recognize the realities of life. Cf. Davies and Allison: "The gospel of the kingdom — in 13.45-6 the kingdom is a pearl — was to be preached to all; but its heralds were also instructed to shake the dust off their feet when they were not received into a house or town (10.14)." We must bear in mind that some hear the gospel[24] only to rebel. Disciples are not called on to keep offering it to those who continue to reject it with vicious contempt.[25] Jesus taught all sorts of people generously, but before Herod he refused to say a word (Luke 23:9). Paul preached to the Jews in Corinth for a time, but in face of persistent rejection and hostility he turned away (Acts 18:5-7; cf. 1 Cor. 2:14-15; Tit. 3:10-11).[26]

With this is linked the command not to throw *pearls*[27] to *pigs*.[28] Again there is the thought of incongruity, of the impossibility of the objects being understood for what they were and of having them treated accordingly. Things of value and beauty will not only not be appreciated by pigs, but will be abused. What is precious is not to be given to people who have no appreciation of it. In a Christian context the *pearls* are apt to be pearls of wisdom, apt pieces of teaching. So far from appreciating pearls, pigs

---

and hold that we have here a mistranslation of an Aramaic word meaning "ring"; a gold ring would effectively stand over against "pearls." Black discusses the suggestion and points out that an attractive saying might be reconstructed: "Give not a (precious) ring to dogs, and cast not your pearls before swine." But he thinks that that may be an interpretation rather than a mistranslation (Black, pp. 146-48). There seems to be no real reason for amending the text.

23. Cf. Hendriksen, "Staying on and on in the company of those who ridicule the Christian religion is not fair to other fields that are waiting to be served, especially in view of the fact that the harvest is plentiful but the laborers are few."

24. Calvin, "Here He means by dogs and swine, those so infected with an impious scorn for God that they admit of no healing" (p. 228).

25. Cf. Bruner, "insensitive evangelism often proves harmful not only to the obdurate whose heart is hardened by the undifferentiating evangelist, but harmful also to the gospel that is force-fed" (p. 275).

26. Quite early the church interpreted the saying in connection with its own liturgical observances: "Let none eat or drink of your Eucharist except those who have been baptised in the Lord's Name. For concerning this also did the Lord say, 'Give not that which is holy to the dogs'" (*Did.* 9:5).

27. μαργαρίτης (3 times in Matthew; 5 times in Revelation; once in 1 Timothy) means the precious stone we call a pearl. The word was used sometimes to denote anything of great worth. An interesting use is for the utterances of a great person: "The mouth that uttered pearls . . ." (*Qidd.* 39b).

28. χοῖρος occurs 4 times each in Matthew, Mark, and Luke and nowhere else in the New Testament. It means a young pig and then is used of pigs generally. These animals were, of course, unclean for the Jews, though here the emphasis is not on that, but on their inability to appreciate the value of pearls.

may well[29] trample them under foot.[30] It is possible that the pigs also *turn* on those who give them the pearls and *tear* them *to pieces,* for a large and unrestrained pig can do considerable damage. But it is perhaps more likely that we should understand the construction as chiastic: the pigs do the trampling and the dogs the tearing to pieces (for the combination of dogs and pigs see also 2 Pet. 2:22).

8. Prayer, 7:7-11

> [7]*"Ask and it will be given to you, seek and you will find, knock and it will be opened to you. [8]For everyone who asks receives, and he who seeks finds, and to him who knocks it will be opened. [9]Or which man is there among you whom his son will ask for bread, and he will give him a stone? [10]Or if he asks for a fish, will he give him a snake? [11]If therefore you, being evil, know how to give good gifts to your children, how much more will your Father who is in heaven give good things to those who ask him!"*

Jesus has set a high standard before his followers in the preceding section; how are they to reach it? Prayer is an important part of the answer, and Jesus goes on to teach significant lessons about praying. Even sinful people know how to do good to their children; how much more, then, may they expect the heavenly Father to do good to his children![31] This is not Jesus' complete teaching on prayer; for that we must remember the importance of forgiving as we pray for forgiveness, of asking in faith, asking in accordance with the will of God (cf. 6:12; 21:21-22; 26:39), and more. Here he is simply making emphatically the central point, that prayer to a loving Father is effective. The point is not that human persistence wins out in the end, but that the heavenly Father who loves his children will certainly answer their prayer.

7. *Ask* is quite general, but the context makes it clear that Jesus is referring to prayer. The general expression shows that no particular kind of prayer is in mind; Jesus is concerned with praying as such and telling his hearers that prayer is efficacious: *it will be given. Seek* is an interesting word in this connection. It can scarcely mean that the praying person does not know where to find what he is looking for; if that were so he would not be praying. The fact that he is asking the Father shows that he knows that what he seeks is within the gift of God. Perhaps the meaning is that

---

29. μήποτε is used to indicate purpose. It generally takes the aorist subjunctive, but sometimes the future indicative, as here. Matthew has it 8 times and Luke 7 out of its 25 New Testament occurrences.

30. ἐν is used here of "means or instrument"; we say "trample with the feet."

31. The Lukan parallel is in Luke 11:9-13. Apart from Luke's "and I say to you," verses 7-8 are identical and there is a close resemblance to verse 11, but there are differences in verses 9-10 where, in place of the son asking for bread, then fish, in Luke he asks for fish, then an egg.

the praying person does not know exactly what he should be praying for, but he knows that the Father will not lead him astray. There is also the thought of prayer with a greater intensity than would be implied when the person is doing no more than asking.[32] And as he seeks the good gift from God, he is to know that he *will find*. For a second time we notice that the answer to prayer is certain. So is it with the third way of looking at praying: *knock*. It is not said at what the praying person should knock, but the imagery is that of a closed door that he cannot open (*NIV* brings this out by inserting "the door" before "will be opened").[33] All who serve God know what it is to be faced with "doors" that are fast closed, and it means a lot that prayer will result in the opening of such doors. The three expressions underline the effectiveness of prayer. Look at it which way you will, it gets things done. All three imperatives are present, underlining the importance of continuous action.[34]

8. *For*[35] introduces a reason. In the heavenly court *everyone who asks receives*, and so with seeking and knocking. God's grace and God's love justify disciples in regarding prayer as a valuable weapon in their fighting the good fight. This verse takes up the injunction of the previous verse almost word for word (there is a change from "it will be given" to *receives*, but otherwise the same verbs are used). The repetition emphasizes the certainty that prayer will achieve the effect that is sought. Carson cites some significant words from Broadus: "One may be a truly industrious man, and yet poor in temporal things; but one cannot be a truly praying man, and yet poor in spiritual things." Prayer is infinitely enriching.

9. *Or*[36] makes more or less the same point in another way. Instead of saying simply what God will do in answer to prayer, Jesus asks a question from a situation in human life. He envisages a son asking his father for *bread* and inquires whether the father will in such a case give his child *a stone*. Jesus is reasoning from the less to the greater: if even an

---

32. Hendriksen holds that seeking means "asking plus acting"; the praying person "must be active in endeavouring to obtain the fulfilment of his needs."

33. Zahn sees the knocking as seeking entrance into the kingdom, and Patte has a somewhat similar idea: "the good things which will be given by God in answer to prayers are themselves certainly related to entrance into the kingdom." But Jesus' saying is more general than that; he is talking about prayer in general. Another way of looking at knocking is found in the Talmud, where we read that Mordecai "knocked at the gates of mercy and they were opened to him" (*Meg.* 12b).

34. Calvin comments, "There is nothing that we do not allow ourselves to ask from God, and if He does not fulfil our stupid ideas, we grumble at Him. So Christ subjects our prayers to the will of God" (p. 231).

35. On γάρ BAGD remarks, "the general is confirmed by the specific" and here "the specific by the general" (1.d). It is not easy to see verse 7 as more specific than verse 8, but there is certainly the note of confirmation.

36. ἤ may be "used w. an interrog. word, mostly after another interrog. sentence" (BAGD, 1.d.δ). The preceding expression is, of course, a statement, not a question, but there is no difficulty in seeing ἤ as helping on an interrogation.

earthly[37] father will give good gifts to his children and not bad ones, how much more will the heavenly Father do so! The question looks for a negative answer:[38] no one would do such a wicked thing. *Stone* is opposed to bread in the temptation narrative as well as here. Perhaps the thought is that the small loaves in common use resembled stones in appearance.

10. *Or* carries on the questioning, simply substituting *a fish* and *a snake* for the bread and the stone of the previous verse. France holds that "a snake might be taken for a fish, particularly the eel-like catfish of Galilee," while Mounce sees in the *snake* "some eel-like fish without scales that, according to Lev. 11:12, was not to be eaten." We cannot be sure which is correct, but clearly there was something that resembled fish but was not and that mocked hunger rather than satisfied it. Again the question looks for a negative answer. The repetition hammers home the point that even in this sinful race there is no tendency to give those we love and who depend on us some unsatisfying or harmful thing when we are asked for something to satisfy a real need.[39]

11. The conditional of the first class assumes the correctness of the supposition, and *therefore* gives a reason for posing it. We should not overlook the way *being*[40] *evil* is slipped into the argument. Jesus brings forward no evidence, but assumes this as so basic that it can be taken for granted, even when he is referring to a good action. As throughout the New Testament, the solidarity of the race in sin is taken as a basic fact: "An illustrious testimony to the doctrine of original sin" (Bengel).[41] There is some emphasis on *you*. This does two things: it differentiates the hearers from Jesus and it conveys the meaning: you, members of a race that is sinful, you know about giving good gifts. For *good* see on 5:45; it here denotes something like "beneficial." Having made the point about earthly parents and their children, Jesus uses a *how much more* construction to bring out the certainty that the heavenly Father (see on 5:45) will give *good things* to those who pray. He lays down no conditions, such as prayer in faith or in accordance with the will of God. Such things are made clear elsewhere and can be assumed. He concentrates on the wonderful truth that the Father gives to those who *ask him*.

---

37. *Man* is not necessary for the sense; "who among you" would have been quite sufficient. But this word puts some emphasis on humanity: if even a member of this human race will act kindly, then — .

38. It is introduced by μή.

39. Turner points out that the anacolouthon here is Semitic (M, III, p. 325).

40. The participle is used with an adjective or a noun sometimes in the sense of an "if" clause, sometimes as "although"; here, of course, it is the latter.

41. Cf. G. Harder, "In contrast to God, who alone is good (Mk. 10:18), men generally are called πονηροί (Mt. 7:11; Lk. 11:13)" (*TDNT*, VI, p. 554). Schweizer finds this "extremely sobering in the face of the widespread romantic belief that man is innately good." Bonnard notes and rejects C. H. Dodd's view that Jesus is talking about something in the heart of people that naturally responds to Christ's teaching.

9. The Golden Rule, 7:12

12 "Therefore all things whatever that you wish that men should do to you, you also do so to them; for this is the law and the prophets."

12. The golden rule is found in some form or other in a variety of religions, mostly in the negative: "Do not do to others what you would not like them to do to you."[42] Jesus, however, enunciates the rule in a positive form, and he appears to have been the first to do so;[43] his followers are to be active in doing good to others.[44] It is a most important rule for disciples. *Therefore* probably refers to the whole of the preceding sermon, not simply to the immediately foregoing.[45] In the light of the whole way of life that Jesus is inculcating this is the rule that his people must obey. At the same time it is very apt in this place; the example of the Father in his goodness in answering prayer is a magnificent incentive to his people to do good to others. *All things whatever* is comprehensive: nothing is excluded from the scope of this rule. The word rendered *wish*[46] is "the popular word" in Hellenistic Greek for "to wish, want" (BDF, 101). *Do* is a general term, but here it obviously has the meaning "do to one's advantage." That is what the disciple should be doing to others. *You* is emphatic; others may not follow this rule, but there is no escaping it for disciples.[47] Jesus rounds this off by saying that to act like this *is the law and the prophets.* This is the customary expression for the whole Old Testament. To say that this rule *is* the law and the prophets means that the rule sums up Old Testament teaching as a whole. Elsewhere Jesus says that the law and the

42. For example, "What you hate, do not do to any one" (Tob. 4:15). The great Hillel, when invited to teach a certain heathen the whole Torah while he stood on one leg, replied: "What is hateful to you, do not do to your neighbour: that is the whole Torah, while the rest is the commentary thereof" (*Shab.* 31a). Many examples may be cited from Judaism, and indeed some are to be found in most religions.

43. Davies and Allison think that "There is much room for doubt about this." But although they cite the rule in many forms, from a variety of sources, they do not cite any example of the positive form prior to Jesus.

44. It is often urged that it matters little whether the golden rule be cited in its positive or negative forms, but this is not so. If we did nothing at all, we would satisfy the negative form! In the great judgment scene in chapter 25 those who are condemned might well claim that they had fulfilled the golden rule in its negative form. Their condemnation lay in the fact that they had failed to do good, not in any evil action that they had carried through. Cf. Bruce: "The negative confines us to the region of *justice;* the positive takes us into the region of *generosity* or *grace,* and so embraces both law *and* prophets."

45. Davies and Allison remark that verse 12 brings "to a climax the entire central core of the sermon on the mount, 5.17–7.11."

46. θέλω. The ἵνα that follows is not telic, but introduces the content of the wish.

47. Ryle speaks of the value of this rule as a daily guide: "It settles a hundred difficult points, which in a world like this are continually arising between man and man; it prevents the necessity of laying down endless little rules for our conduct in specific cases, it sweeps the whole debateable ground with one mighty principle." So also Barclay, "It will be a principle which will dominate his life at home, in the factory, in the bus, in the office, in the street, in the train, at his games, everywhere" (p. 281).

prophets "hang" on the two commandments to love God and one's neighbor (22:40), which is another way of saying the same thing. Both ways of putting it totally exclude selfishness and stress a proper attitude of love and care for others. The person who consistently lives according to the golden rule is keeping all the regulations in Scripture directing one's conduct toward other people.

10. True and False Discipleship, 7:13-27

13"Enter through the narrow gate; for broad is the gate and spacious the road that leads to destruction, and there are many who go in through it. 14How narrow is the gate and constricted is the road that leads to life, and there are few who find it!

15"Beware of the false prophets, who come to you dressed up as sheep, but inwardly they are ravenous wolves. 16From their fruits you will know them. Do people gather grapes from thornbushes or figs from thistles? 17Likewise every sound tree bears good fruit, but the worthless tree bears bad fruit. 18A sound tree cannot bear bad fruit, neither can a worthless tree bear good fruit. 19Every tree that does not bear good fruit is cut down and thrown into a fire. 20So then, from their fruits you will know them.

21"Not every one who says to me, 'Lord, Lord' will enter the kingdom of heaven, but he who does the will of my Father who is in heaven. 22In that day many will say to me, 'Lord, Lord, did we not prophesy in your name, and in your name cast out demons, and in your name perform many mighty works?' 23And then I will say to them plainly, 'I never knew you; go away from me, you who work lawlessness.'

24"Everyone therefore who hears these words of mine and does them will be likened to a wise man, who built his house on rock. 25And the rain came down, and the rivers rose, and the winds blew, and beat against that house, but it did not fall because it had been founded on rock. 26And everyone who hears these words of mine and does not do them will be likened to a foolish man, who built his house on sand. 27And the rain came down, and the rivers rose, and the winds blew, and struck that house, and it fell with a great crash."

The concluding section of the sermon is taken up with impressing on the hearers the difference between real and merely nominal discipleship.[48] In four short paragraphs (vv. 13-14, 15-20, 21-23, and 24-27) Jesus calls for wholehearted commitment to himself and denounces spurious discipleship. He speaks about two ways that lie before people, about the

---

48. "Jesus began his sermon with unqualified tenderness, embracing in the Blessings those who felt least embraceable. He concludes with unqualified toughness, warning us that his sermon is not an intellectual option, a set of suggestions we may take or leave, one philosophy among several others, but that it is the exclusive way to life" (Bruner, p. 282).

importance of living fruitful lives, and about deeds that back up one's words. He concludes with the little parable of the two men who built their houses, one on rock and one on sand, and the fate of such buildings when the time of testing came.[49]

13. Jesus makes it clear that there are two ways in life, and two ways only, that are set before all people; it is thus important that the right choice be made. The section on the two ways is not included in the other Gospels, but it can be found in the ancient Scripture (Deut. 30:19; Ps. 1:6; Jer. 21:8) and in Jewish writings (e.g., 2 Esdr. 7:6-13).[50] It made quite an appeal to the early church, and there are references in early Christian literature (e.g., *Did.* 1:1; *Ep. Barn.* 18:1). Jesus begins with a firm command, *enter*, though at this point he does not say what *gate*[51] is in mind. He says only that it is *narrow;*[52] not until the climax of this saying do we find that it is the way into life. A narrow gate must be sought out: it is not as easily perceived as is a *broad* one. *For* is a causal conjunction; the implication is that something of an effort must be made to enter the narrow gate, for there is another that is much more easily perceived. By contrast, there is a gate that is *broad*[53] and a *road* that is *spacious* (NRSV has "the way is easy," but this is misleading; Jesus is not speaking about ease of passage but commodiousness, a road on which many may be found). Jesus is picturing a scene where the broad road leading to a splendid gate is obvious and easy to be seen, whereas the path that brings the traveler to the unpretentious gate is inconspicuous and is perceived only by those who look for it carefully. But the commodious road *leads to destruction,*[54] a fact that its

49. Luke has parallels to much of this section, but they are spread out and vary in closeness of resemblance; see Luke 6:43-46, 47-49; 13:23-24, 25-27; 4:32.

50. Davies and Allison cite many passages from Judaism and a number from Christian writings. They show that the idea is also found in writings outside Judaism and Christianity, but that the imagery of the gate is much less common.

51. πύλη may be used of a gate or door of many kinds. Thus it is the gate of the temple (Acts 3:10), of a city (Luke 7:12), or of a prison (Acts 12:10). It is also used of the gates of Hades (16:18). It seems to be used of a significant entrance, which may be why it is used here of the entrance into life.

52. στενός is found in this passage and in Luke 13:24 only in the New Testament; there, too, it refers to a narrow entrance into life.

53. πλατύς occurs in this passage only in the New Testament. Some MSS omit *gate* here (notably ℵ* 1646, some OL, and a number of the Fathers) and in the following verse; if they are followed, the word is used of the road ("broad and spacious is the road . . ."). But we should probably read *gate* in both places. Cf. Metzger: "On the whole it seemed best to follow the reading of the overwhelming weight of the external evidence, and to account for the absence of the word in one or both verses as a deliberate excision made by copyists who failed to understand that the picture is that of a roadway leading to a gate." εὐρύχωρος, "spacious," is found here only in the New Testament. "Go in" (enter) is more applicable to a gate than a road, but the meaning is plain enough.

54. ἀπώλεια occurs 18 times in the New Testament, but apart from 5 occurrences in 2 Peter, there are no more than 2 in any one writing (Matthew, Philippians, and Revelation). It may denote the destruction that one brings about (26:8), or the destruction that one experiences, "ruin"; in this sense the New Testament writers mostly use it of eternal loss, as here.

popularity does nothing to alter. But that popularity means that many go through this gate.

14. *How*[55] *narrow* brings us back to the right gate and exclaims at its small dimensions. In contrast to the wide gate this one is narrow; in contrast to the spacious road this road is *constricted*.[56] But though narrow and superficially less attractive than the broad highway, this road *leads to life*. *Life* often refers to life in the physical sense, this earthly, natural life. But in this context it clearly refers to the fuller and more satisfying life, the life that Christ alone brings about, eternal life. We must not press *few* too hard, for elsewhere Jesus can speak of "many" that are saved (8:11; 20:28). In none of these places is he giving an exact estimate of the numbers of saved and lost; in all he is emphasizing God's will to save and the importance of responding to his call. No matter how many are to be seen going along the broad road, it is important to choose the narrow one. That the road that leads to life is narrow explains why so many fail to find it. The thought is that the narrow road is far from an obvious way to go; it must be "found" (cf. vv. 7-8). No one drifts into the narrow way by chance.

Jesus does not explain whether the gate is entered at the beginning or end of the path. Some have held that the way is entered first; the believer proceeds along it until he comes to the gate at the end, through which he passes into the eschatological salvation (e.g., Tasker).[57] Others hold that the gate comes first; on this view we enter the gate right at the beginning (i.e., we commit ourselves to following Christ), after which we pursue the path before us (so Carson, Hendriksen). Another view is that the path and the way are practically the same (so W. Michaelis,[58] and Ridderbos, "The gate is in fact the road, and the road is the gate"). Bruner objects that this view "fails to do justice to the 'way' in the saying and to the (participial) continuing force of the other verbs in the sentences. Matthew's Jesus is appealing *both* for an evangelical decision (the gate) *and* for an ethical endurance (the way). Taken together, then, the narrow gate and the tough

55. Some MSS read "For," but it seems that *How* is the right reading (see the note in Metzger).

56. τεθλιμμένη. The verb occurs only here in Matthew (10 times in the New Testament). It conveys the basic idea of pressing (which can lead to the thought of affliction); here it is that of compression and thus narrowness. The perfect points to a continuing state. It is not the obvious opposite to "broad," and perhaps we should detect an allusion to the persecutions that are part and parcel of the Christian life. The cognate noun is used in conjunction with references to persecution in 13:21 (cf. also 24:9, 21, 29), and it occurs in Acts 14:22, "through many tribulations we must enter the kingdom of God."

57. J. Jeremias says, "the image of the gates has an eschatological character. The narrow and broad gates are the gates to eternal life and eternal perdition, and the sequence πύλη–ὁδός is to be regarded as a popular hysteron-proteron" (*TDNT*, VI, p. 923).

58. Michaelis detects "synonymous metaphors which are not to be interrelated but which stand side by side, supplementing and strengthening one another . . . way and gate are interchangeable in the saying" (*TDNT*, V, p. 71). Lenski understands the gate as "an entrance portal" and the way as "the passageway to which it admits. Both belong to a building and lead to the court from which the rooms are reached."

way are simply the difficult choice for Jesus *and* the constantly challenging decisions for discipleship to him" (pp. 282-83). It appears that in asking our questions we are trying to make Jesus more precise than he chose to be. We may profitably reflect that both the initial commitment to Christ and the subsequent journey of faith are important, and that we may see them both indicated here. But we can scarcely say more. Perhaps we should notice that the word for *road* is that used for the Christians in Acts, namely "the Way" (Acts 9:2, etc.).

15. Having made it clear that those on the narrow way are few in comparison to others who prefer the commodious path, Jesus moves on to speak of teachers who will help or hinder and to warn[59] about people who can be relied on to advocate the wrong way in some shape or form. A prophet was one who could speak directly from God, who could say, "Thus saith the Lord." In a day when it was widely accepted that prophets could speak authoritatively in this way, whether by way of foretelling the future or denouncing evil or commending the good, there must have been a strong temptation for some people to claim direct inspiration, whether they had it or not. *False prophets*[60] were thus people who claimed falsely to speak in the name of God. We have no way of knowing whether Jesus had any precise group in mind (and if so, which); nor can we know whether Matthew had any particular people in mind in recording the words. But the term is wide enough to cover any who[61] falsely claim to set forth the way of God, and the unhappy truth is that the people of God have never lacked false teachers whose emphasis is such as to lead them away from God. Jesus speaks of them as approaching the disciples (the false prophets do not have to be sought out) and presenting themselves as harmless. They appear "in clothing of sheep," which means that they appear as harmless as the most harmless of animals.[62] But the reality is different; they are *ravenous wolves,* animals with insatiable appetites. *Inwardly* differentiates their essential nature from their outward appearance. Jesus is speaking of religious teachers who put on a harmless front to deceive their followers but whose real interest is their own profit. Sheep

59. προσέχω has the idea of "turn (one's mind) to," and thus "give heed to." Used with ἀπό, it conveys the notion "be on one's guard against."

60. Matthew knows of Christian prophets (10:41; 23:34), and Jesus himself could be called a prophet (21:11). There are, of course, many references in the Pauline writings to Christian prophets. There was thus the continuing possibility that prophets might appear and the corresponding possibility that people might falsely claim that they had the prophetic gift. Matthew comes back to false prophets again in 24:11, 24 and in other New Testament writings. The test of whether a prophet is true or false is the way he lives (v. 16).

61. ὅστις (see on 2:6) may differ little from ὅς, but here it "is correctly used in connection with a substantive of indefinite reference" (BDF, 293[2]). It may well have the meaning "who are of such a quality as"; Jesus is drawing attention to the kind of people the false prophets are.

62. Hamann finds as sheep's clothing such things as "great success in gaining a following; a pleasant personality; sincerity; unselfishness, and generally a virtuous life."

they may appear to be, but their inward character indicates that they will always be wolves who try to further their own interests at the expense of those of the flock.

16. How can the followers of Jesus recognize such people? *From*[63] *their fruits;* their *fruits* will in the end betray them. The word "fruit" (like its Greek equivalent) refers in the first instance to the edible product of certain trees, but it is also used figuratively of a variety of produce. Here the thought is that it is not the outward appearance that is important (wolves may be dressed up to look like sheep), but the things the false prophets do, the produce of their manner of thought and life. If the disciples take note of what these false prophets do and refuse to be charmed by their false words, they will recognize them for what they are. We should probably understand their teaching also as part of their *fruits,* for their teaching proceeds from what they are and it is by our words that we will be condemned or justified on Judgment Day (12:37).[64] Jesus illustrates from plant life. He asks whether people get *grapes from thornbushes,* useful fruit from plants that are notable only for their thorns. So with *figs* and *thistles.* To people who lived closer to the soil than the denizens of huge modern cities the illustrations would come with powerful force.

17. From lowly bushes we move to trees, but the basic reasoning remains the same (*likewise* introduces a further but similar point). The argument now concerns the quality of the fruit rather than the kind, and it extends to the tree that bears it. Jesus contrasts the *sound*[65] tree with the *worthless*[66] one. The sound tree produces *good*[67] *fruit,* but not so the worthless one. The worthless tree bears only *bad*[68] *fruit;* the nature of the tree makes any other result impossible.

18. Jesus makes the point a little more strongly by indicating the impossibility of trees bearing fruit that is contrary to their nature. If the

63. ἀπό conveys here "the notion of source" (Robertson, p. 576).

64. Cf. Calvin, "I believe it is wrong when people confine this to our way of life. Often, some of the worst imposters put on a fake holiness. . . . all teaching is to be examined by the Word of God, and so in judging false prophets, the analogy of faith is to be dominant" (p. 238). So also Stott, "In examining a teacher's credentials, then, we have to examine both his character and his message" (p. 202).

65. For ἀγαθός see on 5:45. It means "good" in any one of a variety of ways, physical or moral. Here it denotes the tree that is as it should be, a "healthy" (*GNB*) tree. When the tree is sound, the fruit is good.

66. σαπρός is used of what is decayed and thus rotten, though we cannot think that the tree in question is actually decaying; if so, it would not bear fruit at all. O. Bauernfeind says that the word "contains a critical and adverse but not very precise judgment with a sinister overtone: 'unserviceable,' 'of little worth' " (*TDNT*, VII, p. 96). But it is in a far from healthy condition (diseased? Bauernfeind notes a use for disease in the human body), and this shows up in its inability to bear good fruit.

67. καλός (see on 3:10) is close in meaning to ἀγαθός, but perhaps conveys something of the notion of goodliness of appearance. We can speak of "beautiful fruit," and that is what the term denotes.

68. πονηρός is a general term for "evil" (see on 6:23); as applied to fruit it signifies "bad, worthless."

tree is perfectly healthy, it simply cannot bear the kind of fruit that is natural to the worthless tree. So with the worthless tree; it lacks the ability to bear good fruit (cf. Job 14:4). The point is fairly obvious, but it is important, and Jesus brings it out explicitly.

19. Jesus moves from the fruit of the rotten tree to its fate. In words reminiscent of those of John the Baptist (3:10) he reminds his hearers that people who run orchards do not put up with rotten trees. Such trees take up space, and besides cumbering the ground they may spread their corruption to perfectly sound trees. There is no reason for their continuing to exist and no reason why a competent orchardist should let them continue to grow. *Every* makes it universal; no bad tree is allowed to continue producing its bad fruit. Interestingly, Jesus does not speak of what the tree does, but of what it does not do: in the last resort it is not the tree that actively bears bad fruit that is condemned, but one that fails to produce good fruit.[69] Such a tree *is cut down,* and not only *cut down* but burned as well. *Thrown* may have some notion of violence about it; at the least it marks a decisive rejection. In the case of the orchardist the *fire* is literal; the burning of a worthless tree removes the possibility that it will infect other trees. But *fire* is often used of the fire of hell, and this meaning may be not far away. Jesus is making it clear that discipleship means a great deal more than religious activity.

20. This section of the argument is complete; *so then* brings us to the logical conclusion.[70] The rest of the verse simply repeats the opening part of verse 16. The fruit is the test of the tree; if there is no good fruit there is no good reason for the tree to exist. And the fruit is the test of one who claims to be a prophet. If there is no good fruit there is no good reason for the person to be treated as a prophet.

21. From the broad and narrow ways and from the bearing of good or bad fruit Jesus moves on to the consummation. Just as there are only two ways, so in the end there are only two destinations. This means also that he moves from the way his people can recognize false prophets to his condemnation of such people. When *the kingdom of heaven* (see on 3:2) comes in all its fulness, it will not be people's profession that counts, but their profession as shown in the way they live. *Not*[71] *every one* does not mean that none who use the expression will enter the kingdom: Jesus is not saying that it is a bad thing to say to him *"Lord, Lord,"* but that it is insufficient. He has just made emphatically the point that a person's deeds

---

69. μὴ ποιοῦν κτλ conveys a causal idea: "because it does not bear good fruit."

70. ἄρα, "inferential (illative) particle; in class. usage never at the beginning of its clause." When it occurs at the beginning of a sentence it means "so, as a result, consequently" (BAGD, 4). γέ simply strengthens the word to which it is attached. Moule says that its "exact force is difficult to define. Generally it appears to call attention and lend emphasis to the word or phrase to which it adheres" (*IBNTG,* p. 164).

71. οὐ is here used to negate the single expression that follows. It makes it clear that speaking is not enough.

show what the person is, and he is now saying that words are not the significant thing. It is easy for anyone to profess loyalty, but to practice it is quite another thing. *Says* stands in contrast to *does;* words are not enough. The word *Lord*[72] was used in a variety of ways. Originally it meant the owner of anything (cf. 20:8), but it could be used of important people generally. It thus became a conventional form of address in polite society, very much like our "Sir" (cf. 21:30). The Romans used it of their emperor (Acts 25:26), and the term was in common use of the gods people worshipped (1 Cor. 8:5). When the Old Testament was translated into Greek, *Lord* was employed consistently as the translation for the divine name Yahweh. It was the word the Christians found used of God in their Bible, and accordingly it was very significant when they came to call Jesus by this title. It is a title of majesty. In this Gospel it is used to refer to Jesus only once (21:3), apart from its use as a form of address (which shows that Matthew is not indiscriminately reading back into Jesus' lifetime the title that was so common in the church of his day).

Here, of course, *Lord* could be simply the polite form of address, but since it refers to what will happen on Judgment Day it more likely has overtones of divinity. On Judgment Day Jesus will be seen for what he really is, and the greeting here implies that the people in question will be claiming to belong to him. But their claim will be of no avail, Jesus says, unless their lives back it up. It is doing the will of the Father that matters,[73] not the words we profess. This is not salvation by works: the contrast is not between merit and grace, but between profession and way of life. If people really trust Christ for salvation, their lives will no longer be self-centered; that they belong to the good tree will be made manifest by the fruit they bear. The history of the church is replete with examples of ecclesiastics who made free use of expressions like *"Lord, Lord,"* but whose arrogant and self-centered lives made a mockery of their words. Jesus is not saying that those saved will have earned their salvation, but that the reality of their faith will be made clear by their fruitful lives. We should notice his use of *my Father,* the first use of this expression in this Gospel; Jesus often refers to the Father in such a way as to imply a close personal relationship (10:32-33; 12:50; 16:17; 18:10, 19). His relationship to the Father is not the same as that of others.

22. For the *many* who will rise up cf. 24:11. *That*[74] *day* is not described

72. Κύριος is used in Matthew 80 times. It occurs often in the New Testament (718 times), being noticeably frequent in Luke (103 times), Acts (107 times), and the Pauline writings (275 times).

73. There is a rabbinic saying, "Do his will as if it was thy will," but it is given a different thrust when it continues, "that he may do thy will as if it was his will" ('*Abot* 2:4). Less self-seeking are the words of R. Judah b. Tema, "Be strong as the leopard and swift as the eagle, fleet as the gazelle and brave as the lion to do the will of thy father which is in heaven" ('*Abot* 5:20).

74. ἐκεῖνος is used of Judgment Day a number of times (cf. Luke 6:23; 10:12; 2 Thess. 1:10; 2 Tim. 1:12, 18). The rabbis tended to use the expression of the messianic period or of the world to come (SBk, I, p. 468).

further, but clearly what is meant is Judgment Day, the day at the end of this world's life when all will give account of themselves to God. That the people will make their plea to Jesus shows that he will be their Judge at the critical time (cf. 2 Cor. 5:10). The doubled *Lord* is apparently a way of emphasizing lordship; the speakers insist that they regard Jesus as their Lord. They go on to speak of things done in the name of Jesus that they regard as significant. The question *"did we not prophesy?"* looks for an affirmative answer: there is not a doubt that they did this. The *name* (see on 6:9) stands for the whole person, and actions done *in* the name (which here clearly means something like "with the authority of the name") are listed accordingly as evidence of submission to the lordship of Jesus.[75] Since there is no preposition, the meaning may be "with" the name rather than "in" the name, in which case the claim is that they had the name as the weapon they could wield. These people had been active in the service of God; Morgan says, "they had done everything but the Lord's will," and this is the critical thing. To be active in religious affairs is no substitute for obeying God.

They claimed to have done a number of things. First they asked, *"did we not prophesy?"* The word signifies speaking in the name of God, which may be meant in the sense that they revealed what is hidden or that they foretold the future (their claim would be that they could not do this in the name of Jesus unless Jesus approved). Second, they said that they had *cast out demons*.[76] In secular Greek the word for "demon" could mean a deity. Or it might refer to an aspect of human personality, for example when Plato speaks of the "genius" of Socrates (*Euthyphro* 7.b). But in the New Testament demons were beings who occupied a position somewhere between people and God and were especially linked with Satan. In the Gospels their deeds are evil, and they sometimes bring striking physical limitations to people in whom they make their dwelling. Jesus expelled demons from sufferers on a number of occasions, and exorcisms are here regarded as meritorious works, done in the name and the spirit of Jesus. *Mighty works*[77] are miracles (the term is often used of Jesus' healing miracles), though there is no indication of precisely what form the miracles of the false teachers took. But to do any kind of miracle in Jesus' name is surely something that might be pleaded on Judgment Day? Certainly these teachers thought so. That there were *many* shows that such miracles were done in abundance. The group of three outstanding achievements is

---

75. σῷ puts some emphasis on *your*: "It has more weight than the gen. σοῦ or σεαυτοῦ; it serves to emphasize or to contrast" (BAGD). The triple repetition puts strong emphasis on the way they had appealed to the name of Jesus.

76. δαιμόνιον is a term especially prominent in the Synoptic Gospels (11 times in Matthew, 13 in Mark, 23 in Luke; 63 times in the New Testament).

77. δύναμις, which conveys the idea of power, is the usual word for a miracle in the Synoptic Gospels (John prefers to speak of "works" or "signs"). Matthew has the term 12 times.

pleaded as clear evidence that those who performed them were in good standing with Jesus (*name* is in an emphatic position in each clause).[78] But those who so plead have overlooked the fact that there can be "lying wonders" (2 Thess. 2:9).

23. *Then* (see on 2:7; this is the unclassical use "to introduce that which follows in time," BAGD, 2) leads us into Jesus' rejoinder. He will *say . . . plainly,*[79] which leads into his verdict of total rejection. *"I never knew you"* (cf. 25:12) does not, of course, mean that he was ignorant of their existence, but rather that he never acknowledged them; he never recognized them as what they claimed to be (Knox, "You were never friends of mine"). *You* is in contrast to the threefold "your" of the previous verse. The rest of his rebuke is given in the words of Psalm 6:8. *"Go away from me"* (cf. 25:41) means total rejection ("away from me," *JB*; "out of my sight, you and your wicked ways," *REB*, is more paraphrase than translation, but it brings out the force of the original). *You who work* renders a participle that conveys the meaning of habitual practice; they are not condemned for an occasional error but for consistent wrongdoing. *Lawlessness* is basically the rejection of the law of God. The word is often translated in terms of wrongdoing ("evildoers"), which is, of course, involved. But the term points to a refusal to submit to the law of God;[80] all the wrongdoing follows inevitably from this refusal. The words of these people may be good words, but their lives are lawless. On this passage Diétrich comments, "Verses 21-23 are a dreadful warning: the most orthodox avowals of faith have no value in the eyes of God if they are not translated into concrete obedience to his will. One may with his lips loudly profess his faith in God, and even invoke Jesus as Lord, yet deny him by thoughts, words, and acts."

24. The little parable about the one man building on rock and the other man whose foundation was sand emphasizes the importance of acting in accordance with Jesus' teaching.[81] It is one thing to hear what he said and even approve of it; it is quite another to obey. But it is only obedience that results in solid achievement. *Everyone* makes the application general: taken with the repetition of the word in verse 26 it rules out

---

78. Cf. Gutzwiller, "God who is holy can do holy things with instruments which are not. The ability to drive out demons says nothing about the inner holiness of the broom which God may make use of. Obedience is more important than miracles."

79. It is not easy to find an exact equivalent for ὁμολογέω (a word Matthew has 4 times). It has meanings like "confess" or "declare"; in this context it will be something like the latter; *REB* has "I will tell them to their face." The word is used of the judgment in 10:32; Revelation 3:5.

80. Of the use of this term in 23:28 Davies remarks, "ἀνομία refers not to any outward conduct but to an inner state, a condition of the will" (*SM*, p. 205). That will be so here also. Matthew has the noun 4 times and is the only one of the Evangelists to use it.

81. The passage is similar to Luke 6:47-49, but the similarity is more in the thought than the language. For example, Matthew has 22 words in verse 24 and Luke has 33 in the corresponding section. But only 8 are common.

181

any exceptions. All either respond to Jesus' words or do not; there is no other possibility. *Therefore* is inferential; what follows is an inference from what precedes. Jesus goes on to speak of the person who *hears* his[82] words, and not only hears them but *does them*. "Doing" words is a somewhat curious expression, but clearly it means that the person in view is not content with admiring some outstanding teaching; he makes it his guide and models his life on it. The expression underlines Jesus' earlier call for obedience. He is telling us now the result of obedience. The person who puts his teaching into practice is *likened* (i.e., "declared to be like")[83] to *a wise[84] man*. His wisdom is shown in the fact that he[85] *built his house* (see on 2:11) *on rock*, the most solid of foundations.

25. Any building must face some vicissitudes during its useful life; Jesus therefore proceeds to list a particularly testing time for this house. *Rain*[86] clearly denotes heavy rain, torrential rain, not ordinary gentle rain that would not put a building to a severe test. It was such rain that *the rivers rose*, where *rivers* "are to be understood as the *mountain torrents* or *winter torrents* which arise in ravines after a heavy rain and carry everything before them" (BAGD, 1). Certainly Jesus is speaking of testing torrents. Strong *winds* accompanied the rain, winds that *beat against* the house. The combination of rains, rivers, and winds represent the severest testing the weather can bring to a house. But it survived them all, owing to the excellence of its foundation. First, negatively, *it did not fall* (the verb may be used of structures, "fall to pieces, collapse," Acts 15:16);[87] then, positively, comes the reason, *it had been founded on rock* (the last expression is repeated from v. 24). The foundation is clearly critical. With the right foundation a building may well withstand the severest testing.

26. Attention moves to the foolish and careless hearer of Jesus' teaching. Most of the words are repeated from verse 24, but with the negative *not* inserted before *do them*, with *foolish* replacing "wise," and *sand* substituted for "rock." We should not understand a deliberate choice of sand,

---

82. Davies sees "mine" as emphatic: "Everyone then who hears me, in respect to these sayings" and explains: "In this sense, the ethical teaching is not detached from the life of him who uttered it, and with whom it is congruous. It is personalized in him" (*SM*, p. 94).

83. Some MSS have the active ὁμοιώσω αὐτόν. But the attestation of ὁμοιωθήσεται is superior, and the active may have arisen through scribes conforming this passage to that in Luke 6:47.

84. φρόνιμος (7 times in Matthew, out of 14 times in the New Testament) indicates the man characterized by φρήν, the midriff, which was understood as the center of thought. He is thus the thoughtful, intelligent person. It is wise not only to hear Jesus' teaching but to put it into practice.

85. ὅστις here is qualitative, "who is of such a character as to."

86. βροχή is "a late and rare word" (Allen); it is found twice only in LXX, while it occurs again in the New Testament only in verse 27. It is used of moistening of various kinds. LSJ notes its use for the inundation of the Nile and for irrigation as well as for rain (see also *LAE*, pp. 81-82).

87. There is a play on words with προσέπεσαν . . . οὐκ ἔπεσεν; it is something like "the winds *fell against* the house, and it *fell* not."

but a failure to take seriously the necessity for a solid foundation.[88] The man described is one who hears Jesus and perhaps enjoys the process, but who does not put into practice what he has heard. That man is *foolish* (see on 5:22); he is a stupid person who acts in a stupid way. This is seen in that he builds *on sand*. This last word is used 5 times in the New Testament, mostly of things too numerous to be counted. Here, however, the thought is that a sandy subsoil makes a very poor foundation on which to build a house.

27. The same process of testing that confronted the wise builder tests out the foolish builder; the language is repeated exactly until we come to *struck*,[89] which replaces "beat against." This word can mean a very hard blow indeed, but it is also used in the sense "stumble." Lenski sees this meaning here,[90] but the context seems to favor a hard blow and that, coupled with the action of rain and rivers, was too much for the house with the poor foundation. That house *fell* (it would not be too much to say "collapsed") *with a great crash*. The expression points to complete ruin. For a house built on sand there is in the end no other fate than complete destruction. So it is with anyone who hears Jesus' teaching without heeding it. It is teaching with a strong undertone of warning as well as with much to comfort and inspire. We neglect the warning at our peril.

11. Conclusion, 7:28-29

> [28]And it came to pass that when Jesus had ended these sayings, the multitudes were astonished at his teaching; [29]for he was teaching them as one having authority, and not as their scribes.

Matthew rounds off the section with a few words about the effect of Jesus' teaching. It is clear that many people were impressed not only by what Jesus said, but by the way he said it. His teaching was markedly different from anything to which they were accustomed.[91]

28. It is not easy to know what to do about the recurring expression, rendered in *KJV* with "and it came to pass."[92] Most modern translations

88. "In the natural sphere no man in his senses commits such a mistake. But utterly improbable cases have to be supposed in parables to illustrate human folly in religion" (Bruce).

89. προσκόπτω is an unusual word for the action of the wind. In Matthew's only other use of the verb it refers to striking the foot against a stone (4:6). LSJ gives the meaning as "*strike* one thing *against* another"; clearly it refers to vigorous action.

90. He finds it less vigorous than προσπίπτω in verse 25 and says: "the house on the rock withstood all the pounding of the winds and the waters while the house on the sand gave way as soon as the tempest stumbled against its foundation."

91. There are parallels in Mark 1:22; Luke 4:32. We should also notice John 7:46. Although there are no verbal coincidences there is the thought of the incomparableness of Jesus' teaching.

92. καὶ ἐγένετο. This is the Septuagint's rendering of a common Hebrew construction;

simply ignore it with this justification, that it is not the way we would normally express things. But it is not the way a first-century Greek writer would normally express things either; therefore I have tried to retain the flavor of the Matthean expression by using the traditional English way of rendering it. Here it introduces a formula that Matthew uses at the end of each of Jesus' major discourses (11:1; 13:53; 19:1; 26:1), as a way of transition into his next section. The formula draws attention to the discourses as significant; Matthew insists on the importance of Jesus as a Teacher. He tells us now that Jesus *had ended* his discourse[93] (the verb sometimes has the thought of "accomplish," and there is possibly a hint that Jesus had said all that he intended to say). The effect of what Jesus had said was continuing astonishment[94] among his hearers. The plural, *multitudes*, indicates that this was not the impression of a tiny minority but of large numbers of people. As we saw in 5:1, the sermon was addressed primarily to disciples, but there were others than disciples present. It is the reaction of these others that Matthew now relates. He does not give the impression that Jesus was simply another in a multitude of teachers, some slightly more acceptable than others. Jesus astonished people. There was no one like him. *Teaching* may mean the manner or the content of the instruction. There seems no reason here for restricting it to either. Jesus did not teach in the same way as other Jewish teachers, nor did he say the same kind of things.

29. Matthew explains.[95] *He was teaching*[96] (habitually) as someone who had *authority* ("with a note of authority," *REB*; "like an authority," Moffatt), and this clearly impressed the hearers, for it was not the way *their scribes* taught. It was the scribal habit to appeal to authority, for it was an age in which originality was not highly prized. It was widely accepted that there had been a golden age early in the history of the race and since then history had been all downhill. Those closer to the golden times might be expected to have the rights of it when any dispute arose. There was a widespread respect for age. Thus it was important to cite authorities if one wished to obtain a hearing. But Jesus ignored this scribal commonplace. Where others appealed to authorities, Jesus simply said, "I say unto you," a fact noted in all the Gospels (Mark 3:28; Luke 12:37; John

---

it is especially frequent in Luke. Matthew has it in 8:26; 9:10; 11:1; 13:53; 19:1; 26:1. He usually follows it with the aorist indicative. The construction is discussed in Robertson, pp. 1042-43; Moulton doubts whether it is rightly regarded as a Semitism (M, I, pp. 16-17).

93. The plural of λόγος is used of a discourse or a conversation.

94. ἐκπλήσσω means "strike out of one's senses"; it points to a great deal more than mild surprise. It may refer to astonishment (13:54) or shock (19:25). Perhaps there is something of both here, astonishment at the depth of the sermon and shock at what the judgment implies for the hearers. The imperfect points to continuous action: "they were more and more amazed, their astonishment went on and on" (Plummer, p. 120, n.).

95. γάρ introduces the reason for the foregoing.

96. The periphrastic ἦν διδάσκων puts some emphasis on the continuing nature of the activity.

6:47, etc.; there is a clear and strong note of authority). This should not be taken to mean that there were no new teachings among the rabbis. Of course there were, but they were not typical.[97] New teachings were typical of Jesus, and especially the teaching that made clear his messianic place (vv. 22-23, e.g., would be unthinkable among the rabbis).

97. There is an impressive chain of teaching in *'Abot* 1:1-12 in which we read that each successive rabbi "received the Law" from the preceding one. There was no novelty; the succession guaranteed that the teaching went back to Moses. Daube argues that new teaching might be given by an ordained rabbi, and that the novelty in Jesus' case was that he was not ordained (Daube, pp. 205-16). There may be something in this, but it does not dispose of the difference between the tone of Jesus' teaching and that of any Jewish authority known to us, scribal or rabbinic (compare the difference in tone between, say, the Sermon on the Mount and *'Abot* 1:1-12). Davies and Allison quote a rabbinic saying: Hillel "discoursed of the matter all the day, but they did not receive his teaching until he said, Thus I heard from Shemaiah and Abtalion." That is the authentic rabbinic note. But it is not the way Jesus taught.

Matthew 8

D. JESUS' MINISTRY OF HEALING, 8:1–9:34

In 4:23 Matthew gave a summary of Jesus' ministry as one of teaching, preaching, and healing (in 9:35 he will give a similar summary). Then in the Sermon on the Mount he gave his readers an outstanding example of the way Jesus taught. Now he turns his attention to the healings that were such an important and striking part of his ministry. Jesus displayed power as well as authority as he went about his earthly task. It is noteworthy that Matthew concentrates his accounts of Jesus' miracles into the early days of his mission. He records ten miraculous healings (and some general accounts of many healings) before Peter's great confession at Caesarea Philippi, and one afterward. He has four nature miracles in the earlier period and one in the later time. It seems that Matthew wants to tell us that, once the disciples came to understand that Jesus was indeed the Messiah, the Lord focused his attention on the necessity and the meaning of his suffering and death. Matthew here records ten miracles arranged in three groups, with sections on calling and discipleship in between. The miracles are the following: cleansing a leper, healing the centurion's servant, healing Peter's mother-in-law, stilling the storm, casting out demons from the Gadarene demoniacs, healing the paralyzed man, raising the daughter of Jairus, healing the woman with an issue of blood, giving sight to two blind men, and giving speech to a dumb man. Some scholars are reminded of the ten miraculous happenings at the time of the Exodus and take this as evidence that Matthew saw Jesus as a second Moses. But we should not overlook the fact that Matthew refers to more than the ten wonderful happenings that he singles out (v. 16), and further that he nowhere draws attention to the number ten. We should also bear in mind that ten was a popular number and that there could be any number of reasons for recording ten miracles. In addition, nothing in the narrative points to Moses. Further, these works of mercy are not really parallel to the plagues in Moses's day. It is better to think of Matthew as going on from Jesus' matchless teaching to his matchless power, power over disease and even the forces of nature.[1] Almost all

---

1. Davies remarks that this section (8:1–9:34) "expresses the infinite succour available in Christ in his deeds, just as v.1–vii.28 expresses his infinite demand" (*SM*, p. 90).

the incidents in this section of the Gospel have parallels in Mark or Luke, but not necessarily in the same order. It is clear that Matthew's arrangement here is topical, not chronological.

J. D. Kingsbury examines these chapters and divides them into four main sections dealing with Christology (8:1-17), discipleship (8:18-34), the separation of Jesus and his followers from Israel (9:1-17), and faith (9:18-34).[2] This may be a useful way of dividing the two chapters, but I am more convinced by his conclusion that "Paradigmatically, these chapters set forth for the members of Matthew's church the cost and commitment of discipleship and ways in which they are distinct from contemporary Israel (8:18-22, 23-27; 9:1-17). Paraenetically, they invite these Christians, as persons of faith, to approach the exalted Son of God, under whose lordship and in whose presence they live, and to offer to him their petitions for help in the sure knowledge that he desires to hear them and will employ his divine power to aid them in time of trial and need."[3]

1. Three Healings, 8:1-17

Matthew starts this section with miracles of healings for three people who would all have been considered unlikely from the Jewish point of view: a leper (and thus unclean), a Gentile, and a woman. They bring out something of the compassion and the wide sympathy of Jesus, as well as his power.

a. Cleansing a Leper, 8:1-4

> [1]When he came down from the mountain, great crowds were following him. [2]And look, a leper came to him and bowed low to him, saying, "Lord, if you are willing, you are able to make me clean." [3]And he stretched out his hand and touched him, saying, "I am willing. Be made clean." And immediately his leprosy was made clean. [4]And Jesus says to him, "See that you tell no one, but go show yourself to the priest and make the offering that Moses commanded for a testimony to them."

There is an account of this miracle in all three Synoptists (cf. Mark 1:40-45; Luke 5:12-16), with an interesting mixture of resemblances and differences. Thus there is nothing corresponding to verse 1 in Mark or Luke, Mark differs in his word for "came," and Luke has none. But the leper's words are identical in all three (except that Mark omits Lord). Clearly the story was widely used, and the Synoptists have all told it in their own way. Schweizer points out that when Matthew follows Mark he condenses miracle stories by about 55 percent, controversy stories by about 20 percent, and stories showing Jesus is the Christ by about 10 percent

2. *CBQ*, 40 (1978), pp. 559-73.
3. *Ibid.*, pp. 572-73.

(p. 210). Therefore we should not read too much into his omissions. He may omit not because he disagrees but because he consistently shortens Mark's narratives. Green remarks that in the first three healings there is a common feature: "they are all persons excluded from full participation in Israel's worship."

1. After Jesus had come down from the mountain (evidently the mountain he went up in 5:1), great crowds kept following him. Matthew does not say why, but we are probably meant to see this as the continuance of the state of affairs he described previously (cf. 4:25). In due course he will come to the opposition Jesus faced and his rejection by the Jewish leaders and others, but at this point he is describing happenings in the time of Jesus' great popularity. Matthew uses his "many crowds" expression (see on 4:25) to bring out the fact that Jesus had a large following at this time. *Following* may be used of adherence to Jesus, following him as a disciple, but in such a context as this it means no more than that the multitudes were accompanying him (see on 4:20).

2. For *look* see on 1:20; it is Matthew's favorite way of introducing a note of vividness into his narrative. It does not point to strict chronology and specifically does not mean that the leper came to him just as he came down from the mountain (Luke says that the incident happened "in one of the cities," Luke 5:12). Matthew's arrangement is topical: he is bringing together a number of healing stories and not necessarily saying that they all happened after the Sermon or in the order in which he relates them. It is not known for certain what *a leper* meant.[4] Nowadays "leprosy" denotes a specific ailment, Hansen's disease, but in ancient times, when diagnostic facilities were considerably more limited than those we take for granted, "leprosy" meant not only Hansen's disease but a number of other diseases as well (cf. *GNB*, "a dreaded skin-disease"). Some of them were curable, and thus a procedure was laid down so that when a cure took place the cured person would be inspected by a priest who certified the cure, after which the healed person was restored to the full life of the community. But leprosy as we know it was not curable, and the dreadful physical afflictions in the advanced state of the disease were such as to give the ancients horror at it all. Since no one knew how it could be cured and since its effects were so horrible, the only treatment was quarantine. Lepers were not allowed to live in towns or villages, but had to remain outside centers of habitation (Lev. 13:46). They were required to keep their distance from people, and if they happened to approach anyone they were required to call out "Unclean" (Lev. 13:45). Leprosy was not only a terrible disease, but it was defiling; anyone who had it was ceremonially unclean, cut off from the religious and social life of the community.

4. See the article on leprosy by R. K. Harrison in *NIDNTT*, II, pp. 463-66. Leprosy was so important that the Mishnah devotes a whole tractate to it (*Nega'im*, "Leprosy Signs"). See also the Excursus in SBk, IV.2, pp. 745-63.

On this occasion *a leper* approached Jesus, which must have been a fairly unusual procedure. This man came respectfully and *bowed low*[5] to him. It is uncertain what meaning we are to put into this action. Our problem is that it may be used of the worship of a deity or of a respectful approach to a man (*KJV* has "worshipped" and *NRSV*, "knelt"). If the man was recognizing Jesus as divine, then an act of worship is meant, whereas if his knowledge was more limited he is showing the respect due to a healer from whom he hoped to receive a cure. There is the same ambiguity about *"Lord"* (see on 7:21). He may mean this as a polite form of address to a man ("Sir"), or he may be using it as the right term for one who was more than a man; this ambiguity is often present, for Jesus is frequently addressed by this word in this Gospel by people who believe in him (e.g., v. 6; 15:22; 17:15; only once, however, is he explicitly called "the Lord," 21:3). Matthew does not tell us how the man had come to hear of Jesus, but plainly he knew enough to be impressed with his abilities to heal. He clearly had no doubts about Jesus' healing powers, but he was not so sure whether the Lord would want to heal a person like him. Who would be interested in helping a poor leper? He does not even make a request, but contents himself with the statement, *"if you are willing,[6] you are able to make me clean."* The request is implied both in the man's condition and in his confidence in Jesus' power to heal. He does not speak of being cured but of being cleansed, and this is normally the case. Leprosy was a terrible disease, but it was also a defiling disease. Those who had it were "unclean." Being freed from leprosy was different from being freed from, say, paralysis. It was spoken of in terms of cleansing, not simply of cure.[7]

3. Jesus could simply have spoken the healing words, but we should not miss the compassion implied in that *he stretched out his hand and touched him*.[8] Nobody would touch a leper, for such a touch brought uncleanness (and guilt! Lev. 5:3); people would also fear the possibility of contracting the disease. It must have been years since the man had experienced such contact with anyone who did not have the disease. Jesus' answer is but two words in the Greek (identical in all three Synoptists), but those two words say all that is necessary. The first clears up the matter of Jesus' will; it assures the leper of his willingness. The second removes the leprosy; it is a word of power, a command that the man be cleansed. The cure was instantaneous (*immediately*); the man *was made clean*.

4. Jesus moves on to the procedure that would be necessary to restore

---

5. For the verb προσκυνέω see on 2:2 and 4:9.

6. Cf. BDF, "If you wish (but in modesty I leave that open) . . ." (372[1]*a*).

7. καθαρίζω (7 times each in Matthew and Luke) may be used of physical uncleanness (23:25-26), but also "of the healing of diseases which make a person ceremonially unclean, esp. leprosy" (BAGD, 1.b).

8. Chrysostom asks why Jesus touched the man and answers, "that He might signify by this also, that He is not subject to the law, but is set over it; and that to the clean, henceforth, nothing is unclean" (p. 173).

the healed man to a place in society. *See*[9] is a verb used of ordinary sense perception with the eye, but it may also refer to taking care that something be done, "See to it that you — ." *Tell no one* is a firm prohibition of making the miracle known. This motif is found elsewhere (9:30; 12:16; 16:20; 17:9) and is, of course, well known in Mark. It is unlikely that this is a device the Evangelists have adopted to account for the fact that a greater number did not respond to Jesus during his ministry.[10] It is much more probable that Jesus did not wish people to misunderstand what he was about and to regard him simply as a wonder-worker or the kind of person who would be expected to lead a revolt against the Romans in due course. He thus urged people to keep quiet about the wonderful things he had done for them. Instead of such talk (*but*[11] is the strong adversative) the man must *go;* he should not gossip. The sense of urgency is brought out in some translations, "Don't stop to talk to anyone" *(LB);* "Listen! Don't tell anyone" *(GNB).* Mark tells us that in fact the healed man did not obey this injunction, but spread abroad the fact of his cure, with the result that Jesus could no longer show himself openly and his ministry was accordingly hindered. He is to show himself *to the priest* (Lev. 14:1-2); the article denotes the particular priest, the one who has the responsibility of certifying a cure.

The man is also to *make the offering that Moses commanded* (see Lev. 14:10, 21-22). The word for *offering* is used of gifts of various kinds, but here there can be no doubt that it is a sacrifice that is meant. This could be offered only in Jerusalem, so that the man had a journey before him. This may also be part of the reason Jesus urged him not to talk about what had happened but to go to the priest; there would be a strong temptation to put off the journey and perhaps never get around to it. Matthew is generally supposed to be the most Jewish of the Gospels, but it is interesting that he mentions Moses less than any of the other Evangelists (7 times; Mark has the name 8 times, Luke 10, and John 12). The sacrifice is to be offered *for a testimony to them,* but it is not clear to whom *them* refers. It might be the priests, or "the authorities," or people in general. There is also some doubt about the significance of the *testimony.* It will certainly be a public demonstration of the reality of the cure ("to certify the cure," *REB).* It will also demonstrate the power of Jesus to heal and thus be a witness to Jesus' messiahship. Albright and Mann (and others) find here a proof "of Jesus' allegiance to the Law" *(AB).* On any showing it means that the man would be known to be healed and would be able to resume his place in society without question.

---

9. ὁράω (13 times in Matthew); it is used of physical sight (28:10) and of spiritual perception (5:8), as well as in the sense of taking care to do something.

10. Tasker cites Sanday's verdict that this view is "wrongheaded" and considers it regrettable that some recent scholars have gone along with it.

11. ἀλλά.

b. The Centurion's Servant, 8:5-13

5*And when he came into Capernaum, a centurion approached him, beseeching him* 6*and saying, "Sir, my servant is lying at home paralyzed, suffering great pain."* 7*And he says to him, "Shall I come and heal him?"* 8*And the centurion answered, saying: "Sir, I am not worthy to have you come under my roof; but only say the word, and my servant will be healed.* 9*For I, too, am a man under authority, having soldiers under me, and I say to this man, 'Go,' and he goes, and to another, 'Come,' and he comes, and to my slave, 'Do this,' and he does it."* 10*And when Jesus heard this, he was astonished, and he said to those who were following, "Truly I tell you, with no one have I found such faith even in Israel.* 11*But I tell you that many will come from east and west and sit at table with Abraham and Isaac and Jacob in the kingdom of heaven,* 12*but the sons of the kingdom will be thrown out into the outer darkness; in that place there will be the wailing and the grinding of teeth."* 13*And Jesus said to the centurion, "Go; as you have believed, so be it to you." And his servant was healed at that hour.*

The story of the healing of the slave of the centurion is given at greater length in Luke 7:1-10 (there are also some linguistic parallels in Mark and John,[12] but they come from different stories). An important difference is that right at the beginning Matthew has the centurion meeting Jesus in person and urging Jesus not to come to his house, whereas in Luke he first sends the Jewish elders to make the request and later he sends friends to urge the Master not to come into his house. Some harmonize the two narratives by saying that the man first sent the elders and later went himself; others regard the two narratives as irreconcilable. But as I wrote in my commentary on Luke,

it is better to see Matthew as abbreviating the story and leaving out details inessential to his purpose. What a man does through agents he may be said to do himself. So Matthew simply gives the gist of the centurion's communication to Jesus, whereas Luke in greater detail gives the actual sequence of events. Perhaps we can discern something of the differing purposes of the two Evangelists in their treatment of the messengers. Matthew was concerned primarily with the centurion's faith and nationality; to him the messengers were irrelevant, even a distraction. But Luke was interested in the man's character and specifically in his humility; to him the messengers were a vital part of the story.[13]

---

12. In my commentary on John I have pointed out that there are several significant differences between the Johannine and the Synoptic stories and that they should be regarded as distinct (*The Gospel according to John* [Grand Rapids, 1971], p. 288).

13. *Luke*[2] (Leicester and Grand Rapids, 1988), p. 151.

5. Matthew moves the story to Capernaum (see on 4:13), the place that Jesus made the center of his ministry. There Jesus had contact with *a centurion* (the word occurs 4 times in Matthew, 3 times in Luke, 13 times in Acts, and nowhere else in the New Testament; a synonym is found 3 times in Mark). As the name indicates, the centurion was originally the officer in charge of a hundred soldiers, but in course of time the number varied. From Josephus we learn that there were officers above the centurion, namely the chiliarch and the hegemon (like the colonel and the general?), and the decurion below him (like the NCO?).[14] If we think of him as rather like our captain we will not be far out (Moffatt translates "army-captain"). F. D. Gealy says, "the centurions were the actual working officers, the backbone of the army. The discipline and efficiency of the legion as a fighting unit depended on them" (*IDB*, I, p. 548). This centurion would have been in the army of Herod Antipas; he may not have been a Roman, but he was certainly a Gentile (vv. 8, 10). Every centurion referred to in the New Testament appears to be a worthy man. This man came to Jesus *beseeching* him, which indicates a courteous approach. It may indicate more; Calvin remarks, "before Christ healed his servant, he himself had been healed by the Lord" (p. 247).

6. The centurion uses the polite address *"Sir"* (which in some contexts signifies "Lord"). The word I have translated *servant* means "boy," and it may be used for a young male, a son, a servant, and in other ways. Luke speaks of a slave, and that is probably the way we should understand it here. *Lying*[15] is more literally "thrown," but the word is used of throwing on a sickbed (cf. Rev. 2:22). In this case the lad was *paralyzed*.[16] Matthew uses two expressive terms to bring out the depths of the pain the boy was suffering.[17] Like the leper, the centurion makes no request: he simply states the facts.

7. Matthew says nothing about the Jewish elders and their commendation of the centurion (which Luke sets straight after the words about how ill the boy was). He moves straight from the soldier's request to Jesus' agreement to heal the sufferer (which is implied whether the words are a question or a statement). Most translations take Jesus' words as a statement, "I will come and heal him," and this may be correct. Either way it is clear that Jesus was willing to enter the home of a Gentile (which is

---

14. *War* 5.503. Barclay cites Polybius for the qualities sought in centurions: "They must not be so much venturesome seekers after danger, as men who can command, steady in action, and reliable; they ought not to be over-anxious to rush into the fight, but when hard pressed, they must be ready to hold their ground, and die at their posts." He adds, "The centurions were the finest men in the Roman army" (p. 306).

15. βέβληται; notice the absolute use — it is not necessary to refer to the bed.

16. παραλυτικός, a word used 5 times each in Matthew and Mark and not elsewhere in the New Testament. The word basically signifies "suffering from the relaxing of the nerves of one side" and thus "disabled, weak of limb" (*GT*). It was used widely of crippling diseases. Luke does not specify the nature of the illness, but he says the slave was near death.

17. δεινῶς (elsewhere in the New Testament only in Luke 11:53) means "terribly," "fearfully," while βασανίζω is used of torture, torment, and the like.

striking because the dwelling places of Gentiles were unclean, *Ohol.* 18:7, and thus to enter one would result in contracting uncleanness; cf. John 18:28; Acts 10:28). But if the words are taken as a statement, it is difficult to understand why Jesus uses the emphatic *I* (cf. *JB,* "I will come myself"). It is also difficult to understand why the centurion should have protested as he did in his reply. As McNeile puts it, if Jesus' words "are a direct statement assenting to the request that He would come, the humble answer, with its profound faith, is called forth by no apparent cause." Jesus probably puts the question as an act of courtesy. The centurion would know that Jews regarded Gentile dwellings as ceremonially unclean, and accordingly to ask a Jewish religious teacher to come into his home would put the teacher in a difficult position. If the teacher agreed, he would be open to harsh criticism from stricter Jews; if he did not, he could be accused of not caring about a sick person. Does the centurion want to place Jesus in this position? Jesus asks what he really has in mind.[18] Or is he thinking of something else? It is perhaps worth noticing that the only time Jesus is recorded as actually going to a sick person is the case of the daughter of Jairus. On all other occasions the sick are brought to him. He is never recorded as having entered a Gentile dwelling.

8. The centurion *answered,*[19] again using the polite form of address, then goes on humbly to disclaim worthiness to have Jesus enter his home. The word is used of sufficiency of various kinds, but here it is something like competency that is in mind; *worthy* gives us the sense of it. The centurion disclaims worthiness to have Jesus *come under my roof;*[20] he was not great enough to have Jesus as his guest. Besides, what Jesus is suggesting he considers unnecessary; anyone in authority can issue orders knowing that what he says will be done even though he himself is not present at the scene of operations. *But* is the strong adversative;[21] it introduces something very different from Jesus' suggestion. All that is needed is for Jesus to *say the word,* where the expression is something like "speak with a word" — the word is the instrument "with" which the servant will be healed. The centurion uses a different word for healing than Jesus used,[22] but there is probably no great difference in meaning. Until now

18. Turner understands the words as a question. They are an act of courtesy, taken so that Jesus would not place the officer in the awkward position of either causing him, a Jew, "to offend against the precepts of his own religion" or refusing to open his home to him (*Grammatical Insights,* p. 51). Allen, Carson, and Zahn also detect a question here; that it is a statement is the view of Bonnard, Ridderbos, and others.

19. If δέ were read (with ℵ* B 33 etc.), there would be something of a contrast: far from wanting Jesus to come, he wants something very different. But most MSS have καί.

20. *Roof* is στέγη, "a poetical subst. which has passed into general use in the Κοινή" (MM). BDF considers μου here an example of placing unemphatic words as close to the beginning of the sentence as possible (473[1]).

21. ἀλλά.

22. Jesus used the word θεραπεύω, and the centurion ἰάομαι. The former word carries the idea of service, whereas the latter denotes healing only. But in this context there is not much difference between them.

there has been no example of Jesus healing at a distance, so the centurion's faith was unusually strong.

9. The centurion shows that he is familiar with the concept of authority. His emphatic *I* places him over against Jesus: "Even *I* can secure action at a distance." He does not emphasize his exalted status but speaks of himself as *under* (rather than "in") *authority* (REB, "under orders"). All authority in the army was vested in the emperor, so that the centurion was subject to imperial authority. But when a centurion gave orders he was obeyed because he spoke with the authority of the emperor. This man's reply shows that he had an unusual understanding that Jesus spoke with the authority of God.[23] He would accordingly be obeyed. Though he speaks humbly, the officer shows that he is well aware of what authority means. He goes on to illustrate. He himself has *soldiers* who are subordinate to him, and he knows that when he gives a command it will be obeyed. He instances three commands that he gives: *"Go," "Come,"* and *"Do,"*[24] and in each case he says that the command is obeyed. There is probably no great significance in his moving from *soldiers* to his *slave;* in both cases the point is that the person receiving the order is a subordinate and the centurion knows that he will do what he is told.

10. Matthew records Jesus' astonishment, a very human trait.[25] Faith like this was not to be expected of a Gentile. Jesus did not reply to the centurion immediately, but spoke to the people who were following him (for *following* see on v. 1). *Truly* (see on 5:18) indicates that the saying that follows is important and should be heeded carefully. *With no one* comes first and is given some emphasis. *Such*[26] may be used of quantity or quality; perhaps there is something of both in this passage. *Faith* is one of the great Christian concepts, but it is found only 8 times in Matthew. It points to trust in Jesus and, in a context like this, in his ability and readiness to give help in unexpected ways. *Israel* is here the nation. In all Israel Jesus had seen no faith like that of the centurion (the distance of *in Israel* from *with no one* in the Greek justifies the insertion of *even;* cf. RSV, "not even in Israel"). It is not without its interest that in the whole story nothing is

---

23. "He recognized in Jesus an authentic authority which came to him from the highest source — from God himself" (Diétrich). ἐξουσία is an expressive term; it can signify "the power exercised by rulers or others in high position by virtue of their office" (BAGD, 4).

24. It is not clear why the first and third imperatives are aorist while between them stands a present (all the more so since the present imperative of ἔρχομαι is not common in the Synoptic Gospels). Moule says that "the tense appears to be determined more by the meaning of the verb or by some obscure habit than by the 'rules' of *Aktionsart*" (*IBNTG*, p. 135). Turner sees πορεύθητι as used correctly, "be off!" (M, III, p. 75).

25. Calvin remarks, "Though amazement is not appropriate for God, seeing it must arise from new and unexpected happenings, yet it could occur in Christ, inasmuch as He had taken on our human emotions, along with our flesh" (pp. 249-50). Jesus is twice recorded as being amazed, here at the faith of a Gentile and in Mark 6:6 at the unbelief of some Jews.

26. τοσοῦτος.

said about whether the sufferer had faith or not; it is the faith of the centurion that is brought out.[27]

11. *But*[28] contrasts Israel with the *many* who will come from a variety of places. We should not overlook Matthew's interest in the place of the Gentiles. *I tell you* is another solemn introduction; what follows is important and is not to be overlooked. *Many* is not specific but makes it clear that Jesus is speaking of a large number of people. For *east* see on 2:1; there it signifies a specific point of the compass, but here in conjunction with *west* it points to the whole world (Luke adds "and from north and south," which perhaps makes it a little clearer). The saved, in the end, will come[29] from all over the earth, which clearly means that many Gentiles will be included. It may be significant that the words here used of Gentiles are similar to Old Testament passages referring to Jews (e.g., Ps. 107:3; Isa. 43:5-6; 49:12). Not only will they be included in the number of the saved, but they will enter into bliss, here typified by "reclining"[30] with the patriarchs in God's kingdom. One way first-century Jews had of referring to the coming bliss was to speak of the messianic banquet, an occasion of festivity in the world to come. To recline with the patriarchs was to feast in leisurely manner in the very best company. The patriarchs would undoubtedly be the recipients of God's blessing in the coming world; therefore, to be associated with them was to share the blessing. This is what Jesus speaks of here, as his mention of leisure with the patriarchs and the reference to *the kingdom of heaven* (see on 3:2) clearly show.

12. But that is not the whole story. Another adversative *but* brings us to *the sons of the kingdom* (cf. 13:38). In this unusual expression *son* denotes "one who shares in this thing or who is worthy of it, or who stands in some other close relation to it" (BAGD, 1.c.δ). Jesus is speaking of Jews who, because of the nation's relationship to God, would be expected to feature in *the kingdom* but whose lack of faith means that they forfeit their place. They *will be thrown out*, where the verb may have the notion of some force; at any rate the *sons* will not be able to resist the expulsion. Jesus does not say from whence they will be thrown out, but clearly *the kingdom* is in mind. Their destination is not left in doubt. They will go *into the outer darkness* (an expression found only in Matthew), where *outer* points to the darkness farthest out, farthest removed from the joy and light of the king-

27. Another Gentile, the Canaanite woman, is recorded as having faith that availed for another and as accepting that Jesus healed at a distance (15:28).

28. δέ has adversative force. Luke has parallels to this part of the story in quite another section of his Gospel, 13:28-29, though the word order is different, as is some of the wording. Apparently Jesus used the idea on more than one occasion.

29. ἥκω means "have come" and thus "be present."

30. ἀνακλίνω in the active has the meaning "make to lie upon" (Luke 2:7) and in the passive "recline." In most of its 6 New Testament occurrences it refers to reclining at table, and this is surely its meaning here. *REB* brings this out with "sit with Abraham . . . at the banquet," and *JB* with "take their places with Abraham . . . at the feast. . . ."

dom,[31] and *darkness* contrasts with the light of the kingdom. *In that place* there will be misery, which is described as *the wailing and the grinding of teeth,* a proverbial expression for pain and distress. Matthew uses it a number of times (13:42, 50; 22:13; 24:51; 25:30), but elsewhere in the New Testament it occurs only in Luke 13:28. *Wailing* signifies not only grief but grief loudly expressed, while the definite article "indicates the unique and extreme character of the action" (BAGD); it is not any old wailing that is meant, but the wailing that is associated with final rejection. It will be accompanied by *the grinding of teeth,* another proverbial expression for distress and mostly used in the New Testament, as here, for grief (or possibly anger or vexation) at the final rejection. Some of those who might be expected to respond to Jesus with faith and commitment will not do so, and their failure is shown up by the centurion's faith. The Master leaves his hearers in no doubt that this is a failure with dire and permanent consequences.[32]

13. From the crowds (v. 10) Jesus turns to the centurion. He invites him to return home and gives him the assurance that the boy will be healed. This is linked with the man's faith *(as you have believed),* for trust in Christ is always of the utmost importance. Here the gift is expressly related to the faith: *as* you have believed *so* be it. This probably does not mean that the gift is in proportion to the faith; Jesus does not work that way. We should see rather a causative meaning, "Because you have believed — " (cf. Moffatt, "as you have had faith, your prayer is granted"). The result was that the *servant* was healed[33] immediately *(at that hour),* where *hour* does not mean the spread of time over one twelfth of the day, but something like "moment"; Matthew is describing a cure that took place as Jesus spoke the word.

c. Healing Peter's Mother-in-Law and Others, 8:14-17

> [14]*And when Jesus came into Peter's house, he saw his mother-in-law lying sick with a fever.* [15]*And he touched her hand, and the fever left her; and she got up and waited on him.*
>
> [16]*Now when evening came, they brought to him many who were possessed by demons; and he cast the spirits out with a word, and healed all who were ill,* [17]*in order that what was spoken through Isaiah the prophet was fulfilled, saying,*
>
> "*He himself took our sicknesses and carried our diseases.*"

31. Turner doubts "whether Jesus distinguished betweeen an inner and an outer darkness. More likely he envisaged an ever-increasing intensity of it as the sinner moves further from God's presence"; he goes on to refer to "the outermost darkness of all, the nemesis of blind refusal to believe" (*Grammatical Insights,* p. 59).

32. G. Barth refers to "the problem of Israel rejecting its Messiah and thereby its salvation, so deeply felt and seen by Matthew alone alongside Paul" (*TIM,* p. 112).

33. Jesus had used θεραπεύω for healing in verse 7, the centurion had employed ἰάομαι in verse 8, and now Matthew uses the centurion's word for the consummation.

All three Synoptists tell of the miraculous healing of Peter's mother-in-law (Mark 1:29-31; Luke 4:38-39), and characteristically Matthew's account is the shortest; he has 30 words, Mark has 44, and Luke 38. Almost everything in his account is found in one of the others.

14. Matthew does not say why Jesus went to Peter's[34] home, simply that he did (the other two accounts call the disciple "Simon" and say that the group came from the synagogue). Mark states that they told Jesus about the sick lady and Luke that they asked him about her, but Matthew concentrates on what happened: he goes straight to the fact that Jesus saw her and healed her. This is the only time Matthew tells of Jesus healing without some form of request; elsewhere people approach him. *Lying sick* is more literally "thrown" (as in v. 6; *KJV* renders this with "laid," and *REB* with "in bed"), to which Matthew adds that she had a fever (Luke says it was "a great fever").

15. Matthew informs us that Jesus *touched her hand*[35] (Mark indicates that he "took" her hand, and Luke that Jesus "rebuked" the fever); touching was often for the purpose of healing (cf. Jesus' touching of the leper, v. 3). The result was that the fever *left her;* she was cured immediately. Matthew brings out the completeness of the cure and tells us something significant about the lady when he says, *she got up and waited on him.* Not only was she cured of the fever but she was restored to full strength. And clearly this lady was no malingerer. She did not stay in bed but got up and immediately became busy serving Jesus in some way.[36] The other Evangelists say that she served "them," but Matthew concentrates on what she did for Jesus.

16. The healing of many sick people in the evening is recounted in all three Synoptists, though with not inconsiderable differences.[37] *Evening* may mean the time just before sunset or just after (the context is often decisive). On this occasion we are helped by Mark's information that they had been to the synagogue; in other words, it was the Sabbath. People

---

34. Matthew has the name Peter 23 times, whereas Mark has it 19 times and Luke 18. John uses it 34 times; clearly he was very interested in Peter. But the name Simon is found in this Gospel only 9 times, whereas it occurs in Mark 11 times, in Luke 17 times, and in John 25 times.

35. In Jewish teaching a man should not make contact with a woman's hand, not even to count money from his hand to hers (*Ber.* 61a).

36. διακονέω is a general word for service and is used for a variety of services people may perform for one another. Its original use was for waiting at table, and that is a not unlikely meaning here. The imperfect tense may point to a continuing activity, or more probably it is conative, "she began to wait on him."

37. Matthew tells the story in 36 words, whereas Mark has 46 and Luke 52; but Matthew has only 6 words in common with Mark and 1 with Luke. The resemblance is in content, not language. Attention is often drawn to the opening, where Mark has "Now when evening came and the sun was set." It is suggested that Matthew and Luke had Mark before them and that Matthew took the first expression and Luke the second. Alternatively it is sometimes thought possible that Mark has collated the other two (or the sources on which they relied). But in view of the many verbal differences either hypothesis is hazardous.

would wait until the sun went down and the Sabbath ended before they took up the work of carrying sick folk to Jesus. Matthew does not say who his *they* were; the indefinite plural refers to people in general. Interestingly, he speaks only of demoniacs as being brought, though he refers also to the *ill* as being cured. Many physical ailments were attributed to demons (see on 7:22), but not all; Matthew differentiates the ill from the demoniacs. But it was an important part of Jesus' ministry to cast out demons. Here people are said to be possessed by demons, but it is *the spirits* that are cast out. When it refers to demons, this term is usually qualified by "unclean" or "evil" or by some such word as "dumb"; the general term here means that whatever the alien spirits were, they were expelled. Jesus cast them out *with a word*, a contrast to the techniques characteristic of contemporary exorcists, but characteristic of Jesus (cf. v. 8) and indicative of his supreme power. In addition to dealing with the demons, he *healed all who were ill*. For Matthew's interest in healing see on 4:23. *All* is comprehensive; there was no illness that was beyond Jesus' power. For the expression "had [it] badly" to denote illness see on 4:24; it is a general term covering illness of any sort. Matthew is interested in the fact that Jesus brought healing and not in the precise ailments the patients had.

17. *In order that*[38] indicates purpose; Matthew saw a divine purpose in what Jesus did, a purpose that was foretold in the prophets. Accordingly Matthew appeals to the fulfilment of prophecy again and again (see on 1:22). On this occasion he specifies that the prophecy is in Isaiah, and he proceeds to quote it (Isa. 53:4). If he is quoting from LXX, the quotation is very free;[39] more probably he is using an independent translation from the Hebrew.[40] *He himself* has some emphasis (so Turner, M, III, p. 40). Isaiah 53 is generally understood as setting forth in prophetic form some of the great truths of the atonement for sin brought about by the death of Jesus; it is unusual to see it applied to illness rather than to moral evil. Clearly Matthew saw in the passage scriptural warrant for Jesus' healing ministry. For him it was plain that Jesus' healing came from God, so it was natural to find it prophesied in the Scripture that also came from God. There may be the thought that Jesus in some way took on himself the ailments he cured; healing is at cost. There is certainly the thought that the final answer to sickness is in the cross. As Gundry puts it, "The healings anticipate the passion in that they begin to roll back the effects of the sins for which Jesus came to die."[41] We cannot say that all our sicknesses are due to

---

38. ὅπως, found again in connection with fulfilment of prophecy in 2:23; 13:35. ἵνα is more usual.

39. The only words that are identical are τάς, ἡμῶν, and καί.

40. The Hebrew in this passage, חֳלִי, means "sickness" (Brown, Driver, and Briggs), though it is often translated as "grief" (*RSV*) or "suffering" (*REB*).

41. He also says, "The prophet has in mind the Servant's taking the diseases of others upon himself through his suffering and death for their sin, the root cause of sickness and disease" (*Use of the OT*, p. 230).

personal sin, but we can say that sickness was not part of the original creation[42] and that it will have no place in the final state of affairs. God not only "forgives all your iniquity" but also "heals all your diseases" (Ps. 103:3).[43] In the final salvation there is "no more pain" (Rev. 21:4). *Took* and *carried*[44] are unusual expressions to use of illness; they indicate the complete removal of the sicknesses in question.

2. The Cost of Discipleship, 8:18-22

> [18]*Now when Jesus saw a crowd around him, he gave orders to go off to the other side.* [19]*And a scribe came and said to him, "Teacher, I will follow you wherever you go."* [20]*And Jesus says to him, "The foxes have holes and the birds of the air roosts, but the Son of man has nowhere to lay his head."* [21]*And another of the disciples said to him, "Lord, allow me first to go off and bury my father."* [22]*But Jesus says to him, "Follow me, and let the dead bury their own dead."*

Matthew shares this incident with Luke 9:57-62, but while Matthew is slightly longer in the matter they share, Luke adds a sentence telling about a man who wanted to bid farewell to his family. The paragraph brings out the necessity of wholeheartedness in following Jesus. There were people who were well disposed to him and apparently recognized that his teaching was outstanding, but who were not prepared to make the sacrifices necessary to be real disciples. Matthew leaves his readers in no doubt that Jesus demanded wholehearted loyalty. Some commentators take it that neither of these two men in the end followed Jesus,[45] some that both did, and some that Matthew is giving us an example of one who responded and one who did not. We should be clear that all these are guesses. Matthew is concerned to make clear what Jesus looks for in a disciple; he is saying nothing at all about the ultimate attitude of either of these two.

42. "Man came from God's creative hand, healthy in soul and body" (Gutzwiller).

43. "The violation of the laws of health will inevitably result in physical trouble of some sort, so that we may perhaps discern a certain kinship between sickness and sin. At any rate complete healing, making a person 'every whit whole', involves dealing with both moral and physical disorder. Looked at in this way it is not at all surprising that Christ's atoning work should have as one of its effects a dealing with sickness, even if we do not see the full effects of that here and now" (Leon Morris, *The Cross of Jesus* [Grand Rapids, 1988], p. 93; in this book I have discussed this text, pp. 89-93).

44. λαμβάνω is used in a wide variety of ways, for example, of taking coins from the temple (27:6) and peace from the world (Rev. 6:4). It can mean "take away completely," and this is its meaning here. βαστάζω refers to carrying in a variety of senses; here it denotes carrying disease off so that we see it no more (BAGD, 3.a cites Galen for the use of the verb in this medical sense). Both verbs can have a meaning like "bear the burden of," but "remove" is more likely.

45. Morgan says that, while most people think that neither of these men went on to follow Christ, "We are not told the sequel, and we have as much right to think that they ultimately followed Him, as that they did not" (pp. 86-87).

18. Presumably the healings brought crowds about Jesus. Matthew does not say why the people came, but simply that there was *a crowd* there. Jesus may well have wanted some peace and quietness, and therefore instructed his immediate followers to cross the lake. Nothing is said about how they were to make the journey; the writer apparently assumes that a boat was available, but he says nothing about it. We do not know whose it was or how it came to be put to Jesus' use. Matthew says nothing at all about the reason for the crossing, and it is possible to understand the passage not of a literal crossing of the lake, but in the sense that Jesus is inviting would-be disciples to leave their present places and follow him *to the other side* (as Patte thinks); discipleship means forsaking present securities and adventuring into the unknown. But it is better to think of a real boat and a real voyage (cf. v. 23), with *the other side* signifying the far shore of the lake.

19. Since we read a little later of Jesus embarking, it seems that the people now mentioned approached Jesus before he got away. For *scribe*[46] see on 5:20; this man was obviously well versed in the law and was thus interested in the service of God, but *NEB*'s "doctor of the law" seems to be an exaggeration. Most scribes seem to have been opposed to Jesus, but this one clearly thought highly of him. Matthew may mean us to see this man as in some sense a disciple of Jesus: he does not call him one of "their scribes" (cf. 7:29), and "another of the disciples" (v. 21) may be meant to point back to this man and include him in the number. At any rate the scribe made the approach and addressed Jesus as *Teacher*, a courteous form of address, more or less equivalent to "Rabbi"; it is used by the rich young ruler who, of course, is not said to have followed Jesus (19:16). But in this Gospel it is never used by disciples; it is the form of address used by people who are not well disposed to Jesus, such as Pharisees (e.g., 12:38; 22:16, 24, 36), tax collectors (17:24), Herodians (22:16), and Sadducees (22:24). There does not appear to be any occasion when it is used by a committed follower of Jesus (such people call him "Lord"; see on v. 25). *Follow* may be used simply of coming along behind, but here it has the fuller meaning, "follow as a disciple." *Wherever you go* indicates a readiness to be with Jesus through thick and thin.[47] There is nothing wrong with this profession, but it appears that this scribe had not given sufficient thought to what following Jesus meant. It is possible that he thought of Jesus simply as a teacher and felt that being with him would bring security, the security of being constantly in touch with a reliable teacher.

20. Jesus' reply reflects his poverty and complete freedom from earthly ties. But the emphasis falls on his lack of what most people would

---

46. εἰς is used here in the sense of τις, an infrequent construction in Matthew.

47. Unless we understand the Greek to mean, "whithersoever Thou art [at this moment] departing" (McNeile; so also France). Jesus' reply would then mean that he was not on his way home.

think of as basic, a home. He did not have even the human equivalent of what *foxes* and *birds* possessed. A foxhole is not exactly luxury, but the fox who has it has somewhere to sleep at night. Jesus had no such place. Jesus taught that the *birds* have no need to worry about food — they are cared for by the heavenly Father (6:26). Now he says that they have their places of residence.[48] Creatures of the land and the air have their dwelling places, and in that the Son of man forms a contrast. He *has nowhere to lay his head.* "Laying the head" here stands for owning a place where one may rest; Jesus cannot claim a place of his own where he can sleep.[49] As Schweizer puts it, he was "devoid of all middle-class security." If the scribe wished to follow him, he must bear this in mind. Jesus sat loose to possessions, he had no secure job, and he owned very little. To be the disciple of such a man might well be interesting, but it would be far from comfortable. The scribe's reaction is not given, but certainly the cost of discipleship is brought clearly before him. It is perhaps worth noticing that John uses the verb for *lay*[50] when he is speaking of Jesus bowing his head on the cross (John 19:30); there the Master found the resting place that he did not have throughout his ministry.

This is the first use of *the Son of man*[51] in this Gospel. It is a literal translation of an Aramaic expression commonly used with the meaning "man." It is used over 80 times in the New Testament and, with the exception of Luke 24:7 and John 12:34 (both quoting Jesus) and Acts 7:56, it is always on the lips of Jesus. It was his favorite way of referring to himself. The expression has caused endless comment. Matthew uses it 6 or 7 times to refer to Jesus' earthly mission (8:20; 9:6; 11:19; 12:8; 13:37; 16:13; 18:11 [if this verse is authentic]), 10 times for his rejection and suffering (12:40; 17:9, 12, 22; 20:18, 28; 26:2, 24 [twice], 45), and 14 times for his future glory (10:23; 12:32; 13:41; 16:27, 28; 19:28; 24:27, 30 [twice], 37, 39, 44; 25:31; 26:64). Such a threefold division is to be discerned in the use of the term outside this Gospel as well. The expression was not an accepted messianic designation, which makes Jesus' extensive use of it rather puzzling. There is lowliness about it because the unthinking could see in it no more than the meaning "a man." But there is also greatness, for it is not unlikely that it is derived from the reference to the heavenly being described as "one like a son of man" in Daniel 7:13-14. This points to someone especially close to God and thus has messianic significance. But this does not answer our question, Why did Jesus use the term? I have

---

48. κατασκήνωσις has to do with a place to stay (σκηνή = "tent"); it means "encamping, taking up one's quarters" (LSJ). With birds it seems to mean a place to roost (a nest is a place for breeding). The corresponding verb is used of birds in 13:32.

49. We have already noticed that Matthew's arrangement here is topical, not chronological, and it may well be that this incident comes from a much later time in Jesus' ministry, especially if 9:10 is rightly understood to refer to Jesus' home.

50. κλίνω.

51. ὁ υἱὸς τοῦ ἀνθρώπου.

suggested elsewhere that that was "firstly because it was a rare term and one without nationalistic associations. It would lead to no political complications. . . . Secondly, because it had overtones of divinity. . . . Thirdly, because of its societary implications. The Son of man implies the redeemed people of God. Fourthly, because it had undertones of humanity. He took upon Him our weakness."[52]

21. Another[53] would-be disciple is introduced. Indeed, this man is called one *of the disciples*[54] so clearly that it appears that he had made some form of commitment, though the passage assumes that he was not a disciple in the sense in which the Twelve were. We should bear in mind that "disciple" may be used of people with varying degrees of attachment to Jesus. This man addressed Jesus respectfully as *"Lord"* (or perhaps he meant it in the sense "Sir"). He apparently realized that being a disciple of Jesus meant severing home ties, and he professed himself ready to do this. But before doing so, he made the stipulation that he wanted to *go off and*[55] *bury* his *father*.

He may mean that his father was dead and that he wanted to discharge his family obligations before leaving all for Jesus' sake. The Jews regarded the burial of one's father as especially important (see Gen. 50:5-14; Tob. 4:3; 6:14), and, for example, even a priest, who was normally required to avoid defilement by contact with the dead, was exempted from this requirement on the death of his father (and other close relatives, Lev. 21:1-2). It was accepted that, faced with a burial, a man was exempted from a whole string of important religious duties: the saying of the daily

52. *The Lord from Heaven*[2] (London and Downers Grove, 1974), p. 28. I have discussed the term with references to the literature in pp. 25-28 of that book. See also my *New Testament Theology* (Grand Rapids, 1986), pp. 101-3, 124-25, 159-60, 234-35. The literature on the subject is enormous, but there is a useful summary in Carson, pp. 209-13. Kingsbury sees a minimal significance in the term and finds "this man" to be "its translational equivalent" (*Matthew*, p. 63; see also *Structure*, pp. 113-22). But he does not consider the way the expression is used outside Matthew, nor the fact that in all four Gospels this is Jesus' favorite way of referring to himself. It is not to be understood in isolation as though it were a Matthean construction, Matthew's own way of referring to Jesus. Nor does Kingsbury do justice to what Matthew says, for he argues that in this Gospel "The most striking feature about Matthew's use of Son of Man is that it assumes a totally 'public,' as opposed to 'confessional,' character"; "our conclusion is that 'Son of man' in the first Gospel is the term with which Jesus encounters the world, first Israel and then the Gentiles, and particularly his opponents and unbelievers" (*Structure*, pp. 114, 117). But Matthew gives examples of the use of the term among the disciples, as in 10:23; 13:37 (to name no others). In this Gospel the expression is not "totally 'public.' "

53. ἕτερος can mean another of a different kind (Bruce sees this meaning here, as does Buttrick). But in the New Testament it is often used in much the same sense as ἄλλος, and this is the way it should be taken here.

54. It may be that we should read "one of his disciples" (with C L W Θ etc.; αὐτοῦ is not found in ℵ B 33 etc.). In the days of Jesus his followers would have been designated as his by the insertion of "his" or the equivalent. In later times among the Christians no more was needed than "the" disciples. Matthew often has the earlier use. *AB* emends the text to read "not one," but the reasons are inadequate.

55. Turner considers καί here as final (M, III, p. 334).

prayers, the study of the law, the temple service, the observance of cirum-
cision, the killing of the Passover sacrifice, and the reading of the Megilla
(*Ber.* 3:1; *Meg.* 3b). Burial was normally carried out the day the person died
(Acts 5:6, 10), but mourning customs followed throughout the subsequent
week.[56] Paying proper attention to the last sad rites was considered of
prime importance. If the man's father was in fact dead, it is highly probable
that the son would be caught up in all this. The death of the father meant
that the son's presence at home had a high priority. He would be busy
with funeral arrangements and not speaking to Jesus about discipleship.

So it is much more likely that the man's parent was still alive and
that he was referring to the obligation that rested on a dutiful son to look
after his father in his declining years until his eventual death.[57] He was
saying that he must fulfil his duty to his father, a most important duty. In
that case he was postponing his discipleship, perhaps for several years.
He was saying in effect, "Some day, after my father has died, I will follow
you." There is no way of being absolutely sure which is the right way to
take the words, but it is clear that the man was insisting on a delay before
he took his place with Jesus.

22. *But* is adversative: far from the course the man suggested, he
should follow Jesus immediately. *"Follow me"* is a firm imperative. If the
present tense is to be pressed, it means "keep following me," that is, do
not let even family obligations stand in the way. It is not easy to understand
how *the dead* are to bury other dead people if we take the expression in
the usual way, of the physically dead. But the expression may mean those
who are soon to die (as in 9:24 Jesus says that Jairus's daughter lives when
she is about to leave the realm of the dead). The meaning then is that those
who are preoccupied with the issues of death are the ones to concern
themselves with burials. Or we could understand the words figuratively,
of those who have not attained the new life of the kingdom: "Let the
spiritually dead bury their physically dead ones." Burying the physically
dead is a suitable pursuit for the spiritually dead (for the use of "dead"
in such a way cf. Luke 15:24, 32; Eph. 2:1). What Jesus is saying in this
striking expression is "The claims of the kingdom are absolute and immediate" (Nixon).[58]

---

56. Chrysostom says, "After the burial he must of necessity proceed to inquire about
the will, then about the distribution of the inheritance, and all the other things that follow
thereupon; and thus waves after waves coming in succession upon him, would bear him
away very far from the harbor of truth" (p. 187).

57. K. E. Bailey can say, "The phrase 'to bury one's father' is a traditional idiom that
refers specifically to the duty of the son to remain at home and care for his parents until they
are laid to rest respectfully" (*Through Peasant Eyes* [Grand Rapids, 1983], p. 26).

58. Ryle comments that nothing "has done more harm to Christianity than the practice
of filling the ranks of Christ's army with every volunteer who is willing to make a little
profession, and to talk fluently of his 'experience.' " He goes on to point out that "numbers
alone do not make strength," and advises, "Let us tell them plainly that there is a crown of
glory at the end; but let us tell them no less plainly, that there is a daily cross in the way."

3. *Three Wonders, 8:23–9:8*

For the second time in this section of his Gospel Matthew brings three miracles before his readers. He is emphasizing the authority and the power that were manifest throughout Jesus' ministry.

a. Calming a Storm, 8:23-27

> 23*And when he got into the boat, his disciples followed him.* 24*And look, a great storm arose in the sea, so that the boat was covered by the waves; but he stayed asleep.* 25*And they came to him and woke him up, saying, "Lord, save us, we are perishing!"* 26*And he says to them, "Why are you frightened, you men of little faith?" Then he got up and rebuked the winds and the sea, and there was a great calm.* 27*And the men were astonished and said, "What kind of man is this, that even the winds and the sea obey him?"*

Mark and Luke both share this story with Matthew (Mark 4:35-41; Luke 8:22-25), and as usual Matthew has the shortest account. He has only twenty-one of his seventy-three words in common with Mark and twenty-three with Luke, so the resemblances are not close. And despite the common matter there are not inconsiderable differences on important points. For example, the other two have no equivalent of Matthew's *"Why are you frightened, you men of little faith?"* while they have the boat filling where Matthew has it covered with the waves. There are thus formidable differences as well as agreement on the main happening. The other two have the story in teaching contexts, but Matthew uses it as part of the way in which he brings out the power and the authority of Jesus.[59] In his famous treatment of the story G. Bornkamm stresses its importance for an understanding of Matthew's view of discipleship: "the story becomes a kerygmatic paradigm of the danger and glory of discipleship."[60] He points to the sayings about would-be disciples that precede this miracle (vv. 19-22), to the verb "followed" (v. 23), and to Jesus' "accusing remark" that precedes the miracle (v. 26). And "As the need of the disciples on the sea becomes a symbol of the distresses involved in discipleship of Jesus as a whole, so also in the same connexion the great peace which his word evokes takes on the meaning of the Johannine saying . . . (John 16:33)."[61]

23. Matthew has told us that Jesus had given a command to go to the other side (v. 18); now he tells us that Jesus embarked and that the disciples followed him. *Disciples* here refers to the Twelve, not to all those who followed Jesus, and the possessive *his* is the early use, differentiating

---

59. Barclay holds that Matthew has used the story to bring out an important spiritual truth: the meaning of the story is "that *wherever Jesus is the storms of life become a calm*. It means that in the presence of Jesus the most terrible of tempests turns to peace" (p. 324).

60. *TIM*, pp. 57.

61. *TIM*, pp. 55-56.

the disciples of Jesus from those of other teachers. Notice that Matthew refers not to "a" boat, but to *the boat*.[62] It seems that he had a definite boat in mind, but we have no way of knowing what that signified. On the entering into the boat Hill comments, "the disciples 'follow' Jesus: the story of the storm is concerned with discipleship."

24. *And look* is Matthew's characteristic way of making it all vivid (see on 1:20). Matthew's word for *storm* is unusual;[63] it more commonly refers to an earthquake or the like (the addition *in the sea* makes it clear that a storm is meant). It is a vivid word and, reinforced with *great*, brings out the magnitude of the turbulence. Luke calls this sheet of water a "lake," but Matthew always refers to it as a *sea*. It is about 700 feet below sea level, and the winds sweep down through the steep ravines that run into it to whip up tumultuous and sudden storms. On this occasion the storm was such that the boat *was covered by the waves*, the only place in the New Testament where a boat is said to be *covered* by waves (cf. *REB*, the waves "were breaking right over the boat"; Filson has "submerged by the waves," and *LB* "with waves higher than the boat"). The meaning is that when the boat was in the trough between the waves, those waves towered over it, completely concealing it from view. *But*[64] has adversative force and introduces what is contrary to what might have been expected. And it is certainly surprising that in a storm of the magnitude of that described by Matthew anyone could stay *asleep*. But Jesus had had a very heavy day with healing and teaching, and dealing with potential disciples. Wearied as he was with all his labor, he fell asleep and remained asleep despite the magnitude of the storm.

25. So they came to him (Mark tells us that he was in the stern, sleeping on a cushion) and woke him. Matthew has a terse, three-word expression, "Lord, save, we-perish." Matthew alone has the disciples address Jesus as *"Lord"* here (the disciples characteristically address Jesus as *"Lord"* in this Gospel, as in 14:28; 16:22; 17:4; 18:21, as do those who are

---

62. πλοῖον is noted by BAGD as especially frequent in later times when ναῦς became rare. It may be used of a large seagoing ship (Acts 20:13), but on the Lake of Galilee it would have been a much smaller boat. Matthew generally speaks of *the* boat (8 times, plus 2 v.l.); he has the anarthrous form 3 times. In *Buried History* (the journal of the Australian Institute of Archaeology), vol. 25 (1989), pp. 46-54 there is a report on the discovery in February 1986 of a boat that had been buried in the bottom of the Sea of Galilee. It appears to be from the New Testament period. It measures 26.5 ft. (8.2 m.) in length, 7.5 ft. (2.3 m.) in breadth, and 4.5 ft. (1.4 m.) in height. The stern platform covers a ballast bag of 110-120 lbs. (50-59 kg.), used to adjust the trim of the boat; this was the "pillow" on which Jesus slept (Mark 4:38). With places for two oars a side (there was also a place for a mast) and a steering oar, it had a crew of five; it could carry up to ten passengers. A mosaic in a house in Migdal depicts such a boat.

63. σεισμός, "shaking, shock" (LSJ, which notes its use for earthquakes, but, apart from this passage, not for storms). Matthew has it 4 times and Revelation 7 times, but no other New Testament book has it more than once. In all its other New Testament occurrences it refers to earthquakes. Neither Mark nor Luke uses it of this storm.

64. δέ.

coming to believe in him, 8:2, 6, 8; 9:28, etc.). And he alone has the word *save*. The lack of any mention of what they want to be saved from injects a note of urgency into their plea. The verb *perish* (in Matthew 19 times) is used of disasters of various kinds, which may explain the variety in translations (e.g., REB, "we are sinking"; JB, "we are going down"; GNB, "we are about to die"; Moffatt is precise with "we are drowning!"). The present tense states the process as already in progress; it is a cry of anguish.[65]

26. In Mark and Luke Jesus stills the storm immediately, but Matthew concerns himself first with the words Jesus addressed to the stricken disciples: *"Why are you frightened?"* His word[66] is often used in the sense of "cowardly" or "timid" (REB has "Why are you such cowards?"); it indicates more than a slight nervousness. Some of these people were fishermen, well versed in the storms on the sea of Galilee, and the fact that they were so afraid indicates the magnitude of the tempest. It is also significant that, when the skill of the sailors was unavailing, they called on one whose training had been in the carpenter's shop; clearly he had impressed them so greatly that it was natural to turn to him in a crisis. Jesus goes on to characterize them as *men of little faith* (for this expression see on 6:30; this is the second of Matthew's uses of the term with respect to the disciples).[67] Jesus signifies that, while the storm was no doubt a great one, they might well have trusted more.[68] This may mean either that they should have trusted God or that they should have trusted him. Having dealt with the troubled disciples, Jesus turned to the boisterous winds and the troubled sea and *rebuked*[69] them (for addressing the waves of the sea cf. Job 38:11). This is a somewhat surprising verb and perhaps indicates that Jesus saw an evil force in the tempest that put him and his disciples in peril. He deals with that force as sovereign over it. The result of the rebuke was *a great calm* ("it became perfectly calm," NASB). Matthew does not describe a gradual diminution of the force of the winds and the waves, but a sudden cessation of all the storm's activity, so that everything was peaceful. We are not to think that the storm had blown itself out, but that Jesus had power over the elements and replaced tempest with calm.

---

65. Cf. Moulton, "we recognise in the perfective verb the sense of an *inevitable* doom, under the visible conditions, even though the subsequent story tells us it was averted" (M, I, p. 114).

66. δειλός, again in the New Testament only in Mark 4:40; Rev. 21:8.

67. The combination of cowardice and unbelief is a serious one. Carr points out that these two qualities head a list of those destined for the lake of fire (Rev. 21:8).

68. "Faith chases out fear, or fear chases out faith" (Carson).

69. AS differentiates the verb ἐπιτιμάω from ἐλέγχω (which also means "rebuke") in that it expresses "simply rebuke, which may be undeserved (Mt 16²²) or ineffectual (Lk 23⁴⁰)," while ἐλ. implies rebuke which brings conviction." On *rebuked* McNeile comments, "This is important. The incident is related, not primarily for the sake of recording a miracle, but as an instance of the subduing of the powers of evil, which was one of the signs of the nearness of the Kingdom."

27. *The men* doubtless means the men in the boat at that time. But since this is not the way disciples are generally described, many interpreters have suggested that Matthew's use of the general term means that others than the disciples were in due course impressed. This, of course, did happen, but here Matthew is more probably using the expression "as a foil to the divine figure of Jesus" (Gundry); *the men* stand over against the one whom *the winds and the sea* obey. Matthew certainly contrasts the majesty of Jesus with the powerlessness of his followers. Those in the boat were in no doubt that a mighty miracle had taken place. Some of them, as we have noted, were familiar with the sea of Galilee and its moods, and they knew that this was not the way this stretch of water behaved. They *were astonished* (for the verb see on v. 10), and they expressed their astonishment by asking *What kind of man* Jesus was *that*[70] *even*[71] the elements are subject to him.[72]

b. The Gadarene Demoniacs, 8:28-34

> [28]*And when he came to the other side, to the country of the Gadarenes, two demon-possessed men met him, coming out of the tombs; exceedingly violent, so that no one was able to pass by along that road.* [29]*And look, they cried out, saying, "What have we to do with you, you Son of God? Did you come here to torment us before the time?"* [30]*Now there was at a distance from them a herd of many pigs feeding.* [31]*And the demons besought him, saying, "If you cast us out, send us into the herd of pigs."* [32]*And he said to them, "Go." And they came out and went into the pigs; and look, the whole herd rushed down the steep slope into the sea and died in the waters.* [33]*And the swineherds fled, and when they came into the town they told everything, and what had happened to the demon-possessed men.* [34]*And look, the whole town went out to meet Jesus; and when they saw him, they begged him to leave their region.*

70. BAGD comments on ὅτι: "ὅτι alone is used for εἰς ἐκεῖνο ὅτι *with regard to the fact that*"; here it means *"what sort of man is this* (in consideration of the fact) *that?"* (BAGD, 1.c). But it also notes the possibility that we have here the causal conjunction "because, since," and this seems preferable. Chamberlain says that ὅτι here "seems to introduce a result clause" (p. 192).

71. It would be possible to take the two καί's to mean "both . . . and," but it seems better to take the first in the sense "even" and the second as linking the winds and the sea as the elements that made up the storm.

72. G. Bornkamm has an interesting examination of this incident. He can say: "Matthew is not only a hander-on of the narrative, but also its oldest exegete, and in fact the first to interpret the journey of the disciples with Jesus in the storm and the stilling of the storm with reference to discipleship, and that means with reference to the little ship of the Church." He goes on to speak of "the need of the disciples on the sea" as "a symbol of the distresses involved in discipleship of Jesus as a whole" and to view the peace Jesus brought as evoking the peace we read of in John 16:33 (*TIM*, pp. 55, 56). Early Christians interpreted the story in somewhat this way. For example, Tertullian wrote: "that little ship did present a figure of the Church, in that she is disquieted 'in the sea,' that is, in the world, 'by the waves,' that is, by persecutions and temptations; the Lord, through patience, sleeping as it were, until roused in their last extremities by the prayers of the saints, He checks the world, and restores tranquillity to His own" (*On Baptism*, XII).

This is another story in the triple tradition, and again Matthew has the shortest account and Mark the fullest.[73] The principal difference between Matthew and the others is that he speaks of two demoniacs and they of one. For modern students there is a problem in the demons entering the pigs, and in the end we must remain content with an element of mystery. But since this feature is in all three accounts, we cannot lightly dismiss it. We should notice that demon possession is rare if it occurs at all in the Old Testament, and there are very few examples after the Gospels. In the Bible demon possession is part of the upsurge of evil opposing Jesus in the time of his incarnation.

28. For *the other side* see on verse 18. Matthew explains that this was *the country of the Gadarenes.*[74] There is a problem in that Gadara was about six miles away from the lake and separated from it by the deep gorge of the Yarmuk. But Gerasa was about 40 miles away, so it is unlikely. The third reading, Gergesa, appears to have arisen because Origen suggested it (he does not cite earlier manuscripts for this reading). He argued that the other two readings arose only because Gergesa was a little town, not known to the scribes, who accordingly substituted the names of towns they knew in the region. There is some evidence that Gadara had territory on the shore of the lake,[75] and our best understanding is that Matthew is right in referring to Gadara and that the territory ruled from this city extended to the lake. We lack information about the precise boundaries of the territories claimed by any of the cities in the region, but there is nothing improbable in the suggestion that the sovereignty of Gadara reached the lake and that there was a settlement there with a name that could be corrupted into "Gergesa" and perhaps "Gerasa" (cf. the modern Khersa), so that all three names entered the tradition. We should notice that Matthew does not say that they went to Gadara or Gerasa or Gergesa, but to "the country" of whatever city is to be read (the "town" of v. 34 may refer to a settlement established in the territory of the main city). It was a predominantly Gentile region, as is shown by the reference to the herd of pigs, which would not be found in a Jewish area.

The landing party encountered two demoniacs. This presents us with a problem, in that Mark and Luke speak of only one. It may be that one was more prominent than the other and that Mark and Luke concentrate on this man. A less probable solution is that Matthew is including the

73. Matthew has 135 words, Mark 324, and Luke 293. Matthew has about 50 words in common with Mark and about 40 in common with Luke, so his account is reasonably independent.

74. In all three Gospels there is a textual problem. The name *Gadara* has the best attestation in Matthew (Metzger cites (א*) B C[txt] (Δ) Θ syr[s.p.h]; *Gerasa* is read by it vg cop[sa] syr[hmg2], and *Gergesa* by א[c] C[mg] K L W f1 f12 cop[bo]). We should read *Gadara* in Matthew, though *Gerasa* seems to be the text in Mark and Luke.

75. Josephus says that it lay "on the frontiers of Tiberias" (*Life* 42), which means the sea of Galilee. D. G. Pellett says, "coins indicate its shipping interests, so that the 'country of the Gadarenes' may well have extended to the shore of the lake" (*IDB*, II, p. 335).

demoniac in Mark 1:23-28; he has a much shorter account than Mark, and the suggestion is that he has rolled two exorcism stories into one. But in the end we must confess that we really do not know the reason for the difference. Matthew says that the two were *coming out of the tombs*. They would not have been literally in the tombs; the reference may be to "the little ante-chambers in front of the 'rooms' in which bodies were laid" (Hill). Alternatively, it is possible that some tombs had been abandoned (so Lenski). Matthew tells us that they were *exceedingly violent*.[76] Thus the form their demon possession took made them a menace to society. The result[77] was that *no one was able*[78] *to pass by*. The fierceness of their attacks made it impossible for people to make ordinary use of *that*[79] *road* (which need not mean a well-made road; a place where pedestrians could walk is all that the word necessarily denotes).

29. Matthew's typical *and look* carries the narrative along at a lively pace. The demoniacs *cried out;* the word may be used of unintelligible screaming (cf. *GNB*, "At once they screamed"), but here they scream out meaningful words. *"What have we to do with you?"* translates an expression Matthew uses only here.[80] Literally it means "What to us and you?" and indicates that the speakers see no common ground between themselves and Jesus. The demoniacs have an understanding of the nature of Jesus not very common at the time, for they address him as *Son of God*, though, of course, we have no way of knowing what content they put into the expression. It was not used very often by the Jews as a messianic desig-nation, but in the world of the day the title was common in myths and the like and sometimes was even used of great men. It was an exalted title, and at the very least it shows that the demoniacs sensed that Jesus belonged with God in a way that others do not and that because of that relation he might be expected to do things that ordinary people could not do. This raises the question of the meaning of *here*. Did they mean "here to this earth" or "here to this Gentile land"? Their recognition of Jesus as Son of God makes the former somewhat more likely. They go on imme-diately to refer to *torment before the time;* clearly they think that Jesus may

76. χαλεπός basically means "hard"; AS notes its use for "hard to do or deal with, difficult," "hard to bear," and of persons, "hard to deal with, harsh, fierce, savage." It is the last usage that we have here. It is used elsewhere in the New Testament only in 2 Timothy 3:1.

77. ὥστε is used in its normal construction with the infinitive to introduce result.

78. *REB* and *GNB* have "dared" (which may well express a truth, though it is not what Matthew is saying); ἰσχύω means "to have power, to be able."

79. ἐκεῖνος signifies "where the demoniacs dwelt; the road itself had not yet been mentioned" (BDF, 291[3]).

80. τί ἡμῖν καὶ σοί. It occurs twice in Mark and once in Luke and John (and in several places in LXX). BAGD regards it as a Hebraism that made its way into colloquial Greek with meanings like "what have I to do w. you? what have we in common? leave me alone! never mind!" They say, "It serves to refuse a request or invitation" (*sub* ἐγώ). Turner has an extensive examination of the expression (*Grammatical Insights*, pp. 43-47). He thinks that the context here "demands a meaning like 'Why are you troubling us?' " (p. 43).

well have come *to torment*[81] them. As demons they must expect torment in hell as their ultimate fate, but not torment *here* and not torment now, *before the time.*[82] This last word may be used in a variety of ways, but there is little doubt that here it signifies the end time, the time of judgment with its punishment of wickedness (*NIV*, "the appointed time"), when the devil and his helpers will be cast into hell (25:41). The demons recognized that their ultimate fate would be unpleasant, but they did not want it to come any more quickly than was necessary.

30. Matthew pauses to set the scene.[83] He speaks of some *pigs* some *distance*[84] from them all. There is no indication of how far off they were, but clearly they were not close. Matthew tells us that there were *many* pigs in the *herd;*[85] we are to think of no small number. *Feeding* indicates a normal, peaceful occupation. There was nothing to indicate imminent trouble from the animals.

31. Matthew pictures the demons,[86] not the men, as speaking, though presumably they spoke through the men's lips. There is a note of urgency, but also of respect, as they make their request to Jesus (they *besought him*). Their *if you cast us out* leaves little doubt that they thought Jesus would do this.[87] They request that in that eventuality Jesus would *send* them into *the pigs.* There is no indication in the narrative as to what that meant for either the demons or the pigs, or as to why the demons should make such a request. But we may reflect that unclean animals would be suitable dwellings for unclean spirits.

32. Jesus told them to leave the men. *Go* ("Begone!" *NASB, NEB*) orders them out (though we should probably take this as an imperative of permission); it may be held to imply consent for the demons to do as they had requested, though Jesus says nothing about the pigs. His basic concern was for the well-being of the men. Matthew tells us that the demons *came out*, then that they *went into the pigs*. Again he uses his vivid *and look*, which leads to the information that *the whole herd* bolted. What this meant is difficult to ascertain in an age like ours that does not believe in widespread demon possession. Moreover, this is the one occasion on which demons are said to enter beings other than people. All that we can

---

81. βασανίζω is connected with βάσανος, "a touchstone," a stone used in testing metals. It comes to mean "examine by torture" and thus, as here, simply "torture," "torment."

82. καιρός has sometimes been sharply differentiated from χρόνος, and in reaction to this too much has been made of their similarity; see the note in my *The Epistle to the Romans* (Grand Rapids, 1988), p. 470, n. 64. Here it means "the suitable time," "the right time."

83. δέ here is purely transitional; it has no adversative force.

84. μακράν is the accusative of the feminine of the adjective μακρός; with ὁδόν understood it means "a long way," "far."

85. ἀγέλη is found in the New Testament only in this story (and in the parallels). χοῖρος meant originally a young pig, but it came to be used of pigs generally.

86. This is the only place in the New Testament where the word δαίμων occurs (there are a few examples in late MSS). It does not seem to differ from δαιμόνιον.

87. The construction is εἰ with the indicative. ἐκβάλλω is often used for "throwing" demons out of people.

say is that the entry of the demons into the pigs was followed by a rush *down the steep slope*[88] *into the sea,* where the animals all perished (Mark and Luke say that they "choked," but Matthew says no more than that they died). We can at least say that this visual demonstration of the exit of the demons must have been of great value to the formerly "possessed."[89]

33. Attention moves to *the swineherds* who had been looking after the animals. What had happened not unnaturally scared them, and they took refuge in flight. *The town* means the town that was nearby; *town* does not necessarily indicate a bustling metropolis, for the term could be used of any reasonably sized aggregation of people (Greek does not seem to have a word for a medium-sized town; every place is either a village or a city). *The town* would have been the place where the pigs' owners were and, being the center of population, would be the place to which the herdsmen would naturally go. There they told their exciting story, and told it completely *(everything).* We need not doubt that they told it all in such a manner that they were exonerated from all blame for the loss of the pigs they were minding; they would have insisted that it was all Jesus' fault. An interesting little problem centers on *and.* This word can mean something like "namely," in which case they described "everything, namely what happened to the *demon-possessed men.*" But it is incredible that they omitted the fate of the pigs, and, if we take *and* to mean an addition, the meaning is that their big story was the loss of the pigs, after which they added the healing of the men.

34. For the third time in this story and the fifth time in this chapter Matthew has his vivid *And look.* It is a good story, and he does not let his readers miss its dramatic force. *The whole town* was impressed with the story, and all the people came out to meet Jesus. It might have been expected that they would want to welcome the man who had power over the demons and who had brought such spectacular and unexpected deliverance to the demon possessed in their own area. But this was not the case. They were evidently more concerned with their economic loss. Mark and Luke say that the people came out and saw the healed demoniac, but Matthew omits this. Since he is concerned with Jesus, he speaks only of their meeting with him. They *begged him;* the verb has a note of respect, but also of imploring; they left no doubt as to what they urgently wanted.

---

88. κρημνός is variously understood. *GNB* and *JB* have "cliff," but the pigs would have gone over a cliff, not rushed down it (but perhaps κατά has a meaning like "over and down"). So with *REB*'s "the edge." It seems that Matthew is writing about a steep slope, but not a precipice.

89. Plummer points out that the demons "cannot have intended or expected the destruction of the swine" (p. 133); that would mean the immediate loss of their new home. We have already seen that Jesus could be surprised (vv. 10, 26), and Plummer considers it possible that he had not foreseen the destruction of the pigs. But this does not seem to be what Matthew is saying. Ridderbos thinks that the demons did not take Jesus by surprise; he holds that they hoped to "turn the Gadarenes against Jesus," a hope that was realized. But Matthew is scarcely telling us of a victory of the demons.

The verb is the same as that used by the demons in verse 31 (are we to see this request as having something demonic about it?). They asked him to[90] leave their region. Matthew gives no reason for this, nor does Mark; Luke says that they were very much afraid. This may have been fear of further economic loss, or fear of such an authoritative figure.

The story leaves us with some unanswered questions. We do not know what demon possession really is, though the New Testament examples make it plain that it is hostile to people's best interests; it seems always to involve suffering of some sort. Nor can we know what it means for demons to enter animals, or why, when they do, the animals should behave in the way this story says they did. A difficulty of another kind is why Jesus should have permitted the destruction of the herd of pigs. "Permitted" is the word; there is nothing in the narrative to indicate that Jesus deliberately set out to destroy the animals. Matthew does not say that Jesus told the demons to enter the pigs, nor that he sent the pigs into the lake. But at least we can say that this brought to light the real values of the local people: they valued their pigs more than the healing of the demoniacs. Their request that Jesus leave them makes it plain that they preferred to live on a lower level than the one he was opening up before them. Further, they ignored the benefit conferred on their neighborhood in that two men who had terrorized the district (v. 28) were now normal citizens. How did that compare with the loss of their pigs? And the wonderful thing is the way the compassion of Jesus for those poor, tormented men shines through. Nobody else in their day did anything for them, but Jesus liberated them from their dreadful bondage.[91]

90. ὅπως is here moving into the territory of the infinitive. But there may be some lingering sense of purpose; they made their request in order that they might get him out of the district.

91. Mounce points to modern reinterpretations of the story and comments, "Rather than arguing whether demon possession was a primitive explanation of eccentric behavior or whether it was morally right for Jesus to destroy a large herd of pigs, it is better to hear the story as it was told and come to grips with what it intends to tell us about the authority of Jesus over all the powers of the supernatural realm."

Matthew 9

c. Healing a Paralytic, 9:1-8

¹And getting into a boat, he crossed over and came to his own city. ²And look, they brought to him a paralytic, lying on a bed. And when Jesus saw their faith, he said to the paralytic, "Take courage, my child, your sins are forgiven." ³And look, some of the scribes said to themselves, "This man is blaspheming." ⁴And Jesus, knowing their thoughts, said, "Why are you thinking evil things in your hearts? ⁵For which is easier: to say 'Your sins are forgiven,' or to say 'Get up and walk'? ⁶But so that you may know that the Son of man has authority on earth to forgive sins" — then he says to the paralytic, "Get up, take up your bed, and go home." ⁷And he got up and went off to his home. ⁸And when the crowds saw this, they were awe-struck, and they glorified God, who had given such authority to men.

This is another story that is found in both Mark and Luke, and characteristically Matthew's account is the shortest. He has 126 words, whereas Mark has 196 and Luke 212. His most significant omission is the lowering of the sick man through the roof, which makes such an impressive feature of the other accounts. This healing shows once more the importance of faith. On this occasion, however, Jesus declares the forgiveness of the sins of the patient before the healing. This provokes opposition, and the Master demonstrates his authority to declare sins forgiven by healing the patient. Matthew's abbreviation of the story enables him to put greater emphasis on forgiveness.[1] That for him is the important thing. Until now Matthew has said little about opposition to Jesus, but there is opposition to him in all the incidents related in this chapter.

1. This incident apparently follows on the healing of the Gadarene demoniacs. Thus Jesus got back into the boat[2] for the return voyage. Matthew simply says that *he crossed over* without telling what it was that

---

1. H. J. Held cites E. Lohmeyer, who notes that the story is "written around a clear and dominating centre-piece, the saying about the sin-forgiving power of the Son of Man." He adds his own view, "this is what Matthew is concerned about" (*TIM*, p. 176).
2. For πλοῖον see on 8:23. This one of Matthew's three uses of the term without the article, though here we might have expected it: it was "the" boat in which they had gone across the lake and in which they were now returning.

213

he crossed (cf. 14:34). But the context makes it clear that it is the sea of Galilee that is in mind. Jesus came to *his own city*,[3] which is not specifically named, but which is clearly Capernaum (cf. 4:13). That it was this city rather than Nazareth (where he had lived for so long) that is called *his own* indicates that he now lived in the lakeside city and not simply that he paid it an occasional visit. It was the center for his ministry.

2. For *And look* see on 1:20; it is Matthew's favorite way of introducing a vivid touch. He does not say where in the city the incident took place, but from the other Evangelists we learn that it was in a house. Nor does Matthew say who were bringing[4] the man, but only that the action was performed. The patient was *a paralytic*,[5] which explains why he was being carried. He was *lying*,[6] *on a bed*, where *bed* will mean a portable bed, a "mat" *(NIV)*. None of the Evangelists indicates that either the bearers or the patient asked for healing. Not a word from them is recorded; the plight of the man and what they looked for from Jesus were obvious enough without words. Jesus *saw*[7] *their faith*, though Matthew does not say how he saw it. Mark and Luke, with their fuller narratives, tell us that the bearers made a hole in the roof and lowered the man in front of Jesus, a striking demonstration of their deep conviction that Jesus could and would heal their friend. For *faith* see on 8:10; there as here it is concerned with trust in Jesus as a helper of those in physical need. We would naturally take *their* to refer to the faith of the bearers, but we cannot say that the faith was confined to these friends; it was clearly shared by the paralytic himself. Jesus spoke to him rather than to those who had brought him (though it was *their* faith that he had perceived). He began with encouragement: *"Take courage"*[8] ("Take heart," *NRSV*; Matthew alone has

3. Matthew has πόλις 26 times and Luke 39 (with another 42 in Acts), but Mark and John have it only 8 times each. Matthew and Luke are much more interested in cities. H. Strathmann points out that in LXX and the New Testament πόλις lacks the political significance it had for the Greeks; he gives its meaning as "an 'enclosed place of human habitation' as distinct from uninhabited areas, pastures, villages and single houses." He finds "no sharp distinction between πόλις and κώμη" *(TDNT*, VI, p. 530). Moulton considers this one of the places where the emphasis of ἴδιος "is undeniable" (M, I, p. 90).

4. The force of the imperfect is "they were bringing"; Matthew depicts the action as in progress.

5. For παραλυτικός see on 8:6. R. K. Harrison thinks that Luke's description of this man as παραλελυμένος is "the more technical word," and he holds that the sufferer "was evidently paraplegic." He conjectures that this was caused "by an accident earlier in life or by a bony lesion" and adds, "In any event, organic changes would have taken place in the spinal cord, and it is improbable that they would have been initiated by factors of a psychic nature such as conversion hysteria, which would transmute an emotional state of guilt or conflict into physical symptoms of paralysis or blindness" *(IDB,* I, p. 851).

6. βεβλημένον; for this verb of lying on a sickbed cf. 8:6, 14.

7. εἶδον is used of ordinary visual perception and of sense perception of any kind. But this seems to be the only place in the New Testament where it refers to perceiving faith (though cf. Acts 14:9; it is used of seeing God's kindness, Rom. 11:22).

8. θαρσέω, 3 times in Matthew, twice in Mark, and once each in John and Acts only in the New Testament, means "be cheerful" or "be courageous," either of which is appropriate here.

this word of encouragement), and addressed the man as *"my child,"*[9] a warm and friendly form of address that must have encouraged a man in dire need. Then Jesus said, *"your sins are forgiven,"* words that must have astounded everybody. It is interesting that Jesus begins by ignoring the man's physical need and grants him forgiveness. The tense points to a gift now:[10] Jesus is not pointing to a future time when the forgiveness would take place. *Sins* is a comprehensive term, including all the man's departures from the way of righteousness. Now the man has nothing to fear — all his sins are gone. In the early part of this Gospel we were told that Jesus would save his people from their sins (1:21), but this is the first occasion when we read of his giving anyone forgiveness. Indeed, it is the only occasion in this Gospel when Jesus forgives a specific individual.

3. Again the vivid *And look* introduces something new. What Jesus said set *some of the scribes* (for this word see on 5:20) thinking. They were the experts in the law, and the law was ecclesiastical as well as civil. If there was to be any question of forgiveness they were the ones to decide it, or so they would have thought. They were disturbed by Jesus' words, but they did not speak out against him: they spoke *to themselves.* Matthew is talking about what went on inside them, their inward reflection on a most unusual saying. We should probably discern a note of contempt in *This man* (*NASB* reads "this fellow"), and the most serious accusation possible is expressed in the verb *is blaspheming.*[11] There was a good deal of discussion among the Jews as to precisely what constituted blasphemy, but it was laid down in the Mishnah that " 'The blasphemer' is not culpable unless he pronounces the Name itself" (*Sanh.* 7:5; in 7:4 we find that the punishment for blasphemy was stoning). It would seem that the scribes were enlarging the concept for their own purposes. H. Beyer says, "In the NT the concept of blasphemy is controlled throughout by the thought of violation of the power and majesty of God" (*TDNT*, I, p. 622). As the scribes saw it, for Jesus to forgive sins was to assume the divine prerogative; indeed, in both Mark's and Luke's accounts they go on to ask who can

---

9. τέκνον occurs 14 times in Matthew and Luke, the highest in any one book. It is used of a child in relation to its parents, but also as a form of familiar address to others than children. A number of translations have "my son" here.

10. Some MSS (such as C L W Θ) have the perfect ἀφέωνται, but it appears that ἀφίενται should be read (with ℵ B lat etc.). Turner takes this as a punctiliar present, *"sins receive forgiveness* herewith" (M, III, p. 64). Lenski holds that both forms imply that the sins were dismissed the moment Jesus spoke. He also holds that we should not assume that the man's paralysis was the result of his sin: "The Christian rule of charity holds good also in the case of exegesis, namely, that we should not make any man worse than he may be." He thinks that it is sufficient to hold that the paralysis brought the man's sinfulness to mind. Jesus never says that a specific illness is due to sin (cf. John 9:2-3).

11. βλασφημέω occurs 3 times in Matthew; 4 times is the most it is found in any one book, but the word occurs in 14 books, so the idea is fairly widespread. The corresponding noun βλασφημία is found 4 times in Matthew. The original idea concerned the use of words, insulting words as opposed to εὐφημία, the use of words of good omen. Its meaning was extended to include all words and actions that were to the detriment of deity.

forgive sins but God alone. That was what concerned them. They viewed Jesus as no more than another Galilean, and thus as someone to be understood within ordinary human limits. For such a person to claim to bestow forgiveness was for them nothing less than blasphemy.

4. But though they said nothing out loud, Jesus knew[12] what they were thinking. He first asked them a question, *"Why[13] are you thinking evil things?"* This invites them to examine their motivation. Jesus castigates their thoughts as *evil things*, where *evil* covers a very wide range. It can refer to deeds or actions and is applicable to things and people alike. Here it could possibly be thought to mean the planning of evil deeds, but it is more likely to be confined to thinking badly of Jesus. For *hearts* see on 5:8; Jesus passes by what is merely on the surface and asks about their innermost being. It is there that the trouble lies.

5. Jesus goes on to a further inquiry. He sets forth two statements and asks the scribes which is the easier to affirm. His first is the statement he made when he forgave the paralytic's sins (v. 2), while the second introduces a new dimension into the situation, *"Get up and walk."* The obvious answer is that it is easier to say that sins are forgiven, for it is impossible for the bystanders to confirm or refute what has been said, whereas when a paralyzed man is told to get up and walk anybody can see whether the command is obeyed or not. On a deeper level, however, it is the second statement that is the easier: a healer can say that, but it takes deity really to forgive sins.[14]

6. Jesus makes no pronouncement on which of the two statements is easier to make; he has posed his question and he leaves it there. Now he goes on to demonstrate that he can say both things. He has already pronounced the paralytic's sins forgiven, and he now goes on to heal him. *So that[15]* introduces the thought of purpose; the healing is, of course, in order to overcome the man's disability and open to him a whole new way of living, but it is also in order that the scribes may enlarge their horizon. Some of the translations bring this out by introducing the notion of proof:

---

12. There is a textual problem, with ἰδών read by א C D K etc., and εἰδώς by B f1 565 700 etc. We should probably give the preference to the former as the more difficult reading; it is easier to "know" thoughts than to "see" them. But in practice there is not much difference in meaning.

13. ἱνατί (often written as ἵνα τί) means "in order that what might happen?" and thus "Why?" is meant in the sense of purpose. Matthew has it again in 27:46.

14. Curiously Bruce says, "It is implied that it is easier to forgive than to make a palsied man strong . . . the one is within the power of any man, the other belongs only to the exceptional man." But there is no warrant, scriptural or other, for saying that to forgive sins "is within the power of any man." Any person can, of course, forgive offenses against himself, and he should do so (6:14-15). But he cannot forgive sins against God, and that is what is in mind here. "What was in dispute was not the obligation of men to forgive each other for wrongs done to each other — every devout Jew was aware of that obligation. What was in question was the authority Jesus claimed *from heaven* to remit the sins of men" (*AB*).

15. ἵνα normally introduces a clause of purpose, here the purpose of the action Jesus is about to perform.

"But to prove to you" *(JB)*, "I will prove to you" *(GNB)*. For *the Son of man* see on 8:20; here there can be no question but that it refers to Jesus himself, but perhaps we can say that it refers to him in his "official" capacity. He is the man from Nazareth, but he is also *the Son of man*, and it is as *the Son of man* that he has the right to forgive. In this context his *authority* means his right to forgive. The addition *on earth* brings out two points: the Son of man is not adequately accounted for by his earthly manifestation; there is that about him that refers to heaven, not earth. And even here on earth he has the right to forgive sins. Jesus does not deny the scribes' premise that only God can forgive sins, but he invites them to reflect on what that means in the present situation.

Then introduces what follows next in time (see on 2:7). As often, Matthew uses the present tense for greater vividness. He tells us that Jesus turns to the paralytic and commands him, *"Get up, take up your bed, and go home."*[16] More literally *go home* means "go to your house" (for "house" see on 2:11). Jesus is directing the man to his own familiar surroundings.

7. The man did as he was told. Matthew does not say that he took up his bed (Mark and Luke both include this detail), but concentrates on the fact that the former paralytic got up and went off home. Matthew has a different verb for *went off* from that used in the command, but the meaning is essentially the same. The point being emphasized is that this man who had to be carried to Jesus by four companions was now able to walk back home.

8. Matthew does not tell us what the effect of all this was on the scribes who had been so supercilious when Jesus forgave the paralytic's sins (unless he includes them in *the crowds,* which seems unlikely). As often, Matthew uses the plural *crowds* rather than the singular as he refers to the bystanders generally. These were people who were presumably not particularly well disposed to Jesus (they are not spoken of as disciples or the like). But they were not hostile like the scribes, either. The effect of the miracle on them was that they were *awe-struck.*[17] They reacted as in the presence of God. The healing of a man who had to be carried by four others was not to be taken as commonplace, and the *crowds* recognized this. They recognized the hand of God in it all, and they *glorified* him. They saw that the power that had raised the man from his bed was divine, not human. But they also recognized that God had *given* this *authority to men.* Some understand *authority* in terms of power (*KJV* translates the word here as "power"), but it is not so much naked power as power rightfully

16. The aorist tense is used for the single act of taking up the bed (ἀρόν) and the present for the continuous walking home (ὕπαγε).

17. The verb φοβέω can mean "to be afraid, fear." It is possible that the people were scared at what they saw. But their praise of God makes awe much more likely to be their emotion than fear. Carson, however, argues for the meaning "fear"; he says that people "should fear whenever they are confronted by an open manifestation of God. . . . Such fear breeds praise."

exercised that is in mind. That the authority is given to men does not mean that any person can do what Jesus had just done.[18] There is not the slightest indication that anyone in the crowd thought that. Rather, the thought is that God has been pleased not to keep the power in heaven, but to give it to people here on earth in and through Jesus.

4. Discipleship, 9:9-17

Matthew inserts a little section on discipleship, starting with his own call to be a disciple of Jesus. That leads to a meal that he apparently gave for Jesus and his disciples at which a question of the Pharisees leads to an important saying about Jesus' calling of the disreputable. Discipleship means something very different from anything the Pharisees had imagined.

a. The Calling of Matthew, 9:9-13

> *9And as Jesus passed on from there, he saw a man named Matthew sitting at the tax office; and he says to him, "Follow me." And he got up and followed him.*
>
> *10And it came to pass that as he reclined at table in the house, look! many tax collectors and sinners came and reclined with Jesus and his disciples. 11And when the Pharisees saw it, they said to his disciples, "Why does your teacher eat with tax collectors and sinners?" 12But when he heard it, he said, "Those who are well have no need of a doctor, but those who are sick. 13But go and learn what this means, 'I want compassion and not sacrifice.' For I did not come to call righteous people, but sinners."*

All three Synoptists have the story of the call of the tax collector (who is called Matthew in this Gospel and Levi in the other two), and all three place it immediately after the healing of the paralytic. In all three he is sitting in the tax office when he responds to the call. Matthew and Luke give the story about the same amount of space, but characteristically Mark's account is a little longer.

---

18. Cf. Filson, *men* here "cannot mean that all men have this authority. The authority was given to the man Jesus to exercise on behalf of mankind." Some exegetes hold that Matthew teaches that the church has the power to forgive sins and that this passage points to this power of absolution (cf. also 16:19; 18:18; to which we might add John 20:23). Bruner accepts this view and cites F. W. Beare, "the plural 'men' . . . does not indicate at all that Matthew thinks of this as a *general* authority which God has granted to *all* men. The thought is that the authority of Jesus to pronounce the forgiveness of sins is now exercised by the ministers of his *church*" (p. 333). But despite the confident assertions of such scholars we must face the fact that in the New Testament there is not one example of any church or any Christian forgiving the sins of anyone; if this is what Jesus meant, surely someone would have done it. And Calvin long ago pointed to an important distinction: "This power is quite different from that which was entrusted to the Apostles, and which today the pastors of the Church exercise, for they do not so much remit, as testify that they are remitted, in declaring the mission they are enjoined to fulfil" (p. 260).

9. Jesus went on his way after healing the paralytic[19] and came across "a man sitting at the tax office, Matthew," a word order that adds the name almost as an afterthought. The other two Evangelists call him "Levi" and give the name more prominence, but this writer is not fastening attention on himself. The difference in the name should not concern us, for there were others who had two names (e.g., Simon Cephas = Peter, Saul who was Paul, John Mark, Joseph Barnabas, and Lebbaeus Thaddaeus).[20] The name *Matthew* is found only here in the New Testament in lists of the Twelve (10:3; Mark 3:18; Luke 6:15; Acts 1:13), and in the title of the first Gospel; the *tax office* occurs only in the three accounts of this incident. For the system of tax collection see on 5:46. The taxes in mind here would have been tolls levied on goods passing through or customs duties, so that the toll booth would have been situated in a strategic spot, which may have been on the great road from Syria to Egypt (when Matthew would have collected tolls) or near the lake (when Matthew would have been concerned with customs levied on goods that came across the lake, for the eastern shore lay outside the dominions of Herod Antipas; it was ruled by Herod Philip and thus was another country).[21] The Romans allowed Herod Antipas to collect and use the taxes from this area (Josephus, *Ant.* xvii.318). Matthew does not speak of any preliminary conversation, nor does he say what previous contact he had had with Jesus (though it is probable that he knew Jesus; how could a citizen of Capernaum not know him?) or what knowledge he had of Jesus' teaching. He concentrates on the one central thing: Jesus called him with the words *"Follow me"*; the present imperative seems to indicate a continuing following, and there is no doubt that Matthew is describing a call to discipleship with all that that means. And Matthew obeyed: *he got up and followed him.* He says no more, but concentrates on that one decisive action. Luke brings out a little of its meaning by telling us that he left everything (Luke 5:28), and this is implied here. Matthew left a whole way of life to follow Jesus.[22] Tax collectors were usually wealthy men, for there was ample scope for profit in their business, so Matthew was probably making a great material sacri-

---

19. ἐκεῖθεν occurs 12 times in Matthew, but no more than 5 times elsewhere (Mark). It signifies "from there."

20. W. L. Lane draws attention to inscriptions showing that a number of people had two Semitic names (*The Gospel according to Mark* [Grand Rapids, 1974], pp. 100-101, n. 29). R. T. France takes Levi and Matthew as alternative names of the same man: "Since no Levi occurs in the texts of Mark and Luke, and since the stories told of the calls of Levi and of Matthew are clearly the same, this seems the most economical explanation" (*Matthew: Evangelist and Teacher* [Exeter, 1989], p. 69). Beare argues that the man's name was Levi and that the author of this Gospel substituted Matthew, an obscure member of the Twelve. But France has the better position.

21. A. Edersheim has a useful summary of taxation practices as they concern Matthew (*The Life and Times of Jesus the Messiah,* I [London, 1890], pp. 514-17).

22. Barclay points out that Matthew "lost a comfortable job, but he found a destiny. He lost a good income, but he found honour. He lost a comfortable security, but he found an adventure the like of which he had never dreamed" (p. 339).

fice when he walked out of that office. And the action was final. They would surely never take him back again if he later decided he wanted to return. The fishermen might go back to their fishing, but the tax collector would not be able to return to the levying of customs duties. Anyway, his lucrative post would soon be filled. And if he tried to get another job, who would want to employ a former tax collector? Matthew's response indicated a thoroughgoing trust in Jesus.

10. Matthew's grand gesture in leaving everything was not made in a spirit of grim resignation, as of a man doing what he knew was right but saddened by the cost. He tells of Jesus and others reclining[23] at a banquet and says no more than that, but Luke tells us that it was the new disciple who made "a great feast." Matthew celebrated becoming a disciple with a banquet at which many of the guests were as disreputable as he himself had been. This took place *in the house* (see on 2:11), where the article points to a particular house, probably Matthew's own house (Mark and Luke say that it was).[24] Matthew's characteristic *look* makes it all so vivid: his readers are invited to see it all in their minds' eyes. The guests were not such as might be expected where a religious teacher was the honored guest, but disreputable, *tax collectors and sinners.* The combination points to social outcasts. The tax farmers themselves were not regarded as necessarily unclean, but those they employed to do the actual work were unclean. Tax collecting necessarily brought the collectors into close contact with Gentiles, which, taken in conjunction with the social ostracism imposed by the religious parties, led to their being careless about the niceties of ceremonial uncleanness. They were also seen as following a disreputable profession. *Sinners* were in much the same position. The kind of ceremonial purity that was valued so highly by the Pharisees was such that many people could not attain it and still follow their profession. So they were lumped with the tax collectors as *sinners.*[25] Jesus and *his disciples*

---

23. For καὶ ἐγένετο see on 7:28. It makes a somewhat loose connection with what precedes. Here, as not uncommonly, it is followed by a genitive absolute plus καί with a finite verb.

24. Some interpreters suggest that it was Jesus' own house and that it was he who gave the banquet, inviting many sinners. This cannot be dismissed as impossible, but nothing in any of the Gospels leads us to think that Jesus was wealthy enough to put on a large banquet such as this one clearly was (there were *many* there). A tax collector would have been rich, and we should accept the natural meaning of "the house" and Luke's express statement that it was Matthew who gave the feast. Hill points out that the expression I have translated *reclined with Jesus* "could be understood simply as 'had their meal along with Jesus'"; it seems to mean no more. Bonnard says that the context makes clear that it was Matthew's house and not that of Jesus or Peter.

25. K. H. Rengstorf says that ἁμαρτωλός means "the 'sinner' as a man who forfeits a correct relationship to God by his culpable attitude to the Jewish Law." Here in conjunction with tax collectors it "partly means those who live a flagrantly immoral life (murderers, robbers, deceivers etc.), and partly those who follow a dishonourable vocation or one which inclines them strongly to dishonesty." But for the Pharisees, a person "is not a sinner because he violates the Law, but because he does not endorse the Pharisaic interpretation" (*TDNT,* I, pp. 327, 328).

reclined at table with these people. Some take this as an indication that Jesus was the host, but the words need mean no more than that the people mentioned "had their meal with Jesus" (cf. Hill in n. 24 above).

11. This event scandalized the Pharisees (see on 3:7). They would not have been at the dinner; the house would have been open and they could have come in (like the woman who came into the house of Simon the leper and anointed Jesus as he reclined at a meal, 26:6-7), but Pharisees would not have even entered the house lest they become unclean by contact with some uncleanness.[26] Matthew is probably telling us what happened later when they heard all about it. Interestingly they complained not to Jesus but to *his disciples.* They ask why Jesus engages in table fellowship with *tax collectors and sinners* (they lump these two groups together under one article). This is not so much a question seeking information as an accusation. Sharing a meal was considered a closer association (and therefore more blameworthy) than simply teaching them. A religious teacher might well pass on words of wisdom to sinners (though the Pharisees seem to have been slow to do this). But to eat with them meant to refrain from condemning them; it gave countenance to their laxity. The Pharisees could not understand it. They saw Jesus as claiming to be a religious teacher, and they could not understand how a religious man could associate with irreligious people.[27]

12. *But*[28] sets Jesus over against his Pharisaic critics. Their question was not addressed to him, but he heard what they said and made his response, without waiting for the disciples to think up what they should say. He takes a humble illustration from ordinary life, where it is the *sick,*[29] not the *well,*[30] who need medical help. The application of this to spiritual things is not difficult to find. We should not miss the implied rebuke of the Pharisees. They undoubtedly saw themselves as "well" in the sense that Jesus was using the word, and the tax collectors and sinners as "sick." Why then were these "healthy" people doing nothing to heal the sick? And why can they not see that his concern is to help the sick, not persuade them to continue in their sickness?[31]

13. *Go and learn* does not mean "go off on a journey" but is a call for

26. The rabbinic regulation says, "If tax gatherers entered a house (all that is within it) becomes unclean"; people "may not be believed if they say 'We entered but we touched nought' " (*Ṭohar.* 7:6). Simply to enter the house thus made a person ceremonially unclean. The Pharisees would not do it.

27. "Keep thee far from an evil neighbour and consort not with the wicked" (*'Abot* 1:7) was the rabbinic dictum. The Pharisees would have received repentant sinners, but they would not seek them out. Jesus did. He actively sought sinners to bring them to repentance. This was a new thing in Judaism.

28. δέ is adversative.

29. For κακῶς ἔχω see on 4:24; it is a general term for illness.

30. ἰσχύω signifies "to be in possession of one's powers" and thus "be well."

31. "Jesus speaks as the One who, divinely sent, leads from ruin to salvation by restoring the fellowship with God which was disrupted by sin and penally abrogated" (A. Oepke, *TDNT*, IV, p. 1095).

a genuine effort to understand.[32] Jesus proceeds to quote from Hosea 6:6,[33] where the prophet looks for God's people to show love and loyalty.[34] In the first instance this will mean that they should love the God who loves them so much. But this means also that they should love other people as God loves them. So it is that Jesus looks for the self-satisfied Pharisees to show compassion to the outcasts instead of rejecting them so firmly. He makes that clear when he goes on to outline his own procedure. *I did not come* points to his existence before he "came" to this world and sums up the essence of his mission (cf. 5:17). When he left his heavenly abode to come to earth, this was not in order to congratulate people like the Pharisees who were so well satisfied with themselves and so ready to condemn all who failed to measure up to their finicky standards. Nor indeed was it to deal with people who were genuinely right with God (*GNB* has "respectable people," but it is righteousness, not respectability, of which Matthew writes). Rather, his business was with sinners,[35] those who must produce repentance if they were to be saved. The attitude of the Pharisees was such that these people were left far from God; they made no attempt to bring them near. Since they were ready to let these people die in their sins, their attitude lacked compassion and thus failed to comply with the standards taught by the prophet they professed to honor so highly. This failure meant that in fact the Pharisees belonged among the people Hosea condemned — a startling accusation for these so outwardly religious people! Luke tells us that Jesus came to call the sinful people "to repentance" (Luke 5:32), but Matthew lets this be understood. He leaves his emphasis on the fact that the people Jesus came to call were *sinners*. Later we find that he came to die for them (20:28). Jesus never said that the people in question were anything other than sinful. But that was not the point. The point was that he came to save sinners.[36]

32. This corresponds to a formula used by the rabbis when they wanted someone to look more closely at the text to get its meaning (SBk, I, p. 499).

33. τί ἐστιν is to be understood in the sense "what this means"; the verb "to be" can be used to signify "mean," especially in the expression τοῦτ' ἔστιν. "this means."

34. I have examined Hosea's word (חֶסֶד) in *Testaments of Love* (Grand Rapids, 1981) and point out that it "suggests loyalty and constancy as well as indicating love" (p. 71). It is the attitude proper to partners in a covenant and thus should be manifested by the people who have made a covenant with God. This means those in the new covenant as well as the old. In LXX the word is translated by ἔλεος, a word that generally translated is "mercy" but that seems to have a wider meaning here.

35. Matthew uses ἁμαρτωλός 5 times, 3 in verses 10-13. The Pharisees could signify by the term those who did not observe their regulations, but Jesus means people who really offended God. Such people, however, could be induced to repent and turn from their evil ways. His mission was to bring salvation to such sinners. ἀλλά, which sets the *righteous* over against *sinners*, is the strong adversative. It is not with the righteous *but* with sinners that his mission is concerned. Cf. Robert Munger, "The church is the only fellowship in the world where the one requirement for membership is the unworthiness of the candidate" (cited by C. H. Talbert, *Reading Luke* [New York, 1984], p. 64).

36. We should not understand this to mean that Jesus had no business with those the world sees as righteous. After all, when the prophet cites the Lord as saying, "I want

b. Fasting, 9:14-17

14*Then the disciples of John came to him, saying, "Why do we and the Pharisees fast often, but your disciples do not fast?" 15And Jesus said to them, "Can the wedding guests mourn as long as the bridegroom is with them? But days will come when the bridegroom is taken away from them, and then they will fast. 16And no one puts a patch of unshrunk cloth on an old garment; for it pulls its overlap away from the garment, and the tear gets worse. 17Neither do people put new wine into old wineskins; if they do, the skins burst, and the wine pours out, and the skins are ruined. But they put new wine into new wineskins, and both are preserved."*

A further aspect of discipleship is brought out with a paragraph on fasting, a practice that occupied a large place in the religious observances of some of the Jews (and for that matter other people). Matthew makes it clear that fasting was not a feature of discipleship while Jesus was with his followers, but he leaves the way open for it in the days after Jesus would be "taken away from them." As usual, Matthew's account is shorter than those in Mark and Luke, but he has some touches peculiar to himself (e.g., the reference to mourning in v. 15 where the others have fasting).

14. For Matthew's favorite *then* see on 2:7; it does not point to strict sequence. But it may well be that John's disciples were fasting on a day that the followers of Jesus were feasting (cf. Mark 2:18). Matthew generally uses the term *disciples* (see on 5:1; 8:21) for the disciples of Jesus, but he can use it for the followers of other teachers, such as those of the Pharisees (22:16) or, as here, of John the Baptist. In the word "disciple" there is the thought of personal adherence to a teacher in the pursuit of learning. The Baptist is simply *John* without qualification. There is probably no great emphasis on *we* (despite the use of the pronoun): the pronoun had to be inserted so that John's people could link themselves with *the Pharisees*. Fasting was a common religious practice in the ancient world. The only fast prescribed in the Law was that on the Day of Atonement,[37] but in New Testament times pious Jews fasted every Monday and Thursday, and they might employ the practice at other solemn times. Perhaps we could say that whenever people felt that God should be approached in special humility for help in some time of trouble they saw fasting as the appropriate way. Fasting regularly twice a week and on other occasions as well certainly merits the description *often*.[38] Fasting could be seen as a way of

---

compassion and not sacrifice," he is not saying that people should not offer sacrifice. He is saying that people should do both, but also that God's priority puts compassion first. So here Jesus is not denying that he would ever call "righteous" people; he is saying that his priority is with sinners.

37. We should notice that the prophets insisted that ethical conduct was more important than fasting (e.g., Isa. 58:6-7; Jer. 14:12; Zech. 7; 8:19).

38. After νηστεύομεν some MSS read πυκνά (chiefly ℵ^a and some OL), but this should probably be considered an assimilation to the text of Luke. More difficult is whether to accept

gaining merit before God, and thus it is not surprising that Jesus and his disciples eschewed the practice. But this certainly marked them out as distinctive; John's men say that Jesus' people do not do it (GNB has a strong antithesis, "fast often . . . don't fast at all"). Jesus himself fasted at the time of the temptation in the wilderness, but there is no record of him engaging in the practice subsequently.

15. Jesus countered their question with one of his own. His question looks for a negative answer,[39] and the negative along with the verb *can* points to a complete impossibility. The bridegroom's attendants cannot be fasting while the feasting is at its height! The expression *wedding guests* (more literally "the sons of the bridal hall"[40]) refers particularly to "that group of the wedding guests who stood closest to the groom and played an essential part in the wedding ceremony" (BAGD). These people are necessarily preoccupied with the marriage; that is why they are there, and such practices as mourning are far from their minds. *As long as* is necessary because a wedding feast could go on for several days, but Jesus does not say "as long as the festivities go on" but *as long as the bridegroom is with them;* he concentrates on the presence of the bridegroom. *The bridegroom* (again in 25:1, 5-6, 10; 22:2, and developed toward the close of Revelation) carries on the same imagery,[41] and, of course, John the Baptist spoke of himself as "the best man" and Jesus as "the bridegroom" (John 3:29). *Mourn* points to an activity proper at a funeral (and other sad occasions), but not at a wedding. Bonnard well remarks that the Pharisees and the disciples of John had not recognized that Jesus was the messianic Bridegroom: "their pious sorrow is the sign of their refusal of Jesus and of the true repentance." But "Fasting is not appropriate if the kingdom is being manifested in Jesus' mighty deeds" (Johnson).

But joy in the presence of the bridegroom is not the whole story. Jesus points to a future time when *the bridegroom is taken away.* There can be no doubt that by *the bridegroom* he means himself, nor that *is taken away*[42]

πολλά (with אᵇ C D K L etc.). The word is absent from Mark, and the question is whether copyists put it in to make Matthew's text agree with that of Mark (the word is lacking in א* B etc.) or whether Matthew himself used it. Tasker sees internal evidence as against it "as the question at issue is not the frequency of fasting but the practice of it at all." It is perhaps slightly more likely that we should accept the word.

39. It is introduced by μή.

40. οἱ υἱοὶ τοῦ νυμφῶνος, where "sons" indicates those who are closely involved in the noun that follows. νυμφών (found in the New Testament only in the three accounts of this incident and as a v.l. in 22:10) means "the bridal hall." NASB translates "attendants of the bridegroom"; REB, "the bridegroom's friends"; and NIV, "the guests of the bridegroom."

41. This imagery is used in the Old Testament to refer to God (e.g., Isa. 54:5-6; 62:4-5; Jer. 31:32; Hos. 2:16-20). Jesus' words may be, as Carson thinks, "implicitly christological: he himself is the messianic bridegroom, and the Messianic Age has dawned."

42. ἀπαίρω has no necessary implication of violence, but we should notice that Jesus speaks of being *taken away*, not of "going away"; the expression refers to the crucifixion. France thinks that it perhaps echoes Isaiah 53:8 and that it "suggests a violent end, and the beginnings of official opposition in this chapter would give an early intimation of this eventual outcome."

refers to his death. This is not part of the marriage imagery but an alien element, and it shows us that from quite early in his ministry Jesus faced the fact that it would end in rejection and death.[43] John the Baptist had been put into prison and opposition to Jesus was growing, so it is not surprising that he should think of his death. When the bridegroom is no longer with them the disciples will fast. Cf. Carr, "There is a time of sorrow in store for my disciples when fasting will have a real meaning, *now* in my presence they can but rejoice." Jesus does not command them to fast; he simply prophesies that they will. And they did (cf. Acts 9:9; 13:3; 14:23; 27:9).

16. Jesus brings out another point with a homely appeal to practices in poor households where patching old clothes was a necessary part of life. *No one,* he says, patches *an old garment* by using *a patch of unshrunk cloth. No one* indicates that the practice is unthinkable. There is a play on words in *puts a patch* that is difficult to reproduce in English,[44] but the meaning is not in doubt; Jesus is referring to the process of mending a worn garment.[45] It may signify any garment, but some translations make it specific, such as "coat" *(NEB)* or "cloak" *(JB)*. The point is the wear the garment has had, its raggedness, rather than precisely which piece of clothing is in mind. The wrong patch, Jesus says, is one of *unshrunk cloth;*[46] such cloth was considerably stronger than cloth that had been treated and was used to make clothing. A patch of this kind would be most unsuitable for use *on an old garment,*[47] and Jesus proceeds to explain that such a *patch*[48] on such a garment would mean trouble. When there was any strain the patch would not tear, but the garment would, and the patch would take

43. A. M. Hunter remarks that this saying is "an awkward bit of evidence for those who deny that Jesus could have foreseen the Cross from an early date"; "the saying itself surely cries out to be put early in the story, for it belongs to a time when the lightheartedness of Jesus' disciples betrays no apprehension of danger. In short, the saying proves that in the full tide of the Galilean ministry Jesus faced the probability of death" (*The Work and Words of Jesus* [London, 1950], pp. 93-94).

44. ἐπιβάλλει ἐπίβλημα. The verb may be used of "put or lay upon" in various senses (Matthew's only other use is for arresting a prisoner, 26:50). The noun denotes anything put or thrown on something. In the New Testament it is used only in this saying (and parallels).

45. ῥάκος means a "ragged, tattered garment" (LSJ); it points to a worn rather than to a torn piece of clothing.

46. ἄγναφος (derived from κνάπτω, "to card" wool) means "uncarded, undressed" and thus "new" (so *GNB*).

47. παλαιός means "old," often with the idea that it is worn out or antiquated. ἱμάτιον often means a cloak, an outer garment, but it may be used in the sense of clothing in general.

48. πλήρωμα, which Matthew uses only here, means "that which fills." This could be another name for the patch (as McNeile, e.g., holds), but if so we are left without a meaning for αὐτοῦ (McNeile attaches it to ἱματίου, but its position in the sentence is against this). Michael G. Steinhauser denies that πλήρωμα is synonymous with ἐπίβλημα and translates, "No one puts a patch of unshrunk cloth on to an old cloak; because the patch of unshrunk cloth draws the overlapping section of the unshrunk cloth from the cloak and the tear becomes worse" (*ET,* LXXXVII [1975-76], p. 313). This is an awkward translation, but it does seem to give the sense of it. Many modern translations simply ignore αὐτοῦ.

some of the garment (*its overlap*) with it. Since sooner or later there would be some strain on a garment being worn (the first time it got wet the unshrunk patch would shrink!), this means that inevitably there would be a bigger split. Instead of mending a bad situation, such patching only makes things worse. This homely piece of wisdom would be immediately grasped by Jesus' audience, and it brings out vividly the point that Jesus is not trying to patch up a worn-out Judaism.

17. The same point is made in another way, this time with an illustration from the practice of storing wine. *Neither*[49] introduces another practice people do not follow. The verb *put* lacks a subject, but it is plural, conveying the notion of people in general. Those storing *new wine*,[50] which here means wine that is still fermenting, must take care how they store it. They do not put it into *old wineskins; old* is the word used in verse 16; clearly it points to something close to "worn out." Wine was commonly stored in containers made from the skins of animals.[51] But old skins lose their elasticity; if[52] new wine is stored in such containers, the process of fermentation puts more pressure on the skins than they can sustain, with the result that the skins burst and both wine and skins are lost. *But* (the strong adversative[53] — far from following the procedure that loses both wine and skins) people put *new wine* into *new*[54] *wineskins,* with the satisfactory result that *both are preserved.* The two illustrations effectively make the point that Jesus was not simply bringing in a revised and updated Judaism, or even founding a new sect within Judaism. What he was teaching and doing were such that they could not be contained within the accepted Jewish system; to attempt to confine his followers within the limits of the old religion would be to invite disaster. This did not mean that he was rejecting the Old Testament; he came to fulfil the law and the prophets, not to reject them (5:17). What he repudiated was not Scripture, but the current religious practices allegedly based on Scripture. He did not even repudiate those practices all at once and call on his followers to forsake Judaism. But he did repudiate the suggestion that they should remain confined within the accepted understanding of the old system. His new approach

---

49. οὐδέ carries on the negative, adding another instance of the same kind. Matthew uses the word 27 times, the most in any one book (next is Luke with 19 occurrences).

50. οἶνος means "*wine,* normally the fermented juice of the grape . . . the word for 'must', or unfermented grape juice, is τρύξ" (BAGD).

51. *Wineskins* "were usually made from whole goat hides, the neck and the feet being tied. Naturally an opening was left for the escape of gases formed by fermentation" (J. F. Ross, *IDB*, IV, p. 850).

52. *If* renders εἰ δὲ μή γε, where the negative negates the previous negative (in 6:1 it negated a previous positive): it signifies "but if (they do) not (refrain from putting new wine into old wineskins) the skins burst. . . ." See the note by J. L. Boyer, *GTJ*, 4 (1983), pp. 182-83.

53. ἀλλά.

54. Matthew utilizes two words for *new:* νέος, used with *wine,* strictly means "the new primarily in reference to time, the young, recent" while καινός, used with *wineskins,* signifies rather "the new primarily in reference to quality, the fresh, unworn" (AS). καί is employed to introduce result, "and so" (*NRSV*).

could not be fitted into those old forms. His followers must find new forms or there would be religious disaster.[55] Much the same point is, of course, made in the Fourth Gospel with its account of the changing of the water of Jewish purification into wine (John 2).

5. Three Stories of Healings, 9:18-34

Matthew rounds off his section on healings with another triplet, two of which have two healings. This concludes his making of the point that Jesus had an extensive ministry of healing and that he was able even to raise the dead. Later he has one or two miracles, but this is the section in which he makes his point firmly, after which it needs no further emphasis.

a. A Sick Woman and a Dead Girl, 9:18-26

18*As he was saying these things to them, look, a ruler came to him and bowed down before him, saying, "My daughter has just died; but come and lay your hand on her, and she will live."* 19*And Jesus got up and followed him, and so did his disciples.* 20*And look, a woman who had been suffering from a haemorrhage for twelve years came behind him and touched the tassel of his cloak;* 21*for she said within herself, "If only I touch his cloak, I will be healed."* 22*But Jesus turned and saw her and said, "Take heart, daughter; your faith has made you well." And the woman was made well from that hour.* 23*And when Jesus came to the ruler's house and saw the flute players and the noisy crowd,* 24*he said, "Go away, for the girl is not dead, but asleep." And they laughed at him.* 25*But when the crowd had been put out, he went in and took her hand, and the girl was raised.* 26*And the report of this went out into all that region.*

As is not uncommonly the case, Matthew's account is shorter than that of either Mark or Luke (it is about one third the length of Mark's and about half that of Luke). Even so, Matthew has some details that are absent from the others (e.g., the flute players and the raising of the girl where the others say that she "got up"). This short account includes all the essentials, and the final sentence helps us to see something of Matthew's purpose in recording it all. H. J. Held points out that Matthew's abbreviation of the story of the woman with the haemorrhage (which is in the middle of the story about the girl) is made in such a way as to emphasize the importance of faith. This, he notes, is also true of the little girl, and he goes so far as

---

55. Gundry asks, "if we were to identify the new wine with the gospel and set it in contrast with the old wineskins of Judaistic forms, what could we make of the concern not to let the old wineskins of Judaistic forms perish?" But Jesus is not calling for the old wineskins to be preserved from perishing; he is saying that it is the new wineskins into which the new wine is put that are to be preserved. Ridderbos remarks, "Jesus did not mean to condemn the old forms; He merely said that they had had their time."

to say, "Thus in this instance, too, we see not really a miracle story but a teaching narrative about faith" (*TIM*, p. 180). That may be going too far. but there is no denying the importance Matthew attaches to faith.

18. Matthew alone locates this story: *As he was saying these things* (Mark has Jesus "by the sea,"[56] and Luke says that it happened "when he returned"). For Matthew's characteristic *look* see on 1:20; it introduces a note of vividness. It is not easy to know how to understand the word translated *a ruler;*[57] it certainly means an important man in the community, a leader of some sort, but the term is not precise. Most interpreters understand the man to be a synagogue official, and this is probably correct. Mark calls him a ruler of the synagogue, and this is what Matthew implies.[58] The synagogue was the center of local life, civil as well as religious to use our terms (though first-century people did not put a sharp distinction between the two), and a man who is designated *a ruler*, without any qualification, would have been one of the leaders in the local synagogue. That a member of the local establishment should seek Jesus' aid probably means that he was desperate. It is clear that those in official positions were coming to regard Jesus as a dangerous heretic; thus there is every reason for supposing that a synagogue official would try every other source of help before turning to Jesus. But this ruler approached Jesus courteously: he *bowed down*[59] to him, which certainly indicates respect and may even mean that he worshipped him.

But the first Evangelist's interest is not in the man but in the daughter. There is a problem in that in Mark and Luke the daughter was no more than ill and that while Jesus was on his way to the house news came that she had died. It may be that we should understand Matthew to mean that the man's daughter was as good as dead, a view that was shortly confirmed by news of the actual death. Or once again Matthew may have abbreviated a narrative by running together the opening of a story and

---

56. It is possible to take Mark 5:21 as the conclusion to the previous story and to discern a new beginning, not necessarily in the same place, in verse 22. Mark has such transitions a number of times, for example, 3:20, 31; 10:46.

57. ἄρχων can denote leadership of many kinds, as is indicated by the variety of translations here: "a synagogue official" (*NASB*), "a president of the synagogue" (*NEB*), "one of the officials" (*JB*), "a Jewish official" (*GNB*). εἰς here has the force of the indefinite article (τις) rather than the numeral "one" (BDF, 247[2]). Cf. 8:19.

58. The ἀρχισυνάγωγος was the leading man in the synagogue organization. According to I. Sonne, he "was responsible for maintaining order during the meetings and removing disturbances (Luke 4:13); he was authorized to distribute honors, such as the reading of the Torah, reading from the Prophets, and preaching" (*IDB*, IV, p. 489). There could be a number of officials with this title (Acts 13:15).

59. Matthew alone uses the verb προσκυνέω here (see on 2:2; 4:9). The verb may mean no more than "bow down" and indicate respect. But it can also indicate the worship of a deity (as in 4:10), and it is probable that this is why Matthew uses it so often of Jesus. Even if in a given context respect seems required, this Evangelist is not unmindful of the worship that is due to Jesus. Turner thinks that the imperfect has the meaning "request" here, "as distinct from the aorist which means *worship*" (M, III, p. 65), but this does not seem probable.

the sending of messengers (as he did in the story of the centurion's servant, 8:5-13; in neither passage do the messengers play any significant role for Matthew). The story was one that demanded a raising from the dead, and Matthew makes that clear from the beginning. What mattered to him was that the ruler sought Jesus out and that, even when it was known that his daughter had died,[60] he went with Jesus to his home and saw the miracle of the dead girl brought back to life. So Matthew tells us that Jesus was acquainted with the death of the girl and that Jairus asked him nevertheless to *come* and *lay* his *hand on her* (an action often used in healing) in the assurance that then she would live. *Hand* is singular; one hand is sufficient.

19. There is no conversation or discussion; Jesus simply *got up and followed* the man. *His disciples* went along with him. There is no emphasis on them, for the story is about what Jesus did, but the disciples would be important to Matthew's readers. They saw what happened, and the church owed its knowledge of the miracle to their report.

20. Again Matthew's characteristic *And look* introduces something new (and no doubt unwelcome to the ruler). He speaks of a woman who had severe bleeding over a period of twelve years (the same span of time as the life of the ruler's little girl; Mark tells us that she was twelve years old, Mark 5:42). The woman's disability was not only a physical malady but one that had significant social implications; she would have been ceremonially unclean (Lev. 15:25-27), and therefore cut off from the ceremonial observances of the community. She could not join in worship, and her contact with other people would have been restricted because even a touch from her would make people unclean (Lev. 15:27). It was probably this that made her take the approach she did. She was convinced that one touch of Jesus would bring her healing, and she managed to effect this without drawing anyone's attention. With a crowd of people thronging around Jesus she was able to come up behind him and touch just *the tassel of his cloak*. It is not quite certain what the word I have translated *tassel* signifies here. It is used for the border or edge of something, and thus could mean the hem of Jesus' cloak. But among the Jews it was also used of the tassels attached to their outer garment to remind them to follow the commandments of God (Num. 15:37-38; Deut. 22:12; Jesus rebukes the Pharisees for making their tassels long, 23:5). Since this was a normal part of Jewish dress, we should probably understand the word here to mean one of these tassels. The *cloak* was the outer garment.

21. Matthew explains why the woman did this. She was sure that a touch would bring healing and reasoned that one touch of *his cloak* would be sufficient[61] (cf. 14:36). There seems to be an element of superstition

---

60. Matthew usually has ὅτι after indicatives, but here it precedes an indicative. But its meaning is clear: it refers to what has happened in the immediate past.

61. Burton says of this conditional clause, "The protasis states a supposition which refers to the future, suggesting some probability of its fulfilment" (*MT*, 250). Turner sees more than this. "This kind of conditional clause has almost a temporal meaning ('when' for 'if')

mingled with the faith of the woman, but Jesus did not reject her; he responded to the faith that he discerned. She certainly had the deep conviction that Jesus could cure her. If only she could get close enough to touch him, she would be free forever from her terrible disability. Her mind was clearly running[62] on the certainty of her cure.

22. The other Gospels tell how the woman tried to remain concealed and slip away quietly in the crowd, whereas Jesus insisted that she come forth. Matthew passes over all this and concentrates on Jesus' words to her. Jesus' refusal to let her remain hidden is probably connected with the nature of her complaint. All those who knew her would have known that she was unclean and accordingly would have excluded her from a good deal of the social life of her community. It was important that her cure be widely known, so that she could slip back into normal community and religious life. So Jesus *turned and saw her*; he gave her his full attention. His first word is one of encouragement, which was probably very much needed. The life she had led must have made her a bit scared of being with people, and there may possibly have been the thought that perhaps Jesus would not like what she had done (would he take her cure away?). But Jesus said, *"Take heart"*; he was concerned to encourage her, not dishearten her. He uses the tender address, *"daughter"*; the word could be used of a literal daughter (as in v. 18), but it was also used as a friendly greeting (this is the only woman Jesus is recorded to have called *daughter*).[63] Then he speaks of *your faith*; it is important that the woman understand that she had not been cured by magic of a kind that meant that anyone who touched Jesus would be healed. Her cure had been the result of a mighty power in Jesus, indeed, but it came to her because of her faith, not because of magic in a touch. That her faith *has made* her *well*[64] raises the question of whether the words mean more than physical healing (Bruce gives the meaning as "you are a saved woman"). Healing is certainly prominent, but it is not unlikely that we should understand that a real trust in Jesus was followed by spiritual blessing. The verb is the normal one for "save" (it is used in the message of the angel to Joseph when he said of the child that was to be born, "he will save his people from their sins," 1:21). While it is certainly used of salvation from sickness and the like, it is also used with a deeper meaning when connected with faith. It may well be that Matthew is not unmindful of that deeper meaning and that he recalls that Jesus certainly saved people like this woman from physical ailments, but that this was only part of a fuller and more wonderful salvation. It is difficult to think that the blessing received by even a

---

and represents rather more than mere probability. There was no doubt in the woman's mind. She said to herself, 'After I have touched that garment, I shall receive my healing' " (*Grammatical Insights*, p. 33).

62. The imperfect ἔλεγεν may mean "she kept saying."

63. Bengel argues that the term shows that "she was, therefore, not advanced in years."

64. σέσωκεν.

small faith means no more than physical soundness. At any rate, from that moment[65] the sufferer was made well, the specification of *that hour* making it clear that it was Jesus' saving power that was responsible and not some spontaneous cure.

23. The interruption over, Matthew returns to the story of the ruler and his daughter. He says nothing more about the journey, but goes straight to the point when Jesus reaches the ruler's house. In first-century Palestine burial was normally carried out very soon after death; in this case it is clear that the process was already underway. The professional mourners had not even waited for the father's return to his home. Thus it was that when Jesus reached the house he found some *flute players* and a *noisy crowd*, which we must understand as the normal mourning at a time of bereavement. The Mishnah lays it down that "Even the poorest in Israel should hire not less than two flutes and one wailing woman" (*Ketub.* 4:4); for the daughter of a ruler there would be much more than that. Matthew is referring to professional mourners who were on the job very promptly (cf. Jer. 9:17-18). But relatives and friends would join in with their loud wailing (the *noisy crowd*).[66]

24. Jesus immediately commanded them all to *go away*. He had insisted that the haemorrhaging woman come out into the open; in her case publicity was important. The same consideration that he had shown for her need is now shown to the little girl,[67] but it takes a different form. When she came back from the dead she was not to be confronted with a noisy and certainly confusing group of mourners. Jesus goes on to explain that the girl was *not dead, but[68] asleep*. Some students take this to mean that Jesus had made a diagnosis that assured him that she had not died. But this is surely not Matthew's intention. He is not telling a story of how Jesus woke a girl from a daytime nap, but recounting a miracle of a raising from the dead.[69] For him what we call death is nothing more than sleep (cf. John 11:11); the girl's death, though real, was not permanent. For the people there the girl was dead; all that remained was to go ahead with a decent burial and the proper period of mourning. But Jesus wanted none

---

65. Turner takes σέσωκεν as "a true resultative perfect denoting a past action of which the results still vividly survive": "from that very hour received her wholeness ἐσώθη" (M, III, p. 69). Elsewhere he gives Jesus' meaning as "You have received healing and *are now* in perfect health" (*Grammatical Insights*, p. 33).

66. For an account of mourning and burial customs see Daniel Rops, *Daily Life in Palestine at the Time of Christ* (London, 1961), pp. 328-34. Schweizer says that flute players at funerals "seem to have been employed only in Jewish households" (on v. 18, p. 229).

67. κοράσιον is found 3 times in Matthew, 5 times in Mark, and nowhere else in the New Testament. It is a diminutive of κόρη, "girl."

68. The strong adversative ἀλλά; far from the death they believed to have taken place, she was in what was for Jesus no more than sleep.

69. Cf. Fenton, "the Christians would not have told the story unless they believed that it was a miracle. They understood Jesus to mean 'Death is not the end, because I have come to raise the dead, to awake those who are asleep.' "

of this; he wanted them out of the way. To the mourners this must have seemed stupid, for at this point Jesus had not even seen the girl. They had. So despite the solemn business in which they were engaged, they laughed[70] at this person who, in their view, did not know what he was talking about. Since they had been engaging in loud-voiced mourning, this was quite a shift!

25. Matthew speaks of a *crowd* of people in the house, which makes it clear that the number was not small. But Jesus had his way, and the crowd was removed[71] from the house. Then he entered the house and went to the place where the girl was lying. He took her by the hand (touching the dead meant contracting ceremonial uncleanness; cf. Jesus' healing touch of the leper, 8:3) and raised her. As we have seen, Jesus did a number of cures by taking people by the hand, and for Matthew evidently that was what mattered. Mark and Luke record that Jesus spoke to the dead girl, recalling her from death, but for Matthew the taking of her hand was sufficient. When he did this, the girl *was raised* (or "arose").

26. Matthew rounds off the story with an addition of his own that the news[72] of what had happened spread around. It went out into *all that region*, which indicates that the report was widespread. The incident made a deep impression and was widely spoken of.

b. Two Blind Men, 9:27-31

[27]And as Jesus passed on from there, two blind men followed him, crying out and saying, "Take pity on us, Son of David." [28]And when he had come into the house, the blind men came up to him, and Jesus says to them, "Do you believe that I am able to do this?" They say to him, "Yes, Lord." [29]Then he touched their eyes, saying, "According to your faith let it be done for you." [30]And their eyes were opened. And Jesus said to them sternly, "See that no one knows (of this)." [31]But they went out and spread the news about him widely in all that region.

There are no miracles of the giving of sight in the Old Testament, nor in the New after the Gospels (the restoration of sight to Saul of Tarsus, Acts 9:17-18, is not of the same order). But in Jesus' ministry there are more miracles of the giving of sight than of any other single category. The

---

70. It is not easy to get an adequate English equivalent of καταγελάω; the prefix shows that a meaning like "laughed him down" is required, that is, they "derided him" (cf. LSJ).

71. The verb ἐκβάλλω may here have something of the notion of force. It is unlikely that a crowd of noisy and busy mourners would easily have allowed themselves to be removed from the house that was the center of attention.

72. φήμη is found elsewhere in the New Testament only in Luke 4:14. It means something said (cf. φημί) and thus a report. News like this would, of course, be spread by word of mouth. There is a textual problem: whether we should read αὕτη (with B K L W etc.), αὐτῆς (א C Θ), or αὐτοῦ (D sah. etc.). Metzger explains why we should accept the first reading: "The more difficult expression ἡ φήμη αὕτη appears to have been alleviated by scribes either by reading αὐτῆς ("the news about her") or by substituting αὐτοῦ ("his fame").

giving of sight is a divine activity (Exod. 4:11; Ps. 146:8), and it has messianic significance (Isa. 29:18; 35:5; 42:7). Matthew has a story very similar to this one in 20:29-34 (with parallels in Mark 10:46-52; Luke 18:35-43). In both of Matthew's stories the blind men cried out, "Have mercy on us, Son of David," in both Jesus touched their eyes, and in both their eyes were opened. But this story is located in Galilee, while the later one takes place near Jericho; here the men follow Jesus whereas there they sit by the way. In the later story people told the blind men that Jesus was passing and then rebuked them for crying out, Jesus called the blind men to him (here they follow him into the house), he asked what they wanted (here he questions them about their faith), and the story ends with the blind men following him (here with them spreading the story throughout the region). It seems plain enough that Matthew regarded the two stories as distinct, and that it is the later one that is paralleled in the other Synoptists.

27. *And* links this healing loosely with what precedes, while *passed on* and *from there* are also expressions of a general kind. Matthew is not tieing this story very closely to what has gone before. Matthew often speaks of people following Jesus, and there is frequently an overtone of discipleship. Here the *blind*[73] *men* follow because they want Jesus to give them sight. They were *crying out*,[74] which indicates that they were determined to be heard. *"Take pity*[75] *on us"* does not specify in what way they want the pity to be effective, but for the blind men there is little doubt as to their major concern. *"Son of David,"* a messianic term (see on 1:1), is here used for the first time in this Gospel as a form of address. The men may not have understood all that was implied in the term, but they saw Jesus as a great person and used a suitable designation when they approached him. It may well be that it was their use of this messianic name that caused Jesus to say nothing to them until they got into the house. It is unusual for him to ignore anyone who came to him for help, but to respond to such a term might well have led many of the passers-by to think that he was claiming to be a political Messiah.

28. Jesus was on his way to *the house,* and the blind men followed him there. There is an article: it is *the house* rather than *"a house"* to which Jesus went, and many conclude that it was Jesus' own house. This may

---

73. τυφλός is an adjective, but the masculine is often used as a noun, as here. It occurs 50 times in the New Testament, of which Matthew has 17, just over one third of the whole; he is the most frequent user of the term. On the frequency of eye trouble in Palestine Daniel Rops remarks: "The hot summers, with their brilliant light and their all-pervading dust, caused a great deal of eye-disease; and this is still the case, for at present the ophthalmic hospital of Saint John of Jerusalem treats twenty thousand patients a day" (*Daily Life in Palestine at the Time of Christ* [London, 1962], p. 321).

74. κράζοντες certainly indicates that they were making a noise; Lenski renders "yelling," and Moffatt, "shrieked" (which probably exaggerates).

75. ἐλεέω is usually translated "Have mercy," but "pity" seems more appropriate here; it is not a matter of being merciful to people who deserved harshness but of seeking pity for those in an unfortunate plight.

be so, but we have no way of knowing which house is in mind, or indeed whether he had a house (8:20 does not support the view). Matthew may mean that he went to the house where people had given him lodging. For the word see on 2:11; REB has "had gone indoors." The blind men went in too, and they *came up* to Jesus. We might have expected that they would repeat their plea (it had apparently been continuous as they followed Jesus along the way). But in the house it is the Master who speaks first (unless in compressing his narrative Matthew has omitted some words of theirs). He does not ask them what they want; that can be taken for granted. Instead he asks whether they *believe*,[76] whether they have faith. Faith is being given strong emphasis in this part of the Gospel, for Matthew has just brought out its place in the stories of the woman who came behind Jesus in the crowd and of the man whose daughter was dead. So now what matters is whether these blind men believe that Jesus can *do this*.[77] Neither he nor they spell out that it is a cure for blindness that they want. In the situation that may be taken for granted. They do not hesitate, but reply, *"Yes, Lord."* Their affirmation is definite, and their address is to be understood as "Lord" (as NRSV, NIV, LB) rather than as simply the polite "Sir" (as NEB, GNB, JB). At this point they are giving the term all the meaning they can put into it. They are respectful and certain. We should not overlook the fact that, being blind, they could not have seen anything that Jesus had done. They had had to depend on what people told them. Yet they came through with a definite and positive faith.

29. Once again Jesus heals with a touch. Matthew can use *eyes* for spiritual perception (e.g., 13:15), but here the word, of course, means the physical organs of sense perception. Jesus accompanied his healing touch with some words that underline the importance of faith. We should understand *according to your faith* in the sense "since you have faith" rather than thinking of strict proportionality (the meaning is not "the more faith, the better the result"; cf. 8:13). JB renders, "your faith deserves it," but this makes of faith a merit instead of a trust in Jesus through which God's good gift is received (for *faith* see on 8:10). It is better to understand the words in the sense of REB, "as you have believed, so let it be"; cf. Bruner, "You believe; you have it."

30. The miracle is put very simply: *their eyes were opened.* The verb is used of opening one's mouth to speak (5:2), of opening the mouth of a fish (17:27), and again of opening the eyes of the blind (20:33). In this last sense it means, of course, the giving of sight. Jesus follows this with a firm

76. This is the only place in Matthew where πιστεύω is followed by ὅτι, a construction that points to the content of the faith. Matthew has the verb 11 times: 4 times it is followed by the dative (= accept as true), 4 times it is used absolutely, once each it is followed by ὅτι, εἰς, and ἐπί.

77. Chrysostom comments that to lead them higher, and to teach them how they should think of him, "He did not say, 'Believe ye that I am able to entreat my Father, that I am able to pray' but, 'that I am able to do this?'" (p. 211).

injunction[78] that they keep silent about what he had done for them (cf. 8:4). *Sternly* indicates that Jesus was deeply serious about this: he did not want the men to take his injunction lightly. Matthew does not explain why he was so much in earnest about silence at this point, but he leaves his readers in no doubt that this was the case. "See, let no one know" is a more literal translation of what Jesus said. The command is compressed but the meaning is quite plain.

31. But[79] although Jesus' injunction was made so firmly, it seems that the men's joy at what had happened was too great for them to keep quiet. It was inevitable that some people would know; it is impossible for two blind men to become sighted without those near them knowing that something wonderful had happened. But it was not inevitable that the news should be made known far and wide. These two men had faith, and it was in response to their faith that they were given sight. But they lacked obedience. They did not supplement their deep conviction that Jesus could give them sight with an equally deep resolve to do his will. In the context *they went out* means that they left the house, they went off, but in view of the next words it may be meant to signify that they went out throughout the region. And as they went, they told[80] people what had happened. Matthew expresses this in a way that means something like "they spread him abroad"; it was obviously news that they spread abroad, but they did so in a way that centered on Jesus. The sequel to the miracle meant that Jesus was now known throughout the entire area where the formerly blind men moved.

c. A Dumb Demoniac, 9:32-34

> [32]*And as they were going out, look, people brought to him a dumb man who was demon-possessed.* [33]*And when the demon was cast out, the dumb man spoke. And the crowds were astonished, saying, "Nothing like this was ever seen in Israel."* [34]*But the Pharisees said, "He casts out demons by the ruler of the demons."*

There is a parallel to this story in Luke 11:14-15, and for once Matthew does not abbreviate (he has 38 words and Luke 34). There are minor differences throughout, but the words of Matthew's Pharisees are identical

---

78. It is difficult to find a good translation for the verb ἐμβριμάομαι, which is found 5 times only in the New Testament. It is connected with βριμη, "strength" (AS), and is used for the snorting of horses. When used of people it seems to signify strong emotion, and thus here it signifies a strict charge. Some exegetes suggest that it should be understood in terms of anger, but this does not suit the context here; *sternly* is about as far as we can go. Some translations have "warned" (*NASB, JB*), but it is not easy to understand what the warning could mean.

79. δέ has adversative force, "But, (instead of obeying Jesus) they. . . ."

80. διαφημίζω means *make known* by word of mouth, *spread the news about* (BAGD). We would expect it to have an object like "the news," or "what had happened," but instead we have αὐτόν, "him." It was Jesus they made known.

with those of Luke's crowds except that Matthew lacks the words about Beelzebul (which he has at the end of his similar story in 12:22-24). This, the last in this series of miracles, shows us Jesus doing a healing of a kind different from those earlier in the section.

32. As in verse 31, Matthew speaks of *going out* without specifying from where. But the context shows that it is the house of verse 28 that is in mind. The present tense indicates that the incident happened as they were on their way (*JB*, "they had only just left"). The Evangelist does not say who brought the dumb[81] man (he simply has the verb "they brought"), but he makes it clear that the man did not come by himself as in some other cases. This man was *dumb,* a disability caused by demon possession (see on 4:24); he may well have been deaf as well. Chrysostom says, "the affliction was not natural, but the device of the evil Spirit; wherefore also he needs others to bring him. . . . For this cause neither doth He require faith of him, but straightway heals the disease" (p. 211).

33. Nothing is said about a request for healing; people simply brought the man. Nor is there anything about what Jesus did. With his passion for brevity Matthew assumes that his readers will understand (a) that the man was brought to Jesus in order for his dumbness to be cured, and (b) that Jesus responded to the need. So he simply goes on to the situation when *the demon* had been *cast out* (the verb has the notion of a forcible expulsion; for *demon* see on 7:22). The demons do not readily leave those in whom they have taken up residence; hence the forcible word. Notice that there is no mention of faith, nor any action of Jesus like the laying on of the hand (contrast Mark 7:32-35). The expulsion of the demon is not the same as the cure of a disease (though the verb "heal" may be used of it as well as "expel," 12:22-24). That the man is now said to speak (rather than to hear) shows clearly that he had had a speech disability, though he may have had a hearing defect as well. Those who brought the man to Jesus had presumably expected a cure, but the crowds had not; they accordingly *were astonished* and gave voice to their astonishment, exclaiming that this was a completely new thing for Israel.[82] *Israel* here means the nation (as in 8:10), not the patriarch (10:6). The people are saying that their nation had never seen a miracle like this. We might reason that the raising of the dead is even more stupendous, but these people may not have known of that, and in any case this was "their" miracle: they had actually seen it done.

---

81. κωφός is found 7 times in Matthew, 3 times in Mark, 4 times in Luke, and nowhere else in the New Testament. It has the meaning "blunt, dull," and when used of the senses it may mean "dumb" or "deaf" or both (AS; those born deaf are mostly dumb as well). Here the meaning is clearly "dumb" (and perhaps "deaf" as well), and in 11:5 "deaf."

82. οὐδέποτε ἐφάνη οὕτως, "never was it seen thus"; Matthew has οὐδέποτε in 5 of its 16 New Testament occurrences (it is mostly used with past tenses as here, but cf. the future in 26:33). The verb means "appear, become visible" and is used here with the meaning "happened."

34. But *the Pharisees* (see on 3:7) had their own explanation. They were sure that they were right and Jesus was wrong, and nothing could be allowed to interfere with that basic conviction. They did not deny that something miraculous had occurred; they had seen this just as "the crowds" had done. If something miraculous had occurred and if Jesus was not on the side of the good, then for them the conclusion was obvious — it was by means of[83] Satan that the dumb man was made to speak. They give the evil one the title *the ruler of the demons* (again in 12:24; from Mark 3:22 it seems to be a standard accusation of Jesus' opponents). The Pharisees shut their eyes to the good Jesus does and ascribe it to the working of evil. This calling of good evil is perhaps the greatest blasphemy, the blasphemy that is unforgivable (12:28-32).[84]

He does not confer authority of word because He is the Word.

E. JESUS' SECOND DISCOURSE, 9:35–10:42

Matthew has concluded a major section on Jesus' teaching and another on his miracles, and through the two he has brought out the fact that both word and deed showed his authority. He now moves to a further important topic and tells us that Jesus conferred a certain authority on his disciples. He precedes the second of his great discourses, which will tell us something of what Jesus expects of his followers, with an account of the way Jesus chose twelve disciples and sent them on a mission to preach and to heal. Until now it has been Jesus who has taught and healed, but in the providence of God the followers of Jesus are to be given an important place in the work of the kingdom. The choosing and the sending out of the apostles is the first step; in due time this will be further extended through the work God would do through his church. In this passage we may discern some of the things that Matthew saw as of continuing importance for the ongoing mission of the church.

1. The Harvest and the Workers, 9:35-38

> [35]*And Jesus went around all the cities and the villages, teaching in their synagogues, proclaiming the gospel of the kingdom, and healing every disease and every sickness.* [36]*And when he saw the crowds he had compassion on them, because they were harassed and cast down like sheep without a shepherd.* [37]*Then he says to his disciples, "The harvest is great, but the workers few.* [38]*Therefore pray the Lord of the harvest that he will send out workers into his harvest."*

---

83. The instrumental use of ἐν.
84. Since this verse is omitted in some MSS (D some OL syr[s]), *REB* puts it in the margin; Allen, Zahn, and others likewise reject it. But it has strong attestation and may well be presupposed by 10:25 (Carson); it should be read.

As a whole this section is peculiar to Matthew. Some expressions about Jesus going about preaching are paralleled in Mark and Luke but in different contexts. Matthew is giving a summary of a good deal of Jesus' activity, and he may well have embodied in it isolated sayings from other contexts. Verse 35 is very similar to 4:23, and it may be that the two are meant to bracket the intervening section on the authority of Jesus for teaching and healing. But perhaps it is more likely that for Matthew each passage forms an introduction to an important section on the teaching of Jesus. Here he goes on to bring out the compassion of the Master and his call to prayer for the sending out of those who would bring in the spiritual harvest.

35. The verb *went around* is in the imperfect, pointing to a continuing process (cf. Moffatt, "made a tour"), while the combination of *the cities* and *the villages,* reinforced as it is by *all,*[85] indicates a comprehensive activity. This is what Jesus kept doing. Matthew does not say explicitly that this tour took place in Galilee, but this is to be understood. There is no indication that Jesus journeyed into Judea or the region east of the Jordan. Jesus' tour of the area was one in which he proclaimed *the gospel of the kingdom* and healed all kinds of illnesses (the same program that preceded the Sermon on the Mount, 4:23). The *synagogues* were places of instruction as well as of worship; they were a natural place in which a teacher would do his work. *Their* has no discernible antecedent, but it perhaps distances Jesus from the synagogue establishment: it was *their* synagogue, not his (cf. 7:29; 10:17). For *proclaiming* see on 3:1, and for *the gospel of the kingdom* on 4:23. The good news Jesus brought was about *the kingdom;* Matthew does not say what kingdom or whose, but that Jesus was proclaiming the rule of God is plain enough. And he healed *every disease and every sickness,* which may mean every illness that was brought to him, or "every kind of disease and sickness" (*GNB*). It is a comprehensive expression that brings out Jesus' mastery over all ill health. Matthew has a threefold description of Jesus' ministry: teaching, proclaiming the gospel of the kingdom, and healing.

36. *When he saw the crowds* looks like a reference to a specific occasion, but if so, Matthew does not say when or where. The main thing is that Jesus *had compassion*[86] on them (this is said of Jesus again in 14:14; 15:32; 20:34). In the New Testament this verb is always used of Jesus or

---

85. Matthew has *all the cities* only here; it is not a common expression. He uses κώμη only 4 times (Luke has it 12 times).

86. σπλαγχνίζομαι is found 5 times in Matthew, 4 in Mark, and 3 in Luke only in the New Testament. It is connected with τὰ σπλάγχνα, "the entrails," which were regarded as the seat of the emotions. But in distinction from καρδία, this is "a more blunt, forceful and unequivocal term" (H. Köster, *TDNT,* VII, p. 549). It is *"the seat of the feelings, affections,* esp. of anger" (LSJ). It is significant that whereas when the emotions are strongly involved the Greeks thought of anger, the Christians thought of compassion. This is the only place in the New Testament where the verb is followed by περί (ἐπί is more common).

by Jesus in his parables; it is particularly associated with him. H. Köster comments, "outside the original parables of Jesus there is no instance of the word being used of men. It is always used to describe the attitude of Jesus and it characterises the divine nature of His acts." He finds in Matthew's use of the term "a Messianic characterisation of Jesus rather than the mere depiction of an emotion" (*TDNT*, VII, pp. 553, 554). What we are to see here is not purely human pity, but divine compassion for troubled people. Matthew goes on to use two picturesque expressions to bring out the plight of those who were the object of Jesus' compassion. The translations employ a variety of expressions: "worried and helpless" (GNB); "harassed and helpless" (NRSV, REB, NIV); "distressed and downcast" (NASB); "harassed and dejected" (JB). The imagery is that of shepherdless sheep, sheep wounded and torn either by hostile animals or by thornbushes and the like, and then prostrate and helpless. *Harassed* is probably as good a translation as we can find for the first term, while *cast down* is almost exactly what the second conveys.[87] This picture of people completely without resource is rounded off by explicitly likening them to *sheep without a shepherd,* an expression used of the Old Testament people of God (Num. 27:17; 1 Kings 22:17; 2 Chron. 18:16; Zech. 10:2) Sheep are defenseless animals. Without a shepherd they are vulnerable to any attack. Even without predators they are in trouble if they have no shepherd, for they are not good foragers. They need a shepherd to lead them in green pastures and beside still waters (Ps. 23:2). Goats manage very well by themselves, but sheep do not. Sheep without a shepherd points to people who are in great danger and without the resources to escape from it.

37. For Matthew's characteristic *then* see on 2:7; here it means "next in sequence." *His disciples* is Matthew's characteristic early use; this is what would be said at a time when it was necessary to distinguish Jesus' followers from those of other teachers. *The harvest* may refer to a literal crop of grain or the like, but here it is used metaphorically of people.[88] Jesus does not spell it out, but he is speaking of people who are ripe for inclusion in the kingdom. In that situation it is necessary that something be done to bring them in. A crop of wheat needs workers[89] to bring the grain into the barn; without the laborers the crop cannot be reaped.[90]

---

87. σκύλλω meant originally "to skin, flay" and thus came to be used metaphorically for serious trouble of any kind. The second verb is ῥίπτω, "to throw, hurl," which might be used of violent action (like Judas hurling the money into the sanctuary, 27:5), or of nonviolent action such as the laying of people at the feet of Jesus (15:30). Clearly it means that the people in question are "down," that is, "downcast," "dejected." McNeile thinks that the reference is to the people "*as sheep,* mishandled and lying helpless."

88. Barclay points out that "the orthodox religious leaders" and Jesus saw ordinary people in different ways: "The Pharisees saw the common people as chaff to be destroyed and burned up; He saw them as a harvest to be reaped and to be saved" (p. 365).

89. ἐργάτης can denote any workman, but it is used especially of agricultural laborers.

90. There is a noble rabbinic saying attributed to R. Tarfon, "The day is short and the

Jesus says that in the great harvest of which he is speaking *the workers* are *few*.

38. In that situation action is demanded. Jesus himself could be in only one place at a time; therefore, to reap the harvest he saw, he enlists the disciples to take part in the harvesting. *Therefore* means that the state of affairs indicated in the previous statement demands action. Because there are few workers for the great harvest it is incumbent on the disciples to do something. The particular action Jesus singles out is prayer.[91] In an age like ours we would expect a call to more vigorous and effective action ourselves (and situations continually arise when that is the right course to pursue). But Jesus points to prayer as the really effective thing.[92] No matter how great our personal exertion, we will not be able to gather in the whole harvest. Therefore we are to pray to him who can *send out*[93] the workers who are needed. *The Lord* is used of God in a variety of ways (all of which bring out his superiority); here the term is related to the *harvest*. The harvest is already *his*. But it must be gathered in. It is one of the functions of the workers in God's field that they pray for more workers to be sent into the field. Some exegetes see the thought of judgment here,[94] for harvest is often used in connection with judgment. It has an obvious suitability, with the sickle cutting off the possibility of further growth and development. But in this passage there is nothing to indicate judgment; the thought is rather that of the owner's care for his crop. He takes infinite pains over it.

---

task is great and the labourers are idle and the wage is abundant and the master of the house is urgent" ('*Abot* 2:15).

91. δέομαι, used here only in Matthew but 22 times in the New Testament, means prayer that springs from a sense of need (AS gives the first meaning of the verb as "to want for oneself; 1. to want, need"). To appreciate the need is to be driven to prayer.

92. "The prayer is not to be a substitute for the labor: the disciples were to be reapers as well as praying men. But the work will not be done without prayer" (Buttrick).

93. Carr says that ἐκβάλῃ "denotes the enthusiastic impulse of mission work."

94. Patte asks, "what will be the predominant role? The positive role of a shepherd? Or the judgmental role of the harvesters?" But in this passage Jesus is not speaking about two different roles; he is talking about the care God has for his own and the importance of bringing them home to him.

240

Matthew 10

2. The Mission of the Twelve, 10:1-42

Having given a general introduction to this next section of his narrative, Matthew proceeds to Jesus' summoning of the Twelve and his commissioning of them for the mission to which he is sending them. The other Gospels have no parallel to this charge as a whole, but there are parallels to most parts of it in a number of places in Mark and Luke (see Mark 3:13-19; 6:7-11; Luke 9:1-6; 10:1-15). Matthew speaks of persecutions (e.g., vv. 17-18), which seem to have taken place later than this sending of the Twelve; perhaps he has included instructions given to the disciples on a number of occasions in one compact section. Some of the parallels in Luke come from that Evangelist's narrative of the sending out of seventy (or seventy-two) disciples (Luke 10), an event not mentioned in Matthew or Mark. It is likely that the Twelve would have been included in the seventy, and it would be in line with what we have seen of Matthew's method if he telescoped the instructions given on the two occasions (cf. his omission of the messengers in the healing of the centurion's servant and in the raising of the daughter of Jairus). Or there may be a better explanation of this Evangelist's procedure. I am not so much concerned with how he wrote his Gospel as with its meaning as we have it. He tells us then that Jesus chose twelve men for special service and sent them on a mission; he tells us of instructions that Jesus gave, some of which had a good deal of relevance during the years subsequent to the life of the Master.

a. The Twelve, 10:1-4

1And having summoned his twelve disciples, he gave them authority over unclean spirits, to cast them out, and to heal every kind of disease and every kind of sickness. 2Now the names of the twelve apostles are these: first, Simon, who is called Peter, and Andrew his brother; and James the son of Zebedee, and John his brother; 3Philip and Bartholomew; Thomas and Matthew the tax collector; James the son of Alphaeus, and Thaddaeus; 4Simon the Cananaean, and Judas the Iscariot, who also betrayed him.

Matthew has told his readers how Jesus called five disciples and he has spoken of people following Jesus, but this is the first indication that

241

the Master chose out twelve to be especially close to him. These men were to be especially significant for the whole Christian movement, and through the centuries the Twelve have been held in special honor. But very little is known about most of them; evidently some of them were not memorable men. If this is so, it would accord with the fact that God has often chosen people the world has regarded as insignificant through whom to do his wonderful works.

1. *And* seems a curious way of introducing a new narrative; as in 9:1 it will introduce something new with a loose connection to what precedes (BAGD, 1.5). Jesus called to him *his twelve disciples,* who come before us for the first time as a special entity (until now we have heard of five who responded to the call to be disciples, 4:18-22; 9:9, but there must have been many more). Matthew is the only New Testament writer to use the expression "the twelve disciples" (11:1; 20:17; 26:20), though there are quite a few references to "the twelve." There were many disciples, but twelve were especially close to Jesus and were destined to have a unique place in the church that would emerge in due course. Matthew does not say why Jesus chose twelve, but it is the number of the tribes of Israel and may point forward to the true Israel and the renewal of the people of God that Jesus would bring about (cf. 19:28).[1] To these men Jesus gave *authority*[2] for both exorcisms and healing (Bonnard points out that it is authority for the apostolic mission that is in mind and not an authority for government of the church). Matthew refers to *unclean spirits* again only in 12:43; Mark has 11 such references, and Luke 5. *Unclean* may be used in a cultic sense of that which has no contact with deity, but when used of *spirits* the moral sense is more prominent. These *spirits* are to be thought of as evil. They are opposed to the purposes of God and the welfare of people; the Twelve now have the authority that enables them to[3] expel such evil beings. With that is joined the authority to heal (see on 4:23). The repetition of *every kind* before both *disease* and *sickness* shows that the disciples were equipped with a far-reaching power (the same expression is used of Jesus' healings in 4:23).

2-4. This is Matthew's one use of the word "apostle,"[4] and the only

---

1. *AB* emphasizes the importance of the messianic community: "even if we had no evidence from the OT, the Qumran literature is evidence enough that in contemporary Jewish thinking a Messiah without a Messianic Community was unthinkable."

2. ἐξουσία is here followed by the genitive of that over which the authority is exercised; it may also be used of the one who exercises authority (Rev. 12:10).

3. We might have expected authority ἵνα . . . , but Matthew says ὥστε (which he uses 15 times). He is more interested in the result than the purpose. Burton finds the construction to express "Tendency or conceived result thought of as such" (*MT,* 371), while Moule thinks it "perhaps" indicates purpose (*IBNTG,* p. 140; a number of others hold that this shows that ὥστε can signify purpose). There is some notion of force in ἐκβάλλω; it was not to be expected that the evil spirits would cheerfully and easily leave people they "possessed," but the Twelve had the power to expel them.

4. ἀπόστολος is found once each in Mark and John also, and 6 times in Luke. But it occurs 28 times in Acts and 34 in Paul; it was a significant word in the life of the early church, though apparently not so much so during the lifetime of Jesus. I have examined the word in chapter

use of the expression *the twelve apostles* in the Gospels (it occurs in Rev. 21:14). These men are to be understood as identical with the *twelve disciples* of verse 1 (though "disciple" has a wider significance than "apostle"). They were the leaders in the group that attached itself to Jesus and have always been seen by the church to have great significance. The word "apostle" has a new sense in the New Testament. In earlier times the word was used of naval expeditions, of ships "sent" on a mission, sometimes also of other groups that were "sent," and now and then of the commanders of such groups (the "admiral," for example). Jesus was not simply repeating some earlier practice when he sent out his Twelve; *the twelve apostles*, sent out with Jesus' authority, represent something new in the world of religion. These men were to have a key role in the church that would in due course be set up.

Matthew proceeds to record the names of the Twelve (so also Mark 3:13-19; Luke 6:12-16; eleven are listed in Acts 1:13). He has arranged them in six pairs: the two in each pair are connected by "and" (which may be a reminiscence of their being sent out two by two, Mark 6:7), but the pairs are not connected (except the first two pairs). Matthew begins with *Simon, who is called Peter*, and says that he is *first*, which indicates that he was in some sense the leader (cf. Barclay, "first and foremost"). It can scarcely mean that he was the first to come to Jesus, for Andrew brought him in the first place (John 1:41-42). But we should bear in mind Bengel's reminder that Peter was "first *among* the apostles, not placed *over* the apostles: *in* the apostolate, not *above* it." All the lists have three groups of four, with the same name coming first of the four in each list. No name appears in one four in one list and in another four in another list, though there are variations in order within the fours and some slight variations in the names. In all the lists the members of the first two groups are identical though the order is not the same. Thus in the first four Mark puts *Andrew* in fourth place (as does Acts), while Luke agrees with Matthew in placing him second. In the second four Mark and Luke put *Matthew* before *Thomas*, while in this Gospel *Matthew* follows *Thomas* and has *the tax collector* added; Acts also has this order but does not refer to the tax collector. In the final four *James the son of Alphaeus* is first in all the lists and *Judas the Iscariot*[5] is

---

III of my *Ministers of God* (London, 1964). Many commentators draw attention to the Jewish functionary called the *shaliaḥ* and cite the adage "a man's *shaliaḥ* is as it were himself." But this overlooks the fact that there is no evidence for the *shaliaḥ* as early as the time of Jesus. G. W. H. Lampe says, "The institution which we know in the fourth century almost certainly came into existence later than the time of the New Testament, and the 'shaliachate' in this sense is not likely to have contributed anything to the development of the Christian apostolate" (*Some Aspects of the New Testament Ministry* [London, 1949], pp. 15-16).

5. Matthew has ὁ Ἰσκαριώτης, but Mark and Luke Ἰσκαριώθ. The list in Acts omits the traitor. The meaning of *Iscariot* is disputed. It may be a place name meaning "man of Kerioth" (cf. Josh. 15:25; Jer. 48:24, 41), though some other suggestions are that it is derived from the Latin *sicarius*, referring to a rebellious group, or that it reflects the man's occupation and means "Judas the dyer," or that it signifies "Judas the red-head," or "carrier of the leather

last. All have a second *Simon*, but, while Matthew and Mark call him *the Cananaean*, Luke speaks of him as "who was called Zealot."[6] Matthew and Mark have *Thaddaeus*[7] before *Simon*, but Luke has "Judas, son of James" after him.

It thus transpires that the lists are identical except for the variant descriptions of the second *Simon* and Luke's Judas where the others have *Thaddaeus*. This may be another name for the same man (Chrysostom accepts the identification); Lenski and others think the name "Judas" would have been dropped after the betrayal by Judas Iscariot. Or possibly the exact composition of the Twelve varied a little from time to time. It will be seen that most of these have left very little mark on the history of the church, and it may well be that that was because they were not outstanding people ("They were very ordinary men," Barclay, I, p. 367; "men of obscurity, and of no repute," Calvin, I, p. 290). When Jesus chose his Twelve he did not choose supermen; God does not need outstanding people to do his work, and it seems that, while some of the Twelve were very able men, others were very ordinary.

b. The Charge to the Twelve, 10:5-15

> [5]*These twelve Jesus sent out, after instructing them in these words: "Do not go off on the road to Gentiles, and do not go into any town of the Samaritans;* [6]*but rather go to the lost sheep of the house of Israel.* [7]*And as you go, preach, saying, 'The kingdom of heaven has drawn near.'* [8]*Heal sick people, raise dead people, cleanse lepers, cast out demons; without cost did you receive, without cost give.* [9]*Don't get gold or silver or copper in your money belts,* [10]*or a bag for the journey, or two tunics, or shoes, or staff; for the workman deserves his keep.* [11]*And into whatever town or village you enter, inquire who in it is worthy; and stay there until you leave.* [12]*And when you go into the house, give it your greeting.* [13]*And if the house is worthy, let your greeting of peace come upon it; but if it be not worthy, let your peace return to you.* [14]*And whoever does not receive you or listen to your words, when you go out of that house or town shake off the dust from your feet.* [15]*Truly I tell you, it will be more bearable for the land of Sodom and Gomorrah in the Day of Judgment than for that town."*

---

bag." The first suggestion is probably the best, and it agrees with the fact that Judas's father was also called Iscariot (John 6:71). The aorist participle is used of action future to the time of which Matthew writes, though antecedent to the time of writing (cf. BDF, 339[1]; *MT*, 142).

6. Καναναῖος is not to be seen as "Canaanite" but as a translation of the Aramaic קַנְאָן, and thus means "Zealot"; Matthew and Mark have transliterated, while Luke has translated the word. *NEB* has "Simon, a member of the Zealot party." It is not clear that there was a party of Zealots as early as this; there was hostility to Roman rule, but that those who opposed it were called "Zealots" does not appear to be attested until the war of A.D. 66-70. Some scholars hold that Simon was a member of the resistance movement, but the term may indicate simply that he was zealous for God's law.

7. D and some other MSS call this man Lebbaeus, and the later MSS give him both names.

Having named the Twelve, Matthew proceeds to relate the instructions Jesus gave as he sent them out on a preaching and healing mission. On this occasion they were to confine their labors to Israel, and he expressly forbade them to to beyond Israel's borders, even to the Samaritans. At a later time they would have a wider commission (28:19), but their first venture was to their own people. Matthew was more interested in the instructions Jesus gave the preachers than in the actual trip, for he mentions neither that they departed, nor where they went, nor when they returned.

5. *These twelve* comes first with a certain emphasis: it was the people named, those whom Jesus has chosen and Matthew has called "apostles" (for the only time in this Gospel) whom Jesus now sends forth[8] on a mission. He gives them instructions, where the word *instructing* has a military ring about it; it points to authoritative commands.[9] The first direction Jesus gives is one that confines the apostles to Israel for the duration of this mission. They are not to take *the road to Gentiles,*[10] which places the whole of the Gentile world outside the scope of the work they are now beginning. So with *any town of the Samaritans*. This is Matthew's only use of the word, and he does not use the name "Samaria" at all. Though the Samaritans were not viewed as on exactly the same level as the Gentiles, they still did not belong with the ancient people of God. It was to the Jews that this mission was directed. All this means that on this first mission the Twelve were to work in Galilee; the roads to the north and east led to Gentile territory, while that to the south went to Samaria. Only Galilee was left. In due time the followers of Jesus would preach to people of any nation, but there was a proper order; here they were told to start with the Jews (cf. Paul's practice, Acts 13:46, and his theory, Rom. 1:16; 2:9-10).

6. Instead[11] the Twelve are to *go to the lost sheep of the house of Israel.* Matthew uses a present imperative (whereas he had two aorist imperatives in v. 5); if it is used strictly, it means "keep going." Throughout this mission they are to keep going to Israel. Matthew is fond of the sheep imagery; he has the word *sheep* 11 times in all (elsewhere only John with 17 has it more than twice). Mostly, as here, the usage is symbolical. In John 10 the sheep belonging to the Good Shepherd are the saved; but sheep all too easily go

8. The verb ἀποστέλλω is related to the word ἀπόστολος; it was fitting that the "apostles" should engage in "apostling."

9. παραγγέλλω. AS (*sub* ἐντέλλω) notes that this verb is used "esp. of the transmitted orders of a military commander" (passed along a line of soldiers?). It is used of a variety of people in authority, but the note of authority is constant.

10. Turner takes ἐθνῶν as an objective genitive with the meaning "a way leading to" (M, III, p. 212), but Moule regards the genitive as practically doing the duty of an adjective to give the meaning, "to Gentile parts" (*IBNTG,* p. 38).

11. δέ has adversative force, since it sets the Jews over against all those outside that nation. μᾶλλον (9 times in Matthew; only 1 Corinthians with 10 has more) indicates a preference: rather than going to the Gentiles and Samaritans they were to go to Israel.

astray, and here they are the Israelites who have wandered far from God.[12] This probably does not refer to a part of the nation, for as the prophet put it, "All we like sheep have gone astray" (Isa. 53:6; cf. Jer. 50:6; Ezek. 34, etc.). *The house of Israel* means all the descendants of Jacob; it is a common way of referring to the nation (Matthew has the expression again in 15:24, and "sons of Israel" in 27:9; he has *Israel* 12 times).

7. Again the present imperative seems to point us to continuous action. The message the apostles were to preach was constant: they were not directed to preach a variety of topical sermons but simply to say, "*The kingdom of heaven has drawn near,*" the message of John the Baptist (3:2, where see note) and of Jesus himself (4:17). As we have seen, the message of the kingdom included the thought that Jesus had a special place; so, as the disciples went on this preaching tour, they would be proclaiming their Master. It was not their business to work out the solution to contemporary problems, but to sound out the message Jesus was proclaiming. *Preach* (see on 3:1) came to be used characteristically for the preaching of the gospel, but it cannot have that technical meaning here (Jesus had not yet died and risen). It means here the preaching of the same message as Jesus. The fact that the kingdom was *near* shows that their message concerned a present reality rather than a distant future possibility.

8. The apostles' message was to be accompanied by action, and this is along the lines of what has already been narrated of Jesus. First, they were to *heal sick people* (for *heal* see on 4:23). Jesus does not tell them how they are to do this, simply that it was their task. Presumably they are to follow his example. Most translations have "the sick," and perhaps this is the way we should take it. But since the word lacks the article, it may be that the direction is not that they should heal sick people as a class and thus turn into full-time healers. Rather, they were to preach the kingdom, and as an adjunct to that they were to do some works of healing. So, too, they were to *raise dead people.* Again there is no article, so it is not the dead as a class that are in mind, but those dead people whom they would encounter in the discharge of their commission. There are no recorded examples of their raising dead people (though later some disciples did this, Acts 9:40; 20:9-10), but then there are no recorded examples of their healing sick folk either. We do not know how they did either or how frequently. A similar remark attaches to their cleansing of *lepers;* it is good to know that these needy people came within the scope of their commission, but we have no information about how extensively they performed this task. And, finally, they were to *cast out demons.* Matthew has the word "demon" 11 times, of which 7 refer to these evil spirits being cast out and

12. ἀπόλλυμι (19 times in Matthew, 27 in Luke; next are Mark and John with 10) can mean "lose" (Luke 15:8-9), but also "ruin, destroy" (Mark 1:24) and even "kill" (2:13) or "destroy eternally" (Rom. 14:15). McNeile, Bruner, and others favor "perished" as the meaning here, but "lost" seems more probable, "sheep that have wandered from the fold" (Mounce).

an eighth to a demon going out (17:18; cf. 7:22). Mark records that the disciples cast out demons (Mark 6:13), and Luke that demons were subject to them (Luke 10:17).

Until now the verbs have all been present tense, but now we have two aorists. "You received" points back to what God has already given to them; *give* points forward to their own act of giving. The same adverb[13] is used in both clauses: the way God has treated them is the way they are to treat others. *REB* renders, "You received without cost; give without charge"; this brings out the sense of it nicely, though it translates the adverb in two different ways.

9. Jesus goes on to the way they should look forward to their journey. Normally people make provision for such a trip, but Jesus is telling the disciples that they must go as they are. They are not to *get*[14] a store of money that would enable them to meet the expenses that they thought might well arise as they journeyed. *Gold* might refer to the precious metal in itself, but here it will refer to its use in coins. So with *silver*; it is not the metal in itself that is in mind or its use in ornaments, but coined silver. *Copper* can refer to anything made of copper, but when used of coins, as here, it will refer to coins of least value, small change. The word I have translated as *money belts* is used of girdles in general, though in the New Testament it always refers to the belt of a man or an angel. In this context it clearly is a place in which money can be kept. Jesus sweepingly forbids them to take money, and that of either large or small denominations. It is not money that will sustain them on the journey they are about to make, and they are not to rely on any monetary resource.

10. Nor[15] are they to take *a bag* in which to store possessions. *JB* makes this "a haversack" and *GNB* "a beggar's bag," while *LB* thinks of "a duffle bag." Such translations may be a trifle over-definite; the word is used of a wide variety of bags. W. Michaelis maintains that the bag here is the normal bag a traveler would take in which to store the food he would need for his journey;[16] he denies that we should think of a beggar's

---

13. δωρεάν means "in the manner of a gift"; it points to the freeness with which God had supplied the needs of the disciples, and it formed a model for their own giving,

14. κτάομαι means "procure for oneself, acquire, get" (BAGD); it points to a serious effort to acquire what would be necessary to sustain them on their journey. Gundry and others think that this refers not to money *for* the journey, but to money *from* the journey (cf. Goodspeed, "Do not accept gold . . ."). This is a possible meaning of the verb, but the same verb covers two tunics, shoes, and a staff. Would it be likely that they would acquire these on their journey? Moreover, Mark tells us that Jesus introduced the words with the command that they "take nothing for the journey" (Mark 6:8).

15. In verse 9 μή introduces a negative command, and this is carried on with a string of μηδές. Here we have μή again, after which μηδέ is resumed. But there seems to be no difference in meaning.

16. Michaelis says, "When he put εἰς ὁδόν after πήραν Mt. was undoubtedly thinking of the travelling wallet which would contain what was needed *en route*, not of the beggar's sack which would be empty at the start and filled during the journey" (*TDNT*, VI, p. 121, n. 14).

bag. Jesus is saying that it will not be necessary for them to take provisions for the road. He goes on to say much the same about clothing. His followers should not take *two tunics*. The tunic was the usual undergarment and was worn next to the skin by either sex. It is not certain whether Jesus is saying that they should not wear two tunics at once (perhaps for extra warmth? Josephus speaks of a man wearing two tunics, though he does not say why; *Ant.* 17.136) or that they should go as they were and not take along an extra one. *Shoes* were made of soft leather, whereas sandals were of hard leather.[17] Jesus may mean that they were to wear sandals (as Mark 6:9 says), or perhaps, as some of the poor did, that they were to go barefoot; he may mean that his followers were to identify with these poor. Alternatively, if the difference between shoes and sandals is not in mind, the meaning may be that they should not take an extra pair along with them (*get* seems to mean "get in addition to the pair you are now wearing"). That they were to use some form of footwear seems implied in the instruction to shake the dust off their feet (v. 14). Nor should they take a *staff,* an implement that most people would take when walking.[18] The accumulation of things not to be taken emphasizes the point that they are to go as they are. They are not to make elaborate preparations for their journey.[19] That God would surely supply their need is the unspoken thought, and they are not to rely on their own resources and ingenuity. There may also be a reference to the fact that a man "may not enter into the Temple Mount with his staff or his sandal or his wallet, or with the dust upon his feet" (*Ber.* 9:5). If this is in mind, the meaning is that they must not give even the appearance of doing anything other than serving God.[20]

A reason[21] is introduced. It will not be necessary to take these various precautions, *for the workman deserves his keep* (cf. Luke 10:7). The disciples are workmen for God, and they can rely on their employer to supply the things they need. The *workman* is strictly a farm laborer, a worker in the fields, but from this the word came to be used of workmen of various

17. We see the distinction in *Yebamot* 12:1, where we find that the rite of *halitzah* (Deut. 25:9) is valid if performed with a shoe but not if performed with a sandal unless the sandal has a heel piece. Daniel-Rops distinguishes between the shoe and the sandal (*Daily Life in Palestine at the Time of Christ* [London, 1962], pp. 217-18). LSJ gives the meaning of ὑπόδημα as "sole bound under the foot with straps, sandal," but adds that it may also be used of "a shoe or half-boot, which covered the whole foot."

18. In Mark 6:8-9 the Twelve were to take (αἴρω) a staff and sandals; the difference may be that in Matthew they are not to acquire (κτάομαι) these things. In both accounts Jesus is prohibiting elaborate preparations for their journey.

19. Allen thinks it possible "that Christ wished His missioners to avoid anything that would make them look like ordinary travellers journeying for purposes of trade or pleasure."

20. Cf. Edersheim, "The symbolic reasons underlying this command would, in both cases, be probably the same: to avoid even the appearance of being engaged on other business, when the whole being should be absorbed in the service of the Lord" (*The Life and Times of Jesus the Messiah*, I [London, 1890], p. 643). Against this view is the fact that two tunics are prohibited, as well as staff, shoes, bag, and wallet.

21. γάρ.

kinds. Such workmen would be paid a wage, but they would also be given the food they needed while they were on the job. As they are doing the work they are deserving of their keep.[22] The workman receives his food as of right; it is not a gift, for he has earned it. The Twelve were going out in the service of God; they, too, would therefore merit their food as they labored for their Master. They would not need to pay for it, for he would supply what was needed.

11. Jesus turns to what is to happen when his emissaries reach a *town or village*.[23] Matthew uses the word for *town* (or "city") 26 times, but that for *village* only 4; for the most part he is more interested in the larger centers of population than the smaller (though here, of course, he is saying in effect, "When you enter any inhabited place, large or small"). There was, of course, a long tradition of hospitality in that land, and in any case inns do not seem to have been plentiful. It was natural to expect to stay as guests in private homes. The apostles are to *inquire*[24] about a lodging, where the word signifies careful scrutiny but gives no indication as to how this is to be done. But the point is clear: they are not to choose lodgings haphazardly, but to look carefully for the right person. The householder is to be *worthy* (the word occurs 4 times in vv. 10-13), but worthy of what? *GNB* renders, "look for someone who is willing to welcome you," and this may be the sense of it; in that case it is hospitality that is being stressed. Or it may be people who are willing to welcome the message of the kingdom; if so, it is spiritual fitness that is to be sought. The word does not seem to have the ethical connotation it has with us (people might be "worthy of blows," Luke 12:48). Having found a suitable lodging place, they are told to *stay there until you leave.* The point about remaining in one home is apparently that they could well prolong their stay if they went from house to house, whereas Jesus was sending them on a trip that would embrace a large number of centers of population in a short space of time. They were not to spin it out. Another suggestion is that they might be tempted to move from a less luxurious home to a more luxurious one, but this does not seem as likely.

12. Now come instructions for behavior when they *go into* the place where they are to stay. *The* house will be the house chosen as the result of the scrutiny just described. The travelers are to begin by giving *it* (grammatically the house, but in sense the household) the *greeting.* Mat-

---

22. τροφή is used 4 times in Matthew; it may be used literally of things to eat (as here) or metaphorically.

23. δ' comes rather later in its clause than is usual; it serves to link this with the preceding. On ἦν . . . ἄν BDF comments, "Relative clauses which can be converted into conditional clauses usually make no assertions about concrete realities, but rather general assertions or suppositions, so that ὅς . . . ἄν, corresponding to the ἐάν of the conditional clause proper, appears as a rule" (BDF, 380[1]).

24. ἐξετάζω (twice in Matthew and once in John only in the New Testament) means "scrutinize, examine" and may be used "as legal t.t. *question* judicially" (BAGD).

thew uses the verb for giving a greeting again only in 5:47; it is the usual word and does not denote anything other than the greeting normally used, "Peace be to you."

13. Two possibilities arise from their selection of a house: they may be right or they may be wrong in adjudging the house (i.e., "the household") to be *worthy*. If the household really is worthy, then their *greeting of peace* will be effective; there really will be peace to these people.[25] But this will not be the case if the household *be not worthy*; it is unrealistic to think that the peace of God would rest on such people. It is not easy to see precisely what is meant by their peace returning to them, but clearly it is a way of saying that despite the prayer involved in the greeting there would be no peace for the unworthy householders. The peace of which the apostles were the messengers would not remain with the contemptuous.

14. Jesus gives attention to those who reject the preachers. There will be some people who will not *receive* them, that is, receive them as guests, or welcome them. With the failure to welcome the preachers is coupled a failure to heed their words. These people will not *listen* to them, that is, hear them with understanding and appreciation. Neither the men nor their message is being welcomed. In such a case the preachers are to register what has happened with a small gesture of repudiation. As they leave *that house or town* (rejection might be on a smaller or larger scale) they are commanded to *shake off the dust from your feet*.[26] This seems to mean the dust that clings to the feet, but BAGD notes the view of A. Merx that it means the dust raised by the feet that settles in the clothing. Either way it is clear that it is a symbolic act whereby the unfriendly people are repudiated. It points to the severing of the smallest of ties. The Jews held that even the earth in Gentile lands was unclean, and it was their custom when they returned from abroad to shake from their feet the dust they had acquired when abroad.[27] Jesus is telling his followers to treat the unwelcoming Jews as they would treat Gentiles.

15. For *Truly I tell you* see on 5:18. It introduces a solemn and important statement. Those who reject the messengers of Christ will find themselves in a very difficult situation in *the Day of Judgment* (both nouns lack the article in this technical expression; cf. our "Judgment Day"). *Sodom*

---

25. ἐλθάτω is a 3rd person imperative; the meaning is not "you allow your peace to come . . ." but something like "then may your peace come. . . ." A similar caution is involved in interpreting ἐπιστραφήτω. We are not to think of the apostles as in some way withdrawing their kind words (as *GNB*, "take back your greeting"), but the imperative is rather directed at the words themselves. They will not bring peace on unworthy people. In the similar Luke 10:6 there is a future, not an imperative.

26. ἐκτινάσσω means "to shake off." In Mark 6:11 it refers to shaking the feet, and in Acts 18:6 to shaking clothing. This is Matthew's one use of the word. An example of the practice is given in Acts 13:51.

27. See SBk, I, p. 571. Earth from a foreign country is included in a list of things that convey uncleanness, alongside that from a grave area (*Ohol.* 2:3; *Tohar.* 4:5).

and *Gomorrah*, the cities of the plain, were proverbial for wickedness, and their overthrow showed something of the power of God and the certainty that wickedness could not forever go unpunished.[28] It is perhaps significant that just before their overthrow they had committed a grievous sin against the laws of hospitality (Gen. 19). That it would be *more bearable*[29] for the proverbially wicked cities than for these cities shows the seriousness of their offense: deliberately to reject those who came to them with the message of the nearness of God's kingdom could not go unpunished forever. We should not miss the christological claim that is implied. If the punishment of those who rejected Jesus' followers who brought his message was greater than that of notorious sinners of old, then how great must we understand Jesus to be?

c. Troubles Ahead, 10:16-25

16"*Look, I send you out as sheep in the middle of wolves; therefore be sensible as serpents and innocent as doves.* 17*And beware of men, for they will hand you over to the courts and they will flog you in their synagogues;* 18*and you will be brought before governors and kings for my sake as a testimony to them and to the Gentiles.* 19*But whenever they hand you over, do not worry about how or what you will speak; for it will be given to you in that hour what you are to speak.* 20*For it is not you who will be speaking, but the Spirit of your Father who will speak in you.*

21"*And brother will betray brother to death, and a father his child, and children will rise up against parents and have them put to death.* 22*And you will be hated by all on account of my name; but he who endures to the end, this one will be saved.* 23*And when they persecute you in this town, flee to the next. For truly I tell you, you will not finish (going through) the towns of Israel before the Son of man comes.*

24"*A disciple is not above his teacher, nor a slave above his master.* 25*It is enough for the disciple that he be as his teacher, and the slave as his master. If they have called the head of the house Beelzebul, how much more the members of his household.*"

The next section of the discourse is one that looks beyond the immediate mission on which the Twelve were to be engaged to a time when Christian preachers would be brought before hostile tribunals and undergo severe persecution. Whereas in the earlier section the preachers could expect a fairly friendly reception (they would receive hospital-

28. Cf. BAGD, the city of Sodom was an example "of extraordinary sinfulness" and as such "as proof of the terrible power of God to punish." It mentions an inscription in Pompeii that includes the words "Sodoma Gomora"; this indicates a very widespread reputation for the two cities.

29. ἀνεκτός occurs 3 times in Matthew and twice in Luke only in the New Testament. It derives from ἀνέχω, which in the New Testament is always middle with the meaning "to bear with, endure" (AS).

ity in homes in each place to which they went), now there is the thought of bitter hostility.[30] Matthew has gathered here teachings of Jesus that would be of importance to the Christian preachers of his own day. He seems to have liked to put together sayings that related to similar topics.

16. Matthew's characteristic *Look* (see on 1:20) introduces a note of vividness as we come to a new section of the exhortation. Jesus' *I* is probably emphatic (though Carson doubts this, as does McNeile; Bruce, however, affirms it, and Plummer finds "a notable emphasis on the Sender," p. 151):[31] "it is *I* who am sending you." The preachers are now likened to *sheep in the middle of wolves* (the danger is even clearer in Luke 10:3 with "lambs in the middle of wolves"). Bengel points out that the word is *in*, not "into," for they are already among wolves. Earlier Jesus has likened the hearers to sheep (v. 6, where see note), for they so easily go astray. Here the thought is rather that sheep are defenseless;[32] they have no way of resisting fierce animals like *wolves*.[33] Other than rams (who are so designated) they have no physical equipment designed for offense, and they are in trouble against most predators. *In the middle* puts them squarely in the place of danger; it leaves them no escape route. *Wolves* (again in Matthew only in 7:15) may be used literally or metaphorically. The expression leaves no doubt that there is serious trouble ahead. But there is also encouragement in the expression, for it speaks of no unforeseen tragedy but a difficult time that their Master has known would come and has reckoned with in his plan for them.[34]

But this does not mean that they need not be concerned. They must do their very best in the difficult situations they will meet. They are to be *sensible as serpents*, where the term rendered *sensible*[35] is given various nuances in the translations, such as "wary" (*REB*), "cunning" (*JB*), or

---

30. D. R. A. Hare comments on "how large a proportion of the material in the chapter is concerned with the non-acceptance of the gospel and the hostility with which the missionaries are treated. There is no instruction regarding what is to be done with converts in a successful mission!" (*The Theme of Jewish Persecution of Christians in the Gospel according to St Matthew* [Cambridge, 1967], p. 98).

31. Matthew has ἐγώ 210 times. This is considerably below John's total of 465 and a little below Luke's 215, but more than in any other book. Matthew is fond of this emphasis.

32. "We are not primarily fighters, we are not allowed to be haters, and we cannot even use the arsenal of invective that revolutionary movements find indispensable for motivation; thus in these ways disciples, factually, *are* sheep" (Bruner, p. 380).

33. "*Wolves* seem hardly convertible things; *Sheep* strange missionaries to be sent to them. But so Christ describes their position. And for centuries it was their willingness to die for Christ and men; that was the greatest converting quality in the apostles of Christ" (Glover).

34. Cf. G. Bornkamm, "they are also comforted, for this is no unforeseen disaster, but exposure to danger is involved in the very fact that they are sent out by Jesus. In a series of sayings from v. 11 on Mt. brings out the eschatological significance of the relation of the disciples to the world by clearly contrasting their authority and the persecution which awaits them" (*TDNT*, IV, pp. 310-11).

35. φρόνιμος, from φρήν, "midriff," which was considered the organ of thought, and thus "mind, thought"; φρόνιμος signifies "practically wise, sensible, prudent" (AS).

"shrewd" *(NASB)*. It points to the need for careful thought when confronted with these difficult situations. Disciples are *sheep* indeed, but that does not mean that they are to be stupid. *Serpents* were widely thought to be clever as well as hostile to people (cf. Gen. 3:1).[36] So when confronted with them it behoved the preachers to put forth their best mental effort. But brains are not enough. They must also be *innocent*[37] *as doves*.[38] The dove was thought of as chaste and as faithful to its partner for life, and its gentleness and guilelessness were proverbial.[39] But also on occasion a dove may be thought of as "silly" (Hos. 7:11), so dovelike conduct must be balanced with a figure that brings out the need for wisdom. The Christian preacher must live in such a way as to commend the message, not carelessly as non-Christian people generally do. Cf. Bruner, "If we are to be sheep among wolves — and this *is* Jesus' intention — then we should at least be smart sheep, sheep who use our heads, sheep who don't overestimate the benevolence of wolves" (p. 381).

17. Jesus leaves the metaphors and says *beware of men*, where *men*, of course, is used inclusively to mean "people" and does not signify "members of the male sex." The term is quite general, but in this context it has special reference to people in authority, for it is they who are in a position to bring believers before the courts. *Hand over* (see on 4:12) may be used of various kinds of handing over; it is the usual word for Judas's betraying of Jesus (as in v. 4). Here it has the technical sense of handing over to the court for trial. *Courts* is more literally "sanhedrins," a word that is used for all sorts of councils. Mostly in the New Testament it refers to the great council in Jerusalem, but here it signifies local councils (only here and in Mark 13:9 do we have the word in the plural); a council of twenty-three men was found in each locality. With it is linked *synagogues*, which, as we have seen before, means centers of Jewish life. Synagogues were places of worship, but they were also places of instruction and, as we see here, places where local justice was administered. The court would sit in the synagogue and punishment be inflicted. The terminology shows that Jesus is referring to the Jewish administration of justice, not that of the Gentiles. The offender would be whipped with a scourge of four thongs through which smaller thongs were plaited (*Mak.* 22b). Three judges were required (or, according to another opinion, twenty-three, *Sanh.* 1:2). One man would read passages of Scripture, a second would count the strokes, and a third would give the command before each stroke (*Mak.* 23a). There could be

36. W. Foerster points out the widespread "idea of the cunning and malice of snakes, as indicated in the expression 'to nourish a snake in one's bosom,' related proverbs, and many phrases" (*TDNT*, V, p. 567).

37. ἀκέραιος means "unmixed" and points to single-mindedness in doing the right; "it demands not naivety, but an irreproachable honesty" (France).

38. περιστερά means a pigeon or dove (the ancients apparently did not differentiate closely). "The dove, which fr. the viewpoint of natural science in ancient times, has no bile, was for the early Christians the symbol of all kinds of virtues" (BAGD).

39. See SBk, I, pp. 574-75.

as many as thirty-nine strokes, but no more in a Jewish synagogue (cf. 2 Cor. 11:24).[40]

18. Jesus envisages that his followers will be brought before the highest in the land. *Governors*[41] will stand for the highest officials in any given area (people like Pilate), and the link with *kings* (puppet kings like the Herods, though they were strictly tetrarchs and the like) makes it clear that Jesus is speaking of all the chief people. There would be the strongest possible opposition to his preachers. These expressions make it clear that Jesus is not now referring to the preaching trip on which the Twelve were about to embark, for that would not bring them before governors or kings. He seems to be speaking of what would happen when his followers preached in Gentile lands. When in due course some of his followers would undergo the trials of which he is speaking, this would be *for my sake* and it would be *as a testimony to them*. The authorities would think that they were simply dealing with ordinary lawbreakers, but that would be a superficial view. The prisoners would be people who were there for the sake of their leader, the Messiah, and the trial would not really be an ordinary legal process. It would be an occasion when witness would be borne to the coming of the kingdom and to what that should mean for those who were sitting in judgment on God's messengers. *To the Gentiles* indicates that the testimony would extend beyond the officials of the courts and makes it quite plain that Jesus is now referring to happenings outside Palestine. The sufferings of the disciples would be the means of bringing the essential Christian message to Gentiles, people outside the ancient people of God but within the scope of the Christian message.

19. *Whenever* indicates that the fact is certain, though the time is not. *Hand over*, as in verse 17, refers to the official handing over for trial. Jesus is still concerned with the troubles his followers would have before hostile judiciaries, but now he is concerned with the problems his frequently illiterate followers would face in unfamiliar and terrifying surroundings. He tells them not to *worry* (see on 6:25 for this verb), a thought that receives some emphasis in this Gospel. In this place it means that those who trust the heavenly Father and who are acting in obedience to Christ need not be anxious when they stand before earthly councils. Specifically they need not be concerned about the manner or the content of their defense; they are to give forethought to neither. What they are to say before the great ones might well have been a worry to Galilean peasants, and Jesus' words must have been a very welcome encouragement. This does not, of course, mean that those who speak for Christ on other occasions are spared the necessity of careful preparation and the proper marshalling of their thoughts. Jesus is not speaking about the general conduct of his followers

40. There is a useful account of the Jewish system in *TDNT*, IV, p. 516.
41. ἡγεμών is found in Matthew in 10 of its 20 New Testament occurrences. It can mean a prince (2:8) but more often it is used of governors, often of Pilate.

but of the specific problems facing those who are haled before hostile tribunals. They are not to worry nor to prepare. *It will be given* is another example of the divine passive. God will give them what they need is the thought, and this is spelled out in the next verse with its reference to the Holy Spirit. The gift will be given *in that hour;* they will not know a long while beforehand what to say, but divine inspiration in the law court will enable them to give the witness that God wants them to give.

20. *For*[42] carries the argument along in logical sequence, and *you,* preceded by its negative, is emphatic: "you will not be the speaking ones!" They will, of course, provide the mouth and throat through which the voice will come, but[43] they will not have the responsibility for producing the defense. That will be something *the Spirit of your Father* will do for them. This expression is found nowhere else in the New Testament, but we need not doubt that Jesus is speaking of the one who elsewhere is usually called "the Holy Spirit." This form of expression relates the Spirit more closely to the Father than do other ways of referring to him. Notice further that the Spirit is the Spirit of *your Father.* Jesus often refers to God as his own Father, and it is clear that he stands in such a relationship to God as do none of his followers. But that does not mean that they may not think of God as their Father, too. There is a difference in the relationship, but they are in a very meaningful sense children of the heavenly Father, and it is that Father who will send his Spirit to them to speak in them at this critical time. Matthew says that it is the Spirit who will speak, Mark, that it is "not you who speak, but the Holy Spirit" (Mark 13:11), and Luke, "I will give you a mouth and wisdom, which all your adversaries will not be able to resist" (Luke 21:15). All three assure the followers of Jesus that they will not be left to their own devices in the critical hours of which he speaks. We should not think of disciples in such situations as mere passive instruments; Bonnard points out that "to you" and "in you" are significant, and adds, "the man is never more himself than when the gift of 'the Spirit of the Father' is given him."

21. Jesus is speaking of no minor difficulties but of troubles on a grand scale. He says that family life will be disrupted in the coming trials, and gives examples of the divisions that will occur (cf. Mic. 7:6; Mark 13:12). *Brother* will "hand over" *brother* (note again Matthew's interest in brothers), so that there will be treachery in that place above all where we look for love and loyalty. The verb *betray* is that used of Judas in verse 4 and repeated in verses 17 and 19; the failure of people to be loyal is emphasized, while *to death* indicates a situation of the utmost seriousness. Jesus is not referring to minor troubles that can easily be put right, but to situations of the utmost gravity. There is no more far-reaching consequence of an action than that it leads to death. And it does not stop with fratricidal

---

42. γάρ. We might have expected the finite verb, but we have the participle οἱ λαλοῦντες.
43. *But* is the strong adversative ἀλλά.

strife. *A father* will act in the same way toward a *child,* as will *children* to *parents*[44] as they bring about their deaths. It is impossible to think of any more complete breakdown of the family, the basic unit of society.

22. Jesus turns from family disruption to a universal hatred for his followers. They *will be hated* (see on 5:43), which points to much more than mild opposition,[45] while *by all* indicates wholehearted rejection of the disciples by the communities in which they are found. It cannot mean every individual without exception (for then there would be no point in their preaching), but it does indicate widespread and strong opposition. Christ's people have often faced unreasoning hatred (why should people actually *hate* those committed to love for all?), but it helps to know that the Master foresaw this from the beginning. And the reason for the hatred? *On account of my name!* The name, of course, means all that the person is and stands for (see on 6:9). The persecution and the hatred will arise because of the disciples' connection with Jesus, whose very name indicates that he came to save people from their sins (1:21). Hill thinks that there may be an allusion to bearing the name Christian (as in 1 Pet. 4:14). Either way we see the unreasonableness, the irrationality of the hatred. Of course, through the years Christians unfortunately have sometimes been less than faithful and have acted in anything but the spirit of Christ. But Jesus is here telling them that even when they are completely faithful they cannot expect to be universally liked. There is that about the *name* of Christ that arouses opposition and hatred from worldly people.

In these circumstances of extreme hostility Jesus looks for his followers to be steadfast. They are to *endure* ("stand firm," NIV), which points to a continuing attitude. It is important to make a commitment to follow Christ, but more than that is required. Jesus looks for continuance in the Christian way, a constancy in discipleship even when it is known that the most severe consequences may well ensue. *To the end*[46] means not only to the end of some period of time, but to the end of the trials, the persecutions. It is not good enough for the follower of Jesus to renounce his allegiance somewhere along the line. Real discipleship means perseverance right through whatever trials the world throws in our way. It is *this one,* the perseverer, who *will be saved* (see on 1:21). Salvation may be used in any one of a number of ways (we have seen it used of those saved from illness or the like), but here the word must be given its fullest meaning. Those

---

44. *Rise up* renders the verb ἐπανίστημι (again in the New Testament only in Mark 13:12); it means something like "rise up in rebellion" and here indicates a complete disregard for parental authority. θανατόω means *"kill someone, hand someone over to be killed,* esp. of the death sentence and its execution" (BAGD).

45. The periphrastic tense points to more than a passing whim; there will be continuing hatred. Robertson takes the tense as "expressing continuance" (p. 357); he says that it was "The very failure of the future to express durative action clearly" that led to this periphrastic construction (p. 889).

46. εἰς τέλος lacks the article and could mean simply "finally." But in this context it is more likely to signify the end of the trials in question.

who endure through the persecutions will in the end find themselves in the presence of their Lord forever. There is some emphasis on *this one;* Jesus is not talking about a universal salvation, but about a salvation in which this person, just described, will find blessedness.

23. The thought of the persecution continues, with the instruction not to persist unnecessarily in a situation of persecution. *When* might be translated "whenever."[47] It implies that the persecution is certain; it is the time that is uncertain. It may also signify that the action is repeated — there will be more than one persecution. When a disciple finds one place implacably hostile it is not his function to continue to offer himself for maltreatment and death;[48] needlessly to court martyrdom is not the Christian way. Jesus tells him to seek safety in flight, to *flee to the next*[49] town. The verse is clear up to this point. But the remainder presents us with a very difficult problem.

The statement is important, for it is introduced with *Truly I tell you,* an expression Jesus uses when he is making solemn and significant statements (see on 5:18). But it is not clear exactly what we should understand by "finishing the towns of Israel" and by the coming of the Son of man. *Finish*[50] in this context would seem to mean finish going through the cities and towns of Israel on the preaching trip that the Twelve were about to begin. But it is not easy to see what the coming[51] of the Son of man could mean in this connection. The "coming" normally brings us into the sphere of eschatology and refers to the second coming, the return of the triumphant Lord at the end of the age. While it is not impossible to hold that Jesus referred on occasion to this "coming," that does not seem to be what is in mind here. One possibility is that we should remember that the term "the Son of man" appears to be derived from the vision in which "one like a son of man" "came to the Ancient of Days" (Dan. 7:13). In other words, the coming may be Jesus' coming to the Father rather than to his return to earth at the end of the age. The coming to the Father would then refer to the conclusion of his mission here on earth with the passion and resurrection. There will still be work to do in *the towns of Israel* when that

47. ὅταν.

48. "It sometimes happens that there is more real heroism in daring to fly from danger than in stopping to meet it. To stop and meet useless risks, because one is afraid of being called a coward, is one of the subtlest forms of cowardice; and the desire to be thought brave is not a high motive for courageous action" (Plummer, p. 152).

49. The word is ἑτέραν, which strictly means "the other of two," but in this context surely means "next." The use here "is peculiar" (BDF, 306[2]), but Turner finds it an example of the classical use for "a definite division into two" (M, III, p. 197). Bruce understands the meaning as "not merely to another city numerically distinct, but to a city presumably different in spirit."

50. τελέω (7 times in Matthew out of 28 times in the New Testament) means "bring to an end," "finish," "complete."

51. The verb is ἔρχομαι, which is used for a variety of comings (including that of Jesus at the end of the age, which BAGD sees here).

consummation is reached. Tasker thinks that the reference is to Jesus' coming "in triumph immediately after His resurrection" when he commissioned his disciples to make disciples of all nations (so Mounce).

Others have suggested that Jesus is encouraging the Twelve to move smartly when they go on their mission, for he will be coming along after them and will in due course catch up with them. There are not wanting scholars who think that Jesus is speaking of the Second Advent and that he thought it would come about very shortly. The extreme form of this view is that of A. Schweitzer, who held that Jesus thought that the consummation would take place in his own lifetime.[52] But Matthew was writing quite some time after the words were spoken, and he knew that the Lord had not returned; he cannot have meant that he would. More recent scholars sometimes take the view that Jesus expected the end of all things within a generation or so of the time of speaking and that it is this climax of which he speaks here (e.g., Fenton; Hill, "within perhaps 40-50 years"; and others). Ridderbos thinks of a merging of the sufferings of the disciples preaching to the Jews with the sufferings of the end time: "the sufferings of the Jews in Israel were merely a prelude to and a shadow of the agonies that will have to be endured at the end of the age." Yet another view is that Jesus may be held to "come" in various ways and that a very significant "coming" was that in A.D. 70 when Jerusalem was destroyed. That judgment meant the end of Jewry organized around the temple cultus and formed a terrible judgment on people like those of whom Jesus has been speaking in the previous verses as opposing Christian preachers, punishing them in synagogues and handing them over to Gentiles. Such a view is accepted by Lenski, Carson, and others.

The variety of views shows that a decision on the meaning of the words is not easy. Perhaps there is most to be said for the view that they refer in an unusual way to the climax of Jesus' mission, his coming back from the dead after his rejection by the people ("a reference to the exaltation of the Messiah in passion-resurrection," AB). There is triumph in that coming and there is a further commission to the disciples to take the message over all the earth. On this understanding Jesus would be saying that the disciples are to carry on with the task to which he sent them, and further that they certainly would not have completed it before his work on earth reached its climax.

24. Jesus returns to the thought that it is inevitable that his followers will suffer rejection. He points out that this is the common lot of *a disciple* (for the term see on 5:1; 8:21). Mostly the word is used in this Gospel for the follower of Jesus, but here the term is quite general. Any disciple *is not above his teacher.* In time, of course, he may surpass his teacher and become considerably greater (though this is not a possibility for the followers of the incarnate Lord). But while he is a disciple he is no more than

52. *The Quest of the Historical Jesus* (London, 1911), pp. 357-62.

a learner: the very concept of discipleship means that he cannot be greater than his teacher. The point here is that he cannot expect to be treated better than his master; if the teacher suffers persecution, the disciple can expect nothing less. A second negative carries on the thought. *A slave* is not to be thought of as *above his master*; the very concept of slavery means that the slave occupies an inferior position. He may be a more worthy man, but as a slave he is subordinate. Jesus is saying that in the very structures of society there are some immutables. His followers should learn from this. They cannot expect to be given better treatment than that which their Master received.[53]

25. *Enough*[54] indicates that the disciple must be content with his place. Jesus has just made the point that the disciple is not greater than his teacher, and it follows that he must regard it as sufficient if he can be as his teacher is; he can look for no more. So with *the slave* and *his master*. The slave can share in the glory of the household of which he is a humble member, but no more. While he is a slave he cannot expect to be superior to his owner. That is not the way society works. All this is the way Jesus brings out the inevitability of troubles for his followers. They cannot expect to be regarded more highly than their Master or to secure better treatment. Jesus refers to the fact[55] that his enemies have called him *Beelzebul* (again in 12:24, 27; the form Beelzeboul also occurs, and the Vulgate has Beelzebub), which raises further problems. But whatever the precise form of the name, it certainly indicates rejection. The god of Ekron was called "Baal-zebub" (2 Kings 1:2, 3, 6, 16; the name does not occur in the LXX text), a term that means "lord of flies" and that apparently was a Hebrew pun on the name of a Philistine god. The Jews may have further corrupted this into "Baal-zebul," "lord of dung," which would be a way of further insulting the heathen deity. This name, however, occurs in the Ras Shamra tablets as the name of a Canaanite deity, and it appears to mean "lord of the dwelling" or "lord of the high place" in Canaanite. Taking all this into consideration, it seems likely that the Hebrews took the name of a heathen deity that they could interpret contemptuously as "lord of flies" or "lord of dung" and that they applied to evil beings. In time it came to signify a

---

53. G. Bornkamm remarks, "the title and address of Jesus as κύριος in Matthew have throughout the character of a divine Name of Majesty. The legitimation of this from Scripture is found in Ps. 110.1 (22.41ff.)" (*TIM*, pp. 42-43). On this Kingsbury says, "The effect of Bornkamm's essay was to put an end for all practical purposes to the dispute, as far as Matthew's Gospel is concerned, over whether *kyrios* is a christological title or merely an expression of human respect." He sees the present passage as "enunciating the principle that the disciples and others in Matthew's Gospel who approach Jesus uttering the word *kyrie* are acknowledging thereby that he is a figure not merely of human but of lordly, or divine, dignity" (*Matthew*, p. 104).

54. ἀρκετός occurs in the New Testament twice in Matthew and once in 1 Peter. It is connected with ἀρκέω, "to suffice." ἵνα is here equivalent to the infinitive; it does not have telic force.

55. εἰ ... ἐπεκάλεσαν is a condition of reality, "if (as they have done). ..."

very important demon, probably the being we call Satan.⁵⁶ To apply this name to Jesus was to give him as deadly an insult as they could.

Jesus is saying, then, that his enemies have not only rejected him and his teaching, but have identified him with the leader of the forces of evil. This perverse approach cannot but have its consequences for his followers. He speaks of himself as *the head of the house,* an unusual expression for himself. But its meaning in an ordinary family is clear enough, and the word could be used in parables to refer to God (13:27; 20:1, etc.). It is intelligible as a description of Jesus' position in the little band of his followers. And if the enemies have no more respect for the head than to link him with the forces of evil, his followers can surely expect nothing better. Jesus carries on with the metaphor of the household by calling them *members of his household.*⁵⁷ They are identified with him as those in a household who looked up to the head. Indeed, Jesus says *how much more* will they be reviled. There might be some small respect for the head, but the followers would be isolated and persecuted even more. They are easier to pick on than their leader and will prove irresistible targets. They must expect to be regarded as evil people and persecuted accordingly.

d. Fear and Loyalty, 10:26-42

²⁶"*Therefore do not be afraid of them; for there is nothing covered that will not be uncovered, and hidden that will not be made known.* ²⁷*What I say to you in the darkness, speak in the light; and what you hear whispered, proclaim on the housetops.* ²⁸*And do not be afraid of those who kill the body but are not able to kill the soul; be afraid rather of him who is able to destroy both soul and body in hell.* ²⁹*Are not two sparrows sold for a penny? And yet not one of them will fall to the ground apart from your Father.* ³⁰*But even the hairs of your head have all been counted.* ³¹*Therefore do not be afraid; you are worth more than many sparrows.* ³²*Everyone then who shall acknowledge me before men, I also will acknowledge him before my Father who is in heaven.* ³³*But whoever shall disown me before men, I also will disown him before my Father who is in heaven.*

³⁴"*Do not think that I came to bring peace to the earth; I did not come to bring peace, but a sword.* ³⁵*For I came to divide a man against his father, and a daughter against her mother, and a daughter-in-law against her mother-in-law;* ³⁶*and a man's enemies will be the members of his household.* ³⁷*He who loves father or mother more than me is not worthy of me, and he who loves son or daughter more than me is not worthy of me.* ³⁸*And whoever*

---

56. If it be held unlikely that people would use the name of a demon as an insult, we should probably accept the suggestion that the term was simply "a vulgar insult with no reference to a demon" (McNeile). But a reference to a demon is more likely.

57. οἰκιακός is found in the New Testament again only in verse 36. It means any member of a household and is often used of a member of the family. But it could also be used of dependents, and it is, of course, used in this way here.

does not take up his cross and follow after me is not worthy of me. ³⁹*He who finds his life will lose it, and he who loses his life for my sake will find it.*

⁴⁰*"He who receives you receives me, and he who receives me receives him who sent me.* ⁴¹*He who receives a prophet in the name of a prophet will receive a prophet's reward, and he who receives a good man in the name of a good man will receive a good man's reward.* ⁴²*And whoever in the name of a disciple gives one of these little ones only a cup of cold water to drink, truly I tell you, he will certainly not lose his reward."*

In a further section that apparently gathers teaching given on a number of occasions (the parallels in Mark and Luke are scattered over a wide area) Matthew brings out something of the cost of discipleship and the importance of wholehearted allegiance to Christ. There is a threefold command not to be afraid (vv. 26, 28, 31), which emphasizes that Jesus' followers are to be without fear. They need not be afraid, for (1) every hidden thing will in due course be made public — the disciples will be vindicated (vv. 26-27); (2) their foes can kill the body but no more; they cannot kill the soul (v. 28); (3) the heavenly Father cares for the humblest of his creation (vv. 29-31). To this Jesus adds, (4) he will acknowledge all who acknowledge him (vv. 32-33).

26. *Therefore* introduces a reason. Jesus has made it clear that he himself is not respected by the Jewish authorities. From this it follows that, the disciple not being greater than his Master, those authorities will have no respect for his followers. But he is not dismayed at what evil men are doing and will do to him, and his followers should not fear either. He does not mean that the authorities are men of straw and may safely be neglected. He is well aware that they have power and that they will use it against him and also against his followers. He means rather that his true followers belong with him. He will in due course be vindicated, and so will they. Nothing would be done to his followers that had not been done to the Master, but his triumph is sure, and so is theirs. *For* adds a reason; none of the things people do in secret will remain secret. The plots of the Jewish hierarchy against Jesus (and of all their enemies against the disciples) are in secret, and thus the evil may be made to appear to be the good. But this is temporary. In the end everything will become public. Publicity is an advantage to the good, but it makes things harder for the evil, whose ways must be concealed if they are to be successful. Let the disciples, then, not be afraid but preach openly the things Jesus has committed to them.

27. Concealment is to be no part of the life of the disciples. What Jesus says to them in secret *(in the darkness)* they are to speak *in the light* ("in broad daylight," *REB*); it is not to be concealed; they are to give it full publicity. There are two thoughts here. One is that the followers of Jesus get their message from him; it is not something they have laboriously evolved for themselves. The other is that, having received Jesus' message, they are to give it the widest publicity. The same thought is conveyed in another way with the contrast between what they hear *whispered*[58] (and which is therefore secret) and their proclamation *on the housetops*. The tops of homes were, of course, greatly used in the Palestine of those days, and a housetop made a fine platform for anyone who wanted to bring his message before a large number of people.[59] The expression is a way of saying that the words in question are to be given maximum publicity. It is possible to convey information to a few people secretly, but Jesus' teaching is to be much more widespread than that. He has public proclamation in mind.

28. Again we have an injunction not to be afraid; openness and fearlessness run through this passage. This time the disciples are told not to fear[60] people who can kill[61] the body but can do no more. *Body* may be used of the bodies of people or of animals, alive or dead; in this place it stands for the whole of mortal life, which is put in contrast to *the soul*, that which is more than mortal.[62] The persecutors will be able effectively to bring an end to bodily life, but they lack the power[63] *to kill the soul*. People with this significant limitation are not to be feared. But it is a different matter when attention is turned to God (curiously Bruce thinks "the tempter" is in mind, but the tempter's power avails only to the extent that God permits; McNeile points out that in the parallel passage [Luke 12:5], Jesus speaks of "authority" to cast into hell, an authority that only God has). The Bible never says that believers are to be afraid of Satan. If we are going to be afraid, let it not be of the minor danger that is all that evil people or even Satan himself can bring us, but of the major danger involved in God's

---

58. εἰς τὸ οὖς = "into the ear"; the singular shows that whispering is meant. Jesus is referring to something spoken in such a way that it will be heard only by the one for whom the words are directly intended.

59. The coming of the Sabbath, for example, was announced from the highest rooftop in the town (SBk, I, p. 580). Six blasts were blown on the trumpet, the first for those in the fields to cease work, the second for those in the town and the shops to desist, and so on (*Shab.* 35b).

60. φοβέομαι is here followed by ἀπό (though in v. 26 and later in this verse it takes the accusative). This may be a Hebraism (Robertson, p. 577), though Lenski views it as "indicating a fear that causes one to flee from what is feared." The construction is found elsewhere in the New Testament only in the parallel passage, Luke 12:4.

61. ἀποκτείνω (13 times in Matthew; 74 times in the New Testament) can refer to any way of bringing the life of the body to an end. In this verse it is also used of ending true spiritual life.

62. ψυχή can refer to this earthly life (2:20; Rev. 8:9) or to the soul as the inner life (26:38). It may also signify that part of us which transcends this earthly life and survives death (here). E. Schweizer comments on the present passage: "Here again ψυχή is ultimately life in the authenticity which God intended and which has still to be regarded as bodily life even in hell. Thus man can be presented only as corporeal, but what affects the body does not necessarily affect the man himself, for whom a new body has already been prepared by God" (*TDNT*, IX, p. 646).

63. μὴ δυναμένων: they are not able.

holy wrath against evil.[64] Where they *are not able* he *is able;* his power far surpasses that of anyone or anything else in all creation. And Jesus illustrates that power by saying that God can *destroy both soul and body in hell* (cf. Isa. 10:18). It is perhaps surprising that he should speak of the destruction of the body[65] in hell (for *hell* see on 5:22): the body dies here on earth. But the expression refers to the whole person, and the whole person is body and soul; Jesus is not so much speaking of the particular area in which the body suffers dissolution as of the power of God, a power not limited to this earth (as the power of the persecutors is), but extending to the world to come. The reference to *hell* shows that we are not to understand *destroy* of annihilation. Jesus is speaking of the destruction of all that makes for a rich and meaningful life, not of the cessation of life's existence.

29. The power of God is to be discerned not only in the way he disposes of soul and body and works out his purposes in hell as elsewhere. We see it in his care for even the most insignificant of his works of creation. Jesus draws attention to the *sparrows*[66] that were sold in the marketplace for food.[67] They were very small birds and could command only a very small price: two a penny![68] Clearly they ranked low in the scheme of things and must be regarded as of little importance. But God takes notice of every individual little sparrow. Not one of them falls to earth (Chrysostom has "fall into a snare," but this has no support in the MSS)[69] without[70] the involvement of *your Father.* It is not certain precisely what these last words mean, as is evident from the translations. *NIV* has "apart from the will of your Father" (so *RSV*); *NEB,* "without your Father's leave" (*GNB,* "consent"); *JB,* "without your Father knowing." Any of these might be the right way of understanding the passage. But whatever our understanding of

64. "Two types of *fear* are here contrasted: fear of men is a self-interested cowardice, but fear of God is a healthy response of awe and obedience in the face of the Almighty" (France).

65. Bonnard points out that this does not mean that the body has little importance but rather that "God alone decides the destiny of the whole person."

66. στρουθίον is a diminutive of στρουθός, "sparrow," and thus means "little sparrow"; Jesus cites a very small bird and uses a diminutive even of that! MM cites evidence "that of all birds used for food sparrows were the cheapest." An inscription of the Emperor Diocletian setting out the maximum prices that might be paid for various articles of commerce shows that sparrows were the cheapest of birds used for food (see *LAE,* pp. 272-74).

67. The question is introduced with the emphatic οὐχί, which decisively looks for a positive answer.

68. A different word from that in 5:26. The ἀσσάριον (diminutive of the Latin *as*) was a Roman copper coin of small value, one sixteenth of a drachma, and a drachma was the wage paid to a laborer for a day's work. Coins of various nationalities circulated in first-century Palestine.

69. Another view is that of Barclay: "God marks the sparrow every time it lights and hops upon the ground" (I, p. 401). But Mounce objects that this "removes the idea of martyrdom that is central to the section."

70. ἄνευ, elsewhere in the New Testament only twice in 1 Peter (and a v.l. in Mark 13:2). It means much the same as χωρίς, "without," "apart from."

the point in detail, it is plain that Jesus is affirming that the little sparrows matter to God. People regard them as of trifling worth, but they are part of God's creation and have real value for him. God is not so busy running the universe that he has no time for little birds. Perhaps we should notice that the prophet Amos can ask, "Will a bird fall on the ground without a fowler?" (Amos 3:5, LXX). But the loving care of the heavenly Father forms a strong contrast to the fowler's aim simply to destroy.

30. If God is interested in the smallest of his created beings, he is also interested in the smallest details of the people he has made in his own image. *Your* comes first in the sentence and puts some emphasis on people in contrast to birds, a contrast that is strengthened with *But*. It scarcely seems to matter how many hairs we have on our heads[71] (and we certainly do not have that information ourselves; Bengel points out that we take no notice of hairs "pulled out by the comb"). The word order is "of you . . . even the hairs the head, all (of them)," which draws attention to "all" and thus emphasizes that the Father has complete knowledge of the most insignificant information about each one of his children. The verb *counted*[72] is in the perfect tense, which may signify that the number stays on record; it points to God's continuing interest.

31. *Therefore* introduces the consequence of these evidences of God's care. Since God cares for the humblest members of his creation and since he has knowledge of the most unimportant piece of information about his people, those people need not fear.[73] In this Gospel Jesus often tells people not to be afraid; fear is no part of being a disciple. On this occasion he gives the reason that they matter very much to the heavenly Father; their worth[74] is much more than that of *many sparrows* (*JB* has "hundreds of sparrows"). Since the Father cares for the sparrows, much more will he care for them.

32-33. Positively and negatively Jesus brings out the importance of wholehearted allegiance to him. *Everyone . . . who*[75] indicates a totality: there are no exceptions. *Acknowledge*[76] signifies an open declaration of allegiance (cf. *GNB*, "declares publicly that he belongs to me"; Hill, "affirm

---

71. Turner includes the singular κεφαλῆς among those "Contrary to normal Greek and Latin practice" where "Something belonging to each person in a group of people is placed in the sing." as in Aramaic and Hebrew (M, III, pp. 23, 24).

72. ἀριθμέω occurs only here in Matthew (and once in Luke and Revelation).

73. μὴ φοβεῖσθε may mean "Stop being afraid" or "Do not be in a continuing state of fear"; either way the command makes it clear that the believer should live a life without fear. The verb is in the aorist imperative in verse 26, and in the present in verse 28 as well as here.

74. διαφέρω, literally "carry through," comes to mean "differ"; when one thing differs from another, it may well be in the sense that it is worth more. At any rate this verb is used of such differences.

75. Both πᾶς and ὅστις (see on 2:6) are favorite Matthean words. The combination includes all who are in the class described. οὖν carries the argument along in logical sequence. Jesus has been speaking of the care the Father has for his creation. *Therefore* allegiance to him is important.

76. ὁμολογέω has meanings like "promise" and "agree," but it is also used in the sense of a public declaration and is used especially in this way for confessing Christ. It is usually

solidarity" with). Jesus looks for such a declaration from those who profess to follow him: there is no point in having followers who do not follow. It is one thing to become convinced that Jesus is an outstanding teacher, even that he is the Messiah, and quite another to profess oneself to be his follower in the face of hostile opposition from people in influential places. But to those who acknowledge him publicly in this way Jesus gives the assurance that he will likewise acknowledge them. His *I* is emphatic: they will be acknowledged by none less than he. And this acknowledgment will take place *before my Father who is in heaven*. This obviously refers to God, and it is significant that Jesus refers to him as Father. But when he says *my* Father, he is taking up a special place; he does not stand in the same relationship to God as do others (he never links himself with people in saying "Our Father"). There is an implied claim for himself,[77] and then his addition *who is in heaven* makes clear the greatness of the Father of whom he speaks. The acknowledgment his followers will receive will avail in the highest of all courts.

The obverse of this is that there are those who will *disown* Jesus *before men* here on earth; they will reject Jesus and side with his worldly opponents. The remainder of the saying follows the pattern of the previous one, bringing out the truth that those who disown Jesus here on earth are stuck with the consequences of their choice. They will necessarily find themselves disowned before the heavenly Father. Jesus is pointing out that there are permanent consequences of rejecting him. Those who do this suffer not some slight and temporary inconvenience, but the eternal consequences of rejection by God himself.[78]

34. Up to this point in this Gospel there has been a good deal of comforting teaching (as well as that which challenges) and many kindly actions of Jesus in healing those oppressed in various ways. The previous words would have made it clear that all is not sweetness and light for those who serve him, and this is now made very clear. *I came* is an incidental revelation of something of Christ's person — it is not an expression that would normally be used of anyone else's coming into the world. He had an existence prior to his earthly birth, and his coming to earth was

---

followed by the accusative (as it is in 2 Clem. 3:2 in quoting this saying). Burton includes this among passages with "Future Supposition with More Probability" and notes that it is rare either in classical or New Testament Greek to have the subjunctive without ἄν (*MT*, 307). ἐν ἐμοί is an Aramaism (BAGD, 4).

77. "Again we have a claim which is monstrous if He who makes it is not conscious of being Divine. Who is it that is going to own us or renounce us before God's judgment-seat (32, 33)? Who is it that promises with such confidence that the man who loses his life for His sake shall find it?" (Plummer, p. 157).

78. Robinson denies that this passage has in view arbitrary rewards and punishments: "It is in the nature of things that a man cannot be on both sides at once. If he belongs to Jesus, is one of his friends, holds a place in his company, then it follows that he will admit and even claim his position. If he fails, then by that very act he excludes himself from the divine community whose essential bond is a common love and loyalty to Christ."

for a purpose. It is startling to find him saying that his followers must not think that he came *to bring*[79] *peace to the earth,* an expression that is given emphasis by its repetition. Actually the word *peace* is used very little in this Gospel (only in v. 13 and here), but the general tenor of Jesus' teaching and actions is such as to lead us to expect him to be a bringer of peace. And there is, of course, a most important sense in which he came to bring peace. But the peace he came to bring is not simply the absence of strife; it is a peace that means the overcoming of sin and the bringing in of the salvation of God. And that means war with evil and accordingly hostility against those who support the ways of wrong. So it is that Jesus says that, far from peace,[80] he comes to bring *a sword,*[81] that is, conflict. The *sword* is not, of course, meant literally, but it is an obvious symbol of conflict. It is a stern reminder of the fact that to follow one whom his followers delight to call the "Prince of peace" (Isa. 9:6) sometimes means disunity and conflict. "A *sword* divides; so does the truth which Jesus came to bring. It is more important than family unity" (Argyle). But, of course, his coming presents a challenge to which people respond differently. And emotionally, for some who oppose Jesus do so passionately, as do those who become his followers. And where strong and opposed feelings are held, conflict is inevitable.[82]

35. *For* does not give a reason for the preceding so much as an explanation, "for, you see." Once again we have *I came* with its implication of a previous existence elsewhere. The kind of conflict Jesus has in mind is brought out with references to the family. His coming may well *divide*[83] families (cf. Mic. 7:6). *A man* is used generally, "any man at all." *His father* points us to the fundamental family loyalty. Since the father was the head of his household, the loyalty owed to him was above most loyalties, perhaps above all. To bring division between father and son was to offend against one of the most deep-seated convictions in the minds of Jesus'

---

79. βάλλω is somewhat unexpected for bringing peace, though the verb is, of course, used in senses like "to put, place" as well as the more vigorous "throw." But the meaning is clear enough. The verb is used 34 times by Matthew, where Mark and Luke have it 18 times and John 17. It occurs 28 times in Revelation, but it does not occur at all in Paul or Hebrews or in 1 and 2 Peter.

80. The strong adversative ἀλλά marks the contrast, not peace *but* a sword.

81. μάχαιρα (7 times in Matthew, 29 times in the New Testament) means a large knife or a small sword, a dirk (see AS). Here, of course, there is no particular emphasis on the size of the weapon. It is simply used as a symbol of strife.

82. In a series on "Uncomfortable Words" Matthew Black examines this saying (which he calls "The Violent Word"). He interprets "fire" in the Lukan equivalent as referring to judgment and thinks that Matthew has added "the symbolism of the Sword. The Final Judgment of God on the earth will be by Fire and Sword" (*ET,* LXXXI [1969-70], p. 118). That our understanding of final judgment may be helped by the symbolism of fire and sword is undoubted. But in this passage the subject is division in families, not the final judgment.

83. διχάζω means "to cut into two parts," thus "divide," "set at variance." Moule says of the infinitive here, "its basic, literal, meaning must actually be consecutive" (*IBNTG,* pp. 143-44).

hearers. And just as the son is set over against the father, so *a daughter* is set over against *her mother*. The mother was the important person in the female section of the household, where she exercised a headship corresponding to that of the father over the whole household. Division among the women was another serious split. And it does not stop there. The *daughter-in-law* became a member of a new household upon her marriage, and it would be expected that she would enter fully into her role as a member of her husband's family and that she would look to her *mother-in-law* for guidance and affection. To have division here would leave the bride very much alone.[84] Jesus makes it clear that nobody could reckon that the possibility of division would pass her or him by. The fundamental unit, the family, would be divided, and this might affect anyone.

36. This is summed up in the general proposition that one's *enemies*[85] will be those in one's own *household*,[86] the last place where we would expect hostility. Jesus is emphasizing that from the human point of view following the right way can be a lonely business. Divisions and oppositions may well arise where they are least expected, for it is impossible to predict how people will react to the gospel. And where they oppose it they may oppose it bitterly and extend that bitter opposition to all who have accepted it. "Enemies" is not too strong a word.

37. It is affection that binds households together; thus Jesus moves on to consider the place of love. He assumes that there will be love between parents and children, but claims for himself a higher[87] place in his disciples' affection than that which they accord to their nearest and dearest on earth, and that in a society that held it a dreadful thing to put anyone higher than one's parents. *Loves*[88] is a significant word; it points to the warmest affection. Jesus does not bid his followers love their parents or their children (nor, on the other hand, does he forbid warm affection in the family). He simply assumes that family members will love one another. But he is concerned that they must not value their attachment to the members of their families so highly that he is pushed into the back-

84. There was a rabbinic view that "when Messiah comes" there will be a number of evils, and one of them will be that "daughters will rise up against their mothers, and daughters-in-law against their mothers-in-law" (*Sanh.* 97a).

85. ἐχθρός is connected with ἔχθος, "hatred," and may mean passively "hated," "hateful," or, actively, "hating" (AS). Either way it indicates hostility and thus is the general term for enemy.

86. οἰκιακός, in the New Testament again only in verse 25, signifies any member of a household.

87. ὑπέρ with the accusative is used primarily of place, "over, above, across," but from this it comes to indicate degree, as here.

88. Matthew uses φιλέω 5 times in all (it occurs 13 times in John and 25 times in the New Testament). ἀγαπάω occurs 141 times, so it is much commoner. G. Stählin points out that in nonbiblical Greek φιλέω is the more common word, but this is reversed in LXX (*TDNT*, IX, p. 116). There appears to be little difference in meaning in the two words in the New Testament. I have examined the use of φιλέω in *Testaments of Love* (Grand Rapids, 1981), ch. 11.

267

ground.[89] This has important implications for an understanding of the person of Jesus. No mere man has the right to claim a love higher than that for parents or children; it is only because he is who he is that Jesus can look for such love. The words imply that he is more than a merely human teacher and leader. Of the one who lacks this love for him he says that he is *not worthy of me* (GNB, "is not fit to be my disciple"). We must not forget that Jesus knew what it was to experience misunderstanding in the family, for his own thought him mad (Mark 3:21). Jesus is not asking from his followers something he did not know for himself.

38. The demand for loyalty is further brought out by relating it to taking up a cross (cf. 16:24).[90] For us this is a remote metaphor, but Jesus' hearers were people who had seen men take up their cross (anyone condemned to be crucified was required to carry the cross beam to the place of execution). They knew that when this happened and the man went off with a little knot of Roman soldiers, he was on a one-way journey. He would not be back. Thus, for them, taking up the cross stood for the utmost in renunciation of the claims of self. The person who took up a cross had died to a whole way of life; Jesus demands from everyone who follows him nothing less than a death to self. For *follow*[91] see on 4:20; here it clearly means "follow as a disciple" (*after me* is a glimpse of the way a follower would literally walk behind his teacher).

39. Now comes the tremendous paradox that brings out the truth that the person who concentrates on getting the best, by that very fact loses it.[92] *He who finds* is more exactly "he who will have found,"[93] and *life* (see on v. 28) may be used of the whole of one's earthly existence or of life considered in terms of eternity. This poses something of a problem: Is Jesus speaking of life here and now or of life in eternity? But perhaps we can put the antithesis too strongly; both may be in mind. "Since the soul is the center of both the earthly and the supernatural life, a man can find himself facing the question in which character he wishes to preserve it for himself" (BAGD, 1.d). To *find* life in the sense of the things one

---

89. There is a rabbinic saying about looking for lost property; if a man is seeking "that of his father and that of his teacher, his teacher's has first place — for his father did but bring him into this world, but his teacher that taught him wisdom brings him into the world to come" (*B. Meṣ.* 2:11). But Jesus claims more than this, for he is more than simply a teacher; he is the Savior.

90. Matthew has σταυρός 5 times, which is more than in any other book in the New Testament (Mark and John have it 4 times, and it is spread over the Pauline epistles 10 times; the New Testament total is 27).

91. BDF denies that καί here is equivalent to οὐδέ and gives the meaning as "and yet follows me" (445[3]).

92. "The words about losing one's life to find it are among the most quoted of all Jesus' sayings — six times altogether in the gospels — doubtless because it summed up, in words from his own lips, that aspect of him with which his later followers were particularly drawn to identify themselves" (Green). Cf. 16:25; Mark 8:35; Luke 9:24; 17:33; John 12:25.

93. The aorist participle εὑρών here looks forward to the action that will occur. So with ἀπολέσας.

delights in here and now and without regard to other considerations is to lose it in the deeper sense, both now and in eternity. The verb rendered *lose*[94] can have the sense "destroy"; it points to the total loss of the only life that is worth living in the empty pursuit of that which has no permanence; it cannot last beyond the fleeting hour. The other side of the coin is that the person who counts life well lost in the service of Christ will find life in the fullest sense. That person will live a fuller life here and now and can face eternity without trepidation. *For my sake* is important. Jesus is not suggesting that anyone should weigh up the merits and demerits of life here and now and life in the hereafter and decide for the latter on the grounds that he will get more out of it that way. That is still selfish living and means the loss of real life. The life that matters is the life for the sake of Christ, the life that takes the same road of self-denial as Jesus did and that is concerned not with the benefit that one will be able to secure either here or hereafter, but with the service of God and of one's fellows. It has been suggested that *life* here means very much what we mean by "self"; to concentrate one's best energies on oneself is to destroy oneself, whereas to lose oneself in the service of Christ is to find oneself.

40. From the depths of the devotion required in his disciples and the importance of taking up one's cross and losing one's life for Jesus' sake, the Master now turns to what will happen when people respond to his challenge. He has spoken of the uncertain reception his followers will receive when they go out with the message of the kingdom. They should be under no illusions as to the difficulty of their task and the certainty that there will be people who will oppose them bitterly. But that is not the whole story, and now he speaks of those who will *receive* his disciples, where the verb indicates "receive as a guest, welcome." *You* refers in the first instance to the Twelve, whom Jesus was sending on a mission, but the word surely refers also to all those others who will later go forth in Jesus' name. To receive any such one will result in great blessing, for by that very fact they receive the Master. And not only the Master, but they receive *him who sent me*, that is, the heavenly Father. Notice again the thought of mission: Jesus had been *sent*. The thought is that of the outworking of one great divine purpose in which the Father, Jesus who had been sent by the Father, and the disciples who were being sent by Jesus all had their part. They were so closely connected that any honor paid to the disciples had to be regarded as something that overflowed to Jesus and to the Father.

41. This leads on to a more general statement about a variety of servants of God and a variety of kinds of service. Again we have the thought of receiving a person in the sense of giving a welcome, and this time it is the reception of *a prophet*.[95] The prophets were great figures in

94. ἀπόλλυμι, used, for example, of losing or destroying one of the members of the body in 5:29, 30.

95. *AB* translates "the Prophet" and a little later "the Righteous One," seeing the

269

Old Testament days, and their writings were regarded with reverence and respect and seen as holy Scripture. At an early period in the history of the Christian church there were charismatic figures who also bore the title "prophet," but we have no knowledge of any group of people who bore this title during Jesus' lifetime. We should probably bear in mind that the basic idea in "prophet" is that of a person who speaks directly from God. Others may comment on what God has said, but the prophet can say, "Thus saith the Lord —" (GNB translates "God's messenger"). Such a prophet can arise at any time.[96] Prophets in olden times were often rejected by their hearers, and Jesus recognizes that that was still possible. But it was not inevitable; thus Jesus speaks of a hearer who *receives a prophet,* that is, welcomes the man and his message. *In the name of a prophet* seems to mean accepting a prophet for what he is "as a prophet" (NEB), "because he is a prophet" (REB, NIV, JB).[97] Such a man will receive *a prophet's reward,* the gift with which God rewards the prophet for his faithful service. That gift we now find will be given not only to the prophet, but to the one who accepts the prophet and aligns himself with him.[98]

A similar comment is made about receiving *a good*[99] *man* (*prophet* and *good man* are joined again in 13:17; 23:29). The goodness of this man will be indicated not so much by his ethical uprightness as by his conformity to the law of God. He is the man who accepts the sovereignty of God and accordingly walks in the ways of God.[100] To welcome such a man is to agree with his basic position. It is to recognize the importance of goodness and to be ready to bring about goodness oneself. Such a receptor of a *good man* will be treated as a good man; he will receive the reward (or the wage) befitting the *good man.* Being a true servant of God means among other things being able to perceive the work of God in others and to respond to it.

---

passage as referring to Jesus and the rewards he would give to those who received him. But this is not the way the Greek reads.

96. Another view is that *prophet* refers to any disciple, regarded as a charismatic, one in whom the Spirit dwells. Thus Schweizer thinks that both *disciple* and *good man* refer to the disciple: "The first term refers to the charismatic activity of the disciple, the second one to his obedience towards God's Law as interpreted by Jesus" (NTS, XVI [1969-70], p. 223). But this passage surely means that there is a difference between a prophet, a good man, and one of the "little ones"; that is the thrust of it all.

97. Turner construes εἰς here as causal (M, III, p. 266). "By a usage similar to that with ref. to Heb. םשׁ . . . but also common in Hellenistic . . . of all that the name implies" (AS, 2).

98. μισθός means "wages" as well as "reward," and if this meaning be held to be the right one here, then Jesus will be saying, "he will receive the wage of a prophet, remuneration befitting a prophet."

99. For δίκαιος see on 1:19. The word has about it the air of "rightness," justice, or conformity to the law of God, and it could be translated as "a just man" or "a righteous man." Matthew is very fond of the word, which he uses 17 times. D. Hill argues that in Matthew the term, when linked with "prophets," refers to teachers in the early church (NTS, XI [1964-65], pp. 296-302). But the evidence is not convincing.

100. "To receive a righteous man in the name of a righteous man is to receive him as one who shows the divinely appointed way in his life" (T. W. Manson, *The Sayings of Jesus* [London, 1949], p. 183).

42. From the recognition of what God has done in prophets and good men generally, Jesus turns to the kind of conduct appropriate in his followers when they encounter those who can claim neither status — God's *little ones*. He speaks of giving a drink *in the name of a disciple*, that is, in recognition of the fact that these *little ones* are Christ's (cf. *RSV*, "because he is a disciple"; *REB* is similar). Notice that Jesus is speaking of the smallest conceivable gift to the most insignificant of people. The gift is that of no more than[101] *a cup of cold water*; no smaller gift can easily be conceived. Even the smallest gift, given with the right motive, does not go unnoticed. And the gift is made to *one of these little ones*; to *one* only, and that one from the class of *little ones*.[102] Jesus is not speaking of a small service rendered to a great person, but of a small service rendered to a small person. The word *little* may mean no more than small in size, and some have taken it here to mean "little children." Jesus certainly took a deep interest in children, but in this context it seems clear that he is speaking of insignificant persons who are his followers whether they are children or not. The *little ones* are a class who stand alongside prophets and good men. As O. Michel puts it, "He is referring to people who are present, without disparagement, and without having children in view."[103] The term means those who are insignificant, but it may also refer to those who are without earthly power but who are yet accepted by God (cf. the references to Gideon, Judg. 6:15, and Saul, 1 Sam. 15:17). For those who respond to the smallest needs of the humblest of disciples there will be a *reward*, just as in the case of those who respond to a prophet or a good man. This part of the saying is introduced with *truly*, which invests the words that follow with peculiar solemnity (see on 5:18). This is reinforced by the emphatic double negative,[104] which leaves no doubt about the proposition that follows.

---

101. μόνον is omitted by D syr$^{s.c}$, but it should be read. It is absent from the Markan equivalent (9:41), and the word is certainly Matthean; it is found 7 times in this Gospel, twice in Mark, and once in Luke. It "appears to represent a genuine Matthean touch" (Metzger). The word "water" is omitted; we have simply "a cup of cold — ."

102. Carr points to a gradation, "apostles — prophets — the saints — the young disciples. The simplest act of kindness done to one of Christ's little ones *as such* shall have its reward."

103. *TDNT*, IV, p. 651. The rabbis mostly have a different usage. For them the young or the small are the immature. Cf. R. Jose b. Judah of Kefar ha-Babli: "He that learns from the young, to what is he like? To one that eats unripe grapes and drinks wine from his winepress. And he that learns from the aged, to what is he like? To one that eats ripe grapes and drinks old wine" ('*Abot* 4:20). Cf. SBk, I, p. 592. Michel further says, "Whereas the term 'the small' is used disparagingly in the Rabbis (the immature, those who are not yet great and old), and whereas μέγας has a particular glory in the Greek and Hellenistic world, and μικρός is usually disdained (at best it is only a means and way for the μέγας), the saying on the lips of Jesus seems to point paradoxically to a secret, a concealed inner or future dignity" (*TDNT*, IV, p. 652).

104. οὐ μή (see on 5:18).

Matthew 11

F. RESPONSES TO JESUS' ACTIVITY, 11:1–12:50

Matthew rounds off his account of this second great discourse in words not unlike those of 7:28-29, and proceeds to tell his readers about some of the reactions to what Jesus said and did. Mostly these reactions are unfavorable, and even John the Baptist gives evidence of misunderstanding the Lord to whom he had earlier borne witness. Matthew goes on to tell of unrepentant cities and of opponents like the Pharisees. Throughout these chapters we discern some willful misunderstanding of Jesus and a rising tide of opposition to him. But we should not miss the way Matthew brings out through it all significant teaching about the person of Jesus. In this chapter the question raised by John the Baptist leads to important teaching about Jesus as the Christ, the denunciation of the impenitent cities shows him to be the Judge, and the chapter ends with the beautiful picture of the Savior of the heavy laden.

1. John the Baptist, 11:1-19

1And it came to pass that when Jesus had finished giving instructions to his twelve disciples, he went away from there to teach and preach in their towns. 2Now when John heard in the prison about the works of the Messiah, he sent through his disciples 3and said to him, "Are you the Coming One, or do we wait for another?" 4And Jesus answered them, saying, "Go and tell John what you hear and see: 5blind men receive sight and lame men walk, lepers are cleansed and deaf people hear, and dead people are raised and poor people have good news preached to them; 6and blessed is anyone who is not tripped up on account of me."

7And as these men went away, Jesus began to say to the crowds about John, "What did you go out into the wilderness to look at? A reed shaken by a wind? 8But what did you go out to see? A man dressed in soft clothes? Look, those who wear the soft clothes are in the houses of the kings. 9But what did you go out to see? A prophet? Yes, I say to you, and more than a prophet. 10For this is he about whom it stands written, 'Look, I send my messenger before your face, who will prepare your way before you.'

11"Truly I tell you, there has not arisen among those born of women a greater than John the Baptist; but the least in the kingdom of heaven is greater than he. 12*And from the days of John the Baptist until now the kingdom of heaven suffers violence, and violent men are seizing it.* 13*For all the prophets and the law prophesied until John;* 14*and if you are willing to accept it, he is Elijah who is to come.* 15*Let him who has ears hear.*

16*"To what shall I liken this generation? It is like children sitting in the marketplaces who call to the other children,* 17*saying, 'We played the flute for you, and you did not dance; we wailed, and you did not lament.'* 18*For John came neither eating nor drinking, and they say, 'He has a demon.'* 19*The Son of man came eating and drinking, and they say, 'Look, a gluttonous man and a wine-drinker, a friend of tax collectors and sinners.' And yet wisdom is proved right from her actions."*

This section of the Gospel has no parallel in Mark and, while there is a Lucan equivalent, Luke has a different arrangement and some significant verbal differences. Most scholars find it difficult to understand why the two narratives differ in the way they do, and many deny that there can have been a common source.

1. This verse rounds off the teaching Jesus has been giving, just as 7:28-29 (where see notes) rounds off the Sermon on the Mount. Jesus was constantly teaching, and Matthew notes that the completion of his work in one place was followed by his moving on to continue it in other localities. For *And it came to pass* see the note on 7:28. It is a Matthean characteristic, as is this transition from a discourse section to something of a different kind. Matthew notes that Jesus *finished giving instructions,*[1] and once again he specifies *his twelve disciples* as the recipients. It is characteristic that Jesus' activities are teaching and preaching. This last term has the idea of proclamation (see on 3:1) and is used of proclaiming the gospel (Mark 16:15) and a number of times of proclaiming the good news of the kingdom (cf. Luke 8:1). Here it is the absolute use: Jesus made proclamation, but Matthew gives no indication of the content of the proclamation. *To teach* is a much more general term and covers instruction of various kinds. This took place *in their towns,* where *their* is not defined. But Matthew seems often to use this term to denote the Jews in general, specifically those opposed to Jesus.

2. Matthew turns his attention to John the Baptist.[2] He has already given an account of the ministry of that stern man of the wilderness and has noted his concentration on judgment. He has also made it clear that

---

1. τελέω is here followed by a participle of that which is completed (in 10:23 Matthew used an accusative). Burton calls this "the substantive participle" and points out that though it here agrees grammatically with the subject of the verb, it is logically the object (*MT,* 459). Turner takes it as "a predicate answering to the subject" (M, III, p. 158). διατάσσω points to the giving of orders.

2. δέ is common in Matthew. Here it will have some adversative force as it distinguishes between Jesus and John, to whom the narrative now turns. There are parallels to this section in Luke 7:18-35.

John had recognized Jesus' greatness and found it hard to understand why he should receive a baptism intended for sinners (from the beginning John had had difficulty in understanding a ministry so different from his own). Matthew has also told us that John was put in prison (4:12; Josephus tells us that this was in the fortress of Machaerus, *Ant.* 18.119, situated east of the Dead Sea), and later he has spoken of the question about fasting raised by the Baptist's followers (9:14). Now we are back to the man himself. The name *John* is sufficient; there is no need to explain that it is the Baptist of whom Matthew writes. John, he tells us, was still in prison, and there he heard about what Jesus was doing. Unusually at this early stage, Matthew speaks of Jesus as *the Messiah,* perhaps, as Carson thinks, "in order to remind his readers who it was that John the Baptist was doubting." *Works* is a neutral term and can mean ordinary deeds or miracles or both. There is no indication here of either class, and perhaps Matthew intends that we understand both. John sent a message *through his disciples* (an unusual construction, but quite intelligible). Luke says that he sent two disciples (Luke 7:18), and some MSS have "two" here.

3. John's question raises a problem, for Matthew tells us that when Jesus came to be baptized John had been reluctant, saying that he needed to be baptized by Jesus, not the other way about. He had recognized the greatness of Jesus. Why then should he now be asking, "*Are you[3] the Coming One?*" It is perhaps relevant that Matthew has not reported in the earlier encounter that he had used this precise expression of Jesus. The expression was not a recognized messianic title[4] (though cf. Ps. 118:26; Isa. 59:20). But as John uses it, it seems to have much that force. Since John had given such recognition to Jesus in earlier days, it is a puzzle that he should now be questioning his credentials.

A number of solutions to the problem have been suggested. (1) Some suggest that John himself was in no doubt, but asked the question so that Jesus would reassure his followers. This view was common in the early church and among the Reformers; Ryle accepts it. But it is surely too artificial. (2) Others think that John was just coming to believe in Jesus. He had not recognized him as the Messiah, the reasoning runs, but now in prison he had time to reflect and he was coming to see something of the greatness of Jesus (Fenton accepts such a view). So he began to wonder whether he should give up his own movement and follow Jesus. But this is sheer speculation. There is evidence that John had told people to follow Jesus (3:2, 13-14; John 1:29-34, 35-37; Acts 18:25; 19:4), and there is no

---

3. οὔ is emphatic, and probably ἕτερον also (so Gundry, "Are *you* the Coming One, or should we expect *another?*").

4. Vincent Taylor finds the expression used of Jesus a few times, but says, "Clearly, the title had only a brief and restricted currency in certain circles" (*The Names of Jesus* [London, 1953], p. 79; he cites H. J. Cadbury, "There is no evidence that it was a Jewish or Christian technical term"). The participle is in the present tense, but "In confident assertions regarding the future, a vivid, realistic present may be used for the future" (BDF, 323).

evidence that he had wavered in this. (3) Another view is that prison had had a depressing effect on John. Confinement in Herod's jurisdiction meant a good deal of suffering, and there was no certainty of ultimate release. The suggestion is that all this was too much for John. But nothing that we know about the Baptist suggests that he would have buckled under pressure. Our sources give no indication that he ever did. (4) Some argue that it was not so much John's faith that failed as his patience. John had looked for Jesus to bring in the kingdom of God, but instead of doing this the Master was doing nothing more than move among the people of Galilee, teaching and healing. He was making no attempt to overthrow the rulers of the country and bring in the rule of God. So John, it is suggested, was trying to prod Jesus into decisive action. This must remain a possibility, but it certainly comes short of having been demonstrated. (5) Perhaps John was simply puzzled. He had prophesied such great things about Jesus, and specifically he had spoken of judgment (cf. 3:11-12). But there was no sign of the judgment he expected (it would have been very human for John to have looked for judgment on those who had brought his ministry to a close and made him suffer so many things in jail). Jesus was simply moving among ordinary men and women, teaching them about the things of God and healing their sick. Was this really what the Great One would do?[5] What sort of Messiah was it who refrained from religious practices like fasting (which John's disciples followed, 9:14), consorted with irreligious characters (9:9-13), and left his forerunner to languish in prison?

On the whole this last appears to be the most probable solution. John is asking whether it is this sort of thing that God's Messiah would do, *"or do we wait for*[6] *another?"*[7] Was Jesus, like John, a kind of forerunner? Would a greater come and bring judgment on sinners?

4. Jesus does not directly answer John's question, but he invites the messengers to tell John what was happening. He should draw his own conclusions when he knew what Jesus was saying and doing. *What* is plural: Jesus is drawing attention to a multitude of things, and the addition *you hear and see* makes it comprehensive. It includes both what Jesus taught and what he did, and indeed the expression could be wider, for it could include people's reactions. How they responded might well tell John important things about Jesus.

---

5. Part of the expectation was that the Messiah would free captives (Isa. 61:1; cf. Luke 4:18), and John's failure to secure release may have been a factor in his thinking.

6. προσδοκάω (twice in Matthew) means *"wait for, look for, expect,* in hope, in fear, or in a neutral state of mind" (BAGD). προσδοκῶμεν could be the present indicative (with a future meaning, "Shall we look. . . ?") or the present subjunctive (with a deliberative meaning, "Should we look. . . ?").

7. The use of ἕτερον may mean a Messiah of a different kind (so Mounce); McNeile thinks that this cannot be pressed, but H. W. Beyer says that the word "may involve a more or less pronounced qualitative distinction, in which case the term acquires theological significance." He gives the sense of it here as "the qualities which Jewish expectation attributed to the Messiah might better fit another than Jesus" (*TDNT*, II, p. 702).

5. Jesus begins with *blind men receive sight.*[8] Now no miracle of the giving of sight to the blind is recorded throughout the whole of the Old Testament, nor is there any record of such a miracle performed by Jesus' followers (apart from the falling of scales from the eyes of Saul of Tarsus, removing temporary blindness, Acts 9:17-18, but that is scarcely the same thing). But it is the most frequent healing miracle of any kind among the works of Jesus; he stood out as a healer of the blind. The giving of sight is, of course, mentioned a number of times in Old Testament messianic prophecies, and we can surely say that such healings point to Jesus' messiahship. *Receive sight,* like the other verbs in this sentence, is in the present tense and indicates a continuing process: Jesus is speaking of his habitual activities, not of an occasional (and atypical) happening.

To the healing of blindness is added, *lame men walk,* a conjunction we find also when the blind and the lame came to Jesus in the temple (21:14; sufferers of these groups are joined with others coming to him in 15:30-31). As with blindness, Matthew speaks of the lame more than do others (5 times). To this Jesus adds, *lepers are cleansed;* leprosy was not simply a disease to be cured, but a defilement from which the sufferer must be cleansed (see on 8:2; *NIV* misses this point with "are cured"). It is mentioned in the New Testament only in the Synoptic Gospels (Matthew has it 4 times, Mark 2, Luke 3). *Deaf*[9] *people hear,* to which is added the raising of the *dead.* The word may denote the spiritually dead (Heb. 6:1), but here it clearly denotes the death of the body. Matthew relates no miracles of giving life to dead people (though he tells us that Jesus told his disciples to do this, 10:8), but Luke speaks of the raising of the son of the widow of Nain (Luke 7:11-17; he puts this immediately before his parallel section on John the Baptist). And John, of course, tells of the raising of Lazarus (John 11). The Baptist was to know that even death was subject to Jesus.

The final item on the list is *poor*[10] *people,* who *have good news preached to them.* The poor were important to Jesus, and they feature prominently in the Gospels. They were downtrodden and counted for little in the eyes of the general community. But to Jesus they mattered, and he draws John's attention to this reversal of generally accepted values. It was something new that to such people *good news* was preached. It is possible that we should translate this "the gospel is preached," for the verb is that used

8. Matthew uses τυφλός 17 times, which is more than in any other book; he is very interested in blindness. ἀναβλέπω means "look up, see again" (BAGD) and may possibly indicate that many people were blind not from birth, but as a result of diseases of the eye, which appear to have been common and very serious (see the articles in *ISBE* and *IDB*). But this cannot be pressed, for the verb is used for the cure of a man blind from birth (John 9:11, 15, 18).

9. κωφός may mean "deaf" or "dumb" (see on 9:32), but here the verb makes it clear that it is deafness that is in mind.

10. The word is πτωχός (see on 5:3), connected with πτώσσω, "to crouch, cower," and is used of a beggar, one who has nothing.

characteristically for the preaching of the gospel.[11] But since the Christian gospel in its fulness could not be preached before the atoning death of Jesus that was at its heart, we should probably not understand the verb here in this way. A number of translations capitalize with "Good News," which draws attention to the fact that Jesus' preaching had a special quality about it and that the news he brought was of particular comfort to poor people. John would have known that Jesus was doing these things; indeed, that was part of his problem. But Jesus is using words that will evoke recollections of messianic prophecy: the blind, the deaf, and the lame (also the dumb) are the subject of prophecy (Isa. 35:5-6), as are the poor (Isa. 61:1). Clearly Jesus is drawing attention to wonderful deeds the Messiah would do and adding others (cleansing the lepers, raising the dead). We should also bear in mind that in the relevant scriptural passages there is the thought of judgment as well as that of blessing (Isa. 35:4; 61:2). Judgment was not immediate, but it was not forgotten. If John were to consider these things carefully, he would have the answer to his question.

6. Jesus rounds off his words to John with a benediction on anyone who trusts him. For *blessed* see the note on 5:3; it points to happiness, but not happiness in a general, secular way. It means the joy that comes from the presence and approval of God. And that joy will come on the person who sees Jesus for what he is and not as "a stumbling-block" *(NEB)*. The verb I have translated *tripped up* is a difficult one.[12] It is a passive with a meaning like "is not stumbled, is not tripped up on account of me";[13] Jesus is thus speaking about the person who trusts him (has "no doubts about me," *GNB*) and does not take offense at who he is and what he does. His was nothing like the conventional understanding of the Messiah, and because of this people wedded to traditional ways might well be highly offended by him. Not that way lies the path of blessing. John is being exhorted to trust Jesus and not be tripped up by preconceived ideas of what the Messiah should be like.

7. With this message from Jesus John's men went on their way. But the fact that John had sent this embassy, coupled with the way Jesus replied, might well have given some hearers the impression that John was in the wrong and that Jesus was in some way in opposition to his forerunner. This was far from being the case, however, and without any delay for errors to spread (it was as John's messengers were on their way that

---

11. εὐαγγελίζομαι is used here only in Matthew, and 54 times in the New Testament. Moffatt omits the preaching to the poor here on the grounds that it "seems a harmonistic interpolation from Luke vii.22," but this is a gratuitous assumption. The verb is normally a deponent, but it is usually taken here as a passive with the sense it has in the translation. If it is middle, the meaning is that the poor are preaching the good news and the reference is to the preaching of the disciples. But this is not a likely reading of the passage.

12. σκανδαλίζω, a frequent verb in Matthew (see on 5:29). It is connected with the bait stick of a trap and comes to have the meaning of triggering off trouble in any one of a variety of ways.

13. ἐν is used with a causal significance, "because of me" (cf. 6:7; 13:57).

Jesus took action) Jesus proceeds to bring out something of John's greatness. He *began* to speak (which may mean that there was more to be said,
but at least he was making a beginning), and he did so by asking a series
of questions.[14] Notice that Jesus asks "what?" not "who?" It is what John
stood for rather than what he was to which he directs attention (though,
of course, the questions center on the kind of man John was).[15] To go out
into the wilderness[16] demanded some effort and required some reason. What
was it? Jesus suggests that the object of their contemplation may have
been *a reed shaken by a wind*. The *reed* might be used as a kind of flute, or
it might be a pen (see MM), or a fairly stiff reed might be thought of as
something like a rod (27:29, 30, 48). But here the *reed* is a slight thing that
may be moved about by *wind*. A reed blown here and there by a puff of
wind is the most inconstant and unstable of things. This was obviously
an impossible description of John, for the Baptist was not characterized
by fickleness. He took a firm line in his preaching, and his manner of life
backed up his words.

8. Jesus makes a second suggestion, which he introduces with the
strong adversative;[17] this dismisses the preceding and leads into something new. The question of the previous verse is repeated with a change
of verb.[18] Jesus turns attention to clothing and asks whether they went to
the wilderness to see someone in *soft clothes*. We were told earlier that John
was dressed in camel's hair with a leather belt (3:4); anything less like soft
clothing is not easy to imagine. The translators tend to paraphrase here:
"silks and satins" *(NEB)*, "fancy clothes" *(GNB)*, "fine clothes" *(JB)*, but
these are all interpretations: the word means "soft" (it is sometimes used
in the sense "effeminate"). *Look* is Matthew's word for drawing attention
to some saying; here he cites Jesus' words about the place where *soft clothes*
are to be found, namely *in the houses of the kings*. There is a tendency for

14. There is an ambiguity in that τί might be understood as "what?" or as "why?" and
a further uncertainty as to where the question mark is to be placed. Thus we might translate,
"Why did you go out into the wilderness? To look at a reed shaken by the wind?" And so
with the other questions down to verse 9 (Filson takes this view, and McNeile thinks it more
natural and vivid). Curiously *RSV* begins with "What did you go out to behold?" but in
verse 8 changes to "Why did you go out? To see a man. . . ?" and retains "Why" in verse 9.
The *NEB* has "What" in the first two questions but changes to "Why" in the third (some MSS
put προφήτην before ἰδεῖν, which would require this translation, but Metzger rejects this
reading). Whichever way we take it, the infinitive denotes purpose: "in order to see."
15. Robinson remarks that verses 7-11 "give us the best picture of John that we have.
He stands out as a rugged, fearless, sturdy hero, with the independence and inspiration of
a prophet."
16. ἔρημος is strictly an adjective meaning "solitary, deserted," but BAGD lists it in a
section of which it says, "adj. attributes whose noun is customarily omitted come to have
substantival force and therefore receive the art." (ὁ, ἡ, τό, II.2.b).
17. ἀλλά used "before independent clauses, to indicate that the preceding is to be
regarded as a settled matter, thus forming a transition to someth. new"; here, "you could not
have wanted to see that" (BAGD, 3).
18. In verse 7 we have θεάσασθαι but now ἰδεῖν. The change is probably no more than
stylistic.

the translators to read "palaces," but Jesus' word is that for ordinary houses. Admittedly the houses of kings would be magnificent, but Jesus is not drawing attention to that.

9. Another use of the strong adversative brings us to the suggestion that people may have gone out to see *a prophet*, and to this Jesus appends a strong affirmation, *"Yes, I say to you."* Strong motivation was required to cause people to go out into the wilderness, and the thought that they would see a prophet provided that strong motivation. A prophet was the spokesman of God; among the Jews there could be no higher pedestal on which to place a man. And while there had been many prophets in olden days, the people of that day had never seen one, nor had their ancestors for hundreds of years. So they would flock to see a prophet. Jesus agrees with this estimate of John, but goes on to say that it was not high enough. John was *a prophet* indeed, but he was *more than a prophet*, where the word used indicates "abundantly more."[19] It would have been hard for Israel to think of any man as more than a prophet, and when the word means abundantly more (not just a little bit more) it is clear that John is being given the highest praise.

10. Jesus explains. John's greatness arises because he is not only a prophet but himself the fulfilment of prophecy, the prophecy of Malachi 3:1 (cf. also Exod. 23:20), which Jesus proceeds to quote.[20] This marks John out as the forerunner to the Messiah and thus as greater than those who did no more than prophesy of him. Jesus uses the formula *it stands written*, a formula commonly used in quoting Scripture, which is probably the reason for translations like "of whom Scripture says" *(NEB)*. There is some emphasis on the subject, *I*;[21] it is none less than God himself who sends the messenger.[22] In the original prophecy Yahweh speaks of sending his messenger to prepare the way before him, but in the way Jesus quotes the passage it refers to his own coming; the messenger is sent *before your face* and he is to *prepare your way before you* (note his use of *your* [twice] and *you*). Yahweh is addressing his Messiah. We should not miss the application to Jesus of a passage originally speaking of Yahweh: Jesus is the

---

19. περισσότερον, the comparative of περισσός, which itself means "more than sufficient, over and above, abundant" (AS). This is the one place in which Matthew uses this exuberant word. If it is neuter, it signifies "something more," that is, something beyond a prophet; it then points to John's place in the whole chain of events, including the fulfilment of the prophecy, and not simply to the man himself. If it is masculine, it means "one who is beyond a prophet"; in other words, John is an exceedingly great person.

20. The passage is quoted also in Mark 1:2; Luke 7:27. All three are substantially the same, but there are slight differences from LXX. Evidently they shared a common text form (unless Matthew and Luke both derive the words from Mark).

21. The emphatic ἐγώ is used.

22. ἄγγελος means a messenger and is used of human messengers, such as those sent by the Baptist (Luke 7:24) and by Jesus (Luke 9:52); here it is used of a human messenger sent by God. Mostly in the New Testament it is used of messengers sent by God and of a more than human kind, so the common translation is "angel."

manifestation of Yahweh.[23] *Before your face* means, of course, "before you." The function of the messenger would be to *prepare*[24] *your way before you,* and the passage signified the preparing of the way for the Lord's Messiah. *Way* is often used of a road; when great dignitaries paid official visits at that period, it was usual to pay careful attention to the roads over which they would travel to make sure that all was as it should be. Here the word is used metaphorically; Jesus is speaking of getting people ready for God's Messiah, not of laying down a pavement. Jesus is saying that John had the dignity of preceding the Messiah in order to get ready for his coming. He does not spell this out and says nothing of his own position. But he makes it clear that in the providence of God John the Baptist had a most important role, a role exceeded only by that of the Messiah himself.[25]

11. For *Truly I tell you* see the note on 5:18; the expression draws attention to the following words as important. Here they will be somewhat unexpected, for they are part of Jesus' verdict on John at a time when John has appeared to be less than wholehearted in his following of the Master. Jesus speaks of *those born*[26] *of women,* which, of course, means anyone of the human race. It is not usual to speak of people with the formal term *arisen,* but the verb on occasion is used in the sense "*appear, of prophets*" (BAGD, 2.e); it points to John's greatness. Jesus tells his hearers that in all the human race there has never been anyone greater than John, a verdict that may well have surprised many of his hearers. Despised he may have been by many in contemporary Judaism, but the Baptist was great where it counted, great as God reckons greatness. We have just seen that he was more than a prophet (v. 9) and the forerunner of the Messiah (v. 10); of nobody else in all the history of the race could these things be said. But if it is surprising that John was the greatest man who ever lived, it is even more surprising that *the least*[27] *in the kingdom of heaven is greater than he.* Jesus is not denigrating John but bringing out the wonder of being in the kingdom. Great though he was, John the Baptist belonged to the old order. He proclaimed the need for repentance in view of the coming of Messiah, but his function was preliminary to the Christian era; he was not in that

---

23. Hamann says that the passage "in a veiled way suggests that the coming of God expected in Malachi is fulfilled in the coming of Jesus, and of that coming John is the way-preparer." Lenski regards the translation not as "free" but rather as "interpretative": it gives the meaning of the original.

24. κατασκευάζω is the perfective of σκευάζω, "to prepare," and signifies, "equip, furnish fully" (LSJ).

25. Cf. *Midrash Rabbah, Exodus,* "In the millennium, likewise, when he will reveal himself, salvation will come to Israel, as it says, *Behold, I send My messenger, and he shall clear the way before Me*" (32.9).

26. γεννητός is found in the New Testament only here and in Luke 7:28. Strictly it points to the action of the male parent and means "begotten."

27. μικρός can denote that which is small in size or stature, but may also signify small "in esteem, importance, influence, power . . . *the one of least importance in the Kingdom of Heaven*" (BAGD, 1.c; they also note that F. Dibelius and O. Cullmann "prefer 'youngest', and refer it to Christ"; this view, however, is improbable.

era and therefore was in some sense of lesser stature than those who are in it.[28] John is classed among those who preceded the kingdom. Jesus is speaking of unimportant people who are *in the kingdom of heaven* (for this term see on 3:2), and it is a measure of the greatness of the privilege of being in the kingdom he proclaimed that its humblest member surpasses the greatest of the race. This cannot mean in character or achievement; it refers to privileged position.[29] We learn later that the humility of the little child gives a clue to real greatness (18:4).

12. Jesus looks back to *the days of John the Baptist*. Normally such an expression would refer to a man's whole lifetime, but this cannot be the meaning here, for John was still alive. It refers to the time in the wilderness when he did his effective preaching and established his reputation, the time when he accomplished his life's work. That period had inaugurated an era in which *the kingdom of heaven suffers violence*.[30] This does not mean that John inaugurated the kingdom; that was the work of Jesus, and the words point to what was happening in the ministry of Jesus. It is a very difficult expression and has been understood in any one of three general ways: (1) The kingdom is being violently treated (taking the word as a passive), that is, its messengers and preachers and adherents are rejected with violence, which may refer to activities like those of Herod and of Jewish opponents of the gospel. (2) The kingdom suffers violence in the sense that some who look for it (the *violent men;* people like the Zealots?) are trying to bring it about by violent means; perhaps also they view it as no more than a political kingdom. (3) The kingdom is entered with burning zeal. This may be in the sense, "goes forward with triumphant force" (taking the verb as middle), or the verb may have the meaning *"invite urgently*, of the 'genteel constraint imposed on a reluctant guest'" (BAGD, 2.d). Cf. *NIV,* "has been forcefully advancing" (Carson accepts this sense).[31]

---

28. The disciples of Jesus "are greater, not in their moral character or achievements, but in their privileges" (Johnson). "The thought is that it is better to enter the kingdom than to herald its coming" (Allen). "In the dispensation of promise, his significance was unsurpassed. Nevertheless it was nothing compared to the message brought by the least of Jesus' disciples and followers in the dispensation of fulfillment" (Ridderbos).

29. μείζων is used of the greatness of John in his superiority to all others, and then the same word brings out the greatness of the least in the kingdom.

30. βιάζω may be used transitively, "inflict violence on," or intransitively, "use force, violence." The position is complicated by the fact that the verb may be used as a deponent, so that βιάζεται may be a middle with an active sense (transitive or intransitive), or a genuine passive; it thus may mean "inflicts violence," "uses violence," or "suffers violence." The Mishnah 'Eduyyot 8:7 says that Elijah will come "to remove afar those that were brought nigh by violence and to bring nigh those that were removed afar by violence." This refers to people brought wrongly by violence into the number of the Israelites and those excluded from the number by violence. It is not unlike what Jesus is saying.

31. Stendahl sees the possibilities as "'the Kingdom of Heaven suffers violence (passive) and men of violence grab it' or 'the Kingdom of Heaven manifests itself violently (or: powerfully; reflexive) and keen and daring men take hold of it'. The latter meaning fits better into Mt.'s context, but the former . . . is more natural from a linguistic point of view." Hill puts it this way: "The allusion may be to the opposition of Satan and evil spirits to the

Violent men[32] are those who are carrying out the violence the kingdom suffers. The noun's normal meaning supports the idea that the sense in the earlier part of the sentence is that of evil people harming the kingdom. If this is the way to take it, Jesus is referring to people who do not understand what God is doing in and through the coming of the kingdom. People like those in power in the world of Judaism act violently in *seizing*[33] what they conceive to be the kingdom and in seeking the best for themselves as they reject what God offers in his Christ. Alternatively we may understand the word to mean putting forth one's best effort in the kingdom, snatching people away from evil so that they may have membership in the kingdom. This, however, goes against the normal meaning of *violent men*. We should surely understand this of violent opposition to the kingdom; this means that in the earlier part of the verse "suffers violence" ("has been under violent attack," *AB*) is more probable than "advances strongly." Matthew includes these words of Jesus in a context that speaks of the difficulties of John the Baptist and goes on to refer to people who found themselves unable to agree with Jesus or John. It is much more likely in such a context that Matthew understood the words of the opposition of the evil rather than the progress of the good.[34] We should also bear in mind that in this chapter the Evangelist emphasizes meekness and lowliness rather than aggression; Jesus does not teach that people enter the kingdom by reason of their vigor and aggressiveness.

13. Jesus stresses the preliminary character of the Old Testament

---

Kingdom, or to the violence of Herod Antipas to John; but a more likely explanation is that the reference is either to Zealots who try to bring in the Kingdom by employing force against the Romans, or to Jewish antagonists of Jesus who continued to persecute Christians."

32. βιαστής, which means "violent, impetuous man" (BAGD, who note only three other uses of the term, "all three in a bad sense"). P. W. Barnett argues that the meaning here is people like those who tried to make Jesus king in John 6:14-15 (*RThR*, XXXVI [1977], pp. 65-70).

33. The verb ἁρπάζω, like βιάζω, may be understood in a good sense or a bad sense. It means "seize," and may be used in the sense of stealing (12:29), of taking away by force (13:19; it is used of an arrest in Acts 23:10), or of being caught up for blessing (e.g., Paul's being caught up to the third heaven; 2 Cor. 12:2). Schweizer points out that Matthew's only other use of the verb is for the action of the devil (13:19); he notes that the verb "actually means 'take by force' " and further, "The suggestion that it should be understood in the good sense as the violent struggle of a passionate faith is almost out of the question" (p. 262). E. Moore has examined the use of the two verbs in Josephus (*NTS*, 21 [1974-75], pp. 519-43), and concludes that they are used "especially in combination, to signify the direct employment of physical violence as a means of coercion, and that they carry with them a strong overtone of censure" (p. 540).

34. "Matthew's inclusion of it in a passage explaining the rejection and persecution of those who belong to the kingdom makes it clear that he understood it as describing hostility to the kingdom. From the days of John, there are violence, rejection, and persecution against those who belong to the kingdom and thus against the kingdom itself" (Patte, p. 161). Luke 16:16 resembles this passage, but there the thought is that people press their way into the kingdom. Jesus may have used similar language to bring out different truths, or, as Barclay holds (II, p. 9), there may have been a saying of which Matthew and Luke preserve different parts.

period. Not some but *all the prophets* did their work *until John*, and with them is joined *the law*, the crowning gift of all God's good gifts to his people. This means that the whole of the Old Testament revelation is viewed as preliminary to the coming of Jesus. It is interesting that the Law is said to prophesy[35] as well as the prophets; both had their origin in God and both conveyed the word of God to people. Both indeed conveyed the authentic word of God, but Jesus is saying that both were of limited duration. They both did their work until the coming of John, the herald of the incarnate Son of God in whom came the definitive revelation. *Until* has the force of "up to John but not beyond him." This does not mean that now that John has come the law and the prophets may be discarded. The whole Christian revelation insists on the continuing significance of both law and prophets. But until the ministry of John the law and the prophets were the sum of the divine revelation; nothing could be set alongside them. Jesus is saying that with his coming a new age has dawned. The law and the prophets are no longer the revelation that is the key to everything else. The revelation made in Christ is the key to the revelation in the law and the prophets. The translations draw attention to the difficulties of the verse. Thus *JB* reads, "it was towards John that all the prophecies of the prophets and of the Law were leading"; but this makes John the object of the prophecies, and this is not what Matthew is teaching here or elsewhere. Jesus is the object of prophecy. *GNB* reads, "Until the time of John all the prophets and the Law of Moses spoke about the Kingdom," but this introduces a thought not in the Greek.

14. *If you are willing* draws attention to the importance of attitude (Matthew has the verb "to will" 42 times, which is more than in any other book in the New Testament); Jesus' hearers might not have the will to accept the reality of John's position.[36] They may well have preferred (as we all naturally do) to retain their old securities; it always takes an effort of will to accept something radically new, such as the place of Jesus in the divine economy.[37] Jesus goes on to identify John with *Elijah who is to come*, thus seeing in John the fulfilment of the prophecy of Malachi that Elijah will come "before the great and terrible day of the LORD" (Mal. 4:5; see also Matt. 17:10-13). There is something of a problem in that John denied that he was Elijah (John 1:21), which may mean that, although he fulfilled the prophecy of Elijah's return, he was not the literal, physical Elijah whom

---

35. προφητεύω occurs 28 times in the New Testament, whereas προφήτης is found 144 times; the noun is thus much more common than the verb, which is used 11 times in 1 Corinthians and no more than 4 times in any other book (Matthew, Acts). It means to utter a revelation from God; the prophet could say, "Thus saith the LORD — ."

36. J. Jeremias holds that εἰ θέλετε δέξασθαι "seems to be designed to indicate that this interpretation of the figure of the Baptist is new and that the fulfilment of the Elijah prophecy does not take place in the form of a reincarnation" (*TDNT*, II, p. 937).

37. Calvin comments that by these words, "He reproves their hardness, for they are maliciously blind in clear light" (II, p. 8).

many Jews were expecting. Or it may mean that he did not know that he was the fulfilment of the prophecy. None of us are what we think we are, but what God knows we are. Jesus is saying that John came in the spirit and power of Elijah (cf. Luke 1:17), and his function was to prepare for the coming of the Lord (whether he was aware of this or not).[38] *Who is to come*[39] takes up John's verb (v. 3). Later Jesus will repeat the statement that John is Elijah (17:12).

15. Matthew repeats these words in 13:9, 43, and there are similar expressions in Mark and Luke. The command recurs in each of the letters to the seven churches in Revelation 2–3. In the Synoptic Gospels the words are always on the lips of Jesus, and in Revelation on those of the ascended Lord. The thought in all these passages is that the physical act of hearing is not sufficient. It is more important to take in what is heard, to comprehend it, and to assimilate it.

16. Jesus turns to the people of his day and uses the contrasting emphases in the ministries of John and himself to show the unreasonableness of their refusal to take either preacher seriously. He begins by asking to what he should *liken this generation,*[40] that is, the people living at that time (the word also can be used of people with certain characteristics [cf. 12:39; 16:4] and thus include others). There were, of course, exceptions, but he is referring to the generality of his contemporaries. He answers his own question by saying that these people are *like*[41] *children* he has observed at play. *Children* is strictly a diminutive, meaning "little children,"[42] but in fact the word is used of children of any age (it may even be used of grown men, John 21:5). The *marketplace* was the center of community life (Acts 17:17), a place where people sought work (20:3) and where goods were bought and sold. We notice from this passage that it was also a place where children played. It is not without its interest that Jesus had watched children playing (other religious leaders seem generally to have taken little interest in these young people). So he recalls little folk *sitting* in the public place and calling to their fellows.

17. Jesus uses an illustration from children's games, apparently with

---

38. See further my *The Gospel according to John* (Grand Rapids, 1971), pp. 134-36.

39. μέλλω is used here simply to bring out the thought of the future.

40. ὁμοιόω is a Matthean word (8 times out of 15 in the New Testament; Luke has it 3 times). It signifies "declare to be like, compare." γενέα may mean a clan, or a generation (all those living at a given time), or the time of a generation, or the prevailing and characteristic attitude of a generation. Nixon comments, "*This generation* were the privileged witnesses of the redemptive acts of the new covenant, as had been the generation of the Exodus in the old covenant. . . . They are therefore in a particularly responsible position in their reaction to the gospel." Cf. Ridderbos, " 'This generation' refers not merely to the people of Jesus' day but, more importantly, to all people with their attitude."

41. Matthew and Luke both have ὅμοιος 9 times (and Revelation 21 times). No other New Testament book has it more than twice. It means "like," "similar," mostly, as here, with the dative of the person or thing with which the comparison is made.

42. παιδίον, another Matthean word (18 times out of 52 in the New Testament).

children playing at weddings and at funerals, and with one group complaining that another will never cooperate. *"We played the flute for you,"* they said, where their musical expertise was clearly meant to encourage a merry dance and was not something like a concert piece, played for aesthetic appreciation. But the trouble was that their friends did not cooperate: *"you did not dance."*[43] It was the same when they were glum instead of merry. *"We wailed,"*[44] they said, *"and you did not lament."*[45] Glad or sad, their fellows declined to join in with them.

18. *For* (see on 1:20) introduces the application. John the Baptist *came,* which means more than arrival (cf. v. 11); it points to the whole ministry on which he entered. John's manner of life was ascetic: he was not noted for either *eating* or *drinking.* This does not, of course, indicate that he went without either food or beverages, but it does signify that John was frugal in his dietary habits. He was a serious-minded man, and food played no great part in his manner of life (cf. 3:4). But people did not profit from John's contempt for culinary delicacies. Instead of seeing the serious purpose behind all that he did they preferred to notice that he was different and put the difference down to demon possession: *"He has a demon"* (see on 7:22). The term could be used in a good sense, of a deity (see Acts 17:18), though this is rare in the New Testament; mostly it is used of an evil being who could enter a person and prevent him from fulfilling his proper role in life. So John's asceticism, which delivered him from the love of food that characterized all too many, was ridiculed as the meanderings of a maniac.

19. Jesus speaks of himself as *the Son of man* as he usually does (see on 8:20), and goes on to point out that he was no ascetic like John. When he says that he came *eating and drinking,* we should not imagine that he was claiming to be a gourmet. He is not saying that food and drink were at the center of his life; he is saying that, far from being an ascetic, he ate and drank normally, as other people did. In dietary habits he was a normal member of society. But this did not bring him praise from those who accused the Baptist of being a demoniac. Not a bit of it. *"Look,"* they said (drawing attention to one who was to be an object of scorn), *"a gluttonous man and a wine-drinker."*[46] Since he was not an ascetic, they accused him of eating and drinking to excess. With dietary excesses these people linked bad company; his social habits, they say, were deplorable. Their word

---

43. ὀρχέομαι is used again of children dancing in Luke 7:32, twice of the dancing of the daughter of Herodias (14:6; Mark 6:22), and nowhere else in the New Testament.

44. θρηνέω, here only in Matthew (and 4 times in the New Testament), means "mourn, lament"; it may be used of singing a dirge.

45. κόπτω may mean "cut off," as of branches (21:8); it is used in the middle of beating one's breast as an act of mourning.

46. φαγός (again in the New Testament only in Luke 7:34) means "an eater," "a glutton." οἰνοπότης is a drinker of wine, but taken strictly that meant just about everyone (wine and water were the only beverages generally available). So the term was used to denote someone who drank to excess, a drunkard.

order puts *tax collectors* first, "of tax collectors a friend and of sinners!" As we have seen (on 5:46), *tax collectors* were social outcasts. They were rejected because of their extortionate habits, and this was reinforced by the fact that they were regarded as ceremonially unclean. The nature of their business brought them into such contact with Gentiles that it was thought that they could not avoid becoming unclean. So people, especially religious people, kept as far away from them as possible. Not Jesus. He ate with them, which meant that if they were ceremonially unclean Jesus inevitably contracted defilement. With this Jesus joins *sinners*, a general term, not so much for those who were outrageously evil, but for people who did not bother to observe the details of the ceremonial rules that were the delight of the religious people of the day ("non-observant Jews," *AB*).[47] His opponents evidently reasoned, "You can know a man by the company he keeps!" Thus the people rejected John because he was an ascetic and Jesus because he was not. There was no logic, no reasonableness in their position.[48] They would neither repent with John nor rejoice with Jesus. Filson speaks of a "comfortable evasion of God's urgent claim," and that sums it up. They did not want to reckon with God's claim, and they manufactured reasons for passing it by.[49]

Jesus appends a saying about *wisdom*. This personification may go back to the Old Testament (cf. Job 28; Prov. 1:8), or it may signify the wisdom Jesus passed on to his disciples. In Luke's version this wisdom is vindicated by her children — the lives of those who accept Christ's teaching show that it was excellent. When Matthew says much the same about *actions*, he makes essentially the same point. The wisdom Jesus taught was not meant as a topic for debate in religious or philosophical schools — it was something to be lived out and it is *proved right*[50] in the works his followers do ("results," *NEB*, *GNB*). This is a "by their fruits you will know them" situation; wisdom does not need people to commend her, for the

---

47. I. Abrahams has a chapter on "Publicans and Sinners" in which he draws attention to the combination "publicans and robbers" in rabbinic literature. These, he finds, "were not those who neglected the rules of ritual piety, but were persons of immoral life, men of proved dishonesty or followers of suspected and degrading occupations" (*Studies in Pharisaism and the Gospels,* I [New York, 1967], p. 55). It is probably relevant that Jesus uses the term "sinners," not "robbers," but in any case the important point is that he reached out to people whom the Pharisees and the like excluded from fellowship. They saw them as having no possibility of receiving the blessing of God.

48. Cf. Green, "the Jewish people have never really meant to take the kingdom seriously; they will neither repent with John because it is near, nor rejoice with Jesus because it is here."

49. It is possible also to understand the children who piped and mourned as dictating to the others what they should do and the others as declining. Then the current generation is seen as dictating to John and to Jesus, who both declined to comply (cf. Lenski). But the view in the text is more natural; the people of the day did not demand that John or Jesus should live in this or that way.

50. δικαιόω = "show to be just, vindicate." The aorist is interesting, and is probably gnomic. This use of ἀπό will come under the heading "cause, means or outcome" (BAGD, V).

deeds of those who accept her vindicate her. It is possible to take the *children* as John the Baptist and Jesus (very different as they were, both were actuated by the divine wisdom). But the context seems to imply a distinction between those who accepted Jesus' wise teaching and those who did not.

2. Unrepentant Cities, 11:20-24

> 20*Then he began to reproach the towns in which most of his mighty works had been done, because they did not repent:* 21*"Woe to you, Chorazin! Woe to you, Bethsaida! For if the mighty works that were done in you had been done in Tyre and Sidon, long ago they would have repented in sackcloth and ashes.* 22*Nevertheless I tell you, it will be more bearable for Tyre and Sidon on the Day of Judgment than for you.* 23*And as for you, Capernaum, will you be exalted to heaven? Unto Hades you will be brought down; for if the mighty works that were done in you had been done in Sodom, it would have remained to this day.* 24*Nevertheless I tell you that on the Day of Judgment it will be more bearable for the land of Sodom than for you."*

Matthew shares with Luke a passage in which Jesus speaks of the eternal consequences for some of the cities that rejected him, specifically Chorazin, Bethsaida, and Capernaum. Miracles had been done in those cities, miracles enough to accredit him who performed them, but the people had not responded.[51] Even cities notorious for doing evil will be better off on Judgment Day than the cities that failed to respond to Jesus. Usually Matthew abbreviates, but here his account is longer than that of Luke.

20. Matthew introduces this section with his favorite *Then* (see on 2:7). As in verse 7, Jesus *began* to speak, this time to *reproach*[52] *the towns* in which he had worked. *Mighty works*[53] are miracles (see on 7:22, where the word refers to miracles done by false teachers). It is clear that Jesus had performed a number of miracles, mostly works of healing, and he expected those who saw them to recognize them for what they were, signs that God was at work in their midst. Jesus was not looking for amazement and admiration, but for repentance. That was the first note he struck in his preaching (4:17), and it remained a constant. People will

---

51. N. B. Stonehouse refers to the "once-popular notion that the ministry of Jesus began with nearly universal success" and says, "the extent of his outward success in the springtime of his Galilean ministry seems commonly to have been greatly exaggerated" (*Witness*, p. 148).

52. ὀνειδίζω (3 times in Matthew) may be used of insults (27:44), but it may also be used as here for reproaches that are fully justified.

53. Turner thinks that the meaning is "the cities in which 'his very many mighty works' were performed" (*Grammatical Insights*, p. 34). The superlative can indeed be used in an elative sense, but this is not likely here, for it would imply that all the mighty works were done in these three cities. "Most of his mighty works" is the meaning.

never advance spiritually unless they take the first step of turning away from the evil they have done. The people in the towns of which Jesus is speaking had seen the miracles indeed, but they had not reflected on what those miracles meant for those who saw them. The miracles testified to the presence of the divine in their midst; therefore the people who saw them should have asked themselves how they stood before God. But they did not. They continued on their sinful way without even the beginning of repentance. It was their failure to repent that formed the charge against them, and it runs right through this paragraph. Repentance is important and, it would seem, characteristically Christian in the sense that it was a call for a change of direction of the whole life. For the Greeks the word pointed to a change of mind, which referred to a single idea and might as easily be a change for the worse as for the better. Jesus is calling for a revolution in the whole of life. He is calling for people to change their whole direction away from sin and toward God. We should be clear that it is the orientation of the whole life that is in mind and not simply a being sorry for this or that sinful act. See further the note on 3:2.

21. *"Woe to you"* is not a grim call for vengeance, but an expression of regret (many translations render it as *JB*, "Alas"; *GNB* has "How terrible it will be"); it combines warning and compassion. Jesus is sad about the fate the city has brought down upon itself. *Chorazin* is mentioned in the New Testament only in this passage and the parallel in Luke 10:13. The name does not occur in the Old Testament, and it appears to be cited once only in the Talmud (*Menah.* 85a). There seems to be agreement that it is to be identified with the ruins now called Khirbet Keraseh, about two miles away from Capernaum; if so, it was a town of some importance.[54] It is a reminder of how little we know about the life of Jesus that we have only this one reference to what was evidently an extensive ministry during the course of which a number of miracles were performed (the previous verse states that "most of his mighty works" had been done in these cities). Jesus follows with a similar expression of regret for *Bethsaida*. This was a town (or "village," Mark 8:26) on the shore of the Sea of Galilee (Mark 6:45), just east of the Jordan (some claim that there was another Bethsaida to the west, but this has not been demonstrated). Philip, Andrew, and Peter came from this town (John 1:44), though Peter now had a house in Capernaum (8:14). The fact that three apostles came from this town shows that it was highly possible for people from Bethsaida to repent. Mark tells us that Jesus gave sight to a blind man there (Mark 8:22-26), and Luke locates the feeding of the five thousand with reference to this place (Luke 9:10-17). But it is clear from

---

54. It seems to be the town mentioned in the Talmud (*Menah.* 85a) as famous for its wheat. Among the ruins are those of a synagogue that includes a carved seat bearing an Aramaic inscription, which is perhaps an example of "Moses' seat" (23:2).

this passage that Jesus did many things in Bethsaida that have not been recorded.[55] The reason for the *Woe* is now given as *the mighty works* done in these places. Clearly this means that he had done much more in these places than our records indicate, and equally clearly that he did not regard the miracles simply as wonders to be gaped at. They were works of power, manifestations of the presence of God, and accordingly invitations to people to reflect on how they stood with God and to repent of the evil they had done.

Jesus brings out the enormity of the sin of the people of Chorazin and Bethsaida by calling to mind *Tyre* and *Sidon*, important coastal cities to the north of Israel (Tyre was actually on an island adjacent to the coast). They had been great and powerful cities for centuries, and their proximity to Israel had meant a good deal of contact. Since they were heathen cities their customs offended the Israelites, and the cities thus were well known for their shortcomings. They had been vigorously denounced by the prophets for their wickedness (e.g., Isa. 23; Ezek. 26; Amos 1:9-10). It is against this background that Jesus says that even these cities would have *repented* if there had been done in them the mighty works that Chorazin and Bethsaida had seen (cf. Jon. 3:6-8). *Long ago* points to the longsuffering of God: the resistance to the works Jesus did had been going on for quite some time, such a time indeed that Tyre and Sidon would have been moved by it. *Repented,* as we have seen, means a change in direction of the whole life. Confronted by Jesus, the Tyrians and the Sidonians would long since have responded by grieving over their sins. The use of *sackcloth*[56] *and ashes* was a traditional sign of grief over one's misdeeds. It was an action that conveyed publicly the truth that the wearer was profoundly sorry for what had been done.

22. Tyre and Sidon had not had those mighty works done in them, and they had not repented. But the inhabitants of Chorazin and Bethsaida are informed that, despite this, the lot of those sinners will be preferable to theirs. *I tell you* signifies that the following words are important.

---

55. The name means "House of fishing," which indicates the characteristic occupation of its inhabitants. There is some dispute about the exact location of this town. It is usually accepted that it was Bethsaida Julius, on the shore of the Sea of Galilee to the east of the Jordan where that river flows into the Sea of Galilee. But there is disagreement as to whether there was also a Bethsaida to the west of the river (Mark 6:45 is said to indicate a Bethsaida on the western side); D. F. Payne thinks that a suburb of Bethsaida Julius on the west bank of the Jordan is the best suggestion (*IBD*, I, p. 190). For our present purpose this does not greatly matter; it is enough to know that there was a flourishing center in which Jesus had an extensive ministry, most of which has not been reported.

56. σάκκος (once each in Matthew and Luke, twice in Revelation) means the material out of which sacks were made, rough and dark cloth (cf. Rev. 6:12), and thus suitable for use as garments in times of mourning (cf. 1 Kings 20:31-32). σποδός (once each in Matthew, Luke, and Hebrews only in the New Testament) means "ashes"; its link with sackcloth underlines the unattractiveness that conveyed the idea of mourning. People put ashes on their heads (2 Sam. 13:19), sat in ashes (Jon. 3:6; cf. Luke 10:13), lay in them (Esth. 4:3), and rolled in them (Jer. 6:26).

Nevertheless[57] indicates that despite the fact that they had not repented there was something going for them. God recognized that they were not as incorrigible as these Israelites. *The Day of Judgment* is the day of final judgment when everyone, non-Israelites as well as the people of God, will be called upon to account for the way they have lived their lives. It was a day when most Israelites were sure that they would be much better off than any heathen. Jesus calls on them to think again. For the Tyrians and the Sidonians *it will be more bearable*[58] *than for you*. He does not say that they will not be punished for their sins. He says that on Judgment Day those who have had greater opportunities (e.g., the people of Chorazin and Bethsaida) will be judged more severely than those who have had less.[59] We should not miss the point that Jesus knows how the people of Tyre and Sidon would have reacted had they had the privilege that the cities of Galilee had had. This perhaps has relevance to the problem of those unreached by the gospel.

23. The address is switched to *Capernaum,* the town that figures most prominently in the Gospel narratives. Jesus was there often, and indeed it can be called "his own city" (9:1). Its location is not completely certain (see on 4:13). Instead of pronouncing a "woe" on this city Jesus asks a question (which looks for a negative answer),[60] *"will you be exalted to heaven?"* Evidently the people of Capernaum thought highly of themselves and looked to heaven (see on 3:2) as their ultimate destination. But this did not correspond to the facts, and specifically with the ultimate fate that lay before them. Jesus tells them that it is *Hades*[61] rather than *heaven* to which they must look forward; *unto Hades* comes first in its clause, which gives it emphasis. *Hades,* the underworld, here stands for the lowest possible place, just as *heaven* is the highest possible. It is the place of the departed spirits, but refers to those in torment rather than to those in bliss. Their failure to repent meant that there was no other ultimate fate open to the Capernaumites than Hades (cf. Isa. 14:13-15). *For* introduces the reason, and the conditional implies that the condition has not been fulfilled.[62] *Sodom* was

---

57. πλήν means "only, nevertheless, however, but"; it is "the real colloq. word for this idea" (BAGD, 1.b). *JB* has "and still."

58. ἀνεκτός is connected with ἀνέχω, "to bear up"; it thus signifies "bearable." Cf. Carson, "There are degrees of felicity in paradise and degrees of torment in hell (12:41; 23:13; cf. Luke 12:47-48), a point Paul well understood (Rom. 1:20–2:16)."

59. Bruner remarks, "It is going to go better in the judgment day for notorious pagans than for self-satisfied saints."

60. It is introduced by μή. The text behind *KJV* makes the words a statement: "which art exalted unto heaven," but the attestation is inadequate and transcriptional probability is against it (see the note in Metzger).

61. ἅδης (twice in Matthew, Luke, and Acts, and 4 times in Revelation only in the New Testament) was originally the name of the god of the underworld, then the name of the underworld itself. *NEB* here has "exalted to the skies" and "brought down to the depths," a translation that is suitable for modern doubters but scarcely one that fits the meaning for first-century people who saw heaven and hell as realities.

62. εἰ in the protasis with aorists in both clauses points to a condition contrary to fact:

proverbial for wickedness (10:15; Mark 6:11 t.r.; Luke 10:12; Rom. 9:29; 2 Pet. 2:6; Jude 7), but Jesus says that it was not as firmly set in paths of evil as was Capernaum. It would not have been impervious to the meaning of the mighty works that Jesus did. Capernaum was, and in that lay its condemnation.

24. As in verse 22, *Nevertheless I tell you* leads into a saying that was both unexpected and important. And again we have a reference to the Day of Judgment and to what is *bearable*. Even evil Sodom would do better on the great day than these people in Capernaum who had been confronted with the high point in God's revelation and who had scorned it or been indifferent to it.

3. Jesus' Invitation, 11:25-30

> 25At that time Jesus answered, saying, "I praise you, Father, Lord of heaven and earth, because you hid these things from wise and clever people and revealed them to babies. 26Yes, Father, for so it was well pleasing before you." 27"All things were handed over to me by my Father; and no one knows the Son except the Father, neither does anyone know the Father except the Son, and the one to whom the Son wills to reveal him. 28Come to me, all you who are weary and heavily burdened, and I will refresh you. 29Take my yoke upon you and learn from me, for I am gentle and humble in heart, and you will find rest for your souls. 30For my yoke is easy, and my burden is a light one."

Matthew goes on to tell his readers of a little prayer Jesus offered, followed by some words to his disciples. The section is in three parts. In the first Jesus expresses his thankfulness that the way he teaches is not something that is open only to the learned and intelligent; even little children may apprehend it. In the second he reflects on the relation between the Father and the Son,[63] and then in the third he invites the world's downtrodden ones to find rest and peace in him. There are parallels to the first two in Luke 10:21-22, but the invitation is found in this Gospel only. The whole is in a style akin to that in John's Gospel, which leads some critics to believe that Matthew did not write it. It would be better to conclude that this Synoptic passage shows that Jesus did sometimes teach in the style of our Fourth Gospel.

25. *At that time*[64] locates what follows in the same general period as the preceding, but does not tie it down with precision. It is curious that

---

"If the mighty works had been done in Sodom (as they were not), it would have remained (as it has not)."

63. Kingsbury points out that for Matthew "Jesus is uniquely the Son of God" and that it is in this pericope "that this is most emphatically brought out" (*Matthew*, pp. 42, 43).

64. καιρός (in Matthew 10 times) may indicate a point of time or a period of time; here it is quite general. For ἐκεῖνος see on 3:1.

Matthew says that Jesus *answered*, for there is no question expressed or implied. But Matthew is fond of the verb (he has it 55 times), and it sometimes is equivalent to "said" (Hebraistically), as here.[65] The prayer begins with praise to God.[66] As he usually does, Jesus addresses God as *"Father"* (see on 5:16); we should bear in mind that in this Gospel this term occurs 64 times (a total exceeded in the New Testament only in the Gospel of John, with 137). Sometimes this means a human father, but much more often it refers to God; he may be seen as the Father of people, but here he is the Father of Jesus Christ. Jesus goes on to add the title *"Lord of heaven and earth"* (an uncommon expression, but it is found in Tob. 7:18). Jesus taught his followers to regard God as their Father, not as some remote tyrant, but that does not mean that he thought meanly of him or thought he could safely be neglected. He knew him as the Lord of all that is, in this world and in any other, so that everyone must pay to him the homage due to the Lord of all. On this occasion Jesus' thanks were not on account of the Father's greatness but on account of the way he had made his revelation known. *You hid* does not mean that God completely concealed the things in question from the world's wise ones, but rather that it is in his plan that the way to knowing them is not the way of human excellence or wisdom (cf. 1 Cor. 1:18-19; 2:6-8). As far as human excellence in itself is concerned, these things are hidden, and that by the divine plan. Jesus does not define *these things*, but the expression "must refer, in one way or another, to the secret of the presence of the Kingdom which was the burden of Jesus' preaching."[67] Some interpret it as speaking of eschatological happenings, and others of the knowledge the Son received from the Father and which he passes on to his followers. Or there may be a reference to the mighty works Jesus did and which the Jews in general were unable to understand as signs of kingdom. But all such views surely point to "the presence of the Kingdom," and we will do well to take this as our starting point.

This knowledge, Jesus says, the Father has *hid* from the world's great and wise ones and revealed to the lowliest, those who can be called *babies*. This does not mean that all the *wise* are lost and all the *babies* are saved; it means that the knowledge of God does not depend on human wisdom and education. *Wise and clever people* will sum up the best of human achievers; not by the exercise of their gifts will the presence of the kingdom

---

65. Howard includes the construction in his discussion of "Semitisms in the New Testament." He finds it 45 times in Matthew (15 in Mark, 38 in Luke), and says that the participle "is strictly redundant (in the sense that nothing has been said to which an answer is needed) only in a few places"; in this Gospel he finds it here and in 12:38; (15:15?); 17:4; 28:5 (M, II, p. 453).

66. ἐξομολογέω in the active means "profess, agree" and in the middle "acknowledge, confess," from which it is but a step to "praise."

67. A. M. Hunter, *NTS*, VIII (1961-62), p. 243. His whole article, a reappraisal of Matthew 11:25-30, is very valuable. He argues strongly for the authenticity of the paragraph. H. D. Betz has a useful history of interpretations of the passage (*JBL*, 86 [1967], pp. 10-24).

be detected. It has always been easy for the world's wise ones to trust in their wisdom. They realize how their wisdom makes them superior to the foolish and accordingly come to rely on that wisdom. Their self-sufficiency means that they do not easily come to trust God for salvation. This does not mean that none of the world's wise and clever people will come to know it. In every age there have been wise and clever people who have rejoiced in the revelation Jesus has made known. But the point is that they came to know it by their simple trust in Jesus, not by their intellectual skills and their knowledge of abstruse research methods. And that simple trust is open to the humblest of us all, to the *babies* among us.

26. *Yes* reaffirms what has just been said, while *Father* repeats the characteristic of God that gives confidence. He is loving enough to make his revelation available to the humblest of his people. And Jesus locates this in the divine will: *"so it was well pleasing before you."*[68] We are not to think that some people of little ability chanced to hit on the truth while more able and profound people missed the mark, and that God then accepted what happened. Jesus is saying that the Father planned things this way. He never intended that the knowledge of the kingdom and the like should be such that only the profoundly intellectual could find it. It was his good will that the lowly could find the way, and that if the clever found it, it would be in the same way as the lowly did.

27. Jesus' prayer was a short one, and he now addresses the disciples. *All things* is very general and may conceivably mean the totality of existence or all power and dominion (cf. 28:18; Dan. 7:14), but in the context the emphasis is rather on all knowledge.[69] It is also probably relevant that the power is said to be given to Jesus after the resurrection (28:18). Some commentators also point out that the verb *handed over*[70] is used often of the handing on of tradition; if this is in mind, there will be a contrast between the tradition handed on by the scribes and the knowledge conveyed to the Son by the Father. That knowledge is meant is indicated also by the fact that Jesus immediately goes on to the knowledge he has of the Father and the knowledge of the Father that he reveals. Jesus is claiming real knowledge of God (in contrast to what the teachers of the law claimed to have) and the ability to reveal the Father to other people. Jesus says that *all things* were handed on to him by *my Father* (not "the Father"); he is claiming a relationship to the heavenly Father closer than that held by anyone else.

This is further brought out with the assertion that it is only *the Father*

---

68. εὐδοκία means "goodwill." It is perhaps unexpected to have ἔμπροσθεν, but, as BAGD puts it, "It is a reverential way of expressing oneself, when one is speaking of an eminent per., and esp. of God, not to connect him directly w. what happens, but to say that it took place 'before him.'"

69. Lenski thinks that the reference is to the incarnation, but there seems to be no good reason for taking the words in this way.

70. παραδίδωμι (see on 4:12) is found in this Gospel more than in any other book of the New Testament. It is the usual word for handing on traditions (e.g., 1 Cor. 15:3).

who *knows*[71] *the Son.* There were many in the first century who held that
the essential being of God is quite unknown; he dwells in unapproachable
mystery. It is a quite different thought that the essential being of the Son
is not known. Jesus is not now speaking of the relationship of sonship that
all the people of God may claim: it is not "a" Son of whom he speaks, but
the Son. The Jews, the people of God, had consistently rejected him, so it
was plain enough that they did not know *the Son;* but it is also the case
that the disciples who had responded to his call did not have as yet
anything like an adequate understanding of his person. It was true of
them, too, that they did not really know him, so that it was only the Father
who had real knowledge of him.[72] It is interesting that when Peter came
to know Jesus as he really is, as the Christ, Jesus said that flesh and blood
had not revealed this to him, "but my Father" (16:17). In the Lucan parallel
we have "who the Son is" (Luke 10:22), and that is the meaning: they did
not know who he really was. But the Father did, and it was this that
mattered to Jesus, not the hostility of Jewish leaders. The essential being
of the Son was not obvious to human observation. Who could see in the
carpenter from Nazareth the only Son of God?

To this is added the further thought that no one knows *the Father
except the Son.* The Jews, of course, from their study of the revelation in
the Old Testament, had some knowledge of God, but their knowledge was
imperfect. Jesus is saying that his knowledge of the Father surpasses that
in any revelation made hitherto: he knows the Father as he really is. He
has a knowledge of the Father not shared by any of his contemporaries.
To this he adds, *"and the one to whom*[73] *the Son wills to reveal him."* This does
not mean that those who receive the revelation know the Father in the
same intimate way as the Son does. Knowledge that springs from community of nature is not the same as that which comes from revelation. It
means rather that it is in him that they come to know God. Those who
are willing to receive the revelation in Jesus will have a knowledge of God
not open to anyone else. Notice that the revelation is connected with the
will of the Son.[74] The revelation of the Father does not come by chance; it

71. ἐπιγινώσκει. The verb is sometimes held to have the meaning "know fully, exactly,"
but this is not easy to prove. J. Armitage Robinson has a lengthy examination of this verb
and its cognate noun (*St Paul's Epistle to the Ephesians* [London, 1907], pp. 248-54) in which
he finds γνῶσις to be the wider word with ἐπίγνωσις knowledge directed toward a particular
object. We should notice that in the Lucan parallel the verb is γινώσκω.

72. "The Son is not only the organ of revelation but is himself a mystery to be revealed;
the knowledge of the Father and the knowledge of the Son are two sides of the same mystery,
which is now revealed, and so the Father and the Son in fellowship with one another are
both subject and object of revelation" (N. B. Stonehouse, *Witness,* p. 212). Cf. 16:17.

73. ᾧ ἐάν is general, "to whomever"; Jesus is not claiming to found an exclusive set of
gnostics, people with a special spiritual endowment. His revelation is open to anyone who
comes humbly. It is not easy to get an idiomatic English equivalent, and a number of
translations bring out the universal aspect by rendering with a plural, "those to whom. . . ."

74. The verb βούλομαι (which Matthew uses only twice) signifies a decision of the will,
often after deliberation. There is no thought of caprice.

comes only to those to whom the Son chooses to make the revelation. The saying ascribes to Jesus the critical place in the revelation of the Father.

28. In a section peculiar to Matthew, arising out of this will to reveal, comes the gracious invitation.[75] *Come*[76] *to me* carries on with the thought that it is Jesus only who has access to the Father and to the resources of the Father. It is because he is the only one who knows the Father and because only those to whom he reveals the Father will have knowledge of him that it is so important to give heed to his invitation. The invitation is extended to all the troubled. *All* means that the invitation is universal — none of the troubled are omitted. Traditionally the first invited have been "ye that labor," and there is a good deal to be said for that translation.[77] But Jesus is not here speaking about work but about need. It seems that we should understand the term to mean the *weary*. The present tense points to a continuing state. With them are joined the *heavily burdened*,[78] where there is no qualification added to indicate the nature of the burden. Jesus is calling anyone who is wearied with life's burdens. To all such he says, *"I will refresh*[79] *you."* The verb seems not to imply the rest that is the complete cessation from labor, which is made clear when Jesus goes on to speak of his "yoke," of learning, and of his "burden." The rest in mind is the rest that enables the worker to go back to the task with renewed vigor. We should not miss the point that Jesus says that he will give rest, not that the Father will do this; this is underlined by the use of the emphatic pronoun *I*.

75. Luke T. Johnson makes a number of observations on "this extraordinarily rich passage": "First, because he is gentle and lowly, Jesus personifies membership in God's kingdom (cf. 5:3-5). Second, as Torah revealed God's will, so Jesus reveals the Father to whom he wishes (11:27). Third, in contrast to scribes and Pharisees — the 'wise' from whom the revelation is hidden, 11:25 — Jesus gives a light burden. Fourth, his 'yoke' corresponds exactly to the symbol of Torah as 'yoke of the kingdom of God.' Fifth, as the Pharisees looked to Torah to learn God's ways, so those whom Jesus calls are to 'learn from me.' Sixth, the commandment that, above all, defined Jews in society was the Sabbath observance, which was regarded as participation in God's own Sabbath rest; here, learning from Jesus brings rest for the soul" (*The Writings of the New Testament* [Philadelphia, 1986], p. 190).

76. δεῦτε (which serves as the plural of δεῦρο) occurs in Matthew 6 times out of its 12 New Testament occurrences. It invites people to come.

77. κοπιάω has a meaning like "labor to the point of weariness," and the question is whether we should bring out in our translation the labor or the suffering. Since this context has nothing about work, either for God or people, it seems that we should accept some such meaning as *weary*.

78. φορτίζω is not common in the New Testament (elsewhere only in Luke 11:46). It is connected with φόρτος, a load or burden (used in some MSS in Acts 27:10 of the cargo of a ship). The perfect participle here indicates a continuing burden. Plummer differentiates the verbs: "The one implies toil, the other endurance. The one refers to the weary search for truth and for relief for a troubled conscience; the other refers to the heavy load of observances that give no relief, and perhaps also to the sorrows of life, which, apart from the consolations of a true faith, are so crushing" (p. 170).

79. AS points out that ἀναπαύω in LXX translates 14 different Hebrew words, so it covers a wide range of meaning. MM says that it "is a technical term of agriculture," and the examples it cites show that it is used of sowing light crops, not only of fallowing.

29. The thought is developed in a different way. Jesus speaks of people as his servants and his students. *Take* is a verb with the meaning "take up," "lift up," and *yoke*, of course, is a metaphor from carrying or ploughing; it was also a mark of servitude to a conqueror (Jer. 27:2-7; 28:10). Jesus is inviting people to follow him, to serve him, and to learn from him. In the New Testament *yoke* is always used metaphorically and signifies bondage or submission to authority of some kind. "The yoke of the law" and kindred expressions are common among the Jews (e.g., "He that takes upon himself the yoke of the Law, from him shall be taken away the yoke of the kingdom and the yoke of worldly care," *'Abot* 3:5; cf. Sir. 51:23-27 and the passages listed in SBk, I, pp. 608-10). The rabbis spoke lovingly about "the yoke of the law," and there can be no doubt that for them it was a singular blessing. But their delight in the law was not necessarily shared by the common people, to whom it may well have appeared much more burdensome than the rabbis thought. "The arbitrary demands of Pharisaic legalism and the uncertainties of ever-proliferating case law" (*AB*, p. 146) point to a situation where what was a delight to the legal experts was intolerable to ordinary people.[80] Jesus speaks of scribes and Pharisees as putting heavy burdens on people's backs (23:4), and it is this sort of thing that is in mind. The New Testament believers did not agree with the rabbinic assessment.[81] They took seriously what the yoke of the law meant, and, for example, Paul spoke of bringing Christians under the law as laying "on the neck of the disciples a yoke that neither we nor our fathers were able to bear" (Acts 15:10), and again of not being "entangled in a yoke of bondage" (Gal. 5:1; cf. 1 Tim. 6:1). In contrast with this yoke Jesus is holding out to his followers the thought of a yoke that was easy, not bondage. It was not that he demanded less from his followers, for the Sermon on the Mount shows that he looked for more. But it was of a different kind and in a different spirit so that it was kindly, not a burden.

Jesus further says, *"learn from me."*[82] Throughout this Gospel there is an emphasis on learning, on being a disciple, and the like, and the verb here is cognate with "disciple"; it means "learn through instruction." To be a follower of Jesus is to be a disciple and therefore a learner. It is not enough to indicate that one would like to be a follower of Jesus; to commit oneself to him means to commit oneself to a learning process. This is not meant to scare people or make them think that the way Jesus teaches is much harder than that of the rabbis. Jesus affirms that he is *gentle*[83] *and*

80. This is overlooked by discussions such as that of M. Maher (*NTS*, 22 [1975-76], pp. 97-103), where all the emphasis is put on the rabbinic delight in the law.

81. K. H. Rengstorf speaks of "the point where with perfect clarity the yoke of Jesus and the yoke of a divine dominion conceived in human terms divide with all the sharpness with which the Gospel is distinct from the Law" (*TDNT*, II, p. 901).

82. ὅτι may mean "that": "learn from me that I am gentle . . ."; but *for* seems more probable.

83. πραΰς (3 times in Matthew and once in 1 Peter only in the New Testament) means *"gentle, humble, considerate, meek* in the older favorable sense" (BAGD).

humble[84] *in heart.* This taking of a lowly place is noteworthy. Leaders and teachers have always tended to take a superior place, but Jesus has no need of such gimmicks. He left his place in heaven and on earth took the form of a slave (Phil. 2:7). *In heart* locates these qualities at the center of his being. It was not that he pretended to be humble and made a show of being lowly: he really was lowly, and that at the very center of all that he was. Because of what he is in his innermost being, meek and lowly, those who come to him *find rest.*[85] This does not mean that they are excused henceforth from hard work. On the contrary, to be a follower of Jesus is to enter a way of life that necessarily involves hard work. But there is nothing of the hopelessness about it that characterizes life for far too many of the world's afflicted. The calling must be fulfilled, but there is rest *for your souls* (see Jer. 6:16, and for *souls* on 10:28). That is to say, those who bear Christ's yoke know rest at the center of their being. They do not worry and fuss about what they are doing, for their commitment to their Savior means that they recognize his sovereignty over all and the fact that he will never call them to something that is beyond their strength. Paradoxically those who take Christ's *yoke* on them have rest, rest now and eternal rest in the hereafter.

30. Jesus adds a sentence that shows that the service to which he calls is no difficult and burdensome affair. His yoke, he says, *is easy,* where his adjective[86] signifies what is good and pleasant. He does not call people to a burdensome and worrying existence. Another way of putting it is to say that his *burden is a light one.* The word for *burden* is a diminutive,[87] which helps bring out the thought that his service is pleasant. So with *light* (cf. its use of a light affliction, 2 Cor. 4:17). It adds up to an invitation to service indeed; Jesus is not calling people to lives of careless ease. But it is service for which they will be glad. It will be a delight, not a painful drudgery.[88]

---

84. ταπεινός (here only in Matthew) has a negative connotation in Greek writings generally. We would convey the idea by some such term as "servile"; it "expresses both the low estate of the man who lives in poor and petty relations, esp. the slave, and also the base disposition resulting therefrom" (W. Grundmann, *TDNT*, VIII, p. 2).

85. The word is ἀνάπαυσις, "cessation, rest, refreshment" (AS, who goes on to distinguish this word from ἄνεσις, on which he says, "[lit. the relaxation of the strings of a lyre], prop. signifies the rest or ease which comes from the relaxation of unfavourable conditions, as, e.g. affliction: ἀνάπ. the rest which comes from the temporary cessation of labour"). Tasker thinks that it would be better translated "relief," for Jesus promises not inactivity and repose but "relief from such crushing burdens as crippling anxiety, the sense of frustration and futility, and the misery of a sin-laden conscience" (p. 122).

86. χρηστός, which Matthew uses only here, means both kindly and useful.

87. φορτίον is a diminutive of φόρτος, which means a load, and is often used of a ship's cargo. Jesus does not call people to bear huge burdens.

88. Lenski quotes Bernhard, "What can be lighter than a burden which unburdens us and a yoke which bears its bearer?"

Matthew 12

4. The Use of the Sabbath, 12:1-14

¹*At that time Jesus went through the grainfields on the Sabbath; and his disciples were hungry and began to pluck heads of grain and eat them. ²But when the Pharisees saw this, they said to him, "Look, your disciples are doing what it is not lawful to do on a Sabbath." ³But he said to them, "Have you not read what David did when he and those with him were hungry, ⁴how he entered the house of God and they ate the loaves of offering, which it was not lawful for him to eat nor for those who were with him, but for the priests alone? ⁵Or have you not read in the law that on the Sabbath the priests in the temple profane the Sabbath and are guiltless? ⁶But I say to you, that there is something here greater than the temple. ⁷And if you had known what this means, 'I desire mercy and not sacrifice,' you would not have condemned the guiltless. ⁸For the Son of man is lord of the Sabbath."*

⁹*And he went on from there and came into their synagogue. ¹⁰And look, a man who had a withered hand. And they asked him, saying, "Is it lawful to heal on the Sabbath?" — so that they might accuse him. ¹¹But he said to them, "What man of you will there be who will have one sheep, and if it falls into a ditch on the Sabbath, will he not take hold of it and lift it out? ¹²How much more is a man worth than a sheep! So then it is lawful to do good on the Sabbath." ¹³Then he says to the man, "Stretch out your hand." And he stretched it out and it was restored, whole as the other. ¹⁴But the Pharisees went out and took counsel against him, so that they might kill him.*

In the first days of his ministry it is plain that Jesus won a wide measure of acceptance. He did works of mercy and was a popular preacher. But in the course of time the Jewish establishment came to see that what he was doing and what he was teaching were incompatible with an acceptance of their essential position. So they came to oppose him, and that with a virulence that would eventually lead to his death. In this chapter Matthew has gathered a number of incidents that enable the reader to see the kind of opposition that was aroused and something of the reason for that opposition. He begins with Jesus' attitude toward the Sabbath.

The Jews took Sabbath observance very seriously. Thus when the enemy attacked on the Sabbath in the days of the Maccabees, they let themselves be slaughtered, men, women, and children, rather than break the Sabbath by defending themselves (1 Macc. 2:31-38). At a later time Pompey was able to erect the earthworks that made his siege of Jerusalem successful quite unhindered by the defenders because he did it on the Sabbath (Josephus, *Ant.* 14.63). The Jews were ready to suffer rather than break the Sabbath. It is clear from all four Gospels that Jesus had a continuing controversy with the Pharisees over the right use of the Sabbath, though Matthew's account of it is not extensive; indeed, he concentrates it into the stories in the opening part of this chapter. From the Mishnah and Talmud tractates on the Sabbath it is plain that the right use of this day was of the utmost importance to religious Jews in Jesus' day. Morgan points out that the Sabbath was "the only symbol peculiar to Judaism" (p. 124); he finds sacrifices, circumcision, and the place of the temple in the religions of the peoples around Israel, but the Sabbath was different.[1] To most Jews the Sabbath was a delight,[2] even though there was a mass of regulations, drawn up with the laudable intention of ensuring that the day was kept holy (the Mishnah devotes the whole of *Shab.* 7 to what constitutes work on the Sabbath). Even the Mishnah laments that "the rules about the Sabbath . . . are as mountains hanging by a hair, for [teaching of] Scripture [thereon] is scanty and the rules many" (*Ḥag.* 1:8). Some of these regulations were very curious, and there can be no doubt that taken the way the Pharisees took them they could be extremely burdensome.[3] We should not overlook the fact that Matthew places this section immediately after Jesus' words about his yoke being easy and his burden light. The different attitudes to the Sabbath form an excellent illustration of what Jesus' invitation meant.

But we should not think that the controversy arose because Jesus was trying to relieve people of the mass of regulations. It was not that he thought the Pharisees were too rigorous in their Sabbath observance and was trying to relieve a grievous burden. Rather, he held that they had the

1. This is not to say that no other nation ever had any equivalent of the Sabbath. Special days were observed by a number of peoples, and it is pointed out that the Babylonians in particular had a Sabbath. But the Jewish observation of the Sabbath set them apart from other peoples in New Testament times.

2. C. G. Montefiore says, "in spite of many restrictions and regulations the Sabbath was upon the whole a joy and a blessing to the immense majority of Jews throughout the Rabbinic period" (*The Synoptic Gospels*, I [London, 1909], p. 93).

3. To take an example at random: "If a man took out aught in his right hand or in his left hand, in his bosom or on his shoulder, he is culpable; for this last was the manner of carrying of the sons of Kohath. If [he took it out] on the back of his hand, or with his foot or with his mouth or with his elbow, on in his ear or in his hair or in his wallet [carried] mouth downwards, or between his wallet and his shirt, or in the hem of his shirt, or in his shoe or in his sandal, he is not culpable, since he has not taken it out after the fashion of them that take out [a burden]" (*Shab.* 10:3). If one took all the regulations in this way, it was a tremendous burden even to remember what was and what was not permissible.

wrong idea of the Sabbath altogether. It was a day for honoring God, which meant doing good; thus works of healing were not simply allowed, they were obligatory. It was a day for refreshing people, for meeting their need. But for the Pharisees it was primarily a day for keeping the regulations that expressed their desire to honor God. In this chapter Matthew shows how Jesus taught from the examples of David and of the priests that the right use of the Sabbath is very different from the usage of the Pharisees. Scripture shows the Pharisees to be in error.

1. *At that time* is a very general expression, locating what follows in the general period of the preceding, just as that had been linked with what went before it (so also in 11:25; 14:1). Matthew does not tell us where Jesus was going, only that it was on the Sabbath,[4] the day of rest and worship. The Jews generally and the Pharisees in particular were strict in their observance of the Sabbath. To go astray on the Sabbath was for the Pharisees a matter of first importance. Jesus' journey took him through the fields of grain;[5] Matthew does not say that the disciples were with him, but that can be assumed. He tells us that they were hungry (neither Mark nor Luke includes this; Matthew has the verb "to hunger" more than a third of all its New Testament occurrences; for some reason he is interested in hungry people). So they began to pluck some of the grain and eat it. The fact of their eating shows that they were satisfying a genuine hunger and not wantonly breaking the Sabbath regulations.

2. *But* is adversative: it sets the Pharisees over against Jesus. Matthew does not say how the Pharisees came to be in that particular grainfield, but clearly they were in a position to observe what was done. They complain to Jesus, not the disciples, though it is not said that he was joining in the plucking and eating. But Jesus was the Master; it must be accepted that the disciples were acting with their Master's approval. In any case it was Jesus who was the concern of the Pharisees. And in this instance they were not acting on the basis of reliable reports; they were there and saw it for themselves. They were acting on sure knowledge. They said that what the disciples were doing was not lawful to do on a Sabbath. Travelers were permitted to eat grain from the fields they passed through (Deut. 23:25); it was not the action that was the problem, but the fact that it was done on the Sabbath. As they understood it, plucking the grain was reaping, rubbing it to separate the grain from the husks (Luke tells us that they did this) was threshing, blowing away the husks may well have been interpreted as winnowing, and for good measure they may have seen the whole as preparation of food, which they also regarded as prohibited (all food eaten on the Sabbath had to be prepared on the previous day). That

4. The Aramaic שַׁבְּתָא was transliterated as σάββατα, which was taken as a plural in Greek and a singular σάββατον formed from it (used in v. 2).

5. σπόριμος is an adjective meaning fit for sowing; in the neuter plural it was used for fields of grain.

it was but a small amount did not excuse the disciples, for it was blame-worthy to reap and grind corn of a bulk no more than that of a dried fig (*Shab.* 70b); it would have required a good deal more than that to satisfy a person's hunger.[6]

3-4. Another adversative construction[7] moves the narrative along as Jesus confronts the Pharisees with a question on an apparently unrelated subject. "*Have you not read?*" points them to the Scripture whose authority they were so committed to uphold, though "They had read the letter, without perceiving the spirit" (Bengel).[8] We should perhaps notice that when Jesus is speaking to the people he says, "You have heard" (5:21, 27, etc.), but these men were educated: they would have read for themselves. Jesus refers them to an action of David when he and his men were hungry. This is an argument of a well-known rabbinic type, called *qal wahomer* ("the light and the weighty"); if a thing was true for the less important, then much more was it so of the more important. Here David is the less important and Jesus, the Son of David, the more important. David and his men did not content themselves with the grainfields, but David *entered the house of God*. Not only so, but he and his men[9] *ate the loaves of offering* (1 Sam. 21:1-6),[10] the holy bread. The recipe for the bread and its manner of arrangement Sabbath after Sabbath are detailed in the law (Lev. 24:5-9),[11] where it is specified that this bread "belongs to Aaron and his sons" (v. 9); it was not for others than priests to eat. The singular for *entered* seems to mean that David went into the holy place to get the bread (unless the loaves were those taken out of the holy place and not yet eaten by the priests). He then brought it out, and his little band ate it. They were in need and there was no other bread, so they ate the holy loaves. *For him* fastens the responsibility on David; his men are then joined with him, but Jesus makes it clear that the great David, whom everyone honored, was

6. Carr points out that the Pharisaic interpretation really destroyed the Sabbath. "If sabbatical observances prevented men from satisfying hunger, the Sabbath was no longer a blessing but an injury to man."

7. ὁ δέ, where the article has something of its original demonstrative force and acts as subject; δέ has adversative force.

8. Cf. M. Green, "the Pharisees were so anxious to study what Scripture said that they could not hear what Scripture meant" (p. 125).

9. The plural ἔφαγον (א B 481) is unexpected, for the previous verb is in the singular and we expect this one to agree, as indeed it does in many MSS (as 𝔭[70] C D etc.), and in the parallel passages in Mark and Luke. ὅ is also difficult since the reference is to loaves and we expect a masculine plural; perhaps the meaning is that it is the action, the thing, that is not lawful.

10. It is not easy to translate ἄρτους τῆς προθέσεως. πρόθεσις has the idea of setting forth, and thus presenting, and the meaning appears to be the loaves that were presented to God (*GNB* has "bread offered to God"; *NIV,* "consecrated bread"; *NRSV*'s "bread of the Presence" is not easy to understand; perhaps the idea is that the bread was placed before the Lord and was thus always in his presence).

11. These were very large loaves. G. J. Wenham speaks of them as "huge" and explains that "the figures suggest that about 3 liters or 3½ lbs. of flour went into each loaf" (*The Book of Leviticus* [Grand Rapids, 1979], p. 310, n. 6).

the principal figure in this breaking of the strict provisions of the law. Jesus goes on to make it clear that the bread belonged to the priests alone, the priests of Aaron's line. They alone prepared the loaves, set them out in the sanctuary, and consumed them when the time came for removal and replacement. Eating the holy loaves was a priestly prerogative — laymen were not allowed to do it. But the Scripture, the very Scripture on which the Pharisees professed to rely, did not condemn David or his men. David was not breaking the Sabbath; the relevance of what he did was that the need to satisfy hunger overrode a liturgical provision. His men were not starving, just badly in need of food. This makes a powerful argument: if these men's hunger set aside a divine regulation without blame, how much more should the hunger of Jesus' disciples set aside a rabbinical rule!

5. Verses 5-7 have no parallel in Mark or Luke; Matthew alone has Jesus' citation of the practice of the priests as they offered sacrifice. *Or*[12] introduces an alternative. Again Jesus appeals to Scripture, with *"have you not read. . . ?"* He points his hearers to that reading which brings them knowledge of what God commands. *The law* is, of course, the Pentateuch, the heart of revelation as the Jews understood it. What they read in the law they held to be especially sacred. Daube points out that this argument (which is found in Matthew only) would be of greater weight for Jews than the previous one. In appealing to David Jesus was appealing to an example; the argument is based on an incident, on something that happened. But the appeal to the sacrifices rests on an explicit commandment of Scripture. It is definitely commanded that two lambs be offered on the Sabbath (Num. 28:9-10), so that temple service takes precedence over Sabbath observance.[13] Jesus draws attention to the fact that in the law it was prescribed that every Sabbath the priests should offer the sacrifice of two lambs as well as the normal daily offerings. The command does not specially mention the priests, but since they were the only ones who could offer sacrifices it was they who would work on the Sabbath. The Talmud recognizes that "the sacrificial service supersedes the Sabbath" (*Shab.* 132b). That the priests performed work on the Sabbath — every Sabbath — should give cause for those who reverenced Scripture to think hard about what God meant the Sabbath to be and what people should do to keep it holy. They had too easily accepted views that made the Sabbath a burden and had overlooked the fact that Scripture did not fit into their

12. ἥ is found in Matthew 67 times (next is 1 Corinthians with 49 instances); it is used here "to introduce a question which is parallel to a preceding one or supplements it" (BAGD, 1.d.β).

13. See Daube, pp. 67-71. The technical point is that the incident with David belonged to the *haggadah*, while that of the priests in the temple was an example of *halakah*; it was based on an actual commandment given in Scripture. Daube concludes, "Scripture — thus the argument in Matthew runs — ordains that the observance of the Sabbath must yield to the temple service; *a fortiori* it must yield in the present case, where something greater than the temple demands consideration. There is nothing *haggadhic* about this. The argument is of a kind which no student of *halakha* could lightly dismiss" (Daube, p. 71).

pattern. Jesus speaks of the priests in the temple, and it might be pointed out that the regulations in the Pentateuch concerned the tabernacle; there was no temple in those early days. But, of course, the tabernacle pointed forward to the temple, and what was laid down for the former applied in due course to the latter. Jesus uses a strong and startling word when he says that the priests *profane* (Moffatt, "desecrate")[14] the Sabbath; certainly the physical work they performed was not inconsiderable and far exceeded the small labors of the disciples. But everyone agrees that the priests are guiltless; no blame attaches to them despite their vigorous Sabbath activities.

6. *"But I say to you"* puts some emphasis on what follows. Some MSS read "someone greater than the temple," but it appears that we should read *something greater.* . . .[15] Turner, however, points out that the neuter may be used of persons "provided that the emphasis is less on the individual than on some outstanding general quality" (M, III, p. 21). We should understand this to refer to the nature of the service and the person of Jesus as one sent to bring in the kingdom, to the launching of the saving events. What God was doing in the sending of Jesus far surpassed what he did in setting up the temple worship. The argument is from the less to the greater: the satisfaction of the hunger of David and his men and even the offering of sacrifice by the priests in the temple do not compare in significance with the coming of the Christ to bring salvation. Or, to put it in another way, while it was true that God's presence was to be discerned in the offering of sacrifices in the temple, even more so and in a fuller and deeper way his presence was to be discerned in the mercy at work in Jesus.[16] *Is* indicates a present reality: Jesus is talking about what is really there at that time, not prophesying that some great happening would take place in the future. And just as he speaks of the present time, so he speaks of the present place, here. The Pharisees who criticized were not aware of present realities.

7. Jesus' conditional, *"if you had known . . . ,"* implies that in fact they had not known, and further that they had condemned the guiltless.[17] They prided themselves on their devotion to the law and the prophets, but yet again Jesus complains that they did not really know the writings they claimed as sacred. They had read them, but they had not entered into what they really meant.[18] He quotes Hosea 6:6, exactly as in LXX. *Mercy* in the

---

14. βεβηλόω occurs in the New Testament again only in Acts 24:6. AS derives it from βέβηλος, and this from βαίνω, "permitted to be trodden," and thus unhallowed.

15. μείζων is read by C L Δ f13 etc., but the great majority of MSS have μεῖζον; since this is the harder reading, it is accepted by most scholars.

16. Cf. Birger Gerhardsson, "That which is being contrasted here is, on the one hand, the outward sacrificial service, and, on the other, the perfect spiritual sacrifice that Jesus and his disciples are offering and which is characterized by 'mercy' " (R. Banks, ed., *Reconciliation and Hope* [Exeter and Grand Rapids, 1974], p. 28).

17. εἰ with the pluperfect indicative (aoristic in meaning; cf. BDF, 347[3]) in the protasis and an aorist indicative with ἄν in the apodosis.

18. Literally "what it is," but the meaning is clearly "what it signifies," "what it means."

303

Old Testament often means the compassion of God as it does in the New Testament (Luke 1:50), or of Christ (Jude 21), but here the mercy that people should show one another is what is in mind. Matthew cites the same passage in 9:13, and he has the concept of mercy in 23:23. *I desire* points to the exercise of the divine will.[19] Over against that is set *sacrifice*. The negative does not mean that sacrifice was not really of divine ordinance, but that it could not compare in importance with mercy. It is the practice of compassion that should distinguish the people of God rather than the punctilious observance of outward regulations, no matter how sacred. When we reflect that the performance of sacrifice was at the heart of almost all religion in antiquity, we see the courage and the insight of the prophet that in God's name he could downgrade a practice so universally and so feelingly accepted. But, of course, sacrifice could so easily become merely mechanical and external. Compassion is much more important and much more characteristic of those who really are the servants of God. The compassionate do not rush to condemn people, as these Pharisees had condemned people who were guiltless. Jesus expressly says that the disciples were innocent.

8. *For* introduces a consideration that justifies what has just been said. Jesus uses his favorite self-designation, *the Son of man* (see on 8:20), and declares that he is *lord of the Sabbath* (*NEB*, "sovereign over the Sabbath"). *Lord* is used in the New Testament in a variety of ways, but here there can be no doubt that it refers to the person who has supreme authority. Jesus is saying that he, the Son of man, has complete authority over the Sabbath. Some commentators reflect that son of man[20] in Aramaic may be understood to mean "man" and hold that Jesus is saying that any human being is entitled to modify the Sabbath regulations as seems good. But this understanding of the text misses Matthew's strong christological emphasis. He is saying something important about Jesus. Further, it is more than difficult to hold that Jesus taught that any member of our sinful race is entitled to modify a divine ordinance as he chooses. No. He is saying that he, being who and what he is, can declare what are the rules for observing the Sabbath.[21] It must immediately be added that in the context this does not mean simply that Jesus has the authority to relax harsh restrictions. He, the Lord of the Sabbath, shows what the observing of the Sabbath really means; he determines how the principle of Sabbath observance is to be worked out. He makes the point that Sabbath observance means mercy. He has himself shown mercy to his disciples, and

19. θέλω means "I will"; it is used of the demands God makes on his people, his will for them (see on 1:19).

20. In the parallel passage Mark emphasizes "even of the Sabbath," but Matthew's word order puts the emphasis rather on *Son of man* (BDF, 472[1b]).

21. "If rulings about Sabbath observance are to be made, it is not the Pharisees but 'the Son of Man,' as 'Lord of the Sabbath,' who has authority to say how to observe properly the day of rest" (Filson).

Matthew goes on immediately to the way he will show mercy to the man with the shriveled hand. Sabbath observance led to a full and rich life.

9. Matthew follows the incident in the grainfields on the Sabbath with a healing on the Sabbath. He had taught the right use of the Sabbath from the Scriptures, and he backs that up with teaching about the deeds of mercy that are appropriate on the Sabbath. He is emphasizing the importance of a right use of God's holy day. It is a day on which deeds of mercy are not merely permitted, but required. He begins by saying that Jesus *went on* from there, but since the previous passage has done no more than locate him in a field of grain this does not help us greatly in discerning where the incident took place.[22] But wherever it was, Jesus went into the local *synagogue* (see on 4:23). It was the center of community life, but here it is its function as the place of worship that is in mind. *Their* synagogue means that of the local people. The previous verses have referred to the Pharisees, but it would not be their synagogue.[23] Lacking further information about the locality, we can scarcely say more.

10. Matthew helps us see the scene with his vivid *And look* and his lack of a verb: *And look, a man. . . .*[24] This man had trouble with atrophied muscles in one of his hands (Luke tells us that it was his right hand).[25] Besides the discomfort and unsightliness, this would have made it difficult for the man to earn his living.[26] Matthew pictures the enemies of Jesus as taking the initiative: the man who was in trouble was right there in the synagogue with an obvious need. The man himself apparently did not begin proceedings (none of the three Synoptists says that he asked for healing), but Jesus' opponents were watching him closely to see whether he would heal and so that they might accuse him of healing on the Sabbath (Mark and Luke both say this). The rabbis permitted healing on the Sabbath if life was in danger, and they were fairly liberal in their interpretation: "Whenever there is doubt whether life is in danger this overrides the Sabbath" (*Yoma* 8:6). But if there was no danger there was to be no healing. In this case, of course, there was no danger; the man could well have waited until the next day. Matthew tells us that they led off with a question,

---

22. Matthew uses a number of verbs in a formula, such as "going on from there," "passing by from there," and the like (cf. 4:21; 9:9; 11:1; 13:53, etc.).

23. Mounce, however, holds that it was: "their" synagogue, he says, "refers to the synagogue of the Pharisees (cf. v. 2). It does not reveal a later period in history when Jewish Christians were no longer welcome in local synagogues." We may agree that the expression does not point to a later period without tying it closely to the Pharisees.

24. For Matthew's characteristic καὶ ἰδού see on 1:20.

25. ξηρός means "dry"; it is used of branches or plants (and in 23:15, Matthew's only other use of the word, for dry land). As applied to a hand it seems to indicate that there was a problem with some of the muscles; the hand was "withered" (NRSV), "paralysed" (GNB), "deformed" (LB), "shriveled" (NIV).

26. According to *The Gospel according to the Hebrews* the man said to Jesus, "I was a mason seeking a livelihood with my hands: I pray thee, Jesu, to restore me mine health, that I may not beg meanly for my food" (James, *The Apocryphal New Testament*, p. 5).

almost provoking him to heal the man. He does not say who they were, but Luke speaks of scribes and Pharisees; clearly they were opponents of Jesus who thought that he might well heal the man before him. Matthew records their question, *"Is it lawful to heal on the Sabbath?"*[27] but makes it clear that this was not so much a genuine search after information as the first shot in a battle. They asked so that they might accuse him.[28]

11. *But he*[29] sets Jesus over against his questioners. He counters with a question of his own. *"What man of you. . . ?"* makes it personal. They were ready to accuse him of Sabbath breaking in a situation of their choice; what then would they do on the Sabbath in a situation of his choice? He looks to the future possibility that one of his hearers who owned just one sheep would have it fall into a ditch on the Sabbath. It is his entire flock. What will he do? Will he not[30] lay hold on the animal and haul it out? The Jews in general showed great care for their animals and would take whatever action was necessary to deliver them from such a plight as the one Jesus outlines.[31]

12. With a "How much more" construction Jesus finishes his refutation of the position his opponents were taking up.[32] *A man,* he says, differs from[33] *a sheep,* which means that a man excels a sheep. Jesus simply states the fact as something obvious and does not draw out in what ways the excelling is to be discerned. He draws the important conclusion that if it is in order to help a sheep in trouble on the Sabbath, much more is it right to do so to a man. It is not only a good idea, but it is lawful to do good

27. εἰ is used here as an interrogative particle to introduce the question (which Turner notes as "a Bibl. Greek usage" (M, III, p. 333). τοῖς σάββασιν is a plural; they refer to Sabbaths in general, to the habitual practice, and not to this one occasion. θεραπεύω (see on 4:23) means "to render service," but the kind of service it denotes is usually healing, and this is clearly in mind here.

28. κατηγορέω is used of bringing charges in court, and this may be in their minds. But it is also used of slanderous accusations, and there may be nothing more in it than the hope of discrediting Jesus.

29. ὁ δέ has adversative force.

30. The emphatic form οὐχί stresses the certainty of the action he will take; it "insists on an affirmative answer. . . . Jesus' point is, 'Of course, a man will rescue his sheep on the Sabbath' " (Chamberlain, p. 158).

31. Very strict Jews would not do this, and, for example, the Damascus Document forbids it (see the passage in T. H. Gaster, *The Scriptures of the Dead Sea Sect* [London, 1957], p. 87). But other Jews were more considerate. Some thought that while a man should not actually haul an animal out, he could throw into the pit material like bedding that would enable the animal to scramble out (*Shab.* 128b; there is a discussion of ways of getting animals out of such plights in *Shab.* 117b). Gundry points out that at best the rabbis made it possible for the animal to scramble out itself, but Jesus was addressing a general audience, "who might be expected to disregard the niceties of rabbinic pilpulism."

32. πόσος (which Matthew uses 8 times, more than in any other New Testament book) means "how great," but here, "to what degree? how much?" (BAGD). οὖν is here inferential; it indicates that what follows is an inference from what precedes.

33. διαφέρω means literally "carry through," "carry about" (as in Mark 11:16), from which it comes to mean "differ" and, since when things differ one is normally better than the other, it comes to mean "excel," as here.

to people. His adversaries appealed to the traditional interpretation of the law, but Jesus pointed out that their practice in matters concerning animals contradicted their exposition of the law. The accepted practice in helping animals (which all agree are of less worth than people) leads to the conclusion[34] that on the Sabbath it is quite lawful to do good.[35] This is a general conclusion applying to every Sabbath, and not simply an affirmation that applies only to the specific case before Jesus. For him human need was primary. Even though this man's life was not in danger, Jesus saw no reason why he should suffer for one moment more.

13. There was apparently no rejoinder from those objecting to healing. How could there be to such an argument? With no further discussion in sight Jesus turns his attention to the sufferer. He did nothing like lay hands on him, but he simply gave the command, *"Stretch out your hand,"* a feat that was obviously quite beyond the man in his crippled state. Matthew's use of the present tense *(says)* makes it all the more vivid. Jesus' word of command was a word of healing. The man's withered hand *was restored*, healed in a moment. Matthew brings this out with his addition, *whole*[36] *as the other.* Matthew makes it clear that the man's hand was completely healed, making for a memorable Sabbath.

14. *But* has adversative force; the Pharisees, who had not been mentioned earlier in this incident (indeed, not since v. 2), are set over against Jesus. They had had an effective argument that healing on the Sabbath was to be accepted, but they did not respond. Matthew has an interesting conjunction of activities when he says that they went out of the synagogue and plotted a murder. So can a perverted and legalistic piety blind people. God had done a wonderful thing for the formerly crippled man, but it was not this that impressed them. Rather, they were concerned with a breach, not of the commands of God, but of their own understanding of what the command of God required. It is not said with whom they took counsel, but the expression indicates a determination to explore all the possibilities. Their opposition was so bitter that nothing less than death for Jesus would satisfy them, a curious reaction to a miracle of healing, even if it was done on a Sabbath. And it was a curious action for men who were so keen on keeping the Sabbath lawfully.[37] But, of course, what Jesus did called in question their understanding of the

---

34. ὥστε (in Matthew 15 times, the most in any New Testament book) may introduce an independent clause, as here, to give a meaning like "for this reason." Matthew has this construction again in 19:6; 23:31, but mostly, like other writers, he follows it with the infinitive.

35. καλῶς is an adverb meaning "well, beautifully"; here it signifies "beneficially" and thus "good."

36. ὑγιής means "healthy, sound."

37. Their purpose is brought out in a number of ways. συμβούλιον may mean "counsel" or "council"; here, of course, it is the former, and it indicates a firmness about their decision; it was only the method that was in doubt. κατ' αὐτοῦ leaves no doubt that they were "against" him, ὅπως introduces a clause of purpose, and ἀπολέσωσιν means that that purpose was nothing less than Jesus' death.

law of God,[38] and thus their whole theological position. If his popularity led people to follow him in this, then their leadership was threatened; they could lose everything. More was at stake than the health of an unknown cripple.[39]

5. Jesus Fulfilling Prophecy, 12:15-21

[15]But Jesus knew it and went away from there. And many followed him, and he healed them all. [16]And he gave them strict instructions that they should not make him known, [17]so that what was spoken through Isaiah the prophet might be fulfilled, saying: [18]"Look, my servant whom I chose, my beloved in whom my soul is well pleased; I will put my spirit upon him, and he will proclaim justice to the nations. [19]He will not quarrel, nor will he shout, nor will anyone hear his voice in the streets. [20]A shattered reed he will not break, and a smoking wick he will not snuff out, until he brings out justice into victory. [21]And nations will set their hope in his name.

Matthew inserts a paragraph to bring out the truth that Jesus' messiahship fulfils Old Testament prophecy. In this chapter we have seen unreasoning opposition to him on the part of religious men, and Matthew will bring this out more fully as he unfolds his story. But, though there will be vicious and unprincipled opposition to Jesus, and though he will stoutly resist his enemies, there will be no hitting back at them as one with his unusual powers might conceivably do. Rather, Jesus will take a lowly way, not quarreling with his opposition, nor entering into brawls, verbal or otherwise. Before he develops this theme further, Matthew quotes from Isaiah 42:1-4, a passage that shows that God's servant does not bluster but quietly proceeds on his chosen path, whatever the cost, until the eventual divine victory.

15. *But* has adversative force; Matthew sets Jesus over against the plotters.[40] He tells us that Jesus *knew* (which may mean "came to know") what his adversaries were planning (neither Mark nor Luke mentions this piece of knowledge), but he gives no indication of how Jesus knew it. It would have been obvious in the synagogue that there were people who were opposed to Jesus, but here Matthew seems to be referring to the plot to kill him. Somehow Jesus came to know of this plot. His

---

38. "The argument has the effect of placing Jesus firmly within the Law, rightly understood: he does good on the Sabbath, and so fulfils the will of God, who desires merciful action rather than ritualistic legalism" (Hill).

39. Gutzwiller comments, "They would rather walk over dead bodies than change their path, and they convince themselves that, by doing so, they show service to God. They want to give glory to God and they decide to kill him. It is difficult to know whether this is tragic, ironic, or merely grotesque."

40. Again we have ὁ δέ, where δέ is adversative. ὁ goes with Ἰησοῦς, as normally in this Gospel. Gundry thinks that δέ is used "in order to contrast Jesus' withdrawal with the Pharisees' plot.

reaction was to avoid provocation; he would die courageously when the right time came, but he would not engage in needless provocation of his enemies until his ministry drew to its close. So now he went away from the place where the plotters were, though evidently he did this quite openly (and not by way of hiding from his foes), for many followed him.[41] Since he *healed them all*, it is a fair inference that many came because they had infirmities of one kind or another and wanted his help. *All* indicates that there were no failures; as many as came to Jesus for healing received it.

16. But Jesus did not want undue publicity. Obviously with a large crowd following him a certain amount of publicity was inevitable. But he was no publicity seeker, apparently not because he would be in danger if his enemies knew where he was, but because he preferred to do his work quietly and without fuss. Matthew will quote Isaiah to that effect, and here he says that Jesus gave strict instructions to minimize publicity.[42] The people were not to *make him known*, but Matthew does not say to whom they might take the news. What he makes plain is that Jesus, while ready to heal any in need who came to him, did not want undue publicity.

17. Neither Mark nor Luke quotes the prophecy at this point, but for Matthew it is significant that there is scriptural support for what Jesus is doing (for Matthew's characteristic appeal to prophecy see on 1:22). This is not only the longest quotation from Scripture in this Gospel but it also appears to be very important for Matthew, bringing out as it does essential truths about the kind of person Jesus is and the way his work is done. We should not miss Bonnard's point that the quotation presents us with "an original reinterpretation of messianic authority" (p. 177); in popular expectation messiahs exercised their authority by crushing opposition, but Jesus showed his authority in his concern for the helpless and downtrodden. Matthew's introductory *so that* indicates the purpose; the divine purpose must be worked out through the fulfilment of prophecy. On this occasion the name of the prophet is given (Isaiah; the passage is 42:1-4), as it is not in quite a few of Matthew's quotations. The quotation is not exact; indeed, there are so many variations from LXX that it is clear either that Matthew is making his own translation or that he is citing some other Greek version (the trans-

---

41. There is a good deal of Matthean language here. ἀναχωρέω occurs in Matthew in 10 of its 14 New Testament occurrences. It means "go back, withdraw," often in the sense of withdrawing from danger (Abbott-Smith). Matthew has ἐκεῖθεν 12 times out of 27, and ἀκολουθέω 25 times out of 90, in both cases the most in any New Testament book. Many MSS have ὄχλοι before or after πολλοί, and the word may have fallen out of the text. But it is more likely that it was inserted to agree with a common Matthean expression (4:25; 8:1, etc.).

42. ἐπιτιμάω means "1. *rebuke, reprove, censure*, also *speak seriously, warn* in order to prevent an action or bring one to an end" (BAGD). Abbott-Smith differentiates it from ἐλέγχω in that it expresses "simply rebuke, which may be undeserved (Mt 16[22]) or ineffectual (Lk 23[40]), while ἐλ. implies rebuke which brings conviction." ἵνα indicates purpose.

lation also seems to make use in some places of a Hebrew text that differs from the Massoretic text).[43]

18. Matthew's characteristic *Look* begins the quotation (though it is not found in the Isaiah passage). The person to whom attention is directed is my servant;[44] immediately we have the thought of lowliness, a thought that runs through the passage quoted. Matthew can use terminology like "the Son of David" that directs our attention to the royalty of the Messiah, but here he stresses the servant motif. But *I chose* points us to the divine action that sets this servant apart from all others; God has chosen[45] him for a special task. The lowliness is qualified by the truth that this servant has a divine destiny. And it is followed by the thought of the divine love. *Beloved* is not common in Matthew; apart from this quotation he has it twice only (3:17; 17:5); all three refer to Jesus as beloved by God. The prophecy moves on to God's pleasure in the chosen and beloved servant. *My soul* is, of course, a way of referring to "myself" and refers to a person at the center of his being.[46] The prophecy is making the point that God is delighted in his servant. God says that he will put his spirit on the servant.[47] The Spirit is given in some measure to all who serve God, but clearly here it is envisaged that the servant will have a special endowment. This will enable him to proclaim justice[48] to the nations. The word is in an emphatic position: among the Jews the nations generally were despised since the people of God saw themselves as specially favored. But the prophet regarded all the world's peoples as having worth before God, and it will be the function of the servant of whom he writes to make sure that justice is done for them. This was not a conspicuous feature of Jesus' ministry here on earth, but the salvation he brought about was available to people of all

---

43. Cf. Hendriksen, "It is not a word for word reproduction but the result of profound sympathetic reflection" (p. 519).

44. παῖς, of course, means "child" as well as "servant." BAGD indicates that it is used with reference "to a relation betw. one human being and another" that from the point of view of age may mean "youth," of descent "son," of social position "servant." Here the thought is that of servant.

45. αἱρετίζω is found here only in the New Testament. BAGD gives the meaning of the middle as "choose for oneself." Two other verbs in this quotation are likewise not found elsewhere in the New Testament, ἐρίζω and τύφομαι, and none of the three is found in the LXX version of the prophecy.

46. Turner classes this with other quotations from LXX in which ἡ ψυχή μου = ἐγὼ αὐτός. He adds, "But clearly the contexts intend us to feel the force of the double meaning of נֶפֶשׁ as *soul* and *life*, which cannot be rendered so neatly in Greek" (M, III, p. 43).

47. BAGD understands this use of πνεῦμα "as that which differentiates God fr. everything that is not God" (BAGD, 5).

48. κρίσις is more frequent in this Gospel than in any other New Testament book (12 times). It often conveys the notion of judgment, the passing of a sentence, which leads to the meaning "condemn." But the impartial weighing of evidence means that right is done, and the word is used, as here, for "justice" (cf. Luke 11:42). The servant will make sure that right is done to the nations as well as to Israel. Curiously Moffatt translates the word as "religion" (cf. JB, "the true faith"), but it is justice that it connotes. Cf. Lenski, "*Mishpat*, κρίσις is not 'religion' but 'right' as established forensically at the judgment bar of Jehovah" (p. 473).

nations and by the time Matthew wrote something of a fulfilment of this part of the prophecy was evident.

19. Those who lead the nations are mostly forceful characters, insistent on getting their own way. They tend to quarrel with anyone who hinders them, so sure are they that what they are seeking to accomplish is the right thing for the people they lead. The prophecy points out that God's servant is not set in this mold. *He will not quarrel* means that his mission is one of peace. It does not, of course, mean that he will not strongly oppose those who do evil. But it affirms in strong terms that he will not try to impose his will on everybody regardless of their desires. *JB*'s "He will not brawl" and *GNB*'s "He will not argue" represent different ways of bringing out the servant's quiet approach. *Nor will he shout*[49] carries on with the same idea. He will do his work quietly, making no loud claims to underline his importance. So, too, his voice will not be raised in the streets (*GNB*, "will not . . . make loud speeches in the streets").[50] So far from fanfares and the like, there will not even be a *voice in the streets*. The Lord's work will be done without noise and publicity.

20. And it will be done in gentleness. A *reed* might be used as a flute, a measuring rod, a pen, and in many other ways. But for whatever purpose it was wanted, a whole reed was desirable. Reeds grew plentifully and were cheap. "The reed, growing by millions in every marsh and riverside, was a type of commonplace insignificance" (Glover). The natural thing was to discard an imperfect reed and replace it with a better one. But the Lord's servant does not discard those who can be likened to *shattered*[51] reeds, earth's "broken" ones. A perfect reed is at best fragile, so the imagery emphasizes weakness and helplessness. The same truth is brought out with the reference to *a smoking wick*.[52] A wick that functioned imperfectly was a nuisance: it would not give out good light and its smoldering released a certain amount of smoke. The simple thing was to snuff it out and throw it away. A little bit of flax did not cost much, so replacing it was the normal procedure. It took time and patience and the willingness to take pains to make anything useful out of a bruised reed or a smoking wick. People in general would not take the trouble. In a similar fashion

---

49. κραυγάζω, which Matthew uses only here, may be used of animal noises, of the cries demons make when expelled from people (Luke 4:41), of the angry yells of a mob (Acts 22:23), of the expressions of exultation at the triumphal entry (John 12:13), and of Jesus' calling of Lazarus from the tomb (John 11:43). The common factor seems to be noise: all the passages speak of a loud voice. BAGD gives the meaning here as "cry for help," but this scarcely seems to be correct; the thought is that of quietness rather than of an appeal for aid.

50. πλατεῖα (the feminine of the adjective πλατύς, "broad") is used with ὁδός in the sense "street"; it denotes a broad street as against ῥύμη, "a lane."

51. συντρίβω means "shatter, break in pieces" (Mark 5:4; 14:3). It cannot be used with that full force here, but it certainly makes clear that the reed is not in good shape.

52. λίνον is used again in the New Testament only in some MSS of Revelation 15:6. It means "flax" or "linen" and thus anything made from this material. Here it is clearly a lamp wick.

most of us regard the world's down-and-outs as not worth troubling ourselves over; we do not see how anything can be made of them. But love and care and patience can do wonders, and that is what the prophet is talking about.[53] God's servant will persevere to the end. He will persist until he *brings out*[54] *justice into victory.* The prophet cannot acquiesce in the thought that evil will finally have the victory. For him it is clear that in the end the servant will bring about the triumph of justice.

21. The prophet's horizons are widespread. He is not talking about a petty salvation for one little group, but about what the servant will do for the nations generally. The word for *nations* is that which is often translated "Gentiles," but it seems unlikely that that is the meaning here. The focus is not on nations outside Israel as the people of God, but rather on the nations of the world as a whole. With his broad vision the prophet sees them all as coming within the scope of God's compassionate love and of the servant's saving activity. The *name*, of course, stands for the whole person; the prophet is saying that the peoples will come to trust in God as he is in his essential character. Matthew does not use the concept of hope very often (this is his only use of the verb "to hope"). But it is an important concept in the New Testament generally and in this prophecy in particular. With whatever vicissitudes along the way, in the end the peoples of the world will come to see that the one in whom they must put their hope is the servant of God, the emissary of love who effectively brings salvation to the downtrodden. And he does it in lowliness. That the servant himself takes a lowly place matters to Matthew. Indeed, this prophecy sums up a good deal of his understanding of the work Jesus would do and the way he would do it.

6. *Conflict with the Pharisees, 12:22-37*

> [22]*Then a blind and dumb demoniac was brought to him; and he healed him, so that the dumb man both spoke and saw.* [23]*And all the crowds were astonished and they were saying: "Can this be the Son of David?"* [24]*But when the Pharisees heard it, they said, "This fellow does not cast out demons except by Beelzeboul, the ruler of the demons."*
>
> [25]*But he knew their thoughts and said to them, "Every kingdom divided against itself is ruined, and every city or house divided against itself will not stand.* [26]*And if Satan casts out Satan, he is divided against himself; how then will his kingdom stand?* [27]*And if I cast out demons by Beelzeboul, by whom do your sons cast them out? Therefore they will be your judges.*

---

53. GNB discards the imagery to bring out the meaning with "He will be gentle to those who are weak, and kind to those who are helpless."

54. This is an unusual use of ἐκβάλλω, which normally has a meaning like "throw out, discard" or perhaps "drive out," often with the notion of force. Here the thought is rather "to cause to proceed to its goal" (AS). Matthew uses νῖκος only here.

28*But if I cast out demons by the Spirit of God, then the kingdom of God has come upon you.* 29*Or how can anyone enter the strong man's house and seize his goods unless he first binds the strong man? Then indeed he will plunder his house.* 30*He who is not with me is against me, and he who does not gather with me scatters.*

31*"For this reason I say to you, every sin and blasphemy will be forgiven men, but the blasphemy of the Spirit will not be forgiven.* 32*And whoever speaks a word against the Son of man, it will be forgiven him; but whoever speaks against the Holy Spirit, it will not be forgiven him, neither in this age nor in that to come.*

33*"Either make the tree good and its fruit good, or make the tree rotten and its fruit rotten; for the tree is known by its fruit.* 34*You offspring of snakes, being evil how can you speak good things? For out of the abundance of the heart the mouth speaks.* 35*The good man brings good things out of his good treasure, and the evil man brings evil things out of his evil treasure.* 36*But I say to you, that every careless word that men shall speak, they will render account for it on the Day of Judgment.* 37*For by your words you will be justified, and by your words you will be condemned."*

Matthew narrates the casting out of a demon that resulted in speech and sight being given to the sufferer. But this provoked a controversy with the Pharisees; evidently they were set to oppose him whatever he did. Jesus pointed to the weakness in their argument that he was in league with the evil one, and he went on to give significant teaching about the nature of good and evil and the importance of doing what is right. Throughout this whole section Matthew is concerned with the opposition of two kingdoms strongly opposed to one another, that of Satan (v. 26) and that of God (v. 28). The length of the section is noteworthy. Matthew is usually very concise, but he evidently regards this passage as very important and he treats it more fully than is his custom.

22. For Matthew's use of *then* see on 2:7; it does not necessarily signify that what he next narrates took place immediately after the preceding, merely that it was later in time. Luke speaks of Jesus' healing a dumb demoniac, but only Matthew says that the man was *blind* as well. This man was brought to Jesus, though none of the Evangelists says who brought him (but being blind and dumb he certainly needed help).[55] There is no indication how Jesus performed the healing, whether with laying on hands or with a word or in some other way. Matthew concentrates on the fact of healing, without specification of the means; indeed, few healings are described as briefly as this one; the Evangelist seems to be more intent on the controversy to which the incident led than on the healing itself. It

---

55. There is characteristic Matthean language here. This Evangelist uses δαιμονίζομαι (see on 4:24) 7 times, τυφλός 17 times, and κωφός 7 times, in each case the most in any New Testament book.

is unusual to have a demoniac described as healed (though cf. 17:18; perhaps also we are meant to see a link with v. 15); more commonly the demon is said to be "cast out." But Matthew has other things to say, and he moves through this healing quickly: it is really the trigger for the discussion that follows. Matthew specifies that the man both *spoke and saw;* the cure was complete.

23. The people who witnessed the cure *were astonished.*[56] Characteristically Matthew says that *all* had this experience, and he uses the plural for *crowds* (the combination *all the crowds* occurs here only in this Gospel). Matthew emphasizes the impact of what Jesus had done; not just a handful of the people were affected but *all the crowds.* This is the one place in his Gospel where Matthew says that Jesus had this effect on the crowds. He is describing something very unusual, which may explain the strong reaction of the Pharisees and the discussion that followed. The response of the people is crystallized in a question: *"Can this be the Son of David?"* The question is worded in such a way as to indicate a measure of perplexity, but also to open the door to an interesting possibility.[57] Jesus was so unlike what they expected in the Messiah, but could he yet really be the Son of David? Like the Pharisees they probably did not look for the Messiah in such a person as the Man from Nazareth, but unlike them they were open-minded enough to ask the question. They are clearly using the expression "Son of David" (see on 1:1) as equivalent to "Messiah," and they are so impressed by the miracle they had witnessed that they wonder whether they are in the presence of the Messiah.

24. *But* is adversative and sets the Pharisees in contrast to the crowds. Unlike the crowds they were not puzzled: they were sure that Jesus was evil, and they gave expression to this conviction by explaining how Jesus cast out demons. *This fellow*[58] is contemptuous; their statement is confident. They are sure that the only way Jesus can cast out demons (for this term see on 7:22) is with the help of one they name as *Beelzeboul* (see on 10:25) and describe as *the ruler of the demons.* Jesus is in league with the powers of evil, they say, and because the prince of the forces of evil is at work in him he is able to do things that ordinary people cannot do. They were spectators of some of the wonderful things that God did through Jesus and were perverse enough to ascribe these divine works to the forces of evil. The same charge is made in 10:25.

25. Matthew tells us that Jesus *knew their thoughts;* he may be ascribing supernatural knowledge to the Lord or he may mean that Jesus had the

---

56. ἐξίστημι occurs here only in this Gospel. It means "to put out of its place" and thus "to drive out of one's senses, to amaze."

57. It is introduced by μήτι, which often looks for the answer "No" but which may be used "in questions in which the questioner is in doubt concerning the answer" (BAGD, which classes this question in the latter category). *NASB* renders, "This man cannot be the Son of David, can he?"; Filson, "Is this perhaps the Son of David?"; and *NRSV,* "Can this be. . . ?"

58. οὗτος.

314

normal human capacity for penetrating to some extent into what others have in mind (people sometimes say, "I know what you're thinking!"). Whichever it was, Jesus was aware that they ascribed his good deeds to Satan, so he pointed out that the facts were all against it. He starts with the general proposition that a divided group, be it a kingdom or a house or a city, is impotent; it cannot overcome its opponents. In this Gospel *kingdom* mostly refers to the kingdom of heaven, but here it clearly refers to the ordinary kingdoms of the earth. If a kingdom is united it may well set forth its aims, but if it is divided the factions waste their energy in disputing with those who ought to be their allies. The result is disaster for the kingdom.[59] There is no future for a kingdom divided against itself, and the same is true for smaller groupings (Jesus retains the same expression for divided against itself but changes *ruined* to *will not stand*). Factional strife and division are just as fatal to success in the smaller sphere of a city or household as in the larger affairs of a kingdom; it will always prevent the group from standing firm and holding its ground whatever the ground may be. This is an elementary piece of the wisdom of this world, and Jesus is suggesting that the Pharisees are naive if they think that Satan is not well aware of it.

26. From his hypothetical kingdom or city or family Jesus moves to Satan and looks at what would happen if what the Pharisees were saying were in fact correct. His conditional is put positively: "If it were really to happen — ."[60] If it is by Beelzeboul that Jesus casts out devils, then Satan is in effect casting himself out: he would then be enabling Jesus to deliver people from his own power. That would mean hopeless division in the ranks of evil, with demon ranged against demon. In that case how could Satan effect his purpose? Satan would be removing Satan from the afflicted man and thus diminishing his sphere of influence while delivering the man over into the sphere of goodness. It is not to be presumed that Satan is stupid: the Pharisees were taking up an impossible position. Theoretically, of course, it might be argued that Satan could allow the expulsion of one demon in order to effect some diabolical purpose, but this would be met by the fact that Jesus kept on expelling demons; he carried on an unrelenting war against all the demonic forces.

27. *And* adds another to Jesus' objections to the Pharisaic position, "introducing someth. new, w. loose connection" (BAGD, 1.5). The conditional construction is the same as that in verse 26, and again it is put strongly to indicate what consequences would follow if it were the case. *I* is emphatic: Jesus is stressing that it is the things that he, being who and what he is, does. It prepares for the contrast that follows. "Let us suppose for a moment that you are right," he is saying, "then what follows in the case of other exor-

---

59. ἐρημόω is used here only in Matthew. It is cognate with ἔρημος (see on 3:1) and conveys the thought of being made a desolation: it points to total loss.

60. εἰ with the indicative; the condition is obviously false, but if it were true then what follows must necessarily be the case.

cists?"[61] There were apparently many who claimed to cast out demons, and some of them could be characterized as *your sons*. The expression is important, and it is set forth in a way that gives it emphasis: "your sons, by whom do they cast out?" Matthew is fond of the word "son," which he uses more often than in any other New Testament book (89 times). It most often denotes the male child of a parent, of course, but it may be used also in the sense of a pupil, one who was a son in the sense of deriving his academic being from his tutor (cf. Sir. 7:3); it may be used here in the sense that the people of whom Jesus was speaking derived their spiritual being from their Pharisaic tutors. The only possible logic behind the Pharisaic position was that a mere human could not overcome a demon. If Jesus did have such a victory, therefore, it would show that he had aid from a superhuman source, and in their hostility their logic led them to hold that that source could only be Satan. But they had spoken hurriedly; they had not stopped to reflect that some of their own people claimed to cast out demons.[62] The Pharisees would have vehemently denied that their sons were in league with the evil one, but they had not realized that such exorcisms said something about Jesus also. Therefore *they will be your judges*; your own sons will prove you wrong! The logic of a Pharisaic denial that their followers cast out demons through the evil one meant that Jesus did not use the powers of evil either. Their sons would be able to testify to the fact that casting out demons was not a work of Satan. They would "judge" them for ascribing to Satan what they, the exorcists, knew came from God.

28. *But if* introduces the contrary position. *I* is the emphatic pronoun again, and the construction assumes that Jesus does in fact cast out demons by the Spirit of God. Jesus invites his hearers to reflect on the implications of this fact. Nobody disputes the fact of his exorcisms; the only question is the source of his power. For *Spirit* see on 1:18; here *the Spirit of God* precedes *I*, though "I" precedes "by Beelzeboul" in verse 27; the effect is to give strong emphasis to *the Spirit of God* (in the parallel passage Luke has "the finger of God" [Luke 11:20; cf. Exod. 8:19; 31:18]; both ways of putting it emphasize that the power is from God). If, as Jesus says, his power came from the Spirit of God, then there are implications. *Then*[63] there *has come upon you*[64] nothing less than *the kingdom of*

---

61. Cf. Chamberlain, "For the sake of the argument, Jesus assumes as true the Pharisees' statement that he casts out demons by Beelzebub to prove them wrong" (pp. 195-96).

62. Josephus testifies to exorcisms in his day (*War* 7.185); he says that the practice goes back to Solomon's time and goes on to describe an exorcism he himself had witnessed (*Ant.* 8.45-49). A demon is cast out in Tobit 6:16-17; 8:1-3. Cf. Acts 19:13. For Jewish ideas about demons see SBk, IV.1, pp. 501-35.

63. ἄρα (which Matthew uses 7 times, second in the New Testament only to Romans, with 11) is an inferential particle "in class. usage never at the beginning of its clause . . . 3. in the apodosis of conditional sentences, to emphasize the result, *then, as a result*" (BAGD).

64. φθάνω, here only in Matthew, can mean "come before," but it may also signify "come upon" with the idea of confrontation or hostility.

God.[65] This expression (found again in 19:24; 21:31, 43; Matthew mostly has "kingdom of heaven") is put last in the sentence, a position that gives it emphasis. The coming of the kingdom is to be discerned in Jesus' defeat of the demons. Mostly Matthew speaks of the kingdom as future, but here it is a present reality.

29. Or[66] is a disjunctive particle that introduces an alternative way of looking at the facts. Jesus puts this in the form of a question; he asks how anyone can[67] take possession of the goods of the strong man unless he first binds him. He speaks of entering the man's *house* (for *house* see on 2:11), which, of course, would be the part of his possessions that he would guard most closely. Jesus does not explain who he means by the *strong man*,[68] but it seems clearly enough to be a designation of Satan; the alternative is to regard Jesus as speaking in parabolic fashion of any mighty man here on earth (as Isaiah does, Isa. 49:24-25). Such a man's possessions are safe until he is overcome. In that case we are to think of Satan as being in much the position of the strong man; therefore the two interpretations come to much the same in the end. Jesus asks how anyone can *enter the strong man's house and seize[69] his goods* unless he first *binds the strong man,* which means that he must overcome him. While he has any strength left the strong man will resist being bound, and when at length he is bound that in itself is clear proof that he has been defeated. When that happens his house and all that is in it is at the mercy of the conqueror: he *will plunder[70] his house.* The picture is that of a tyrant in complete and utter defeat.

30. The illustration has brought out the point that Jesus is engaged in a struggle with a powerful enemy. Now he goes on to the point that in this struggle there is no neutrality. In any moral issue we are forced to

---

65. Patte thinks that the kingdom of God in this Gospel refers "to an aggressive manifestation of the *power of God* which asserts itself against satanic and demonic powers." He contrasts this with "the kingdom of heaven," which "refers to the *authority of God* — an authority which, at present, is not imposed upon people through the use of power but which people (should) recognize and acknowledge in the meekness and mercy of the Father and the Son" (p. 177). This is an interesting distinction, but it does not seem to be demonstrated in the way Matthew actually uses the two expressions. From the same evidence Albright and Mann find that " 'Kingdom of God' in the Matthean tradition is applied to the Father's reign after the judgment of the End, and 'Kingdom of heaven' to the continuing community of The Man, lasting up to the time of the judgment" (p. 155). For Lenski the sense of the two expressions "is quite the same" (p. 480). According to Fenton, it is used as a contrast to the kingdom of Satan (v. 26).

66. ἤ is a Mattheanism (67 times in Matthew; next most frequent is 1 Corinthians with 49 occurrences).

67. For δύναμαι see on 3:9; with the negative it points to the sheer impossibility of taking the goods of the strong man without taking measures to counter his strength.

68. Matthew uses ἰσχυρός only 3 times. The adjective may refer to physical strength or to moral or spiritual power. It is used of divine strength as well as of human might.

69. ἁρπάζω means "to seize," often with the notion of the use of force.

70. διαρπάζω is a strengthened form of the verb rendered "seize" earlier in the verse. It means "plunder thoroughly." NEB has "ransack," and JB "burgle."

take sides. I may have little power to influence the outcome, but if I do nothing I am saying in effect, "As far as I am concerned the tyrant can do as he wishes." So Jesus says of anyone who does not side with him in his conflict with evil that this person *is against me*. His influence, however great or small it is, is not thrown into the cause of good and therefore it helps the cause of evil.[71] The same point is made with gathering and scattering. The imagery is apparently taken from tending flocks. Animals tend to scatter, and if any given person takes no part in gathering the scattered members he in effect scatters them; by doing nothing he casts his vote in favor of scattering.

31. There are consequences of this impossibility of neutrality. *For this reason* links what follows closely to the preceding, and *I say to you* lends a certain solemnity to the words. *Sin* (see on 1:21) is here linked with *blasphemy*.[72] When Jesus says that every sin and blasphemy *will be forgiven*[73] he does not, of course, mean that these sins are not serious or that they will automatically be set aside. They will be forgiven in the normal way of forgiveness when the sinner repents and seeks pardon in penitence and lowliness and faith. Sins of this kind are serious; if they are not repented of and forgiven, they will have eternal consequences. But they are forgivable.

Jesus contrasts this with another sin that he calls *the blasphemy of the Spirit*, a sin that will not be forgiven. We must understand this in the context of the Pharisaic attribution to Satan of the good deeds Jesus was doing. The sin that cannot be forgiven is not to be understood as the utterance of any particular form of words. It is impossible to hold that any form of words is unforgivable, granted that the sinner subsequently repents and turns to God. Jesus is talking about the set of the life, not any one isolated saying. When a person takes up a position like that of the Pharisees, when, not by way of misunderstanding but through hostility to what is good, that person calls good evil and, on the other hand, makes evil his good, then that person has put himself in a state that prevents forgiveness.[74] It is not that God refuses to forgive; it is that the

---

71. Barclay illustrates: "We may take this saying and apply it to ourselves and to the Church. *If our presence does not strengthen the Church, then our absence is weakening it*" (II, p. 44).

72. This is Matthew's first use of βλασφημία, a term he will use 4 times in all. Its use is similar to that of the verb βλασφημέω (see on 9:3). It denotes abusive speech of all kinds, slander, defamation, and the like. Religiously it signifies all kinds of speech derogatory of the deity.

73. ἀφίημι is another favorite Matthean word: Matthew has it 47 times whereas no other book has it more than Mark with 34. It has a wide range of meanings, such as "let go," "send away," "cancel," and others, but it is the characteristic word for "pardon," "forgive." While other words such as χαρίζομαι or ἀπολύω may be used for "forgive," the one we meet again and again is ἀφίημι.

74. Buttrick quotes Whittier,

What if thine eye refuse to see,
    Thine ear of Heaven's free welcome fail,
And thou a willing captive be,
    Thyself thine own dark jail?

person who sees good as evil and evil as good is quite unable to repent and thus to come humbly to God for forgiveness. And there is no way to forgiveness other than by the path of repentance and faith.[75] As I have written elsewhere, "They called good evil. People in such a situation cannot repent and seek forgiveness: they lack a sense of sin; they reject God's competence to declare what is right. It is this continuing attitude that is the ultimate sin."[76]

32. *And* links on a further proposition, and *whoever*[77] makes it general. The offenses of which Jesus proceeds to speak are, on the surface of it, purely verbal: both refer to what the sinner says. First, there is a reference to speaking against *the Son of man* (see on 8:20), which in Jesus' teaching is a solemn way of referring to himself, but referring to himself in his messianic function (not as people in general understood messiahship, but as Jesus understood it). People may oppose him, and they may speak strong words *against*[78] him in ignorance (cf. Acts 3:17). But there is no reason why a person who sins in this way should not later repent and find forgiveness in the way he finds forgiveness for any other sin. After all, it was not obvious to everybody that Jesus was the Son of God; it was possible for people to make a mistake about his Person.

But blasphemy against the Holy Spirit is another matter. To deny that God was at work in the exorcism that had just amazed the crowds (vv. 22-23) was inexcusable. This is more than merely verbal, more than a difference of opinion. If it were no more than a matter of words or opinions, there is no reason why it should not be forgiven following due penitence. Carr points out that the Pharisees might have had a conscientious difference from Jesus over the observance of the Sabbath, but "now they have no excuse." They are objecting to what was obviously a good deed and ascribing it to the evil one. The context here is that of people ascribing to Satan deeds done by the Son of God in the power of the Holy Spirit. This makes it difficult to hold, as some suggest, that the sin against the Spirit is post-Pentecostal sin.[79] Jesus is not prophesying about the

---

75. H. W. Beyer says of this sin, "It denotes the conscious and wicked rejection of the saving power and grace of God towards man" (*TDNT*, I, p. 624). See further my *Spirit of the Living God* (London, 1960), pp. 48-49. Filson comments, "though he is 'Son of Man,' human in lot and situation but destined for triumph and glory, forgiveness and eternal salvation are open to those who blasphemously berate him. But he knows the Spirit directs his life; to call these Spirit-effected healings the work of Satan reveals the speaker's hopeless bankruptcy."

76. *Luke, An Introduction and Commentary*[2] (Leicester and Grand Rapids, 1988), p. 231. Cf. Robinson, "The only 'Spirit' that can cast out devils is manifestly the 'holy Spirit'. To call this evil is to confuse all moral and spiritual issues, to identify God with Satan. This is an attitude which makes a return to God, a genuine repentance, impossible, and in no circumstances can he who is guilty of it be forgiven" (p. 113).

77. ὅς ἐάν.

78. κατά is used here "in a hostile sense" (BAGD, I.2.b), or, perhaps better, "after words and expressions that designate hostile speech" (BAGD, I.2.b.β).

79. "The possibility of this sin thus arises only with the Pentecostal era when the Holy

future, but speaking to people who had just ascribed to Satan a marvelous work of the very Spirit of God. In that good work Jesus said that nothing less than the kingdom of God had come upon them, so that they were refusing to accept the divine rule. To call good evil in the way they did is evidence of "the lie in the soul," a complete perversion of values. And since the Spirit is especially characteristic of the new life Christ offers, to reject that new life[80] is to reject the divine Spirit. It is to set oneself in opposition to the very Spirit of God. People who take up such a position make themselves unforgivable; in maintaining that goodness is satanic they place themselves outside the possibility of salvation.[81] Jesus brings out the seriousness of all this by declaring that such people will not be forgiven, *neither in this age*[82] *nor in that to come*. This does not, of course, mean that some of those who are not forgiven in this world may hope for forgiveness after death. Such a possibility is not contemplated. The meaning is something like "neither in time nor eternity; never!" The blasphemy against the Spirit has eternal as well as temporal consequences. Those who commit this sin cut themselves off from forgiveness here and now and from forgiveness in eternity.[83]

33. Jesus sees two possibilities for trees:[84] they may be *good* or *bad*. It is not easy to understand why the verb *make* is used; the sense appears to be something like "Suppose a tree is good, then its fruit will be good."[85] But *make* may be used to provoke people to action. In the context Jesus is saying that in the end there are two kinds of people. Those who are like

---

Spirit has been poured out by Jesus on the disciples and has become their indwelling possession" (O. Procksch, *TDNT*, I, p. 104).

80. Carson says, "The distinction between blasphemy against the Son of Man and blasphemy against the Spirit is not that the Son of Man is less important than the Spirit, or that the first sin is prebaptismal and the second postbaptismal, still less that the first is against the Son of Man and the second rejects the authority of Christian prophets. Instead, within the context of the larger argument the first sin is rejection of the truth of the gospel (but there may be repentance and forgiveness for that), whereas the second sin is rejection of the same truth in full awareness that that is exactly what one is doing — thoughtfully, willfully, and self-consciously rejecting the work of the Spirit."

81. Cf. Alan Richardson, "to reject the inbreaking Aeon (the Kingdom of God) and to dismiss the signs of its arrival — such as the exorcisms which demonstrate the overthrow of Satan's counter-kingdom — as the work of Beelzebub, is to reject the salvation which God is bringing and is in fact to be guilty of unforgivable sin against the New Age" (*An Introduction to the Theology of the New Testament* [London, 1958], p. 108).

82. αἰών occurs 8 times in Matthew. It may be used, as here, for this present age, the whole time of life on earth. This is set in contrast to the age to come, the age that comprises all future time, the era that will be ushered in by the coming in triumph of the Messiah and that means the reign of God.

83. There are Old Testament examples of sin that cannot be forgiven (e.g., Num. 15:30-31; 1 Sam. 3:14).

84. Matthew is fond of the disjunctive ἤ (see on v. 29). It is used here of opposites that are mutually exclusive (either . . . or), but it may also be found with expressions that are similar or supplement one another (as in 5:17).

85. The reasoning may be, "In your thinking make the tree good and its fruit will be good, make it evil and evil fruit follows."

good trees produce good fruit, whereas those who are like rotten trees produce rotten fruit. For *good* see on 3:10. Jesus is saying that a good tree and good fruit go together, so that if the tree is sound there will be nothing wrong with the fruit. The alternative is for the tree to be *rotten*,[86] in which case its fruit will also be *rotten*. The fruit shows what kind of tree the tree is. The pious professions of those who opposed Jesus cannot hide the fruit in their lives, fruit of hatred, intolerance, injustice, and the like. What they did showed what kind of people they were.

34. John the Baptist used the expression *offspring of snakes* to describe the Pharisees and Sadducees who came to his baptism (3:7, where see note). Jesus takes up the same words to bring out the venomous nature of the opposition with which he was confronted, and their oneness with those who had opposed God's messengers in previous generations. They bewailed the opposition and frustration the prophets had encountered, blissfully unconscious of the fact that they themselves were reproducing the same attitude toward Jesus. They are *evil* (a term Matthew has 26 times, which is exactly twice as often as the next highest use, Luke with 13),[87] and therefore they are simply unable[88] to say *good things* (for *good* see on 5:45). It is with the tree and the fruit as with the fathers and their offspring. Being what they are, they can produce only rotten fruit, or follow in the steps of their impious forebears. From another angle Jesus brings out the importance of the source when he proceeds to affirm that what one says proceeds from *the abundance of the heart*. *The heart* is used here as an inclusive term to denote "the seat of physical, spiritual and mental life . . . as center and source of the whole inner life, w. its thinking, feeling, and volition" (BAGD, 1 and 1b). It is what the heart is full of (*abundance*) that determines what anyone says. People do not speak out of character.

35. In this verse *good* is used 3 times and *evil* is also used 3 times, the repetitions serving to underline the contrast. It is essentially the same point that has just been made in the previous verse, but emphasized for its importance. The *good man* is the man of inner excellence, the man whose goodness is not merely on the surface but at the center of his being. He produces *good*[89] *things* from his *good treasure* (see on 6:19). The word signifies what is valuable, but also where one keeps what is valuable. Either meaning is possible here: Jesus may be saying that it is from the things he values that the good man produces his good things, or he may mean that

---

86. Matthew has σαπρός 5 times out of its 8 New Testament occurrences. It means "decayed, rotten," and may be used of fish (13:48) as well as of trees. It certainly brings out the uselessness of the tree in question.

87. Notice how Jesus slips in *being evil* in the same way as in 7:11; for him this is a fundamental truth; it can be assumed, it is not necessary to prove it.

88. The verb is δύναμαι (see on 3:9). It points to the power to do (or with the negative, as here, lack of power to do) certain things.

89. *Good* here is not καλός as in verse 33, but ἀγαθός (see on 5:45). If it differs from the former term, it will signify inner excellence as against excellence that shows itself in outward appearance. Evil in this verse is the word used in verse 34, not that in verse 33.

he gets them from his innermost storehouse, his heart. In the end there is not a great deal of difference. What the good man produces is what he values, and it comes from the center of his being. So with *the evil man*. In both cases what one brings forth proceeds from what one is at the core of one's being. *The evil man* produces *evil* just as surely as the good man produces goodness. One's deeds accord with what one is essentially. A good person does not do good sporadically or haphazardly, but habitually, and so with the evil person. Our deeds are a reflection of what we are, and they show what we really value, deep down. And, of course, we can produce from our treasure only what is there.

36. The words about the way speech reflects character are found only in Matthew. *"But I say to you"* puts emphasis on what follows: it draws attention to it as significant. Jesus emphasizes the importance of what people say by speaking of *every careless word* they utter. When people speak lightly without paying serious attention to what they are saying, the *careless*[90] *word*, the word uttered without any thought of the effect it will have on other people, then that word shows something of what they are, deep down (objection may legitimately be made to *JB*'s "unfounded"; Jesus is talking about words that certainly have a foundation, even though this is not realized). This makes it more significant than the person uttering it may think, and it will be taken into account on Judgment Day. Jesus is saying that in the end we must all give account of ourselves and that words we take lightly will then be seen to have meaning, for they show what we are in our innermost being.

37. *For* introduces the reason; people's words will be of the utmost significance when the judgment takes place.[91] *Justified* means "declared to be righteous"; the verb is used in the strict sense of obtaining the verdict when brought to judgment. It is not common in the Gospels, being found twice in Matthew, 5 times in Luke, and not at all in the other Gospels. But Paul uses it 27 times, and for him it is a very important concept. It brings out the truth that our salvation has a legal aspect and that we are saved in a manner that accords with right, not simply because God is stronger than the devil and overcomes every force of evil (though that, of course, is also true and is taught in the New Testament). We should not understand the Evangelists to be in contradiction of Paul; it is simply that they have different ways of describing what Christ has done in bringing us salvation, and the way used here is more characteristic of Paul than of Matthew. Jesus is not, of course, saying that in the end the only thing that matters will be our words, that our deeds do not matter in comparison with what we say. That is completely false. What Jesus is saying is that at the judg-

---

90. ἀργός (from ἀ privative + ἔργον, "work") means "inactive, idle, worthless." *REB* has "thoughtless"; *GNB*, "useless."

91. γάρ is rendered *For*. ἐκ more commonly means "out of," but here it is used "of the underlying rule or principle *according to, in accordance with*" (BAGD, 3.i).

ment what we are is what matters, and that our words, especially those to which we give no particular thought, reveal what we are. The other side of this particular coin is, of course, that where our words do not lead to our justification they lead to our condemnation (cf. Luke 19:22, "Out of your own mouth will I condemn you"; cf. Prov. 18:21). As is true throughout the New Testament, there are just two ultimate possibilities.

7. The Sign of Jonah, 12:38-42

38Then some of the scribes and Pharisees answered him, saying, "Teacher, we wish to see a sign from you." 39But he answered them, saying, "An evil and adulterous generation seeks a sign, and no sign will be given it except the sign of Jonah the prophet. 40For as Jonah was in the belly of the sea monster for three days and three nights, so the Son of man will be in the heart of the earth for three days and three nights. 41The men of Nineveh will rise up in the judgment with this generation and will condemn it, because they repented at the preaching of Jonah; and look, something greater than Jonah is here. 42The queen of the South will rise up in the judgment with this generation and will condemn it, because she came from the ends of the earth to hear the wisdom of Solomon; and look, something greater than Solomon is here."

It is curious that after the miracles that Matthew has just recorded (vv. 13, 22-23) people should be asking Jesus for a *sign*. But since both Mark and Luke tell us that they were "testing" (or "tempting") him, we should not take this to be a sincere request. It leads Jesus to point out their failings as a generation; compared with even some Gentiles from earlier days they were found wanting. Perhaps (as Bruner thinks) they held that a sign "was a divine credential. It was proof or documentation that a person truly spoke for God." He goes on, "The difference between a sign and a miracle was that signs were believed to be delivered immediately from heaven, while miracles were done here on earth, mediately, through people and things . . . a sign appeared in or from the sky; a miracle happened on earth" (p. 466). There may be something in this, but "the sign of Jonah" does not fit the definition, nor do the "signs" done by R. Jose and R. Eliezer as noted on verse 38.[92]

38. *Then* is often used in Matthew without any great precision, indicating simply that something happened at a later time (see on 2:7), but it is not unlikely that on this occasion it points to something that followed pretty closely. Although the verb *answered* may be used somewhat loosely, the fact that these men *answered* Jesus seems to indicate a response to what

92. Glover comments, "It does not occur to them that what they ask for is before their eyes; and what they need, is not light, but sight. More than His deeds, Himself is the great sign, than which none could be greater or more Divine."

he had just said. The *scribes* (see on 5:20) were the experts in the law, scholars whose field was the study of Scripture; here as often they are linked with the *Pharisees* (see on 3:7). As Matthew speaks of some of them, it seems that this was an informal group, and not anything in the way of an official delegation. This little group addressed Jesus courteously as *Teacher* (for this term see on 8:19; it corresponded to the title "Rabbi"), and said that they wanted to see *a sign*[93] from him. They do not explain what they mean by *a sign*, but it is clear that they were asking him to accredit himself by doing some striking miracle; apparently they did not regard his miracles of healing as meeting their need. After all, in antiquity there were many "healers" who did things that ordinary folk could not understand but who in the end proved to be no more than charlatans. The Pharisees had already ascribed some of Jesus' work to Beelzeboul (v. 24). They were asking him now for something that unmistakably came from God. In the Old Testament sometimes such signs were given (Exod. 4:8-9; Isa. 7:11), but they were God's good gift, not the result of a demand from unbelieving sceptics. The Pharisees evidently saw a "sign" as a miraculous happening produced on demand to prove that God was with a person.[94] Could Jesus produce evidence that it was God who was enabling him and not some unusual human power or some demonic force? In that they were testing him out (Mark 8:11), it is plain that they did not expect him to come up with anything that would satisfy them. The kind of miracle they were demanding Jesus consistently refused to perform. His miracles were always directed toward the fulfilling of a need felt by those for whom the miracle was performed. Jesus was no circus performer, gratifying the appetite for wonders on the part of people who were not serious about spiritual things. From the beginning he refused to demand that God should do miraculous things for him (4:5-7).

39. Jesus' strong reaction demonstrates his abhorrence of the showmanship his inquisitors were seeking. He castigates them as *an evil and adulterous generation*,[95] where *generation* extends the scope of his condem-

---

93. σημεῖον occurs 13 times in Matthew (17 in John). It may be used of a distinguishing mark (26:48; 2 Thess. 3:17), but in the New Testament it is more commonly used of a miraculous sign of some sort (John uses it of Jesus' miracles, as deeds that have important spiritual significance). In the Synoptic Gospels it is more commonly used of miracles demanded of Jesus that he refused to perform. Paul finds the seeking of signs characteristic of Jews (1 Cor. 1:22).

94. Josephus says that Theudas persuaded his followers to go with him to the Jordan. Theudas said "that he was a prophet and that at his command the river would be parted and would provide them an easy passage" (*Ant.* 20.97). It was this kind of sign that Jesus was asked to produce. That the rabbis thought such signs occurred is made clear from Talmudic stories about rabbis a little later than Jesus' time. Thus we read that the disciples of R. Jose b. Kisma said to him, "Master, give us a sign." He refused at first, but then turned the waters of the grotto of Paneas into blood (*Sanh.* 98a). When R. Eliezer's arguments were not accepted he moved a tree a hundred cubits (according to another report, four hundred cubits), made a river flow backwards, and did other curious things (*B. Meṣ.* 59b).

95. K. H. Rengstorf remarks that the demand for a sign "is more an assault on God's

nation beyond his immediate questioners to the sum total of the contemporaries they represent. They are evil (see on 6:23), for their profession of religion is joined to a massive selfishness whereby they impose their own rules on God, and adulterous, for they have turned their proper relation of fidelity to God into spiritual adultery;[96] their demand[97] for a sign showed their failure to trust God and their readiness to try to impose on him a miraculous act of their own choosing where they should have been content with faithful service. People who serve God in faithfulness may indeed see signs, but sensation-seeking unbelievers will not see them. Signs are granted to faith, so how can the faithless ever see them?

"*No sign will be given it,*" Jesus says, where *given* points to the fact that "signs" are not to be obtained by aggressive demand; if they come at all, they are the gift of God. And in this case there will be no such gift; *the sign of Jonah the prophet* is sufficient. Jesus is saying that Jonah himself is the sign,[98] which means that it is what is recorded of the man that constitutes the marvel. It is in vain for the people who confront Jesus to look for a sign; the sign they need is there, in the book of the prophet that they value so highly.

40. Jesus explains. It was not the whole life of the prophet that was significant but the fact that he was three days *in the belly*[99] *of the sea monster.*[100] As we count time, *three days and three nights* points inexorably to three periods of twenty-four hours each; we thus have a problem with the use of this expression for the time between Jesus' death and resurrection: the period from toward the middle of the day on Friday (when he was crucified) to early on Sunday morning (when he was seen alive) comes

---

freedom in so far as it lays upon God its own basic principles concerning what may be and what may not. In the last resort this is what makes of those who demand a sign . . . a γενεὰ πονηρὰ καὶ μοιχαλίς . . . a society which breaks away from God by emancipating itself from Him in its judgment and acts" (*TDNT,* VII, p. 236). A little later than Jesus' time Josephus writes of the Jews: "that period had, somehow, become so prolific of crime of every description amongst the Jews, that no deed of iniquity was left unperpetrated, nor, had man's wit been exercised to devise it, could he have discovered any novel form of vice" (*War* 7.259). There is evidence that the generation was literally adulterous (e.g., *Ps. Sol.* 8:11), but Jesus is speaking of spiritual things.

96. Interestingly there was a Jewish idea that the Messiah would come in such a generation (see SBk, I, pp. 641-42).

97. The verb is ἐπιζητεῖ, on which Gundry comments, "he prefixes a perfective ἐπί to ζητεῖ with the result that the meaning 'seeks' is intensified to something like 'insists on.' "

98. The genitive τὸ σημεῖον Ἰωνᾶ seems to be a genitive of apposition, "the sign that is Jonah." Matthew has προφήτης 37 times (next highest is Acts with 30). His preponderance is perhaps connected with his interest in the fulfilment of prophecy, though here it is the experience of the prophet rather than his predictions that is primarily in mind.

99. κοιλία is used of the digestive organs and more generally of the inward parts of the body; it may be used, for example, of the womb (19:12). Here it denotes the stomach. ὥσπερ indicates correspondence: "just as." On the relevance of Jonah, Bengel comments, "it was as much believed that he would not return from the fish, as it was that Jesus would not return from the heart of the earth; yet both of them did return."

100. κῆτος is found here only in the New Testament. It means "any sea-monster or huge fish" (LSJ).

short of what we understand by three days and three nights. But the Jews did not reckon as we do: they counted the day on which any period began as one day, and they did the same with the day on which the period ended. Thus we have Friday, Saturday, Sunday, three days; it does not matter that neither the Friday nor the Sunday was complete.[101] According to the method of counting in use at the time, this is the period during which Jesus would be in the heart of the earth. Matthew elsewhere speaks of Jesus as rising "on the third day" (16:21) and "after three days" (27:63); there is no reason to think that he sees any difference between these expressions.[102] However we understand it in detail, the expression indicates that after the crucifixion Jesus will be three days in the tomb.[103]

41. Jesus turns to those associated with Jonah, and refers to the inhabitants of Nineveh,[104] who, he says, *will rise up in the judgment.* The verb is often used of a literal rising (26:62), and is not uncommonly used of rising from the dead (e.g., 1 Thess. 4:16), but here it seems to refer to initiating a process of judgment (perhaps standing up to make an accusation in court?). Jesus speaks of *the* judgment, that is, the judgment at the end of the world, the judgment that counts.[105] In that judgment the Ninevites will confront *this generation* (i.e., the people living at the time Jesus was speaking) *and will condemn it.* This does not mean that they will issue edicts in the manner of judges, but long ago their conduct had set a standard that the current generation should have attained but did not. Jesus further explains that this condemnation will arise from the fact that the Ninevites *repented* (see on 3:2) because of[106] Jonah's preaching. The word Jesus uses for *preaching* means strictly the proclamation of a herald.[107] The point of the word is that a herald was not given latitude to vary the proclamation in any way; it was not for him to improve on it by substituting what he regarded as better words or better news. His task was

---

101. The rabbis said, "A day and a night make an 'Onah and a part of an 'Onah is as the whole"; and again, "The part of a day is as the whole day" (SBk, I, p. 649).

102. οὕτως (in Matthew 32 times, which is more than anywhere else in the New Testament) corresponds to ὥσπερ at the beginning. καρδία (see on 5:8) can refer to the innermost part; J. Behm explains it as "the inward part, the bosom, of the earth" (*TDNT,* III, p. 613). Or it may signify *"heart* in the sense *interior, center"* (BAGD, 2).

103. In the Lucan equivalent of the saying there is no reference to the resurrection, and Jonah himself seems to be the sign, probably with reference to his preaching. But there is no question that in Matthew the resurrection of Jesus is stressed.

104. ἄνδρες strictly means males, but here it signifies inhabitants generally. The word is not common in Matthew (8 times; Luke has it 27 times). Νινευίτης, "Ninevite," is found in the New Testament only here and twice in Luke.

105. "In its individualizing use (the article) focuses attention on a single thing or single concept, as already known or otherwise more definitely limited. . . . The art. takes on the idea of κατ' ἐξοχήν 'par excellence' " (BAGD, II.1.a.α).

106. εἰς here has "the Semitic causal sense . . . they repented because of the preaching of Jonah" (M, III, p. 255).

107. κήρυγμα. In view of its common use in modern discussions of the New Testament it comes as something of a surprise that it occurs only 8 times in the New Testament, 6 times in Paul and once each in Matthew and Luke.

simple — to say what he was told to say. This formed a good word for the message God gave to his preachers, and it is used in this sense here: Jonah did not compose a message of his own, but he told the Ninevites what God told him to say. Confronted with the word of God, the Ninevites responded with wholehearted repentance. The people of Jesus' day should likewise have responded to his message with repentance, but they did not. And their guilt was all the more serious because *something greater* than Jonah is here. We might have expected the masculine "someone greater," but the neuter points to God's whole work in Jesus, the sending of his Son, the decisive provision for the salvation of repentant sinners, the bringing in of the kingdom. All this represents something far greater than the coming of a Jewish prophet to the ancient city of Nineveh. We should notice two contrasts: the Ninevites repented and the people of Jesus' day did not; and again, the Ninevites were confronted with Jonah, these Jews with someone far greater.

42. The same construction is repeated with an appeal to another Gentile. Jesus cites Scripture to show that on a second occasion, in strong contrast to the Jews of his day, a Gentile responded to the teaching of a Hebrew man of God. *The queen of the South*[108] is not defined more closely, but clearly Jesus is referring to the Queen of Sheba, who came from a distant land to listen to Solomon (1 Kings 10:1-10). The verb for *rise up* is changed from that used of the Ninevites in the preceding verse, but the sense appears to be much the same. Like the conduct of the Ninevites, what she did will form a condemnation of the current generation, for she went to great lengths to hear the wisdom of a mere mortal and they refused to be impressed when confronted with something greater than Solomon. *The ends of the earth* means that she came a long way to meet Solomon; it is generally agreed that Sheba was in the region we now call Yemen, and with conditions of travel in King Solomon's day that meant a long and difficult journey. In some ways she forms a more impressive example than the Ninevites, for they responded to a man who came and preached to them on their own home turf, whereas she embarked on a lengthy journey to hear Solomon. But she made it in order to hear the wisdom she regarded as outstanding. Yet the men of Jesus' day refused to be impressed with the presence of the greatest of all. Wisdom may be used of the best human sagacity or of a good gift of God (1 Cor. 2:6-7, 13). Solomon was proverbial for wisdom, but his wisdom was not to be compared to what had happened with the coming of Jesus. And yet the people of that generation would not believe.[109] They had merited a greater condemnation. We

108. νότου lacks the article as regularly with the points of the compass (BDF, 253[5]). But there may here be some influence from the Hebrew construct state.

109. Cf. Calvin, "It will be well to consider this antithesis. A woman, quite uneducated in the school of God, came from a distant land to learn from Solomon, an earthly king. The Jews, pupils of God's Law, reject His highest and indeed unique Teacher, the Head of all the prophets" (II, p. 59).

should notice these points of comparison: the queen came from a long distance whereas the Jews did not have to travel, she responded but they did not, and she was confronted with Solomon but they with a greater than Solomon.

8. *The Return of the Unclean Spirit, 12:43-45*

> 43"But when an unclean spirit goes out from a man, it goes through waterless places looking for rest, and does not find it. 44Then it says, 'I will go back to my house from which I went out.' And when it comes, it finds it empty, swept, and tidied. 45Then it goes and takes along with it seven other spirits more evil than itself, and they come in and settle down there; and the last state of that man is worse than the first. So will it be with this evil generation."

Jesus underlines the impossibility of being neutral on moral issues with a little story about a man who is forsaken by an unclean spirit who has taken possession of him. But simply to be rid of the spirit results in a vacuum that in the end will be filled in an undesirable manner. The paragraph follows on from verse 32 in Luke's version, and it certainly continues to bring out the thought that the power of God is needed to defeat evil. And it hammers home the lesson that one cannot be neutral toward Jesus. The attempt at neutrality ends with the coming in of the equivalent of seven devils, so that the person finishes in a worse state than at first.

43. *When* has the meaning "whenever";[110] Jesus is speaking of what may be expected to happen from time to time. The spirit is described as *unclean,* an expression that originally pointed to what cultically might not be brought into contact with the deity, but that came to be used in a moral sense. Thus an "unclean" spirit was an "evil" spirit. In the Gospels such spirits are often said to reside in people, and Jesus not infrequently casts them out. The spirit in this little story leaves voluntarily and wanders about looking for rest. *Waterless places* reflects the idea that demons were wont to frequent dry and desert places (cf. Isa. 13:20-21; 34:14; in Tob. 8:3 an expelled demon fled to "the remotest parts of Egypt"). It is not clear why the spirit should seek *rest* (or "a resting-place," *REB*), but presumably spirits, like people, may seek respite from whatever it is that spirits do. But this spirit was unable to find the rest it sought.

44. The spirit soliloquizes. It can still refer to the man it left as *my house* (see on 2:11). No one else has taken up residence, so the man still is

---

110. ὅταν is "a temporal particle . . . of an action that is conditional, possible, and, in many instances, repeated" (BAGD). It is especially common in the Gospels (which range from 17 occurrences in John to 29 in Luke), but the highest number elsewhere in the New Testament is 12 in 1 Corinthians.

open for the spirit's reoccupation. The spirit returns[111] and finds its former home *empty, swept, and tidied,* a very satisfactory situation for a homeless spirit. It is *empty,*[112] so there is no barrier to the spirit's return. But if it is empty, it is not desolate; the man has evidently been busy on himself so that the place vacated by the spirit may now be said to be *swept and tidied.*[113] Jesus is talking about a pleasant, moral reformation, but with the man thinking that he is still in control of himself and with no reference to the Spirit of God. The man is empty; he is open to invasion from all kinds of evil, and in fact the original spirit comes back with reinforcements.

45. *Then* (see on 2:7) takes us to the next stage in the process. The spirit goes off and takes along with it *seven other spirits,* described as *more evil than itself. Along with it*[114] associates the newcomers with the original demon; the picture we get is of one of willing cooperation in taking over the empty man. That there are seven of them may be significant; seven is the number of perfection, and while that is a strange category to apply to evil spirits the point may be that the takeover is made by the most appropriate number of demons. The newcomers are worse than the first demon; the man is not simply reverting to his previous state, but has more demons and of a more evil type. The eight evil spirits go into the man and settle down;[115] henceforth he will never be free of evil spirits. His *last state*[116] is worse than anything earlier. It is not without its interest that when the first spirit left the man, he was better off than he had been previously. He was able to set himself in order. But there was no dynamic about the change, no new power that would enable him to escape being demon-ridden. And his lack of spiritual resources left him open to a worse fate than he had known previously.[117]

Jesus rounds off the story by driving home the application to his hearers. *So* ("as it was with the spirit-ridden man") *will it be* with those before him. They had seen him cast out a demon, he had refuted the

---

111. The participle ἐλθόν is more or less equivalent to a conditional: "if it comes and finds — ."

112. σχολάζω, again in the New Testament only in Luke 11:25 (the parallel to this story) and 1 Corinthians 7:5. It is used of people, where it means "to be at leisure" (curiously, as it seems to us, this is the root from which we get "school"). It is also used of things in the sense "to be unoccupied, empty."

113. σαρόω means "to sweep," and the perfect indicates a completed job. κοσμέω signifies "to order, arrange" (it is used in Homer of marshalling armies). So it gets meanings like "adorn, furnish" (AS).

114. μεθ' ἑαυτοῦ.

115. κατοικέω (see on 2:23) conveys the notion of permanent residence; the demons have no intention of moving on in due course.

116. τὰ ἔσχατα, "the last things," the final state of affairs, here compared with the former state of the man.

117. "There is a terrible persistence in wickedness: it returns, and the soul not indwelt by the rightful Tenant is always beleaguered. Reformation is never enough . . ." (Buttrick). Cf. Filson, "The power of God, and not merely the skill of trained counsellors, is needed to resolve the deep-seated crisis which evil brings to man."

suggestion that he did this by Beelzeboul and had pointed out that the Spirit of God was at work in him, he had pointed out that it is unforgivable to blaspheme the Holy Spirit, he had made it plain that they were in the presence of something greater than Jonah or Solomon, and he had told his little story about the man from whom the unclean spirit went out. In his casting out of the evil spirit that started this chain of events (v. 22) Jesus had bound the strong man. Clearly he was now pointing out the danger in which his conversation partners stood. They had been confronted with divine power, and if they tried to live empty lives, lives that did not replace evil by the presence of the Holy Spirit, there was nothing before them but the grimmest of prospects. If it continued on its self-opinionated way, the generation that refused the opportunity presented to it by the appearance in its midst of the very Son of God, the generation already characterized as "evil and adulterous," faced a future that was bleak indeed.

9. Jesus' Family, 12:46-50

46While he was still speaking to the crowds, look, his mother and his brothers were standing outside, trying to speak to him. 47And someone said to him, "Look, your mother and your brothers are standing outside, trying to speak to you." 48But he answered, saying to the man who spoke to him, "Who is my mother? And who are my brothers?" 49And he stretched out his hand toward his disciples and said, "Look! My mother and my brothers. 50For whoever does the will of my Father in heaven, he is my brother and sister and mother."

Jesus' earthly family seem not to have understood exactly who he was and what his mission demanded. John tells us that his brothers did not believe in him (John 7:5), and Mark that on one occasion his family (or perhaps his friends) tried to seize him because they thought he was beside himself (Mark 3:20-21). There may well be something of the same attitude here. They were probably moved, not by any spirit of opposition, but by concern; they seem to have wanted to preserve him from unfortunate consequences (as they saw them) of what he had been doing. At any rate they appear to be claiming special treatment on account of their family ties, and Jesus makes it plain that in his ministry his relation to his family is different from what it had been in the days of his growing up. At the same time we must bear in mind that Jesus is not so much downgrading loyalty to a human family as insisting on the importance of loyalty to God.

46. Jesus' family seem to have tried to claim him while he was still[118]

---

118. ἔτι means "yet, still"; BAGD notes that it may be used "in positive statements, to denote that a given situation is continuing" (1.a).

speaking to the crowds (characteristically Matthew has the plural). The *brothers* should probably be understood as children of Joseph and Mary born subsequent to the birth of Jesus. After the doctrine of the perpetual virginity of Mary made its appearance, there were conjectures that these were children of Joseph by a former marriage or cousins. But since there is no support for such views in the New Testament, we should take the natural understanding of the words. The impression Matthew gives is that the family felt that they had prior rights; they could interrupt him in the middle of a teaching session, and he should stop what he was doing and come to them. This might arise out of the very strong family loyalty that was universally accepted: a dutiful son and brother would not leave his family in order to teach the crowds. Matthew is quite interested in the family. We have already noticed that he uses "brother" more often than in any other book in the New Testament apart from Acts (he has it 39 times, the same number as in 1 Corinthians; Acts has it 57 times). John exceeds his total of 64 for "father," but nobody else does, and his 27 uses of "mother" is ten more than the next most frequent users (Mark and Luke). It is quite in keeping with this that he draws attention to Jesus' family at this point and very significant that he records the words that set a firm limit to any family claim on Jesus. On this occasion the family were outside (unable to get closer because of the crowds?), but were trying to speak to him.

47. They were able to get a message to him. Someone (there is no indication who managed to get through) told him that both his mother and his brothers were trying to talk to him. The verse simply repeats the statement of the previous verse. Some MSS omit it (ℵ* B L etc.), but it seems required for the sense and may well have been omitted by the eye passing from the last word in verse 46 to the identical word at the end of verse 47. We should accept it (Metzger's committee indicated no more than "a certain amount of doubt" about it).

48. Jesus answered the implied request with a couple of questions of his own, the first relating to his mother and the second to his brothers. The mother as the matriarch is singled out, but the two questions basically ask the same thing: In the light of the ministry he is exercising in the name of God, what do ordinary family ties mean? Must Jesus forsake the service of the heavenly Father in order that he may please his earthly family?

49-50. Jesus proceeds to answer his own question. He acccompanies it with the action of stretching out his hand and pointing at his disciples. Matthew frequently uses *Look* for greater vividness (see on 1:20), but here it may well be used in the sense "Look at these people" (the ones to whom he is pointing). Jesus transfers the name *mother* to those whom he respects and loves as a mother, or perhaps those who respect and love him as a mother would. This is an unusual way of using "mother," but it is a not uncommon way of using *brother.* Jesus is saying that those with whom he is closely associated in the service of God have become "family" to him.

331

He spells this out. *Whoever*[119] means anyone at all: the way into the heavenly family is open wide and there are no restrictions on who may enter. When he speaks of "doing the will" of the Father,[120] Jesus is not opting for salvation by works, but pointing to the importance of conforming to God's way and not imposing one's own pattern on heavenly things. It is relationship to the heavenly Father that constitutes membership in the family. *He* is emphatic, "he and no other"; he is the whole family, *brother and sister* (who appears for the first time in this paragraph) *and mother.* Jesus is not saying that earthly familial ties are unimportant, only that they are not all-important. Doing the will of God is all-important.

This chapter has drawn attention to a variety of ways in which Jesus was opposed. Matthew has made it clear that his Lord faced constant and bitter and unjustified hostility from people who ought to have been giving him a welcome.[121] Even Jesus' own family did not understand him. But the chapter ends with the firm reminder that there were those who, despite all the opposition, committed themselves wholeheartedly to Jesus.

119. ὅστις (see on 2:6). The term is frequent in Matthew; here its force is heightened with the addition of ἄν.

120. Matthew speaks of God as "Father" 44 times in all, which compares with 5 in Mark, 17 in Luke, and 42 in Paul. Only John has it more often (122 times). It means a lot to Matthew that God is a Father to believers. It is a tender word and speaks of love and care on the one hand, and love and devotion on the other.

121. Cf. Gutzwiller, "throughout this whole passage there is a warning, a deep seriousness. Man faces the decision either to accept Satan and become possessed by him, or to accept God and be called into his love" (p. 147).

Matthew 13

G. Teaching in Parables, 13:1-52

This chapter marks something of a turning point for Matthew. Until now he has pictured for us Jesus teaching in synagogues, but here he speaks of him as teaching on a beach. Increasingly Jesus will forsake the synagogue and teach the people out of doors. A further change is the use of parables. Previously there has been some teaching of a parabolic nature (e.g., 7:24-27), but the fully developed parable appears here for the first time. A parable may take the form of a story or a simile or a metaphor; it is an appeal from what people know in the realm of ordinary life to truths Jesus wants to teach in the spiritual life, in the classic definition "an earthly story with a heavenly meaning." Sometimes details in a parable are significant, but mostly there is one great truth that takes hold of us; as Barclay puts it, Jesus' parables "were designed to make one stabbing truth flash out at a man the moment he heard it" (II, p. 63).[1]

But perhaps we learn best what a parable is by looking at the way Jesus used it rather than by trying to produce a satisfactory definition. Parables formed an important part of Jesus' teaching, and it is significant that no other New Testament character is recorded as having told as much as one parable. The parabolic method is Jesus' own.[2] Parables were, of course, known outside Jesus' teaching; there are parables in the Old Testament, and the rabbis told parables.[3] But nobody used the method as

---

1. C. H. Dodd has a well-known definition of a parable as "a metaphor or simile drawn from nature or common life, arresting the hearer by its vividness or strangeness, and leaving the mind in sufficient doubt about its precise application to tease it into active thought" (*The Parables of the Kingdom* [London, 1936], p. 16). There is an extensive literature on the parables, but perhaps particular mention should be made of J. Jeremias, *The Parables of Jesus* (London, 1954); K. E. Bailey, *Poet and Peasant* (Grand Rapids, 1985); J. C. Little, *ET*, LXXXVII (1975-76), pp. 356-60; LXXXVIII (1976-77), pp. 40-44, 71-75; M. Black, *BJRL*, 42 (1959-60), pp. 273-87.

2. Filson comments, "The Synoptic Gospels contain about five dozen separate parables; the Gospel of John has almost none of these; the rest of the N.T. offers no real parallels. This is fatal to the idea that the early Church created the parables; no one in the Church even attempted to rival Jesus in this teaching method. He used parables not only to illustrate and clarify truth but also to capture the imagination, direct the will, and lead to obedience."

3. It was said of R. Meir that in his public discourses "a third was *Halachah*, a third *Haggadah*, and a third consisted of parables" (*Sanh.* 38b). But not many early parables are

---

effectively or as extensively as Jesus did. To this day his parables are known and loved the world over, but who can name even one parable from his contemporaries? Jesus used the method apparently in order to convey his teaching vividly and to stimulate his hearers to think, with the result that those who apply themselves learn to their profit, whereas those who do not never find the truths Jesus is teaching (cf. vv. 11-15). The use of parables teaches not only the lesson of the individual parable, but also the importance of thinking about spiritual things.[4]

Matthew at this point relates seven parables, beginning with the parable of the sower, perhaps to show what a parable is. It is given importance by being followed by an explanation of Jesus' purpose in using parables and then an explanation of this parable. The other six are divided into two groups of three, separated by an explanation of the parable of the weeds. Each of the last six is introduced by "the kingdom of heaven is like — " (all seven are often called "parables of the kingdom," but we should respect Matthew's usage; he does, however, speak of "the word of the kingdom" in his explanation of the first, v. 19). Four of them are found in this Gospel only (the weeds, the pearl, the hidden treasure, and the net). It is often said that Matthew has gathered these parables, though they were spoken originally at different times. This may be so, but verse 53 seems to mean that Jesus gave them as a coherent series.

1. The Parable of the Sower, 13:1-9

> [1]On that day Jesus went out of the house and sat by the sea. [2]And great crowds were gathered around him, so that he got into a boat and sat down, and all the crowd stood on the beach. [3]And he told them many things in parables, saying, "The sower went out to sow. [4]And as he sowed, some seeds fell beside the path, and the birds came and devoured them. [5]And others fell on the rocky places, where they did not have much soil; and immediately they sprouted because they had no depth of soil. [6]But when the sun rose they were scorched, and because they had no root they withered away. [7]And others fell among thornbushes, and the thornbushes grew up and choked them. [8]And others fell on good soil and produced a crop, some a hundredfold, some sixtyfold, and some thirtyfold. [9]He who has ears let him hear."

This well-known and much applied parable is drawn from the processes of agriculture, which would have been very well known to Jesus'

---

recorded; according to Strack and Billerbeck only one (told by Hillel) survives from pre-Christian times (SBk, I, p. 654).

4. "The form had already been established; what Jesus did was to take it and make such wide and varied use of it that he gave the parable as a method of teaching renewed vitality. In fact, he perfected the form so well that Christians were reluctant to use it thereafter, knowing they could never be as effective as he was" (AB, p. CXXXII).

hearers. For that matter even modern city-dwellers can understand it. It makes effectively the point that the one message can produce different results in different hearers. It is common in recent discussions to have it said that the parable is concerned simply with eschatology: it stresses the greatness of the coming kingdom in contrast to the present small beginnings. Perhaps this view does not give sufficient attention to such facts as the absence of any reference to the kingdom in this parable and the amount of attention that is given to the variety of ways in which the seed may come to nothing.

1-2. *On that day* connects the following session of teaching with the preceding time of discussion with the Pharisees and scribes. Jesus went out of the house where he was; it is probably significant that Matthew uses the same verb here as that in the opening of the first parable where the sower *went out* to sow. Later in the chapter the sower of the good seed is the Son of man (v. 37). Clearly Matthew wants the reader to see that it is Jesus who is the sower. Having gone out of the house, Jesus made his way to the shore of the lake (it is not necessary to add the name; there was only one lake that could be meant). There he *sat down*, which is the posture for teaching and indicates that he was getting ready to teach the crowd. This is supported by the fact that large numbers of people came around[5] him: clearly they saw that he was going to teach. But there is a limit to the number of people who can crowd on a beach with comfort to the teacher, so Jesus got into a boat and sat there, while the people stood on the shore. Mostly in this Gospel lengthy pieces of teaching are addressed to disciples, but this one is aimed at the crowds.[6]

3. It was apparently quite a long discourse, for Jesus told[7] them *many things*. This is Matthew's first use of the term *parable* (though, as we have noted, some of the teaching he has recorded is of a parabolic nature, e.g., 7:24-27). There are several parables in this chapter, but we cannot be sure that they were all spoken on this one occasion. It seems more likely that Matthew has given us the information that it was a long discourse, making extensive use of parables, and that he has given us a sample of what Jesus said and added other parables. The word "parable" is hard to pin down. We use it mostly for a story taken from this life that conveys spiritual truth, and it certainly is used in this way. But it may also denote a short, pithy saying, a wise saying. Not much, however, turns on our definition. It is more important to notice what Jesus said and what it means to us.

---

5. συνάγω is a favorite word of Matthew's (24 times out of 59 in the New Testament). It means "gather together" and may be used of things or of people. πρός means "to"; the people gathered "to" Jesus.

6. αἰγιαλός, "shore, beach," occurs again in Matthew only in verse 48. εἰστήκει is pluperfect, with the meaning "stood," "were standing."

7. Tasker, however, thinks that ἐλάλησαν may be an inceptive aorist meaning, "he began to speak." Tasker adds, "It was the first time Jesus embarked on this policy."

The first parable[8] begins with the information that the sower[9] went out to sow. In agriculture as we know it, this would mean that the land had been prepared by ploughing or digging, but in Palestine it was common for the sower to sow his seed first and then plough it in (I have observed this process quite recently, so it has persisted through the centuries). P. B. Payne has produced evidence that both practices were in vogue: sometimes farmers ploughed the land first to clear it of weeds, sometimes they did it after sowing to put the seed underneath the soil, and sometimes they did it both times.[10]

4. In the process of sowing the seeds fell into a variety of situations with diverse results for the crop. Jesus begins with those seeds that fell on hard places. In those days plots of ground were not, of course, fenced off, and people seem regularly to have gone on their journeys through the fields as well as around them. There were paths that ran through the fields, and when the sower was scattering his seed it was inevitable that some of it would fall on or close beside such paths.[11] Since there was no soft soil there in which the seeds might sink, they remained where the birds[12] could reach them and they were speedily devoured.[13]

5. *Others*[14] fell into stony ground.[15] This will mean not ground littered with stones, but ground where the bedrock came close to the surface, with the result that these seeds had no depth of soil. There would have been a small amount over the bedrock, but not enough to sustain full growth. This did not stop a promising beginning, for *immediately* these seeds *sprouted*.[16]

---

8. This is Matthew's first use of παραβολή, a term he will use 12 times in this chapter and 5 times in the rest of his Gospel. In LXX it translates the Hebrew מָשָׁל, which is from a root meaning "to be like," and which means a wise saying: it may be a cryptic one-liner or a more extensive expression; it often signifies an enigmatic figure of speech. There is not much that is of the same sort as Jesus' parables, but the expression introduces us to a class of sayings that convey truth vividly and in a manner that requires the hearer to think.

9. Matthew uses the participle ὁ σπείρων, "the sowing one"; such a participle often conveys the thought of the person who does the action continually. *NIV* has "farmer," but the word means "sower" (who may or may not be a farmer).

10. "The Order of Sowing and Ploughing" (*NTS*, 25 [1978-79], pp. 123-29).

11. παρὰ τὴν ὁδόν may be understood as meaning on the edge of the path or perhaps on the land immediately beside the path. In either place it would not be ploughed.

12. πετεινός signifies "winged"; in the neuter it refers to "a winged thing," and thus "a bird."

13. κατεσθίω occurs only here in Matthew (and as a v.l. in 23:13). AS regards it as a "perfective" compound of ἐσθίω, with the meaning "eat up," "devour."

14. ἄλλα strictly means "others of the same kind," and while there is no particular emphasis on that here, that is surely the meaning. Matthew follows it with δέ (and so throughout the parable), whereas Mark and Luke prefer καί; he is making a slight contrast between one group of seeds and the others.

15. πετρώδης (πέτρα, εἶδος) = rocklike, stony; it occurs in the New Testament only in this parable in Matthew and Mark. Matthew has the plural, "stony places," but Mark the singular, "the rock" (in the interpretation he has the plural).

16. ἐξανατέλλω (only in this parable in Mark elsewhere in the New Testament) means "to spring up"; coupled with the adverb this means that the plant was quick-growing. Minus the ἐξ the same verb is used of the sun's rising in verse 6.

"Because"[17] is unexpected; but the shallow soil would have warmed quickly and encouraged rapid growth. But in that it had *no depth of soil* there was no future for any plant in this position.

6. *When the sun*[18] *rose* is not to be taken with strict literalness: the sun rose every day, and the meaning is not that the plant withered the day after the seed was sown; the reference is rather to hot days that came early in the plants' life. When this happened the little plants *were scorched*[19] and *withered away*.[20] Where the previous verse said they had no "depth of soil," this one says they had no *root*; but this amounts to much the same. Plants that grow in rocky places seem all right at first, but they soon wither away. Lacking abundance of soil the roots cannot develop, and plants with defective root systems are not equipped to stand hot weather. They wither away.

7. Jesus moves on to seeds that lodged where thorny bushes were growing.[21] The point about these plants is that they were sturdy, robust plants, not easily to be defeated in the struggle for life. The plants as such would be ploughed in with the good seeds, but they would have their own seeds or pieces of roots that would enable them to spring into growth. So the good seeds found intense competition for the nourishment in the soil, and the thorny plants were too strong. They *choked* out the new plants by preventing them from getting the nourishment they needed.

8. Finally we come to the seeds that fell on good soil (for *good* see on 3:10). Matthew uses this word *good* more than do other writers; it has the notion of "beautiful" about it. Good seed going into good ground bears[22] a good crop. The magnitude varies from *a hundredfold* (cf. Gen. 26:12) down to *thirtyfold*. The first mentioned is an extraordinary crop, but even thirty-fold is very good.

9. This verse is identical with 11:15 (where see note). Jesus invites his hearers to think through what he has said. It is a responsibility easily overlooked. Great words like "repent," "believe," and "do good" strike a chord, but in every age it has been easy not to take care how or what we hear.

17. διὰ τό with the infinitive "expresses cause" (Chamberlain, p. 108).

18. This is the one place in Matthew where ἥλιος occurs without the article; the meaning, of course, is "the" sun.

19. καυματίζω (once each in Matthew and Mark and twice in Revelation) signifies "burn, scorch."

20. ξηραίνω, from ξηρός, "dry," signifies "to dry up, wither."

21. Strictly ἐπί means "upon," but Jesus is not speaking of seeds that were caught on the thorns. Rather, the meaning is "up to," "near." ἄκανθα (ἀκή, "a point") means prickly plants in general; it does not denote any one particular plant.

22. If the imperfect ἐδίδου is used strictly, it means that the seed once sown (aorist, ἔπεσεν) kept on bearing.

2. *The Purpose of the Parables, 13:10-17*

> [10]*And the disciples came and said to him, "Why do you speak to them in parables?"* [11]*But he answered them, saying, "Because to you it has been given to know the mysteries of the kingdom of heaven, but to them it has not been given.* [12]*For whoever has, it will be given to him, and he will have in abundance; but whoever does not have, even what he has will be taken away from him.* [13]*For this reason I speak to them in parables, because seeing they do not see and hearing they do not hear, nor understand.* [14]*And there is be fulfilled in them the prophecy of Isaiah that says,*
>
> *'You will hear and hear and will not understand,*
> * and you will see and see and will not perceive.*
> [15]*For this people's heart has become dull,*
> * and with their ears they scarcely hear,*
> * and their eyes they have shut,*
> *lest they should see with their eyes,*
> *and hear with their ears,*
> *and understand with their heart,*
> *and turn, and I should heal them.'*
>
> [16]*But blessed are your eyes because they see, and your ears because they hear.* [17]*For truly I tell you, that many prophets and righteous men have wanted to see the things that you see and have not seen them, and to hear the things that you hear and have not heard them."*

Although Matthew has recorded only one parable prior to this one, he tells us that the disciples came to Jesus and asked him why he taught in parables. Clearly he had used the method much more than Matthew records. The explanation is given in terms of prophecy: Jesus points to Isaiah 6:9-10, a passage that tells of the way people refused to accept divine direction. He is saying that although the people heard the words, they did not understand them and did not want to understand them. That was the fault of the people in Isaiah's day, and it was the fault of the people in Jesus' day.

10. *The disciples* lacks any indication as to whose they were, but there is no doubt that Jesus' disciples are meant. They *came*[23] to him and asked, *"Why do you speak to them in parables?"* where *them* evidently refers to people as yet uncommitted to Jesus. We may understand *speak* in the sense "keep speaking"; it certainly means more than that Jesus had told one parable. Commentators differ as to whether parables were meant to make the truth plain and simple or whether they were a way of making a veiled witness to truth. Paradoxically there is truth in both suggestions, but

23. For the meaning of προσέρχομαι and its unexpected frequency in Matthew see on 4:3; for *the disciples* see on 5:1.

338

certainly in the present passage the emphasis is on hearers who did not understand. As Patte says, the disciples' question "presupposes that the crowds — together with the readers — do not understand this kind of speech" (p. 186). The parable is a powerful method of teaching, but perhaps some measure of commitment is required in hearers if they are really to understand what a parable is saying. It is a fallacy that everyone can understand a parable. Did David understand Nathan's parable, even though it referred directly to him? An unexplained parable is usually open to interpretation in any one of a number of ways,[24] and those who lack devotion to Jesus may be relied on to go astray even when they hear the very stories that convey truth so vividly to disciples. Jesus expressly speaks of those who *know the mysteries of the kingdom of heaven* as those who understand. If someone does not know the great basic truths of the kingdom, what is he to make of the parables that set it forth or indeed of other parables? Commitment to Jesus is the prerequisite for a true understanding of his parabolic teaching.

11. *But he answered*[25] puts a difference between Jesus and the disciples. The doctrine of election lies behind these words. It is not a merit in the disciples that they understand where others do not; their comprehension is due to the fact that God has chosen them and given them the gift of understanding. They have received a gift that outsiders have not received (*to you* is emphatic), and the perfect tense signifies that the gift remains with them.[26] This is Matthew's one use of the word *mystery* (which is found 20 times in the Pauline corpus). It signifies something that people could never work out for themselves, which is why it is a "mystery."[27] But in the New Testament it usually carries the further thought that that which people can never work out for themselves God has now made known to them (it is not without its interest that some

24. Once a parable is divorced from its setting, "an ingenious mind can make a parable mean almost anything" (Melinsky, p. 49). McNeile can say, "If the parable transparently teaches a single truth, modern writers ought to be agreed upon what it is. But they are not" (p. 195), while Mounce, after a survey of critical opinions on the parable of the sower, states, "This rather widespread disagreement on how parables should be understood argues the fragile nature of critical conjecture" (pp. 129-30).

25. δέ sets Jesus in contrast to his questioners: they were puzzled, "But he — ." ὅτι may be taken as recitative (as by *NASB, REB,* etc.) or causal *(KJV, JB).* The latter is probably to be preferred, for "because" follows aptly on "Why?" and ὅτι does not seem to be used in the recitative sense after the words that precede it here (Carson cites D. Wenham for the point). If the word is taken as recitative, the reason for the parables will be that given in verse 13.

26. "The disciples receive far more frequent special instructions in Matthew than in any other Gospel," which means that "the disciples often fail to understand, but that they come to understand through Jesus' explanation (13:51)" (U. Luz, in Stanton, pp. 102-3). He also says, "discipleship is always related to the teaching of the historical Jesus" (p. 105).

27. Some commentators make a great deal of the fact that there was a group of "mystery religions" that had secret rites into which converts were initiated. It is certainly the case that there were such religions, but there is no evidence that either Jesus or the early church was interested in them.

translate it by "secret" [e.g., *NRSV*] and some by "open secret" [e.g., Moffatt]). Jesus is saying that the truths about God's kingdom were not known to people in general. Nobody could know such truths unless they were revealed to them. This had happened to the disciples (which was why they were disciples), but the crowds had not responded to the revelation; they were still ignorant of the mysteries of the kingdom (for *the kingdom of heaven* see on 3:2). Now the most significant truth about the kingdom was the place of Jesus in it. It was precisely because they had accepted the revelation that Jesus was the Messiah who would bring in the kingdom that the disciples were able to understand and respond to the teaching in the parables. And it was because people like the Pharisees had not accepted it that they did not understand.[28] Jesus does not explain who he means by *them*, but clearly it is the multitudes who came to hear him but who did not commit themselves to his cause. They had heard Jesus' words, but they had not apprehended the revelation.

12. The words of this verse (repeated with small alterations in 25:29; it is found also in Mark 4:25; Luke 8:18; 19:26; the repetition shows that it is an important saying) are an occasion of offense for some people, who consider it grossly unfair that more should be given to the rich and that the poor should be stripped of what little they have. And that, of course, is unfair, but it is not what Jesus is speaking about. He is referring to spiritual truth; he has just drawn attention to the importance of God's gifts of grace, and he now emphasizes the importance of human responsibility. When anyone uses the spiritual truth he has, that truth grows. More is added to it. By contrast, if he does not use it, he finds that it vanishes away little by little (Plummer says, "the purpose is educational to disciples, and disciplinary to those who refuse to become disciples," p. 189). The principle is capable of application in many areas of life (the achievement of sports people, for example).[29] But Jesus was not speaking of such areas; he was referring to a spiritual truth of permanent importance.[30] He confines himself to saying *whoever has*, without specifying what it is that he

---

28. Cf. G. Bornkamm, "They are enabled to understand the parables of Jesus in a different way from the people, for the parables mediate to them more than a general understanding of the nature of the βασιλεία; they point them to the incursion of the divine rule in the word and work of Jesus" (*TDNT*, IV, pp. 818-19). Hill says, "the 'secret' is the purpose of God concerning his Kingdom — that it is inaugurated in the person, words and work of Jesus of Nazareth"; he cites Bonnard for the further point "that it is established only after loss and disappointment."

29. Cf. Buttrick, "A man who exercises his strength increases it: such is his due reward. A man who neglects his muscles loses them: such is his proper penalty. We ourselves would not deeply wish it otherwise. The universe, meaning the very rule of God, is not a moral topsy-turveydom, but a rectitude in love."

30. This is an example of a conditional relative clause; such clauses "usually make no assertions about concrete realities, but rather general assertions or suppositions" (BDF, 380 [1]).

has, but in a land where the very poor had nothing at all it was enough to separate the haves from the have nots. The person who responds will receive much more. The saying is an encouragement to those who have committed themselves to following Jesus. They have made a good beginning and have received blessing and understanding; therefore they will receive more. It has nothing to do with the selfishness that aims only at piling up earthly goods.[31] But the saying is a warning as well as an encouragement. The person with little and who does nothing with that little will find that his little disperses.

13. That is the reason,[32] Jesus says, that he speaks[33] to them in parables (cf. Mark 4:33-34). Many think that Jesus would not have used parables (or any other method) "in order that" people would not understand. There is a sense in which this is true, but it is not the whole truth, for the whole truth includes election and the complete purpose of God. We must bear in mind that everything that is has its place in the purpose of God, who created it all. The disciples were not disciples because, left to themselves, they had decided that this would be a good thing. They were disciples on the Gospel view because God had chosen them. And it was in the outworking of this divine choice that they came to see Jesus for who he was and for what he was doing in bringing in the kingdom of God. They could understand the parables because of the insight that God gave them, but God did not give this insight to those who rejected Jesus. The word of God is always effective: it brings enlightenment or judgment — enlightenment to the disciples, judgment to those who rejected Jesus. It was in this sense that it was the divine purpose that they should not understand. If people rejected the Christ and set themselves in opposition to God, how could they understand the teaching that came from God through the Christ?

There is a certain emphasis on the word *parable:* "that it is in parables that I speak to them." Jesus proceeds, *because seeing they do not see,* a Hebraic construction signifying that, while there is a sense in which they certainly see, there is a more meaningful sense in which they do not see at all. Gutzwiller draws attention to Augustine's remarks about a man who looks at beautiful writing in a foreign tongue; he may admire the calligraphy, but the meaning he cannot appreciate. So when a person who rejects Jesus hears parables. He may find things in them that he can appreciate and

---

31. περισσεύω means *"to exceed a fixed number or measure"* (*GT*) and thus "to be in abundance" or "to have in abundance." Matthew has the verb 5 times, which is the same number as in Philippians and more than in any book other than 2 Corinthians, which has it 10 times.

32. διὰ τοῦτο means "on account of this," "therefore," and may be used "in real and supposed answers and inferences" (BAGD, B.II.2). Here, of course, the real reason follows.

33. λαλέω is used for speaking in parables as in verses 3 and 10; it recurs in verses 33 and 34. ὅτι may mean "that" or "because," probably the latter. Mark and Luke have ἵνα, but we should not think Matthew is softening the point; after all, he proceeds to use the same quotation to make the same point and what he has said in verses 11-12 agrees with this.

admire, but their essential meaning he cannot attain.[34] So is it with hearing. The repetition indicates that the people in question are shallow. They have the habit of seeing and hearing without appreciating the real significance of what they have seen and heard. This is brought out in the final expression, *nor understand;* they have no comprehension of what their sense perception has brought them.

14. Characteristically Jesus sees a fulfilment of prophecy, and he specifies that the words he quotes were spoken by Isaiah before going on to cite the passage he has in mind (for fulfilment of prophecy in this Gospel see on 1:22).[35] The quotation, which is as in LXX, opens with the accusation that the people addressed will not respond to what they hear.[36] They will not understand what they are hearing, which evidently means that they will have their minds so made up and will be so set in their ways that when they hear the word of God that challenges them to new thinking and new ways of living they simply do not understand it. They interpret what they hear in terms of they have always thought and done. So will it be with what they see. There will be no shortage of things they see, but there will be no perception.[37]

15. There is a change of approach. In the previous verse the people are addressed ("you will hear," etc.), but now God describes them. *For* gives a reason for the foregoing. The *heart* stands for the whole of the inner being (see on 5:8), thought, will, and feelings, but here the emphasis is on thought. They have become sluggish[38] in the way they think. So they hear new teaching from God but do not take it in nor model their lives on it. The same truth is put in terms of their ears and their eyes. With their ears

34. Matthew uses βλέπω 20 times, which is more than in any other book (17 times in John is next). It is used of perception with the eyes, but also sometimes of mental perception (e.g., 22:16).

35. ἀναπληρόω is found only here in Matthew (his usual word is πληρόω). The compound has the meaning "to fill completely"; G. Delling understands the meaning here to be that the prophecy "is 'fully actualised' in the rejection of Christ's message and work" (*TDNT*, VI, p. 306). This is also Matthew's only use of προφητεία, which here means the prophetic words rather than the gift of prophecy or the prophetic activity. The same prophecy is cited again in Acts 28:26-27.

36. ἀκοῇ (see on 4:24) is literally "with hearing"; here the thought is something like "no matter how often you hear." The problem is not that the people will not hear the message: they will hear it again and again (cf. *NIV*, "you will be ever hearing"). But they will not act on it. καί here has the sense "and yet," while *not* is the emphatic double negative οὐ μή. The construction reflects the Hebrew infinitive absolute and results in "Greek that was possible, however unidiomatic" (M, I, p. 76).

37. Again there is the emphatic double negative. The verb is ἴδητε, which may be used in the sense "see," but also, as here, with the meaning "perceive"; it is set over against βλέψετε rather than as an example of what that verb means.

38. παχύνω is found in the New Testament again only in Acts 28:27 in quoting the same Isaiah passage. It derives from παχύς, "thick," and has the meaning "to thicken, fatten" and in the passive "to grow fat." Metaphorically it signifies "to make dull or stupid" (AS); here it signifies that the people have become sluggish in their reasoning processes ("their minds are dull," *GNB*).

they scarcely[39] *hear,* while as for their eyes, they have shut them. This is probably to be understood as a stage worse than the preceding. It would be possible to have a problem of partial deafness, but the shutting of the eyes is a deliberate refusal to see.

The prophet brings this out with a series of clauses introduced with *lest.*[40] He traverses the ground he has covered, mentioning the eyes, the ears, and the heart (the last-mentioned is singular, though referring to many, a Semitic construction, M, III, p. 23). Those to whom the prophetic words come make sure that they are not disturbed by it. At the end of the quotation the prophet comes to what God would do if the people responded. Their response is that they should *turn* ("be converted," JB), which signifies an alteration in the whole direction the life is taking. It is a turning away from worldliness and self-centeredness, a turning to God. And when that happens, God heals.[41] Sin is a disease, and the people of whom Jesus speaks decline to be healed of it. Using the imagery of eyes that refuse to see and ears that refuse to hear, he rebukes people who refuse to heed God's gracious invitation and choose to go their own way. So, Jesus says, is it with the people of his day. They are the very fulfilment of the ancient prophecy.

16. *But* is adversative; it sets the disciples over against the people that fulfil the prophecy. For *blessed* see on 5:3; it points not only to a happy state but to one in which the blessing of God is operative. The word *your* comes first in the Greek, which gives it emphasis. Jesus is not pronouncing a blessing on the human race at large or on the Jews as the people of God. He is singling the disciples out; they have received and continue to receive a blessing from God. The reason? Their eyes see and their ears hear. As throughout this passage, this refers to spiritual perception; the disciples are perceptive in spiritual things whereas the evil generation with which Jesus was confronted was not.

17. *For* introduces a reason for this blessedness and one that might not have occurred to them, namely that what they are seeing and hearing is that to which prophecy has been pointing throughout the centuries. Many of God's great ones would have liked to have taken part in the events then taking place; the disciples should be mindful of their very great privilege. *Truly* (see on 5:18) adds solemnity to what Jesus is saying; this is a reliable saying. Primarily in mind with *prophets* are the great prophetic figures of the Old Testament, though the word is broad enough

39. The adverb is βαρέως, "heavily," "ponderously," and thus "with difficulty"; real hearing, hearing with understanding, has become difficult for them.

40. μήποτε (see on 4:6) is a conjunction denoting a negative purpose: "in order that . . . not." They do not understand what God is saying, partly, at least, because they do not want to hear. They are comfortable in their selfishness and do not wish to be disturbed by the kind of thing God would say about them.

41. ἰάομαι is used of healing in the physical sense (8:8, 13, etc.), but also, more rarely, of deliverance from spiritual ills (1 Pet. 2:24).

to include any who have received the prophetic gift. They are the mouthpieces of God here on earth, and they speak words that can be relied on. They live close to God and have insight into the ways of God. With the prophets are linked *righteous men* (see on 1:19). These will be people who lacked the prophetic gift, but who nevertheless served God well in their generation. Such giants of faith from of old would have liked to see and hear what the disciples see and hear, but did not attain that blessing. Jesus is saying that his mission in the world is the culmination of the purpose of God made clear in prophecies from of old. The servants of God in olden times may have looked for these days and desired to be involved in them. But that was not their privilege. Let the disciples accordingly appreciate what God is doing before their very eyes.

3. The Meaning of the Parable of the Sower, 13:18-23

18"*You, therefore, listen to the parable of the sower.* 19*When anyone hears the message of the kingdom and does not understand it, the evil one comes and snatches away that which was sown in his heart; this is he who was sown beside the path.* 20*But he who was sown on the rocky places is the person who hears the word and immediately receives it with joy;* 21*yet he has no root in himself but is temporary, and when there is trouble or persecution on account of the word he immediately takes offense.* 22*But he who was sown among the thorns is the one who hears the word, and the worry of the world and the deceitfulness of wealth choke the word, and it becomes unfruitful.* 23*But he who was sown on the good earth is the one who hears the word and understands it; who indeed bears fruit and produces, some a hundredfold, some sixtyfold, and some thirtyfold.*"

It is often said that the interpretations given in the Gospels are those of the early church rather than of Jesus. These interpretations not infrequently contain an element of allegory, and it is urged that a parable is used to convey one point strongly and that therefore allegorical interpretations are to be rejected. There is something to this approach, for it is important to understand that Jesus' parables are not to be taken as allegories, with a detailed explanation required for each several point. But it is possible to go too far in the other direction. Allegory was used in the Old Testament and also in the New Testament period; it is not wise to affirm dogmatically that Jesus never used it. Why not? We should further notice that to dismiss the interpretations given in the Gospels as erroneous and due to the early church rather than to Jesus comes up against the difficulty that in that case Jesus' closest followers did not understand what he was teaching. It seems preposterous that they should all be completely wrong and that twentieth-century scholars should alone at last have discovered what Jesus meant. We should also bear in mind that the fact that an interpretation has a certain suitability and value in the life situation of the early church does not mean that it does not go back to Jesus. We cannot take up the position that Jesus could speak only to the needs of his day. His teaching has enriched the church through the centuries; every age has found it relevant.[42]

18. We might well translate "Hear the parable" (as many translations do), but this overlooks the fact that Jesus begins with an emphatic *You* (cf. Knox, "The parable of the sower, then, is for your hearing"). Jesus has made the point that the parables are meant to conceal truth from those who lack genuine religious seriousness (like his scribal opposition), and he proceeds to set his close followers apart from that kind of approach to religious truth. The parable may go over the heads of Jesus' enemies and of the careless crowd, but those who have committed themselves to Jesus will not remain in ignorance. *Therefore* conveys the reason: because of their privilege in knowing "the mysteries of the kingdom of heaven" (v. 11) in contrast to the careless crowd they are to know what the parable signifies. In modern times the parable is often called "the parable of the soils," but Jesus calls it *the parable of the sower*. In interpreting it Calvin warns us that we should not think that Jesus meant that only one seed in four will bring forth fruit, or that the four reactions are the only ones ("there is no mention here of the despisers who openly repulse God's Word," II, p. 71). We should be on our guard against looking for information the parable does not purport to give.

19. Jesus begins with the careless hearer.[43] This person hears what is said,[44] indeed, but without any comprehension; he hears a parable but does not perceive the spiritual truth it conveys. When this happens the devil[45] becomes active. He *snatches*[46] what has been sown in this hearer's

---

42. Cf. Philip Barton Payne, "The Authenticity of the Parable of the Sower and its Interpretation," in R. T. France and David Wenham, eds., *Gospel Perspectives*, I (Sheffield, 1980), pp. 163-207. He finds evidence that both the parable and its interpretation are authentic. Bonnard favors the view that the interpretation is that of the early church and not Jesus himself, but he adds that the more important question is not that. Rather, it is whether the passage identifies the sower and his decisive word with the historic person of Jesus, "which is certainly the case" (p. 197). Filson is doubtful as to whether Jesus spoke these words, but "the explanation, if not original with Jesus, catches the meaning" (p. 160). Cf. Gundry, "The singularity of the expressions in Jesus' teaching may derive, however, from the singularity of the parable itself and therefore carry little weight concerning the authenticity or inauthenticity of the interpretation" (p. 261).

43. παντός will be used in the sense " 'any one' no matter who" (Robertson, p. 744). The two participles in the genitive are probably to be taken as a genitive absolute (so Robertson, p. 1105). The present depicts the action as in process; the evil one snatches away the word while the person is still listening to it.

44. λόγος means not a word simply, but here the whole message that tells of the kingdom (see on 3:2). We often have "of God" added to specify which kingdom is in mind, but in this context that is not necessary.

45. πονηρός is used in Matthew twice as often as anywhere else in the New Testament (26 times; Luke has it 13 times). It may be used of evil actions or of evil people, and here *the* evil one clearly designates Satan.

46. ἁρπάζω conveys the notion of violence, "snatch," "seize." Cf. BAGD, "*snatch, seize,* i.e. take suddenly or vehemently . . . of seed already sown *tear out.*"

heart. The verb *sown* is in the perfect, which points to a firm lodgment; perhaps we can say that the seed is beginning to put down roots. The implication of *heart,* which refers to a person's innermost being, is that Jesus is speaking of something more than mere outward hearing. The word points to a certain receptiveness; this person is not hostile to the message. The hearer knows that there is some spiritual truth here intended for his profit, but since he does not act on it, he soon finds that what he heard is lost. The failure to attend to the message and to find out what it means results in total loss, first of the message and ultimately of the hearer. Jesus explains, *"This is he who was sown beside the path."* In the parable he had the neuter plural, proper to seeds, but in the interpretation he emphasizes the people who respond to the seeds in such different ways (cf. *JB,* "this is the man who received the seed on the edge of the path"). *Beside the path* reproduces the language of the parable.

20. In the previous verse we moved from the neuter ("that which was sown") to the masculine, but here we have the masculine throughout. He who was sown *on the rocky places* stands for the person who receives the word straightaway and does so *with joy;* the picture is one of happy enthusiasm. Unfortunately, as we shall see, it is all too shallow, but the joy and the enthusiasm are to be noted.

21. *Yet* marks something of a contrast with the preceding; despite the joy and the initial growth the end result of this piece of sowing is tragic. It is put in two ways: the man *has no root in himself* and he *is temporary.* The lack of root points to the real problem: like seed in a place that lacks depth of soil, this superficial hearer lacks depth. With that is joined *but is temporary* ("has no staying-power," *REB*).[47] Jesus explains this by referring to the time of testing that will surely come to all believers. Sooner or later all face *trouble*[48] such as *persecution;* there is no easy way for the servant of God. When trouble of this sort comes to the shallow enthusiast, the pretty bubble is burst and the profession of loyalty is exposed for the sham it is. *Immediately,* the same word as that used for the joyful reception of the word in verse 20, signifies that the test shows the person up straightaway; he is no more than a fair weather adherent. Most translations say that he "falls away" (so, e.g., *NRSV, NEB*), but there is something more than falling. He *takes offense.*[49] That is to say, he comes to regard adherence to Christ as something of a trap; if it means persecution he wants nothing

---

47. ἀλλά is the strong adversative; far from being deep-rooted and therefore well established, he is temporary. πρόσκαιρος (in the New Testament once in each of four books) signifies "for a time, temporary, transient."

48. Matthew uses θλῖψις 4 times. The word denotes heavy pressure and is used, for example, of treading out the grapes, when there is pressure to the point of bursting. It links naturally enough with διωγμός (here only in Matthew, 10 times in the New Testament). This points to a specific trouble, that of persecution.

49. σκανδαλίζω connects with σκάνδαλον (see on 5:29), the bait stick of a trap. When the animal or bird touches the σκάνδαλον, it is trapped. The word often means "cause to sin" or the like.

to do with it. He is repelled. The time of trial means the end of this person's adherence to Christ.

22. Again we have the masculine, with its emphasis on *he who*. The one sown *among the thorns* is one who really listens to the word. He is no hardened rejector, nor a man given to shallow enthusiasm. But his attention to the word has to be understood in the light of the other truth that he is caught up in the affairs of this life. Jesus specifies two things that especially preoccupy him. *The worry of the world*[50] is something with which every reader can empathize. It is one of the conditions of living here on earth that we do not know what a day can bring forth, and it is another of those conditions that we can always think of something that threatens us and of something that we would like but do not have. It is possible to be so taken up with the contemplation of the threats and opportunities of life that the word from God that we receive and welcome does not get sufficient attention. Jesus says that these worldly concerns *choke*[51] the word. One life can hold only so many things, and he is referring to a life that is so full of worry that there is no room for serious attention to the word of God. With worry Jesus links *the deceitfulness of wealth.*[52] To the poor riches seem desirable possessions that liberate the holder from many worries, and, of course, there is an element of truth in this. But things are not always what they seem (cf. Phillips, "illusions of wealth"); riches also bring problems. There is, for example, the problem of holding on to them, for there are always those who try to rob the owners in one way or another. And there can be an insidious consequence of being wealthy; the rich may so enjoy having riches that they find themselves caught up in the pursuit of more wealth and end on a treadmill, rich, but never rich enough.[53]

23. Finally Jesus comes to the seed that fell in a good place. Again we have the masculine, as the emphasis is placed on the person who receives the seed rather than the seed itself. The seed that fell into good soil finds its meaning in the person who *hears the word and understands it;* this is not a careless and unheeding person, nor one whose life is distracted by other considerations. The person receives the word with intelligent appreciation and acts on it. The result is that he indeed[54] *bears fruit and*

---

50. μέριμνα occurs here only in Matthew; it signifies "care, anxiety" and the like. In Mark and Luke the word is plural, but to Matthew the worry of being in the world is one whole rather than a group of unconnected worries. *World* is the translation of αἰῶνος, "age" (see on 12:32); it includes the whole of this earthly life. Here there is probably also a contrast with "the age to come."

51. συμπνίγω means "(crowd together and) choke" (BAGD). It may be used of people crowding together (Luke 8:14), but here of the crowding that squeezes out the life.

52. ἀπάτη can mean deceit or, as here, deceitfulness. πλοῦτος occurs only here in Matthew. It denotes external possessions of any kind, "wealth," "riches" (it can be used of spiritual possessions, Rom. 2:4, etc.).

53. Calvin envisions a universal application: "There is no-one who has not a huge crop, a veritable forest, of thorns. . . . Hardly one in ten will take the trouble to cut back the thorns, let alone root them out" (II, p. 72).

54. δή occurs here only in Matthew. It is a particle that never comes first in its clause;

produces.[55] There are three groups, those that produce a hundredfold, those that produce sixtyfold, and those that produce thirtyfold. Commentators disagree as to whether these figures are an exuberant exaggeration to bring out the bountiful nature of the crop or whether they are meant to be taken literally. Without knowing the seed, it is not easy to be dogmatic. Maize, for example, might well produce a hundred or more seeds, though with wheat that is not quite so likely. But in any case Jesus is making the point that in good ground carefully nurtured seeds will produce an abundant harvest. It may also be significant that not all produce the same amount; there are different responses that are accceptable.

√4. The Parable of the Weeds, 13:24-30

> [24]He put another parable before them, saying: "The kingdom of heaven is likened to a man sowing good seed in his field. [25]But while men were sleeping, his enemy came and sowed weeds in the middle of the wheat, and went away. [26]When the grain sprouted and produced a crop, then the weeds appeared too. [27]But the slaves of the householder came and said to him, 'Sir, did you not sow good seed in your field? Whence then does it have weeds?' [28]And he said to them, 'An enemy did this.' And the slaves say to him, 'Do you want us, then, to go off and gather them up?' [29]But he says, 'No, lest as you gather up the weeds you root up the wheat with them. [30]Let them both grow together until the harvest; and at harvest time I will say to the harvesters, "First gather the weeds together and bind them into bundles to burn them up, but gather the wheat into my barn."' "

This parable is found only in Matthew, who has it as the first of a series of parables specifically said to refer to the kingdom of heaven. It has a strong eschatological emphasis, even though it says important things about the admixture of those who belong to the kingdom and those who do not in the time before the end. It is a story that people who lived close to the land could well appreciate.

24. Jesus *put another parable before them.*[56] *Them* will mean the people generally, not the disciples (cf. vv. 34 and 36). For *the kingdom of heaven*

---

it indicates that something is definitely established, here "he is just the man who" (BDF, 451 [4]); they add, "good classical usage."

55. Matthew has two words, καρποφορεῖ and ποιεῖ, whereas in both Mark and Luke there is only the former. The former verb means "bears fruit" and is used both literally and metaphorically; the latter simply means "makes," but it is used of the ordinary processes of plant life (cf. 3:10). Here it is used of the differentiation between what one seed produced and another.

56. παρατίθημι signifies "put or place before," here in the way of teaching. Carr points out that in Homer the usual meaning was for setting food before a guest, a use that continued and that we find in Mark 6:41; Luke 11:6, and elsewhere. Matthew uses the verb only twice. ἄλλος is a common Matthean word, occurring 29 times, a total exceeded only by John with 34. It normally signifies another of the same kind.

see on 3:2; it is a major thrust of Jesus' teaching as recorded in this Gospel. And it is a theme that recurs throughout the rest of this chapter. It was important that Jesus' followers should have a good grasp of teaching on this subject. Jesus likens[57] the kingdom to a man[58] sowing his crop. Jesus specifies that he sowed *good seed*,[59] his word for *good* being that used for the *good* ground in the preceding parable; it indicates careful choice of the right seed for his purpose. Matthew is fond of referring to fields, and he has the word *field* more than anyone else in the New Testament (16 times).

25. There is some adversative force in *But*;[60] over against the careful preparation for a good crop there comes the evil act of an enemy. He moved while people were asleep and thus could do what he wanted unobserved. He proceeded to sow[61] weeds[62] right where the crop was growing. *In the middle* does not, of course, mean that the sowing was confined to the center of the field; rather, it signifies that it extended through the crop. We find now that the crop was wheat (darnel looks much like wheat, which would make the second sowing difficult to detect). The enemy sowed and departed.

26. Nothing the intruder had done was obvious until the grain began to grow.[63] When the ears of wheat began to appear and the plants *produced a crop*, literally "made fruit,"[64] it became obvious that some of the plants were not wheat. Before that the weeds appeared as wheat.

27. The slaves would have been more closely occupied with the management of the field than their master,[65] and thus it was they who

---

57. ὁμοιόω is used 8 times in Matthew, just over half its 15 occurrences in the New Testament. It means "to declare to be like."

58. It was not necessary for Matthew to include the word ἀνθρώπῳ (the article with the participle would have been sufficient). He may be giving some emphasis to the fact that it was a *man* sowing, but there seems to be no reason for this, and in any case what would it mean? There is probably no more to it than that Matthew is fond of the word and uses it often (112 times; no other book has it so often).

59. This is Matthew's first use of σπέρμα, a word he will use 7 times in all. It is interesting that he has recounted the parable of the sower without using the word once. σπέρμα is used of the seed of plants, of male semen, and of descendants.

60. δέ.

61. This is the one place in the New Testament where the verb ἐπισπείρω is found. It mostly seems to mean "sow again," "sow with fresh seed." MM notes the use of the cognate noun for re-sowing or second crops. ἐπί has the force of "upon," "over."

62. ζιζάνια, which is usually understood as darnel, a troublesome weed that resembles wheat (*REB* translates "darnel").

63. *Grain* renders χόρτος, which properly means "an enclosed place" and thus a place for feeding. It is an easy step to "fodder," and in the New Testament that seems to be its usual meaning (in Matthew's other two uses of the term the meaning appears to be "grass," 6:30; 14:19). Here it refers to the seed that will in due course produce fodder. βλαστάνω has the meaning "sprout" (it is used of Aaron's rod, Heb. 9:4). While this is included here, the meaning is clearly more than sprouting: the seed produced plants that could be recognized.

64. Black takes "made fruit" as a Semitism, found in both Hebrew and Aramaic (Black, p. 101).

65. He is here called the οἰκοδεσπότης, the master of the house or householder (Matthew

first came to recognize what had happened. They used the respectful *"Sir"* in their address (the appropriate way for slaves to speak to their owner) and asked him whether he had not sowed good seed (they will mean "caused good seed to be sowed"; it was they, not he, who had done the actual sowing). The answer to their question was not in doubt,[66] so they proceed to another asking where the weeds came from. Their *then* really means "therefore": in view of the fact that you had only good seed sown, what is the origin of the weeds?

28. There may be some adversative force in the master's answer,[67] as he responds to the bad news brought by his slaves. His answer is prompt and accurate as he recognizes the hand of *an enemy* in what had happened. Actually he says "a hostile man," and while "man" is redundant (the adjective is often used by itself with the meaning "enemy"), it may put some emphasis on the fact that what had happened was of human origin. They were not faced with some curious plant mutation or with a supernatural intervention. The slaves respond (the tense of the verb changed to the present for greater vividness) with another question: they wonder whether he would like them to gather up the weeds. Their immediate reaction is that the weeds must be removed and destroyed.

29. *But he* has adversative force. The householder rejects the argument of his slaves with a firm *"No."*[68] He gives a reason.[69] It would be difficult to pull out the weeds without rooting up some of the wheat with them.[70]

30. The householder had a better idea: "Leave them alone."[71] They can grow side by side without detriment to the wheat right up to harvesttime.[72] Then he will issue an instruction to the reapers[73] that Jesus cites as it will be given. When the crop is reaped, the first thing that is to be done is to take the weeds out and burn them. The owner gives priority to getting rid of the weeds; he perhaps reasons that it will not matter greatly if a little of the wheat is pulled up with them at that time, for it could be separated off with little difficulty. The weeds are then to be tied in bundles and burned. *The wheat* has some emphasis from its position; it is the wheat that is important, and the wheat will be gathered into the barn.

---

has the word in 7 of its 12 New Testament appearances). The word refers to him in connection with his household rather than with his field (though that, of course, would be included).

66. The emphatic οὐχί emphasizes that a positive answer is expected.

67. δέ seems to have that meaning here.

68. οὔ is accented; it means "no" rather than "not." Matthew, with 4 uses of the word, equals 2 Corinthians as having the most in the New Testament.

69. μήποτε conveys the idea of purpose, "in order that you may not. . . ."

70. ἅμα is normally an adverb meaning "at once" or "together" (e.g., Rom. 3:12) or "at the same time" (e.g., Acts 27:40). Here it is an improper preposition with the dative, the only place in the New Testament where this occurs.

71. ἀφίημι (see on 12:31) conveys the notion of "let," "allow."

72. θερισμός means "harvest," here referring to the act of harvesting and the time this is carried out (in 9:37-38 it is the crop).

73. θεριστής, "reaper," "harvester," is found again in the New Testament only in verse 39.

Carson makes an important point when he draws attention to the large number of commentators who interpret this parable of the church. But we should be clear that Matthew nowhere equates the kingdom with the church, and he explicitly says that this parable concerns the kingdom. Carson says, "The parable does not address the church situation at all but explains how the kingdom can be present in the world while not yet wiping out all opposition. That must await the harvest. The parable deals with eschatological expectation, not ecclesiological deterioration." If we so choose, we may reflect that the situation described in the parable is much like what we see in our church, but we should not take this as Jesus' meaning. He is talking about the kingdom.[74]

5. More Parables of Growth, 13:31-33

> 31He spoke another parable to them, saying: "The kingdom of heaven is like a mustard seed that a man took and sowed in his field. 32It is the smallest of all the seeds; but when it is grown, it is larger than all the garden plants and becomes a tree, so that the birds of the air come and roost in its branches." 33He spoke another parable to them: "The kingdom of heaven is like leaven, which a woman took and put into three measures of flour, until it was all leavened."

Jesus continues with his parables. Matthew has two of them that bring out the thought of growth before he goes on to the interpretation of the parable of the weeds. These parables are important. Over against the mighty numbers of the worshipers of heathen gods and even of the Jews who acknowledged the true God, those who proclaimed the kingdom were a tiny minority. Jesus teaches them not to be hypnotized by size. These tiny beginnings would grow into something greater by far than any of the religions found in the disciples' contemporary world.

31. The formula Matthew has already employed in verse 24 is varied slightly[75] to introduce another parable of growth, this one contrasting the smallness of the seed with the greatness of the plant. Again the parable is introduced with a reference to *the kingdom of heaven*. The kingdom has many aspects, and the theme is developed throughout this chapter. This time it is *like a mustard seed*[76] that *a man took and sowed*. We notice again Matthew's frequent use of *man*. *Took and sowed* may be a Semitism, or it

---

74. Stendahl favors the view that the parable refers "to the situation which applies in Jesus' earthly ministry, where the ultimate dividing line is not yet drawn," rather than to church discipline.

75. In verse 24 the verb ὡμοιώθη was used, while here the formula is ὁμοία ἐστίν, but there seems to be no significant difference. This new formula is used in introducing the other parables in this chapter.

76. κόκκος means a seed or grain; MM notes its use for pine cones, so it does not necessarily denote a small seed, though, of course, it does here. σίναπι is the mustard plant.

may point to an element of deliberation and purpose. It is not usual to sow just one seed, perhaps especially if it is a very little seed, and if, as here, it is sown in a field rather than a garden.[77]

32. That mustard is *the smallest of all the seeds* does not mean that nowhere is there any smaller seed. It is a way of saying that among all the seeds mustard is a very little seed indeed. It was popularly held to be the smallest of the seeds (Lightfoot cites evidence that the size of the mustard seed "passed into a common proverb," 2, p. 215; indeed, Jesus himself used it that way when he spoke of faith like a grain of mustard seed, 17:20). We should understand Jesus as appealing to this well-known view rather than to his having surveyed all the seeds and come up with the conclusion that there is none smaller than this (in fact, some seeds are smaller). The point of the parable is that this very little seed grows into a sizeable plant, one larger than all the plants of the garden,[78] and indeed in its mature state becomes *a tree*[79] (it can grow to a height of 8 to 12 feet). Jesus passes over the various stages of its growth; for this parable they are irrelevant. He is concerned with the contrast between the tiny seed and the mature majestic plant. *So that* introduces the thought of result;[80] the consequence of the great growth of the plant from the tiny seed is that birds[81] come and roost[82] in its branches (cf. Dan. 4:12, 20-21; Ezek. 31:6). The little detail about the birds roosting fills out the picture of the seed growing into a tree; in the end the mustard plant fulfils all the functions of a tree. This points up the strong contrast between the tiny seed and the tree that is the end result of the seed. The kingdom may be considered insignificant in its beginnings and was doubtless despised by many in Jesus' day because of this. But in the end its growth would be extensive; it would be a very great kingdom indeed. There is also the thought of the continuity between the seed and the grown plant; it is from the mustard seed and that seed only that the mustard plant grew. So it is from Jesus and his little band that the mighty kingdom of heaven would emerge. And if we can reason from the connection with all the nations in the Ezekiel passage, there will be representatives of all peoples in the kingdom.

33. Jesus moves to a twin parable conveying much the same teaching (this one is not in Mark, but it is found in almost identical words in Luke). He repeats the formula of verses 24 and 31 as well as the reference to *the*

---

77. Cf. Bonnard, "As often, the Matthean parable does violence to agricultural reality in order to bring out the unexpected and paradoxical character of Jesus' action."

78. μεῖζον has some emphasis from its position. λάχανον is connected with λαχαίνω, "to dig," and points to plants that are the result of digging, that is, garden plants.

79. δένδρον occurs in Matthew in 12 of its 25 occurrences; it is quite a Matthean word; it signifies a tree over against smaller growths.

80. Robertson sees "actual result" here (Robertson, p. 1000).

81. πετεινόν is the neuter of the adjective meaning "winged"; used as a noun it means "winged thing" and thus "bird." The addition τοῦ οὐρανοῦ makes it clear that birds are meant — "winged things of the sky."

82. κατασκηνόω is connected with σκηνή, "a tent," a place to lodge.

kingdom of heaven. This time he gives us a picture of a woman at work preparing food. Bread was normally baked in homes, not obtained from bakers' shops, and Jesus pictures a woman occupied in this task. Most translations refer to her as using "yeast," but this is not strictly accurate. *Leaven* was a piece of last week's dough, which certainly made this week's dough rise, but was not strictly "yeast."[83] Some exegetes hold that leaven must be taken as a symbol for evil on the grounds that this is the way it is to be understood in the Old Testament (Morgan, for example). But this is not invariably the case, for leaven was sometimes specified for use in sacrificial offerings (Lev. 7:13; 23:17-18). That in some contexts it may be used as a symbol for evil forces does not mean that in others it cannot stand for what is good. We should take this parable as making much the same point as the previous one; they reinforce one another. Jesus speaks of the woman as putting[84] her piece of leaven *into three measures of flour*[85] (the quantity used by Sarah, Gen. 18:6; Gideon, Judg. 6:19; and Hannah, 1 Sam. 1:24) until the whole was leavened. The leaven was but a small amount, but in time it changed the large quantity of flour. Like the previous parable this one brings out the contrast and the continuity between the small beginnings of the kingdom and its great consummation. The little group of disciples might be despised as preaching a kingdom too insignificant to be noticed, but as surely as a tiny piece of leaven had its effect on a large mass of dough, so surely would the kingdom have its effect throughout the world. The parable also makes the point that the power that effects the change comes from outside the dough; the mass of dough does not change itself.[86]

83. See the article by C. L. Mitton, *ET*, 84 (1972-73), pp. 339-43. A. R. S. Kennedy says, "The leaven both of OT and of NT may be assumed to have always consisted of a piece of fermented dough from a previous baking. There is no clear trace, even in the Mishnah, of other sorts of leaven, such as the lees of wine or those enumerated by Pliny (*NH* xviii.26)" (*DB*, p. 573). J. D. Douglas speaks of "fine white bran kneaded with must," "the meal of certain plants such as fitch or vetch," and "barley mixed with water" as ways in which leaven might be originated (*IBD*, II, p. 891). Bread could be made from yeast or leaven, but the continuing use of leaven from batch to batch opened up the way to corruption and infection. The annual destruction of all leaven (Exod. 12:14-15) thus had hygienic as well as religious significance.

84. ἐνέκρυψεν strictly means "hid," but here there is no notion of deliberate concealment; it means no more than "withdrew from sight." The verb occurs here only in the New Testament.

85. ἄλευρον means wheaten flour, normally used in baking bread. σάτον (elsewhere in the New Testament only in Luke 13:21) was a measure usually understood as roughly equivalent to a peck and a half. The precise size of a σάτον is not clear, but three of them make a large amount (*NEB* has "half a hundredweight"; *GNB*, "forty litres"; *NIV*, "about half a bushel or 22 liters"). Gundry thinks that this was "the largest amount of dough a woman could knead" and estimates that it was enough for about a hundred people (Schweizer also thinks that it would feed a hundred, p. 306; Fenton makes it 160), whereas Mounce thinks it would be enough "to feed a large family" (p. 132). Carson has a long note in which he draws attention to the difficulties in working out the amount and the very varied estimates scholars have achieved. That it was a large amount is clear, but we cannot say how large.

86. "Leaven had a bad press in Judaism. . . . So the hearers would be surprised to find Jesus using leaven as an image of the Kingdom. Yet, on second thoughts, that is just what

6. Parables in Prophecy, 13:34-35

> [34]All these things Jesus spoke to the crowds in parables, and without a parable he spoke nothing to them; [35]so that it might be fulfilled which was spoken through the prophet, saying, "I will open my mouth in parables, I will utter things secret from the foundation of the world."

At this point Matthew inserts a characteristic appeal to prophecy. He finds not only individual events in Jesus' life and ministry to be fulfillments of prophecy but also the parabolic method.

34. *All these things* signifies the totality of the preceding section of teaching about the kingdom with its series of parables. The aorist tense in the first *spoke* views that teaching as a whole, but it should not be pressed to mean that it was all given on one occasion (though, of course, it is not inconsistent with that view). The second *spoke* is in the imperfect tense and has the force "he used to speak"; it points to the habitual mode of teaching. Matthew is not saying that Jesus never taught in any other way than by using parables, but he certainly maintains that this was his common practice, and perhaps also that this was the way he taught about the kingdom. The crowds could so easily understand plain teaching on the kingdom in a political sense, but parables made this much more difficult.

35. The purpose[87] is to show that Jesus' use of parables was in order to fulfil prophecy, this particular prophecy being contained in Psalm 78:2[88] (for Matthew the whole Old Testament comes from God and is thus prophetic; for him there is no problem in seeing prophecy contained in a Psalm, and in any case Asaph is expressly said to have prophesied, 1 Chron. 25:2, and to have been a seer, 2 Chron. 29:30). In this context *parables* indicates wise sayings of a pictorial kind in general and is not to be limited to the stories with which we are familiar from Jesus' teaching. From his affirmation of his intention to speak in this way the Psalmist goes on to affirm that what he will say[89] has been *secret from the foundation*

---

his followers must have seemed to respectable Jews. Common uneducated fishermen and farmers, carpenters and women, tax-gatherers and disreputable characters — it would all seem rather distasteful. . . . But God is like that. He takes distasteful characters and transforms them, and then transforms society through them" (M. Green, p. 138).

87. ὅπως is a Matthean word (17 times; next highest is Acts with 14). It may be used as an adverb, but more commonly it is a conjunction indicating purpose. It mostly follows an aorist (though here an imperfect) in a formula indicating the fulfilment of Scripture (as in 2:23; 8:17; 12:17 t.r.). For the formula see on 1:22.

88. Some MSS read "Isaiah the prophet" (א* Θ f1 f13; Zahn accepted this reading, and Fenton thinks that it may be original; *NEB* accepts it), and Jerome speaks of reading "Asaph." The difficulty with the former is, of course, that the words do not come from Isaiah. This inclines some to accept it as the harder reading, but we must also bear in mind a tendency in scribes to insert the name of a well-known prophet, and this probably explains the reading. "Asaph" would have been inserted by some scribe who knew where the words came from.

89. ἐρεύγομαι is scarcely elegant, having the meaning "belch," and thus comes to signify "utter forcibly," "blurt out."

of the world. That is to say, he intends to utter no commonplace, but things that God has revealed. That they have never been known from the beginning of the world[90] indicates that they are not attainable by human search. Asaph picks out significant points in the history of Israel and shows that the divine purpose has been worked out despite the rebelliousness of the people. Just as God's salvation was made clear in Asaph's interpretation of history, Matthew is saying, so is God's salvation brought out in the parables of Jesus.

7. The Meaning of the Parable of the Weeds, 13:36-43

36*Then he left the crowds and went into the house. And his disciples came to him and said, "Explain for us the parable of the weeds of the field."* 37*And he answered, saying, "He who sows the good seed is the Son of man;* 38*and the field is the world; and as for the good seed, these are the sons of the kingdom; and the weeds are the sons of the evil one;* 39*and the enemy who sowed them is the devil; and the harvest is the end of the age; and the reapers are the angels.* 40*Therefore as the weeds are gathered together and burned in fire, so will it be at the end of the age.* 41*The Son of man will send his angels, and they will gather out of his kingdom all the things that cause sin and the people who commit lawlessness.* 42*And they will cast them into the blazing furnace; there there will be weeping and grinding of teeth.* 43*Then the righteous will shine like the sun in the kingdom of their Father. He that has ears, let him hear."*

For a second time Jesus explains the meaning of a parable; on the first occasion it was in response to a question from the disciples as to why he used this method, this time it is in response to their request for an explanation. His reply has a marked eschatological emphasis and makes it clear that he is speaking about what will happen at the end of the age. Then God's righteous purpose will be vindicated and wickedness will receive its fitting recompense.[91]

36. Matthew's favorite *Then* carries us along to the next item in the sequence. As often, this Evangelist speaks of *the crowds,* and he says that at this point in his teaching Jesus left them[92] and went into *the house* (he

---

90. καταβολή is not a common word in the New Testament (11 times, 2 in Matthew). It "is a t.t. for the *sowing* of the seed, for begetting" (BAGD, 2); here, of course, it is rather the casting down of the foundation stone. κόσμου is read by some MSS (ℵ*·c C D L W etc.), but even if it is not read it is implied. Carson, however, takes the passage in the sense "the foundation (of the nation)."

91. As with the parable of the sower, many critics see the interpretation as the creation of the church. But we should bear in mind Hill's point that "parable and interpretation belong, and stand or fall, together. . . . The point of the interpretation, then, is exactly that of the parable itself: only God himself may distinguish the good from the evil: it is God's business alone to decide who belongs to the Kingdom" (p. 235).

92. *KJV* has "Then Jesus sent the multitude away," which is a possible understanding of the Greek. Either way Jesus retired into quietness.

355

had gone out of *the house* in v. 1). Matthew thus takes up the private instruction of those committed to Jesus as against Jesus' public preaching to the crowds. Some students view this as the center point of this Gospel: until now Jesus has been largely engaged in teaching the people generally, but from now on he concentrates on the disciples. Since Matthew puts no emphasis on the words, we can scarcely regard it as his intention to mark the major turning point in his account of Jesus' teaching, but there is undeniably a change of emphasis from here on. Matthew tells us that the disciples approached Jesus and asked for an explanation of the parable of the weeds.[93]

37. Matthew has his common formula for a reply ("having answered he said"), and he reports Jesus' explanation. His series of *ands*[94] links statements that explain the features of the parable in detail. He begins with the man who sows the good seed, who is *the Son of man* (see on 8:20); the seed is *good* (as in v. 24). If the present tense is significant, it may be meant to indicate that the sowing goes on; Jesus is not speaking of a once-for-all piece of sowing, but indicates that he is continually active in his field.

38. *The field is the world* indicates that the good seed is widely distributed. *World* is a term that may have any one of several meanings, but here it clearly denotes the entire population of this inhabited globe. Jesus is speaking of no narrow particularism. It is interesting that *the good seed* is not the words that tell of the kingdom, but *the sons*[95] *of the kingdom*, the people who receive and respond to the word. They are characterized by their relationship to the kingdom; they belong to the kingdom. The weeds also belong — to the evil one! Jesus makes a sharp distinction: in the end people belong either to the kingdom or to Satan.

39. *The enemy* (see on 5:43) picks out the the devil (see on 4:1) as THE foe of God and of good (for that matter of people, too, but this is not stressed in this parable). Satan then brings evil people into God's good world. But they can flourish only for a time, for *the harvest* is coming. It is defined as *the end of the age,* where *end* points to the consummation,[96] and

---

93. διασαφέω is found in the New Testament only in 18:31 and here (it is connected with σαφής, "clear," AS) and signifies "make clear." Evidently the disciples were puzzled by some aspects of the parable at least.

94. ὁ δέ, "and he" or "but he," may have adversative force or may simply carry the narrative along. Taking notice of it makes for untidy English but retains the flavor of the original.

95. Matthew uses υἱός 89 times, which is more than anyone else. The use here with the genitive of a thing is probably a Semitism, indicating someone who shares in the nature of the thing. So sons of the kingdom are characterized by their membership in the kingdom — they are "kingdom people." In 8:12 this expression is used of those who might be expected to be "kingdom people" but are not.

96. συντέλεια is used of "*a joint payment* or *contribution* for public service; hence, generally, joint action (Plat.) 2. in late writers (Polyb., al.), *consummation, completion*" (AS). Matthew has the expression συντέλεια (τοῦ) αἰῶνος 5 times (40, 49; 24:3; 28:20); elsewhere in the New Testament it occurs only in Hebrews 9:26. MM notes the use of συντέλεια for "consummation," and LSJ finds a use for "*the consummation* of a scheme."

age to this whole life. The word may be used of any age, the past, the present, or the future, but in a context like this the present age is clearly in mind; Jesus is speaking of the end of this life as we know it. The picture of harvest is carried on, with the reapers defined as *the angels*.[97] The angels are associated with the consummation elsewhere (16:27; 24:31; 25:31). Jesus assigns to them an important part.

40. *Therefore* leads us to the consequence of the picture Jesus has painted. Since things are to take place as outlined in the parable, there will be the equivalent[98] of the burning of the weeds. The parable led up to the point where the weeds were gathered and burned, and life in this world leads up to *the end of the age* (in v. 39 neither noun had the article; here both have it, but there seems to be no difference in meaning). Jesus is talking about "the end of time" *(REB, JB)*, the completion of all that is involved in this age.

41. For *the Son of man* see on 8:20; at the end of the age he will have the supreme place. Some emphasis is put on *send* by placing it first in the sentence; Jesus is not referring to some function that the angels will naturally perform, but one that they will carry out only because it is he who will send them to do it. They will gather (the same verb as in vv. 28 and 30) the evil people out of the Son of man's kingdom, an expression that indicates that in the end his kingdom will embrace all people, evil as well as good. There is no escaping his rule. *His kingdom* is not a common expression (though cf. 16:28; 20:21; Luke 22:29-30; John 18:36; Col. 1:13, etc.). The ultimate sovereignty is more usually ascribed to the Father, but it is clear that the Son is one with him in the final rule. The reaping process will include gathering *the things that cause sin*[99] as well as the people who do lawless things. In the final state of affairs those traps will be taken away completely. Jesus speaks of people who do *lawlessness*,[100] where the reference will be to the law of God. In this life there are people who overlook or defy the divine law, but that is not permanent: it lasts only for the here and now. The expression reminds us of the importance and the permanence of the divine law. For the thought of the whole parable cf. Zephaniah 1:3.

42. In words reminiscent of Daniel 3:6 Jesus speaks of the fate of the lawless ones. The angels will *cast*[101] *them into the blazing furnace* (lit. "fur-

---

97. For ἄγγελοι see on 1:20. The construction here is a preceding anarthrous predicate that according to Colwell's rule will mean "the angels," not "angels" *(JBL,* LII [1933], pp. 12-21). That is to say, it is "the" angels as a definite group rather than beings who have the general quality of being angels.

98. ὥσπερ is used as the protasis of a comparison, the apodosis being introduced here by οὕτως (32 times in Matthew); it signifies "just as."

99. τὰ σκάνδαλα, for which see on 5:29. It points to the things that trap people and lead them into captivity to sin.

100. ἀνομία is found 4 times in Matthew, but not again in the Gospels or Acts. It can mean "lawlessness" or "a lawless deed."

101. βάλλω is a vigorous word for consigning evildoers to their final place. Matthew uses the verb 34 times, which is more than in any other book.

nace of fire"), which fits in with other passages using the imagery of fire for the final destination of the wicked.[102] In that place *(there)* there will be misery, symbolized by the specification of *weeping and grinding of teeth*.[103] This expression occurs 6 times in Matthew, once in Luke, and nowhere else in the New Testament. It leaves no doubt about the unhappiness of the final state of the lost.[104]

43. At that time (see on 2:7 for Matthew's frequent *then*) *the righteous will shine*. Here *the righteous* are those accepted as righteous on the last great day; the term points to their acceptability, not to their meritorious achievement. *Shine* represents a verb found here only in the New Testament; the comparison to the sun brings out the radiance of the life to which they have come (cf. Dan. 12:3). For *kingdom* see on 3:2; it is mostly in this Gospel the kingdom of heaven, with now and then the kingdom of God, but this appears to be the only place where God's fatherhood is linked with the kingdom. It perhaps brings out the thought that the one who will rule us through eternity is a father to us. The kingdom is not harsh authority but fatherly love. For *He that has ears* see on 11:15. It is an injunction to the listener to understand what he hears.

8. Three Short Parables, 13:44-50

[44]*"The kingdom of heaven is like treasure hidden in the field, which a man found and hid, and from joy over it he goes off and sells all he has and buys that field.* [45]*Again, the kingdom of heaven is like a merchant looking for fine pearls;* [46]*and when he had found one pearl of great price, he went away and sold all he had and bought it.* [47]*Again, the kingdom of heaven is like a dragnet cast into the sea and catching fish of every kind.* [48]*When it was filled, they drew it up on the beach; and they sat down and gathered the good ones into baskets, but the bad they threw away.* [49]*So will it be at the end of the age; the angels will go out and separate the wicked from the righteous,* [50]*and will throw them into the blazing furnace; there there will be weeping and grinding of teeth."*

Matthew proceeds to record three little parables each of which starts with "the kingdom of heaven is like — ." The first two stress the value of the kingdom, and the third the finality of the separation that will take place at the end of this age. All three are found only in this Gospel.

102. πῦρ is used here "of fire that is heavenly in origin and nature. . . . Fire appears mostly as a means used by God to execute punishment. . . . Quite predom. in connection w. the Last Judgment" (BAGD, πῦρ, 1.b).

103. κλαυθμός occurs 7 times in Matthew out of 9 times in the New Testament, while for βρυγμός the figures are 6 out of 7; it always occurs in the phrase we have here.

104. Lenski quotes Trench that whatever the precise meaning of these words, "this at all events is certain, that they point to some doom so intolerable that the Son of God came down from heaven and tasted all the bitterness of death that he might deliver us from ever knowing the secrets of anguish, which, unless God be mocking men with empty threats, are shut up in these terrible words" (Lenski, p. 539).

44. Jesus likens the kingdom to a man who finds *treasure* (see on 6:19) *hidden in the field. Treasure* might denote the place where valuables are kept (2:11), but here it is the valuable thing itself. In a day when places for keeping things safe that we take for granted (like the safe deposits in banks) did not exist people had to make their own arrangements. One method they employed was to bury their valuable possessions (as did the unprofitable servant who hid his talent, 25:25). If anyone did this before going off on a journey and failed to return, the possessions remained there and might be found later through a chance discovery like that in this parable. So too, in frequent wars, people would hide valuables to keep them from looting soldiers, and sometimes the owners would not survive. The *field* might be a piece of ground used for growing crops or grazing animals, but the term sometimes denotes country as opposed to city, so we cannot insist on the location being a farm or the like. When anyone found treasure like this, the legal position appears to have been that the finder was entitled to keep it.[105] But acquiring legal title to such a find was not always straightforward. If the finder was an employee, his employer could argue that he was acting as his agent, especially if the employer happened to own the land where the find was made. And if he was his employer's agent in "lifting" the treasure, then the treasure belonged to the employer. This will be the reason the man hid the treasure instead of "lifting" it straightaway; if he "lifted" it before the field was his, it might be argued that when he did the "lifting" he was acting as the owner's agent. By buying the land before "lifting" the treasure, he removed all possibility of dispute. It is in this connection that we should understand the man's buying the field (that he had to sell all he had to buy it indicates that he was a poor man). Sometimes it is objected that it was not a very honest thing for a man to do to buy up a field in which he knew there was treasure. But in the first instance, Jesus does not say that he kept his knowledge hidden; we cannot say for sure that he did not disclose it. And in the second, the legal position was that the find belonged to him, but buying the field was the surest way of making his possession absolutely secure.[106] In any case Jesus is not dealing with the morality or the legality of the man's action, but making the point that there can be treasure such that it is worth selling everything in order to possess it. So with membership in the kingdom.

Jesus says that the man was very happy over his discovery; finding treasure must surely be a joyful experience. The Greek here could mean "in his joy" *(NRSV)* or "joy of it" (i.e., the treasure; cf. Knox, "for the joy

---

105. "Ownership of landed property is acquired by means of money, deed and possession . . . objects which are usually lifted can be acquired by *hagbahah* only" (*B. Bat.* 86a); *hagbahah* is defined in these terms: "(Lit., 'a lifting'), a legal form of acquisition consisting in the lifting up of the object to be acquired" (Soncino *B. Bat.*, p. 784). This means that in a case like that of buried treasure the man who found it had only to "lift" it to acquire legal title to it.

106. See the discussion by Derrett, *Law*, pp. 1-16.

it gives him"), but in practice there is no significant difference. The man's joy leads him to go off and buy the field, even though this means that he must first sell *all he has.* Jesus is not saying that a man may buy his way into the kingdom; that would fly in the face of all his teaching. The selling of *all he has* is rather a way of bringing out the truth that one should count all well lost for the sake of the kingdom.[107] It may not appear to be riches from the world's point of view, but membership in the kingdom has superlative value.

45. *Again* is used often when a speaker takes up a formula he has used previously. Jesus moves to another parable of the same sort, this time referring to *a merchant*[108] on the lookout for *fine pearls.*[109] Whereas in the previous parable the man apparently stumbled across the treasure by accident when he had no such thing in mind, in this story the man knows quite well what he wants and is definitely on the lookout for the best in the way of pearls (Bruce speaks of the kingdom here as "the object of *systematic quest* and *venturesome faith*). Nevertheless there is still some element of the unexpected in his discovery: "this pearl he did not expect" (Hamann).

46. The quest is successful and the merchant finds just *one pearl,* but it is *of great price.*[110] He acted as decisively and at the same cost as the man in the previous parable. He went off, *sold*[111] everything,[112] and acquired that wonderful pearl. The story is teaching us much the same as did the previous parable. Again we see that it is well to take decisive action while the opportunity is there, and that no cost is too great when it is a matter of gaining the kingdom. The sacrifice of all that a man has is not too much. But in this second parable there is the further point that, whereas the man with the treasure could sell part of it and still be wealthy, the man with the pearl must retain it; his delight was in possessing it, not in the profit he could make from it.

47. With this third parable comes a change of direction. Instead of a

---

107. "When a man will venture nothing for Christ's sake, we must draw the sorrowful conclusion that he has not got the grace of God" (Ryle, p. 152).

108. ἔμπορος (from πόρος, a journey) points to a traveler or a merchant; it meant a *"wholesale dealer* in contrast to κάπηλος 'retailer' " (BAGD). In contrast to the poor man who sold all he had to buy just one field, this man would have been wealthy.

109. *Fine* translates καλός (see on 3:10), which has about it the notion of the beautiful as well as the good (which is especially appropriate here). μαργαρίτης is found 3 times in Matthew, once in 1 Timothy, and 5 times in Revelation only in the New Testament; it cannot be said to be widely used. It means "a pearl" and points to what is of great value. In antiquity pearls were regarded as especially valuable, and they are often classed with gold.

110. πολύτιμος, only twice elsewhere in the New Testament, signifies "valuable," "very precious."

111. The verb is changed from πωλέω in verse 44 to πιπράσκω, a less common verb. But the change appears to be mainly stylistic; there is no significant difference in meaning. The perfect is used in much the same sense as the aorist (BDF, 343[1]).

112. McNeile points out that the expression is "πάντα ὅσα, 'all his possessions,' not πάντας ὅσους, 'all the pearls that he had.' "

third story about the worth of the kingdom we have one that, like the parable of the weeds, tells us about the intermingling of good and bad at the present time and the certainty of their separation at the end of the age. Fisherfolk from around the Sea of Galilee would appreciate the reference to the *dragnet*,[113] which must have been commonly used in that stretch of water. This story differs from both of the previous parables in that, whereas they were concerned only with acquiring one valuable thing, this one speaks of acquiring a host, comprising both what is valuable and what is valueless. There is no discrimination about netting fish; everything in the area, good and bad alike, is caught up.

48. Putting out the net is the first process, but then comes the drawing of it in with all the fish enclosed. The net is said to be *filled*; there has been a good catch. It is drawn up *on the beach*, so Jesus is speaking of the hauling in[114] of the fish at the end of the operation. Sitting was apparently the normal position for the sorting operation, when they *gathered the good ones into baskets* (it is not without its interest that the same verb is used of gathering the evil "out of" the scene in v. 41 and of the good "into" their place here).[115] The bad[116] were discarded; they simply *threw* them *away*. They had no value, so what else could fisherfolk do with them?

49. *So will it be at the end of the age* is repeated exactly as in verse 40 (where see notes). Again *the angels* are seen in their function at the end of time. They will *go out*, but nothing is said about the place from which they will make their exit. It is possible that we should understand some such words as "from heaven," but more probably the verb means that they will "make an appearance" or perhaps that they will commence their task. That task is described as separating[117] *the wicked from the righteous*. The former term refers, of course, to those who have lived evil lives and have not repented and sought the divine forgiveness. *The righteous* are those who are accepted by God, those who are adjudged as in the right when they are judged before the divine tribunal. It is easy to misinterpret this

---

113. σαγήνη (here only in the New Testament) appears to have denoted a seine type net, with ropes at the top and weights at the bottom to keep it vertical. One end could be secured to the shore while a boat dragged the other end through the waters in the shape of a semicircle (the maneuver could be employed, of course, from two boats). When the fishermen went ashore and hauled in the net, all the fish enclosed were trapped. See C. G. Rasmussen, *ISBE*, III, p. 524.

114. ἀναβιβάζω occurs here only in the New Testament.

115. The neuter τὰ καλά is to be noted (ἰχθύς is masculine): "good things." Are we to understand this to mean "good fish" or were other things than fish included in what was caught in the net? ἄγγος means a "container" and could be a vessel of any sort. But fish seem normally to have been put into baskets.

116. τὰ σαπρά; the word means "decayed," "rotten," but this can scarcely be the meaning when used of fish brought directly from the sea. It will mean fish whose use was prohibited (Lev. 11:10-12), useless fish, fish unsuited for the market.

117. The verb is ἀφορίζω, "to mark off by boundaries" (AS), but here it signifies taking the wicked out from among the righteous. Cf. 25:31-32.

361

as though Jesus were talking of an ethical virtue and holding that those who have attained this virtue by their own efforts are righteous.[118] But throughout this Gospel there is an emphasis on the "little ones," the "poor," those who have no merit of their own, and it is those of whom Jesus speaks here. Those who are finally *righteous* are those who realize their own shortcomings and rely on God's mercy.

50. This verse is identical with verse 42. See the commentary there.

9. The Householder, 13:51-52

51"Have you understood all these things?" They say to him, "Yes." 52And he said to them, "Therefore every scribe who has become a disciple in the kingdom of heaven is like a man who is a householder who brings out of his treasure things new and old."

Matthew rounds off the teaching session with a little section on understanding Jesus' teaching and the importance both of the new and the old teachings. This is found only in Matthew's Gospel.

51. This is the end of a solid session of teaching, and Jesus asks the disciples whether they have understood. They are in no doubt that they have understood, and they reply briefly, *"Yes."*[119] This may perhaps be a trifle glib, for there is evidence in the remainder of the Gospel that their understanding was somewhat imperfect. But Jesus raises no question, and we may be sure that, with whatever uncertainty there may have been about details, they had understood the main thrust of what Jesus had said. At any rate there were no questions.

52. Since the meaning of this little parable is not as obvious as is that of some of the other parables, there have been many interpretations (see Carson). We should probably reject interpretations that see a class of Christian scribes or that see Jesus as the householder. It is more likely that he is adding a little postscript about the happy state of the well-instructed disciple. *Therefore* connects with the preceding; because of their understanding certain things follow. For *scribe* see on 5:20; mostly in the Gospels it is used in a pejorative sense for learned people who strongly opposed Jesus and whose understanding of the real meaning of the law was superficial. But here it is not such scribes who are in mind, but one whose studies proceed from a genuine humility and lead him into a true understanding of the things of God. Jesus speaks of him as having *become a*

---

118. But cf. G. Schrenk, "There is a deep gulf between the NT δίκαιος and the Greek ideal of virtue, which isolates man in independent achievement" (*TDNT*, II, p. 187). See further my discussion of the righteousness terminology in *The Apostolic Preaching of the Cross*[3] (London and Grand Rapids, 1965), chs. VIII, IX.

119. ναί occurs 9 times in Matthew; it is the normal particle of affirmation.

disciple[120] *in the kingdom of heaven,* which points to the truth that the scribe in question has not only applied himself to the teaching Jesus has been giving but has also committed himself to all that the kingdom stands for. Jesus likens such a person to *a man* (notice Matthew's fondness for this word; he could have made the point by referring only to a householder, and most translations omit *man*) *who is a householder,*[121] and thus a significant person, one with possessions. *Treasure* may denote the container in which valuables are kept or the treasure itself (as in v. 44); here it clearly refers to the container. The good householder has in his treasure box some new things and some old things: he despises neither the new nor the old as such. It is the temptation of both the radical and the conservative to value the one too highly and the other too lightly. Jesus is pointing out that there are fresh insights that are of value and that there are also teachings that have stood the test of time. If the word order is significant, the new matters more than the old and Jesus is saying that the new teachings his followers are embracing do not do away with the old teachings (those in the Old Testament), but are the key to understanding them. The new age has dawned, and it is only in recognition of that fact that the old can be understood in its essential function of preparing the way for the new.

IV. THE END OF JESUS' MINISTRY IN GALILEE, 13:53–18:35

Although Matthew has not tried to disguise the fact that there was some opposition to Jesus from the first, his book so far has been mostly concerned with the wonderful teaching of Jesus and with the way people flocked around him to hear him teach and to see the miracles he did. But this did not last. Matthew now makes it clear that the opposition grew. There were still faithful and loyal followers, but in these chapters he tells us of people who failed to respond in the right way. We see the opposition growing and becoming increasingly bitter; in time it would lead to the cross. Matthew begins with two stories of rejection: the rejection of Jesus by the people of Nazareth and the rejection of John the Baptist, slain at the hands of Herod. These two stories make a fitting introduction to the next section of this Evangelist's narrative.

120. μαθητευθείς (the verb occurs in the New Testament only 3 times in Matthew and once in Acts). *KJV* translates "is instructed," and this indeed brings out some of the meaning, for the word certainly contains the thought of being taught. But there is also the thought of commitment, of having been "discipled." Cassirer renders, "when a teacher of the law becomes a learner in the kingdom of heaven."

121. οἰκοδεσπότης is another Matthean word (7 times in this Gospel out of 12 New Testament occurrences). Some translations make him the "owner of a house" (as *NIV, GNB*) or "head of a household" *(NASB).*

A. A PROPHET WITHOUT HONOR, 13:53-58

53And it came about that when Jesus had finished these parables, he went away from there. 54And when he had come to his hometown, he taught them in their synagogue, so that they were astonished and said, "Where did this man get this wisdom from, and the miraculous powers? 55Is not this the carpenter's son? Is not his mother called Mary, and his brothers James and Joseph and Simon and Judas? 56And his sisters, are they not all with us? Where then did this man get all these things?" 57And they took offense at him. But Jesus said to them, "A prophet is not without honor except in his own hometown and his own household." 58And he did not do many miracles there on account of their lack of faith.

All three Synoptists tell of a visit Jesus paid to his hometown, though neither Matthew nor Mark mentions its name, and only Luke says that it was Nazareth. It is not certain that the visit in Luke is the same as that in Matthew and Mark: it seems to be located earlier and contains an account of Jesus' sermon in the synagogue that is lacking in Matthew's account, as is the attempt to throw Jesus over a cliff. Earlier Matthew spoke of Jesus as going away from Nazareth (4:13), which might refer to an earlier visit. All the accounts agree that Jesus received a poor reception in his hometown. Luke has far and away the longest narrative, including as it does Jesus' sermon in the synagogue. As is usual, Mark's narrative is longer than that of Matthew (127 words, compared to 106). But Matthew has the essentials; he makes it clear that the people of Nazareth were astonished at Jesus' wisdom and his miraculous powers. But they still rejected him.

53. For *And it came about that* and its place as marking the end of a major discourse and a transition to another section see the note on 7:28. The construction is often used to carry the narrative along in Luke (and in the Old Testament), but Matthew has only five examples; this one points to the end of the teaching session in which Jesus had told *these* parables, that is, those Matthew has just narrated. Jesus *went away from there*, which means that he left the place by the sea (v. 1) where Matthew locates the teaching of the parables. He gives no indication of whether Jesus embarked on a preaching tour, or whether he decided to rest for a time or engage in some other activity. Matthew simply marks the end of the parable session and moves on to Jesus' visit to Nazareth.[122]

54. Jesus came to his *hometown*.[123] Matthew says nothing about what

---

122. μεταίρω is not a common word, being found elsewhere in the New Testament only in 19:1. AS gives its meaning as "to remove" and notes that "to depart" is unclassical. ἐκεῖθεν is a favorite Matthean word (12 times).

123. πατρίς is strictly the feminine of πάτριος, but it is used to mean one's "fatherland," "home land," or, as here, "hometown."

he did there until he went to the *synagogue* and began to teach (the imperfect is probably inceptive; so *NIV*, "began teaching"). The synagogue (see on 4:23) was the center of community life; this is Matthew's last mention of a synagogue (though he has a couple of references to what went on "in synagogues," 23:6, 34); from this point on Jesus' ministry was carried on outside official Judaism. The synagogue exercised a variety of functions; in a small town like Nazareth it would be especially important. Here what is to the fore is the fact that it was a place for teaching, and Matthew is interested in Jesus' function as teacher. He does not tell us how Jesus came to be teaching, but it was common for synagogue officials to invite visitors to teach, and they would certainly be interested to hear what one of their own people had to say. Matthew does not tell us what Jesus said, only that it impressed the hearers, with the result that they *were astonished*.[124] They were impressed by two things: Jesus' *wisdom* and his *miraculous powers*. They asked where he got these things from: he certainly did not get them from Nazareth. The question of origin was important for them: Did these things come from God? Or were they of human or even demonic origin? *Wisdom* is a word covering a wide range, from shrewdness in ordinary daily life to "mental excellence in its highest and fullest sense" (AS); in the New Testament it is used of purely human wisdom but also of the divine wisdom and the wisdom God gives to people. The Nazarenes spoke of *this* wisdom, so it was wisdom that Jesus demonstrated in his teaching that impressed them. He was wise beyond the possibilities of a village sage, and they recognized this. With this they join *miraculous powers* (or "mighty works," "miracles"),[125] which presents us with a problem because Jesus did not do many such works in Nazareth (v. 58) and none is recorded up to this point. It may be that Jesus did do something that astonished them (and which the Gospels do not record), or, more probably, they may be referring to what they had heard about him. They are not denying that Jesus had *wisdom* and *miraculous powers*; they only question the source.

55-56. They explode in a series of questions stressing the fact that Jesus was no more than "one of us." The questions are expressed in such a way as to look for the answer "Yes." There may be a note of contempt in their use of "this" in their first question, for the term often conveys the notion of "this fellow." They start with his parentage as they knew it, asking "Is he not *the carpenter's*[126] *son?*" (Mark has "Is he not the car-

---

124. ἐκπλήσσω properly means "to strike out, drive away," but comes to mean *"to strike with panic* or *shock, to amaze, astonish"* (AS).

125. The word is δύναμις, commonly used in the Synoptic Gospels for Jesus' miracles. It points to the power that enabled him to accomplish things beyond the reach of ordinary mortals.

126. τέκτων (used elsewhere in the New Testament only in Mark 6:3) could be used of any craftsman, but it is mostly used for a worker in wood, a carpenter. MM cites a passage

penter?"), and move on to speak of his mother, whose name is *Mary*. For good measure they add *his brothers* and give their names. They go on to *his sisters*, though without giving their names. But they are *all with us*.[127] That is the point. Jesus comes from a village family, and that is proved by the fact that the father and mother, the four boys, and the girls are all well known to the speakers and perhaps still living there. There is no denying that Jesus did not belong with the higher-ups. He is a villager, they are saying, just like them. They ask where he got *all these things*. In view of his family connections, they are reasoning, his rightful place was in their own community, doing the things that villagers did. He had no business teaching people and doing miracles. In their minds they cut him down to size.

57. And because they saw him as no more than another villager like them, they *took offense*[128] *at him*.[129] He did not fit into their categories, so they rejected him. This led Jesus to speak about the way *a prophet* is commonly treated. Matthew is more than a little interested in prophets; he uses the word "prophet" more often than does any other writer in the New Testament (37 times; next is Acts with 30). It refers to the great religious leaders who spoke the word of God, not by way of reinterpreting words spoken previously, but as those in direct touch with God who passed on what God said. It is used of the great religious figures of the Old Testament who set forth the way of God, and it is used of John the Baptist (14:5; 21:26). Here in what may have been a proverbial saying Jesus clearly uses it of himself. This is an important claim, for, apart from John the Baptist, there had been no prophet for centuries. Jesus had immediate communion with the Father, and he could and did authoritatively set out what God said. But what God says is not immediately obvious to people in general, nor is it often palatable. So a prophet is often rejected. Jesus points out that this is particularly true of those who know him best, those *in his own hometown* and especially those of *his own household*. Like Jesus' own earthly family, they find it difficult to think that one of their own

---

where it is used of a sculptor but agrees that it mostly means a carpenter. There is no reason for seeing any other meaning here. Albright and Mann translate "builder," and say that the word "has a wide range of meanings, from a shipbuilder to a sculptor, but it generally indicates a craftsman of considerable skill. The word can even be used of a physician" (pp. 172-73). Moffatt has "joiner."

127. πᾶσαι is feminine, "all the sisters." On πρὸς ἡμᾶς Turner remarks, "instead of class. Attic παρ' ἡμῖν, marking the Hellenistic preference for accus." (M, III, p. 273).

128. The verb is σκανδαλίζω, the one that speaks of the bait stick of a trap, which when touched by an animal or bird sets the trap in motion. They viewed Jesus as someone who meant trouble, and they saw no further ("by refusing to believe in him or by becoming apostate fr. him a person falls into sin," BAGD, 1.b). G. Stählin points out that in the Gospels this verb is always used for "the reason for going astray or falling, the reference in each case is to Jesus"; he goes on to say that the expression is the opposite of believing in him (*TDNT*, VII, p. 349).

129. Causal use of ἐν.

could possibly be different. He grew up with them, he belongs to them, he cannot be different from them. It is sobering to reflect that what is true of prophets in general Jesus experienced too.

58. The story concludes with the sad comment that Jesus *did not do many miracles* in Nazareth. This is seen by many as a contradiction of Mark, who says that Jesus could not do any miracles there. But this is not quite accurate. Mark goes on to say, "except that he laid his hands on a few sick people and healed them" (Mark 6:5). Matthew incidentally does not mention these healings. Both Evangelists are saying that in his own hometown Jesus met with unbelief and that he did not do many miracles, though he did do some.[130]

130. The question of the limitation posed by unbelief is a difficult one. We cannot say that Jesus never healed unless the patient had faith, for there was the lame man in John 5 who knew nothing about Jesus, not even his name. There is similarly no room for faith in the story of the raising from the dead of the son of the woman of Nain; Jesus met the cortège, stopped it, and called the young man back from the dead, but nobody is said to have believed in him. We could similarly cite the healing of the Gadarene demoniac and other miracles. We may say that Jesus commonly worked his miracles in an atmosphere of faith and that normally only those with faith were in a position to receive healing at his hands. But at Nazareth we are dealing with outright rejection and hostility; we cannot expect miracles in such an atmosphere.

Matthew 14

B. The Death of John the Baptist, 14:1-12

¹At that time Herod the Tetrarch heard the report about Jesus. ²And he said to his servants, "This is John the Baptist; he has risen from the dead, and therefore miraculous powers are at work in him."

³For Herod had arrested John, bound him, and put him in prison because of Herodias, the wife of his brother Philip. ⁴For John had said to him, "It is not lawful for you to have her." ⁵And he wanted to kill him, but was afraid of the people, for they held him to be a prophet.

⁶But when Herod's birthday came, the daughter of Herodias danced before them and pleased Herod. ⁷Therefore he promised with an oath that he would give her whatever she asked. ⁸Prompted by her mother, she said, "Give me the head of John the Baptist here, on a plate." ⁹And although the king was grieved, because of the oaths and the guests he commanded it to be given. ¹⁰And he sent and had John beheaded in the prison. ¹¹And his head was brought on a plate and was given to the girl, and she brought it to her mother. ¹²And his disciples came and took the body and buried it; and they came and told Jesus.

Matthew follows his account of Jesus' rejection by telling us of the way John the Baptist was put to death. He has given an account of John's ministry in chapter 3, and he has mentioned him briefly in 4:12; 9:14. He has told his readers also of John's imprisonment, of the questions he asked of Jesus, and of Jesus' response (11:2-19). Now he rounds it all off by telling how John's death came about.[1]

1. *At that time* (again in 11:25; 12:1) is an indefinite expression, indicating that what follows took place at around the time of the events just described, but without attempting any precision. Matthew has the name *Herod* (for the Tetrarch) 4 times in this chapter, but not elsewhere (it is used for King Herod throughout ch. 2). *Tetrarch*[2] means strictly "ruler over a fourth part," but it was also used to denote petty rulers of various kinds

---

1. See Harold W. Hoehner, *Herod Antipas* (Cambridge, 1972), pp. 110-71 for a good account of the problems relating to the Herods and John the Baptist.
2. τετραάρχης from τετράς, "four," and ἀρχή, "rule," thus "ruler of a fourth part." It is used only here in Matthew, and 3 times elsewhere in the New Testament.

(*NEB* has "Prince Herod"). It denoted a status below that of ethnarch (2 Cor. 11:32), which in turn was below a king. Precisely what the reasons were for bestowing any of these titles and the exact differences they denoted are not now clear; probably the size of the territory to be ruled and the measure of independence the Romans allowed were significant factors. There seems to have been a certain fluidity in the use of the titles; natural human vanity meant that, for example, tetrarchs liked to be called "king" and flattering courtiers were always ready to oblige. People in general may well have used the term "king" of their ruler (Mark speaks of "King Herod" here, and Matthew calls him "the king," v. 9). Archelaus, though an ethnarch, is said to "reign as king" (2:22; see also Josephus, *Ant.* 18.92). King Herod the Great in his will divided his kingdom into three parts; the title Ethnarch was given to Archelaus who ruled over Judea, and Tetrarch to Herod Antipas and Herod Philip. Herod Antipas, the Tetrarch mentioned here, thus ruled one of three parts (not four, as his title suggests); he was Tetrarch of Galilee and Perea 4 B.C.–A.D. 39, and accordingly the ruler over the region in which Jesus lived out most of his life. Herod heard *the report about Jesus.*[3] Matthew does not say who brought the report, but obviously any tetrarch would have sources of information about what went on in his region.

2. Herod reacted by speaking to "his boys."[4] *This is John the Baptist* (for this expression see on 3:1) is a curious reaction. It would seem that Herod had been unwilling to kill John but had been maneuvered into it, and that he still had a conscience about it. He evidently had regarded John as a real prophet and had had a deep respect for him. He should have known that John could not be identified with Jesus, for the ministries of the two had overlapped and Jesus had been active at the very time that Herod had imprisoned John. But he was probably not well informed about what must have seemed unimportant movements at the grass-roots level. In any case superstition and a bad conscience make a strong couple, and they led Herod into this curious affirmation. He goes on to say that *"he[5] has risen from the dead."[6] Therefore* introduces the reason, but the logic of it is far from obvious. If in fact John had come back from the dead, that scarcely seems to be a reason for him to exercise *miraculous powers,* all the more so since John did no miracle (John 10:41). But it is perhaps not too big a step from a man miraculously alive to a man working miraculously; that he was now alive when everyone knew that he had been killed may

3. ἀκοή (see on 4:24) here denotes "what is heard," "a report." The definite article indicates "the" news about Jesus; Herod heard the definitive story. The absence of the article with Ἰησοῦ is unusual in this Gospel.

4. τοῖς παισὶν αὐτοῦ. Clearly the word here refers to servants, apparently those especially close to the ruler.

5. αὐτός puts emphasis on the subject, "he and no other"!

6. ἐγείρω is used of a variety of risings; it is often used of resurrection from the dead. ἀπό is not the usual preposition in such cases (which is rather ἐκ, as in the Markan equivalent of this saying), but it is found again in Matthew in 27:64; 28:7.

have seemed to Herod to mean that he had miraculous power.[7] Herod does not say "he does miracles," but "miracles are at work in him"; clearly the miracles made a deep impression.

3. Now Matthew slips in an account of the events that led up to the death of John. His account is very much shorter than Mark's, but he has the essentials and the reader has a well-rounded account of John's death even if we must look elsewhere for many details. Herod[8] had *arrested* John, we read, *bound* him ("he had him chained," *GNB,* is too explicit; there is no mention of chains), and imprisoned him. He did this *because of Herodias.* This lady was a granddaughter of Herod the Great, being the daughter of his son Aristobulus. She married her uncle Herod Philip (who is to be distinguished from the tetrarch Philip, Luke 3:1), who was half brother to Herod Antipas.[9] Herod Philip and Herodias had a daughter, Salome. Herod Antipas married a Nabatean princess (whose name is not known), the daughter of King Aretas, but he and Herodias fell in love. They agreed to marry, and Herodias left his half-brother Herod Philip (as Matthew says, she was *the wife of his brother Philip;* she was also his niece). The daughter of Aretas got wind of what was happening and fled to her father, who promptly went to war with Herod and defeated him (which provoked Roman intervention).[10] It was a tangled and complex situation, but what is clear is that the marriage of Herod Antipas and Herodias was contrary to Old Testament law (Lev. 18:16; 20:21).

4. Matthew has explained that John's imprisonment was on account of Herodias, but he has not explained how this came about. Now he tells us that the Baptist had said or, better, "used to say"; the tense is imperfect,[11] *"It is not lawful for you to have her."* The marriage was a clear breach of the law of God, but the Herods had little regard for the laws of God and their marriages and intermarriages make a bewildering pattern.[12] They saw themselves as above the laws that governed their subjects. Not so John.

---

7. For δύναμις see on 7:22; here the definite article points to the miracles of which Herod had been hearing, not theoretical miracles.

8. Ἡρῴδης lacks the article in verse 1, but has it here and in verse 6; "the" Herod, mentioned above. A number of MSS read τότε here, but this is a frequent Matthean word and it may well have been inserted to make clear that "the situation reflected in ver. 3 antedates that of verses 1 and 2" (Metzger). But this is sufficiently indicated by the use of the aorist in the sense of the pluperfect (*MT,* 48); the word should probably not be read.

9. There is a certain confusion in the use of names. Ridderbos says of Herod Philip, "Josephus then calls him by his first name and Matthew and Mark by his second. The same thing in fact happened with the name Herod Antipas, but in reverse order; in the New Testament he is always called Herod, while elsewhere he is called Antipas."

10. Josephus describes these happenings in *Ant.* 18.109-15; in the following section (116-19) he tells of Herod's execution of John the Baptist.

11. Bruce speaks of this as a "progressive imperfect, with force of a pluperfect." But it certainly indicates more than a solitary utterance.

12. Thus Herodias married her uncle Herod Philip and had a daughter Salome. Later Salome married Philip the tetrarch, half brother to Herod Philip. She thus became both aunt and sister-in-law to her own mother!

This man boldly pointed out that the laws of God are as binding on the highest in the land as on anyone else, and he was fearless in his denunciations of evil in high places as in low.

5. Grammatically *he wanted* could refer to John, but the sense makes it clear that Matthew is referring to Herod.[13] We should probably understand this of his initial reaction, for the whole of the present story, and especially verse 9, makes it clear that at this point he was very unwilling to have John executed. This lack of desire was reinforced by the fact that he *was afraid of the people.*[14] Herod may have been more superstitious than religious, but that was not the case with all his people. There were those who could recognize[15] a prophet when they saw one. They recognized that John certainly brought a message from God and that he was rightly called a prophet. Herod might take many actions of which his people did not approve, but he was sensible enough to realize that there was no point in antagonizing them over a man like John. We should bear this in mind when it is contended that there is a contradiction between Matthew and Mark. Matthew, it is said, has altered Mark's story that Herodias wanted to kill John but could not because Herod saw him as a righteous man and therefore protected him, into another story that it was Herod who was the main opponent of the Baptist. But surely the situation that both Evangelists envisaged was that there was hostility from both husband and wife in the palace. Herodias took strong exception to what John had said about her marriage and, careless of the consequences, wanted his execution. Herod also wanted to kill John, but he was not careless of the consequences. He hesitated, for he knew the sort of man John was and was afraid of the reaction from the people if such a holy man were executed.

6. In the modern world birthday celebrations are accepted as important and enjoyable social occasions, but this was not the Israelite custom. Of this present passage F. B. Knutson says, "When Herod celebrated his birthday he was acting in accord with a Hellenistic custom; there is no evidence for the celebration of birthdays in Israel in pre-Hellenistic times" (*ISBE*, I, p. 515). It seems that at first there was a celebration of the birthday only of someone who had died, but in later times this was extended so that there were celebrations of the birthdays of living persons.[16] Herod,

---

13. θέλω (see on 1:19) signifies the action of the will. Herod did not go through with the suggestion, but this is what he wanted to do.

14. ὄχλος means a "crowd" and is often used in this Gospel of people gathered together. But here it does not mean a specific gathering, but the people as a whole, assembled or not. Filson comments, "throughout the story Herod acts in fear and cowardice; he fears John; he fears the Jews who approve John's preaching; he fears to break an unholy oath; he fears to seem weak before his guests; he fears Herodias, whose merciless scheming and hatred are apparent."

15. ἔχω is used here in the sense "consider, look upon, view" (BAGD, I.5; cf. 21:26). ὡς may introduce the characteristic quality of a person, thing, or action (cf. "did not glorify God as [ὡς] God," Rom. 1:21; "condemned as [ὡς] a sinner," Rom. 3:7).

16. There were two words in use: "The distinction between τὰ γενέσια, the commemora-

more of a Hellenist than a Jew, clearly celebrated his birthday with gusto. It is somewhat surprising that *the daughter of Herodias* featured in a public dance of this kind; we would expect that there would be dancing, but it would come from paid performers, not from a princess. This may be the point of the word order: "there danced the daughter of Herodias" with its emphasis on what was actually done.[17] Salome danced *before them*,[18] which makes it plain that it was a public performance. Some dancing meets with approval in Scripture, such as that at the time of the deliverance from Egypt (Exod. 15:20). The Jews also found acceptable the dancing of the maidens at the end of the ceremonies of the Day of Atonement (*Ta'an.* 4:8). But there is something repulsive about a princess performing before a crowd of (presumably) drunken men. However, whatever our scruples, the dance pleased Herod (*REB* has, Herod "was delighted").

7. For this reason[19] he made an extravagant promise, and made it sure by swearing *an oath*. It is not clear why he used an oath; it certainly was not necessary in such a situation. His promise was far reaching: he said he would give her *whatever she asked* (Mark adds that he added, "up to half of my kingdom").[20] The scarcely sober ruler was in earnest about expressing his appreciation of the dancing.

8. But how to take advantage of it? This must have been puzzling as well as exciting for the girl, so she consulted her mother (Mark tells us that she did this; Matthew as usual abbreviates the narrative). It was on her mother's prompting[21] that she asked for *the head of John the Baptist*. Nothing in the narrative indicates that the daughter had any particular animosity against John, but clearly John's accusation had rankled with Herodias more than it did with Herod, and she was able to communicate

---

tion of the dead, and τὰ γενέθλια, the birthday feast of a living man, disappears in late Greek" (MM, which draws attention to examples in the papyri cited in *LAE*, p. 371). The word here is γενέσια, again in the New Testament only in the parallel in Mark 6:21. The plural is usual for a festival, and γενεσίοις γενομένοις is "apparently a dat. absolute" (M, III, p. 243; no other example of the construction appears to be cited from the New Testament).

17. ὀρχέομαι is used 4 times only in the New Testament, here and in Mark 6:22 of Salome's dancing, in 11:17 and in Luke 7:32 of children at play. We have no information about the nature of the dance (the "seven veils" and other suggestions are no more than conjecture), but there is no reason to question Filson's reference to "the no doubt immodest and provocative dance of her daughter."

18. ἐν τῷ μέσῳ, "in the middle"; this scarcely means "in front of the whole group" (*GNB*), but it certainly signifies that the performance was public.

19. ὅθεν means "from where" and may be used of place (25:24, 26), but also, as here, logically: "from which fact."

20. The verb is the middle, αἰτήσηται. J. H. Moulton draws attention to the distinction made by Blass, that "αἰτοῦμαι was used in business transactions, αἰτῶ in requests of a son from a father, a man from God and others on the same lines." Of the middle here Blass says, "the daughter of Herodias, after the king's declaration, stands in a kind of business relation to him," and Moulton comments, "so that the differentia of the middle cited above will hold" (M, I, pp. 160-61).

21. προβιβάζω (here only in the New Testament) is causal of προβαίνω and means "*to lead forward, lead on*; metaph., *to induce, incite, urge*" (AS).

enough of her anger to her daughter to get her to make the request. Some commentators hold that Matthew shifts the blame to Herod's shoulders, whereas Mark makes Herodias the more guilty party. But it is clear from this verse that the proposal for John's execution came from Herodias, not Herod. It was on her urging that Salome specified that she wanted the head *here* (Mark has "at once") and that she wanted it *on a plate*,[22] which seem unusual specifications. Perhaps Herodias feared that Herod would vacillate if he were given the opportunity; after all, his heart was not in it and he did not want to execute John. So the girl says that she wants the head here and now, while her *on a plate* spells execution.

9. The request was far from pleasing to *the king* (this is the only place where Matthew gives him this title);[23] Phillips brings out something of his consternation by translating, "Herod was aghast at this"; alternatively we could understand the meaning as "stricken with grief." Clearly the request was totally unexpected and totally unwelcome. It was no part of Herod's plan to see John dead. But two things weighed with him: *the oaths* and *the guests*.[24] Matthew has referred to only one oath, but there is nothing surprising in the tetrarch's repeating what he had said;[25] his promise was effusive. And while Herod was in many respects an evil man, he did not want to go back on sworn oaths, especially oaths sworn before so many guests.[26] So the oaths and the guests were decisive. He gave the necessary order.[27]

10-11. Herod *sent* and *beheaded* John, there, where he was in the prison. It was against Jewish law to execute a man without a trial, and beheading was not a Jewish form of execution, but Herod could be careless of Jewish law and customs. Josephus tells us that John was imprisoned at Machaerus, and since there was a palace there, evidently that was where the birthday feast and the execution took place. And, as the girl[28] had requested, the head was brought[29] on a plate and given to her. Not sur-

---

22. πίναξ properly signifies something flat like a board; here a *plate* seems the meaning (cf. Luke 11:39).

23. "Since he was called 'king' only by courtesy, Matthew's use of the title here has a touch of irony: a king made the tool of a woman" (Lenski, p. 559).

24. τοὺς συνανακειμένους, "those who reclined with him," that is, at table.

25. Or this may be an example of the "allusive" plural, which "is sometimes used when a class or variety rather than number is stressed" (M, III, p. 25).

26. Derrett points out that there were ways in which Herod might have been released from his oath (*Law,* pp. 339-58). But he evidently preferred not to use them.

27. κελεύω means "to command" ("mostly of one in authority," AS); the verb here has no object, but it is easy to understand "it."

28. κοράσιον is used in the New Testament only in Matthew (3 times) and Mark (5 times); it is the diminutive of κόρη and is used of Jairus's daughter (9:24, 25), who was about age 12 (Mark 5:42). Hoehner estimates that Salome would have been "twelve to fourteen years old" (*Herod Antipas,* p. 156). At this age it would have been natural for her to consult her mother as to what to ask.

29. The verb for "bring" is φέρω: "On the bringing in of a head at a banquet cf. Diog. L. 9,58 — the presence of a severed head did not necessarily disturb the mood at a meal. Appian . . . relates concerning Antony that he had the head of Cicero placed πρὸ τῆς τραπέζης" (BAGD, 4.a.α).

prisingly, she gave it to her mother. It had been the mother's idea, and it was the mother above all who wanted John dead.

12. Matthew rounds off the narrative with John's disciples providing for his burial and then letting Jesus know what had happened. We have met John's *disciples* before, namely when they came to Jesus with John's question (11:2). On this occasion they were apparently not hindered in taking John's body and making arrangements for its burial. We are not told where the burial was carried out, only that it was done (the MSS are divided on whether to read they buried "it" or "him," but there is no great difference). The burial completed, they came and told Jesus. Matthew does not say why they did this, but they would certainly have realized from Jesus' answer to John's question that he was very much in sympathy with John, much more so than, say, the Jewish hierarchy. And Matthew may be saying that some at any rate of John's followers now considered Jesus to be their leader.

C. SOME MIRACLES OF JESUS, 14:13-36

Matthew has sounded the note of rejection, both of Jesus and of John the Baptist, and sad notes will be struck more frequently as his narrative proceeds. But all is not doom and gloom, and he now lets us see Jesus still at work and finding acceptance among the people. He relates a number of miracles, including the feeding of the five thousand, walking on the water, and some healings. Despite the rejections, it is still the same Jesus of whom Matthew writes, the Jesus who does wonderful things.

1. The Feeding of the Five Thousand, 14:13-21

13*Now when Jesus heard this, he went away from there privately by boat to a deserted place; and when the crowds heard of this, they followed him from the towns on foot.* 14*And when he came ashore, he saw a great crowd, and he had compassion on them and healed their sick.*

15*Now when evening came, the disciples approached him, saying, "The place is remote and the time is already late; send the crowds away so that they may go off to the villages and buy themselves food."* 16*But Jesus said to them, "They have no need to go away; you give them something to eat."* 17*But they say to him, "We have here nothing but five loaves and two fish."* 18*But he said, "Bring them here to me."* 19*And he told the crowds to recline on the grass, took the five loaves and the two fish, looked up to heaven, gave thanks, broke the loaves, and gave them to the disciples, and the disciples to the crowds.* 20*And they all ate and were satisfied; and they took up what remained over of the broken pieces, twelve baskets full.* 21*Now those who ate were about five thousand men, apart from women and children.*

All told there are six accounts of miraculous feedings in the Gospels, two each in Matthew and Mark and one each in Luke and John (15:32-39;

Mark 6:30-44; 8:1-10; Luke 9:10-17; John 6:1-15). Loaves and fish often appear in the art of the early church. Clearly the early church was very interested in this aspect of Jesus' ministry. Perhaps this was because believers remembered that God had fed his people with manna in olden days in the wilderness (this is brought out in the discourse in John 6 immediately after the story of the feeding of the five thousand), and they looked forward to the messianic banquet at the end of the age. John says that the miraculous feeding took place near the Passover (John 6:4), so it happened about a year before Jesus' crucifixion. The feeding of the five thousand is the only miracle of Jesus (apart from his resurrection) that finds a place in each of the four Gospels; clearly it was a story that appealed to the Evangelists. We should bear in mind that it was concerned with bread, the basic food. In modern times we have so many other foods that we scarcely realize how central bread was to life in Bible times. But for people then bread was desperately important; it can stand for "necessary food" (e.g., Gen. 3:19, where *NIV* translates the Hebrew for "bread" as "food"; so also in Gen. 28:20 and elsewhere). Similarly the end of a period of drought is signaled by the Lord providing "bread" (Ruth 1:6). Times of trouble may be brought out with expressions like "bread of adversity" (Isa. 30:20) or people seeking for bread (Lam. 1:11). God's provision for his people is spoken of as "bread from heaven" (Neh. 9:15), while blessing may be described as a plentiful supply of bread (Prov. 28:19). A miracle that meant multiplying bread was thus especially significant; it pointed to God's giving his people abundance of blessing.

We should notice that this incident introduces a section in which Matthew brings out the disciples' shortcomings and their failure to understand what Jesus was doing and to believe in him (vv. 15, 26, 30; 15:16, 23, 33; 16:5, 22; 17:4, 16). It is often said that Matthew glosses over the failures of the disciples, so this series of statements should be borne in mind.

The miracle has been understood as a "miracle" that took place in people's attitudes. When the small boy gave his lunch to Jesus, this reasoning runs, he shamed those many who were keeping the food they had brought with them well hidden lest they have to share it. Now they brought it out and shared, and behold! there was enough for all and plenty over. Another suggestion is that we should understand a token meal, something like Holy Communion (indeed, Gundry speaks of Jesus as "the host at this 'Lord's Supper,'" p. 293). But neither suggestion does justice to what the Evangelists say. Any fair exegesis of the Gospels leads us to see a striking miracle wherein the incarnate Son of God multiplied a small amount of food so that there was abundance for the crowds. "It is impossible to reduce the event to ordinary human dimensions. It stands as witness to the fact that God can and does supply human need in the way he sees best" (Melinsky).[30]

---

30. Plummer points out that the supernatural in this story "is confined to what was absolutely necessary, and goes no further. If an exhibition of power had been the main

13. Verses 3-12 have been a parenthesis in which Matthew responds to Herod's view that in Jesus' ministry John the Baptist had been raised from the dead by explaining how that great man died. We should take what he writes now as following on from verse 2 rather than from the immediately preceding. When Jesus heard of Herod's reaction to his ministry, he withdrew[31] from there. Matthew does not say where he went, but it was to *a deserted place* and, since he and his followers went there *by boat*, clearly it was on the other side of the lake (Matthew often has the definite article with "boat," but not here). The destination was *deserted* ("a remote place," REB; not "a desert," for there was grass there, v. 19) and they went *privately*, so evidently they were looking for a place where they could be alone. But such hopes were to be disappointed. Evidently they spoke of their destination, and *the crowds* heard it. They were just as determined to be with Jesus as he and the disciples were to be alone. So the people *followed him*. The Sea of Galilee is not a huge area of water, and it would be fairly obvious from the direction the men in the boat took where they would come to land. The people were *from the towns*, which indicates that the word had spread from the center at which Jesus embarked to other towns. The people went *on foot*; there was no transport, and they evidently had no access to boats.

14. The result was that when Jesus *came ashore*[32] he found a large group of people instead of the solitude for which he had crossed the lake. Matthew ignores the disciples at this point and concentrates on what Jesus saw and did. He saw large numbers of people, and he *had compassion on them*;[33] Jesus was deeply moved at the plight of the afflicted and the poor. So on this occasion he *healed their sick*.[34] Matthew does not qualify this in any way, but leaves the impression that Jesus healed all who were unwell in that crowd. Mark tells us that Jesus taught the people "many things," and Luke that he spoke about "the kingdom of God," but Matthew concentrates on the healing.

15. Matthew moves to the coming of evening, which we must not put

---

purpose, something much more striking might have been wrought. The food might have come down visibly from heaven. It might have been not only multiplied, but distributed miraculously. Ten times the amount that was required might have been provided, and it might have been of a much richer quality" (p. 204).

31. "Went away" translates ἀναχωρέω, which Matthew has in 10 of its 14 New Testament occurrences. It signifies "go away," "withdraw," and is often used of a withdrawal that avoids danger (cf. 2:12-14; 12:15, etc.).

32. ἐξέρχομαι means "go out," but here clearly it is going out of a boat that is meant. The participle is singular; presumably the disciples disembarked at the same time, but Matthew says nothing about that. He concentrates his attention on what Jesus did.

33. For σπλαγχνίζομαι see on 9:36. It is a strong term; Barclay translates here, "He was moved with compassion for them to the depths of His being." Matthew often speaks of "crowds" in the plural, but here ὄχλος is in the singular.

34. For θεραπεύω see on 4:23. ἄρρωστος occurs only here in Matthew (5 times in the New Testament). It derives from ἀ privative and ῥώννυμι, "to strengthen," and thus signifies "feeble, sickly."

too late because of the events that took place after this; late afternoon will be the meaning — perhaps it was after the normal time for the evening meal.[35] *The disciples* is a general expression and could refer to any follower of Jesus, but here it clearly refers to the Twelve (or some of them; Luke has "the Twelve"). These men saw that the day was wearing on, and it seemed that neither Jesus nor the crowd was preparing to bring things to an end, so they took the initiative. They pointed to both place and time: the place was *remote* and the hour was *already late.*[36] They thought it would be prudent to do something about bringing proceedings to a close so that the people would be able to get something to eat. There might not be supplies enough in the villages round about to meet the needs of so many people, but there would, they thought, be better prospects than in a place totally bereft of shops. So they make their suggestion in the form of a command, *"Send the crowds* [this time the word is plural, as often in Matthew] *away."* They consider it important that the people get away from their lonely situation *so that* (the conjunction indicates purpose) *they may go off to the villages and buy themselves food.* We do not know exactly where they were, but it seems that there were no large centers of population nearby. The disciples thought that villages, however, would provide what was needed. Considering the size of the crowd this might have been a trifle optimistic, but at least it was a start; where they were nobody could buy food, but some of them at least would be fed if they went to the neighboring hamlets. And if they spread out, perhaps not too many would go to any one village? Since they speak of buying food,[37] it would seem that people either had not brought food with them or had eaten all they had brought. The disciples were probably hungry themselves, and they knew that many people in the crowd would be more than ready for food. It was therefore important that they be transferred to places where their need could be met.

16. *But* has adversative force; Jesus rejects the suggestion that he should dismiss the crowd. There is no need for that. Matthew's account is shorter than those of Mark and John and not much longer than Luke's, so that there is very little in this account that is not found in the others, but *"They have no need to go away"*[38] is such a touch; only Matthew records these words. The disciples can do better than sending people off, Jesus says, and he goes on, *"You give them something to eat"*;[39] *give* is a command,

---

35. ὀψία occurs in Matthew 7 times, exactly half its New Testament total of 14. He always has it in the expression "when evening came."

36. *Remote* renders ἔρημος, for which see on 3:1; it points to a deserted place ("desolate," *NASB*) where there was no prospect of local help. παρέρχομαι means "to go by, pass by"; it is used of people passing by (8:28), of heaven and earth passing out of existence (5:18), and of the passing of a whole generation (24:34), but this is the only place where Matthew has it of the passing of time.

37. This is Matthew's one use of βρῶμα, and he has it in the plural, "foods"; this, however, does not appear to differ significantly from the singular.

38. ἀπέρχομαι is a favorite word of Matthew's (35 times).

39. ὑμεῖς is emphatic: *You* give them what is necessary.

not a suggestion. Jesus does not say what is to be eaten or how the disciples are to obtain it. He simply turns their attention away from the hopelessness of the situation and their easy solution and invites them to think how they could help.

17. *But* is another adversative conjunction setting the disciples over against Jesus as they reject the suggestion. Matthew uses the present tense *they say*, which gives greater vividness. They explain the slenderness of their limited resources, and they start with a negative "We have not here — "[40] after which they add their exception, "except five loaves and two fish." The "loaf" would have been quite small, perhaps the size of a bun. Five of them might well be eaten in one meal, and the two fish would go with them. In John 6:9 we learn that Andrew told Jesus that a small boy had this food. How did Andrew know? John does not tell us, but the small amount looks like his mother's provision for a small boy's lunch and it is tempting to think that the boy had offered it to Jesus, there being nothing to eat in their deserted situation and no possibility of buying anything. John tells us that the loaves were "barley loaves" (John 6:9), the food of the poor.

18. The disciples had put forward their evidence of this meager supply as a way of indicating the impossibility of their doing anything, but Jesus thinks of it as the basis for action. For the third verse in succession we have an adversative *But* as Jesus rejects the position the disciples were taking up. Without giving any indication of what he was about to do, he told them to bring the food to him, a little detail found in this Gospel only.

19. There is an authoritative note about Jesus' verb for *told*.[41] He is now taking over the situation and giving instructions as to how it is to be resolved. The people are to *recline*[42] *on the grass.* We do not know what their posture was up to this point, but reclining would indicate preparation for a meal. Then Jesus *took* the loaves and the fish. Until now he has given orders but other people have done what had to be done; now Jesus is beginning to act. Looking up[43] to heaven was a normal attitude for prayer (cf. John 17:1), so it was appropriate as Jesus *gave thanks*,[44] the normal

40. ἔχω is common in Matthew (75 times). Here it has no object. It is followed by εἰ μή, "if not, except."

41. The verb is κελεύω, "of verbal orders in general" (AS); it is a command, not a suggestion.

42. ἀνακλίνω occurs again in 8:11, once in Mark, 3 times in Luke, and nowhere else in the New Testament. It means "recline" and does not seem to differ significantly from ἀνάκειμαι. Reclining was the normal posture at a banquet, and France thinks that this may hint at a formal banquet. Though the meal was simple (bread and fish were the food of the poor), this is a formal occasion looking forward to the messianic banquet. Translations like *GNB*, "sit down," miss this point.

43. Matthew has ἀναβλέπω three times, and in both the others it refers to blind people receiving sight. But the word also means "to look up," and there is no doubt that that is the meaning here.

44. The verb is εὐλογέω, which we might translate "blessed." But if we do we should be clear that this does not mean that Jesus imparted a blessing to the bread (Moffatt errs here

Jewish practice before a meal. So was breaking[45] the bread, though this was normally a symbolic gesture and here it is evidently a way of breaking the bread and the fish into pieces for distribution to the multitude. A number of scholars draw attention to the resemblance of the words to eucharistic language (the verbs "took ... blessed ... broke ... gave" occur in the narrative and in every communion service known to us), but this cannot refer to a celebration of Holy Communion. Jesus had not yet instituted that ordinance, there is no use of wine, and fish have no place in the eucharist.[46] Matthew is describing a meal. He tells us that when Jesus had broken the loaves and the fish, he *gave* the pieces to the disciples, and the disciples passed them on to the people.[47]

20. So everybody ate,[48] where *all* makes it clear that the whole multitude was included. That they *were satisfied*[49] shows that Matthew is not talking about a symbol or a token repast. It may not have been a banquet (bread and fish were the food of the poor), but it was a full and satisfying meal (M. Green says, "Those who merely *touched* a crust of bread during the Feeding were filled," p. 149; but that is not what Matthew is saying). This is further underlined with the information that the disciples took up what had not been eaten (John has the information that this was done in response to a command from Jesus). All four Evangelists tell us that what was over amounted to *twelve baskets full.*[50] It would seem that each of the

with "blessed them"). It is a way of referring to a prayer of thanksgiving. One of the oldest forms of prayer among the Jews is the "Eighteen Benedictions," a series of prayers of thanksgiving, each of which begins with "Blessed art Thou ..." and goes on to mention that for which thanks is being given. In the Mishnah we find that the blessing to be said over bread was "Blessed art thou who bringest forth bread from the earth" (*Ber.* 6:1). From the Talmud we find that "A man is forbidden to taste anything before saying a blessing over it" (*Ber.* 35a).

45. κλάω, "break," occurs 14 times in the New Testament; they all refer to the breaking of bread, and most of them are accompanied by a verb expressing the giving of thanks. Matthew does not specifically mention the fish as being broken, but since Jesus took them along with the loaves the presumption is that he shared them too (as Mark says he did, 6:41).

46. But we may say, as Diétrich does, "This brotherly love feast anticipates the Lord's Supper, and beyond that Supper the great gathering of the children of God at the banquet of the Kingdom."

47. Glover comments, "there is *one Mediator who wins God's gifts;* there are many mediators who distribute them."

48. The verb ἐσθίω is used 65 times in the New Testament, of which Matthew can claim 11. Moulton says of it, the verb "is very obviously durative. ... The root *ed* is so distinctly durative that it forms no aorist, but the punctiliar φαγεῖν (originally 'to divide') supplies the defect. It will be found that φαγεῖν in the NT is invariably constative: it denotes simply the action of ἐσθίειν seen in perspective, and not either the beginning or the end of that action" (M, I, p. 111).

49. The verb χορτάζω (connected with χόρτος, "an enclosure," then "a feeding place," and so "food") is used properly of animals with the meaning "to feed, fatten" (AS). It thus comes to signify a satisfying meal.

50. Each of the Evangelists uses the word κόφινος for "basket." It is often said that this term denotes a small container for goods that a traveler might take with him over against σπυρίς or σφυρίς, which is said to be large and able to hold a man (Acts 9:25). But the difference between the two words appears to refer to material, not size. A κόφινος was rigid (made of

apostles had a basket and filled it (the baskets were *full*). So there was an abundant meal, but also there was no waste.

21. Matthew gives us the total of those who ate.[51] He gives an approximation only (*about*), which is to be expected. Who would have laboriously counted the full total? Interestingly he gives the count of *men*; for first-century Jews it was the number of adult males that mattered. The word for *five thousand* is used in each of the four Gospels for the number of this crowd, and for nothing else. Matthew specifically excludes women and children from the total.

2. Peter Walking on Water, 14:22-33

> ²²*And immediately he made the disciples embark in the boat and go before him to the other side, until he had sent the crowds away.* ²³*And when he had sent the crowds away, he went up into the mountain by himself to pray; and when evening came, he was there alone.* ²⁴*Now the boat was already many stadia distant from the land, tossed by the waves because there was a head wind.* ²⁵*In the fourth watch of the night he came to them, walking on the sea.* ²⁶*But when the disciples saw him walking on the sea, they were frightened and said, "It's a ghost!" And they cried out in fear.* ²⁷*But Jesus straightaway spoke to them, saying, "Take courage, it is I, don't be afraid."* ²⁸*Peter answered him, saying, "Lord, if it's you, tell me to come to you on the waters."* ²⁹*And he said, "Come." And Peter got down from the boat and walked on the waters and came to Jesus.* ³⁰*But when he saw the wind boisterous he was afraid, and beginning to sink he cried out, saying, "Lord, save me."* ³¹*And Jesus at once stretched out his hand and took hold of him, and says to him, "Man of little faith, why did you doubt?"* ³²*And when they got up into the boat, the wind dropped.* ³³*And those in the boat worshipped him, saying, "Truly you are the Son of God."*

Matthew, Mark, and John follow the feeding of the five thousand with the striking story of Jesus walking on the water. Matthew adds to this, as the others do not, the story of Peter's success and failure in attempting to do the same thing. Many expositors see in these stories no more than acted parables that teach us God's care when in difficulties and the importance of faith when the winds blow hard. But while we may thankfully appropriate these spiritual teachings, such understandings are not exegesis; they proceed from the presuppositions of the expositor.

22. We learn from John's account that some of the people who were there when the five thousand were fed were so impressed that they tried

---

wicker?), while a σφυρίς was flexible (made of hemp or the like?). See further my note in *The Gospel according to John*, p. 345, n. 25.

51. οἱ ἐσθίοντες is present, "the eaters"; we might have expected a past tense, but Matthew is concentrating on the number, not the precise stage of the meal.

to make Jesus king (John 6:15). This was evidently the reason that he packed the disciples off straightaway and sent them away to the other side of the lake. It was important that the Twelve be not involved in king making and, indeed, that the whole project be squashed without delay, and Matthew stresses this.[52] He is quite clear that Jesus was determined to get the disciples out of the way without delay, and this will be the point also of his sending them *to the other side*.[53] No destination is given; the important thing was that the disciples be gotten out of the way until he had dismissed (for the verb see on 5:31) the crowds (characteristically plural).

23. Jesus finished the task of sending the people away, then went up into the mountain (see on 5:1; it is a Matthean word) to pray. After the big day with the crowds Jesus turned to his Father in prayer; the infinitive will indicate purpose. This was done privately; Matthew has two expressions, *by himself* and *alone*, so that he is emphasizing that what took place was between Jesus and his Father only; Matthew is not referring to any public expression of devotion. The day had been wearing; Jesus found solace in quietness with the Father.[54]

24. Matthew turns his attention to the disciples. The boat (see on 8:23) was making progress, and when he takes up the story it was quite a long way from land — *many stadia* in fact. A *stadion* was about 600 feet (LSJ makes it 606.75 feet; this was about 185 meters); John tells us that the disciples had gone 25 to 30 *stadia*. The greatest width of the lake is 61 *stadia*, but their crossing would have been shorter, even though we do not know their exact route. But clearly they were well into their journey, though with quite a way still to go. The distance was compounded by the weather: a strong wind was blowing, and they were *tossed by the waves*[55] and facing a *head wind*.[56] Matthew is describing a situation in which the sailors were in some difficulty with the head wind and a rising sea. Matthew does not say how long they had been making the crossing, but they had started right after the meal finished (v. 22), so they had been battling against the elements all night. They must have been very weary.

25. The Romans divided the night (the time between 6 p.m. and 6

---

52. He says that Jesus did this εὐθέως, that he constrained (ἀναγκάζω, "*compel* by force or persuasion" [AS], used here only in Matthew; it signifies strong action and means more than giving gentle advice) the disciples to go (they may well have been sympathetic to the king makers), and that that meant that they should *go before him* (the verb is προάγω).

53. πέραν means "*on the other side, across* (usually with the idea of water lying between)" (AS).

54. Argyle quotes some words of William Temple: "The right relation between prayer and conduct is not that conduct is supremely important and prayer may help it, but that prayer is supremely important and conduct tests it."

55. βασανίζω may be used in the sense "torture," and from that it comes to signify any severe distress. Here the waves are pictured as harassing the sailors. κῦμα, "wave," is used only 4 times in the New Testament, 2 in Matthew.

56. ἐναντίος, here only in Matthew, has the meaning "over against, contrary" and thus signifies a wind dead against the travelers.

a.m. on our system) into four "watches,"[57] and the Jews into three. Mostly in the New Testament the term refers to the Roman system (cf. Mark 13:35), and this is obviously the meaning of the *fourth* watch, there being no such watch in the Jewish system. The fourth watch would cover the time "between three and six o'clock in the morning," as *GNB* translates. Somewhere in this period Jesus came to the disciples *walking on the sea*.

26. *But* will have some adversative force; it sets the agitation of the disciples over against the calm of Jesus as he walked on the sea[58] in the midst of the storm. The disciples were agitated[59] and scared. They could not envisage any mortal doing what Jesus was doing, so they gave their verdict, *"It's a ghost!"* What else?

27. Jesus recognized that they were scared and immediately took steps to calm them. He said first, *"Take courage,"* where the verb is one normally used in the New Testament of being cheerful (see 9:2, 22). In all three Gospels Jesus identifies himself with the words *"it is I,"*[60] employing the emphatic pronoun commonly used in the Greek translation of the Old Testament where God is the speaker. The expression is sometimes used in the Old Testament where God is revealing himself, such as "I am who I am" (Exod. 3:14). Its use on the lips of Jesus at this point might perhaps be said to be natural under the circumstances. The disciples were scared and in need of reassurance; it was important that they should know right away that the one they were seeing was no ghost, so Jesus identifies himself. But the expression has overtones of deity, and who but God could walk on the stormy waters? At the least Matthew is giving us a hint that Jesus was more than a mere man. *"Don't be afraid"* is a note of reassurance that runs right through this Gospel (1:20; 10:26, 28, 31; 17:7; 28:5, 10). Matthew likes to make the point that Jesus' own need never fear.

28. The incident with Peter is related in this Gospel only and is part

---

57. φυλακή is used 10 times in Matthew; it signifies "a guarding, a guard," as in Luke 2:8. It is used of those who guard (Acts 12:10), or of the place where the guarding is done, that is, a prison (as in vv. 3 and 10), or, as here, of the time when the guarding or watching was done.

58. In this verse *on the sea* translates ἐπὶ τῆς θαλάσσης; it is not clear why Matthew here uses the genitive, whereas in verses 25 and 29 it is the accusative. BAGD speaks of the accusative as being used "w. motion implied" (ἐπί, III.1.a.α), but motion is just as much implied in verse 25, where they see the preposition as "answering the question 'where?'" (I.1.a.α).

59. Matthew uses the verb ταράσσω, which is used of disturbing, stirring up, primarily in a physical sense, but also metaphorically of the mind (AS), the sense in which it is used here; they were "troubled," "disturbed." So it was that they "cried out from fear" (ἀπὸ τοῦ φόβου). Their cry (κράζω) will have been an inarticulate shriek.

60. ἐγώ εἰμι. This expression may well be no more than a means of self-identification, but it is used in John's Gospel a number of times when Jesus is giving teaching about his special functions — "I am the Good Shepherd," "I am the bread of life," and so on. Such expressions are not found in the Synoptic Gospels, but the present expression is suggestive. Filson remarks that the statement "implies that the speaker has authority and embodies God's power and claim. Jesus brings the answer to their need if only they perceive and believe that in him God is at work to save them" (p. 173). Cf. also Hill, "not 'It is I', but 'I AM', the Living One, master of wind and wave."

of Matthew's portrait both of that impetuous disciple and of Jesus, the sustainer of his people. It is characteristic that it is Peter[61] who calls out to Jesus. He addresses him with the respectful, *"Lord"* (see on 7:21), which here will have a full meaning, addressed as it is to one who walks on water in the middle of a storm. *"If it's you"* betrays some element of doubt, though the construction suggests reality.[62] *"Tell me"* is authoritative and sits well with the address "Lord" as Peter asks Jesus to give the necessary command. Peter has no word like "to walk," but speaks generally of coming to Jesus. It is interesting that Peter is of the opinion that if this really is Jesus, then he will enable his servant to move on the face of the waters.

29. Jesus gives a one-word command, taking up Peter's verb, *"Come"* (an ingressive aorist, "Start to come"). And Peter did. He *got down*[63] *from the boat and walked* (the aorist says nothing about duration as an imperfect would; it simply points to the fact as having occurred)[64] *on the waters.* There is no indication of how far Peter's remarkable walk went, but wherever Jesus was his servant managed to come to him. The preposition could mean "to" or "toward" Jesus, but the fact that when Peter began to sink Jesus took hold of him means that Peter was pretty close. We usually remember that Peter's faith failed and that Jesus drew attention to this. But we should bear in mind that it took courage for the apostle to venture on the water at all.

30. *But* has adversative force; over against the wonderful fact that Peter walked on the water Matthew sets this new fact: Peter's attention moved from Jesus to the storm.[65] Matthew says, *he saw the wind,* which means, of course, that Peter saw the effects of the wind; he perceived the wind; with the movements of the waves and boat, the spray and the feel of the wind, there was no doubt that it was *boisterous.*[66] As Peter perceived all this, it came home to him that to be on the water in a storm like the one he was experiencing and to be outside the boat was to be in a position of some danger. The result was that Peter became *afraid* (Phillips, "he panicked"), and the onset of fear was accompanied by the beginning of sinking.[67] Peter's shifting of concentration from Jesus, who could enable

---

61. Πέτρος has the article here and in every reference in Matthew from this point on (apart from "Simon Peter," 16:16, and "You are Peter," 16:18), although it never has it in the preceding passages.

62. εἰ with the indicative.

63. καταβαίνω. It is used of the coming down of rain (7:25, 27), of people from a mountain (17:9), of an angel (27:42), and of the Holy Spirit (3:16).

64. Tasker denies that Peter walked on the water "even for a brief moment," maintaining that the aorist is inceptive, "began to walk." This seems a curious reading of the Greek, but even if we accept it, Peter did commence walking.

65. The present participle βλέπων means something like "as he saw"; the switch of attention from Jesus to the storm coincided with Peter's inability to stay on top of the water.

66. Some MSS say no more than that he saw the wind (א B* 073 33 cop), but there is good support for adding ἰσχυρόν (B² C D K L P f1 f13 etc.).

67. ἀρξάμενος may be "beginning over against continuing" or "beginning over against completion."

him to overcome difficulties, to the difficulties in which he found himself, was disastrous. So he cried out for help. *Save* can refer to deliverance in any one of a variety of ways; here clearly it means "save from sinking."

31. And Jesus did. *At once*[68] he *stretched out his hand and took hold of him*. He could have delivered his servant by simply speaking, but Jesus' firm grip must have been very reassuring to the sinking apostle. The other verbs around here are in the aorist tense, but Matthew uses the present *says to him* presumably for greater vividness. Jesus bestows on Peter the epithet *"Man of little faith"* (for this term see on 6:30; this is the only place where it is used of one individual; elsewhere it refers to disciples as a whole). *"Why did you doubt?"*[69] Jesus asked him. The leading apostle might have been expected to trust more wholeheartedly, more especially since he had already taken some steps in his alien environment. He was learning that problems arise when doubt replaces trust.

32. Matthew does not say that Peter ceased to sink and resumed his place on top of the water, but that is implied. The two of them proceeded to get up into the boat, and then the wind dropped.[70] Matthew does not say that Jesus caused the wind to cease its raging, but he may imply that this happened.

33. Matthew rounds off the story with the effect all this had on the rest of the apostolic band (Calvin thinks that those in the boat includes not only disciples, but also "sailors and other passengers," II, p. 154). The experiences of seeing Jesus walk on the water and then of seeing him call Peter to walk there and of delivering that disciple when his faith failed made a profound impression; as a result they *worshipped* Jesus. For the verb see the notes on 2:2; 4:9. It betokens the worship that should be offered to deity and thus shows us the effect the incident had had on those who saw it all. They gave utterance to what it all meant to them with *"Truly you are the Son of God."* *Truly* is a strong affirmation of certainty.[71] They leave no room for doubt. They affirm that Jesus is *the Son of God*,[72] which means that they are putting him in the highest place, though it is not easy to see precisely how they would have understood the expression at this

---

68. εὐθεώς is a favorite Matthean word (he has it in 11 of its 33 New Testament occurrences). It indicates that Jesus did not delay; he acted promptly to deal with Peter's predicament.

69. διστάζω occurs in the New Testament again only in 28:17. Turner sees the aorist here as conveying the meaning "get into a state of doubting" (M, IV, p. 33). Matthew refers to lacks in the faith of the disciples again in 16:8; 17:20; 21:20; 28:17.

70. The aorist participle implies that they got into the boat first, and then the wind dropped. The tempest raged all the time they were on the water. The verb κοπάζω (elsewhere in the New Testament only twice in Mark) means "to grow weary," an interesting word to use of the wind.

71. ἀληθῶς occurs 3 times in Matthew (and 18 times in the New Testament). In LXX it renders אָמֵן and means "truly," "surely."

72. The lack of articles in θεοῦ υἱός does not mean "a son of a god" but is an example of Colwell's rule, that the preceding anarthrous predicate is definite: the meaning is "the Son of God."

time (after the resurrection it would have had a fuller significance for all Christians). But at least they are saying more than that Jesus is one among many whose godliness entitles them to be classed as "sons of God." They are saying that Jesus is uniquely related to the one God.

3. Jesus Healing, 14:34-36

> 34And they crossed over and came to land at Gennesaret. 35And when the men of that place recognized him, they sent into all that region and brought all that were sick to him. 36And they besought him that they might only touch the tassel of his cloak; and as many as touched were healed.

Matthew shares with Mark 6:53-56 information about a series of healings in Gennesaret. It is one of a number of passages in which this Evangelist speaks of numbers of people being healed from a variety of illnesses, but without reference to any one specific cure.

34. *They crossed over.*[73] That they *came to land* indicates that they reached the shore, and *Gennesaret* indicates their place of arrival, though since the name refers to "a coastal plain about 5 km. (3 mi.) long and 1.5 km. (1 mi.) wide, extending from Magdala to just S. of Capernaum,"[74] we cannot say that Matthew places the point of arrival with any great precision. It is enough for him that Jesus reached the western shore in an area that was fertile and well populated.

35-36. Whatever the precise point of disembarkation it was a place where Jesus was known. Thus *the men of that place* (which here appears to indicate a general area rather than a particular town) recognized Jesus and took action to secure what benefits they could for their own particular region. They sent word throughout the area that Jesus was there, with the result that *all that were sick*[75] were brought to him. Matthew does not say that these senders of good tidings said anything about healing: they just let people know that Jesus was there. But the result was that all the region's sick folk were brought to him, and this leads us to another of Matthew's quick and summary accounts of large numbers of healings. He does not describe any particular cure (he never does in his accounts of large numbers of healings); evidently it was not any one healing that stood out, but it was important that his readers should see that Jesus, in this time when there was such opposition to him, continued to to do good works.

When the people came, they *besought* Jesus that they might *only touch*

---

73. διαπεράω is used twice each in Matthew and Mark and once each in Luke and Acts, so it cannot be said to be frequently used in the New Testament. It signifies "pass over," "cross over." ἐπί may be used of motion across (so v. 25) or "motion that reaches its goal completely" (BAGD, III.1.a.β).

74. W. W. Buehler, in *ISBE*, II, p. 443.

75. For κακῶς ἔχειν see on 4:24; to "have it badly" is a general term covering all sorts of complaints.

the tassel of his cloak (it is not certain whether the word means "edge" or "tassel"; see on 9:20). We read elsewhere of a woman who was healed when she touched this tassel (or edge; 9:20), but it is not common. Matthew does not say that Jesus gave permission, but he apparently did, for the account goes on to speak of those who touched it. Whether it was the "edge" or the "tassel," it meant that only this marginal contact with Jesus, when done in faith, brought about healing. And *as many as touched were healed.*[76] The *cloak* was the outer garment. Matthew makes it clear that Jesus had total control over sickness; he thoroughly healed all who came to him.

76. διασῴζω is found only here in Matthew (and only 7 more times in the New Testament). It signifies "to bring safely through a danger . . . of sickness, *to recover*" (AS).

Matthew 15

D. OPPOSITION AND LOYALTY, 15:1–16:12

Matthew continues his story of the growing opposition to Jesus, but he interweaves heartening evidence of loyalty from those who appreciate him. The Pharisees are his principal opponents in this section.

1. Blind Leaders of the Blind, 15:1-20

¹Then Pharisees and scribes from Jerusalem come to Jesus, saying, ²"Why do your disciples break the tradition of the elders? For they do not wash their hands when they eat bread." ³But he answered them, saying, "And you, why do you break the commandment of God on account of your tradition? ⁴For God said, 'Honor your father and mother' and 'Let him who speaks evil of father or mother be put to death.' ⁵But you say, 'Whoever says to his father or mother, "Anything of mine that might have benefited you is a gift [to God]," ' ⁶is not to honor his father. You have nullified the word of God because of your tradition. ⁷Hypocrites, well did Isaiah prophesy about you, saying,

⁸'This people honors me with their lips, but their heart is far away from me. ⁹In vain do they worship me, teaching as doctrines men's commandments.' "

¹⁰And he called the crowd and said to them, "Listen and understand: ¹¹not that which goes into the mouth defiles a man, but that which goes out of the mouth, this defiles a man."

¹²Then the disciples came and say to him, "Do you know that the Pharisees took offense when they heard this saying?" ¹³But he answered, saying, "Every plant that my heavenly Father did not plant will be rooted up. ¹⁴Leave them alone. They are blind guides of blind men. And if a blind man guides a blind man, they will both fall into a ditch."

¹⁵But Peter answered him, saying, "Explain this parable for us." ¹⁶And he said, "Are you without understanding even now? ¹⁷Do you not perceive that everything that goes into the mouth passes into the stomach and goes out into the latrine? ¹⁸But the things that go out of the mouth come from the heart, and these defile the man. ¹⁹For out of the heart go evil thoughts, murders, adulteries, fornications, thefts, perjuries, blasphemies. ²⁰These are

the things that defile the man. But to eat with unwashed hands does not defile the man."

"The tradition of the elders" arose because pious Jews were very careful about keeping the law. They saw the law as God's greatest gift to the human race and regarded it as a wonderful privilege that the Jews, the people of God, had received it. They considered it important that they should treasure the law and practice its every provision. So they studied it with diligence; the Mishnah and the Talmud reveal the closeness of their study and the detail into which they went. They were anxious not to break any of its provisions, and this led to a mass of definition and interpretation. Exactly what had to be done to keep a given law? When two provisions of the law did not obviously agree, which had the preeminence?

To take an example of the kind of reasoning that went on, there is a command, "let no man go out of his place on the sabbath day" (Exod. 16:29). The words were an instruction to the people in the wilderness as they went out to gather the manna that fell from heaven. On the day before the Sabbath a double portion was provided, but there was none on the Sabbath, and the people were told that they must not go out on that day. But in later generations pious souls felt that there was something permanent about this command, as there was about every provision in the law. They interpreted this passage to mean that one must not go out of a house on the Sabbath carrying a burden of any sort.

But what if one wished to do a good deed on the Sabbath, such as making a gift to the poor? The Mishnaic tractate *Shabbath* begins with a situation where a householder wants to give something to a poor person on the Sabbath. If the householder stood inside his house and put his gift outside or if the poor person, standing outside, reached inside and took up the gift, in either case there was a transgression: a person had carried something out of a house on the Sabbath. The pundits decided that the way to do the good deed was this: neither person should cross the boundary carrying the gift. But if the poor man stood outside and reached his hand inside and if the householder then placed his gift into the poor man's hand, the poor man could withdraw his hand and neither had transgressed (the forbidden act had not been completed by either one). The same result was, of course, obtained if the householder stood inside and held his hand containing the gift outside so that the poor man, standing outside, could simply receive the gift (*Shab.* 1:1). In this case there is no transgression: neither man has carried the burden across the line. Apply such casuistry to the whole of the Pentateuch and there is a marvelous field for "the tradition of the elders." Since the solutions offered to the problems that were discerned were often far from obvious, the experts had a magnificent field over which to roam. Some of their traditional interpretations were undoubtedly beneficial, but some produced extraordinary results. Jesus draws attention to some of them.

Matthew proceeds to a controversy that arose between Jesus and some Pharisees who had evidently come to provoke an argument. The discussion turned on the failure of Jesus' disciples to keep the tradition of the elders in that they ate food without first engaging in a ceremonial washing of their hands. Jesus began by making it clear that the tradition that meant so much to the Pharisees was not to be accorded uncritical acceptance, for it could and sometimes did lead people to disobey the commandments of God. Having made this point, he turned to the question of unwashed hands and pointed out that defilement comes not from overlooking some physical regulation about ceremonial cleanliness but from the evils that people conjure up in their innermost being. In this passage Jesus addresses three distinct groups: the legal visitors (vv. 1-9), the people (vv. 10-11), and the disciples (vv. 12-20). Mark's account is much fuller and deals with several Pharisaic practices, whereas Matthew concentrates on the one issue of eating with unwashed hands.

1. With a characteristic *Then* (see on 2:7) Matthew moves on to the next stage of his story. This brings us to a group of *Pharisees and scribes* (the only place in Matthew with this order; his habit is to speak of "scribes and Pharisees"). They were *from Jerusalem,* which is not quite what we expect in Galilee. Matthew's word order, moreover, puts some emphasis on *Jerusalem:* there came to Jesus "from Jerusalem Pharisees and scribes." Coming from the capital, the holy city, into this rural area, they would have been regarded as especially authoritative. It was not to be expected that people from the great city would make their appearance in such a remote area. Matthew also makes it clear that they came *to Jesus.* It was not that they were paying a pastoral visit to Galilee and happened to come across Jesus; it seems that they had come expressly to confront him. That they would come from so far in order to oppose him tells us something of the reputation that Jesus had built up and something also of the measure of the hostility of the Pharisees (for these religious teachers see on 3:7). They were accompanied by *scribes* (see on 5:20; most scribes were Pharisees, but there were many Pharisees who were not scribes), or legal experts. They would feel that they were well equipped to cope with whatever they would encounter in the northern area.

2. They come right to the point with a question about *the tradition of the elders,* though interestingly they do not complain about Jesus' attitude to the tradition but about the practice of his disciples (cf. 9:14). This does, of course, imply an accusation against Jesus, for it was he who taught his followers to do these things. Indeed, the scribes would probably have regarded teaching people to disregard the tradition as much more serious than an occasional breach oneself. Teaching people to act contrary to the tradition meant a systematic and thought-out practice. It meant breaking the tradition as a matter of principle, not as a thoughtless aberration in a moment of weakness. Therefore to speak of the practice of the disciples implied a serious accusation against their Master. The disciples, the accusers affirm, break[1] the tradition[2] of the elders.[3] This was a body of teaching handed down from the religious leaders of the past. (Indeed, REB emphasizes the time element and ignores the people involved by rendering it as "the ancient tradition.") Some of it was concerned with the way those leaders had understood passages in Scripture, especially passages whose meaning was not obvious or was ambiguous. It also gave guidance as to how passages that might be construed in more than one way were to be understood. In origin the tradition was praiseworthy and useful, but through the years, with the contributions of many teachers, some with less insight than others, it had come to amount to a very burdensome body of doctrine. Its huge volume meant that by New Testament times even to know what it comprised was a difficult chore, while to obey all its multitudinous regulations was too big a task for most people. The Pharisees and their adherents were distinctive in their regard for and their attempt to put into practice this vast body of tradition, and for them it was unthinkable that a religious teacher should take the traditions lightly. They could not understand why Jesus should allow his disciples to break any of the traditions. That amounted to being irreligious, and for a religious teacher that was a contradiction in terms.

The particular tradition that they took up with Jesus was that concerned with the washing of hands before eating. This was not a matter of personal hygiene but of the removal of ceremonial defilement. In the law it was prescribed that the priests must wash their hands (and feet) when they were ministering (Exod. 30:17-21), but the tradition extended this to all people and was concerned with removing ceremonial defilement in-

---

1. The verb παραβαίνω, found only in Acts 1:25 outside this passage in the New Testament, has the meaning "go by the side of, stand beside" and thus "overstep, violate, transgress" (AS). The disciples transgress the tradition. The present tense points to their continuing practice.

2. παράδοσις, "a handing down or over" and thus "a tradition" (AS), is used in the Gospels only 3 times by Matthew and 5 times by Mark, all with reference to the Jewish traditions. It may be used in this way in Paul, but that apostle also used it of Christian traditions (1 Cor. 11:2, etc.). Among the Jews it was held that "Moses received the Law from Sinai and committed it to Joshua, and Joshua to the elders. . . . They said three things: Be deliberate in judgement, raise up many disciples, and make a fence around the Law" ('Abot 1:1). R. Akiba explained this last point: "The tradition is a fence around the Law" ('Abot 3:14). The point of this is that the tradition was seen as a protection for the law; anyone who kept the tradition would not come anywhere near breaking the law. How false this view was is clear from the incident we are considering. Danby takes the law Moses received as "The 'Oral Law,' " and further notes that "the traditions of the elders" were "rules of Jewish life and religion which in the course of centuries had come to possess a validity and sanctity equal to that of the Written Law" (Danby, p. 446, n. 2).

3. πρεσβύτερος is the comparative of πρέσβυς, "an old man"; it was used of age, but more significantly "Of dignity, rank or office" (AS). It might refer to civic or religious leaders, and to those of the past or of the present. Among the Jews it was often used of the great ones of the past who had given authoritative interpretations of the meaning of Scripture and of religious duties, and also of lay leaders in the synagogues and the like. Later, Christians took up the term and employed it for leaders in the local churches.

curred in daily life.[4] The Pharisees discerned a great number of "unclean" things that one might encounter in the ordinary course of life and that might easily be touched with the hands. The contact made the hands unclean, and if unclean hands touched food, that, too, became unclean. When it was eaten the whole person was made unclean. To avoid such a dreadful happening the strict upholders of the traditions had evolved a ritual washing that removed defilement, and they practiced it scrupulously before eating. So important was this that a whole tractate of the Mishnah is devoted to it (called *Yadaim*, "Hands"). Water must be poured over the hands up to the wrist (*Yad.* 2:3; a different opinion prescribes only parts of the fingers, *Hul.* 106b; Scriptural justification for the practice was somehow derived from Lev. 15:13). Defilement could be removed only by running water (hence the pouring). But Jesus' followers did no such thing, and the Pharisees ask the reason for their practice.[5] Eating bread, of course, refers to eating food in general; the Pharisees are speaking about the ordinary meals people ate day by day, whatever the food might be.

3. Matthew uses an adversative conjunction to set Jesus over against his interrogators[6] and goes on to his normal formula for "having answered, said." Jesus made no attempt to defend the practice of his disciples. That might well have invited the kind of argument that the Pharisees loved and in which they excelled. In any case he probably thought that failure to observe a ridiculous scribal regulation needed no defense. Instead he went to the root of the matter by drawing their attention to the fact that sometimes their tradition, which was intended to help people keep the law of God, could lead them to break that law. Their concentration on the tradition could lead them to neglect the law of God, and not only to neglect it, but to engage in practices that involved breaking it. His reply emphasizes *you:* they have been complaining about his disciples, but what about themselves? And his *break* is the same verb as that used in the previous verse by the Pharisees when they complain of the disciples breaking the traditions. But then he introduces a contrast: where they speak of "the tradition of the elders" he speaks of *the commandment[7] of God*, a much more serious matter. And they break God's commandment *on account of*[8] their *tradition.* Jesus is not saying, "Despite your tradition you break the law of God." He is saying, "*Because* of your tradition you break the law of God." He does not speak of "the tradition of the elders" as the Pharisees had just done, but of "your tradition," the tradition they

---

4. See F. Hauck, *TDNT,* IV, pp. 946-48 for these washings. He points out that the washing of hands before meals "goes back to regulations imposed by Hillel and Shammai" (p. 946).

5. *When* is ὅταν, "whenever"; the washing in question should take place every time food is eaten.

6. ὁ δέ marks the contrast.

7. ἐντολή signifies an authoritative injunction and is especially used of the divine commandments.

8. διά with accusative "to indicate the reason" (BAGD, B.II.1).

had accepted and made their own. They could not evade responsibility by saying that others had compelled them.

4. Jesus proceeds to draw attention to one of the ways they broke the commandment and precedes it with, *"For God said."* Since the divine origin of the commandment is important, he does not allow it to drop out of sight. What God has said is not to be put on a level with what even godly scribes laid down and handed on from one to another. The commandment he selects for attention is that which commands the Israelites to honor their parents. The Jews commonly respected their parents, but Jesus points out that this attitude was due not to a scribal requirement, but to a divine command. God, no less, has prescribed that proper respect be paid one's parents (Exod. 20:12; Deut. 5:16). With this he links a further prescription that anyone who *speaks evil*[9] of parents shall be put to death (Exod. 21:17; Lev. 20:9).[10] Scripture leaves no doubt that parents are to be honored, and that extends even to the way people speak of their parents.

5. *But* is adversative and *you* is emphatic; Jesus is setting the Pharisees in contrast to God, whose words he has just quoted. "God said . . . but you say" means that the words of God stand in opposition to the words of the Pharisees. *Whoever* is general, "anyone at all." This "anyone" is pictured as addressing either father or mother and announcing that he has made a gift to God of anything that the parent might be expected to get from him.[11] *Gift* comes first in this expression, which gives it emphasis, and while it may be used of gifts in general, in the New Testament it is used mostly for gifts made to God. In his version of the incident Mark at this point has *korban*, a transliteration of a Hebrew word meaning "offering" and always used in the Old Testament of offerings to God.[12] What

---

9. κακολογέω (here only in Matthew; 4 times in the New Testament) means "to speak ill of, abuse." Some translations render it "curse," but the term is a wide one and covers smaller offenses than cursing.

10. τελευτάω (4 times in Matthew) means "to complete" and is often used of the completion of the life, that is, death. Here all doubt is removed with the addition of θανάτῳ, a somewhat Hebraistic construction.

11. Such vows were in fact made. The Mishnah speaks, for example, of a problem faced by a man at Beth Horon "whose father was forbidden by vow to have any benefit from him." In due course the man came to give his own son in marriage and wanted his father to share in the festivities. So he tried to make a temporary gift of the courtyard and banquet to a friend, only for the purpose of having his father come to the banquet. The Sages, however, decided that this was not a valid gift (*Ned.* 5:6). The incident shows further that it was not necessary for the son actually to give the gift to the temple; he could retain the use of it as long as it was withheld from the person(s) specified in the vow.

12. In a Glossary of Hebrew terms appended to Herbert Danby's translation of the Mishnah we find: "KONAM. A word substituted for Korban (lit. 'an offering', i.e. sacred as an offering dedicated to the Temple), the usual term introducing a vow to abstain from anything, or to deny another person the use of anything." The tractate *Nedarim* makes it clear that anything vowed to the Lord, even rashly, could not be put to any other use. A rash vow might then take up resources that should have been used to support aged parents. The Mishnah contains provisions whereby such a rash vow may be annulled "by reason of the honour due to father and mother" (*Ned.* 9:1), but this appears to be later than New Testament times.

the child is telling the parent in this saying is that he has decided to give as an offering to God what the parent might have expected would be given to him or her in old age. *Anything of mine* is comprehensive.[13] The son is vowing away all that he might have used to support his parents.

6. This verse begins with the emphatic double negative with the future, which is here used in the sense of an imperative.[14] *Honor* is the word used in the commandment. Since what should have been used for parental support has been irrevocably vowed to God, there is nothing left for the parents (the better MSS omit "and his mother," but the words are surely implied), and thus they are not honored. The tradition about the rash vow is honored, but the commandment of God is not kept. Jesus puts the responsibility on his hearers (and those who like them are tied to the tradition): *"You have nullified[15] the word of God,"[16]* no less, by your scrupulous observance of *your tradition*.

7. *Hypocrites* (see on 6:2; *AB* has "Shysters!") is very much a Matthean word and one that was used a number of times of the Pharisees (22:18; 23:13, 15). Its appropriateness here arises from the fact that these opponents of Jesus professed a deep concern for the service of God and took issue with him over the way his disciples took lightly the traditions that seemed to the Pharisees essential to that service, but they used those very traditions to nullify the express commandment of God. They allowed the use of Korban to override one of the Ten Commandments. This leads to the application to the hypocrites of some words of Isaiah; indeed, Jesus says that Isaiah prophesied about them. This striking way of putting it does not, of course, mean that Isaiah did not mean to sting the people of his own day when he spoke these words or that he had primarily in mind people who would live centuries later. Rather, Jesus is saying that the prophet's words fit the people who are opposing him so mindlessly, whatever other applications the prophet may have intended.[17]

---

13. ὃ ἐάν is general and signifies "whatever"; it thus points to the whole of what might otherwise have been given to the parents.

14. Burton remarks, "the thought requires the Imperative sense, and in view of the frequent use of οὐ μή with the Future in an imperative sense in the Septuagint, and its occasional use in classical Greek, the possibility of it can hardly be denied" (Burton, 67). Cf. *REB*, he "must not honour. . . ," *NIV*, "he is not to 'honor . . .'"; "need not honor" *(NRSV)* is not strong enough, "for the point is that the man was legally *prohibited* from doing so" (Tasker, p. 148).

15. ἀκυρόω (once each in Matthew, Mark, and Galatians only in the New Testament) means "revoke, invalidate" (κῦρος, "authority") (AS). MM notes its use in the papyri in the sense "revoke" etc.

16. τὸν λόγον seems to have better attestation (א¹ B D Θ etc.) than the variants τὸν νόμον and τὴν ἐντολήν; it also has transcriptional probability, for we expect something about law or command.

17. Matthew uses the verb προφητεύω only 4 times (he has the corresponding noun 37 times). This is not his usual formula for quoting a prophet, but he makes the point firmly enough that Isaiah spoke these words and that they referred not only to people in the prophet's own day but to those confronting Jesus.

8. *"This people*[18] *honors me with their lips,"* God says, referring to people who say the right things though without really meaning them. Matthew uses the word for *lips* only here; it can, of course, refer simply to that part of the human body, but here it signifies the organ of speech. The people in question honor God in that they say all the proper things. But this is all a matter of outward profession. *Their heart* is not in it. The heart (for this term see on 5:8; the singular is the Semitic use for something that belongs to each person in a group, a construction "Contrary to normal Greek and Latin practice," M, III, p. 23) points to the inward part, the center of one's being. Deep down, where it counts, the people gave no honor. On the contrary, their heart, God says, *is far away from me.* Despite their good words they were lacking in good works. They were far away from God where it counts, in the heart.

9. *In vain*[19] is their worship. The people of whom the prophet speaks went through the motions of worship, evidently performing the outward ritual as they should, but quite oblivious of the fact that punctilious performance of rites and ceremonies is no substitute for genuine, inward devotion. We might have expected that this would be followed with some reference to the importance of the inward or to that of godly living, the fruit of true worship. But the interest of Isaiah (and of Jesus as he quoted the prophet) was in what their instruction brought about in other people; the emptiness of their worship is seen in what they teach others to do. *Doctrines* is from the same root as *teaching;* the expression means literally "teaching teachings").[20] The prophet points out that the people of whom he complains inculcate *men's commandments* as their doctrines. People who genuinely worship God will proceed to teach what God has commanded; the fact that these people teach what is of human origin demonstrates that their worship is a sham. Jesus' charge against the Jewish scholars was that in the last resort they were substituting manmade regulations for the divine commands. Their motives may possibly have been excellent, but the results were deplorable.

10. Jesus then *called the crowd.* It would seem that the people had stood back while the Pharisees confronted Jesus, possibly as a mark of respect for these teachers from Jerusalem, possibly because they felt that questions like that of ceremonial uncleanness were not for the likes of them. Let the experts look to such matters! But there was something in

18. λαός occurs 14 times in Matthew, twice each in Mark and John, 36 times in Luke, and 48 in Acts. It can be a general word for "people" and may mean no more than a crowd (27:25), the populace at large (27:64), or the people as opposed to their leaders (26:5). But it may also mean specifically "the people of God" (2:6).

19. μάτην (again in the New Testament only in Mark 7:7) is the accusative of μάτη, "a fault, folly," and is used in the sense, "to no purpose" (AS).

20. διδάσκω occurs 14 times in Matthew (17 times each in Mark and Luke, and 9 times in John). With this frequency of the verb it is curious that the noun διδασκαλία occurs only here and once in Mark in the Gospels (Paul has it 19 times). It may mean the act of teaching or the content, what is taught.

the question being discussed that was important for the lowliest worshiper, and Jesus intended the people who were there to understand the significant thing about uncleanness. It was important for the people (and, for that matter, for the Pharisees themselves) to understand that in their concern for ceremonial purity the Pharisees were missing what was important about uncleanness. Breaking their pettifogging rules did not make people unclean in the sight of God, but they should not think that therefore it was impossible to become unclean before God. It was all too possible, and the people should understand what caused it. So Jesus calls them to *"Listen and understand."* He wants them to hear what he has to say and to think hard about it, an injunction that is certainly justified by the novelty of the truth he is about to enunciate.

11. *Not* comes first with a certain emphasis: "it is *not* this that the Pharisees have emphasized so much that brings defilement." That would have been a revolutionary statement for pious Jews of the time; for them careful ritual washing as a preliminary to eating was part of life. How else could one avoid eating something that had been defiled by contact with unclean hands? To say that nothing that goes into the mouth *defiles*[21] *a man* cut across all the rules of defilement to which they had been accustomed all their lives; it challenged the accepted religious way of looking at a wide range of practices.

Jesus looked at those practices from a different perspective, which he proceeds to contrast with the accepted Jewish way. His *but* is a strong adversative, "but, on the contrary"; he is not introducing a comparatively minor modification of the Jewish practice but advocating something radically new. It is *that which goes out*[22] *of the mouth* that *defiles a man.* Jesus is warning that defilement is not something that may be casually acquired by physical contact (and which may easily be removed by appropriate ritual practices). It is something that affects the person at the root of his or her being. When one is evil there, then the words that come out of the mouth reveal the inner corruption. People should take more notice of the significance of their words than of the possibility that their hands may have made contact with a source of ritual defilement. Words that go out of the mouth are more likely to indicate defilement than food that goes in.[23]

12. Matthew alone records the reaction of the Pharisees to Jesus'

21. κοινόω (5 times each in Matthew and Mark) is used in the classics for "to make common," and in LXX and the New Testament for "to make ceremonially unclean, to profane" (AS).

22. ἐκπορεύω (which Matthew has 5 times) can mean the going out of people to meet John the Baptist (3:5), of demons (17:21), of people leaving a city (20:29), and of words spoken by God (4:4).

23. Gundry comments, "Thus the cleansing of all foods does not countermand the law, but intensifies it by transmuting the dietary taboos into prohibitions against evil speech, just as the so-called antitheses in the Sermon on the Mount did not destroy the law, but fulfilled it" (p. 306).

saying. Not surprisingly the Pharisees took umbrage at a statement that
so radically rejected a practice that had been dear to them all their lives.
And it is not surprising either that they seem to have made their protest
to the disciples rather than to Jesus himself. At any rate it is *the disciples*
who came to Jesus and *say* (the present gives greater vividness) that the
Pharisees *took offense*[24] at what Jesus had said. These religious experts
found Jesus' dictum a hard saying, something they could not accept and
to which they took strong exception.

13. Jesus' reply proceeds from scathing contempt for the position of
the Pharisees. *But* is an adversative conjunction and sets Jesus over against
the Pharisees. He proceeds to a horticultural metaphor to bring out his
total rejection of their position, and speaks of the fate of plants that the
heavenly Father did not plant.[25] Whether the *plant* refers to the teacher or
the teaching, Jesus is saying that the heavenly Father (see on 5:16) has
revealed truths; his word may denote the truths themselves or the people
to whom the truths have been revealed. Either way the point is that what
God has made known is the significant thing. What God has not made
known and what people like the Pharisees teach so confidently and
authoritatively has no future. Because it is not divine truth it will not last.
In due course it will be *rooted up*, another horticultural metaphor, this one
speaking of plants torn up by the roots. This signifies final and complete
destruction. In this way Jesus makes clear his contempt for the teachers
who so confidently claimed to know the ways of God, but who had not
been "planted" by the God to whom they so brazenly appealed. So far
from being reliable expositors of the kingdom of God, the Pharisees were
not even in the kingdom.

14. *"Leave them alone,"*[26] Jesus says. People in general might look up
to them and regard them as reliable religious guides, but the disciples
should not share such attitudes. They are to keep away from the Pharisees
and leave them unheeded; teachers like these could not lead them nearer
to God; they could only becloud the issues. Jesus characterizes them as
blind guides of blind men. Eye diseases were common in first-century
Palestine, and the resulting blindness meant that blind beggars were not

24. The verb is σκανδαλίζω (see on 5:29); it means "to cause to be caught in a trap" or
"to fall" in any one of a variety of ways. It may mean "to cause to sin" (5:29-30), but here it
is rather (in the passive) "be given offense," "be offended." G. Stählin denies that this means
"feeling hurt"; rather, "the primary meaning is 'deep religious offence' at the preaching of
Jesus, and this both causes and includes denial and rejection of Jesus" (*TDNT*, VII, p. 350).

25. φυτεία is found here only in the New Testament; it signifies "a planting" and thus
"what is planted," a garden plant, not a wildflower. φυτεύω is more frequent (11 times), but
occurs only twice in Matthew; it means "to plant."

26. ἀφίημι (which Matthew uses 47 times; see on 12:31) has a meaning like "let go,"
"send away" and is used in a variety of ways for "sending away." Thus Matthew utilizes it
for permitting an action (3:15), going away from fishing nets (4:20), letting a man take a piece
of clothing (5:40), forgiving sins (6:14-15), and so on. Here clearly it means that the disciples
are not to be unduly concerned by what the Pharisees said; they are to "forsake," "leave
alone" such religious teachers.

uncommon. Blind people were often in need of guides, but people who were themselves blind were not of much use as guides to others.[27] Indeed, Jesus says, where a blind man is acting as guide to another blind man, they are both certain to end up in *a ditch*.[28] Disaster is necessarily the ultimate outcome of such a situation. Here, of course, the meaning is metaphorical, and we should not miss the point that *blind guides* is a devastating description of the Pharisees, men who prided themselves on their enlightenment. We should not miss either the force of Jesus' future tense, which gives an air of prophetic certainty. He is not speaking of a hypothetical possibility but of a certainty. Those who follow blind guides are headed for disaster; the Pharisees of whom Jesus speaks specifically cannot lead people to spiritual profit. This is all the more devastating in that Jewish teachers sometimes claimed to be guides to the blind (cf. Rom. 2:19; Luke has a reference to blind guides of the blind in a very different context, Luke 6:39).

15. Characteristically it is Peter who responds, asking Jesus for an explanation.[29] Peter is referring to what Jesus has said about uncleanness (v. 11) and finding it not at all obvious. This is not really surprising, for, though he would never have accepted all that the Pharisees said about uncleanness, the view that defilement can arise from eating or drinking what has been touched by unclean hands was so much part of his heritage that he would not find its total abandonment easy (cf. Diétrich, "There is something so revolutionary in his attitude that their minds have difficulty in following him"). We should notice further that Peter speaks of this saying as a parable; a parable is not necessarily a story, but may simply be a wise saying.[30]

16. Again the Evangelist has the adversative conjunction,[31] this time to set Jesus over against the disciples; clearly Peter is not alone in seeking the information, and Jesus' plural recognizes that he is the spokesman for the group. Plainly Jesus thought that those closest to him ought to have picked up his meaning. He asks the question, *"Are you without under-standing even now?"*[32] The disciples had been with Jesus for quite some

27. There are textual problems relating to this verse. τυφλῶν is omitted by B D and some other MSS, and the position of ὁδηγοί varies. But the longer reading best accounts for the variants, which leads Metzger to accept it. There is no significant difference in meaning.

28. βόθυνος occurs again in 12:11; Luke 6:39 only in the New Testament. It signifies "a pit," "a ditch."

29. φράζω, elsewhere in the New Testament only as a variant reading in 13:36, has a meaning like "tell, declare, explain."

30. Stendahl remarks that Peter's use of the term "parable" here "may well remind us of how bold Jesus' interpretation was felt to be, since we would hardly find 11 to be a parable or an enigma."

31. δέ as in verses 3, 5, 13, and 15.

32. Matthew uses ἀσύνετος only here; it conveys the idea of a lack of discernment or understanding. ἀκμήν occurs nowhere else in the New Testament. It is the accusative of ἀκμή, "a point," used as an adverb, "at the present point of time, even now, even yet" (AS). καὶ ὑμεῖς puts emphasis on *you*.

time; they had seen what he did and heard what he taught. They ought to have had more understanding than is implied in Peter's request.

17. Jesus' explanation begins with a question, the construction showing that he expects the answer "Yes." "Don't you perceive — ?" he begins, where his verb[33] points to mental activity. They ought to have been able to think through their problem. His *everything* is comprehensive; Jesus allows of no exceptions. Everything, then, that goes into[34] the mouth has one destination, *the stomach.* Jesus passes over the digestive processes (which formed no part of his reasoning) and comes to the point that the end product of the process passes out[35] of the body *into the latrine.*[36] The body uses what it needs and discards the remainder. Nothing remains of any "defiling thing" that may have entered it.

18. It is otherwise with what goes out of the mouth. The things anyone says come *from the heart,* the innermost being, and *these*[37] *defile the man.* It is a profound revolution in religious thinking when Jesus transfers the source of defilement from the merely outward to the state of the heart. At one stroke he removes the necessity for a multiplicity of regulations to cover a variety of situations and concentrates on an attitude that will take care of them all.

19. *For*[38] introduces a reason for the preceding statement. *Out of the heart* comes first with emphasis; this is the real source of the problem. Jesus proceeds to a list of evils that proceed from this source. He starts with *evil thoughts,*[39] which, of course, can lead to all sorts of evil deeds; such evils are far worse than any defilement that may result from the accidental contact of the hands with any one of the multiplicity of objects the scribes perceived as unclean. Matthew proceeds to a series of offenses arranged in the order in which they come in the Ten Commandments. They are all plural: Jesus is speaking of the many sins people commit. Matthew uses the word *murders* only here. *Adulteries* and *fornications*[40] between them cover the full range of unlawful sexual activities, involving either married or single

33. νοέω. It is connected with νοῦς, "the mind."

34. In verse 11 Jesus used εἰσέρχομαι for what goes into the mouth, but now his verb is εἰσπορεύομαι. There seems to be no difference in meaning; the variation is stylistic.

35. ἐκβάλλεται, "is thrown out" or "is expelled."

36. ἀφεδρών means "a privy," "a latrine." Cf. Lenski, "An ἀφεδρών is not a 'draught' or a 'drain' but a place to which one retires (ἀπό) and sits down (ἕδρα, seat)" (p. 592).

37. κἀκεῖνος (in Matthew again only in 23:23) can denote "what is relatively more distant" or, as here, "what is relatively closer" (BAGD).

38. γάρ.

39. διαλογισμός means "thought," "reasoning," and the adjective πονηρός (see on 6:23) "evil." The combination adds up to "evil plans."

40. μοιχεία is found in the corresponding passage in Mark 7:22, in the story of the woman caught in adultery that has been appended to John 7 (John 8:3), and nowhere else in the New Testament. It differs from the following term, of course, in that it involves a sin against the marriage tie. πορνεία (3 times in Matthew and 25 times in the New Testament) strictly means "fornication" (the use of the prostitute, πόρνη), but it comes to be used for sexual sin of any kind.

people. Such sins proceed from evil desire within the persons concerned
and defile them much more than any ritual transgression can possibly do.
Jesus proceeds to *thefts*,[41] which are obvious examples of evil that can
proceed from premeditation. So with *perjuries*, literally "false witness,"[42] a
sin that should be taken more seriously than it always is. Perjury, being false
testimony that involves the name of a god, is taken as serious by people in
all sorts of cultures. There is little future for society if testimony supported
by an appeal to the deity cannot be relied upon. But to make a difference
between sworn and unsworn testimony such that the former must be true
while the latter need not be is to make the kind of pedantic distinction of
which Jesus complains in the Pharisees. Unsworn testimony must be just
as reliable as testimony on oath if a good deal of our social fabric is to hold
together. It is important that we can trust what people say, and where we
cannot life becomes a precarious affair. The last item on Jesus' list is
blasphemies,[43] which may be used in the sense of slanders against our
fellows (the other items in the list are offenses against our fellow citizens).
But the word is also used of offenses against God, and it would be unwise
to exclude them in this context, especially in view of the fact that the word
is plural. It would not be in the manner of Jesus to split hairs, declaring that
some forms of blasphemy were acceptable and some were not. Clearly he
is saying that any form of blasphemous speech, whether the object is God
or people, is blameworthy and that, issuing from the heart, it defiles the
person. We should not, of course, hold that this is the complete list of sins
that defile, so that if we can avoid what Jesus has just named, we will be in
the clear (to take up such a position is to make much the same error as that
of the Pharisees). The list is no more than a sample of the evils that proceed
from the heart. All sin defiles, and we should understand Jesus to mean that
his followers must avoid evil of any sort. To follow the example of the
Pharisees and concentrate on avoiding ceremonial defilement is to waste
time and energy. Much more important is the avoiding of evil deeds, which
really do defile the doers.

20. *These are the things that defile,* and it is the intention behind them,
the purpose formed in the heart, that is the most serious thing, serious
though the actual sin may also be. For the most part ceremonial defilement
must have been accidental — people did not try to be defiled. But sins like
those Jesus has mentioned are done with serious intent or with loss of
self-control. It is this kind of thing that really defiles. Bonnard points out
that Jesus is not differentiating between an internal and an external form

41. κλοπή, again in the New Testament only in Mark 7:21, means "theft" of any kind
(LSJ even notes its use for theft from authors, plagiarism).

42. ψευδομαρτυρία. Mark's list is longer than Matthew's, but he does not include "false
witness."

43. βλασφημία (4 times in Matthew) can mean "slander" (12:31), and it is translated that
way here by NRSV and other translations. But it is also used of impious words uttered against
God; Phillips renders here "blasphemy," and Goodspeed, "impious speech."

of piety but is speaking of something quite different: his teaching "presupposes that man is not pure in himself; if that were the case he would only have to keep himself from the world's impurities; but he is evil precisely in his interior, in his heart from which go out (v. 19) all his crimes" (p. 229). Eating *with unwashed hands*[44] was not, of course, the only way of contracting ceremonial defilement, but it is the one in question, and, of course, what Jesus says about this path to defilement applies equally well to other paths. By putting his emphasis on "the heart" Jesus is drawing attention to the fact that wickedness takes its origin in our innermost being. He is warning his followers against letting their personal desires and lusts be the guide to their conduct.

2. The Canaanite Woman, 15:21-28

> [21]*And Jesus went out from there and went away into the regions of Tyre and Sidon.* [22]*And look, a Canaanite woman from those parts came out and shouted, saying, "Have mercy on me, O Lord, Son of David; my daughter is wickedly demon-possessed."* [23]*But he answered her not a word. And his disciples came and requested him, saying, "Send her away, because she keeps shouting after us."* [24]*But he answered, saying, "I was not sent but to the lost sheep of the house of Israel."* [25]*But she came and knelt before him, saying, "Lord, help me."* [26]*But he answered, saying, "It is not good to take the children's bread and throw it to the dogs."* [27]*But she said, "Yes, Lord, for even the dogs eat the scraps that fall from their masters' table."* [28]*Then Jesus answered her, saying, "O woman, your faith is great; be it as you wish." And her daughter was healed from that hour.*

From a story of unremitting hostility Matthew turns to one of outstanding and unexpected trust. This is one of very few stories of healings of people outside the Israelite nation, and it presents Christians with a problem in that Jesus seems to take up a harsh attitude toward the suppliant woman.[45] Mark has this story too, though with differences. But in both it is clear that the woman had exceptional faith and that her persistence received its due reward. H. J. Held views this story as an example of Matthew's ability to stress the importance of faith when he has a fuller account than that of Mark as well as when his is shorter. He points out that for Mark it is the fact of the healing that matters, but "In Matthew the whole narrative is directed towards this last sentence (i.e. 'your faith is great; be it as you wish') which has a majestic note about it. . . . In Matthew only the fact and power of faith are expressed" (*TIM*, p. 199; cf. also pp. 239-41, 275-96).

---

44. ἄνιπτος, "unwashed," is found again in the New Testament only in Mark 7:2.

45. Albright and Mann comment, "Both the silence of Jesus and the near-desperate cry of the disciples are interesting in the light of commentators' assertions that this gospel (in contrast with the supposedly earlier Mark) treats Jesus and his disciples with increased reverence."

21. Matthew tells us that Jesus *went out,* but he does not say from where he made his exit. Perhaps he had been in a house, but none is mentioned. Perhaps the thought is that he left Galilee, that he went out of his own country. He *went away,*[46] which may mean that after the encounter with the scribes and Pharisees mentioned earlier in the chapter Jesus deemed it politic to move into the adjoining territory for a time. He went into *the regions*[47] *of Tyre and Sidon,* the area to the north of Galilee. These were Phoenician cities on the Mediterranean coast, but they controlled territory inland. Matthew does not indicate with any precision just where Jesus went in this territory (nor does Mark). Sidon was about twenty-five miles north of Tyre, and that city was much the same distance from Jesus' Galilean haunts, so this represents a considerable journey on foot. The round trip could have taken months, which is suggested by the references to sitting on the green grass (14:19) and on the ground (15:35), that is, the difference between spring and late summer. Mark tells us, as Matthew does not, that Jesus went into a house and did not want anyone to know where he was, but he could not be hidden. The desire for privacy suits Matthew's narrative well, but this Evangelist does not mention it. It is enough for him that Jesus was in this foreign territory and that there he met the woman to whom he goes on to refer.

22. Matthew's favorite *And look* (see on 1:20) introduces the lady who is to be the significant figure in the story he is about to narrate. She was *a Canaanite*[48] and thus a member of a race that goes back to c. 3000 B.C. Tyre and Sidon were great trading centers, and from them the Canaanites traveled far and wide. They were a cultured race, and, for example, the first-known alphabet comes from Canaanites working with Egyptians in the mines of the Sinaitic peninsula. A woman about whom we know nothing apart from what is told in this story *came out,* which appears to mean that she left her house and sought Jesus out (if we understand the Greek as "came out of those parts" [Moffatt], the meaning will be that she met Jesus in the border area). *From those parts* does not locate her precisely, but it does indicate that she belonged to the general area. That she *shouted*[49]

46. The verb is ἀναχωρέω, "to go back, withdraw," "freq. in sense of avoiding danger" (AS); "The connotation of 'taking refuge' from some peril will suit most of the NT passages remarkably well" (MM).
47. τὰ μέρη, "the parts." The word can denote the part as opposed to the whole (Luke 11:36) and be used in other ways, but Matthew generally has it in the sense here, the regions belonging to a province or city (cf. 2:22; 16:13). The expression indicates that Jesus went into Phoenician territory, not just to the border.
48. Χαναναῖος is found only here in the New Testament. It denotes "belonging to the land and people of Canaan, Canaanite" (BAGD). *AB* renders "Phoenician" and points out that "the native name" of a Phoenician "was in the Greek *Chananaios.*" Carr notes that the expression rendered "the land of Canaan" (Josh. 5:12) appears in LXX as the land "τῶν Φοινίκων." It is clear that the people could be called either "Canaanites" or "Phoenicians."
49. κράζω may mean that she shouted or that she cried out or spoke loudly. Whatever the precise way in which we should understand the verb, clearly the woman was not speaking calmly in an ordinary voice.

probably means that she was agitated and spoke in an excitable way, while the imperfect tense indicates that she kept shouting. She said, *"Have mercy on me"*; or perhaps we should translate, "Take pity on me." Whichever way we take it, she was not claiming a reward for merit, but looking for a boon for which she could claim no worthiness. But if she claimed nothing for herself, she discerned greatness in Jesus. She greeted him as *"Lord"*[50] and went on, *"Son of David,"* an expression Matthew has 8 times in refer- ring to Jesus (as well as once of Joseph). It speaks of a descendant of the great King David and came to be used of the Messiah, viewing him as a great warrior like David, one who would establish a mighty kingdom. It is curious to find the title being used by a Canaanite woman for whom an Israelite ruler would presumably have no attraction. Perhaps she thought that it would be as well to address the one from whom she was looking for help in terms that he would recognize as signifying greatness. Or better, in view of the faith that this narrative shows she possessed, she had come to accept Jesus as Messiah.

She goes on to detail her need. She speaks of *my daughter,* but gives no indication of her age. Nor indeed does she indicate her problem with precision. The girl, she says, *is wickedly demon-possessed,* but says nothing about the way the demon possession was manifested. Elsewhere there are references to demoniacs who were deaf or dumb or blind (9:32; 12:22), and it is clear that a variety of physical complaints were ascribed to demon possession. This woman gives no indication as to the way her daughter was troubled, but she does emphasize the extent; she was *wickedly* possessed.[51] The mother is making it plain that the daughter is in a pitiable plight.

23. Jesus said nothing to her, which is very unusual; he usually responded to any appeal for help, and indeed sometimes he took the initiative and helped before a request was made to him. Matthew empha- sizes his silence by saying that Jesus did not answer *a word,* but he gives no reason for this. His disciples apparently had no doubts: the woman was a Canaanite, not a Jewess, and to them her crying out was nothing but a nuisance. So they came up to Jesus and asked[52] him to send the woman away. They give a reason for asking: *"she keeps shouting after us."* They repeat the verb used in verse 22 of the shouting, but add a new element in that they view themselves as included in its scope; she is

---

50. Κύριε is not to be understood as no more than a polite greeting (like our "Sir," which *REB* translates here and in v. 27). In this context it will have its fullest meaning.

51. κακῶς δαιμονίζεται. Matthew has the adverb κακῶς 7 times, which is more than in any other New Testament book. He commonly speaks of very sick people as "having badly," but this use is not quite the same. It may mean "cruelly demon-possessed" (*NASB*) or "tormented by a devil" (*REB*), or, as in the translation I have suggested, there may be the thought of evil in conjunction with the activity of the demon.

52. ἠρώτουν is imperfect, which seems to mean "they kept asking"; they pressed their request.

shouting not only at Jesus, they think, but at them.[53] They apparently felt that she was calling on them to do something, and they did not appreciate such a request from one who was both a woman and a Canaanite. Yet we should bear in mind that they do not say that Jesus should do nothing for her and that their words could, and probably should, be understood in the sense "Give her what she wants and send her off!" Cf. *JB*, "Give her what she wants."[54] They wanted to be rid of the woman and her embarrassing noise, but there is no indication that they did not want her daughter to be healed. This is supported by the fact that the disciples had never seen Jesus turn away anyone genuinely seeking his help; they would not have expected him to do it now. Mark has neither the silence of Jesus nor the suggestion of the disciples; we owe them both to Matthew.

24. Another piece of information we owe to Matthew is Jesus' reference to his mission to Israel. *But* has adversative force; it sets Jesus over against the disciples. Our best understanding of the next words is that they are are a response to the disciples' suggestion that Jesus should grant the woman her request. How could he do this when his mission was to Israel? He speaks of being *sent,* another example of his consciousness of mission. His time here on earth was not his own, but he had been sent by the heavenly Father for a specific purpose. That purpose he sought to accomplish, and his whole life was given over to its fulfilment. He speaks now of his mission as only *to the lost sheep of the house of Israel,*[55] an expression that may be taken in more ways than one: it may mean "all the house of Israel," regarded as lost, or "those from the house of Israel who are lost." During his time on earth Jesus did not go to Athens or Rome or Alexandria, indeed to any of the places that we might have anticipated. Apart from very occasional trips like this one (which did not interfere with his discharge of his mission) he spent all his time in Galilee and Judea. There are mysteries here that we cannot solve, but while Jesus came to make that atonement for sin which would mean salvation for people in any place throughout this whole wide world, he did not come to engage in a worldwide mission of healing or the like. His earthly mission was to the Israelites, here described as *lost sheep.* The word *sheep* is used frequently in metaphorical senses, usually to bring out thoughts like the timidity or stupidity or idleness of those described, or to depict them as followers of a leader. Among Christians it is sheep as the followers

53. ὄπισθεν means "from behind"; apparently the little group was moving, and she kept following and calling out to them "from behind."

54. Their verb ἀπολύω is used of sending away satisfied in 18:27; Luke 2:29.

55. οὐκ . . . εἰ μή excludes from the scope of the mission all those not designated. G. Strecker pointed out that some have argued from this expression that Matthew's church was Jewish-Christian, but the saying "rather corresponds to his historical reflection: only for Jesus, and thus for the disciples in the lifetime of Jesus, is this restriction valid. Only during the life of Jesus is the proclamation directed exclusively to the people of Israel" (Stanton, p. 72).

of the Good Shepherd who are most significant. But here the sheep are *lost* in the sense that they are spiritually astray, alienated from God. For *house* see on 2:11; here it stands for "nation," a not uncommon use. *Israel* is the nation regarded as the people of God. Jesus is saying that his mission was to the ancient people of God,[56] and the Gospels show us quite clearly that this was the way it was worked out. His contacts with Gentiles were very few, and his preachers were sent only to Israel (10:5-6).

25. Once again *But* has adversative force. Over against Jesus with his words about a mission to Israel is this Gentile earnestly seeking healing for her daughter. That *she came* is a little puzzling, but perhaps she had not been close to Jesus until now; after all, she had been shouting, which may indicate distance as well as urgency. Now she came and *knelt*[57] *before him.* Her attitude gave expression to the deep reverence she had for Jesus. Then she put her plea in the simplest form, *"Lord, help*[58] *me."* Again she addresses Jesus as *"Lord"* and pleads nothing but her need.

26. Jesus' answer is on the surface a harsh one.[59] He appeals to family life with the reminder that *the children's bread* is to be used for *the children* and not thrown *to the dogs.* For *good* see on 3:10; the word has the meaning "Ethically, *good,* in the sense of right, fair, noble, honorable" (AS); it is used of the "good works" people should do so that others may glorify their heavenly Father (5:16). *Take* here means "take away," "deprive"; it points to an injustice if children are deprived of their food. Children are the helpless members of the family; senior members must see to it that their needs are met. *Dogs*[60] here are clearly house pets; they must be fed, but not at the expense of the children. There are priorities that must be observed. The expression is apparently a harsh one, but, as Barclay reminds us, "The tone and the look with which a thing is said make all the differ-

---

56. "Jesus wished the woman to understand that His activities were circumscribed not only by the inevitable limitations of His manhood, but by the specific part that He had been called to play during His brief earthly life" (Tasker, p. 150).

57. προσκυνέω is often used in the sense "worship," which may well be the meaning here; after all, the woman had spoken of Jesus as "Lord" and as "Son of David," so she clearly had a high view of his person. But in this place it appears that some bodily expression of worship is meant, so perhaps "knelt" is right. Turner regards the imperfect as important; he holds that it indicates that the meaning is *"request . . .* as distinct from the aorist which means *worship"* (M, III, p. 65).

58. βοηθέω, here only in Matthew, means "help," "come to the aid of" and may be used of helping in need of various kinds.

59. There is textual variation, with some MSS reading ἔξεστιν, to give the sense "it is not lawful," and there are other readings. But there seems to be no doubt that we should read ἔστιν καλόν both because of its superior attestation and because it is the harder reading.

60. κυνάριον (found in the New Testament only in this narrative and the Markan equivalent) is a diminutive of κύων and may signify a house dog in contrast to a dog of the streets, but it is also used with no diminutive force. Mostly in Scripture dogs are pariah dogs, but this cannot be the meaning here, for such dogs would not be allowed in a house where they could pick up scraps (though John W. Klotz thinks "scavenging dogs" are meant, *BEB,* I, p. 100). The meaning must be house dogs. That such dogs were kept in Israel is clear from the Mishnah (*B. Qam.* 5:3; such a dog must be kept on a chain, *B. Qam.* 7:7).

ence. Even a thing which seems hard can be said with a disarming smile. We can call a friend 'and old villain', or 'a rascal', with a smile and a tone which takes all the sting out of it and which fills it with affection. We can be quite sure that the smile on Jesus' face and the compassion in his eyes robbed the words of all insult and bitterness" (pp. 134-35). Filson also points to the importance of tone and facial impression. He also says, Jesus' "blunt answer is not a literal statement, calling her and her countrymen dogs, but a parable or proverbial statement used to make clear that his work is with his own people."[61]

27. Another adversative *But* introduces a different point of view. The woman begins tactfully with *"Yes, Lord."* She agrees with what Jesus has just said; how could anyone possibly disagree with it? The needs of the children must be met, and care for the dogs must not interfere with this necessary duty. But this is not the whole story. *For*[62] is important; it draws an inference. The little dogs, the dogs that belong in the household, have their place, too. They eat *the scraps*[63] *that fall from their masters' table.* The *table* here obviously is a table on which a meal is spread, and that the dogs eat what falls from the table shows that they have their recognized place in the house. Those who own dogs make sure that they are fed. This neat answer[64] shows that the woman was not presuming on her position. She knew that she did not belong to Israel and thus had no claim as belonging to the chosen people. But surely there would be crumbs!

28. For Matthew's *Then* see on 2:7; "having answered, said" is an Aramaism, common in this Gospel (see the note on 3:15). *O* is not a common form of address in this Gospel (twice only).[65] *Woman* is not a harsh or cold form of address, as we see from the fact that Jesus is here using it in granting her request (he uses it also in his words to his mother from the cross, John 19:26). Matthew uses the word *great* quite often (20 times), but only here does he link it with *faith;* he has it in an emphatic position so that the greatness receives some stress ("Only she and another Gentile, the centurion at Capernaum [8:10], are praised publicly for their faith by Jesus," Hamann, p. 169). It is interesting that Jesus does not

61. Beare insists on taking the saying in the harshest possible way. Jesus replies "more brutally," "the offensive words are unrelieved." Beare speaks of "the brutality" and "the incredible insolence of the saying." But this unsympathetic literalism is surely not the way this Gospel is to be interpreted. Barclay and Filson are much nearer to the mind of Matthew.

62. γάρ; translations like "but" (*GNB*) miss the point that the woman is drawing an inference from what Jesus has said, not opposing him.

63. ψιχίον is the diminutive of ψίξ, "a crumb," so it points to "a little crumb," a very small piece indeed.

64. "Curiously felicitous combination of ready wit, humility and faith: wit in seizing on the playful κυνάρια and improving on it by adding ψιχία, humility in being content with the smallest crumbs, faith in conceiving of the healing asked as only such a crumb for Jesus to give" (Bruce).

65. BDF points out that it may be used in a polite, unemotional manner, but "There is a stronger emotion in Mt 15:28 . . . which announces an immediate reward" (BDF, 146 [1 (b)]).

commend the woman's persistence or her humility; it is her faith that is basic.[66] She believed in Jesus, and in the end she obtained her petition. Jesus says that it will be *"as you wish"*; the woman's deep desire was granted. Matthew tells us that the girl was healed immediately. He never gives an indication of the nature of the illness; for him two things were important: the faith of the Canaanite woman and the immediacy of the cure of her daughter. As with another Gentile, the centurion whose slave was sick, there is healing at the request of another than the sufferer, healing at a distance, and a commendation of the Gentile's faith.

3. The Feeding of the Four Thousand, 15:29-39

29And Jesus went away from there and went along the Sea of Galilee. And he went up into the mountain and sat there. 30And great crowds came to him, bringing with them lame, crippled, blind, dumb, and many others; and they put them down at his feet, and he healed them, 31so that the crowd was astonished when they saw dumb people speaking, cripples whole, lame walking, and blind seeing; and they glorified the God of Israel.

32But Jesus summoned his disciples and said, "I have compassion on the crowd because they have stayed with me for three days already and have nothing to eat; and I do not want to send them away fasting, lest they faint on the way." 33And the disciples say to him, "Where will we get in a wilderness so many loaves to satisfy so many people?" 34And Jesus says to them, "How many loaves do you have?" And they said, "Seven, and a few little fish." 35And having told the crowd to recline on the ground, 36he took the seven loaves and the fish; and when he had given thanks, he broke them and kept giving to the disciples, and the disciples to the crowds. 37And all ate and were satisfied, and they took up what was left over of the broken pieces, seven baskets full. 38Now those who had eaten were four thousand men, apart from women and children. 39And when he had sent the crowds away, he got into the boat and came to the districts of Magadan.

Matthew has another of his little sections on healing, in which he speaks briefly of great numbers of people coming to Jesus and being healed of a variety of complaints. He goes on to speak of Jesus as taking pity on the crowds in the wilderness with no access to food. As he had done before, he multiplied a small amount of bread and fish and made it sufficient for a large crowd, the number being given as four thousand people. Discussions of the passage raise the possibility that we have here nothing more than a variant account of the feeding of the five thousand, but this is not what Matthew is saying. He clearly regards the two incidents as distinct: the numbers of people are different in the two incidents,

---

66. Matthew has πίστις only 8 times; it is comparatively rare in the Gospels (Mark 5 times, Luke 11 times, John 0). But it is found 243 times in the New Testament.

as are the quantities of food and the amounts left over; the words for "basket" are different; the people in this incident had been with Jesus for three days (v. 32) whereas in the earlier incident they had just gone around the lake to head him off (14:13-14); and the times appear to be different, the earlier feeding being when the grass was green (Mark 6:39), that is, in spring, while here there is no mention of grass and the ground appears to be hard (v. 35); in other words, it is late summer.[67] The feeding of the five thousand is found in all four Gospels, but this miracle is related only in Matthew and Mark.

29. Jesus *went away*[68] from the place where the previous incident took place and returned to Galilee, where Matthew specifies that he went *along the Sea of Galilee* (see on 8:24). This is a common way of referring to this sheet of water, but Matthew uses it elsewhere only in 4:18. This Evangelist says that Jesus went along the shore or perhaps simply came to the shore. Matthew does not indicate whether it was the eastern or western shore of the sea, but Mark 7:31 says plainly that Jesus came to Decapolis, Gentile country to the east of the sea (Matthew's reference to "the God of Israel," v. 31, looks like the utterance of Gentiles). We should probably understand that Jesus came down from Phoenicia to the eastern side of the sea, thus remaining in Gentile territory. This means a continuing work among Gentiles, including healings and the feeding of the four thousand.[69] Jesus went up into *the mountain* (see on 5:1), which may refer to a particular mountain, but perhaps the expression means no more than "the hilly country." That Jesus *sat* means that he took up the normal posture for teaching, though Matthew does not say that he taught, only that he healed. Since, however, the people were with him for three days (v. 32), it would seem that he engaged in teaching as well as healing.

30. Characteristically Matthew has the plural *crowds* as he speaks of large numbers of people coming to Jesus. He speaks first of the well, then of the afflicted that they brought with them, clearly seeking healing for their suffering friends.[70] Matthew specifies some of the ailments and starts

---

67. Tasker also discerns a difference in "the spiritual lessons which Jesus seems to have wished His disciples to learn from them. . . . Although both miracles are performed in the same way, and are signs that Jesus possesses supernatural power over created things, in the first story He seems to be concerned that the disciples should understand how utterly dependent upon Him they must always be, if they are to do what He would have them do, and in the second story He seems to be indirectly reproving them for their lack of sympathy with the needs of the Gentile world" (p. 154).

68. μεταβαίνω (5 times in Matthew, the most in any New Testament book) means "to pass over from one place to another" and here "with reference to the point of departure only, to withdraw, depart" (AS).

69. "From the time of St. Augustine the suggestion has been known that the Feeding of the Five Thousand represents Christ's communication of Himself to the Jews, and that of the Four Thousand represents His self-communication to the Gentiles" (Alan Richardson, *The Miracle-Stories of the Gospels* [London, 1959], pp. 97-98).

70. ἔχοντες μεθ' ἑαυτῶν is a somewhat curious way of putting it, but clearly the meaning is that the healthy brought with them those with impaired health.

407

with the *lame*.[71] For *blind* see on 9:27; the Gospels have more examples of Jesus' giving sight to the blind than of any other kind of healing, which is all the more striking in that there are no accounts of the giving of sight to the blind anywhere else in Scripture (the restoration of sight to the temporarily blind Saul, Acts 9:17-18, is the nearest we come to it). In the Old Testament the giving of sight to the blind is something God does (Exod. 4:11; Ps. 146:8). For *dumb* see on 9:32; the word may mean "deaf" as well as "dumb," but since Matthew goes on to speak of the cured here as speaking (v. 31) there is no doubt that "dumb" is correct in this place. To these specific infirmities Matthew adds *and many others,* indicating that a great variety of complaints was represented in the crowds who came to Jesus. The word I have translated *put,* and which *NEB* renders "threw,"[72] means "to throw, cast, hurl" (AS), though presumably here it signifies a more gentle depositing than Judas's hurling of the thirty pieces of silver into the sanctuary (27:5) or than that of the passengers who threw the cargo into the sea to lighten the ship in a storm (Acts 27:19). They put the sufferers *at his feet* (where they would have his full attention), and *he healed them* (for *healed* see on 4:23).

31. The result[73] was that *the crowd* (singular here as it is 19 times out of its 49 occurrences in this Gospel) *was astonished;* they recognized Jesus as a charismatic figure. Matthew particularizes by referring to the cures of each of the classes mentioned in the previous verse. *Dumb people speaking* indicates that these folk were not simply deaf (though, of course, they may well have been both; some MSS have "hearing and speaking"). Matthew speaks of the crippled as *whole*[74] and of the *lame* as *walking.* Both forms of impairment of limbs were cured. So with the *blind seeing.* Matthew makes it clear that Jesus' healings were not confined to any narrow range of disabilities; whatever the physical problem, he solved it. The result was that people *glorified* Israel's God. This is the one place in Matthew where we find *the God of Israel* (see also Luke 1:68; Acts 13:17). The genitive denotes a special relationship. It is the God who has chosen a people for himself that the people glorify. We should understand the words as an expression of thanks and praise.

32. There is not much adversative force in *But;*[75] it simply moves the narrative along to the next stage. Jesus *summoned his disciples* (see on 5:1; 8:21). This is the one place (together with its Markan equivalent) in which

---

71. χωλός signifies "lame," "crippled"; the term may be used of the hands as well as of the feet. κυλλός means "club-footed and bandy-legged" and more generally "deformed, contracted" (LSJ). It is not easy to distinguish between the two words, and we can scarcely say more than that Matthew is referring to deformities of various kinds.

72. ῥίπτω.

73. For ὥστε see on 12:12.

74. ὑγιής, again in Matthew only in 12:13 (of a hand); it signifies "healthy," "whole."

75. ὁ δέ.

Jesus says, "*I have compassion*"; all the other occurrences of the verb (for which see on 9:36) are in the third person. It signifies that he was very deeply moved by the plight of the people.[76] The verbs are in the present tense: "they are staying with me throughout three days and they have not what they may eat."[77] The people had evidently not come prepared for as long a stay as it had turned out to be. The meaning is not that the crowds had been fasting for three days, but that during that time they had exhausted their food supply. Now Jesus says that he does not want[78] to send them off without something to eat.[79] It would be a long way home for some of the people, and without food it would be a distressful journey. Jesus cares for them. They had come to him for help, and he is not willing to send them off in such a way that they would end up fainting (Hendriksen, "lest they collapse") on the way.

33-34. The disciples do not discuss the plight of the people, nor do they dispute Jesus' estimate of what might happen on the journey home. They concentrate on the problems of supply, asking where[80] in a remote wilderness (see on 3:1) they would get enough loaves to satisfy[81] the needs of so many people.[82] Clearly the number of people was large and the food supplies were small. For the disciples this was a problem of some magnitude, and obviously they saw no way of solving it. Granted their situation and the size of the crowd, they regarded themselves as confronted with a hopeless situation. But Jesus proceeds to look at their resources, inquiring as to how many loaves they had. "*Seven*" is their reply, to which they add, "*and a few little fish.*"[83]

76. Bonnard remarks, "Jesus is not a stirrer of crowds; he does not use them; he welcomes them, brings them together and feeds them" (p. 236). Ryle points out that "of all the feelings experienced by our Lord when upon earth, there is none so often mentioned as 'compassion' . . . this was the distinguishing feature of His character."

77. προσμένω, here only in Matthew, means "to wait longer, continue; remain with" (AS). The nominative ἡμέραι τρεῖς is unexpected; for the duration of time the accusative would be usual. Turner suggests that we should supply a main verb such as εἰσιν and add καί (M, III, p. 231). Moule includes this in a section on "peculiar uses, which it is difficult to justify grammatically" (*IBNTG*, p. 31). "That this is the true reading is guaranteed by the unusual construction, the accusative being what one expects" (Bruce).

78. οὐ θέλω puts the emphasis on the will.

79. νῆστις occurs in the New Testament only here and in the Markan equivalent. AS says that it is chiefly poetical and that it derives from νη-, a negative prefix, and ἐσθίω; it thus means "not eating," that is, "fasting." μήποτε (see on 4:6) is here used "denoting purpose . . . oft. expressing apprehension" (BAGD, 2.b.α).

80. πόθεν is used of location, "from what place?" There is no verb in the clause; the disciples say simply "Whence to us?"; in other words, "Where will we obtain. . . ?"

81. The verb is χορτάζω, a verb properly used of animals — "to feed, fatten" — and in late Greek of persons with the meaning "*to fill* or *satisfy* with food" (AS).

82. Matthew uses τοσοῦτος both for the number of people and the number of loaves; the problem is to fit the number of loaves to the number of eaters.

83. ἰχθύδιον, found elsewhere in the New Testament only in Mark 8:7, is a diminutive of ἰχθύς. The fish were little ones. Or perhaps, as Bengel thinks, they speak disparagingly of their supply, for the diminutive is not used in verse 36.

35. Jesus took charge with a command[84] that the people *recline*[85] *on the ground*, as they did at the earlier miraculous feeding (14:19). Once again the setting for an act of heavenly magnificence is one of earthly lowliness.

36. As he had done in the previous miracle of feeding, Jesus *took* the loaves and the fish (which may mean that he took them from the disciples or that he took them into his hands preparatory to asking the blessing). Interestingly Matthew now speaks of "fish," not "little fish"; we should understand that, while the fish were small, there is no particular emphasis on size. Jesus gave thanks (which means much the same as "said the blessing" in 14:19) and *broke*, which was the customary action when prayer was offered at the beginning of a meal. Matthew does not supply an object, so we are left wondering whether the fish as well as the bread were broken. The verb is in the aorist, which points to a single significant action, in contrast to *kept giving*, which points to a continuing action. This verb, too, has no object, but it would seem that the fish are included as well as the loaves. As in the earlier miracle, Jesus kept giving to the disciples, and they to the crowds.

37. Matthew tells his readers that *all ate*, which makes it clear that Jesus provided for the whole group; none was omitted. And all *were satisfied*, which means that they had an ample meal (the same verb is used as in v. 33). Matthew is not referring to a token meal or a snack. He adds that there was a substantial surplus; *what was left over of the broken pieces* essentially repeats the language of 14:20, but the size of the surplus here is *seven baskets full*.[86] But both indicate that the meal was more than adequate. Jesus provided for the needs of all the people and more.

38. *Now*[87] leads into a statement about the number of the eaters. As in the story of the feeding of the five thousand, it is the number of men that is specified; women and children are expressly excluded. Matthew tells us that the number of adult males was *four thousand men* (this number is mentioned in the New Testament only with reference to this miracle and in Acts 21:38). This was *apart from*[88] *women and children*. The last word is a diminutive and strictly means "little children," but there is no empha-

84. Matthew employs παραγγέλλω again only in 10:5. It has a military ring (of passing a command "along" a line of soldiers) and points to an authoritative command.

85. ἀναπίπτω, here only in Matthew, is used of the beloved disciple's leaning back on Jesus' breast at the Last Supper (John 13:25), but it is more commonly used of reclining for a meal, at table (Luke 11:37, etc.), and here on the ground.

86. It is impossible to compare the surplus here with that in the earlier feeding, for the word for *basket* here is σφυρίς while in 14:20 it was κόφινος. The distinction between the two words is not that of size, but of material; the earlier word denoted a basket of some rigid material (wicker?) whereas that used here is of a more flexible material (perhaps hemp). Since we do not know how big any of the baskets was, we cannot compare the quantities of their contents.

87. οἱ δέ has no adversative force; it simply carries the narrative along.

88. χωρίς (3 times in Matthew) is used as in 14:21 to distinguish the number of men from others.

sis here on size. Matthew is simply concerned to bring out that the number he has cited is that of adult males.

39. Jesus *sent the crowds away* (the same verb and the same process as in 14:15, 22). Evidently he did not simply walk away from people at the end of a session of teaching and healing, but in some more or less formal manner he "dismissed" his congregation. On this occasion he embarked in *the boat* (see on 8:23); again *boat* is preceded by the definite article, which may point to a definite boat, perhaps one owned by someone connected with the apostolic band. He went off, though Matthew tells us nothing about the voyage, only that he ("he," not "they"; he concentrates on the movements of Jesus) came *to the districts*[89] *of Magadan.* The location of this town is unknown (as is the case with Mark's "Dalmanoutha," which may be a variant name for the same place, or there may have been two towns close together), and there are variations as to its spelling in the MSS. Some have identified it with Magdala (see *BEB*, 2, p. 1375), but there seems to be no good reason for this.

---

89. ὅριον occurs 12 times in the New Testament, 6 being in Matthew. The word means "a boundary," but in the New Testament it is always used in the plural with reference to the area enclosed in the boundaries; hence "districts," "regions."

Matthew 16

The opposition of the Pharisees to Jesus continues. On this occasion they are joined by the Sadducees. This is part of the way Matthew brings out the growth of hostility on the part of those opposed to Jesus. And here it leads to Jesus' denunciation of the "leaven" of these two groups. We should not miss the point that Jesus has only just returned to Galilee from Gentile territory and that this opposition leads him to go away from Galilee again (v. 5; he returns in 17:22).

4. The Leaven of the Pharisees and the Sadducees, 16:1-12

¹*And the Pharisees and Sadducees came, and testing him they asked him to show them a sign from heaven. ²But he answered them, saying, "When it is evening you say, 'Fine weather; for the sky is red'; ³and in the morning, 'Stormy today, for the sky is red and dark.' You know how to interpret the appearance of the sky, but the signs of the times you cannot. ⁴An evil and adulterous generation looks for a sign, and a sign will not be given it except the sign of Jonah." And he left them and went away.*

⁵*And when the disciples came to the other side, they had forgotten to take bread. ⁶And Jesus said to them, "Look out and beware of the leaven of the Pharisees and Sadducees." ⁷And they reasoned among themselves, saying, "It is because we did not bring any bread." ⁸But when Jesus knew this, he said, "Why are you reasoning among yourselves, you men of little faith, about having no bread? ⁹Do you not yet understand? Do you not remember the five loaves of the five thousand and how many baskets you took up? ¹⁰Nor the seven loaves of the four thousand and how many baskets you took up? ¹¹How is it that you do not understand that it was not about loaves that I spoke to you? But beware of the leaven of the Pharisees and Sadducees. ¹²Then they perceived that he had not told them to beware of the leaven of loaves, but of the teaching of the Pharisees and Sadducees.*

Matthew relates another incident in which Jesus' enemies ask him for a "sign" (see 12:38-40 and the notes on that passage). This leads into a warning against the teaching of these leaders couched in terms that the disciples at first misunderstand.

1. For *Pharisees* and *Sadducees* see on 3:7; they were the principal religious and political parties among the Jews and together "they represent official Judaism in its entirety" (Hill). Here they are linked under one article, so Matthew is depicting them as united on this occasion. They were far from friendly with one another, and it is a measure of their hostility to Jesus that they combined on this occasion in an endeavor to discredit him (they came together to hear John the Baptist [3:7] and are linked again in vv. 6, 11, and 12). They had little in common, but it could be said that they both stood for the old ways as against Jesus, whom they saw as a dangerous innovator. They apparently reasoned that it was better to combine to discredit him; that done, they could resume their normal opposition to each other with which they were familiar and which represented the old paths. Matthew has 14 references to the Sadducees (Mark and Luke 1 each, Acts 5, and they are mentioned nowhere else in the New Testament); it accords with his interest in this group that he alone mentions them in connection with this incident. This is the only place in the New Testament where they are mentioned outside Judea. They were a comparatively small party with a great interest in the temple. The two groups came *testing* Jesus, where the verb mostly has a bad meaning, testing with a view to failure.[1] It signifies that they were not sincere in their seeking a sign. They evidently thought that Jesus could not produce it, and their intention was not so much actually to see a sign as to show people that Jesus could not produce one. On an earlier occasion "scribes and Pharisees" had come to Jesus asking for a sign with much the same motivation (12:38-39, where see notes). Now they made a request[2] for *a sign* (see on 12:38) *from heaven.* In the Synoptic Gospels the word is mostly used in the sense of wonderfully impressive miracles accrediting the person who performed them (whereas in John they are actions pregnant with meaning, wonderful deeds certainly, but with deep spiritual significance). Jesus was asked for such a sign on a number of occasions, but he consistently refused to give it. *Heaven* (see on 3:2) may mean the sky or the divine abode, and sometimes it comes close to signifying God himself. Here the demand for *a sign from heaven* means that they want a miracle with divine significance, a miracle that will show beyond all contradiction that God is with him (see on 12:38). They demand that Jesus accredit himself by performing some spectacular marvel. It might reasonably be argued that Jesus' miracles of healing were signs from heaven, but that was not the way his enemies saw them. They wanted something spectacular, not healings that others also claimed to do.

2. *But* has adversative force; far from giving the sign they asked, Jesus answered in the following way. There is textual doubt about his answer.[3] As it stands, Jesus refers to the ability of his contemporaries to

---

1. The verb is πειράζω, for which see on 4:1.
2. ἐπερωτάω, 25 times in Mark, but only 8 times in Matthew. It is often used of asking a question, but in late Greek it may signify to ask for something, as here.
3. The words from *When it is evening* to the end of verse 3 are absent from some

predict the weather. *When it is evening*[4] a *red* sky indicates that *fine weather*[5] is on the way, according to the accepted dictum in Palestine of that day (and elsewhere, as our saying "A red sky at night is the shepherd's delight" indicates).

3. But the same astronomical feature coming at a different time of day has a different meaning. Early in the day the weather-wise see much the same phenomenon as indicating that stormy weather is on the way.[6] *The sky is red* repeats from the previous verse the expression indicating fine weather but with the addition *and dark*.[7] Jesus compliments his conversation partners on their ability to forecast the weather but links that with their inability to discern the great events that were taking place in their midst. *The signs of the times* are sometimes understood as referring to the signs that indicated that the end of all things is at hand (so BAGD, 1), but "end" scarcely seems justified here. In the Old Testament there are references to "the day(s) of visitation" (as in Isa. 10:3; Hos. 9:7) and to "the time of their visitation" (Jer. 10:15) or "the year of their visitation" (Jer. 11:23), and *the times* here may well have such a meaning. In the person of Jesus God was visiting his people, but the Pharisees and Sadducees were quite unable to perceive what was happening right there, where they were. There may also be a reference to the restless spiritual and political currents that would in time bring disaster to the nation. *You cannot* points to complete disability. They were quite imperceptive, totally lacking in spiritual discernment.[8] "The proof that they cannot discern the 'signs' is that they ask for a sign (v. 1)!" (Carson).

---

important MSS, such as א B X f13 syr^c.s sah boh Origen, and there is no Marcan equivalent. But they are read by C D K L f1 33, and indeed by the great majority of MSS. Many scholars regard them as a variant of Luke 12:54-56 (though we should notice that there are significant differences in wording). Their attestation is impressive, and those who favor acceptance point out that the words may well have been omitted by scribes in lands like Egypt where red sky in the morning does not mean that rain is imminent. Metzger cites both views but gives no verdict; UBS marks its uncertainty by giving it a D rating. In the end it seems that we must remain uncertain: the support for the reading is far from negligible, but the MSS that omit it are important. We should, however, bear in mind Ridderbos's point about the disputed words: "To explain how they could have been added, however, would be as hard as to explain how they could have been omitted" (Ridderbos, p. 293, n. 37).

4. ὀψία occurs in this Gospel only in the expression ὀψίας γενομένης (7 times).

5. εὐδία (εὐ + Διός, gen. of Zeus), here only in the New Testament, has a meaning like "calm" and points to good weather. The one-word forecast is followed by the justification, introduced by γάρ. πυρράζω connects with πῦρ, "fire"; the sky is red like fire.

6. πρωΐ means early in the morning. χειμών occurs twice in Matthew and no more than once in any other book. It can mean rainy and stormy weather or winter, the season of bad weather.

7. στυγνάζω (in the New Testament only here and in the Marcan parallel) is connected with στυγνός, "sombre, gloomy, sullen," and signifies "to have a sombre, gloomy appearance" (AS). It is translated as "threatening" (*NASB*), "has a threatening look" (Cassirer), "overcast" (*NIV, JB*).

8. They should know "that abounding sin like that of their generation was a sign of approaching doom, and that goodness and greatness like His were signs sufficient of His mission from on high" (Glover).

4. A *generation*[9] here signifies the people alive at that time. He castigates it as *evil*, for it has turned away from goodness and right. It is also *adulterous*,[10] for it is false to its vows; it professed to be the people of God but walked in the ways of the evil one. It *looks*[11] *for a sign*; it directs its energies to sign-seeking. But, Jesus says, this is all in vain; the generation in question will not get the sign it seeks.[12] The only *sign* it seeks will be *the sign of Jonah* (a prophet mentioned in the New Testament only by Matthew [5 times] and Luke [4 times]; each time the name is used in connection with the Jews' demand for a sign). At this point Jesus says no more, but in 12:38-40 he makes it clear that the sign of Jonah was that prophet's reappearance after being in the belly of the great fish for three days and three nights. The resurrection of Jesus would be a sign comparable with this. But the point is not elaborated. Jesus leaves them to think over *the sign of Jonah*. Matthew says simply that Jesus left them.

5. The construction here is not quite as smooth as we might have expected, but the sense is clear. The little group went *to the other side*, clearly the other side of the lake. Matthew says nothing about how they crossed or why, simply that they did so. And it was only when they got there that the disciples realized that they had forgotten all about the need to take some bread with them.

6. Jesus proceeded to give them a warning. *"Look out"* translates a verb often used of bodily vision (as in 2:2), and sometimes of perceiving with the mind (9:2). But it is also employed to bring out the meaning "beware," "take heed."[13] The warning is emphasized by adding *"beware"*; Jesus leaves no doubt but that those who follow the Pharisees and Sadducees are in no good state. He goes on to concentrate his warning on *the leaven* of these parties (for *leaven* see on 13:33). *Leaven* was a piece of last week's dough used to make this week's dough rise, and it lends itself to metaphorical uses for something that works away unseen but in the end produces considerable effects. It may be used of a moral tendency, normally in the New Testament for an evil tendency (cf. 1 Cor. 5:6-8; Gal. 5:9), although the parable of the leaven is an exception (13:33). Jesus is warning his hearers to be on their guard against the insidious and pervasive influ-

---

9. γενεά occurs 13 times in Matthew and 15 times in Luke, but no other book has it more than 5 times (Mark, Acts). It may mean all those descended from a common ancestor, a clan (Luke 16:8?), or all those living at a given time (11:16) or period of time (Luke 1:50). Matthew uses it of generations (1:17), and of the people alive in his time (24:34). He frequently characterizes the generation as evil (12:39, 41, 42, 45; 17:17; 23:36).

10. μοιχαλίς is strictly a noun meaning "adulteress," but it is here employed as an adjective.

11. ἐπιζητέω is the " 'directive' of ζητέω," meaning "to inquire for, seek after" (AS). The thought is of wholehearted concentration.

12. "The band of disciples must be on their guard against a self-conscious religiosity that demands guarantees, when it is God's desire to break in unexpectedly through the fixed notions of their system" (Schweizer, pp. 333-34).

13. The verb is ὁράω. It is used in this sense with μή and the subjunctive in 8:4; here with the imperative.

ence that the Pharisees and Sadducees represent (in the Marcan equivalent we have "the leaven of the Pharisees and the leaven of Herod" [Mark 8:15], which is difficult but also points to evil influence; Lenski points out that one of Herod's wives, Mariamne, was a daughter of the high priest and reasons that the high-priestly party, the Sadducees, "must thus be classed as Herodians," p. 608).[14]

7. Evidently the minds of the disciples were running on their recent discovery that they had no bread. For them this was evidently the important thing (a dozen young men looked as if they were beginning an involuntary fast, and that for hearty appetites is a factor of some importance). They evidently found Jesus' saying difficult, and they discussed[15] it among themselves. Without coming up with any recorded conclusion about its meaning, they felt that it had something to do with their failure to remember the bread (what else would "leaven" be about than bread?).

8. *But* will have adversative force; Jesus is set over against the disciples. Matthew does not say how he came to know what they were saying, but there would have been loud voices among the Twelve, and there was no reason for keeping the discussion secret. So he asked a series of questions that would take their minds off speculation about their lack of loaves. His first question looks for the reason for their discussion among themselves, and the form of address, *"you men of little faith"* (see on 6:30 for this expression), indicates a shortcoming in that most important aspect of being disciples, trust in the Master. We might have expected that Jesus would complain about their lack of understanding, but it is not this that concerns him. Faith is the critically important thing. Those who wholly trust God will not enter into the kind of error Jesus is castigating. He does not go into what they have been saying, other than that they had been speaking about their lack of bread.

9-10. Jesus' next question implies that the disciples ought to have been more understanding than they were; *not yet* indicates that they had been with Jesus long enough to be past the kind of reasoning they had just indulged in. They should have grown in understanding. His verb[16] signifies "perceive with the mind," "understand." Then he invites them to engage in another mental process, that of memory; he asks whether they remember the first of the miracles with the loaves, the five loaves and the five thousand men, and how many baskets of food had been taken up. He repeats the process with the seven loaves and the four thousand

---

14. W. Lane comments, "The figure of leaven thus describes the disposition to believe only if signs which compel faith are produced" (*The Gospel according to Mark* [Grand Rapids, 1974], p. 281). This would fit both the Sadducees and the Herodians.

15. διαλογίζομαι means "to balance accounts" and then "to consider, reason" (AS). In this context it points to discussion. ὅτι may be understood in more ways than one. It may be recitative, simply introducing the words the disciples said (so *NRSV, NASB, UBS*³; cf. BDF, 480[6], "with reference to the fact that"), or it may introduce a direct question, as in Turner (M, III, p. 49). But it is better to take it as causal (as *KJV, NEB*, etc.).

16. νοεῖτε.

men. He uses the same word for *how many* in the two questions, but changes the words for *baskets* as in the original accounts of the two miracles. The reminder of these two outstanding miracles should relieve the minds of disciples concerned about feeding a dozen or so people.[17]

11. In the light of the two miraculous feedings Jesus asks how they could have misunderstood his words in the way they did. The memory of the ample supplies received on those previous occasions should have taken their minds off current bread shortages. In any case it is not easy to see how they got from "the leaven of the Pharisees and Sadducees" to their own lack of loaves. Jesus repeats his warning exactly as he had given it earlier (v. 6).

12. *Then* (see on 2:7) they understood. The reminder of Jesus' provision for the multitudes and the repetition of his warning against "the leaven of the Pharisees and Sadducees" enabled them to recognize that Jesus was not speaking about bread,[18] but warning them against the teaching of these groups. It is curious that *teaching* is singular when followed by *of the Pharisees and Sadducees*, for the two groups had many differences and in fact were strongly opposed to one another. Thus the Pharisees put a great deal of emphasis on the "tradition of the elders" with its stress on the written and oral law, whereas the Sadducees would accept nothing but the law written in the Bible. The Sadducees were politicians; they were a comparatively small, but wealthy, aristocratic party, very anxious to work with the Romans. The Pharisees were not politically minded but would live under any government that allowed them to practice their religion. But in different ways both were conservative, and over against Jesus and his followers they might be said to be united and form a unit. At the very least they were linked by their inability to see that Jesus was the Messiah, by their hatred of him, and by their determination to overthrow his teaching if they could.[19]

E. THE CHRIST MADE KNOWN, 16:13–17:13

Matthew has told the story of a group of people who followed Jesus of Nazareth, at first with somewhat dim perceptions of who he was and what

---

17. Argyle remarks, "The thought is: 'The feedings of the five thousand and four thousand are symbolic of my teaching which is all-sufficient for you. You do not need the teaching of my enemies, and you must beware of it.'" But there is no mention of the "leaven" of Jesus, nor any reference to his teaching. We may agree that the two miraculous feedings teach important spiritual lessons, but at this point it is rather the fact of their showing Jesus' capacity to supply bread than these lessons that is to the fore.

18. There is a difficult textual problem with τῶν ἄρτων, read by א[c] B L 892 sah etc., τοῦ ἄρτου by C K W etc., τῶν Φαρισαίων καὶ Σαδδουκαίων by א* syr[c] etc., while D Θ and others omit. It is possible that this last was the original reading with the others as expansions, but it is also possible that the scribes thought the words superfluous and omitted them. With Metzger's committee it seems best to accept τῶν ἄρτων.

19. Bruce remarks, "The *dogmas* and *opinions* of the two parties in question were not the worst of them, but the spirit of their life: their dislike of real godliness."

he taught. As the story has unfolded the disciples have learned more and more about Jesus, but they have still not given expression to anything that shows any real appreciation of who he was and what it was that he had come to accomplish. Matthew now tells his readers of how they came to know Jesus explicitly as Messiah, and how that knowledge was given content because of Peter's misunderstanding and then because of the vision we know as the Transfiguration.

1. Peter's Confession, 16:13-28

13Now when Jesus came into the district of Caesarea Philippi, he asked his disciples, "Who do men say that the Son of man is?" 14And they said, "Some say John the Baptist, others Elias, and others Jeremiah or one of the prophets." 15"But you," he says to them, "who do you say that I am?" 16And Simon Peter answered, saying, "You are the Messiah, the Son of the living God." 17And Jesus answered him, saying, "You are blessed, Simon Barjona, because flesh and blood did not reveal this to you but my Father who is in heaven. 18And I say to you: You are Peter, and on this rock I will build my church, and the gates of Hades will not overpower it. 19I will give you the keys of the kingdom of heaven, and whatever you bind on earth will have been bound in heaven, and whatever you loose on earth will have been loosed in heaven." 20Then he admonished the disciples that they should tell no one that he was the Messiah.

21From then Jesus began to show his disciples that it was necessary for him to go off to Jerusalem and to suffer many things from the elders and chief priests and scribes, and be killed, and on the third day be raised. 22And Peter took him aside and began to remonstrate with him, saying, "God forbid, Lord; this will never happen to you." 23But he turned and said to Peter, "Go away behind me, Satan. You are a trap to me, because you are not thinking the thoughts of God but those of men."

24Then Jesus said to his disciples, "If anyone sets his will on coming after me, let him deny himself, and let him take up his cross, and follow me. 25For whoever sets his will on saving his life will lose it; but whoever loses his life for my sake will find it. 26For what will a man be profited if he gains the whole world and loses his life? Or what will a man give as an exchange for his life? 27For the Son of man will come in the glory of his Father with his angels, and then he will recompense each person according to his behavior. 28Truly I tell you, there are some of those standing here who will not taste death until they see the Son of man coming in his kingdom."

The little group were in Gentile country with no crowds coming to them for teaching and for healing. This doubtless gave them the opportunity for quiet reflection. Jesus took advantage of the situation first to clarify their thoughts about his person, and then to teach them some important truths about messiahship and about being disciples of the Messiah. Shortly he would set out for Jerusalem (19:1); Matthew is telling us about a little interval for quiet reflection away from the crowds. This was a significant time, a time when it would be made clear to the disciples who Jesus was and what that meant in terms of rejection and suffering and death. They would be taught also a little of what discipleship means.[20]

13. At this point Matthew puts his emphasis on the Master. *Jesus came*, he says, when it is clear that the whole band came. But in this section it is what Jesus says and does that dictates the action. He came to *the district* (literally "the parts"; see the note on 2:22) *of Caesarea Philippi*. This city was situated about twenty-five miles north of the sea of Galilee at the foot of Mount Hermon, which was largely pagan territory. One of the sources of the Jordan issues from a cave near this city, and there was an ancient shrine in the cave. When the Greeks came they dedicated the shrine to "Pan and the Nymphs"; they called the cave "Paneion" and the area "Paneas." In 20 B.C. Augustus gave the district to Herod the Great and built a temple of white marble in honor of the emperor at Paneas. When Herod died in 4 B.C. the area became part of the tetrarchy of Philip, and this man rebuilt the city. He called it Caesarea in honor of the emperor Augustus and added "Philippi" (which distinguished it from Caesarea on the Mediterranean coast and, of course, honored Philip himself).[21] Jesus asked the disciples a question about what people thought of him. There is no indication of why he did this, and nothing in the narrative leads up to it. But he asked them who *men* (i.e., people in general) said *the Son of man* was. This, of course, was Jesus' favorite self-designation (see on 8:20), and it is clear that he was asking a question about how he himself was regarded by people outside his circle, not inquiring about how they interpreted Daniel 7:13. This is clear from Mark and Luke, neither of whom has "the Son of man," but simply "who I am" (a number of MSS import "I" into Matthew and there is considerable textual variation, but whichever reading we adopt, it is clear that Jesus is asking who people think he is). Some scholars hold that Jesus would not have put the question in this form, for by calling himself "the Son of man" he was asserting his messiahship. But this title (which he had used before, 8:20; 9:6, etc.) was not an accepted title of the Messiah; it was simply the way Jesus referred to himself. The objection lacks validity.

14. They reported a variety of opinion, but did not include any hostile views. They concentrated their answer on people who in some sense approved of Jesus, and even among them they found different views, though in one way or another all the views mentioned affirmed that Jesus

---

20. "Here we reach the crisis, the turning-point in the ministry of Jesus. He knew what lay before him. He knew because he planned the future, with his own death at Jerusalem. He had therefore to secure some representatives whom he could leave behind him to carry on his work" (Robinson).

21. See Josephus, *Ant.* 15.363-64; 18.28; *War* 2.168, and the articles in *ISBE*, I, p. 569 and *IDB*, I, p. 480.

was a prophet. Some people[22] thought that Jesus was *John the Baptist*, as Herod did (14:2, though at first he appears to have rejected the view, Luke 9:9). John had made a profound impression, and apparently there were some who thought that his death at the hands of Herod could not be the last of him. A second group regarded *Elias* as more likely. This is the Greek form of Elijah, and these people evidently saw Jesus as the fulfilment of the prophecy that Elijah would appear again (Mal. 4:5). It is not clear why others thought of him as *Jeremiah* (we owe this information to Matthew; neither Mark nor Luke mentions him). In the Hebrew Scriptures Jeremiah is said to be listed first in some groupings of "the latter prophets," and he may have been considered the typical prophet.[23] Perhaps, too, those who held this view remembered Jeremiah's prophecies of doom and held that Jesus was Jeremiah all over again because of what he had to say about the future of the nation (cf. 11:21-24). There is Jewish teaching that Jeremiah will come, together with Isaiah, before the coming of the End (2 Esdr. 2:18). And Judas Maccabaeus before his battle with Nicanor saw a vision of "a man who loves the brethren and prays much for the people and the holy city, Jeremiah, the prophet of God" (2 Macc. 15:14; in the vision Jeremiah gave him a golden sword). *One of the prophets* is a loose, general category. The people who held this view were not prepared to identify Jesus with any particular prophet, but they held that he was great enough to be numbered among the prophets. They may have agreed with the previous groups that he was the reincarnation of some great prophet of earlier days, or they may have thought of him as a new member of the prophetic band. Clearly many people were impressed by Jesus and saw him doing the kind of thing they thought prophets would do. It is also clear that there was a good deal of discussion and that people held very varied opinions of him.

15. *But you* are two important words: *But* is adversative and marks a contrast, while *you* is emphatic (the question is identical in Mark and Luke). Jesus turns attention away from the general public with its casual contacts and its imperfect loyalty and understanding and asks how it was with the men who were his closest followers (Jesus did not ask Peter for his personal view). They had left all and followed him. They had been with him now for quite some time. They had seen what he did and they had heard what he taught. In the light of all this, how did they view him? We are apt to concentrate our attention on Peter as we reflect on this passage, but we should not forget that he is the spokesman for the Twelve as he answers a question addressed to them all.

---

22. οἱ μέν occurs here only in Matthew (though ἃ μέν etc. are found). ὁ μέν . . . ὁ δέ signifies "the one . . . the other," but here we have οἱ μὲν . . . ἄλλοι . . . ἕτεροι. There can be little difference in meaning between the last two.

23. His sufferings may also have been important. Tasker comments, "of all the historical characters of the Old Testament Jeremiah approximates most closely to Jesus as an outstanding example of patient endurance of undeserved suffering" (p. 157).

16. As Peter speaks for the whole band on this significant occasion, Matthew gives him his full name, *Simon Peter* (which he does only here in his Gospel, though cf. 4:18; 10:2). Peter's reply is, *"You are the Messiah,"* words that are found in all three Synoptists (Mark has no more, but Luke adds "of God"; for *Messiah* [= Christ] see on 1:1). It is unlikely that this is the first occasion on which the apostles thought of Jesus as Messiah; some such idea was surely in their minds from the beginning, and it was because they saw Jesus in this capacity that they left their homes and followed him. But as they lived and worked with him, their understanding of "Messiah" enlarged. We see this in the way Peter continued: he went on to say that Jesus was *"the Son of the living God"* (for *Son of God* see on 8:29; cf. 26:63). Jesus was God's Anointed One, the One who was sent to do God's will in a special way. It may not be easy to understand precisely what Peter thought the Anointed One would be and do (even with his insight that he was God's Son), but he was certainly giving voice to an exalted view of Jesus. He could not have ascribed a higher place to him. His words bring out the essential being of our Lord in the most comprehensive expression in the Gospels.

17. Matthew introduces Jesus' response with his "having answered, said" construction, so frequent in this Gospel. Matthew is the only one to report this response (Mark and Luke move immediately to Jesus' instruction not to tell anyone about his messiahship, which Matthew has in v. 20). Jesus tells Peter that he is *blessed* (see on 5:3), a word that signifies godly felicity. It means not worldly happiness (as "fortunate," *AB*, might indicate), but religious delight; nor does it signify gloomy piety but rather holy joy. This is the one place in the New Testament where Peter is accorded his full family name, *Simon Barjona*, "son of Jona."[24] Jesus follows his pronouncing of a blessing on Peter with the reason for it. He begins by denying that what that apostle has just said is the end result of some splendid human effort; *flesh and blood* means any human being over against God or angels or demons (*NEB*, "mortal man").[25] It is important to realize that this knowledge is not due to human cleverness or even profound spiritual insight. Jesus says that it is the product of divine revelation (cf. 11:25-27), for the source of Peter's words was *"my Father who is in heaven."* There is intimacy in the expression *"my Father"* (the Jews spoke of God as "Father," but they preferred the plural *"our Father"*); Jesus' relationship to God is not the same as that of anyone else; he is saying something about himself as well as about the source of Peter's information. We should also notice that he accepted Peter's use of the word "Messiah"; mostly he declined to use the word (presumably because it would arouse misunderstanding of what he was and had come

---

24. In John 1:42 he is "son of John." His father may have borne two names, or perhaps Ἰωνᾶ is a contraction of Ἰωάνης. Jona is a very infrequent name, and it is possible that "son of Jona" means "someone very like Jona."

25. The expression means "*man* w. strong emphasis on his ephemeral character, his shortsightedness and moral weakness" (BAGD, αἷμα, 1.a).

421

to do). But popular misconceptions would not flourish in the little apostolic band, and he accepts the title there.

18. *And I* follows the revelation made by the Father with a solemn statement from Jesus himself. He uses the emphatic pronoun, which in this context means "I, the Messiah"; it marks the following words as important. Peter has made a significant statement about Jesus: Jesus proceeds to make a significant statement about Peter. When he goes on to say *"You are Peter,"* his *You* is also emphatic: "You, the man who has just made this important statement, you to whom my heavenly Father has revealed this great truth." We should not understand the words to mean that Jesus was giving the name at this point; that would more likely be in the form "You will be called" (cf. John 1:42); rather, Jesus was drawing attention to the significance of a name already familiar. He proceeds to make his point with a play on words: the Greek words for *Peter* and for *rock* are related.[26] If a difference is intended here, the massive live rock will be the declaration, the great truth now revealed, that Jesus is the Messiah, over against Peter, the man who received the revelation.

"On this rock I will build my church"[27] is a saying that has caused endless controversy in the church's history. The big question is the meaning of *this rock*. Does it mean the man Peter? Or the faith Peter has just professed? Or is it the teaching of Jesus (as in 7:24)? Or Jesus himself? Each of the views has been argued passionately by some exegetes, often maintaining at the same time that other views can be espoused only by people who refuse to accept the plain meaning of the Greek. Clearly this is a place where we must tread carefully and keep in mind the possibility of interpreting the passage in ways other than the one that appeals to us.

Some scholars, especially from among the Roman Catholics, have insisted that Jesus is saying that Peter is the rock on which the whole church is to be built, and accordingly that only the church that can claim to be built on the apostle is the true church. But it is not easy to establish that the whole of the early church was built on the foundation of Peter, and what are we to say of the descendants of the non-Petrine churches?

---

26. Πέτρος and πέτρα. This latter means "*a rock,* i.e. a mass of live rock as distinct from πέτρος, a detached stone or boulder" (AS). Turner remarks, "The name of the apostle Πέτρος, if it actually means *rock* and corresponds to Aram. Κηφᾶς, cannot be connected directly with πέτρος, since this was out of general use; it does not mean *rock* but is a masculinizing of πέτρα" (M, III, p. 22). Elsewhere Turner cites this pun as part of the evidence that Jesus spoke in Greek on occasion (*Grammatical Insights,* p. 181), though the pun, of course, is possible also in Aramaic. There is no evidence that Peter was called Kephas until Jesus gave him the name. Indeed, "There is no evidence that anyone had the name Peter before Christian times, either in its Greek form or in Aramaic, Cephas. In fact it is not a name at all, but a nickname, and it should really be translated 'Rock'" (Fenton).

27. The imagery of the foundation is used in different ways. Thus Jesus himself is the one foundation (1 Cor. 3:11), and again the church is built on the foundation of the apostles and prophets (Eph. 2:20). Believers themselves lay up a good foundation (1 Tim. 6:19), while God's strong foundation stands (2 Tim. 2:19), and from another point of view repentance and faith form the foundation (Heb. 6:1).

And so in later times with, for example, the churches of the Reformation that separated from the churches that professed a connection with Peter. Are we to say that because they understand this passage in a different way they are no part of the true church? Moreover, the statement that the rock is Peter is true only as we keep in mind what that apostle has just said; it is not Peter simply as Peter but Peter who has confessed Jesus as the Messiah who is the church's foundation on whom the church is to be built. We must not separate the man from the words he has just spoken.[28] From the earliest times it has been recognized that Peter's faith is important for an understanding of the passage. Thus Chrysostom cites the words "upon this rock will I build my Church" and immediately goes on, "that is, on the faith of his confession" (p. 333). Any interpretation that minimizes the importance of the faith that found expression in Peter's words is to be rejected. Barclay puts it this way: Jesus "did not mean that the Church *depended* on Peter, as it depended on Himself, and on God the Rock, alone. He did mean that the Church *began* with Peter; in that sense Peter is the foundation of the Church" (II, p. 156). And we must bear in mind that while the name Peter is connected with "rock" it is not easy simply to equate the two, for *rock* here is feminine, not masculine.[29]

We should also bear in mind McNeile's point that to address Peter as *this* would be strange immediately following the direct address *"You are Peter."* Why would Jesus not continue with something like "and upon you I will build my church"?[30] *This* would be more natural if Jesus were addressing the whole group rather than Peter himself. And if Peter was here given the chief place, the question of the disciples just a little later as to who would have that place (18:1) is inexplicable. They at any rate knew nothing of Peter as the supreme pontiff. So it is argued that the church is built on Peter's confession of the truth that Jesus is the Messiah, the truth that the Father has revealed to Peter. Against this is the emphasis on Peter himself in the incident. So perhaps it is better to think of the church as built on Peter as the man who has received the revelation.

---

28. As Hill, for example, does. He says, "Attempts to interpret the 'rock' as something other than Peter in person (e.g. his faith, the truth revealed to him) are due to Protestant bias"; he makes no attempt to give a reason for separating the words of the confession Peter has just made from the man who made them. And it leads him to say things like "Peter has authority to make pronouncements (whether legislative, as 'chief rabbi' . . . or disciplinary) and these will be ratified by God in the Last Judgment" (on v. 19). Peter! The Peter of verses 22-23; 18:21; Gal. 2:11-14 the chief rabbi with his pronouncements ratified by God at the last judgment?

29. It is sometimes said dogmatically that Jesus spoke in Aramaic in which there is no distinction of gender, but it must be borne in mind that Jesus may well have spoken in Greek (see n. 26 above). In any case it is a Greek text that we must expound, and it is hazardous to rest its meaning on a hypothetical Aramaic original.

30. Cf. Ryle, "To speak of an erring, fallible child of Adam as the foundation of the spiritual temple, is very unlike the ordinary language of Scripture. Above all, no reason can be given why our Lord should not have said, 'I will build my Church upon *thee*,' if such had been His meaning, instead of saying, 'I will build my Church upon *this rock*.'"

Others argue that we should put the words in the context of Matthew's Gospel as a whole. They point out that Jesus likens the person who hears his words and builds on them to a man building on rock (7:24-25).[31] Throughout this whole Gospel the teaching of Jesus is taken with the utmost seriousness, and there is never a hint that his followers can take it lightly. This does not mean that people are expected to earn their salvation by keeping Jesus' teachings; his atoning death is as clear in this Gospel as in the others. The whole of his teaching is to be taken into account. This includes his teaching that the lowly will be blessed (cf. the beatitudes in the Sermon on the Mount). In this way the view that the teaching of Jesus is in mind runs into that which holds that Jesus himself is the rock (cf. 1 Cor. 10:4; 1 Pet. 2:6-8) or the foundation (1 Cor. 3:11; 2 Tim. 2:19).

Thus it seems that there is truth in more than one way of looking at the words. There is no doubting that Peter is assigned a preeminence (which we see clearly in the early chapters of Acts), but it is not an absolute preeminence and we must be careful in defining it. In any case there is no mention of any successors of Peter; whatever position is assigned to him is personal and not transmissible to those who would succeed him. Jesus is speaking of the apostle and not of those who followed him.[32]

The word *church* has also caused much disputation. Since it occurs in the Gospels again only in 18:17, many scholars hold that Jesus could not have used the word. Its occurrence here, they think, is a case of Matthew's reading back onto the lips of Jesus an expression that would justify the existence of the church in his day. But this is surely unjustified. The word we translate as *church* could be used of almost any assembly; it is used, for example, of the rioting Ephesians in Acts 19:32, 40. Granted that Jesus intended his followers to continue after his death as a coherent group, there is no reason why he should not have used the word occasionally. If he was the Messiah he would be linked with a community that followed his teachings.[33] This would be the more likely in that the word

31. Gundry emphasizes this: "In accord with 7:24, which Matthew quotes here, the πέτρα consists of Jesus' teaching, i.e., the law of Christ. 'This rock' no longer poses the problem that 'this' ill suits an address to Peter in which he is the rock . . . we are free from the necessity of appealing to Aramaic in order to explain away the usual distinction between Πέτρος, 'detached stone' (hardly a firm foundation), and πέτρα, 'bedrock.' The two words retain their peculiar Greek connotations, for Matthew's Jesus will build only on the firm bedrock of his law (cf. 5:19-20; 28:19), not on the loose stone Peter" (p. 334).

32. The early church knows nothing of a personal headship over the church possessed by Peter. He, together with John, was "sent" by the church (Acts 8:14), he is called by the church to give an account of himself (Acts 11:1-18), it is James, not Peter, who presides over the council in Jerusalem (Acts 15), and Paul rebukes him sharply (Gal. 2:11-14). That Peter was a great apostle, widely honored in the early church, is clear. That he was the earthly head of the church is not.

33. Cf. Albright and Mann, "It is hard to know what kind of thinking, other than confessional presupposition, justifies the tendency of some commentators to dismiss this verse as not authentic. A Messiah without a Messianic Community would have been unthinkable to any Jew."

was used in the Greek translation of the Old Testament for the people of God, whether assembled or not. In the New Testament the word is mostly used of the local church, but in Ephesians particularly it refers to the whole church universal (as also in some passages in the earlier letters, e.g., 1 Cor. 12:28).[34]

Jesus goes on to say, "*the gates of Hades will not overpower it.*" The word *gate* is normally used in the New Testament for some impressive gate, such as the gate of a city (Luke 7:12), of the temple (Acts 3:10), or of a prison (Acts 12:10); it may indicate the gate to life (7:13-14). *Hades* is the underworld, the place of the dead; it may be contrasted with heaven (11:23). That the *gates . . . will not overpower* the church is a little puzzling, since we think of gates as part of the defense rather than as a weapon of offense. But gates were important parts of fortifications in the first century and were usually flanked by bastions. Wooden gates would be overlain with bronze. They thus lend themselves to the imagery of strength. The gates of Hades were probably regarded as especially strong (did not they keep in all the dead?). The expression may, of course, be metaphorical (cf. "powers of death," *REB*). Jesus is then saying that the gates of Hades are not strong enough to prevail against his church; that church will never die. There may also be the thought that though Hades is strong and the dead do not come back from it, it is not strong enough to contain Jesus and it is not strong enough to contain the Christian dead. Whether we can understand all the detailed imagery or not, it is clear that Jesus is giving his followers the assurance that nothing in this world or the next can overthrow the church.[35]

19. Jesus continues with the promise that he will make Peter a gift, where the future tense probably points to the time subsequent to the resurrection (about which Jesus is about to speak, v. 21). He says that he will give Peter *the keys of the kingdom of heaven.*[36] The kingdom, of course, is not to be identified with the church. The kingdom has reference to the divine rule; the church to the people of God. They are closely related, but not identical. The key lends itself to metaphorical uses (e.g., the key of knowledge, Luke 11:52). It is an obvious symbol for admitting people through a door, but it was also used for exercising authority (the steward rather than the porter). We should understand it here in close connection with Peter's confession of faith: it was on the basis of his confession and not on that of personal abilities that Peter was given the keys. In the Lucan passage the lawyers were excluding people from the knowledge of God

---

34. Carson has a useful note on the word's etymology and usage, and the significance of the words it translates in LXX. He thinks that it is "entirely appropriate" in this passage "where there is no emphasis on institution, organization, form of worship, or separate synagogue."

35. Cf. these words about God from ancient times: "thou hast power over life and death; thou dost lead men down to the gates of Hades and back again" (Wisd. of Sol. 16:13).

36. Many see an allusion to Isaiah 22:22. Jesus has the key of David and the keys of death and Hades (Rev. 1:18; 3:7).

by their handling of Scripture. Later in this Gospel Matthew will report that Jesus spoke of the scribes and Pharisees as shutting up the kingdom before people and thus preventing them from entering (23:13). Peter, by contrast, was to open the way. We see him doing this in Acts 2 and 3, where his preaching brought many into the kingdom, and in Acts 10, where he opened the way for the Gentile Cornelius to come in. We should see another aspect of the use of the keys in Acts 8:20-23, where he is excluding an impenitent sinner. And while the gift of the keys indicates that Peter is clearly given a certain primacy, we should not exaggerate this. The right to bind and loose, here connected with the gift of the keys, is given to the disciples as a whole in 18:18; thus we are not to think of Peter as elevated to a plane above all the others.

The metaphor of binding and loosing was used by the rabbis for declaring forbidden or permitted.[37] There is a strong opinion that the Christians thought rather of excluding from and admitting to the Christian community. This may be correct, though we should bear in mind that *whatever* is neuter both times and that this fits better with things than with people. If we take this seriously, the saying means that the Spirit-inspired church will be able to declare authoritatively what things are forbidden and what things are permitted. The Jews held fast to the law of Moses, but this was not to be binding on the new community in the sense in which the Jews understood it; Jesus was telling Peter how it should make decisions about what is permitted and what forbidden. We should also notice that the verbs of binding and loosing are both future perfect, a tense about which France says: "as the future perfect sounds as stilted in Greek as in English, the tense is apparently deliberate" (p. 256). With respect to its significance in this passage Chamberlain remarks: "This is wrongly translated 'shall be bound' and 'shall be loosed,' seeming to make Jesus teach that the apostles' acts will determine the policies of heaven. They should be translated 'shall have been bound' and 'shall have been loosed.' This makes the apostles' acts a matter of inspiration or heavenly guidance." He adds, "This incorrect translation has given expositors and theologians a great deal of trouble" (p. 80).[38]

In the end we must be guarded in our understanding of this passage,

---

37. G. Dalman makes this clear, though he thinks that the Christians used it in the different sense of exclusion from the community and admission to it (*The Words of Jesus* [Edinburgh, 1902], pp. 213-17). F. Büchsel takes up much the same position. He understands "the customary meaning of the Rabbinic expression" as "to declare forbidden or permitted," but here and in 18:18 "even if we cannot say more, the weight of probability is definitely in favour of the interpretation: 'to impose and remove the ban' " (*TDNT,* II, pp. 60, 61).

38. Turner also understands the meaning as "Whatsoever thou bindest shall already have been permanently bound," and says of this passage, "It takes away the responsibility of human choice, and therefore uninformed choice, and represents St. Peter as acting in these solemn binding and loosing matters always under the infallible guidance of the Holy Spirit" (*Grammatical Insights,* p. 80). A similar comment should be made about the use of the perfect tenses in connection with the forgiveness of sin and the reverse in John 20:22-23.

for there are several possibilities, and whichever view we adopt we must agree that there are quite good reasons why other people hold other opinions. But on the whole it seems that the right to "bind" and "loose" refers primarily to the regulation of conduct, while the keys point to admission and exclusion. The new community, while regarding itself as God's Israel and retaining the Old Testament Scriptures, did not think of itself as nothing more than a variant of Judaism. Living by the same Scriptures and serving the same God, but rejecting the Jewish way of life, meant that there would be a continuing need for guidance in understanding what was permitted and what was forbidden. Jesus is saying that that guidance would be given to Peter and (a little later he adds) to the other apostles. Good reasons may be brought forward for holding that Jesus meant that the new community would exercise divinely given authority both in regulating its internal affairs and in deciding who would be admitted to and who excluded from its membership.

20. Matthew rounds off the episode, as do Mark and Luke, with Jesus giving the disciples firm instruction to tell nobody that he was the Messiah. Matthew's favorite *Then* (see on 2:7) moves on to the next point. Jesus gave the Twelve firm instruction that they were not to disclose the conversation. There is some emphasis on *he* in the expression *that he was the Messiah: he* and no other *was the Messiah*. This was a fact, and he had admitted it among the disciples. But the term could all too easily be misinterpreted and understood, for example, in political terms. If the disciples had gone out proclaiming that Jesus was the Messiah, both they and their hearers would have thought of a glorious, conquering Messiah. They would have looked for armies and bloodshed and victories. To know that Jesus was the Messiah was one thing; to understand what messiahship really meant was quite another. To have proclaimed Jesus' messiahship would have been to invite misunderstanding. Better by far for Jesus to get on with the completion of his mission and to keep the knowledge that he was the Messiah within the inner circle. The disciples are to follow the same path as the Master: he knew he was the Messiah, but he did not proclaim it publicly; they are to take up the same position.

21. *From then* marks the incident as of critical importance; it changed the whole thrust of Jesus'[39] instruction of the Twelve. Now that it was clear that the little band had come to understand that Jesus was indeed the long-promised Messiah, he proceeded to teach them something of what messiahship meant. For the Jews in general, and presumably for the Twelve up to this point, being Messiah meant unadulterated glory. The Messiah might encounter opposition and even hardship, but this kind of thing was no more than an unpleasantness that must be passed through

39. A few MSS (notably ℵ* B* boh) read "Jesus Christ," an expression found very rarely in the Gospels (1:1, 18; Mark 1:1; John 1:17; 17:3). It may perhaps be the right reading here, for a solemn name would suit a solemn passage. It would also recall that Peter has just called Jesus the Christ.

on the way to majesty and splendor. For Jesus suffering was the essence of messiahship, and from this point on he brings it out again and again (cf. 17:9, 12, 22-23; 20:18-19, 28; 21:38-39; 26:2). Learning this was a lesson the disciples found very hard indeed. This may be the point of Matthew's *began;* it would be a long, slow process, but Jesus began it right after Peter made his magnificent affirmation, and the others presumably acknowledged its truth.[40] He told them that *it was necessary* for him to suffer, and we should take notice of the way he puts it. He does not simply prophesy that he will die, nor does he even say that, on the whole, this seems to be an advisable procedure. He says it was *necessary*[41] for him to *go off to Jerusalem.* Most of his ministry, as Matthew records it, had been spent in Galilee and adjacent regions. But now a divine necessity takes him to Jerusalem (cf. 23:37; Luke 13:33-34) for the climax of his ministry. There he must *suffer,* a word that can cover a variety of unpleasantnesses,[42] and *many things* indicates that the suffering will be no light affliction. Jesus makes no mention of what the suffering entails, but specifies that it will come from *the elders and chief priests and scribes.* The conjunction is a comprehensive term for the Jewish leadership, and the single article that precedes the list classes them as a united group. The conjunction can scarcely be anything other than the Sanhedrin, the supreme legislative body among the Jews. There were local elders in local governing bodies and synagogues, but those in Jerusalem would be members of the Sanhedrin. It is the same with *chief priests* (for the term see on 2:4); strictly it denoted the ecclesiastic holding the highest position, but it came to be used of others in the high-priestly family (unfortunately there is no information about which others).[43] *Scribes* (see on 2:4; 5:20) were men learned in the law; they formed an important part of the Sanhedrin. What Jesus is saying is that the highest court in the land will inflict suffering on him. Not only will he suffer pain, but he will *be killed.* The disciples are to be in no doubt as to the outcome of the sufferings he describes.

40. Cf. Plummer, "The 'began' is important. We have here a summary of what went on for some time, and neither Mt. nor Mk. tells us at what point Peter drew upon himself Christ's terrible rebuke" (p. 232). Plummer thinks that it would have been after Peter had had time to think over "this new and amazing teaching respecting the Messiah."

41. δεῖ, which Matthew uses 8 times. See 26:54 for another statement of the inevitability of the cross. Bonnard remarks that this verb does not point us to "the individual or heroic determination of Jesus, nor to the increasing opposition of his enemies, very real though that was, nor to a blind fate, nor to the arbitrary inscrutability of a distant divinity, nor to the psychological or religious needs of the Jews or of men in general, but to a plan of God, certainly impenetrable for unbelievers, but perceptible to faith . . ." (p. 247).

42. πάσχω, which Matthew uses only 3 times (out of 40 New Testament occurrences). It is mostly used in the way it is here, without a defining word.

43. According to BAGD the term covers also "adult male members of the most prominent priestly families." J. Jeremias, however, gives a list of "The Chief Priests and Chief Levites" almost all of whom are priests (*Jerusalem in the Time of Jesus* [London, 1969], p. 160). He gives the title of each as "The Captain of the Temple," "The director of the weekly course," etc.

But this is not the end. On the third day he will *be raised*. The verb is one regularly used for being raised from the dead, and the passive is important. Jesus does not say that he will rise, but that he will be raised, that is, the Father will raise him (the New Testament does sometimes say that Jesus will rise,[44] but it is more common to have the passive in this way). For *the third day* see on 12:40; according to the normal Jewish way of counting time it was the third day on which Jesus rose. Jesus simply makes the statement and does not elaborate, and apparently the disciples did not take it in; their attention was concentrated on the suffering and death, which they could not fit into their understanding of what it means to be the Messiah.

22. Characteristically it is Peter who initiates the disciples' reaction, probably all the more so since he has just received Jesus' commendation and his promise of an important role in the future. He *took him aside*,[45] which indicates a friendly attitude (though perhaps *NEB*'s "took him by the arm" is a trifle too definite). That he further *began to remonstrate with him* carries on with the superior attitude (*began* may mean that he only made a start). Peter is now assuming that he knows better than Jesus does what the Master should do. He does not accept what Jesus has said and presumes to criticize him for saying it. *"Lord"* is a respectful form of address, but *"God forbid"* is a strong repudiation of what Jesus has just prophesied.[46] Peter has just given expression to the conviction that Jesus is the Messiah and has been praised by Jesus for this. He has seen something of Jesus' greatness, and because he has seen that greatness it is inconceivable to him that Jesus would undergo the humiliation of which he has just spoken. For Peter it is unthinkable that the one he has just pronounced "the Messiah, the Son of the living God" should be rejected and killed. How could the Jewish nation reject the Jewish Messiah? So he says forthrightly, *"this will never happen to you"*; his double negative is very emphatic (and with the future indicative rather than the aorist subjunctive even more so).

23. *But* has adversative force and sets Jesus at odds with what Peter

44. *AB* asserts, "The NT writers always speak of Jesus as 'being raised' by the Father, or in the power of the Spirit, never that he raised himself," but this is not accurate. In the Marcan parallel we have ἀναστῆναι, and see 1 Thessalonians 4:14; cf. Romans 14:9.

45. The verb is προσλαμβάνω, only here in Matthew. It means "to take in addition" and "to take to oneself." It is not easy to see what it signifies here. McNeile thinks that it may be redundant, "But it may mean literally that Peter 'drew Him to him,' with a gesture implying protection if not superiority." It may indicate an attempt to speak of Jesus privately (though Ridderbos denies this). It is used of Priscilla and Aquila "taking to themselves" Apollos to help him acquire a better understanding of the Christian way (Acts 18:26). Cf. Romans 14:1; 15:7.

46. ἵλεως is found in the New Testament again only in Hebrews 8:12. It has a meaning like "propitious," "merciful" and with ἔστω ὁ θεός understood signifies, "May God be merciful, spare you this!" But it can scarcely mean "God bless you, Master!" (Goodspeed). It is used in LXX to render חָלִילָה in the sense "far be it from — ." *JB* renders "Heaven preserve you, Lord," and *NIV*, "Never, Lord."

has just said. Evidently he had been facing away from Peter, but he now turns to him and in unusually strong words utters a vigorous repudiation of Peter's pious petition. *"Go away"* is more forceful than elegant,[47] while *behind me* consigns him to an insignificant place where he can be ignored. Most surprisingly of all Jesus addresses his follower as *"Satan,"* an address unparalleled in the New Testament. It expresses vividly Jesus' rejection of Peter's suggestion. Peter's words are not what might have been expected from the man to whom the revelation of Jesus' messiahship had been made; they are a suggestion emanating from Satan himself. We are to understand that Jesus' death was so central to God's plan that to try to avoid it was to do the work of none less than the evil one himself.[48] Indeed, Peter was taking up essentially the position of Satan in the temptation narrative. The evil one had tried to get Jesus to take the easy, spectacular way and to avoid the path of suffering, and that in essence was what Peter was advising.

Jesus goes on to say that Peter was *a trap*[49] to him. The apostle's well-meant suggestion, if adopted, would lead Jesus seriously astray and turn him away from that death which was to be central to the gospel he came to establish. The trouble was that Peter was not thinking in the right way. *The thoughts* is really a general term meaning more literally "the things"; Peter's mind was not set on the things of God. *But* is the strong adversative[50] — far from the things of God ("You are not on God's side," *AB*), Peter's mind was set on purely human ways of thinking. It comes naturally to us to think of glory and honor, of comfort and security. We find it difficult to understand things from the perspective of the righteous God who loves righteousness (Ps. 11:7). Peter had had his view that Jesus was the Messiah confirmed; in the light of that he found it incredible that this would entail rejection and suffering and death.

---

47. ὑπάγω. BAGD notes that it is not found at all in Acts, Paul, and Hebrews and says, "it tends more and more to mean simply 'go' in colloq. speech." MM cites its use in the vernacular for "go away." The word was addressed to Satan when he tempted Jesus to earthly greatness (4:10), but here it is followed by ὀπίσω, "behind," on which Barclay says: "His command to Peter is: 'Begone *behind me!*' that is to say, 'Become my follower again.' Satan is banished from the presence of Christ; Peter is recalled to be Christ's follower" (II, p. 166). This is an interesting thought, but we must remember that in many MSS of Luke 4:8 ὕπαγε ὀπίσω μου is applied to Satan.

48. Ryle reasons from the strength of the language Jesus uses in rebuking Peter that "there is no doctrine of Scripture so deeply important as the doctrine of Christ's atoning death" (p. 200).

49. Most translations have "stumbling block" or the like (so *REB, NASB, NIV*), but a σκάνδαλον was the bait stick of a trap, the mechanism that triggered off the trap when a bird or animal touched it. MM argues that the corresponding verb means " 'I set a trap for' rather than 'I put a stumbling-block in the way of.' " Lenski notes the explanation that "adds the thought of 'impediment' which leads to 'stumbling block' (R.V.)." But he goes on, "Here it is important to retain the original meaning. One may *fall* over a stumbling block and yet may rise again. But this is not the case with a *skandalon*, for merely to touch the bait affixed to it would spring the trap, and Jesus would be *caught* in its death grip" (p. 641).

50. ἀλλά.

24. *Then* (see on 2:7) here means "next in sequence"; having vigorously set aside Peter's unwelcome and worldly suggestion, Jesus now addresses the disciples as a whole. He has told his followers that he must suffer and now, in words similar to those in 10:38-39, he goes on to say that those who follow him must likewise expect suffering. He puts the resolution to be a disciple hypothetically but positively,[51] and speaks of *anyone,* which makes the words refer to any would-be disciple whatever. *Sets his will* is important; the prospective disciple must exercise his will; nobody becomes a follower of Jesus by drifting into it. There must always be the wholehearted decision. *Coming after me* could mean simply walking behind Jesus as he moved along the road, but in a context like this there is no doubt that it means "be a disciple," "be a committed follower." Such a person must *deny*[52] *himself.* The natural tendency of the race is to affirm oneself, to concentrate on what serves one's own interests, to make oneself as prosperous as one can. Jesus calls on all his true followers to renounce such self-interest (*NEB,* "leave self behind"). It is not easy to understand that we must concentrate on meeting the needs of others rather than promoting ourselves (which is why people make utterances like the one Peter had just made).

Jesus brings out the truth that he is looking for the utmost in self-denial by saying that the disciple must *take up his cross.*[53] We minimize the force of this with sayings like "We all have our cross to bear." Jesus was not talking about minor discomforts. Those who heard him utter these words knew what taking up a cross meant; they knew that it was the prelude to that person's crucifixion. Jesus was speaking about a death to a whole way of life; he was talking about the utmost in self-sacrifice, a very death to selfishness and all forms of self-seeking.[54] We should not miss the force of *his cross:* there is a cross for every servant of God. And when we come to *follow,* we should not miss the present imperative: "let him keep on following me." Jesus is talking about a discipleship that is a whole way of life.[55] Taking up a cross is not something that can be done once and for all and gotten out of the way (Luke has "take up his cross daily," Luke 9:23).

25. Jesus gives a reason;[56] *whoever* makes the statement general. Jesus is enunciating a principle of universal application. Paradoxically anyone

---

51. εἰ with the indicative.

52. Chamberlain sees perfective force in the verb ἀπαρνέομαι, "I deny utterly" (p. 134).

53. Matthew is interested in the cross; he has σταυρός 5 times (Mark and John both have it 4 times; Paul has it 10 times but no more than 3 in any one epistle).

54. MM quotes a prayer from the 4th-5th century A.D.: "O God of the crosses that are laid upon us, help thy servant Apphouas," where "God is apparently thought of as at once the sender and mitigator of trials" (Ed.).

55. Mounce comments that the construction used here "would suggest definitive action in the decision to enter into a life of discipleship and the necessity of continuing faithfulness in following through on a daily basis."

56. Introduced by γάρ.

at all who *sets his will on saving his life will lose it*. As in the previous verse there is emphasis on the action of the will. To set one's will on saving the life is self-defeating. *Life*[57] may be understood as the soul (so Calvin, II, p. 195), in which case Jesus is saying that to concentrate on saving one's own soul is to lose it; the follower of Jesus must be outgoing. Or it may be life here and now but life in its most meaningful sense.[58] And, of course, it is not impossible that Jesus had both senses in mind, for what he says is true of both. If we regard life as no more than this ordinary, physical life, if we spend our time and our resources on getting as much out of this life as we can, Jesus is saying, we lose life in its more important sense.[59] To spend oneself trying the get the best one can out of this present life, the here and now, is to lose life in the fullest sense. Jesus is not saying that anyone who concentrates on his own selfish concerns will be punished by having his life taken from him. He is saying that, by the very fact that he concentrates on his own selfish concerns, that person has lost life in the best and fullest sense. He exists, but does not live. Jesus is speaking of the person who puts his emphasis on all that increases the sum of things he finds attractive. It is the selfishness that makes one's personal happiness the ultimate criterion. That, Jesus says, is self-defeating; to concentrate on saving the life is to lose it. It is otherwise with anyone who *loses his life for my sake*. Again there is the *whoever* that makes the words universal. But this time it is not only the will to lose one's life that Jesus is speaking of, but actually losing it.[60] This is the complete opposite of willing to save one's life. Jesus is not talking about some masochistic activity; he is not referring to someone who has such a poor self-esteem that his life crumbles. He is referring to the person who *loses his life for my sake*, the one who puts the service of God's Messiah before all else, who counts all well lost for Christ's sake and who consequently devotes all his time to serving Christ and other people for Christ's sake. That person will *find* life. He now finds that the life he lived before giving up all for Christ was not really life at all. Full and abundant life is the life of service, the life in Christ, the life that takes anyone out of concentration on merely selfish concerns and puts ultimate meaning into life.

57. ψυχή (see on 10:28) may refer to the soul or to life in its fullest sense.

58. Beare notes that the word is "used in two senses — that of mere physical existence and that of the true and essential self, the 'soul.'" Diétrich comments, "The words of verses 24-25 should be taken literally in the first instance: Jesus is preparing his Apostles for the possibility of martyrdom. They have a secondary meaning which is spiritual: to live life for God it is necessary to consent to the death of the self."

59. Cf. E. Schweizer, "Life, then, is not just a natural phenomenon. Man lives it. If he is not aware of this, and regards life only as a natural phenomenon, he interprets it in a definite way, namely, in such sort that he misses what ought to be his life. Nor can there be any substitute for it. He has already lost his life" (*TDNT*, IX, p. 645). Filson comments, "To sacrifice permanent spiritual welfare for temporary physical safety or comfort is a bad bargain (Jesus gave a place to common sense)." The man who does this "has no business sense!"

60. The verb is ἀπόλλυμι, "to destroy utterly, destroy, kill" (AS). It points to a thorough-going renunciation.

26. Jesus drives home his point with a couple of questions. The first appeals to the profit motive and compares the value of the whole world and that of a person's life (*KJV* has "soul" here, as do some of the modern versions, e.g., *NIV, ASV; NEB* has "at the cost of his true self"; cf. Moule, "in exchange for himself," *IBNTG*, p. 185). What is the profit[61] in an exchange where one gains the maximum imaginable at the cost of one's life? Indeed, it is more than the maximum imaginable, because there are no circumstances in which anyone could gain the whole world. *World*, of course, means this world with all its riches, and *the whole* means all of it (cf. H. Sasse, "to gain possession of everything that man can control," *TDNT*, III, p. 888). Put one's life in the balance against this, and the life wins out. The magnitude of the loss is brought out by a second question in which Jesus asks what anyone would give *as an exchange for his life*, where the language of commerce is used ("What could a man offer to buy back his soul once he had lost it?" Phillips).[62] But the language of commerce is not applicable when we are talking about one's life. Nothing in the world of commerce has a value comparable to that of one's life, his essential being. One's life is in a different world; nothing can compensate for its loss. Allen thinks that Jesus is speaking about martyrdom, and, of course, what he says has relevance where martyrdom is a possibility. But the saying is of wider application. It is possible to lose one's life in the highest sense while yet continuing in existence.

27. Jesus further brings out the point by referring to eschatological values. In due course this world with all its values will be done away, and in the world to come the profits made in the here and now will be seen for the shoddy things they are. This is the third consecutive verse with an opening *For;* Jesus is following a tightly reasoned argument. The giving of an exchange for life in this world is nonsense, for in due course this world will be replaced by something new. *The Son of man* is, of course, Jesus' favorite way of referring to himself (see on 8:20). He does not say when or where he will come, but clearly he has ceased to speak of the ordered life of the present world and is speaking of the end of that ordered life. The end will be ushered in by the coming[63] back to this earth of the Son of man. He will then be coming *in the glory of his Father*, an expression that brings out the oneness of the Father and the Son and also something of the brilliance that will attend the second coming. That will not be in

---

61. ὠφελέω (3 times in Matthew) is connected with ὄφελος, "advantage." Jesus' question means "Where is the advantage?" "What is the profit?"

62. ἀντάλλαγμα means "*an exchange*, the price received as an equivalent for an article of commerce" (AS). It is found in the New Testament only here and in the Marcan equivalent. The word is also found in Sirach 26:14, "there is no ἀντάλλαγμα for a disciplined soul."

63. *Will come* is not a simple future, but μέλλει . . . ἔρχεσθαι. μέλλω may be used to "denote "an action that necessarily follows a divine decree *is destined, must, will certainly*" (BAGD, 1.c.δ) ἔρχομαι is used of "coming" in various ways, among them "*appear, make an appearance, come before the public.* So esp. of the Messiah" (BAGD, I.1.a.η).

the lowliness that characterized his first coming to this earth, but in glory and splendor. This is further brought out with the addition *with his angels*. We should probably understand *his* to refer to the Son's angels rather than those of the Father, but there is probably no great difference. In that new world it is hard to think of any division of glory into that of the Father and that of the Son.

Then leads us to what is next in sequence. Jesus speaks of the judgment wherein each will receive the appropriate requital.[64] His behavior is the sum of his achievement; it includes all that he has done.[65] Jesus makes it clear that there will be a final reckoning and that those who have exchanged their essential being, their "life," for ephemeral profit or pleasure will receive the recompense that is due. In the end there will be a righting of all wrongs.

28. *"Truly I tell you"* (see on 5:18) marks out the words that follow as especially solemn and significant. Jesus goes on to say that there are some of his present audience *(those standing here)* who[66] will not undergo death[67] before the coming of the Son of man *in his kingdom*[68] (there are many references to the kingdom in this Gospel, but few that refer to it as "his" kingdom; though cf. 13:41; 20:21). Some interpreters have understood this to mean that the end of the age would come about during the lifetime of some of Jesus' hearers. But it seems unlikely that Jesus would mean this; he consistently refused to set dates, and in any case he said explicitly that he did not know when the End would come (24:36). In his commentary on the equivalent passage in Luke Alfred Plummer lists seven principal ways of understanding the passage that have been put forward: (1) the transfiguration, (2) the resurrection and ascension, (3) Pentecost, (4) the spread of Christianity, (5) the internal development of the gospel, (6) the destruction of Jerusalem, and (7) the second advent. He points out that the passage assigns special privilege to those standing there over against people in general, and in his judgment that rules out all except the first and the sixth; he prefers the sixth.[69] He may be right, but we must bear

---

64. ἀποδίδωμι is a favorite word in this Gospel (18 times, next is Luke with 8). It points to paying exactly what is due and is used of wages, debts, oaths, and so on.

65. πρᾶξις (here only in Matthew) means "a deed," but here it is not any single deed that is in mind, but the sum total of all his deeds.

66. οἵτινες perhaps means "who are of such a kind as to"; but probably the form should not be pressed and we should understand it as "who."

67. γεύω is used of tasting in the literal sense, but it is not uncommonly used metaphorically as in the present passage. The double negative οὐ μή is emphatic. Schweizer says, "possibly he takes the saying about 'not tasting death' in the sense that the disciple of Jesus can die secure in the knowledge that death has been overcome and that he will be raised" (p. 347).

68. "In quick succession the first evangelist has written about the Father of the Son of man, the angels of the Son of man, and the kingdom of the Son of man — a Christological emphasis hard to overestimate" (Gundry, p. 341).

69. *A Critical and Exegetical Commentary on the Gospel according to S. Luke* (Edinburgh, 1928), pp. 249-50.

in mind that the Son of man comes in many ways. There is a good deal to be said for a reference to the events linked by the death and resurrection of Jesus and the coming of the Spirit that led on to the preaching of the gospel and the growth of the church. That was a decisive coming, of permanent significance to the church.

Ridderbos reminds us that prophecy "often compresses the distinct phases of the future into a unity." He further points out that "Whenever He (i.e., Jesus) told the disciples about His exaltation, He spoke *either* of His resurrection *or* of His coming again." He holds that "coming in his kingdom" is a compressed way of referring to the whole exaltation and that it was not until after the resurrection that the disciples would see that there were two parts to the coming in of the kingdom. They would see the early manifestation in the resurrection and what followed immediately, though the final fulfilment of the words is yet future. Some such understanding of Jesus' words is surely required.

Matthew 17

2. The Transfiguration, 17:1-13

¹*And after six days Jesus takes Peter and James and John his brother, and brings them up into a very high mountain by themselves.* ²*And he was transfigured before them, and his face shone like the sun, and his clothes became white as the light.* ³*And look, there appeared to them Moses and Elijah, talking with him.* ⁴*But Peter answered Jesus, saying, "Lord, it is good that we are here; if you wish, I will make three shelters here, one for you and one for Moses and one for Elijah."* ⁵*While he was still speaking, look, a bright cloud covered them, and look, a voice from the cloud, saying, "This is my Son, the beloved, in whom I am well pleased; listen to him."*

⁶*And when the disciples heard this, they fell on their face and they were greatly afraid.* ⁷*And Jesus came to them and touched them and said, "Get up and don't be afraid."* ⁸*And when they raised their eyes, they saw nobody but Jesus himself alone.*

⁹*And as they were going down from the mountain, Jesus commanded them, saying, "Tell the vision to no one until the Son of man has been raised from the dead."* ¹⁰*And the disciples asked him, saying, "Why therefore do the scribes say that Elijah must come first?"* ¹¹*And he replied, "Elijah indeed comes, and he will restore all things.* ¹²*But I tell you, that Elijah has come already, and they did not recognize him, but did to him whatever they wanted. So also the Son of man will suffer at their hands."* ¹³*Then the disciples understood that he had spoken to them about John the Baptist.*

This incident is related in all three Synoptists, though not in John, perhaps because he prefers to bring out the point that the glory was everywhere in Jesus' life. Whereas Matthew normally abbreviates matter he shares with Mark, on this occasion he is significantly longer (most of the added matter is in vv. 6-8). There are individual differences, such as Matthew's information that when they heard the heavenly voices the disciples fell on their faces, or Luke's recording of the fact that the conversation between Jesus and the heavenly visitants concerned Jesus' death. The central truth, that Jesus was transfigured, is common to all three, though it is not easy to see exactly what that means. But at least Peter, James, and John saw a transformed Jesus, one who for a short time appeared in heavenly glory. After Jesus' teaching on taking up the cross, it may be that the vision provided some encouragement for the disciples. But we should also see the incident as having significance for Jesus himself. Only a few verses back he has spoken of the suffering and death that he faced; now the heavenly Father gives Jesus the assurance that what he is doing is pleasing in his, the Father's sight. That will help him as he goes forward.[1]

Many recent scholars have regarded the story as originally a resurrection story, and Rudolf Bultmann, for example, asserts this strongly.[2] But despite the firmness with which this view is held by some, it is hard to understand why. As Stendahl says, "The prevailing interpretations of the story as a post-resurrection appearance projected back into the ministry of Jesus hardly account for many of its precise details." The story does not read like a postresurrection story and nothing in it indicates that Jesus was already risen, quite apart from the "precise details" to which Stendahl draws attention.[3]

1. Matthew and Mark both locate the next incident *after*[4] *six days* (Luke has "about eight days"). Time links like this are not common in the Synoptic Gospels (before the passion narratives), and this may indicate that the two incidents should be taken together. Jesus has made it clear to the disciples that he must suffer in the fulfilment of his vocation. Now in the vision on the mountain he receives the assurance that the path on which he has embarked is the right one. Matthew has a series of present tenses (which makes for a vivid narrative) as he tells his readers that Jesus took[5] a small company of his apostles up a high

1. A. M. Ramsey views the transfiguration "as a mirror in which the Christian mystery is seen in its unity. Here we perceive that the living and the dead are one in Christ, that the old covenant and the new are inseparable, that the Cross and the glory are of one, that the age to come is already here, that our human nature has a destiny of glory, that in Christ the final word is uttered and in Him alone the Father is well pleased. Here the diverse elements in the theology of the New Testament meet" (*The Glory of God and the Transfiguration of Christ* [London, 1949], p. 144). He also says, "the Transfiguration meant the taking of the whole conflict of the Lord's mission, just as it was, into the glory which gave meaning to it all" (p. 146).

2. He does not see any necessity to argue the case, but lays it down as he begins his discussion of the transfiguration that "It has long since been recognized that this legend was originally a resurrection story" (*The History of the Synoptic Tradition* [Oxford, 1963], p. 259).

3. There is a very useful discussion of the incident by Walter L. Liefeld in R. N. Longenecker and M. C. Tenney, eds., *New Dimensions in New Testament Study* (Grand Rapids, 1974), pp. 162-79. Liefeld argues that the story has typological and eschatological significance, but further, "the transfiguration is not basically either typology or eschatology, but *revelation*. If the one who receives the divine designation is truly at once Messiah, Son of Man, beloved Son of God, and Servant, whose mission is to suffer, it is not surprising if more than one aspect of his person and work should be seen in his transfiguration" (p. 178).

4. μετά is a favorite word with Matthew; he has it 70 times, which is more than in any other New Testament book.

5. Matthew is fond of παραλαμβάνω, which he has 16 times. It signifies "to take along with one."

mountain. This is the only place where Matthew links Peter, James, and John, but the other Gospels make it clear that the three formed something of a unit and that they were especially close to Jesus. In the Greek they are linked by a single definite article; Matthew regards them as in some sense a unity. To *John* he adds the description *his brother;* perhaps in these early days John was of rather less stature than James. Jesus then took these three up *a very high mountain.* There has been a good deal of speculation as to which mountain this was. The traditional site is Mt. Tabor, but most scholars agree that this is not likely to be correct: it is too far away from Caesarea Philippi and, moreover, it seems to have been occupied at the time, which would mean that it was not a good place for the solitude Jesus sought. A spur on Mt. Hermon is more likely; other suggestions include Mt. Miron and Jebel Jermak, but we have no means of knowing for sure. Jesus took them to a place where they could be *by themselves;*[6] this was to be a special occasion, and Jesus avoided publicity. Luke tells us that Jesus went up the mountain to pray (Luke 9:28). He also speaks of the disciples as being asleep (Luke 9:32); thus it appears that the transfiguration took place at night (they went down the mountain the next day, Luke 9:37).

2. There on the mountaintop Jesus *was transfigured.* There is a variety of translations; for example, *GNB* reads "a change came over Jesus," and Cassirer, he "was transformed." I have retained the conventional and somewhat obscure word *transfigured* because in fact we do not know exactly what happened, and this word at least brings before us the truth that Jesus underwent a unique transformation before the disciples. Matthew selects two features of this change, the first being that Jesus' face *shone like the sun.* This is a detail we owe to Matthew; Mark says nothing about Jesus' face, and Luke tells us that while Jesus was praying the appearance of his face "became other"[7] but he does not tell us in what way it was "other"; only Matthew speaks of it as shining.[8] He goes on to say that Jesus' clothing[9] *became white as the light.* The shining of the face indicates unusual radiance. It is perhaps curious that his clothing became *white as the light,* for we do not normally regard light as being white (though we can use the expression "white light"). The meaning appears to be that even Jesus' clothing became splendid in appearance. J. Behm understands this as the "transformation from an earthly form into a supraterrestrial," and he explains further, "Before the eyes of His most inti-

6. κατ' ἰδίαν, "privately"; "where they could be alone" *(JB)*.
7. τὸ εἶδος τοῦ προσώπου αὐτοῦ ἕτερον.
8. When Moses returned from Mt. Sinai with "the two tables of the testimony," the skin of his face shone (Exod. 34:29-30). Paul points out that this "glory" was fading, and he contrasts it with the glory of the new covenant (2 Cor. 3:7, 11).
9. The word is ἱμάτια, the plural of the word for the outer garment, the "cloak." In this context it will mean clothing in general and not any particular article (though, of course, the cloak would have been especially prominent). In any case a person wore only one cloak; the plural must refer to other articles of clothing.

mate disciples the human appearance of Jesus was for a moment changed into that of a heavenly being in the transfigured world."[10]

3. A characteristic Matthean *And look* draws attention to the astonishing appearance[11] of two great Old Testament figures, *Moses and Elijah*.[12] Matthew does not say how the apostles recognized them, but the important thing is not how they knew, but that it was these people who talked with Jesus and not some of their own contemporaries. Moses, of course, was the great lawgiver, and Elijah an outstanding figure among the prophets. The two represent a way of saying that the whole of the Old Testament revelation found its fulfilment in Jesus.[13] None of the conversation is recorded, though Luke tells us that it concerned Jesus' death, which was soon to take place in Jerusalem.

4. A typical Matthean "having answered said" construction introduces a typical Petrine initiative. Peter *answered* Jesus, which is somewhat curious since Jesus is not said to have spoken to Peter; that apostle "answered" the situation in which Jesus was appearing. Peter spoke to Jesus, not to the heavenly visitants, and addressed him reverently and appropriately as *"Lord"* (in Mark the address is "Rabbi," and in Luke "Master"). He went on to say that it was *good* that they were where they were, and to make a suggestion. *If you wish*[14] defers to what Jesus thinks is good and proper, and Peter goes on to suggest the construction of *shelters* for Jesus and the heavenly visitors. *I will make* characteristically thrusts Peter into the forefront of the proposed action (some MSS read "we will make" [cf. *KJV*], but this reading is unlikely to be correct). It is not clear what *shelters* means,[15] but

10. *TDNT*, IV, p. 758. Behm sees this in "the context of apocalyptic ideas," and he says further, "What is promised to the righteous in the new aeon . . . happens already to Jesus in this world, not as one among many others, but as the bearer of a unique call."

11. The verb is ὤφθη, used as the aorist passive of ὁράω. This passive means "*become visible, appear*. . . . Mostly of beings that make their appearance in a supernatural manner, almost always w. dat. of the pers. to whom they appear" (BAGD, 1.a.δ). The verb is singular, agreeing with the nearest subject.

12. In later Judaism there was the expectation that great ones would return in the end time. For example, God is reported to have said to Moses: "Moses, I swear to you, as you devoted your life to their service in this world, so too in the time to come when I bring Elijah, the prophet, unto them, the two of you shall come together" (Deut. Rab. 3:17). According to J. Jeremias, this is the only reference to the joint coming of Moses and Elijah in all the rabbinic literature (*TDNT*, IV, p. 855, n. 96). There was, of course, a widespread expectation that Elijah would come (see *TDNT*, II, pp. 931-34).

13. Cf. McNeile, "The vision thus represents the quintessence of Christian teaching on the relation of the Old Covenant to the New. The glory of the former lies in the fact that it is contained in, and transcended by, the latter" (p. 251).

14. εἰ θέλεις, a conditional of the first class, may hint that Peter thinks that this is in fact Jesus' will ("if, as appears to be the case. . . ," BDF, 372[1] [a]; they also think that the expression may be equivalent to "please," 372[2][c]), but more probably it indicates that if it really is Jesus' will then certain consequences follow.

15. σκηνή (here only in Matthew, 10 times in Hebrews) basically signifies a "tent" (so GNB, JB here), but the term comes to mean other forms of shelter, and on the mountain Peter can scarcely mean "tents" in the ordinary sense of the term. Where would he get the material? He must have in mind some structure of timber and leaves, perhaps "huts."

since temporary shelters were used at the Feast of Tabernacles some scholars hold that we should see the Tabernacles motif here. Be that as it may, clearly Peter was envisaging a lengthy stay on the mountain for the heavenly visitors and wished to provide suitable lodging places. He says nothing about shelters for himself and his earthly companions; perhaps that is to be understood, or he may have in mind that they would remain in the open. Luke tells us that Peter did not know what he was saying, and his suggestion is certainly incongruous (cf. Bruce, "The whole scheme a stupidity").

5. *While he was still speaking* means that the next phase of the action did not wait until Peter was finished with his suggestion; it went right on while he was still bringing out his idea for the huts. *A bright cloud*[16] came over the area. The traditional translation is something like "overshadowed," but since the cloud was full of brightness there is no thought that it cast a shadow; it covered them with light rather than with shade (*NIV* has "enveloped"). Here it is surely symbolic of the divine presence.[17] It is not clear whether we should understand the cloud as enveloping them all or whether this refers only to Jesus together with the heavenly visitants. But since the voice came to them *from* or "out of" the cloud, perhaps we should understand that the three disciples saw the cloud come upon Jesus and the heavenly visitants who were thus drawn into the immediate presence of God. Matthew's characteristic *and look* (the third use of the expression in this vivid narrative) introduces the high point: first there were the heavenly visitants, now *a voice from the cloud*. He does not say whose voice it is, but the fact that it comes from the cloud, taken together with its reference to Jesus as *my Son,* shows plainly that it is the voice of God (and the words spoken are very similar to those God spoke at the baptism of Jesus, 3:17). Matthew does not say how it was made clear that *This* refers to Jesus, but clearly that is his meaning. The divine voice speaks of the Son as *the beloved.* This may mean "my own dear Son" (*GNB*), but more probably it is a messianic title; the Messiah is "the Beloved."[18] Matthew tells us (as the others do not) that the voice went on, *"in whom I am well pleased,"* which may well signify, "I take pleasure in him."[19] At the very least it indicates warm approval and makes it clear that the Father

---

16. φωτεινός is connected with φῶς, "light," and indicates that this cloud brought radiance rather than darkness. A. Oepke holds that the term "expresses the kindly nature of the encounter with God in the NT, though against the background of the divine majesty" (*TDNT,* IV, p. 908). νεφέλη means "*a cloud* (single and specific as opp. to νέφος, a great indefinite mass of vapour)" (AS).

17. ἐπισκιάζω often means "cast a shadow (σκιά) upon (ἐπί)," but it may be used of the presence of God as in Exodus 40:35.

18. J. Armitage Robinson has made out a convincing case for taking ὁ ἀγαπητός as a distinct title and not simply "a mere epithet of υἱός" (*St Paul's Epistle to the Ephesians* [London, 1907], pp. 229-33). In Luke the Son is called "My Chosen One."

19. The aorist εὐδόκησα is unexpected; we might have anticipated the perfect. See the note on the similar expression in 3:17 and the reference there to Burton's view that it means "I have become well pleased."

is setting his seal of approval on the Son in his earthly mission. The heavenly voice concludes with the command, *"listen to him"* (cf. Deut. 18:15). His credentials are unrivaled; mortal people should take heed to all that he says.

6. Matthew adds (as the others do not) that at the sound of the voice the disciples *fell on their face,* and further that *they were greatly afraid* ("fell on their faces in terror," *REB*). Prostration (falling on the face) was characteristically used for taking up a lowly position before God or on occasion before a great man. It was a sign of humility and devotion. Fear is not infrequently used to denote a deep reverence before God, but it may also be used of fear generally. Since Jesus counseled them not to be afraid, on this occasion we should understand the term to refer simply to being scared. The three disciples were going through an awesome experience; it is not surprising that they were very frightened.

7. We owe to Matthew the information that when the disciples were distressed in this way Jesus reassured them. He *came*[20] *to them and touched them* (this verb can be used for fastening oneself to, clinging to, but clearly here no more than physical contact). Matthew does not indicate why he did this, but the disciples had been through a very trying experience and one in which they had been on the frontier of the supernatural. The three had had a wonderful blessing, but they had evidently had a feeling of the uncanny as they had had this contact with another order of being, and this human touch must have been very comforting. They realized that the Master was still with them and that he felt for them. He told them to get up and stop being afraid. Clearly the wonderful episode had had its terrifying aspects, but it was now over and they must get on with the business of living. Their experience on the mountain had doubtless been wonderful, both for what it was in itself (people do not usually experience such a close presence of God or hear his voice so audibly) and for what it told them about Jesus. They had thought enough of him to leave "home and toil and kindred," but they could not have known that he stood in such a close relationship to the heavenly Father.

8. The disciples had fallen with their faces to the ground (v. 6), and evidently they did not raise their eyes until Jesus touched them and spoke to them. Now that they did, they found that the wonderful experience was over; the heavenly visitants had gone, and so had the cloud. They were with *Jesus himself alone.* This puts the emphasis on Jesus and on the absence of anyone else. They saw that he alone was there, he and no other.

9. Matthew moves to the descent from the mountain. As the little party went down, Jesus gave them firm instructions[21] to keep quiet about

---

20. προσέρχομαι is a distinctively Matthean word (see on 4:3).

21. ἐνετείλατο signifies "commanded"; Jesus was not making a request. AS says of the various words for commanding, κελεύω means "*to command* of verbal orders in general; παραγγέλλω *to charge,* esp. of the transmitted orders of a military commander; ἐντέλλω points rather to the contents of the command."

what they had seen on the mountain. *No one* comes first in its clause with a certain emphasis; they are to tell no one at all.[22] *The Son of man* refers to Jesus in his divine mission, a mission that would involve death and then resurrection, to which he alludes here. The passive *raised* looks to the action of the Father in bringing his Son back from the dead.[23] Jesus looks through death to the certainty of the resurrection (which, of course, implies that his death will take place along the way). By referring to the resurrection he concentrates on the ultimate triumph.[24]

10. The disciples reply with a question, where we might have expected them to make some comment on the vision or the need for silence. But instead they ask why *the scribes say that Elijah must come first.*[25] *Therefore* is not what we expect, and it is not easy to see its force in this place. Perhaps it arises because they had just seen Elijah in the vision and were interested in his further activities. The disciples would have had a problem in that the prophecy said that Elijah would precede the Messiah and "restore all things"; why therefore should the Messiah suffer? Moreover, Jesus had just spoken of his resurrection, which, of course, implies a preceding death. If the Messiah was going to die, where did Elijah fit into the picture? Other passages show that Elijah was in people's minds (16:14; John 1:21), so there would be interest in him. For whatever reason the disciples want to know about him, and in any age there is curiosity about a worthy from the past who is said to be about to reappear on earth. It is interesting that they refer to the teaching of *the scribes* when they might well have referred to the prophecy of Malachi 4:5 that was the origin of the teaching of the scribes. But since these men were the religious experts, their teaching about important religious matters would be respected by people like the disciples. Their word *must*[26] indicates a compelling divine necessity; in the view of the learned scribes it was in the divine will that Elijah would precede the Messiah. In view of the prophecy this required no profound insight, but perhaps the disciples want to reinforce their own position by reference to accepted authorities. They do not say who Elijah is to precede, but the prophet speaks of "the great and dreadful day of the

---

22. Moulton lists this use of the aorist imperative preceded by μή as one where the appropriate response would be "I will avoid doing so"; that is, the aorist means "Don't start" rather than "Stop doing" (M, I, p. 125).

23. This is Matthew's one use of ἐκ νεκρῶν (though he has ἀπὸ τῶν νεκρῶν, 14:2; 28:7; there appears to be no real difference).

24. "For why should He deprive others of this same remedy? More, why should He expressly forbid them to say what they had seen before His resurrection, save because the fruit of the vision would come after His death? I have no doubt that Christ wanted to testify that He was not dragged unwillingly to death but went to it of His own free will, to offer the sacrifice of obedience to His Father. The disciples did not think of this until after Christ had risen" (Calvin, II, p. 197).

25. Plummer conjectures that the scribes may have used the absence of Elijah as an argument against Jesus' messiahship; they may have asked, "How can He be the Messiah, when Elijah, who is to precede the Messiah, is not yet come?" (p. 240).

26. δεῖ.

Lord" and this is easily understood of the coming of the Messiah. After Peter's confession narrated in the preceding chapter and now the splendid vision on the mountain, none of them would have had any doubts but that Jesus was the Messiah. But where was Elijah? The scribal interpretation of the prophecy was clearly widely known, but these disciples had not seen a fulfilment. Had Elijah come unnoticed? Were the scribes wrong? They ask Jesus to clear up the point for them.

11. It may be a little too strong to translate "But he replied,"[27] but there is certainly some adversative force as Jesus speaks to the puzzlement of the disciples out of his own clarity and knowledge. *"Elijah indeed[28] comes,"* where the present tense is used to refer to something that is past; it brings out the continuing validity of the prophecy (the present is not infrequently used in "confident assertions regarding the future," BDF, 323[1]), and the aorist in the next sentence points to the fact that Elijah has already come. The future, *he will restore,* indicates a future aspect of the work that prophet has inaugurated. *Restore* signifies a bringing back to a former state of affairs, and *all things* shows that the restoration will be thoroughgoing (*REB*'s "will come and set everything right" misses the restoration idea). The thought is apparently that sin has corrupted and ruined the creation, but Elijah's function is to usher in the events that will (through the atoning work of Jesus) restore the pristine blessedness. A less likely view is that we may understand the words to mean that Jesus accepts this as a fair statement of what the scribes taught. However, John did not in fact restore all things; that was still future.[29]

12. Jesus goes on to make plain that the prophecy about Elijah has already been fulfilled: *"Elijah has come already,"* but the surprising thing is that *they did not recognize him.* Jesus does not say who *they* were, but evidently it is people at large who are in mind, perhaps particularly the Jewish leaders; there was no general recognition of Elijah. The great prophet had come among the people unrecognized and therefore without receiving the welcome he would surely have had if they had known who he was. *But* is the strong adversative,[30] "but, on the contrary." They ill-treated him, and this is described in the words *did to him whatever they wanted* ("worked their will upon him," *NEB*). The verb *did* is neutral and may be used of doing good (7:12), or evil as here. *To him* is really "in him," a somewhat unusual construction that perhaps means that what they did had its effects not only around the prophet but "in" him (though the

27. The sentences are linked with ὁ δέ.

28. μέν (20 times in Matthew) relates to a following δέ and is used to distinguish "the word or clause with which it stands from that which follows" (AS).

29. Tasker comments, "The words of Jesus in verse 11 are best understood as a recognition by Him that what the disciples have said is a true statement of what the scribes were teaching. They are not an indication that He agrees with it. On the contrary, in verse 12 He implies that the scribal tradition is wrong" (p. 165).

30. ἀλλά.

preposition may simply be equivalent to the dative). *Whatever they wanted* indicates that they acted toward him as though there was nothing to be considered but their own will. They did not realize that they were answerable to God for their mistreatment of God's own messenger to them.

The ill treatment afforded the prophet is the measure of the ill treatment Jesus himself will in due course receive; *so*[31] *also* links the fate of *the Son of man* with that of the prophet. *Will suffer* is not a simple future,[32] but a compound that expresses the certainty of the outworking of a divine purpose. The suffering of the Son of man will be the doing of evil by wicked men, but God will use it to bring his purpose to pass, and this means that there is a certain inevitability about it. *At their hands* is more literally "by them"; the expression sheets home their responsibility. They are not to be thought of as spectators watching while the Son of man suffers, but as the perpetrators of a grievous wrong, those who will bring the suffering about. The scribes on whose interpretation of Scripture the disciples had relied so much were wrong about Elijah and wrong about the Messiah. They thought of both in terms of earthly glory and victory. They did not understand that the purpose of God in both was worked out in terms of lowliness and suffering. There is glory on the mountain of transfiguration, but it is a glory that meant suffering for the Baptist and would mean suffering for Jesus.

13. Following the explanation came understanding, though it is not easy for us to see how Jesus' words would convey to the disciples the information that he had been speaking of John the Baptist. Perhaps there had been no other religious figure of importance in recent times, at least among those known to the disciples, who had been mistreated in the way Jesus had indicated. Or perhaps he said more than Matthew has recorded. Or the disciples may have recalled that Jesus had identified John with Elijah (11:14). For whatever reason, they now understood that the prophecy about Elijah had its fulfilment in John the Baptist and that that great man's treatment at the hands of the authorities set the pattern that would in due course receive further fulfilment in Jesus.

F. THE CHRIST AT WORK, 17:14–18:35

Matthew has practically concluded his account of Jesus' public ministry in Galilee. He will shortly move on to the Master's move to Jerusalem for the final showdown and the passion and resurrection (19:1). But before he does this, he gives his readers one final glimpse of Jesus at work.

31. οὕτως is a Matthean word (32 times, which is more than in any other New Testament book; 1 Corinthians has it 31 times). It indicates that Jesus' treatment will be just like that of Elijah.

32. The expression is μέλλει πάσχειν, where μέλλω is used to denote "an action that necessarily follows a divine decree *is destined, must, will certainly . . . he is destined to suffer*" (BAGD, 1.c.δ).

1. Casting Out a Devil, 17:14-20

14*And when they came to the crowd, a man came to him, falling on his knees* 15*and saying, "Lord, take pity on my son, for he is a lunatic and suffers grievously; for frequently he falls into the fire and frequently into the water.* 16*And I brought him to your disciples, and they could not cure him."* 17*But Jesus answered, saying, "O faithless and perverse generation, how long shall I be with you? How long shall I put up with you? Bring him here to me."* 18*And Jesus rebuked it, and the demon came out of him, and the boy was cured from that hour.* 19*Then the disciples came to Jesus privately and said, "Why could we not cast it out?"* 20*And he says to them, "Because of your small faith. For truly I tell you, if you have faith like a mustard seed, you will say to this mountain, 'Move from here to there,' and it will move; and nothing will be impossible for you."*

All three Synoptists tell us that immediately after the wonderful experience on the mountain Jesus and the three were confronted with a situation in which the rest of the band had been unable to cure a lunatic (or epileptic) boy. In sharp contrast to the glory on the mountain is the scene of frustration and defeat that awaited Jesus and the three when they came down and were immediately confronted with a demoniac — a veritable "coming down to earth" experience. Although on an earlier occasion the disciples had had power over demons (10:1), this time the nine were powerless. But the Jesus who had been so wonderfully transfigured on the mountain was well able to cope with the problem on the plain. He reasserted his authority over the demons (for the last time in this Gospel) and gave some significant teaching on the importance of faith. Matthew greatly abbreviates Mark's narrative, but he stresses the disciples' lack of faith as Mark does not.[33]

14. Matthew does not tell us where this incident happened; he simply says that *they* (evidently Jesus and the three) *came*[34] to the crowd (Matthew prefers to speak of "crowds," but on this occasion he has used the singular; Mark and Luke both note that it was a great crowd). He says that a man *came*[35] to Jesus and fell on his knees, a piece of information found in this Gospel only. The attitude is that of one who is respectful and who is seeking a favor.

15. He addresses Jesus respectfully as *"Lord,"* as befits his kneeling

---

33. J. Wilkinson has an interesting discussion of the incident (*ET*, LXXIX [1967-68], pp. 39-42). He examines the boy's symptoms and accepts the view that he suffered from epilepsy, but he does not find this incompatible with his being demon possessed.

34. Actually ἐλθόντων has no subject, but the context shows that it refers to Jesus and his three disciples. It is a genitive absolute without the subject being expressed, a construction that Robertson says is "a very frequent idiom in the papyri" (Robertson, p. 513). Moulton also finds the construction frequent in the papyri, though rare in the New Testament (M, I, p. 74).

35. προσέρχομαι is a favorite verb of Matthew's; see on 4:3.

posture. He asks Jesus to *take pity* on his son (5 times Matthew records people as asking Jesus to take pity on the sufferer when they come for healing). Actually he says "the" son, that is, the son in his family. He speaks of the boy as *a lunatic*,[36] which most modern interpreters take to mean "epileptic" (so, e.g., *NRSV, NIV*), for the boy's symptoms are those which we associate with that complaint. Some translations retain "lunatic" (as *JB*, Phillips, and, of course, *KJV*; Carr says, "the child was a possessed epileptic lunatic"!). Mark and Luke both speak of the boy as possessed by "a spirit" (Mark adds that it is a "dumb" spirit). All three bring out the fact that it was a very serious case, Mark and Luke by describing convulsions and Matthew by saying that the boy *suffers grievously*[37] ("has such terrible fits," *GNB*), and further that he falls into *fire* or *water*. These falls are cited as indicating epilepsy, which, of course, they might; but they are also congruous with lunacy. The falls happened often, and since the boy was still alive we may presume that there was good family care.

16. The father says that he had brought his boy *to your disciples*, where *your* distinguishes Jesus' disciples from those who learned from other teachers; *disciples* does not necessarily confine the reference to the Twelve, but they must have been primarily in mind. Unfortunately the disciples were not able to *cure him*. This verb is of interest since it is mostly used of curing people from illnesses of one sort or another, whereas demons are said to be "cast out" (both Mark and Luke mention that the man asked them to cast out the spirit, but they could not do it). Matthew seems here to regard the problem as one of sickness. But the main point is that the boy remained in his unhappy condition. The disciples could not provide the answer, and the father now looks to Jesus to do what his followers could not do.

17. *But* has adversative force and sets Jesus over against his powerless followers. He came down the mountain and "found Himself confronted by that helpless boy, by that helpless father, by that helpless age, by those helpless disciples" (Morgan, p. 225). Matthew introduces his words with his frequent "having answered, said" and tells us that Jesus complains not only about the powerless disciples and the crowd looking on, but about the whole *generation*. *O* (elsewhere in Matthew only in 15:28) may be used in address or as an exclamation; not much turns on which we accept in the present case. It may perhaps indicate emotion or it may be no more than a stylistic element.[38] *Generation* (see on 16:4) refers to all the people

---

36. He employs the verb σεληνιάζω, which is connected with σελήνη, "moon," and is thus etymologically equivalent to our "lunatic." It occurs elsewhere in the New Testament only in 4:24 (where see note). Most scholars take it to refer to epilepsy, on the ground that in antiquity epileptics were understood to be "moonstruck."

37. κακῶς πάσχει. Matthew often has κακῶς ἔχω (see on 4:24), but this expression occurs here only in the New Testament. It indicates not only that the ailment was severe but that the boy suffered a good deal.

38. Horsley cites J. A. L. Lee for the view that ὦ is "primarily a feature of higher style.

alive at that time, at least in Galilee. Jesus castigates them in two ways: they are *faithless* and they are *perverse*. The former term[39] points to their wrong attitude toward God; throughout Scripture people are urged to trust God, and when they do that nothing is impossible to them (cf. v. 20). The fact that nobody in the crowd, including some of his own disciples, could bring about the lad's cure is evidence for Jesus that they were lacking in the faith through which God delights to work. They are also *perverse*,[40] which may mean that they are "twisted" in their thinking, "distorted" in their spiritual attitude. With such a fundamental imbalance they were quite unable to do things like cure the troubled boy.

Jesus asks *how long*[41] he is to be confronted with this sort of problem. He asks first how long he is to be with people like this, which gives us a little glimpse of how trying it must have been for such a one as Jesus to be set in the middle of such spiritual pygmies. A second question refers to "putting up with"[42] people like this. The two questions bring out something of the trial it was for Jesus to be constantly confronted by people who were not fully sympathetic with what he was doing. His words are apparently directed at the crowds and the disciples; they can scarcely be aimed at the father, who was trying to do the best he could for his boy. It seems that the father and others had left the scene of the attempted cure and rushed to meet Jesus when they saw him approaching. The Master was thus some way from the boy, so he called on them to bring him to him.

18. When the boy arrived, Jesus took firm action. He *rebuked*[43] *it*.[44] It was important to cure the boy, but it was also important to make it clear that evil in any form is to be opposed. Although no emphasis is put on *it*, for example, by calling the spirit "unclean" or "evil," it was clearly seen as one who brought harm to the boy. For that it was rebuked. Matthew does not say that Jesus told the spirit to come out of the boy. That may be

---

Its chief effect in all places [in the NT] is to give a formal and elevated tone" (*New Documents*, 5, p. 57).

39. ἄπιστος, here only in Matthew, occurs 23 times in the New Testament. It can denote what is incredible (Acts 26:8), and when used of people signifies "without faith," "unbelieving." It may be used of unbelievers as opposed to Christians (1 Cor. 6:6).

40. Jesus uses the perfect passive participle of the verb διαστρέφω, which means "to distort, twist." L. Hartman sees a reminiscence of Deuteronomy 32:5 (LXX) with its reference to "a crooked and perverse generation" and comments: "it seems to me that this allusion is an instructive example of how something is implicitly communicated by an allusion which can be understood only by someone aware of the original context and its interpretation" (*L'ÉSM*, p. 147).

41. ἕως πότε = "until when?" and thus "how long?"

42. ἀνέχω, here only in Matthew, has the meaning "hold up," but in the New Testament it is always used in the middle with the meaning "endure, bear with."

43. ἐπιτιμάω can mean "to honor" or "to admonish," but in the New Testament it more commonly has the meaning "to rebuke," as here.

44. αὐτῷ is ambiguous; it could be masculine or neuter, but there seems to be no doubt that here it is neuter. There appears to be no reason for Jesus to rebuke the boy or the father; it is the spirit that is the object of his displeasure.

447

implied, or perhaps the rebuke was sufficient. The result was that the spirit left the boy and its departure meant healing. Mark says that the demon convulsed the boy when Jesus commanded it to come out of him, so that people thought that he was dead until Jesus took him by the hand and raised him. But Matthew concentrates on the simple fact that the boy[45] *was cured from that hour.* Again Matthew refers to a cure even though the expulsion of a demon is in mind. And the cure was instantaneous ("at that very moment," *GNB*). The lack of any delay stresses Jesus' mastery over demons and disease.

19. Matthew's favorite *Then* (see on 2:7) carries the narrative along, and it is supplemented by another Matthean word translated *came to* (see on 4:3). The expression for *privately*[46] is used 6 times in Matthew and 7 in Mark, but only sporadically throughout the rest of the New Testament. These two Evangelists are more than a little interested in what went on outside the public gaze. The disciples were evidently chagrined at their failure to deal with the demon. They had received power to do this on an earlier occasion (10:1, 8), and clearly they had expected success this time too. Their *we* is emphatic: "Why could not *we* cast it out?" Their expression *could not*[47] shows that they recognized that they lacked the power. Earlier it was said that they did not have the power to heal (v. 16), here that they were unable to cast the demon out.

20. We could translate *And he* as "But he":[48] Jesus is set in contrast to the powerless disciples. In one concise expression Jesus explains it: *"Because of your small faith."* This is the one place in the New Testament where the word *small faith* occurs (though the corresponding adjective is found 4 times in Matthew and once in Luke). In view of the fact that Matthew is often accused of softening hard words about the disciples we should notice that more than anyone else he preserves the information that Jesus found his followers lacking in that most important quality — faith.[49] By *small faith* he is probably referring to the poor quality, the poverty of their faith, for he goes on to speak of even a very little real faith as able to move mountains. Perhaps the disciples had been treating their power to cast out devils as a new possession of their own — a kind of magic — they would go through their routine and the devil would come out! But that is not the way it was. There was nothing in the disciples

---

45. Earlier he was called υἱός (v. 15), but here he is παῖς. The former term denotes a male offspring, whereas the latter may be used of either sex. AS says that the former term is used "with emphasis on the privileged position of heirship; π. refers to both age and parentage, but with emphasis on the former" (*sub* παῖς). There will be no significant difference here; the change is stylistic.

46. κατ' ἰδίαν.

47. οὐκ ἠδυνήθημεν.

48. ὁ δέ.

49. Matthew has πίστις 8 times and πιστεύω 11 times. He connects faith with healing (8:10; 9:2; 15:28, etc.) and with the miracle of the fig tree (21:21), and he says that it is a quality that the Pharisees lacked (23:23).

themselves that overcame demons. It was God who in every case gave the power, and it was necessary for them to look to him and to act in humble faith. Jesus speaks of faith *like a mustard seed* (see on 13:31 for this smallest of seeds), an expression that clearly had become proverbial for the smallest thing. Jesus is saying that even a little faith would enable the disciples to do what they had just proved they could not do. It is not necessary to have great faith; even a small faith is enough, as long as it is faith in the great God.[50]

Jesus illustrates. He envisages a disciple telling a mountain to move and says that it will happen. The moving of mountains was proverbial among the Jews for accomplishing something of very great difficulty (e.g., it was said that Rabbah was "an uprooter of mountains," *Ber.* 64a; one who saw Resh Lakish in debate "would think that he was uprooting mountains and grinding them against each other," *Sanh.* 24a). The expression should, of course, be understood metaphorically.[51] Through the centuries pious souls have never been conspicuous for transferring physical objects such as literal mountains, but there are many instances on record where mountainous difficulties have been removed by the exercise of faith. Then Jesus makes a staggering promise: *"nothing will be impossible for you."* This is comprehensive; Jesus sets no limit to what can be done by the person of faith.[52] We should perhaps reflect that if there is no limit to the power the person of faith can exercise, Jesus says nothing about that person's knowledge. It is possible to misunderstand the will of God and to try to move a mountain that should not be moved. In that case the believer will be disappointed.[53] Jesus is not dealing with such cases. He is not trying to cover every eventuality. He is saying that there are infinite resources open to the believer, and he is calling on those who follow him to exercise the faith they have.[54]

50. Hamann thinks that the comparison of true faith to a mustard seed indicates "both the apparent insignificance of faith in itself and yet also its great potential. The power of life in the seed and the power of faith both come from God himself."

51. Ridderbos points out that "it is not the task of faith literally to move mountains. That is irrelevant, however. Jesus was not speaking of the task of faith, nor of the direction in which it must be exercised, but only of its power. This power is unlimited because it is based on God's omnipotence."

52. M. Green points out that the story was both embarrassing and encouraging for Matthew's church, "For Jesus had permanently ascended up a mountain, and had left them to carry on his work. Were they powerless? It was attributable to lack of faith . . . the more settled and established a church becomes, the more it needs to learn afresh that it can achieve precisely nothing without sincere dependence on the Lord."

53. Cf. Calvin, "He does not mean that God will give us whatever comes heedlessly into our minds or mouths. In fact, since there is nothing more contradictory to faith than the foolish and unconsidered wishes of our flesh, it follows that where faith reigns there is no asking for anything indiscriminately" (II, p. 210).

54. Some MSS include verse 21 (rendered in *KJV* as "Howbeit this kind goeth not out but by prayer [and fasting]"). But it is omitted by ℵ B Θ 33 syr^c.s etc., and there seems to be no good reason for holding it to be part of the true text. It seems to have been imported into Matthew's text from Mark 9:29.

2. A Prophecy of the Passion, 17:22-23

22And as they were gathering in Galilee, Jesus said to them, "The Son
of man will be delivered into the hands of men, 23and they will kill him,
and on the third day he will be raised." And they were very sad.

Matthew has already twice recorded Jesus' prediction that he will be
killed in Jerusalem and once that he will rise again (16:21; 17:12; the
frequent statement that this is the second prediction of the passion is thus
inaccurate). Now he has another such prophecy, but this time it is not
related to a specific context, other than that it was spoken in Galilee.

22. This passion prediction took place *as they were gathering in Galilee*.
Matthew does not tell us who *they* were, but we must believe that the words
were spoken to the Twelve. It is highly unlikely that Jesus would have given
teaching like this to people outside the inner circle. That they were gathering
in Galilee tells us that it took place before Jesus moved up to Judea, but there
is no more indication of time than that and no more indication of place than
that it was *in Galilee*. The group was *gathering*, but the word is very general
and tells us little.[55] Jesus apparently did not wait for them all to assemble (it
was not "when they had gathered"). No reason is given for his choice of time
and place; Matthew simply records the prediction. He tells us that Jesus
spoke to them; evidently he took the initiative, for there is no indication that
he was replying to a question or a remark that any of the disciples made. He
began with *the Son of man*, his normal way of referring to himself in the
fulfilment of his messianic vocation. The Son of man, then, *will be delivered*,[56]
where *will be* is not the simple future but the compound used in verse 12
(where see note; see also on 2:13), which is often used to denote "an action
that necessarily follows a divine decree *is destined, must, will certainly.*"[57] The
passive is often taken as "the divine passive," signifying that it is really God
who delivers him up, a truth that Paul brings out (Rom. 8:32). This delivering
up will be *into the hands of men*, where the verb perhaps is used in the more
or less technical sense of handing over to the courts. The arresting officers
are not defined and the whole prediction is left very general. But it is plain
enough that Jesus says that he will be given over into the power of those
who are no more than men (and evil men at that!).

23. Jesus makes it plain that he is not facing some minor discomfort.
Those evil men *will kill him*, so he is facing the end of his life here on earth.
But that is not the end of the matter; *on the third day he will be raised*. For

---

55. Tasker thinks that συστρεφομένων means "that the disciples of Jesus, including others
in addition to the Twelve, were beginning to assemble in groups in preparation for the journey
to Jerusalem" (p. 169), that is, for the Passover. Zahn sees rather a meaning like "they crowded
around him" (p. 569, n. 17; Metzger is similar), Ridderbos that "Jesus continued to seclude
Himself with His disciples," and Hendriksen that "they were moving about together."
56. For παραδίδωμι see on 4:12.
57. BAGD, *sub* μέλλω, 1.b.δ.

on the third day see the note on 12:40; it is consistently said that that will be the day on which Jesus' resurrection would take place. Here, as often, he does not say that he will rise but that he *will be raised*, using the expression that brings out the action of the Father. Jesus is in no doubt that he will die, but in no doubt either that death will not be the end. The Father will raise him, and that speedily, for it will be as early as *the third day*. For Christians through the centuries (and even for these very disciples sometime later), this has been the heart of the faith. But at that time the disciples were more impressed by the words about death than by those about resurrection. So Jesus' words grieved them, and that in much more than a slight degree. They were *very sad*.

3. *The Temple Tax, 17:24-27*

> 24*And when they came to Capernaum, the collectors of the didrachmas approached Peter and said, "Does not your teacher pay the didrachmas?"* 25*He says, "Yes." And when he came into the house, Jesus spoke to him first, saying, "What do you think, Simon? From whom do the kings of the earth receive customs duties or tribute? From their sons or from outsiders?"* 26*And when he said, "From outsiders," Jesus said to him, "Then the sons are free.* 27*But lest we be a snare to them, go to the sea, cast a hook, and take the first fish that comes up, and when you have opened its mouth you will find a stater; take it, and give it to them for me and you."*

This paragraph is found in Matthew only. It indicates Jesus' view that in the light of his relationship to the heavenly Father he was under no obligation to pay the temple tax, but also the fact that while he was here on earth he submitted to the regulations that people in general were bound to observe. After the destruction of the temple in A.D. 70 the Romans made the Jews pay the temple tax to Jupiter Capitolinus; some scholars connect the story with the Christians' attitude to that tax. This, however, seems fanciful, as do other attempts to see it as concerned with the payment of taxes by Christians to the civil authorities. It makes a lot more sense to understand it as fitting in with the Palestine of Jesus' day.

24. The little group proceeded to Capernaum (see on 4:13). This is Matthew's last reference to the city that had been so important throughout Jesus' ministry. There *the collectors of the didrachmas* came to Peter. It is not clear why they approached him rather than Jesus; perhaps it was the custom not to approach a rabbi directly, and they saw Peter as the person who would be involved in handling day-to-day matters like settling taxes. The *didrachma*[58] was the amount the Jewish adult male would pay each year for

---

58. δίδραχμος (only in this passage in the New Testament) is an adjective meaning "worth two drachmas"; the neuter is used in the sense "a double drachma." This was roughly equivalent to the Jewish half shekel and amounted to approximately two days' pay for an

the upkeep of the temple. The impost was based on the provision that each man should pay a half shekel for the upkeep of the tabernacle in the wilderness (Exod. 30:11-16), though the tax itself was of much more recent origin.[59] It was paid by Jews outside Palestine as well as those in the holy land, and provided a significant part of the revenue that kept the temple going with all its functions. So important was it that the Mishnah devotes a whole tractate to it *(Sheqalim)*. From it we learn that pledges for the tax might be exacted from "levites, Israelites, proselytes, and freed slaves, but not from women, slaves, or minors" (1:3). Priests did not pay it (1:4); Gentiles or Samaritans were not allowed to pay it (1:5). Those who collected this tax approached Peter with a question that assumes that Jesus would in fact pay the tax (Patte says, "They anticipate a negative answer" [p. 246], but he has not paid sufficient attention to the form in which their question is couched; it looks for a positive answer).[60] Evidently it was due but had not yet been paid, and they were giving Peter a gentle reminder that something ought to be done.

The tax men inquired whether *your teacher* paid the tax. We should understand this as a polite request that the tax be paid, but a dispute could have been raised by it. It seems that Jesus and his followers were living on the gifts of well wishers (Luke 8:3), and they may possibly have been exempt. There is also the question of whether it would be right to pay tax out of gifts given for their maintenance. The priests in the temple service were certainly exempt from the tax, and others occupied solely in God's service apparently could claim exemption. The collectors would not have been learned people, so that any objection would have to be referred to the authorities in Jerusalem. There could be a lengthy and possibly acrimonious dispute, which was not in keeping with Jesus' approach.[61]

25. Peter agreed that Jesus did pay the didrachma; *he says* is in the present tense, which gives greater vividness (curiously Cassirer has "It is true that he does not"; Peter's answer is a one-word affirmative). It would be expected that the apostle would proceed to take the matter up with

---

ordinary workman. H. Hamburger conveys the information that when half shekels were not in circulation the tax was paid in didrachmas, but by New Testament times these, too, had gone out of circulation, so that the Jew would pay two Roman denars or else use one tetradrachma or one Tyrian shekel for two people *(IBD,* III, p. 810). Josephus attests the paying of the didrachma *(Ant.* 18.312).

59. There is a useful account in R. Banks, *Jesus and the Law in the Synoptic Tradition* (Cambridge, 1975), pp. 92-94. Banks brings out the diversity in attitudes to it: "The Sadducees took exception to it, probably because of its recent origin, while the Qumran covenanters felt bound to pay the levy only once, thus more correctly interpreting its alleged biblical precedent" (p. 92). He points out that most Jews of the time paid the tax.

60. The reference to those who collected *the didrachmas* is intelligible, relating to the continuing collection of these coins. It is not so easy to understand why the plural is used in the question about Jesus, for he would have paid only one didrachma. Perhaps the word is simply repeated from the beginning of the verse. Or there may be the thought of the coins paid year after year. Perhaps more probably people may have referred to the tax generally as "paying the didrachmas" (so Lenski, p. 673).

61. See further *NIDNTT,* III, pp. 752-54; Derrett, pp. 247-65.

Jesus, but when he came into the house to which they were going Jesus took the initiative ("forestalled him," *REB*).[62] He asked Peter's opinion and addressed a question to him, calling him *Simon* as he usually did (it was Jesus who gave Simon the name Peter, but only once is he recorded as having addressed him as Peter, Luke 22:34). He went on to ask whether in Peter's judgment earth's kings get their taxes from their sons or those outside their families. Many translations have something like "The citizens of the country or the foreigners?" and record Peter's answer as "The foreigners" (so *GNB*). But this is not really the alternative, and it does not correspond to reality.[63] Conquerors, of course, have always shamelessly plundered conquered peoples, and some of them may perhaps have been able to make do with this source of revenue, but *the kings of the earth* in general certainly have always taxed their own people and have never been in the luxurious position of being able to finance their activities solely from taxes levied on foreigners. Such translations do not pay enough attention to the language Jesus uses. He speaks of *their sons*, which draws attention to the male members of the royal households (and would probably include all in those households): the contrast is not between citizens and foreigners, but between those of the royal household and those outside.[64] Kings regularly tax their citizens, not their families. Jesus speaks of different kinds of taxes,[65] but he does not seem to be defining narrowly two kinds of taxes; he is using the words to refer to taxes in general.

26. Peter's reply[66] gives the expected *"From outsiders,"* whereupon Jesus points out the consequence, *"Then[67] the sons are free."* The logical result of the reasoning Peter has pursued is that the king's sons (and, of course, their dependents) are in a different relationship to taxes than the population in general; they are free from the obligation. Those who belong

62. προφθάνω is found only here in the New Testament (φθάνω with much the same sense is more frequent); it means "to anticipate."

63. Gundry well remarks that the incident hardly implies "that Matthew is teaching Christians to pay civil taxes to the Romans as well as the religious tax for the Jewish Temple; for he brings in payers and nonpayers of civil taxes only as an analogy for the religious tax in question. The contrast between the king's sons and those belonging to others is not a contrast between citizens and noncitizens. Citizens paid taxes, too. It is a contrast between members of royal households and all other subjects and implies that Jesus' disciples belong to God's household, but unbelieving Jews do not" (p. 357).

64. ἀλλότριος signifies "other" (cf. ἄλλος); AS points out that it is opposed to οἰκεῖος. MM cites a papyrus that says "know then that a strange woman is made his heir." This clearly shows its use for those outside the family. It is, of course, used in other senses, but the contrast here is surely between family and nonfamily.

65. τέλος means "end," but it is also used, mostly in the plural, for customs duties, tolls levied for the passage of goods. κῆνσος is a loanword from the Latin *census* and refers to a poll tax, the payment of tribute.

66. εἰπόντος δέ is a genitive absolute minus its subject (see on v. 14 above); variants supply τοῦ Πέτρου or change the word to λέγει.

67. ἄρα, which Matthew uses 7 times, is an "illative particle, expressing a more subjective or informal inference than οὖν" (AS). γε is an enclitic particle that puts emphasis on the word to which it is added.

to the king's household are exempt from the king's taxes. Since Jesus was in a special sense the Son of God, he was exempt from taxes to be paid to the temple of God, and by extension his close servants were exempt too.

27. But exemption from the requirement to pay taxes was not the only element in a complex situation. If Jesus paid the tax he would be putting himself in the same position as others; he would be classing himself as an "outsider," not as a "Son," and that impression should be avoided. If he refused to pay the tax, he would give the impression that he rejected the temple and all that it stood for, whereas the Gospels make it clear that he did no such thing.[68] Moreover, there were the people entrusted with the obligation to collect the taxes to consider. Had Jesus insisted on his rights, those men would not have been able to collect the tax from him. Jesus did not intend to *be a snare to them*,[69] to lead them into sin in some way, though it is not clear precisely how a refusal to pay would cause the collectors to sin. It is salutary to notice that in that situation Jesus gave thought to the position in which the tax collectors found themselves and the effect his actions would have on them. As Meir puts it, "Jesus is interested in something more than theoretical rights. If the sons are free from tax, they are not free from the claims of love, even love of enemies" (cf. Green, "Payment is an expression of pastoral concern"). A refusal to pay would put the tax collectors in a difficult position. We do not know exactly what would have followed, but they would probably have had to appeal to their superiors (the authorities in Jerusalem?), who would have been most unlikely to have been sympathetic to Jesus. When the result came back, it would surely be that they must take the money from Jesus, even though he maintained that he was not liable to pay. The collectors would thus be placed in an awkward position, and in the end they might find themselves constrained to take action they were not convinced was right. Perhaps this was the sin (as Derrett holds).[70] Alternatively the sin might be that which resulted from the effect on the tax collectors (and all who knew what he had done) if Jesus refused to pay the tax. They would conclude that he rejected all that the temple stood for and accordingly turn away from him and his message of salvation.

To prevent any such unfortunate consequences Jesus took action that would satisfy the tax collectors without using money given by supporters for the maintenance of the little band. He instructed Peter to do some

68. H. Montefiore says that to refuse to pay the temple tax "would give the impression that Jesus disapproved of all Temple worship. What the Pharisees demanded as a legal due, Jesus gave as a free-will offering of the heart" (*NTS*, XI [1964-65], p. 71).

69. The verb is σκανδαλίζω; most translations render it in some such way as "lest we give offense to them." But this verb has the idea of entrapment (see on 5:29). The thought is not that the tax collectors be offended, but that they be tripped up, entrapped, led into conduct that was sinful. Knox renders, "we will not hurt their consciences."

70. N. J. McEleney says that Derrett's explanation " — Jesus saves the tax collectors from the sin of forcing him to pay when he need not — is an unsupported supposition and does not convince" (*CBQ*, XXXVIII [1976], p. 186, n. 51). There is, of course, no specific information on the point, but perhaps it is unwise to dismiss Derrett so hastily.

fishing with a hook (the only reference to catching fish with a hook in the New Testament; elsewhere a net is spoken of). He is to take the first fish he catches and open its mouth, and there he will find a *stater*.[71] Derrett argues that the fish in mind would have been a catfish, which scavenges near landing places, is without scales, and thus is not to be eaten by Jews. It grows to a length of four feet or more. It has a large mouth and, according to Derrett, would be attracted by a bright disk, which when taken into the mouth "might easily be caught in the framework of the hinder part of the mouth" (p. 259).[72] A stater was enough to pay the temple tax for two people, and it seems to have been often used in this way. "Found" money did not belong to anyone, so there was no barrier to Peter's paying the tax with it. The little group's meager store of money would then not have been used to pay taxes. It is also possible that the use of a "found" coin, while it satisfied the tax collectors, did not involve any admission that Jesus was liable to pay the tax; it was not "his" money.[73] Jesus tells Peter to give the coin to the collectors *for me and you*.[74]

Matthew does not tell us that Peter actually caught the fish in this way and paid the tax. His interest was not so much in the act as in the fact that Jesus spoke in the way he records. That Jesus was in the relationship of Son to the heavenly Father was for Matthew the important thing. Many commentators find the story difficult and rationalize in one way or another. Thus Melinsky thinks that Jesus' words to Peter "may have been a humorous way of saying, 'Get on with your fishing and the tax will look after itself.'" But if this is what Matthew meant, he has recorded it in a very strange way. It is better to understand him to mean that there would be a real coin in the mouth of a real fish.

71. A στατήρ was worth four drachmas and was thus equivalent to the temple tax for two men. "It was minted at Antioch, Caesarea in Cappadocia and in Tyre" (*IBD*, II, p. 1022). It is mentioned in the New Testament only here. Gutzwiller comments: "God needs no one and nothing. If he gives, the giving is his right and his free choice. The tax-money in the fish's mouth, rather than in the hand of man, shows God's sovereign freedom: he takes where he will and gives to whom he will" (p. 202).

72. "The *clarias macracanthus*, or 'St. Peter's fish,' common in the Sea of Galilee, is certainly able to accommodate coins in its ample mouth" (*AB*).

73. Chrysostom comments: "See how He neither declines the tribute, nor simply commands to pay it, but having first proved Himself not liable to it, then He gives it: the one to save the people, the other, those around Him, from offense" (p. 359). "The collectors were doubtless as well satisfied with this coin as they would have been by a coin obtained from a patron: but charity money had not been used, and the important admission had not been made" (Derrett, *Law*, p. 258). As to the other disciples, Derrett thinks that since God had showed the way for his Son and for Peter those who gave money to the little band would now give for their temple tax; alternatively the collectors may have been glad to escape from an embarrassing situation and would not have pressed the matter further.

74. The preposition rendered *for* is ἀντί, which is normally the preposition for substitution, "in place of." Turner points out that the half shekel was a redemption tax (Exod. 30:11); thus he refuses to accept "on behalf of" as a separate meaning for ἀντί: "the sole significance of the preposition in each New Testament context is that of substitution and exchange" (*Grammatical Insights*, p. 173).

Matthew 18

4. Life in the Messianic Community, 18:1-35

For the last section of his narrative before going on to Jesus' departure for Judea Matthew has a discourse of Jesus on what it means to live as servants of the Messiah. He stresses the importance of lowly people in the kingdom. The values of the kingdom are not those of the world. Uprightness and a readiness to forgive others are important. There is disagreement as to whether Matthew has combined statements of Jesus made on a number of occasions or whether this chapter formed a connected whole from the first. There is disagreement also as to where the divisions in the chapter ought to be made. All in all it seems better to take it as Matthew has given us and study it as one piece of teaching.[1]

> [1]At that time the disciples came to Jesus, saying, "Who then is greatest in the kingdom of heaven?" [2]And he called a little child, and stood him in the middle of them, [3]and said, "Truly I say to you, unless you are turned and become like little children, you will certainly not enter the kingdom of heaven. [4]For whoever humbles himself as this little child, this person is the greatest in the kingdom of heaven. [5]And whoever receives one such little child in my name receives me. [6]But whoever makes one of these little ones who believes in me to sin, it were better for him that a heavy millstone were hung around his neck and he were drowned in the depths of the sea. [7]Woe to the world because of the things that lead people to sin. The things that lead to sin must come, but woe to the man through whom the thing that leads to sin comes.
>
> [8]"And if your hand or your foot leads you to sin, cut it off and throw it away from you; it is better for you to enter life crippled or maimed rather than having two hands or two feet to be thrown into the eternal fire. [9]And if your eye makes you sin, pluck it out and throw it away from you; it is better for you to enter life having one eye than having two eyes to be thrown into the hell of fire.

1. Davies is impressed by the didactic tone of the passage and says that the chapter as a whole "constitutes what may be described as an incipient manual of discipline" (*SM*, p. 292). G. Bornkamm similarly regards it as a "Rule for the Congregation" (Stanton, p. 86).

10"See that you do not despise one of these little ones, for I tell you that their angels in heaven continually see the face of my Father who is in heaven. 12What do you think? If a man has a hundred sheep, and one of them goes astray, does he not leave the ninety-nine on the hills and go and keep looking for the one that strayed? 13And if it happens that he finds it, truly I tell you, he rejoices over it more than over the ninety-nine that did not go astray. 14Just so it is not the will of your Father in heaven that one of these little ones should perish.

15"And if your brother sins against you, go and reprove him between you and him alone. If he listens to you, you have won your brother. 16But if he does not listen, take with you one or two more in order that every matter should be established on the testimony of two or three witnesses. 17But if he refuses them, tell it to the church; and if he refuses even the church, let him be to you like the pagan and the tax collector.

18"Truly I say to you, whatever you bind on the earth will be bound in heaven, and whatever you loose on the earth will be loosed in heaven.

19"Again, I truly say to you, that if two of you agree on earth about any matter that they may ask, it will be done for them by my Father who is in heaven. 20For where two or three are gathered in my name, I am there in the middle of them."

21Then Peter came and said to him, "Lord, how often shall my brother sin and I forgive him? Up to seven times?" 22Jesus says to him, "I do not say to you, up to seven times, but up to seventy-seven times.

23"For this reason the kingdom of heaven may be likened to a king who wanted to settle accounts with his servants. 24And when he had begun to reckon, there was brought to him a debtor owing ten thousand talents. 25And since he did not have the money to repay, the lord commanded him to be sold, and his wife and his children and all he had, to repay the debt. 26Therefore the servant fell down and prostrated himself, saying, 'Have patience with me and I will repay you all.' 27And the lord of that servant, moved by compassion, released him and forgave him the debt. 28But when that servant went out, he found one of his fellow servants who owed him a hundred denarii; and he took hold of him and began to choke him, saying, 'Pay back what you owe.' 29Therefore his fellow servant fell down and besought him, saying, 'Have patience with me and I will repay you.' 30But he would not, but he went off and threw him into prison until he should pay back what was owed. 31When therefore his fellow servants saw what had happened, they were very sorry and went and told their lord all that had happened. 32Then his lord summoned him and says to him, 'You wicked servant, I forgave you all that debt because you appealed to me; 33and was it not necessary for you also to have had mercy on your fellow servant, even as I also had mercy on you?' 34And his lord was angry and handed him over to the torturers, until he should repay all that was owed. 35So also will my heavenly Father do to you unless you each forgive his brother from your hearts."

As he finishes his account of Jesus' Galilean ministry, Matthew records a discourse some of which is not recorded in Mark and/or Luke and some of which is recorded but not in the same context. He begins with a section on the importance of lowliness. Mark tells us that the disciples were disputing about who would be the greatest (Mark 9:34); Jesus' teaching about lowliness responds to this. He goes on to the importance of avoiding evil and of being forgiving to other people.

1. *At that[2] time[3] the disciples* is general enough to signify any followers of Jesus, but in this context it surely means the Twelve. *Came* (see on 4:3) may indicate a more or less formal approach, and this is favored by the nature of the question they put to Jesus. They seem to have become increasingly sure that Jesus was the Messiah, which meant that the messianic kingdom was just around the corner, and that in turn meant for them that the top places in the kingdom were up for grabs. So they ask a question about the greatest in the kingdom.[4] Jesus has said some unexpected things about what being Messiah meant and about the kingdom. The disciples wonder who will be the great ones in the kingdom of which he spoke, so they ask a question to find out. They use the comparative of the adjective meaning "great," so that their question strictly means "Who is greater — ?" But the comparative is often used in the sense of the superlative, and there is no reason for doubting that here they are looking for the name of the person who would be second to Jesus when the kingdom was established. Barclay remarks, "the very fact that they asked that question showed that they had no idea at all what the Kingdom of Heaven was" (II, p. 192).

2. Jesus did not answer immediately or in the way the questioners expected. He called *a little child[5]* and *stood him* in the middle of the group. Surrounded by grown men, the child must have looked insignificant, which of course is Jesus' point.[6]

3. Jesus prefixes his comment on the child with *"Truly I say to you"*

2. ἐκεῖνος is a favorite Matthean word (see on 3:1).

3. Strictly Matthew says "hour" (ὥρα), but this word may be used for almost any period of time. Here it surely tells us that what follows took place at about the same time as the events narrated at the end of the last chapter. Carr supposes that Jesus and Peter "were alone when the last incident happened, they had entered the house (probably Peter's) and were now joined by the other apostles who had been disputing on the way." Filson sees the connection this way: "if sons of the Kingdom are free and the full Kingdom will be so great a privilege, who will have top rank in it?" (p. 198).

4. It is introduced naturally enough by τίς, but ἄρα is perhaps not so much to be expected. It perhaps arises out of Peter's role in the immediately preceding incident. That showed Peter in a prominent position. Would that be reflected in the kingdom?

5. παιδίον is strictly a diminutive, but the word is used of children generally. Here, however, the child must have been a small one; a big child would have obscured the point Jesus is making.

6. "The child is weak, small, basically helpless, and unimportant in comparison with grown-ups. It is dependent on others; the younger it is the more dependent. This objective insignificance of the child, not any particular characteristic of children, is set forth as the way in which disciples are to think of themselves" (Hamann).

(for which see on 5:18). It is a solemn opening and emphasizes that what follows is important; it is to be heeded carefully. Mark and Luke tell of Jesus taking a child, and Mark of setting him in the middle and taking him into his arms; they also tell us (much in the manner of v. 5) of teaching that Jesus gave on that occasion. But Matthew alone has the words about being *turned* and becoming *like children.*[7] *Be turned* can refer to any one of a variety of turnings, but in this context it will signify a change of direction of the whole life, a conversion.[8] This is further described as becoming *like little children;* adults tend to leave childlike ways behind them (and some such ways certainly ought to be abandoned; children can manifest qualities like pride, selfishness, and temper),[9] but Jesus is pointing out that there are some things to be learned from small children. He seems to be referring to the insignificance and unimportance of children as the ancient world saw them, perhaps also to qualities like trustfulness and dependence.[10] Adults like to assert themselves and to rely on their own strength and wisdom. This attitude is impossible for those who wish to enter the kingdom. We should notice further that Jesus does not answer the set terms of the question. He does not concern himself with relative positions and who will have the top job when the kingdom comes: he speaks of the more basic problem of getting into the kingdom. His emphatic double negative rules out the possibility of even entering the kingdom for those seeking great things for themselves. He does not talk about eminence in the kingdom at all; without genuine humility it is impossible even to get into it, and for humility the question of personal preeminence does not arise.

4. That humility is foremost in Jesus' mind is now made clear. *Whoever* makes the following statement quite general; what Jesus says is of universal relevance. And he does not think of any quality in the child other than humility; it is the one who *humbles himself as this little child* who is *the greatest in the kingdom of heaven.*[11] We should not take this to mean

---

7. Patte comments, "people — that is, would-be disciples — are not spontaneously like children. They must *become* like children by turning away from what they are, by humbling themselves. Self-denial, giving up what one is, is a prerequisite for participating and being great in the kingdom" (p. 248).

8. G. Bertram draws attention to the use of the verb in the classics for "the moral walk and inner turnings" (*TDNT*, VII, p. 714). Tasker objects to the translation "turn," maintaining that it is best to take the verb στραφῆτε "as a strict passive, for the change that is necessary before a man becomes as a little child is not something that he can bring about by himself. It is in fact a new birth, which we are told in John iii.3-6 is supernatural" (p. 175).

9. Fenton remarks that the child is the symbol of humility "not because a child is humble (most of them are not), but because a child has no status in society." He cites Galatians 4:1.

10. Melinsky speaks of "unselfregarding trust in God, like that so shatteringly displayed by young children towards their elders."

11. Cf. Robinson, "It is not merely the simplicity of the child that Jesus has in view, it is even more the fact that he is starting life afresh, with no preconceived notions; the saying means much the same as the Johannine 'Ye must be born again' " (p. 152).

"humbles himself as this little child humbles himself" but rather "humbles himself until he becomes like this little child." Humility was a quality Jesus himself displayed (Phil. 2:8) and which he looks for in his own. It is not a quality that comes easily and naturally to people like us; a person must work at being really humble. In modern Western societies children are often seen as very important, but in first-century Judaism they were not (other, of course, than that a man who had many children was seen as richly blessed; children formed an important indication of divine approval). In the affairs of men children were unimportant. They could not fight, they could not lead, they had not had time to acquire worldly wisdom, they could not pile up riches, they counted for very little. To speak of them as humble is surely a reference to their small size rather than any intellectual or spiritual virtue. Their smallness made them very humble members of society. Thus when Jesus says that his followers must humble themselves *as this little child,* he was not uttering a truism, but making a most unexpected pronouncement.[12] He draws attention to *this little child,* the concrete embodiment of childhood standing there in their midst. In the previous verse Jesus spoke of children generally, as the plural shows; now he refers to the child standing there.

The kingdom of heaven is not like earthly kingdoms. In earthly kingdoms military might or earthly wealth is what counts. It is the ability to overthrow others or to outsmart them or to outbid them that matters. The person who asserts himself is the one who gets on. But Jesus' kingdom is quite different. Paradoxically it is the person who is like the little child who is the greatest. Being in the kingdom does not mean entering a competition for the supreme place, but engaging in lowly service. True greatness consists not in receiving service but in giving it. The genuinely humble person is the one that really counts in that kingdom. The humble person is *the greatest.*

We should not overlook the fact that this implies reliance on the love and the grace of God. Jesus does not emphasize these qualities at this point, but they are implied. The little child can do nothing to bring about his status; all that the child is and has comes from someone else. Jesus' followers are not great achievers who carve out for themselves a niche (or a cave!) in the kingdom of heaven. For all that they have and all that they are they depend on the heavenly Father.

5. A different aspect of the kingdom is now brought out, but one in which the child is still important. Jesus speaks of anyone[13] who welcomes[14]

---

12. Cf. W. Grundmann, "Jesus is speaking to adults. He is conscious of their lost childlikeness before God. He thus gives humility a special nuance. It is to become a child again before God, i.e., to trust Him utterly, to expect everything from Him and nothing from self" (*TDNT,* VIII, p. 17).

13. ὅς ἐάν here will have much the same meaning as ὅστις in verse 4; both signify "whoever."

14. δέχομαι (which Matthew uses 10 times; Luke has it 16 times) means "receive hospitably," "welcome."

one such little child. The numeral *one* indicates the minimum, the smallest possible number of children, and *such* widens the thought to include children in general, not only the child there in the middle. To receive even one of them hospitably is important. It is the habit of the world to serve the great and the popular, but for the follower of Jesus the priority must be to receive and welcome the world's little people. Jesus says further that the reception is to be *in my name*,[15] where the *name* is used "of all that the name implies, of rank, authority, character etc." (AS; cf. "believe on the name" and similar usages; see further the note on 6:9). Jesus speaks of the disciple as receiving the little child because that is what Jesus would do and therefore it is what Jesus would want his servant to do too. And when that happens, Jesus says, "me he receives." In the Greek "me" comes first, which gives it emphasis, "no less than me." What started this whole discussion off was the question "Who is greatest in the kingdom of heaven," but this leads to the surprising statement that one receives Jesus by receiving just one little child like the one in the midst. The kingdom is not to be envisaged in the way the disciples had been thinking of it.

6. From the privilege Jesus moves to the responsibility. Just as receiving the little child properly brings such a great reward, so acting against the interests of the child brings a severe punishment. Another *whoever* shows us that Jesus continues to deal in sweeping generalities; this is what happens universally, not simply in the isolated instance of the one little child in the middle of the group of disciples. He speaks of one who *makes one of these little ones . . . to sin.*[16] The verb with its idea of entrapment indicates that the person in question is leading the little one into something that that little one does not properly understand. The little one is deceived into committing sin, and sin involves dreadful penalties that the sinner cannot escape. Jesus does not specify any particular sin; the meaning will be any sin, for all sin draws people away from Christ. The person responsible for this outrage will be in a serious plight. Jesus does not say precisely what this plight is, but he brings out its seriousness by saying that it would be better for the person to be drowned. That means a sentence of death, which is the ultimate penalty in human affairs. Jesus speaks picturesquely of the person having *a heavy millstone*[17] tied around his neck and for him then to be *drowned in the depths of the sea.*[18] Jesus is speaking of a fate the person cannot possibly escape.

15. ἐπί means "on the ground of," "on the basis of."

16. The verb is σκανδαλίζω (see on 5:29), which speaks of setting off the bait stick of a trap and thus ensnaring.

17. μύλος ὀνικός, where the adjective means "pertaining to an ass." Grain was often ground in a small mill worked by hand, but Jesus is referring to a stone too heavy to be manipulated by the human hand and thus requiring the service of an animal like an ass. It would be very weighty and would ensure that the person around whose neck it hung went to the bottom of the water.

18. καταποντίζω signifies "to throw into the sea" and thus to sink or drown in the sea. πέλαγος (again in the New Testament only in Acts 27:5) means "the deep sea"; when combined with θάλασσα it points to the depths of the sea ("far out in the open sea," McNeile), not

We should notice that Jesus does not here speak of children generally, but of one little one *who believes in me*. The question arises whether he is still speaking of children or whether the "little ones" are now the unimportant people who believe in him. Most commentators agree that the "little ones" include not only small children but all lowly believers (Johnson holds the "little ones" to be "not merely children but the 'weaker brethren' who did not understand the implications of their faith," but there seems to be no reason for limiting the expression in this way). The word *little* is sometimes used of importance in this world rather than age, for example, in the expression "both great and small" (cf. Acts 8:10). This view is assisted by the fact that the little one in question is said to *believe* in Jesus. The addition *in me* makes it clear that it is faith in Christ that is in question, faith that trusts in him alone, centers its trust in him.[19] We should understand Jesus to be referring to lowly disciples, those who claim nothing great for themselves but trust him for all things; they are God's little people.

7. Matthew tells of Jesus' words denouncing those who lead others into sin, a passage found only in this Gospel. *Woe*[20] is to be understood as an expression of regret and compassion (see on 11:21); Jesus is not exulting in the punishment that must come, but he is making it clear that punishment will come (*woe* is a verdict as well as an expression of sorrow). The person who leads others to sin is storing up grievous trouble for himself. *The world* here denotes earth's people, those who sin and those who lead them to sin;[21] unhappiness is inevitable for both. The sinner is in trouble because of the evil he does, and the person who leads another into sin is in a worse position, as Jesus is now saying. The world being what it is and people being what they are, it is inevitable that *the things that lead to sin* (Phillips, "pitfalls") will make their appearance. But that they are certain to come does not excuse the person who brings them about. A second *woe* brings out the certainty of that person's unhappiness in due course. Jesus does not speak of the man who leads another to sin, but of the man *through whom* the enticement to sin comes. The evil is almost seen as having an independent existence and as coming on the scene *through* the offender; his offense is in facilitating the coming of the entice-

---

shallow water where the person might possibly escape. Josephus tells us that the Galileans on occasion used drowning as a method of execution (*Ant.* 14.450).

19. This is the one place in the Synoptic Gospels in which there is an explicit reference to believing in Christ (it also occurs in some MSS of Mark 9:42). It is, of course, implied in many places, but it comes to expression only here.

20. οὐαί occurs 12 times in Matthew, 15 times in Luke, 14 times in Revelation, and only 4 times elsewhere in the New Testament. It is a strong expression of regret, usually for the punishment that sinners are inevitably drawing down on themselves. Here it is followed by ἀπό, which introduces the reason.

21. τὰ σκάνδαλα (see on 5:29) are the things that entrap; there is always something of deceit about sin. People would not want to commit sin if they realized just what sin is and what its inevitable consequences are. Thus those who sin are entrapped.

ment, not in originating it. There is more to evil than the wrong deeds of the sinner.

8. Jesus moves from provocation to sin to the importance of avoiding sin of any kind. These words are much the same as those in 5:29-30 (where see notes). He makes the supposition[22] that one's *hand* or *foot* leads one into sin. Jesus does not define how this should take place, but leaving it general covers all the ways in which one of these members of the body should occasion evil. If that takes place, he enjoins a drastic remedy: *cut it off and throw it away.* In other words, get rid of the source of the sin. Jesus is not, of course, counseling his followers to engage in mutilation of the body. He is using picturesque language to make clear that he looks for a complete and thorough repudiation of evil. He underlines his point by saying that it is better[23] to be alive with an impaired body than to be destined for hell. He speaks of entering *life,* where he means more than this earthly existence which we share with all others; the sinner obviously has already entered this life. He is speaking about the life that really matters, the life of the world to come (cf. Cassirer, "where true life is to be found").[24] It is better to make sure of that life, even if it means some impoverishment in this life; he specifies being *crippled or maimed.* There is not a great deal of difference in the meanings of the two words; both point to a grievous handicap. But better that than having the normal equipment of two good hands and two good feet to be lost eternally. For *thrown* see on 10:34; it speaks of vigorous action. *Eternal fire* is, of course, used metaphorically in an expression that brings out the painfulness of the lost in their eternal lostness. Jesus leaves his hearers in no doubt as to the seriousness of the eternal state of sinners.[25]

9. Jesus repeats the thought, shifting attention from the hand or foot to the *eye,* a member of the body that we all tend to value very highly (and one in which Matthew is very interested; he uses the word 24 times, which is more than in any other New Testament book). But he has already recorded an example of the way it can lead to sin (5:29) and spoken of the importance of a healthy eye (6:22). Again he speaks of getting rid of the offending member; better to pluck the offending eye out and hurl it away than to retain it as an occasion for sin. As in the preceding verse, we should

22. The conditional clause is introduced by εἰ; this does not tell us whether or not the condition is fulfilled, but it puts the condition strongly enough that we can see what should be the consequence if the event were to take place.

23. καλόν is an example of the positive used in the sense of the comparative (cf. M, III, p. 31).

24. Cf. AS, "ζωή, is life *intensive,* 'vita quâ vivimus,' the vital principle; βίος, life *extensive,* 'vita quam vivimus,' . . . in cl., ζ., being confined to the physical life common to men and animals, is the inferior word (cf. *zoology, biography*). In NT, ζωή is elevated into the ethical and spiritual sphere" (*sub* βίος).

25. Matthew uses πῦρ 12 times, which is more than in any other New Testament book apart from Revelation (26 times). Mostly he employs it to bring out the thought of the eternal destiny of the wicked. Thus here it is *eternal fire.*

not take Jesus' words as advocating literal self-mutilation. He is saying that his followers should take decisive action to be rid of sin. *"Throw it away"* is another vigorous expression; the offending member is not to be lingered over but to be decisively repudiated. The rest of the verse repeats verse 8 (with the necessary modifications for "eye" over against "hand" or "foot") until we come to the final expression, where *the hell*[26] *of fire* replaces "the eternal fire." There is no essential difference; *hell* indicates place, whereas "eternal" points to the unendingness.

10. Jesus returns to the subject of the *little ones*, first calling on his hearers to *See,*[27] where his verb calls for concentrated effort. People are not to despise even *one of these little ones* (France reminds us that "one individual can conveniently be ignored in one's care for 'the church'"). Here again it is uncertain whether the *little ones* are children or lowly disciples (his "common people").[28] Either makes good sense, and the following reference to *angels* does not clear it up. Perhaps we should understand Jesus to be speaking first of the children that started him on this section of teaching, but now to be using words that have relevance to all his lowly followers. *For* introduces the reason. *Angels* (see on 1:20) are heavenly beings, but *their* poses a problem. Jacob referred to an angel who had had concern for him (Gen. 48:16), while in the book of Daniel it seems that each nation has its angel (Dan. 10:13) and in Revelation we are introduced to the angels of churches (Rev. 1:20). Perhaps we should notice further that angels are said to have carried Lazarus to Abraham's bosom (Luke 16:22) and to rejoice over one sinner who repents (Luke 15:10). Angels are apparently active in and about the affairs of people. It is possible that here guardian angels are meant (*NEB* translates "guardian angels"), with a particular angel watching over each *little one*. But if this were meant, it would point to something so significant that we would expect references to guardian angels elsewhere, and we do not find them.[29] Calvin regards the suggestion that guardian angels are in mind as "weak" and prefers the idea that "to the angels is committed the care of the whole Church and that they succour individual members so far as their necessity and situation demands" (II, p. 218). We can say no more than that the passage looks like a reference to guardian angels but comes short of proof, and in any case we have no further information on who such angels are

26. *Hell* translates γέεννα, for which see the note on 5:32.
27. ὁράω may be used of bodily vision (Mark 8:24) or of perception with the mind (9:2). Here it is rather in the sense "take heed, beware."
28. Hillel was a great and good teacher, but he could say of the people of the land, the common people, that one of them "cannot be saintly" (*'Abot* 2:6). Jesus' attitude is a long way from this.
29. Some point to Peter's "angel" in Acts 12:15, but this is not very convincing; it refers to some being that could be mistaken for Peter, and there is no reason to think that a guardian angel would look like those he guards. Others draw attention to Tobit 5:6, 21, but it is not said that this angel is "his" angel; and in any case the angel is no more than a being who looks after him on one particular journey.

or what they do.[30] Certainly the angels to whom Jesus refers are *in heaven;* he further says that they *continually see the face of my Father* (for *Father* see on 5:16). Perhaps our insertion of "guardian" before angel is misleading: the angels of which Jesus speaks do not "guard" the little ones, but bring their situation before God. He is using picturesque language to bring out the truth that God in heaven is aware of the situation here on earth of even the lowliest of his people.[31] We should notice *my:* the relationship of Jesus to the Father is something special. The whole expression is surely a way of saying that these angels have immediate access to God; indeed, some translations concentrate on this (as *GNB,* "are always in the presence of my Father"); any act to the detriment of the little ones would not go unnoticed in the highest place of all. The little ones matter to God.[32]

12. *"What do you think?"* (more literally, "what does it seem to you?") invites the hearers to reflect. Jesus is now not laying down a firm assertion of his own but calling on those listening to him to work something out for themselves. He refers to a man who owns a flock of *a hundred sheep* of which *one goes astray.* Such a man does not reason that 99 percent of his flock are safe and well and that on the whole he has no reason for alarm. Jesus asks whether he does not[33] leave the ninety-nine where they are *on the hills* (and presumably far from shelter) and *keep looking* (the change of tense from the future to the present points to the continuous effort of seeking) *for the one that strayed.* Though only one is missing, the shepherd's whole routine is altered. He concentrates all his energy on recovering that lost one. He is prepared to leave the ninety-nine at some risk in order to ensure the safety of the one that strayed.

13. The opening words are equivalent to "if in fact he finds it."[34] Another *"truly I tell you"* introduces a statement that is very important. The joy that results from finding the lost exceeds the joy of knowing that

30. Carson endorses Warfield's suggestion that what is meant is the spirits of the "little ones" after their death, but there is a problem with the present tense. Jesus appears to be speaking about heavenly representatives now. Jesus may well be saying that the "little ones" are not to be despised, for they will in due course enjoy the glory of being with the Father in heaven. This would be an unusual meaning for *angels,* but Carson thinks that it would not be an impossible one. But it is more likely that Jesus is saying that little ones should not be despised because right now their plight is drawn to the attention of God himself.

31. G. Kittel comments, "recollection of the angels τῶν μικρῶν τούτων who constantly behold the face of God serves to describe the all-embracing love of God to which these μικροί are important, and thus to drive home our human responsibility to regard them as important too" (*TDNT,* I, p. 86).

32. Some MSS read verse 11 (as D K W X and many later MSS). But this cannot outweigh its omission from ℵ B L* Θ etc. and the likelihood that it was borrowed from Luke 19:10 to make a good connection between verse 10 and verses 12-14 (so Metzger).

33. οὐχί, the emphatic negative, makes it clear that a positive answer is expected for the question.

34. γίνομαι is used with the infinitive following "to emphasize the actual occurrence of the action denoted by the verb"; here "= if he actually finds it" (BAGD, I.3.e). Palestinian shepherds did not always find lost sheep; a sheep might be killed by wild animals or fall over a precipice or wander too far away to be found.

ninety-nine are safe. The shepherd *rejoices* ("is more delighted," *REB*) over this one, Matthew reports, *more than*[35] *over the ninety-nine that did not go astray.* Jesus is not saying that the shepherd does not rejoice over those who are safe, nor does he say that the heavenly Father is less than delighted over disciples who are safe in the fold. But he points out that there is a peculiar joy over bringing one that is lost safely into the fold. The flock then has not lost one of its members.[36]

14. *"Just so,"*[37] Jesus goes on, God does not will that any of the little ones should perish. The expression about the will is more literally "it is not will before your Father," which is a reverent way of referring to what God does. Sometimes the expression is used also of what great men, and especially kings, do. Dalman says, "it comes to pass that in Egypt men spoke only 'in the presence of the king,' not 'to' him"; he cites a similar form of expression in Esther and Daniel.[38] The expression is thus equivalent to "God does not will." Jesus goes on to use words that put all *these little ones* under God's care. He does not will the perishing of any one of them.[39]

15. Jesus moves from the brother who offends to the brother who is sinned against.[40] Again he raises the topic with a hypothetical *if;*[41] Jesus gives no indication of the probability of this occurring. He simply raises the possibility and tells his followers what they are to do if it happens. There is a difficult textual problem as to whether we should read *against you* or omit the words.[42] If we accept them, Jesus is referring to what to

35. μᾶλλον is the comparative of μάλα; it may be used of increase, when it means "more," or of preference, with the meaning "rather."

36. The second-century Gnostic Gospel of Thomas has the story of a shepherd who left ninety-nine sheep in the wilderness and tired himself out looking for the hundredth that was lost. But that sheep was "the largest" and was loved more than the others (107). Schweizer comments, "This change totally perverts the meaning of the parable; that a single particularly devout person is worth more than ninety-nine average Christians is precisely the position Jesus attacks" (p. 368).

37. οὕτως is used often in Matthew (32 times); it may refer to what precedes or to what follows. It indicates that the joy of the heavenly Father is like that of the successful shepherd.

38. G. Dalman, *The Words of Jesus* (Edinburgh, 1902), p. 212.

39. ἀπόλλυμι means "ruin," "destroy," and covers all sorts of destruction. Here it is eternal loss that is in question.

40. The passage is often said to reflect later church discipline, but Filson remarks: "The passage is Jewish and early in character; the only basis for assigning it a late origin is the use of the word *church,* which here means not the later hierarchical Church of Gentile Christianity, but the local group of believers in which two disciples are at variance. Nothing justifies the view that Jesus could not have spoken the words" (p. 201).

41. ἐάν with the subjunctive raises the possibility but gives no indication of the likelihood. Matthew has ἐάν 66 times.

42. εἰς σέ is read by MSS like D K L X Δ Θ etc., but is omitted by ℵ B f1 etc. The words may have been omitted by scribes who wanted to make the passage apply to all sin, or they may have dropped out accidentally. But it is also possible that they were not originally in the text and were put in by scribes who wanted something parallel to verse 21. Metzger's committee enclosed the words within square brackets, and most students would think that fair enough. It is impossible to be sure of the original reading.

do when another believer (a *brother;* see on 1:2) does something that we can only regard as sin against us, as wronging us in some way. If not, he is speaking of what we are to do when another believer sins in any way. In either case we are first to take the matter up with the sinner. *"Go"* means taking the initiative; the person in the clear is not to wait for the sinner to come to him. The next part of the Greek is not easy to translate, as is shown by the variety of renderings that have been accepted; for example, *NIV* reads, "go and show him his fault"; *REB,* "take the matter up with him"; and *JB,* "have it out with him." I have translated *reprove him,* for that is what the verb often means.[43] Jesus seems to be saying that the first thing the believer should do is try to get the offender to see his sin for what it is. He is not advocating the harsh attitude his people sometimes take up nor the very light attitude that is also common. Jesus specifies that this should be done *"between you and him alone."* There should be no attempt to bring all this out into the open. It is a matter between the offender, the offended, and God, and if the sinner can be persuaded to repent and seek forgiveness, the whole affair is over. *"If he listens to you,*[44] *you have won your brother."* The brotherly relationship was disrupted by the sin; now it is restored. Instead of a lost brother there is a restored brotherhood.[45]

16. But this technique is not infallible. There is the possibility that the offender will not alter his ways.[46] He may refuse to take any notice when the brother sinned against points out his fault. The sinned against is to try again; it is important to win the brother back if that can be done. So he is to take with him[47] a small number of others (*one or two* does not specify the number, but clearly a small group is meant; the matter is to be kept as quiet as possible). It would seem that after he has resisted the quiet approach of one brother it is unlikely that he will respond to others. The purpose[48] of the *one or two more* is that the situation should be *established on the testimony of two or three witnesses.* There is a reference to Deuteronomy 19:15, which regulates evidence in a court of law. Nobody is to be convicted on the evidence of a single person; everything must be attested by two or, better, three witnesses. Where it is important to have the exact words attested, there must be two or three people who can vouch for what was

43. ἐλέγχω is assigned four meanings by AS: "1. in Hom. *to treat with contempt* 2. *to convict* 3. *to reprove, rebuke* 4. *to expose.*" MM cites examples to show that in the papyri it can have the meaning "to convict," but also "expose, set forth." The usage of the verb allows for more than one translation.

44. Again the conditional is introduced with ἐάν; there is no indication of the likely outcome.

45. Bruce asks, "gained as a *friend,* as a *fellow-member* of the Kingdom of God, or as a *man* = saved him from moral ruin?" and answers, "All three alternatives find support. Is it necessary or possible to decide peremptorily between them?"

46. Yet another ἐάν introduces the possibility with no indication of probability.

47. Matthew has παραλαμβάνω 16 times, whereas it occurs more than 6 times in no other New Testament book; it signifies "take along with." Similarly he has μετά, "with," more than in any other book (70 times; Acts has it 65 times).

48. ἵνα introduces a clause expressing purpose.

said. Jesus is not, of course, talking about a trial, and in any case the *one or two more* are not witnesses of the offense; they can testify only that they have tried to help the offender. Jesus is saying that the church must not apply less stringent tests than the courts. It must not be slipshod.

17. *"But if*[49] *he refuses*[50] *them."* Jesus is speaking of someone who is set in his ways: he will take notice neither of his brother nor of the small delegation from the brotherhood. The fact that he is said to refuse them shows that the small delegation is not intended only as witnesses; its members will be trying to win over the offender. In the event of obduracy they will indeed function as witnesses, but Jesus is speaking of the possibility that the sinner may hear them. It sometimes happens that a wrongdoer will take more notice of two or three (especially if they are people worthy of respect) than he will of one, especially if the one is a person with whom he has had a difference of opinion.

In the event of continuing obduracy they are to *tell it to the church.*[51] The use of this term (again in the Gospels only in 16:18) appears to many scholars to be an indication that the passage is late and that it reflects Matthew's interest in the church rather than the actual teaching of Jesus. Those who are convinced that Jesus could not have used the term must, of course, construct some such hypothesis, but why should he not? The term is met with often in the Greek Old Testament, where it is used for the people of God, assembled or not assembled. It can mean any group of people, and we should not be misled by later ecclesiastical uses (*AB* translates here with "community"). If Jesus meant his followers to be a continuing group, then there seems to be no reason why he should not occasionally refer to them with the word "church."

This appears to be another attempt to win the offender over. The imperative *"tell it to the church"* is singular ("say to the church" with something implied like "the whole story"); Jesus envisages the brother who initiated the process as telling the local church as a whole what had happened. "Church" can mean the whole body of Christians, but it can also refer to a local group, and that is surely what is meant here. Yet this is still by way of appeal, for Jesus goes on to what is to be done if he does not heed the church. The implication is that the church will try to bring him to his senses. When the offender sees that the whole group of believers opposes his behavior, surely he will repent? But the possibility remains that he will not. In that case he has cut himself off from the group of people

49. Another ἐάν with the subjunctive leaves all the possibilities open. This time it is accompanied by δέ, which has adversative force; the sinner should repent, *but.* . . .

50. παρακούω (in the New Testament only here and in Mark 5:36) has the meaning "to overhear," "to hear amiss" or "imperfectly," and then to hear without heeding (see AS). This last is the meaning here.

51. The Qumran community had a similar threefold procedure: "let him rebuke him on the very same day lest he incur guilt because of him. And furthermore, let no man accuse his companion before the Congregation without having first admonished him in the presence of witnesses" (*The Community Rule* V-VI; Vermes, p. 80).

who have eschewed the kind of conduct that he has followed and from which he refuses to depart. *"Let him be to you"* indicates that in the end the believer must accept the reality of the situation. The person has done what he should not have done. He has remained obdurate against the pleadings of a brother, of two or three brothers, and now of the church as a whole. He has taken the role of *the pagan and the tax collector.*[52] Both these expressions stand for people outside the people of God, people who have sinned and not repented, and that is the position of the sinning brother. He has made his choice, and the brother sinned against must respect his decision. It is usually said that the passage speaks of excommunication from the church, but that is not what the text says; *to you* is very personal. Whatever be the case vis-à-vis the church, to the brother against whom he has sinned he is as an outsider.

18. Another solemn introduction (for which see on 5:18) brings us to a solemn and significant saying. The words are very similar to those in 16:19, except that there the verbs are in the singular since they are addressed to one individual, Peter, while here they are in the plural, embracing believers as a whole, the entire church. As we observed in the earlier passage, the probability is that we should understand the "binding" and "loosing" as declaring forbidden or permitted. That would certainly fit this context, where the church in the last resort has to say whether what the offender has done is forbidden to the Christian or whether it is permitted. To the church as a whole there is committed the responsibility of declaring what conduct is forbidden to the believer and what is permitted. This was very necessary in a situation where the Jewish Scriptures were accepted as the Scriptures of the believers, but where the Jewish interpretation was rejected, as were many Jewish practices that those who performed them alleged were based on Scripture. The church as a whole should decide such matters, Jesus is saying. And again we must bear in mind that the verbs are future perfect: "shall have been bound" and "shall have been loosed." Jesus is not giving the church the right to make decisions that will then become binding on God. Such a thought is alien from anything in his teaching. He is saying that as the church is responsive to the guidance of God it will come to the decisions that have already been made in heaven. In John 20:22-23 it is made clear that this is because of the gift of the Holy Spirit. Jesus is not saying that the church will be full of natural, human wisdom. He is referring to decisions made in the light of the guidance of the Spirit of God.

19. Next Matthew has a little section on prayer (which is not paralleled in the other Gospels). *Again* links this on as a fresh start;[53] it is not a continuation of the teaching he has just been giving. Yet once more we

---

52. These are terms that Jewish people would use rather than those in the church in which Matthew was writing. They point to a Palestinian origin of the saying.

53. Turner sees it as an Aramaism giving the meaning "then verily I say to you" (M, IV, p. 32).

have the emphatic introduction "*I truly say to you*" (not all MSS include the *truly*, but the meaning will be much the same even if we omit it); we are at the end of Jesus' teaching in Galilee, and there are some very important statements yet to come. This one has to do with the practice of prayer.[54] Jesus envisages two or three of his followers here on earth as agreeing on some *matter that they may ask*. There are some matters that an individual follower of Jesus will think it important to pray about, but occasions arise when a small group are agreed on the importance of some petition and offer it together.[55] *Matter* is a very general word and opens up a wide scope for prayer; it is reinforced by *that they may ask*.[56] Jesus is saying that the agreement of even two of his followers to pray will bring great results. Of course there is a problem in that we do not always receive the answers we expect to our prayers, corporate or individual. We must bear in mind that there are other conditions, such as praying in faith, praying in the name, praying in accordance with the divine will, and so on. Jesus is not putting in all the qualifications that apply to praying, but simply making it clear that God is always ready to hear the united prayers of even two of his little ones. Prayer is effective, not because of the power or the number of the praying people, but because the answer is given by "*my Father who is in heaven.*" Prayer is offered to a mighty God, one who commonly does his greatest work on earth in response to the prayers of his humble people.

20. Something of the reason follows.[57] *Two or three* once again brings before the reader the smallest possible group; the apparently insignificant matter to God. *In my name*[58] may mean "calling on my name" or "with me as their reason for assembling." The "name" will stand for the person; it is not simply pronouncing the name of Jesus, but in order to worship Jesus, to be with Jesus, or the like. *There*, Jesus says, in that very place, he is *in the middle of them*. The rabbis could say, "if two sit together and words

---

54. This is disputed by J. D. M. Derrett in an article in *ET*, 91 (1979-80), pp. 83-86. He points out that the context deals with offenses, not prayer, and argues that the "two or three" are arbitrators, one from each of the opponents in the dispute and the third from the church if the two could not resolve the dispute. To him the passage "means that unofficial dispute-settlers, peacemakers, perform a divine function. The Christian, submitting to Christian discipline, has faith that the arbitrators whom he has partly chosen for himself, supplemented perhaps by one chosen by the Church, will act as colleagues of Christ himself, and therefore he will believe that their solution is his will" (p. 86). But there is nothing to indicate that the passage refers to a judicial dispute. The verb "ask" is often used of asking in prayer (7:7-11; 21:22, etc.).

55. Ridderbos notes that this "does not mean that any two people who agree will have their prayer answered, even if they disagree with all the other members of the church. It means rather that if for some reason no more than two believers are present at some time or place, they still can be certain that they will receive God's special help" (p. 340).

56. οὐ ἐάν is very general, "whatsoever"; it means that there is a great variety of things that may legitimately be prayed for.

57. Introduced by γάρ. Turner notices this as one of only four places in the New Testament where the clause introduced by οὖ precedes the main clause (M, III, p. 344).

58. εἰς τὸ ἐμὸν ὄνομα may reflect the Hebrew לְשֵׁם.

of the Law (are spoken) between them, the Divine Presence rests between them" (*'Abot* 3:2). For Christians, coming together in the name of Jesus replaces coming to study the law, and the presence of Jesus is "the Divine Presence."

21. For Matthew's *Then* see on 2:7. Peter, as often, is the leader in approaching Jesus and on this occasion in putting a question to him, and the incident is recorded only here. He uses the respectful form of address, "*Lord,*" and inquires about the frequency of forgiveness required in a disciple.[59] Peter has learned that it is important to forgive, so he has made some progress. But surely, he apparently reasons, there must be a limit? How long must one keep on forgiving? He talks about a *brother* (see on 1:2 for Matthew's interest in brotherhood) sinning against him,[60] so he is thinking primarily about what happens within the circle of Jesus' followers (*brother* can mean "brother-man," but that does not seem to be the meaning here). This accords with the fact that a few verses back Jesus has been talking about one brother sinning against another (v. 15). Peter asks whether forgiving[61] such offenses *seven times* is sufficient.[62] There was a rabbinic view that one need forgive only three times: "If a man commits a transgression, the first, second and third time he is forgiven, the fourth time he is not forgiven" (*Yoma* 86b). Peter more than doubled this quota of forgivenesses. Peter has clearly learned something from Jesus. He understands now that retaliation is not the right path for a disciple; rather, forgiveness is a quality to be prized. But he sees this as something that should be practiced in moderation. Surely forgiving the same person seven times would be enough?[63]

22. There is no conjunction linking this verse on to the preceding, and the asyndeton adds force to the abrupt reply. Jesus is not concerned with a petty forgiveness that calculates how many offenses can be disregarded before retaliation becomes acceptable. For him forgiveness is wholehearted and constant. He rejects Peter's *seven times* with decision. *But* is the strong adversative,[64] "far from that"; no satisfactory line of conduct for the believer is to be found along the path of calculating numbers of offenses. For Peter's *seven times* Jesus substitutes *seventy-seven times* (or "seventy times seven," as *REB, GNB,* etc.; either way a lot of

59. ποσάκις = "how often?" is found again in the New Testament only in 23:37 and Luke 13:34.

60. "Against" is εἰς; the sin is directed "to" the brother (cf. Luke 17:4; 1 Cor. 6:18).

61. The question about forgiveness is cited as an example of "Parataxis in interrogative sentences under the influence of Semitic usage" (BDF, 471[2]).

62. ἕως is used here "of degree and measure, denoting the upper limit . . . *as many as seven times*" (BAGD, II.4).

63. Many commentators regard Peter as having too great a readiness to be unforgiving, but Calvin remarks, "the number seven is to be taken as meaning a great number, and the adverb 'seven times' is equivalent to saying, 'How frequently, Lord, do you want us to be reconciled to sinners? For it is absurd and useless for them to find us reconcilable repeatedly' " (II, p. 234).

64. ἀλλά.

forgiving is meant).[65] This, of course, is not counseling an essay in arithmetic so that the seventy-eighth offense need not be forgiven. It is a way of saying that for Jesus' followers forgiveness is to be unlimited. For them forgiveness is a way of life. Bearing in mind what they have been forgiven, they cannot withhold forgiveness from any who sin against them.

23. Jesus underlines his teaching with a parable, found only in this Gospel. *For this reason* brings out an implication of the preceding. Forgiveness is important in a sinful world where all people are sinners, in the first place because we are all in need of being forgiven, and in the second, because people keep on sinning against us so that we ourselves are constantly confronted with situations in which the followers of Jesus are required to forgive. Because of his teaching on forgiveness (and to bring out something of its basis), the kingdom may *be likened*[66] to *a king*[67] who decided to have a day of reckoning.[68] A king would have many officials who handled money in the various departments of state. This king decided it was time to see how they had managed the money that had been entrusted to them. The word rendered *servants* is the ordinary word for "slaves," but in accordance with the usage of the time it was commonly applied to those who served the king. These people would not have been slaves in our sense of the term, but responsible officials in high office.

24. As he initiated the process, *there was brought to him a debtor owing ten thousand talents.* That he *was brought* may indicate a certain unwillingness on the part of the man in question (he certainly had good reason for avoiding the reckoning!), or even that he had already been arrested. That he was *a debtor* indicates that he was legally obliged to pay the money to the king. It is possible, as Derrett holds, that the practice of tax farming is in mind (*Law,* pp. 32-47), in which case the man had bid a large sum for taxing rights and had not been able to produce the money.[69] A *talent*

---

65. Chamberlain says the ending -κις is "a multiplicative and answers the question 'how often' "; here "seventy times seven" (p. 111). Moulton, by contrast, sees an allusion to Genesis 4:24 and holds that that means "seventy-seven times" (M, I, p. 98). Turner accepts this and explains the meaning as "70 times (and) seven" (M, III, pp. 187-88). Argyle asserts, however, that "the Greek cannot bear that meaning." The decisive argument for *seventy-seven* times is that the expression reproduces Genesis 4:24 (LXX), where it is the translation of a Hebrew expression that means "seventy-seven times." If Jesus had that passage in mind he is opposing to the limitless vengeance of Lamech a demand for limitless forgiveness in his followers.

66. ὁμοιόω occurs 8 times in Matthew out of 15 in the New Testament. It means "liken" in the sense "declared to be like" rather than "made like" (as a context like this makes clear).

67. Actually Matthew says "to a man a king"; he is fond of ἄνθρωπος, which he uses 112 times (Luke has it 95 times). He follows it here with ὅς, while in an identical construction in 22:2 he has ὅστις; clearly he makes no distinction betwen the two pronouns. And equally clearly ἄνθρωπος is here equivalent to an indefinite adjective.

68. *Wanted* renders ἠθέλησεν; "he set his will" or "he made up his mind"; it points to a settled decision.

69. Josephus tells of a certain Joseph who heard that 8,000 talents was bid for certain taxing rights and who countered by bidding twice that (*Ant.* 12.175-76). He immediately made himself liable for the huge amount of 16,000 talents. The man in the parable may possibly have found himself in a similar situation.

represented a large sum of money. It was actually a measure of weight, the largest weight in use among the Jews (though its precise size is not known).[70] When used, as here, for amounts of money, it was gold or silver or copper that was weighed. In the parable it is not specified which metal the talent comprised of gold or silver, but either way *ten thousand*[71] of them represented a huge sum of money (his debt "ran into millions," *NEB*). Jesus is speaking of a vast sum; the man must have been a high official on special service to have been entrusted with such an amount (or perhaps the tax farmer over an especially rich province; Josephus speaks of the taxes from Palestine as amounting to 8,000 talents, *Ant.* 12.175; he also says that Antipas received 200 talents as taxes from Perea and Galilee and that Archelaus got 600 talents from his area, *Ant.* 17.318-20).

25. Evidently the venture on which the man had been engaged had failed dismally, and on the day of reckoning he *did not have the money to repay*.[72] There is no information about the enterprise in which he had been engaged and on which he had had such spectacular losses (if he was a tax farmer such factors as drought or a financial depression might make it impossible to raise the amount of money for which he had contracted). There is no indication as to whether the failure had been due to incompetence or dishonesty. The point of the parable lies elsewhere: it is the absence of the money and not the reason for its absence that matters for this story. The king (from this point on called *the lord,* a title that emphasizes that he had full rights; it is the natural correlative of "slave," which is used for the subjects of the king) took seriously the man's inability to pay what he owed. So he issued a command that the defaulter be sold into slavery, and for good measure *his wife and his children* too (cf. Exod. 22:1 [*RSV*]; 2 Kings 4:1; Neh. 5:5; Isa. 50:1). Even when we add the proceeds from *all he had,* it is unlikely that the proceeds of the sale would come anywhere near meeting the liability involved in the ten thousand talents that were missing. The point is that the man was being punished for his offense, not that he was fully reimbursing the king for what he had lost. The sale was a gesture, not a settlement. To us it seems unfair that the *wife* and the *children* should be sold, too; but in the thinking of the time they

---

70. E. M. Cook says, "The weight of the Greco-Roman talent . . . ranged from 26.4 kg. (58 lbs.) to 37.8 kg. (83 lbs.) in different periods. It is not known what standards prevailed in NT Palestine" (*ISBE*, IV, p. 1055). E. R. Sellers adds, "In NT times as money the talent was equal to six thousand drachmas" (*IDB*, IV, p. 511).

71. μυρίος is an adjective used in the sense "numberless" (1 Cor. 4:15; 14:19). The plural here is usually taken to mean ten thousand, but obviously no precise figure is being given. Jesus is simply speaking of a very large sum of money. "The sum is made up of the highest number used in arithmetic and the largest monetary unit employed in the ancient Near East" (Schweizer, p. 377). Several commentators suggest that "a billion" would give the thrust of it.

72. The verb is ἀποδίδωμι; it is used of rendering what is due in a variety of circumstances. It runs through this story, being used twice in this verse and again in verses 26, 28, 29, 30, and 34.

belonged to the man, and if he was to be sold it was natural that they should be sold as well. The man had run up a huge debt; he must pay a huge penalty. Imprisonment for debt was apparently well known in the Greco-Roman world. It prevented the defaulter making his escape and, of course, it encouraged his relatives and friends to raise the money to free him. But in this story the amount is so huge that raising it in order to free him does not come into consideration. His being sold is no more than punishment.

26. All this spelled disaster for the unfortunate debtor. With such a huge debt hanging over his head and with all his assets lost to him there was no chance of his ever being free again. Everything was lost. Justice was of no use to him, so he wholeheartedly went for mercy. He *fell down and prostrated himself,* where either verb would have given the information but the combination emphasizes that he took up a lowly position. It is not quite certain what his lowly posture was, for some translate "fell on his knees" *(NIV, NRSV, GNB).* The second verb is often used for the posture of worship (though also for homage paid to human superiors), and in view of the customs of the day it seems that prostration is perhaps more likely than kneeling. After all, the man's case was desperate, and he would certainly exercise all the diplomacy of which he was capable. The imperfect tense indicates that he kept pleading; his was no half-hearted plea. He entreated his lord, *"Have patience with me."*[73] *All* comes first in its clause, thus acquiring some emphasis. It is, of course, the wrong term and the wrong emphasis for the realities of the debt. One who was bankrupt would never succeed in repaying a debt of the magnitude of that with which the man was faced *(repay* is the same verb as the one the king used, v. 25). But his plight was desperate; he was ready to promise anything.

27. The king was a compassionate man, and Jesus employs a verb that indicates that he was deeply moved in his pity.[74] The king is here called "the lord of that slave," a title that brings out the fact that he had the right to dispose of the defaulter as he chose. But as his initial anger drove him to harshness, so now his compassion led him to act forgivingly. He did more than the man asked. The debtor had requested no more than time to pay, but the king gave him complete freedom. He *released* the man; prison no longer hung over his head. And he *forgave him the debt.*[75] The king set no conditions. The man had asked for forbearance and volunteered to repay the debt (even though it was so large that there was no possibility of his ever doing so). But the king ignored all this. He freely

73. μακροθυμέω strictly = "be long tempered"; it is the opposite of being short tempered. It can be used in the active sense of "persevere," but also passively, as here, "be patient," "long-suffering." In the present case there was certainly scope for long-suffering.

74. σπλαγχνίζομαι; see on 9:36.

75. δάνειον is found here only in the New Testament; strictly it means a loan. It is perhaps worth noticing that the verb ἀφίημι (again in vv. 32 and 35) is used 47 times in Matthew, which is more often than in any other New Testament book.

forgave. That was all. There were no conditions and no hesitation. It was an act of pure grace.

28. But just as the defaulter had owed money, so money was owed to him. When he *went out*, that is, from the presence of the king, *that servant*, the one whose huge debt had been remitted, *found one of his fellow servants*, one who was on the same level as he, one who shared with him in serving the king. Jesus does not say whether the man happened to encounter the fellow servant or whether he went looking for him; *found* could be used in either sense, but it seems more likely that he sought the man out. This man *owed him* money, but whereas the debt he had just been forgiven was so large that its extent could scarcely be computed, this debt was certainly small enough to be understood, *a hundred denarii* (a denarius was a Roman silver coin; it was the wage an ordinary laborer was paid for a day's work; there were 6,000 denarii to a talent). The wages for a hundred days' work cannot be said to be insignificant, but clearly, compared to the first man's debt, this man's was a mere trifle. But the man to whom the money was owed was most anxious to get his money back; he was greedy and grasping as well as extravagant. He laid hands on the debtor and indeed began to choke him; clearly he took him by the throat,[76] a hostile and threatening act, to enforce his demand for repayment.[77] He uses the same verb toward his fellow servant as the king had used toward him.

29. The resemblance continues. *Therefore* is used as in verse 26, and so is the verb for *fell down*, while *fellow servant* corresponds to "servant" in the earlier verse. *Besought* is the word of one taking a lowly place and asking for a favor, while the words of the request are identical with the words of the man to whom they are addressed with the solitary exception that whereas this man promised no more than to repay (which may mean that he would repay some or repay what he could), the other had specifically said that he would repay "all." There is this difference that, whereas the first man's undertaking was one that he could not possibly have fulfilled, this man's was more realistic. It was not impossible that in due course he would be able to raise the money.

30. But whereas the petition was to all intents and purposes identical with the earlier request, the response is diametrically opposite. *But* is adversative; it introduces matter contrary to what we might expect. He *would not*, where the verb refers to the action of the will; the imperfect tense points to continuing action: he continued in his opposition to the petition; his will was set against clemency. The second *but* is the strong adversative (as in v. 22); far from forgiving, he did the very opposite. He went off and *threw* (the verb indicates vigorous action) his fellow servant *into prison*. Since the unfortunate man was to be there until he repaid the

76. This was not unknown among the Jews: "If a man seized a debtor by the throat in the street . . ." (*B. Bat.* 10:8). Was this standard practice in dealing with defaulting debtors?
77. εἴ τι ὀφείλεις, where εἴ τι is equivalent to ὅ τι (see BDF, 376).

debt and since in prison he had no opportunity to earn the necessary money, his outlook was bleak. Jesus is depicting for us a horrible example of an unforgiving, though forgiven, man. It is the height of ingratitude and injustice.

31. Attention moves to the other servants of the king, here described as the *fellow servants* of the man just thrown into jail. When they saw what *had happened,*[78] they were *very sorry,* an expression that evokes a variety of translations (e.g., "very upset," *GNB;* "greatly distressed," *NIV;* "deeply grieved," *NASB).* However we translate it, it clearly points to a deep feeling of grief. The imprisoned man may or may not have been popular, but there was no doubting that he had been treated very shabbily. So these servants went to the king (still spoken of as *lord;* that was his relation to all the other people concerned in this story). They explained[79] to him *all that had happened;* they left him in no doubt but made a clear and full explanation of the whole situation.

32. *Then* is a frequent Matthean word (see on 2:7); it indicates that what follows came next in sequence. *His lord* is another reminder of the relationship in which the king stood to him; *says* is present for greater vividness, and *"You wicked servant"* leaves no doubt as to the king's opinion of his conduct. *Wicked* is very much a Matthean word (see on 6:23, where it is translated "evil"); with its connotation of evil it is a very fitting term to apply to this harsh and unforgiving man (*REB* renders "you scoundrel").[80] The word order in the Greek is "all that debt[81] I forgave you," which puts the emphasis on *all:* all that immense amount! And the man had done no more than appeal to his lord! He had said he would repay, but he had in fact repaid nothing, and everyone knew that it was impossible for him to repay everything as he had said he would. He had been the recipient of extraordinary grace.

33. And those who receive extraordinary grace should act in accordance with the grace they receive. The king asks whether the servant ought not to have had mercy on his fellow (the form in which the question is put looks for an affirmative answer).[82] Most translations have something like "ought you not — ?" which makes for better English, but the king says something stronger than that. He sees it as *necessary*[83] that the forgiven man act like a forgiven man, namely in forgiving others. *You also* underlines the point: "you, you who have been forgiven, you who have received

---

78. τὰ γενόμενα, an expression found twice in this verse and rarely elsewhere in the New Testament.

79. διασαφέω, elsewhere in the New Testament only in 13:36, means "to make clear, explain fully" (AS).

80. "The king denounces the servant as wicked — not because he has mishandled the money given to him but because he has mishandled the forgiveness given to him" (Meier).

81. This is the one occurrence of ὀφειλή in Matthew, but it is the sixth occurrence of words from the ὀφειλ- stem in this passage.

82. It is introduced by οὐ.

83. ἔδει.

such striking generosity, 'you too' should have been generous." The king says that the man should have had *mercy*. We might have expected him to say something like "you should have cancelled the debt," but he refers to mercy as the attitude that should have guided the thinking and the actions of a man who had been the recipient of such signal mercy. The king speaks of mercy on *your fellow servant*, putting the emphasis on his relationship to the man he had condemned rather than on that to his sovereign. *I also* does not mean "I, in addition to others" but "even I," "I, for my part."[84] And the king goes on to remind the man that he had received *mercy* (rather than strict justice).

34. Not surprisingly the king *was angry*, and equally unsurprisingly he took action against the man who refused to forgive. He handed him over to *the torturers* (a word found only here in the New Testament). This certainly means that he was put in jail, and some interpreters hold that "jailor" is all that the word means. But the root is connected with torture, and an angry king would not hesitate to employ torture to punish someone with whom he was very angry (we should not, of course, reason that God tortures sinners; this is simply part of the detail of the story). Whichever way we understand it, the man was to remain there until his entire debt was discharged. He would not be freed if a token amount was paid. This means that he would never get out.

35. Jesus does not always make an application of the truth taught in his parables, but on this occasion he does. *So* does not mean "exactly like this," but it does mean that the severity we discern in the punishment of the man in the parable is all that unforgiving sinners can look for from the hand of God. God might, of course, be more merciful than the king, but that is not the point. The point is that the man deserved no more; any unforgiving sinner, by the fact that he refuses to forgive, is inviting God to withhold forgiveness from him. Jesus refers to God here as *"my heavenly Father,"* stressing his special relationship to God and at the same time something of the majesty of God. The certainty that God will be our final Judge underlies the statement that he will *do* to the unforgiving as they have done to others. The lesson that is driven home is that the followers of Jesus must *each* (the word is important; there are no exceptions) *forgive.* And the final expression brings home the truth that we must forgive wholeheartedly, not grudgingly. It is easy to skimp on forgiveness, refraining from outward evidence of an unforgiving heart but nursing up a grudge against one who has offended us. "Forgive us our trespasses as we forgive them that trespass against us" is a prayer that we must pray with due searching of heart.

84. The placing of κἀγώ immediately alongside σέ places the two in strong contrast.

Matthew 19

V. JESUS' JOURNEY TO JERUSALEM, 19:1–20:34

Matthew has completed his account of what Jesus did and taught in Galilee, and his narrative moves on to the climax at Jerusalem. Apparently Jesus continued to teach as he went. Matthew has recorded Jesus' teaching about divorce, the danger of riches, and other topics, and he finishes this section with the giving of sight to two blind men near Jericho. Luke has a much longer account of this journey (Luke 9:51–19:44), and it is not easy to relate what he says to what the other Evangelists say. What is clear is that on his way to Jerusalem Jesus gave his disciples significant teaching as he prepared them for the path they would tread when his time on earth was completed.

A. TEACHING ABOUT DIVORCE, 19:1-12

¹And it came to pass when Jesus finished these words, he went away from Galilee and came into the region of Judea beyond the Jordan. ²And great crowds followed him, and he healed them there.

³And Pharisees came to him, testing him and saying, "Is it lawful for a man to divorce his wife on every ground?" ⁴But he answered, saying, "Have you not read that he who created them from the beginning 'made them male and female?'" ⁵And he said, "'For this reason a man will leave his father and mother and will be joined to his wife, and the two will become one flesh.' ⁶So then they are no longer two, but one flesh. Therefore what God has joined together, let man not put apart." ⁷They say to him, "Why then did Moses command to give a certificate of divorce and send her away?" ⁸He says to them, "Because of your hardness of heart Moses allowed you to divorce your wives; but from the beginning it was not so. ⁹But I say to you, that whoever divorces his wife, except for fornication, and marries another commits adultery." ¹⁰His disciples say to him, "If this is the case of a man with his wife, it is not advisable to marry." ¹¹But he said to them, "Not all people have the capacity for this saying, but only those to whom it is given. ¹²For there are eunuchs who have been so from their mother's womb, and there are eunuchs who were made eunuchs by men, and there are eunuchs who made themselves eunuchs for the kingdom of heaven's sake. Let him who can accept this accept it."

Once more Jesus confronts a wrong understanding of the meaning of God's law. Just as in the Sermon on the Mount, he shows that it is not enough to keep the letter of the law. The law allowed divorce, and some pious Jews availed themselves wholeheartedly of this provision. Jesus invites his hearers to reflect on what the law actually means and to recognize the sanctity of marriage. The fact that divorce was possible did not mean that it was to be sought. Rather, it was to be seen as a desperate last resort; every effort must be made to save a marriage.

1. Once again Matthew employs his unusual *And it came to pass* (see on 7:28). Here as elsewhere it marks the end of one of his discourses and the transition to the following narrative. On this occasion he tells us that Jesus *went away* (the same unusual verb as in 13:53, where see note) *from Galilee*. He does not draw attention to it, but this is Jesus' final withdrawal from the place where he has had the major part of his ministry. He now goes to Judea; there is no return to Galilee until after the resurrection (28:16). Mark and Luke both speak of Jesus as going into Judea, but neither says anything about leaving Galilee. This, however, is important for Matthew, and he includes it. He also tells us that Jesus came into Judea *beyond the Jordan*. Since Judea lay to the west of the Jordan, this raises a problem. It may mean that he traveled to Judea by way of the region to the east of the Jordan (as Jews commonly did; it enabled them to avoid going through Samaritan territory). In favor of this is the fact that Jesus passed through Jericho on his way to Jerusalem (20:29). Or, as Argyle thinks, Matthew may be using *Judea* loosely, to include Perea as well as the territory to the west of the Jordan; this would be supported by the fact that many Jews in fact lived in Perea. But it is more likely that Matthew is saying that Jesus' first entrance into the province of Judea was by way of the area beyond the Jordan.

2. The entrance into Judea was in no sense a withdrawal from public ministry, for Jesus was accompanied by *great crowds* (Matthew's usual plural). There are two points to be noticed. One is that whereas Mark says no more than that crowds went with Jesus, Matthew has a characteristic *followed him*; this Evangelist delights to use an expression that is also used of those who followed him in the sense that they became disciples in doing so. The other is that Jesus *healed them*. He has said nothing about there being sick people in the crowds, but that may be assumed; therefore Matthew goes on to record Jesus' healing activity (Mark says no more than that he taught the people as he usually did).

3. Now some Pharisees (see on 3:7; here the word lacks the article, so it is "some Pharisees" rather than "the Pharisees") came to Jesus (the verb may indicate something of a formal approach; see on 4:3). They came with a question, but they were not genuinely looking for information; they were *testing* Jesus, posing a question that they hoped he would not be able to answer satisfactorily. It was a question about divorce to which widely different answers were given, and at the very least the Pharisees might expect that whatever position Jesus took up he would antagonize those

who held strongly to other positions. It was accepted throughout Judaism that a man had the right to divorce his wife, though a woman had no such right to divorce her husband. In some circumstances she could petition the court, and the court might direct her husband to divorce her, but even then the actual divorcing was done by the husband. The husband was given the right by an express provision of the law (Deut. 24:1-4); the Pharisees' question was not whether a man had the right to divorce his wife, but rather what grounds justified him in proceeding to divorce her. They ask whether it is lawful for him to divorce her *on every ground* (*NEB* translates, "on any and every ground"; *JB*, "on any pretext whatever"; and Moule says that the meaning is "on the ground of any cause," *IBNTG*, p. 59).[1] The question in the rabbinic schools revolved around the meaning of "because he has found some indecency in her" (Deut. 24:1). The term "indecency" is not defined in this passage, but it is unlikely that adultery was in mind since the penalty for adultery was death (Deut. 22:22). However, the strict school of Shammai understood the passage to refer to adultery; they saw that as the only ground that justified divorce. But the more lenient school of Hillel interpreted the words more widely; they held that the words about indecency were fulfilled, for example, if a wife did no more than spoil her husband's dinner. A little later Akiba interpreted the words "if she finds no favor in his eyes" to mean that if he found someone prettier he could proceed to divorce her (Mishnah, *Giṭ.* 9:10; for an account of a discussion in the schools see Talmud, *Giṭ.* 90a). With such a variety of opinions the subject of divorce was a veritable minefield; thus the Pharisees may well have thought that it did not matter greatly which way Jesus answered; he would offend many people whatever he said. Even Jewish men who had no intention of divorcing their wives might be expected to defend strongly their right to do so.[2]

4. Jesus declined to go along with the accepted rabbinic methods of understanding the question; he did not side with any of the disputants. But by appealing to the creation he was making use of a rabbinic method

---

1. Patte cites Schweizer and Bonnard for the meaning "for any reason a man wishes," and accepts it himself (p. 279, n. 4). Turner understands the question as "Is there *any* ground on which it is lawful for a man to divorce his wife?" He goes on, "Jesus's strict ideas on the indissolubility of marriage were well known. The Pharisees were not attempting to inveigle him into taking sides in a rabbinical dispute so much as betraying surprise that he was stricter even than the school of Shammai" (*Grammatical Insights*, p. 61). The Pharisaic practice may be illustrated from Josephus. He was a Pharisee who divorced his wife, apparently for no great cause: "I divorced my wife, being displeased at her behaviour" (*Life* 426). He could write, "He who desires to be divorced from the wife who is living with him for whatsoever cause — and with mortals many such may arise . . ." (*Ant.* 4.253).

2. With divorce so easy for a man it might have been expected that there would be a great deal of it, but according to I. Abrahams this was not the case (*Studies in Pharisaism and the Gospels*, 1st ser. [New York, 1967], pp. 66-78). He says that most Jews married young and that "Jewish sentiment was strongly opposed to the divorce of the wife of a man's youth" (p. 68). In the Talmud we read, "If a man divorces his first wife, even the altar sheds tears" (*Giṭ.* 90b).

of disputation, namely, "the more original, the weightier." This meant that what happened as early as the creation narrative was weightier than what Moses said considerably later (though, of course, it did not do away with the Mosaic regulation; that regulation was still part of the law and was to be respected, but it must be interpreted in the light of the more original statement). Jesus then referred his questioners to the creation, in which presumably God could have created the race in any one of a great variety of ways. But *from the beginning* God chose to make them *male and female* (Gen. 1:27). Chrysostom comments: "if it had been His will that he should put this one away, and bring in another, when He had made one man, He would have formed many women" (p. 382). Our sexuality is of divine ordinance; it is intended to be exercised in monogamous relationships.

5. To this passage Jesus joins another (*And he said* refers to Jesus, not the Father, who is not said to have uttered the first words quoted), that which speaks of a man leaving his parents and "cleaving" to his wife (Gen. 2:24). The verbs point to strong and decisive action.[3] When a man marries, he is entering into a new and very intimate relationship that takes precedence over all previous ties. To leave one's parents in antiquity was thought of as a most unnatural thing to do; family ties were of the greatest importance. But the creation ordinance put the marriage tie above all other relationships, even family relationships. One must abandon one's home and family as a new home is set up. Man and wife belong together, bound more closely together than any other two persons.

The Scripture says further, "*the two will become one flesh.*" This refers to the sexual act, which unites husband and wife in the most intimate fashion. Paul can object to consorting with harlots because it involves becoming "one flesh" (1 Cor. 6:16), a relationship that befits a husband and his wife only. Jesus cites Scripture, then, to bring out the truth that marriage is more than a casual arrangement for the convenience of the two parties. It is the closest of earthly unities, and must be understood so.

6. Jesus underlines the closeness of the unity. *So then*[4] the married couple are *no longer* what they were, two isolated and separate individuals; they are now bound in the closest and most intimate of human relationships and are in fact *one flesh.*[5] The followers of Hillel and Shammai and

---

3. *Leave* is the translation of χαταλείπω, which can mean "abandon"; it is certainly no half-hearted action. χολλάω means "to glue, cement" (LSJ), and points to no half-hearted union.

4. ὥστε, which Matthew has 15 times, more than in any other New Testament writing, indicates the logical consequence, "for this reason," "it follows that — ." Here it is followed by the indicative rather than the infinitive, which puts some emphasis on the actuality of the result.

5. "*One flesh* vividly expresses a view of marriage as something much deeper than either human convenience or social convention, and this is drawn out by Jesus' ringing pronouncement (rightly and magnificently emphasized in the marriage service), *What God has joined together, let not put man asunder.* To see divorce as *man* undoing the work of *God* puts the whole issue in a radically new perspective" (France).

of other disputants in this subject were all losing sight of this central truth. Marriage is not to be understood as a casual union, subject to the whims and desires of the lordly male. It is a close and binding union, the closest of unions known on this earth. It must accordingly be treated with respect and even reverence. Jesus draws an inference from this. Because marriage is what it is, because God has created the union, *let man not put apart* those whom God has joined. Jesus is not siding with any of the disputants, an act that would have meant antagonizing the adherents of other positions (as the Pharisees had hoped he would do). Rather, he was rejecting them all and calling on his hearers to take seriously the Scripture that they professed to respect. If they did this they would realize that marriage was a much more binding relationship than they were making it. The typical attitude of the people of his day had reduced a God-given unity to a casual union, dissolvable at the whim of the male. This was not what Scripture meant when it spoke of what God did at the creation.[6]

7. This was not quite what his interrogators were looking for; therefore they came up with a further question. What Jesus had said looked suspiciously like a prohibition of all divorce, and that suited none of them. So they pose a question reminding Jesus that divorce was due to what Moses, the great lawgiver, said: *"Why then did Moses command to give a certificate of divorce and send her away?"* They go beyond Scripture, for Moses did not *command* divorce. He pointed to current custom and did something to regulate it (he said, "When a man . . . writes her a bill of divorce . . ."). But this is a long way from commanding. The Pharisees assume that the dissolution of marriage was part of the will of God in instituting the married state. This Jesus denies. The *certificate of divorce* was the document the Jews currently used; its content was regarded as important. It must include the provision that the woman is now free to marry ("The essential formula in the bill of divorce is, 'Lo, thou art free to marry any man,'" *Giṭ.* 9:3). Provided it was properly drawn up, witnessed, and served in the due legal manner, that was all that was required. Jesus' questioners, who understood the legal position perfectly, did not understand why divorce should not take place, if not according to the teaching of one rabbi, then certainly in accordance with the teaching of another.

8. Jesus corrects them. Moses did no more than allow divorce (he did not command it). And he *allowed* it *"Because of[7] your hardness of heart."*[8]

---

6. It is perhaps surprising that little notice appears to have been taken of God's words "I hate divorce" (Mal. 2:16). The index to Danby's translation of the Mishnah does not include a reference to the verse and that to the seventeen-volume Soncino translation of the Talmud refers to only one passage.

7. πρός with the accusative can take this meaning; BDF, 239(8) notes it as a classical usage.

8. JB has "because you were so unteachable." But it is not their failure to understand that is in question, but their failure to do what they should have done. Phillips paraphrases with "because you knew so little of the meaning of love." This is scarcely a translation, but it is a suggestive thought.

In Moses' day divorce evidently did need regulation. It would seem that prior to the regulation in Deuteronomy women were in a more than difficult position. It was possible for a husband to reject his wife and put her out of his house. But if she tried to contract marriage with another man (and there was little future in a patriarchal society for a woman not attached to some man), then a mischievous husband could claim that she was still his wife. Legally there was nothing she could do about it. When Moses took note of the ills that could be done toward women and provided for divorce, he was giving the repudiated wives a little measure of protection. Until the husband gave the wife a "certificate of divorce" she was still his wife, and he still owed her the duty that any husband owed his wife. When he had given the certificate, she was no longer his wife and he had no claim on her. Her position might still be difficult, but at least she was freed from any arbitrary reclaiming of her by her former husband.

Permission for divorce, then, was a concession made because of men's hard hearts. It was not part of the original provision of marriage. This was no concession to any human weakness, but God's provision whereby a man and a woman should live together and produce a family. *From the beginning* marriage was a holy estate into which a man and a woman would normally be called. Nobody should enter this holy estate with the reservation that if difficulties arose there was abundant provision for divorce. That was simply a desperate provision where hearts were hard, not a regular part of the matrimonial scene.

9. *But* has adversative force; over against the Mosaic provision for divorce because of hard hearts Jesus sets his own verdict. For a husband to divorce his wife and marry another woman means that he *commits adultery;* his second marriage violates the creation ordinance and thus is no marriage. Jesus leaves his hearers in no doubt but that marriage is meant to be for life and that contemporary Jewish discussions about when a divorce is properly carried out and when it is invalid are wide of the mark. Such discussions proceed from a view that marriage is a human device that may easily be set aside. But when we realize that it is God's will for people, marriage must be seen in another light.

Jesus does allow for an exception, *except for fornication.*[9] This repeats the position he took up in the Sermon on the Mount (see the discussion on 5:31-32). As we saw in the earlier passage, *fornication* strictly means sexual relations between unmarried people. But the term was used more widely than that and came to signify irregular sexual unions of all kinds (*NIV* reads, "except for marital unfaithfulness"; *GNB* has, "even though she has not been unfaithful"). In this passage it will signify adultery

---

9. There is a complicated textual problem with μὴ ἐπὶ πορνείᾳ read by ℵ C³ K L etc., and παρεκτὸς λόγου πορνείας by B f¹ boh etc., a reading that Metzger thinks has probably been assimilated to that in 5:32. There are other problems, but the important point is that there is no real doubt that the words about fornication are to be accepted.

because it refers to the actions of married people. We have seen that sexual relations mark a close and peculiar intimacy. When a married person engages in this action, Jesus says, then "hardness of heart" has come into the picture again and, the marriage having been irreparably destroyed, divorce is permissible. There is a problem with this in that the exception is not found in Mark or Luke. Precisely opposite conclusions have been drawn from this. Some students hold that Jesus did not use the words and that Matthew has inserted them because this was the custom in his church (or for some similar reason). But it is also possible to reason that it was so widely accepted that adultery was a sufficient cause for divorce that it did not need stating; it could simply be assumed, and Mark and Luke are doing just that. In fact, among the Jews of the time divorce on the grounds of adultery was not simply permitted — it was required (see the note on 5:32, n. 122). Thus there are good reasons for accepting the exceptive clause as part of Jesus' teaching. But we should be clear that he is not setting up a new set of regulations and providing for all the exceptions that a law must take note of. He is laying down in strong terms the permanent nature of the marriage tie in the face of a society where a marriage could be dissolved at any time a husband chose to write out a few lines containing the necessary formula, sign it before witnesses, and hand it to his wife. Jesus is saying that this is no way to treat a divine ordinance. He is not defining under what circumstances a divorce may or may not take place.[10]

10. Matthew adds a section (vv. 10-12) to which the other Gospels have no parallel. Evidently Matthew felt that Jesus' teaching on this subject was so far-reaching and so different from that of his contemporaries that it was important for him to add something about the Master's further teaching when the disciples expressed a problem. Not only Jesus' antagonists but his disciples are staggered by this teaching. The disciples are impressed by the problems they see when a marriage is under strain if this teaching is carried through. If there is no relief from the strain and no possibility of divorce, then life is going to be very difficult indeed. *The case*[11] *of a man with his wife* strikes the disciples as difficult. It would mean that no matter what the wife did, no matter how badly the marriage was going, there could be no divorce. So they suggest to Jesus that if this is the way of it, *it is not advisable*[12] *to marry*. The disciples envision problems in maintaining the marriage relationship with this hanging over their heads. They probably had no intention of making use of the provision for divorce, but they found it comforting that the provision was there in case of need.

---

10. Carson has a full and helpful discussion of the problems in this verse (pp. 413-18). Tasker makes some good points about the place of divorce in the modern church (pp. 181-83).

11. αἰτία, which Matthew uses 3 times, has a variety of meanings including the technical sense of an accusation, a reason for a judicial verdict (e.g., 27:37; John 18:38). It is suggested that here it might be taken in the sense "the relationship of a man with his wife." BDF takes it as a Latinism = *causa* (5[3b]).

12. οὐ συμφέρει. The verb is often used of what is profitable or expedient.

11. Jesus' reply may mean that the teaching he has just given is indeed beyond some people's capacity.[13] There are people who simply cannot live up to all that this teaching involves. If we take the words this way we must be on our guard, for Jesus never gives countenance to the idea that among his followers there will be a spiritual elite, people who will live constantly on a high spiritual plane and will be of a different grade in the kingdom of heaven from that occupied by ordinary people. All his followers are sinners, and all have need of forgiveness. But here he is recognizing that not all in fact manage to reach the same standard. Without watering down the truth that all are equal in the kingdom, Jesus recognizes that there will be different levels of achievement. So some will have more fulfilling marriages than others; some will profit more from the grace freely proffered to all than others will. Alternatively, *this saying* may refer to the words of the disciples, that it is better not to marry. In that case Jesus is saying that this is true for some people, though it is a way of life that not all can follow. But some do, and in the next verse he goes on to look at them.

12. Jesus illustrates by referring to *eunuchs.* To belong to this group of people is not normally regarded as highly desirable (among the Jews eunuchs could not become priests, Lev. 21:20; they could not even enter the congregation, Deut. 23:1), but Jesus points out that there are some who *from their mother's womb* have been in this state; they have never had sexual capacity. This does not refer necessarily to literal eunuchs, men who have been physically castrated, but to those with a genetic defect. The second category does refer to castration. In the world of the first century quite a few men had been emasculated by people in high places. This might be done as a punishment, or to provide safe people to work in harems and the like. It was a fact of first-century life. Jesus goes on to point out that there are some *who made themselves eunuchs for the kingdom of heaven's sake.* Through the centuries there have always been some who have foregone the delights of marriage in order that they may discharge specific tasks for *the kingdom of heaven.* Jesus himself was not married, nor was John the Baptist.[14] Not many have taken these words literally, as Origen did when he castrated himself. But through the centuries many have turned their backs on all that marriage means because only so could they pursue their particular vocation in the service of God. Jesus is not saying that this is a higher calling than others or that all his followers should seek to serve in

---

13. χωρέω is used of literal, physical capacity, as, for example, of the house where people were listening to Jesus and there was no more room for more (Mark 2:2). Here, of course, it refers to spiritual capacity.

14. Lenski sees the words as referring to all believers: "As they have done with regard to other natural desires, so thay have put also the desire of sex under complete subjection because of their spiritual life in the kingdom" (p. 739). But, while it is true that believers subject sex as everything else to the lordship of Christ, that scarcely fits the words used here. Jesus is speaking of total abstinence from sex.

this way; that would be a contradiction of his appeal to Genesis 1–2. He is simply saying that the claims of the kingdom override all other claims and that some are called to serve in the path of celibacy (just as others are called to serve in marriage). There is no one path of service, but whatever a person's calling is, grace will be given so that that calling may be fulfilled. And in this context it means that grace will be given to those called to serve God in the married state so that they will be able to fulfil their calling. He invites his hearers to *accept* the teaching as they have the ability (his word for *accept* is the same as that translated "have the capacity" in v. 11).[15]

B. JESUS AND THE CHILDREN, 19:13-15

> [13]*Then little children were brought to him so that he might lay his hands on them and pray; but the disciples rebuked them.* [14]*But Jesus said, "Let the little children come to me, and don't forbid them, for of such is the kingdom of heaven."* [15]*And when he had laid his hands on them, he went away from there.*

Jesus had a great interest in children. We have already noticed that he used one small child as a model to drive home some important spiritual truths (18:2-6, 10), and now we see the same interest and concern. We should not take this too calmly, as though it might be expected in a religious teacher. It is not easy to think of Muhammad as concerned for little children, or Gautama the Buddha. But the Gospels make it clear that there were often children around Jesus. He observed their games (11:16-17), spoke of them in his teaching, and clearly was genuinely interested in them.

13. *Then* should link this on to the preceding section as the next happening in time, and this indeed may be the way to take it. But Matthew uses the word so often that we cannot insist on this (see the note on 2:7). The word Matthew uses for the children is a diminutive and strictly means *little children*, but it is often used of children in general, so that we cannot insist that they were very small. All three Synoptists tell us that children were brought to Jesus, Mark and Luke say that this was in order that he might touch them, but only Matthew tells us that this meant laying his hands on them[16] and only he tells us that those who brought them wanted Jesus to pray. This tells us a lot about Jesus and about the parents of the

15. Gundry understands the last injunction to mean that "Jesus' true disciples live as eunuchs after they have had to divorce their wives for immorality" (p. 382). But there is no reason for thinking that these words refer to divorced people only. Moreover, the position scarcely does justice to the words *for the kingdom of heaven's sake.* Jesus is surely speaking of a voluntary effort with a view to setting forward the kingdom rather than to a rule regulating the conduct of all divorced males, whether they have the capacity to live the single life or not.

16. J. Jeremias cites rabbinic sources that tell of the "beautiful custom in Jerusalem" on the Day of Atonement of bringing children from one to twelve years old to the scribes for them to lay their hands on them and pray for them (*Infant Baptism in the First Four Centuries* [London, 1960], p. 49).

children; they were all ready to give time for the spiritual welfare of the little ones. We also learn something about the disciples; they wanted none of it.[17] Clearly they did not share Jesus' attitude to children, and they could not understand why the Master should be bothered by these small people. So they *rebuked* those who brought the children (grammatically the words could mean that they rebuked the children, but this seems very unlikely).[18]

14. *But* is adversative; it sets Jesus over against the disciples, and his attitude in contrast to theirs, as he instructed the disciples to allow the children to come to him (Mark tells us that Jesus was indignant with them, but Matthew omits this). *"Don't forbid them,"* he said, making it clear that the attitude of the disciples was the wrong one. He goes on to say, *"of such is the kingdom of heaven."* He had earlier said that one must be like little children if one is even to enter the kingdom of heaven (18:3), but this expression goes beyond that. It means that the kingdom is made up of people like these little ones, or perhaps that the kingdom belongs to people like them. Either way Jesus is asserting that children are important. The attitude of the disciples toward them was all wrong.

15. Jesus did as he was asked and *laid his hands on them.*[19] Matthew does not specifically say that he prayed, but we must surely understand that he did this. He had been asked to do so, and he had rebuked those who tried to keep the children away from him. So, of course, he would have prayed for them. Then, Matthew tells us, he *went away* from that place. Since he has not told us where they were, we cannot say anything about his destination.

C. TEACHING AND TRAVELING, 19:16–20:34

Matthew carries on with his story of Jesus' journey, a narrative that is mostly concerned with teaching Jesus gave as he went. There are some happenings, like the coming of the rich young man to him and the healing of a couple of blind men, but mostly Matthew is concerned at this point with the teachings that Jesus gave as he journeyed on to Jerusalem.

1. The Peril of Riches, 19:16-30

> [16]*And look, one came to him and said, "Teacher, what good thing shall I do so that I may have life eternal?" [17]But he said to him, "Why do you*

---

17. Hill comments on the disciples' "lack of understanding of Jesus' ministry; they were annoyed that he was being stopped on his way to Jerusalem. Were they hastening him onwards to the city in the hope that he would make a triumphant messianic display there?"

18. Moffatt translates, "The disciples checked the people," but ἐπιτιμάω means more than "checked." The word signifies "rebuked."

19. Green says that "the Jewish practice of taking children to a rabbi to have his hands laid on them" was one that "was interpreted not as conferring a blessing, but as asking one from God."

ask me about the good thing? One there is who is good; but if you wish to enter into life, keep the commandments." ¹⁸*He says to him, "Which?" And Jesus said, "You shall not murder, You shall not commit adultery, You shall not steal, You shall not bear false witness,* ¹⁹*Honor your father and mother, and You shall love your neighbor as yourself."* ²⁰*The young man says to him, "All these I have kept. What do I still lack?"* ²¹*Jesus said to him, "If you want to be perfect, go, sell your possessions and give to the poor, and you will have treasure in heaven; and come, follow me."* ²²*But when the young man heard this saying, he went away grieved, for he had many possessions.*

²³*But Jesus said to his disciples, "Truly I tell you that only with difficulty will a rich man enter the kingdom of heaven.* ²⁴*Again I say to you, it is easier for a camel to go through the eye of a needle than for a rich man to enter the kingdom of God."* ²⁵*But when the disciples heard this, they were greatly astonished and said, "Who then can be saved?"* ²⁶*And Jesus fixed his gaze on them and said, "With men this is impossible, but with God all things are possible."*

²⁷*Then Peter answered, saying, "Look, we left everything and followed you; what then will there be for us?"* ²⁸*And Jesus said to them, "Truly I say to you that in the renewal, when the Son of man will sit on the throne of his glory, you who have followed me will also sit on twelve thrones, judging the twelve tribes of Israel.* ²⁹*And everyone who has left houses or brothers or sisters or father or mother or children or lands for my name's sake will receive a hundredfold and will inherit life eternal.* ³⁰*But many who are first will be last, and the last will be first."*

Following the failure of the rich young man, Matthew now has a little section on wealth and its hazards in which he brings us some of Jesus' teaching both on riches and on the unimportance of worldly affluence in the kingdom of heaven.

16. Matthew cannot be said to have exerted himself to give us information about the man who came to him, confining himself to the single word *one*. Since the Greek word is masculine, we can say that the person who came was male, but that is all. Mark tells us that he came running and that he knelt before Jesus, from which we may perhaps deduce that he was both eager and devout, while Luke has the information that he was a ruler. Matthew tells us that he came up to Jesus and addressed him as *"Teacher."* Sometimes a good deal is made of the fact that Mark and Luke both have "Good teacher" while Matthew omits the adjective. But we should bear in mind that the man goes on to ask the "teacher" what *good thing* he should do to gain eternal life. It is no ordinary teacher who could answer that question, so perhaps Matthew's omission is not as significant as some suggest. The man then inquired how he could have *life eternal.* His *"what good thing shall I do?"* shows that he was firmly of the opinion that the way into life with God is the path of doing good in some form.[20] His problem apparently was that, although he had paid strict attention to the commands of God, he still felt that he was coming short in some way. He apparently thought that there must be something he could do to make good the deficiency of which he was so conscious. He may have been unsure of what *good* is essentially, what the nature of the *good* that God demands is.[21] Or he may have been convinced that the way into the eternal life he sought was through some outstandingly meritorious action, and he was not conscious of having performed any such action, or at least any that would merit the reward of *life eternal*. By this he clearly meant life in the age to come, life in the final kingdom that God would set up. He was clearly very different from the childlike people that Jesus has been commending. He was sure that entrance to eternal life was within his grasp if he only knew how to go about it. "This young man stands in stunning contrast to those to whom, according to Jesus, the kingdom belongs" (Carson; he adds, "This may help explain Matthew's wording").

17. The man was on the wrong track, and Matthew's introductory *But* may be meant to set Jesus' answer in opposition to the question. Jesus countered with a question inquiring why the man asked him *about the good thing*,[22] and he went on to say, *"One there is who is good."* The man has inquired about the *good thing* he should do in order to obtain eternal life, so Jesus takes up his term and asks why he speaks of the *good thing*. This does not mean that Jesus agrees that people are saved by meritorious deeds. At this point he is simply concerned with the man's terminology and what it meant.

Matthew has omitted to say that the man addressed Jesus as "Good teacher" (as both Mark and Luke assure us), which perhaps makes it a little harder to see the relevance of these words. But clearly Jesus was bringing home to the inquirer the fact that he was not using his words carefully enough; the Master was now making him think about what he

20. Such a view may be found within Judaism. We read, for example, of a man speaking of the giving of alms "in order that through it I may merit the future world" (*Rosh. Hash.* 4a). More generally we read, "All is foreseen, but freedom of choice is given; and the world is judged by grace, yet all is according to the excess of works (that be good or evil)" (*'Abot* 3:16). See also SBk I, pp. 808-10.

21. Hamann points out that in Amos 5 we read "Seek good, and not evil, that you may live" (v. 14), but also "Seek me and live" and "Seek the LORD and live" (vv. 4, 6). He suggests that "life is related to good and God . . . interchangeably." Really to seek good is to seek God. The young man may not have been aware of this.

22. "It was not a simple question, as the ruler thought: two points are raised: (1) What is 'the good?' (2) How to enter life eternal. Then again the answer to the first is partly left to inference, and the answer to the second lies deeper than the young ruler's thought had gone. (1) There is one only who is good, therefore (the inference is) 'the good' can only be the will of God. (2) Then the way to enter into life eternal is to keep God's will as expressed in the commandments. Jesus shows that here too the questioner had not thought deeply enough. Keeping the commandments is not external observance of them, but being in heart what the commandments *mean*, and what the will of God is" (Carr).

was saying. There are practically no examples in Jewish writings of a teacher being addressed as "Good"; the man was engaging in thoughtless flattery, and he had not considered the implications of the term he was using. Now Jesus reminds him that there is only one who is really good and invites him to reflect on what he has just said. This does not mean that Jesus was denying that he was divine; he was not discussing that question, and if he had meant that he was not "good" he would surely have said that he was a sinner. He did not. He simply asked the man to reflect on the implications of "good." Then he moved on to the man's spiritual need and began with the commandments. God has made himself known, and the commandments he has given show people the way to life.

18-19. The man asks,[23] *"Which?"*[24] Jesus specifies, referring to the commandments to abstain from murder, adultery, theft, and false witness, to which he adds that for honoring parents (placing this commandment outside its proper order fastens attention on it and gives it emphasis), and one from outside the Ten Commandments, *"You shall love your neighbor as yourself."* Those from the Ten are reported in Mark and Luke, but only Matthew has that to love one's neighbor. He has cited it before (5:43), and he will do it again when he reports Jesus' summation of the commandments (22:39); clearly it means a good deal to him. It is noteworthy that all the commandments Jesus cites have to do with the way we treat other people; he stresses the importance of the ethical ("the most suitable specimens for shewing, in a practical form, what it meant to live the life of God," McNeile).[25] The young man was probably thinking in terms of some highly "spiritual" process and would have been disappointed in such prosaic expressions of the religious duty.

20. For the first time Matthew refers to the questioner as *the young man* (neither Mark nor Luke tells us that he was young). Since the term covers a range of ages, we can say no more than that he had not reached mature years. We discover something of his spiritual lack when he says that he has kept[26] all these commandments (in the Greek the word for *all* comes first, which gives it emphasis). He follows this facile assumption with the further question, *"What do I still lack?"* ("What more do I need to

23. The verb is in the present tense, though Jesus' response is in the aorist, a phenomenon that is repeated in verses 20-21.

24. His word is ποίας. Strictly this interrogative signifies *"of what quality or sort"* (AS); Barclay translates, "What kind of commandments?" The questioner may be thinking that for life eternal there must be some special commandments, and he was not aware which they were. But the word is used widely (cf. 22:36), and we cannot insist on this.

25. The omission of any reference to the commandments about God is explained by Hendriksen thus: "It was not necessary for Jesus to include the commandments relating to man's duty with respect to God; for, failure to observe the second table implies failure to observe the first: 'He who does not love his brother whom he has seen cannot love God whom he has not seen' (1 John 4:20)."

26. The verb is φυλάσσω, which has the basic meaning of "guard." But it can have the idea of keeping a law or the like from being broken and thus of "observing" it.

490

do?" *JB*). Despite his misconception about his standing as a keeper of commandments, he was clearly conscious that something was missing. Without being able to put it all into words, he knew that his spiritual makeup was defective, and he was looking to Jesus to show him how to put it right.

21. It would seem that the young man was somewhat disappointed. He had come to Jesus looking for a brilliant new insight into the ways of God, a challenge that would stir the blood, some great deed to be done, after which his claim on eternal life would be certain. Instead all that had happened was that he had been referred to the commandments, old stuff that he had been keeping for years ("from my youth" is added in the other two accounts).

But now Jesus makes him face up to his real situation. First he puts the supposition, *"If you want to be perfect"* ("If you wish to be complete," *NASB*),[27] where the thought is that of wholeheartedness in God's service. The young man had a felt need (v. 20); Jesus points him to wholeness, completeness. Some interpreters have seen a reference to a double standard in which Jesus asks for much from some disciples and rather less from more ordinary followers (e.g., Gutzwiller, p. 227), but there is no justification for this. The outworking may differ from one disciple to another, but wholeheartedness is required of all. The young man has shown that he is not content with a conventional goodness, so common in nominally religious people. He wanted something more than that. So Jesus says, *"go, sell your possessions and give to the poor"* (Glover remarks, "He who chose Calvary for Himself is apt to prescribe sacrifice to others"). This is a demanding enough challenge for anyone seeking to do more than what is conventional (though it is one that has sometimes been met!). The poor in a first-century city were poor indeed, and often lacked what we would call the necessities of life. For a wealthy person to sell everything and give to the poor was to do something about meeting a very real need.[28]

Bonnard points out that there are several ways of understanding the connection between the two commands. The meaning might be "Sell in order to follow me" (with the emphasis on following), or "Sell and in addition follow me" (where the two are set side by side), or "Sell first, choose poverty; then quite naturally you will follow me" (where the emphasis is on choosing poverty). He prefers the first, probably correctly. The result of this, Jesus says, would be that the young man would

---

27. εἰ with the indicative seems to imply that this is what he does want. θέλεις points to the action of the will, while τέλειος (3 times only in this Gospel) means that which has reached its aim. When used of people it mostly signifies the attainment of full physical development, but it can be used of ethical development, as when it conveys the idea of "*complete, perfect* (expressing the simple idea of complete goodness, without reference either to maturity or to the philosophical idea of a τέλος)" (AS). In *AB* it is translated "true," and this is explained as "true to God, true to the Covenant."

28. In the early church people sometimes sold their goods to give to others (Acts 2:44-45; 4:32). But this was an optional thing, not a requirement laid on all (Acts 5:4).

have treasure where it really counts, *in heaven*. This does not mean that getting into heaven is a matter of rewards for meritorious acts. It means rather that the young man of this story was quite unaware of his failure to keep the commandment to have no other God but the one true God. He had made a god of his wealth, and when faced with the challenge he could not forsake that god. If his attitude to the true God had been such that he could have dispensed with his riches, then he would have had treasure in heaven, whether he gave them all away or not. But the challenge to get rid of them all showed that he did not have the right attitude to God. God demands undivided loyalty from those who would be his.[29] *"Come, follow me,"* Jesus went on. This is the challenge he had previously made to the fishermen as they were at their nets (4:19) and to Matthew as he sat at his place of work (9:9). They did not have the riches of this young man, it would seem, but they left what they had and followed Jesus. They were prepared to sacrifice everything; that is the path of the service of God.

22. But this young man could not rise to such a challenge. He had looked for something demanding, prepared to do some great deed. But when he was faced with a really great deed, getting rid of all his wealth, the only thing he could do was go away grieving (contrast the man in the parable who in his joy sold everything, 13:44).[30] Matthew explains that the reason for his sorrow was that *he had many possessions*. His wealth stood between him and the service of God. Ryle comments on the dangers of wealth and says, "Well may the Litany of the Church of England contain the words, 'In all time of our wealth, good Lord, deliver us'" (p. 242).

23. *But* will have some adversative force, indicating that Jesus stands over against the man who has gone away. Doubtless the conversation had left them wondering about wealth. What did it all mean? It was widely accepted that wealth was a wonderful blessing; it was a sign that God approved of a person and prospered that person's business affairs. But now Jesus had told this man to get rid of his wealth. Were their ideas all wrong? Jesus proceeds to tell them that a wealthy person will enter the kingdom only *with difficulty*.[31] This does not mean that he will not enter at all. But it certainly means that wealth, so far from being an unmixed blessing, poses a problem for all but the flippant.[32] It is all too easy for

29. "The kingdom demands man's first allegiance, and a rich man's first allegiance is usually given to the acquisition or maintenance of his wealth. Loyalty to the kingdom cannot take second place" (Melinsky).

30. The word for *grieved* is λυπούμενος, "being distressed" or "grieved."

31. δυσκόλως derives from δυσ-, which gives the idea of difficulty, and κόλον, "food." It thus has a meaning connected with difficulty in satisfying with food, and thus generally "with difficulty."

32. Cf. Robinson, "It is sometimes supposed that he (i.e. Jesus) condemned riches on economic grounds; it was a bad thing for property to be concentrated in the hands of a few, and would lead to oppression of the less privileged people. But that is not his real objection. He considers far less the harm that a man's money may do to others than the fatal injury which it inflicts on himself. To be rich is an appalling peril. . . ."

most of us to be so wrapped up in what we own that we find it difficult to face the prospect of doing without it. In the abstract we approve of the challenge; we recognize that people we regard as rich all too easily come to rely on their wealth. But seeing that that applies to us, too, is another matter, and that is the difficulty the young man encountered. Whatever our wealth, great or small, it can tempt us to self-sufficiency, and Jesus is saying that this is a special temptation to the wealthy. He does not say that wealth excludes people from the kingdom (e.g., he welcomed Zacchaeus, Luke 19:1-10), but he does say that it makes it hard for them.

24. Matthew uses *"again"* reasonably often (17 times), but this is one of only two places where he has it with *"I say to you"*; it has a meaning like "furthermore" and builds on the preceding statement, while giving the new words a certain emphasis. That it would be hard for a rich man to enter the kingdom was a devastating thought, and Jesus now underlines it with a humorous reference to *a camel*[33] going through *the eye of a needle.*[34] There have been attempts to understand this of a small gate called "the eye of the needle" that was not meant for the passage of large animals but through which a camel might be coaxed to go; but this is surely wrong-headed. Apart from the fact that no real evidence appears to be cited for such a gate, this supposition misses the point that Jesus is simply using humor to drive home his point. Where the people of his day saw riches as a manifest sign of the blessing of God, he saw wealth as a hindrance to spiritual progress. The rich man has strong temptations to concentrate on his riches, to the detriment of his spiritual welfare.[35] In this Gospel *the kingdom of God* occurs rarely (see on 12:28); we should understand it as equivalent to "the kingdom of heaven," which is Matthew's preferred expression.

25. *But* has adversative force: the disciples stand over against the Master in this matter. They shared the common attitude and found Jesus' words difficult to accept. Matthew uses a very strong expression to bring out the extent of their astonishment.[36] They were not merely mildly sur-

---

33. Some MSS read κάμιλος, "a heavy rope, a cable," rather than κάμηλος, "camel," but there seems to be no doubt that "camel" is correct. "Cable" is apparently an attempt to make the proposition a little more possible (Howard remarks, "we may preserve for the museum of exegetical curiosities the Byzantine invention of a κάμιλος 'cable' to be an improvement on κάμηλος," M, II, p. 72). But we should understand Jesus to be speaking of the largest animal found in Palestine in that day and the smallest opening in common use; he is referring to sheer impossibility.

34. There are textual difficulties, but it seems that Matthew uses τρύπημα, Mark τρυμαλιά, and Luke τρῆμα for the "hole" in the needle (in each case the word appears only here in the New Testament). Matthew and Mark have ῥαφίς for *needle*, while Luke uses βελόνη, but there does not appear to be a significant difference.

35. "It is noticeable that Christ's tone is much more severe in reference to wealth than to wedlock. Eunuchism for the kingdom is optional; possession of wealth on the other hand seems to be viewed as all but incompatible with citizenship in the kingdom" (Bruce).

36. ἐκπλήσσω signifies "to strike out of one's senses," and it is reinforced here by σφόδρα, "exceedingly," a term that Matthew uses 7 times (nobody else in the New Testament has it more than once). The imperfect here points to a continuing state.

prised: this view of riches cut clean across the ideas that the disciples had accepted without question all their lives. Was it not obvious from the very fact of their wealth that the rich were the objects of God's approval? Their riches were surely the sign of his blessing? While there were occasional holy men who were accepted as holy despite their poverty (like John the Baptist), this was not carried over into life as a whole. The occasional exception did not invalidate the rule, and that the blessing of God meant earthly prosperity was the accepted rule. So the disciples burst out in an incredulous question, *"Who then can be saved?"* If those on whom the blessing of God so manifestly rested were to have such difficulty in entering the kingdom, what would be the plight of lesser mortals? It was all very puzzling; despair appeared to be in order.

26. *Jesus fixed his gaze* on them, which means more than a casual glance.[37] He looked hard at them all as they were experiencing such difficulty in coming to grips with his meaning. He recognized their problem and assured them of two things: the first was the sheer impossibility of any human activity bringing about the salvation of a rich man (or, for that matter, any man); the second, the truth that God is not limited as people are.[38] It is, of course, true that a poor man is just as unable to bring about his salvation as a rich man,[39] but that is not in question at this point. Jesus is dealing with the fact that in the opinion of most people of his day, the disciples included, the rich were so obviously blessed by God that they must have his approval and therefore were obviously the ones who would be signally blessed in the kingdom. It is this truism that had to be demolished. When salvation is viewed as Jesus saw it (and as he has outlined it in his teaching in ch. 18), then it is clear that it depends on the action of God, not the achievement of the creature. And, of course, it is harder for a rich man to become like a little child (18:3-4) than for a poor man, who has so much less evidence of his ability to cope. But what is of overwhelming importance is that the power of God is not limited; he can bring about the salvation of anybody.

27. Typically it is Peter who responds to what Jesus has said. It may be that the apostle was looking for a reward for himself and his companions,[40] but it is perhaps more likely that he was uncertain. "If it is true that a person can gain salvation and enter the kingdom only by God's power, then could the disciples be completely sure that they were saved? They

---

37. ἐμβλέπω has a meaning like "fix one's gaze upon" (BAGD).

38. δέ marks the antithesis between men (who cannot) and God (who can).

39. "The rich man who owns a lot and the poor man who wants a lot are two peas in a pod and fall under the same condemnation" (Hamann).

40. McNeile finds here "Another mistake of the chief apostle, a self-complacency which the Petrine tradition in Mk. faithfully records: 'we at any rate have thrown off the fetters of wealth.'" He goes on to suggest that Peter's question "heightens the self-centredness." Diétrich comments, "The question of Peter is somewhat naïve. He thinks that he has 'left everything' (vs. 27). His denial some weeks later will show that he also is not free from human attachments. He has not measured the cross which awaits him."

had indeed given up everything, but had they really done all that was necessary? What was in store for them?" (Ridderbos, p. 360).[41] "Look" makes for a vivid opening, drawing attention to what the apostle has to say, and Peter's "we" is emphatic; he differentiates the little group that was close to Jesus from all others. He draws attention to the sacrifices that they had made. They had *left everything*, which makes it clear that they were not people who spent a few days with Jesus and then went back to their homes. And it forms a contrast with the rich young man a few verses back who went away grieved (v. 22). They had cast in their lot with their Lord, and that meant leaving behind them all that they had. They had *followed* Jesus, had become disciples in the fullest sense of the word. Matthew alone records that Peter finished with the question, *"what then[42] will there be for us?"* Peter expects that there will be a reward of some sort, but he does not know what it will be.

28. More commonly Jesus speaks of the cost of discipleship and refers to taking up one's cross and the like. But while that is an important part of what being his follower means, it is also true that those who follow him will receive the fullness of the divine blessing. And now it is this idea of the glorious state into which the followers of Jesus are called that receives the emphasis. *"Truly I say to you"* is the emphatic introduction we have seen so often that marks what follows as important and worthy of being pondered very carefully. Jesus goes on to refer to *"the renewal,"*[43] which here denotes the renewal of all things that was looked for in the messianic age at the end of this world. Jesus makes this clear by referring to his own function at the time of which he speaks. He uses his favorite self-designation, *"the Son of man"* (see on 8:20), and says that he will be sitting on *the throne of his glory.* This expression may be understood as "his glorious throne," but it seems probable that we should discern a reference to the glory that will be his at that time and of which the throne will be a symbol rather than solely to the throne.

At that time the Twelve will have a significant part to play. Jesus takes up Peter's words and speaks of them as *"you who have followed me"*: it is their attachment to Jesus that is the important thing. And they will

---

41. We should also bear in mind Michael Green's comment: "It is easy for us to sneer at the question, but which of us has given up what the disciples had? Perhaps that is why Jesus gives no rebuke but rather encouragement to the twelve" (p. 188).

42. ἄρα is inferential, "consequently." Peter is looking for what the Twelve could reasonably expect as the consequence of what they had given up for Jesus.

43. παλιγγενεσία, which signifies "rebirth," "new birth," "regeneration." Philo uses it for the renewal of the world after the Flood (*Vit. Mos.* 2.65), and Josephus for the return of the nation from exile (*Ant.* 11.66), but mostly it is used for something more radical than that. T. W. Manson shows that the term is used by the Stoics for "the beginning of a new cycle in the cosmic process," that is, a new cycle in an endless series of repetitions. The Jews used it for the end of the universe as we know it and the beginning of a new era, "a new era that is really new, a new creation" (T. W. Manson, *The Sayings of Jesus* [London, 1949], p. 216). In the New Testament it is used only here and in Titus 3:5 (where it refers to personal regeneration). Here it refers to cosmic renewal, "the world that is to be" *(NEB).*

also sit on *thrones*, symbols of high station, and they will be *judging the twelve tribes of Israel*. It is impossible to be certain of what this means in detail. That there will be judgment at the end of this world is frequently taught in the New Testament, but mostly it is the Father or the Son who is thought of as the Judge. But the Twelve fit into that picture somewhere. At the Last Supper Jesus said that he would appoint a kingdom for the apostles and that they would sit on thrones judging the twelve tribes (Luke 22:28-30). So the thought is not an isolated one in this passage. But it is not easy to work out from these references precisely what the Twelve would be doing. Judging is sometimes used in the sense of ruling, and we cannot rule out such an understanding of the present passage. We can scarcely say more than that the Twelve would share in the activities of that glorious time, that they would enjoy kingly state, and that they would engage in some way in the ordering of the affairs of the twelve tribes.

29. From the Twelve Jesus moves on to consider all who have made sacrifices for him. He speaks of those who leave possessions (*houses, lands*), or family members (*brothers, sisters, father, mother, children*, all one's immediate family).[44] He is not speaking of people who have left these things or these people because of some preference of their own for the wilderness or the solitary life, but who have left them *for my name's sake*. As we have seen, the *name* stands for the whole person (see on 6:9); Jesus is speaking of those who recognize him for what he is, God's Messiah, and who accordingly are quite prepared to give up whatever is necessary in order to fulfil their vocation as his followers. These people, he says, will not in the end find that they have entered an impoverished existence. Jesus is not calling people away from everything that makes life enjoyable. He is calling them to make sacrifices indeed, but to make sacrifices in a worthwhile cause, and one that in the end will bring a rich reward. He is not suggesting that they serve him simply in order to obtain a reward; if they do, they have not escaped the worldliness he calls them to abandon. But the reality is that when they respond to his call they enter an abundant life in which they *will receive a hundredfold*. This, of course, is not to be taken literally (one cannot have a hundred fathers!); it points to uncountable blessings. He does not say what it is that they will receive so abundantly, but clearly it points to a rich reward (Was it Hudson Taylor who said that he had never succeeded in making a sacrifice for God? Every time he gave up anything for God he found so much blessing that he felt himself better off rather than worse off for having given up whatever it was). And especially wonderful will be the inheriting of *life eternal*. This means, of course, life that never ceases, but more than that it means life

44. Kenneth E. Bailey comments, "It is nearly impossible to communicate what all of this means in our Middle Eastern context. The two unassailable loyalties that any Middle Easterner is almost required to consider more important than life itself are *family* and the *village home*. . . . Surely the shock of the passage cuts deeply into the presuppositions of any culture" (*Through Peasant Eyes* [Grand Rapids, 1983], p. 169).

of a particular quality, life that is appropriate to the age to come. The most wonderful gift that comes to those who obey the call of Christ is that they share in life of the highest quality.[45]

30. All this points to a reversal of the generally accepted order of things (cf. 20:16). Those who are highly esteemed and held to be *first* in this world's order of things will end up *last*, in the worst possible position. The point is that they have put their whole effort into earthly success without reference to the more worthwhile life of service to which Christ is calling them. Inevitably when the time comes that earthly success is seen for the tawdry and temporal thing it is, they will rank with the *last*.[46] That is what they have qualified for, and that is where they will be. The corollary of that is that those who are *last* here and now will often be found to be among the *first* in the life to come. They have not accepted the false values of the world but have set their sights on the service of God and of their fellows no matter what the cost to themselves, and they reap the consequences accordingly. The words are a strong warning against being deluded by earthly ideas and standards and shutting one's ears to the call of God.

45. Lenski points out that we have here "both a markedly different verb and an object so great that it cannot be classed with any blessing bestowed in this life. This alone is enough to indicate that life eternal is not a reward for forsaking relatives, property, or for enduring other afflictions for Christ's sake" (p. 761).

46. Allen points out that the connection of these words with the preceding is obscure. He takes them as "a rebuke to the self-complacent spirit implied in S. Peter's words: 'It may be difficult for the rich to enter into the Kingdom, but we who have left all are in no danger of exclusion.' Christ's words are a warrant for this confidence, and at the same time a rebuke and a warning."

Matthew 20

2. The Parable of the Workers in the Vineyard, 20:1-16

¹"For the kingdom of heaven is like a householder who went out early in the morning to hire workmen for his vineyard. ²And having agreed with the workmen for a denarius per day, he sent them into his vineyard. ³And he went out about the third hour and saw others standing in the marketplace idle; ⁴and to them he said, 'You, too, go into the vineyard, and I will give you whatever is right.' ⁵And they went off. And he went out again at about the sixth and ninth hour, and did likewise. ⁶And about the eleventh hour he went out and found others standing; and he says to them, 'Why do you stand here idle all day long?' ⁷They say to him, 'Because no one has hired us.' He says to them, 'You go into the vineyard, too.' ⁸Now when evening had come, the owner of the vineyard says to his manager, 'Call the workmen and pay them the wage, beginning with the last and (proceeding) to the first.' ⁹And those hired at about the eleventh hour came and received a denarius each. ¹⁰And when those who were first came, they thought that they would receive more; and they also received a denarius each. ¹¹And when they had received it, they grumbled at the householder, ¹²saying, 'These last worked one hour, and you made them equal to us who have borne the burden of the day and the burning heat.' ¹³But he answered one of them, saying, 'Friend, I do you no wrong. Did you not agree with me for a denarius? ¹⁴Take what is yours and be off. I want to give to this last man as I gave to you. ¹⁵Is it not lawful for me to do what I want with what is mine? Or is your eye evil because I am good?' ¹⁶Even so, the last will be first, and the first last."

Matthew adds a parable that underlines the lessons taught in the preceding passage. Jesus has been speaking of the dangers of riches and warning his followers against giving themselves over to the pursuit of personal gain. He has spoken of first who will be last and last who will be first, and he does so again in verse 16. This shows plainly that Matthew intends this parable to underline the point he has just made. With the new parable, then, we should probably see a continuing reference to the problems associated with Peter's question (19:27). Peter and the rest of the Twelve have indeed left all for Christ, but they must not think that their

498

priority in time gives them an overwhelming advantage.[1] The new parable impresses these lessons, but adds an even more important one — God acts toward us in sheer grace. There is no question of salvation being an arithmetical process, adding up the good deeds and the bad ones and coming out with salvation or loss according to whether the balance is on the credit or debit side. That is not the way to understand the dealings of a gracious God.

1. *For*[2] links what follows to the preceding. It is because of what Jesus has just said about those who would follow him giving up everything for the kingdom of heaven's sake and because of the reversals implied in the first being last and the last first that Jesus proceeds to this parable. He speaks about *a householder*,[3] which many translate as "landowner" (e.g., JB) or "farmer" (Phillips). In our compartmentalized society these words refer to different functions, but in first-century Palestine it would not be at all strange for a man who owned his house to own land as well and use it, if only on a small scale, for farming activities (though this man was not farming on a small scale, as we observe from the number of laborers he hired). The man in this parable owned a *vineyard*. Jesus speaks of a time when the grapes were ripe and the time had come to pick them. The man went out *early*,[4] which would be usual in order to be sure of getting the workmen and also of getting a whole day's work out of them.[5] Jesus does not say where he went to, but the normal place for hiring workers appears to have been the marketplace, and that is where he would have gone (cf. v. 3). We should probably understand the day laborers as being somewhat indigent. Those who belonged to a household, such as slaves and hired servants, had the security of membership in a household unit, but agricultural laborers working for a daily wage had nothing of the sort.[6] They depended for their livelihood on being hired each day.

2. The householder apparently had little difficulty in getting work-

---

1. Cf. Carr, "Not only will the disciples not be the only called, but they may not reach a higher place or a higher reward than some who follow them at an apparent disadvantage. . . . But they must beware of a spirit very prevalent among hard workers, and not think too much of their own labours, or be displeased because others are equally rewarded."

2. γάϱ.

3. The word is οἰκοδεσπότῃ, "the master of the house." It is here preceded by ἀνθϱώπῳ, which like the usage in 18:23 is equivalent to the indefinite pronoun, and which KJV renders as "a man that is an householder."

4. Moule remarks that ἅμα πϱωΐ "makes ἅμα practically equivalent to a preposition and πϱωΐ practically equivalent to a noun." He understands the meaning to be "at dawn" (*IBNTG*, p. 82), that is, "with the early morning."

5. The Talmud says that the workman's day lasted from the rising of the sun until the rising of the stars; the laborer would go to the field during his employer's time, but come home in his own time (*B. Meṣ.* 83b). This means that his time of work began when he was hired in the marketplace and ended in the field when the stars appeared.

6. Horsley cites G. E. M. de Ste. Croix for the view that "the hired labourer was despised in antiquity and that his status 'was as low as it could well be — only a little above that of a slave, in fact' " (*New Documents*, 4, p. 97).

men, and he came to an agreement with them that they should work for
a denarius per day (this appears to have been the normal pay for a day's
work [Tob. 5:14; a drachma was equivalent to a denarius]). There would
probably have been no difficulty in negotiating such a deal, for it meant
normal pay for normal work. With agreement reached he sent them off to
his vineyard.

3-4. Either he could not at first get all the workmen he needed or
else he decided later to hire some more so that the work would be done
more quickly. So he went out *about the third hour,* that is, the third hour
after sunrise. The day was divided into twelve parts, each called an hour,
with the day beginning at sunrise and the night at sunset (the night seems
to have been divided, not into hours, but into three or four watches). The
length of an hour varied throughout the year as the days grew longer or
shorter, but people evidently saw that as no handicap. In any case,
measurements of time were always approximate in the absence of anything equivalent to our watches and clocks to measure time accurately.
So with about a quarter of the daylight hours gone the householder went
out again. He found potential workmen *standing in the marketplace idle.*
Evidently they were looking for work but had somehow escaped his
notice when he made his first foray. Perhaps they came to the marketplace
later.

So he approached them to secure them as laborers. There is no
specific offer of a job, nor is there any indication of haggling over terms
or even of coming to an acceptable agreement (as in the case of the first
workers). The householder simply addressed them[7] and directed them to
go into his vineyard. He named no specific figure as the wage, but said
that he would *give whatever is right* ("pay you a fair wage," *REB, GNB*).
The workmen apparently were ready to leave it to the owner (they were
too late to claim a full day's wage). They probably understood him to
mean that he would pay the right proportion of a denarius.[8]

5. Evidently this was enough, for the workmen *went off.* The householder repeated the process at three-hour intervals. We get a picture of a
man who wanted a good deal of labor for his vineyard, but who could
not get it all on any one occasion; therefore he made repeated visits to the
marketplace, and as he found them he directed workers to his vineyard.

6. That the man kept coming and looking for workmen even toward
the end of the day perhaps indicates that he wanted to complete his grape
harvest that day; grapes will not keep indefinitely, but must be harvested
soon after they ripen. There is a slightly longer conversation with those

---

7. καὶ ὑμεῖς puts some emphasis on *you* in addition to others.

8. There is no suggestion that they haggled; they apparently simply wanted a job and
agreed to work for whatever was right. Barclay remarks, "A man is not a Christian, if his
first concern is pay. That is what Peter asked: 'What do we get out of it?' The Christian works
for the joy of working and the joy of serving God and his fellow-men. That is why the first
will be last and the last will be first" (II, p. 249).

hired at *about the eleventh hour.*[9] By this time the working day was almost over, and it is somewhat surprising that there should still be potential laborers *standing* and evidently seeking employment. The fact that they were still there perhaps indicates that they desperately needed work. This time there is no immediate offer of employment, but an inquiry as to why these men had been standing *idle all day long.* There might have been something detrimental to good workmanship in people who were idle throughout the day. At any rate the man thought it well to inquire before proceeding further.

7. But the reason is simple: no one had hired them. Jesus does not explain how they had come to miss the householder with his continuing offers of work, but the point of the story is not that. It is rather that right up to the eleventh hour the man was ready to take on workmen and that at that very time he sent his final batch to the vineyard. Once more there is no discussion about their pay. There is the simple instruction, *"You go into the vineyard, too."*[10] Nothing is said about remuneration. There is no agreement as for the first workmen, nor assurance that the man would pay what is right for the second (and presumably also for those at the sixth and ninth hours, for the owner dealt "likewise" with them, v. 5). Obviously there was an understanding that these last workmen would be paid, but there is nothing to show how much they would get.

8. When the working day came to its end, the workers had to be paid (Lev. 19:13; Deut. 24:15). So *the owner* summoned his *manager.*[11] He instructed him to *"Call the workmen and pay them the wage."* This seems to be standard procedure, but that may not be the case with the direction to begin with *the last* and go on to *the first.* However, that is the order in which these workmen were to be paid.

9. The men who had worked for only one hour were doubtless pleasantly surprised at getting a full day's wage. They could not have known what they would get. They had not made a bargain with their employer, but had been content to trust him to do what was right. So their one hour's work resulted in the wage appropriate to a full day of work. That he had paid the full day's wage probably indicates a genuine concern for the needs of others. It can scarcely be due to a desire to be rid of money! We must assume that that householder knew that a poor man and his dependents needed the money if they were to have even the necessities of life. There is compassion behind the payment.

9. The Greek says simply τὴν ἐνδεκάτην, but clearly ὥραν must be understood.

10. καὶ ὑμεῖς puts some emphasis on *you;* in addition to those others, *you, too.*

11. *Owner* renders κύριος, mostly rendered "Lord" in the New Testament, but here used in the sense of the owner of property. ἐπίτροπος is not the owner but someone who looks after property or the like on behalf of the owner. It may signify a manager, a foreman, a steward, or looking a little higher, a guardian, or higher still, a governor. Here it is the man who had the responsibility of looking after the day-to-day business of running the vineyard (and possibly other affairs of the owner). *NIV* has "foreman," and *JB* "bailiff," but this latter conveys the wrong nuance.

10. Nothing is said about those who came at the intermediate times, but we are left to presume that they also got the full day's wage. The story moves to the men who had worked all day. They were the spectators of this generosity and, forgetting that they had made a formal agreement with the employer, expected that they would receive more.[12] It is an obvious piece of reasoning: they had worked longer hours and done more work, so they deserved more pay. But it did not work out like that. They received the denarius they had agreed on, that and no more.[13]

11. Receiving their pay under those circumstances was not a matter of rejoicing. They felt that they had not been treated fairly (had they not done twelve times as much as the latecomers?), and so they *grumbled*.[14] The verb is in the imperfect tense, which indicates a continuing process; the grumbling went on.[15]

12. Their complaint amounted to this: they had not been treated fairly. The latecomers *worked one hour*,[16] so their contribution to the work in the vineyard was miniscule. But when it came to pay, they were made *equal* to those who had done most of the work. Is it significant that they complain, *"you made them equal to us,"* not "You made us equal to them"? They were jealous of what had been given to these others; they envied the generosity of the owner to people who had no merit. And it was not only a matter of time spent working; the conditions in which the work was done were also a consideration. The grumblers bring this out by saying that they had *borne the burden*[17] *of the day and the burning heat*.[18] The thrust of the complaint is thus twofold: the latecomers did very little work, and what they did they did under the best conditions in the cool of the day (*NIV* says that their complaint was that they had endured "the burden of

12. In indirect speech the future λήψονται retains the tense of the original speakers.

13. καὶ αὐτοί is the use of the emphatic pronoun, which puts some emphasis on *they*, *they* as well as those who were paid ahead of them.

14. γογγύζω is the muttering that goes through a group of discontented people; it indicates displeasure, or complaint. Here it is followed by κατά, which denotes the object of the complaint.

15. Glover comments: "There are, perhaps, as many murmuring elder brothers as there are repenting prodigals" and goes on, "whenever complacency, disparagement, discontent, enter the soul, then it begins to decline; and *the first* are becoming *last*, till they fall below the level of those they despise, and the publican and the harlot enter the kingdom of heaven 'before,' i.e. in front of them."

16. ποιέω is used here in the general sense of doing whatever had to be done; I have translated it "worked." The same verb is used later in the verse with the double accusative (*made them equal*).

17. βαστάζω is used of carrying literal burdens, for example, a water jar (Mark 14:13). It comes to be used for enduring hardship and difficulty of various kinds, here the burden of the day's work (that done by the latecomers being no more than a tiny fraction of what had to be done). βάρος may be used of a literal burden, but in the New Testament it is used metaphorically of a variety of hardships.

18. καύσων is connected with καίω, "to burn." It signifies the burning part of the day, the time when the sun was at its hottest. It was also used for the hot east wind, the sirocco, and some accept this meaning here.

the work and the heat of the day," while *REB* prefers "sweated the whole day long in the blazing sun"). Surely those who had done a full day's solid work under the worst conditions of the day as well as during the more comfortable hours should be paid more than those who had done very little and had done that little in comparative comfort? It wasn't fair.[19]

13. But this argument did not impress the owner. He is not pictured as addressing the group, but he spoke to one of the grumblers, and in what he said we understand why he had acted as he did. He addressed him as *"Friend,"* a form of address used in this Gospel only in friendly remonstrance (22:12; 26:50). On his side there was no malice or hard feeling; the man who had worked for him all day was his friend. Then he pointed out that there was no injustice: *"I do you no wrong."* When a man makes a solemn agreement and keeps to his side of the bargain, there should be no thought of injustice. This man had made a legal agreement with his workmen; they would work for a day, and he would pay them a denarius.[20] That was what they did and what he did. Where is the injustice? The fact that he chose to be generous to other people gave these men no new rights. Their discontent was due to envy, not to the overlooking of any of their rights.

14. So he told him to *take* what he had earned and what accordingly belonged to him, and *be off* (like the hypocrites in 6:2, 5 he had received what was due!). He had made a legal agreement, and both sides had kept to the bargain. There was nothing more to be said along those lines. The householder further explains that he wants *to give* to the latecomers just what he had given to those who were there earlier. This is not a question of a legal undertaking or of striking a bargain; the man says simply, *"I want to give."*[21] He chose to be generous to those who came late on the scene. This did not mean that he was compelled to be generous to those who had worked all day.

15. Two more questions finish off the owner's little speech. He asks whether it is not *lawful* for him to use his own money as he chooses.[22] If

---

19. France reminds us that our natural sympathy with this position is revealing; he quotes R. H. Stein: "It is frightening to realize that our identification with the first workers, and hence with the opponents of Jesus, reveals how loveless and unmerciful we basically are. We may be more 'under law' in our thinking and less 'under grace' than we realize. God is good and compassionate far beyond his children's understanding!"

20. The question *"Did you not agree. . . ?"* is introduced with οὐχί, which looks for a positive answer. What other answer could be given? Here it is said that they agreed δηναρίου, but the meaning appears to be the same as in verse 2, where it is preceded by ἐκ.

21. θέλω points to the action of the will; this is what the man has set himself to do. And he says he wants *to give* (δοῦναι), not "to pay"; the same verb was used in verse 4 of the payment to those taken on at the third hour and "likewise" (v. 5) may imply that the same was done for those who came at the sixth and ninth hours. But in all these cases there is an element of gift, even if not quite as much as with the last comers. They all differed from those who had come first and worked all day.

22. Buttrick points out that this "does not mean that God is a God of capricious whim and fiat mind. It means that he has his own criteria which we, in mortal sight and selfish aim, cannot comprehend."

people are going to stick by the requirements of the law, he will fulfil his obligations, and indeed he had done so. He had not skimped in paying any of those with whom he had had an agreement for a denarius. It could not be denied that he had acted within the law. And as for the others? "God is not answerable to man for what he does with his rewards" (Fenton). All that we have we receive from his mercy. With that the householder joins the question whether those who objected to what he had done had an evil eye. We saw in an earlier passage that in first-century Palestine the word *eye* was used in ways quite different from our usages, and specifically that people talked about an "evil eye" (6:22-23). The evil eye was sometimes thought of in terms of miserliness, and that may well be in mind here. The grumblers were not complaining of some evil action that the householder had done; they were not saying that they had been cheated out of the wages they had agreed on. They were objecting to an act of sheer generosity that he had displayed toward other people (Phillips translates, "Must you be jealous because I am generous?").

This is a very important parable. It is possible to interpret it in terms of Israel and the Gentiles (as Gundry, e.g., holds). The vineyard is often used as a symbol for Israel (e.g., Isa. 5:1-7); those who take the parable this way argue that Israel is like the men who worked all day, while the Gentiles are symbolized in those who came later and were admitted by God's grace. Others point out that there is always a tendency for those who have been followers of Christ for a long time to be suspicious of those who come later. This applies to Jews and Gentiles, but it also applies to the Twelve and to later believers, and it is not difficult to see this tendency at work in the church of all ages. The parable warns us that priority in time means little.[23] But it seems better to interpret the parable as putting emphasis on the truth that God acts in grace toward us all. There is a tendency in the human race to think of salvation in legal terms. There is no heresy as widespread as the one we can put simply as "If I live a good life, I will go to heaven when I die." It is natural for us to think that we can earn our salvation. But the consistent teaching of Scripture is that we are sinners; we all fall short of the standard we ought to have attained, and thus we have no claim on salvation. But as in this parable the workers who came late had no claim on a full day's wage though they got it, so sinners have no claim on salvation. Salvation is always a work of grace.

---

23. "The parable, as originally spoken, can hardly have had any other object than that of warning Christ's first disciples, that others who should become His disciples at a later date would also be partakers of privileges equal to theirs who had first joined Him" (Allen). Cf. Argyle, "For Matthew the vineyard is the Christian community and those who join it late will be treated as equal in privilege with those who join it early. In the intention of Jesus the parable simply illustrated the teaching that the gift of eternal life is not the reward of human merit but the free gift of divine grace." Hill similarly says, "its main concern is to declare the sovereign grace and good-will of God. . . . It is addressed to those who resembled the grumblers, those who (like the Pharisees) criticized the acceptance of the despised, the outcasts and sinners, into the Kingdom of God."

That God does not treat us on the basis of justice is a fact for which sinners must be truly grateful. The parable emphasizes the place of grace (eleven twelfths of what the last comers received was unearned!).

I do not know of any way of bringing out the point of this parable better than referring to a parable uttered by the rabbis (as far as our information goes, it was later than New Testament times, but, of course, we have no way of knowing how long it was passed on by word of mouth before it was recorded). It concerns a king who hired workmen to work in his vineyard. One of them worked skillfully, and the king took him by the hand and spent most of the day talking with him. When the laborers were paid, this man received the same as the others. They grumbled and said, "We toiled all the day, whereas this man toiled for two hours, and yet the king has given him his full wage!" The king said to them, "What cause have you for grumbling? This man in two hours did more good work than you in a whole day" (*Eccl. Rab.* 5.11.5; McNeile cites it from Jer. *Ber.* 2:5c, and it is found also in *Cant. Rab.* 6.2.6). Clearly the story made quite an appeal to the rabbis, and we can understand that. The natural man assumes that reward is geared to merit. Jesus is pointing out that God does not deal with us on the basis of merit but of grace.[24] The love of God in all its fulness is poured out on sinners, and they receive infinitely more than they deserve. The parable underlines the truth that God's way is always the way of grace.

16. *Even so* aligns the next piece of teaching with the parable, as Jesus repeats essentially what he had said in 19:30. Because God acts in grace and we so easily think in terms of merit, there will be many surprises for us all in the end when God's will is seen in its final working out. Human rankings will avail nothing at that time, and there will be those we have made *last*[25] who will be *first,* and, of course, the reverse phenomenon will also take place.[26]

3. A Prediction of the Passion, 20:17-19

> [17]*And as Jesus was going up to Jerusalem, he took the twelve disciples apart privately and said to them on the way,* [18]*"Look, we are going up to Jerusalem, and the Son of man will be delivered up to the high priests and scribes, and they will condemn him to death,* [19]*and they will deliver him up to the Gentiles to mock and to flog and to crucify, and on the third day he will be raised."*

24. T. W. Manson has a worthwhile comment: "God's love cannot be portioned out in quantities nicely adjusted to the merits of individuals. There is such a thing as the twelfth part of a denar. It was called a *pondion*. But there is no such thing as a twelfth part of the love of God." *The Sayings of Jesus* (London, 1949), p. 220.

25. ἔσχατοι has the article and thus is the subject in the first clause.

26. Many MSS add "for many are called, but few chosen," but the words are omitted by ℵ B L Z sah boh etc. It seems probable, as Metzger says, that copyists inserted them from 22:14, where they conclude another parable.

Commentators routinely copy from one another the statement that this is Jesus' third prediction of his passion, but Matthew has already recorded three such predictions (16:21; 17:12, 22-23; cf. 10:38); this is his fourth. An exception is Plummer, who notes that this is the fourth and thinks that there may have been others (p. 275). The repeated predictions show that Jesus had no doubts about what awaited him in Jerusalem as the culmination of his mission and the climax of the opposition of those who rejected him. And his inclusion of the resurrection in this prediction shows his firm conviction that the Father would ensure his ultimate triumph. On this occasion there is greater detail regarding what will happen to Jesus: he will be condemned by the Jewish leaders, he will be handed over to the Gentiles, he will be mocked and flogged and crucified (only Matthew records Jesus' explicit prediction that his death will be by crucifixion).

17. Matthew locates this prediction on the journey to Jerusalem, but he gives no indication as to just where it took place, nor of any happening that may have called it forth. He simply says it took place *as Jesus was going up*[27] *to Jerusalem.* The whole band of disciples were, of course, going up to the city, as were multitudes of pilgrims; but when Matthew says simply that Jesus was going up, he puts emphasis on the leader. Mark has a striking picture of Jesus striding ahead and of the disciples following amazed and afraid. Matthew says nothing of this, but clearly he envisaged unusual circumstances such that taking the disciples apart was a significant action. Evidently others were traveling along the way (there would be pilgrims going up to observe the Passover in the capital city), but Jesus did not want his prediction to become public property. He *took the twelve disciples apart privately.*[28] Matthew says explicitly that this happened *on the way* (the others do not mention this). It was as they were going to Jerusalem that this prediction was made.

18. *"Look"* (see on 1:20) is Matthew's way of drawing attention to what follows. Jesus reminds his followers that their destination was *Jerusalem.* They were going up at the time of one of the great festivals of the Jewish liturgical year, and the expectation would be that they were facing a time of celebration and rejoicing. But Jesus says that *"the Son of man"* (his name for himself in the fulfilment of his messianic vocation) *"will be delivered up*[29] *to the high priests and scribes."* Both terms have par-

---

27. ἀναβαίνω (9 times in Matthew) is often used of going up to the capital. Jerusalem was, of course, on high ground.

28. All three Synoptists have the verb παραλαμβάνω (which Matthew uses 16 times) with the meaning "take along with oneself," but only Matthew has κατ' ἰδίαν.

29. παραδίδωμι (31 times in Matthew; no other book has it more than Mark's 21 times) means "to hand over, deliver up" and is often employed as a technical term for handing over into custody (e.g., Acts 8:3). It is used in a variety of ways for the "delivering up" of Jesus for his atoning death. Thus Judas handed him over (26:25), as did the chief priests and elders (27:2), and the people of Jerusalem (Acts 3:13). From another angle it was Pilate who delivered him up (27:26). We are quite ready to condemn these evil and weak people, but we had our

ticular meanings (see on 2:4), but the combination (with no article before *scribes* so that the two are something of a unity), together with the reference to a judicial condemnation, shows that the Sanhedrin, the highest court of the Jews, is in mind. Not only will Jesus appear before them, but these people, the religious leaders of the nation, *will condemn him to death,* where the verb points to the exercise of judicial power, not to a lynching. Under Roman domination the Sanhedrin had no power to put anyone to death, but that did not stop them sentencing people to this punishment. They would then hand over to the Romans those they held to be guilty, and these rulers of the nation would decide whether the sentence would be carried out or not. Jesus is speaking here of the part the Jewish authorities would play in bringing about his death.

19. He moves to the next stage in the drama. The Jewish leaders will *deliver him up* (the same verb as in v. 18) *to the Gentiles.* Jesus does not specify which Gentiles, but in the circumstances of the time there could be no doubt but that he meant the Romans. He goes on to specify three things these people will do. They will *mock,*[30] which fits the practices of the day (there was no tradition that a prisoner should be treated kindly), but it was not an invariable accompaniment of condemnation and it speaks of another piece of bitterness in the sufferings Jesus would undergo. Flogging was the normal prelude to crucifixion, though it could, of course, be used as the proper and adequate punishment for some offenses. Since it was a very brutal practice, it was no light punishment in itself. But here it is the prelude to execution, as the addition *to crucify him*[31] shows. Jesus leaves no doubt that he was facing the ultimate in rejection by his people and in suffering at the hands of the Gentiles who ruled them. Matthew is the only one of the Evangelists who tells us that Jesus specifically prophesied that he would be crucified. This was a form of death normally reserved for slaves, criminals, and other despised people (a Roman citizen could not be crucified).

But that is not the whole story. As he has done before, Jesus goes on to predict his resurrection. This will take place *on the third day* (for this expression see on 12:40; it was the third day according to the Jewish method of counting, even if some modern people have difficulty with the expression). Jesus does not say that he will rise, but that he *will be raised.* As is the normal (though not invariable) way of putting it, the resurrection

---

part in it too, for he was delivered up for our sins (Rom. 4:25). In a little glimpse of what happened from the heavenly point of view we find that the Father did this (Rom. 8:32), while according to one of the most moving passages in Scripture, the Son gave himself up (Gal. 2:20).

30. εἰς τό seems here to indicate purpose (cf. Turner, M, III, p. 143).

31. Crucifixion was widely used by the Romans (and other nations) as a method of inflicting the death penalty. The Jews officially accepted burning, stoning, strangling, and beheading as methods of execution (*Sanh.* 7:1), but under the Romans they were not permitted to put anyone to death (John 18:31). Jesus' words thus indicate that it will be the Romans who will be his executioners.

is attributed to the activity of the Father. He will set his seal on the saving death of the Son of man by raising him from the dead.

4. Places for the Sons of Zebedee, 20:20-28

20Then the mother of Zebedee's sons approached him together with her sons, and she knelt and made a request. 21And he said to her, "What do you want?" She says to him, "Say that these two sons of mine will sit on your right hand and on your left in your kingdom." 22But Jesus answered, saying, "You do not know what you are asking. Can you drink the cup that I am going to drink?" They say to him, "We can." 23He says to them, "My cup you will indeed drink, but to sit at my right hand and at the left is not mine to give, but is for them for whom it has been prepared by my Father." 24And when the ten heard it, they were indignant at the two brothers. 25But Jesus summoned them and said, "You know that the rulers of the nations exercise lordship over them, and their great men exercise authority over them. 26It will not be so among you, but whoever wills to be great among you will be your servant, 27and whoever wills to be first among you will be your slave; 28even as the Son of man did not come to be served but to serve, and to give his life a ransom for many."

Consistently Jesus had taught his followers that there was no place for pride and self-seeking of any sort in the life to which he called them (equally consistently they failed to learn the lesson!). Matthew brings this out by following the prediction of the Messiah's sufferings and death with the story of the Zebedee family's petition for the highest places in the kingdom of which Jesus had taught so much. We need not think that the request was made immediately after Jesus' prediction of his passion, but it must have been at about that time, for it took place during the journey to Jerusalem. It shows a complete failure to understand the essential thrust of Jesus' teaching. It was not a minor misunderstanding, but an error at the heart of what service in the kingdom means.

20. *Then* (see on 2:7) can signify next in sequence, but it is also used more loosely for sometime later, and that will be the meaning here. Mark tells us that James and John, the sons of Zebedee, came to Jesus with the request, but Matthew assures us that their *mother* was with them, and the way Matthew puts it, that she took the leading role in the petition they offered.[32] She may have been the sister of Mary the mother of Jesus,[33] in

---

32. Many commentators say that Matthew is altering what Mark says in order to minimize criticism of the brothers, but "The suggestion is interesting solely as an example of ignorance of the ways and manners of mothers anxious for their sons" (AB).

33. At the crucifixion Matthew mentions Mary Magdalene, Mary the mother of James and Joses, and the mother of Zebedee's sons (27:56). Mark has Mary Magdalene, Mary the mother of James and Joses, and Salome (Mark 15:40). John has the mother of Jesus, her sister, Mary the wife of Cleopas, and Mary Magdalene (John 19:25). A comparison of Matthew and

which case she would probably have been urging the claims of the family. The verbs translated *knelt* and *made a request* are both feminine participles, so that it was the lady who was foremost in bringing the request. She took up a respectful, even reverent, posture[34] and indicated that she had a request to make. At this point she did not say what she wanted, but *made a request*.[35] This action appears to mean that, in deference to the position of a great person, she was seeking Jesus' permission before presenting her petition.

21. Jesus accordingly asked what she wanted; his verb is singular, so at this point he is confining the request to the lady and not associating her sons with her. She asks for an assurance[36] that her two sons would sit at Jesus' *right hand* and at his *left*[37] in the kingdom. Next to the ruler, these were the two places of highest honor. Luke tells us that at about this time the members of the little band were expecting that the kingdom was about to be set up (Luke 19:11); perhaps they thought that that was why Jesus was going up to Jerusalem. It would seem that the Zebedees wanted to be ready when that kingdom came into being. There is faith in their request. The kingdom had not yet been established in the way the Zebedees looked for it, and there was no sign of such a kingdom. But despite the lowliness of Jesus and of the entire little band the Zebedee family were so sure that the kingdom would eventuate that they were already putting in their claims for the best places when it came. We must deplore the self-seeking implicit in their desire to get the chief places for themselves, but at the same time we should appreciate their deep conviction that in the end Jesus would certainly establish the kingdom.

22. But for all their confidence in Jesus they were on the wrong track. *But* has adversative force and sets Jesus over against the suggestion just made. The mother had asked the question, but the sons were more nearly

Mark makes it likely that the mother of Zebedee's sons was called Salome, and John's account makes it seem that this lady was the sister of Jesus' mother. If this is the way the passages should be understood, James and John would be cousins of Jesus. J. A. T. Robinson says, "This cannot be more than a hypothesis," but that it is supported by the fact that on the cross Jesus committed Mary to the care of the Beloved Disciple (*The Priority of John* [London, 1985], pp. 119-20).

34. προσκυνέω is often used in the sense "worship," and it is employed for the worship of God (4:10). But it is also used for actions conveying deep respect for humans (18:26), and this seems to be in mind here. Bengel remarks, "From the adoration and discourse of this woman, it is evident that she entertained a high idea of our Lord's majesty, but possessed very little knowledge."

35. αἰτοῦσά τι ἀπ' αὐτοῦ, "asking something from him."

36. She says εἰπέ; the kingdom was not yet a reality, but she looks forward to its coming and asks Jesus to speak now the command that would give the Zebedees what they doubtless saw as their rightful places when the kingdom came.

37. εὐώνυμος strictly means *"of good name* or *omen, well-named"*; it was used as a euphemism "to avoid the ill-omen attaching to the left" (AS). There is, of course, no suggestion that its use in the New Testament is influenced in any way by omens; it is interesting that a term with such an origin had passed into general speech. ἀριστερός, which is also a euphemism (meaning "better"; see LSJ), is used for "left" in Matthew only in 6:3.

concerned, and it is to them that he addresses his answer. He goes on to say, *"You do not know what you are asking."*[38] They were clearly viewing the kingdom in terms of the contemporary understanding of splendor; Jesus would reign, they thought, over a realm much like that of the Romans, only more glorious. Despite all the teaching Jesus had given, they had still not realized that the kingdom meant lowliness, sacrifice, and rejection in this world. Who would ask for places of honor in such a kingdom? Who *could* ask for places of honor in it? To ask the question is to show that one has not understood what the kingdom is; it is impossible to seek greatness for oneself in it.

Jesus goes on to ask, *"Can you drink the cup that I am going to drink?"*[39] He does not explain what this means, but the *cup* is used in the Old Testament with associations of suffering and sometimes of the wrath of God (e.g., Ps. 75:8; Isa. 51:17, 22; Jer. 25:15-16). All four Gospels use the term when they are recording what Jesus said of his sufferings in Gethsemane and at the time of his arrest (26:39; Mark 14:36; Luke 22:42; John 18:11). It is clear that the term was often used for suffering and the like, but it is not so clear why the sons of Zebedee were so ready to express their willingness and their capacity to endure it. *"We can,"* they said, without hesitation, without understanding, and without seeking clarification of exactly what the *cup* involved. That they claimed too much was made plain when they ran away in Gethsemane (26:56). And yet — in due course they did drink the cup, James by martyrdom (Acts 12:1-2) and John by exile to Patmos (if, as seems probable, he was the John who wrote Rev. 1:9).

23. Jesus agrees that they will drink his *cup*, even though they do not understand what it implies. Their knowledge of the kingdom and of what following Jesus meant would be considerably enlarged, and that in the not-too-distant future. In the end they would be ready to eschew self-seeking and be ready to endure whatever suffering was required of them as humble members of the kingdom. That would happen, although at this time they did not understand it. But the chief places in the kingdom are another matter. Jesus says that gift *"is not mine to give."* That is the prerogative of the Father, and Jesus says that it has already *been prepared* for them. If it has already been prepared for certain people, then obviously Jesus could not now give it to others, no matter how worthy. We should notice again *"my Father."* Jesus has just announced that he will be crucified and, in the context of a request for the highest places in the kingdom from

---

38. In verse 20 the verb for "asking" is in the active but here it is in the middle. The general rule is that the middle αἰτέω is used "of requests in commerce and so as a rule in the NT; the active is usually used for requests addressed to God" (BDF, 316[2]). Lenski thinks that the mother here "asks devoutly as one asks of God," while Jesus uses the middle, "for this asking was really in the nature of a business transaction" (p. 787).

39. The verb is not the simple future, but μέλλω πίνειν; there is a sense of inevitability about Jesus drinking the cup.

people who ought to have known better, he still speaks of God in terms of the closest intimacy. He knew that he would undergo agonizing sufferings, but he faced them with trust in his loving Father.

24. Not unnaturally the action of the Zebedee brothers did not please the rest of the apostolic band. They *were indignant*.[40] The two were stealing a march on the others, some of whom doubtless had their eye on the same positions. It was a source of indignation that the Zebedees had tried to get in first.

25. Jesus approved of neither the actions of the two nor those of the ten; thus he called them all to him to teach them yet once more that it is lowliness, not self-assertion, that is important in the kingdom. The two were wrong, but then so were the ten. *"You know,"* he says, appealing to what is common knowledge and something that does not require demonstration. He refers to rulers of *the nations*, where his word is that commonly used for "the Gentiles" (as indeed a number of translations render it here). But it seems that Jesus is speaking about what happens in nations generally (*NEB* has "in the world"); he is not contrasting Jews with Gentiles. And in the nations *rulers* commonly *exercise lordship over them*. The world is apt to reason: "What is the point of being a ruler if you can't act like one?" So rulers all too easily come to tyrannize over their subjects. And *great men* who are not quite in the positions of being rulers are still quite ready to make use of whatever *authority* they can exercise.[41] It is the way of the world to look for the highest possible place and to take delight in making full use of the authority that that place gives. In political life the world over and the centuries through humility is seen as a handicap, not a virtue. Jesus draws attention to a well-known fact of life. It scarcely needs adding that he is not objecting to constituted authority as such; there must be people in authority if there is to be ordered government. He is objecting to the misuse of power that so easily comes about.

26-27. There is no connective, and the abrupt transition from the world to the group of Jesus' followers helps to show that the two are quite different. Disciples are not meant to be the world in all its self-assertion all over again. So Jesus says quite definitely, *"It will not be so among you."* The future tense lays down what is to happen; it is to be understood as having the force of a command (cf. M, III, p. 86). *But* is the strong adversative; the followers of Jesus will be far from adopting the worldly approach. Anyone among them who *wills to be great* may recognize that there will be those among the followers who, like the sons of Zebedee, have visions of doing more than the humdrum things in which so many find contentment. They may want more than what someone has called "the

40. ἀγανακτέω is connected by AS with the ideas of "much" and "grieve," but the strong grieving is linked with reproach and thus signifies "be indignant." MM cites the word from the papyri with this meaning.

41. κατεξουσιάζω occurs only here and in Mark 10:42 in the New Testament. The verb is rare; "scarcely to be found in secular Gk" (BAGD). It is not cited in MM or *New Documents*.

flim-flam of respectable Christianity." But those who are moved by such feelings are not to think that their place is to be like that of some earthly lord, sitting at the top of the heap and directing other people. Rather, the person who wants eminence in the kingdom is to take the path of lowliness and humility.[42] Jesus takes that to the limit by saying that the one who *wills to be first* in the brotherhood *will be your slave.*[43] In the ancient world there was no one lower than a slave; the slave's "whole life is lived in service for which he can claim neither credit nor reward" (Robinson). Jesus could scarcely use a more graphic term to bring out the lowliness his people must seek. It is in lowly service that Christians find their true fulfilment. They follow a Master who took the form of a servant and lived all his earthly days in humble obscurity. The way forward for them is in humility and lowliness. To set one's heart on eminence is to lose the heart of the Christian way. This does not, of course, mean that among the followers of Christ there are to be no leaders, none in high places. It means that those who take the lead among them are to be humble, people seeking not personal success but the opportunity of doing lowly service.

28. This line of reasoning is clinched by an appeal to what Jesus himself was doing. He uses his title *"Son of man"*; his messianic function is involved; this is the climax of what he came to do. He *did not come* (the words do not prove that Jesus was conscious of existing before he appeared in this world, but that is the natural way to understand them; cf. 5:17, etc.) *to be served but to serve.* This is the very antithesis of what the sons of Zebedee wanted. They viewed themselves as the kind of people who would be right at the top in the kingdom. Jesus is saying that he sought no such place for himself. He sought the path of lowly service.[44] He underlines this by saying, *"and to give his[45] life a ransom[46] for many."*[47] The word *ransom* took its origin from the practices of warfare, where it was the price paid to bring a prisoner of war out of his captivity. It was used of sacral manumission of slaves, a process

42. Chrysostom comments: "Nothing is higher than lowliness of mind, and nothing lower than boastfulness" (p. 402).

43. McNeile considers the choice of words significant: "as πρῶτος is higher than μέγας, so is δοῦλος lower than διάκονος."

44. The verb διακονέω was used of waiting on someone at table, and from that came to denote lowly service in general. Jesus is using an interesting term to state quite firmly that he sought no great place for himself, but chose to serve in a humble capacity.

45. αὐτοῦ is to be seen here as a "strengthening of the reflexive" (BDF, 283[4]).

46. λύτρον was a well-known concept, often used of the sacral manumission of slaves (see MM and *LAE*, pp. 319-30). It occurs only here (and in the parallel in Mark 10:45) in the New Testament, but the corresponding verb λυτρόω is found 3 times, as is the noun λύτρωσις. More frequent is ἀπολύτρωσις (10 times).

47. ἀντὶ πολλῶν, "in the place of many"; ἀντί is the normal preposition for substitution (cf. Moule, *IBNTG*, p. 71). F. Büchsel says that here "ἀντί means 'for' in the sense of 'in place of' rather than 'to the advantage of'" (*TDNT*, IV, p. 342). Robertson says that this passage and Mark 10:45 "teach the substitutionary conception of Christ's death," not because ἀντί of itself means 'instead,' which is not true, but because the context renders any other resultant idea out of the question" (p. 573). Many commentators assert that "many" here is equivalent to "all," but the absence of the article is perhaps against this.

wherein the slave went through the solemn rigmarole of being sold to a god "for freedom."[48] In effect this meant that, while the slave technically belonged to the god, as far as people were concerned he or she was free. This forms a vivid illustration of one aspect of Christ's saving work. Sinners have become the slaves of sin (John 8:34), and they cannot break free. But Christ has paid their ransom price, and now they are free indeed. "The ransom saying undoubtedly implies substitution. For, even if the ἀντί be translated 'to the advantage of,' the death of Jesus means that there happens to Him what would have had to happen to the many. Hence He takes their place" (Büchsel, *TDNT,* IV, p. 343).[49] There may well be a reference to Isaiah 53, though there is no exact quotation (Gundry brings out this point; he also says that the words rendered *a ransom for* "establish the substitutionary value of the sacrifice given in service").

5. Two Blind Men of Jericho, 20:29-34

> 29*And as they were going out of Jericho, a great crowd followed him.* 30*And look, two blind men sitting by the wayside heard that Jesus was passing by, and cried out, saying, "Take pity on us, Lord, Son of David."* 31*But the crowd admonished them so that they should be silent; but they cried out all the more, saying, "Take pity on us, Lord, Son of David."* 32*And Jesus stood still and called them, and said, "What do you want me to do for you?"* 33*They say to him, "Lord, that our eyes may be opened."* 34*And Jesus, moved with compassion, touched their eyes, and immediately they received sight and they followed him.*

Matthew moves on in his account of Jesus' journey to Jerusalem and tells the story of two blind men who received their sight as the Master was leaving Jericho. There are problems in relating this to what we read in the other Gospels. Matthew has two blind men, whereas Mark and Luke have but one, whom Mark names as Bartimaeus. Our first two Gospels have the miracle as Jesus was leaving Jericho, but Luke has it as he was arriving. We may or may not be able to reconcile the accounts, but some things should be said. If there were two men, one of them may well have been more prominent than the other and attracted more attention, so that it was possible to write the story concentrating on him.[50] It does not seem

---

48. Deissmann documents this (*LAE,* pp. 319-30).

49. See further my *The Apostolic Preaching of the Cross*[3] (London and Grand Rapids, 1965), pp. 11-64; *The Atonement* (Leicester and Downers Grove, 1983), pp. 106-31. Hamann says, "The sentence makes three assertions about the ransoming death: it was a voluntary death, it was a vicarious death (a substitutionary death, a death by proxy — see Rom. 3:24; 2 Cor. 5:21; Gal. 1:4), and it has a universal character" (p. 206). Mounce remarks, "It would be difficult to express the substitutionary nature of Jesus' death in clearer language."

50. Tasker holds it "equally probable that two men were in fact given back their sight,

to make a great deal of difference whether it took place as Jesus was arriving at Jericho or leaving, and in any case there is a complication in that there were two Jerichos (Josephus, *War* 4.459), the site of Old Testament Jericho, which had been overthrown, and the site nearby of the rebuilt Herodian Jericho. It is not impossible that the miracle was performed as Jesus was leaving one Jericho and approaching the other. We should not miss the point that this story follows immediately on the sayings about Jesus' saving death. He used his great powers, not to save himself, but to heal a couple of apparently quite unimportant blind men.

29. Since Matthew has given us few details of Jesus' journey, we are left wondering about his precise route. But at this point he is certainly within the borders of Judea, with Jerusalem no more than about fifteen miles away. Matthew locates the happening as they were leaving Jericho. He says that *a great crowd* was following Jesus (usually he uses the plural "crowds," but here the word is singular). There would have been many pilgrims going up to Jerusalem for the Passover, and, since Jesus was known to many from Galilee, there is nothing surprising in their attaching themselves to him as they all journeyed on to the same destination.

30. Matthew's vivid *"And look"* (see on 1:20) invites the reader to contemplate *two blind men sitting by the wayside.* It is not said that they were begging, but that is not improbable (and Luke says that was what his blind man was doing). The blind had no other way of earning a living, and with crowds of people going up to Jerusalem for the feast there was always the possibility of help coming from well-disposed worshipers. They *heard* from some of the crowd that *Jesus was passing by.* Evidently they knew something of Jesus, and specifically they knew that he had brought healing to many. So they did not waste their opportunity — they would probably never get another. They *cried out;* there is no indication of how far they were from Jesus, and they probably did not know. But shouting was the way to get his attention, so that was what they did. They did not specify that they wanted him to give them their sight, but asked him to *take pity* on them, as did the two blind men in 9:27 (which some think is a doublet of the present story), the Canaanite woman (15:22), and the man Jesus encountered at the foot of the mountain of the transfiguration (17:15). It is not certain whether we should include *"Lord"* as part of the true text here (as it is in v. 31), but this seems likely.[51] They further greeted him as *"Son of David,"* a messianic title (see on 1:1),[52] which

---

but that the Petrine tradition of the story known to Mark concentrated attention solely upon one of the beneficiaries, who may have been personally known to Peter" (p. 196). It might support this that the name Bar-Timaeus is given only in Mark.

51. It is read by $\mathfrak{p}^{45vid}$ C K W X etc., but there are many variants. Evidently copyists bore in mind the similar passage, 9:27, and the accounts in Mark and Luke. It is impossible to be sure of the true text here, but on the whole it seems that κύριε should be read.

52. Grosheide says that " 'Son of David' is never used elsewhere as a mere title of honor. To conceive it as such therefore is pure speculation"; he argues that the view that "Son of David" is not a messianic title is "untenable" (pp. 374, 375).

Matthew records a number of times. It is of interest that Jesus does not reject it, though it was uttered loudly in the presence of a large crowd (earlier he had discouraged talk of his messiahship; cf. 9:30). He was going to Jerusalem to die, and he would die as the Messiah. The title indicates that the blind men thought highly of Jesus and saw in him someone who could deliver them from their blindness if he only would. But they realized, too, their lowly place, so they asked for his pity.

31. *But* has adversative force; it sets the unsympathetic crowd over against the noisy blind men. The people wanted to see and hear Jesus, not to be disturbed by these men shouting out for pity. They *admonished*[53] the blind men with a view to[54] their being quiet. But they were totally unsuccessful. The blind men were highly motivated and they were persistent. When they were rebuked, they reacted by crying out *all the more.*[55] They said the same words as before (this time there is no textual doubt about *"Lord"*; REB has "Sir," but where the men are addressing the *Son of David* "Lord" is more likely than "Sir"); they wanted the Lord, the Son of David, to take pity on them, so they kept repeating their plea.

32-34. In the end they were successful; Jesus halted his progress[56] and *called them.* He asked them what they wanted and received the answer, *"Lord, that our eyes may be opened."*[57] The greatest thing that could be done for them was that they be given sight. And Jesus responded. He was *moved with compassion* (see on 9:36 for this illuminating expression); the crowd had been ready to silence these men and keep them out of the way, but Jesus was too compassionate for such harsh treatment of people in need. He has just been teaching his followers the importance of lowly service, and he now gives an example of it. For a moment he ignores the great crowds of people thronging around him and concentrates on two insignificant men in need. He *touched their eyes,*[58] as he had touched people in his healings a number of times. Thus Matthew reports him as touching a leper (8:3), Peter's mother-in-law (8:15), and the eyes of blind men (9:29), in each case with healing following. Sometimes people touched his clothes and received healing (9:20-21; 14:36). On this occasion the immediate sequel to the touch was that the men *received sight.*[59] Matthew also records that they *followed him.* This may mean no more than that they joined the

---

53. ἐπιτιμάω is mostly used in the New Testament in the sense "rebuke." AS points out that it expresses "simply rebuke, which may be undeserved (Mt 16²²) or ineffectual (Lk 23⁴⁰)" over against ἐλέγχω, "which brings conviction" (sub ἐλέγχω). Here the rebuke has no effect.

54. ἵνα indicates purpose.

55. According to Howard, this is the only place in the New Testament where μεῖζον has the meaning "more" (M, II, p. 165).

56. ἵστημι is used in the aorist with the meaning "stand still," "halt."

57. This may well be an example of imperatival ἵνα.

58. The word here is ὄμμα (again in the New Testament only in Mark 8:23). It is usually regarded as a poetic word, but MM cites it from the papyri.

59. ἀναβλέπω means "to look up"; it is also utilized in that sense in 14:19. But it is also used often, as here, for the recovery of sight of the blind (so in 11:5).

crowd behind Jesus as he journeyed on, but it is more likely that Matthew uses the term here of a more meaningful following; he sees the two as becoming disciples. Schweizer considers this so important that he heads his discussion of the whole story, not "Two Blind Men Receive Sight" but "Two Blind Men Follow Jesus." He expressly understands *they followed him* to mean "the men joined Jesus as disciples" (p. 399).[60]

---

60. Michael Green has an apt comment: "The request of the disciples (for top places in the Kingdom) shows their blindness: the request of the blind men shows their vision — of who Jesus is and what he can do" (p. 196). Diétrich also links the two: "It is easier for Jesus to give sight to the blind who believe in him than to make the scales fall from the eyes of his disciples who do not know to what degree they are still blind."

Matthew 21

VI. JESUS' MINISTRY IN JERUSALEM, 21:1–25:46

Matthew has finished his accounts of Jesus in Galilee and Jesus on the way to Jerusalem. He moves on now to how the Lord came to the capital city and what happened thereafter. There are a few accounts of happenings, but mostly this section of the Gospel is concerned with the teaching Jesus gave in Jerusalem.

A. Beginnings, 21:1-27

Matthew begins this section of his narrative with an account of Jesus' entry into Jerusalem in triumph, together with what happened immediately after that.

1. The Triumphal Entry into Jerusalem, 21:1-11

> ¹And when he drew near to Jerusalem and came to Bethphage to the Mount of Olives, then Jesus sent two disciples, ²saying to them, "Go into the village opposite you, and straightaway you will find an ass tied up and a colt with her; loose them and bring them to me. ³And if anyone says anything to you, you will say, 'The Lord has need of them.' And immediately he will send them." ⁴Now this happened so that what was spoken through the prophet might be fulfilled, saying,

> ⁵"Say to the daughter of Zion,
>   'Look, your King is coming to you,
> Meek and mounted on an ass,
>   and on a colt, the foal of a beast of burden.' "

> ⁶And the disciples went and did as Jesus had instructed them; ⁷they brought the ass and the colt, and they put their cloaks on them, and he sat on them. ⁸And the great crowd spread their cloaks on the road, while others cut branches from the trees and spread them on the road. ⁹And the crowds who went ahead of him and those who followed were shouting, "Hosanna to the son of David; blessed is he who comes in the name of the Lord; hosanna in the highest!" ¹⁰And when he entered Jerusalem, the whole city was stirred

517

up and said, "Who is this?" [11]*And the crowds said, "This is the prophet Jesus, who is from Nazareth of Galilee."*

All four Gospels tell us that when Jesus came up to Jerusalem for the last time during his public ministry he was greeted by a large and enthusiastic crowd. This is somewhat surprising, for during the immediately preceding days there has been quite an emphasis on the fact that at this time Jesus concentrated largely on teaching his disciples (there has also been a marked growth of opposition to him on the part of people like the Pharisees). Nothing prepares us for this outburst of enthusiastic support from the general public. We should probably understand that among the crowd who came up to Jerusalem to celebrate the Passover[1] there were many who had been impressed by his teaching and his miracles. The Roman occupation cannot have been popular, and some patriotic souls must have thought it possible that Jesus would form the spearhead of a movement in opposition. So people cheered him with enthusiasm.

In John's Gospel the story begins, not with Jesus sending for the donkey, but with crowds of people taking palm branches and going out to meet Jesus,[2] shouting "Hosanna." John appears to be saying that the excitement was begun by enthusiastic pilgrim crowds already in Jerusalem and by those from the neighborhood of Jerusalem who had been impressed by the raising of Lazarus. In passing we should notice that the Synoptists have made it clear that Jesus could expect only opposition and death when he went up to Jerusalem, but they have not given attention to the question, Why then did he go up? In the deepest sense they have made it clear that this was to fulfil the purpose of God, but they have not brought out the human circumstances that led him to go up at just this time. John supplies that reason — Jesus went up to help his friends at Bethany when Lazarus was ill. The fact that he brought Lazarus back to life after he died explains why so many of the Jerusalemites were ready to welcome Jesus when he came to the city. Miracles done in the backwoods of Galilee would not impress them, but a raising from the dead in their own backyard at Bethany was quite another matter. What he had done in Bethany had clearly become known, at least in some quarters in Jerusalem.

Some commentators suggest that these two accounts are in contradiction, but this does not appear to be the case. If we accept what John is saying, it would seem that when Jesus saw that these people were trying to make a political messiah out of him he sent for the donkey, as the

---

1. Some scholars have held that the triumphal entry took place at the Feast of Tabernacles (so Hill, following T. W. Manson), or the Feast of the Dedication (B. A. Mastin, *NTS*, 16 [1969-70], pp. 76-82). Such views remain possible, for Matthew does not specifically identify the feast, but it is more likely to be Passover, as John clearly indicates (cf. John 12:1).

2. Josephus tells of the people of Antioch going out to meet Titus and welcome him into their city (*War* 7.100-103). Going out to welcome an eminent person was thus not unknown.

Synoptists tell us he did, in order to show by his symbolic action that he was not the potential overthrower of the Romans that the crowds would dearly have loved to see. No, he was the Prince of peace.[3] However we relate the Synoptic accounts to the Johannine record, the important thing is that the crowds were engaging in unwise political enthusiasm, but Jesus came to Jerusalem, not as the leader of a revolt against Rome but as the King of peace.

1. Matthew has recorded Jesus' departure from Jericho, and now we find that he was getting near to Jerusalem. *Bethphage* (the name apparently means "House of Unripe Figs") was a village whose precise site is not now known. Both Mark and Luke link it in this narrative with Bethany and mention it first, so it was probably to the east of that village. The Jews regarded it as the outer limit of the area of Jerusalem (the loaves of Lev. 23:17; 24:5 "were valid whether made in the Temple Court or Bethphage," *Menaḥ.* 11:2; Bethphage is seen as the outer limit of Jerusalem also in *Pes.* 63b; 91a; *Menaḥ.* 78b, etc.). The location is further described as *the Mount of Olives*, just to the east of the city. At this point Jesus *sent two disciples* on an errand. None of the Evangelists tells us which two were sent.

2. They were to go to *the village opposite*, which is not named in any of our sources. It may have been Bethany, but we cannot be sure. There, Jesus says, they will find *an ass tied up and a colt[4] with her.* That they will find the animals *straightaway* seems to mean that they would be near the entrance to the village (Luke in fact says that they will find them as they enter). Jesus anticipates no trouble in their identifying the animals. Matthew is the only one who tells us that there were two animals; both Mark and Luke refer only to "a colt." He tells them to *loose them* and to *bring them* to him.

3. It is unlikely that a stranger might walk into a village, untie an animal, and walk off with it without being challenged. So Jesus tells them what to do should anyone question them. *You will say* is a future with imperative force (Mark in fact has an imperative). The password is *"The Lord has need of them."* "Lord" is patient of more than one meaning. It could mean the owner of the animals, but against this is the fact that, though Luke has the same expression at this point, a little later he says that the owners ("lords") questioned the disciples when they came for the animal; there was more than one owner, and the owners were with the donkey, not where the donkey was to go. It could mean God, for the animal was to be used in God's service, but it is not easy to see how those standing

---

3. "Jesus' reaction was a prompt repudiation of the crowd's acclamations. . . . He could not escape, as he had done after feeding the crowd in Galilee, and so, to show that he was not accepting the rôle of a military Messiah, but coming in peace, he *sat* on an *ass* . . ." (J. N. Sanders, *A Commentary on the Gospel according to St John*, ed. and completed by B. A. Mastin [London, 1968], p. 288).

4. πῶλος signifies "a foal, colt," initially used of a horse, but later of other animals as well (AS). Here clearly it refers to the colt of an ass.

near the donkey could have understood this. Another possibility is that "Lord" means Jesus himself (cf. GNB, "the Master"); if this is the way of it, we should notice that he says "the" Lord, not simply "our" Lord; it is the Lord of all that is in mind. This cannot be ruled out, but Jesus did not usually apply this word to himself. All in all it seems better to understand the words as a prearranged password. This means that Jesus had somehow made an arrangement with the owners of the animals. None of the Evangelists gives any indication who the owners were or how the arrangement was made. But that it was made shows clearly that Jesus had had more dealings in and around Jerusalem than Matthew has so far indicated. He has written of Jesus only in his Galilean ministry (apart from his visit to John the Baptist and the temptation narrative, and neither of those took him to the capital city). From John's Gospel we learn that Jesus had been to Jerusalem on a number of occasions and had had an important ministry there, and it would seem that it was on such occasions that he made the acquaintance of people like the owners of the animals he was now borrowing. There still remains the mystery of how on the journey from Galilee Jesus was able to make the arrangements about the animal, but if he had been in Bethany for some days that is not an insuperable problem. He tells the disciples that when they say the words he has given them, anyone who questions them will not only permit them to take them but *will send them*. Evidently the owners were cooperating fully in Jesus' plan. Of course the words about sending back may be part of the message delivered by the two disciples, in which case it means that Jesus will send the animals back when he has finished with them.[5]

4-5. Characteristically Matthew sees a fulfilment of prophecy in all this (as does John; see John 12:15), and only in this Gospel do we find it said that Jesus did what he did in fulfilment of the prophecy of Zechariah 9:9 (Buttrick speaks of this as "sheer insight"). He has his characteristic formula for introducing fulfilment of Scripture (see on 1:22), and though he speaks of what was spoken through *the prophet* he actually combines words from two prophets, Isaiah 62:11 and Zechariah 9:9. The Isaiah passage is addressed to *the daughter of Zion*,[6] an expression that means the inhabitants of Jerusalem, and it goes on to refer to "your salvation" as coming, which enables Matthew to move over smoothly into the Zechariah passage, where we read of *your King* as coming. Obviously there is no great difference; the King brings salvation, and it matters little which the prophet chooses to say is coming.

But the important point in the prophecy is that this King is *meek*.

---

5. Mark has, "and he will send it back here again immediately."

6. Zion was a Jebusite stronghold that David captured and that he made the royal residence (2 Sam. 5:7, 9). The "city of David" in time was known as Zion (1 Kings 8:1), and eventually the term became indistinguishable from Jerusalem (e.g., Isa. 4:3-4). The expression "daughter of Zion" came to mean the population of the city (e.g., Isa. 1:8), the meaning it has here.

When the prophet says that he comes riding on *an ass*,[7] he is contrasting him with "the chariot," "the war horse," and "the battle bow" (Zech. 9:10). It is the fact that the King is a man of peace that is distinctive. In antiquity a king would not normally enter his capital riding on a donkey. He would ride in proudly, on a war-horse, or perhaps he would march in at the head of his troops. An ass was the animal of a man of peace; it would be used by a priest or a merchant or an eminent citizen. But the ass Jesus rode was no well-bred animal meant for the convenience of the wealthy (cf. Judg. 5:10). It is specifically called *a beast of burden;* it was a lowly animal. A king on an ass was almost a contradiction in terms, though, of course, sometimes in times of peace a king would use an ass (cf. 1 Kings 1:33). That Jesus rode into the city in the way he did was a significant affirmation of his character and his purpose. The pilgrims might shout their acclaims and think of a king who would fight against the Romans and throw them out of the country, but Jesus viewed himself as the King of peace. He had accepted the salutation "Son of David," and there is no doubt that he agreed that he was the messianic King. But he did not interpret messianic kingship as most of his contemporaries did. He did not view it in terms of armies and battles and conquests. He saw it in terms of peace and love and compassion. Riding on an ass was important. The mention of the prophecy that was fulfilled right at the beginning of this incident (and not after Matthew has related what happened) may be meant to indicate that Jesus consciously fulfilled the words of the prophet. This does not mean that the disciples understood what Jesus was doing; John explicitly tells us that they did not until Jesus was "glorified" (John 12:16). But Jesus knew what he was about, and his action proclaimed boldly to all who had eyes to see that Jesus was indeed the Messiah, but a Messiah of a very different stamp from any that the deliriously happy crowds had imagined.

6-7. The disciples did as they had been instructed. They went off and got the donkey. Matthew sees a literal fulfilment of the prophecy, which speaks of *an ass* and also of *a colt*.[8] It seems likely that the prophet was speaking of one animal but refers to it twice, varying his description the second time.[9] Matthew can scarcely mean that Jesus sat on two animals; he is simply saying that Jesus fulfilled all that the prophet had foretold.

---

7. Our translation would perhaps lead us to think that Zechariah was talking of two animals, but his Hebrew parallelism means that he was speaking of one animal that he first describes as "an ass" and then as "a colt, the foal of a beast of burden" ("Only one animal is intended," Joyce G. Baldwin, *Haggai, Zechariah, Malachi* [London, 1972], p. 166). Nixon comments, "it may be assumed that he mentions the mother because she would be needed to calm the colt in the crowd." "The sight of an unridden donkey colt accompanying its mother has remained common in Palestine up to modern times" (Gundry, p. 409). Ridderbos holds that Matthew did not add this touch to make his story agree with Zechariah 9:9, "Rather the colt apparently could only be taken if its mother went with it" (p. 380).

8. As indicated in n. 4 above, the word πῶλος means "a foal, colt." ὑποζύγιος literally means "under a yoke"; it signified a beast of burden of any sort, here obviously an ass.

9. Gundry discusses the passage in *Use of the OT*, pp. 197-99.

Some scholars say that Matthew has misunderstood Zechariah and thus introduces two animals, but it borders on impertinence to suggest that Matthew, of all people, should not be able to discern the force of Hebrew parallelism. Moreover, the writer came from a culture that knew more about riding on asses than do modern New Testament scholars — people actually rode asses in those days. Mark tells us that the animal had never been ridden (Mark 11:2), and Matthew may be indicating that it was still with its mother; if so, it would explain the two animals, for the mother's presence would help to calm the colt being ridden for the first time, and that in the middle of a noisy demonstration. Before that, though, the disciples put their cloaks[10] on the ass to serve as a saddle; then Jesus sat on the animal. *He sat on them* means, of course, that he sat on the cloaks, not the animals; it is not easy to see why some commentators affirm so dogmatically that Matthew is speaking of the impossible situation of sitting on two animals; as Plummer puts it, "the Evangelist credits his readers with common sense. The sarcasm of Strauss is misplaced" (p. 286). Tasker similarly warns against "unintelligent exposition. The authors of Scripture did not write nonsense, and Jesus did not ride on two animals at once!" (p. 198). Matthew does not actually say that Jesus rode the animal into Jerusalem, but that is clearly what he meant.

8. Matthew often refers to the crowds that were found around Jesus, and frequently he has the plural. On this occasion he has an expression for *the great crowd* that he uses nowhere else.[11] The people then *spread their cloaks on the road,* clearly to make a kind of ceremonial carpet over which the King should ride (cf. 2 Kings 9:13). The thought will be the same when others *cut branches from the trees* and spread them on the road. Both groups were concerned to do honor to Jesus and welcome him into the city.[12]

9. Matthew goes on to the acclamations that were a feature of the excitement. He speaks of two crowds, one ahead of Jesus and one behind. The one will doubtless be pilgrims going up to Jerusalem for the Passover (whose enthusiasm was perhaps generated because they had heard his teaching and seen his miracles in Galilee), and the other is probably mainly local, those who lived in the capital city and its environs (and who had been there when Jesus raised Lazarus from the dead or had heard of it). Characteristically Matthew has the plural form *crowds* for both. His verb *were shouting* is in the imperfect tense, which indicates that the shouting kept on

---

10. ἱμάτιον is often used, especially in the plural for clothes in general, but there is no reasonable doubt that in this passage it is used in the strict sense of the outer garment, the cloak.

11. ὁ πλεῖστος ὄχλος. Strictly πλεῖστος is the superlative of πολύς and means "most." It signifies a very large crowd. In employing the unusual expression perhaps Matthew wants to indicate that it was the largest crowd.

12. John tells us that palm branches were used (John 12:13), and these seem to have been associated with celebrations of victory (1 Macc. 13:51; 2 Macc. 10:7). The people may well have been greeting Jesus as a national liberator.

for quite some time. The picture we get is one of great excitement. Evidently there were many Galileans who had thought of Jesus as the Messiah and were disappointed that in his own area he made no public declaration of who he was and of his determination to establish a kingdom that would throw the mighty Romans out of the land. But they had heard his teaching and they had seen him do miracles. As a result they had hoped that he would proclaim himself King, and they were prepared to follow him if he did. Now they thought he was going to fulfil their hopes, and they were ecstatic at the prospect. They took no notice of the significance of the lowly animal on which he was riding nor of the prophecy he was fulfilling.

The crowd shouted, "Hosanna[13] to the Son of David"; this must be understood as an expression of exultation and honor. Matthew has just told his readers that two blind men used the title "Son of David," and we must see the same messianic significance here. The crowds were exultant that Jesus was symbolically declaring his messiahship (and they took insufficient notice of the significance of his riding on a donkey).

They follow this with, "blessed is he who comes in the name of the Lord" (cf. Ps. 118:26).[14] To come "in the name" of anyone was to come in some sense representing him and to come in order to set forward his purposes. The crowds proclaim Jesus as God's representative, one who would set forward the divine purpose. Luke and John both include "the king" in this part of the crowd's cry, and although Matthew does not use the expression, it is implied. It was because they foresaw a Galilean King that the crowd of pilgrims got so excited. They cried "Hosanna" once again, and this time added "in the highest."[15] It is an enthusiastic cry and probably means that Jesus is to be praised everywhere, right up to heaven itself.

13. This appears to be a transliteration of the Hebrew הוֹשִׁיעָה נָּא or perhaps of its Aramaic equivalent, both of which are strong appeals to hear. The expression occurs in Psalm 118:25, where it is usually translated "Save now" or the like. Because we do not find the Greek form ὡσαννά in LXX, some interpreters suggest that it was coined by the Christians (e.g., Edwin D. Freed, *Old Testament Quotations in the Gospel of John* [Leiden, 1965], pp. 71-72). Our problem is that here it is clearly an acclamation, whereas the form of the word (and its use in the Old Testament) would lead us to expect it to be a petition (*AB* has "O Son of David" and comments, "a cry to the anointed king for deliverance"). Of course we might understand it as a prayer addressed to Jesus, asking him to save the people; but this would face the difficulty of the addition *in the highest*. It could be a prayer asking God to save Jesus (cf. "God save the King"), but the same objection could be raised. It is not unlikely that the term had come to be used conventionally, as an acclamation, and that people who used it had no clear meaning in mind other than that of generally giving honor. Augustine thought it indicated "rather a state of mind than having any positive significance" (*Homilies on the Gospel of John* 51.2 [NPNF, 1st ser., VII], p. 283). Or, as J. A. Fitzmyer says, it is "a spontaneous cry of greeting or a cry of homage" (G. F. Hawthorne and O. Betz, eds., *Tradition and Interpretation in the New Testament* [Grand Rapids, 1987], p. 115).

14. Turner cites κυρίου here as an example of the omission of the article with what comes near to being a proper noun (M, III, p. 174).

15. ὕψιστος is a superlative that lacks a positive. Matthew uses it only here (Luke has it 7 times). It is a somewhat poetic word and may be used of heaven or of God himself (Mark 5:7).

10. The acclamation had evidently started some distance from Jerusalem as the procession wound its way to the city. The noisy group attracted so much attention that *the whole city was stirred up* (cf. 2:3).[16] Though a large crowd was evidently involved, Matthew concentrates his attention on Jesus and says that *he* entered the city. And, of course, the Jerusalem mob was interested in the question, *"Who is this?"* Jesus had been in the capital city a number of times (as John in particular makes clear). But clearly Jesus was not as well known in that city as he was among the Galilean pilgrims. Those who made their homes in the metropolis would tend to take little notice of a "prophet" from the remote countryside even if he visited their city from time to time.

11. The crowds of pilgrims were ready to respond, and they spoke of their hero as *"the prophet Jesus."* They may have meant the great prophet like Moses who was to arise in the last time (Deut. 18:15), and that this prophet was Jesus. The Twelve knew more than this, for Peter had saluted Jesus as "the Christ, the Son of the living God" (16:16); some of those outside the inner circle probably knew about this, but the crowds in general would not have known. For them *prophet* was the highest accolade they could give, and they gave it cheerfully. And probably with some local pride they added that he was *"from Nazareth of Galilee."* Most of them did not come from Nazareth, but most did come from Galilee, and for them the Galilean prophet was a most important figure. It is interesting that they use this designation, for Jesus had left Nazareth before he began his public ministry and as far back as 4:13 Matthew has said that he left his native village and came and lived in Capernaum. But the place of one's birth is always important, and clearly the crowd associated Jesus with Nazareth. That was the place that spontaneously came to their lips when they were asked who Jesus was. It is worth noting that it was the crowd's view that Jesus was a prophet who would presently save him from being arrested (v. 46).

2. The Cleansing of the Temple, 21:12-17

> *12And Jesus entered the temple and threw out all who sold and bought in the temple, and he overturned the tables of the money changers and the seats of those who sold the doves. 13And he says to them, "It stands written, 'My house shall be called a house of prayer'; but you are making it a robbers' cave."*
>
> *14And blind and lame people came to him in the temple, and he healed them. 15But when the high priests and the scribes saw the wonderful things that he did and the boys who were crying out in the temple and saying,*

---

16. σείω is a strong and vivid word; it may be used of earthquakes (cf. 27:51; Heb. 12:26; we get our word "seismic" from it). Matthew is the only one of the Gospel writers to use the verb.

"Hosanna to the Son of David," they were indignant, 16*and they said to him, "Do you hear what these are saying?" But Jesus says to them, "Yes. Did you never read, 'Out of the mouth of infants and those giving suck you have brought perfect praise'?"* 17*And he left them and went outside the city to Bethany, and he lodged there.*

All three Synoptists have this story of Jesus driving the traders from the temple precincts at this point, the end of his public ministry, whereas John has a similar story at the beginning (John 2:13-17). It is perhaps significant that in both traditions the temple cleansing comes at the beginning of Jesus' first visit to Jerusalem. It is usually assumed that the action took place once only, and argument centers on whether John or the Synoptists have it in its correct place. But against this are the many differences. First, there is the fact that John has the story in a large block of non-Synoptic matter (in John 1–5 nothing occurs in the Synoptic Gospels except the ministry of John the Baptist, and this is so different that there is no question of dependence either way). Then there are the many differences in the narrative. John has a reference to oxen and sheep and to a whip made of cords, none of which is in the Synoptists. And where they are talking about the same thing, the words are mostly different: the word for *money changers* is different (though in a second reference John also has the Synoptic word), as is that for *overturned*.17 John speaks of the money as being poured out and says that Jesus commanded the traders to take their things away, while none of the Synoptists mentions this. The Synoptists all tell us that Jesus quoted Isaiah 56:7, but John does not say that he cited Scripture at this point. He does, however, say that the disciples remembered the words, "Zeal for your house will eat me up" (Ps. 69:9), which is not found in any of the Synoptic accounts. There are other differences from Mark in parts of the story that Matthew does not reproduce. So many differences in a very short narrative make it unlikely that the Synoptists and John are describing the same event. And we must bear in mind that the Synoptists omit the whole of Jesus' early ministry in Jerusalem. There seems to be no good reason why they should take this one solitary incident from those days and include it in their accounts as far away from its rightful place as possible. We should also bear in mind that if Jesus did throw the traders out in the early part of his ministry, it is not at all unlikely that they would return in due course. Nor that Jesus should repeat his action.18

17. For *money changers* Matthew has κολλυβιστής (from κόλλυβος, a small coin charged as a fee for exchanging money) while John has κερματιστής (John has Matthew's word in v. 15) from κερματίζω, "to cut small"; it strictly means someone who changes large money into small. Matthew's word for *overturned* is κατέστρεψεν, John's is ἀνέτρεψεν.

18. Diétrich comments, "The violence of this scene often shocks gentle spirits," but she also says, "Let us be thankful that the Gospels have preserved this story for us. Gentleness does not exclude firmness, and love sometimes demands the most unyielding severity."

We often put all our emphasis on "cleansing" and do not make so much of the fact that it was the "temple" to which Jesus went. France says of our usual description "the cleansing of the temple" that it "misses much of the significance of this event. It is the sequel to and culmination of the deliberately symbolic entry to the city; we see now how the Messiah stakes his claim in the central shrine of his people." It is important that Jesus came to the temple and acted there as one who had authority, even though this greatly displeased those who were responsible for the day-to-day administration of the place of worship.

12. It is usually assumed that Matthew is saying that the cleansing of the temple took place on the same day as the triumphal entry. But the fact is that this Evangelist simply omits any note of time. He does not indicate when this took place (which, of course, is the case also with the cursing of the barren fig tree, the next incident that he relates). He simply tells us that Jesus *entered the temple*, which, of course, means that he entered the temple precincts. The temple contained the court of the Gentiles (that area beyond which Gentiles could not go), the court of the women (beyond which women could not go), the court of Israel (beyond which laymen could not go), the sanctuary (beyond which priests could not go), and the holy of holies. The traders would have been at work in the outermost court. The money changers performed a useful, even a necessary function because worshipers came with a variety of coinage. Many commentators say that they had to change the money because so many coins bore the emperor's image or a heathen symbol of some sort, but this overlooks the fact that offerings were required to be made in Tyrian coinage (*Bek.* 8:7). No reason is given for this, but it is not hard to conjecture that it was because Tyrian coins were so reliable: the men of Tyre were traders, and they insisted that their coins should be of the correct weight and that they should have the right amount of silver or gold in them. Whether that was the reason or not, worshipers had to make their offerings in Tyrian currency, and the money changers performed a necessary function. So did the sellers of sacrificial animals and birds. It was not practicable for people coming from all over the Roman world to bring their beasts or birds with them. If they were to offer sacrifice, there had to be some place where they could purchase them. But the point is that that place did not have to be within the temple precincts, and it is to this that Jesus was objecting. So he *threw out* the traders,[19] and *overturned the tables* so necessary to the money changers and *the seats* of the dove sellers. This effectively stopped the trading and brought about the fulfilment of Zechariah's prophecy that a day would come when "there shall no longer be a trader in the house of the LORD of hosts" (Zech. 14:21), though Matthew does not draw attention to this particular fulfilment of prophecy. It is often suggested that

19. One article covers both πωλοῦντας and ἀγοράζοντας; Matthew is not making a distinction between them, but regarding them as one company of traders.

Jesus was protesting against dishonest trading practices. That such practices did at times exist[20] and that Jesus would have opposed them is beyond doubt, but Matthew is describing a protest against the practice itself, against the buyers as well as the sellers. It was wrong for this to go on in the temple precincts. That he accomplished this single-handedly seems to imply that he had a mighty ally in the consciences of the traders. Deep down they knew that what they were doing was not right.

13. Jesus justified what he had done and gave his reason for doing it with a citation of Scripture (Isa. 56:7; the *robber's cave* is a description from Jer. 7:11). The temple was meant as a place of worship;[21] Matthew omits the words "for all the nations" (as does Luke; Mark includes them). The omission fastens attention on the importance of prayer (and since the Gentiles could go no further than the outermost part of the temple precincts, the court of the Gentiles was important). But using the outer court for trading meant that if a Gentile came to the temple to pray, the only place he could do it was in the middle of a busy bazaar. And while Israelites could go into the inner courts, they had to pass through the trading section there, and there is little doubt that the noise from the traders would penetrate the inner courts enough to interfere with quiet worship. The traders had put profit above worship (McNeile, "the Lord does not speak of noise and distraction, but wickedness"). And when Jesus speaks of *a robbers' cave*,[22] he indicates not only that they were trading in the wrong place, but that they were trading dishonestly.[23] They were bringing their sharp practices into the holy precincts.

14. Mark and Luke end their treatment of Jesus in the temple with the expulsion of the traders, but Matthew goes on to speak of his further contact with some of the people there. At this point this Evangelist is apparently not greatly concerned with chronology but with giving a short account of some important facts. Mark says that Jesus looked around the temple and went out of the city. On the following morning as he came from Bethany he cursed the fruitless fig tree before going on to drive the traders from the temple. The next day he and the disciples saw the fig tree withered. Matthew telescopes much of this. He has the facts but is not

20. The Mishnah refers, for example, to an occasion when Simeon ben Gamaliel found a pair of doves being sold for a golden denar (worth twenty-five silver denars). He took vigorous action, with the result that "the same day the price of a pair of doves stood at a quarter-*denar* each" (*Ker.* 1:7).

21. "It should be noted moreover that the Prophet uses the word prayer for the whole worship of God" (Calvin, III, p. 5; he refers to Ps. 50, "where God relates all the exercises of devotion to prayer").

22. σπήλαιον denotes a "cave" that may be used for any one of a variety of purposes. Thus it might be a tomb (John 11:38), or a place of refuge (Heb. 11:38: Rev. 6:15). Here there is no emphasis on a cave as such; it is simply a place where dishonest men might gather (*GNB*, "hideout").

23. ὑμεῖς is emphatic, "you, who listen to me"; Gundry notes that it "stands in terrifying isolation" (p. 412).

527

interested in precisely how much time elapsed between one incident and another. Now he notes that *blind and lame* people came to Jesus in the temple. Matthew says nothing about their requests for healing or any conversation Jesus may have had with them. At this point his interest is in the reaction of the Jewish leaders to what Jesus was doing, and he simply says that Jesus *healed them* (Matthew's last mention of Jesus healing). They were in need; he met that need. This stands in striking contrast to the attitude of the men of Qumran: the blind and the lame were explicitly excluded from their assembly (*The Messianic Rule* II, Vermes, p. 120), and when they went out to war these people were not to enter their camp (*The War Rule* VII, Vermes, p. 132).

15. The healings did not go unobserved, and Matthew proceeds to the reaction of *the high priests and the scribes.* Both terms indicate members of the group in question; Matthew is not talking here about a solemn session (as in 20:18) but about priestly and learned figures whom one might well expect to encounter in the temple. Until now Matthew has referred to the high priests only three times, but from this point they figure increasingly in his narrative, being mentioned 32 times from this point on. The high priests and the scribes, Matthew says, *saw the wonderful things*[24] *that he did,* evidently the healings just spoken of. Matthew adds that there were *boys*[25] acclaiming Jesus. Once again we notice Jesus' attraction for little children; it is significant that on a day of such high drama Jesus should find time for children. They were using the acclamation *"Hosanna"* (see on v. 9) and speaking of Jesus as *"the Son of David."* We have seen that this was a messianic term (see on 1:1); it is unlikely that the children understood all that the term signified for their elders. But the priestly and academic people knew what it meant, and it annoyed them that children, however innocently, were using such a term for Jesus. In any case, in the usages of the time such exalted personages would not have cared greatly for children. So it does not surprise us that they *were indignant.* It was bad enough to have the enthusiasm of the crowds at Jesus' entry to the city, but it was worse to have him invade the temple precincts (their own special territory) and destroy a lucrative source of income, and it was intolerable that there, in the temple courts, he was doing his miracles and now being acclaimed by children (who knew no better!) in messianic terms.

16. They asked Jesus whether he heard what the boys were saying. Their implication is that if he did, he, being a religious teacher of sorts, ought to put a prompt stop to it. It is not without its interest that they picked on the easiest target they could find — little children. They had no criticism of the unholy traders who defiled the sacred place, but they

24. θαυμάσιος is the adjective of θαῦμα, "a wonder"; it is found only here in the New Testament. It indicates that what Jesus had been doing was miraculous.
25. τοὺς παῖδας is masculine; Matthew could have used τὰ παιδία, as in 18:3; 19:14, etc.

objected to the praises of children. *But* has adversative force; Matthew sets Jesus over against them. He agrees that he has heard the boys, but then questions the leaders about their knowledge of Scripture. *"Did you never read"* means, of course, "read in Scripture," and Jesus goes on to refer them to Psalm 8:2. The passage is cited from the Greek version, which indicates that the praise of God from little children is perfect praise.[26] God does not need the choirs of mighty temples or the gifts of outstanding musicians (though, of course, he accepts these when offered in the spirit of devotion and lowliness). The praise of little ones is perfect praise. The terms Jesus chooses points to the youngest children;[27] even these offer worthwhile praise.

17. That ended the incident. After this memorable day, Matthew says, Jesus *left them* and went off to Bethany. That was the village in which his friends Mary, Martha, and Lazarus lived. The probability is that he lodged with them, though, of course, we cannot be sure of this. Luke tells us that through these days Jesus taught in the temple by day but at night lodged on the Mount of Olives (Luke 21:37). This may mean that he bivouacked there, or, since Bethany was in that area, he may have stayed with his friends. With the Twelve all there, it may well be that they could not all find room in a house and some may have camped out.[28]

3. The Fig Tree, 21:18-22

> [18]In the morning, as he returned to the city, he became hungry. [19]And when he saw a fig tree by the roadside, he went up to it and found nothing on it but leaves only; and he says to it, "No longer may there ever be fruit from you!" And at once the fig tree withered away. [20]And when the disciples saw this, they were astonished and said, "How did the fig tree wither away at once?" [21]And Jesus answered them, saying, "Truly I tell you, if you have faith and do not doubt, not only will you do what was done to the fig tree, but if you say to this mountain, 'Be taken up and be thrown into the sea,' it will happen. [22]And all things whatever that you ask in prayer, if you believe, you will receive."

Matthew shares the story of the fig tree with Mark, and as is usually the case his account is shorter. Thus Mark says that this happened on the

26. The Hebrew appears to mean that "by the mouth of children and infants God has erected a bulwark which is designed to silence his adversaries" (A. Weiser, *The Psalms* [London, 1962], p. 141).

27. νήπιος signifies "an infant," while θηλάζω indicates "to suckle, suck." In those days a child would often remain breast-fed for longer than with us. A mother addressed her son during the persecutions leading up to the Maccabean era in these terms: "I carried you nine months in my womb and suckled you (θηλάσασαν) for three years . . ." (2 Macc. 7:27).

28. The verb is αὐλίζομαι, which properly means "to lodge in a courtyard (αὐλή)" and thus "camp in the open." But the word was used simply of lodging, wherever one's bed might be. MM notes its use for the lodging of a wayfaring person.

day after the triumphal entry, that they "passed by" (coming from Bethany?), that it was not yet the time for figs, and that it was Peter who drew attention to the withered tree, none of which is in Matthew. Mark makes it clear that this happened on the day after the triumphal entry, but as we have seen, Matthew omits a good deal of information about chronology in this part of his book: he concentrates on what happened, not on when it took place. We should understand this story as an acted parable: the fig tree in leaf gave promise of fruit but produced none. The result was that it was accursed. Those who profess to be God's people but live unfruitful lives are warned.[29] This will have special relevance to the Jews of Jesus' day, who viewed themselves as the chosen people, as those to whom God had committed his law and as the servants of God in a way people of no other nation were. But they were not bringing forth fruit worthy of such a position.

18. *In the morning*[30] Jesus and his followers went back again into the city. Matthew tells us nothing about the mealtime habits of the little band, so we do not know what breakfast arrangements they had or even whether they had any breakfast. If they did, it could not have been much, for on his short walk to Jerusalem (less than two miles) Jesus *became hungry*. Matthew does not say anything about the dietetic state of the apostles, but it is not unlikely that if Jesus was hungry they were too. Matthew concentrates on Jesus.

19. Still omitting anything having to do with the disciples, Matthew tells us that Jesus saw *a fig tree by the roadside* (Mark says that it was at a distance, but Matthew leaves out unnecessary details; that it was *by the roadside* indicates that it was not part of anyone's property). When he came near the tree, he found no fruit *but leaves only*. This is unusual.[31] If a fig tree is in leaf, it is to be expected that it will be bearing figs. Until they are ripe the taste may not delight the gourmet, but the fruit is edible (Mark tells us that it was not the time of fruit as yet, so this is all that could be expected). The point here is that the tree gave every outward sign of bearing fruit but in fact bore none.[32] The tree "stood out because it was in

---

29. Hill thinks that this parable was "meant to be interpreted as a prophetic action prefiguring the judgment brought by the Messiah upon the Jewish nation and the strictness of Jewish religion, neither of which bore the fruit which by right was expected from them — they gave promise of fulfilment but in fact produced nothing!" Of the view that it is a dramatization of the parable in Luke 13:6-9 he says, "that story is governed by the theme of delay in judgment, whereas this miracle is concerned with immediate judgment."

30. πρωΐ means "early"; it points us to the next morning.

31. Cf. R. K. Harrison, "When the young leaves are appearing in spring, every fertile fig will have some *taksh* on it, even though the season for edible figs (Mk. 11:13, AV) has not arrived. When the leaves are fully developed the fruit ought to be mature also. But if a tree with leaves has no fruit, it will be barren for the entire season" (*ISBE*, II, p. 302; he explains *taksh* as "underdeveloped fruit" that nevertheless "is often gathered for sale in the markets").

32. W. E. Shewell-Cooper comments, "the fruit often starts to be ready before the leaves and this is especially true in the case of an early variety. Anyway, our Lord who made the

leaf. Its leaves advertised that it was bearing, but the advertisement was false" (Carson). Unusually Jesus addressed the tree and pronounced a sentence: the tree will *no longer*[33] bear fruit, not forever.[34] Matthew tells us that the fig tree *at once withered away.* There is a problem in that Mark tells us that Jesus and the little band went on their way and that it was the next morning when they found the fig tree withered away. But, as we have seen, in this part of his narrative Matthew is very concise and specifically ignores chronology. He gives no indication of the time when the cleansing of the temple took place,[35] nor of that when the blind and the lame came to him in the temple and were healed, nor when Jesus went to Bethany, nor when he came to the fig tree (other than that it was "early"). By narrating the withering of the tree immediately after Jesus spoke, Matthew avoids another note of time and keeps this section of his narrative short.[36]

20. Not unnaturally the disciples *were astonished*[37] at this (Mark does not mention their astonishment; he simply says that Peter drew attention to the tree). They asked Jesus how it happened, unless we take the words as an exclamation, "How the fig tree withered at once!" Either way of taking the Greek is possible. Clearly the disciples were impressed by the miracle.

21. Matthew has been abbreviating, but he makes this part of his narrative longer than that in Mark (Mark has no more than, "He says to them, 'Have faith in God,'" before going on to the words about the mountain). The words are important and are introduced with the emphatic, *"Truly I tell you"* (see on 5:18). Jesus is telling his followers about the importance of trust; he puts the truth positively, *"if you have faith,"* and then negatively, *"and do not doubt."* Trust in God is stressed throughout the New Testament ("faith" is mentioned 243 times and the verb "to believe" 241 times); it is often used of a quality of life that brings salvation, serenity, and the like, but here it is related to what the disciple can accom-

---

trees would certainly know whether this particular type should have been fruiting or not. He certainly would not have been looking for the fruits long before their proper time" (*Plants and Fruits of the Bible* [London, 1962], p. 26).

33. μηκέτι, "no more," "no longer," here only in Matthew. Burton points out that "the Imperative Subjunctive" is "rare in the third person" (167).

34. εἰς τὸν αἰῶνα is a not uncommon expression, but Matthew has it only here (and as a v.l. in 6:13). John has it 12 times.

35. On which Stonehouse comments, "If it be granted that Matthew does not fix the exact point after the entry when the temple was cleansed, one will be prepared to recognize that the position of the story of the cursing of the fig tree, following the cleansing of the temple, does not necessarily fix its order of occurrence" (*Witness*, p. 161).

36. Ridderbos comments on the withering of the tree "immediately": "This does not mean that it became barren at once, but merely that it began to wilt from that moment on" (p. 390). The word "is associated with delay for a month" (MM), so we cannot press it. Robinson points out that Mark's account "leaves open the possibility that the words of Jesus have been misunderstood, and that he saw as he looked at the tree that it was soon to die." Matthew leaves no such misunderstanding possible.

37. Matthew has θαυμάζω 7 times; Mark has it 4 times, and only one of these refers to astonishment at a miracle.

plish. In human strength, very little can be done, but when the disciple trusts God wholeheartedly and without doubting, then great things are possible. Jesus says that in that case the disciples would do not only *what was done to the fig tree*, but they would also be able to move mountains. He puts it graphically, picturing the disciple as speaking to *this mountain* (apparently the Mount of Olives), commanding it to be raised up and be thrown into the sea, with the result that the command would be obeyed. Jesus had earlier said much the same thing in slightly different words (17:20; see the note there for Jewish use of the expression), and the meaning here, as there, will be metaphorical. There is no record of any disciple ever moving a literal, physical mountain; for that matter, Jesus himself is not said ever to have done such a pointless thing. But throughout the history of the Christian church mountainous difficulties have often been removed when people have prayed in faith. There can be no doubt that it is this to which Jesus is referring.

22. There is a very similar promise, and again it is related to faith. This time, however, Jesus is not referring to moving mountains but to making requests. Prayer is concerned with a good deal more than making requests of God, but that is certainly part of what it means. Jesus encourages his followers to make their requests in faith (*"if you believe"*), and his *"all things whatever"*[38] makes the promise limitless in the possibilities it opens up. The proviso *"if you believe"* excludes the bringing of purely selfish requests, for they are no part of the outworking of faith. But Jesus is saying that the believer who looks to God for anything at all in the path of Christian service can be confident of an answer to prayer: *"you will receive."*

4. The Question of Authority, 21:23-27

23And when he had come into the temple, the high priests and the elders of the people approached him as he was teaching and said, "By what authority are you doing these things? And who gave you this authority?" 24But Jesus answered them, saying, "I, too, will ask you one question, which if you tell me, I, too, will tell you by what authority I do these things. 25The baptism of John: where did it come from? From heaven or from men?" But they reasoned among themselves: "If we say, 'From heaven,' he will say to us, 'Then why did you not believe him?' 26But if we say, 'From men,' we are afraid of the crowd; for they all hold John to be a prophet." 27And they answered Jesus, saying, "We do not know." He also said to them, "Neither do I tell you by what authority I do these things."

The question of proper authority was important for the Jews of the day. They held that they were the people of God, and they therefore

38. πάντα ὅσα ἂν opens the door to its widest extent; nothing is excluded.

detested their Roman overlords. Of necessity they submitted to them, but they did not believe that the Romans had the right to govern them. They were God's own people, and their human lords were God's high priest and those associated with him in the appointed assemblies, the great Sanhedrin and the lesser councils throughout the land. People like John the Baptist and Jesus presented problems because they did not fit into this picture. They were not like the Romans, who ruled unjustly but had the military backing that enforced their demands. And they were not like the high priests and other officials, who because of their official position were regarded as authoritative persons by official Judaism. What authority, then, did they have?

It was also a day when originality was not highly prized. In the rabbinic schools it was necessary to cite some previous rabbi if one wished to obtain a hearing. Authority was always clothed with some external justification. But Jesus simply appeared and taught. The Jewish authorities saw no justification for him to do this. He had no authority that they could discern, and they were the people who authorized teachers. So they asked him for his credentials.

23. Once more Matthew has dispensed with any indication of when the incident he is about to narrate took place. He simply locates it when Jesus *had come into the temple.* It is natural to hold that it followed on from the story of the fig tree, but we are left to deduce this; Matthew does not say so. But the temple courts were the natural place for teaching to take place, and Matthew is about to tell us something of the teaching Jesus gave in Jerusalem, so it was only to be expected that Jesus would make his way to the temple. There *the high priests and the elders of the people* encountered him.[39] For *high priests* see on 2:4; the term often included others than the reigning high priest, but it is not clear how many others and precisely who. In this context it is plain that people of the high-priestly family and party are meant, men who were committed to upholding the status quo in the temple and, as far as they could, elsewhere as well. *The elders* might denote any senior citizens, but in a context like this the meaning will be eminent laymen, probably those who held membership in the Sanhedrin. They would have been committed to much the same positions as those held by the high priests. The separate articles with the two groups may mean that the men came from two significant classes of Jews. Luke's inclusion of "the scribes" makes it seem like an official delegation from the Sanhedrin, and that may be Matthew's meaning (G. Bornkamm holds that Matthew prefers to refer to the Sanhedrin in this way, without mention of the scribes, *TDNT*, VI, p. 659, n. 46). As they approached him, Jesus *was teaching,* but they apparently were not greatly concerned at interrupting him. For that matter, he was probably not greatly

---

39. For προσέρχομαι see on 4:3. Matthew is not describing a chance meeting, but a deliberate confrontation of Jesus.

concerned at being interrupted; his teaching would have been very informal. Luke says that he was teaching "and evangelizing," "preaching the
gospel," that is, bringing God's good news to the people around him.

The men come with a twofold question about authority. They ask first,
"By what authority are you doing these things?" and second, *"who gave you this
authority?"* They do not explain what they mean by *"these things."* The
expression is very general and may cover the triumphal entry, the driving
out of the traders, and the healings in the temple. Certainly these were
significant happenings, and in the view of the questioners they should not
be done without authority of some kind. What authority?[40] The groups
associated with the questioners had not given Jesus any authority, so they
are intrigued. Their second question implies that nobody could assume
authority. There had to be some superior person or institution that gave
anyone the authority to act in ways like those Jesus had just demonstrated.

24. The questioners doubtless thought of themselves as taking action
from a position of strength. Jesus must, they would have reasoned, cite
some source of authority, and since they represented temple authority, it
could not be any authority that justified him in taking action in the way
he did in the place he used. Any human authority he claimed must necessarily be inferior. And if he claimed to have God's authority, they would
be able to accuse him of blasphemy. But Jesus was not disposed to answer
along the lines they expected. He doubtless could have cited his authority,
but that would have led to endless argument since his opponents would
not have conceded that he had the authority he claimed. So Jesus
countered with just one question of his own, and promised to answer their
two questions if they would first answer his.[41] His use of *"these things"*
shows that he understood what the questioners meant by this expression
even though they have not defined it.

25. *"The baptism of John,"* he says, and leaves the expression without
syntactical connections. It stands there in lonely isolation, thus marking it
out as something he views as significant and important. He asks where it
came from and suggests two possibilities: *"From heaven"* and *"from men."*
This was not a red herring to lead them away from their questions, for if they
had answered it honestly they would have had the answer to their own since
John had borne witness to Jesus. But they found the question a difficult one
to answer. They do not seem to have been concerned with the truth or
otherwise of either of Jesus' alternatives. Their reasoning covers the consequences of each of the possible answers, and they give no attention
whatever to the actual source of John's baptism. They reasoned *among
themselves;* this was not for public hearing. They saw straightaway that if

---

40. ποῖος often has very little qualitative force in the New Testament, but Chamberlain
finds it here: "By what sort of authority do you do these things?" (p. 209).

41. Twice Jesus employs the emphatic κἀγώ: "You have asked questions, *and I, too,* will
ask one. You answer, *and I, too,* will answer."

they said, *"From heaven,"* they had lost their case. Jesus would immediately ask why they did not believe him; and, of course, had they believed him they would not have been engaging in the inquisition that was their present task. They would have become followers of Jesus. That was unthinkable for these men, so there was no trouble in rejecting that as a possible answer.

26. The alternative was to say, *"From men,"* but when they examined the consequences of such an answer they immediately realized that it was one that was impossible for them to give. John the Baptist had made a profound impression on a large segment of Judaism. There had been no prophet in the land for centuries, and John had come in the tradition of the ancient prophets, calling everyone back to repentance and the seeking of forgiveness of all their sins. Many had responded, and it is clear that even those who did not do this were impressed by the man. Almost everyone would have agreed that he was a prophet, and how could anyone speak of a martyred prophet as *"from men"?* To make such a statement would be to provoke a riot. They were afraid of the consequences of such a bold rejection of the common opinion.

27. The inevitable answer was: *"We do not know."* It was not that they were ignorant of what was involved, nor that they did not have a strong opinion of their own about John. It was that neither answer was practical politics. Jesus had challenged them, and they had declined the challenge.[42] So Jesus declined to tell them anything about his authority. We ought not to think that he was evading the question, or that he was uncertain of the source of his authority. He knew very well, and in proper circumstances he would answer. But these were men who had been asked a question to which they knew the answer, but who refused to give it because they were afraid of the consequences. Why should a teacher like Jesus answer the loaded questions of men like these?

B. Teaching in Parables, 21:28–22:14

Matthew proceeds to narrate three parables that Jesus taught. He has given a number in the earlier part of his Gospel, and as he comes to the end of Jesus' public ministry he puts before his readers further examples of Jesus' skill in telling such stories.

1. The Parable of the Two Sons, 21:28-32

28*"But what do you think? A man had two sons, and he went to the first and said, 'Son, go work today in the vineyard.'* 29*But he answered, saying,*

---

42. "Actually this is no escape from their dilemma, for they thereby confess incompetence to judge one who except for Jesus has been the most prominent preacher of their day. If they cannot tell whether God was at work in John the Baptist, they are not competent to question and judge Jesus" (Filson, p. 226).

'I won't,' but afterward he changed his mind and went off. [30]*And coming to the other, he said the same thing. But he said, 'I will, sir,' and yet he did not go.* [31]*Which of the two did the will of his father?" They say, "The first." Jesus says to them, "Truly I tell you that the tax collectors and the harlots go into the kingdom of God before you.* [32]*For John came to you in the path of righteousness, and you did not believe him; but the tax collectors and the harlots did believe him; but you, when you had seen this, did not repent afterward so as to believe him."*

This homely parable (found in Matthew only) brings out the importance of doing what is right and not merely talking about it. It leads naturally enough into a castigation of those who had heard John but had not obeyed him. There are some confusing textual variants, with three main groups of MSS.[43] One has the first son saying "I won't" but changing his mind and going, with the second saying "I will" and doing nothing (so ℵ* C* K W etc.). A second reverses the order of the two, with the first agreeing to go but not going and the second refusing but then changing his mind and going (B Θ 700 etc.; this is supported by urging that if the first son went there was no need for the second to go, but this is not conclusive since we do not know how much work there was to do). The third group has the first son saying "I won't" but in the end going, and the second saying "I will" but not going; but in this group the answer to the question "Which did the will of the father?" is "the second" (D some OL syrˢ). We can surely dismiss the third group as making nonsense of the parable,[44] but it matters little which of the first two we accept. With either of them the general sense of the parable is clear: it is not enough to say "I will"; we must put our good intentions into effect.

28. Jesus begins this parable by inviting his listeners to put on their thinking caps. This follows very naturally on the preceding paragraph, but Matthew gives no indication as to whether the parable was told immediately after the incident of the question about Jesus' authority or on some other occasion. Jesus goes on to speak of a man with two sons who came to the first (often understood as the elder) and said, *"Son,*[45] *go*

---

43. The variants are discussed in Metzger, pp. 55-56.

44. One way of making sense of it would be to regard verbal rejection of authority as worse than actual disobedience. There is a story in *Exodus Rabbah* 27.9 of a man entrusting a field to others. Several refused to have it, but one accepted it, agreeing to the condition that he should till it. But when he got the field, he did not do so. This is likened to Israel accepting the law when the other nations would not. The fact that the nation did not keep the law as it should did not alter the fact that it accepted it, which was more than any other nation did. So here, the son at least agreed to do something even if he did not live up to his undertaking. But this view comes up against the fact that the other son did indeed go and (presumably) do what was required.

45. τέχνον denotes a child (of either sex), but the context can make it clear whether it is a male or female child; clearly the one who was asked to work in the vineyard was a boy. The vocative may be used "as an affectionate address to a son" (BAGD, 1.a.β).

work today in the vineyard." "The" vineyard is, of course, the one belonging to the speaker. He does not specify what he wants done with the vines, but that would be plain enough to any son of the house, who would know what was required.

29. Most uncharacteristically for a son in first-century Palestine, this lad gave an unqualified refusal. "I do not will" is the thrust of his reply. But that is not the whole story, for he *changed his mind* (the word is sometimes used in the sense "repent," a nuance that may not be out of mind in a parable of this kind). Jesus does not say that this son actually did the required work in the vineyard, but clearly the fact that he *went off,* following the reference to the change of mind, means that this is what he did.

30. Exactly the opposite is true of the other son. The father came to him and *said the same thing.* It cannot be argued that some difference in the instructions brought about different results. The command was the same both times. But if the command was the same, the response was very different. This son was quite agreeable with his *"I will, sir."*[46] But his actions did not match his politeness. Despite his agreement[47] he stayed away from the vineyard. His words were good, but his actions did not match his words.

31. Jesus asked his hearers who did the will of the father (and incidentally we see him involving his audience in a very effective way of teaching). There could, of course, be only one answer (despite the scribes, who produced the variant reading "the second"!), and they gave it. Cf. France, "what counts is not promise but performance." Jesus proceeded to apply his little parable to the contemporary situation. He introduced it with the emphatic *"Truly I tell you"* that so often opens his very serious statements, and went on to refer to *"the tax collectors and the harlots,"* descriptions that were almost proverbial for wicked people outside the number of true servants of God (though it is unusual to find these two linked in this way). The whole manner of life of such people cut them off from the kind of religious observance that was the heart of religion for people like the Pharisees. Quite often, of course, these rejects from polite society lived up to the worst their detractors expected from them. But this was not inevitable, as the numbers of such people who accepted Jesus' teaching showed. And now he says that these people *"go into the kingdom of God before you."*[48] This does not mean that ethical considerations do not apply and that the worst of sinners keep on with the worst of their sins in the kingdom. It means that sinners like official Judaism's outcasts could

46. His ἐγώ, used without a verb, indicates an affirmation of the instruction just given: "I will" or "Yes"; it is a polite acceptance of the command. κύριε is a respectful form of address (cf. 7:21).

47. καί is used in the sense of καίτοι, "and yet."

48. "Comparison = exclusion may be contained in the verb, or rather its preposition, Mt 21:31 προάγουσιν ὑμᾶς '. . . go into the Kingdom, but you do not' " (BDF, 245a[3]).

respond to the message of the kingdom much more readily than sinners whose sins were cast in the conventional mode that brought no rebuke from the religious establishment.[49] *Go* means progress; it means that they left their gross and obvious sins for the sake of the kingdom. They entered the kingdom *before you*, which refers to the representatives of the high priests and elders of the people (v. 23). The conventionally religious who cause no scandal and go through the outward motions of religious observances can fail to respond to the demand for wholehearted repentance and complete dedication to the service of God that Jesus demanded. Matthew usually has "the kingdom of heaven," but here *the kingdom of God* (see the note on 12:28).

32. Jesus makes sure that there is no misunderstanding of his words by referring explicitly to the reactions of the people he has just mentioned to the preaching of John the Baptist. John *"came to you,"* he says; the Baptist's message was not something hidden and known only to the select few. It had been widely and publicly proclaimed; if John's locale had been in the wilderness it was not a hidden locale, and we are explicitly told that people from Jerusalem and all Judea as well as the region of the Jordan went out to him (3:5). Jesus' interrogators had known what John demanded all right. But they did not respond. They did not *believe*. People whom they despised, *the tax collectors and the harlots*, were more open to John's message. They *did believe him*, which means that they responded to his call for repentance and amended their whole way of living and of approach to God.[50] Clearly the change was evident, for Jesus says, *"you had seen this."* But even the evidence of what a true response to John's preaching could do in people's lives did not produce a change in the conventionally religious. They *did not repent afterward*, that is, after they had seen what repentance effected in the lives of those who responded to John; they did not believe John. Repentance and believing John are closely connected; had they produced the one they would have produced the other, but they produced neither.[51]

2. The Parable of the Tenants, 21:33-46

> [33]*"Listen to another parable. There was a householder who planted a vineyard, and put a fence around it, and dug a winepress in it, and built a tower, and let it out to vine growers, and went abroad. [34]When then the*

---

49. Chrysostom brings out the point by referring to a notorious harlot "from Phoenice" who was converted and transformed (p. 412).

50. It also seems to mean that John baptized repentant harlots. To admit women to such a religious rite would have been unusual among the Jews, and, of course, this attitude was carried further by the Christians (cf. Gal. 3:28).

51. Burton classifies τοῦ πιστεῦσαι as an "infinitive of result" and renders "did not even repent afterward, so as to believe him" (Burton, 398). Moulton says that this infinitive "gives rather the content than the purpose of μετεμελήθητε" (M, I, p. 216).

time of fruit bearing approached, he sent his slaves to the vine growers to receive his fruit. 35And the vine growers took his slaves; they beat one, and they killed another, and they stoned another. 36He sent again other slaves, more than the first, and they did the same to them. 37But last of all he sent his son to them, saying, 'They will respect my son.' 38But when the vine growers saw the son, they said among themselves, 'This is the heir; come on, let us kill him and take his inheritance.' 39And they took him, and threw him out of the vineyard, and killed him. 40When therefore the owner of the vineyard comes, what will he do to those vine growers?" 41They say to him, "He will bring those bad men to a bad end, and he will let out the vineyard to other vine growers who will pay him the fruits at the proper times." 42Jesus says to them, "Did you never read in the Scriptures, 'A stone which the builders rejected, this has become the head of the corner; from the Lord this came about, and it is astonishing in our eyes'? 43Therefore I tell you that the kingdom of God will be taken away from you, and it will be given to a nation that produces its fruits. 44And he who falls on this stone will be crushed; and whomever it falls on it will pulverize." 45And when the high priests and the Pharisees heard his parables, they recognized that he was speaking about them; 46and when they sought to arrest him, they were afraid of the crowds because they held him to be a prophet.

The second parable in the series underlines both the iniquity of the Jewish establishment and the peril in which they had placed themselves by their continuing refusal to walk in the ways of God. Jesus speaks of a man who let out a new vineyard to tenants and put up with an astonishing sequence of evil deeds until the culmination, when they killed his own son. This brought about a full and final punishment of the sinners. The warning to those who even as he spoke were plotting his death is clear.[52] The parable takes up a theme found in the Old Testament (e.g., Ps. 80:8-16; Isa. 5:1-7), and it has a considerable allegorical content. Thus the owner of the vineyard stands for God, the vineyard for Israel, the fruit for righteousness, the tenants for the nation's leaders, the slaves for the prophets, while the son, of course, is Jesus. Tasker remarks that in this parable "Jesus indirectly, but none the less certainly, teaches that He is the Messiah acting by divine authority and destined in obedience to the divine will to be slain outside the vineyard of Israel" (p. 204).[53]

33. Jesus introduces this parable with an invitation to hear it, and

---

52. Some view the parable as largely or wholly the creation of the church, but as Filson says, "The parable is not what the Apostolic Age would have produced. It offers no real doctrine of atonement or clear mention of the resurrection; its atmosphere is not post-Easter. It can best be understood as coming in essentials from Jesus" (p. 228).

53. "A parable like this shows how restrictive it would be to assume that a parable always has one point. The word 'parable' means 'a throwing together' for comparison. Very often there is one main point in the comparison, but there may well be more. In this case there clearly is" (M. Green, p. 206)

proceeds to refer to *a householder*[54] who *planted a vineyard.*[55] From the subsequent description and happenings it is clear that this was an investment, not a project in which the man planned to take a personal part. Vineyards were an important feature of first-century Palestinian life; Jesus speaks of a process that would have been well known to his audience. This was a new vineyard, set up on new land. Being new, it involved some uncertainty as to how well it would work out, but the householder did all that he should have done to ensure a good vineyard. He fenced it off, which would protect it from wild animals and the like. He *dug a winepress.* This meant two basins cut out of rock, or if out of soil, lined with rocks and sealed with plaster; one would have been lower than the other, and they would have been connected by a channel. The grapes were thrown into the upper basin and trodden under foot, with the result that the juice flowed into the lower where it began the process of fermentation. He also *built a tower,* which would enable a watchman to survey the vineyard and the surrounding terrain so that he could take action against marauders, human or animal.[56] Then he let the vineyard out to *vine growers.*[57] That he *went abroad* does not necessarily mean that he went to another country (though that is not unlikely), but it certainly indicates that he was at quite a distance from his new investment.

34. We do not know the terms under which the vineyard was let out to the tenants, but it would have been natural for the terms to include a payment at the time that the grapes were ripe. In a new vineyard there would not be very much yield until the fourth year and no great profit until the fifth. Vines take time to establish themselves and must be supported with stakes, trained, and pruned (the Mishnah provides that the owner and the tenants must share in the expenditure for the stakes, *B. Meṣ.* 9:1). It was important that the owner make clear his position as owner by sending to receive the agreed amounts at the stated times.[58] People could establish title to a vineyard if they could show that they had had undisputed possession of it for three years (Mishnah, *B. Bat.* 3:1). The owner was establishing his position by collecting his rent, even if it was no more than a nominal amount, during the years that the vineyard was

---

54. As in 13:52; 20:1 Matthew reinforces οἰκοδεσπότης with ἄνθρωπος, which is more or less equivalent to the indefinite pronoun.

55. The Mishnah tractate *Kil'ayim* has detailed regulations governing vineyards, specifying such matters as minimum size, spaces between rows, etc.

56. H. N. Richardson defines a watchtower as "A structure from which a certain area of land could be guarded." He says further, "In present-day Palestine watchtowers are usually round and may be as high as ten feet. Often they consist of two levels — a ground level, where there will be living quarters, and the top level, surrounded by a low wall, from which there is a good view of the entire field" (*IDB*, IV, p. 806). In biblical days it is likely that the tower would have been much like this.

57. γεωργός means someone who works the land, a farmer. But in this context it refers to those who are competent in working with grape vines, *vine growers.*

58. J. D. M. Derrett has an informative study of this parable (Derrett, pp. 286-312) in which he emphasizes that this had to be done so that the owner could establish his title.

being established. Indeed, the tenants might even claim that on balance he owed them money for such items as the purchase of stakes. The amount to be collected by the owner would not have been much, but it was important that it be collected, for unless this was done the people who were occupying the land and working it would be establishing a claim of their own to the land. So at *the time of fruit bearing*[59] he *sent slaves* to *receive his produce,* the agreed share of what the vineyard had produced.

35. Evidently the tenants had already decided that they were going to make the vineyard their own. The man who had set it all up was at a distance, and they may well have thought that if they gave him enough trouble he might let the vineyard go. Whether that was the reason or not, they made a start by ill-treating the slaves sent to collect the rent, beating,[60] killing, and stoning[61] them. There is no uniformity in what they did, but the various misdeeds combined to make it clear that they had paid no rent. They may well have been preparing for a claim in due course that they had forcibly repelled people who were trying to rob them. Mark and Luke differ in that they report that one slave was sent each time, but Mark adds after the third that the owner sent "many others." What all are saying is that a succession of emissaries was sent to collect the rents that were due, and all were rejected with violence.

36. The householder repeated the process, perhaps (as Derrett thinks) at the time for payment in the second year. This time he took the precaution of sending *more than the first,* but to no avail. The tenants treated the larger delegation in the same way as they had treated the first slaves. Their rejection of the owner's claim is definite and vigorous.

37. Whether this was in the same year or the following year is not clear. But finally the owner *sent his son* (in Mark and Luke he is said to be "beloved"; cf. 3:17). In real life, of course, this is unlikely. The owner would have had the law on his side, and he would have taken strong action to eject his defaulting tenants. But Jesus is telling a story that would illustrate the way a compassionate and loving God acts toward sinners, not the way a businessman would act to protect his investment.[62] So the owner sent his son, saying, *"They will respect my son."* He knew that his slaves had

---

59. Both Mark and Luke say "at the time," but Matthew adds τῶν καρπῶν, "of the fruits," which in a vineyard would be the vintage. Even though there would be little vintage if any at this early stage, this was the time to look for rent. And, of course, even in a vineyard there might be small amounts of other crops, planted between the rows, especially in the early years.

60. δέρω properly means "to skin, flay," but the weakened sense of "beat" is found in later Greek (cf. *New Documents,* 4, p. 66).

61. The procedure is given in the Mishnah: "The place of stoning was twice the height of a man. One of the witnesses knocked him down on his loins; if he turned over on his heart the witness turned him over again on his loins. If he straightway died that sufficed; but if not, the second (witness) took the stone and dropped it on his heart. If he straightway died, that sufficed; but if not, he was stoned by all Israel" (*Sanh.* 6:4).

62. Cf. Hendriksen, "it is a parable depicting *sin most unreasonable* and *love incomprehensible!*" (p. 783).

541

been rejected with force and his rights totally disregarded. Apparently he was reasoning that slaves are one thing, the son of the house quite another.

38. But the tenants persisted in their violent opposition to the owner's just claims. They may have thought that the appearance of the heir on the scene indicated that the owner was dead and now the son had come to take possession. Or perhaps that the father had transferred the title to the son. Or they may have reasoned that if they treated the son badly, the father, who was still at a great distance, would think that he had had enough problems with his troublesome vineyard and would desist from his claim. Whatever the reasoning behind it, they decided in the end to *kill him and take his inheritance.* It was unthinkable to them that the owner, who had been given so much trouble, would bother to press his claim.

39. So they *took* the son and *threw him out of the vineyard.* This was probably important, for they were going to kill him; if they had shed his blood in the vineyard, it would have become an unclean area and they would have problems in disposing of their produce. This would be so even if they killed him in the vineyard without actually shedding blood and then carried him out.[63] So they got him outside the vineyard first, and then *killed him.* From their point of view their title was now secure. They had never paid rent for the vineyard, they had been in it a number of years to secure their claim, and they were sure that the owner, who had never been back since he established the vineyard, would not care (and perhaps not dare) to prosecute his claim. The vineyard was theirs.[64] They would claim that the dead man had come to make an unjust claim to their vineyard and that all they had done had been to repel a robber.

40-41. But the vine growers in the story had reckoned without their host. He was not the man to let this final horror go unpunished, a fact that Jesus brings out with an appeal to his audience. He speaks of the time when *the owner of the vineyard comes,* which makes it clear that he will come. He asks his listeners to tell him what the owner will then do, to which they reply, *"He will bring those bad men to a bad end."*[65] He will also

---

63. The corpse would render unclean all the land it "overshadowed" (Mishnah *Ohol.* 2:1). There are also bothersome regulations about a "grave area" (*Ohol.* 18:1), some of which might be applicable. Mark says, "they killed him and threw him out," which probably means that they gave him a mortal wound while still in the vineyard but carried him out before he died (so Derrett, p. 307).

64. In the Talmud there are examples of people claiming possession of land they had worked for three years (e.g., *B. Bat.* 35b). In one case a man mortgaged an orchard for three years, but when he came to get it back the mortgagee said, "If you will sell it to me, well and good, and if not, I will suppress the mortgage deed and say that I purchased it outright" (*B. Bat.* 40b). This is, of course, blackmail, but the point is that when the mortgage deed could not be produced the man who had worked the land for three years could indeed claim that the orchard was his.

65. There is a vivid wordplay with κακοὺς κακῶς, on which MM comments, "It seems clear that the collocation κακοὺς κακῶς ἀπολέσθαι, starting as a literary phrase, had been perpetuated in common parlance, like our stock quotations from Shakespeare" (*sub* κακῶς). ἀπολέσει means that he will totally destroy them.

pursue his original plans for the vineyard. He will find other tenants who will *"pay him the fruits at the proper times."*[66] There is no difficulty on the part of the hearers in bringing the story to its appropriate close. No one could countenance the wicked behavior of the people who tried to steal the vineyard and in the process did bodily harm to quite a few slaves and even killed some of them. Bonnard declines to press the imagery of the vine, finding the stress laid on the son and the vine growers (p. 317). It is this that is the culmination of the parable.

42. Jesus drives the point home with a quotation from Psalm 118:22 (there are other important "stone" passages in Isa. 8:14-15; 28:16). This quotation is found in all three Synoptists at this point (also in Acts 4:11 and 1 Pet. 2:7); clearly it was thought very important in the early church. He introduces it with *"Did you never read in the Scriptures,"* a question that underlines the importance of Scripture, assumes that his hearers ought to be familiar with their Bibles, and moves straight to the relevant passage. Building with stone was, of course, a common practice, and clearly *the head of the corner* was the most important stone in the building (cf. *GNB,* "turned out to be the most important of all"). But we do not have enough knowledge of the way people built in that day to be quite sure which stone it was. It may have been a large stone laid in the foundation at the corner of two walls. In such a place it provided a foundation that could be built on and it also set the position for two walls and therefore for the whole building. The other suggestion is that it was at the top of the walls, binding two walls together and thus marking the consummation of the builders' task. On the whole it seems more likely that the stone in the foundation is meant, but we cannot be sure. The Psalm speaks of an unexpected revolution: a stone[67] that the builders thought they could not use — it was unsuitable and they rejected it — in due course became the most important stone in the building. Luke stops his quotation at this point, but Matthew and Mark add the next verse, which tells us that it was *from the Lord* that *this*[68] *came about.* We have moved now from the astonishing reversal to the truth that God is working his purpose out through it all. That it *is astonishing* to human eyes emphasizes the truth that created beings cannot understand the way the Creator works.

43. *Therefore* draws the logical inference from all this. We have seen the way the Lord works, and we must now notice the way this works out in our day. Jesus goes on to say that *"the kingdom of God"* (for this expres-

---

66. Since the future indicative may have a final sense, Moule finds it difficult to know whether we should understand the meaning here to be "who shall render . . ." or "so that they may render . . ." (*IBNTG,* p. 139).

67. λίθον ὅν is an example of the attraction of a subject into the case of the relative (BDF, 295).

68. We expect the neuter ("this thing") but have the feminine αὕτη; it is usually explained as a literal translation of the Hebrew, where the feminine has the same function as the neuter in Greek.

sion see on 12:28) *"will be taken away from you."* Jesus is addressing representatives of the Jewish hierarchy, and it is to them that he addresses this dreadful truth. The Old Testament Scriptures with all their wealth of promise had been addressed to the Jewish people. But they had not responded as they should — witness the way they treated most of the prophets. Isaiah was doubtless very popular when he prophesied of the deliverance God was about to give, but the rejection of Jeremiah was a much more typical reaction to the teaching of the prophets.[69] And now at last God had sent his beloved Son; they had rejected him throughout his ministry, and now they were about to hand him over to the Romans to be executed. The *kingdom* would be taken away from them and given to those who would respond to it more adequately, those who would produce *its fruits.* Jesus is telling his hearers that deeds speak louder than words and that their failure to respond to all that God has done for them will reap its inevitable reward. That did not mean that God would not establish his kingdom. He would do so, but with people who live fruitful lives. The words foreshadow the appearance of the Christian church.

44. It is not certain on textual grounds whether we should read this verse.[70] But if we do, we return to the stone imagery (in words reminiscent of Dan. 2:34, 44-45) and carry on with the thought of rejection. Those who do not appreciate the place of the stone face retribution in more ways than one. The stone is clearly a very large and solid one. Anyone who falls on it *will be crushed,* while the person on whom it falls will be *pulverized.*[71] Morgan points out that there is a difference here: "Fall on it — and there is a touch of mercy even here — and you will be broken, but the broken man can be healed. But let it fall on you, and you will be ground to dust, and there is no healing then" (p. 262).

45. Earlier the *high priests* were linked with the scribes (v. 15) and with the elders of the people (v. 23). Now they are linked with *the Pharisees* (Luke has "the scribes" at this point, but since many of the scribes were Pharisees there is no conflict). This is a notable coalition, for the Pharisees and the Sadducees (to which party most of the high priests gave their allegiance) were for the most part bitterly opposed to one another. But they had both felt the lash of Jesus' denunciation, though in different ways. The Pharisees had been meticulous in their observance of rites and ceremo-

---

69. Plummer remarks, "Deeply as the Jews lamented the cessation of Prophets after the death of Malachi, they generally opposed them, as long as they were granted to them. Till the gift was withdrawn, they seem to have had little pride in this exceptional grace shown to the nation, and little appreciation of it or thankfulness for it" (p. 297).

70. The verse is omitted by some important MSS, D 33 it[mss] syr[s] etc., but is read by ℵ B C K L X etc. Those who reject it point out that it might well have been imported from Luke 20:18, but against this is the fact that a copyist's eye might well have slipped from αὐτῆς at the end of verse 43 to αὐτόν at the end of the disputed verse, omitting everything in between. We should probably accept it.

71. λικμάω mostly means "to winnow," but the meaning "grind to powder" of AV is not excluded by MM, which cites Deissmann, *BS,* pp. 225-26 in support.

nies and had overlooked the more important matters to which the law of God pointed. The high priests were more concerned with politics, with preserving their places at the head of the nation in collaboration with the Romans, than with the niceties of religious observance. Both professed to be the servants of God, but neither was able to discern the Son of God for what he was when he came. Both became bitter opponents of Jesus, and within a few days of this piece of teaching they would succeed in having him put on a cross. Matthew tells us that they discerned the thrust of the parables (which mean primarily the two Matthew has just recorded) and saw accordingly that Jesus was opposing them and condemning their practice.

46. They would have liked *to arrest him,* but the crowds of people in Jerusalem for the feast presented them with a problem. Matthew has recorded Jesus' triumphal entry into Jerusalem no farther back than the beginning of this chapter, and it is clear that at this time Jerusalem contained a large number of his enthusiastic followers. These were people who *held him to be a prophet.* How do you arrest a prophet in the middle of crowds who are enthusiastic about him? No immediate answer appeared to this question; therefore the enemies of Jesus did nothing for the time being. But this did not mean that their opposition was any the less. It meant only that they were biding their time. As soon as they had a convenient opportunity, they would strike.

Matthew 22

3. The Parable of the Wedding Feast, 22:1-14

¹*And Jesus answering spoke again in parables, saying to them,* ²*"The kingdom of heaven is like a king who made a wedding feast for his son.* ³*And he sent his slaves to call those who had been invited to the wedding, and they would not come.* ⁴*Again he sent other slaves, saying, 'Say to those who were invited, "Look, I have prepared my banquet, my oxen and fattened beasts have been slaughtered, and all things are ready. Come to the wedding."'* ⁵*But they did not care and went off, one to his farm, another to his business;* ⁶*and the rest laid hands on his slaves, ill-treated them, and killed them.* ⁷*But the king was angry, and he sent his troops and destroyed those murderers and set their city on fire.* ⁸*Then he says to his slaves, 'The banquet is ready, but those who were invited were not worthy;* ⁹*go therefore to the road intersections, and as many as you find invite to the wedding.'* ¹⁰*And those slaves went out into the highways and gathered together all whom they found, both evil and good; and the wedding was filled with guests.* ¹¹*But when the king came in to see the guests, he saw there a man not wearing a wedding garment.* ¹²*And he says to him, 'Friend, how did you come in here not having a wedding garment?' But he was speechless.* ¹³*Then the king said to the servants, 'Bind him feet and hands, and throw him out into the outer darkness; there there will be wailing and gnashing of teeth.'* ¹⁴*For many are called, but few chosen."*

The third in this trilogy of parables further hammers home the danger in which the members of the ecclesiastical establishment had placed themselves. It is not enough to have accepted the invitation to the marriage feast — one must also go to the marriage. The parable is not unlike that in Luke 14:15-24, and many commentators assume that it is a variant of the same parable. But there are some not insignificant differences. Matthew's story is related after Jesus had reached Jerusalem, Luke's while he was still on the journey. Matthew's parable concerns a king making a wedding feast, it speaks of the kingdom of heaven, it lists oxen and fattened beasts as food items, it refers to many slaves as going with the invitations, has no equivalent of the excuses that form the central feature of Luke's story, has slaves insulted and killed by the potential guests, has the king sending armies to deal with the rejectors of his invitation, and has an addendum about a man with no wedding garment. Luke's story arises from a remark made by a fellow guest at a dinner Jesus attended, it refers to a man (not a king) who put on a big dinner, it says nothing about the food, has only one slave inviting the guests to turn up, makes a feature of the excuses the guests made for not coming, and has the slave going out twice to bring in the outcasts. Add to that the fact that there is very little agreement in wording. There are obvious resemblances between the two parables, but not enough to say that they are variants of the one story. Rather, they are variations on a theme that a teller of parables might well make on different occasions, before different audiences. Is anyone prepared to say that Jesus used each of his parables on only one occasion? Surely one of the advantages of the parabolic method is that the parables can be adapted to new situations. And if and when Jesus repeated a parable before a different audience, is there any reason why he should not have modified it to suit its new application? It fits the facts better to take this as another parable embodying features Jesus had used before than to take it as a second form of the same parable, modified in transmission.[1]

1. There have been no previous words that Jesus was *answering*, but Matthew is fond of the verb (which he has 55 times) and he may have it in mind that Jesus was responding to the hostility of the high priests and Pharisees who wanted to arrest him. *Again* adds this to the previous parables and completes the trio.

2. For *the kingdom of heaven* see on 3:2. This time it is likened[2] to *a king*[3] giving a *wedding feast*[4] *for his son* (sons feature in all three of the parables in this group). The use of the singular may point us to *the* son, the one who would in due course succeed him (it is unlikely that a king would have only one son). Any royal occasion would be notable, but the wedding of the son would be especially significant. Jesus says nothing about the preparations that went into the making of the feast, but it would be expected that the king would put on a magnificent banquet (and it would also be expected that people would be very glad to receive an invitation and would make a point of being there). Many see an eschato-

---

1. The rabbis sometimes told parables about banquets. For example, there is one about a king who invited people to a banquet without fixing a time. The wise waited outside the palace in their wedding garments whereas the foolish went about their work, reasoning that they would have time to change. But the king suddenly called them in and the wise enjoyed the banquet while the fools without proper clothes stood watching (*Shab.* 153a).

2. Lenski understands the aorist as "spoken from the standpoint of the end of the world when the earthly history of the kingdom will be complete as here portrayed" (p. 847). The aorist is used also in introducing parables elsewhere (13:24; 18:23).

3. Once more Matthew uses ἄνθρωπος ("a man, a king") as equivalent to the indefinite pronoun.

4. γάμος may mean a wedding or a wedding feast. It is used here in the plural (again in vv. 3, 4, and 9), but there does not seem to be any difference from the use of the singular in verses 8, 10, 11, and 12.

logical significance in this parable and draw attention to the messianic banquet that was so much part of Jewish tradition. But no one seems to have found a *wedding* feast as part of the eschatological expectation, so the application to the end time must be seen as uncertain.

3. At the time when the banquet was about ready, the king *sent his slaves* to tell the guests that it was time to come. This presupposes a previous invitation that had been accepted.[5] There would be many slaves (over against the singular "slave" in Luke's parable), partly because of the number of guests and partly because this befitted royalty. It seems that a second invitation to a feast was usual (cf. Esth. 5:8; 6:14). In a day when people had nothing equivalent to watches and when banquets took a long time to prepare, it was obviously a very helpful thing to be notified in this manner. From the *Midrash Rabbah* we find that there was another reason: "None of them would attend a banquet unless he was invited twice" (*Lamentations* 4.2; to explain this the *Midrash* tells a story of a banquet to which an invitation was sent by mistake to an enemy whose name was very similar to that of a friend; there were disastrous consequences when the enemy, once invited, refused to leave the feast, while the host insisted that he go). So the customary second invitation went out. But on this occasion *they would not come.*[6] This was something completely unnatural; in real life a royal invitation is not refused, and people are very glad to be present at a royal banquet. We should not miss the point that Jesus regards the actions of the high-priestly party as completely unnatural. When they were summoned by the King of heaven, they should surely have complied with his gracious invitation. But they did not. Their outward profession was a long way from the glad acceptance of the ways of God that was looked for from men in their position.

4. There had to be some mistake; the guests had been invited, and they would surely come. So the king sent *other slaves.* This time they had a specific message from the king that said, first, that the great feast[7] had been *prepared;* second, that *oxen and fattened beasts*[8] had been butchered for the occasion; and third, that *all things are ready.* Nothing could be more explicit.[9] So, the assurance having been given that everything had been

5. τοῖς κεκλημένοις means "to those who had been invited"; it points to a previous activity.

6. οὐκ ἤθελον ἐλθεῖν: their wills were set against coming.

7. ἄριστον properly denotes an earlier meal than does δεῖπνον (= dinner); the corresponding verb is used of breakfast (John 21:12; cf. v. 4), though the Pharisee's invitation to Jesus employing the same verb (Luke 11:37) looks more like the midday meal. We should probably understand here a meal during the day rather than an evening meal, but not much depends on the word, for wedding feasts often went on for days, and this would certainly be true of a royal wedding.

8. σιτιστός, a rare word (found here only in the New Testament), is connected with σιτίζω, "to fatten"; it could signify any animals, but animals especially fed and thus in prime condition. NRSV has "fat calves," but this is a trifle more definite than the Greek.

9. We should notice the perfects ἡτοίμακα and τεθυμένα and the adjective ἕτοιμα. The perfect κεκλημένοις makes it clear that the invitations still stand.

done to ensure that the guests would have a magnificent banquet, the king concludes with *"Come to the wedding."*

5. But all to no avail. The guests *did not care,*[10] an incredible attitude to take up in the face of a royal command and the almost sacred duty of complying with an accepted invitation. But this group of people were too concerned with their own affairs to respond to the king's invitation. Jesus illustrates with two concerns, which we are expected to regard as typical. In the parable in Luke the invitees all make excuses (Luke 14:18), but these do not bother; they just go off to pursue their own concerns. One prospective guest went off *to his farm.* In the Lukan parable this was to look over his newly purchased field; Jesus does not say in this parable what it was that took the man to the farm, but it will be some concern of this sort. Whatever it was, it was surely something that might easily have been held over. So with the second and *his business.*[11] No urgency is suggested, and this, too, looks like an excuse. Jesus is citing typical shallow excuses to bring out the point that the impolite guests had no real reason for staying away from the banquet. They simply did not care.

6. *The rest* leads into an account of those who took hostile action and did not simply go about their own affairs; the expression indicates that there were quite a few of them. They treated the king's messengers with scant respect. First, they *laid hands on his slaves.* In no society is it considered good manners to lay hands on people who come bearing a warm invitation, even if one does not intend to accept it. Then two things are said about what they did to the slaves sent to them with the message of goodwill. The first is that they *ill-treated* them, a term that covers a wide range of unpleasantness.[12] The second is that they *killed them.* This does not necessarily mean that they did this to all of them, but it was a dreadful crime to do it to any. There was nothing more serious they could possibly have done than to take away these men's lives. Their easy assumption apparently was that they themselves were in no danger: they could do to the king and his messengers anything they wished and do it with impunity. They had no respect for the king and no fear of him.[13]

7. But they had not thought hard enough about *the king;* they had

---

10. ἀμελέω is seen by MM as a "common vernacular word"; it cites its absolute use from a papyrus of 73 B.C. It signifies "have no care for," "be neglectful of."

11. ἐμπορία (here only in the New Testament) can mean business of any sort. It is connected with πόρος, "a journey," which reminds us that many merchants in antiquity wandered from place to place in pursuance of trade. But the word is used of settled businessmen as well as those who journeyed.

12. ὑβρίζω is connected with ὕβρις, "pride," "insolence." The verb has meanings like "outrage, insult, treat insolently"; it stands for an attitude that treats the objects as absolutely worthless.

13. It is sometimes objected that in real life people would not kill messengers simply because they did not want to go to a feast. But Josephus tells us that the Israelites did precisely this to those whom King Hezekiah sent to invite them to join him in the feast of the Passover (*Ant.* 9.265).

not allowed for the fact that he was not the kind of man to take a snub lightly, nor did they reckon with the way their refusal would inevitably be regarded. "For a subject to scorn the summons to the royal feast implied disloyalty and rebellion" (Carr). The king was very displeased and *sent his troops*,[14] which in this context will denote not an army but a detachment of soldiers, sufficient to deal with the offending guests. Jesus speaks of them as *murderers* and says that *their city* was *set . . . on fire*. This envisages the insulters as being concentrated in one city, and that not the place where the feast was to be held. It would, of course, take time for this to take place, and other events occurred before the destruction of the city. But Jesus takes to its conclusion his account of the fate of those who rejected the king's invitation before returning to the subject of the feast. We should not miss the point that the language is very much like that of Old Testament passages dealing with judgment.[15]

8. The narrative becomes vivid with the use of the present tense, *he says*, as Jesus moves on to a further instruction the king gave to *his slaves*. A wedding is an important occasion, and the celebrations are not to be cancelled just because some ill-mannered guests refuse the invitations and must be dealt with. The king reminds some of *his slaves* that *"the banquet is ready,"* a fact that has emerged as early as verse 4. Normally the guests would even then be reclining at table and consuming the magnificent repast. But *"those who were invited were not worthy,"* which, considering what they had done to the messengers, is a considerable understatement.

9. *"Go therefore,"* says the king, *"to the road intersections,"*[16] which seems to mean the places where the main highways go out from the city to the country, evidently places where poor people tended to congregate. Such people would not expect to find themselves as guests at a royal banquet, but the king is determined that the wedding feast go ahead, and that means that there must be guests to fill the places. Poor people at the road junctions are unlikely to refuse such an invitation. So the king instructs his slaves to invite *"as many as you find"* in these places to come to the wedding.

10. The slaves did as they were instructed. In the parable in Luke the slave had to go out into the country because he could not get enough

14. στράτευμα can denote an army (Rev. 9:16), but it is also used for "a body of soldiers" (MM).

15. Some commentators see a reference to the fall of Jerusalem in A.D. 70 and regard this Gospel as written after that date. Gundry, however, points out that this would imply that the mission to the Gentiles did not begin till that date, but "that implication would disagree with (Matthew's) own theology of evangelism in 28:19-20"; Gundry thinks that the background is rather Isaiah 5:24-25. Those who identify what is said with the destruction of Jerusalem do not generally notice that Jerusalem was not in fact burned, though the temple was (see Introduction, II. Date).

16. ἐπὶ τὰς διεξόδους τῶν ὁδῶν. AS gives the meaning of διέξοδος as "a way out through, an outlet," while GT takes it as "lit. *ways through which ways go out*" and thus *"places before the city where the roads from the country terminate,* therefore *outlets of the country highways,* the same being also their *entrances."* MM approves this and suggests " 'the *issues* of the streets,' " i.e. where they lead out from the city into the country."

guests in the city, but in this parable one trip secured all that were needed. The slaves went out *into the highways*[17] and enlisted *all whom they found, both evil and good*. In the application this means that Jesus accepts people the Jewish establishment would regard as evil and therefore totally unacceptable. Of course, those who accept Jesus' invitation do not stay evil, but the point is that Jesus welcomes people that the high priests did not want to include among God's own. *The wedding was filled with guests;* in the end the king's purpose was worked out, and Jesus leaves his hearers to see that God's purposes will take effect; in the end those he calls will be present at his heavenly feast.

11. The parable could have ended at this point (as Luke's parable in fact does). Indeed, many scholars hold that as Jesus taught it the parable does end here; they contend that Matthew has tacked on the bit at the end about the man without the wedding garment.[18] Sometimes they hold that this is another of Jesus' parables, sometimes that it emanates from Matthew or the early church. But the fact is that, as we read this Gospel, this section certainly belongs to the parable of the wedding feast. The story Matthew relates has a further point to make. Patte notes that tensions like that between verses 10 and 11 occur elsewhere in this Gospel, and "such tensions signal that at such places in the text Matthew conveys major points (convictions) that are surprising for the readers because they involve a view unknown to them — a view that Matthew strives to convey to them. In brief, the concluding verses, 22:11-14, should be considered an integral part of Matthew's parable; they express its main point" (p. 301).[19] Jesus says that the king *came in to see the guests*. We know little about customs at wedding banquets in first-century Judaism, but this seems eminently reasonable, all the more so since the king would not have known whom his slaves had brought in. So he came in to make his presence known and to see for himself who had come to the feast. He found a man *not wearing*[20] *a wedding garment*. The precise meaning of this is not known, but obviously a marriage is a time when most people would wear appropriate clothing (cf. Isa. 61:10; Ezek. 16:10). In this case, when a king took all sorts of poor people right from the streets into the banqueting hall, it is not impossible that he made available suitable clothing and that this man did not bother to make use of what the king provided (though

17. τὰς ὁδούς.

18. Fenton, for example, says simply, "Matthew inserts two more parables into Mark — the marriage feast and the wedding garment." He does not bother to discuss the view that these verses are part of one parable.

19. Bruce remarks that this paragraph "would form a suitable pendant to any parable of grace, as showing that, while the door of the kingdom is open to all, personal holiness cannot be dispensed with."

20. οὐ with the participle rather than μή is unexpected; BDF finds it due to "the preference for καὶ οὐ instead of καὶ μή . . . and to the emphasis on the negation" (430[1]). Robertson says that this "lays emphasis on the actual situation in the description (the plain fact) while the second instance (i.e. μή in v. 12) is the hypothetical argument about it" (p. 1138).

evidence that this sort of thing was done in ancient times is lacking; Lenski, however, draws attention to Gen. 45:22; Judg. 14:12, 19; 2 Kings 5:22; 10:22; Esth. 6:8; 8:15; Rev. 19:8, 9; p. 857). Whether that was the way it was or not, the words imply that suitable clothing was available and this man had not made use of the opportunity.

12. The king greeted him as *"Friend,"* a form of address found elsewhere in the New Testament only in 20:13; 26:50. In all three passages there is something ironical about the greeting, for the "friend" in each case is doing something short of a friendly action. But *"Friend"* is a kindly word, and there is something of an appeal about it. The king goes on to ask how the man came in without the right garment, but the offender has nothing to say.[21] Quite plainly he knew that he could have had the right clothing but had declined to wear it.

13. It is puzzling that the man had come to the feast but had not made use of the appropriate clothing as the other guests had done. Commentators give a good deal of attention to the significance of the robe, some seeing in it meritorious works, others imputed righteousness or the righteousness that comes as a consequence of God's saving work in the sinner, and so on. It is wiser to avoid speculation since the narrative gives no hint of a particular meaning we should attach to it. But in this parable the king is a strong personality, one who tolerates no nonsense. The man has no business being where he is, clothed as he is. So the king gives a command to his *servants* ("servants" this time, not "slaves"), directing them to tie the man up, both *feet and hands* being specified, after which he is to be thrown *into the outer darkness,* an expression often used to denote the uncomfortable lodging of those who are rejected.

14. Jesus rounds off the parable with a reason for the rejection of this man. *Many are called* classes him with the other guests; they had all heard the gracious invitation of the royal host, and they were all where they were because of his generosity. But Jesus sounds a warning. Those who hear God's call and know of his grace must not think that a call is the same as a response. While many indeed hear the call, *few* are *chosen.*[22] In interpreting this we must bear in mind that Hebrew and Aramaic both lack comparative forms of the adjective. Comparisons are expressed by using expressions like "large" and "small," sometimes "many" and "few." It is possible to understand this passage to mean that the elect are fewer in number than those called; the actual number of the elect is then not in mind.[23] Jesus is not saying whether the elect will be a tiny remnant or not; he is saying that not all the called will be finally chosen.

---

21. The verb φιμόω derives from φιμός, "a muzzle"; in the face of such a question from such a source he was "muzzled."

22. Patte points out that these words apply to the parable of the two sons just as much as to this one, which is one of the reasons for regarding verses 11-14 as part of the original parable (p. 306, n. 26).

23. Ben F. Meyer has argued the case for this view in *NTS,* 36 (1990), pp. 89-97. He

This is an expression of the doctrine of election that we find in one form or another throughout the New Testament. The Jews could say, "All Israelites have a share in the world to come" (*Sanh.* 10:1), but Jesus rejects such views. The gospel invitation goes far and wide, but not everyone who hears it is one of God's elect. We know those who are elect by their obedient response. Perhaps it is worth noticing here that this doctrine is also found in Paul, but that he expresses it differently. For him the "call" is the effectual call, so that it is enough for him to speak of people as being called by God. "Call" in his writings means much the same as "chosen" here.[24]

C. PHARISEES AND SADDUCEES, 22:15–23:17

Throughout his ministry Jesus often came into conflict with the religious establishment, especially the Pharisees, for they were deeply interested in religious matters and felt that Jesus was destroying the very basis of their divinely established religion. The Sadducees were also opposed to Jesus, but more from political motives (though, of course, they objected to his religious teaching as well). They apparently thought that Jesus might be aiming at revolution in due course, and even if he was not, his followers might take it into their heads to proclaim him as Messiah and try to oust the Romans, which would destabilize the political equilibrium and might well upset their privileged position. Matthew proceeds at this point to relate some incidents that bring out the nature of the opposition Jesus encountered from these groups and the way he met it.

1. Attempts to Trap Jesus, 22:15-46

> [15]Then the Pharisees went off and took counsel so that they might trap him in what he said. [16]And they send to him their disciples, together with the Herodians, saying, "Teacher, we know that you are true and that you teach the way of God in truth, and do not care about anyone because you do not have regard to anyone. [17]Tell us therefore, what do you think? Is it proper to give poll tax to Caesar or not?" [18]But Jesus perceived their malice and said, "Why are you testing me, you hypocrites? [19]Show me the coin

---

says, "I am arguing that, as in LXX Num 26.56, πολλοί and ὀλίγοι are used in Matt 22.14 as correlative comparatives to mean 'more numerous' and 'less numerous' " (p. 95). J. Jeremias similarly says that "many" here is used in the sense of "the totality": "Mt. 22:14 contrasts the totality of those invited with the small number of the chosen" (*TDNT*, VI, p. 542). It would probably be better to say "the smaller number."

24. Robinson points out that we should not think of God as unreasonable in first inviting people and then rejecting them: "It is not as if God were represented as summoning A and B by name, and then later casting them off. The call is the universal appeal which comes through the public preaching of the gospel, and if there are comparatively few of the hearers who accept it with all their heart and soul, God is hardly to be blamed for the rejection of the rest."

used for the poll tax." And they brought him a denarius. ²⁰*And he says to them, "Whose likeness and inscription is this?"* ²¹*They say to him, "Caesar's." Then he says to them, "Render therefore to Caesar the things that are Caesar's, and to God the things that are God's."* ²²*And when they heard this, they were astonished; so they left him and went away.*

²³*On that day Sadducees, who say that there is no resurrection, came to him and questioned him,* ²⁴*saying, "Teacher, Moses said, 'If a man dies not having children, his brother shall marry his widow and raise up seed to his brother.'* ²⁵*Now there were seven brothers with us; and the first married and died. And since he had no seed, he left his wife to his brother.* ²⁶*Likewise also the second and the third, and so on to the seventh.* ²⁷*Last of all the woman died.* ²⁸*In the resurrection therefore whose wife of the seven will she be? For they all had her."* ²⁹*But Jesus answered and said to them, "You go astray, not knowing the Scriptures nor the power of God;* ³⁰*for in the resurrection they neither marry nor are given in marriage, but they are like angels in heaven.* ³¹*But concerning the resurrection of the dead, have you not read what was spoken to you by God:* ³²*'I am the God of Abraham and the God of Isaac and the God of Jacob'? He is not the God of the dead but of the living."* ³³*And when the crowds heard this, they were astonished at his teaching.*

³⁴*Now when the Pharisees heard that he had silenced the Sadducees, they were gathered together,* ³⁵*and one of them, a lawyer, asked a question, testing him:* ³⁶*"Teacher, which is the great commandment in the law?"* ³⁷*And he said to him, "You shall love the Lord your God with all your heart and with all your soul and with all your mind.* ³⁸*This is the first and great commandment.* ³⁹*And a second is like it, You shall love your neighbor as yourself.* ⁴⁰*On these two commandments hang all the law and the prophets."*

⁴¹*Now while the Pharisees were gathered together, Jesus asked them,* ⁴²*saying, "What do you think about the Messiah? Whose son is he?" They say to him, "David's."* ⁴³*He says to them, "How then does David in the Spirit call him 'Lord,' saying,* ⁴⁴*'The Lord said to my Lord, "Sit at my right hand until I put your enemies under your feet"'?* ⁴⁵*If therefore David calls him 'Lord,' how is he his son?"* ⁴⁶*And no one could answer him a word, neither did anyone dare any more to ask him a question from that day.*

Matthew narrates a series of attempts to trap Jesus. Pharisees and Sadducees came up with trick questions, questions that they thought would compel answers that would put Jesus in trouble with his followers or with the Roman authorities.

15. The Pharisees led off the process. *Then* may mean that their first attempt followed immediately on Jesus' telling the parable of the wedding feast, but Matthew's *Then* (see on 2:7) is not always so precise; it may mean no more than sometime later. If it did follow on from the parable, it was no hasty question that they put to Jesus. They *went off and took counsel* (as they had done on another occasion, 12:14). Clearly they had learned

554

ATTEMPTS TO TRAP JESUS

enough about Jesus to respect him and did not want to make a half-baked attempt to refute him. So they went off and thought about it and took advice. They wanted to *trap*[25] *him,* and on this occasion the trap had nothing to do with the way Jesus practiced his religion but concerned what he said.

16. The leaders do not take part in the process themselves, but *send* (Matthew uses the present tense to give greater vividness) some of their *disciples,* people who were learning the Pharisaic way. Students would do very well for this task. They were joined by *the Herodians,* a party about which nothing is known except what can be deduced from the name.[26] The name assures us that they were people attached to the Herods, and we are probably right in assuming that when many opposed that dynasty these people supported it. There will always be time servers who do what they think will please those in authority, and it would seem that the Herods were not free from such followers. But *Herodians* as such are not mentioned outside the New Testament, and in it only here and in Mark 3:6; 12:13 (Luke has the incident but does not mention the Herodians). The delegation began with a little flattery. They address Jesus with the respectful *"Teacher"* and go on to say, *"we know that you are true."* The adjective is that normally used for truthful statements, but we have a problem in putting it into English because we do not usually speak of people as being "true." Translations accordingly have "You are truthful" *(NASB)* or the like, or paraphrase with "you are an honest man" *(JB),* "a man of integrity" *(NIV).* The statement means that Jesus has truth in his very being; he can be relied upon to say what is right, and he will not bend his statement to fit it in with what other people would like to hear. Not only is he "true" in himself, but, they say, *"you teach the way of God in truth."* They recognize that Jesus is a reliable teacher when he speaks about the things of God: not only does he speak the truth as he knows it (and from the Pharisaic point of view that might be very imperfectly), but what he says about *the way of God* is true, an interesting concession from those who opposed him. They go on to say that he does not *care about anyone.* This does not mean that he is inconsiderate, but that he is no time server: he tells the truth regardless of what people think and regardless of whether what he says pleases them or not. He is no respecter of persons.[27] The tempters thus manage to say four things about Jesus in short compass: he was sincere, faithful to the truth, fearless, and no respecter of persons.[28]

---

25. παγιδεύω is connected with παγίς, "a snare," "a trap."

26. But they "were presumably pro-Roman and their presence accentuates the political trap which the question is supposed to be" (Stendahl).

27. οὐ γὰρ βλέπεις εἰς πρόσωπον ἀνθρώπων, "for you do not look at face of men." This recognizes that Jesus did not consider "face" as important as most people do.

28. Bruce points this out and comments on the questioners, "They demanded more than they were ready to give, whatever their secret leanings; no fear of them playing a heroic part."

17. *Therefore* is important; because Jesus is the kind of man they have just said he is, because he does not kowtow to anyone in high place (and they will have in mind more particularly the Romans), they look to him to give an honest answer. They proceed to ask, *"Is it proper to give poll tax to Caesar or not?"* This is often translated "Is it lawful. . . ?" and if this is the way the Jews understood it, they were asking whether it was in accordance with the law of God to pay Roman taxes (*GNB* renders, "Is it against our Law to pay taxes to the Roman Emperor?"). Since some Jews held that the law of God forbade the payment of taxes to Gentiles (cf. Deut. 17:15), the questioners may have been sounding Jesus out on his attitude to that question. But this may give the wrong nuance, for the verb does not have in itself the significance of "lawful."[29] The question may refer to what is proper rather than what is lawful. The questioners proceed to ask whether they should *give poll tax*[30] *to Caesar.* Their verb is not without its interest; they themselves are not allowing the possibility that the money was really due to Caesar. Anyone who paid this tax was in their view "giving" money away, not paying a legitimate impost. Nobody likes paying taxes, but in the first century *poll tax* was especially unpopular.[31] Customs duties were disliked, but at least on paying them one got something, the right to take goods to their destination. But with the poll tax there was no such benefit. It was a tax that simply removed money from the citizen and transferred it to the emperor's coffers with no benefit to the citizen. And if it were retorted that it paid the expenses of government, the answer would surely be that no Jew wanted Roman government and every Jew would be happy to dispense with it.

In this situation it would have seemed to the questioners that Jesus could not win. The question is framed in such a way that the answer is expected to be "Yes" or "No." If Jesus said "Yes," presumably the Herodians would agree, but he would alienate many religious Jews who saw support for the Romans as intolerable. If he said "No," he would satisfy the Pharisees, but be in trouble with the Roman authorities. Either way the situation in which he was growing in popularity among the populace and was left unhindered by the Romans would be changed, to their way of thinking, for the better.

18. Jesus was not deceived for one moment by their flattery; he perceived that their question was actuated by *malice*[32] and that they were not seeking for information but *testing* him.[33] And in view of all this it is

---

29. ἔξεστιν means "it is permitted, it is possible, proper" (BAGD).

30. For κῆνσος see *New Documents,* 3, pp. 70-71.

31. The rabbis could say, "do not seek to evade poll tax, lest they discover you and deprive you of all that you possess" (*Pes.* 112b). Clearly the tax was not popular.

32. The word is πονηρία, "evil," "wickedness" (the cognate word πονηρός is that from which we pray to be delivered in the Lord's Prayer, 6:13). *NIV* has "evil intent."

33. πειράζω is often used in the sense of applying a test with a view to the person failing; it can thus mean "tempt" (so *KJV* here).

not surprising that he addressed them as *hypocrites* (see on 6:2). They are not genuinely seeking an opinion from Jesus; they speak flattering words to him and proceed to ask a question aimed at destroying him. That is not the action of honest men but of hypocrites.

19. Jesus asks them for the coin used in paying the poll tax, the Roman denarius (Knox, "Shew me the coinage in which the tribute is paid"). This was a silver coin and was the amount a laborer would be paid for a day's work. The poll tax was paid with this coin, which for the Jews added insult to injury. They did not care to use a coin that carried a human likeness and would have avoided anything to do with it if they could. It is quite in keeping with this attitude that when Jesus asked them to produce the coin they evidently had to send away for it (they *brought* it). A Jew would not be likely to carry such a coin with him when he came to the temple.

20-21. With the coin before them, Jesus asked, "*Whose likeness*[34] *and inscription* is this?" *They say* (the continuing use of the present tense makes for a vivid narrative), "*Caesar's.*"[35] With a Roman coin that was not a difficult question to answer. But Jesus' comment on what they said is a classic.

First, let us notice that he said *render*, whereas they had said "give" (v. 17); we might translate it "pay."[36] But however we translate, the important point is that it has a meaning like "pay what is owing"; the word acknowledges that there are some things that are due to Caesar[37] and what is rightfully due should be paid by all citizens. The coin before them belonged to Jesus' questioners, and the fact that they used Caesar's coins (however unwillingly) was in itself an admission that they owed certain duties to Caesar.[38] "No man should think he is giving less service to the one God when he obeys human laws, pays tax, or bows his head to accept any other burden" (Calvin, III, p. 26). Since Jesus said quite plainly that they should pay Caesar what they owed to Caesar, there was no possibility of an accusation before the Romans. Whatever is due to the emperor must be paid. But Jesus did not say only that. He reminded his hearers that in addition to their obligations to the state they had obligations to God, and those, too, must be rendered. We are at one and the same time citizens of

34. εἰκών can denote a likeness in any one of a variety of ways. It may, for example, refer to an image. Here, of course, it is the likeness stamped on a coin.

35. A Roman denarius of the day had the inscription "TI CAESAR DIVI AUG F AUGUSTUS," that is, "Tiberius Caesar, son of the divine Augustus, Augustus" (see the reproduction in *IDB*, 3, p. 433, no. 29).

36. They used the verb δίδωμι, Jesus ἀποδίδωμι. Chrysostom drew attention to the change of word: "this is not to give but to render"; he further says, "it is possible both to fulfill to men their claims, and to give unto God the things that are due to God from us" (p. 427).

37. "This coin represented Roman organization, security of person and property, facilities of transit, and other beneficent elements of stable government" (Plummer, p. 305).

38. "By this apparently simple action, Jesus says: 'I do not possess the coin used to pay the tribute; *you*, who seem so troubled about it, do carry and use the coin'" (Meier).

some earthly state[39] and citizens of heaven; the obligations of neither may be neglected. And as we reflect on what Jesus said, we are made to realize that there are limitations to *the things that are Caesar's.* People must never allow their obligations to the civil state to encroach on their payment of *the things that are God's.* For serious-minded people this is an important limitation on the rights of the state. The most significant part of life is that which belongs to God; rendering to God what is God's is accordingly the most important duty we have. We should be clear, too, that Jesus is not saying that we can divide life into separate compartments so that God has nothing to do with that section which belongs to Caesar. The obligation to God covers all of life; we must serve Caesar in a way that is honoring to God.

22. The hearers *were astonished.* They had evidently come to this interview with high hopes. They had a good question, and they saw no way that Jesus could answer it without alienating somebody. And if he refused to answer, that, too, would give them a satisfying victory, for they would be able to accuse him of avoiding difficult issues that they had to face. But Jesus had answered their question, and he had answered it in such a way that neither the palace nor the temple could say that he had short-changed them. It was an astonishing answer, and therefore they were amazed. There was nothing for them to do but to leave him and go away.

23. With the Pharisees discomfited, the way was open for somebody else to try. That same day (only Matthew tells us this) some Sadducees brought a problem to Jesus. The Sadducees (see on 3:7) were the aristocratic, high-priestly party, strongly opposed to the Pharisees and probably gratified that they were unable to trap Jesus. But they were also strongly opposed to Jesus and the growing group of enthusiasts associated with him. Their cooperation with the Romans meant that they were suspicious of any movement that might disturb the current political setup, so they would like to have Jesus discredited. They rejected all teaching of a life after this one (Josephus, "The Sadducees hold that the soul perishes along with the body," *Ant.* 18.16; cf. *War* 2.165) and evidently felt that in this area they had a strong position; as far as they could see, there was nothing about a resurrection from the dead in the Old Testament Scriptures, and specifically in the law.[40] They perhaps regarded this as some new-fangled teaching brought in from Persia after the Old Testament Scriptures were written.[41] So they now came to Jesus with a question about life after death that they evidently were sure he would not be able to

---

39. Barclay comments, "failure in good citizenship is also failure in Christian duty. Untold troubles can descend upon a country or an industry when Christians refuse to take their part in the administration of the country, and leave that administration to selfish, self-seeking, partisan, and unchristian men" (II, p. 303).

40. The Samaritans denied the resurrection for the same reason (*Sanh.* 90b).

41. They also rejected the existence of angels (Acts 23:8), but it is difficult to understand why and how they did this in view of the emphasis they put on the books of the law and the fact that angels are mentioned there (e.g., Gen. 16:7-11; 28:12).

answer. Daube regards this as an example of questions of "vulgarity," a name given to questions designed to ridicule a rabbi rather than to obtain information (and among the rabbis, as here, directed against belief in resurrection; Daube, pp. 159, 160).

24. As the Pharisees had done, they address Jesus as *"Teacher";* their approach is a polite one. They appeal to Scripture, and specifically to a passage spoken by Moses. There could be no doubt about the authenticity of such a passage, and they would have felt that they were on very safe ground. They point to a passage providing that when brothers live together and one of them dies childless, his brother should marry the widow[42] and the child of this new union would be regarded as the son of the deceased; thus his name would be carried on (see Deut. 25:5-6; the quotation is not exact). This was a very old custom, as we see from its being practiced in patriarchal times (Gen. 38:8), but most interpreters agree that it was not widely observed in the first century. The Sadducees are not objecting to the custom; they simply point out that Moses authorized it and thus they find sound justification for its continuance.

25-27. They point to an unfortunate family of which they have knowledge (or perhaps to a hypothetical situation) in which there were *seven brothers.* They speak of them as *with us* (only Matthew has this detail; Gundry holds that it "makes an actual case out of one that might be only theoretical," p. 445), so they are claiming knowledge of the facts. In the normal fashion *the first married,* but unfortunately he *died* before begetting a child. Mark and Luke tell us this, but only Matthew puts it in the form *he left his wife to his brother.* The process was repeated with brother after brother, no son being born to any of them, and each marrying the lady as the law provided.[43] The Sadducees make it clear that all seven married her, and they round off the story with the death of the woman.

28. Now comes what they saw as the unanswerable question: "when the dead all rise, *whose wife . . . will she be?"* They point out that *"they all had her."* The legal requirements had been scrupulously fulfilled. There was no way of saying that any one of the seven had no claim to her. For the Sadducees it doubtless reduced the doctrine of resurrection to an absurdity. No brother could claim an exclusive right to her, and it was evidently preposterous to think that she could have seven husbands in heaven (while the Jews permitted polygamy, they did not allow polyandry). There was no answer to their question.

42. The word ἐπιγαμβρεύω is cited by LSJ only from biblical passages, but they note ἐπιγαμβρεία as meaning "connexion by marriage." MM notes it only in passages in LXX. In this context becoming related by marriage clearly refers to the marriage of a man to his deceased brother's wife. Since the word does not occur in the Deuteronomy passage, the Sadducees are giving the sense of it.

43. Chrysostom is sure that the Sadducees made up the story; in real life, he points out, "the third would not have taken her, when he saw the two bridegrooms dead" (in case the third did, Chrysostom repeats the comment with the other brothers), and he goes on to point out that the Jews did not always keep this law (p. 428).

29. Jesus begins his reply with the firm affirmation *"You go astray."* His verb[44] may be used of literal straying from the right path (18:12), but it is also used metaphorically of those who have strayed from the truth. Lenski takes the verb here to be middle, which would give the sense "you are deceiving yourselves" (p. 871). He may well be right, for they were drawing from the Scripture a conclusion that was not there (levirate marriage does not teach us about the truth or otherwise of resurrection). The Sadducees are basing their line of reasoning on Scripture, but they have not taken up a genuinely scriptural position; therefore[45] they are in error. They did not really know *the Scriptures*. It is one thing to be able to quote passages that one thinks support one's preconceived position and quite another to understand and follow the teaching of Scripture. To understand and to yield oneself to what Scripture says is quite different from quoting passages in the way the Sadducees were doing. And just as they do not really understand Scripture, so they do not know *the power of God*. The question of the resurrection from the dead is not one to be solved by citing a convenient passage from somewhere in the Bible; it demands that we recognize God's power to do what he wills. There is a play on words here that is important. The verb the Sadducees have used for "raise up" (v. 24) is connected with the noun "resurrection," the "raising up" of the dead.[46] The Sadducees were interested in marriage as the way of "raising up" descendants for a man who had died without issue so as to perpetuate his name (Deut. 25:6); Jesus points to the fact that this limits the power of God. God can "raise up" people by way of resurrection; the man's name does not need to be perpetuated, for he himself will be "raised up." The Sadducees are limiting the power of God by the way they understand "raising up." We must not so interpret Scripture as to put a limit to the power of God. That is what the Sadducees were doing.

30. *For* introduces the reason; *the resurrection,* of course, refers to the general resurrection at the last day (and not to risings from the dead like that of the daughter of Jairus). Jesus does not demonstrate that the resurrection will take place, but this form of expression simply takes it for granted. It is basic that there will be the raising from the dead of those who have died through the centuries. The Sadducees were assuming that if there is life in heaven it will, of course, be much like life here, doubtless with the ills taken away and the good things multiplied. They thought that marriages would continue there as here. But here marriages are necessary; the race must be propagated, and the family is the environment in which this is brought about. But we must not assume that what is needed here on earth will also be needed there in heaven. Jesus informs the

44. πλανάω, which Matthew has 8 times, the same number as Revelation, and more than in any other New Testament book.

45. We should understand the participle as causal; cf. *NIV,* "because you do not know the Scriptures."

46. The verb is ἀνίστημι and the noun ἀνάστασις.

Sadducees that there will be no marriages[47] in heaven. Life there will be of a different order, with *angels* giving us the pattern. It is the life of the angels rather than the life of people here and now that shows us what heaven will be like. We know little about angels, but this saying of Jesus makes it clear that they do not live in families as we do. He does not say that we will be angels but that we will be *like angels*.

31. Jesus moves from an explanation that may have been beyond the Sadducees to work out for themselves to an understanding of the text of Scripture that they ought to have been able to manage because in rejecting other authorities they made Scripture central; it was Scripture only to which the Sadducees appealed. The Pharisees thought of Scripture as the words of God himself, but for the understanding of Scripture they had an extensive oral tradition. The Sadducees rejected all of this tradition. For them the Bible, the Bible only, was the word of God. Very well then. Let them consider what the Bible says. Notice that Jesus speaks of what Scripture says *to you*. Scripture, of course, says the words to everyone, but it is important for these Sadducees to notice that the following passage speaks to them directly on the subject they had chosen to debate with Jesus, *the resurrection of the dead*.[48]

32. And Jesus does not cite some obscure passage that might well be overlooked by ordinary people (even by high priests and their associates as they went about the complex business of running the temple!). He draws their attention to words spoken by God himself and very much quoted by religious and patriotic Jews: *"I am the God of Abraham and the God of Isaac and the God of Jacob"* (Exod. 3:6). The threefold repetition is most impressive, and presumably the Sadducees, like many others, had been so attracted by the majesty of the words and what they told them of the experiences of the patriarchs that they had never stopped to think of the implications of the saying. So Jesus points out that the present tense is important. Neither the Sadducees nor anybody else said that "God was the God of Abraham, etc." If there is no afterlife, they should have said that when they referred to the patriarchs and their God. The fact that they all took it for granted that God *is* the God of the patriarchs tells us something about the patriarchs as well as about God. He is *the God . . . of the living*, and in this context the living must be Abraham, Isaac, and Jacob.

33. Matthew does not tell us what the Sadducees said in response to this; perhaps they said nothing at all. What could they say? Jesus' citation of the well-known passage was so unexpected and his short interpretation of it so convincing that they must have found themselves without a retort

47. γαμέω is the verb normally used of a man marrying a woman (though it can be used of a woman marrying, as in 1 Cor. 7:28, of a woman as well as a man, and of both sexes, as in 1 Cor. 7:9-10). γαμίζω normally refers to giving a woman in marriage. The two words make it clear that in heaven neither sex will seek marriage.

48. In the New Testament the general resurrection is often spoken of as ἀνάστασις ἐκ τῶν νεκρῶν; resurrection is "from the dead" (but cf. Rom. 1:4; 1 Cor. 15:12, etc.).

(in the next verse we find that they had been "muzzled" by Jesus' words). But if Matthew says nothing about the Sadducees, he does say something about *the crowds* who watched and listened throughout the exchange. They *were astonished;* they had doubtless heard the Sadducees before, and possibly they had heard them bring forth the same little story (it has all the hallmarks of a favorite controversial sally). Now to hear the Sadducaic position demolished in such short order was nothing less than astonishing. The astonishment was directed at *his teaching,* but in the context this will mean mostly at the riposte he had directed at the Sadducees.

34. *The Pharisees* had tried to trap Jesus in his speech (v. 15) without success. But now that they heard that the Sadducees had been *silenced* (the word means "muzzled"; it indicates clearly that they did not know what to say),[49] the Pharisees reviewed the situation. They *were gathered together,*[50] which looks like a more or less formal assembly. The impression Matthew gives is that the discomfiture of the Sadducees signaled to the Pharisees that there was a new situation, and it seemed well to them that they should get together and consider what they ought to do. But if that is what is meant, Matthew is not very interested in the Pharisaic discussions. He goes on immediately to a question asked by one of them. It was not the discussion but the sequel that was important.

35. Matthew says that *one of them* now put another question to Jesus (so the Pharisaic inquisition was still on the job), this one described as *a lawyer.*[51] From the form of the question we might be ready to think it was a genuine quest for information, but since Matthew expressly says that the lawyer was *testing him* we must view this as another attempt to entrap Jesus. The restless attempts to trick Jesus into an answer that would discredit him either with the authorities or with the general public continued. His opponents never learned that they were on a futile quest.

36. Once again we have the polite address, *"Teacher";* throughout this series of attempts to entrap and discredit Jesus there is the outward form of politeness. The lawyer proceeds to ask, *"which is the great commandment in the law?"* (Mark has "the first commandment," but this will mean much the same, "the first in importance").[52] The rabbis divided the command-

---

49. ἐφίμωσεν from φιμός, "a muzzle"; the verb is used in its literal sense in Deuteronomy 25:4 (LXX).

50. ἐπὶ τὸ αὐτό is used in the sense "together," as in Acts 1:15 etc. MM notes the use in the papyri.

51. νομικός, here only in Matthew but 6 times in Luke, means, of course, "learned in the law." The law in question was the law of Moses. Mark has "one of the scribes," but the meaning will be much the same, for the scribes were experts in the law. Luke has Matthew's word. Some MSS omit the word in Matthew, and this, taken in conjunction with the fact that Matthew does not use the word elsewhere, leads some to omit it. But the attestation is strong, and there is no reason why Matthew should not use a word once only. It should be accepted.

52. Howard regards Matthew's form as "quite clearly a much less idiomatic translation of the Aramaic (which has no degrees of comparison)" (M, II, p. 30). In Aramaic "the great" could mean "the greatest"; μεγάλη here means "great as compared to the other commandments," "the greatest."

ments in the law into the light and the weighty. They did not mean that some commandments were so slight that they could be neglected. All the commandments were God's, and therefore all were to be treated with full seriousness. But obviously some commandments were more important than others; the command to do no murder is more important than that which prohibits boiling a kid in its mother's milk (Deut. 14:21). That opened up the way for speculation as to which of all the 613 commandments that the rabbis found in the law was to be regarded as the greatest of them all. This is another question that must have looked to the questioner as though it should give matter for argument and controversy no matter what answer Jesus gave. There is no objective yardstick for measuring one commandment against another, so that whatever commandment Jesus selected for the first place would certainly have been placed lower by others.[53] The lawyer was initiating a discussion that might lead anywhere and that in his view would certainly provide a strong possibility of damaging Jesus' reputation.

37-38. It is not unlikely that Jesus' hearers were expecting one or other of the Ten Commandments, those that had been written by the finger of God and that, as a group, stood out over all the other commandments. But Jesus did not select one of those. Instead he chose the commandment to love God, the commandment that must have been most familiar of all to his hearers, for it was recited every day by the pious Jew: *"You shall love the Lord your God with all your heart and with all your soul."* Thus far the words are identical with those in Deuteronomy 6:5 (cf. Deut. 11:13), but whereas that passage goes on "and with all your might" Jesus proceeds, *"and with all your mind."* We should not make too much of this difference, for both ways of expressing it make the point that love for God should be wholehearted, involving all that we have and all that we are (the threefold *all* is important). Mark interestingly has the three expressions in Deuteronomy, but he inserts "with all your mind" before the third. *"This is the first and great commandment,"* Jesus says (in Mark's version the questioner asked, "Which is the first commandment of all," so that Jesus' summary includes the expressions used in the two Gospels).

39. Jesus was asked for but one commandment, but he goes further and adds *"a second"* that, he says, *"is like it."* Wholehearted love for God means coming in some measure to see other people as God sees them, and all people as the objects of God's love. Therefore anyone who truly loves God with all his being must and will love others, and this is expressed in the commandment, *"You shall love your neighbor as yourself,"* a commandment that is repeated in the Pentateuch (Lev. 19:18, 34).[54] The term *neighbor*

---

53. The rabbis could select other commands than those chosen by Jesus. Thus in reply to the question, "What short text is there upon which all the essential principles of the Torah depend?" the answer is Proverbs 3:6, "In all your ways acknowledge him, and he will make straight your paths" (*Ber.* 63a).

54. The combination was not unknown in Judaism; thus we find, for example, "Keep

is somewhat elastic, but Jesus certainly meant more than loving the person next door (though people sometimes find it easier to love the neighbor understood as an abstract subject than the objectionable person next door who is all too concrete a reality!). It seems that the Jews tended to understand by the *neighbor* one's fellow Jew and to leave open the possibility of extending a thoroughgoing hatred to "lesser breeds without the law." But there cannot be the slightest doubt that Jesus is extending the term as widely as it can be extended; he is saying that one must love one's fellow human being. The two great commandments go together (if anyone says he loves God and hates his brother he is a liar, 1 John 4:20).

40. Jesus rounds this discussion off with the point that, rightly observed, these two commandments involve the whole law.[55] Not only the law, but the prophets as well *hang* on these two commandments.[56] Anyone who loves God and people wholeheartedly is not going to come short in religious observances, nor in doing what is proper to other people. In short, when anyone loves in the way Jesus says, there is no need for a host of hair-splitting definitions of when an obligation has been discharged and when it has not. As I have written elsewhere, "Jesus swept aside all such pettifogging nonsense with his revolutionary insistence on the centrality of love and for good measure he added that the teaching of the prophets is included in this command. At one stroke he did away with any understanding of the service of God that sees it as concerned with the acquiring of merit or with an emphasis on liturgical concerns. What matters can be summed up in one word: love."[57] This does not, of course, mean that all other commandments may be ignored and that all that one must do is love. The commandments of God are serious and must be observed. But Jesus is saying that it is only when we love that we can truly obey them and that without love we do not really understand what the commandments mean. In one way or another all the commandments are expressions of God's love. Love is the thrust of them all, and it is only as we love that we fulfil them.

41. It would appear that Jesus' summary of the law and the prophets

---

the Law of God, my children. . . . Love the Lord and your neighbor" (*Test. Iss.* 5:1-2; see also 7:6; *Test. Dan* 5:3; cited from Charlesworth, pp. 803, 804, 809). It should be added that the date of the *Testaments* is uncertain, and it is quite possible, as some scholars think, that these references are due to Christian influence. But, of course, Luke tells us of a lawyer who gave much the same summary (Luke 10:25-28).

55. There is a well-known passage in which a man told Hillel that he would become a proselyte if Hillel taught him the whole Torah while he stood on one foot. Hillel replied, "What is hateful to you do not to your neighbor: that is the whole Torah, while the rest is the commentary thereof" (*Shab.* 31a). It is an interesting summary, but it is negative in form and it omits any reference to God.

56. "As a door hangs on its hinges, so the whole OT hangs on these two comm." (BAGD, κρεμάννυμι 2b). Cf. G. Barth, the two commandments "are not only the greatest, but the whole law and the prophets 'hang on them'. . . . They are the basic norms, in the performance of which all others are performed, they are the essence of the law" (*TIM*, p. 78).

57. Article on "Love" from the forthcoming *Dictionary of Jesus and the Gospels*.

was such that it cut short any attempt the Pharisees might have contemplated to start a discussion on the relative merits of this or that commandment. What Jesus said was so unexpected and yet so convincing that nitpicking criticism was for the time out of the question. Jesus used the occasion to ask a question of his own. Matthew links it with the foregoing by saying that it was *while the Pharisees were gathered together.*[58]

42. *"What do you think[59] about the Messiah?"* is a question that might cover a very wide field, but Jesus narrows it immediately with *"Whose son is he?"* He is asking a question about ancestry; a query about the Messiah's sonship might be understood in the sense that Jesus is looking for information about his father. But among the Jews *son* was used more widely than in many modern communities, and this question was meant in the sense, "Who is the great man from whom the Messiah is descended?" For the Pharisees this was an easy question, and they gave the expected answer, *"David's";* in a community with vivid messianic expectations there was no doubting that the Messiah would be "Great David's greater Son."

43. Matthew keeps the narrative vivid with another present tense (*says*) as he informs his readers how Jesus proceeds to the telling question. He does this by citing the opening words of Psalm 110 (the verse from the Old Testament most frequently quoted in the New Testament) and asking how this fits into generally accepted ideas of sonship. He accepts the Davidic authorship of the psalm, which, of course, would not have been doubted anywhere in first-century Judaism (the psalm is headed "A Psalm of David").[60] And he accepts that David wrote the psalm under the leadership of the Spirit of God; the psalm is inspired Scripture. Further he regards the psalm as messianic; it teaches something about the Messiah who would come in due course and is not to be confined to statements about David. All this would have been common ground between Jesus and the Pharisees, and so far there would have been no problem. But Jesus draws attention to the fact that David calls the Messiah *"Lord"* (thus conceding his own inferiority to the Messiah).[61]

44. Jesus proceeds to quote the relevant words in the psalm (the

---

58. The perfect participle συνηγμένων points to a continuing assembly; it was not a casual contact where a few Pharisees happened to be in the same place.

59. We have here the impersonal use of δοκεῖ, "What does it seem to you?" (as in 17:25; 18:12, etc.); Matthew uses it with a personal subject in 3:9; 6:7, etc.

60. Derek Kidner points out that before the discovery of the Qumran scrolls there was a tendency "to date the psalm in the Maccabaean era (2nd century B.C.), and even to find the name of Simon, the Maccabaean High Priest and political leader, in the initial letters of the verses, with a little rearrangement." He also points out that H. H. Rowley "saw in verse 4 David's oracle to Jebusite Zadok, adopting him as Israel's High Priest, while in the rest of the psalm Zadok addressed David, newly enthroned at Jerusalem." In modern times, he says, most critics see it as "an enthronement oracle for either David or one of his successors" (*Psalms 73–150* [London, 1975], p. 392, n. 1). In the first century everyone accepted the psalm as Davidic.

61. Cf. Kidner, "while other psalms share with this one the exalted language which points beyond the reigning king to the Messiah, here alone the king himself does homage to this personage" (*Psalms 73–150,* p. 392).

quotation is almost exactly as LXX). *"The Lord"* refers to God himself (the Hebrew is יהוה); the psalm is proceeding to give a divine utterance. When David says that God spoke *"to my Lord,"* he is clearly referring to someone greater than himself (Knox translates, "the Lord said to my Master"), and this is surely the Messiah. David is recording a prophecy of the greatness of his descendant, whom he recognizes as greater than he. The prophecy refers to the Messiah as sitting on the right hand of God, that is, in the highest place of all, in the place where it counts above all. And while he sits there, God himself will defeat all his enemies; that they are to be put under his feet indicates that they are to be thoroughly subjugated to him.[62]

Jesus' contemporaries seem to have thought of "the Son of David" as a Messiah like David, one who would sit on David's throne, make warlike conquests as David did, and in general be David all over again. Jesus rejected that idea. "At the very least Jesus declares the freedom of the Messiah to establish the Kingdom by another path than the political and military methods of David. The Messiah can be and will be the Suffering Servant rather than the military conqueror and earthly king" (Filson, p. 240; Filson thinks that Jesus rejected the "Son of David" idea, but it is more correct to say that he reinterpreted it).[63]

45. *Therefore* links what follows with the quotation: because this is what Scripture says (and Scripture must be accepted, is the reasoning), then certain things follow. The important one is that David recognizes the Messiah as his *"Lord."* Now comes the unanswerable question, unanswerable on the Pharisees' premises, *"how is he his son?"* It was widely accepted that the greatest times had been in antiquity and that history had been all downhill since the early golden age. In a family the father was the great person, and it was axiomatic that his sons were less significant than he. In a society that held views like this the great king David was held to be certainly greater than his descendants. If the Messiah was to be among those descendants, then, of course, on Pharisaic premises, he must be inferior to David. But David speaks of him as *"Lord,"* which means that he must be greater. This presented the Pharisees with a difficult conundrum to which they found no answer.

We should not think of this as no more than an exercise in debating skills. There was a widespread idea that the Messiah was "the Son of David," and that meant for first-century Jews that he would be someone in David's mold. They recalled that David had been a mighty warrior and

---

62. There is a textual variant in that the best text appears to read "under (ὑποκάτω) your feet" (א B D etc.) while some MSS have "footstool" (ὑποπόδιον) (W 0138 etc.). It seems clear that some scribes altered "under" to agree with the text of the psalm. The meaning is much the same.

63. Cf. Plummer, "Christ's argument is seriously misapprehended, when it is supposed that He criticized the assertion that the Messiah is the Son of David as *untrue*. He criticized it as *inadequate*" (p. 310). Ridderbos comments, "He would not remain bound to the limits posed by His human descent" (p. 420).

that in his day Israel's conquests had been extensive. But Jesus was not that sort of Messiah. For him being Messiah meant being a teacher, and being a redeemer, one who would die for others, not one who would head up great armies and slaughter people. By drawing attention to a defect in the way the Pharisees understood the relationship of David to David's Son, Jesus was encouraging his hearers to think again about what Messiah meant. There were many things the Pharisees did not understand about messiahship.[64] Let his hearers then not trust those blind guides.

46. That finished the questioning session. The Pharisees, the Herodians, and the Sadducees had all tried to put questions to Jesus that would embarrass him and put him into disfavor with the people or the governing bodies or both, and while it could not be said that he had failed to answer, it could be said that he had produced answers that left him unscathed and caused the people to marvel at him. He was more admired when they finished than when they started on this exercise. So it is no surprise that, finding they could not answer the question he had put to them, none of them dared any more to question him. This was a game in which they thought they held all the advantages (how could a layman from rural Galilee compete with the professionals who had been through the schools in Jerusalem?). But in the end they had been defeated.

---

64. "It was fundamentally because they had the wrong conception of the Messiah, thinking of Him as a human warrior rather than as a divine Saviour, that they failed to see Him in Jesus" (Tasker, p. 213).

Matthew 23

2. Jesus' Denunciation of the Pharisees, 23:1-39

[1]*Then Jesus spoke to the crowds and to his disciples,* [2]*saying, "The scribes and the Pharisees have taken their seat on the chair of Moses.* [3]*Therefore do and observe the entirety of the things they tell you, but do not do according to their works, for they say and do not do.* [4]*And they tie up loads that are heavy and hard to carry and put them on men's shoulders, but they themselves are not willing to move them with as much as their finger.* [5]*But all their works they do in order to be seen by people; for they make their phylacteries broad and their tassels long;* [6]*and they love the chief couch in the banquets, and the chief seats in the synagogues,* [7]*and the greetings in the marketplaces, and to be called 'Rabbi' by men.* [8]*But don't you be called 'Rabbi,' for one is your teacher, and you are all brothers.* [9]*And do not call anyone your father on the earth, for one is your Father, the heavenly One.* [10]*And do not be called instructors, for one is your instructor, namely Christ.* [11]*But he who is greatest among you will be your servant;* [12]*and he who will exalt himself will be humbled, and he who will humble himself will be exalted.*

[13]*"But woe to you, scribes and Pharisees, hypocrites, because you shut up the kingdom of heaven before men, for you do not enter yourselves, nor do you allow those who are entering to enter.* [15]*Woe to you, scribes and Pharisees, hypocrites, because you travel over sea and land to make one proselyte, and when he becomes one, you make him twice as much a son of hell as yourselves.* [16]*Woe to you, blind guides who say, 'Whoever swears by the temple, it is nothing; but whoever swears by the gold of the temple is bound.'* [17]*You fools and blind! For what is greater, the gold or the temple that sanctifies the gold?* [18]*And, 'Whoever swears by the altar, it is nothing; but whoever swears by the gift that is on it is bound.'* [19]*Blind men! For what is greater, the gift or the altar that sanctifies the gift?* [20]*Therefore he who swears by the altar swears by it and by all that is on it.* [21]*And he who swears by the temple swears by it and by him who dwells in it.* [22]*And he who swears by heaven swears by the throne of God and by him who sits on it.*

[23]*"Woe to you, scribes and Pharisees, hypocrites, because you tithe mint and dill and cummin, and you have neglected the weightier matters of the*

law, justice and mercy and faithfulness; but these you ought to have done, without neglecting the others. 24*Blind guides! You strain out the gnat but gulp down the camel.* 25*Woe to you, scribes and Pharisees, hypocrites, because you clean the outside of the cup and the dish, but inside they are full of robbery and self-indulgence.* 26*Blind Pharisee! First clean the inside of the cup, so that its outside may become clean too.*

27*"Woe to you, scribes and Pharisees, hypocrites, because you are like whitewashed tombs, which indeed appear outwardly beautiful but inwardly they are full of dead people's bones and all uncleanness.* 28*So you also appear outwardly to men as righteous, but inwardly you are full of hypocrisy and lawlessness.* 29*Woe to you, scribes and Pharisees, hypocrites, because you build the tombs of the prophets and decorate the monuments of the righteous,* 30*and you say, 'If we had lived in the days of our forefathers, we would not have been their partners in shedding the blood of the prophets.'* 31*So then you testify against yourselves that you are sons of those who murdered the prophets.* 32*And you — fill up the measure of your fathers.* 33*You snakes! You brood of vipers! How will you escape being sentenced to hell?* 34*Therefore I am sending to you prophets and sages and scribes; some of them you will kill and crucify, and some you will flog in your synagogues and persecute from town to town.* 35*So that there will come upon you all the righteous blood that has been shed on the earth, from the blood of righteous Abel to the blood of Zechariah, son of Barachiah, whom you killed between the sanctuary and the altar.* 36*Truly I tell you, all these things will come on this generation.*

37*"Jerusalem, Jerusalem, you who kill the prophets and stone those who are sent to you, how often would I have gathered your children together, in the way a hen gathers her chickens under her wings, and you would not.* 38*Look, your house is left to you desolate.* 39*For I tell you, you will not see me any more until you say, 'Blessed is he who comes in the name of the Lord.' "*

There is nothing comparable to this sustained denunciation of the scribes and Pharisees in any of the other Gospels. Both Mark and Luke tell us that Jesus made some criticisms of these religious leaders after the question-and-answer session narrated in chapter 22 (Mark 12:38-40; Luke 20:45-47), but in Matthew the denunciation is much more sustained. From it we learn something of the superficiality that characterized all too many of the Pharisees. We know from the rabbinic writings that not all Pharisees were like this, but we must bear in mind that the rabbinic writings let us see the Pharisees as they saw themselves; they do not give us any picture of the Pharisees as the people they despised saw them. We must remember, too, that Jesus was on the spot and we are not. We should also bear in mind that Jesus is not saying that all Pharisees at all times came under his condemnation; he is referring specifically to certain Pharisees of his own day. It is, moreover, not at all impossible that the people Jesus encountered as he went about his mission, largely in rural areas, did not feel the same way about the Pharisees as those later representatives of the party whose teachings are recorded in the Mishnah and the Talmud.[1] Jesus knew what the people that he encountered were like, the Pharisees as well as others.

This chapter brings us to understand that the Pharisaic system, like any system that puts its emphasis on rules and regulations, all too easily degenerated into the observance of requirements that were doubtless intended to help people along the road to godliness but that could become ends in themselves. When this happened, there was the appearance of godliness, but not the reality; the correct performance of outward rites and the firm hold on orthodox teaching became ends in themselves, and genuine piety suffered. There is a danger in the whole Pharisaic method.[2] Stendahl remarks that Jesus "taught with prophetic consciousness in a nation where he found the strongest resistance among those who were its spiritual leaders."

According to many modern scholars, this chapter tells us more about the church in Matthew's day than it does about Jesus. They assume that the Evangelist has put on to Jesus' lips words that apply to conditions late in the first century when the church and the synagogue were often at odds. But, as Carson says, "Even if we assume that Matthew's choice of what he includes largely reflects the situation at the time he wrote, it is naive to think twentieth-century scholars can reconstruct the situation in detail." We should also bear in mind that there are vigorous denunciations of the Pharisees in Luke's Gospel, and it is not easy to argue that Luke was reflecting the same situation over against the synagogue as was Matthew.[3] It may also be observed that in the later writings like the Mishnah and

1. It is true that there are denunciations of hypocrisy in Jewish writings (e.g., *Yoma* 86b), so that later teachers at any rate were aware of the temptation. I. Abrahams tries to refute the criticisms of the Pharisees by citing the examples of Gamaliel, Hillel, and Aqiba (*Studies in Pharisaism and the Gospels*, 2nd ser. [New York, 1967], pp. 30-32). But this is to miss the point. No one doubts that there were some great and good Pharisees, but it is quite another thing to say that the average Pharisee in Jesus' time made the same impression on lowly people as did some of the great leaders.

2. France speaks of "the faults inherent in the Pharisaic approach to religion even at its best. Even the most scrupulous of Pharisees followed a system which tended to understand righteousness in terms of more and more minute legal prescriptions, and which could therefore dangerously distort the whole question of what it means to please God." Diétrich points out that "Jesus addressed these reproaches to the most 'churchgoing' believers of his day," and Fenton aptly reminds us that in reply to anyone who complained of this section of his Gospel, Matthew might well have used the words of Nathan: "You are the man" (p. 365).

3. Mounce remarks, "a Jesus who is not allowed by his critics to say anything contrary to their tastes will be a Jesus quite different from what we should expect to find in history" (p. 222). He reminds us that A. M. Hunter lists as examples of the "astonishing variety of the portraits of Jesus which our learned men have given us": Renan's "Amiable Carpenter," Tolstoi's "Spiritual Anarchist," Schweitzer's "Imminent Cataclysmist," Klausner's "Unorthodox Rabbi," and Otto's "Charismatic Evangelist" (*The Work and Words of Jesus* [London, 1950], p. 14). We must all beware of making a Jesus who fits our own prejudices.

the Talmud there is undeniably a concern for the minutiae. While there are some great passages in these writings, far too much is taken up with things of no great consequence.[4]

1-2. *Then* (see on 2:7) does not always denote strict sequence in this Gospel, but the probability is that this denunciation of a piety that was nothing more than a firm performance of the externals took place soon after the events narrated in the previous chapter (and this would be supported by the abbreviated accounts in Mark and Luke). Jesus addressed his remarks to *the crowds and to his disciples.* He has some strong denunciations of the Pharisees, but he is not so much criticizing them as drawing his hearers' attention to the kind of lives they should be living. He is warning them not to adopt the superficial and hypocritical approach that was unfortunately so characteristic of the Pharisees. As often in Matthew, *crowds* is in the plural and refers to potential disciples. The people as a whole were not yet ready to follow him, but they were much more open than the Pharisees and the Sadducees. Throughout his ministry the *crowds* did not give him wholehearted support, but they listened to him and were glad to see him do miracles of healing; there is no reason for doubting that many from among them in time came to follow Jesus. In this context the crowds will refer to the large numbers who had come to Jerusalem for the Passover; many of these would have been Galileans who had some knowledge of what Jesus had taught and done in their area. But we must not think of the entire group as sympathetic to Jesus, for he goes on to denounce the scribes and Pharisees, where his use of the second person seems to mean that they were there in the audience. For *disciples* see on 5:1; 8:21; they were people who had cast in their lot with Jesus and looked to him for teaching. In other words, Jesus was now talking to a sympathetic audience, not to people trying to trap him as in the previous chapter. He began by speaking of the *scribes* (for which see on 2:4; 5:20) and the *Pharisees* (see on 3:7).[5] Not all the scribes were Pharisees, but we

---

4. This chapter is sometimes included among the great discourses of this Gospel, but we should bear in mind that Matthew does not append to it "and it came to pass, when Jesus had ended these sayings," which we find in 7:28; 11:1; 13:53; 19:1; 26:1. It is also perhaps relevant that whereas in the major addresses he speaks primarily to the disciples with the crowds, perhaps as part of the outer circle, here part of the discourse is addressed to the scribes and Pharisees and part to Jerusalem. It is, of course, possible to include this with the next two chapters to make chapters 23–25 the final discourse (as some scholars do), but this ignores the fact that Matthew says that before the words of chapter 24 Jesus went out of the temple and on his way (24:1); he further says that the discourse that followed was delivered on the Mount of Olives (24:3). Clearly Matthew does not regard what follows in chapter 24 as the same discourse as in this chapter. In any case, there is an abrupt change of subject matter. It would be possible to see chapters 23–25 as a section given over to teaching, but this is not the same as calling it one discourse.

5. There are separate articles with γραμματεῖς and Φαρισαίοι; thus the two are not regarded as one group (as they usually are in this Gospel; this is the one place in Matthew where the two expressions have separate articles); "the two classes are distinguished" (Robertson, pp. 758-59).

should understand most of those mentioned here as belonging to that party, for throughout the chapter they are included in the same denunciations. In speaking of *scribes* Jesus is referring to learned men (i.e., men learned in the Scriptures) who taught the law, and in speaking of *Pharisees* of those who were not necessarily teachers but who took their religion very seriously and made strenuous endeavors to perform their obligations before God. The fact that they were all too often superficial should not blind us to the other fact that often they tried hard to do what they conceived of as their duty as servants of God.

The first thing Jesus says about these religious people is that they *have taken their seat*[6] *on the chair of Moses*. This does not refer to any particular piece of furniture, but to the teaching office. *Chair*[7] here refers to the teaching office as something that carried on from generation to generation. Moses was the great teacher of Israel, and his legacy, the law, was the object of continuing study. That they *have taken their seat* on Moses' chair means that they have taken it on themselves to teach authoritatively in the tradition of Moses (as they saw it).[8] There is some emphasis on *Moses;* he was the great lawgiver, and his teaching had to be respected throughout the generations. The scribes and the Pharisees were not evolving new schools of interpretation but trying hard to make clear what Moses had said, and, where there were problems, in helping people understand what actions were called for on their part as they tried to put into practice the things that Moses commanded. They were held to be authoritative in their teaching, and the Mishnah can even say, "Greater stringency applies to [the observance of] the words of the Scribes than to [the observance of] the words of the [written] Law" (*Sanh.* 11:3).

3. *Therefore* draws a conclusion; because these people were expounding what Moses had said, they must be heard with interest and attention. But, as Bengel points out, only when expounding Moses; "This particle

---

6. The aorist ἐκάθισαν is unusual; there is no reference to a definite point in the past. It may be equivalent to the perfect, but the emphasis is surely on the present state of affairs.

7. καθέδρα can refer to any seat (Matthew has used it of the seats of the dove sellers, 21:12), but it sometimes has specific seats in mind, such as the judge's seat (see BAGD). MM cites its use for the sophistical chair occupied by Nicagoras in the third century A.D., a chair whose holder, they say, "ranked above the other professors." The term has influenced our language in various ways; for example, "cathedral" refers to the place of the bishop's "seat."

8. Some scholars have drawn attention to a prominent stone chair found in excavations of some synagogues (later than New Testament times) and suggest that the law of Moses was expounded from such a seat in Jesus' day. But D. E. Garland is surely right in rejecting such an idea here. He says that, while there may indeed have been such a seat, Jesus "was not referring to a physical sitting but to the collective symbol of their legal authority" (*ISBE,* III, p. 425). Similarly H. C. Kee says that here "Moses' seat" is to be seen "as the symbolic locus of authoritative interpretation of Torah (with its implicit links to oral law, or at least to legal tradition going back to Sinai)" (*NTS,* 36 [1990], p. 15). So Beare: "It is simply a metaphor; the scribes and Pharisees are those responsible for declaring to the people what the law of Moses requires of them." The rabbis could say, "every three [judges] which have risen up as a court over Israel are like to the court of Moses" (*Rosh. Hash.* 2:9); in other words, the decisions of each such court are to be accepted just as were the words of Moses.

limits the expression" so that it does not cover Pharisaic traditions.[9] "*Do and observe*" puts some emphasis on the importance of putting into practice the things the Pharisees were teaching. Carson, supported by Jeremias, holds that the words are "biting irony, bordering on sarcasm" (p. 473). This is possible, but it seems more likely that Jesus is differentiating between the words of the Pharisees and their deeds. His complaint is not that these men were false teachers; they were orthodox and they were rightly drawing people's attention to the things that Moses had taught and that were of permanent importance for the people of God. "*The entirety of the things they tell you*" is more literally "all things whatsoever they say to you"; it amounts to a wholehearted endorsement of the teaching of the Pharisees over against their practice. They studied the law of Moses closely and expounded it in great detail. There was nothing wrong with this part of what they were doing, and Jesus commends it. Of course, when they went beyond the law of Moses they could and did go wrong, and Jesus criticizes them for it (e.g., 15:12-14). Here, however, he is commending their upholding of what Moses taught.

But it was otherwise with the way they lived. Jesus' followers are not to do[10] *according to their works*. Their condemnation is summed up in the words "*they say and do not do*." It has always been the temptation of the religious to put emphasis on their teaching and to take more lightly the obligations to live out the precepts they inculcate. It so easily becomes a habit to live in such a way as to sustain or acquire a reputation for piety, without giving heed to what we are deep down. So Jesus warns his hearers that they should not live in the way the Pharisees lived, though they should take careful note of what the Pharisees taught. When the Pharisees brought out the significance of the teaching of Moses, they were doing something of great importance for the people of God. What they were teaching was both meaningful and creditable: they should be heard. But when they acted hypocritically, that was another matter: they should not be imitated or followed.[11]

4. Jesus begins his catalogue of the wrong things they do with the way they burden those who listen to them. Tying *up loads* points to the preparation of loads that animals or slaves might be involved in carrying; the loads had to be tied into secure packages before they were taken away. But this could be done carelessly, in which case the loads might be both heavy and unwieldy — awkward to carry as well as weighty. Jesus speaks

---

9. So also Gundry: "'All things whatever' does not include their interpretative traditions, but emphasizes the totality of the law. 'Therefore' establishes the qualification" (Gundry, p. 455).

10. If the words are used strictly, μὴ ποιεῖτε will mean "stop doing"; it will indicate that Jesus' audience had been in the habit of viewing Pharisaic practice as a godly model. Jesus tells them not to do this.

11. "They did not (in God's sight) do what they appeared to do. Though they scrupulously observed their own rules, their motive and manner deprived their actions of all value" (McNeile).

of the burdens the Pharisees and their aides prepared for people as both
heavy and *hard to carry*.[12] That is to say, they so interpreted the law of Moses
that the people who heeded them found themselves required to perform
some very burdensome duties in the service of God (by contrast Jesus
could say to his followers, "my burden is a light one," 11:30). But the
Pharisees themselves had no will to engage in such arduous activities. The
regulations they evolved for ritual purity were much harder for people in
trades and similar walks of life than for the more leisured and scholarly
Pharisees.[13] Jesus says that they would not use *as much as their finger*, which
is about as small an effort as one can readily make. The way the law was
interpreted meant that there was a multitude of ways of mitigating hard
requirements that were not known to ordinary people, but that men like
the Pharisees practiced assiduously.

5. The condemnation is that they do *all their works* (not for what they
avail in the service of God, but) *in order to be seen by people*. This is, of
course, the perennial temptation of the religious person, and Jesus has
earlier warned against it (6:1-6); it is so easy to do the things that one
thinks will bring one a reputation for piety, and the Pharisees succumbed
to that temptation. By contrast Jesus expects his followers so to live that
they bring glory, not to themselves, but to God (5:16). Many of the things
the Pharisees did were undoubtedly worthy, but they did them with their
attention fixed on what people would think of them. They did them for
show, and such deeds are not meritorious in the sight of God. Jesus gives
examples with their *phylacteries* and their *tassels*. The phylactery[14] was a
little box containing verses from Scripture (Exod. 13:1-10, 11-16; Deut.
6:4-9; 11:13-21; phylacteries discovered at Qumran show that there was
some variation in the texts used). It is generally identified with the *tefillah*
and was worn by adult males at daily morning prayers (at home or in the
synagogue) in literal fulfilment of passages in the law (Exod. 13:9, 16; Deut.
6:8; 11:18); it seems that some Jews wore them also outside the hours of
prayer. Discoveries of *tefillin* at Qumran and Murabbaʿat indicate that the
one on the forehead tended to be rectangular, and that there was considerable variation in size. The making of the phylactery broad will thus refer
to using a phylactery that spread further across the forehead and accord-

---

12. βαρέα indicates that the loads are weighty. There is textual doubt about καὶ
δυσβάστακτα; it has impressive support from MSS like B D K W, but the words are omitted
by L f¹ 892 and others. The disputed words might well have been introduced from Luke
11:46, but on the other hand they might have been omitted by a copyist's eye passing from
one καί to the other. Metzger rejects the words, but his committee favored including them
within square brackets.

13. "Considerable social tension between the scribes and the people at large is implied
in this saying" (Hill).

14. φυλακτήριον occurs only here in the Bible. The word is connected with φυλάσσω, "to
guard," and there may be the thought of safeguarding, regarding the phylactery as in the
nature of a charm. Two of them were worn, one on the forehead and the other on the upper
left arm (and thus near the heart). See the article by R. L. Omanson in *ISBE*, III, pp. 884-85.

ingly was more prominent than those normally used, rather than one with a bigger box. The *tassel* (see on 9:20, where we find that Jesus himself wore this) was sometimes used of the edge of something, but it was also used of tassels attached to the outer garment to remind people to follow God's commandments (Num. 15:37-38). The tassel was not necessarily ostentatious, but to make the tassel big was to make sure that everyone one met would know that one took God's commandments with full seriousness. Jesus mentions two outward actions that the Pharisees could and did perform to give their piety public display.

6. In keeping with this general attitude they *love* the things that get them in the public eye. Jesus speaks of *the chief couch in the banquets*. At such significant meals the tables were apparently arranged in a U shape, with the most important places at the junction of the two arms. People reclined on couches, leaning on the left elbow and with the head toward the table; food would be taken with the right hand. The chief place was that at the center of the *triclinium* (couch for three) at the head of the table, and this would be taken by the host. The most honored guests would share his *triclinium*, and the others would take their places in descending order of importance. The Pharisees, Jesus says, loved to secure the place they considered most important at such banquets. To be in the place of honor meant that one was seen to be an important person.

Not a great deal is known of synagogues in first-century Palestine. Indeed, H. C. Kee says: "there is simply no evidence to speak of synagogues in Palestine as architecturally distinguishable edifices prior to 200 C.E." Prior to that people met for worship indeed, but in buildings indistinguishable from private houses or "as space set aside in public buildings."[15] Not surprisingly our information about the interior setup of such synagogues is limited, but it seems that there was a platform from which services were conducted, Scripture was read, and preachers delivered their sermons. There appear to have been some seats behind the officiants, facing the congregation, for people not leading the service, and, if so, they would have been regarded as important places. Whether these seats were there or elsewhere, Jesus' words make it clear that some prominent seats were regarded as *the chief seats* and that the Pharisees liked to be seen occupying such seats.

7. The Pharisees also liked *greetings in the marketplaces*, which evidently points to something more than the normal method of greeting people encountered in the everyday course of business. The marketplace was, of course, the place where people gathered together, the public place in any town or village. Jesus was referring to some elaborate form of greeting that conveyed the idea that the greeted person was someone of

---

15. *NTS*, 36 (1990), p. 9. W. S. LaSor and T. C. Eskenazi say, "It may be that distinctive synagogue buildings in the Holy Land were not really common until after the destruction of the temple" (*ISBE*, IV, p. 678).

importance.[16] To be in the public eye in such a capacity was highly desirable from the Pharisaic point of view. So with the title *"Rabbi."*[17] Dalman points out that the word was used in other ways than for a teacher. It could denote a master over against a slave, it could mean a prince, indeed he finds it used of the king of Israel, where it "is considered the equivalent of the royal title." He says that anyone so addressed "is thereby acknowledged to be the superior of the speaker."[18] We are so accustomed to using it as the title of a teacher that we tend to miss the greatness implied by the word. To be called "Rabbi" in public meant that there was open recognition of the status of the man so honored; he was regarded as an outstanding teacher of the law.

8. *But* has adversative force: Jesus sets his followers over against people like the Pharisees of whom he has been complaining. He has shown them the kind of conduct he deplores in people accepted as religious leaders but who do not live up to the things they teach; his followers are not to be like that.[19] Specifically he says that they should not *be called* *"Rabbi,"* a title that sets the holder off from lesser mortals. Jesus' followers did not have teachers that ranked with the Jewish rabbis, and they must not act as though there were outstanding people among them to whom they must give heed. *"One is your teacher,"* Jesus says, and that has its implications for all his followers. It does not mean, of course, that none of them can ever learn from any of the others. The very fact that the books of the New Testament were ever written is testimony to the fact that some Christians were able to teach others. And, of course, in every age there have been some Christians who have been able to give instruction to others. It must always be the case that some will know more than others and that they will have the duty of passing their knowledge on to others. Jesus is saying that among his followers there is to be no such system as that among the Jews, with the "great ones" expounding the law authoritatively and the rank and file permanently occupying an inferior place. Christians have but one teacher, and they must not expect that in due course others will emerge who will eclipse him and establish their own ways of understanding what God wills for his people. There is and can be only one Jesus. The corollary of this is that *"you are all brothers."* Brothers are equal, and they cannot be arranged in a hierarchy. Over against Jesus they all hold inferior rank, and none of them is in a position to lord it over the others.

---

16. "In Oriental etiquette, the inferior had the prior obligation to greet his superior with a salutation whose length indicated the superior's importance. The Pharisees wish to receive salutations and titles, not give them" (Meier).

17. The lexicon tells us that the word is "from רַב 'lord, master', רַבִּי 'my lord', properly a form of address, and so throughout our lit., then an honorary title for outstanding teachers of the law" (BAGD, *sub* ῥαββί).

18. Dalman, p. 334.

19. ὑμεῖς is emphatic; Jesus' hearers are to be markedly different from the Pharisees.

9. There are problems related to this verse. The first we notice is that *father* linguistically might refer to the father in a family or to a teacher as the master of his students. But it is unlikely that the reference here is to the family. The context is concerned with teaching and the like. Elsewhere Jesus insists that honor be given to our earthly fathers (15:4; 19:19). It is perhaps worth noting at this point that even when we are thinking of family loyalties our heavenly Father is to be given our first loyalty. In every age there have been people who have put family ties above everything else. Jesus denies that this is legitimate in the case of his followers.

But it is more likely in a context dealing with teaching that we should understand the term as a singular that corresponds to "the fathers," an expression the Jews often used for the great ones of the past (one of the tractates of the Mishnah is entitled *'Abot,* "Fathers,"), especially those who taught Israel the right way. No teacher seems ever to have been addressed as "Father" *(Abba),* and it is not easy to find a reference to a teacher simply as "father," though Elisha used the term of the departing Elijah (2 Kings 2:12). It is sometimes prefixed to the name of a teacher, such as "Abba Chilkiyya" and others (Dalman, p. 339), while the epithet "the fathers of the world" is used of Shammai and Hillel (*'Eduy.* 1:4). This would fit the context with its emphasis on teaching and on the right place for the teacher. There is, of course, a sense in which a Christian may be spoken of as "father" to other believers (or for them to be called his children, e.g., 1 Cor. 4:15; 1 Tim. 1:2), but in the New Testament the term is not used as a title, nor is it to be employed in any spirit of superiority. We are all brothers and sisters and belong to one family with one Father, the *heavenly* Father. The adjective enables us to grasp something of his surpassing excellence and to recognize that Jesus is not speaking of some light and unimportant person. There is some emphasis on *your;*[20] whatever be the case with others, the followers of Jesus are such that they recognize that they have but one Father.

10. Jesus continues his instruction not to seek high places for ourselves with *"do not be called instructors."*[21] This is really another way of saying what he has already said in verse 8 (and some have suggested accordingly that the verse should be deleted; but the words are textually sound and should be retained). Apart from the fact that a new word is used for "teacher" the verse does no more than underline and emphasize the teaching given in the earlier verse. This time Jesus names *Christ* ("Messiah," here used as a name rather than as a title) as the one teacher of the disciples, as he did not in the earlier expression. But all that that means is that what was implied there is made explicit here.

---

20. Moule sees emphasis on ὑμῶν, "for *you* there is only *one* Father" (*IBNTG,* p. 166).

21. καθηγητής is found only in this verse in the New Testament. It signifies "a guide, teacher." MM cites it from the papyri, and it is used in an inscription on a memorial to a teacher (*New Documents,* 4, p. 156).

11-12. Throughout his teaching Jesus insists that his followers must be lowly. He set the example himself, for in his whole life he forsook the corridors of power and was content to be a lowly teacher, mostly in the remote rural areas of the province in which he lived. He has earlier taught plainly that his followers must tread the lowly path, and he has linked their service with his own, going on to say that he would give his life a ransom for many (20:26-28). The theme of lowliness is now resumed as part of the contrast with the Pharisees that must mark the lives of the servants of Jesus. If they are seeking to be great, they are not to look for the kind of prominence that Jesus has denounced in this discourse. For them to be great is to take the place of a *servant* (earlier he has taught that they must be like little children, 18:4). It is in giving service, not in receiving adulation, that true greatness consists.

Jesus explains that there will be some reversals of what people have thought they have achieved. The person who *will exalt*[22] *himself will be humbled.* It is important to be clear on this because the disciples were accustomed to a society in which people like the Pharisees who exalted themselves were thought certain to be accepted by God as the truly exalted ones. But God does not see them as they see themselves, and in the end such people will *be humbled.* The other side of that coin is that the person who takes the lowly way here and now will in due course *be exalted.* This does not, of course, mean that the ambitious person must take care to serve his stint in a lowly place here and now in order to make sure of a good reward in the hereafter. There is no humility in such an attitude. Jesus is looking for genuine lowliness, the attitude of the person who is not seeking personal gain of any sort, but simply the opportunity of doing service. It is that that matters, and it is that that he could not find among the Pharisees of his day.

13. Jesus proceeds to a vigorous denunciation of his religious opponents in a series of seven woes, with which we should perhaps compare the six in Luke 11:42-52. They are far from being identical, but they show us plainly that the denunciation of the Pharisees was not a peculiarity of Matthew's account. These are addressed specifically to the *scribes and Pharisees,* so some of them must have been in the crowd. Jesus pronounces a *woe* on these people, pronouncing them *hypocrites* in a refrain that runs through this chapter (vv. 15, 16, 23, 25, 27, and 29). For *woe* see the note on 18:7; as pointed out there, it is an expression of both compassion and regret. We are not to understand it as a way of exulting over the fate of evildoers in any of its occurrences in this Gospel. Jesus uses it by way of making it clear that the fate of the people in question is a terrible one. But he is not rejoicing over their final overthrow. He is stating the way things are, and at least in some places the word contains something of appeal.

---

22. The future is a little curious; perhaps it is "occasioned by the reference to the future of the disciples" (BDF, 380[2]).

Surely they will turn from their evil way? With this expression which makes it so clear that an unpleasant fate awaits those who continue to live as the Pharisees do, there is something of an explanation. They are *hypocrites* (see on 6:2), people who act a part. It is a word that denies that those so described are sincere: they do what they do for its effect on those who observe them, not because deep down they think of it as right.

In the case of the Pharisees and their scribes there is the very serious accusation that they *shut up the kingdom of heaven before men*. They were in reality effectively shutting people out of God's kingdom at the same time that they claimed they were helping them into it; in that lay their hypocrisy. The verb *shut up* indicates a firm closing.[23] Jesus has been proclaiming *the kingdom of heaven* and has won disciples. It might have been thought that prominent among these would be people like the Pharisees because they had given so much time and energy to the study of Scripture. They should have been aware of the ways of God there made known to people and of the prophecies that were being fulfilled in the life and work of Jesus. But they shut their eyes to these things; they took no notice and thus declined to enter the kingdom.[24] Worse, they did not *allow* others to go in. There were people in Galilee and Judea who heard Jesus gladly and were ready to respond to his teaching. But some of them had respect for the scribes and the Pharisees, the respected teachers of Israel, and when these revered leaders tried to discredit Jesus, they believed them. They had been in the process of entering,[25] Jesus says, but the religious leaders stopped them.

15. Some MSS have the words that lie behind verse 14 in *KJV*, but there are good reasons for seeing them as an interpolation in this Gospel. They are not found in the best witnesses for the text, and where they are included, some MSS put them before verse 13 and some after. They seem to have been copied by scribes from Mark 12:40 or Luke 20:47.

Jesus repeats his proclamation of *woe* to the religious leaders, and this he time turns his attention to their activities in making converts. He says that they put in tremendous efforts to do this; they *travel over sea and land*, which, in a day when travel was not nearly as easy as it is today, meant going to a good deal of trouble. The expression was evidently proverbial for making a big effort to bring about a desired result. They speak of doing all this just to make *one proselyte*.[26] The term, used only here in the Gospels, means a convert to their religion. Throughout history the Jews at some times have been very loathe to make converts while at other periods they have been active. There is general agreement that at

23. κλείω is connected with κλείς, "a key"; it is used of shutting up a door and locking it. The thought is not that the door may be easily opened, but that it is firmly closed.
24. We should notice the emphatic ὑμεῖς: "*You*, you of all people" are not entering.
25. The present participle εἰσερχομένους "amounts to an impf." (M, III, p. 81), perhaps "those who were trying to enter."
26. For the trouble people might go to in making a proselyte see Josephus, *Ant.* 20.38-48.

this time they were very active, and Jesus is saying that in his day the Pharisees at any rate were keen to make converts. Even one convert was highly prized. But being a proselyte of the Pharisees meant that the person was instructed in Judaism according to Pharisaic understanding of that faith. And since the convert presumably knew little or nothing about Judaism other than the instruction he was given by those who converted him, he was a convert to Pharisaism. He knew nothing of any other way of understanding Scripture, so that any door that might have opened to him for a fuller knowledge of God was closed from the beginning. By indoctrinating with their own errors minds that knew nothing of the new religion other than what they taught them the Pharisees ensured that the proselytes were twice as sure of finishing up on the wrong track as they were themselves. It has often been demonstrated that a new convert may be fanatically zealous for his new faith, far more zealous than those who have accepted it all their lives. Jesus speaks of the convert as *twice as much a son of hell* as his mentors, a vivid way of saying that he had all the characteristics of a denizen of the place of torment ("a person belonging to, worthy of, and bound for hell," Hendriksen). It was the saddest of fates for a person who had evidently felt some attraction to the revelation God had made in the Scriptures, and there is a consequent guilt in those who could and should have led him to a better understanding of what God had done for him.

16. A shortened *woe* (only this one lacks the address "scribes and Pharisees, hypocrites") leads to a denunciation of *blind guides*. Jesus has earlier used this expression to describe Pharisees who took offense at his teaching (15:14). On that occasion he warned that if the blind lead the blind, both will surely fall into a ditch. Now he turns his attention to specific examples of Pharisaic blindness, namely those concerned with the swearing of oaths.[27] In the Sermon on the Mount Jesus discouraged this whole practice (5:34-37), teaching his disciples that they should always tell the truth, so that it would not be necessary for them to back up what they were saying with an oath. But if we can go by rabbinic literature, the swearing of oaths was commonplace among the Jews. A whole tractate of the Mishnah is given over to the subject *(Shebu'ot)*, with, of course, the corresponding section of the Talmud. This tractate goes into a bewildering variety of forms of oaths, their validity and their invalidity,[28] and this

---

27. "The intention behind the rulings of the scribes here under criticism was a good one: they were against insincere oaths and this led them to discourage oaths by the most holy things, allowing such by what appeared more removed from the centre of holiness" (Stendahl).

28. For example, if a man said, " 'I swear that I will not eat this loaf! I swear that I will not eat it! I swear that I will not eat it' and he ate it, he is liable only on one count. Such is reckoned 'a rash oath', for which a man is liable to Stripes if he uttered it wantonly, but, if unwittingly, to a Rising and Falling Offering. For 'a vain oath', if it is uttered wantonly, a man is liable to Stripes, but if unwittingly, he is not culpable" *(Shebu. 3:7)*. If you take this kind of regulation and definition through an entire tractate, you have an enormous volume

makes it clear that the topic was both difficult and of enormous interest for what went on in daily life. Jesus gives an example. To swear *by the temple* meant nothing; the oath was not binding. But to swear *by the gold of the temple* was binding. We lack specific information on this point in the Jewish writings, but there is nothing improbable about it. The distinction is the kind of distinction that was very common in the rabbinic writings.

17. Jesus adds to the description of the Pharisees in verse 16 as *blind* the new one that they are *fools*. Both descriptions are apposite in such a situation. It is preposterous to think that God is going to be concerned with the precise form of words a man uses in swearing an oath, so that he would take seriously an oath sworn by the gold of the temple, but would not regard an oath by the temple itself in the same way. To maintain such a distinction is both foolish and blind. Anyone who does so takes insufficient notice of the fact that God demands complete truthfulness in his people so that any pledge is to be discharged. We cannot escape any legitimate pledge by quibbling about the form of words in which the pledge is expressed, oath or not. Jesus further points out that the distinction is illogical. Gold is not a sacred object by itself; there is no reason for regarding an oath sworn by gold as having any particular validity. It could be argued that "the gold of the temple" is different; it has been put into the holy place for the service of God, but it is the temple that makes the difference, not the gold in itself.

18-20. Jesus attacks a similar quibble on the difference between swearing[29] by the altar and by some gift that is offered on the altar. It is not easy to follow the reasoning by which the difference could be made, but we need be in no doubt but that casuists were capable of coming up with a difference.[30] The result was that to swear by the altar meant nothing; the oath was not binding. But to swear by some gift that had been made holy by being placed on the altar was binding. Again Jesus points to a flaw in the reasoning by which the Pharisees overlooked the fact that *the altar that sanctifies the gift* is surely greater than *the gift* it has sanctified. Jesus sweeps away the whole argument by saying that to swear by the altar is to swear by everything on it.

21-22. Jesus carries on in the same strain. An oath by the temple was not regarded as binding.[31] But Jesus sweeps away the quibble. To swear

---

of requirements for oaths. The unfortunate result of all this was that "By subtle distinctions the Pharisees have succeeded in making perjury legitimate" (Diétrich).

29. The aorist ὀμόσας (v. 20) is used of "the class of those who do the action," the point being that it refers to "those who once do the act the single doing of which is the mark of the class" (Burton, *MT*, 123, 124). There is no emphasis on a past action.

30. There might possibly be the thought that a creditor might have a claim to something a worshiper brought to offer, such as gold or the gift on the altar, whereas no creditor could have a claim on the temple or the altar.

31. In the Mishnah we find that an oath "by heaven and by earth" is not binding, but an oath "by *Alef-Daleth*" (the first two letters of *Adonai* = "Lord") is binding, as is an oath "by *Yod-He*" (the first two letters of the sacred name YHWH) (*Shebu.* 4:13).

by the temple is to swear *by it and by him who dwells in it.* That which makes a temple a temple is that it is the abode of the deity worshipped therein. If there is no deity, there is no temple. Therefore a man may not claim that he is not bound by his oath because he swore by the temple and not specifically by God. If he swore by God's temple, then he swore by God, because it would not be a temple at all apart from the fact that God chooses to dwell in it.

It is the same with an oath by heaven. For the Jews this was not a binding oath; the Mishnah specifically excludes it from having binding force. So Jesus points out that this is mere casuistry: an oath *by heaven* is an oath *by the throne of God and by him who sits on it.* People cannot escape the force of their oaths by wording them in such a way that, while they sound impressive, they lack the precise wording that makes them valid. This may serve in human courts, but it is quite invalid where God himself is concerned. Of course, for followers of Jesus it is not necessary to swear an oath at all, and he has already made it clear that they are expected to tell the truth at all times without the necessity of an oath to enforce truth (5:33-37).

23. Jesus reverts to the fuller formula, *"Woe to you, scribes and Pharisees, hypocrites,"* and proceeds to the way these people went about their tithing. Tithing was an old custom (Gen. 14:20) and the law laid it down that a tenth should be given to the Lord (Lev. 27:30-33; Num. 18:21, 24; Deut. 12:5-19; 14:22-29, etc.), which presumably means a tenth of all one's income.[32] Tithes were paid to the Levites (Num. 18:21), who in turn paid to the priests a tithe of the tithes they received (Num. 18:25-28). The Pharisees evidently took the practice very seriously and carried it through in minute detail. They paid to the Lord a tenth of small garden plants like *mint and dill and cummin.*[33] This indicates a determination to fulfil the tithe regulations with minute accuracy — not the smallest plant was to be overlooked (Luke says that they tithed "every herb," 11:42); everything that belonged to the Lord was scrupulously to be paid to him. The tithing of small herbs was probably going farther than the tithing laws intended, but there was nothing wrong in doing it (as Jesus agrees). The trouble was that in their concern that these small matters be properly attended to, the Pharisees neglected weightier matters that were much more important. These more important duties were made much more plain in Scripture

32. The rules governing tithing are not gathered together conveniently for us although many are found in the Mishnah tractate *Ma'aserot,* the opening words of which say, "A general rule have they laid down about Tithes: whatsoever is used for food and is kept watch over and grows from the soil is liable to Tithes." It is not easy to fit together all the pieces of information that have come down to us; evidently the way tithing was carried out was well known to the participants; therefore they had no need to have it described in full.

33. W. E. Shewell-Cooper discusses these plants in *Plants and Fruits of the Bible* (London, 1962), pp. 68-69, 79. The tithing of vegetables was the rabbinic rule (*Yoma* 83b), but this was not laid down in Scripture. The rabbis specifically required the tithing of *dill* (*'Abod. Zar.* 7b) and cummin (*Dem.* 2:1).

than the minutiae on which the Pharisees concentrated their attention. So Jesus selects the qualities of *justice* (Gen. 18:19; Prov. 21:3, etc.), *mercy* (which is said again and again to have been shown to his people by God and which God likewise requires of them, Mic. 6:8; LXX has the same word as that used here), and *faithfulness* (Prov. 28:20; Hab. 2:4). Calvin sums this up with "Briefly, then, the sum of the Law comes back to love. . . . Christ typically refers the real test of sanctity to brotherly love" (III, p. 57; Luke, of course, has "the love of God" in his equivalent of this statement, 11:42); Robinson explains this wording as "possibly due to an alternative rendering of the original Aramaic"). It is fatally easy to be preoccupied with minutiae and to overlook what is important. That was the error of the Pharisees. Jesus does not find fault with them for what they did, but for what they left undone.

24. Again these *guides* are castigated as *blind* (cf. v. 16); for all their zeal they cannot perceive the right ways of God. With a humorous illustration Jesus pictures them as straining out *the gnat*,[34] the point being that this little organism was "unclean" (Lev. 11:41) and therefore should not be consumed. But these same people gulped down *the camel*, the largest of the beasts normally found in Palestine (and in addition also ceremonially unclean, Lev. 11:4).[35] They were pernickety in complying with the regulations about the smallest matters, but were capable of quite neglecting much more important matters, things like those Jesus has just mentioned; "in their eagerness to avoid a tiny defilement the Pharisees are polluted by a huge one" (Johnson).

25. The fifth *woe* contrasts the inward and the outward. The Pharisees were meticulous with outward things, things that people could notice and that would impress on observers just how pious the Pharisees were.[36] They were not so careful about things that people could not see and measure. So Jesus speaks of them as cleaning *the outside of the cup and the dish*. The *cup* was the ordinary utensil for drinking, and the *dish* was that on which food was served.[37] The outside of these useful articles was carefully cleaned, but the inside was quite another matter. On the inside everything was the proceeds

34. ὑλίζω means "to strain," and with the prefix διά "to strain thoroughly" (διϋλίζω occurs here only in the New Testament); it signifies the act of straining a liquid through gauze or the like, a practice apparently employed to make sure that small sources of defilement would be removed before one drank. κώνωψ is a "gnat, mosquito," according to BAGD, which also raises the question whether it may be "a certain worm found in wine" mentioned by Aristotle. Whatever the precise meaning, it was proverbial for smallness of size.

35. This saying may translate an Aramaic pun between קַלְמָא and גַּמְלָא (so Moule, *IBNTG*, p. 186 and others).

36. Jacob Neusner draws attention to disputes between the Shammaites and the Hillelites about the cleansing of cups: the Hillelites held that the outside was always unclean and that it was important to clean the inside, whereas the followers of Shammai favored the cleansing of both outside and inside (*NTS*, 22 [1975-76], pp. 486-95). But Jesus is not dealing with a minor ritual matter. He is concerned with the inward cleansing of people.

37. παροψίς (παρά, "beside" + ὄψον, "food") signified "a side-dish of dainties" and later the dish itself (AS).

of *robbery and self-indulgence* ("full of what you have obtained by violence and selfishness," *GNB*). In Luke's form of the saying it is the Pharisees who are full of robbery and evil, but Matthew seems to be speaking rather of what they obtained by their wrong acts. "These people ate and drank luxuriously things which they secured by acts of violence and wrong. What they put in their cups was contaminated by the source from which it had come, and it was useless to polish the outside of the vessel, and so meet the demands of the traditional Law" (Robinson). That the containers are *full* points to good measure; Jesus is not complaining of an occasional lapse but of the habitual activity of these religious leaders. *Robbery* is a startling accusation;[38] the practices in which they engaged meant that they took from others that to which they were not entitled. We do not know enough about the scribes and Pharisees of Jesus' time to be specific about this charge, but in all ages there have been people who were scrupulous about outward religious obser-vances but who did not allow their profession of piety to hinder them from making unjust profits at the expense of other people. The scribes and Pharisees of Jesus' day were evidently not above this. With it Jesus joins *self-indulgence.*[39] The Pharisees were outwardly religious, but this did not mean that they were in any degree given to self-discipline. They apparently did not allow their religious observances to interfere with their comfort. Jesus is saying that their attention to the outside of the cup and the plate is useless because all that is in these vessels has been contaminated by the way it was acquired. No amount of attention to ceremonial detail can compensate for dishonesty and self-indulgence.

26. For the fifth (and last) time in this chapter Jesus uses the adjective *blind,* this time in the singular as he addresses himself to one typical Pharisee. He returns to the metaphor of *the cup* and urges the Pharisee to clean its *inside.* But the application of the metaphor is uppermost rather than the metaphor itself, for Jesus goes on to say that *the inside* is to be cleaned so that the *outside may become clean too.* It is not the case that the cleaning of the inside of a cup makes the outside clean too, but when a person is made clean in his innermost being this is necessarily reflected in that person's outward actions. The Pharisees are being taught that their method is all wrong. In the case of a person, to concentrate on the outward does nothing for the inward, whereas to make sure that the inward is clean means that the outward will also be clean. That follows inevitably.

---

38. ἁρπαγή, "pillage, plundering, robbery" (AS), is connected with ἁρπάζω, "to seize, carry off by force." There may be some notion of the use of force, though, if so, we do not know what it was. But some of those in high position in any society have never been guiltless of using unfair pressure to gain their own ends.

39. ἀκρασία means "want of power," thus "want of power over oneself," "lack of self-control." *NEB* renders, "which you have filled inside by robbery and self-indulgence," and Argyle comments, "just as a ritually clean vessel may be full of poison, so a ritually clean person may be full of *robbery and self-indulgence!*" This is an important truth, though the passage seems rather to be referring to the things obtained by robbery and self-indulgence, as we noted above.

27. The next *woe* likens the scribes and Pharisees to *whitewashed tombs,* which refers to the customs of burial. People were not necessarily buried together in cemeteries; isolated graves might be found in all sorts of places. A grave might not be well kept after a long lapse of time (the relatives of the buried person might all die themselves), and the grave could easily become inconspicuous. People not familiar with the locality but passing through on the way up to Jerusalem for a feast might well accidentally make contact with such a grave, and the contact would make them ceremonially unclean (see Num. 19:11-22; v. 16 explicitly says that anyone who touches a grave is unclean for seven days). As a help for such pilgrims (and others) tombs were whitewashed on the fifteenth of the month Adar, a month before Passover; the tombs would then be conspicuous and anyone passing through would be warned (see Mishnah, *Ma'as. Sh.* 5:1; *Sheqal.* 1:1; etc.), even though they had little local knowledge. The care with which such tombs were whitewashed made them *beautiful,*[40] but it did nothing for the fact that inside such tombs there were *dead people's bones and all uncleanness.* Nothing could be more "unclean" than the inside of a tomb. To the objection that the whitewashing of tombs was in order to make them plainly visible and that this is not a good illustration of hypocrisy it may be retorted that the point is the contrast between the exterior (white, cared for, and beautiful) and the interior (total uncleanness).

28. The application, like that in the previous "woe," brings out the fact that the outward appearance of the Pharisees bears no resemblance to their inward state. There is nothing wrong with Pharisaic externals: the Pharisees *appear to men as righteous.* But their inward state is quite another matter. Jesus picks out *hypocrisy* and *lawlessness* as qualities that characterize them inwardly in full measure but that are not necessarily obvious to people who observe them. The charge of *hypocrisy* runs through this chapter, but *lawlessness* is an interesting and ironical addition. The Pharisees were punctilious in observing the law as they understood it. But their concentration on the externals to the neglect of demands like justice and mercy and faithfulness meant that in the last resort they followed their own inclinations, not the law of God. They rejected the divine demands in the place where those demands were most significant, in the region of the heart. Because in their innermost being they refused to submit to the law of God, in the fullest sense of the term they were lawless.

29. The final *woe* concerns the attitude of the Pharisees to the great prophets of the past. These outwardly godly people honored the memory of the prophets but continued in the sins that the prophets denounced.

40. Some deny that whitewashing made tombs *beautiful* and suggest that what is meant is the plastering of urns or other containers for bones. Gundry sees a reference to "decorative plastering" as in Proverbs 21:9 LXX, and says forthrightly, "there is no allusion to whitewashing tombs" (p. 466). But he does not explain how a reference to the whitewashed tombs could be so definitely excluded when Jesus is speaking just before Passover to people who must have seen such tombs on their way to Jerusalem.

"You build the tombs of the prophets," Jesus says, which indicates that the prophets had not been greatly honored in the manner of their burial. To make up for what their ancestors had failed to do for those great men of the past the Pharisees and their allies had done what they could to bring respectability and even honor to the burial places where the bodies of the prophets had been interred. In doing this the intention of the Pharisees was clearly to honor the prophets. And coupled with that, Jesus says, *"you decorate the monuments of the righteous."* This will refer to upright and God-fearing citizens, people who are rightly honored for their whole-hearted service of God but who were not the vehicles of the direct divine message to the people of their day as were the prophets. Just as with the prophets, the Pharisees took little notice of *the righteous* who lived in their own day (as witness their attitude to Jesus and the godly men in the apostolic band). But they gave outward evidence of honoring the great ones of the past in decorating their *monuments.*[41] This last word often means a "tomb" (e.g., 8:28; 27:60), and that may be its meaning here; in that case it is no more than a stylistic variant of the term used earlier in the verse. But it seems better to regard the change as significant, in which case Jesus is pointing to different ways of honoring *the righteous* from those used with the prophets. But in both cases the important thing is that the scribes and Pharisees took up a stance with regard to the great ones of the past that indicated their applause for the work they had done.

30. And in thus doing honor to the memory of the prophets the Pharisees said the right words. They affirmed that had they lived *in the days of* their *forefathers* they would have had no share *in shedding the blood of the prophets.* With the advantage of hindsight they can see the slaying of the prophets for the evil thing it was. Their building of the tombs seems to be a way of proclaiming how much better they were than those who put the prophets to death. And there is no reason for doubting that they sincerely thought that had they been alive at the time when the prophets were killed they would have had no part in those evil deeds. The trouble was that they had not realized the radical nature of the obedience to God that the prophets had demanded, nor had they realized their own imperfect adherence to the ways of God. Now that the prophets were safely out of the way and they could no longer hear the thunderbolts those great men hurled at conventional religiosity, they could safely applaud all that the prophets had said, quite oblivious of the fact that their lives gave daily evidence that the kind of thing the prophets denounced lived on. Their hypocrisy consisted in the fact that while they gave outward evidence of devotion to the prophets, they took the strongest action against those who stood in the tradition of the prophets, Jesus and his followers.

41. κοσμέω has the meaning "to order, arrange, prepare" and then "to adorn, furnish" (AS). μνημεῖον signifies "memorial" and thus "monument," but it often means specifically the burial monument, the tomb. Herod erected "a memorial of white marble" at the entrance to David's tomb (Josephus, *Ant.* 16.182), which may be an example of what is in mind.

586

31. What the Pharisees were saying was in fact a testimony against themselves, even though they did not realize it. In Luke's similar saying (Luke 11:47-48) Jesus asserts that they give their consent to what the former generations did, for where their forefathers killed the prophets this generation completes the work by building their tombs. While it is not spelled out in quite the same way here, it is this kind of thing that Jesus is saying. The actions of the Pharisees at the tombs of the prophets does not show them to be better men than those who killed those great men of God. Rather, it aligns them with those who put those prophets into their tombs: the prophet killers and the prophet buriers belong together. Their very preoccupation with the tombs shows that their real interest is in the interment of those men who spoke from God, not in heeding the messages they gave. Their actions show that they are the true sons of the murderers of God's messengers. There is a solidarity between the killers of the messengers and those who attended to their tombs.[42]

32. *And you* is an emphatic expression; it sheets home Jesus' accusation. He is not referring to some hypothetical speakers about the prophets, leaving everyone to guess who they are. He is speaking about people he is addressing then and there. Their consistent opposition to what God has spoken through the prophets in earlier days and what he is now saying through his Son has hardened them, so that there is now no prospect of their repenting and turning away from the ways Jesus has been denouncing. So he says, *"fill up the measure of your fathers"* ("Go on, then, and finish what your ancestors started!" *GNB*). There is irony here: go on as you are going and take the inevitable consequences, is the thought. There have always been those who opposed the word of God spoken through his messengers, and these Pharisees are simply continuing it. Let them see that as they proceed along their chosen course they will be completing the task that their forefathers began when they refused the word of God through the prophets and put them to death.

33. Jesus addresses them as *"You snakes"* and then as *"You brood of vipers."* We should probably not try too hard to distinguish between the two expressions. *Snakes* is a term that covers a wide variety of reptiles, and while *viper* apparently in strictness refers to "a constrictor snake" (LSJ), in this context there will not be much difference from *snakes*. *Brood of vipers* is repeated from the denunciation of John the Baptist (3:7; only Matthew tells us that Jesus repeats John's words). The whole expression means "snakes and sons of snakes"; the words and works of the Pharisees of Jesus' day show their genuine kinship with the *vipers* who had put the prophets to death in earlier days. These Pharisees who have no difficulty

---

42. "They witness against themselves that they are the physical sons of the prophets' murderers. What they do not realize is that they are the spiritual sons also" (Nixon). J. D. M. Derrett argues that there is the idea of compensation for blood guiltiness: "To spend money on a tomb, when that money was incapable of being paid as compensation, would have been correct practice at Jewish law" (F. L. Cross, ed., *Studia Evangelica*, IV [Berlin, 1968], p. 192).

in understanding that those who ill-treated the prophets in earlier days were destined for hell are invited to reflect on their own position. If those who opposed the prophets were so clearly *sentenced to hell,* then how are contemporary followers of the persecutors and executioners of the prophets to escape the same sentence?[43]

34. *Therefore* seems to mean something like "because this is the way it has happened again and again," "because God's sending of his prophets and the like has never been welcomed." That God has sent his messengers is a truth that is plain throughout the Old Testament (cf. 2 Sam. 12:1; for the repetition, Jer. 7:25-26; 25:4). The emphatic *I* here seems to mean God the Father; there is a sense in which Jesus sends out his messengers (the very word "apostle" means "messenger"), and grammatically he could be saying that he himself is sending people. But it fits the context better to understand Jesus as speaking in God's name and identifying himself with God's continuing activity: God has sent messenger after messenger and they have consistently been rejected, as the Pharisees well know. Jesus is saying that God will continue to do this, even though their rejection at the hands of the present generation is as certain as it was with their predecessors in earlier days. God's messengers are not all alike. There will be *prophets,* men who can say authoritatively "Thus saith the LORD" and pass on to the people of their generation the authentic message of God. There will be *sages,* wise men who have studied the sacred writings and made that message their own. They, too, can pass on to their generation the authentic word of God, not because they have direct inspiration (for they do not have it), but because in a lowly and reverent spirit they have studied the revelation made through others until they are able to pass it on without distortion. There will be *scribes,* learned men, men who write, men who teach, and they, too, will speak the authoritative word they have learned from the prophets. Through them all the message that God sends to a given generation will be made plain.

But the sad thing is that, just as the prophets and their message were rejected in days of old, so these godly men will be rejected in the days to come. God's messengers have never been warmly received by any generation, and Jesus is saying that it is not to be expected that this will happen in the days that lie ahead. He is sheeting home to the scribes and Pharisees he has been denouncing the behavior of which he is speaking; now he says to them explicitly: *"some of them you will kill and crucify."* The Jews did not themselves crucify people at this period, but, as in the case of Jesus himself, they may have brought about crucifixions by getting the Romans to perform the deed (in Acts 2:36; 4:10 the Jews are said to have crucified Jesus, though it was the Romans who actually performed the execution).

---

43. Moulton translates, "how are ye to *flee from* the judgement of Gehenna?" and adds, "The thought is not of the inevitableness of God's punishment, but of the stubbornness of men who will not take a step to escape it" (M, I, p. 116).

It is religious people like those he is confronting who will take the lead, and they will bring about the deaths of some of God's messengers. Crucifixion was not the only way of executing them, but it was a particularly horrible way and it would happen. Some would get the lighter punishment of being flogged *in your synagogues*. We tend to think of the synagogue as being a place of worship, and so it was. But it was also the center of community organization; the ordered life of the community flowed around the synagogue. Community discipline was administered from it, and clearly it is this that is in mind at this point. The local council could order floggings of up to thirty-nine lashes (cf. 2 Cor. 11:24). They would also *persecute* some of the messengers *from town to town*. The verb *persecute* covers a wide variety of harassments, but whatever it may mean in detail it certainly denotes hostile action, while *from town to town* makes it clear that the messengers will be continually pursued as they carry out their mission. They will not be able to flee from one town and be assured of respite in the next one but will be harried from place to place. Jesus is speaking of a recurring and vigorous hostility. Paul's account of his hardships (2 Cor. 11:21-27) shows us something of what Jesus is forecasting.

35. *So that*[44] indicates that the divine purpose will be worked out in and through this human rejection of God's messengers. When Jesus declares that *all the righteous blood* will *come upon* his hearers, he seems to be saying that the culmination of the whole process of God's sending his messengers has arrived. Through the ages God has sent his prophets, sages, and the like, and he will continue this through the ministry of the apostles and other Spirit-led people in the church. But the high point of it all is in the sending of his Son. This means that those who reject him will be guilty of an especially serious sin; this is the climax of all the opposition to the messengers of God. So Jesus refers to the shedding of the blood of righteous men through all the generations. He specifies *the blood of righteous Abel,* the first righteous man to be recorded in Scripture as having been killed by a wicked man, and goes on to *the blood of Zechariah, son of Barachiah.* This appears to be the death recorded in 2 Chronicles 24:20-21,[45] which in the order of books in the Hebrew Bible (the Law, the Prophets, then the Writings of which 2 Chronicles is the last book) is the

---

44. ὅπως is often used by Matthew to indicate the divine purpose, as in things happening "in order that" Scripture may be fulfilled (2:23; 8:17, etc.).

45. There is a difficulty in that in 2 Chronicles Zechariah is said to be the son of Jehoiada; therefore a number of other Zechariahs have been suggested. But none of them has any plausibility. It seems better to think of this Zechariah as being named from his grandfather rather than his father. That this was sometimes done is clear from the fact that the prophet Zechariah is called "the son of Berechiah, son of Iddo" in Zechariah 1:1, but the same man is also named from his grandfather; he is "the son of Iddo" in Ezra 6:14. Apparently the same procedure is followed in the case of the Zechariah of this passage also. Another view is that the man had two names. Lenski accepts Luther's suggestion that Jehoiada also had the name Barachiah (Ryle is another to accept this view), and he cites the son of Joash who had the name Gideon and also Jerubbaal (Judg. 8:29, 32; Lenski, p. 920).

last martyrdom recorded in Scripture. In 2 Chronicles it is a particularly heinous crime, for the murder took place "in the court of the house of the LORD" (2 Chron. 24:21), which will mean much the same as Jesus' words, *between the sanctuary and the altar.* Both are ways of saying that the slaying occurred in a very holy place. *Whom you killed* unites the people Jesus is addressing with the killers of an earlier age in a solidarity of guilt. Jesus is saying that the guilty generation he is addressing will be liable for all kinds of blood guiltiness, for they have taken no notice of holy things as they reject the messengers of God. We will see them presently using the Sanhedrin, the highest religious court in the land, to bring about their purpose in having Jesus crucified. People who could perpetrate such a blasphemous crime are the most guilty people of all time.

36. Jesus rounds off this denunciation with a solemn assurance. *"Truly I tell you"* (see on 5:18) introduces a weighty utterance and one that his hearers do well to take with the utmost seriousness. *All these things* sums up all the crimes of which Jesus has been speaking. They all involve blood guiltiness, and it is this that will be laid to the door of the people he is addressing. All this guilt will be laid on *this generation.* There is to be no doubt that Jesus' hearers are guilty and that they will have to give account of themselves before God.[46]

37. This address closes with a lament over Jerusalem,[47] the last words Jesus addresses to the crowds in this Gospel. The lament is almost word for word the same as that in Luke 13:34-35, but where Luke places it earlier Matthew makes it Jesus' last words to Jerusalem. The city is the one that was chosen long ago as the place where the temple of God should be built and that should be the center of government for the people of God. There are many expressions of affection for this city above all others (for just one example, cf. Ps. 137:5-6). For Jesus, as for every other Jew, Jerusalem was special. It was tragic in the extreme that this city should bring down upon itself, in addition to its rejection of God's messengers through the centuries, the guilt of rejecting God's own Son. We are not to think that Jesus took this calmly. It grieved him deeply that this city above all cities should embrace the guilt that it would presently incur by its part in the execution of the Son of God, the last one God would send to her.

Jesus speaks first of what the inhabitants of the city have done in the past. Jerusalem is the city that kills the prophets and stones God's messengers (the present participles point not to an occasional aberration, but

---

46. It is not without its interest that the later rabbis could say that the first temple was destroyed because of "idolatry, immorality, bloodshed." When asked why the second was destroyed their answer was, "Because therein prevailed hatred without cause. That teaches you that groundless hatred is considered as of even gravity with the three sins of idolatry, immorality, and bloodshed together" (*Yoma* 9b). This is an interesting later commentary from leading Jews on the Judaism of the New Testament period.

47. This is the only place in this Gospel where Matthew uses the form Ἰερουσαλήμ; elsewhere he always has Ἰεροσόλυμα.

590

to the continuing practice). This does not mean that Jesus rages against the city; rather, he regards it tenderly, and asks *how often* he would have *gathered* her children. Unless the words are spoken (from the divine perspective) of the whole history of Israel, this indicates that Jesus had more contacts with Jerusalem than Matthew has expressly noted (John makes this very clear). None of the Gospels, of course, is a full account of the life of Jesus, and it is not surprising that Matthew should omit Jesus' earlier visits to the capital. The saying he now records goes beyond what any prophet could have said. In particular, we should not overlook the christological implications of the words: "Jesus' longing can only belong to Israel's Savior, not to one of her prophets" (Carson); Jesus implies a special place for himself. There is compassion in his words, and it is very moving to find him likening his desire for the city's inhabitants to that of a hen[48] gathering her chickens.[49] There are the thoughts of the helplessness of the chickens, of the care of the mother hen for them, and for their safety under her wings. All this applies to Jerusalem. Jesus is saying that he had had a deep affection for the inhabitants of this holy city and that he had wanted them to commit themselves to his care. Under his wings they would have found safety. But the final condemnation is put in the simple words, *"you would not."* The words mean "you were not willing"; the will of the inhabitants was directed elsewhere. They could join with the Galilean pilgrims in welcoming Jesus at the triumphal entry, but this was no more than a passing enthusiasm. When matters got serious they did not will to seek the shelter that he offered them. They preferred to send him to the cross.

38. Matthew's characteristic *"Look"* (see on 1:20) highlights the words that follow. *"Your house is left to you desolate"* points to the city's final destruction.[50] When the Romans captured Jerusalem in A.D. 70, the city was reduced to a desolation; Jesus' words were prophetic. *Your house* has a family ring about it. Jesus could have spoken of the nation, but he prefers the city as the place where the people of God live and are one family under the heavenly Father. Some commentators have seen a reference to the temple, but it is more likely that Jesus has the whole city in mind. That it is *desolate* means more than that there is widespread destruction; it means that God has forsaken it. He no longer dwells with a people that has persistently refused him.

39. *For* introduces the reason, and *I tell you* comes with solemn

---

48. ὄρνις signifies "bird" and may refer to cock or hen; what the bird is doing here shows that a hen is meant.

49. In 2 Esdras God is reported to have said, "I gathered you as a hen gathers her brood under her wings" (2 Esdr. 1:30; the passage goes on to refer to the sending of the prophets and to their being slain).

50. ἔρημος means "solitary, deserted," and the corresponding verb carries the force "to lay waste, make desolate." The word is omitted by a few MSS, notably B. But this may be an assimilation to Luke 13:35; it should be accepted here.

emphasis. *"You will not see me any more"*[51] marks the end of Jesus' earthly ministry. He has come to the city for the last time and, though there was something of a welcome when he entered it, that was no more than a momentary enthusiasm. It was not a lasting reception of what he was and what he stood for. The inhabitants had had their last opportunity of welcoming Jesus, and they had refused to accept him. There would not be another chance. Jesus speaks of a time when they would utter the words of Psalm 118:26. Some students hold that this refers to the triumphal entry, when in fact these words were uttered by the crowds (21:9). But it is more than difficult to think that Matthew would use words that naturally refer to the future if he is referring to what he has described as having happened earlier. He is surely referring to some future happening. It is better to take the words as pointing to an eschatological reality. When the final kingdom is set up in all its glory, Jesus will be greeted as him *who comes in the name of the Lord.* Not until then will the inhabitants of Jerusalem recognize the reality of the divine visitation that took place when Jesus came to them.

---

51. *AB* translates "from this moment" and comments, "The Greek is far stronger than the usual English translations."

Matthew 24

D. THE OLIVET DISCOURSE, 24:1–25:46

The last of Jesus' major discourses in this Gospel is largely concerned with judgment and the conduct expected of the follower of Jesus in view of the coming judgment. There is a problem for the student in that sometimes what Jesus says refers to the coming judgment on Jerusalem, a judgment that was consummated in the destruction of the city in A.D. 70,[1] and sometimes what he is saying refers to the judgment at the end of the age.[2] We may well argue that there is a theological unity between the two judgments, and that some of what Jesus says could apply equally well to both. The first of these is a judgment that followed the rejection of Jesus in his earthly ministry, and the second is the judgment that will follow the preaching of the gospel throughout the world.[3] But we should not approach these chapters with the conviction that everything in them applies to only one of these judgments.[4] The intermingling of prophecies referring

1. It is often urged that what Matthew says about the destruction of Jerusalem must have been written after it. But this is to overlook the fact that the details mentioned in this Gospel are not such that they can have been derived only from a knowledge of that destruction. B. Reicke can say, "An amazing example of uncritical dogmatism in New Testament studies is the belief that the Synoptic Gospels should be dated after the Jewish War of A.D. 66-70 because they contain prophecies *ex eventu* of the destruction of Jerusalem by the Romans in the year 70" (D. E. Aune, ed., *Studies in New Testament and Early Christian Literature* [Leiden, 1972], p. 121). He proceeds to examine the passages and to argue that they do not "indicate any historical knowledge of the first Jewish war and its results" (p. 133).

2. Ryle remarks, "let us remember that the first coming of the Messiah to *suffer* was the most improbable event that could have been conceived, and let us not doubt that as He literally came in person to suffer, so he will literally come again in person to *reign*" (p. 314).

3. Cf. Tasker, "As the language in which these events is expressed is partly literal and partly symbolic, and as Jesus would seem to have regarded both of them as 'comings' in judgment, scholars have found it extremely difficult to say with any degree of certainty which parts of the chapter contain an answer to the question of the disciples *When shall these things be?* (viz. the destruction of the temple buildings mentioned in verse 2), and which parts are a response to their supplementary question *And what shall be the sign of thy coming, and of the end of the world?*" (Tasker, p. 223).

4. France takes verses 1-35 to apply to the judgment of Jerusalem and verses 36-51 to that connected with the parousia (p. 333). J. Marcellus Kik takes verse 34 as the point of division: everything up to that point he sees as referring to the generation alive when Jesus came and everything after that to the second coming (*Matthew Twenty-Four, An Exposition*

to the events leading up to A.D. 70 with those applying to the end of all things makes this discourse particularly difficult to interpret. The exegete must always exercise proper caution. Matthew shares a good deal of his material with Mark or Luke or both, but he has significant variations in those passages and there is a not inconsiderable amount that he alone contributes (especially in ch. 25).

Some commentators take the whole discourse to refer to a single judgment. They hold that Jesus confidently expected his return within a comparatively few years and that there would be a judgment on Jerusalem as part of the judgment of the whole world. But the language used is against this. Far from promoting speculations that he would soon return in glory, Jesus seems to be discouraging this kind of thing (cf. vv. 6, 8, 14, and 23-28). And we should not overlook the important fact that he said quite plainly that he did not know the date of his coming back (v. 36). If he did not know it, how could he say confidently that it would occur within a few years?[5]

1. The Destruction of the Temple, 24:1-2

> [1]And when Jesus had gone out of the temple he went on his way, and his disciples came to him to show him the buildings of the temple. [2]But he answered them, saying, "Do you not see all these things? Truly I tell you, there will certainly not be left here a stone upon a stone that will not be thrown down."

All three Synoptists tell us that this important discourse was triggered by a comment made to Jesus about the stones with which the temple was built. The temple was an important and beautiful building, and plainly the Jews were very proud of it. But Jesus was more interested in the service of God than the beauty of the place of worship, and he immediately prophesied the destruction of the magnificent edifice.

1. Matthew makes a break between this narrative and the preceding by telling his readers that Jesus *had gone out of the temple* (where his previous teaching had been located). There appears to be symbolism in this: Jesus now leaves the temple for the last time; he abandons it. Matthew omits the story of the widow's mite (Mark 12:41-44), an omission that has the effect of showing that what he now says is the sequel to the lament over Jerusalem at the end of chapter 23. It is not clear why *his disciples* drew attention to the great stones in the building (Mark says that one of them did this, and Luke has the indefinite "some"), for Jesus had been in the temple before and

---

[Swengel, Pa., 1948], p. 9). But it is more than doubtful whether the chapter can be divided up so neatly.

5. For an excellent discussion of the problems in interpreting this chapter see Carson, pp. 488-95.

indeed had evidently been teaching there during the last few days. Perhaps it was not so much an attempt to show him something that they thought he had not seen before, as a companionable remark about the wonder of the temple's construction, more especially, as Morgan holds (p. 281), in the light of Jesus' lament over the city (how would such a solidly built city be destroyed?). There were some very large stones in the temple Herod built; Josephus says in one place that they measured twenty-five cubits in length, eight in height, and twelve in width (*Ant.* 15.392), and in another he gives the dimensions as forty-five by five by six (*War* 5.224). This historian is somewhat prone to exaggeration, but even allowing for that, the stones were evidently remarkable enough to merit a comment. In any case, the temple was a beautiful building with its white marble and its gold over-lays.[6] There is a rabbinic comment: "He who has not seen the Temple of Herod has never seen a beautiful building" (*B. Bat.* 4a).

2. The disciples were doubtless moved by admiration for the magnificent building, and they probably expected some expression of appreciation from Jesus. *But* (there is adversative force in the conjunction) they got nothing of the sort. Instead Jesus invited their attention to *all these things*[7] and went on to prophesy solemnly the total destruction of the temple. He uses the emphatic *"Truly I tell you,"* goes on to employ the emphatic double negative, and supplies the detail that *a stone will not be left upon a stone.*[8] Jesus is making clear that, while the temple was undoubtedly a wonderful building, the disciples should not be beguiled by its beauty. What matters is that God's people should live godly lives. When they do not, disaster in some form is inevitable. For the Jews that was going to include the destruction of their beautiful place of worship.[9]

2. The Beginning of the Troubles, 24:3-14

> [3]*And when he was seated on the Mount of Olives, the disciples came to him privately, saying, "Tell us, when will these things happen, and what will be the sign of your coming and of the consummation of the age?"*

6. To cite Josephus again, "being covered on all sides with massive plates of gold, the sun was no sooner up than it radiated so fiery a flash that persons straining to look at it were compelled to avert their eyes, as from the solar rays. To approaching strangers it appeared from a distance like a snow-clad mountain; for all that was not overlaid with gold was of purest white" (*War* 5.222-23).

7. The question in the form οὐ βλέπετε looks for a positive answer: "Do you not see. . . ?"

8. The emphatic double negative οὐ μή removes all possibility of one stone being left on another.

9. Mounce comments, "Critics who think that the bulk of Matthew comes from the early church rather than from Jesus himself are hard pressed to explain why there is no mention at this point of the burning of the Temple. A *vaticinium ex eventu* (prophecy after the event) would not have omitted such a specific item." Nor would such a prophecy omit other information we find in Josephus about the siege, such as cannibalism (he has a terrible story about a woman who killed her baby, roasted him, and ate him; *War* 6.208) and the dreadful conflicts among the defenders.

4And Jesus answered them, saying, "Take care that you be not led astray. 5For many will come in my name, saying, 'I am the Messiah,' and they will deceive many. 6And you will hear of wars and rumors of wars; see that you are not troubled, for it is necessary that these things happen, but the end is not yet. 7For nation will be raised up against nation, and kingdom against kingdom, and there will be famines and earthquakes in many places. 8But all these things will be the beginning of birth pangs. 9Then they will hand you over to trouble, and they will kill you, and you will be hated by all the nations on account of my name. 10And then many will be entrapped, and they will hand one another over and hate one another. 11And many false prophets will arise and will deceive many people; 12and because lawlessness will be increased, the love of many will grow cold. 13But he who endures to the end will be saved. 14And this gospel of the kingdom will be proclaimed in all the world as a testimony to all the nations, and then the end will come."

3. Evidently nothing more was said at the temple, and the little band went on their way to the Mount of Olives. Both Matthew and Mark tell us that Jesus *was seated* on that mountain, the posture of a teacher, and Mark adds that they were opposite the temple. Doubtless the view helped them remember the strange words that Jesus had said, and *the disciples* pursued the matter (Mark particularizes with Peter, James, John, and Andrew; we are probably not being unfair to the other eight if we say that the subject was taken up by the leading disciples). Both Evangelists indicate that this was done *privately*; this was not a subject for public teaching. Had Jesus taught such things publicly there might well have been a furor, but for the disciples it was important in later years to remember that Jesus had prophesied the destruction of the temple forty years or so before it occurred. They asked specifically for two pieces of information: the time when all this would happen, and what *the sign of your coming*[10] *and of the consummation of the age*[11] would be. It would seem that the disciples thought that the two were to be closely connected.[12] The form of their question indicates that Jesus had spoken more about eschatology than is recorded. There is nothing to be surprised at in this, for it was an age when all sorts of speculations about the Last Things were in vogue and throughout his ministry Jesus said things that indicated an interest in the topic. He knew that he would not be with the disciples much longer;

10. παρουσία is found 4 times in Matthew (again in vv. 27, 37, and 39) and nowhere else in the Gospels. It signifies a "being present" and thus "coming." It is used for the visit of an important person like a king (it is cited, e.g., from a papyrus that mentions a visit of King Mithridates, *New Documents*, 4, pp. 167-68), and it becomes the usual word in the Epistles for the "coming" of Jesus at the end of the age. The other Gospels have the question as to when "these things will be," but only Matthew refers to Jesus' coming.

11. "The consummation of the age" is found 5 times in Matthew (see on 13:39).

12. In the best text there is one article to govern both *your coming* and *the consummation of the age*; they are parts of a connected whole.

therefore he told them plainly about some significant eschatological happenings.

4. All three Evangelists tell us that Jesus' opening remark was to warn the disciples against being *led astray*. When we survey the history of the church, we are reminded that eschatology is certainly a subject on which it is easy to err. Throughout the centuries people have held with the utmost tenacity to a wide range of views on this subject. In our own day there are doughty exponents of pre-, post-, and a-millenarianism to remind us that all the mysteries have not yet been solved and that differing views are still strongly held. Perhaps we should notice Jesus' care for the future conduct of his followers. We should not think of this passage as simply a demonstration of Jesus' power to forecast the future; it was a series of prophecies designed to help believers.

5. Jesus' next words make it clear that the main problem his first followers would confront would be people who would claim to be *the Messiah*. Ever since the incident related in 16:13-20 the disciples had known that Jesus was the promised Messiah, but their faith was going to be severely tested in the days that lay ahead. It would be difficult for them to cope with the loss of their leader when Jesus was crucified, and even after the resurrection confident eschatological speculations would be put forward. Jesus says that there will be *many* with whom the disciples will have to cope, and that they will come *in my name*. This expression is used a number of times with reference to genuine followers of Jesus, for they came in his name to set forward his purposes. But in this place the meaning is rather that they will claim for themselves the name *Messiah*, Jesus' own title. Mark and Luke both mention that the false teachers will say, "I AM." This probably means "I am he" and will be another way of claiming to be the Messiah, but we should not overlook the fact that there is a hint of the divine name about this form of speech and that Jesus may well be warning that some of these people will come close to claiming deity. This will surely be a reference to the last days, for there is little evidence that any of the turbulent men so active preceding the fall of Jerusalem ever claimed to be the Messiah. Some claimed to be prophets, but that is not the same thing.

And not only will they claim the title, but they will *deceive many*. The fact that God's true Messiah has come will not prevent false teachers from arguing persuasively that they are the Messiah, and convincing many. This will be confusing for ordinary followers of Jesus, and it is important that his apostles be clear on the truth: there is but one Messiah, and Jesus is he. They must expect that there will be people who will claim to be the Messiah and that they will attract large followings. But in the face of this they must retain a firm hold on the truth. Jesus is preparing them for the difficult days that lie ahead.

6. Those difficult days will see happenings that will include *wars and rumors of wars*, but apparently Jesus' followers will not be caught up in these conflicts, for he says only that they *will hear*[13] of them. The *rumors* point to a very disturbed populace; even when there is no actual conflict people will still be talking as though hostilities were occurring (unless we take the meaning as *GNB*, "the noise of battles close by and the news of battles far away"). In those troubled times Jesus' followers are to *see* to it that they *are not troubled*.[14] In an atmosphere created by the horrors of war and abuzz with rumors of more wars it is easy to be worried and thrown off balance. Jesus is telling his followers that they must not let themselves be caught up in the general disquiet; they are to be sure that they are not gripped by the panic that will take a firm hold on other people.[15] They have one thing going for them that the general public has not: they know that God is over all and that his purpose will in the end be worked out. This is the significance of *it is necessary*.[16] Although in a time when people are caught up in war and when other wars are rumored it seems that evil is in control, this is illusory. God is in control, and all apparent triumphs of wrong will in the end be seen to fit into his perfect plan. The wars and the like of which Jesus speaks are events that must happen, but they do not mean *the end* of all things. That end will take place in the way and time that God wills, but the conflicts of which Jesus speaks are no more than part of the preliminaries. *The end is not yet.*

7. The strife will be on the grand scale, *nation against nation, and kingdom against kingdom*. It may be that this means no more than that there will be the normal conflicts of interest that through the centuries have led to war after war. But it is also possible that the passive, *will be raised up*, is significant and points to forces at work beyond the control of the nations. This is certainly the case when we move to *famines* and to *earthquakes*. Famines were beyond the control of kings, as, of course, were earthquakes. But these form part of the general unsettlement that will characterize the end time. *In many places* means that the disasters in question will be widespread.

8. Jesus places the happenings of which he has been speaking in their proper place in the scheme of the last things. *All these things* is comprehensive; the totality of the tumults and troubles does not mean simply an especially disastrous period in the history of the race. It means the beginning of the process that will usher in the final state of affairs; it is *the beginning of birth pangs*[17] (*REB* brings out the meaning with a little addition,

---

13. μελλήσετε ἀκούειν adds a touch of certainty; the wars and the like *will* take place.

14. θροέω is connected with θρόος, "a tumult." In the New Testament it means *"to be troubled,* as by an alarm, *alarmed"* (AS).

15. Jesus "certainly does not intend either to justify war or to invite us to resign ourselves to evil. He simply states that in a world in revolt against God, a world of hate and violence, such explosions are in the logic of things, and should not trouble our faith" (Diétrich).

16. δεῖ conveys the thought of a compelling divine necessity. The text says no more than δεῖ γενέσθαι, "it is necessary to happen," but a number of MSS supply πάντα (C W etc.). In English we need something like "these things."

17. ὠδίν means "birth pain"; it is used mostly of the pains that accompany the physical

"first birth-pangs of the new age"). Among the Jews there was a widespread expectation that before the Messiah came to set up the kingdom of God in a form that would last forever there would be trouble on the largest possible scale. The powers of evil will not give up without a struggle, and thus there will be disaster after disaster. Jesus is pointing to this period which was so widely expected and speaking of it in traditional language.

9. Jesus moves from what the Jews in general expected to the way these happenings will affect his followers. In a little section largely peculiar to Matthew (though cf. Luke 21:12), *they* are introduced without explanation, but clearly he is speaking of people in places of authority, people in a position to take decisive action and who will take action against the disciples. They *will hand you over* (for the verb see on 4:12; it is used with special frequency in this Gospel, 31 times in all) *to trouble.*[18] This signifies that people in authority will take the initiative against Jesus' followers; they must expect special trouble in the last days and not simply the suffering they will share with all people, such as the famines and earthquakes of which Jesus has just spoken. They will suffer because of who they are — Christians, and their suffering will be no insignificant discomfort but the trouble that crushes. That *they will kill you* does not mean that all Christians will be killed but that some of them certainly will. And they will all be the objects of a hatred that will be universal. It is one of the things that puzzle Christians in every age that, although they are doing their best to love God and their neighbor and to put love into practice by ministering to whatever needs they discern in those they encounter on their way through life, they are so often the butt of ridicule and the objects of hatred. Jesus is saying that this will be especially the case in the last days. Perhaps the issues will be more clearly drawn then. Whether that is the reason or not, Jesus' followers are clearly warned that the end time will mean serious trouble for them. They *will be hated*[19] not because of anything that they will have done, but *on account of my name;* they will suffer persecution simply because they bear the name "Christian." In an evil world they must expect to suffer for what they are, not for what they have done.

10. Matthew now has a little section not found in the other Gospels (vv. 10-12). In those difficult circumstances *many will be entrapped.*[20] The

---

birth of a child. But the word is also employed "of the 'Messianic woes', the terrors and torments traditionally viewed as prelude to the coming of the Messianic Age" (BAGD). G. Bertram points to the use of the term in Judaism for the "woes" of the Messiah and says of this passage, "The woes precede the new birth of the world" (*TDNT*, IX, p. 672).

18. *Trouble* is θλῖψις, pressure to the point of bursting; it signifies no minor discomfort but the trouble that crushes. See on 13:21.

19. Johnson cites Tacitus, who speaks of Christians as "a class hated for their abominations." What happened in first-century Rome will be widely repeated in the end time.

20. For the verb σκανδαλίζω see the note on 5:29; it is especially frequent in this Gospel.

meaning is that they will be caught in the situation in which their Christian profession will be the accusation against them (cf. Lenski, "be caught so as to have their faith killed, like an animal that springs a trap . . . ; not 'shall stumble' [our versions], for one may quickly recover after stumbling," p. 933). These people will encounter disaster: they had professed to be Christians because of the peace and joy they sought in a difficult world, and instead they find persecution. In such a situation nominal Christians readily find the faith a trap and seek to get out of it promptly. *GNB* paraphrases with "will give up their faith," and *NRSV* with "will fall away." That certainly is the outcome, and they will go so far as to *hand one another over* (the verb is that used in v. 9); we could translate "betray one another" (as several translations do). So far from fulfilling their function as the servants of God they will actively assist the evil people in authority by handing over to them those with whom they had been associated in the church. The final disaster for those who formerly professed the Christian faith is that they will *hate one another.* Those who had been taught to love as Christ had loved them will degenerate into living in hatred. If this passage refers to the siege of Jerusalem, it is worth noticing that Josephus gives vivid pictures of the hatred and strife that characterized those days.[21]

11. In the early church prophets were very significant figures (they are ranked second to apostles, 1 Cor. 12:28). Clearly they were valued very highly and their words listened to with close attention. Accordingly it is a disastrous situation when *false prophets* make their appearance, and in that there will be *many* of them Jesus is speaking of no small trouble in the church. The inevitable result, given the church's estimation of the prophets, is that they will *deceive many people.* Jesus' followers were accustomed to valuing the prophets highly; until a false prophet discredited himself, therefore, he was going to be heard and heeded, and he was going to lead simple people astray.

12. In that situation *lawlessness* will abound.[22] With the increase of evil both inside and outside the church many people will choose to go their own way. It is possible to put too much stress on the letter of the law and thus to descend to legalism. But the opposite error can cause much wider devastation. When people refuse to submit to law and each person does what is right in his own eyes, moral disaster follows (as is abundantly documented in many lands in modern times).[23] It is basic to the Christian

---

It refers to triggering off the bait stick of a trap, but many prefer to translate it "stumbled," "offended," or the like.

21. Thus he speaks of the Zealots who killed the brave "from fear" and the nobility "out of envy" and who pursued private quarrels in order to exterminate their enemies (*War* 4.357-65).

22. πληθύνω means "increase, multiply"; the thought is that in the days of which Jesus is speaking lawlessness will not simply increase a little: it will be multiplied.

23. "'Lawlessness' does not mean apostasy from Pharisaic literalism in obeying all the commandments of the Mosaic Law, but a way of life that refuses to recognize any divine

way that the follower of Jesus must be humble, must say "No" to self (16:24). To acknowledge no law is to place oneself outside the sphere of those who are Christ's, so it is not surprising that in an atmosphere of lawlessness Jesus says, "*the love of many*[24] *will grow cold.*" Jesus does not here speak either of love to God or of love to people; in this context the noun probably means both.[25] But real love is impossible for the lawless person. By definition the lawless person is motivated by personal, selfish concerns, not by any regard for others or for the rules that govern our intercourse with one another. So with the upsurge of lawlessness there is a cooling off of love. The one necessarily involves the other.[26]

13. All this, however, should not daunt the true follower of Christ. "*He who endures*[27] *to the end will be saved.*" Saving faith is known not by some firm declaration or a well-intentioned beginning, but by endurance. The words, however, are not to be thought of wholly as an injunction to constancy. They are that, but they contain also a valid and valuable promise: the person described *will be saved*. The power of God is such that he can and will sustain his faithful servants through whatever trials they may be called upon to endure.

14. Mark has a parallel to verse 13, but not to this verse (nor has Luke). The church's missionary task is very important for this Evangelist. For the third and last time in his Gospel Matthew speaks of the proclamation of the *gospel of the kingdom* (for this expression see on 4:23). He has first spoken of Jesus as proclaiming this gospel (4:23; 9:35), but now it is a task for his followers. *Gospel*, of course, means "good news." The good news that God has established his kingdom through what his Son has done for sinners is a message that must be taken to the ends of the world. So Jesus now says that it will be *proclaimed* (the word is that used for a herald passing on the message that has been committed to him) *in all the*

---

law, which is identical for Matthew with a way of life in which one's neighbor no longer has any legal claim" (Schweizer, p. 451).

24. The article τῶν πολλῶν, "the many," indicates the majority; cf. Moffatt, "most of you."

25. This is the one occurrence of ἀγάπη in Matthew, but the corresponding verb is more frequent (8 times). It does not signify the reaction produced by an encounter with the beautiful or the attractive. It is first God's love for those he has made, a love that persists despite the unworthiness of sinners. Then it is the sinner's response to God's love for sinners. Thus it denotes the love that proceeds from a loving person, in the first instance from God, but then in those who respond to God's love. They become in their measure loving persons. The word may be used for their love for God or for their love for other people.

26. Verses 10-12 "are peculiar to Matthew and list most of the spiritual disasters which can come on the Christian community — apostasy, treachery, internal hatred, heresy, lovelessness" (Nixon).

27. The verb is ὑπομένω, which, Trench says, Chrysostom contrasts with μακροθυμέω in this way: "a man μακροθυμεῖ, who having power to avenge himself, yet refrains from the exercise of his power; while he ὑπομένει, who having no choice but to bear, and only the alternative of a patient or impatient bearing, has grace to choose the former." Trench himself holds that "The man ὑπομένει, who, under a great siege of trials, bears up, and does not lose heart or courage" (Trench, pp. 195, 198).

world. At a time when his followers were confined to a little group of people mostly in Galilee with a few in Judea, Jesus looked to the gospel message as good news that would be taken throughout the whole world.

It is perhaps somewhat unexpected that the proclamation is to be done *as a testimony,* but we must bear in mind that throughout the New Testament the gospel is always the good news of what God has done. It is never simply a challenge for people to do something for themselves. There is, of course, a challenge in living out the Christian life, but the essence of the gospel is what God has done in Christ. Christian salvation calls for endurance, as this passage makes abundantly clear, but in its essence it is not anything that people do. It is what God in Christ has done. The death of Jesus was to be an atoning death, a death in which he would deal with the problems of human sin and be (as Matthew has earlier reported) "a ransom for many" (20:28). The proclamation of the gospel is the bearing of testimony to that great fact. And this is to be done in no minor way but *to all the nations.* The followers of Jesus must not lose sight of the fact that their Savior, during his life on earth, spoke of carrying the gospel to every nation. Christianity must always be a missionary faith.

All this is spoken in an eschatological context. Jesus has been speaking of the importance of being prepared for all manner of troubles before the end of this age. Now he says that the missionary task must be carried out, *and then the end will come.* Strictly this verb means something like "will have become present," "will have made its appearance."[28] Jesus has foretold grievous trouble for his followers in the days ahead. But he does not let them forget the certainty of final triumph.

3. The Climax of the Troubles, 24:15-28

15"*Therefore when you see the 'abomination of desolation' spoken of through Daniel the prophet standing in the holy place (let the reader understand),* 16*then let those in Judea flee to the mountains,* 17*let him who is on the housetop not come down to fetch the things in his house,* 18*and let him who is in the field not turn back to take up his cloak.* 19*But woe to pregnant women and to those with babies at the breast in those days.* 20*But pray that your flight be not in winter nor on a Sabbath.* 21*For then there will be great distress, such as has not been from the beginning of the world until now, and will not be again.* 22*And unless those days were shortened, no one would have been saved. But for the sake of the elect those days will be shortened.* 23*Then if anyone says to you, 'Look, here is the Messiah,' or 'Here he is,' do not believe him.* 24*For false Messiahs and false prophets will appear, and they will perform great signs and wonders so as to lead astray,*

---

28. ἥκω is a perfect with a present meaning, "to have come, be present" (AS). In one way or another in every occurrence of the verb in this Gospel there is the thought of the last things (8:11; 23:36; 24:50).

if that were possible, even the elect. *25Look, I have foretold it for you.* *26If therefore they say to you, 'Look, he is in the wilderness,' do not go out; or 'in the inner rooms,' do not believe it.* *27For just as the lightning comes out from the east and flashes to the west, so will the coming of the Son of man be.* *28Wherever the corpse is, there the vultures will gather."*

Jesus has spoken of the troubles through which his followers would have to go as well as of the importance of the proclamation of the gospel of the kingdom and of the certainty of final triumph. Now he turns his attention to the happenings at the destruction of Jerusalem.

15. *Therefore* connects with the preceding statement and leads into what follows. It is because the end will certainly come that the disciples are to be on their guard. *When*[29] has the force of "whenever"; Jesus is giving no indication of the exact time when what he speaks of will take place. It will surely happen, but it is the occurrence and not the precise timing that occupies his interest. The *abomination of desolation* is an expression that recurs in Daniel with some variation in wording (8:13; 9:27; 11:31; 12:11), where most scholars agree that there is a reference to the desecration perpetrated by Antiochus Epiphanes when he built an altar to Zeus in the temple and offered swine and other unclean animals on it as sacrifices (cf. 1 Macc. 1:41-61).[30] It may refer here to the Romans with their standards; they certainly brought *desolation* to the land (cf. Luke 21:20). There has been a good deal of dispute about the precise meaning of the expression in this context, but there can be no doubt that Jesus was referring to some "abominable" thing, that is, something that brought or would bring defilement to the temple. It would stand *in the holy place,* that is, the temple. At the siege of Jerusalem many horrific things took place as zealous Jews fought over the temple and defilement of some sort certainly took place. The reference seems to be to something of this sort rather than to what the Romans did when they captured it, for by that time it would be too late to flee; there were opportunities earlier. *"Let the reader understand"* is a little parenthesis inserted at exactly the same place in Mark's account (Mark 13:14); it will refer to the reader of Daniel, not to the reader of the Gospel in which the words occur. It encourages the reader to think hard about the words: "it means, Look more deeply into this, because what is said is less than what is meant" (Fenton). Our problem is that with our background it is not at all easy to understand what the expression means. Perhaps Jesus meant that nobody will be able to understand the prophecy fully until the event of which he speaks takes place. But clearly he is saying that there will be some sacrilegious hap-

---

29. ὅταν is a "temporal particle, with a conditional sense, usually of things expected to occur in an indefinite future" (AS).

30. *AB* translates "the abominable sacrilege," which omits the idea of desolation. It also states, "It was common practice then and for long centuries before, to assert sovereignty over a nation by dethroning its gods and replacing them by those of the conqueror."

pening that will pollute and empty the holy place and that his followers should take notice of it when it occurs.

16-18. That is to be the signal for those of them in Judea to take refuge in flight. There is the thought that the city faces destruction; thus it will be a very unsafe place in which to be. Jesus says that they should make for *the mountains,* presumably because mountains have always been a refuge for those harried by armies. The terrain makes pursuit difficult, and there are greater possibilities of survival. It is sometimes urged that this injunction was fulfilled when the Christians fled to Pella at the time of the Jewish revolt, as the historian Eusebius reports (*Eccl. Hist.* 3.5.3), but it is objected that Pella is not in fact in the mountains but at the foothills. There are serious doubts whether the Christians in fact did flee to Pella at that time (see Hendriksen, p. 858, for the difficulties in the way of the Pella hypothesis). Jesus is saying that flight will be important in those days, but Pella is not what he is speaking about. Jesus goes on to underline the urgency of flight in that trying time. He speaks of anyone *who is on the housetop,* a place that was important in family life in first-century Palestine. Houses had flat roofs, and these were used as part of the living quarters of a house. While doubtless they would be uncomfortable during the hottest hours of the day, they would form a cool living room on hot evenings. If a man was taking his ease on his housetop and there received the signal that the dangerous time had come and that he should lose no time in escaping, it would be natural for him to think of some of his valued and easily portable possessions and to go down into the interior of his house to fetch them.[31] Jesus tells them not to do it. The danger he prophesies is great; the need for flight is urgent. No time should be lost. Better to lose one's portable possessions than one's life. Carson thinks that the meaning is that the man is to run from rooftop to rooftop to get out of the city with the utmost speed (Josephus speaks of people avoiding the streets by leaping from roof to roof [*Ant.* 13.140], so the method was used).

There is a similar urgency for the man *who is in the field* when he gets the news. Presumably he is at work, for what else would he be doing in the field? The natural thing would be for him to take off his *cloak* before he started work and leave it at the side of the field (or even at home before he started out), and since it was an important part of his clothing he would want to snatch it up before he left. But Jesus warns him not to be concerned about clothing. It is better to concentrate on saving his life.

19. In a similar strain is a remark about women. Jesus says nothing about their flight, but pronounces a *woe* on those who are *pregnant* and those *with babies at the breast.* It would be difficult for women to make a

---

31. We would have expected a reference to the things "in" (ἐν) the house rather than "out of" (ἐκ); there may be the thought that he would want to take them "out of" the house. Moule speaks of "a 'pregnant' sense" for the preposition here and explains: "to take *from* his house the things which are *in* it" (*IBNTG,* p. 74).

speedy getaway, and exceedingly difficult for the two classes of which he speaks. Jesus does not tell them what they should do, but he indicates that there will be difficulties for them. They are warned. They, of course, would be in a worse position than that of the men just described. They could not leave their burdens behind as the men could.

20-21. A word in the same strain now comes for all the people. Flight *in winter* would be difficult, for winter weather could create all manner of hindrances. The disciples could do little about such conditions if they met them, but they could *pray* that they would not face the necessity of such a flight. With that Jesus joins, *nor on a Sabbath.* The regulations about "a Sabbath day's journey" would make for a difficulty of a different sort; journey on a Sabbath would present a problem for Jewish Christians, and Sabbath-observing Jews would make things difficult for hurrying Christians.[32] These are ways of underlining the difficulties of flight when the time comes. But we must not miss the point that even should the critical time come on the Sabbath instant flight is imperative. Something of a reason appears with the information that *then* (see on 2:7 for this word; here it locates what follows at the same time as the preceding) *there will be great distress,* where the term indicates very serious trouble, pressure to the point of bursting (see the note on 13:21; Phillips translates "misery"). This is underlined with the information that it will be of a magnitude unparalleled in the entire history of the world; such trouble has never been, nor will it be equalled thereafter.[33]

22. This verse is usually taken with the preceding, and this may be the way to understand it. But it makes a good deal of sense to take it as resuming the line of reasoning from verse 14 and applying primarily to the end time (though, of course, it has an application to the fall of Jerusalem also). The reference to *the elect* seems to take us beyond Judaism,[34] and again "all flesh" (*no one* is literally, "all flesh will not — ") surely means more than Judaism. It is further brought home by the neces-

---

32. Most commentators think that Matthew records the words because Jewish Christians in the congregations for whom he wrote would wish to observe the Sabbath day limit for travel. But Meier says, "the context speaks of external circumstances which will make flight difficult, not impossible. The various dispute stories in Mt do not favor the view that Mt's church still scrupulously observed the Sabbath, even when it meant endangering life (cf. 12:1-14)." Robert Banks points to the fact that flight on the Sabbath in emergencies may not have been condemned by rabbinic teaching and takes the meaning here as "shutting of gates of the cities, difficulty in procuring provisions, etc." (*Jesus and the Law in the Synoptic Tradition* [Cambridge, 1975], p. 102). G. Barth agrees that there is no evidence that contemporary Jews would have regarded flight on the Sabbath as a sin; he cites E. Hirsch, "A Christian congregation fleeing on the Sabbath would have been as recognisable in Palestine as a spotted dog"; there would be danger "from the side of the hate-charged Jews" (*TIM*, p. 92).

33. There is an unusual piling up of negatives — οὐδ' οὐ μή — that makes for a very emphatic negation.

34. Although, of course, the term could be used by the Jews; for example, "The blessing of Enoch: with which he blessed the elect" (1 Enoch 1:1).

sity for it to be *shortened*,[35] for without this *no one would have been saved*. In this context *saved* is not to be understood in the sense of receiving eternal life, but saved from death here on this planet. An interesting feature of this shortening is that it is *for the sake of the elect*. God's people bring a certain mercy to the people around them; while the unrepentant do not share in the ultimate salvation, yet something of good comes to them because of the presence of the elect in their communities. Jesus does not indicate how the time of trouble will be shortened, but we are doubtless to see the hand of God in this.[36]

23-25. *Then* does not necessarily denote "immediately after," and it may well be that there is an interval of time at this point, perhaps even a considerable interval.[37] In times of trouble people tend to look for some kind of deliverer; Jesus foretells that in the troubles of which he is speaking there will be those who proclaim that *the Messiah* has come. They will not lack confidence, for they will point him out with *"Look, here is the Messiah,"* or in another place they may say, *"Here he is."* This may indicate fickleness as people shift from one they regard as Messiah to another, or it may mean that different people will put forward rival claimants to messiahship. Either way the followers of Jesus are not to give credence to the claims. How could they? For them it is a fundamental article of faith that Jesus is the only Messiah. All others of necessity are false. But *false Messiahs* will appear, and so will *false prophets*, who may be prophets attesting one or other of the false Messiahs or who may be claiming to have the gift of prophecy as they pursue some career of their own.[38] These false religious figures, apparently both Messiahs and prophets, will do miracles in support of their claims. *Signs* is a term used often in John's Gospel for the miracles of Jesus, but not so in the Synoptics. As John uses it, it indicates that the miracles are meaningful; the person who contemplates them in faith will see the hand of God at work and understand that God is saying

---

35. Enoch has a reference to shortening the days: "In respect to their days, the sinners and the winter are cut short" (1 Enoch 80:2).

36. It is not without its interest that according to Josephus, Titus saw the hand of God in the capture of Jerusalem. When he entered the city Titus is reported to have been impressed by the strength of the fortifications and to have said, "God, indeed, has been with us in the war. God it was who brought down the Jews from these strongholds; for what power have human hands or engines against these towers?" (*War* 6.411).

37. Chrysostom remarks, "Here, as I have often said, the word, 'then,' relates not to the connection in order of time with the things before mentioned. At least, when He was minded to express the connection of time, He added, 'Immediately after the tribulation of those days,' but here not so, but 'then,' not meaning what should follow straightway after these things, but what should be in the time, when these things were to be done, of which He was about to speak" (p. 458). Since Greek was his native language, this is an important observation.

38. For example, Josephus tells of an Egyptian false prophet who gathered a following of about 30,000 and led them to the Mount of Olives, preparatory to an attack on Jerusalem. But Felix's Romans routed these optimists, killing and imprisoning many, though the Egyptian himself managed to escape with a few followers (*War* 2.261-63; cf. Acts 21:38).

something to him in the miracle. Here the meaning seems to be that those who see the false religionists performing their miracles will discern that what they are seeing is more than human. This will be reinforced in that what they do are *wonders,* happenings that cannot be understood on the basis of merely human powers. There is something more than the merely human at work. They will be correct in seeing this, but, whereas they will be persuaded that they are seeing the power of the one true God, in fact it will be the power of the evil one, the enemy of God. But their miracles will be convincing. They will impress *even the elect.* Since the elect are God's own, and are kept by the power of God, it will not be possible for them to be led away by these charlatans. But Jesus brings out the impressive character of the things they will do by saying that if it were possible to lead the elect astray, they would do it. However, he knows what they will have to go through, and it will be a further strength to them that he has foretold that all this will come to pass. When it happens they will surely remember his prophecy, and this will help them not to be unduly impressed.

26. *Therefore* leads on to a consequence of Jesus' having foretold all this. Since he has assured them of the coming of false teachers, they must not be unduly impressed by those who will claim to know precisely where the Messiah is located. There will be some who will say that he is *in the wilderness.* John the Baptist had made his appearance in the wilderness, and other holy men sometimes made such places their dwellings as they sought to escape the corrupting influences of urban society (cf. the Qumran community). There might thus be some plausibility in claiming that the Messiah was in some remote locality. Others might go to the other extreme and say that he is *in the inner rooms.* But since the inner rooms of a house were the less accessible rooms (and might even be used as storerooms), this way of locating him, too, put him out of the reach of ordinary people.[39] Those trying to lead them astray will be claiming that they have special knowledge; whereas ordinary people do not know where the Messiah is, they do. If people will only trust them, they will lead them to him. Jesus says definitely, *"do not believe it."* His followers must not be led astray in this way.

27. The coming of the Messiah will not be some secret thing such that only those with special knowledge will be able to say where the Messiah is. Jesus likens his coming to *the lightning.* Nobody needs to be told where the lightning is. When it flashes, the whole sky is lit up from east to west. The coming of the lightning is a coming that thrusts itself on our notice; we cannot overlook it. *The coming of the Son of man* will be like that. It will be open and public; nobody will need to be told about it.

---

39. Carr thinks that "lecture rooms" are meant, giving the meaning, "whether the false Christ come like John the Baptist in the desert, or like a great Rabbi in the schools of the synagogue, be not deceived."

28. It is not easy to see the connection of this saying with the immediately preceding. Perhaps the thought of judgment follows hard on that
of the coming of the Son of man. These words are found also in Luke 17:37
in a passage dealing with the coming of the kingdom and the consequent
judgment and that has a number of affinities with this discourse. The
words may well be a known proverbial saying, bringing out the truth that
it is the dead body and not something less that attracts vultures (*KJV* has
"eagles," but eagles are not eaters of carrion, nor do they gather in flocks).
The thought will be that the spiritually dead inevitably attract judgment.

4. The Coming of the Son of Man, 24:29-51

29"*And immediately after the distress of those days the sun will be
darkened, and the moon will not give its light, and the stars will fall from
heaven, and the powers of the heavens will be shaken.* 30*And then the sign
of the Son of man will appear in heaven, and then all the tribes of the earth
will lament, and they will see the Son of man coming on the clouds of heaven
with power and great glory.* 31*And he will send his angels with a loud
trumpet, and they will gather his elect from the four winds, from one end
of the heavens to the other.*

32"*Learn the parable from the fig tree; when its branch has already become
tender and puts forth leaves, you know that summer is near.* 33*So you too,
when you see all these things, know that it is near, right at the doors.* 34*Truly
I tell you, this generation will not pass away until all these things happen.*
35*Heaven and earth will pass away, but my words will not pass away.*

36"*But as for that day and hour, no one knows, not even the angels of
heaven, nor the Son, but the Father only.* 37*For as the days of Noah, so will
be the coming of the Son of man.* 38*For as they were in those days before
the Flood, eating and drinking, marrying and giving in marriage, until the
day Noah entered the ark,* 39*and they knew nothing until the Flood came
and took them all away, so will the coming of the Son of man be.* 40*Then
two men will be in the field; one is taken and one is left.* 41*Two women will
be grinding at the mill; one is taken and one left.* 42*Watch therefore, because
you do not know on what day your Lord is coming.* 43*But know this, that
if the householder had known in what watch the burglar was coming, he
would have kept watch and would not have allowed his house to be broken
into.* 44*For this reason you also be ready, because the Son of man is coming
at an hour you do not expect.*

45"*Who then is the faithful and sensible slave whom the master has
appointed over his household to give them their food at the proper time?*
46*Blessed is that slave whom his master will find so doing when he comes.*
47*Truly I tell you, he will appoint him over all his goods.* 48*But if that wicked
slave says in his heart, 'My master is delayed,'* 49*and begins to beat his
fellow slaves, and eats and drinks with drunken fellows,* 50*the master of that
slave will come on a day that he does not expect and at an hour that he does*

*not know, 51and he will cut him in two and give him a place with the
hypocrites. There will be the wailing and the grinding of teeth."*

The remainder of the chapter is taken up with the coming of the Son
of man back to this earth[40] and with the kind of conduct required in his
followers in view of the certainty of that coming. No indication is given
as to the time of that coming, and indeed Jesus specifically says that he
does not know this (v. 36). But he does know that many people will go on
living as though this life is all that there is and their personal success is
all that matters. Such attitudes are not for the followers of Jesus. They are
to have much more of a sense of purpose. Jesus, who is aware of current
eschatological speculations, proceeds to give what information his followers need about the End. Much of the language is the apocalyptic
language of the prophets (e.g., Isa. 13:19-22; 34:4; Dan. 7:13-14; Zech.
12:10-14), and of such passages it has been said, "It is important to remember that all these natural portents in the apocalyptic literature are signs of
God's power and overruling providence; they are a terror only to the
faithless" *(AB)*. Jesus speaks of some happenings that could be terrifying,
but because God is in them and God is working out his loving purposes
they are an encouragement to his people, not a reason for them to be afraid.

29. Jesus has spoken of troubled times that will precede the end of
all things, and he now goes on to speak of what will follow *the distress* he
has earlier mentioned (vv. 9 and 21; for the meaning of the word see the
note on 13:21). He speaks of significant celestial phenomena in language
reminiscent of Old Testament passages but without specifically quoting
them (e.g., Ezek. 32:7; Joel 2:10). The most striking thing is that neither *the
sun* nor *the moon* will give any light: the whole earth will lie in darkness.
With that is joined disturbance in *the stars*, for they *will fall from heaven*
(Matthew has the word for *star* 5 times, which is more than in any other
New Testament book). That the stars will fall means that starlight is affected as much as is sunlight and moonlight. There is to be no source of
light here on earth in that day. It accords with what will happen to sun,
moon, and stars that *the powers of the heavens will be shaken*. The word for
heaven is singular in the reference to the stars, but plural where the powers
are spoken of, but there does not seem to be any great significance in this
(Matthew uses both forms with no apparent difference of meaning). Jesus
does not say what these *powers* are, but in the first century it was widely
accepted that there were many heavenly beings and that on occasion they
might make their present felt on earth. Jesus is saying that, whatever the
powers of the heavens may be, they are subject to God, and that at this

---

40. Unless we assume, with Tasker, "that the events described in the symbolic language
of Jewish prophecy in verses 29-31 would take place directly after the downfall of Jerusalem"
(p. 225). Part of this section may refer to that event, but certainly the bulk of the rest of the
chapter is concerned with Jesus' second coming.

time, that of the return of the Son of man to this earth, their power will be disturbed. Whatever functions they may be exercising at the time will be affected by the great fact that the Son of man is coming back to this earth to bring an end to the current system and to inaugurate the reign of God over all the earth.

30. Matthew's favorite *then* (see on 2:7) brings us to the central happening: *the sign of the Son of man will appear in heaven.* It is not completely clear what is meant by *the sign.*[41] It may be some outward sign (Chrysostom thought it would be the cross, p. 459, as did others in the early church). *REB* renders "the sign that heralds the Son of Man," a translation that at any rate makes clear the function of the sign even if it does not tell us what it is. Or it may simply mean the coming of *the Son of man* himself, a view that is supported by the fact that neither Mark nor Luke refers to *the sign;* they both say, "they will see the Son of man." Whatever it is, the *sign* will appear in the sky and will be clear enough to be recognizable, for it will have its effect on *all the tribes of the earth* (a point mentioned by Matthew only; he also is the only Evangelist to speak of the trumpet call). We would have expected a reference to "the nations," and perhaps that is the sense of the term in this context (*NIV,* "all the nations of the earth"). If it is used strictly it will point to smaller groups than nations, but either way the whole of earth's population is in view. They will not rejoice at the coming of the Son of man, but *will lament* at it. They will recognize that this coming is decisive and that it spells the end of their comfortable securities. Jesus does not say whether they will immediately recognize that he has come for judgment and that accordingly they will face the penalty for their misdeeds, but clearly there is something about the coming that will make them uncomfortable. In words reminiscent of Daniel 7:13 Jesus goes on to tell us that he will appear, and that is the important thing. He is speaking of his coming back to this earth, a return that will be so striking that it will leave no doubt as to his majesty. *The clouds* are often associated with the presence of the divine, and that will be their significance here. This is further made clear by the addition of *with power and great glory.* Jesus is speaking of the majestic appearance of a King, the very antithesis of his first coming, a lowly coming in the form of a servant.

31. The majestic appearance of the King will spell deliverance for the servants of God. He will send *his angels* (cf. 25:31; 2 Thess. 1:7) *with a loud trumpet.* This detail is peculiar to Matthew, but we must remember that

---

41. The genitive τοῦ υἱοῦ is ambiguous. It may indicate "the sign which is the Son of man" (cf. "the sign of Jonah," 12:39), or "the sign belonging to (or referring to) the Son of man." T. F. Glasson argued from the normal Greek usage of σημεῖον and from its conjunction here with "trumpet" that the word should be understood as "standard" or "ensign" (*JTS,* n.s. XV [1964], pp. 299-300). Carson accepts this view. It is used in LXX of the serpent Moses put on a pole in the wilderness (Num. 21:8), and of the ensign the Lord will raise before the nations (Isa. 11:12).

Paul speaks of "the last trumpet" (1 Cor. 15:52) and says that a trumpet call will herald the coming of the Lord (1 Thess. 4:16). The coming of the King and his angels is to be no hole-in-the-corner affair, but a coming that will be known immediately throughout the earth. The angels will be sent to *gather his elect*; the messengers of heaven will gather up the saints of earth. Jesus brings out the truth that not one of them will be overlooked; the angels will gather them *from the four winds*, which is expressive enough as a reference to the whole earth, but here it is reinforced with *from one end of the heavens*[42] *to the other*. Jesus' followers are encouraged by the certainty that on the last day not one of God's people will be missing.

32. Jesus turns from the signs that will precede his coming to the kind of conduct that is appropriate in his servants as they await him. As he has so often done throughout his ministry, he proceeds to teach by means of a parable, this one not so much a story (as many of them were) as a command to pay attention to the significance of the way *the fig tree* grows (REB, "Learn a lesson from the fig tree"). Most trees in first-century Palestine, we are told, kept their leaves throughout the year, but not the fig tree. This tree sheds its leaves in winter, but year by year the miracle takes place in spring. The *branch*[43] becomes *tender*[44] (the reference will be to the change that takes place when the sap rises in the spring) and *puts forth leaves*. There are other ways of knowing that the winter has come to an end, but anyone who has grown trees knows how satisfying it is to see the new leaves make their appearance. There is then no doubt that the harsh days of winter are gone and that *summer is near*. The fig tree does not bring the summer, but the appearance of its new leaves is a sure and certain indication that summer is now at hand.

33. The followers of Jesus are to be no less discerning than the orchardist. When the tokens of which he has spoken make their appearance, they are commanded, *"know that it is near"* (it is also possible to take the Greek in the sense "you know"); the imminence is underlined with *right at the doors*. It is also possible to understand the meaning as "he is near" (so NRSV), but this does not seem nearly as probable as "it"; the reference is to the whole series of events, not simply to the central person.

34. The solemn *"Truly I tell you"* (see on 5:18) introduces an important statement. Unfortunately there are problems relating to the meaning of this statement, the most important being the significance we should attach to the words *this generation*, the generation that will not *pass away* until the occurrence of *all* the things of which Jesus has been speaking. On the

42. Turner takes the plural οὐρανοί as "following a Jewish idea," but "In the material sense of *sky* the sing. predominates," this being one of the few "exceptional plurals" (M, III, p. 25).

43. κλάδος means "*a young tender shoot* broken off for grafting; then *a branch*" (AS; it is connected with κλάω, "to break").

44. ἁπαλός (again in the New Testament only in Mark 24:32) means "tender" and is "a favorite expression w. plants" in Theocritus (BAGD).

surface of it, the meaning is that he will be returning in glory during the lifetime of people then living, and indeed some exegetes hold to this view, claiming that Jesus thought that he would reappear on earth not so long after his death, perhaps at the fall of Jerusalem, to usher in the end of the world, which, of course, means that he was mistaken. In view of the fact that two sentences later he says that he does not know when it will occur (v. 36), this appears to be an erroneous interpretation of the words. A better view is that *all these things* refers to the distress indicated in verses 4-28, which must occur before Jesus comes again but which does not mean that his coming will follow immediately.[45] A difficulty with this view is that it is not easy to see why *all these things* should include the events of verses 4-28, but not those of verses 29-31. So others have suggested that the *generation* is the Jewish nation (it means "not just the first generation after Jesus but all the generations of Judaism that reject him," Schweizer, p. 458; so also Ryle, Hendriksen, and others) and point to its continuation through the centuries. Others think that the reference is to the human race,[46] but this view has little to be said for it.

We should notice that in the Old Testament the term is sometimes used for a kind of person, as when we read of "the generation of the righteous" (Ps. 14:5) or "the generation of those who seek him" (Ps. 24:6). From passages like this some have taken Jesus to mean that the church will survive to the end (e.g., Green). But the term is used also of the wicked, as when the Psalmist prays, "guard us ever from this generation" (Ps. 12:7); or it may refer to "the generation of his wrath" (Jer. 7:29). If this is its meaning, Jesus is saying that this kind of person, "this generation," will not cease until the fulfilment of his words.[47] It is perhaps relevant to notice that a little earlier Jesus said of people to whom he was speaking, "you killed" Zechariah (23:35), a statement that implies the solidarity of the race through the years. Mounce draws attention to the phenomenon of multiple fulfilment. He points out that the "abomination of desolation" had one fulfilment in the desecration effected by Antiochus Epiphanes and another in the destruction of Jerusalem by the Roman armies. "In a

45. Thus Carson says, "all that v. 34 demands is that the distress of vv. 4-28, including Jerusalem's fall, happen within the lifetime of the generation then living. This does *not* mean that the distress must end within that time but only that 'all these things' must happen within it." Calvin comments, "Christ uses a universal term, but does not apply His words in general to all the afflictions of the Church, but simply teaches that in one generation events would establish all He has said" (III, p. 97).

46. *NIV* mg. has "race." A. R. C. Leaney notes that the equivalent saying in Luke means "mankind" (*A Commentary on the Gospel according to St. Luke* [London, 1966], p. 263). So also W. J. Harrington, "Luke may well have taken 'this generation' in the broad sense of 'mankind'" (*The Gospel according to St Luke* [London, 1968], p. 242).

47. Lenski is forthright in rejecting the view that the words refer to the people then living: that they refer to "those living at the time when Jesus spoke, is untenable. A look at the use of *dor* in the Old Testament and at its regular translation by γενεά in the LXX reveals that *a kind* of men is referred to, the evil kind that reproduces and succeeds itself in many physical generations" (p. 952).

similar way, the events of the immediate period leading up to the destruction of Jerusalem portend a greater and more universal catastrophe when Christ returns in judgment at the end of time." Right up to the time when *all these things happen* there will be people of the same stamp as those who rejected Jesus while he lived on earth.

35. Jesus makes a further statement that underlines the certainty and the permanence of what he is saying. *Heaven and earth* have lasted through many human lifetimes and stand for what is permanent. We know that they are not unchangeable and that, for example, through the centuries storms, earthquakes, erosion, and other forces have changed the face of the earth to some extent. But for all that, we speak easily of "solid earth" and view it as one of life's permanencies. So also with the sun, moon, and stars. But, Jesus now says, all these things will *pass away,* and in doing so they form a contrast to his saying. His *words will not pass away.* This implies a far-reaching claim about his person, as well as about the end of the world. What he says will in the end have its fulfilment.

36. Wth such firm and detailed prophecies of the end of the age it seems natural to most of us to look for the date, and through the centuries there have never been lacking those who felt that it was possible to work out that date, sometimes exactly, sometimes approximately, referring only to a general period. But all such efforts are wrecked on this saying of Jesus. It is both clear and emphatic. *That day and hour* defines the measures we use in fixing a date, but that *no one knows* firmly excludes the possibility of doing so. One would have thought that *no one* is definite enough to make clear the impossibility of all date fixing. It shuts out the whole human race from the knowledge in question.[48] But Jesus goes further. *The angels* do not have this knowledge; even in heaven the knowledge is not shared. And what surprises us even more is that *the Son*[49] himself did not share the secret. The only person who knows, Jesus says, is *the Father only.* Nothing could be more explicit.

37. Up to this point Mark's narrative has been on all fours with that of Matthew, but now Matthew includes a section to which Mark has no parallel (Luke has much of the content of this section, but in a different context, Luke 17:26-36). Jesus proceeds to bring out what this means for those who would live the life of service to God by pointing out what had happened in a critical period long ago. There is a resemblance of the coming of *the Son of man* to the coming of the Flood. The time until then is likened to *the days of Noah.* We are not told how long it took Noah to

---

48. Glover finds value in this: "No day is named, that every day may be hallowed by the sense of the possibility of its being the day of His Advent. It helps to hallow each day of life, to realize that before its close we may be in the presence of Christ's glory."

49. Apparently it surprised some in the early church too, for οὐδὲ ὁ υἱός is omitted by many MSS. But it is read by ℵ*·b B D Θ etc. And, as Metzger comments, "The omission of the words because of the doctrinal difficulty they present is more probable than their addition by assimilation to Mk 13.32."

build his ark, but with all that had to be put in it, it must have been quite large and must accordingly have taken quite some time to build. But when Noah and his family and the animals entered the ark, the Flood came very swiftly. The emphasis is on the suddenness of the deluge. "*So,*" Jesus says, "*will be the coming of the Son of man.*" We get the picture of a long time of waiting and of a sudden act at the conclusion.

38. Jesus refers to life in the pre-Flood days. The Old Testament informs us that the people of that day were sinners, and indeed that it was their exceeding sinfulness that brought down the Flood on them. But Jesus refers to none of this. He reminds his hearers that life before the Flood was in many respects like life in their own day. People were engaged in *eating*[50] *and drinking,* they were *marrying and giving in marriage* (the verbs normally used of the man and of the woman respectively). We should notice that there is nothing sinful in the activities Jesus mentions; these actions are the stuff of life.[51] No community could exist without them. And these actions continued right up to *the day Noah entered the ark.*

39. The people could see Noah building his ark, and doubtless, human nature being what it is, some mocked him. But *they knew nothing;* they did not share in Noah's wholehearted commitment to the service of God, so they did not know what was coming on the earth. They disregarded what Noah said to them, doubtless believing firmly that their views were just as valid and just as likely to be correct as those of the ark maker. But such convictions did not avail when *the Flood came and took them all away.* The purposes of God are worked out quite irrespective of what puny humans think about them. Jesus is saying that people will in this way continue to be about their normal business right up to the time of his coming. That will be the critical point; after that it will be too late, just as it was too late for the antediluvians when the Flood came. *The coming of the Son of man* will be just as abrupt, just as unexpected, just as decisive as the coming of the Flood was.

40-41. Two pictures of the activities that will be going on at the time of Jesus' return bring out the importance of being ready and also of the fact that some will not be ready and will miss the glories of the great day. The first picture is of two people *in the field.* Presumably these will be men at work on their land. No distinction is made between them; their circumstances are the same. But *one is taken,* to share in the blessings of being with the Lord (it is possible to understand *taken* in the sense "taken for punishment," but this seems less likely). But there is also *one* who is *left.* In both cases the verb is in the present tense, which makes it all very vivid. The reality is that some will have lived with no thought for the things of

---

50. This is the one example of τρώγω in the New Testament outside the Fourth Gospel. Properly it denotes noisy eating by animals, but it is also used of human eating.

51. Bonnard comments, "Contrary to certain Jewish ideas of the time, Matthew does not insist on the extraordinary laxity of the conduct of the Noachian generation."

God; in that day they will, of course, have no part in the things of God. The story is repeated with *two women*. They, too, will be going about their normal duties, on this occasion *grinding*[52] *at the mill*, a regular part of normal life for women of that day. The reference is to a hand mill that the women used each day to grind the grain required for the day's food. Here, too, there is separation: *one is taken and one is left*. In both the field and the mill the emphasis is on division. The coming of Jesus marks a complete and permanent division. Jesus makes clear that the coming of the Son of man does not mean that all indiscriminately will enter into the joys of that day. Those who have chosen to live without God will find their choice respected when the great day comes. It will be the portion of the godless to be without God.

42. In the light of this certainty Jesus calls on his followers so to live that they will be ready when the great day comes. He says, *"Watch therefore,"* where his verb looks for his followers to live such lives that whenever he comes they will be prepared, and the present tense conveys the meaning "Keep watching." *Therefore* links the demand to the uncertainty that attaches to the time of the coming. If people knew just exactly when the coming would take place, they could delay preparations until just before the time. They do not know, and *therefore* they must live in constant readiness. Jesus underlines the point with *"you do not know on what day your Lord is coming."* Ignorance of the day is one of the conditions of living here and now.

43. A homely illustration underlines the point. The hearers do not know at what hour their Lord is coming, but they do know[53] what they would do if a certain situation arose in their normal course of life. Burglaries, alas, do happen from time to time, but what makes them possible is that the burglar does his work unknown to the householder. He chooses a time when he will not be expected and thus can get away with his nefarious business. If the time of his coming was known, even in general terms,[54] the householder would be ready for him. A *watch* would be about three hours on the Jewish system and about four hours as the Romans ordered things. Thus Jesus is not arguing for a position in which the householder knew the exact time when the burglar planned to do his breaking in.[55] He is saying that if the man knew approximately when the burglar would come, he would keep

---

52. The participle in this construction "is not good Greek" (BDF, 418[2]). But the meaning is clear.

53. γινώσκετε might be indicative, "you know," or imperative, "know." Either makes good sense.

54. φυλακή (see on 14:25) signifies a "watch"; both Jews and Romans divided the night (the time between 6 p.m. and 6 a.m. as we count time) into "watches," the Romans having four and the Jews three. On either system a "watch" lasted for hours.

55. The verb διορύσσω literally means "to dig through," a process obviously applicable to houses made of mud bricks, though, of course, it was used of any method of "breaking and entering." MM cites the verb from a papyrus dated 260 B.C. where the meaning is to break into a house.

watch and protect his goods; he could safely neglect watching at all other times. Since he does not, he must take reasonable precautions at all times or run the risk of losing his valuable goods. Constant readiness is his only safeguard. The point is that no one knows even approximately when the Son of man will return. There is no particular "watch" that we may keep and be sure that Jesus will come within those limits.

44. *For this reason* carries on the chain of the argument: because disciples are in essentially the position of the householder and do not know when the coming is to be. Jesus therefore calls on his followers (his *you* is emphatic) to be *ready* at all times, and again he repeats the reason; it is *because* they do not know the time of the return that they must live in a state of constant preparedness. Jesus says once more, "*the Son of man is coming."* He leaves no doubt about the fact. That is a certainty on which they may reckon. But the timing of it all is another matter. The *hour* of the coming is one that they *do not expect.*

45. Jesus turns attention from the duty of watchfulness in view of the uncertainty of the hour to the fate first of the servant who is ready when his master comes and then to that of the one who is unprepared. Jesus does not nominate the servant who is ready but asks who he is. This is a way of inviting his hearers to reflect on their own state of readiness. He designates this servant as *"the faithful[56] and sensible slave."* Jesus is taking his illustration from a household where there are many slaves, one of whom is put in a responsible position while his master is away. He does not owe his position to his own deliberate choice: his master *has appointed* him *over his household.* But being there, he is responsible. It is his task to be sure that the members get *their food,*[57] and get it *at the proper time.*[58]

46-47. This slave does what he should. He does not know when his master will return, but apparently that does not concern him greatly. He works at the task committed to him so that whenever the master chooses to come back all will be in order. When the master comes back and finds him working at the things at which he should be working, then that servant's lot is *blessed* (for this term see on 5:3). The solemn *"Truly I tell you"* (see on 5:18) emphasizes that the following words are significant. The master will reward the slave by setting him in the most responsible position in the estate — he will be appointed *over all his goods.* The reward for faithful service is the opportunity of serving in a higher and more responsible place (not ease and rest forevermore).

---

56. The adjective πιστός is applied to a slave in an epitaph cited in *New Documents*, 2, p. 53.

57. This will be the "consecutive or final sense" of τοῦ — the infinitive with the meaning "in order to give them food." Turner says that the construction "belongs to a higher level of the Koine" and is mostly found in Paul and Luke in the New Testament (M, III, p. 141).

58. "It will be noticed that the lesson is most practical. The servant is not required to abstract himself from all business, and stand day and night looking out over the road" (Robinson).

48. But that slave's accomplishment is not the only possibility. There-fore Jesus proceeds to refer to another slave, this one at the opposite pole of character and achievement. *If* introduces a hypothetical case; Jesus is not speaking of something that actually happened. He designates him as *"that wicked slave,"* so he lacks the moral fiber of the first slave (but Jesus does not speak of him as actively rebelling). He reasons within himself; *in his heart* signifies "in his innermost being"; this is not what he says to other people, but the thinking that governs his actions. *"My master is delayed"* (is there perhaps a hint that Jesus' coming will be delayed also?) sums up the situation for him. He does not ask how long the delay will be, but seizes on the fact that he will not have to give account of himself for quite some time. He acts for all the world as though the delay had somehow removed all possibility that his master would ever come back.

49. Now we observe the kind of man he is. Knowing that there is no possibility of being called to account speedily, he *begins* to act unjustly. He takes advantage of his temporary superiority *to beat his fellow slaves.* They were really on a level with him, his fellows. But he has temporary author-ity, and he uses it to inflict punishment on them. To this strain of cruelty he adds that of self-indulgence and proceeds to eat and drink *with drunken fellows.* This speaks of dissoluteness as well as lack of care in discharging his function.[59]

50. The slave in temporary charge has failed to reckon with the fact that his charge is indeed temporary. His conduct is on the basis that the master's absence will continue indefinitely. He has not reckoned with the basic fact that inevitably his master will come back. Jesus speaks of him not simply as the householder or the master of all, but as *the master of that slave;* he had a relationship to the slave who was neglecting his duties. He *will come on a day that he does not expect* (in view of the conduct of his slave he could scarcely do anything else). This is emphasized with the addition *at an hour that he does not know.* Jesus is underlining the truth that delay does not mean cancellation. The master may have been away for longer than this particular servant expected, but that did not mean that he would never come back. The application to the coming of the Son of man is obvious.

51. The illustration ends with the unhappy fate of the wicked slave. *"The master,"* Jesus says, *"will cut him in two."*[60] This cannot be meant literally (the man is still alive in the next clause), but clearly it stands for severe punishment, perhaps a heavy beating. The master will also put him *with the hypocrites* (for this word see the note on 6:2; in the Lukan version of the saying the word is "unbelievers," Luke 12:46). It is not at first easy

59. Meier makes an application to a particular group of Christ's servants: "if the church leader forgets that all his power is derivative and is conferred only for a time and for the good of others, the 'servant' will turn into a 'cleric.'"
60. The verb is διχοτομέω (δίχα, "apart" + τέμνω, "cut"). Such a punishment is indicated in Hebrews 11:37 (though with a different verb).

to see why this should be his fate. But perhaps we should bear in mind that throughout this Gospel *hypocrites* come in for severe condemnation; Jesus has left no doubt that their ultimate fate will be a most unhappy one. This man who pretended to be a capable overseer of a whole household and who proved to be inefficent and interested only in his own self-indulgence belongs with them. *The wailing and the grinding of teeth* is a proverbial expression that Matthew uses quite a number of times, but that is rare elsewhere in the New Testament. It stands for the anguish and suffering of those who are finally lost (see on 8:12).

Schweizer regards the fact that this chapter about the followers of Jesus follows the severe denunciation of the Pharisees in the previous chapter as important. "Chapter 23 pronounces judgment on Pharisaic Judaism in harsh and oppressive terms; chapter 24 pronounces judgment in equally harsh terms — but this time on the community of Jesus" (p. 464). It is important to understand that Jesus does not set a high standard for people like the Pharisees and a lower one for those who have given their allegiance to him. All those who profess to serve God must accept the truth that that service must be wholehearted and that in due course they will have to give account of themselves to one from whom nothing is hidden.

Matthew 25

5. The Parable of the Ten Girls, 25:1-13

1 "Then the kingdom of heaven will be like ten girls who took their torches and went out to meet the bridegroom. 2Now five of them were foolish, and five were sensible. 3For when the foolish took their torches, they did not take any oil with them. 4But the sensible ones took oil in the flasks with their torches. 5Since the bridegroom was delayed, they all nodded off and slept. 6Now in the middle of the night a cry went up, 'Look, the bridegroom! Go out to meet him.' 7Then all those girls woke up and trimmed their torches. 8But the foolish girls said to the sensible ones, 'Give us some of your oil, for our torches are going out.' 9But the sensible ones answered, saying, 'There will not be enough for us and you. Better go to the sellers and buy for yourselves.' 10But while they were going to make their purchase, the bridegroom came, and the girls who were ready went in with him to the wedding, and the door was shut. 11Later the other girls came, saying, 'Sir, sir, open up for us.' 12But he answered, saying, 'Truly I tell you, I don't know you.' 13Watch therefore, because you know neither the day nor the hour."

Jesus continues to teach his followers the necessity of continual readiness as they await his coming again. From the emphasis he put on watchfulness he clearly regarded it as very important. Some explanations of this parable contain considerable elements of allegory,[1] and it is not difficult to interpret the bridegroom as the Messiah,[2] his delay in coming as the delay in the Parousia, and so on. One may discern some elements of allegory, but this does not mean that this passage is not a genuine parable, nor that Jesus did not intend some of its details to be understood allegorically. Allegory was widely used, and there is no reason at all for holding

1. The early church delighted to interpret the parable allegorically. Chrysostom, for example, says, "By lamps here, He meaneth the gift itself of virginity, the purity of holiness; and by oil, humanity, almsgiving, succor to them that are in need" (p. 470).
2. Hill points out that "the representation of the messiah as bridegroom is unknown in the OT and in the literature of late Judaism (except Pesik. 149a), and it makes its first appearance in 2 C. 11.2; therefore it seems improbable that Jesus' hearers would have applied the figure to the messiah." But he goes on to argue that whether we accept this allegorical understanding or reject it, "the essential point of the section is the same: 'Be ready.'"

that he rejected it and refused to use it. But this story makes excellent sense if taken as what it purports to be, a parable. Our interpretation is handicapped by the fact that we do not have complete information about wedding customs in first-century Palestine. Nobody seems to have thought it worthwhile to set down in detail what was normally done; after all, why should anyone do this? Everyone knew what happened in a wedding. So we are left with stories like the present one, which tell us some of things that were done and leave us to guess at others.

1. *Then* is a favorite Matthean conjunction (see on 2:7). Some translations bring out the temporal connection with "At that time" *(NIV, GNB).* We are to understand that this parable was delivered on the same occasion as the teaching Matthew has recorded at the end of chapter 24, and that it refers to the time of the Lord's return. For the last time in this Gospel we have the expression *the kingdom of heaven* (see on 3:2). The general idea of God's rule will be before us throughout this chapter, but the precise expression introduces this parable and is not used again. Jesus says that this kingdom *will be like*[3] *ten girls*[4] with *torches*[5] who were going out to meet *the bridegroom.*[6] This makes clear that Jesus is speaking of a wedding.

3. Matthew makes a good deal of use of the verb ὁμοιόω; he has it 8 times whereas Luke uses it only 3 times; nobody else has it more than once. To introduce parabolic teaching he sometimes has the aorist "was likened" (13:24; 18:23; 22:2), but he has the future in 7:24, 26; 11:16 as well as here. There does not appear to be any significant difference.

4. παρθένος is used 4 times in this Gospel and twice in Luke. It means "a virgin" (and on occasion may be used of men, Rev. 14:4). In this parable there is no particular emphasis on virginity, so I have translated παρθένος as "girls." But they would have been virgins; married women were not attendants of the bride in weddings of that time. These girls would have helped in the dressing of the bride and acted as her attendants. When the bridegroom came, they would have formed part of the procession to his home for the feast.

5. It is not certain how we should understand λαμπάδας here. Traditionally this has been understood as "lamps" (which may be what the word means in Acts 20:8), but against this is the fact that λαμπάς means "torch" (Carr says that this is "the only meaning that the word bears in Greek literature early or late"); the word for "lamp" is λύχνος (5:15 etc.), while "lantern" is φανός. We should also bear in mind that ordinary lamps gave inadequate light for an outdoor procession, that they would be easily blown out in even a light breeze, and that they would hold enough oil for hours of burning. J. Jeremias cites evidence that in modern times in wedding processions in Palestine light is given by "long sticks, around the tops of which are wrapped rags completely soaked with olive oil" (J. McDowell Richards, ed., *Soli Deo Gloria* [Richmond, 1968], p. 84). It seems likely that this was the custom in antiquity and that we should understand the term in this way here. Lightfoot cites a passage from R. Solomon referring to "Ismaelite" weddings where the bride is preceded by "about ten wooden staves, having each of them on the top a vessel like a dish, in which there is a piece of cloth with oil and pitch: these, being lighted, they carry before her for torches." Hamann is another who appeals to modern Palestinian customs and insists on torches as the meaning. He points out that the girls would not recline at the feast (only men did this). They would "dance for the groom and his guests as long as their torches permit" (p. 249).

6. Some MSS read καὶ τῆς νύμφης (D X Θ f1 etc.). This reading is scarcely enough to outweigh the majority, but it is accepted by some scholars on such grounds as that the *girls* would be the bride's attendants, not those of the bridegroom. A difficulty is that, while there would be maidens waiting on the bride and going with her to the bridegroom's home, we know of none who would be going out to meet the couple. Allen calls it "a natural but thoughtless interpolation."

Not much is known of the actual wedding ceremony in first-century Palestine. It was preceded by a betrothal that was much more binding than is an engagement in modern societies. It was really the first stage of marriage, and it took divorce proceedings to dissolve it. At the end of the betrothal period the marriage took place, on a Wednesday if the bride was a virgin and on a Thursday if she was a widow (*Ketub.* 1:1). The bridegroom and his party made their way to the home of the bride, or to some other place; there is a record of a wedding in which two parties, one of the bridegroom and his friends and the other of the bride and her people, went out to meet each other at an unspecified place (1 Macc. 9:37-39). When the two groups came together the wedding took place. After this there was a procession, generally to the home of the bridegroom, where feasting took place that might go on for days. The processions often took place at night, when *torches* made for a spectacular display. Clearly this is presupposed in Jesus' parable. The *ten girls* were involved in going out *to meet the bridegroom,* which makes it appear that they belonged to the bride's party. They would then have had their place in the procession to the bridegroom's home for the feast.

2. The girls fell into two groups, *five* of them in each, though there appears to be no particular significance to the fact that the same number were in each group; it seems to be no more than a convenient division. The important thing is that some of them were *foolish* (Moffatt, "stupid"), and some were *sensible.* Matthew has an interest in people who behaved foolishly, and he has half the occurrences of the adjective *foolish* in the New Testament.[7] But he is also interested in the *sensible,* and interestingly he also has exactly half the New Testament occurrences of this word.[8] Jesus sets the scene, then, with a wedding procession in prospect and a group of girls waiting to take part in it with *torches* for the procession, and the information that some of them were more stupid than the others.

3. *For* introduces the evidence for judging some of them to be foolish and some wise. They all had *torches* and to that extent were prepared, but *the foolish* took no *oil* with them. Jeremias points out that it was necessary to pour oil on the rags at the end of the torches to get them to burn brightly, but these girls had not bothered to bring the necessary oil. He says, "their negligence can no longer be judged as lack of foresight excusable by the unexpectedly long delay of the bridegroom. It must be judged as inexcusable, punishable carelessness."[9] The rags would have been oily to start

---

7. μωρός is found 6 times in this Gospel and 6 times in all the rest of the New Testament. AS notes that it is properly used "of the nerves, *dull, sluggish,*" and that it is used also "Of the mind, *dull, stupid, foolish.*"

8. φρόνιμος occurs 14 times, 7 being in Matthew. AS defines its meaning as "practically wise, sensible, prudent." He can say that φρόνησις may be differentiated from σοφία and σύνεσις as denoting "practical, σύνεσις critical, both being applications of σ. in detail" (*sub* σοφία).

9. *Soli Deo Gloria,* p. 86.

with, but in a society where people set little store on punctuality and where preparations for a wedding were extensive and time-consuming this might well not be enough. It was foolish to think that the amount of oil the rags in a torch could hold would be sufficient.

4. *But* is adversative; it sets *the sensible* over against the foolish and particularizes by referring to the *oil*. These girls apparently reasoned that there was no way of knowing when the bridegroom would make his appearance and that he might well be late. In any case, if we are thinking of *torches*, oil was needed to ensure a bright and lasting flame. So *the sensible* took oil *in the flasks*.[10]

5. *The bridegroom* was late. No reason is given for this, and none, of course, is necessary. The bridegroom would take his time, as everyone knew. A wedding was important. Everything else would be set aside for it. And since nobody expected punctuality, no great attention would be paid to getting through the preliminaries smartly. The bridegroom was in no great hurry, so the ten girls waited. Evidently all their preparations had been made, and there was nothing for them to do but wait. So *they all nodded off and slept*.[11] This is not regarded as reprehensible; Jesus speaks no word of blame for the sleepers. In the circumstances to sleep was a good idea. All their preparations had been made, and from the time the bridegroom made his appearance they would be kept busy for a long time. To sleep while they could was an opportunity not to be missed.

6. The night was well on before *the bridegroom* made his appearance. Several translations say that he arrived "at midnight" (NIV, NRSV, etc.), but the expression may not be as definite as that: *in the middle of the night* is the sense of it. The bridegroom had not actually arrived as yet, but he had been sighted and *a cry went up*.[12] *"Look, the bridegroom!"* indicates that someone in the place where the ten girls were had sighted the approach of the party. So the command is given, *"Go out to meet[13] him."* The bride-

---

10. ἀγγεῖον (in some MSS ἄγγος) is used here only in the New Testament; it means "*vessel* for holding liquid or dry substances" (LSJ). MM notes its use in the papyri for containers for a number of things, one use being to hold oil. *NIV* has "jars," and *GNB* "containers."

11. Matthew has two words for sleeping, νυστάζω and the more usual καθεύδω (the former occurs twice in the New Testament, the latter 22 times). There does not appear to be any great difference in meaning; the expression may be rendered "slumbered and slept," as in the *KJV*. But there is a difference in tense. Robertson remarks, "When the aorist and the imperfect occur side by side, it is to be assumed that the change is made on purpose and the difference in idea to be sought. In juxtaposition the aorist lifts the curtain and the imperfect continues the play." Here he takes ἐνύσταξαν as ingressive, "fell to nodding," and ἐκάθευδον as meaning "went on sleeping" (p. 838). Most translations ignore the difference (e.g., *NIV*, "became drowsy and fell asleep").

12. The perfect γέγονεν is used in the sense of the aorist ἐγένετο (BDF, 343[3]).

13. The expression is εἰς ἀπάντησιν αὐτοῦ, "for meeting of him." The noun is often used for the arrival of great people; MM notes its use for magistrates and the like and comments, "The word seems to have been a kind of t.t. for the official welcome of a newly arrived dignitary — a usage which accords excellently with its NT usage." Here it points to the bridegroom as the important man.

groom is the center of attention: they should give him the appropriate welcome.

7. *Then* is used with precision; the shout got immediate action. At this point there is no difference among the ten. *All* of them *woke up,* and all got to work on their *torches.* This probably entailed putting more oil on the oily rags to make sure that the torch would burn steadily and give out its maximum light.

8. Now the difference between the two groups begins to appear. It is not necessary to hold that the torches were kept burning during the time the girls were sleeping. A torch would hold only a small amount of oil, and it could be consumed between the time of the shout and the arrival of the bridegroom. *The foolish girls* now found themselves in trouble, for their torches were *going out* (the present tense indicates that the torches were even then going out; it was not a matter of "our torches will soon go out"; they were going out right then).[14] There would be no place in a torchlight procession for girls whose torches gave no light. But there was no immediate panic because there were other girls there who had oil. So they asked them to give them some of their oil. To the careless girls that must have seemed the obvious solution.

9. But it did not appeal to *the sensible* girls. They were not sure whether the supply would be adequate for them all. There is a textual problem relating to the negative, and this affects the sense of their reply.[15] Thus they may be saying definitely, "there is not enough" (*GNB;* so also *REB,* "there will never be enough"). Alternatively they may be hesitant; if the other reading be accepted, they are saying no more than "Perhaps there will not be enough" (*RSV*). On the whole it seems that they are saying that there certainly won't be enough oil if it is split up among them all, but even if the "Perhaps" version be accepted as their meaning they are not prepared to take the risk that none of them would see the procession out.

But there is no such ambiguity about their suggested line of action. "*Better go*[16] *to the sellers,*" they say, "*and buy for yourselves.*" Evidently it

---

14. Chamberlain gets a lot out of the tense: "The present tense tells you that the lamps are still burning but getting very dim and, no doubt, smoking badly" (p. 70). Carr says that in the sixth-century Codex Rossanensis there is a picture in which "Three of the foolish virgins hold torches nearly extinguished, but still burning."

15. The clause is introduced with μήποτε, but this is followed either by the simple negative οὐκ (with ℵ A L Z f13 etc.) or the more emphatic double negative οὐ μή (B C D K etc.). On μήποτε BAGD says, "Somet. the negation is weakened to such a degree that μήποτε introduces someth. conjectured *probably, perhaps*"; it suggests that with the reading οὐκ the translation should be "perhaps there might not be enough." But if the reading with the double negative οὐ μή be accepted, "The tone is sharper"; it translates "certainly there would never be enough" (4). Turner sees here "a cautious statement" (taking the negative οὐκ, M, III, p. 98).

16. μᾶλλον has the meaning "more, rather"; here "the negative can be unexpressed, though easily supplied fr. the context: πορεύεσθε μ. (do not turn to us) *rather go*" (BAGD, 3.a.β). The significance of the construction, according to Blass, is, go "here and there, wherever you may find one" (BDF, 336[1]).

was quite possible to buy oil in the middle of the night, though, of course, it might mean routing the sellers of oil out of their beds and getting them to open up their stores, which would have been safely locked up for the night.[17] All this would take time and may explain why the foolish girls did not suggest this to one another in the first place. It is possible to argue that the girls with the oil ought to have been kinder to those without and to have shared what they had. To this more than one thing might be said. One is that the possibility that there would not be enough oil to get any of them to the banquet was evidently real ("enough for one cannot be made to do for two," Glover). It would have been silly to have excluded them all, foolish and sensible alike, from the festivities. The bridegroom had to be welcomed ("if *all* the torches went out, the procession would be a disaster," Mounce). Another is that a parable does not cover all the options. It is there to teach a specific lesson, and in the case of this parable it is the lesson of being ready. A story about sensible girls who shared their oil and stayed with the foolish in being unable to go to the banquet might have taught a lesson about being ready to sacrifice for the improvident. But it would not have taught the necessity for being ready, and that is the point of this story.[18] Jesus is teaching the importance of watchfulness, not going into all the possibilities in the life of the believer. And in the sense of being ready for the coming of the Christ being ready is not something that can be shared or passed on. It is an individual matter.

10. The delay was fatal. *But* is adversative: what happened was not that they came back quickly with enough oil, *but* that while they were still on their journey *the bridegroom came.* Jesus omits all that followed until they went into the place where the feast was to be held. He says nothing about what happened when the bridegroom arrived, nor about the procession for which the torches were required. His hearers were well enough versed in what went on at weddings to understand this for themselves. He goes immediately to the time when *the girls who were ready went in with him to the wedding.* Their forethought was justified, they had the oil they needed, and they took their appointed place in the wedding festivities. That *the door was shut* indicates that at this wedding feast, at any rate, there was a time to join the festivities and those who were not there when the time expired were totally excluded.

11. In time the careless ones evidently got their oil (or did they fail

---

17. Unless, as A. W. Argyle believes, shops would be open at all hours: "There was nothing to prevent a business, with sufficient staff to work night and day shifts, from keeping open for all day and all night, and these could well include not only shops that catered for victuals but those which supplied oil — in fact the same shops might do both" (*ET,* LXXXVI [1974-75], p. 214). Even if a shop did not do this regularly, it might when a wedding was on and the whole community was going to be up through the night.

18. Cf. M. Green, "there are some things you cannot borrow. You need to possess them for yourself" (p. 240). Buttrick points out that "we should not impose theological meanings on this particular verse." But he goes on, "Yet the fact remains that spiritual preparedness cannot instantly be shared."

to get it and simply turn up, late for the banquet but hopeful?) and arrived at the banqueting hall. They called to the bridegroom, which is interesting, for one would think that it would be someone else who would have the responsibility for keeping the door. But the story is about the bridegroom and the ten girls, so it is what the bridegroom says and not what some subordinate does that is important. "*Sir, sir,*"[19] they say, using a respectful form of address. It could be understood to mean "Lord, lord" and was a suitable form of address to the Son of God (it is used, also in a context of rejection, in 7:21). Jesus may be using the term with a glance at the time in the future when it was to him as Lord that petitions must be addressed. The girls in the parable plead, "*open up for us.*" They have no lack of desire to be numbered among the guests. And they are there, on the spot. Presumably they had been invited earlier and they are sure that there must be a place for them. The door shut in their faces is mystifying. There must be a way for them to get it. So they plead to the bridegroom.

12. *But* is adversative; far from opening up as they request, the bridegroom utters words that make it clear that they will be firmly excluded from the rejoicing throng. "*Truly I tell you*" (for which see on 5:18) is a solemn beginning and emphasizes that the words that follow are important. "*I don't know you*"[20] is devastating. They had been expecting to be on center stage with their torches in the procession. But their failure to be ready when the time came meant that they were excluded finally. If we reason that no bridegroom would say that he did not know some of the invited guests, we miss the sting in the story. Jesus is not telling a story about something that actually happened; he is warning people of the dreadful fate of those who know that they should be watching for the coming of the Son of man but who do not do this. Thereby they exclude themselves from any place among the people of God. The Savior cannot recognize them among the saved. While there was time they shut themselves out. There is no way by which they can now come in.

13. Jesus hammers home the lesson of it all. "*Watch therefore,*" he says, employing a verb that he has used twice before in this discourse (24:42, 43; the call for watchfulness runs through this whole address). It is important. And he repeats that his hearers "*know neither the day nor the hour*" (cf. 24:36, 38, 44, and 50). It is a condition of life here on earth that we cannot know how long it will last, and it is similarly a condition of life in the kingdom of God that we cannot know when that kingdom will be consummated here on earth.

---

19. κύριε, κύριε.
20. This may be "not a judicial penalty for arriving too late, but an inference from the late arrival that those without cannot belong to the bridal party" (Bruce). But, more probably, it may also be a formula for disowning those outside the closed door. "He will deny that there is any bond, any personal relationship, between Him and them. . . . He has nothing to do with them" (Ridderbos).

6. The Parable of the Talents, 25:14-30

14"For it is like a man going abroad, who called his own servants and handed over his property to them. 15And to one he gave five talents, to another two, to another one, to each according to his own ability; and he went on his journey. 16At once he who had received the five talents went and worked with them, and he gained another five. 17Likewise he who had the two gained another two. 18But he who received the one went away and dug in the ground, and hid his master's money. 19Now after a long time the master of those servants comes and settles accounts with them. 20And he who had received the five talents came and brought another five talents, saying, 'Sir, you handed over to me five talents; look, I have gained five talents more.' 21His master said to him, 'Well done, good and faithful servant; you were faithful over a few things, I will appoint you over many things; enter the joy of your master.' 22And he also who had the two talents said, 'Sir, you handed over to me two talents; look, I have gained two talents more.' 23His master said to him, 'Well done, good and faithful servant; you were faithful over a few things, I will appoint you over many things; enter the joy of your master.' 24But he also who had received the one talent came and said, 'Sir, I knew that you are a hard man, reaping where you did not sow and gathering where you did not scatter. 25And being afraid I went off and hid your talent in the ground; look, you have your own.' 26But his master answered him, saying, 'You wicked and lazy servant, you knew that I reap where I did not sow, and gather where I did not scatter. 27You ought therefore to have put my money with the bankers, and when I came I would have received my own with interest. 28Take therefore the talent from him, and give it to him who has the ten talents; 29for to everyone who has will more be given, and he will have abundance; but from him who has not, even what he has will be taken from him. 30And throw the unprofitable servant into the outer darkness; there will be wailing and gnashing of teeth.' "

There are resemblances between this parable and that narrated in Luke 19:11-27; indeed, some scholars see the two as differing forms of the same parable. But the differences in the two accounts are formidable; therefore it is better to see them as two distinct parables, though with the same basic theme of servants trading with their master's money. But in Matthew the amounts are large, while in Luke they are quite small; in this Gospel the amounts vary from servant to servant, in that one they all receive the same amount. Luke's story brings in a reference to a man receiving a kingdom and to the attitude of his subjects, whereas that in Matthew concentrates on trading. The story in Luke teaches that all the servants of God have one basic task, that of living out our faith; this one starts with the fact of the different gifts to be found in God's servants and brings out the way they use (or do not use) those gifts.

14. The story starts rather abruptly with *"For it is like"* without any explanation of what *it* signifies. But since the story follows on a parable explicitly said to refer to "the kingdom of heaven" (v. 1), there is no reason for doubting that *it* carries on the teaching about the kingdom (*GNB* makes this explicit with "At that time the Kingdom of heaven will be like — "). The preceding parable has taught the importance of being ready; this one carries on that theme by showing what readiness means.[21] The kingdom, then, is likened to *a man going abroad.*[22] This man was obviously a man of means, and he wanted to have his money used profitably while he was away. He summoned *his own servants*[23] and passed over to them the money he wanted them to invest while he was away.

15. That the money was calculated in *talents* presents us with a problem, for a talent was a measure of weight,[24] not a specific unity of currency. It was the largest weight in normal use (see on 18:24), and when used for money it might refer to either gold or silver or copper.[25] Attempts to render the equivalent in modern monetary terms run up against difficulties: we do not know exactly what weight the talent was in Palestine in New Testament times, nor do we know whether gold or silver or copper is in mind here, and, of course, with inflation and the like modern currencies vary in worth. All that we can say is that *five talents*[26] represents a considerable sum of money, *two* was not a small amount, and *one* was a sum not to be disregarded. The fact that different amounts were allotted to different servants seems to mean that the master thought one of them distinctly more able than the others, the second one to be a man of some ability, and the third to be distinctly less capable than the first two. No instructions are recorded, and we are left to understand that the master wanted the servants to use their own initiative. He wanted them to trade as best they could with the money he had left with them, but he did not want to tie them down with binding instructions when he could not tell what conditions would be like throughout his absence. Having allotted his money as he saw best, he went off.

21. Cf. France, readiness "is not a matter of passively 'waiting', but of responsible activity, producing results which the coming 'master' can see and approve. For the period of waiting was not intended to be an empty, meaningless 'delay', but a period of opportunity to put to good use the 'talents' entrusted to his 'slaves'."

22. δῆμος means "district, country, land" (LSJ), and ἀποδημέω, "to be away from one's land" and thus "to be abroad," "to go abroad."

23. ἰδίους puts some emphasis on the fact that they were his "own" servants; he did not choose some external financial house, but entrusted his money to those who were his own. δοῦλος normally signifies a "slave," but that can scarcely be the meaning here, for these men were able to enter financial arrangements involving quite large sums of money.

24. From this parable we have derived the use of "talent" to indicate abilities of various kinds, but we should be clear that the word had no such associations for Jesus and his hearers. It was simply a unit of weight.

25. The fact that the third servant buried ἀργύριον (v. 18) may indicate that in this story the talents were of silver. But the word may be used generally of "money," so this is not conclusive.

26. *REB* improves the occasion with "five bags of gold," while *GNB* suggests "five thousand silver coins."

16. There is a little problem related to the way we should take *at once*. Since there is no punctuation in our oldest MSS, it is possible to take it as the last word in verse 15 (as *KJV*, "and straightway took his journey") or as the first word in verse 16 (as most modern translations).[27] The sense seems to require this latter view; if we accept it, Jesus is saying that the first servant immediately set to work. He does not say what that servant did, and it is of no great importance. What matters is that he *worked*[28] *with them*. This signifies that he put them to good use in some way. In time diligence was rewarded, for the *five talents* entrusted to him became ten. His activity resulted in the doubling of his original capital.

17. There is little to be said about the second servant. He was also a diligent worker, and he *likewise*[29] doubled his original capital. He gained but two talents, but then his base was narrower than that of his colleague who had gained five. Both had done well; both had doubled the amount entrusted to them.

18. The third servant was a very different kind of person ("a mouse-minded man," Meier). The word *But*, which introduces this section of the story, has adversative force; this man forms a contrast to those mentioned earlier. Jesus says nothing about his reasoning at this point, but simply that he hid the money. Not for him the labor of buying and selling, working and making a profit. He simply *dug* a hole and *hid his master's money*.[30] This was a not uncommon way of hiding objects for safekeeping in antiquity (cf. 13:44). If it was carefully done, nobody other than the person who dug the hole would know where it was and what was in it. Jesus does not indicate at this point why the man did this (laziness? fear?). The important thing for this man was that the money was secure and that he could produce it when the time came. Keeping it in this way meant that there was no possibility of loss, but it also meant that there was no possibility of gain.

19. The period of the master's absence is not specified, but it was *a long time*; it was this that enabled the first two servants to increase their capital by 100 percent. The master then *comes and settles accounts*[31] *with*

---

27. Metzger points out that elsewhere in Matthew εὐθέως (or εὐθύς) always goes with what follows; he further remarks: "there is no point in the master's departing immediately; there is much point in the servant's immediately setting to work."

28. The verb is ἐργάζομαι; it can refer to any one of a variety of ways of working; it gives no indication of the precise way in which this servant went about his task. Modern translations supply the lack in a variety of ways: "traded with them" (*NRSV*), "invested his money" (*GNB*), "employed them in business" (*REB*), etc.

29. ὡσαύτως, "in the same way"; that is, he did the same as the first slave in increasing the money he was working with by 100 percent.

30. "He kept it in a manner which revealed his real attitude toward the gift and the Giver: he buried it. He thus was like one who had no gift at all; but it was he himself who made himself thus. In this he is a picture of all those in the church who for any reason refuse to use the gifts of Christ in his service" (Lenski, p. 976).

31. συναίρω means "to take up together," but in conjunction with λόγον it is used of settling accounts. MM finds "numerous examples" of the expression used in this sense in the papyri.

them (the present tenses introduce a note of vividness). The day of reckoning had come.

20. The first to give account of himself was the first to have received the money. After the one sentence with the vivid present tenses the past tenses are resumed. The man who had been entrusted with *five talents* brought his original sum plus the money he had gained and explained to his master that he had made a gain of *five talents*. In both clauses he puts emphasis on the amount: "*Five talents* you gave me; look, another *five talents* I have gained."[32]

21. His master commended this servant. First he says simply, "Well," which we normally put into English with *"Well done,"* but which could be taken in some such sense as "It is well." Or we could understand it as an interjection, "Bravo!" (BDF, 102[3]). However we take it, it is a mark of approval. This is something the master understands and approves. He goes on to salute the servant as *good and faithful,* an expression that approves both his character and his diligence; he had been all that the master expected (Cassirer translates, "excellent and trustworthy servant"). The master goes on to develop the thought of faithfulness. The servant, he says, has been *faithful over a few things.* Clearly Jesus wants his hearers to understand that the master was a very rich man. While we do not know exactly how much five talents were worth in our money, it seems clear that it was a considerable sum. But the master can speak of it as no more than *a few things.* Now that the servant has proved himself in what the master regards as a comparatively lowly piece of service, further doors of opportunity will be opened to him. *"I will appoint you over many things"* indicates that the faithful servant will be rewarded with a position that will give him more scope for the use of the abilities that he has shown he possesses. Once again Jesus is teaching that the reward for good work is the opportunity of doing further work. *"Enter the joy[33] of your master"* may be understood in the sense of REB, "share your master's joy."[34] Whether that is the way to take it or not, it clearly means that the servant has received the warm approval of his master and that his future is one in which joy will be prominent.

22-23. The process is repeated with almost identical wording in the

---

32. He speaks of five ἄλλα τάλαντα, "five other talents"; the word ἄλλα preceding πέντε τάλαντα gives the expression some emphasis; not only did he bring the original talents, but also "others," talents he had gained, not talents he had been given.

33. Moffatt has "share your master's feast," and Ridderbos favors the meaning "banquet," but χαρά does not mean "feast"; it means "joy." Granted that a great feast loomed large in common eschatological speculations, this is not the word for the feast, but for the joy that went with it. BAGD notes the suggestion that "festive dinner, banquet" is meant (2.c), but asks, "but would this have been intelligible to Greeks?"

34. Diétrich finds an eschatological reference: "This is the joy of the Kingdom, of the Messianic banquet. The faithful worker participates in the joy of the Master; this is his supreme reward." Cf. McNeile, "the joy that your Lord gives, and shares with you, is a unique expression for the bliss of the divine Kingdom."

case of the servant who had been given *two talents*. The man reports as his predecessor had reported with the one change of *two talents* for "five talents," and he receives his commendation in exactly the same terms. It is noteworthy that though he had gained but *two talents*, his praise is in words identical with that given the man with five. They had both doubled the sum entrusted to them, and they were both congratulated for doing so. The actual size of their gain was not as important as the fact that each had doubled the amount entrusted to him.

24. Finally there came *also* the man *who had received*[35] *the one talent*. He used the same polite address as the other two, *"Sir,"* but diverges by going into a description of his owner. He says, *"I knew that you are a hard[36] man"*; he puts this forward to excuse his failure to do anything with his talent, but in doing so he takes away some of his defense. If he knew that his master was a *hard man*, he knew also that he had been expected to do something profitable with the money entrusted to him. He explains something of what hardness means in this case. *"Reaping where you did not sow"* means that the master had the habit of enjoying a crop on which he had expended no labor. *"Gathering where you did not scatter"* probably has much the same meaning; it refers to the winnowing process at the end of harvest (as it does in 3:12), plying the winnowing shovel to scatter the mingled chaff and grain and thus separate the two. The sowing and the scattering refer to the processes that began and completed the getting of a crop. The master, this man says, profited from sowing and winnowing where he had not gone through the hard work of using the plough and plying the winnowing shovel. The picture this servant draws is of a man with an eye to business; he picked up profits in all sorts of places and not only those that resulted from his own hard work.

25. All this is said to explain his reaction to being left to look after a *talent*. He says that he was *afraid*, evidently afraid that if he used the money in business undertakings as his fellow servants were doing he would lose it and thus make himself liable to punishment. So, he says, *"I hid your talent in the ground."*[37] This made him certain of losing noth-

---

35. Is there any significance in the fact that the perfect tense is used of this man's having received the talent: εἰληφώς? The aorist λαβών is used of the man with the five, while the verb is left to be understood in the case of the man with two talents. The man who got the single talent had it remain with him. Moulton says that "the rather more emphatic perfect suits the situation of v.25 better" (M, I, p. 238). Cf. Bruce, "εἰληφώς, the perfect participle, instead of λαβὼν in ver. 20, because the one fact as to him is that he is the man who has *received* a talent of which he has made no *use*."

36. σκληρός means *"hard* to the touch, rough, harsh"; when used of people it signifies "hard, stern, severe" (AS). Hendriksen points out that in modern English we have taken over the word in "arteriosclerosis," "hardening of the arteries" (p. 882, n. 823).

37. Among the rabbis it was held that hiding money in the ground was the safest thing one could do. "Samuel said: Money can only be guarded [by placing it] in the earth" (*B. Meṣ.* 42a). A footnote in the Soncino translation says, "Otherwise the bailee is guilty of negligence — In ancient days there was probably no other place as safe." It goes on to quote Josephus, who refers to what "the owners had treasured up under ground against the uncertain fortunes of war."

ing,[38] but it also meant that when he was face to face with his master he could say nothing better than *"look, you have your own."*

26. *But* is adversative; far from accepting the explanation, the master was about to rebuke his servant. He did this, calling him both *wicked* and *lazy.* It was a wicked thing to receive money from his master and fail to use it to the best advantage, whatever his motive. But in any case, his motive was something for which he could be blamed, and the master says that he is *lazy.*[39] He let a natural disinclination for work cooperate with a dislike for getting some gain for his master, with the result that he did nothing. He felt that his preservation of the talent was something for which he should receive credit. He did not realize that anyone with a talent must use it. The master accepts the description of himself as reaping what he did not sow and gathering what he did not winnow,[40] but interestingly he drops the word "hard" that the defaulter had applied to him. It may well be that he is not saying that he really is the kind of man he has been said to be, but saying that if the third servant really thought that he was like that he would have acted in a different manner. What the servant had done was not in accordance with a genuine belief that his master reaped where he did not sow, gathered where he did not winnow.

27. The master points out how easily the servant could have made some gain, even if he mistrusted his own ability to trade profitably. *"You ought"* is a strong term;[41] the master is thinking of the easiest possible way of getting a profit, and at the very least this is something that the man was under an obligation to do. So he says that the servant should have *put* his *money*[42] *with the bankers,*[43] a procedure that he could have undertaken with safety and no great personal exertion. The result would have been that his master[44] would have profited from the *interest* earned. As it was, he got his money back, but nothing more.

---

38. Schweizer has an apt comment, "Jesus is saying that a religion concerned only with not doing anything wrong in order that its practitioner may one day stand vindicated ignores the will of God" (p. 473). Ryle cites Richard Baxter: "To do no harm is the praise of a stone, not of a man."

39. Patte comments that the Greek word ὀκνηρός "is derived from a verb that means 'to hesitate' (e.g., because of fear), a meaning that is quite appropriate in view of the explanation the servant gives of his action" (p. 352, n. 23).

40. "His acceptance supports the authenticity of the parable. Early Christians would hardly have made up such a description of Jesus, even in a parable" (Gundry, p. 508).

41. ἔδει means "It was necessary"; the master is not thinking of something that might possibly be done, but of something that *must* be done.

42. τὰ ἀργύρια will refer to the coins that make up the amount; the alternative reading τὸ ἀργύριον views the money as a whole. The use of this expression favors the view that the talents were of silver but does not prove it, for the term may mean simply "money."

43. Βαλεῖν τὰ ἀργύριά μου τοῖς τραπεζίταις: "throw my money to the money-changers" (the people who sit at tables). These were people who changed money from one currency to another, charging a fee for the service. They also seem to have loaned money at interest; that will be the meaning of τόκος here. It is from such activities that modern banking evolved; hence the translation.

44. His ἐγώ is emphatic.

28. Having rebuked his servant and made it clear why he was being blamed, the master proceeds to the action required in that situation. *"Take therefore the talent from him,"* he says. *Therefore* is important. The master is not acting in an arbitrary fashion. The man has had the money for quite some time and has shown that he has no intention of making any use of it. Left with him it would stay buried in the ground. But money should be used, and *therefore* it was necessary to take the money away. *"Give it to him who has the ten talents,"* he goes on. That man has shown that he knows how to use money profitably. He will make the best use of it, and therefore it should be left with him.

29. This verse largely repeats the words of 13:12 (where see the comments), and the small alterations make no difference to the sense. Jesus is not countenancing business practices that enable the wealthy to become wealthier at the expense of the deserving poor. He is laying down a principle of the spiritual life, a principle of great importance. Anyone who has a talent (using the word in the modern sense) of any kind and fails to use it, by that very fact forfeits it. By contrast, anyone who has a talent and uses it to the full finds that that talent develops and grows.[45] This is a law of the spiritual life, and we neglect it at our peril. The parable illustrates both possibilities. The servants who used what they had saw it grow; the one who refused to use what he had lost it. Jesus' followers are warned.

30. The servant who failed to use the talent entrusted to him is now characterized as *unprofitable.*[46] He has had control of a full talent and has buried it. He has failed completely when he had the opportunity to do something useful.[47] So he is consigned to *the outer darkness,* where *there will be wailing and gnashing of teeth.* With one exception, this expression combining the thoughts of punishment and of deep grief is found in Matthew only (see the note on 8:12). It stands for complete and final rejection and for unceasing sorrow and regret. We should bear in mind that this is not here pronounced over someone who has done some particularly heinous crime. It is the final result for the man who had only one talent and who steadfastly refused to use it.[48]

---

45. "Good living is not negative or static; faithful use of one's gifts, large or small, increases them, brings recognition, and opens the door to greater usefulness, but lazy disuse is blameworthy abuse of one's privileges and will mean the loss of one's gifts and place in the Kingdom" (Filson).

46. ἀχρεῖος is literally "useless" (ἀ-privative plus χρεῖος, "useful").

47. "The man who is punished is the man who will not try" (Barclay, II, p. 357).

48. D. C. Steinmetz speaks of God's judgment as shown in this parable as "mercifully severe," and explains, "The swift justice meted out to the lazy servant puts a merciful end to any notion that the disobedient and the dishonest will be able to blackmail their way into the Kingdom of heaven by manipulating the goodness of God or playing on divine pity. God's goodness is too clever to be taken in by such nursery tricks. Divine pity will forgive sins, but it will not condone them" (*Interpretation,* XXXIV [1980], pp. 175, 176).

7. *The Sheep and the Goats, 25:31-46*

31*"But when the Son of man comes in his glory, and all the angels with him, then he will sit on his glorious throne; 32and all the nations will be gathered before him, and he will separate them from one another, as the shepherd separates the sheep from the goats; 33and he will put the sheep on his right, and the goats on his left. 34Then the king will say to those on his right, 'Come, you who are my Father's blessed ones; inherit the kingdom prepared for you from the foundation of the world. 35For I was hungry and you gave me food, I was thirsty and you gave me drink, a stranger was I and you welcomed me, 36I was naked and you clothed me, I was sick and you visited me, in prison was I and you came to me.' 37Then the righteous will answer him, saying, 'Lord, when did we see you hungry and feed you, or thirsty and give you drink? 38And when did we see you a stranger and welcome you, or naked and clothe you? 39And when did we see you sick or in prison and come to you?' 40And the king will answer them, saying, 'Truly I tell you, insofar as you did it to one of the least of these my brothers, you did it to me.'*

41*"Then he will say to those on the left too, 'Go away from me, you cursed ones, into the eternal fire prepared for the devil and his angels. 42For I was hungry and you gave me nothing to eat, I was thirsty and you gave me nothing to drink, 43a stranger I was and you did not welcome me, naked and you did not clothe me, sick and in prison and you did not visit me.' 44Then they also will answer, 'Lord, when did we see you hungry or thirsty or a stranger or naked or sick or in prison, and did not do service to you?' 45Then he will answer them, saying, 'Truly I tell you, insofar as you did not do it to one of the least of these, you did not do it to me.' 46And these will go away to eternal punishment, but the righteous to life eternal."*

This passage is often described as a parable, but Jesus does not use this term for it. This, of course, is not decisive (he does not describe the story of the talents as a parable either, but most of us are happy to refer to it in this way). But this concluding part of the discourse reads like a description of what will happen on Judgment Day rather than like another parable.[49] It puts strong emphasis on the truth that ultimately every person on earth will be called upon to account for his or her use of the opportunities of service experienced through life.[50]

49. Cf. Hill, "Although the story is often referred to as a parable, it cannot really be classified as such. . . . The story seems to be a picture of the Last Judgment, an eschatological vision."

50. Perhaps we should notice, however, that Albright and Mann deny that the topic is Judgment Day. They assert, "If we make this a scene of final judgment, we miss the point entirely. . . . It is precisely in the consummation of his ministry, in the seal of death, and in resurrection-glory, that men will be separated by the response they make, or do not make, to that central, crucial event" (*AB*, pp. 308-9). But it is more than difficult to accept this. That Jesus' death and resurrection mark a separation between people is clear enough. That those events can be described in the language of this chapter is not.

Up to this point in the discourse Jesus has been teaching about the responsibility of disciples and, with the emphasis on being ready for the coming of the Lord, implying the thought of judgment.[51] But now there is explicit treatment of the judgment of the nations. Not only is the concept of judgment made explicit but the horizon is extended worldwide. Jesus makes it clear that on Judgment Day there are going to be some surprises. There will be people who will be rewarded for doing kind things to the Lord, only to find that what they did to all kinds of insignificant people were kind things done to the Lord who was in them. So also others will be punished for failing to make use of their opportunities to serve lowly folk, and for thereby failing to make use of opportunities to serve him.[52]

The passage deals only with works, which are seen as the test of whether one is saved or not; nothing is said here about grace or faith or Christ's atoning work. But we must bear in mind that this picture of Judgment Day does not give us a full account of everything that has to do with salvation; it does not include, for example, the fact that from the beginning of his Gospel Matthew has been writing about one who will "save his people from their sins" (1:21; cf. also 11:25-30; 20:28). This passage deals with the evidence on which people will be judged, not the cause of salvation or damnation.[53] That grace is not part of the present picture does not mean that it is any the less significant. We must bear in mind that it is common to the whole scriptural picture that we are saved by grace and judged by works (for this latter point cf. 16:27; Rom. 2:6; 2 Cor. 5:10, etc.). The works we do are the evidence either of the grace of God at work in us or of our rejection of that grace.[54]

It is sometimes suggested that this is so different from anything else in Jesus' teaching that it cannot really be his. To this Manson retorts, "Whether or not it belongs as a whole and in all its details to the authentic teaching of Jesus, it certainly contains features of such startling originality that it is difficult to credit them to anyone but the Master Himself" (*Sayings*, p. 249). Perhaps we should notice especially the place Jesus assigns here to the Son of man; in the characteristic Jewish teaching about the Last

51. This is the continuation of a topic that has featured throughout this Gospel. Thus Plummer draws attention to "the separations of the wheat from the chaff (iii.12), of the sincere from the hypocrites (vi.2, 5, 16), the wise builder from the foolish (vii.24-27), the wheat from the tares (xiii.30), the good from the bad fish (xiii.48, 49), the profitable from the unprofitable servants (14-30); and now we have the final separation of the sheep from the goats (31-46). The principle of separation throughout is the relation in which those who are judged stand to Jesus Himself" (p. 348).

52. This judgment scene "tells me that I am accountable. I am free to live my life just as I please, but at the end I shall have to give account to the one who gave me my life" (M. Green).

53. Nixon remarks of these kindly deeds, "presumably they are the outcome of a living faith and not the basis of acceptance."

54. Schweizer regards 20:1-6 and 25:31-46 as "the two limiting statements of the New Testament, which protect us against righteousness through works on the one hand and righteousness through intellectualized theology on the other" (p. 480).

Judgment the Judge is God, not the Messiah.[55] It is new and distinctive teaching that the Judge on the last great day will be none other than the Messiah, the Son of man himself.[56]

31. The previous section has ended with those who had used their talents well being praised and given the opportunity for wider work while the one who refused to use his talent was consigned to the outer darkness with its wailing and gnashing of teeth. Jesus goes on from there to give a fuller picture of our responsibility, a picture of Judgment Day. He looks to the time *when*[57] *the Son of man comes in his glory,* a thought that has been with us in one way or another throughout this whole discourse. Jesus' whole earthly life had been one of lowliness and service; now he looks forward to a coming that will be strikingly different. He does not define *in his glory,* but clearly he means that when he returns at the end of this age he will come in majesty and splendor. His servants must not be misled by his readiness to take the lowly place and think that that is his only place. His second coming will be strikingly different. He will come in power and majesty to inaugurate the final state of affairs. He will not be alone, but *all the angels* will be with him. His kingly state is brought out by the reference to his sitting on *his glorious throne.* GNB understands this to be his "royal throne," while NIV refers to "his throne in heavenly glory"; both are ways of bringing out the splendor of the Son of man. JB has "his throne of glory," which means that it is his glory that is itself his throne.

32-33. That *all the nations*[58] will come before him[59] makes it clear that Jesus is speaking of the final judgment of the whole race. In the end each of us must stand before Jesus to give account of what we have done. He does not go into detail, but says that he will "separate them from one another."[60] He takes an illustration from the pastoral processes and says the separation will be like that when *the shepherd separates the sheep from*

---

55. There is something of an exception in 1 Enoch, where "the Elect One" is on the throne of glory judging (1 Enoch 61:8) and "the Son of man" performs much the same function (1 Enoch 62:5). But such views are distinctly exceptional, and in any case "the Lord of Spirits" (God) keeps intervening. G. F. Moore has a useful survey of Jewish ideas on the subject (Moore, II, pp. 295-309).

56. There is a very useful discussion of the passage by G. E. Ladd in R. N. Longenecker and M. C. Tenney, eds., *New Dimensions in New Testament Study* (Grand Rapids, 1974), pp. 191-99.

57. ὅταν is indefinite, "whenever." Jesus is speaking of a time that is not known to his followers.

58. πάντα τὰ ἔθνη seems clearly to mean the whole race, but Green holds that "the reference must be to Gentiles as opposed to Jews." Such views seem to contradict the meaning of the Greek.

59. The verb is συνάγω; later in this discourse it is used in the sense "receive hospitably" (vv. 35, 38, 42), whereas here it has the more general sense of "gather together." Matthew uses the verb 24 times (Acts with 11 times is the next highest total in any New Testament book). Although the subject is the neuter plural ἔθνη, the verb is plural; in the New Testament this normally takes place with a personal subject.

60. αὐτούς is masculine; it is not a matter of separating the nations from each other, but people.

the goats (cf. Ezek. 34:17). These were the most common of the smaller domestic animals, and of the two *the sheep* were prized the more highly. The two groups of animals would graze together, but in due course *the shepherd* would separate them out (most commentators agree that the goats were more sensitive to cold than the sheep, so that at the end of the day the separation had to be made, the goats being put in a warmer place to keep both groups comfortable through the cooler hours of the night). Thus Jesus is referring to a well-known pastoral practice. His hearers would be well aware of separation into two sharply different groups. He gives no explanation as to why these names are chosen for the groups, but it emerges that those called *sheep* are those who receive a favorable judgment and those called *goats* are those regarded unfavorably. It accords with this that *the sheep* are on *his right* and *the goats*[61] on *his left*, for the right-hand side was generally seen as the favored side; for example, to be at the ruler's right hand was to be in the place of highest honor the ruler could give. The *left* was thought of as the side of ill omen (see the note on 20:21), so it is the appropriate place for the less favored *goats*.

34. Since "the Son of man" will have come in glory and it is he who will be sitting on "his glorious throne" (v. 31), it will be he who is now called *the king*. This appears to be the only passage in which Jesus refers to himself as *king*. At the time he was speaking he might well be "despised and rejected of men," but in due course he will be sovereign over all. It is he who will pronounce the verdicts over those in either group. First he speaks to those *on his right*. He calls on them to *"come,"* and he addresses them as *"my Father's blessed ones."*[62] *"Inherit the kingdom,"* he says to them, where his verb draws attention to a significant aspect of their salvation.[63] Something that is inherited comes to one as a gift, not as the result of one's own earnings, and that may be why the word is used of the life of the world to come. Dalman can say, " 'To possess one's self of the future age' is a very popular Jewish expression, whose use from the end of the first century onwards can be demonstrated" (Dalman, p. 125; he proceeds to cite examples). The use was congenial to Christians, all the more so since

61. In verse 32 Matthew has used ἔριφος for "goat," but here he has the diminutive ἐρίφιον. There does not, however, appear to be a difference in meaning (though Bengel remarks, "Although giants, they will be kidlings").

62. εὐλογημένοι is the perfect passive participle and points to a state of continuing blessedness. τοῦ πατρός signifies "of the Father"; this seems to mean that the blessed ones are those who belong to the Father, "the participle being in effect a substantive" (Bruce). McNeile stresses this: " 'Ye blessed ones' is absolute, followed by 'who belong to My Father' "; he complains that the translation " 'ye blessed of My Father' obscures this." But it is also possible to take this genitive to denote the agent (BDF, 183), "blessed by my Father," and many translations and commentators in modern times understand the construction in this way.

63. κληρονομέω (3 times in Matthew, 18 times in the New Testament) is the normal word for inheriting possessions (e.g., Gal. 4:30; MM gives examples of this use from the papyri). But it also comes to be used of secure possession in general and among the Jews especially of a place in the messianic kingdom.

their heavenly possessions came to them as the result of a death, the atoning death of their Savior.

What they are to inherit is *the kingdom*, which signifies a sure and accepted place in the kingdom of God rather than that they are to be kings themselves (they are "made" a kingdom, Rev. 1:6, where we find that they are also "priests"). And the kingdom they will inherit is no afterthought, but one *"prepared[64] for you from the foundation[65] of the world."* This strong expression brings out the truth that this has always been in the plan of God. Jesus is not speaking of some afterthought, but of what God had always planned to bring about, and that will come to its consummation at the end of this age. He leaves "the sheep" in no doubt but that they are entering into a glorious destiny. This should not be overlooked when we come to consider the words commending those who go into the kingdom. Some interpret the passage as though those on the King's right merited their salvation by their good works, but here we have the kingdom prepared for them by God before ever they were born. We should not miss the implication that they are God's elect.[66]

35. He goes on to speak of some of the things they have done in their lives on this earth. Four times this list is repeated in this and the following verses (it "is clearly meant to be remembered as a guide to practical discipleship," France). We should not understand this in the sense that these good works have earned them their salvation; grace is as important throughout this Gospel as anywhere in the New Testament. Jesus is not saying that these are people whose good lives have earned them salvation as their right. He is saying that God has blessed them and brought them into his kingdom, and he proceeds to cite evidence that shows that they do in fact belong in that kingdom.[67] Their lives are evidence that God has been at work in them. *"I was hungry,"* he says, *"and you gave me food,"* a kindly action for which the world has always provided scope. So with being *thirsty* and the need for something to *drink.* The *stranger* is always in a somewhat difficult position, and in first-century Palestine, with its lack of facilities like the hotels that in modern times we so easily take for granted, this was especially the case.

---

64. The perfect participle ἡτοιμασμένην points to something prepared long ago that continues in the state of preparedness.

65. καταβολή may be used of a literal foundation of a building. As the foundation is the beginning of an edifice, the term lends itself to the beginning of anything, here the beginning of the whole creation.

66. "Before the good deeds of these 'sheep' are mentioned (verses 35, 36) emphasis is first of all placed on the fact that the basis of their salvation, hence also of these good deeds, is their having been chosen from eternity" (Hendriksen, p. 888).

67. Cf. Hamann, "I can say: 'It has rained *for* the atmospheric conditions were right for rain', or 'It has rained *for* the streets are wet'. The 'for' in one case gives the reason for the rain, and in the other case, the evidence for it. It is in the second sense that the *for* of verse 35 must be understood. The Judge points to the works of verses 35 and 36 — he might have mentioned other works as well — as evidence for the position assigned to the sheep" (p. 256).

Where would a *stranger* lodge when he came to an unfamiliar place? The Old Testament knows of a man who prepared to spend the night in the town square (Judg. 19:15; cf. Job 31:32); thus a *stranger* could not rely on facilities for temporary lodgings. If he was not to spend the night in the open air, someone would have to take him into a private home. This was done among the Christians (Acts 10:23; Heb. 13:2, etc.), who seem to have taken the duty of hospitality very seriously. Bonnard takes the word to mean exiles from their own country and thus people without rights and without protection. These, too, would be people who were very needy and obvious candidates for the kind of help that the King now praises. So now Jesus commends those who *welcomed*[68] him when he was in need of a place. They offered him hospitality when he needed it.

36. There were other ways in which these "sheep" on the right had helped their Lord. When he was *naked*[69] they *clothed* him. Nakedness in first-century Palestine indicated poverty, the inability to buy clothes (not some form of exhibitionism, as we might suppose in modern times). When he was *sick* they *visited* him. Those without medical skills might not be able to do much for a sick person, but at least by paying him a visit they were able to convey something of their interest and their sympathy. And when he was *in prison* they *came* to him. First-century prisons were grim places; they were meant as places of punishment, and the idea of treating prisoners as normal human beings would have been regarded with astonishment. It was thus a kind act to visit people in prison. Any prisoner was a needy person; these people saw this and did what they could. Jesus does not say what these people did when they came to him in prison, but the fact that they came was in itself striking; most people avoided prisons like a plague.

37-39. But all this is news to the "sheep," and they say so. They are now called *the righteous;* what God has done in them has transformed them[70] into people who are acceptable in his sight and who accordingly do deeds like those Jesus has listed. They ask when they did all these things; they go through Jesus' list and inquire when they did each of them, listing them one by one. Their surprise (and that later of those who were rejected) is not unimportant. It shows clearly that their salvation did not depend on their good works; for in doing those works they must have

---

68. συνάγω means "to bring together," and indeed it has just been used in that sense (v. 32); it was also used of the master of the servants who "gathered" ("brought together") where he did not "scatter" (vv. 24 and 26). But the verb was also used of bringing people together as host and guest, the sense in which it is used here. *NIV* has "invited me in"; *JB*, "made me welcome"; and *REB*, "took me into your home."

69. γυμνός means "naked," but it is also used in the sense "poorly dressed" (BAGD; it also recognizes a use for "without an outer garment"). *NIV* reads "I needed clothes," while Cassirer has "poorly clad."

70. "The righteous are those who have God's verdict in their favor. . . . The entire doctrine of justification by faith through the atoning merits of Christ is contained in οἱ δίκαιοι" (Lenski, p. 993). So also Hill, "the deeds which achieve acceptance (according to Matthew) are not the 'works of the Law', done to win justification; they are the outcome of faith and love."

known that they were doing things that other people did not do. But clearly their kindness to the needy was not in order to gain a reward and merit salvation, but was part of the way they lived in response to what Christ had done in and for them.

40. Again there is the royal title *the king* in Jesus' reply. His answer begins with the solemn *"Truly I tell you"* (see on 5:18); what follows is an important and serious statement and is to be given good heed. *Insofar*[71] as they did the good deed *to one of the least*[72] *of these my brothers* (REB, "one of my brothers here, however insignificant"), they did it to him, he says. Throughout his earthly life Jesus had never sought to be in a lofty and comfortable position. He lived "despised and rejected of men," as the prophet put it (Isa. 53:3), and his followers must not forget it. It is natural to the human race to seek what is comfortable and to be ready to serve only the great. But Jesus' ministry was to the poor and the outcast (cf. 11:5; Luke 4:18), and now he is saying strongly that the ministry of his followers is likewise to be to the needy. Two ways of understanding *the least of these my brothers* have won wide acceptance. One is to bear in mind that elsewhere Jesus' *brothers* are his disciples (12:48-49; 28:10); Jesus may be asserting that the test will be the way people have reacted toward his lowly followers. They do not seem to be in the least important, but their relationship to Jesus is significant. This accords with such teachings as that on giving a cup of water to the "little ones" (10:42; cf. also 18:6, 10, 14). To receive a disciple is to receive Jesus (10:40). The other is to say that *brothers* includes anyone in need; in this case the test is the way they behaved toward lowly people in general. In either case the test is the way people behave toward needy people whom they do not suspect of having any great importance. To act in this way shows what they are. What they did to those needy ones they did to Jesus. The former is probably the way we should understand the words, but that does not give the follower of Jesus license to do good deeds to fellow Christians but none to outsiders. Such an attitude is foreign to the teachings of Jesus. Everyone in need is to be the object of Christian benevolence.[73]

41. *Then* introduces what is next in sequence. Following the commendation of those who have responded to Christ's love and who have lived in the way he taught them there is an address to *those on the left.*[74] Whereas he had invited those on the right with "Come," the king begins his address to these sinners with *"Go away from me,"* and he greets them as *"you cursed ones"*[75] (Chrysostom remarks, "no longer of the Father; for not He laid the

71. ἐφ' ὅσον, "to the degree that."
72. Robertson says, "There must be a special reason" for the construction used here (the adjective with an article of its own following the noun); "the adjective is added as a sort of climax with a separate article" (p. 776).
73. Calvin comments, "Only the faithful are expressly commended to our pity here," but he goes on to say, "there is a common tie that binds all the children of Adam" (III, p. 117).
74. καί adds this group to the preceding: he spoke to these people too.
75. καταράομαι occurs only here in Matthew (in the New Testament it is found in five

curse upon them, but their own works," p. 476). The nature of the curse is brought out with their destination; they are to go *into the eternal fire prepared for the devil and his angels*. Whereas the righteous go into the kingdom prepared for them before the foundation of the world (v. 34), those rejected go into a fire prepared not for them, but for the devil and his angels. The symbolism of fire is sometimes associated with God (Heb. 12:29) or his servants (Heb. 1:7), but more commonly it is the destination of the evil. Thus we read of a vision of a lake of fire and brimstone into which the devil was thrown, together with the beast and the false prophet (Rev. 20:10), and which is to be the place where everyone whose name is not written in the book of life will eventually come (Rev. 20:15). In line with this the *fire* of hell is often said to be the destination of those who do not accept the salvation of God (5:22; 18:8, 9). Here *his angels* is linked with *the devil* and refers to Satan's helpers. Scripture tells us little about them, but there is no reason to think of Satan as a solitary figure. There are, of course, evil angels as well as good ones. Angels are included among the beings that might try to separate us from God (Rom. 8:38); they could be objects of worship, which means that they are opposed to the one God (Col. 2:18). There are angels that sinned (2 Pet. 2:4; Jude 6), and angels are associated with the dragon who is equated with the devil (Rev. 12:7-9). Jesus is now saying that those on his left at the judgment will find their eternal habitation in the place where the evil are, Satan and all those associated with him.

42-43. Jesus goes through the list of the things that those on the right have done, but this time prefixed by the negative in each case. When he was hungry they did nothing for him, and so with all the items in his list. We get a picture of people who were wrapped up in their own concerns and indifferent to the plight of sufferers around them. Throughout this list *GNB* has "would not," but that is not what Jesus is saying; more than intention is involved. They "did not" do these things.

44. These people will be just as surprised as those in the other group. They are not conscious of ever refusing to give food to Jesus when he was hungry or water when he was thirsty, and so through the entire list.[76] Jesus does not go through the whole list again, but summarizes with a list that includes all the things on the previous lists, omitting only the verbs that indicate the way the need was or was not supplied. This time he sums it all up with *did not do service*.[77] These people were not conscious of having failed to render service of any kind to Jesus. They had not realized that their failure

---

books but once only in each of them). On the word here Moulton says, "the perfect κατηραμένοι has the full perfect force, 'having become the subjects of a curse'; and this makes the predicate translation (RVmg 'under a curse') decidedly more probable" (M, I, p. 221).

76. Glover remarks, "the wicked know not their evil. They remember some neglect and harshness, but it was only of a Lazarus at their gate. Had they seen the King there, their best had been His. They discover with horror that all their sins against their brethren are reckoned by the Master as against Himself."

77. The verb is διακονέω, which initially denoted the service of a table waiter but later came to be used of service of many kinds, especially service in a lowly place.

to serve the needy was important. We should notice that their condemnation (like that of the foolish girls in the preceding parable) is expressed not in terms of their having done some awful crime, but in terms of their failure to do what is right. Sins of omission can be very important.

45. The king's answer parallels that to the people on his right (v. 40). The words are almost identical, except that here they are preceded by the negative in the last two clauses (Jesus also omits the reference to his "brothers" in this place, saying no more than *the least of these*). Throughout this judgment scene it is made clear that the service of the lowly, the insignificant, the unimportant in this world's eyes is in the last resort the test of discipleship. To fail this test is sheer calamity.

46. Jesus rounds it all off by telling his hearers what the eternal destiny of each of the two groups will be. *"These,"* he says (i.e., those of whom he has just been speaking, the people who did not do service to the lowly), *"will go away to eternal punishment."*[78] Many in modern times strongly oppose the doctrine of eternal punishment (and none of us really likes it), but Hamann points out that "The net result of the elimination of the teaching of eternal punishment from the Bible would be the loss of the Gospel. Not too many people would be overly upset at the alternatives of eternal life and annihilation. . . . So to eliminate eternal punishment is to extract the teeth of the Law and its presentation of a holy God. The blessing of the Gospel can be retained only if the Law is seen as the completely serious will of the holy God, to whom sin is grievous rebellion, requiring his punishment if it is not forgiven" (pp. 256-57). In contrast, the destination of *the righteous* (the word used in v. 37) is to be *life eternal.*[79] The same adjective is applied to both the punishment and the reward. Jesus is not speaking of some small experience that would be but for a moment, but of that which has no end. He leaves his hearers in no doubt as to the solemnity of what he is saying. Eternal issues are involved, and this is so for both those on his right hand and on his left.

It is worth reflecting that this is Jesus' last teaching to his disciples in this Gospel; Matthew proceeds from this to the story of the passion. He leaves with his followers the teaching that in daily life the way they treat the lowly, the needy, and the unimportant is of the greatest significance. Not for them is it to flatter the great and to seek to ingratiate themselves with the wealthy and the powerful in this world. They will serve their Master when they serve "the least of these."

---

78. κόλασις is found again the New Testament only in 1 John 4:18. According to AS, Aristotle differentiates the word from τιμωρία "as that which, being disciplinary, has reference to the sufferer," while τιμωρία, "being penal, has reference to the satisfaction of him who inflicts." He adds that in late Greek the distinction is not always observed. It would be pressing the word unduly to make a distinction here. It is punishment simply as the consequence of sin that is in mind.

79. The adjective is αἰώνιος, "pertaining to an age"; in a context like this the age in question is the age to come, the age that is without end.

Matthew 26

VII. THE PASSION STORY, 26:1–27:66

The climax of each of the four Gospels comes with the accounts of the crucifixion and resurrection of Jesus. Each Gospel has its own way of presenting the facts, and we need all the accounts. The Synoptic Gospels for the most part tell us about the Jewish role in the death of Jesus, whereas John gives a fuller picture of the Roman involvement. For the most part Matthew's account is similar to what we find in Mark, though, of course, he puts his own stamp on what he has written and he includes some details that the others do not have — for example, the words about the more than twelve legions of angels that Jesus could have called to support him and the account of the death of Judas. A significant feature of his passion narrative is that, while it is much the same as that in Mark, he uses direct rather than indirect speech.[1] On this Stendahl comments, "it is not a merely stylistic feature. Jesus is in command: he gives the orders; here is the Messiah who knows what is going to happen and 'speaks it into effect'." For Matthew it is important that Jesus is in control throughout those events that culminated in his death and led on to his resurrection. Sometimes Matthew expresses the thought by emphasizing what God is doing, but this is essentially the same thought. He starts this early with Jesus' prophecy that the Son of man was to be "handed over to be crucified" (v. 2), where the implication is that God is at work. So also there is the reference to "my time" (v. 18). We see Jesus in charge also in the fulfilment of his prophecy that he would be deserted (v. 31) and that Peter would deny him (v. 34), in the tearing of the temple veil (27:51), in the earthquake and the raising of the saints (27:52-53), and in the resurrection (ch. 28). Matthew is sure that the hand of God is to be seen in all of this. He is not narrating simply what some evil people did to a good and compassionate man.[2]

---

1. See N. A. Dahl, *NTS*, II (1955-56), p. 30.
2. See further my *New Testament Theology*, pp. 132-35. G. Barth sees Matthew's passion narrative in this way: "For Matthew the Passion of Jesus is not merely the gateway to glory, but the Passion and resurrection are two sides of one event in which Jesus takes the place of sinners and 'fulfils all righteousness', brings God's judgment to victory" (*TIM*, p. 147). This scarcely finds a place in J. L. Houlden's study of the passion and resurrection narratives

A. PRELIMINARIES, 26:1-5

> *¹And it came to pass when Jesus had finished all these sayings, he said to his disciples, ²"You know that after two days the Passover is coming, and the Son of man will be handed over to be crucified."*
>
> *³Then the high priests and the elders of the people were gathered in the palace of the high priest who was called Caiaphas, ⁴and they consulted so that they might arrest Jesus craftily and put him to death. ⁵But they said, "Not during the feast, lest there be a tumult among the people."*

1. Matthew moves from the lengthy discourse he has just recounted to the passion narrative with a short transitional section. For his unusual *and it came to pass* see the note on 7:28. It is Matthew's way of marking the passing from a major discourse to the narrative that follows. Matthew notes the completion of *all these sayings*, which will refer to chapters 23–24; there is possibly also a reference to chapter 22, but there is a change of scene after that. Whichever way we take it, Matthew marks the end not only of one discourse but of Jesus' teaching ministry. The word *all* is probably significant; it does not occur in any of the previous occurrences of the formula at the close of a discourse. But this is not only the close of one discourse; it is the close of Jesus' recorded teaching. No more discourses are to be recorded, and Matthew moves to the story of Jesus' death. This little section is peculiar to Matthew; the other Synoptists go straight to the Passover.

2. We should notice that from the beginning Matthew uses direct speech as he tells us that Jesus locates what is happening with reference to *the Passover,*[3] which was *two days* away. The day began at sunset and the Passover meal was to be eaten on the following Friday night, so, depending on the time of day, Jesus would have been speaking on the Tuesday or Wednesday of that week, as we count time. But he says nothing at this point about the feast itself; he simply uses it as a date as he moves on to speak of his approaching death. The Passover was the great feast that commemorated the deliverance of the Israelites from Egypt. A central feature of the observance was the offering of a lamb or kid in sacrifice, and, after the ritual disposition of parts of the animal, the eating of the carcass in companies of ten or more in private homes. From early days the feast was joined with the Feast of Unleavened Bread; the combined observance lasted a week. All this made Passover an especially suitable time for Jesus to lay down his life for his people. The thought of a sacrifice leading to the freedom of the people of God from their slavery in Egypt

---

in Matthew and Mark (*Backward into Light* [London, 1987]). He says, "I have found myself (there is no denying) awarding prizes to Mark and presenting Matthew as, however understandably, the villain of the piece, inferior and even reprehensible at almost every turn" (p. 66). It is curious that a scholar who can find such riches in Mark should fail to appreciate the greatness of what Matthew has done.

3. τὸ πάσχα. Matthew uses the term 4 times, all in this chapter (vv. 17, 18, and 19).

was in the air at the time when the greater sacrifice that would set people free everywhere was to be offered. Jesus uses his favorite title for himself, *the Son of man*, and says that he will be *handed over*[4] (for this verb see on 4:12) *to be crucified.* The verb indicates two things: the initiative will be taken by the Jews, who will do the handing over, but the death sentence will be carried out by the Romans, who in any case were the only people who could perform a crucifixion in Judea at that time. The expression indicates that Jesus was well aware of the schemes of his enemies and of the inevitable outcome. This prediction of the passion is found only in Matthew. It is not without its interest that Jesus accurately fixes the time of his death as after two days, while his enemies say that it will be after the feast, that is, more than a week away (v. 5).

3. For Matthew's frequent use of *Then* see on 2:7; here it does not indicate close sequence. Rather, it locates the plotting of the high-priestly party in that general period. Matthew speaks of *the high priests,* a term that signifies a number of high ecclesiastical officials and members of high-priestly families (see on 2:4). With them are joined *the elders of the people,* the important lay representatives who formed an important part of the Sanhedrin. Though Matthew does not use the term, it would appear that he has in mind the Sanhedrin, though probably not a formal session. It reads as though the more influential members, clerical and lay, met unofficially to decide what should be done about Jesus. It is noteworthy that in this meeting of Jesus' adversaries there is no mention of the Pharisees, who had been his principal opponents throughout his ministry (they are mentioned again in this Gospel only in 27:62). This accords with the fact that the Pharisees were deeply religious people, whereas in the passion narrative Jesus is most strongly opposed by the aristocratic Jewish establishment, people who were interested in political realities and in fitting in with the Roman overlords. The scribes do not feature largely in these chapters either (only in v. 57; 27:41); there is very little discussion of Scripture and the like, in which they were experts. This group met in the high priest's *palace.*[5] Matthew goes on to tell his readers that this man's name was *Caiaphas* (who was high priest from A.D. 18 to 36).[6] He has used the

---

4. παραδίδοται is a present tense used with a future meaning (cf. Moule, *IBNTG,* p. 7; Moule cites Moulton, who notes that "such Futural Presents differ from the Future tense 'mainly in the tone of assurance which is imparted' ").

5. The word is αὐλή, which properly denotes a courtyard but which on occasion means the house to which the courtyard is appended. MM finds nothing in the *Koine* to indicate that the word can mean a house, but here it must denote the residence; such a meeting would not take place in an open courtyard. We could translate "house" (so *REB*), but the high priest would not have lived in the kind of house ordinary people used, so *palace* is surely the sense of it.

6. Barclay points out that in the period 37 B.C.–A.D. 67 there were 28 high priests, so that Caiaphas's tenure "was an extraordinarily long time for a High Priest to last, and Caiaphas must have brought the technique of co-operating with the Romans to a fine art." But that meant that he must be careful. "Let there be any rioting and very certainly Caiaphas would lose his position" (II, p. 362).

expression "high priests" a number of times, but always until now in the plural. This is his first mention of the official high priest, and Matthew tells us who he was. He is the only Evangelist to tell us that the meeting was held in the high priest's home.

4. They *consulted*,[7] but their consultation had a base aim (which may justify *NIV*'s "plotted"). They consulted *so that they might arrest Jesus*, where the construction indicates purpose[8] (*GNB*, "made plans"). Arresting Jesus was not going to be straightforward; they might have been able to count on people like the merchants whose trade in the temple courts had suffered at the hands of Jesus, and there were people in the Jerusalem mob who could be manipulated. But there were also many pilgrims from Galilee in the city for the feast, and they might not be pleased to find the teacher from Nazareth under arrest. So they reasoned that they must approach the task carefully, or, as Matthew puts it, *craftily*.[9] They were not concerned only to arrest Jesus and thus remove him from moving among the people; Matthew tells us plainly that they wanted to *put him to death*. They wanted to be rid of him once and for all.

5. But this was not a straightforward affair. The Passover was almost on them and Jerusalem would be full of pilgrims, many of whom might be reckoned as supporters of Jesus. So they planned not to take action *during the feast*.[10] The Passover commemorated the deliverance of the people from Egypt back in the days of Moses. The people made preparation for it by clearing all leaven out of the houses; then on the fourteenth day of the month Abib they solemnly slew a lamb or a kid for sacrifice in the temple and threw the blood on the altar. They took the carcass home and roasted it; it formed the main feature of a meal in the evening, which was taken reclining, a symbol of the rest God gave his people. For seven days they ate unleavened bread. All this meant that there was high excitement among the people; this was one of the year's highlights. Devout people would not want to be distracted from their religious observances by a public arrest with all its consequences, and Jesus' supporters from Galilee might be expected to be outraged. To send a posse to arrest Jesus openly was out of the question. The Sanhedrin agreed that there must not be *a tumult among the people*.

---

7. συμβουλεύω means "to advise, counsel," and in the middle "to take counsel." This is what the group did. Moulton takes the middle as signifying "they counselled one another" (M, I, p. 157). *NIV* says that they "plotted," and *JB* that they "made plans."

8. ἵνα with the subjunctive.

9. δόλῳ; the word could mean "a bait" or "a snare," but in the New Testament it is used more in the sense of "deceit" or "cunning." BAGD understands the meaning here as "*by cunning or stealth.*"

10. J. Jeremias argues that the expression should be translated, "festal assembly, festal crowd" (*The Eucharistic Words of Jesus* [Oxford, 1955], p. 48). He regards the expression as indicating that the arrest should be made quietly, away from the festal crowds.

B. Jesus and His Followers, 26:6-30

Having made it clear that Jesus' enemies were plotting his death, Matthew gives us a little glimpse of the Master's last activities among his followers. There is the anointing at Bethany, expressing love and devotion right at the time when the religious leaders of the people were giving vent to hatred and planning murder; the contrast is striking. Matthew goes on to Judas's betrayal of his Lord and to the last meal that Jesus would have with his disciples before his death.

1. The Anointing at Bethany, 26:6-13

6When Jesus was in Bethany, in the house of Simon the leper, 7there came to him a woman who had an alabaster flask of very costly perfume and poured it over his head as he reclined at table. 8And when the disciples saw it, they were indignant and said, "Why this waste? 9For this could have been sold for a high price and given to poor people." 10But, aware of this, Jesus said to them, "Why are you bothering the woman? For she has done a beautiful thing for me. 11For you have the poor with you always, but you do not have me always. 12For when this woman poured this perfume on my body, she did it to prepare me for burial. 13Truly I tell you, wherever this gospel is preached in all the world, what this woman has done will also be told as a memorial for her."

There is a story of the anointing of Jesus by a woman in each of the four Gospels, and many modern scholars believe that they all refer to the same anointing. But Luke's story comes earlier in the ministry and is performed by a sinful woman; there are too many differences to regard this story as referring to the same event as the one the others describe. The other three accounts all seem to refer to the same anointing, one carried out by Mary of Bethany in the period shortly before Jesus was arrested. Matthew's is the shortest of the three accounts (he has 109 words, Mark 124 words, and John 142 words), and his account is very similar to that of Mark, while John has details that the others do not mention.

6. Matthew locates the incident *in Bethany* but says nothing of precisely when it took place or why Jesus was there. John dates his incident of anointing six days before the Passover and says that the triumphal entry took place the next day (John 12:1, 12); neither Matthew nor Mark mentions when the incident took place. John tells us that the home of Martha and Mary was in Bethany (John 11:1); presumably it was the house where they lived that was called *the house of Simon the leper* (for leprosy see the note on 8:2). Since people were very fearful of leprosy and had no way of curing it, quarantine was the normal requirement: those with this disease must stay away from other people. Therefore *Simon* could not have had the disease at this time; he may have been cured of it (as we saw in the

646

earlier note, some of the diseases included under the general name "leprosy" were curable; or Jesus may have healed him). Even after his cure he would have still been known as *the leper*. Alternatively he may have been dead at this time, but the house was still known by his name. None of the Evangelists tells us why Jesus was in this home, only that he was there. In John's account we find that Lazarus and his two sisters were there, so it is possible that *Simon* was their father. Jesus was there for a meal, for Matthew speaks of him as reclining at table (v. 7). John tells us that Martha was serving at the meal and that Lazarus was there (John 12:2).

7. Matthew now says that *a woman* (whom he does not name but who John tells us was Mary, John 12:3) *came* to Jesus. She had *an alabaster flask*[11] *of very costly perfume*[12] that she proceeded to pour over his head as he *reclined at table*. Unguents were used among the Jews much more freely than in modern Western societies (cf. Ps. 23:5). For example, it would be expected that when a guest came for a meal, oil would be provided to be put on his head (Luke 7:46). The use of this costly unguent rather than the cheap oil that would be more commonly used is a mark of devotion. Mary did not regard Jesus as a casual, run-of-the-mill guest but as a very special person; for him a very costly offering was just right.[13] Kings were anointed (e.g., 2 Kings 9:6), and it may be that this was in the woman's mind. We should also remember that "Messiah" means "anointed one," and that she may have been giving symbolic expression to her conviction that Jesus was indeed the Messiah.

8. The significance of the beautiful action was lost on the hardheaded disciples.[14] They may not have known precisely what the perfume was, but the costly container indicated something of value and the fragrance would have reinforced this. They might have appreciated the depth

---

11. The word is ἀλάβαστρον, meaning "alabaster" and then what is made of alabaster, "an *alabaster flask* for ointment, a vessel w. a rather long neck which was broken off when the contents were used; a container for spikenard ointment" (BAGD). The expensive container would be used only for expensive perfume. Matthew does not say how the perfume was poured out, but Mark tells us that the woman "broke the alabaster flask"; that is, she broke the long neck that was normally a feature of such a flask and that had to be broken to get the unguent out. *NEB* has "a small bottle," which *REB* changes to "a bottle"; both miss the fact that Matthew is speaking of an expensive container.

12. μύρον means "sweet oil, unguent, perfume" (LSJ). It has often been translated "ointment," but this is misleading; we use "ointment" for a solid that is smeared on, whereas μύρον denotes a liquid, something that can be poured. It is clear that the perfume used on this occasion was very valuable.

13. John tells us that the perfume was "pistic nard." The meaning of the adjective is not known for certain, but clearly the expression indicates that this was not a usual perfume to be used for ordinary dinners. It was something special.

14. The failure of the disciples is a continuing feature of the passion narrative. Here they lack understanding of the beautiful action of anointing; a little later we will read of Judas's treachery (vv. 14-16), of the "Is it I?" questions (vv. 22 and 25), of Peter's boastful self-confidence (v. 33), a confidence shared by them all (v. 35), of the failure to watch in Gethsemane (vv. 40-45), of the flight of the disciples (v. 56), and of Peter's denials (vv. 69-75). It is a sad and sorry story.

of devotion that would make such a gift to their Master, but in fact they were concerned more with what the gift was worth and what they could have done with the money it represented. Mark says that "some" were indignant, Matthew refers to "the disciples" as having this emotion,[15] and John speaks of Judas Iscariot as leading the complaint and goes on to point out that he was the man who kept the money box and would have the disposal of what was put in it; John says that he was dishonest and pictures Judas as looking for some personal profit (John 12:4-6). Matthew tells us that the disciples proceeded to explain their sense of outrage: *"Why this waste?"* they asked. The perfume was very costly; it represented a considerable expenditure, and pouring it out was from their point of view nothing but a *waste*. What use was it to anybody when it was recklessly poured out like this?

9. They explain. *"This"* (Mark and John both have "this perfume," but Matthew contents himself with the pronoun) *"could*[16] *have been sold for a high price."*[17] The disciples mostly came from humble homes and their life-styles since they became associated with Jesus were of the simplest, as, of course, was that of the Master himself who set the example. They were unaccustomed to extravagance and must have been easily shocked by it. For them the beauty of the woman's action and the wealth of devotion to which it gave expression were of no consequence. They looked at the material profit that might have been made, and for poor men that was the important thing. And, of course, they could give their verdict a pious twist. If the perfume had been left in their hands, they could have sold it rather than have the woman throw it away, and the money from its sale would have made a generous gift *to poor people*.

10. It is not made clear where and to whom the disciples made their comment, but it appears as if it was meant to be kept among themselves. But Jesus was *aware* of the way they were reasoning, and he rebuked them. *"Why are you bothering*[18] *the woman?"* he said. He was not indifferent to the plight of the poor; after all, was he not poor himself? But he appreciated the love and devotion that found expression in this very unusual and

---

15. ἀγανακτέω signifies "to be indignant, vexed" (AS). Bruce comments, "Probably all the disciples disapproved more or less. It was a *woman's* act, and they were *men*. She was a poet and they were somewhat prosaic."

16. Robertson points out that verbs of obligation and the like are used in the imperfect when the obligation is not met. "The Greeks (and the Latins) start from the past and state the real possibility or obligation, and the reader, by comparing that with facts, notes that the obligation was not met. The English and the Germans start from the present and find trouble with this past statement of a present duty (an unfulfilled duty)" (p. 886).

17. From John 12:5 we learn that Judas evaluated the perfume at 300 denarii. Since a denarius was the daily wage of a laborer, this represented the best part of a year's wages. It was a costly gift.

18. It is not easy to arrive at a precise English equivalent. κόπος can mean "a beating" or, more generally, "trouble," while παρέχω means "supply, provide." Jesus is saying something like "Why are you providing troubles for the lady?"

unconventional way. So he goes on to explain to the malcontents, *"she has done a beautiful[19] thing for me."*

11. Jesus draws a deduction from what the woman had done.[20] He points out that *the poor* are *with you always* (cf. Deut. 15:11). He is not saying that we should constantly make this an excuse for doing nothing about poverty. After all, in his last recorded piece of teaching he has pointed to the importance of helping the needy (25:31-46). He is saying that it is possible to do good to them at any time (Mark records Jesus as saying this, but Matthew's shorter version omits the words). On occasion other challenges may reach his followers, and while they do not justify a continuing neglect of the poor, they can justify doing something else before continuing to help those in want. That is the case in the present situation.

12. Now comes a most unexpected explanation. Notice again that Jesus uses *For;* what the woman did arose out of an unusual perception of the situation he was in, and that perception must be given its due outlet. In pouring *this perfume on my body,* he says, *"she did it to prepare me for burial."*[21] Carson draws attention to Daube's point that this anointing "'prepares' him for his burial after dying the death of a criminal, for only in that circumstance would the customary anointing of the body be omitted." Jesus was aware of the fact that in a few days he would be hanging on a cross, though the disciples had no idea that such a shocking happening lay in the immediate future. Mary may have had such insight. She could not have been unaware that Jesus was in great danger; the highest in the nation were vigorously opposing him, and it was far from impossible that they would put him to death. Was this the last time he would be with her? It is not impossible that she had a premonition that never again would she have the opportunity of performing such an action, in which case she was doing it as her part in honoring Jesus as he went to death.[22] It is also possible, of course, that she had no such premonition

19. χαλός means "good" as well as "beautiful"; therefore some interpreters prefer that translation here. But it appears that Jesus is not speaking of the action as morally upright but rather as a beautiful expression of devotion.

20. Many modern translations omit *for* here and at the beginning of verse 12, and in so doing obscure some of the reasoned argument Jesus is making. There is a reason why he did not conclude that there was an urgent use of the price of the perfume for the poor, and there is a reason why the woman poured the perfume on Jesus.

21. ἐνταφιάζω signifies "prepare for burial" or "bury." It is used of burying in John 19:40, but here it must mean "prepare for burial" (as it does in Gen. 50:2, where it refers to Jacob's being prepared for burial in Egypt, though he was buried in Canaan). It was customary for unguents and spices to be wrapped around a corpse when it was buried, and Jesus is saying that Mary has done her part while he was still alive.

22. Cf. Lightfoot, "She, and she first, believes that Christ should die; and, under that notion, she pours the ointment upon his head" (p. 341). Hendriksen also thinks that this is possible: "The view, accordingly, that Mary's *conscious* purpose was to prepare Jesus for burial must not be ruled out" (p. 901). Lenski says, "only on the supposition that Mary knew that she was now anointing the body of Jesus for its burial is the tremendous praise accorded her act by Jesus himself justified" (p. 1010).

and that Jesus was interpreting her action in the light of his own knowledge of what would happen.[23]

13. For *"Truly I tell you"* see the note on 5:18; it is an expression used often in this Gospel for emphasis. The words that follow are important and are to be given good heed. *"Wherever this gospel is preached in all the world"* is an interesting statement in this context. Jesus was about to go to his death, and he knew it. But he spoke of *this gospel* as something that would be proclaimed very widely, indeed throughout the world, and thus much more widely than his hearers could possibly have realized at the time the words were spoken. *Gospel* is a significant word here. Jesus knew that his death would not mean the end of the movement he had started, but in a very meaningful sense its beginning. The "good news" that he had come to bring involved his death, and the dark days that lay immediately ahead for the disciples did not alter that basic fact. So Jesus now looks through the atoning work he would accomplish on the cross to the proclamation that would follow and that would go right through the world.

And when that is done, he said, *"what this woman has done will also be told as a memorial for her."* The woman's action had made no sense to the disciples, but it would be another story for the movement that Jesus had begun. Mary would be remembered far and wide for this action specifically. It will be her *memorial.*[24] Curiously both Matthew and Mark have this saying but do not name the woman, whereas John names her but does not have this saying.

2. Betrayal, 26:14-16

> [14]Then one of the Twelve called Judas Iscariot went to the high priests [15]and said, "What will you give me, and I will betray him to you?" And they set for him thirty silver pieces. [16]And from that time he looked for an opportunity of betraying him.

14. All four Gospels tell us that it was *Judas Iscariot*[25] who betrayed Jesus into the hands of his enemies. We should understand that with Jerusalem thronged with pilgrims, including many who had come up from Galilee for the Passover, an open arrest was fraught with danger. Who could tell what the public reaction might be? The high-priestly party did

23. Johnson thinks that "many of the common people wished Jesus to take over political control of the nation" and that in this incident "The woman may even have hoped to force Jesus' hand"; in his opinion the anointing "suggests the hope of a revolt or *coup d'état*." But this seems farfetched.

24. μνημόσυνον is connected with the idea of memory; it often signifies a monument by which some great one of the past is remembered. Mary will be remembered not by some stone obelisk, but by this beautiful and loving action.

25. This is Matthew's first mention of this disciple since he was mentioned in the list of the Twelve. For the meaning of Ἰσκαριώτης see the note on 10:4.

not want to provoke a riot, but they did very much want to remove Jesus from the scene. At this point all three Synoptists speak of Judas as *one of the Twelve;* it is as though this heightened the evil nature of his act. It was not some casual contact, a person from the crowd, but one of the little group of Jesus' closest followers who was involved. Both Luke and John link Satan with the act of Judas; they see the forces of evil as at work in the betrayal. Matthew in common with the other Evangelists makes it clear that the initiative came from Judas; it was not that the enemies of Jesus made inquiries among the disciples, looking for a weak one who might be their tool. Rather, Judas sought them out.

No indication is given in any of the Gospels as to why Judas took this action, and there have been suggestions that absolve him of treachery. Thus some have conjectured that, knowing the powers Jesus possessed and impatient at the delay in establishing the kingdom, he thought that he would put his Master in a position where he would have to put forward his unusual powers and in that way destroy the opposition and set up the kingdom for which so many patriotic Jews were looking. Another view is that Judas was really one of the violent men who were looking for ways of getting rid of the Romans at whatever cost. On this view he had followed Jesus because he thought that the man from Nazareth would in due course lead a successful rebellion against Rome. When he found that Jesus was a man of peace, he was disillusioned and took the action that would get rid of him. A third view regards him as disillusioned; he had come to the conclusion that Jesus was bound to fail and he betrayed him to save himself. A fourth view sees him as coming to realize that Jesus had chosen the path of suffering rather than militant leadership against the Romans and as rejecting such an approach. But such views are mere speculation. There is no indication in any of our sources of any motive other than that of money.[26] That seems clear enough in Matthew; while Mark and Luke speak of money only after Judas has made it clear that he wants to hand Jesus over to his enemies, it is mentioned immediately after that; and there is no real doubt in any of our sources that money mattered to Judas. The sequence of stories may be significant.[27] Matthew has just told the story of the pouring out of the costly perfume, and John tells us in connection with this that Judas was the treasurer of the little band and that he had wanted to get control of the money that might have been theirs had the perfume been sold (John 12:4-6). Disappointed of gain from one source, he now sought it from another. Matthew does not specify the person(s) to whom Judas went, speaking only of *the high priests;* the precise

26. Carr thinks that "His worldly hopes fell altogether at the thought of 'burial.' . . . The motive that impelled Judas was probably not so much avarice as disappointed worldly ambition."

27. " 'Then' (τότε) is meant to imply that the anointing led directly to the betrayal" (Plummer, p. 356).

manner of the approach was not important, but it is plain that Judas went to the enemies of Jesus.

15. Matthew alone has the question, *"What will you give me, and I[28] will betray him to you?"* He is clear that Judas was looking for money in return for handing Jesus over[29] to his enemies. This initial request for money we find in Matthew only, as also the fact that the amount the high priests paid Judas was *thirty silver pieces.* Mark and Luke both say that when the high priests heard that Judas was willing to betray Jesus, they were glad and promised him money. But whoever raised the question of payment first, it is clear that the betrayal and its price were agreed upon. What is a trifle more difficult is when the money was paid. Matthew appears to say that it was paid then and there, Mark and Luke only that the amount was agreed. It was certainly paid early, for Judas had it shortly after the arrest, when he hurled it into the holy place (27:3-5). But since neither Mark nor Luke indicates when the money was paid, there is no real reason for doubting Matthew. At the same time we should notice that his verb does not necessarily mean that the money was paid then and there; it could mean that they set the price, or that the amount was agreed on (though even if we accept the meaning "set," we could understand this to mean that they set the money down before Judas).[30]

16. That was the critical moment. Now Judas was committed to betrayal; all that remained was to find the best time for it. *From that time* indicates that Judas started immediately. *He looked* is in the imperfect tense (in all three Synoptists) and indicates a continuous search: Judas kept looking. What he sought was *an opportunity,* a convenient time[31] for his task. The money was being paid for the right choice of time and place.

28. The καί in κἀγώ is an example of " 'Consecutive' καί" with the meaning "and so, so" (BDF, 442[2]). Judas uses the emphatic pronoun for "I," as if to say, "I, one of his disciples" (and thus well able to betray him).

29. For the verb παραδίδωμι see on 4:12; it can denote a handing over in any one of a variety of ways. Judas is speaking of passing information on to the high-priestly party that would enable them to arrest Jesus in some place of solitude, away from the crowds.

30. The verb is ἵστημι, the meaning of which is "put, place, set" (BAGD). Most modern translations understand this statement to mean that they put the money down then and there and thus paid Judas: "they counted out for him thirty silver coins" *(NIV);* "they weighed him out thirty silver pieces" *(REB).* Cassirer, however, renders, "They fixed the price they would pay him." Whichever way we take it, Matthew seems to be saying that it represented the fulfilment of prophecy (see Zech. 11:12). We should not miss the further point that it was also the price of a slave, the price to be paid when one's ox gored a slave (Exod. 21:32). Argyle points out that the expression is ambiguous so that either meaning is possible; perhaps we should accept both.

31. εὐκαιρία (εὐ + καιρός) means a "good" or "suitable" time. The wrong time could have provoked a riot with incalculable consequences. The chief priests want it all to be done quietly; a suitable time meant a time when Jesus would be away from his supporting crowds (Luke says this expressly, Luke 22:6).

3. The Last Supper, 26:17-30

17Now on the first day of unleavened bread the disciples came to Jesus, saying, "Where do you want us to prepare for you to eat the Passover?" 18And he said, "Go into the city to so-and-so and say to him, 'The teacher says: My time is near; at your house I am keeping the Passover with my disciples.'" 19And the disciples did as Jesus told them, and they prepared the Passover.

20Now when evening came, he reclined with the Twelve. 21And as they were eating, he said, "Truly I tell you, that one of you will betray me." 22And they were very sad and began to say to him, each one, "Is it I, Lord?" 23But he answered, saying, "He who dipped his hand in the dish with me will betray me. 24The Son of man goes just as it stands written about him, but woe to that man through whom the Son of man is betrayed; it would have been better for him if that man had not been born. 25Judas, who was betraying him, said, "Is it I, Rabbi?" He says to him, "You said it."

26And as they were eating, Jesus took bread; and when he had given thanks, he broke it, gave it to his disciples, and said, "Take, eat; this is my body." 27And he took a cup, and when he had given thanks, he gave it to them, saying, "Drink from it, all of you. 28For this is my blood of the covenant, which is poured out for many for the forgiveness of sins. 29But I say to you, I will certainly not drink from now on of this fruit of the vine until that day when I drink it with you new in the kingdom of my Father." 30And when they had sung a hymn, they went out to the Mount of Olives.

Of great importance for the church through the centuries has been the service of Holy Communion. It is observed by practically all Christians, and always has been. The ritual and ceremonial may vary, but all Christians find this service especially solemn and especially significant. In this section of his Gospel Matthew tells us how the service was begun. He locates it in the Passover celebration and describes a very simple rite — the breaking and sharing of bread and the sharing of wine from a single wine cup.

17. *The first day of unleavened bread*[32] presents us with a problem in that all three Synoptists clearly regard this meal as the Passover (vv. 2, 18, 19; Mark 14:1, 12, 14; Luke 22:1, 7, 8, 11, 13, 15; Mark and Luke underline this by saying that it was the day on which the Passover was sacrificed), but in John the Last Supper was held before the Passover (John 13:1, 29; 18:28). A number of positions have been advocated to solve this problem.

1. The two accounts are in conflict, and the Synoptists are to be preferred (so Fenton).

2. The two accounts are in conflict, and John is to be preferred (so McNeile).

3. The Last Supper was a Passover meal as in the Synoptists, and John's account can be reconciled with this (so Carson, France).

4. The Passover was observed as in John, and the Synoptists can be reconciled with this (e.g., Carr).

5. There were different calendars in use; John is giving the story in accordance with the official calendar (the one used in the temple) and the Synoptists in accordance with the calendar Jesus and the disciples were using (Nixon favors this position).

It seems to me that the best solution is the last mentioned. Perhaps I may refer to the discussion of the problems in my *The Gospel according to John* (Grand Rapids, 1971, pp. 774-86). There I have cited evidence to show that there is good reason for thinking that different calendars were in use at that time (we know that the men of Qumran used a different calendar from that used by the temple authorities in Jerusalem), and that we pay most respect to the evidence if we hold that Jesus and his disciples were following a calendar that differed from that in use by the temple authorities and that meant that the little band observed the Passover a day earlier than those who ran the temple.[33] That will explain the absence of all mention of the lamb or kid (either could be used, *Pes.* 8:2) from the accounts, though it was the central feature of the normal observance.

The disciples take the initiative by asking Jesus where he wants them to prepare[34] for the feast. They imply that Jesus had this in mind and that he knew where they would be enjoying the meal that evening. There would be preparations like arranging for the food to be used at the feast, arranging the tables for the meal, and so on.[35] Presumably nothing had been said about the location until now as part of the way Jesus and his little group kept themselves out of the way of the enemies who were trying to arrest him and put him to death. But action had to be taken now.

18. Jesus directed them to go into Jerusalem to a certain man whose name is not given;[36] Mark and Luke both tell us that the man would be carrying a water pot (this was distinctive, for a man would normally carry a water skin; women used water pots). Matthew does not say whom he sent, but Mark says that he sent two of the band, and Luke that they were Peter and John. Jesus had evidently made the arrangement and kept it secret so that, for example, Judas would not be able to betray him prematurely. He would go to his death, but it would be in his chosen time, not when Judas chose to hand him over to his enemies. They were to follow

32. Matthew has the plural τῶν ἀζύμων, but this is another example of the practice of using the plural to denote a feast. The Passover victim was killed on the afternoon of 14th Nisan (Exod. 12:6) and eaten that evening. This was followed immediately by the Feast of Unleavened Bread, which lasted for seven days (Exod. 12:15); but often "the feast of unleavened bread" denoted the Passover plus the seven following days, an eight-day festival. That is the way it is used here.

33. A. Jaubert has made the case for holding that Jesus and the disciples used the same calendar as did the Qumran community (*La Date de la Cène* [Paris, 1957]). Albright and Mann favor this understanding of the evidence *(AB)*.

34. Burton cites this as an example of the Deliberative Subjunctive preceded by θέλεις, and he points out that "No conjunction is to be supplied in these cases" (171).

35. For the usual arrangements see SBk IV.1, pp. 41-42.

36. The expression is πρὸς τὸν δεῖνα, the only place in the New Testament where it occurs.

the man and say to the householder: *"My time*[37] *is near,"* words that occur only in this Gospel. They are to go on, *"at your house I am keeping*[38] *the Passover with my disciples."* The Passover was normally a family meal, but these Galileans would have been a long way from their families and it made sense for them to make up a company for their Passover.

19. The disciples did as Jesus had told them.[39] We are given no details, but what had to be done they did. They made things ready for the feast.

20. Evidently Jesus remained where he was, away from the city, until the time for the feast in the evening. When that time came he went to the house where the preparations had been made, and Matthew tells us that he *reclined with the Twelve*. In Old Testament times people seem to have sat down for their meals (e.g., Judg. 19:6), but by New Testament times they had adopted the Greco-Roman habit of reclining. They would lean on the left elbow with the head toward the table and the feet away from it; the right hand was free to take the food. They used triclinia, couches for three. The tables were arranged in a U shape, with the principal couch at the junction of the two arms. In this case Jesus was in the place of the host, namely in the center of the triclinium at the head.

21. It may well be that the group talked about a number of things, but Matthew begins with Jesus' announcement of his betrayal. This was not right at the beginning, for it took place *as they were eating*, and the meal would have been preceded with the saying of a blessing. But Matthew passes over all that took place until the time when Jesus made his startling announcement. He prefaced it with the solemn *"Truly I tell you"* (see on 5:18); what he was about to say was important, and he did not want any of them to miss it. He went on, *"one of you will betray me."* The betrayal in one sense was past; Judas had made his arrangement with the high priests. But Jesus is pointing out that his actually being handed over to his enemies was future. It must have come as something of a shock to Judas to hear these words, but since Jesus did not denounce him he was still safe and could go ahead with what he had planned.

22. Not surprisingly the disciples *were very sad*[40] at this piece of information. What is more surprising is that this started them off asking, *"Is it I,*

---

37. καιρός is often used in much the same sense as χρόνος, but it can signify the appropriate time for anything. Here G. Delling holds that, while the saying would be obscure to the host, "it shows how consciously Jesus grasps and subjects Himself to the καιρός which is given by God's will." He goes on to say that "this resolve to be ready for death, and to die, is taken in accordance with the καιρός, with the demand of God for decision" (*TDNT*, III, p. 460).

38. The verb is ποιῶ, "to do, make." It is used "of meals or banquets, and of festivities of which a banquet is the principal part" (BAGD, I.1.b.ζ). The use of the present for a future action makes it a little more vivid. Turner understands it to mean "I am about to celebrate" (M, III, p. 63).

39. Matthew uses the verb συντάσσω, which he has again in 21:6 and 27:10; it occurs nowhere else in the New Testament. It means "to prescribe, ordain, arrange" (AS).

40. λυπούμενοι σφόδρα, where the verb carries the meaning "be distressed, and σφόδρα is Matthew's word for "very much, exceedingly" (he has it in 7 of its 11 New Testament occurrences; nobody else has it more than once). Rieu translates "sick at heart."

Lord?" We might have expected them to look around the table and wonder which of the others would do this dastardly thing, but instead they all looked at themselves, wondering, "Will I do this?" Perhaps they were thinking of some involuntary act of betrayal. At the same time we should notice that their question is put in a form that expects a negative answer: "Surely, not me?"[41] It is clear that Jesus' statement was shattering; nobody had expected that there would be treachery in this tightly knit little group. Specifically Judas seems to have covered his tracks pretty well. "When our Lord said, 'One of you shall betray Me,' no one said, 'Is it Judas?' " (Ryle).

23. Jesus gives a hint. The guilty person is one *"who dips his hand in the dish with me."* But this surely means no more than that it is one of the present company. The custom was to put food in a large dish within reach of all, and not in individual plates as with us. With a company of thirteen there would be more than one dish, but Jesus probably does not necessarily mean that his hand would be in the dish at the same time as that of his betrayer, but simply that the betrayer was one of the same dinner party.[42] The point of Jesus' words seems to be that to eat together was an outward sign of friendship. The Psalmist was dreadfully unhappy when the man "who ate of my bread, has lifted his heel against me" (Ps. 41:9). It was a shocking thing that the enemy, the one who would hand him over to his enemies, came from Jesus' twelve closest associates.

24. Jesus proceeds to make two things clear: one is that his death has its place in the will of God and thus nothing has been done to him outside the divine purpose, the other that this does not palliate the guilt that rests on the person who is to be his betrayer. For the former point Jesus refers to Scripture. He uses the term *"the Son of man,"* his favorite way of referring to himself in the discharge of his divine calling, and says that he *"goes just as it stands written about him."* His verb may be used of various kinds of departures,[43] but here it clearly refers to his death. That death will come about *"just as it stands written[44] about him."* Jesus does not cite any partic-

---

41. μήτι ἐγώ εἰμι; Chamberlain points out that, while μή is used to introduce a question expecting a negative answer, μήτι may be used"; he cites John 4:29, where the Samaritan woman asks, "Might this be the Messiah?" Of the verse we are discussing and verse 25 he says, "The context must decide the exact emotion that μήτι reveals in the one who asks the question" (pp. 207-8). Translations have renderings like "Surely not I, Lord?" *(NIV)*, "Surely you do not mean me, Lord?" *(REB)*.

42. Some commentators urge us to take notice of evidence that shows that in the Qumran community there was a hierarchic order in taking food. Albright and Mann note the suggestion of F. C. Fensham that "Judas, by not waiting his turn, deliberately denied the leadership of Jesus in the community, and so — to Jesus — marked himself as being in rebellion" *(AB)*. But it is difficult to find such hierarchical practices among the Twelve.

43. ὑπάγω used intransitively means "to go slowly away, withdraw oneself, depart" (AS). Matthew uses it 19 times (a total exceeded in the New Testament only by John with 32), and often of normal departures, as in 5:24; 13:44. It may be used euphemistically of the dead, as it is here (cf. our reference to someone who has died as "the departed").

44. καθὼς γέγραπται. The perfect is often used in citing Scripture; it points to the fact that what is written there is of continuing force.

ular passage, but indicates that his death will be in accordance with prophecies made centuries before. He is making it clear that his death would not take place because he had strong enemies who were weaving a plot from which he could not escape. His death would take place because it was in the will of God, and it would take place in the way that lay before him because that, too, was in the will of God.[45] Jesus is sure that the divine purpose was to be worked out in his death just as it had been throughout the days of his life.

Jesus adds a solemn remark about the seriousness of what the betrayer was doing. It would have been *"better for him if that man had not[46] been born."*[47] We are to understand that Judas's sin was serious. It is true that God used that sin to bring about his own purpose, but that did not make it any the less a sin. Judas was not compelled to betray his Master; that was his own deliberate choice. But having made his choice, he is obliged to suffer the consequences. It is a very serious thing to betray the Son of man.[48]

25. Matthew adds that Judas joined in the questioning as to who would be the betrayer (a piece of information we find in this Gospel only). He asks the same question as the other disciples, "Surely, not me?" The only difference is that he calls Jesus "Rabbi"[49] rather than "Lord" or "Master." He prefers to address him as a teacher rather than as his Lord. Matthew has not recorded any answer that Jesus gave to the disciples who had asked this question earlier, but he does respond to Judas, *"You said it"* (*you* is emphatic). This is a way of expressing an affirmative. Jesus is saying in effect, "It is just as you have said." Jesus did not take the initiative in

45. JB renders "the Son of man is going to his fate," but this is misleading. Jesus is not talking about a blind fate, but about the firm determination of a loving God to bring about salvation, even at cost. Some commentators also miss the point. Thus Kingsbury speaks of the Jewish leaders as bringing about Jesus' death, and goes on, "Ironically, what also happens is that God turns Jesus' death to advantage for all humankind, for through his death, Jesus atones for sins . . ." (*Matthew as Story*, p. 93). But Matthew is not writing about a God who has to wait for evil people to do their worst and who then manages to "turn to advantage" what they have done. The God about whom Matthew writes adumbrated his purpose in the prophets and carried it out in Jesus.

46. Normally in conditionals of this kind we would expect the negative to be μή; instead we have οὐ, which makes it somewhat more emphatic.

47. Moulton remarks, "We might speak thus of some villain of tragedy, *e.g.* 'A good thing if (nearly = that) there never was such a man.' Transferred as it is to a man who is actually present, the saying gains in poignancy by the absence of the contingent form" (M, I, p. 200).

48. Robinson remarks, people "are responsible for what they have made of themselves. . . . It is because the act is the natural outcome of his whole nature that the man falls under sentence; it is what Judas is, not what he does, that dooms him. . . . It is impossible not to feel that Jesus speaks with a certain deep sympathy; in spite of his character and his deed, Jesus loved Judas."

49. In this Gospel Judas is the only one to call Jesus "Rabbi" (he does it again in v. 49). In Mark the address is used a number of times, but the word does not occur in Luke. In John it occurs 8 times, all in addresses to Jesus. In those two Gospels it appears to be an acceptable way of addressing Jesus, but Matthew's usage is different. Further, he reports Jesus' direction to his followers not to use the word of one another (23:8).

accusing him, but when Judas put it that way he could only agree. In view of the way Judas framed his question (looking for a negative answer) he must have been somewhat surprised at Jesus' reply. We should probably understand that it was the fact that Jesus made Judas aware of the fact that he knew him for a traitor that precipitated the events leading to the crucifixion. We have already seen that the authorities wanted to wait until the feast was over (v. 5); with Judas on their side as their secret ally they would then be able to arrest Jesus quietly and put him to death at their leisure. But now Judas knew that he was exposed. He had to act quickly if he was going to betray Jesus at all.

26. Holy Communion has occupied a large place in the life of the church, and often it has become the vehicle for very elaborate ceremonial. But in origin it was a very simple observance, though a very solemn one, as Matthew makes clear. His account is often said to be "more liturgical" than the others, or we meet with comments like "The original Words of Institution have been somewhat expanded in liturgical use" (Schweizer, p. 490). But the fact is that we have no knowledge of any Christian liturgies as early as this writing. There may have been some. Or the first Christians may have preferred to use extempore worship. We simply do not know. That it took worship seriously is clear, but the way it conducted its worship and the forms it used are not. Confident assertions about liturgical forms are out of place.[50]

Matthew tells us that the service we know as Holy Communion began *as they were eating,* which means that Jesus began it in the context of a meal, not as a separate piece of religious ceremonial.[51] He *took bread,* not any special bread, but the bread they were using for the meal. It is uncertain whether they would have been using leavened or unleavened bread, but it is clear that in the service of Holy Communion the Eastern Church has always used leavened bread, and this was the case in the West also until getting on toward A.D. 1,000 (the earliest example of unleavened bread cited in *The Oxford Dictionary of the Christian Church* is in Alcuin, A.D. 798). Jesus "gave thanks" over it (*REB* reads "having said the blessing").[52]

---

50. For example, when Schweizer says, "Here the change took place under the influence of the Eucharistic celebration, in which the minister distributing the bread and wine stands facing the recipient and addresses him" (pp. 490-91). As early as this was there a person who could be described as "the minister"? Did such a person hand both bread and wine to the individual communicant? Or did one person administer the bread and another the wine? Or were the elements passed from one to another? Were there words spoken at the distribution or was it done in silence? We should not base our exposition on the assumption that we know the answers to such questions.

51. Fenton sums up in this way: "The separation between *body* and *blood* suggests sacrifice, because in the Old Testament sacrifices the blood was separated from the body; and here also Jesus says that his blood is *blood of the covenant, which is poured out for many for the forgiveness of sins.* Therefore by these words concerning the bread and the wine, Jesus is saying that his coming death will be a sacrifice offered to God, by which a new *covenant* between God and man will be established."

52. The verb is εὐλογέω, "to speak well of, praise" (cf. Luke 1:64). If it is understood

He would, of course, have broken bread and given thanks at the beginning of the meal, but he was now starting something new and it was appropriate that this new observance be marked off with a new beginning, a special thanksgiving. Then he *broke it,* a not uncommon action when a prayer is said over bread that is to be eaten, but this was done when people were commencing their meal. That Jesus performed the action when the meal was well underway marked it off as an unusual and significant action. Since Jesus is about to speak of this bread in terms of his body and since that body was about to be broken on the cross, there is a special suitability about breaking the bread in this observance. He proceeded to give it to the disciples; they were all meant to eat some of the bread.

Jesus told them to *eat* (Matthew is the only Evangelist to record this command; Mark has "take," which may imply eating), and went on to some words that have caused endless controversy: *"this*[53] *is my body,"* words that are identical in all three Synoptists. We should perhaps notice that the bread was one of the three things to be explained at the Passover celebration (the other two were "Passover" and "bitter herbs," *Pes.* 10:5), so that some words about bread would be natural in the context. These words have sometimes been made the basis for some "realistic" views of the presence of Jesus in the bread; indeed, the consecrated bread has been regarded as in some sense the body of Jesus.[54] It is difficult to know how this could have been understood at this first service, for the body of Jesus was there, before the disciples. The meaning of the words seems to be given by Paul, "As often as you eat this bread and drink this cup, you proclaim the Lord's death until he comes" (1 Cor. 11:26). Jesus is certainly saying something about his death and about his broken body, but there is no warrant for saying that the bread is that body in any realist sense. That it proclaims the Lord's death is clear, and we may certainly say that sacramentally it enables believers to partake of all that that death means, to feed on him "in their hearts by faith with thanksgiving," as the Book of Common Prayer puts it. We should not miss the point that Jesus commanded his followers to perform actions that brought before them his death, not anything in his life.[55]

---

in the sense of "bless," we should be clear that it does not mean to impart a blessing to the bread (in the New Testament sense how can an inanimate object be "blessed"?). It means to say a prayer beginning, "Blessed art Thou, O Lord," and going on to the matter for which thanks are given. See the note on 14:19. We should also bear in mind that when Paul is giving an account of the institution of the Holy Communion he uses the verb εὐχαριστέω, which clearly means "give thanks" (1 Cor. 11:24).

53. The neuter τοῦτο is doubtless due to assimilation to σῶμα.

54. Hill brings out some of the difficulties involved in the words: "In the Aramaic there would be no copula, though it would be implied. To insert *is* suggests a relationship of identity which there is no reason to assume, whereas the rendering 'represents' may convey only a purely figurative suggestion." He favors Moffatt's "Take this, it means my body."

55. Cf. Carson, "What is certain is that Jesus bids us commemorate, not his birth, nor his life, nor his miracles, but his death."

27-28. There are similar words about the wine. Jesus *took a cup,* and though Matthew does not mention the contents specifically (but cf. v. 29), the meaning is a cup containing wine.[56] He "gave thanks"[57] over the cup and said to those present, *"Drink from it, all of you";* once again it is only Matthew who records the command. He tells us, too, that Jesus went on to say, *"this is my blood of the covenant,*[58] *which is poured out for many for the forgiveness of sins."* The same should be said about realistic understanding of the wine as of the bread. Jesus is certainly calling on his followers to drink the wine reverently, and he is saying explicitly that it points them to the meaning of his death. It is thus to be received solemnly and thankfully, but not as though Jesus were somehow physically identified with it. He speaks of his blood as *"my blood of the covenant,"*[59] which takes up a thought that is important throughout the Old Testament; indeed, those writings might well be called those of "the Old Covenant," for the covenant God made with Israel was central. Everything centered on that.

In the making of that covenant, blood was thrown on the people (Exod. 24:8), a most uncommon procedure. Indeed, blood was put on people in only two other places in the whole Old Testament, the consecration of the priests (Lev. 8:22-24) and the cleansing of the leper (Lev. 14:14, 25). In both it seems that the action signifies cleansing from earlier defilement and consecration to a new life of service to God. Again, God could say to his servant, "I have given you as a covenant to the people, a light to the nations" (Isa. 42:6), and Zechariah can report God as speaking of "the blood of my covenant with you" (Zech. 9:11). All this indicates that the covenant with God was central to Old Testament religion; it dominated the relationship of Israel to Israel's God. But the tragedy is that Israel did not keep the covenant; it persisted in the ways of sin and thus forfeited the blessing. So the prophet Jeremiah looked forward to the time when God would make "a new covenant" (Jer. 31:31). That is important for an understanding of Jesus' words here.

56. J. Jeremias draws attention to rabbinic passages that show that on ordinary days bread and water formed the principal items in the diet. Wine was used at festivals (*Eucharistic Words,* p. 28).

57. The verb is εὐχαριστέω (from which we get our word "Eucharist"); it is commonly used in the sense "give thanks" and has much the same sense as εὐλογέω in the previous verse. We should be clear that both words have to do with thanksgiving and that neither means the conveying of a "blessing" to an object.

58. καινῆς is read by A C D K W etc. It is probable that it should not be read. That the reference is to the new covenant of Jeremiah 31 is clear from the fact that Jesus goes on to speak of the forgiveness of sins.

59. There is a problem in translating διαθήκη, for the word in Greek writings generally means a "last will and testament" whereas in the Greek translation of the Old Testament it is used constantly to render the word for "covenant." This, of course, raises the question whether we should speak of "the Old Testament" and "the New Testament" or "the Old Covenant" and "the New Covenant." Ancient Israel was bound to Yahweh by a covenant (Exod. 24; cf. v. 8), and it is one of the key themes throughout the Old Testament. See the chapters on "Covenant" in my *The Apostolic Preaching of the Cross*[3] (London and Grand Rapids, 1965) and *The Atonement* (London and Downers Grove, 1983).

When Jesus spoke of his blood as blood "of the covenant," he was surely claiming that, at the cost of his death, he was about to inaugurate the new covenant of which the prophet had spoken. This was a big claim. Jesus was saying that his death would be central to the relationship between God and the people of God. It would be the means of cleansing from past sins and consecrating to a new life of service to God. It would be the establishing of the covenant that was based not on people's keeping it (Exod. 24:3, 7), but on God's forgiveness (Jer. 31:34).

Jesus goes on to speak of his blood as *poured out,* which is a vivid way of referring to his death. His time on earth is drawing to a close, and he is facing a violent death. But this death, he says, is *for many,* which means that it is a vicarious death.[60] It is also *for the forgiveness of sins* (cf. 1:21; 20:28). This is central to the covenant he was about to inaugurate. Jesus had taught people a good deal about the way they should live their lives in the service of God, but he had also spoken of their need for divine help and forgiveness. Now he makes it clear that that forgiveness would be brought about by his death.[61] Neither Matthew nor Mark nor Luke has the command to continue the observance, but Paul has it (1 Cor. 11:23-26), and this is supported by the practice of the church from the earliest times.

29. *But* has some adversative force: the death of which Jesus has been speaking will inaugurate a whole new religious world. One of the significant things about that world is that the kind of table fellowship Jesus had enjoyed with his disciples is coming to an end. Never again in this life would Jesus drink with them at table, for he was about to go to his death. His *"But I say to you"* is like the "Truly I say to you" that we have met so often, though it lacks the "Truly." We should, however, understand it as putting some emphasis on the words that follow; they form a significant statement. His use of the emphatic double negative *(certainly not)* rules out entirely any possibility of the drinking of which he speaks, while *from now on* marks the present moment as a critical divide. The disciples did not know it, but they were at a decisive moment; things would never be the same for them. Jesus speaks of *"this fruit[62] of the vine,"* which clearly means

---

60. Matthew has περὶ πολλῶν, where περί is "actually for ὑπέρ" (BDF, 229[1]). Turner agrees and says that D reads ὑπέρ (M, III, p. 269). The two prepositions appear to have the same meaning in Ephesians 6:18, 19; cf. also Hebrews 5:1, 3. Meier remarks, " 'many' does not mean some as opposed to all, but rather, according to Semitic usage, the mass of mankind as opposed to the one who is making the sacrifice."

61. Jeremias argues that in these words "Jesus speaks of Himself as the paschal lamb," and further, that "By comparing Himself with the paschal lamb, Jesus describes His death as redemptive" (*Eucharistic Words,* pp. 145, 146). He also says, "by their eating and drinking the disciples are not only to be given a share in the blessing pronounced by Jesus as the Paterfamilias, but also to receive a share in the redemptive work of the Saviour" (p. 159). Nigel Turner examines Jeremias's view that Mark (followed by Matthew) reproduces a traditional form of the words of institution older than that which underlies Paul's words in 1 Corinthians 11:23-25 and dismisses the idea (*JTS,* n.s. VIII [1957], pp. 108-11).

62. The word is γένημα, "fruit," "produce" (to be distinguished from γέννημα, "offspring"). It is used in the Markan and Lucan parallels to this saying and again in the New

"wine," and says that he will not drink it any more until he drinks it *"with you"* (a little touch found only in Matthew) *"new in the kingdom of my Father."* Mark shares with him the word *new*, but Luke speaks only of the kingdom. Jesus is looking forward to the end of this world system and the setting up of the perfect kingdom of God. Then, and not till then, he will have table fellowship with the little group. The words mark a solemn farewell to the familiar intercourse they had been having during the time of Jesus' ministry here on earth, but also are a sure indication that at some unspecified time in the future that fellowship will be renewed.

30. The meal concluded with the singing of a hymn. It was the custom at Passover to use Psalms 113–118, which were called the "Hallel," and it is not improbable that Jesus and his little band sang one or more of those Psalms on this occasion. Psalms 115–118 seem to have been sung at the end of the meal.[63] It would form a fitting conclusion to their meal together. Then they went to *the Mount of Olives*. This was to the east of Jerusalem; somewhere on its slopes lay the village of Bethphage. It was a requirement that people who came up to Jerusalem to observe the Passover must stay within the city limits throughout that night, and Bethphage was regarded as the outermost limit of Jerusalem. This may be why Jesus went to the Mount of Olives, though none of the Gospels tells us specifically that this was the reason.

C. JESUS BROUGHT TO TRIAL, 26:31–27:26

There are some very difficult problems attaching to the way Jesus was tried and executed. There were two jurisdictions, the Roman and the Jewish, and both had their part to play. The problem was that it was the Jews (or some of them) who wanted Jesus executed and it was the Romans who had the power to do this. The Jews had to determine in legal fashion that Jesus ought to die and then find some way of convincing the Romans to carry out the death sentence. We will look at the problems involved a little later. But here as we consider the general subject of "Jesus brought to trial," we should bear in mind the complexity of the situation. Matthew is concerned with both Jews and Romans and, more importantly, with the fact that God was working his purpose out through the actions of both good men and bad. This part of our story begins with what happened in the garden of Gethsemane.

Testament only in Luke 12:18; 2 Corinthians 9:10. Luke, of course, speaks of the cup twice, once before the bread and once after it; his parallel to this saying comes in the reference to the earlier cup.

63. Bengel thinks that they may have recited it rather than sung it, and comments, "Our Lord is frequently said to have prayed while on earth; never to have sung." But ὑμνέω scarcely fits in with this; it means "to sing."

1. Jesus in Gethsemane, 26:31-46

31*Then Jesus says to them, "You will all be brought down because of me this night, for it stands written, 'I will strike the shepherd, and the sheep of the flock will be scattered.' 32But after I have been raised I will go before you into Galilee." 33But Peter answered and said to him, "Though all will be brought down because of you, I will never be brought down." 34Jesus said to him, "Truly I tell you, in this night, before a rooster crows, three times you will deny me." 35Peter says to him, "Even if I must die with you, I will certainly never deny you." And all the disciples said likewise.*

36*Then Jesus goes with them to a place called Gethsemane, and he says to the disciples, "Sit here while I go over there and pray." 37And taking Peter and the two sons of Zebedee, he began to be sorrowful and distressed. 38Then he says to them, "My soul is very sorrowful, to the point of death. Stay here and watch with me." 39And he went on a little and fell face downward, praying and saying, "My Father, if it is possible, let this cup pass away from me; nevertheless not as I will but as you will." 40And he comes to the disciples and finds them sleeping, and says to Peter, "So you did not have strength to watch with me for one hour? 41Watch and pray lest you enter into temptation; the spirit indeed is willing, but the flesh is weak." 42Again, a second time he went away and prayed, saying, "My Father, if this cannot pass away unless I drink it, may your will be done." 43And he came again and found them sleeping, for their eyes were heavy. 44And he left them again, and went away, and prayed the third time, saying again the same words. 45Then he comes to the disciples and says to them, "Sleep on now and take your rest! Look, the hour has come and the Son of man is betrayed into the hands of sinners. 46Get up, let us go. Look, he who betrays me is close."*

Matthew brings out something of the poignancy of what was happening in a little passage that brings out clearly both the fact that Jesus knew what was about to happen and the incomprehension of the apostles. At this time they were sure they would never fail Jesus, and they affirmed this in strong terms. But in Gethsemane immediately afterward they failed him. Clearly in this trying hour Jesus looked for his closest followers to support him in their prayers, but found them wanting. Instead of watching with him and praying, they fell asleep. Jesus was left to bear the strain and the suspense alone.

31. Jesus was not taken by surprise by the happenings of that night, though the disciples were apparently quite unaware that anything out of the ordinary was happening. But before they had any inkling that there was trouble ahead, Jesus gave them a warning. Indeed, it was more than a warning; it was a prophecy that they would be found wanting, and that very soon. It would take place *this night* (Mark has the same prophecy, but only Matthew has *this night*, which brings it into their immediate future).

It is not easy to find an adequate translation for the verb I have rendered *brought down*.[64] Some translations have "fall away" *(NIV)*; others, "lose faith" *(REB, JB)*; and still others, "take offence at me" (Cassirer). But Jesus is not saying that they will really fall away or abandon faith in him. He is indicating that they will have a grievous lapse, even though it will be a lapse out of character. They will fail him (only Matthew sheets this home with *because of me* here and "because of you" in v. 33). But that does not mean that they will cease to be disciples or that they will no longer trust him or for that matter that they will be offended at him (cf. Lenski, "The disciples took no offence because of Jesus. . . . They were simply caught [trapped] and overwhelmed by what happened to Jesus," p. 1034). Out of fear they will run away.

Jesus sees this as a fulfilment of Scripture (with the perfect tense again indicating something written a long time ago, but of continuing force). He cites Zechariah 13:7[65] to bring out the point that the striking of *the shepherd* means trouble for *the sheep*. The disciples will be in no great physical danger, and their flight will deliver them from whatever danger there will be. But Jesus himself will be "struck," and the effect of that will be the scattering of his little band. This is written in Scripture, so it must be fulfilled. But there is comfort in that thought, too, for it makes clear that what will happen will be in fulfilment of the divine purpose.

32. Jesus goes on to refer to his resurrection, which must have seemed puzzling to the disciples, for he had not spoken of his death (only that someone would *strike* him). As is usual, he does not say that he will rise, but that he will be raised. Occasionally the New Testament says that Jesus rose from the dead, but it is much more usual to have it said that the Father raised him, and this passage is in keeping with that thought. Then, Jesus says, he will *"go before you into Galilee."* Most of the resurrection appearances took place in or near Jerusalem. But Matthew insists on Galilee. He has the angel instruct the women to tell his disciples to go into Galilee (28:7), informs his readers that Jesus told them the same thing (28:10), and goes on to recount an appearance there (28:16-17). So here he records Jesus' prophecy that he would see his followers in that region. The figure of the Palestinian shepherd who would go before his sheep while they followed him (cf. John 10:4) is thus very appropriate here. The Good Shepherd will die, and his sheep will be scattered, but in due course he

64. The verb is σκανδαλίζω, for which see on 5:29. It denotes the setting off of the bait stick of a trap and thus bringing someone into trouble. We can scarcely say, "you will be trapped" (though Lenski does: "all you shall be trapped," p. 1033), but there is something of the significance of getting into serious trouble unintentionally and unexpectedly. There is probably also the thought that their Lord, of whom they thought so highly, would be the occasion of the trouble that lay ahead.

65. In Zechariah the verb is in the imperative, on which Carr comments, "Both Hebrew and LXX have imperative for future." The use of the first person singular here makes clear that it is God who takes the action (*GNB* has "God will kill the shepherd"). Cf. Isaiah 53:10, "it was the will of the LORD to bruise him; he has put him to grief."

will lead them again, though we should not press the word to mean that he will actually walk at their head to Galilee. The meaning is that he will be in Galilee before them, but the word Jesus uses evokes thoughts of the care of the shepherd for his flock. It is not without its interest that in the subsequent discussion the disciples ignore this saying. They are so taken up by the words about trouble that they overlook those about reassurance.

33. Characteristically it is Peter who responds to Jesus' words, and equally characteristically it is he who boasts that whatever be the case with others, he will not fail his Lord; Jesus could rely on him. He uses Jesus' verb, allowing indeed that *all* might well be *brought down* on account of their allegiance to Jesus,[66] but affirming stoutly that he *"will never[67] be brought down."* Since he did not know what he would be called upon to go through, it was a thoughtless and foolish boast, but it reflects the deep-seated loyalty in the heart of this disciple and his determination at the time he spoke to be faithful, whatever the circumstances.

34. But Jesus was not deceived. He repeated his warning, this time making it personal to Peter and detailing the exact manner in which his disciple would come short. *"Truly I tell you"* is the solemn introduction, emphasizing the truth and the importance of the words that follow, which we have seen so often in this Gospel (see on 5:18). Peter is warned that Jesus is about to utter an important saying, one to which he will do well to give good heed. *In this night* locates the coming offense with exactitude: Jesus is not speaking of something that might (or might not) occur in the distant future. This is made a little more definite with *before a rooster[68] crows* (all four Gospels have the prophecy about the rooster, Mark in the form "before a rooster crows twice"). The day was, of course, regarded as beginning at sunset, so that the crowing of the rooster would occur during the day in which Jesus was speaking. The ancients took a lot of notice of the crowing of the cock, and indeed the third of the four watches into which the Romans divided the night was called "cockcrow." Here it will be the actual crowing of a rooster that is meant, not the third watch. Before cockcrow, then, Jesus says to Peter, *"three times you will deny me"* (or *"disown me,"* as *NIV, REB,* MM, etc.).[69]

35. This prediction evokes a strong contradiction from the leader of

66. Burton takes εἰ here with the future indicative as indicating "what is regarded as certain or likely to occur" (285).

67. Peter uses the emphatic pronoun ἐγώ and also the strong term οὐδέποτε; it is a very emphatic declaration of his position.

68. Jews were forbidden to keep fowls in Jerusalem (*B. Qam.* 7:7; McNeile speaks of "a single passage in *Bab. Kam.* 82b" and says that it "gives an ideal and fanciful regulation," but he does not notice the passage in the Mishnah). In any case this would not apply to the Romans.

69. ἀπαρνέομαι is found 4 times each in Matthew and Mark, 3 times in Luke, and nowhere else in the New Testament. It signifies "deny utterly" (LSJ). Matthew uses it of denying oneself when one takes up one's cross to follow Jesus (16:24), but his other three uses of the term are in this chapter, referring to Peter's denial of Jesus.

the disciples. He does not know what the situation of which Jesus is speaking will be, but he postulates the worst possible scenario: *"Even if I must[70] die with you."* As it turned out, with soldiers coming to arrest Jesus later in the night, that is what the situation must have appeared to be, and Peter was found wanting. But at this moment his strong loyalty to Jesus made him incredulous. He is emphatic: *"I will certainly never[71] deny you."* Peter did not know the depths of which he was capable and saw it as unthinkable that he should ever deny Jesus. And in this he was not alone. We think of Peter's denial because he was the outstanding leader in the Twelve and because he was so vehement in his affirmation that he would never do any such thing. But he was not alone in this. *All the disciples said likewise,* so apparently their affirmations of loyalty were just as firm and their subsequent falls just as great. Matthew is making the point that all the disciples said that they would not deny Jesus, and later he will tell us that all of them did. He is bringing out the facts that Jesus' closest followers all made protestations of loyalty, but that when the testing time came all were found wanting. Throughout his ordeal Jesus was alone.

36. Another *Then* (for this term, so frequent in Matthew, see on 2:7) moves us on to the next stage in the narrative.[72] We do not know exactly where the little band was during the affirmations in the previous paragraph, but it was somewhere on the Mount of Olives (v. 30). Now Matthew states that they went *to a place[73] called Gethsemane[74]* (only Matthew and Mark have the name). A traditional site is pointed out on the Mount of Olives, and it may be correct, but certainty is impossible. Evidently the place was one that Jesus and the Twelve frequented (cf. John 18:2; Bonnard thinks that it may have belonged to a disciple or a friend of Jesus), for Judas was able to lead the soldiers there in due course.

Jesus had not come to this quiet spot in order to engage in some light conversation. This was to be his last period of freedom in his life here on earth, and he was facing rejection and an agonizing death. So he told the disciples to sit where they were, *"while[75] I go over there and pray."* The

---

70. δέη points to a compelling necessity.

71. He uses the emphatic double negative οὐ μή.

72. Plummer speaks of "a tragic irony" in the placing of our Lord's agony right after the boasting of the apostles: "The Apostles are so sure of their own strength that they will not allow the possibility of failure, even when they are forewarned of it by Christ. The Son of Man is so conscious of the weakness of His humanity that He prays to the Father that He may be spared the approaching trial. He feels the need of being strengthened by prayer" (p. 368).

73. Matthew and Mark call it a χωρίον, which means "a place," but then also "an estate, property, piece of land" (AS). Luke says no more than that it was a "place" (ἐπὶ τοῦ τόπου), while John says that it was a κῆπος; his word may be understood as "garden," "orchard," or "plantation" (LSJ).

74. Γεθσημανί, which AS derives from the Hebrew for "oil-press." Presumably this means that there were olive trees growing there, so that the idea of an orchard (or garden) receives support.

75. Burton sees "the accurate translation" of ἕως with the aorist subjunctive here as "till I pray" or "have prayed" (325).

important thing is that he saw the need for quiet prayer, time alone with his Father, before the terrible ordeal he was facing.

37. But Jesus did not immediately separate himself from the whole band. He took *Peter and the two sons of Zebedee* with him (Matthew has this way of referring to James and John in 20:20; 27:56). In view of what lay ahead of him it is not surprising that Jesus should *be sorrowful and distressed* (Mark also has this piece of information, but it is not in the other Gospels). It is not clear how this was expressed, but Matthew makes it clear that Jesus was deeply stirred at the prospect of what lay before him.[76] Cassirer translates, "a feeling of great distress and desolation began to fill his mind."

38. Jesus' deep anguish comes out in the further words spoken to Peter and the sons of Zebedee. In words reminiscent of Psalm 42:6, 11; 43:5 Jesus speaks of his *soul*[77] as *very sorrowful;* the addition *to the point of death* indicates that this is no normal perturbation, but something that goes very deep (cf. Jonah 4:9; Rieu, "My heart is heavy to the point of death"; *REB,* "my heart is ready to break with grief"). It is *"anguish that threatens life itself"* (Hill). Matthew does not leave his readers to think that Jesus was troubled in the same way as we all are from time to time. In Gethsemane he underwent a most unusual sense of being troubled that we must feel is connected not only with the fact that he would die, but that he would die the kind of death he faced, a death for sinners. Jesus was a brave man, and lesser people by far, including many who have owed their inspiration to him, have faced death calmly. It is impossible to hold that it was the fact of death that moved Jesus so deeply. Rather, it was the kind of death that he would die that brought the anguish. In due course Matthew will record the cry from the cross that says the Father had forsaken Jesus at the point of death (27:46; Paul says, "him who knew no sin he made sin for us," 2 Cor. 5:21). Jesus would be one with sinners in his death, he would experience the death that is due to sinners, and it seems that it was this that brought about the tremendous disturbance of spirit that Matthew records.

In his anguish Jesus calls on the three: *"Stay here and watch with me."*[78]

---

76. λυπέω is connected with λύπη, "grief," "sorrow," and signifies "to be sorrowful." Mark does not have this verb but ἐκθαμβέω, "to be amazed" (another meaning of the verb is "to be terrified"). Both have ἀδημονέω in the next clause, a verb that means "be in anxiety, be distressed, troubled" (BAGD). J. B. Lightfoot says of this word, "It describes the confused, restless, half-distracted state, which is produced by physical derangement, or by mental distress, as grief, shame, disappointment, etc." (*Saint Paul's Epistle to the Philippians* [London, 1908], p. 123). MM cites the word in the papyri in the sense "excessively concerned" and holds that it "would suggest originally bewilderment." The combination makes it clear that Jesus was in great distress of spirit.

77. Apart from passages where ψυχή means "life" (and where Jesus speaks of laying down his life, as 20:28; John 10:15) Jesus speaks of his "soul" again only in John 12:27.

78. Turner finds significance in the tenses: "*do not go away* μείνατε ὧδε (constative), but *continue to watch* γρηγορεῖτε" (M, III, p. 77).

Mark has the same verb *watch*, but only Matthew has the words *with me*, Jesus' appeal to the three to share with him in this difficult time. Clearly he wanted to feel their fellowship with him in the great crisis that was so near. It is perhaps a little puzzling that he went on a little as he prayed, but perhaps Matthew wants us to understand that the three were near enough to provide company and support while Jesus prayed a prayer that only he could pray. There is a sense in which he had to be alone in prayer, for only he could pray the prayer he prayed. But there is also a sense in which he could have been encouraged by the support of his closest followers nearby. He does not ask them to pray, but to *watch*.

39. Jesus *went on a little* (Luke tells us that he went "about a stone's throw" away). He *fell face downward*,[79] an expression that means that Jesus adopted the lowliest posture for this very significant prayer. He began with the warm and tender approach, *"My Father"* (cf. "Our Father," 6:9); even in this time when it would seem that he was abandoned to ignominy and death Jesus knew that his Father was near (see on 5:16 for the importance of "Father" in this Gospel). Only in Matthew, and only here, do we find the address *"My Father"* (Mark has the Aramaic form "Abba," which has much the same meaning; Luke has simply "Father"); it mattered to this Evangelist that in this critical moment Jesus' warm relationship to the Father was clear. *If it is possible* precedes the substance of the prayer and makes clear that Jesus was not pressing for anything that was against the will of the Father. The question at issue was not whether Jesus should do the Father's will, but whether that necessarily included the way of the cross. The kind of death he faced was the kind of ordeal from which human nature naturally shrinks; thus we discern here the natural human desire to avoid it. But we discern also Jesus' firm determination that the Father's will be done. So he prays for the avoidance of the death he faced, but only if that accorded with the divine plan.

The petition is *"let this cup pass away from me."* In the Old Testament the "cup" has associations of suffering and of the wrath of God (e.g., Ps. 11:6; Isa. 51:17; Ezek. 23:33), and we should observe the same kind of symbolism here (*GNB* reads "this cup of suffering").[80] Jesus' death meant

---

79. ἔπεσεν ἐπὶ πρόσωπον, literally "fell on face"; it indicates prostration, the adoption of the lowliest position of all. Only Matthew has the reference to the face; Mark speaks of his falling "on the ground," while Luke speaks of his falling to his knees. This is the only occasion on which Jesus is said to have prostrated himself.

80. C. E. B. Cranfield examined the Old Testament use of "cup" and rejected the view that it is simply a metaphor for suffering. "Surely we must go further, and say that in the O.T. the metaphorical use of 'cup' refers predominantly to God's punishment of human sin." The cup from which Jesus shrinks "is the cup of God's wrath against sin" (*ET*, LIX [1947-48], p. 138). Similarly L. Goppelt says, "The ineffable sorrow and anguish . . . which gives rise to the request that what is approaching might pass from Him is not fear of a dark fate, nor cringing before physical suffering and death, but the horror of One who lives by God as being cast from Him at the judgment which delivers up the Holy One to the power of sin . . . the approaching passion is not fate but judgment" (*TDNT*, VI, p. 153).

suffering, and because it was a death for sin, there are associations of the wrath of God connected to it. We are not to think of Jesus facing death with the passionate longing for martyrdom that has characterized fanatics throughout history. The death he faced was a horrible death, and he experienced the natural human shrinking from undergoing such an ordeal. So he prayed that if it were possible it might be avoided.

But the final petition of the prayer rests in the will of God. Jesus is not seeking to impose his will on the Father (*"not as I will"*), but to accept the will of the Father (*"but as you do"*). Throughout his whole life he had sought only to do the will of the Father. Before he was born it was said, *"you will call his name Jesus; for he will save his people from their sins"* (1:21), and throughout his life he had steadfastly moved toward the accomplishment of the divine will. As he now faces the climax of it all, he insists that it is the will of the Father that is his chief concern.

40. Jesus returns to *the disciples,* an expression that is broad enough to include the entire eleven, but that here seems to refer to the three who were closest to him. It is one of the saddest things in the Gospel accounts that in this critical time, when Jesus was so disturbed in the face of the ordeal that confronted him, and when he had appealed to the three who were closest to him on earth to watch with him, they were so far from understanding the situation that they went to sleep. But Jesus did not upbraid them. He addressed Peter (though the plural verbs show that the words are meant for all of them) with a question that hints at something of an excuse for them. *"So,"* Jesus says, *"you did not have strength to watch with me for one hour?"* (in the next verse we notice his comment on their willingness of spirit). The first verb is one that is often used of physical strength (e.g., Luke 16:3), and perhaps Jesus is pointing to the physical weakness of his closest followers. They had professed their loyalty and their readiness even to die for Jesus (v. 35). But when the first test came, they were tired and lacked the strength *to watch* with Jesus even for *one hour.* This last expression is sometimes used to denote a short interval of time, but it may also signify that Jesus had been praying for an hour. The situation was serious, and prayer for an hour is by no means impossible.

41. Despite all the excuses that might be made for them, Jesus goes on to exhort the sleepers to keep awake and to pray. *"Watch"* is the same verb as Jesus used in verse 38; they had failed to obey, but it is important and he renews the command. This time he adds, *"and pray,"* for they need the help that only God can give; prayer recognizes the limitations of the human frame and seeks divine assistance. Both verbs are in the present imperative, which points to continuing action. Jesus urges them to pray so that[81] they may not be led into *temptation,* or, as JB and others under-

---

81. ἵνα may introduce the content (= "that," as in 24:20) or the purpose (= "so that," as in v. 5) of their prayer.

stand it, "not to be put to the test."[82] Jesus may be saying that they should pray so that they may not be brought into temptation like the one to which they had just succumbed, or he may be pointing to some sharp test that might arise in the future and urging them to pray that they might not have to face it.[83] The former view seems better. And it accords with the following expression, as Jesus goes on to say, *the spirit indeed is willing, but the flesh is weak.* That will have reference to the current situation. Jesus recognizes that the disciples wanted to do as he had asked, but that they were not strong enough. Their physical bodies let them down. It has well been remarked that just at the time when Jesus was showing the victory of spirit over flesh, the disciples were manifesting the victory of flesh over spirit. But Jesus' words will also have relevance to what his followers would face in the future. Because of the frailty of human nature there is the constant need for prayer. A willing spirit is not enough; it must be supplemented by prevailing prayer.

42. Jesus resumed his prayers. Matthew brings out the fact that this was the continuation of what he had been doing previously, with his *again* backed up with *a second time.* As on the first occasion he addresses God with the familiar *"My Father,"* but there is a small advance in the content of the prayer. Whereas previously Jesus had prayed, "if it is possible, let this cup pass away from me," now he says, *"if this cannot pass away unless I drink it."* There is the recognition that the drinking of "this cup" is indeed the Father's will.[84] In the former prayer there is a reference to the will of Jesus, but not in this one. The writer to the Hebrews says that the Son "learned obedience from the things he suffered" (Heb. 5:8); perhaps we see here something of what that means. *"May your will be done"* is a further submission to the will of the Father (and a further reminiscence of the Lord's Prayer, 6:10). That is what Jesus had come to do, and he would do it even though at this moment he was vividly conscious of what it would mean.

43. Matthew says that Jesus *came again,* which appears to mean that he came back to where the three were supposed to be watching and praying (v. 41). But as before, they were asleep, and Matthew explains that this was because *their eyes were heavy.*[85] He does not record any conversation, and perhaps no words were spoken. Mark says that they did not

---

82. πειρασμός may be used simply of a test, or of a test with a view to the person not passing the test, that is, temptation. We have the same problem in understanding the relevant petition in the Lord's Prayer (6:13).

83. "As events proved it was not the Father's will to spare either Him or them, but want of prayer deprived them of the spiritual victory which He won" (McNeile).

84. The condition is introduced with εἰ followed by the indicative. There is a clear indication that this is in fact the Father's will.

85. Their eyes were βεβαρημέvοι (Mark uses καταβαρύνω). We are to understand that the disciples were very sleepy; they "could not keep their eyes open." The pluperfect indicates that their eyes were "weighed down"; "Here the participle is virtually an adjective, referring only to the existing result and not also to the time of weighing down" (Moule, *IBNTG*, p. 19).

670

know what to answer Jesus, which may mean that there was conversation that Matthew has not recorded, or perhaps that they did not reply to a reproachful glance from Jesus. But Matthew does not bother even to mention that Jesus woke them.

44. Once more Jesus *left them* and went away to pray. Matthew tells us two things: Jesus prayed *the third time*, and he used *the same words*. Matthew is the only Evangelist to tell us that Jesus prayed the third time, although Mark probably implies this when, after recording that Jesus found the disciples sleeping on the second occasion, he immediately adds, "he comes the third time" (Mark 14:41). On the second occasion Jesus had expressed submission to the Father's will, and this is reaffirmed with his third time of praying.

45. For the third and final time Jesus comes back to the disciples. Matthew does not say explicitly that they were asleep again, but that seems to be the situation, for Jesus says to them, *"Sleep on now and take your rest!"*[86] This is surely a gently ironical comment on their continuing sleepiness.[87] They had persisted in sleeping when they should have been praying. But this is not a way of encouraging them to be wakeful and prayerful. The time for prayer is past, and Jesus says, *"Look, the hour has come."* He does not define *the hour,* but clearly it is the decisive hour, the hour when the action that meant the salvation of sinners throughout the world would have its beginning. He lets them see something of what that means with *"the Son of man is betrayed into the hands of sinners."* Ten times in this chapter Matthew uses this verb "betray" (Mark in the equivalent chapter has it 7 times, and Luke 5 times); he will not let his readers overlook the dreadful fact of treachery among the followers of Jesus. And he characterizes the Jewish leaders, high priests, and other leaders of the people as *sinners.*[88] Jesus would go to his death in accordance with the will of his Father, but that excuses neither his follower who handed him over, nor the religious leaders who bought his arrest.

46. *"Get up, let us go"* is not a call to run away. Jesus had fought the battle as he spent the time of waiting in fervent prayer. Now events would take their course. He is telling the disciples that their time for sleep is over; he (and they) would move on. He explains, *"Look"* (for this frequent term in Matthew see the note on 1:20), *"he who betrays me is close."* Matthew

86. A number of translations take this as a question; for example, *NIV* has "Are you still sleeping and resting?" But "still" is not a very natural meaning of λοιπόν; the word rather looks to the future, "For the future, henceforth" (AS).

87. Calvin understands the words as ironical and adds that this is their meaning: "So far I have wasted my words on you, I shall now cease urging you. But however much I may let you sleep, the enemy will not allow it you, but will force you to watch against your will" (III, p. 155).

88. Diétrich asks, "Who are the 'sinners' into whose hands the Son of Man is betrayed?" and answers, "An Apostle, the leaders of Israel, a Roman magistrate — the religious authorities and the secular authorities, the 'qualified' representatives of a humanity which does not want God."

does not explain how Jesus knew this, but he had made it clear that Jesus knew that he was being betrayed, and presumably the arresting posse was making some noise as they approached in the darkness. Jesus had no difficulty in interpreting the sound.

2. Jesus Arrested, 26:47-56

47*And while he was still speaking, look, Judas, one of the Twelve, came, and with him a great crowd with swords and clubs from the high priests and elders of the people.* 48*Now he who betrayed him had given them a sign, saying, "Whomever I shall kiss is he; lay hold on him."* 49*And he went up to Jesus straightaway and said, "Greetings, Rabbi," and he kissed him tenderly.* 50*But Jesus said to him, "Friend, do what you are here for." Then they came and laid hands on Jesus, and held him fast.* 51*And look, one of those with Jesus stretched out his hand, drew his sword, and hit the slave of the high priest, cutting off his ear.* 52*Then Jesus says to him, "Put your sword back into its place; for all those who take the sword will perish by the sword.* 53*Or do you think that I cannot petition my Father, and he would provide me now with more than twelve legions of angels?* 54*How then would the Scriptures be fulfilled that it must be thus?"* 55*In that hour Jesus said to the crowds, "As against a robber did you come out with swords and clubs to arrest me? Daily I sat in the temple teaching, and you did not take hold of me.* 56*But all this has happened so that the Scriptures should be fulfilled." Then the disciples all left him and ran away.*

Matthew proceeds to the story of the arrest. He lets his readers see that Jesus is clearly in command of the situation: he has already told the disciples what is happening; now he proceeds to rebuke first Judas, then the disciple who used his sword to strike the high priest's slave, and then the crowds who had come to arrest him. This is not the behavior of some terrified fugitive but of a lordly person, serene in his doing of the will of God.

47. All three Synoptists tell us that Judas and those he was guiding to the spot came up while Jesus was still speaking, and all three remind their readers that he was *one of the Twelve,* a fact that emphasizes the enormity of his offense. This was not some member of the general public who happened to know Gethsemane, but one of Jesus' chosen band.[89] It is noteworthy that not one of the Evangelists attempts to blacken his character or use some abusive term of him. They simply tell us what he did and let that suffice. Evidently Jesus had persisted in his praying until the last possible moment and had rejoined the eleven only when the arresting party was close at hand. Mark and Luke also single out Judas,

---

89. "Repeated not for information, but as the literary reflection of the chronic horror of the apostolic church that such a thing should be possible" (Bruce).

672

and Mark as well as Matthew says that he *came*. In using the singular verb and adding that *a crowd*[90] was *with him*, they put their emphasis on what Judas was doing rather than on the enemy who actually performed the arrest, though they do, of course, go on to the arrest. Only Matthew says that the crowd was *a great* one. They were armed with *swords and clubs*, so they were prepared to counter any opposition they might meet. They came *from the high priests and elders of the people*, which appears to mean that they were official representatives of the Sanhedrin. Though there is mention of a *crowd*, we are not to think of this as an irresponsible assemblage of people; rather, it is a large group of people sent with the highest authority possible for the Jews. Some of the Jerusalem rabble may well have heard that something was going on and have attached themselves to the official party, but basically the group would have been the temple police.

48. It seems clear that their intention was to arrest Jesus only, and not any of the Twelve, and this posed a problem. Even though there would have been moonlight at Passover, it would have been dark in Gethsemane and the disciples would be there, so how were they going to know which was Jesus? Judas (identified as *he who betrayed him*; the tenth use of this verb in this chapter) had foreseen this problem and *had given them a sign*, a means of identifying the man they had come to arrest. He said that he would *kiss* Jesus (cf. *REB*, "The one I kiss is your man"). The kiss was a not unusual form of greeting, used, for example, between a host and his guests (Luke 7:45), or between rabbis,[91] or between a rabbi and his disciple. It was used by the early Christians (1 Thess. 5:26). There is no information about how widely it was used by Jesus and his disciples, but there is no reason for thinking that they would have suspected anything about it. But it was a greeting of friendship, and to use such a friendly salute in this traitorous fashion has always seemed heinous to Christians. Judas adds, "*lay hold on him.*" There was no real need for such words; the whole purpose of the expedition was to take Jesus into custody, and there was no doubt that when the temple police were sure which one of those who confronted them was Jesus they would arrest him. But Judas had to be sure. He was now in the camp of the enemy and wanted to be certain that the deed was done. There may also be a fear that Jesus would seek safety in flight. Judas was not to know that Jesus had no such intention, and he was guarding against a possibility he thought not unlikely.

---

90. Kingsbury takes a simplistic view of Matthew's use of *crowd*. He speaks of the crowds in this Gospel as of "a single, 'flat' character. They are not rich in traits, and the ones they possess tend not to change until the end of Matthew's story, when they suddenly appear with Judas to arrest Jesus" (*Matthew as Story*, p. 24). But by what process of thought are we to identify the crowd that came with Judas with, say, the crowds that came to hear Jesus preach (5:1) or those who were filled with awe and glorified God (9:8)?

91. Thus it is recorded that Rabban Gamaliel kissed Rabbi Joshua on the head (*Rosh. Hash.* 2:9).

49. So Judas *went up to Jesus straightaway*. Prompt action would get the whole affair over quickly. He used the normal word for greeting people (cf. Luke 1:28 and the mocking greeting in 27:29), and addressed Jesus as *"Rabbi"* (as he had done in v. 25, where see note). He also *kissed him tenderly* (or perhaps "effusively"; should we bear in mind Prov. 27:6?).[92] It is possible that we should see more than a greeting here. Moses Aberbach is cited in *AB* for the information that "in any group of teacher and disciples the disciple was never permitted to greet his teacher first, since this implied equality. Judas' sign, therefore, was not only a final repudiation of his relationship with Jesus and a signal to the mob, but also a studied insult."

50. *But* will have adversative force; it sets Jesus over against the traitor. Jesus greets Judas as *"Friend"* (for this term see on 20:13); it is a term used in this Gospel with an ironical twist. Judas ought to have been a real friend to Jesus, and he had just kissed him, a friendly act. But in reality he was far from being a real friend, for his kiss was the means of handing his Master over to the enemy. There is a problem relating to Jesus' next words.[93] They may be a question or a statement, but in view of Matthew's picture of Jesus as master of the situation it seems more likely that Jesus is telling Judas to get on with the job of betrayal and arrest, rather than inquiring why he is there (cf. Moffatt, "My man, do your errand"). At any rate, after his words to Judas the arresting officers came up to Jesus, *laid hands* on him, and *held him fast*. Having found their man, they were taking no chances.

51. All four Gospels tell us that there was a brief and ineffectual show of resistance from Jesus' supporters, with one man wielding his sword and cutting off the ear of one of the arresting party. John alone tells us that it was Peter who used the sword, and he further names the man who was hit as Malchus. Luke joins John in saying that it was the right ear of the high priest's slave that was cut off, and he also records that Jesus healed the man. Matthew links this with the preceding with his characteristic *And look*,[94] and he goes on to say that the disciple *stretched out his hand* (NIV

---

92. There is a question as to whether we should say more than "kissed him." BAGD gives the meaning of καταφιλέω (the verb used here) as simply "*kiss* τινά *someone* in greeting or in farewell." MM cites passages of its use where D. S. Sharp says the stress is laid "not on kissing fervently, but on the very fact of kissing at all." On the other hand, they cite a passage where it is used of a kiss "in a passion of gratitude." AS gives the meaning, "to kiss fervently, kiss affectionately." But Matthew has used the verb φιλέω in verse 48, and we need a reason for the change of verb in this verse. It appears that Judas was overplaying his part.

93. ἐφ' ὅ πάρει, literally "upon which you are present." This may be a statement, in which case we should understand an imperative, "Do that for which you are here" ("do what you came for," *NIV*). Or it may be a question, "For what are you here?" ("why are you here?", *RSV*). The problem with this way of taking it is that ὅ is a relative pronoun, not an interrogative. The words are found in Matthew only. This Evangelist shows a particular interest in what Jesus said in the garden and records other sayings that occur nowhere else (vv. 52, 53, 54).

94. Matthew frequently connects his sentences with δέ (cf. vv. 48 and 50), but that

has "reached for his sword, drew it out"). But it is not easy to grasp the significance of this.[95] That he *drew his sword*[96] is more obvious, after which he *hit the slave*[97] *of the high priest* and cut off *his ear* ("an illustration alike of the misunderstanding as to the nature of Jesus' work and of the futility of the disciples at violence," Robinson). All four Gospels tell us this. D. Daube argues from the fact that slitting an ear disqualified a man from being a high priest to the thought that here the high priest is being insulted through his slave.[98] There may be something in this, but it seems to go against all the probabilities. Peter was not a skilled swordsman, the ear is a very small target, the light must have been poor, there was excitement in the air, and, from Peter's point of view, an imperative need to deliver his Master and escape. It is much more likely that Peter struck a lusty blow in the general direction of the enemy but managed to inflict only minor damage.

52. Jesus promptly intervened.[99] It may well be that this quick action prevented Peter from being arrested. A man who wielded a sword against the officials arresting Jesus was an obvious candidate to be taken into custody along with him. But Jesus called on Peter to put his sword back where it belonged, a command given in other words in John. Then Matthew proceeds to report words of Jesus not found elsewhere. First he says, *"all those who take the sword will perish by the sword."* Peter saw the use of his sword as the way of deliverance from the present trouble, but Jesus viewed it as out of character with all that he stood for. It was, moreover, the means of bringing trouble to the user. Peter was overlooking the fact that people who are hit with a sword have the very nasty practice of retaliating in kind; in the end the user of a sword is apt to finish his days on the end of someone else's sword. The warlike will perish at the hands of the warlike, and this is a most unfitting end for those who are servants of the Prince of peace. Jesus' repudiation of force and his acceptance of the way of the cross are important for his followers. It comes naturally to us to seek to impose our will on others. But that is not God's way. His way is the way of the cross with its repudiation of compulsion and its call for us to trust him.

---

would imply some adversative force; here he is linking evil to evil, the wrong act of Peter to that of Judas; καί is thus more natural.

95. We should notice, however, that it is a not infrequent biblical idiom (see Gen. 3:22; Exod. 8:6, etc.). A number of times it is used of taking a weapon (Gen. 22:10; Judg. 3:21; 15:15; 1 Sam. 17:49). In the Synoptic Gospels it is used of Jesus stretching out his hand to heal (e.g., 8:3; 14:31) and of his inviting a man with a deformed hand to stretch it out (12:13).

96. μάχαιρα meant a large knife or a short sword (the word for a large sword was ῥομφαία; cf. Luke 2:35).

97. All four Gospels say that it was *the* slave, not *a* slave, of the high priest, but with our ignorance of the high priest's household we cannot tell whether this is significant or not.

98. *JTS*, n.s. XI (1960), pp. 59-62. He says, "It was a very well-chosen insult, the wound was of a type which, had it been inflicted on the servant's master, would have forced him from office" (p. 61).

99. Matthew has his characteristic τότε, "then," and he uses the historic present.

53. In any case, Peter has overlooked a most important matter. *"Do you think. . . ?"* introduces a question the apostle might well have asked himself before he acted. He had been with Jesus for quite a long time now; did he really think that his Master was defenseless? In the face of Judas and the arresting posse Jesus had offered up no prayer. Did Peter really think that he could not ask the heavenly Father for help? And if he did seek such help, would it not be given? Jesus says that the Father would then provide him with *more than twelve legions of angels* — a legion for Jesus himself and one for each of the eleven apostles! Since a legion consisted of 12,000 foot soldiers besides a number of horsemen, twelve legions of any sort of troops would surely be more than adequate to cope with the motley group that confronted the little band, but this number of *angels* meant people superbly equipped to defeat any puny earthly force. Jesus makes it clear to his servant that if force were needed there were better means of providing it than resorting to the puny efforts of a man who could do no better than slice off a slave's ear.

54. But there were other considerations than fighting off the enemy. Jesus draws attention to the importance of the fulfilment of Scripture. If the Father were to send an overwhelming force of angels, Judas and the enemy with him would be decisively repelled. But what of the divine purpose? God had caused many things to be written in Scripture that were fulfilled in the life and work of Jesus (Matthew has faithfully chronicled a good number of them), and especially is Scripture to be fulfilled in Jesus' death. The Master now confronts his hearers with the impossibility of his being given earthly deliverance in such a way that the prophecies in Scripture would not be fulfilled. The purpose of God was in those prophecies, and that purpose would inevitably come to its appointed conclusion. *"It must be thus,"* Jesus said, where his *must* is a strong term, allowing of no exception. What was taking place was fulfilling the divine purpose, a purpose that must necessarily come to pass.

55. Jesus has something to say to *the crowds* as well as to his well-meaning followers. All three Synoptists have the words, *"As against a robber did you come out with swords and clubs. . . ?"* (the words could be a statement rather than a question). Clearly this impressed the early church. Everybody knew the kind of thing Jesus did. His teaching and his healings were done openly and publicly, and to class him as *a robber* was ridiculous, even if we understand the term in some such sense as "terrorist" (Josephus uses the term of "brigands" who were put down by the Romans [*Ant.* 20.160-72]; the word is used of those who were crucified with Jesus, 27:38). Why, then, did this motley group come out furtively in the nighttime to arrest[100] him? It was an inexplicable procedure if justice was the prime consideration. He reminds them that he was not unknown. *Daily* points to a

---

100. συλλαμβάνω means "to bring together, collect," but is used not infrequently in the sense "to collect a person," that is, to take a prisoner.

habitual action, *the temple* to a public and unexceptionable place, and *teaching* to a lawful and recognized activity. Jesus had not been a difficult person to find. Throughout the days leading up to that feast he had been in plain view and the arresting posse could have taken him at any time. They had not done so because the authorities feared the people, but that is just the point Jesus is making. Those in whose hands he now was were not interested in justice. They wanted simply to get him out of the way and were prepared to stoop to any means to bring that about. *"You did not take hold of me,"* he says. If they had been honest in what they were doing, they would have proceeded against him publicly. Since a criminal would hide away out of the public gaze, it was fair to arrest such an offender wherever he might be found. But there was something wrong with authorities who treated an honest religious man as though he were nothing more than a brigand.

56. Again Jesus speaks of the importance of the fulfilment of Scripture. He had stressed this to his followers in rejecting the way of force; now he reminds his captors of the same thing. They thought that they were being clever in arranging his arrest in this secluded place away from all but a handful of his followers. But in treating him as a malefactor they were simply doing what the Scripture had long ago foretold. He was "numbered with the transgressors" (Isa. 53:12). Foolish and wicked men can never overthrow the purposes of God.

This was the last straw for *the disciples.* They must have been staggered by all that was going on. They had evidently had no inkling of the plot that had been laid, they were surprised that Judas led the arresting posse to Jesus, they saw Peter's unsuccessful attempt at resistance by violence and heard Jesus' repudiation of it, and now Jesus, instead of doing something miraculous, was reasoning calmly with the people who held him. This was no place for the followers of Jesus, and there appeared to be nothing more they could do, so they *all left him and ran away. All* is significant; there was not one of his intimate followers who was prepared to suffer alongside his leader. At this time of crisis they simply ran off. They left Jesus to suffer alone.

3. Jesus Tried before Caiaphas, 26:57-68

> ⁵⁷Now those who had taken hold of Jesus brought him to Caiaphas, the high priest, where the scribes and the elders were gathered together. ⁵⁸But Peter was following him at a distance up to the high priest's courtyard, and he went inside and sat with the servants to see the end.
>
> ⁵⁹Now the high priests and the whole Sanhedrin were looking for false testimony against Jesus in order to put him to death. ⁶⁰And they did not find it, though many false witnesses came forward. Finally two came forward ⁶¹and said, "This fellow said, 'I can destroy the temple of God and within three days rebuild it.'" ⁶²And the high priest stood up and said to

677

him, "Do you answer nothing? What are these men testifying against you?" [63]But Jesus remained silent. And the high priest said to him, "I charge you on oath by the living God that you tell us whether you are the Messiah, the Son of God." [64]Jesus says to him, "You said it. Yet I say to you: Hereafter you will see the Son of man sitting at the right hand of The Power and coming on the clouds of heaven." [65]Then the high priest tore his robes and said, "He has blasphemed. Why do we still have need of witnesses? Look, you have now heard the blasphemy; [66]what do you think?" And they answered, saying, "He is worthy of death." [67]Then they spat in his face and struck him; and others slapped him, [68]saying, "Prophesy to us, you Messiah. Who is it who hit you?"

None of the Evangelists gives us a full account of the judicial process that led to Jesus' death. The story is a complicated one, arising as it does out of a situation in which there were conflicting jurisdictions. When the Romans conquered a country they normally allowed much of the local administration to continue. It obviously made things easier all around if people could continue to a large extent with the judicial institutions with which they were familiar. But the Romans had to exercise a certain caution lest their supporters in the conquered nation be removed by a judicious use of the local courts on the part of those opposed to Rome. So, while the Romans allowed the conquered peoples a good deal of latitude, the conquerors kept the death penalty in their own hands and reserved the right to take over any case at any stage they chose.

In the case of Jesus the situation was complicated by the fact that the Jews saw him as guilty of a religious crime (claiming to be the Messiah, the Son of God, and thus being a blasphemer), but the Romans, who alone had the power to impose the death sentence, would not recognize this as a crime. They could be induced to execute Jesus only by a demonstration that he had committed what they recognized as a serious offense — for example, setting himself up as a King in opposition to Caesar. In what follows Matthew shows us how the Jewish authorities came to condemn Jesus according to their own law and then how they brought a charge before the Roman governor that was not their real grievance but that would induce Pilate to crucify Jesus.

The trial of Jesus thus took place in two main stages: that before the Jews and that before the Romans.[101] In following it through we have a problem in that none of the Gospels attempts a full account; each of the Evangelists has particular aspects of the story that he wants to bring out and he omits what is not relevant to his purpose. Thus John tells us little about the Jewish section, preferring to concentrate on what happened

---

101. A. N. Sherwin-White has a chapter entitled "The Trial of Christ in the Synoptic Gospels" (*Roman Society and Roman Law in the New Testament* [Oxford, 1963], pp. 24-47). He argues for the essential historicity of the Synoptic accounts.

before the Romans. Luke omits the night session and takes up the story with what happened when it was day (Luke 22:66). Matthew and Mark tell us of activities during the night, when the Sanhedrin examined the case.[102] But we can say that it was the aristocratic Jewish party, the high priests and their allies, who took the initiative. Had they been content with a smaller sentence they could have confined themselves to Jewish processes, but they wanted the death sentence that the law did not allow them. There thus had to be two main stages in Jesus' trial. We come now to the first of them, the trial before the high priests and the Sanhedrin.

There is a further problem in that there were a number of illegalities in the Jewish trial. Thus in capital cases "they hold the trial during the daytime and the verdict must also be reached during the daytime. . . . a verdict of acquittal may be reached on the same day, but a verdict of conviction not until the following day. Therefore trials may not be held on the eve of a Sabbath or on the eve of a Festival-day" (*Sanh.* 4:1). These requirements were not fulfilled. Again, the witnesses do not seem to have been interrogated as the law provided. Further, Jesus was convicted of blasphemy even though he did not actually use the sacred name, and the law required that the name of God be pronounced if there was to be blasphemy ("'The blasphemer' is not culpable unless he pronounces the Name itself," *Sanh.* 7:5). It was required that witnesses be examined carefully (*Sanh.* 5:1); if it was decided that there was a case, the arguments for acquittal must be considered first (*Sanh.* 5:4). But two things may be said about all this. One is that our written sources are later than New Testament times, and customs may have altered during the intervening period; rabbinic sources may not accurately reflect the legal position in the New Testament period. The other is that breaches of the law could be covered by the reasoning, "the hour demanded it"; in times of emergency the letter of the law might be overridden in order that the spirit of it might be upheld.[103]

Of course it is possible that we are mistaken in speaking of a Jewish "trial." What took place before the high priest and the Sanhedrin may well have been something in the nature of a series of more or less informal discussions. In the end they had to bring charges before the Romans, and they may have been basically concerned with that. Against this view, however, is the fact that the high priest persisted until he could find Jesus guilty of blasphemy and stopped there, whereas this was not a charge that would carry weight with the Romans. In the end we shall probably have

102. Sherwin-White reminds us that Roman officials started work very early in the day: "Hence there was every reason to hold the unusual night session if they were to catch the Procurator at the right moment" (*Roman Society and Roman Law*, p. 45).

103. Dalman draws attention to a number of actions that were approved despite being contrary to rabbinic rules and even to the law of Moses because of the pressure of circumstances (*Jesus-Jeshua* [London, 1929], pp. 98-100). D. R. Catchpole asserts, "the debate about illegalities should be regarded as a dead end" (*The Trial of Jesus* [Leiden, 1971], pp. 268-69).

to conclude that the evidence is not clear enough for us to be sure whether this was the first stage of a Jewish trial carried out with some irregularities or whether it was no more than a preliminary discussion on the best way of bringing a formal accusation before Pilate. "The Jewish trial" is, however, so usual and convenient an expression that it is best to continue to use it, despite the doubts.

57. Whether it was a formal trial or an informal inquiry, the first step was to bring Jesus before the Jewish authorities, and that was what *those who had taken hold*[104] *of Jesus* did. Matthew says that they brought him to *Caiaphas*, the second and last use of this man's name in this Gospel (see the note on v. 3). This will reflect the fact that it was Caiaphas who was the instigator of Jesus' arrest. He was the leading Jew in cooperating with the Romans, and there is no reasonable doubt that he was anxious to ensure that Roman rule continued untroubled so that his own position would remain secure. The Jews held that the high priesthood was a lifetime appointment, which meant that Annas, father-in-law to Caiaphas and still alive and vigorous, was the legitimate high priest. But the Romans took it upon themselves to depose and appoint high priests, which made for an anomalous situation. Many Jews probably held that Annas was still the legitimate high priest, but with the Romans in effective control of the country there was no way in which he could function. So Caiaphas, the appointee of the Romans, was the high priest in fact if not with full legal right.

Matthew tells us that *the scribes and the elders were gathered together.* This appears to be a reference to the Sanhedrin, the highest council in the land. It had seventy-one members *(Sanh.* 1:6), the high priest being its president. In earlier times its membership seems to have been largely aristocratic and Sadducean, but later Pharisaic scribes became members. *The elders* here points to lay members of the Sanhedrin. Under the Romans the Sanhedrin had a good deal of power and in secular as well as in strictly religious affairs. There were smaller sanhedrins each with twenty-three members, set up in towns with at least 120 adult male Jews *(Sanh.* 1:6), but the great Sanhedrin in Jerusalem was the important one. Trials in capital matters could take place only during daylight hours *(Sanh.* 4:1) and might not be held on the eves of festivals or sabbaths *(ibid.).* The Sanhedrin seems to have met somewhere in the temple area, so this gathering in the high priest's house would have been an informal assembly.

58. There had evidently been no pursuit of the disciples. Peter was thus able to follow the posse that had taken Jesus. It seems that he was motivated by curiosity; why had Jesus been arrested? What would happen now? He apparently was not hindered from entering *the high priest's court-*

---

104. Moule points out that there is a slight ambiguity here; οἱ δέ might mean "And they, seizing Jesus . . ." or "And those who had seized Jesus" *(IBNTG,* p. 123). But the difference is not significant.

yard,[105] where he was able to sit with *the servants*. Apparently there was no difficulty in doing this, though, as later events made clear, Peter did not think it advisable to be identified with the prisoner. But apparently this did not present him with a problem, at least at the beginning. He was not there to mount a rescue attempt, but only *to see the end*. He was interested to find out what would be the conclusion to those terrible moments in the garden.

59. How much of what went on Peter was able to make out is not made clear. Presumably it was not much. The deliberations of these great folk would have taken place out of the hearing of people like servants (and others who wandered into the courtyard). Peter clearly did not hope to get information about the way the debate went on, but if he remained where he was he could expect to find out what the final verdict was. Matthew speaks of *the whole Sanhedrin*, which we should not press to mean that not one member was absent, but rather see as telling us that all the constituent elements of the assembly were represented. When Jesus was arrested and taken before the Sanhedrin, we would expect that that would be for trial, with the evidence pro and con carefully considered. But it turns out that nothing of the sort was in mind. The gathering was there for one purpose only — to find a suitable legal form for putting Jesus to death. Caiaphas and his cronies were not particularly scrupulous about the method, for Matthew says right at the beginning that they were *looking for false testimony*.[106] We should not press this to mean that they wanted only false testimony; true testimony that accorded with their purpose would doubtless have been acceptable. But it apparently did not occur to them to get testimony as to what had actually been said and done. They were not interested in the facts; they were interested in a condemnation. So they looked for the kind of testimony that would enable them *to put him to death*.[107] In Matthew's view that could only be *false testimony*, so that is what he calls it.

60. Matthew greatly abbreviates this section of his narrative. He has but 36 words in verses 60-62, whereas Mark has 66 in the corresponding passage; for some reason Matthew hurries over this part of the story as he tells his readers that the kind of testimony the Jewish leaders wanted proved difficult to come by. One would have thought that if the testimony was to be false there would be no great difficulty in persuading someone to present it. There was no lack of readiness to help, for *many false witnesses came forward*. But the authorities could scarcely say to them, "This is what we want to hear from you." And not being sure of what was expected, the false witnesses were not able to come up with what the authorities

105. The word is αὐλή; in verse 3 it was used of the high priest's residence, but here it has its proper sense of "courtyard."

106. ψευδομαρτυρία in itself points to testimony that is false, and it is backed up by κατά; it was to be testimony "against" Jesus.

107. ὅπως conveys the notion of purpose, "in order that — ."

were looking for. Presumably part of the trouble at least lay in getting the agreement among the false witnesses that would stand up in a court of law (two witnesses at least were required, and it is specifically said that no one is to be executed on the testimony of one witness, Deut. 17:6). In the end[108] two witnesses were found who were apparently held to be of a different caliber: Matthew does not say that they were "false," and the high priest called on Jesus to reply to them as he had apparently not done to the earlier witnesses.

61. Their testimony concerned something they held that Jesus had said. They refer to him contemptuously as *"This fellow"*[109] and proceed to affirm that they had heard him say: *"I can destroy the temple of God and within[110] three days rebuild it."* Mark has the saying in a fuller form, "I will destroy this temple that is made with hands and in three days I will build another not made with hands" (Mark 14:58). This appears to be a distorted recollection of a saying found only in John. That Evangelist notes that in the early part of his ministry the Jews asked Jesus for a "sign" that would justify his action in cleansing the temple (John 2:18). He replied, "Destroy this temple, and in three days I will raise it up" (v. 19), a saying that would be easy to misunderstand and not too difficult to distort. Our best conjecture is that the false witnesses had heard and misunderstood what Jesus was saying and that they now reproduced it in a garbled form. John explained for his readers that Jesus was speaking, not of the physical temple at Jerusalem, but of "the temple of his body" (v. 21), but it was not the concern of the Sanhedrin at this time to inquire into what Jesus meant by the words; it was enough for them that there were witnesses who could testify that Jesus had spoken words that might be understood as blasphemous. We should also bear in mind that Jesus had said that the temple in Jerusalem would be destroyed (23:38; 24:2), though these sayings contain nothing about either his doing anything in the destruction, nor about it being rebuilt. It appears that these witnesses are reporting an imperfect recollection of what Jesus had said some time before.

It is not easy to see why this brought satisfaction to the authorities. They might have regarded it as an outrageous claim, but it is not obvious that it merits the death sentence; since it ends with the temple fully restored it seems harmless enough. Perhaps they held that the words were demeaning to *the temple of God* and therefore demeaning to God himself. In the ancient world in general it was held to be a very serious matter to treat a place of worship with anything other than respect, even if one did not practice the worship to which it was dedicated. The words point to

---

108. ὕστερον seems to separate these two from the earlier witnesses.

109. οὗτος, which may be used "W. a connotation of contempt" (BAGD, 1.a.α); "Here the witnesses sneer at Jesus' claims" (Chamberlain, p. 47).

110. Διά with genitive "Unclassically for a period within which something takes place . . . 'within three days' " (BDF, 223[1]).

the kind of flashy and spectacular miracle that Jesus persistently refused to perform. It is quite out of character for Jesus to make such a claim.

62. Jesus apparently did not think this testimony worth refuting, so he said nothing (cf. Ps. 38:12-14; Isa. 53:7). But this did not suit the high priest, who tried to get him to respond. He *stood up,* which is unusual for the president of any assembly; apparently he wanted these words to be given all the emphasis he could give them. He asked Jesus, *"Do you answer nothing?"* and proceeded to a further question, *"What are these men testifying against you?"* Clearly Caiaphas felt that he was making progress with this accusation, and he was nettled that Jesus did not respond. Perhaps he felt that although the two false witnesses had not said anything that in itself justified the death sentence, any response Jesus might make would be bound to make things worse for him, and therefore he tried to goad him into saying something.

63. But the high priest's urging had no more effect than the original testimony. Presumably Jesus thought that the words were quite irrelevant. At any rate, he *remained silent.* At one stage or another of his trial each of the four Gospels says that he remained silent. Evidently his silence made quite an impression; the normal thing would be for an accused person to oppose every accusation and assert his innocence. But Jesus' attitude to this tribunal was different from that of most of those who came before it. He had fought his battle in Gethsemane and had recognized that the will of God was that he should die at the hands of the Romans, die the death that would mean forgiveness of sins to the many. So what did it matter that these men, whom everybody there knew to be lying, made false assertions about what he had said on some earlier occasion? There was nothing to be said; therefore he remained silent.

But this did not suit Caiaphas. He was no further ahead on his quest for a condemnation of Jesus. We owe to Matthew the information that he took the unusual step of putting Jesus on oath[111] as he asked him a question on his own initiative. He called on Jesus to swear *by the living God,* as solemn an oath as could possibly be sworn. And the question he wants Jesus to answer under this solemn oath is *"whether you are the Messiah, the Son of God."* In Mark the question refers to "the Messiah, the Son of the Blessed One," and in Luke simply to "the Messiah." But the essential meaning in all three ways of putting it is the same. The difficulty is that there were different ways of understanding messiahship, and for that matter being the son of God. Jesus had avoided such terms during his ministry, presumably because they could easily be misunderstood. The high priest wants Jesus to state on oath whether or not he is the Messiah, and he wants it to be clear

---

111. ἐξορκίζω, found here only in the New Testament, means "(. . . mostly = ἐξορκόω 'cause someone to swear') *adjure, charge under oath*" (BAGD). The Mishnah provides that a man may put another man on oath by saying, "I adjure you," to which the response is "Amen" and the man is duly sworn (*Shebu.* 4:3).

that the sense in which he is using "Messiah" in the question concerns the Messiah's relationship to God. The high priest cannot get the condemnation he wants from the words of the witnesses, so he will try to get it from the words of Jesus himself. His *you* is emphatic and probably indicates some contempt for the prisoner who was before him.

64. The high priest, acting in his official capacity, was asking a question on a religious matter, and that, for Jesus, was a very different matter from that of a group of liars who were trying to malign him. So he responded. His reply begins, *"You said it."* It was a difficult question to answer because his understanding of Messiah and that of the high priest were so different. To say either "Yes" or "No" could be misleading. So he says in effect, "That is your word, not mine" (Melinsky, "Yes, but not in the way you mean"). But the effect is, "I would not have put it that way, but since you do I cannot deny it" (cf. Rieu, "The words are yours. This much I add to them . . ."). *"Yet,"*[112] he goes on, *"I say to you"* (which puts emphasis on the words that follow), *"Hereafter you will see the Son of man sitting at the right hand of The Power and coming on the clouds of heaven."* *Hereafter* may mean "from this point on" or "at a later time";[113] it may signify that a turning point has been reached; the Son of man has lived in obscurity, but after the events now set in train he will return to his heavenly glory. Or it may be used of what is to happen at a good distance from "now," that is, at a later time. Plummer takes the meaning as "henceforth" and says that it "seems to mean that their condemnation led to His glory; there was not merely sequence, but consequence. He who now stands before their judgment-seat will then be seated on the clouds, invested with Divine Power, and ready to judge them" (p. 379). The trouble with this is that, while within a few days Jesus would have risen from the dead and thus have entered into his glory, neither Caiaphas nor any of his other hearers would at that time see Jesus in glory and *coming on the clouds of heaven.* To insist that the expression must be taken to mean "from now" overlooks the fact that neither the friends of Jesus nor his enemies could see the change of which he speaks beginning "now." While seeing the roots of the change in what was to happen immediately, it appears that the complete fulfilment of what Jesus is saying belongs to the future.

---

112. On πλήν BAGD remarks, *"only, nevertheless, however, but* (πλήν is the real colloq. word for this idea . . .)" (1b). Moulton regards the word as significant. He inquires whether σὺ εἶπας may be understood in the sense "That is right," and says that πλήν here "is not satisfied by making the phrase a mere equivalent of 'Yes' " — it means *"You* say it" (M, I, p. 86). Turner agrees with this (*Grammatical Insights,* pp. 72-73). D. R. Catchpole, however, argues strongly that the expression is "affirmative in content, and reluctant or circumlocutory in formulation" (*NTS,* XVII [1970-71], pp. 213-26; the words quoted are the final words). Bruce held that πλήν means "nay more: I have something more startling to tell you." Tasker thinks that the words "suggested that He and Caiaphas would understand the terms contained in the question very differently" (p. 254). Cf. the use of the same expression to Pilate (27:11).

113. ἀπ' ἄρτι means "from now on" (BAGD, ἄρτι, 3).

With *the Son of man* Jesus uses his favorite name for himself with reference to his mission on earth.[114] He says that he will be *sitting at the right hand of The Power*, that is, in the place of highest honor in the court of God. God is often said to be powerful, but it is not often that he is called simply *The Power*, as here (and in the equivalent in Mark). This was the kind of reverent periphrasis that was often used in order to avoid pronouncing the divine name, and it would thus be readily recognized by his hearers as meaning God. Jesus is clearly claiming a relationship to God such as is shared by no other. He adds, *"coming on the clouds of heaven,"* in which he looks forward to the consummation of the age and the place he will have in that great day. These last words were very important for Caiaphas. It was not blasphemy for anyone to claim to be the Messiah (it might be mistaken, but it was not blasphemous), and there was a sense in which a man might be called a son of God (cf. 2 Sam. 7:14; 1 Chron. 22:10). But what Jesus had now said went far beyond that.

65. In fact this gave Caiaphas all he needed. These words represented a far-reaching claim; the ordinary first-century Jew would not concede anything remotely resembling what Jesus had just said. He had affirmed a kinship with God closer by far than any human could possibly claim in the judgment of Caiaphas and his helpers. So at these words *the high priest tore his robes*, an act that signified horror at what he had just heard and vigorous repudiation of the man and his words (was it because words were regarded as blasphemy that clothes were torn in 2 Kings 18:37? cf. Acts 14:14). A high priest must not normally tear his clothes, not even in mourning for the dead (Lev. 21:10-11); it was an action reserved for extreme cases, and, of course, blasphemy was such an extreme case. Caiaphas went on to say, *"He has blasphemed"* (only Matthew records this verdict). According to the Jewish law recorded in the Mishnah this was incorrect — blasphemy involved the use of the sacred name of God, the name we transliterate as Yahweh. The Mishnah is explicit on this: " 'The blasphemer' is not culpable unless he pronounces the Name itself" (*Sanh.* 7:5).[115] Jesus had not used that name; thus according to the Jewish law what he had said might be inadvisable, but it was not blasphemy. But we have seen that this tribunal was looking not for justice but for a guilty verdict; so what Jesus had said sufficed them. Caiaphas led them in viewing the words as blasphemy, and he went on to ask what more was needed. There was now no necessity for calling witnesses: *"you have now heard the blasphemy."*

114. Meier reminds us that at Caesarea Philippi the titles "Messiah" and "Son of God" had been applied to Jesus and that "Jesus, while not rejecting those titles, emphasizes that they need to be completed by another title, Son of Man. With Peter, the title is meant to supply the missing element of the cross. With the high priest, who is quite sure Jesus will die, the title supplies the missing element of exaltation out of death, cosmic rule, and coming as final judge."

115. When sentence is to be given on such a sinner the chief witness was called on to say expressly what he heard, "and he says it; and the judges stand up on their feet and rend their garments, and they may not mend them again" (*Sanh.* 7:5).

66. After that, sentencing became a formality. *"What do you think?"* asked the high priest; in other words, "What is your verdict?" He was met by a chorus, *"He is worthy[116] of death."* Once blasphemy was established there was no question about the sentence: "He who blasphemes the name of the LORD shall be put to death" (Lev. 24:16). The law was quite clear, and the Sanhedrin had no hesitation.

67-68. Some very unedifying scenes followed. In the context it seems that the words that follow refer to members of the Sanhedrin; in Luke 22:63 it seems that the guards are meant, but Matthew here implies that some at least of the members of the Sanhedrin joined in. It is possible to make out some form of defense of the conduct of the assembly up to this point. They had been led by the high priest, they had heard Jesus say things that doubtless shocked them, and when Caiaphas said that this was blasphemy they were not disposed to argue. They gave sentence as it was written in Scripture. But from our perspective there was no excuse for their spitting in Jesus' face (cf. Isa. 50:5-6) and hitting him.[117] No matter how serious the crime, no matter how guilty the prisoner, it seems to us that there could be no justification for the judges behaving in this manner. The slaps followed by a call to Jesus to prophesy may mean that they challenge Jesus to name them, or the meaning may be as in Luke, who tells us that they blindfolded Jesus, then hit him and demanded that he, as a prophet, should say who it was who struck the blow (Luke 22:63-64). But there may be more to it than we see. Perhaps, as Patte thinks (p. 374), we should see in these actions the denial of Jesus' claims: the spitting on him refutes the claim that he has authority, the blows show that he has no power, and the failure to prophesy as to who hit him is for them clear proof that he has no gift of prophecy about what will happen in the future. Derrett goes further; he maintains that something like this was necessary: "had the elders not struck Jesus or at least spat on him (we are told they did both), they could not have cleared themselves from the implications of condoning his (apparently) outrageous behaviour, which every pious Jew must abhor" (*Law,* p. 408). It is, of course, possible that Matthew has left the Sanhedrin and is referring to the conduct of the servants. But if so, it is somewhat curious that he has given no explicit indication. On the whole it appears that we should understand this scandalous behavior to be a vigorous repudiation of Jesus and all he stood for.

4. Jesus Denied by Peter, 26:69-75

> [69]*Now Peter was sitting outside in the courtyard; and a slave girl came up to him and said, "You, too, were with Jesus the Galilean."* [70]*But he*

---

116. The word is ἔνοχος; BAGD explains it as "= ἐνοχόμενος *caught in.*" They go on to give the meaning as "subject to" (Heb. 2:15), but "mostly as a legal term, *liable, answerable, guilty.*" Here it is used "to denote the punishment . . . *deserving of death.*"

117. κολαφίζω strictly means "strike with the fist" (κόλαφος = "knuckle," i.e., closed fist); ῥαπίζω is rather "to slap."

denied it, saying before them all, "I don't know what you are saying." 71And another girl saw him when he had gone out into the gateway, and she says to those who were there, "This man was with Jesus the Nazarene." 72And again he denied with an oath, "I do not know the man." 73And after a little time those who were standing around came and said to Peter, "Certainly you also are one of them, for your speech makes it clear." 74Then he began to curse and to swear, saying, "I do not know the man." And immediately a rooster crowed. 75And Peter remembered the saying of Jesus, who had said, "Before a rooster crows, you will deny me three times." And he went outside and wept bitterly.

The mockers have denied that Jesus can prophesy. Immediately after their words Matthew records the fulfilment of Jesus' prophecy that Peter would deny him three times before cockcrow. That Peter denied Jesus three times is told us in all four Gospels, but there are quite a number of differences in the accounts. Thus John puts quite an interval between the first and second denials (John 18:17, 25), and Luke says that about an hour elapsed between the second and third (Luke 22:59), while the others mention nothing of either interval. But a little reflection enables us to say that there is no likelihood that the three denials went off in close succession. Matthew and Mark recount them together, but there is nothing unlikely in seeing them spread out over quite an interval of time, nothing unlikely either in the Synoptists telling of all the denials in one paragraph. All three agree that the first person to challenge Peter was a slave girl, but after that there are differences. But we should not think that on each occasion everyone was silent but one speaker. There was a group of servants gossiping around a fire, and nothing is more likely than that when one made an accusation against Peter others took it up. The main thing is the impressive agreement that three times the leading man in the apostolic group said that he did not know Jesus.

Why did Peter deny Jesus? He may have been in some danger, but there is little to indicate this. When the enemies came to Gethsemane, they arrested Jesus but they did nothing more; no action against the apostles is recorded. Even when Peter cut off the ear of one of them, there seems to have been no retaliation. All the hostility of which we read was directed against Jesus, not against those who followed him. But with Jesus in the hands of people who were clearly determined to have him executed, evidently Peter thought this was no time for taking risks. He made sure of his safety by denying any connection with Jesus.

It is remarkable and significant that the story of the denials should have been recorded at all. When the Gospels were written, Peter was regarded as the leading apostle, the chief man in the church. It would have been very natural to pass over in silence this man's fall from grace. But all four of our Gospels recount it. They do not do this by way of demoting Peter, for in due course he repented, was reinstated, and continued in a

687

position of leadership. But the church knew that its leader was a fallible sinner like all others and that he had had a dreadful fall. The church knew, too, that he had repented and by the grace of God had gone on to greater and better things. Moreover, there cannot have been others of Jesus' followers in the group in the courtyard. It would seem that Peter himself is the origin of the story. He knew how badly he had fallen, and he confessed it before the church.

69. Matthew has already told us that Peter had followed Jesus and was in the courtyard of the high priest's house (v. 58). Now he returns to the leading man among the Twelve. He tells us that as Peter was sitting there,[118] *a slave girl* accosted him. Notice that this challenge was as gentle as could be imagined. It was not a man but a woman, not a mature woman but a girl, not a free woman but a slave. Perhaps it was the very gentleness of it all that led Peter astray in the first instance. We must bear in mind that Matthew's account is abbreviated, and, for example, he does not tell us as Mark does that Peter was warming himself, or as Luke does that the slave girl looked at him attentively, or as John does that she was the doorkeeper. Throughout the denials Matthew sticks to the main facts; we find many details only in the other Gospels. The slave girl said, *"You, too* [in addition to whom?][119] *were with Jesus the Galilean."* She made no accusation of rebellion, blasphemy, or the like; she simply said that he was with Jesus.

70. But Peter was not going to be known as belonging to Jesus, not in that group of hostile Jerusalemites and in the very courtyard of the leader of Jesus' enemies. *He denied it* and did so publicly, *before them all.* But on this first occasion he did not deal with what the girl actually said; he contented himself with *"I don't know what you are saying."* Her words seem clear enough, but Peter prefers to find it a mystery why she should say such a thing. He takes refuge in an evasion rather than in an outright denial of what she had said, and this is psychologically plausible. But what is clear is that he refused to identify himself with Jesus, and that was effectively a denial.

71. But evidently the encounter made Peter feel uncomfortable; therefore he left the warmth of the fire and removed himself to *the gateway.* This was clearly the main entrance, and it would have been an elaborate affair (*NRSV* has "the porch"); certainly it was an area where people might still gather and where Peter would still be able to pick up the gossip as he tried to find out what was happening to Jesus. But again he struck trouble, and again it came from a slave girl (Mark seems to imply that it was the same girl, but Matthew says it was *another*). This one did not speak to

118. The clauses are connected with an adversative δέ; Peter's faithlessness is contrasted with Jesus' faithfulness.
119. Gundry thinks that the meaning might be "Even you," or " 'You as well as those who fled,' or 'You as well as the disciple who influenced the maid to let Peter in the door' (John 18:15-16)" (p. 548). Or, of course, it might mean "You as well as Judas."

Peter, but to the other people there. *"This man,"* she said (and the expression may be contemptuous, "This fellow"), *"was with Jesus the Nazarene."*[120] Again there is no accusation of any crime; it is just that he was an associate of Jesus.

72. Peter's denial this time is more emphatic. He denied *with an oath;* clearly he felt that something more than his bare word was needed. And he went further in his statement, *"I do not know the man."* Now he says not only that he does not know what the girl is talking about, but that he does not know Jesus. Embarked on this course of denial he is led further into evil; the first denial involved a lie, the second time Peter perjured himself. The first was no more than a declaration that he did not know what the girl was talking about; the second was a clear repudiation of Jesus.

73. *A little time* later (Luke says that it was about an hour, Luke 22:59) some bystanders renewed the charge. They *came*[121] and spoke to Peter. They speak confidently with their *"Certainly,"* their *"you also,"*[122] and their reference to Peter's accent. We do not know in what way Peter's speech differed from that of the Jerusalemites, but there is no reason for doubting that there were Galilean characteristics that this apostle shared.[123] That he spoke with such an accent did not, of course, prove that he was a follower of Jesus, for there were many Galileans who opposed him. But people like these bystanders have never been noted for their logic, and it was enough for them that Peter's speech differed from their own. That, they thought, made it *clear*[124] that he was a supporter of Jesus.

74. Peter may have become a little rattled at this third accusation, or it may have been the kind of men who made it together with their seriousness that bothered him. For whatever reason, his reaction is much more vigorous than in the face of the previous two. This time *he began to curse and swear,*[125] evidently trusting that vigorous and earthy language might persuade his hearers that he had nothing to do with Jesus, Galilean though he might be. His statement, *"I do not know the man,"* is as thorough a repudiation as could be conceived; not only does he not follow Jesus, he is saying, but he has no knowledge of him whatever. It is a comprehensive repudiation of the prisoner being unjustly condemned and rudely mocked.

120. She actually says, τοῦ Ναζωραίου. There are problems with this designation (see the note on 2:23), but there is no doubt that in the New Testament it signifies "from Nazareth."

121. The verb is προσέρχομαι, "to approach," "come to"; it points to a definite approach to Peter.

122. ἀληθῶς, "truly," "surely" (AS). καὶ σύ puts emphasis on *you.*

123. The Judeans were contemptuous of the way Galileans spoke. There are many examples given in 'Erub. 53a, 53b; for example, from the way one Galilean spoke the Judeans could not be certain whether he meant "wool," "a lamb," "an ass," or "wine" (53b).

124. δῆλος signifies "visible," and then "clear to the mind." AS differentiates it from φανερός as referring not to the outward appearance, but "with ref. to inner perception, *evident,* known, understood."

125. His first verb is καταθεματίζω (connected with ἀνάθεμα), his second ὀμνύω, "affirm on oath." The probability is that Peter was calling on God to punish him if what he said was not true.

And *immediately a rooster crowed.* Jesus' prediction was fulfilled to the letter.

75. Matthew does not have Luke's statement that Jesus looked at Peter at this moment (Luke 22:61), but he makes it clear that the crowing of the rooster brought home to Peter the fact that what Jesus prophesied had indeed taken place. He had been so confident that he would never deny his Lord, and now he had done so three times. Matthew joins Luke in saying that Peter *went outside* (the courtyard was no longer a place for the heart-broken apostle) *and wept bitterly.*[126] But we should understand Peter's tears as an expression of grief and repentance; by the following Sunday he was back with the followers of Jesus. It was his loyalty to Jesus, not his temporary repudiation of his leader, that showed the real Peter.[127]

---

126. κλαίω means "to wail" and is used "of any loud expression of pain or sorrow" (AS).

127. Plummer records a comment of Isaac Williams: "It is a matter worthy of the deepest consideration, that not only is so very little told us of the Saints of God, but what is recorded is for the most part to their prejudice . . . we may humbly venture to think that this melancholy failure in one so eminent and favoured was permitted to occur to afford us encouragement and hope in similar derelictions and temptations. And that as our Lord could not afford us an instance of human infirmity in Himself, He has given it to us in the person of the most exalted of His pastors: that all may fear, and none may presume, and all may hope" (pp. 383-84).

Matthew 27

5. Jesus Handed Over to the Romans, 27:1-2

1When it was early morning all the chief priests and the elders of the people took counsel against Jesus so as to put him to death. 2And they bound him, and led him away, and handed him over to Pilate the governor.

As we saw earlier, it was the Romans who had the power to put people to death. Since the Jewish leaders wanted to have Jesus executed, they had to bring him to the Roman authorities and persuade them to carry out the execution. They had reached the limits of what was possible within their own jurisdiction, and the story now moves to what they could persuade the Romans to do.

1. The Jewish leaders acted in *early morning*. As the Roman officials tended to do their business in the early part of the day, it was necessary to move promptly. Moreover, *early morning* means daylight hours; it was required in Jewish trials that the sentence be given in the daytime, not at night. It was also required that the verdict not be given until the second day the accused was before the judges, but time was pressing and apparently nobody raised this objection. Even if there was not the time to comply with all the regulations, at least it was something that the assembly convened again during the daytime and thus gave a semblance of legality to what was being done. *All the chief priests* indicates a full assembly of ecclesiastical dignitaries,[1] while *the elders of the people* points to the eminent laypeople who formed part of the highest Jewish assembly in the land. Matthew is talking about an official meeting of the Sanhedrin. That they *took counsel*[2] may mean that they discussed the accusation made against Jesus, but if so, that they took counsel *against* him shows that they had no intention of coming to an unbiased conclusion; they "met together to plan

---

1. J. Jeremias gives a list of the "chief priests" (*Jerusalem in the Time of Jesus* [London, 1969], p. 160).

2. συμβούλιον is a rare word, but MM is able to cite it from the papyri. Deissmann cites Mommsen, "It appears that the word συμβούλιον is, properly speaking, not Greek, but is formed in the Graeco-Latin official style, in order to represent the untranslatable *consilium*" (*BS*, p. 238). It can mean "council" or "counsel"; the expression may thus mean "held a council" or "took counsel."

the death of Jesus" *(REB)*. Alternatively the expression may mean that they "met in full council" (Rieu). However we translate, Matthew is telling us that the Sanhedrin gathered in the morning to ratify the decision made during the night (the basic discussion was the one that took place during the previous night); they met to frame the accusation they would bring to the governor. Their discussion was *so as*[3] *to put him to death*. Matthew conveys the meaning that the assembly had no intention of reaching any other verdict. Rieu translates, "the Chief Priests and Elders of the people met in full council to decide on measures against Jesus that would ensure his execution"; while this goes beyond the Greek at some points, it does give the sense of it all.

2. It is not clear why they *bound* Jesus,[4] for he had not tried to escape or to put up resistance. It may have been standard procedure (John tells us that they bound Jesus at the time of his arrest [John 18:12], and either that he was still bound or bound again when he was sent from Annas to Caiaphas [John 18:24]). They *handed him over,*[5] which appears to mean that from this point he was in the custody of the Romans; now everything depended on what the Roman authorities decided. We should notice a literal fulfilment of Jesus' prophecy (20:18-19) that he would be "handed over" to the chief priests and scribes and that they would "hand him over" to the Gentiles. The Roman governor at this time was *Pilate;* he held the position for about ten years, which was longer than the normal term for a governor. From this Sherwin-White concludes that Tiberius must have been satisfied with the way he managed affairs.[6] An inscription from Caesarea shows that his title was "prefect." Prefects were army officers "'placed in charge' *(praefecit)* of difficult or isolated districts."[7] Such a governor was often a military man (as Pilate was), and his primary responsibility was that of maintaining order; he "supervised rather than managed the government as an executive" (Sherwin-White). We see something of this in the trial of Jesus, where the prosecution was not initiated by Roman officials, but by Jewish leaders (the Romans would have called

3. The conjunction ὥστε mostly signifies result, "so that," but it may be that here it indicates intended result or purpose (so BAGD, 2b). Burton regards ὥστε with the infinitive as standing "in definite apposition with συμβούλιον, defining the content of the plan, rather than expressing the purpose of making it" (371). If we bear in mind the usual significance of the word, Matthew will mean that putting Jesus to death was the result of the deliberations. But here it seems that the many scholars who favor purpose as the meaning are right.

4. *GNB* has "put him in chains," but there is no reference to chains; we do not know with what he was bound.

5. The verb is παραδίδωμι, which can mean "betray" and which Matthew has used so freely of Judas's betraying of Jesus. Is he hinting now that the Jewish leaders were betraying Jesus by giving him into the custody of the Romans?

6. See *ISBE,* III, p. 868.

7. Sherwin-White in *ISBE,* III, p. 979. He also points out that the term "procurator" (= "agent") was used of people the emperor appointed to be his agents in the provinces and that this title was later given to governors such as Pilate. It is often used anachronistically of this man.

them *delatores*). They argued the case before Pilate, though, of course, it was he who made the final decision.

Pilate had his limitations as a governor. Josephus records an occasion when this man sent troops to Jerusalem with standards displaying images of the emperor (earlier governors had respected Jewish scruples and refrained from bringing images into the holy city). The Jews protested strongly. At first Pilate refused to withdraw them, though he later gave way (*Ant.* 18.55-59). He also ran into trouble when he constructed an aqueduct to bring water to Jerusalem but paid for it out of temple funds. There was a strong protest against the use of temple funds for such a project, and Jews were killed in the protest (*Ant.* 18.60-62). Such incidents indicate that Pilate was apt to act somewhat hastily, though he tried not to antagonize the Jews unduly and he could be constrained to change his mind. It was before this man that Jesus was now brought for trial.[8]

6. The Death of Judas, 27:3-10

> [3]Then when Judas, who betrayed him, saw that he was condemned, he was filled with remorse and brought the thirty silver pieces back to the chief priests and elders, [4]saying, "I sinned; I betrayed innocent blood." But they said, "What is that to us? See to it yourself." [5]And he hurled the money into the temple and departed; he went away and hung himself. [6]But the chief priests took up the money and said, "It is not lawful to put it into the temple treasury, since it is blood money." [7]So they took counsel and bought with it the potter's field for a burial place for foreigners. [8]Therefore that field was called "Field of Blood" to this day. [9]Then was fulfilled that which was spoken through Jeremiah the prophet, saying, "And they took the thirty silver pieces, the price of him who was priced, whom some of the sons of Israel priced. [10]And they gave them for the potter's field as the Lord directed me."

Before moving on to the treatment of Jesus at the hands of the Romans Matthew finishes the story of Judas. He tells of that man's remorse and suicide and of the curious mental processes of the hierarchy who had not scrupled to use the money at their disposal to procure the arrest of Jesus so that he could be killed, but who did scruple to put this same money back into the temple treasury. Characteristically Matthew sees a fulfilment of prophecy in their ultimate use of the funds. The incident is found in this Gospel and in Acts 1 only. Stendahl thinks that Matthew's

---

8. "It is remarkable that the Gospels, while not hiding the weakness and injustice of Pilate, do not give such a black impression of his character as we derive from Josephus and Philo. There does not seem to have been any inclination in the first Christians to exaggerate the misdeeds of either Judas or Pilate. They are not represented as monsters of wickedness any more than the Apostles are depicted as models of saintliness and wisdom" (Plummer, p. 385).

placing of the death of Judas at this point "indicates that he understands
the decision of the Sanhedrin as the crucial one" (in v. 3 Jesus is already
spoken of as "condemned").

3. It was now apparent that Jesus was not going to put forth any of
his powers to deliver himself from his enemies. He had been condemned
by the Jews and handed over to the Romans, and he had not tried to
prevent any of this. So it was quite clear that what Judas had done had
led inexorably to the condemnation of Jesus. Matthew has his characteristic *Then* (see on 2:7), which this time does seem to denote sequence. It was
after Judas had seen that Jesus *was condemned* that the rest followed. The
condemnation by the Jews was not final, for only the Romans could put
Jesus to death, but once the Jews had agreed on their course of action it
was apparent that his execution would follow in due course. Once again
Judas is characterized as *who betrayed him;* we have seen that he used this
verb 10 times in the previous chapter, and he will use it twice more in this
chapter of Judas (and 3 times of other ways of delivering Jesus up; all told
Matthew uses the verb 31 times).

Judas *was filled with remorse*[9] as he now realized what his conduct
had led to. If he had been motivated by a desire to precipitate action that
would lead to Jewish independence, he now saw that nothing of the sort
was going to happen. If, as we have seen, he had simply tried to get what
he could out of it all, then he now saw that the damage he had done was
out of all proportion to the small gain he had made. Interestingly, the result
of his remorse was a return to the Jewish leaders,[10] bringing with him the
thirty silver pieces they had paid him for the betrayal. They, of course, were
religious leaders as well as politicians, and it may be that in his spiritual
anguish Judas was looking for guidance and help. If so, he was to be
bitterly disappointed, for these men were not particularly interested in
helping people like Judas. Their minds were set on getting Jesus executed,
and that was not yet accomplished.

4. Judas's confession, *"I sinned,"* shows that he had come to appreciate
something of the enormity of the evil thing he had done.[11] He spells it out
with, *"I betrayed innocent blood."* Most translations read, "I have sinned,"
but Judas's use of the aorist tense rather concentrates attention on the one
great act of sin rather than on the man's general sinfulness (Moffatt renders,
"I did wrong"). The enormity of his betrayal of Jesus had come home to his

---

9. The verb is μεταμέλομαι, which is often difficult to distinguish from μετανοέω, but
O. Michel comments, "μετανοεῖν implies that one has later arrived at a different view of
something (νοῦς), μεταμέλεσθαι that one has a different feeling about it (μέλει)" (*TDNT,* IV,
p. 626). Whether or not we can distinguish between the two verbs, the context here makes
it clear that Judas was motivated by remorse rather than by genuine repentance.

10. The linking of ἀρχιερεῦσιν καὶ πρεσβυτέροις under a single article points to the
Sanhedrin, the two groups forming one assembly.

11. "The element of past time is absent from the aorist participle especially if its action
is identical with that of an aorist finite verb" (BDF, 339[1]; here "in that I").

conscience, and it is this that he is now confessing.[12] But those who had paid the bribe to get Jesus into their hands were the wrong people to bring spiritual comfort to this remorseful sinner. They disclaim responsibility. *"What is that to us?"* they ask. It is a question to which they might well have given attention, for it was a very great deal to their discredit that they had paid money for the arrest of a man who was innocent and whom they were in the process of handing over to the Romans for execution. Their *you* is emphatic; they are saying that Judas's conscience is a problem for him alone. People like the Jewish leaders had much more important things to bother about than that. To their eternal discredit these spiritual leaders of the people thought of Judas as a tool that had served its purpose and could be discarded, not as a man in desperate spiritual need.

5. So Judas *hurled the money into the temple*, or perhaps we should translate, "threw the coins down in the temple" (cf. *NRSV*).[13] We do not know exactly where Judas was when this conversation took place; if he was in the temple, then *NRSV* could give the sense of it. Rieu points to a pious act with "Whereupon Judas left the money as an offering in the Temple," but this seems very unlikely. The language seems to point to an irrational act of throwing the coins with some force into some holy place nearby, but not where Judas was at the point of his act.[14] There is nothing to indicate an exercise in piety, only a reckless desire to repudiate his evil act. Then he went off and committed suicide by hanging.[15] It is this, rather than the linguistics in verse 3, that makes it clear that Judas was remorseful rather than repentant. We might contrast him with Peter. That apostle had likewise sinned grievously, but he was moved by genuine repentance that led to amendment of life rather than to the further sin of suicide.

6. The hurling of the money into the temple presented the ecclesiastics with a problem. They gathered up the coins but immediately realized that they could not put them into the *temple treasury*.[16] Judas's words had

12. "Not, I have blundered, or have been mistaken, or foolish, or wrong; not I have attempted to hurry this Messiah to declare Himself, but, 'I have sinned' " (Morgan, p. 310).

13. εἰς should be read with א B L Θ etc., though ἐν is found in A C W etc. If the term is used with precision, ναόν denotes the sanctuary proper (while ἱερόν includes all the temple precincts). It may be that Judas threw the money down somewhere in the temple area, but ναόν makes it appear that he threw the money into the holy place, perhaps even that he ran there and threw it down.

14. This would be supported by the use of εἰς rather than ἐν.

15. Moulton sees ἀπήγξατο here as the clearest example of the reflexive middle in the New Testament, but adds, "even here one may question whether the English intransitive *choke* is not a truer parallel than the reflexive *hang oneself*" (M, I, p. 155). For the problems in relating this account to that in Acts 1:18-19 see the discussion in Carson, pp. 561-62. M. Green can say, "It is not very difficult to reconcile those two accounts. Judas went and hanged himself: then either his corpse rotted and fell, or the rope broke and he fell and his insides were ruptured and gushed out. Either Judas had already acquired this field previously, or the priests bought the field in Judas' name with the money which was still legally his and which they could not receive back into the treasury because it was blood money" (p. 267).

16. The word is κορβανᾶς, found here only in the New Testament (the cognate word for a gift is found in Mark 7:11). Josephus uses it for the temple treasury in *War* 2.175.

made it clear that this was the money they had paid to get him to betray Jesus and not some other money that he had come by in some lawful and honest fashion. They regard it as *not lawful* and explain that these coins are *blood money*. Since they were the price paid to secure a death (and they must have known that the death in question was the death of an innocent man), it was not right that it should be put into a treasury dedicated to holy uses. It is not without its interest that apparently they had not scrupled to take the money out of the temple treasury to bring about Jesus' death, but they now had tender consciences about putting it back! To them it was no crime to use it to bring about a death, but it was a crime to put it into their treasury when it had been used for the purpose for which they expended it.[17]

7. *So they took counsel* (the same noun and verb as used in v. 1 for their plan to put Jesus to death). The result of their deliberations was that the money was used to buy some land that they call *the potter's field* and that was thenceforth to be used as a cemetery for foreigners, perhaps people who were not numbered among the people of God and who made no attempt to live according to the law, more probably Jews from other lands who died while in Judea.[18] We have no way of knowing which field was *the potter's field* or why it was given this name, apart, of course, from the obvious connection of some kind with a particular potter.

8. Matthew says that it was on account of this *(Therefore)* that the field was given the name *"Field of Blood."* The land was purchased with money that had come from the price paid to have Jesus delivered up to death, and it was hurled into the temple by a man who proceeded to go and hang himself. Since it was clearly associated with violent death, the name is not surprising. And Matthew indicates that the name stuck; that was what the field was called *to this day*.

9-10. Characteristically Matthew sees a fulfilment of prophecy in these happenings. But he presents his readers with a problem in that he says the words were *spoken through Jeremiah the prophet* when in fact they appear to be a rather free citation of Zechariah 11:13 with the addition of some words that seem to have been derived from Jeremiah (see Jer. 18:2-3; 19:1-13; 32:6-15; this prophet speaks about potters and about buying a field). The explanation may be that Matthew was making a composite quotation and considered the parts that came from Jeremiah significant enough for him to cite that prophet as his authority. He is including words from Zechariah, but he is pointing his readers to Jeremiah. Another view

---

17. Calvin comments, "If blood money may not be deposited in the sacred treasury, how could they draw it in the first place, for their only wealth came from the temple offerings and what they are now hesitant to put back in as polluted could have been taken from no other source? Is not the pollution from their own hands?" (III, p. 176).

18. There is rabbinic authority for the use of ill-gotten gains for public benefit; for example, money that has been stolen and that cannot be returned because the owners are not known may be used for wells and the like (*B. Qam.* 94b).

starts from the fact that Jeremiah came first in rabbinical lists of prophets and, as Lightfoot puts it, "When . . . Matthew produceth a text of Zechariah under the name of *Jeremy,* he only cites the words of the volume of the prophets under his name who stood first in the volume of the prophets" (p. 363; he cites Luke 24:44 as another example of this sort of thing, for there "Psalms," the first book in the third division of the Hebrew Scriptures, is used to include all that follows).[19] It is also possible that Matthew was using a book of Testimonies, a collection of proof texts from the Old Testament.[20] While many scholars agree that such books existed, it is not certain how they were cited. In our present state of knowledge there is nothing improbable in thinking that such a collection may well have been headed by some words from Jeremiah and thus be cited by his name, even though it contained words from other prophets as well (Robinson thinks that the quotation is probably from "a book of 'Testimonies' "). But for our present purpose the important thing is not the precise source from which Matthew derived the words, but the fact that for this Evangelist God was causing prophecy to be fulfilled even in such a detail as the disposal of the money the Jewish leaders paid Judas to betray his Master.

The passage in Zechariah is itself difficult. The Hebrew text signifies "Throw it to the potter" *(NIV),* but many translators think that the Hebrew is defective at this point and prefer the reading in the Syriac, "Throw it into the treasury" *(NRSV).* In either case there is some irony about the "thirty shekels," which is described as "this lordly price at which I was valued by them" *(NRSV).* Whichever reading we accept and however we understand the message of Zechariah to his readers, Matthew is saying that the use of the money paid to Judas took place in accordance with the words of the prophecy; the purpose of God was not overthrown in the deeds that Zechariah was recording, and it was not overthrown in the actions of Judas and the Sanhedrin that disposed of his bribe money. "In Zechariah the payment of thirty pieces of silver was made in order to get

19. E. F. Sutcliffe draws attention to a number of lists of the prophets in which Jeremiah comes first, and argues that Matthew's meaning is "in the prophets" *(JTS,* n.s. III [1952], pp. 227-28).

20. Albright and Mann draw attention to collections of this kind at Qumran and to the possibility that such collections existed among the Christians *(AB,* p. XXXVII). Similarly Filson remarks, "it is possible that some Christian listed in a very early document the passages which Christian teachers saw fulfilled in the work of Jesus." He goes on, however: "But this cannot be proved. . . . The solid truth in the theory is that the earliest Church made constant use of the O.T. and used it to show that the coming and work of Jesus fulfilled prophecy" (p. 8). Gundry examines the hypothesis *(Use of the OT,* pp. 163-66) and concludes that "the Testimony Book is a partially confirmed hypothesis which disappointingly explains little or nothing." But he does not examine its bearing on the question we are discussing here. G. D. Kilpatrick finds an indication of a testimony book in the use of Zechariah 9:9 independently in Matthew and John for the entry into Jerusalem, though he doubts whether these Evangelists had more than the Greek Bible itself *(The Origins of the Gospel according to St. Matthew* [Oxford, 1946], p. 66).

rid of Israel's Shepherd. That same price was paid to get rid of Jesus who is Israel's Shepherd. At such a miserable price the Jews valued Jesus and gladly paid it to get rid of him" (Lenski, p. 1083). The prophecy cited ends with the words, *"as[21] the Lord directed me."* These are important for Matthew. He is recording the fulfilment of the Lord's purposes.

7. Jesus before Pilate, 27:11-26

> [11]And Jesus stood before the governor; and the governor questioned him, saying, "Are you the King of the Jews?" But Jesus said, "You are saying it." [12]And when he was accused by the high priests and elders, he answered nothing. [13]Then Pilate says to him, "Do you not hear how many things they testify against you?" [14]And he did not answer him, not even a single word, so that the governor was greatly astonished.
>
> [15]Now at festival time the governor was accustomed to release to the crowd one prisoner whom they wanted. [16]They had then a notable prisoner named Barabbas. [17]When therefore the crowd had gathered, Pilate said to them, "Whom do you want me to release to you: Barabbas, or Jesus who is called Messiah?" [18]For he knew that they had handed him over out of envy. [19]But as he was seated on the judgment seat, his wife sent to him, saying, "Have nothing to do with that righteous man; for I have suffered many things in a dream today on account of him. [20]But the chief priests and the elders persuaded the crowds that they should ask for Barabbas and destroy Jesus. [21]And the governor answered them, saying, "Which of the two do you want me to release to you?" And they said, "Barabbas." [22]Pilate says to them, "What therefore will I do with Jesus who is called Messiah?" They all say, "Let him be crucified." [23]But he said, "What evil did he do?" But they shouted all the more, "Let him be crucified." [24]But when Pilate saw that he was getting nowhere, but that rather a tumult was starting, he took water and washed his hands before the crowd, saying, "I am innocent of the blood of this man; you see to it." [25]And all the people answered, saying, "His blood on us and on our children." [26]Then he released Barabbas to them, but Jesus he scourged and handed over to be crucified.

Matthew proceeds to what happened when Jesus came before Pilate, the governor and the man who could determine whether Jesus was executed or not. He makes it clear that there was little in the way of a formal trial and concentrates on the fact that Pilate does not seem to have thought Jesus guilty of any crime, but that there was unrelenting pressure from the Jewish leaders to bring about his crucifixion. He mentions Pilate's attempt to get Jesus freed by utilizing the custom of releasing a prisoner at Passover and the failure of this ploy. He tells of the dream of Pilate's wife and of Pilate's washing his hands of the whole affair as in the end

---

21. καθά, here only in the New Testament, means "according to what things."

he did what the Jewish leaders wanted. There was not much in the way of a formal trial, but then, that was not strictly necessary. A Roman governor in a province had considerable latitude and was able to pursue justice in almost any way he thought suitable. He would take into consideration all the facts of the situation and act as he saw fit.

We should bear in mind that Pilate was in a difficult situation. He was answerable to the Emperor Tiberius, a man who would show no mercy to a governor who condoned treasonable activities; it was dangerous for him to take a soft line where treason was alleged. But on the other hand, Tiberius could take a strong line against a governor who treated his subjects badly.[22] Thus when Jesus came before him, he had to be on his guard against doing anything too harsh or too lenient.

11. After the interlude about Judas, Matthew returns to the narrative he had left at the end of verse 2, where Jesus was handed over to Pilate. Now Matthew says that Jesus *stood before the governor.*[23] Nothing is said about the formalities of a trial, and at this point Matthew does not mention any formal accusation; Luke, however, tells us that Jesus was accused of sedition (Luke 23:2). None of the Gospels gives a complete account of what happened when Jesus stood before Pilate, and John in particular gives more information about the discussion on kingship that took place between the governor and the prisoner (cf. John 18:33-38). But Pilate had been informed of the views of the Jewish authorities, and he began by asking, *"Are you the King of the Jews?"* Evidently this is the form in which the Jewish leaders expressed Jesus' claim to messiahship or, perhaps better, the way in which they led Pilate to understand it (cf. 2:2; Jews would say "King of Israel," as in v. 42). Pilate's question is identical in all four Gospels: in all four it is the first thing he said when confronted with Jesus, and in all four *you* is emphatic. Clearly one sight of Jesus was enough to tell this experienced governor that this was no terrorist, no leader of a revolt aimed at overthrowing the Romans. Pilate would also have known that Jesus had no high position, no wealth, no soldiers, a preposterous position for anyone claiming to be a king. Except that he now used the present tense instead of the aorist Jesus made the same reply to this question as he had earlier done to Caiaphas's question as to whether he was the Messiah (26:64): *"You are saying it."* Either "Yes" or "No" would have been misleading. Had he said "Yes," Pilate would inevitably have understood that Jesus was claiming to be an earthly king and that he was

---

22. Indeed, in the end it was Pilate's heavy-handed putting down of a Samaritan disturbance that led to his recall to Rome; an imposter gathered people, saying that he would show them some sacred vessels that Moses had hidden. The gathering appears to have been harmless, but some of the people had weapons and Pilate killed a number of them. The Samaritans complained to the legate of Syria, Pilate's superior, who regarded the incident as so serious that he sent him to Rome to give account of himself to the emperor (Josephus, *Ant.* 18.85-89). This ended Pilate's governorship.

23. ἡγεμών is a general term for a leader and might be used of a governor who was a proconsul, propraetor, legate, or procurator. An inscription shows that Pilate was a prefect.

indeed the rebel the Jewish leaders claimed he was (*NIV*'s "Yes, it is as you say" is a trifle too definite). But to say "No" would negate the fact that he was indeed King, King in the kingdom of God. So his answer means that he was indeed a king, but not in the sense that Pilate used the term.[24]

Three times Jesus has used much the same words to say "You say so" — when Judas asked whether he was the betrayer (26:25), when Caiaphas asked whether he was the Christ (26:64), and now when Pilate asks whether he is King of the Jews. As Patte puts it, this means "that as Jesus does not need to reveal to Judas that he will betray him, so he does not need to reveal to the high priest that he is the Christ and to Pilate that he is the King of the Jews, because they already know it (or should know it)" (p. 378).

It seems clear that Matthew is following his customary practice of abbreviating the narrative. If all that happened was that Pilate asked whether Jesus was king of the Jews and received an affirmative answer, even a hesitant one, surely the trial would have been over and Pilate would have given a sentence that would have gotten rid of this "king." But John tells us of a discussion between Jesus and Pilate about the nature of kingship in which Jesus made it clear that he had no intention of fighting against the Romans.

12. Now we come to the accusation that we would expect. The Jewish leaders kept accusing him (the present infinitive points to a continuous process);[25] they could not, of course, hand a man over to the Romans without laying charges against him. Matthew does not bother to say what these charges were; he leaves his readers to reason from such facts as Jesus' admission that he was the Messiah (26:63-64) and Pilate's question whether he was a king. There is not much doubt about the nature of the Jewish accusations, and Matthew does not stay to spell them out. All the more so in that Jesus *answered*[26] nothing. In all the accounts of his trial he remained silent at some stage. Matthew lets us see that he was not in the slightest concerned about the matters the members of the Sanhedrin raised. The specific allegations did not matter; they were determined to have him executed, and to refute their accusations was irrelevant. If those charges were shown to be false, they would raise others. They were not

24. Turner sees the emphasis here as "*You* are saying this, not *me.*" He goes on, "For the meaning 'yes,' the personal pronoun *su* is pointless. In splendid isolation, the pronoun places full responsibility on the questioner ("you"), dissociating Jesus from the assumptions of the question, neither affirming nor denying" (*Grammatical Insights*, p. 73). It is also possible to take Jesus' words as a question to Pilate: "Do *you* say so?"

25. "The high priests and elders" is an expression that is covered by one article. This probably means that there are not two groups but one: it is the Sanhedrin that is making the accusations.

26. The verb is the middle ἀπεκρίνατο, which is striking because Matthew so constantly uses the passive form. E. A. Abbott argues that the middle here has the sense "make a formal defence" (*Johannine Grammar* [London, 1906], p. 392).

concerned with justice but with an execution. In the trial before the Sanhedrin Jesus was silent when a variety of allegations were made, but he spoke when the high priest put to him a question he was perfectly entitled to put by virtue of his office. Similarly, he responded to Pilate when the governor asked the question he was bound to ask because of his office.[27] But when Pilate drew attention to the accusations of these Jewish officials it was another matter; he did not reply to Pilate then.

13. Jesus' silence provoked an intervention from *Pilate*. He could probably not understand why any prisoner should make no attempt to refute accusations brought against him, especially when, as in this case, the prisoner would be executed if he was convicted. So he interjected a question of his own: *"Do you not hear how many[28] things they testify against you?"* Clearly the Jewish authorities were casting their net as widely as they could.

14. But just as Jesus did not answer the Jewish leaders, so he *did not answer* the Roman governor. Neither Pilate nor the Sanhedrin was interested in what Jesus had come to teach and to do, and Jesus was not concerned to waste time over the kind of accusation that was being brought against him. He did not answer, *not even a single word.*[29] None of it had any relevance to the truth of the situation, so why should Jesus concern himself with what they were saying? Prisoners on trial for their life normally must have been very vocal; they would have tried to refute any and every accusation brought against them. This kind of accusation, alleging crimes that involved the death sentence, would normally have elicited a vociferous defense. So Pilate *was greatly astonished.* This was clearly not going to be the sort of trial to which he was accustomed.

15. Now Matthew tells us that there was a custom that a prisoner be released *at festival time.*[30] The custom is not attested outside the Gospels, but there is nothing unlikely about it since in the ancient world prisoners were sometimes released as a gesture of goodwill. There is, moreover, a provision in the Mishnah that a Passover sacrifice might be offered "for one whom they have promised to bring out of prison" (*Pes.* 8:6), which

27. That Jesus answered Pilate was important. Sherwin-White makes it clear that when an accused person refused to defend himself he was regarded as guilty and sentence was passed against him (*Roman Law,* pp. 25-26).

28. πόσος can signify "how great" as well as "how many," and the expression may refer to the weight of the accusations rather than the number. Either way Pilate is pointing to the seriousness of Jesus' situation. But the likely meaning, *how many things,* makes it probable that the governor is concerned that many accusations are being made against the prisoner and no defense is being produced.

29. ῥῆμα means a "word" and then a "saying," but it comes to be used also for what is the subject of speech, "a thing"; thus here it might be understood in the sense, "a charge" (so *NIV*).

30. κατὰ δὲ ἑορτήν might mean "at every feast," but despite the absence of the article, we should probably understand it to mean "at this feast," that is, at Passover time, which John says was the case (John 18:39). John also says that Pilate said, "You have a custom," which makes it seem that it was a Jewish practice that the Romans were prepared to continue.

701

may well be an echo of the custom. Matthew tells us that the custom was to release, not a prisoner whom the governor selected, but one whom the crowd chose. There is no information about how the choice was normally made, but if what happened on this occasion is any guide, it was done by the crowd shouting for the man they wanted.

16. At that time[31] *they* (the term is not explained, but evidently it means the Romans) *had* a prisoner whom Matthew calls *notable*.[32] His name, according to most manuscripts, was *Barabbas*, but there is manuscript evidence for the name "Jesus Barabbas."[33] This presents us with an interesting textual problem. If the reading "Jesus Barabbas" was original, the reason for its absence in most MSS would be that reverence for the name of the Savior caused many scribes to shrink from including it as the name of a criminal. If it was not original, why did some MSS include it? If we are impressed by the consensus of the MSS we will omit it, but if we give the deciding vote to what the scribes were likely to have done we will include it (the word "Jesus" is included in *GNB, REB, NRSV,* and Rieu, but omitted in *RSV, NIV,* and *JB; JB* has a note that the reading "appears to have its origin in an apocryphal tradition"). Verse 20 is hard to reconcile with the reading "Jesus Barabbas" here. *Barabbas* is an Aramaic expression meaning "son of a father," so it is not unlikely that it was preceded by a name. Sometimes great rabbis were called "father," and it is possible that Barabbas was the son of such a scholar. But if that scholar's name was "Jesus," we may well ask why it has left no trace in the textual tradition of the other three Gospels. It is also relevant that so many MSS of this Gospel do not have the name, and it is not found in any of them in verses 20, 21, and 26.

17. The way Matthew puts it, *When therefore the crowd had gathered,* it appears that not many people were about when the members of the Sanhedrin brought their prisoner to Pilate. But in due course the Jerusalem mob made its appearance. Pilate saw in this an opportunity. He took

---

31. τότε here has the meaning "at that time" rather than "next in sequence," which it often has in this Gospel.

32. His word is ἐπίσημος (σῆμα means "a mark"); it can have a meaning like "bearing a mark" and may be used of money, "stamped." In the New Testament it occurs again only of Andronicus and Junia(s), who are said to be "notable among the apostles" (Rom. 16:7). Here, of course, the word means "marked" in a different way; as a leader in an insurrection he had made his mark.

33. Ἰησοῦν Βαραββᾶν is read by Θ f1 700* syrs and has patristic and versional support. The bulk of the MSS lack Ἰησοῦν, including ℵ A B D K L W, most versions, and patristic citations. Metzger discusses the problem and concludes that this reading, found "in several witnesses of the Caesarean text," was known to Origen. That scholar rejected it on the grounds that "in the whole range of the scriptures we know that no one who is a sinner [is called] Jesus" (Metzger, p. 67). Westcott and Hort have a valuable note in the Appendix to their *The New Testament in the Original Greek* (London, 1907), Appendix, pp. 19-20; they reject the reading and, impressed by the paucity and inferiority of the witnesses known to them, say, "it cannot be right" (p. 20). It may be relevant that the name "Jesus" is not given to Barabbas in any text of Mark, Luke, or John.

advantage of the presence of the people and the nearness of the feast to suggest that according to the custom he release a prisoner, and he nominated two: *Barabbas, or Jesus who is called Messiah* (if the longer reading be accepted, the question asks which "Jesus" he shall release, "Jesus Barabbas or Jesus called Christ"). No indication is given why only these two prisoners should be considered for release. We may conjecture that Barabbas would have had popular appeal, for Mark tells us that this man had been involved in a rebellion in which he had committed murder. It is possible that the reason why the crowd was there was that supporters of Barabbas had come together to ask for Barabbas to be the man released at the customary amnesty at Passover. For whatever reason, a crowd was assembled, and Pilate put to them the choice of Barabbas or Jesus. He may have thought that since Jesus had committed no crime and since he was said by some at least to be the Messiah, the people would want to have him set free. But perhaps he did not give sufficient consideration to the fact that a Jerusalem crowd was unlikely to call for a Galilean to be released when some of their own people were in custody. And it may well be that the Jewish leaders had made sure that some of their supporters were in the crowd urging the people to call for Barabbas. By adding that Jesus was *"called Messiah,"* Pilate was quietly urging a consideration that he might well have thought would weigh heavily with many in the crowd. No answer from the crowd is recorded at this point; it may be that Pilate put the alternatives before the people and allowed them time to think about it.

18. Matthew adds that Pilate was not taken in by what the Jewish leaders were saying. He knew that it was not consideration for the security of Roman rule that had motivated them, but *envy.*[34] Their envy at the success of Jesus in Jerusalem during the past few days would have reinforced their long-standing hatred of him. It may well be that Pilate knew of this and reasoned that since the leaders were jealous of Jesus' popularity with the crowd, he must have sufficient support among the people for them to ask for his release. Ordinary people would surely side with Jesus rather than with a criminal like Barabbas. So he put the choice before them, thinking that in this way he would be able to release Jesus. If the leaders were jealous of Jesus' popularity with the crowd, then the "Messiah" must have sufficient support in the crowd for them to ask for him to be set free.

19. Now comes an interruption. Matthew alone tells us that Pilate's wife[35] sent him a message *as he was seated on the judgment seat.* She clearly regarded it as urgent, for to interrupt the governor while he was in the

---

34. The word is φθόνος, which some take here to mean "malice" or, as Cassirer, "spite." But it seems rather that the Jewish leaders were envious of Jesus' popularity with the common people.

35. Christian tradition has named this lady Claudia Procla, or simply Procla (or Procula). She is said to have been or to have become a Christian, and the Eastern church has even canonized her as a saint.

act of judging was obviously a serious matter. She urged him that he *"Have nothing to do"*[36] with Jesus, whom she describes as *"that righteous man"* (this appears to be a messianic title in Acts 7:52; cf. 1 John 2:1). She gives as the reason that she had *suffered many things in a dream* because of him, but she gives no indication of the nature of her sufferings nor of why she felt that her husband should have no dealings with the man. But since people in antiquity took a good deal of notice of dreams, it is not surprising that Pilate's wife felt that her dream was of some importance. And if it was important, she would believe that she should lose no time in communicating the fact to her husband. She would not have been able to enter the court, but she was able to send a message to the judge. We may well feel that it is astonishing that an aristocratic Roman lady should intercede on behalf of a Galilean peasant. She had clearly been deeply impressed by her dream, and she did what she could. The incident is often dismissed as legendary,[37] a view on which our verdict will depend on our understanding of Matthew's method. There is this in favor of accepting it, that Pilate went to a good deal of trouble for the friendless Galilean when it would have been easy for him to agree with the suggestions of the Jewish leaders. It may be that his efforts on behalf of Jesus owed something to this domestic message. The wife speaks of her dream as having occurred *today,* which probably indicates that she slept on after her husband went to work. As we have seen, Roman officials tended to begin their day early, so there is no great problem with this.[38]

20. The crowd was not left to make up its mind by itself. The crowd never is. There are always people who try to manipulate public opinion, and in this case they were *the chief priests and the elders,* the Jewish leaders who had brought the accusation against Jesus. There was no doubt which answer they wanted. Matthew gives no indication as to the methods employed to convince the crowds, but tells his readers that they were successful. The crowds were persuaded.[39] The leaders left the people in no doubt as to what this involved; they should *ask for Barabbas,* and that meant that they should *destroy*[40] *Jesus.* They were left with the clear un-

---

36. μηδὲν σοὶ καὶ τῷ δικαίῳ ἐκείνῳ, "nothing to you and to that righteous man"; it is a way of saying that he should repudiate any dealings with the righteous man in question. There is a good deal to be said for *NIV*'s translation, "that innocent man."

37. But Bonnard views the way the lady speaks of her dream as "typically Hellenistic"; he contrasts the dreams in chapters 1 and 2 (p. 397).

38. France holds that "Matthew has clearly inserted this verse together with vv. 24-25 in order to heighten the impression of Jesus' legal innocence — even a pagan woman can see it! But while she is open to the voice of God (from whom dreams come; *cf.* 1:20; 2:12, 13, 19, 22), the Jewish leaders are deaf to it."

39. Turner takes this as an example of the perfective aorist, "they succeeded in persuading," and contrasts Acts 13:43, "where Paul and Barn. could only *urge*" (M, III, p. 72).

40. ἀπόλλυμι is used of destruction of various kinds. Thus it is used of the loss of an eye (5:29), of burst wineskins (9:17), and of many other forms of destruction. Here it is employed to signify death.

derstanding that they were not only to seek freedom for Barabbas, but death for Jesus.

21. The time for reflection being up, Pilate asks the people for their choice. He is called *the governor*, designated by his office in the asking of this significant question. He is said to have *answered them*, a form of expression that seems to indicate that from the sounds emanating from the crowds outside Pilate realized that the people had had long enough to make up their minds (or have them made up for them!). So he asked the people *which of the two* they wanted him to release. There was apparently no hesitation as they called out, *"Barabbas"* ("They preferred the man of violence to the man of love," Barclay, II, p. 399).

22. On hearing this answer Pilate may well have felt that the authorities had persuaded the mob to ask for a terrorist to be released without their understanding what this meant for the fate of one of their own people who was guiltless. At any rate, he went on to ask what they wanted him to do with Jesus.[41] *Therefore* is important: Pilate is inquiring about what the answer the crowds had just given meant for Jesus; what is the consequence of their decision. He speaks of *"Jesus who is called Messiah,"* which seems to be a way of reminding them that Jesus was highly thought of, at least in some circles. A person who was called *Messiah* with the meaning that term had for loyal Jews had much going for him. Did these clamorers for Barabbas realize what they were doing to a man whom many of their own compatriots saw as the *Messiah?* They did. Matthew says, *"They all say"* (notice that the decision is unanimous — as far as the crowd went there was no dissenting voice): *"Let him be crucified."* This is the first use of this verb in the passion story (Jesus had used it earlier in prophecies, 20:19; 23:34; 26:2), but Matthew will use it 6 times in this chapter. It shows here that the mob were well aware of what was involved and were content to clamor for the spectacle that a crucifixion afforded. It is not at all surprising that they went along with what their leaders urged rather than accept the suggestion of the Roman governor. Subject peoples will normally prefer the advice of their own leaders to that of the conqueror where they have a choice. It is perhaps worth reminding ourselves that right from the beginning Matthew has written of the Messiah (1:17). But he here makes it clear that there is more to being Messiah than possessing Davidic descent.

23. Pilate made one more ineffectual attempt. The *But* with which Matthew begins this verse is adversative; it sets Pilate over against the mob. *"What evil did he do?"*[42] asked the governor. Crucifixion was a dread-

---

41. Literally "What shall I do Jesus?" Chamberlain points out that "Verbs of doing good or evil may take a double accusative" (p. 38); in English we insert "with" or "to." Moule remarks that "The Dative and Accusative also overlap mysteriously" (*IBNTG*, p. 43, n.).

42. It is not easy to bring out the force of the γάρ in a translation, but the conjunction means "for" and looks for a reason for the foregoing. Pilate could see none, and he asked for one now.

ful penalty, and even though the age was accustomed to it, it was a way of dying that should surely be used only as a punishment for some serious offense. As far as Pilate could see, Jesus had done nothing wrong. No crime had been demonstrated by his accusers. But it was useless to ask the mob for reasons. Their worst passions had been aroused, and they were baying for blood. They *shouted all the more*, repeating their demand, "*Let him be crucified.*" The question of what to do with Jesus was not to be settled by reasoned examination of the evidence. It had been decided by mob hysteria.

24. Only Matthew has this incident.[43] He pictures for us an increasingly frustrated Pilate. Evidently the governor had been acting on the assumption that releasing Jesus would be no great problem. The chief priests were clearly determined to get him executed, but they were jealous of him (v. 18), and in a situation like this, with high officials being jealous of a man who held no office, it must have seemed obvious to Pilate that Jesus had strong support among the people. Why else should they "envy" Jesus? The governor would have had his informers who kept him abreast of what was going on in the realm over which he exercised authority, and accordingly he would have known of those who on Palm Sunday shouted their acclamations of Jesus. But he did not reckon sufficiently with the facts that the crowd now before the praetorium were the Jerusalem mob, not the Galilean pilgrims who shouted for Jesus, and that the mob's sympathies were with the freedom fighters, not with a religious figure like Jesus. So Pilate's well-meant attempts to have the people clamor for Jesus' release misfired and he was left with the mob's demand that the Galilean be crucified. Apparently he saw no way of getting around that; mob passions were high and to oppose the crowd would have been to stir up opposition. Since he had no great stake in Jesus' release, that meant that Jesus' execution was inevitable. But Matthew makes it clear that the governor had not wanted this by recording Pilate's washing of his hands in front of the crowds, together with his words, "*I am innocent*[44] *of the blood of this man;*[45] *you see to it.*" The washing of the hands as a gesture to indicate one's innocence of an offense was a Jewish custom (Deut. 21:6-9; Pss. 26:6; 73:13),[46] although Plummer finds it also in Virgil and

---

43. Many critics therefore regard it as inauthentic. But as Carson points out, it fits in with Pilate's repeated attempts to release Jesus. "He sent him to Herod (Luke), suggested that the paschal amnesty be applied to him, proposed a compromise with a scourging (Luke), tried to turn the case back to the Jewish authorities (John), remonstrated before pronouncing sentence (John)," as well as here washing his hands. It fits the general picture.

44. ἀθῷος (ἀ-privative + θωή, a penalty) means first "unpunished" (MM cites examples of this use from the papyri), and then, as here, "innocent."

45. If δικαίου be read (with ℵ K L W), Pilate takes up the word used by his wife to describe Jesus (v. 19). But it should probably not be accepted.

46. "The irony of this allusion is that Pilate follows a ritual designed to dissociate Israel itself from the consequences of blood-guilt" (Green). Calvin asks, "How can he scrub off the stain of his crime with a few drops of water, when no expiation could have cleared it?" (III, p. 187).

Ovid (p. 391). Pilate apparently used it as something that would be comprehensible to those who saw it; in any case, his words are plain enough.[47] He clearly regarded Jesus' death as the crime of murder, and equally clearly he did not wish to be held responsible for it. In this, of course, he was mistaken. He did not have the primary responsibility (that lay with the Jewish leaders). But in the last resort it was Pilate who said "Crucify" or "Release," and there was no way he could avoid responsibility for that. The picture we get is that of a mob out of control and baying for blood, and in that emotional atmosphere a governor who was not thinking clearly and who was ready to take the easy way out.[48] He tried to evade accountability for a decision that in the last resort was his and his alone. *"You see to it,"* like the hand-washing, is an attempt to evade a responsibility that could not be shrugged off. The very similar words the Jewish leaders spoke to Judas (v. 4) did not exonerate the chief priests, and these words do not exonerate Pilate.[49]

25. The mob cheerfully accepted the responsibility, saying, *"His blood on us,"* and for good measure adding, *"and on our children."* Most translations insert "be" and make the words a prayer, but perhaps we should understand them as a statement: "the responsibility is ours" (so France). This can mean only that they did not take seriously any suggestion that Jesus was an innocent man. Nobody calls down on his children the responsibility for the unjust killing of a righteous person. It would seem that the mob had been completely taken in by the propaganda of the high priests. After all, the high priests were the religious leaders. They of all people could be expected to know the truth about Jesus, and they had taken the initiative in handing him over to the Roman authorities and clamoring for the death sentence. Pilate had held before them the possibility of releasing Jesus and executing Barabbas, but they themselves had been largely responsible for overturning that suggestion. They had yelled for Barabbas to be free. They had yelled for Jesus to be crucified. They had caused the Roman governor to do something he did not want to do. They must have felt on top of the world. What did it matter that they should be charged with responsibility for what they had brought about? They had been successful, and for all the good it would do, they were happy to relieve Pilate of the responsibility.

47. The apocryphal Gospel of Peter opens with "But of the Jews none washed their hands"; according to this tradition they made no attempt to evade responsibility.

48. "The possibility of riot in an overcrowded Jerusalem was always present. In such circumstances the governor might all the more readily bow to the demands of the crowd. From his point of view the death of one man was the lesser evil" (*AB*).

49. Matthew does not record any formal sentence. Vincent Taylor says that Luke is the only Evangelist to do so (and even this is left in doubt, for his ἐπέκρινεν [Luke 23:24] may mean no more than that Pilate decided on an execution). This he thinks is explained only partly "by the Christian conviction that responsibility lay primarily with the Jews . . . but rather, as the consistent use of παραδίδωμι shows, by the belief that, as the Suffering Servant, Jesus is 'delivered up by the determinate counsel and foreknowledge of God' (Ac. ii.23)" (*The Gospel according to St. Mark* [London, 1959], p. 584).

This verse has been greatly misused throughout the centuries, being made a proof text to justify all manner of horrific practices against the Jews. But we should bear in mind that this was no more than a thoughtless assumption of responsibility by an unruly mob. They had no authority to commit their nation for the evil thing that they were doing. And even if they could do this, they could not bind God to punish subsequent generations of the chosen people. Evils have been perpetrated against the Jews through the centuries, and in some places they still are. But Scripture gives us no justification for any such thing. It is relevant that *all* the first Christians were Jews; the writer of this Gospel cannot possibly have meant that punishment for this mob's outrageous behavior would fall on every Jew in every place at every time.[50]

26. It remained only to put the sentence into execution. Pilate *released Barabbas to them,* an expression that indicates that the mob received that murderer into their number. But *Jesus he scourged.* Matthew dismisses this horror in a single word. Scourging was the normal preliminary to crucifixion, and it was a horrible punishment in itself. It was inflicted with multi-thonged whips, each thong being laced with pieces of metal or bone. Josephus speaks of a certain Jesus, son of Ananias, who was "flayed to the bone with scourges" (*War* 6.304).[51] Men sometimes died under scourging, and it is not difficult to understand why. Matthew devotes to this horror no more than one word, and he will later do the same with crucifixion. None of the biblical writers dwells on the dreadful sufferings Jesus endured. Popular piety in modern times, both Catholic and Protestant, often does. We sing hymns like "O Sacred Head, Sore Wounded," and listen to sermons in which we are harried with emphasis on the "bitter pains" that Jesus endured. But the biblical writers are much more interested in the meaning of Jesus' death than in enlarging on the suffering he endured.

Not as much is known about crucifixion as we might have expected. Indeed, the Gospel narratives appear to be the fullest accounts we have from antiquity of this method of execution. Ancient writers regarded it as the most shameful of deaths, and they refused to dwell on it. All the more was this the case in that it was regarded as the appropriate method of execution for slaves and criminals, and it was used extensively for this purpose.[52] Important people might be executed, but it was done decently,

---

50. Glover understands the words as a prayer answered partly in the destruction of Jerusalem. "But it was also answered in a different sense from that in which it was offered — by the mercy, which sprinkled the saving blood of Christ on that nation and on mankind."

51. C. Schneider says that scourging "was so terrible that even Domitian was horrified by it. . . . We know little about the details. The number of strokes was not prescribed. It continued until the flesh hung down in bloody shreds" (*TDNT,* IV, p. 517).

52. A good modern survey of what is known about the subject is found in Martin Hengel, *Crucifixion* (London, 1977). He entitles his chapter 8 "The 'Slaves' Punishment," and begins with, "In most Roman writers crucifixion appears as the typical punishment for slaves" (p. 51). He also says, "crucifixion was practised above all on dangerous criminals and members of the lowest classes" (p. 88).

perhaps by beheading. So for the most part we are left to guesswork. Crucifixion was carried out in a variety of ways. It might be done on a cross in the shape Christians have conventionally adopted, but again the "cross" might be in the shape of an I or a T or an X. The object of the exercise was to kill a person, not to conform to any standard form of cross.[53] The person being crucified was fastened to the cross with cords or nails. There was a projection called the *sedile* that the crucified person straddled; this enabled him to take some of the weight off his arms (when John tells of the legs of those with Jesus being broken, John 19:31-33, he points to the removal of this slight alleviation and to the hastening of death as a consequence). In 1968 some archaeologists discovered the remains of a young man who had been crucified between A.D. 7 and 66 (judging by the pottery in the find). His forearms were nailed to the cross and his legs were bent at the knees and broken. An iron nail was driven through both heels together (the legs were twisted to make this possible).[54]

It is not known what caused death. The body would have been weakened by the scourging, and further by prolonged exposure, and both the respiration and the circulation would have been affected. One suggestion is that the combination of all this brought on heart failure; another, that the brain would be damaged through the reduced supply of blood that reached it. Whatever the reason, death was sure, and it might take a long time.

D. THE DEATH OF JESUS, 27:27-66

Each of the Evangelists tells the story of Jesus' death in his own way, though Matthew keeps fairly close to Mark's account. But he has a few details that we find in this Gospel only, and we will note them as we come to them. We may divide his account into three sections in which he deals successively with the mockery Jesus underwent before being crucified, the actual crucifixion together with what happened while Jesus hung on the cross, and the reverent burial his followers brought about.

1. The Mockery, 27:27-31

27Then the governor's soldiers took Jesus into the praetorium and gathered the whole company to him. 28And they stripped him and put a scarlet cloak on him, 29and they plaited a crown of thorns and put it on his head, and a reed in his right hand. They knelt before him and mocked him,

---

53. "The form of execution could vary considerably: crucifixion was a punishment in which the caprice and sadism of the executioners were given full rein" (Hengel, *Crucifixion*, p. 25).
54. See the articles "Jesus and Jehohanan" by J. H. Charlesworth, *ET*, LXXXIV (1972-73), pp. 147-50; and "Crucifixion in Ancient Palestine, Qumran Literature, and the New Testament" by Joseph A. Fitzmyer, *CBQ*, 40 (1978), pp. 493-513.

*saying, "Hail, King of the Jews." ³⁰And they spat on him, and took the reed
and hit him on the head. ³¹And when they had mocked him, they took off
the cloak and dressed him in his own clothes, and led him away to crucify
him.*

Curious as it seems to us, Matthew says very little about the crucifixion. We regard it as the central happening, but Matthew uses only a
participle to describe it all! His description singles out three things: the
division of Jesus' clothes (in accordance with Scripture), the inscription
over his head that proclaimed him King, and the mockery, before and after
he was put on the cross, in which ironically a number of things are said
in jest that in fact express profound truths. Bonnard underlines this aspect
of Matthew's treatment of the crucifixion.

The decision that Jesus be crucified having been taken, he was given
over into the hands of the soldiers. They would look after him until he
was taken out to the place of execution and then carry out the sentence
of crucifixion. While they were waiting, they amused themselves with
some horseplay. The prisoner had been found guilty of being a king; very
well, they would pay homage to the king in their own way. Matthew
makes more of this mockery than does any of the other Evangelists. He
has 64 words to Mark's 49, while Luke, of course, does not mention it at
all (he has another account of mockery, namely when Jesus was before
Herod), and John deals with it very shortly. It is important for Matthew's
purpose, and he lets us know what the soldiers did.

27. *The governor's soldiers* were, of course, members of the Roman
legion. Since Jesus was out of the control of the Jews, from this point on
the Romans dictated all that was done. It is possible that Matthew is
mocking these mockers. Patte reminds us that "Mockeries, like caricatures,
involve portraying a person by selecting a few *actual* characteristics of that
person and excluding his or her other characteristics." He sees mockery
in Matthew's reference to "soldiers of the governor." "Matthew expects
his readers to perceive not only that the soldiers are insensitive and cruel
in their treatment of Jesus but also that the soldiers are ridiculous and thus
wrong in their assessment of Jesus. . . . The soldiers, apparently under the
political authority of the Roman governor, are actually under the authority
of the Jewish people whose orders they will carry out by crucifying Jesus"
(Patte, pp. 381, 382).

The soldiers then *took Jesus into the praetorium,*⁵⁵ which presents us
with a small difficulty. The word referred to the official residence of the
governor, but it is not known where Pilate resided when he came to
Jerusalem. He lived in Caesarea, where his real praetorium was, but the

---

55. The πραιτώριον is the transliteration of the Latin word *praetorium,* which denoted
the headquarters in a Roman camp; from that it came to be used of the palace or the official
residence of a Roman governor.

name was given to whatever residence he used while he was in Jerusalem. Some commentators hold that this would have been Herod's palace, others that it would have been the tower of Antonia. Whichever it was, it would seem that there was attached to it a place where soldiers could be garrisoned, and it was to this part of the palace that Jesus was taken. *They gathered the whole company*[56] *to him*, which will signify all the garrison at the residence (Moffatt translates "regiment"; *RSV*, "battalion"; and *NRSV*, "cohort"; all bring out the point that it was a recognized military term). Matthew is saying that all the legionaries at the praetorium gathered for some fun at the expense of the condemned prisoner.

28. Their horseplay centered around the fact that Jesus had been convicted of being a king. Matthew is describing a highly ironical situation; the soldiers went out of their way to produce trappings of royalty as a means of ridiculing one who was to be crucified as a King, whereas he really was King in a fuller and wider sense than they had any idea of. They decided that his clothing was not suitable for royalty, so they took it off[57] and replaced it with *a scarlet cloak*[58] (only Matthew has this detail; Mark speaks of their clothing Jesus with purple, the color of royalty,[59] but he does not mention the cloak). Since this kind of cloak was used by military officers, there would have been no great difficulty in getting one, perhaps an old one, discarded by an officer. The point of it was apparently that the color was somewhere near purple, the color of royalty.[60] By getting a cloak of a color not quite that of royalty the soldiers were mocking Jesus' claim to be a king.

29. A crown was needed for a king, so these funny fellows got some thorny material and plaited a crown out of it.[61] They pressed this on Jesus'

56. σπεῖρα, "In our lit. prob. always *cohort*, the tenth part of a legion" (BAGD). That means 600 soldiers, which seems too many for the present passage. The term was also used of a maniple, which comprised 200 men, and that is more likely. The article points to "the" company, the one stationed there (cf. Josephus, *War* 5.244).

57. That is, if we accept the reading ἐκδύσαντες with most MSS (headed by א*,b A K L W). But ἐνδύσαντες is read by א B syrˢ and some other MSS. Metzger regards the latter as "a correction." The clothing sequence here is not clear. If we accept the former reading, Jesus would have been stripped for the scourging (v. 26), then dressed in his own clothes after it, and stripped again, at least partially, before being clothed with "royal" garments. If we accept the latter, he was still naked after the scourging and was now clothed with the χλαμύς, which probably means in his own clothes except for the outer garment, for which the soldiers used the χλαμύς (see next note).

58. A χλαμύς was a short cloak worn by military officers and others in high position. κόκκινος, *scarlet*, was a color produced by a dye made from the dried bodies of a scale insect found on oak trees.

59. For the significance of purple see *New Documents*, 2, p. 25.

60. Calvin points out that where Matthew has "scarlet" Mark has "purple," and proceeds, "but we need not sweat over this. It is not likely that Christ was dressed in a precious robe: we may gather it was not real purple but something that had a resemblance to it, as a painter imitates the real thing in his pictures" (III, p. 190).

61. Strictly στέφανος meant a garland or chaplet used at festivals or as a mark of victory for the winners at the Games; however, it could be used of a royal crown (for which διάδημα

head, which would have both mocked his kingship and increased his sufferings. For a scepter they put *a reed in his right hand.* So they had all the outward trappings of royalty, but every one a piece of cruel mockery. They carried this further in that they *knelt before him* (only Matthew tells us this), a parody of the respect routinely offered to a king. Only Matthew speaks of the *reed;* accompanied by the kneeling, it points to all the outward trappings of royalty. Evidently he took this whole episode seriously; it was a dreadful part of what they had done to his Master. Mark and John join Matthew in telling us that they greeted Jesus with *"Hail, King of the Jews,"* but only this Evangelist includes the information that the mockery included the soldiers kneeling before their helpless captive. *Hail* could be used in ordinary greetings, but it was also a proper method of saluting royalty (cf. "Hail, Caesar"); *GNB* substitutes "Long live the King of the Jews" to bring out the force of it (cf. Phillips, "Hail, Your Majesty, King of the Jews!").

30. Their contempt for their captive is shown by the facts that they *spat on him* and that they *hit him on the head* with *the reed* they had given him for a scepter. There would have been no serious physical violence about this part of the incident, but there was contemptuous mockery of all that Jesus stood for. The soldiers make it clear that nobody should take seriously the bedraggled figure in their charge (cf. Isa. 50:6).

31. How long the mockery lasted we do not know. But it could go on only until the time came for the crucifixion. When that time approached, the soldiers removed the cloak and put Jesus' own clothes back on him. The fun was over and the serious business was about to begin. They *led* Jesus off *to crucify him.* There would not have been as many involved in the actual crucifixion as in the mocking (normally four soldiers crucified a man), but it would have included some of the same men.

2. The Crucifixion, 27:32-56

> ³²*And as they were going out, they found a man of Cyrene named Simon; him they compelled to carry his cross.* ³³*And when they came to a place called Golgotha, which means "Place of a Skull,"* ³⁴*they gave him wine mixed with gall to drink; and when he had tasted it, he would not drink it.* ³⁵*And when they had crucified him, they divided his clothes, casting lots,* ³⁶*and they sat down and watched him there.* ³⁷*And over his head they put the written charge against him:* "THIS IS JESUS THE KING OF THE JEWS." ³⁸*Then they crucify with him two bandits, one on the right hand and one on the left.* ³⁹*And the passersby jeered at him, shaking their heads* ⁴⁰*and*

---

was more usual). H. St. J. Hart argued that the crown of thorns was meant as a "radiate" crown, one with spikes radiating outwards and that signified that the ruler was divine (see *JTS*, n.s. III [1952], pp. 66-75). But it is simpler to understand the crown here as an implement of torture.

saying, "You who destroy the temple and build it in three days, save yourself! If you are the Son of God, come down from the cross." [41]*Likewise also the chief priests, mocking with the scribes and elders, were saying,* [42]*"He saved others, himself he cannot save. He is the King of Israel; let him come down now from the cross, and we will believe in him.* [43]*He put his trust in God; let him deliver him now if he wants him; for he said, 'I am God's Son.'"* [44]*And the brigands who were crucified with him were upbraiding him in the same way.*

[45]*And from the sixth hour there was darkness over all the land until the ninth hour.* [46]*And about the ninth hour Jesus cried out in a loud voice, saying, "Eli, Eli, lema sabachthani"; which means, "My God, my God, why did you abandon me?"* [47]*But when some of those standing there heard it, they said, "This man is calling for Elijah."* [48]*And immediately one of them ran and took a sponge, filled it with sour wine, put it on a reed, and gave it to him to drink.* [49]*But the rest said, "Let be. Let us see whether Elijah is coming to save him."* [50]*But Jesus cried out again with a loud voice and yielded up his spirit.*

[51]*And look, the curtain of the temple was torn in two from top to bottom, and the earth was shaken, and the rocks were split;* [52]*and the tombs were opened, and many bodies of the saints that were asleep were raised;* [53]*and after his resurrection they came out of the tombs, went into the holy city, and appeared to many.* [54]*But when the centurion and those who were with him watching Jesus saw the earthquake and the things that happened, they were very much afraid, and said, "Truly this was the Son of God."*

[55]*Now there were there many women watching from a distance, who had followed Jesus from Galilee, providing for him;* [56]*among them were Mary Magdalene, and Mary the mother of James and Joseph, and the mother of Zebedee's sons.*

In the crucifixion narrative Matthew follows Mark closely. There are a few details that he alone has, but for the most part he tells the same story as his fellow Evangelist. The narrative is strictly factual. There is no attempt to play on the heartstrings of the readers, but a plain account of what happened. A noteworthy feature of Matthew's account is the large number of places where the language echoes Old Testament passages; they show us that Matthew sees the fulfilment of Scripture in what took place that fateful day. Through all the posturing of the Jewish leaders, the blustering of the Roman governor, and the yelling of the Jerusalem mob the divine purpose was worked out.

32. Matthew does not define his *they,* but clearly he is still referring to the military personnel charged with responsibility for carrying out the execution. Somewhere along the way to the place where the crucifixion was to take place they came across *a man of Cyrene named Simon,* and they pressed him into service by making him *carry* Jesus' *cross.* It was customary for the condemned person to carry the cross beam of his cross to the place of execution, and John tells us that as they went out Jesus was carrying his cross. But evidently the burden was too great for him to bear. He had been subjected to a great deal of stress. He had been up all night and had undergone the agony in the garden, the various sessions with the Jewish authorities, and the mockery of a trial before Pilate. He had endured the scourging, which, as we noted before, could be a very brutal affair. He had been mocked and hit by the soldiers. It may well be that Jesus had been more severely treated than the others who were crucified with him. Whether that is the reason or not, he needed help (we cannot think that the soldiery who had carried out the mockery of which we have just been reading would have allowed him to have help if it had been at all possible for him to bear the burden himself). They themselves, of course, would not perform such a service, so they *compelled*[62] a passerby to carry the cross beam. In all three Synoptic accounts it appears that this was a chance meeting; Simon just happened to be there at the time. Mark tells us that this man was "the father of Alexander and Rufus," evidently people known in the church of his day, and probably Christians (would the Evangelists bother naming people like this unless they were Christians? Did what he heard and saw that day lead Simon to become a follower of Jesus?). He and Luke add the information that Simon was coming from the country (or possibly from the field). That he was *a man of Cyrene* may mean that he was a Gentile, but more probably that he was a Jew of the diaspora, now in Jerusalem for the Passover festival. He may, of course, have been resident in Jerusalem at this time; we have no way of knowing.

33. They came to a place *called Golgotha,*[63] which Matthew explains means "Place of a Skull." This does not help us much in identifying the place. It has been suggested that the place of crucifixion was a hill in the shape of a skull (one reason for favoring "Gordon's Calvary"). This may have been the case, but (despite many of our hymns and our constant references to "the hill called 'Calvary' ") there is no evidence in any of the Gospels that the place of crucifixion was a hill. It has been suggested that skulls from executed criminals were left there, but it is highly improbable that the Jews would have allowed parts of unburied bodies to lie around. In any case, if this were the reason, it would be "the place of skulls," not "of a skull." Further, we must not overlook the fact that there was a garden there (John 19:41), and it is impossible to think that skulls were left lying around in a garden. The name of the place is well documented in the Gospel tradition, but with the information at our disposal we are not able to identify it with any certainty.

---

62. The verb is ἀγγαρεύω, for which see the note on 5:41. It signifies the pressing into public service of anyone at all.

63. This is the transliteration of the Aramaic גֻּלְגָּלְתָּא = Hebrew גֻּלְגֹּלֶת, meaning "skull" (2 Kings 9:35). Our word "Calvary" is from the Latin word for "skull," *calvaria*. The neuter relative ὅ is unexpected since τόπος is masculine, but it may refer to Κρανίου, which is neuter, or the two words may be taken as a unity and seen as a neuter place name.

34. When they reached the place of execution, they offered Jesus *wine mixed with gall*.[64] This appears to be a reference to a custom mentioned in the Talmud: "When one is led out to execution, he is given a goblet of wine containing a grain of frankincense, in order to benumb his senses, for it is written, *Give strong drink unto him that is ready to perish, and wine unto the bitter in soul*. And it has also been taught: The noble women in Jerusalem used to donate and bring it" (*Sanh.* 43a; the passage quoted is in Prov. 31:6). The alternative is a reference to the ordinary sour wine used by the soldiers, and Carson suggests that this wine had been made so bitter that Jesus refused to drink it; it would then have been part of the soldiers' mockery of their prisoner (so also Gundry, "the offer of the bitter drink is not an act of mercy, but an act of mockery" (*Use of the OT*, p. 202).[65] That Jesus *tasted it* but then refused to drink it seems to mean that he preferred to keep his senses undulled as he came to the supreme moment when he would give his life as a ransom for the many (cf. 20:28).

35-36. It is noteworthy that Matthew dismisses in a single word one of the most dreadful ways of dying people have ever devised, and that word is a participle forming a subordinate clause.[66] In this he is doing the same as the writers of the other Gospels; as we noticed earlier, none of them tries to harrow the feelings of his readers by going into detail about "what pains he had to bear." Popular Christian piety through the ages has not followed this example, and many have attempted to bring out what we owe to our Savior by dwelling on his sufferings for us. But what mattered for the New Testament writers was that in his death Jesus dealt with our sins; they try to bring out the meaning of his death and leave their readers to work out for themselves that crucifixion was such a painful way of dying.

Having performed their task, then, the soldiers proceeded to divide up his clothing. Those crucified were crucified naked, and their clothing was a perquisite of the soldiers who performed the execution. Matthew says no more than that they did this by *casting lots*. He reports this in the words of Psalm 22:18, without indicating that he is quoting Scripture, but since he is so fond of seeing the fulfilment of Scripture this can scarcely

---

64. There is a reminiscence of Psalm 69:21 (for "poison" the Greek has χολήν). Mark refers to ἐσμυρνισμένον οἶνον, but Plummer thinks that Matthew is "not out of harmony" with this. He says, " 'Gall' (χολή) is a vague word for drugs with a bitter taste, and the meaning in each Gospel is that the wine was drugged" (pp. 394-95).

65. A further suggestion is that of J. Jeremias (*Eucharistic Words*, p. 167, n. 6), that Jesus' refusal to drink was due to the fact that he had taken a vow of abstinence (Mark 14:25). But whatever those words of Jesus mean, it is pushing them too far to say that they ruled out this numbing drink. It is much more probable that he refused to die with his senses dulled by a soporific. Lightfoot thinks that Mark is describing the normal custom, wine mixed with frankincense or myrrh, and Matthew what was actually given in this case, sour wine, mixed with gall to give it a more bitter taste (p. 366). Mounce adds, "If those who gave Jesus the wine were soldiers, then the myrrhed wine (supplied by the women?) was made bitter (another cruel joke?) by the 'gall' . . . added by the executioners."

66. He says no more than σταυρώσαντες, "having crucified."

715

be accidental. John notes that they divided the clothes into four parts, one for each of the four soldiers involved in the execution, and that the gambling was done over the tunic, which was seamless and thus more valuable (John 19:23-24). Matthew adds that they *sat down and watched him*. Presumably they waited until he died and thus made sure that there was no rescue on the part of his followers. A crucified man might be taken from his cross and revived; the guard ensured that nothing of the sort occurred in the case of Jesus. None of the other Evangelists has this small point.

37. The *charge* against Jesus was affixed to the cross over his head. This is sometimes used as a proof that his cross was in the conventional shape and not, for example, a T-shaped cross. But this is not conclusive, for with a T-shape the body would hang down sufficiently to enable the placard to be affixed above the head. It seems that the *charge* was not invariably affixed to a cross, but it was not unusual. Each of the Gospels differs slightly from the others in the wording of the *charge*: Mark has "the King of the Jews"; Luke, "This is the King of the Jews"; and John, "Jesus of Nazareth, the King of the Jews." The gist is the same in all of them, of course, and in any case John tells us that the inscription was in Hebrew, Latin, and Greek, so there was room for small variations. The writing made clear to anyone who could read the identity of this crucified person and the reason for his execution. We notice again that the Gentile inscription refers to "the King of the Jews," where the Jewish form would be "the King of Israel."

38. *Then* moves us on to the next part of the story to which Matthew draws attention; it does not mean that this happened immediately after the events he has just narrated. Jesus was not crucified alone, but two others underwent this form of execution at that same time. Matthew says that they were *bandits*;[67] clearly they were convicted criminals, and with one on Jesus' *right* and the other on his *left* he was in the middle of criminals when he was executed. The prophet had spoken of him as being "numbered with the transgressors" (Isa. 53:12), and the position of his cross gives meaning to the fulfilment of this prophecy (though Matthew does not specifically draw attention to it).

39-40. In Matthew's account Jesus is mocked[68] (cf. Ps. 22:7) by three groups of people: the *passersby*, the chief priests and their allies, and those crucified with Jesus (Tasker calls them "ignorant sinners," "religious sinners," and "condemned sinners," p. 265). In addition to suffering crucifixion Jesus had to put up with the mocking of thoughtless onlookers. The

---

67. The word is ληστής; it may mean a robber or a brigand. Here it is rather the latter and may point to a member of the resistance movement. Luke uses the term κακοῦργος, "malefactor."

68. J. A. Fitzmyer has drawn attention to the fact that the Temple Scroll from Qumran, dating from the end of the second century B.C., speaks of the crucified as "accursed by God and men" (Deut. 21:23 speaks only of being accursed by God). He finds this to be "an interesting illustration of the derision of Jesus" in this passage (*Crucifixion*, p. 512).

passersby were people who had no business at the place of the crucifixion but who saw what was going on and joined in the general abuse of the man on the central cross. It is possible that Matthew's choice of the term is reminiscent of Lamentations 1:12: "Is it nothing to you, all you who pass by? Look and see if there is any sorrow like my sorrow. . . ." Probably many of these people had been in the crowds that clamored for Jesus' death; having done what they could to bring about his crucifixion, it is not likely that they would pass by the spectacle of the execution.[69]

They *jeered at him*, where the verb is one that is more usually translated "blasphemed." It seems best not to translate it that way here because the people in question did not consciously regard Jesus as the Son of God and therefore were jeering rather than blaspheming as they understood the situation. But Matthew's choice of word is the right one, for what they were doing was indeed blasphemy, even if they did not fully understand what they were saying. The reason why they shook their heads is not clear, but it indicates at least that they were entering wholeheartedly into what they were doing; their words were accompanied by what they regarded as suitable gestures. They picked up the accusation that Jesus had said that he would *destroy*[70] *the temple and build it in three days* (cf. 26:61). As we noted earlier, Jesus had not said this, but the accusation evidently persisted. A garbled version of what Jesus had said had clearly gained currency, and it was now hurled at him as he hung on the cross. *"Save yourself"* is a call to the one who, they said, had claimed great things for himself to do something much smaller, but which they considered more relevant to the plight in which he found himself. *"If you are the Son of God,"* they say, where interestingly they repeat the words of Satan at the temptation (4:3, 5). Their conditional points to something they are admitting for the sake of the argument, "If you are the Son[71] of God," then prove it by coming down from the cross.[72] It is indeed blasphemy when mortals in this way dictate to the Son of God how he should exercise his divine sonship.

41-42. The mockery is continued by *the chief priests* and their associates; Matthew alone records that with the *chief priests* were *the scribes and elders* (Mark has "the scribes"; elsewhere in chs. 26 and 27 *scribes* are mentioned only in 26:57) and thus brings out the complete rejection of Jesus by official Judaism. It is surprising that people of this eminence should be present at a crucifixion, and the fact that they were is an indication of the depth of their hostility and vindictiveness toward Jesus. The

---

69. "These probably were not chance passers-by but people who deliberately followed the procession out of the city to enjoy the spectacle of an execution" (Ridderbos).

70. BDF notes that the present participle here is equivalent to the conative imperfect, "who would destroy . . . build" (339[3]).

71. We should view this as an example of Colwell's rule that the preceding anarthrous predicate is definite; despite the lack of the article υἱός is definite — "the" Son, not "a" Son.

72. "We hear in their taunt an eerie reprise of Satan's 'If you are Son of God, throw yourself down' (4:6)" (L. T. Johnson, *The Writings of the New Testament* [Philadelphia, 1986], pp. 180-81).

717

taunts of the general public were directed straight at Jesus, but it is in character that these aristocratic folk did not address the sufferer, though no doubt they made sure that the words were loud enough for him to hear. They spoke ostensibly to one another, not to him, as they joked among themselves. *"He saved others,"* they said, *"himself he cannot save."* The opening words are amply documented in this Gospel; again and again Matthew has recorded Jesus' saving acts (e.g., 9:21-22; 14:30-31). And there is a profound truth in their next words, though they were quite unaware of it. If he would bring salvation to others, then *himself he cannot save.* They were witnesses of the greatest saving act in the history of the world and indeed had taken a leading part in the events that brought it about, but they were quite unaware of its significance.[73] Matthew seems once more to be mocking the mockers.

They move from salvation to kingship. Sarcastically they say, *"He is the King[74] of Israel"* — a King on a cross? Put there by his loyal subjects? From their point of view it was fantastic, and yet once again they have given expression to an important truth. He was and is the King of Israel, his rejection by his own nation notwithstanding. They go on to challenge him to show the power he claimed to have by coming down from his cross. Then, they said, *"we will believe in him."*[75] They probably would not have, for they did not believe when the resurrection took place. But in any case (to quote words I have written elsewhere): "their outlook was wrong. They said they would have believed He was the Son of God had He come down from the cross. We believe He was the Son of God because He stayed up."[76]

43. Matthew adds a further statement that is not in the other Gospels. In words reminiscent of Psalm 22:8 these mockers bear witness to the fact that Jesus *put his trust[77] in God;* even his foes could testify to that. Trust in the heavenly Father had characterized Jesus throughout his whole life. But then they go on to show that they know as little about the character and

---

73. "His willing acceptance of suffering to further in death the purpose for which he had lived is an idea they cannot grasp" (Filson).

74. This is another example of the preceding anarthrous predicate being definite (as in v. 40); it is "the King," not "a King."

75. This is the only example in the Gospels of πιστεύω ἐπί — accusative of person (elsewhere the construction occurs 4 times in Acts and twice in Paul only in the New Testament). The idea is that of faith on the basis of, faith resting on. Moule holds that it "possibly retains a sense of movement, metaphorically" (*IBNTG*, p. 49).

76. *The Story of the Cross* (London, 1957), p. 100. Kingsbury notes that Jesus "does not even have at his command sufficient power to get himself down and so prove this messianic 'claim' (i.e., that he was 'King of the Jews,' v. 37) for which he is being executed" (*Matthew*, p. 36). But this is not what Matthew is saying. He records Jesus' words about access to more than twelve legions of angels (26:53). It is not lack of power to come down from the cross that keeps Jesus there in Matthew's account; it is his will to save others.

77. Burton cites this as an example of the perfect "used when the attention is directed wholly to the present resulting state, the past action of which it is the result being left out of thought" (75).

the purposes of God as they do about those of Jesus. *"Let him deliver him now if he wants him,"* they say. Despite the Scriptures that they studied so assiduously and reverenced so wholeheartedly, they had not penetrated to the great truth that the purposes of God are often worked out through suffering.[78] They could not understand that God was really working out his purpose of salvation through the sufferer on the cross. They conclude with, *"for he said, 'I am God's Son.'"* They had correctly discerned that Jesus claimed a special relationship to God, though it is not clear to what occasion or to what speech of Jesus they are referring.

44. Briefly Matthew records mockery from a third source, those who were crucified with Jesus. He says no more than that *the brigands* who were crucified on either side of him *were upbraiding him in the same way.* It is curious that men in the same plight should join in the mockery, but we should bear in mind that *brigands* were probably freedom fighters and may well have been exasperated with people like Jesus who were strong enough critics of the establishment but did nothing to help those who risked their lives against the enemy. They had also doubtless heard something of the miracles of Jesus and might well feel inclined to say, as Luke reports one of them did, "Are you not the Christ? Save yourself — and us!" (Luke 23:39). But Matthew makes little of the incident. He says nothing about the words *the brigands* actually used, or indeed about anything they said apart from the fact that they were *upbraiding*[79] Jesus and thus joining in the general chorus of his enemies. Matthew is making the point that on all sides there was antagonism as Jesus went to his death. Luke tells us that one of these men was repentant and rebuked the other for his upbraiding of Jesus. It may be that both did this at the beginning but that one, impressed by the way Jesus bore it all, repented and found forgiveness. Or Matthew may be referring to only one of the criminals crucified with him.[80]

45. All three Synoptists tell us that there was darkness over all the land *from the sixth hour*[81] (i.e., noon) *until the ninth hour* (3 p.m.). This cannot be explained as an eclipse, for it was Passover time and with a full moon an eclipse is not possible. It has been suggested that the darkness was due to a sandstorm, but this is unlikely; nothing in the passage indicates sand.

78. They may well have been thinking along the lines of the writer of *The Wisdom of Solomon*: "if the righteous man is God's son, he will help him, and will deliver him from the hand of his adversaries. Let us test him with insult and torture. . . . Let us condemn him to a shameful death, for, according to what he says, he will be protected" (2:18-20).

79. The same verb, ὀνειδίζω, is used in Psalm 69:9 (LXX).

80. This may be an example of the plural "used in the NT for one person or thing in both a Semitic and a normal Greek manner," as Turner holds (M, III, pp. 25, 26); Robertson, however, denies this (p. 409).

81. Matthew is not saying that Jesus was crucified at noon; it is not certain exactly when he was nailed to the cross. Mark says that it was at "the third hour" (Mark 15:25), but John says that Jesus was still before Pilate at "about the sixth hour" (John 19:14). We should understand that both times are approximate (people did not rush to a sundial to find the exact time) and that probably Jesus was crucified in the middle to late morning.

We should understand the darkness as supernatural, leading up to the time when the Son of God breathed his last. It was not a local phenomenon, peculiar to Jerusalem and its immediate environs, for all three Synoptists tell us that it was *over all the land* (the word could mean "all the earth," but the land of Israel seems more likely). They clearly mean that it was not a natural phenomenon but the result of divine intervention. Matthew is probably mindful of the darkness mentioned in Exodus 10:22 and Amos 8:9. Darkness is sometimes associated with the end of all things (cf. 24:29), and accordingly it has been suggested that we are to see such a meaning here. But nothing in the context leads us to think that Matthew has eschatological considerations in mind; furthermore, we should remember that the darkness was followed immediately by the cry of dereliction, which does not fit an eschatological situation. Darkness is associated with judgment in several places in Scripture (Isa. 5:30; 13:10-11; Joel 3:14-15, etc.), and it appears that we are to understand it here as pointing to God's judgment on sin that is linked with the cross.

46. Then at *about the ninth hour* Jesus died. Matthew and Mark both tell us that Jesus uttered a loud cry.[82] The words, which seem to be a mixture of Hebrew and Aramaic,[83] form the opening of Psalm 22 and are slightly different in Mark, where they are more clearly Aramaic. It may be that Jesus quoted the Psalm in Hebrew and that Mark put it into Aramaic, the language of the people. But it is likely that a dying man would use his own language rather than another, and this favors Aramaic as original. Since they are the only words Matthew and Mark record Jesus as speaking from the cross, they must be taken as very significant for these Evangelists (there are six other sayings, but they are all in Luke and John). Speaking loudly as he did, Jesus evidently meant the words to be heard.

There is no great difficulty in translating Jesus' words (as Matthew did for his non-Hebrew-speaking readers): *"My God, my God, why[84] did you abandon[85] me."* But understanding what they mean is a much more difficult problem.[86] For some modern readers the words are so shocking

82. Matthew uses the compound verb ἀναβοάω (an unusual word, here only in the New Testament; MM cites only one example; LSJ says that the meaning is *"cry, shout aloud,* esp. in sign of grief or astonishment"). He reinforces it with φωνῇ μεγάλῃ.

83. Matthew gives the cry in the words: ηλι ηλι λεμα σαβαχθανι. The first word ηλι is a transliteration of the Hebrew for "my God," and this is repeated. Then comes λεμα σαβαχθανι, which is Aramaic.

84. Matthew has ἱνατί and Mark εἰς τί, but there is no great difference in meaning. Matthew has the rare θεέ; Carr thinks that this may be the only example of this vocative of θεός.

85. The verb is ἐγκαταλείπω; it means "1. *leave behind* . . . 2. *forsake, abandon, desert"* (BAGD). On the force of the aorist Turner comments, "the present results of the action are much in mind" (M, III, p. 72).

86. The Jewish understanding of the words is perhaps given by R. Levi, who said of Esther in the inner court of the king's house, "When she reached the chamber of the idols, the Divine Presence left her. She said, *My God, my God, why hast thou forsaken me?"* (*Meg.* 15b). But Jesus is not taking the words in this way.

and so different from anything Jesus said throughout his ministry that they feel it is impossible to accept them.[87] One way of doing this is to point out that the Psalm that begins in this way goes on to praise God for deliverance as the Psalmist says, "From the horns of the wild oxen you have rescued me . . . in the midst of the congregation I will praise you" (vv. 21-22). The suggestion is made accordingly that in his hour of need Jesus was reciting a psalm that brings comfort and that we are to understand from the words quoted that he went through the whole psalm. To this it may well be retorted that if this was the case almost any other verse in the whole psalm would convey the meaning better than those Jesus actually quotes.[88] But in any case it is perilous to argue from the use of one verse that Jesus was quoting the whole psalm; indeed, he may not have been quoting at all. Many religious people express their thoughts in the language of Scripture, and it is possible that Jesus was doing just that.

Another view is that Jesus was mistaken: in this desperate hour he felt abandoned, but, of course, God had not really forsaken him.[89] But it is almost blasphemous to say that we know the situation, and specifically the relationship between Jesus and the Father, better than he did. It is better to face the words honestly and to accept the fact that this was part of the putting away of sin.[90] There must always be mystery here. We who are finite and sinners do not understand, and cannot even begin to understand, how evil appears to a holy God. The prophet Habakkuk could say in his prayer, "Your eyes are too pure to behold evil, and you cannot look on wrongdoing" (Hab. 1:13). And the apostle Paul adds, "him who knew no sin, he [i.e., the Father] made sin for us" (2 Cor. 5:21); and again, Christ became "a curse for us, for it is written, 'Cursed is everyone who hangs on a tree'" (Gal. 3:13). When we put such passages of Scripture together, it seems that in the working out of salvation for sinners the hitherto

87. Many cite T. R. Glover, "I have sometimes thought there never was an utterance that reveals more amazingly the distance between feeling and fact" (*The Jesus of History* [London, 1917], p. 192). But we must not read back our experiences of spiritual weakness into the dying moments of Jesus. Beare takes notice of only two possibilities: Matthew may "intend to convey to us that the last words of Jesus were a cry of despair" or that he thought of "Jesus as having in mind the entire Psalm." But this is surely inadequate.

88. Cf. H. Maynard Smith, "the awful cry which startled the onlookers cannot be reconciled with a devotional exercise" (*Atonement* [London, 1925], p. 155). Barclay says, "on a cross a man does not recite poetry to himself, even the poetry of a psalm; and besides that, the whole atmosphere of the darkened world is the atmosphere of unrelieved tragedy" (II, pp. 406-7).

89. One form of this is put forward by R. Menzies: "this cry was wrung from the soul of Jesus by the *unresponsiveness* of men" (*ET*, LXV [1953-54], p. 183). But Jesus is not complaining about the unresponsiveness of men; he is concerned with the fact that it is God who has abandoned him.

90. Cf. J. Moltmann, "Not until we understand his abandonment by the God and Father whose imminence and closeness he had proclaimed in a unique, gracious and festive way, can we understand what was distinctive about his death. Just as there was a unique fellowship with God in his life and preaching, so in his death there was a unique abandonment by God" (*The Crucified God* [London, 1974], p. 149).

unbroken communion between the Father and the Son was mysteriously broken. It is surely better to accept this, knowing that we do not understand it fully, than to attempt some rationalization of the saying so that it becomes more palatable to the prejudices of modern Westerners.[91]

But abandonment is not the whole story. We must bear in mind that Jesus cried out, *"My God, my God."* The human Jesus felt and gave expression to the abandonment, but he also retained his trust. "My" points to a continuing relationship; according to Bengel, he "adds 'My' with confidence, patience, and self-resignation." E. Stauffer has further pointed out that there can be a crying out after God as well as a crying to God for help.[92] In the anguish of godforsakenness Jesus still cries out in trust. The human Jesus might still be puzzled ("Why. . . ?"). But he trusts, and we should not miss this aspect of the cry of dereliction.

47. Despite the loudness of Jesus' cry, it was not understood. In Hebrew the word for "my God" is not so very different from the word for "Elijah," and some of those near the cross thought that Jesus was *calling for Elijah.* That prophet, of course, had not died in the usual way but had been taken up into heaven in a whirlwind (2 Kings 2:11). He came to be viewed as a worker of miracles and one who might conceivably come to the help of the oppressed on earth.[93] This does not mean that any of the bystanders held that Elijah would come to help Jesus, but only that they thought that Jesus might have hoped for help from the prophet. They were convinced that Jesus was in a situation from which he could not have escaped and could not escape; therefore it was only logical that he should appeal to some heavenly being to help him. So far were they still from understanding what was happening before their very eyes.

48. Perhaps with some confused idea that Elijah might respond and that if he did it would be well to be on the right side, *one of them* (which may mean one of the spectators or one of the soldiers) took action to help Jesus. *Immediately*[94] he *ran,* showing that he was in haste to do what he could (and would be seen to be in haste), and filled *a sponge* with *sour wine.* The *sour wine* was the ordinary cheap beverage that the soldiers used, and it would have been available there where the soldiers were at work. He *put it on a reed* (John says that he put it on hyssop). It has been objected

---

91. Cf. Green, "the overwhelming probability is that (these words) were remembered, and not the work of subsequent devout reflection." I have examined the saying at greater length in *The Cross in the New Testament* (Grand Rapids and Exeter, 1965), pp. 42-49; *The Cross of Jesus* (Grand Rapids and Exeter, 1988), pp. 67-83.

92. He speaks of Jesus as going through "the lowest depth of human need" and goes on, "This depth, however, is the inferno of dereliction. From it He cries as only a man can cry, with full and final force. Yet the ἐβόησεν is no longer a crying to God for help and recompense; it is a crying after God Himself" (*TDNT*, I, p. 627).

93. See *TDNT*, II, p. 930 for the development of such ideas among the Jews.

94. εὐθέως, which Matthew uses 11 times. Mark is fond of saying that things happened "immediately," but for this he uses εὐθύς, which he has 42 times. But despite this fondness for indicating haste he does not do it here.

that a crucified person was too high above the earth for this to take place, but it must not be forgotten that a cross need not be very high (and, we are told, normally was not, except for especially heinous prisoners). All that was necessary was to get the crucified person's feet off the ground, and he would die. Thus *a sponge . . . on a reed* was quite adequate for the purpose. This man then gave Jesus a drink (and thus fulfilled Ps. 69:21).

49. But giving a drink was a one-man affair. *The rest* discouraged him; they preferred to see whose side Elijah was on before they started helping the crucified.[95] Their use of the present tense *is coming* indicates that if there was to be help from that source it would have to be quick, but the notion of futurity is conveyed with the unusual future participle of the verb "to save."[96] They put in general terms the possibility that the prophet will come "saving" Jesus (Mark has "come to take him down," Mark 15:36). The "Wait and see" attitude apparently was the popular one, for we hear no more of any activity on the part of the bystanders. Some commentators (e.g., Schweizer) regard this whole incident as a further piece of mockery. They may be right, but the way Matthew has put it, it seems rather that one person at any rate was trying to help the sufferer by giving him a drink and that the others were simply waiting to see what would happen.

50. *But,* in Matthew's characteristic way, is adversative and sets Jesus in contrast to these uncommitted watchers. Both Matthew and Mark say that Jesus gave a loud cry, though neither indicates what he said. It seems likely that this is the cry that John reports immediately before Jesus' death, "It is finished" (John 19:30). If so, it points to the completion of the saving work that Jesus came to do. He had taught and he had healed and he had set the example in his own life, and now he gave his life "a ransom for many" (20:28). With that loud cry Jesus *yielded up*[97] *his spirit.* None of the Evangelists uses any of the usual ways of saying that Jesus died, and this may be part of the way they bring out the truth that there was something in his death that set it apart from all other deaths. There appears to be an element of voluntariness (cf. Chrysostom, "for this cause He cried with the voice, that it might be shown that the act was done by power," p. 521). Most of the crucified were in a state of absolute exhaustion at the end, but Jesus' utterance of a loud shout does not comply with this and supports the view that to some extent his death was voluntary. To the end all four

95. Moulton comments: "In Hellenistic Greek the imperative 1st person is beginning to be differentiated from other subjunctives by the addition of ἄφες" (M, I, p. 175); the meaning is "Let us see." ἄφες is singular, though it is to be taken with the plural ἴδωμεν. It would, of course, be possible to take ἄφες as addressed to the man giving the drink, followed by "Let us see. . . ."

96. BDF points out that the future participle is used to convey the idea of purpose in classical Greek, but that, apart from Luke, it is found in the New Testament only here (418[4]).

97. The verb is ἀφίημι, which is used 142 times in the New Testament but only here in the sense "die." Mark and Luke both make use of the verb ἐκπνέω, while John has παρέδωκεν τὸ πνεῦμα.

Evangelists refrain from trying to harrow our feelings; they tell their story simply and let the facts speak for themselves.

51. Matthew's characteristic *And look* (see on 1:20) makes for a vivid introduction to what follows, as the Evangelist goes on to speak of some unusual happenings that accompanied the death of Jesus.[98] He starts with the temple and speaks of *the curtain,* which appears to mean the curtain that separated the holy of holies, into which even the priests might not go (except the high priest, and he only one day in the year), from the holy place, into which only the priests might go (most interpreters accept this view, for the meaning is surely that by the death of Jesus the way into the holiest has been opened). Alternatively it might signify the curtain that separated the holy place to which priests had access from the adjoining court to which lay Israelite men were admitted (McNeile favors this view on the grounds that it must have been visible to people in general and not only to the priests; Ridderbos also thinks of this curtain). Either way the thought is of judgment on the temple, and Matthew is indicating that symbolically the way into the holy place was opened by the death of Jesus (cf. Heb. 10:19-20). He emphasizes this truth by saying that the curtain was *torn in two from top to bottom,* which indicates more than a minor tear. He is speaking of a bisected curtain, a curtain that no longer functioned to keep what lay on the other side of it a secret from all those outside. Religion was never to be the same now that Jesus the Messiah had died for sinners. This phenomenon, Matthew says, was accompanied by an earthquake, *the earth* being *shaken* and *the rocks split.* He leaves his readers in no doubt that what had happened was no minor event, but, in the literal sense of the word, earth-shaking.[99]

52. Up to the tearing of the temple curtain Matthew's narrative has run parallel to that of Mark, but with the earthquake he is using material not found in Mark, or, for that matter, anywhere else. This continues with his reference to the opening of *the tombs.* This would not be surprising in an earthquake; indeed, it is not easy to see how it could possibly be avoided. Rock tombs were not like graves where bodies would be buried under mounds of earth. Normally these rock tombs were above the surface, and when the earth shook great strains would be put on them. Many would burst open in a large earthquake. But Matthew is not speaking of the natural consequences of a big earthquake, for he goes on to say, *many*

---

98. Albright and Mann comment, "It is certainly no service to scholarship to find in these verses an imaginative piece of fiction on the part of the evangelist, or simply an attempt to garnish the account of the passion with improbable details." They go on to say, "At the time of the death of Jesus a new community was born" (*AB*).

99. For earthquakes in the Jerusalem area see *ISBE,* II, pp. 4-5; this article refers to an earthquake that damaged the temple in A.D. 33. In the Talmud we read that the doors of the temple opened by themselves forty years before the destruction of the city (*Yoma* 39b). Allen cites this passage and others from Josephus and Jerome, and says, "A cleavage in the masonry of the porch, which rent the outer veil and left the Holy Place open to view, would account for the language of the Gospels, of Josephus, and of the Talmud."

bodies of the saints that were asleep were raised. The normal New Testament position is that the faithful departed will be raised at the last great day when this earthly life as we know it will give place to the life of the new order in the new heavens and the new earth. But Matthew speaks of some being raised at the time of the crucifixion, information that we find in none of the other Gospels, and indeed nowhere else at all. Donald Senior regards this as important, for it indicates "an implied soteriology." Matthew is telling his readers something about salvation. "It is the *death* of Jesus which triggers the resurrection of the saints — this is the new feature Matthew brings to the synoptic tradition."[100]

53. But he goes on to say that *after his resurrection they came out of the tombs,* so that their rising may possibly not be connected with the earthquake. We could put a full stop after *were opened* (there is no punctuation in the oldest MSS) and understand the breaking of the tombs as occurring on Good Friday and the rising of the saints on Easter Day. Carson cites J. W. Wenham for this view and says: "On the one hand, Jesus' sacrificial death blots out sin, defeats the powers of evil and death, and opens up access to God. On the other, Jesus' victorious resurrection and vindication promise the final resurrection of those who die in him." This may be the way of it, but perhaps we should bear in mind that we too easily separate the death and the resurrection of Jesus and tend to attribute some things to the one and others to the other. There may be some scope for this, but the two go together. The death of Jesus was that of one who would in due course rise again; the rising of Jesus was the rising of one who had died for sinners. The one would be meaningless without the other. It seems that here Matthew has the great death-and-resurrection in mind and links his raising of the saints to the whole happening. Thus he mentions it when he speaks of the death of Jesus but goes on to what he says happened at the time of the resurrection: some of *the saints that were asleep . . . came out of the tombs.* Nobody else mentions this, and we are left to conclude that Matthew is making the point that the resurrection of Jesus brought about the resurrection of his people. Just as the rending of the temple curtain makes it clear that the way to God is open for all, so the raising of the saints shows that death has been conquered. Those so raised went into Jerusalem and *appeared to many.* Since there are no other records of these appearances, it appears to be impossible to say anything about them. But Matthew is surely giving expression to his conviction that Jesus is Lord over both the living and the dead.[101]

54. Matthew returns to the time when Jesus died and gives us the reaction of *the centurion and those who were with him.* Mark and Luke speak

---

100. *CBQ, XXXVIII* (1976), p. 328.

101. To Buttrick the words express the faith that "God watched his Son on the Cross; God wrote in darkened sky and torn mountains his judgment on our wickedness, and his love for Christ; and God proved himself then and there the Lord of death and life."

of the reaction of *the centurion*, but only this Evangelist includes his associates, evidently the soldiers who had actually performed the crucifixion and who were watching the sufferer. *The earthquake* and its accompaniments impressed them, and they linked these happenings with Jesus, for not only were they *very much afraid* (the earthquake by itself would have caused fear) but they went on to say, *"Truly this was the Son of God,"*[102] the same confession as that made by the disciples earlier (14:33). Their *Truly* points to certainty; they were not making a tentative suggestion (cf. *GNB*, "He really was the Son of God!"). They understood that the death of Jesus showed him to be *the Son of God*, and this is important. Even to these Gentiles it was clear that there was something in the death of Jesus, together with the attendant phenomena, that showed that he was not just another man. He had a special relationship to God, and it was important for Matthew that this be made clear.

55-56. Matthew rounds off his account of the crucifixion by telling his readers of the presence of a group of ladies. All the Gospels tell us that women were present to the end, but after Peter's threefold denial of Jesus the only male disciple mentioned is "the disciple whom Jesus loved," and he only in the Fourth Gospel. Against the background of the failure of the male disciples the devotion and the courage of the women shine out. Matthew says that there were *many* of them, and that they were watching *from a distance* (cf. Ps. 38:11). It may not have been safe to go too close to that execution where Jesus' enemies were in control, and it may not have been proper for ladies to be close to a crucifixion; they may also have chosen not to be associated in any way with the mockers. For whatever reason, they kept their distance, but they remained there to the end, demonstrating by their very presence their continuing loyalty to their crucified Lord. It is worth noticing that there is no mention of any woman at any time taking action against Jesus; all his enemies were men. Matthew says that these women *had followed Jesus from Galilee*, where *followed*, as often in this Gospel, has the nuance of being followers, disciples, and *from Galilee* shows that their following was constant. They had come a long way in their service and obviously at some personal sacrifice, for the way was long and it took time. Matthew also says that they had come *providing for him*. The expression might be understood as "serving him,"[103] but in this context and taking into consideration what we learn from other passages (e.g., Luke 8:1-3) it appears that Matthew is referring to the way these women provided the penniless Jesus with what he needed for survival. Matthew proceeds to mention three of them. He does not indicate why he picked these three, but evidently they had some importance for Matthew or his readers or both. *Mary Magdalene* (listed also by Mark and

---

102. With θεοῦ υἱός we have another example of the anarthrous predicate preceding the verb: it denotes "the" Son, not "a" Son.

103. διακονέω often has this meaning.

John as having been at the crucifixion) is prominent in the resurrection narratives, but apart from that we know little about her. But obviously she was devoted to Jesus, and it is interesting that Matthew names her first. He has another *Mary*, this one *the mother of James and Joseph* (Mark has James and Joses), but unfortunately we have no other information about her or her sons. *The mother of Zebedee's sons* has appeared before in this Gospel (cf. 20:20-21). Since two of her sons, James and John, were among the Twelve, she was an important person among the followers of Jesus (she is apparently the Salome whom Mark mentions). These women then, and others, were faithful to the end and watched the last moments of their Lord.[104]

3. The Burial, 27:57-66

> [57]*Now when evening had come, a rich man from Arimathea named Joseph, who was himself a disciple of Jesus, came;* [58]*this man approached Pilate and requested the body of Jesus. Then Pilate commanded that it be given.* [59]*And Joseph took the body, wrapped it in clean linen,* [60]*and put it in his own new tomb, which he had hewn in the rock. And when he had rolled a big stone to the door of the tomb, he went away.* [61]*Now Mary Magdalene and the other Mary were there, sitting opposite the tomb.*
>
> [62]*But the next day, that is, after the Preparation, the chief priests and the Pharisees were gathered with Pilate.* [63]*And they said, "Sir, we remember that that deceiver said while he was alive, 'After three days I will be raised.'* [64]*Command, therefore, that the tomb be made secure until the third day, lest his disciples come and steal him and say to the people, 'He was raised from the dead,' and the last error will be greater than the first."* [65]*Pilate said to them, "Take a guard; go, make it as secure as you know."* [66]*And they went off and made the tomb secure, having sealed the stone, together with the guard.*

Matthew prepares us for the resurrection narrative by recounting the way Jesus' burial was carried out and the precautions that were taken to ensure that nobody stole the body out of the tomb. We might have expected family members to arrange for the burial, or if not, then some of his close followers, but Matthew brings into the narrative Joseph of Arimathea, who went to see Pilate to get permission to bury Jesus and then placed him in his own tomb. This was an action of some generosity, for a rock tomb was expensive, and it was not permitted to bury a criminal in a family grave (*Sanh.* 6:5; cf. Daube, pp. 310-11); the tomb could probably not be used afterward for anyone else. Matthew goes on to tell us that the

---

104. Diétrich comments that Jesus gave women "their human dignity. He revealed to them the grace of pardon. He provoked in them a gratitude and a love which were unflagging. Prior to Jesus, women were regarded as inferior beings, religiously speaking."

Jewish leaders recalled Jesus' prophecy that he would rise from the dead and persuaded Pilate to secure the tomb until the third day after the crucifixion.

57. Nothing further could be done until those on the crosses died, but according to Jewish law they could not be left on the crosses overnight (Deut. 21:22-23); the Romans would be happy to leave the bodies on their crosses indefinitely as a warning to others, but Josephus tells us that even the bodies of crucified malefactors were taken down and buried before sunset (*War* 4.317). But burial had to be completed by sunset, for that marked the beginning of the Sabbath, on which no labor should be performed (specifically a corpse might not be moved on the Sabbath, nor even any member of it, *Shab.* 23:5). Thus *evening* would be late afternoon according to our way of reckoning time. Then a certain *Joseph*,[105] described as *a rich man* (in mentioning this Matthew may be drawing attention to the fulfilment of Isa. 53:9) *from Arimathea*, makes his appearance in the narrative. He is mentioned in all four Gospels in connection with the burial of Jesus, but in none of them does he make his appearance before that time (John says that he was a secret disciple, John 19:38). It is not without its interest that the crucifixion that sent most of Jesus' followers into hiding had the opposite effect on Joseph and brought him out into the open. We have no information about how he came to hear Jesus and became *a disciple*,[106] as Matthew tells us he was; John also has this information, and adds, "secretly for fear of the Jews" (John 19:38). Luke informs us that he was "a councillor," which presumably means a member of the Sanhedrin, and that he had not agreed to the plan to have Jesus executed (Luke 23:50-51). The location of *Arimathea* is not known; it has been thought to be identical with Ramathaim (1 Sam. 1:1), but this does not help us much because the site of that city is not certain. The same is true of other suggested identifications. Wherever it was, it would seem that he had left it and moved to Jerusalem; otherwise why would he have a rock tomb near that city?

58. One might have thought that someone from Jesus' family or from his close followers would have been making funeral arrangements, for the Jews took very seriously the importance of a decent burial. But it was this man Joseph who took the initiative. Since Jesus had been crucified, it was necessary to get permission from the Romans before access to the body would be permitted. Joseph went to the top and *approached Pilate*. That he was able to speak to the governor gives us some indication of his importance. He asked for the body of Jesus, and Pilate gave him permission.

---

105. τοὔνομα (= τὸ ὄνομα) ᾽Ιωσήφ is an accusative of respect: "with respect to name Joseph."

106. It is not certain whether we should read ἐμαθήτευσεν, "was a disciple," or ἐμαθητεύθη, which may have the same sense (the verb having become a deponent) or may be meant as "was made a disciple" (as in 28:19; see BDF, 148[3]).

Mark adds that Pilate was surprised that Jesus had died so soon and that Pilate checked with the centurion to make sure that he was in fact dead (Mark 15:44). When this had been verified, he *commanded that it be given*.

59-60. Joseph then *took the body* (John says that he was accompanied by Nicodemus, who brought spices for the burial, John 19:39), which presumably means that he took it down from the cross (Mark and Luke say explicitly that he took it down, Mark 15:46; Luke 23:53). He *wrapped it in clean linen*; Mark and Luke say that the body was wrapped in linen, but only Matthew specifies, what the others presumably left to be understood, that it was *clean* linen, which "suggests the respect and reverence with which he performed the burial" (Filson); it probably means that this linen had not been used before. The tomb was Joseph's *own new tomb* (only Matthew tells us that it was *his own* and that *a big stone* was needed to close it). This did not mean of itself that Joseph would have had to have another tomb hewn out for himself, for a rock tomb was normally large enough to hold several bodies. But since Jesus had been condemned as a criminal, Jews would not allow other bodies to be buried there; therefore Joseph would in fact have had to have another tomb made for himself. Matthew says that the tomb was *new*, and both Luke and John add that nobody had been buried in it. The burial was completed by rolling *a big stone to the door of the tomb*, the normal way of closing a rock tomb.

61. Matthew rounds off this section of his narrative with the information that two Marys, *Mary Magdalene* and *the other Mary*, were there. Apparently the burial was carried out by the men, for the women are not said to have done anything and apparently were simply *sitting opposite the tomb*[107] to watch what was done. Matthew does not say so, but it is clear that the burial had to be hurried because at sundown it would be the Sabbath, and the beginning of the Sabbath severely limited what could be done. The women would have been observing the scene and planning to come back after the Sabbath to complete anything that was lacking for a fitting burial. Matthew does not explain who *the other Mary* was, but we should understand her to be "the mother of James and Joseph" (v. 56).

62. In a paragraph peculiar to this Gospel Matthew turns now to the opposition (his *But* will have adversative force as he turns from what Jesus' friends did to the activity of the enemy). The story of the guard at the tomb is often assailed as a fictitious invention of the early church, but we must bear in mind that from the earliest days of the church the resurrection of Jesus was at the center of the proclamation (as Acts makes clear). Had the authorities been able to point to a body in the tomb where Jesus was placed on Good Friday, that preaching would have been shown to be

---

107. The word for *tomb* here is τάφος; Matthew uses it 6 times in all, and it is found elsewhere in the New Testament only in Romans 3:13. It does not seem to differ in meaning from μνημεῖον (37 times in the New Testament), which the other Evangelists prefer (and which Matthew also employs, as in v. 60; 28:8).

ridiculous. Though they could not have known how central the preaching of the resurrection would be, there is nothing outrageous in the suggestion that the Jewish leaders would have taken precautions to see that the body of Jesus remained where it was buried. Some such happening as Matthew relates here must have taken place. He speaks of the *next day* and calls it the day *after the Preparation,* but he does not say that that day was the Sabbath. Perhaps he did not wish to speak openly of the holy day in connection with the kind of activity he was about to describe. *The Preparation* was the day when people prepared for the Sabbath, that is, Friday.[108] On this Sabbath, then, *the chief priests and the Pharisees* met with Pilate. There is no mention of the elders, so Matthew is not speaking of an official delegation from the Sanhedrin. But both *the chief priests* and *the Pharisees* were religious personages, and they may have been expected to be interested in what Jesus taught and how they might combat it. The word rendered *were gathered* is often used to describe the coming together of assemblies,[109] and it hints that there was something formal and solemn about this meeting with Pilate.

63. We have seen that on a number of occasions Jesus had prophesied that he would rise from the dead. His disciples seem consistently to have misunderstood these prophecies, and there is no evidence that they had them in mind at this time. But his enemies did remember them, and they ascribed to Jesus' followers better memories than they apparently had. These Jewish leaders did not anticipate a resurrection; they speak of Jesus as *that deceiver* when they are referring to his predictions of his resurrection (incidentally, a marked contrast to the polite "Sir" with which they address Pilate).[110] But they recalled Jesus' prophecies and feared that the disciples might attempt to stage a mock resurrection by causing Jesus' body to disappear. They had taken notice of exactly what Jesus had said, they recalled the interval of *three days* that he had mentioned, and they have the passive *be raised* (not "I will rise"),[111] which refers the resurrection to the action of the Father. They knew exactly what they were up against, even though it does not seem to have occurred to them that what Jesus had thus prophesied would in fact take place. Some commentators say that Jesus' predictions that he would rise always took place among his followers and that the Jewish leaders would not have known this. But in the first place, one such prediction was specifically made in their hearing

---

108. I have discussed the term in *The Gospel according to John* (Grand Rapids, 1971), p. 776, n. 97.

109. συνάγω is used in something of that sense in 2:4 and other passages. Matthew uses it 24 times, which is more than twice as often as the next frequent user of the word in the New Testament (Acts with 11).

110. "As events turned out, it was the priests and the Pharisees who proved to be deceivers of the people, by their persistent assertion after the resurrection that the disciples of Jesus had stolen His body" (Tasker, p. 268).

111. ἐγείρομαι is the present tense, used in the sense of the future.

(12:40), in the second there is nothing against the suggestion that this may have happened on other occasions, in the third place the leaders would certainly have heard reports spread by Jesus' hearers, and, fourthly, Judas may have given them such information.

64. They were probably uneasy that the body had been given to friends of Jesus for burial, so they wanted to make sure that no one removed the body from the tomb where it had been placed. Accordingly they asked Pilate to take steps to ensure that the body was not stolen. *"Command,"* they say, for it was only the governor who could order troops to be stationed at the tomb. There was, of course, no reason why they should not have put some of the temple police there, but evidently they felt that some Roman soldiers would be preferable. In any case, once they had handed Jesus over to the Romans he would have been removed from their control and they might not have any rights at the sepulchre. *Therefore* looks to Jesus' prophecies. They are not saying that there was a danger that the ordinary kind of grave robber would remove Jesus' body (and they probably would not have been greatly concerned had this taken place). But because of the prophecies they wanted a guard. They wanted the tomb to be *made secure;* they did not specify that they wanted soldiers to be there, but security demanded no less. They wanted help *until the third day,* for that was the time specified in the prophecies, and if the disciples stole the body after that time they could point out that Jesus' words had not been fulfilled. But if the body was stolen within that time, the disciples could claim that *he was raised from the dead.* It is, of course, true that the disciples would have had a difficult time claiming a resurrection when all they had was a dead body, but the leaders did not want to give them the opportunity. If such a claim were made, they thought, *"the last error*[112] *will be greater than the first."* Presumably they saw Jesus' claim to messiahship as the first error and a claim to resurrection as a possible last. They were castigating his teaching and specifically they called his prophecy of his resurrection an *error* and held that a claim to resurrection would be an even greater error. They did not consider for a moment that there was any element of truth in what Jesus had said.

65. Pilate responded to their plea in words that may be understood in more ways than one. The verb seems to be an imperative with the sense *"Take a guard"* (literally, "Have a guard," i.e., "I grant you a guard"), but it could be understood as an indicative, in which case it would mean, "You have a guard of your own"; in other words, "Rely on your own temple guard" (M. Green takes the words in this sense, p. 288). It seems probable that we should take the words in the former sense (they would not need Pilate to tell them that they had the temple guard).[113] In 28:11-14 it appears

---

112. *Error* here (πλάνη) is cognate with that for "deceiver" in verse 63 (πλάνος).

113. κουστωδία is the transliteration of the Latin *custodia,* "a guard." In the New Testament it is used only in this incident (v. 66; 28:11). It would not be a natural way of referring

that they are answerable to Pilate. He tells them to go off and to *make* the tomb *as secure*[114] as they can. Presumably this means that they are to choose the best dispositions of the force to guard against the possibility they foresaw.[115] With a free hand in this matter they would not be able to complain that Pilate had let them down if things went wrong.

66. Matthew rounds off this section of his narrative with the Jewish leaders happy and secure. They *went off,* away from Pilate, and proceeded to do as he had suggested. They *made the tomb secure,* and Matthew tells us that they did this, *having sealed the stone.* That was the important thing. If the stone was not moved, there could be no ill-founded rumor of a resurrection. They had the stone sealed and they had *the guard,* so from their point of view all was well. They had neatly defeated any attempt the disciples might make to empty the tomb and to start stories of a resurrection.

But in doing this they did more than they knew. They ensured that there could be no nonsense about disciples stealing the body when in due course Jesus did rise from the dead. The precautions of his enemies would underline the truth of his resurrection. It is not without interest that, after all their precautions to ensure that the body was not stolen, in the event they themselves spread reports that that had indeed happened; they said that his disciples had stolen the body. Justin tells us that in the middle of the second century the Jews were still claiming that the disciples had stolen the body (*Trypho* 108), despite the fact that the Jews themselves had made it clear that there was no possibility of the body of Jesus being stolen. On the third day the tomb was empty; the only question was how this came about.

---

to the temple guard, but it was the term a Roman would use of his own soldiers. That a Roman detachment is meant is clear in *The Gospel of Peter,* which says, "Pilate gave them Petronius the centurion with soldiers to watch the sepulchre" (8:31).

114. The verb is ἀσφαλίζω, used three times in this incident and again in Acts 16:24 only in the New Testament.

115. He orders, "make it as secure *as you know.*" Translations tend to say, "as you can" (e.g., *NRSV,* "make it as secure as you can"; the mg. has "you know how," but this inserts a "how" that is lacking in the Greek).

Matthew 28

VIII. THE RESURRECTION, 28:1-20

Each of the Evangelists has his own way of treating the resurrection of Jesus; thus there are some not inconsiderable differences between the accounts in our four Gospels. But with all their differences there are some things common to them all. One of these is that each tells of something completely unexpected. It is clear that, despite the teaching of Jesus, his followers had no expectation that he would rise from the dead. The resurrection came as a wonderful surprise. The accounts in our four Gospels are notoriously difficult to reconcile,[1] but this underlines the truth that they are independent and that there is no attempt to reproduce some official party line. Each of the Evangelists tells the story as best he knows without trying to harmonize it with what somebody else says. But with all the differences Diétrich points out that "Three elements, nevertheless, are common to all four Gospels — the empty tomb, the announcement of the Resurrection to the women, and the meeting of the disciples with the Risen One." In addition to these three features Matthew's account includes stories of the women seeing an angel and later meeting Jesus, of what happened to the guard the Jewish leaders had posted, and a very important account of the great commission Jesus gave to his followers to take the gospel throughout the entire world. He ends his Gospel on the note of world evangelism in obedience to the last commandment of Jesus Christ.[2]

A. The Women at the Tomb, 28:1-10

1But after the Sabbath, as it began to dawn on the first day of the week, Mary Magdalene and the other Mary came to see the tomb. 2And look, there

---

1. But not impossible. B. F. Westcott, for example, drew up a tentative timetable of the events on that first Easter morning in which he was able to list all the appearances known to us (*The Gospel according to St. John*, II [rpt. Grand Rapids, 1954], pp. 335-36). More recently John Wenham has made a thorough examination of the problem and come up with a solution (*Easter Enigma* [Exeter, 1984]).

2. D. Wenham has a useful discussion of this chapter in his article "The Resurrection Narratives in Matthew's Gospel" (*Tyndale Bulletin* 24 [1973], pp. 21-54).

was a great earthquake; for an angel of the Lord came down from heaven and went and rolled away the stone and sat on it. ³And his appearance was as lightning, and his clothing white as snow. ⁴And from fear of him the guards trembled and became like dead men. ⁵And the angel answered the women, saying, "Don't you be afraid, for I know that you are looking for Jesus, who was crucified. ⁶He is not here, for he has been raised, as he said; come, see the place where he lay. ⁷And go quickly and tell his disciples that he has been raised from the dead; and look, he is going ahead of you into Galilee. You will see him there; look, I have told you."

⁸And they went away from the tomb quickly with fear and great joy, and ran to tell his disciples. ⁹And look, Jesus met them and said, "Greetings." And they came to him, took hold of his feet, and worshiped him. ¹⁰Then Jesus says to them, "Don't be afraid; go, tell my brothers to go into Galilee, and there they will see me."

When he comes to the resurrection narrative Matthew begins with the effect the appearance of an angel had on the guard. Like the other Evangelists, he indicates that Jesus' first appearance was to some women. But unlike them he says that the angel who came and rolled the stone from the tomb told these ladies to tell the disciples that they should go into Galilee and that Jesus would meet them there, an instruction that Jesus himself repeated when he met them as they went to tell the disciples what they had seen.

1. Matthew's *But* has adversative force as he sets the holy women over against the guards the Jews had set over the tomb. He moves to the time *after*[3] *the Sabbath.* He is not speaking of the time immediately after the Sabbath, for that would commence at sunset; he is going on to early morning, *as it began to dawn;* the women would not have been able to do much at the tomb during the hours of darkness, and in any case there would have been no sense of urgency once the body of Jesus had been placed in the tomb. Matthew says that *Mary Magdalene and the other Mary* came to the tomb, but the only indication as to their reason was that they came *to see* it. Mark tells us that when the Sabbath was over they bought spices, and both Mark and Luke say that they brought their spices to the tomb, evidently to complete the burial that had been done in haste on the Friday. Presumably Matthew omits the reference to the spices because he

---

3. ὀψέ, which Matthew uses only here, is an adverb meaning "late" and may be used of the evening (e.g., Mark 13:35). But it can also be used as an improper preposition with the meaning "after" (BAGD, 3). The question is, Which is the usage here? Moule points to the two possibilities, "after the Sabbath" and "late on the Sabbath" (*IBNTG*, p. 86), and Robertson cites examples elsewhere of both uses, "after" and "late on" (pp. 645-46). McNeile says that it probably means "late on the Sabbath" and that Matthew is using the Roman way of starting the day at dawn rather than the Jewish way of starting it at sunset, but this involves too many improbabilities. The grammar is difficult, but it is best to understand Matthew to be saying that the women's action was after the Sabbath; he then goes on to specify that it was dawn on the first day of the week (thus indicating how long after the Sabbath it was).

knows (as the women probably did not) that there was a guard at the tomb that would have prevented them from using their spices anyway; the whole reference to spices was for him irrelevant. John informs us that Nicodemus had used a large quantity of spices at the burial, but even so the women would have wanted to bring their tribute (just as in our day no matter how many wreaths there may be at a funeral we still want to make our own contribution). Matthew concentrates on the fact of the resurrection and simply says that the women *came to see the tomb*. It is enough for his purpose that they were there.

2. Matthew's characteristic *And look* (see on 1:20) introduces a note of vividness;[4] he wants his readers to see the scene at the tomb. He says that there was *a great earthquake* (for "earthquakes" in Palestine see the note on 27:51; only Matthew has this reference). *For* introduces a reason for this one: *an angel of the Lord came down from heaven.*[5] It is not easy to be clear on just what happened when the women came to the tomb. Matthew has one angel, Mark speaks of a young man sitting on the right-hand side (Stendahl thinks that he is the angel in Matthew, for "angels had no wings in the 1st cent."), Luke has two men in dazzling clothes, while John refers to two angels in white. It seems clear that all these are references to angels; the small differences should not disconcert us unduly. Each of the Evangelists is saying in his own way that when the women came to the tomb they encountered an angelic visitation.[6] It is not surprising that they speak of what happened in slightly different ways, for different people may well have had different perceptions.[7] The important thing is that there were unusual angelic visitations and what the angels said concerned Jesus' rising from the dead. The angel of whom Matthew writes *went and rolled away the stone* from the tomb. It appears that he made contact with the earth at some place other than the tomb and that from there he *went* to the place where Jesus had been buried. That he *rolled away the stone*, of course, was not in order that the risen Jesus might get out, but that the women might get into the tomb. Matthew implies that Jesus had already

---

4. Matthew has καὶ ἰδοὺ 6 times in these 20 verses; clearly the whole marvelous time was vivid to him.

5. Hill comments, "The angel at the Birth and at the Resurrection is a witness to the event, explaining its meaning and assigning to others a precise task." The expression "the angel of the Lord" occurs elsewhere in this Gospel only in 1:20, 24; 2:13, 19. It is a common expression in the Old Testament, but in the New it is found again only twice in Luke and 4 times in Acts.

6. Meier asserts that "the angel of the Lord" here is "actually, God himself in visible form," but this is an unwarranted assumption.

7. W. Temple comments, "It is not to be presumed that angels are physical objects reflecting rays of light upon the retina of the eye. When men 'see' or 'hear' angels, it is rather to be supposed that an intense interior awareness of a divine message leads to the projection of an image which is then experienced as an occasion of something seen and heard. That divine messengers were sent and divine messages received we need not doubt; that they took physical form so that all who 'saw' anything must 'see' the same thing we need not suppose" (*Readings in St. John's Gospel* [London, 1947], p. 380).

risen; the rolling away of the stone was to let the women see that the body was no longer there. They had been there on the Friday and seen Jesus buried, and unless the stone was rolled away they would surely think that his body was still there, inside the tomb. Mark tells us that as they came to the place they discussed the problem of rolling the stone away, as well they might, for it was a great stone (27:60). But when they arrived, they found their problem solved; the angel had done it for them, and having rolled the stone away he *sat on it*. What had been an insuperable obstacle for the women was no more than a place to sit for the angel.

3. Matthew inserts a little comment about the way the angel looked. He speaks of *his appearance*[8] and compares it to *lightning*. This undoubtedly signifies that it was impressive, but it is not easy to understand exactly what it means. Perhaps we can say that the angel was "striking" to look at. His *clothing*[9] was *white as snow*; this description has become conventional for that which is very white, but it is used of clothes only here in the New Testament (and only once of anything else, with reference to hair, Rev. 1:14). We are left with the impression of an august personage.

4. And the angel certainly made that impression on *the guards*.[10] They were supposed to keep the tomb safe from disciples who might try to steal the body, and they may well have been prepared to repel any such attempt. But an angel coming from heaven and rolling back the huge stone was another proposition altogether. They had never seen such a being, and not surprisingly they *trembled*[11] at the sight. Matthew is not saying that they were slightly disturbed, but is speaking of an experience that overwhelmed them with fear; they were caught up in a terror that paralyzed them. That they *became like dead men* points to the paralysis that overtook them when they were face to face with an angel. They had probably been prepared to face human opposition of some sort; why else would they have been assigned their task? But a striking heavenly visitant who manipulated the great stone with ease and whose appearance was like nothing they had ever seen was something else altogether.

5. But the angel's business was not with those irrelevant guards. He ignored them and addressed the women. Matthew says that he *answered* them. They are not recorded as having said anything he might answer, but he responded to their situation. They had come to do something about burying a dead body and there was no dead body; there were guards, armed men, though they were trembling and afraid. The angel answered

---

8. εἰδέα (connected with εἶδον) refers to what is seen; it occurs here only in the New Testament.

9. ἔνδυμα signifies "what is put on" and thus "clothing"; in the New Testament it is used only by Matthew (7 times) and Luke (once).

10. That seems to be the way we should translate οἱ τηροῦντες, but the emphasis is on their function as watchers rather than on that of guarding the tomb.

11. σείω was used of the earthquake (27:51; should we say that the guard "quaked"?) and of the whole city being agitated (21:10). It signifies thoroughgoing agitation.

the women's unexpressed fears with *"Don't you be afraid."* Fear in the presence of a denizen of another world is natural enough,[12] but the angel had come to help the women, not to terrify them, so he begins by calming their fears. He goes on to encourage them by assuring them that he knows all about their mission: *"you are looking for Jesus, who was crucified."*[13]

6. *"He is not here"* tells them that their search is a vain one; no more should they look in a tomb for Jesus. *"He has been raised,"* where the passive points to the truth that the Father raised his Son. The angel goes on, *"as he said,"* which should remind them of the predictions that Jesus had made and that apparently none of his followers had taken as they were meant. But the predictions were important, and the angel draws their attention to them. They were not facing a situation in which Jesus had undergone a totally unexpected fate and had then experienced an unanticipated deliverance. He had prophesied both his death and his resurrection, and it was important that his followers should come to understand that the wonderful happening that had just taken place was in fact no more than what Jesus had prophesied during his lifetime. The angel backs up his statement that Jesus had been raised by inviting them to *come* and to *see the place where he lay.* This might not perhaps give an infallible proof of what the angel had said, but at least it would make clear that there was no point in concentrating their attention on the tomb. They could see for themselves that Jesus was not there; then perhaps they would take to heart what the mighty angel had told them.

7. From reassuring the ladies the angel turns to commissioning them to do something. *"Go quickly,"* he says; the good news is not something to be hugged to oneself. They are to be the messengers to the *disciples,* which, while it refers to all who follow Jesus, in this place signifies particularly the eleven. We might have expected that the good news would be given first to Peter or John or some other member of the eleven. But God's ways are not our ways, and the message was given first to a couple of women, people who did not rate highly in first-century estimation. This was not the only place in which the Christian message cut across the accepted idea of the time, specifically in connection with the way women were viewed. These two ladies then were told that they should tell the disciples two things: first, that Jesus *"has been raised from the dead"* and, second, that *"he is going ahead of you into Galilee,"* a meeting that he had prophesied before his death (26:32). This does not mean that he is even now on his way to Galilee, but is a prophecy that he is going to be in Galilee before them. This is the second time the angel has said that Jesus has been *raised;* it is

---

12. This may be the point of the emphatic *you:* μὴ φοβεῖσθε ὑμεῖς. Fear is the reaction to be expected from the enemies of Jesus in the presence of angelic beings, but there is no reason for his followers to be afraid.

13. Interestingly he uses the perfect participle ἐσταυρωμένον, which would normally indicate that he continues in the capacity of the crucified one. They were looking for a crucified man instead of a risen one.

important for the women to be clear on this. And it is of interest that he tells them to assure the disciples that *he is going ahead of them into Galilee* (the use of the present tense for a future event makes it more vivid and certain). In Luke and John there are appearances of Jesus in and around Jerusalem, but of course John also has the story of the miraculous catch of fish, and that took place in Galilee. Matthew puts more emphasis on Galilee than does any of the other Evangelists. The disciples would have to walk to Galilee, so there was no problem about Jesus being there before them. The angel completes his message with *"look, I have told you."* He had done all he could for them. The rest was up to them.[14]

8. The women made haste to do what they were told. They *went away from the tomb quickly;* the place of death no longer had any meaning for them. That they went *with fear* indicates that they were in the grip of the awe that had been aroused in them by their contact with the visitant from another world. But they were not simply scared; they went with *great joy.* They had come to that place mourning the death of their great leader and dear friend; they went away knowing that he was dead no longer. Well might their emotion be *great joy.* They had been told to go quickly and tell the disciples, and they took the injunction literally. They *ran to tell his disciples.* Such good news should be spread abroad quickly, so they certainly made haste. *His disciples* is a general term and is broad enough to cover all those who had given him their allegiance. While the news of the resurrection would in due time be conveyed to all his followers, in this place it appears that the term is used especially of the eleven. They were closest to Jesus, and it was important that they learn at the soonest possible moment that their Master had conquered death. For some reason that is not disclosed to us the news was first given to the women and the first appearances of Jesus were to women. But the disciples were not to be overlooked, and these ladies were commissioned to bring them the good news. We should not overlook the fact that in Matthew the only appearance of the risen Jesus in Jerusalem was to the women, while from there he goes on to speak of appearances in despised Galilee. Both point to a rejection of accepted values. "Galilee of the Gentiles" (4:20), of course, fits in with the emphasis on the Gentiles that was to intensify from the time of the resurrection on.

9. The women had had the great blessing of contact with an angel and of being charged with an angelic message to the disciples. But there was something even greater in store for them, for as they went *Jesus met them* (only Matthew has this information; John has a story of an appearance to Mary Magdalene at the tomb, but only Matthew tells us of an appearance to the women as they went on their way to obey the angel's com-

---

14. It is possible that *his disciples* here means his followers as a whole. Jesus appeared to small numbers in Jerusalem, but Paul speaks of an appearance to more than 500 people (1 Cor. 15:6), and this may well have been in Galilee.

mand). They had been last at the cross and first at the tomb, and now they are the first of whom Matthew writes that they had the joy of seeing their Lord. From what the angel had told them they would have expected that no one would see Jesus until the appointment in Galilee. But now as they went on their way to do as the angel said, *look* (the word makes it vivid), there was Jesus before them. Matthew says little about the manner of the meeting, simply that *Jesus met them*. It is not easy to convey the force of his greeting in English. I have tried with *"Greetings,"* but this is not a usual way of greeting someone we meet, though it was quite a normal thing to say in the first century. The *Basic English* translation renders it literally, "Be glad"; *GNB* reads "Peace be with you," which was a normal Jewish greeting and may convey something of the meaning. But it was not what Matthew wrote. However, we should not engage in a lengthy discussion of this word as though it were important. The women clearly were not concerned with such matters. They were simply filled with joy at seeing Jesus himself, so they *came to him*. Evidently when they sighted him on the way, there was still a little distance between them. So they came right where he was. They *took hold of his feet,* an act of homage. Carr cites a clay cylinder of Cyrus in which that great king says of subject kings, "they brought me their full tribute and kissed my feet." In thus taking hold of his feet the women symbolically recognized Jesus' kingship; indeed, it may indicate that they had come to realize that he was more than mortal. However much or little they had understood who he was before, the fact that he was now risen from the dead made it clear to them that he was more than any mere man. So they prostrated themselves before him and held his feet. In including this detail Matthew makes it clear that Jesus' risen body was a real body — the Evangelist is not describing a vision. Matthew also says that they *worshiped him*.[15] This means that they now regarded him as divine.

10. *Then* (see on 2:7) here means "next in sequence." Jesus apparently was not going to spend a lot of time with them at this point. He accepted their worship and then proceeded to reassure them and to repeat the angel's command. *"Don't be afraid"* is a word of reassurance in the exciting but highly unusual situation in which the ladies found themselves. They had been told by the angel that Jesus was alive, and now they had had this confirmed by seeing and hearing him for themselves. They could recognize something of what all this meant and gladly accept it. But it was still something outside human ken; it is a natural thing to be at least a little frightened of the supernatural. Jesus addressed himself to this natural feeling and told them not to be afraid.

---

15. προσκυνέω is sometimes used of the reverence paid to humans "who, however, are to be recognized by this act as belonging to a superhuman realm" (BAGD, 1). But mostly it is used of worshiping deity, whether the true God or the gods of the heathen. The important thing is that it ascribes deity to the object.

Just as the angel had done, he told them to take the good news to his followers. Here he calls them *"my brothers."* It is just possible that he is referring to his human brothers, but this is not likely. He had spoken of those who gave their allegiance to him as his family (12:50; 25:40), and it seems that it is this kind of thinking which underlies these words. Jesus is asking the women to go to the disciples and tell them *to go into Galilee.* Most of Jesus' ministry had been exercised in Galilee; thus it was natural that he would expect his followers to go there and that he would be ready to meet them there. So he says, *"there they will see me."* Neither the angel nor Jesus said where he would meet them in Galilee, and Galilee covered quite an area. But Jesus had spent most of his life there and most of his public ministry. Those who had followed him would know the places he was accustomed to frequent. At any rate neither the women nor the disciples seem to have raised any query about this.

B. The Soldiers Silenced, 28:11-15

> ¹¹*While they were on their way, look, some of the guard came into the city and told the chief priests all that had happened.* ¹²*And when they had met with the elders and had worked out a plan, they gave a considerable sum of money to the soldiers* ¹³*and said, "Say that his disciples came by night and stole him while we were sleeping."* ¹⁴*And if this should come to the governor's ears, we will persuade him and free you from anxiety.* ¹⁵*And they took the money and did as they were told. And this report has been spread abroad among Jews until this day.*

Matthew turns from the joy of the followers of Jesus to the problem facing the Jewish authorities and the guard. That the guard should say exactly what they knew about what had happened was unthinkable, so the authorities had to concoct a story that would limit the damage as they saw it. Matthew proceeds to outline this piece of skulduggery. This part of the story is, of course, in Matthew only; the others do not tell us anything about the guard.

11. *While they were on their way* indicates that the women were already on the path of obedience, and it transfers attention from the prompt action of the followers of Jesus to the prompt action of his enemies. Matthew has his characteristic *look* (see on 1:20) as he introduces this second group into the action. *Some of the guard* (what happened to the others? Matthew says nothing about them) *came into the city* and sought out *the chief priests.* They might have been expected to go to their own officers, but Pilate had placed the guard at the disposal of the Jewish authorities (27:65) and accordingly it was to them that they reported. In any case, they may well have hesitated to go to their own officers because they would have to confess that they had not prevented the removal of the body from the tomb. It is true that the body had not been stolen, but it might have been difficult to convey the truth of what had happened to sceptical Roman officers. Perhaps it was better to postpone facing certain military punishment as long as possible and to try any other course that seemed open. In any case, the Jewish authorities had been the ones who had understood the necessity of the guard, and some of the guard accordingly thought that the first approach should be made to the *chief priests*. Perhaps the reason that only some of them came was that the others did not consider it proper to approach the Jewish authorities. For whatever reason, this was the action they took. They *told the chief priests all that had happened*. It would be interesting to know what is comprised in Matthew's *all*. We know that they saw the rolling of the stone away from the entrance to the tomb and that this had the effect of making them "like dead men" (vv. 2-4). But did they see Jesus? Were they aware that the one who had been buried in that tomb was now alive? We cannot be sure of this. But it is clear that they had seen enough to know that something most unusual had happened and that after the angel had left them there was no body in the tomb. And that certainly was matter enough for a serious and disturbing report to be brought to the Jewish authorities.

12. The chief priests regarded this as a matter that they should not handle on their own. So they met[16] with *the elders* and discussed the situation. They came up with *a plan*[17] that involved bribing the guard. Matthew says that they gave *a considerable sum of money* to the soldiers, and this must indeed have been the case. The guards had been through a harrowing experience that must have left a deep impression on them, but they were to keep quiet about all this. More. They were to say that they had slept on the job, a dereliction of duty that Roman officers would take with the utmost seriousness. A "substantial bribe" *(REB)* was going to be needed to persuade them to do as the chief priests wanted.

13. The story they were to put out was simple. They had to say that they slept while on duty and that Jesus' *disciples came by night and stole him*.[18] It is ironical that the Jewish authorities themselves were now causing the story to be put out that they had caused the guard to be set in order to prevent. They had feared that the body might be stolen and resurrection stories circulate on the basis of an empty tomb. They were now ensuring that precisely those stories were circulated, the only difference being that

---

16. The verb is συνάγω (for which see the note on 27:62). It is used for the gathering of formal assemblies, but also for gatherings of almost any kind (of the mob, 27:17). We should not understand this as a formal assembly, but rather as an informal consultation.

17. συμβούλιον may be used of a council, but here it seems clear that the plan that was formulated is in mind.

18. Chrysostom pours scorn on the idea that they stole him; he speaks of the guards as men who "are not even able to make up a falsehood" and goes on to refer to the disciples as "men poor and unlearned, and not venturing so much as to show themselves. . . . And how should it enter their minds to feign such a thing, men who were well content to be hidden and to live? . . . they were timorous . . . when they saw Him seized, all rushed away from Him" (p. 530).

behind the stories was a risen body instead of a stolen body. The Jesus whom they had caused to be slain and put into the tomb was now a living reality; all their bribes and lies could do nothing to alter the facts.

14. The guards must have taken some persuading to say that they had slept on the job. That was a serious offense and could bring down on them the heaviest of penalties. Moreover, they were to say that their slumbers had enabled the followers of Jesus to steal his body, though if they were asleep when the nefarious deed was done it is not easy to understand how they would know what had happened.[19] The guards were thus placing themselves in a hazardous position by putting out the story the chief priests had concocted. But they were also in a hazardous position if they did not do this. There was no denying that they had been put on guard to prevent the theft of a body. There was no denying that the body had been in the tomb when the stone was sealed. There was no denying that the body was no longer there. So on any showing they had failed as guards. They could, of course, have told of the coming of the angel and of what he had done. But who would believe them? Angels are not often seen by mortals, and this could well sound like a story concocted to cover up their failure. So they ran a risk. But they may well have thought that if they did as the chief priests suggested, at least they would have some people in high place who had an interest in making sure that their story was accepted.[20] If they refused, they were on their own. There is also the fact that Pilate was no willing partner in the execution of Jesus. The posting of the guard was not his idea, and he might not have been particularly distressed if he heard that the Jewish authorities had been discomfited in the end. Further, the chief priests said that if their tale came *to the governor's ears*[21] they themselves would ensure that the guards came to no harm. It appears that the Jewish authorities felt that there was a good chance that Pilate would not hear of this at all. After all, his residence was at Caesarea, and he would be going there soon after the conclusion of the feast. The probability was that the guards would not be accused of any dereliction of duty, and there was no reason for the governor to know anything about what had happened. The soldiers of the guard would be without any *anxiety*[22] over the matter. The priests were telling the soldiers that a cover-

19. Bruce comments, "The lie for which the priests paid so much money is suicidal; one half destroys the other. Sleeping sentinels could not know what happened."

20. Cf. Nixon, "If they were Roman soldiers, Pilate may have handed over responsibility for them on this duty to the Sanhedrin, and therefore he might be persuaded not to punish this offence of sleeping on duty."

21. ἐὰν ἀκουσθῇ ἐπὶ τοῦ ἡγεμόνος, "if it be heard upon the governor," is an unusual expression. But despite the awkwardness, if we try to put it literally into English there is no real doubt as to what it means. *GNB* has, "if the Governor should hear of this." It is possible that we should take it in the sense "if it comes to a hearing before the governor," but this seems less likely.

22. ὑμᾶς ἀμερίμνους ποιήσομεν is another awkward expression: "we will make you without care." But the meaning is clear enough.

up was both possible and necessary. There is a contrast between the emphatic *we* and *you:* "*We* will persuade him, and *you* will be without a care!"

15. The soldiers were grateful to take the money and be safe from any military charge. *They took the money and did as they were told.* For both the Jewish authorities and the soldiers this must have seemed a good solution to a very awkward situation. Both were involved in a lie and both were involved in bribery (the one giving, the other receiving). But the soldiers realized that they could be free from unpleasant disciplinary action, and the chief priests that they had a story that might account for the facts. Of course, had the resurrected Jesus made appearances among the people, the story could not be believed; but if he did not, they were in a good position. At least it cannot have been easy for them to think of a better solution. And, Matthew tells his readers, *this report has been spread abroad*[23] *among Jews* (there is no article; it is not "the" Jews)[24] *until this day* (cf. Rieu, "this story has been current in Jewish circles ever since"). And not only to the time of writing of this Gospel, for as we saw earlier, Justin speaks of it as still being repeated by the Jews in the middle of the second century (see on 27:66). That neither the Jews nor anybody else could produce the body of Jesus is of the utmost importance. Could this have been done, the story of the resurrection would have been exploded in a gale of laughter. But despite all their precautions, including the setting of a guard of soldiers, no body was ever produced. The empty tomb has always been important for Christians.

C. The Great Commission, 28:16-20

> [16]*But the eleven disciples went into Galilee, to the mountain that Jesus had appointed them.* [17]*And when they saw him, they worshipped, but some hesitated.* [18]*And Jesus came and spoke to them, saying, "All authority has been given to me in heaven and on earth.* [19]*Therefore go and make disciples of all the nations, baptizing them in the name of the Father and of the Son and of the Holy Spirit,* [20]*teaching them to observe all the things I have commanded you; and look, I am with you all the days to the end of the age."*

In his concluding paragraph (which is peculiar to this Evangelist) Matthew tells of Jesus' meeting his disciples in Galilee and of the charge he gave them to make disciples of all the nations and to baptize them in

23. Turner takes διεφημίσθη as a perfective aorist, "in which the emphasis is all on the conclusion or results of an action" (M, III, p. 72).

24. It is agreed on all hands that this is a very "Jewish" Gospel; most commentators hold that Matthew was writing for a Jewish-Christian church. It is accordingly surprising that this is the only place in this Gospel where the word "Jew" occurs, apart from the expression "King of the Jews," which is found 4 times. John's Gospel is very different; it uses the term "Jew" 71 times.

the name of the Trinity. Many scholars have raised doubts over parts of this section, particularly over the use of the Trinitarian formula for baptism. But the arguments are all subjective: there is nothing else with which to compare the passage, and textually it is well attested. And it is very important. As Johnson puts it, "No part of the Bible, with the possible exception of the letter to the Romans, has done more to give Christians the vision of a world-wide church. It has sent them to all nations, bearing the message of salvation through Christ, with which are linked the responsibility and privilege of obeying his words." We must bear in mind that the picture of Jesus as a Jewish rabbi, with a little group of disciples around him, traveling in leisurely fashion in rural Galilee contrasts sharply with the missionary-minded church that we find in the early chapters of Acts. From the beginning the church exercised a missionary function and sought to make disciples out of those who listened to its proclamation. Why this sudden and dramatic change? Surely it is the fact of the resurrection of Jesus, coupled with the charge the risen Lord gave to his followers to make disciples of all nations.

16. The adversative *But* sets the disciples over against the Jews and the intrigues about the guard over the tomb. This is a different kind of story. "The Twelve" have now become *the eleven disciples,* and we find that, in obedience to the command passed on through the women mentioned earlier in this chapter, they *went into Galilee.* In the other Gospels the appearances are mostly in Judea, but Matthew has nothing to say about appearances in that region, apart from the brief appearance of Jesus to the two Marys. But this Evangelist has depicted the greater part of Jesus' ministry as being in Galilee, perhaps to indicate that the task the risen Christ assigns to his followers is continuous with the ministry he exercised when he was here on earth. Matthew goes on to say that the eleven went *to the mountain that Jesus had appointed*[25] *them.* We have no way of identifying this mountain, but the disciples were familiar with Galilee and we need not doubt that there was no problem for them with appearing at a mountain that is unknown to us.

17. When the women saw the risen Jesus they worshipped him (v. 9), and now the eleven disciples did the same. Jesus told the women that the disciples would see him in Galilee (v. 10), and now we read that they did see him. Worship was the natural response to the realization that the Jesus who had meant so much to them throughout his earthly ministry was stronger than death and was alive again. Matthew goes on to say, *but some hesitated,* the meaning of which is not immediately obvious. Many translations have "some doubted," and this may indeed be the meaning, but "hesitated"

---

25. τάσσω is used of various kinds of appointing; here it clearly refers to a command given by Jesus, though there is no indication of when the command was given. BAGD notes that the middle is here used in the sense of the active, and that πορεύεσθαι is to be understood (2.b).

744

seems more likely (so *JB*).[26] It can scarcely mean that the hesitators were included among the worshipers; Matthew is saying that there were those who worshiped and there were those who hesitated. But why did they hesitate? Perhaps they were not sure that the person they were seeing was the one who was crucified. Perhaps they were not sure that Jesus really was risen; they may have wondered whether they were seeing a vision, not a real person. Perhaps they were not sure that it really was Jesus who was before them (cf. *LB*, "some of them weren't sure it really was Jesus!"). We must bear in mind that they were not alone in having difficulty in recognizing Jesus. The two who walked with him to Emmaus did not know who he was (Luke 24:16; cf. vv. 37, 41), and the disciples in the boat did not recognize the risen Jesus on the shore (John 21:4). But in any case we may ask, Who has perfect faith? We should bear in mind that even one of the eleven, Thomas, not only doubted but roundly denied the resurrection when told about it by the ten (John 20:24-25). It is surely not surprising that when the whole body of the followers of Jesus knew that he had been crucified, that he had died, and that he had been buried in a sepulchre, some should have difficulty with the thought that now he was alive again.

This raises another question. It is difficult to think that the hesitation was coming from the eleven, considering all that had happened to them during the recent past. It may well be that others than the eleven were present, perhaps even the group of more than 500 of whom Paul writes (1 Cor. 15:6). This would give more scope for people who believed and people who doubted than if the group had been limited to the eleven who had been closest to Jesus. France argues strongly that only the eleven were present, but it is not easy to see how the hesitators could have been some of the eleven after the dramatic removal of Thomas's doubts (John 20:24-29).

18. Jesus was evidently at a little distance from the group, for he *came.* But perhaps this means that he took up a position from which he could easily address the whole group.[27] First he made clear that in his risen state he was in a situation very different from that when he had been the penniless preacher and healer they knew so well. *"All authority*[28] *has been given to me,"* he said, which points to an end to the time when he was "a man of sorrows, and acquainted with grief . . . stricken, smitten of God, and afflicted" (Isa. 53:3-4, *KJV*). Now he has received the fullest possible authority, for it is authority *in heaven and on earth.* He is making clear that

26. Cf. Stonehouse, "The word 'doubt' is of course not the equivalent of stark unbelief. In the only other instance of the use of this verb in the New Testament, in Mt. 14:31, it expresses Peter's lack of an adequate faith when he started to meet Jesus upon the water" (*Witness*, pp. 179-80).

27. O. Michel regards verses 18-20 as very important; they are "the key to the understanding of the whole book" (Stanton, p. 35). This may be something of an overstatement, but there can be no doubt that they put the capstone on all that has gone before.

28. ἐξουσία is connected with ἔξεστιν and thus means "*freedom of choice, right* to act, decide, or dispose of one's property as one wishes" (BAGD, 1). It comes to mean "*authority, absolute power*" and is used here "of Jesus' absolute authority" (BAGD, 3).

the limitations that applied throughout the incarnation no longer apply to him. He has supreme authority throughout the universe.

19. We might have expected that this would lead on to his disclosure of some of the ways in which that authority would be exercised, but instead Jesus goes on to its implications for those who follow him. *Therefore* leads on to the fact that this has consequences for those who follow him here on earth. Because he is who he is[29] and because he has the full authority he has, they are commissioned to *"go"*[30] (which forms a contrast with "do not go," which had earlier been his direction with respect to the Gentiles, 10:5) and *"make disciples."*[31] In this Gospel a disciple is both a learner and a follower; a disciple takes Jesus as his teacher and learns from him, and a disciple also follows Jesus.[32] The life of a disciple is different because of his attachment to Jesus. The Master is not giving a command that will merely secure nominal adherence to a group, but one that will secure wholehearted commitment to a person. In the first century a disciple did not enroll with such-and-such a school, but with such-and-such a teacher. Jesus' disciples are people for whom a life has been given in ransom (20:28) and who are committed to the service of the Master, who not only took time to teach his disciples but who died for them and rose again. Those who are disciples of such a leader are committed people. And, of course, this is the kind of disciple that he looks for his followers to make. They are to make disciples *of all the nations,* which points to a worldwide scope for their mission. It took the church a little time to realize the significance of this, and in the early chapters of Acts we find the believers concentrating on proclaiming their message to the Jews. But there seems never to have been any question of admitting Gentiles, the only problem being on what conditions.[33]

29. Graham Stanton discovers general agreement "that these verses are crucial for Matthean Christology" but wide difference on their precise meaning. Specifically he objects to Kingsbury's view that that they express a "Son of God Christology." He goes on, "Unless one accepts Kingsbury's view that the title Son of God is the central christological title in Matthew, this seems to be a lop-sided interpretation of the closing verses. Surely it is more plausible to see a cluster of related Matthean themes in this passage" (Stanton, p. 5).

30. *"Go"* translates the participle πορευθέντες. From this fact some have drawn the conclusion that Jesus did not command his followers to go; all that they were to do was make disciples of such people as they happened to encounter. But where a participle is linked in this way with an imperative, it shares in the imperative force (cf. 2:8, 13; 11:4; 17:27). Jesus was commanding his followers to go as well as to make disciples, though the emphasis falls on the making of disciples.

31. In BDF, 148(3) we find that μαθητεύειν meant first "to be a disciple" (27:57 v.l.), then it became a deponent (13:52; 27:57 v.l.) and "from this there developed a new active 'to make a disciple of'." Mounce translates "a learner," and explains, "A disciple is not simply one who has been taught but one who continues to learn."

32. M. Green comments, "The apostles are called not to evoke decisions but to make disciples. And that is an altogether tougher assignment" (p. 300).

33. D. R. A. Hare and D. J. Harrington argue that we should take *all the nations* here to mean all the Gentiles but not the Jews (*CBQ,* XXXVII [1975], pp. 359-69). But they seem to have been answered by J. P. Meier, who maintains that *all the nations* means all the nations of the world including Israel (*CBQ,* XXXIX [1977], pp. 94-102).

Jesus goes on to speak of *baptizing* these new disciples *"in[34] the name of the Father and of the Son and of the Holy Spirit."[35]* This expression has caused endless controversy among exegetes. There are two separate problems, the institution of baptism as a rite of initiation for disciples, and the use of the Trinitarian formula. On the former question it is pointed out that Jesus did not habitually engage in baptism as John the Baptist, for example, did. Throughout his ministry he did not call on his followers to baptize those who wished to become adherents. From this it is argued that baptism was a rite established by the church, and the command to continue it is viewed as having been read back onto the lips of Jesus. But against this is the fact that baptism was part of church life from the very first. On the Day of Pentecost Peter preached to the crowd in Jerusalem, and when they asked, "What shall we do, brother men?" he responded without consultation and without hesitation, "Repent and be baptized" (Acts 2:37-38). We have no knowledge of a time when the church was without baptism or unsure of baptism. It is difficult to explain this apart from a definite command of Jesus.

The words referring to the Trinity are another matter, but we must bear in mind that the faith mentioned in verse 18 "naturally issues in the concept of the Trinity" (Johnson).[36] We must bear in mind as well that in the early church there are references to baptizing in the name of Jesus (e.g., Acts 8:16; 19:5). Bonnard notices this difficulty, but immediately adds, "one cannot doubt that the Trinitarian formula was already there in germ in Paul" (p. 416; similarly Allen remarks, "the conception Father, Son, and Holy Spirit is clearly as ancient as the Christian Society itself"). Such passages, however, may not give the formula used in baptizing, but be a short way of differentiating Christian baptism from the other baptisms in the ancient world. For that matter the words about the Trinity are not necessarily meant to be used as a formula,[37] though in the history of the church they have often been so used and they form a fitting part of

---

34. Turner insists that εἰς here has its proper sense and is not to be taken as equivalent to ἐν; it refers to "baptism *into* the name, i.e. a relationship as the goal of baptism" (M, III, p. 255).

35. C. K. Barrett points out that Eusebius quotes the passage in the form "Go ye into all the world and make disciples of all the Gentiles in my name," which omits the reference to baptism and to the Trinitarian formula. But he points out that no trace of this reading is found in any MS of Matthew or indeed in any writing other than that of Eusebius. He finds it "very difficult to believe that if this (the short reading) is what Matthew wrote, not one copy of his unaltered MS succeeded in escaping revision" (*The Holy Spirit and the Gospel Tradition* [London, 1947], p. 103).

36. Meier points out that the expression has implications for our understanding of the Godhead: "one could hardly imagine a more forceful proclamation of Christ's divinity — and, incidentally, of the Spirit's distinct personality — than this listing together, on a level of equality, of Father, Son, and Spirit. One does not baptize people in the name of a divine person, a holy creature, and an impersonal divine force."

37. "The mistake of so many writers on the New Testament lies in treating this saying as a liturgical formula (which it later became), and not as a description of what baptism accomplished" (*AB*).

baptismal services.[38] That the early followers of Jesus thought of God as triune seems clear from the passages that speak of the three together (e.g., Rom. 8:11; 1 Cor. 12:4-6; 2 Cor. 13:14; Gal. 4:6; Eph. 4:4-6; 2 Thess. 2:13, etc.). That God is a Trinity is a scriptural idea.[39] Jesus spoke a good deal about the Father, but not so much about the Holy Spirit, and he did not link himself with the two in a way comparable to the formula we have here. This being so, it is perhaps not surprising that many modern scholars assert that Matthew is here reading the custom of his church back onto the lips of Jesus. But there is no objective criterion to decide the point. If we hold that Matthew gives a reliable picture of the life and teaching of Jesus, we will say that the formula that has come to mean so much to the Christian church goes back to Jesus himself and to those days when he had risen from the dead and was giving direction to his followers for the times ahead when they would have to manage the affairs of the church without his visible presence. If we think that Matthew is reflecting the life of the later church in which he lived, then here as elsewhere we will think that he has made use of ecclesiastical formularies.[40] We should notice that the word *name* is singular; Jesus does not say that his followers should baptize in the "names" of Father, Son, and Holy Spirit, but in the "name" of these three. It points to the fact that they are in some sense one.

The mention of the Spirit is viewed by some critics as nonhistorical, but we should not overlook the fact that there is some reference to the Spirit in both the Lukan and the Johannine resurrection accounts. Luke tells us that the risen Jesus spoke of sending "the promise of my Father on you" (Luke 24:49), a promise that was fulfilled with the coming of the Spirit on the Day of Pentecost, while John records the risen Jesus as saying, "Receive the Holy Spirit" (John 20:22). There is nothing improbable in Matthew's recording words referring to the Holy Spirit in this context. We should remember also that the Spirit is mentioned in connection with Jesus' own baptism; indeed, we have a Trinitarian passage there (3:16-17).[41]

---

38. Tasker points out that the baptism Jesus here initiates is not a reversion to the practice of John the Baptist (or of what he and his disciples had done in earlier days, John 4:1-2). "It was essentially a *new* sacrament, by which men and women were to come under the influence of the Triune God, to be used in His service. The words *in the name of the Father, and of the Son, and of the Holy Ghost* are therefore both emphatic and essential to the text. Without them, the reference to baptism would be indeterminate and conventional" (p. 276).

39. McNeile denies that the threefold name points to a late date. He reminds us that Jesus spoke of "the Father" and "the Son," while "the Holy Spirit" is an Old Testament expression. He draws attention to the fact that Paul often "brings the Three into juxtaposition."

40. D. Wenham remarks, "the Trinitarian tendencies of the early church are most easily explained if they go back to Jesus Himself; but the importance of the point for our study is that it means that Matthew's reference to the Trinity in chapter 28 is not a white elephant thoroughly out of context. Whether a formula or not, whether *ipsissima verba* or evangelist's paraphrase, the Matthean command may be regarded as the crystallization of ideas that are present as well in the resurrection accounts of Luke and John" (*The Resurrection Narratives*, p. 53).

41. Kingsbury says, "even as the resurrected Son of God, he remains the crucified Son

20. Baptism is not the be-all and end-all; it is no more than the beginning. The new disciple is to be baptized, but he or she is also to be taught[42] *"to observe all the things I have commanded you."* The church's teaching function is thus of great importance. We teach because Jesus commanded us to teach, and there is no way of diminishing the importance of an activity that owes its origin to the command of our Lord himself. But Jesus is not speaking about education for education's sake. He speaks of the taught as "observing" what Jesus has commanded. In other words, Jesus is concerned with a way of life. As we have seen throughout this Gospel, he continually urges his followers to live in a manner pleasing to God. He has objected to the sterile legalism of many in his day and has gone beyond the letter of the law to the things that are rightly seen as arising from its spirit. So there is to be instruction and there is to be purity of life. We should not miss the significance of *all the things.* Jesus is not suggesting that his followers should make a selection from his teachings as it pleases them and neglect the rest. Since the teaching of Jesus is a unified whole, disciples are to observe *all* that this means.

The final promise is introduced by Matthew's characteristic *"and look"* (see on 1:20); *NIV* translates with "and surely," which conveys some of the reassurance the term implies here. The Gospel ends with Jesus' breathtaking promise that he is with his followers *all the days*[43] *to the end of the age.*[44] He does not say "I will be with you," but *"I am with you,"* and his *I* is emphatic, "no less than I." Bruce sees this expression as "conveying the feeling of certainty, but also spoken from the eternal point of view, *sub specie aeternitatis,* for which distinctions of here and there, now and then, do not exist." In other words, the disciple is not going to be left to serve God as well as he can in the light of what he has learned from the things Jesus has commanded. The disciple will find that he has a great companion as he goes on his way through life. This tells us something about Jesus. The Jesus of whom Matthew writes is no small Palestinian figure, but a mighty Person who is with his followers wherever they may be. And this, he says, will last through time. He is not speaking of a temporary residence with first-century disciples, but of a presence among his followers to the very end of time. This Gospel opened with the assurance that in the coming of Jesus God was with his people (1:23), and it closes with the promise that the very presence of Jesus Christ will never be lacking to his

---

of God ('the one who has been, and remains, the crucified'; 28:6; 27:54)" (*Matthew*, p. 57). This is surely the basis for making disciples and baptizing them.

42. *Baptizing* and *teaching* are two more participles dependent on μαθητεύσατε; the force of all this is given by Carson: it is "to make Jesus' disciples responsible for making disciples of others, a task characterized by baptism and instruction" (p. 597).

43. Moule says that the accusative πάσας τὰς ἡμέρας "perhaps strictly = *the whole of every day*" (*IBNTG*, p. 34).

44. ἕως τῆς συντελείας τοῦ αἰῶνος. For this Matthean expression see the note on 13:39. The thought is not only temporal but includes that of the completion of the purpose of God.

faithful follower. This does not, of course, mean that Jesus has not been with his people hitherto; he has made it clear that where two or three are met in his name he is there, right in the middle of them (18:20). But when Matthew draws his Gospel to its close, he has nothing in the way of an ascension account. He emphasizes the importance of his continuing presence and concludes his Gospel with the magnificent assurance to the followers of Jesus that that presence will never be withdrawn; he will be with them always, to the end of the world and to the end of time.

General Index

Index of Authors

Index of Scripture References

DAT